DIMENSIONS OF TAX D

'Like the Meade Report, the Mirrlees Review is an impressive study and will be a standard reference for years to come.... The two volumes produced by the Mirrlees Review provide valuable policy analysis and demonstrate the vitality of modern public economics. They are worthy successors to the Meade Report and represent a new landmark in the field.'

Prof Sir Tony Atkinson

'A major study of utmost political relevance.'

David Walker, *Prospect Magazine*

'The Mirrlees Review offers a blueprint for simpler, fairer, and more efficient taxation. Taking up its proposals is a better use of government time than trying to alter the past.'

Editorial, *Financial Times*

'The outlines of what... a reforming chancellor might do were recently set out in an extraordinary review of the tax system led by Sir James Mirrlees of Cambridge University for the Institute for Fiscal Studies. Published last autumn after nearly five years' work... it is the most comprehensive and devastating indictment of the current situation.... For the main part it is hard to disagree with Mirrlees.'

Will Hutton, *Observer*

DIMENSIONS OF TAX DESIGN

The Mirrlees Review

Chair

SIR JAMES MIRRLEES

Editors

Stuart Adam, Timothy Besley, Richard Blundell, Stephen Bond, Robert Chote, Malcolm Gammie, Paul Johnson, Gareth Myles, and James Poterba

for the

Institute for Fiscal Studies

OXFORD
UNIVERSITY PRESS

OXFORD
UNIVERSITY PRESS

Great Clarendon Street, Oxford, OX2 6DP,
United Kingdom

Oxford University Press is a department of the University of Oxford.
It furthers the University's objective of excellence in research, scholarship,
and education by publishing worldwide. Oxford is a registered trade mark of
Oxford University Press in the UK and in certain other countries

First published 2010
First published in paperback 2017

Impression: 1

Published in the United States of America by Oxford University Press
198 Madison Avenue, New York, NY 10016, United States of America

British Library Cataloguing in Publication Data
Data available

Library of Congress Cataloging in Publication Data
Data available

ISBN 978–0–19–955375–4 (Hbk.)
ISBN 978–0–19–879519–3 (Pbk.)

Printed and bound by
CPI Group (UK) Ltd, Croydon, CR0 4YY

Contents

Preface to the Paperback Edition

Since the first edition of *Dimensions of Tax Design* was published much tax policy has changed. Internationally the Organisation for Economic Co-operation and Development's (OECD) major project on international corporate taxation—Base Erosion and Profit Shifting—represents one of the biggest cross-national tax projects in recent decades. It flowed from growing concern about, and focus on, perceived inequities in (low) levels of tax payments by some large companies. Combine that with concerns about the ability of some very high income individuals to minimize their tax payments and tax has never been so much at the forefront of public debate.

At the same time in the UK we have seen increases then reductions in the top rate of income tax, very big changes to the taxation of savings and pensions, big cuts in the effective taxes on driving, increases in VAT rates, and cuts in rates of corporation tax. Some of these changes have been consistent with a rational approach to tax policy, some have not.

What we still have not had is anything approaching a clear strategy for a tax system. Reform still occurs piecemeal, mistakes and about-turns are too frequent, and the complexity is ever increasing. Nor do we have a good public debate about or understanding of the tax system. Given that in most developed countries around 40% of national income is taken in taxes this is an extraordinary, and potentially dangerous, situation.

Dimensions of Tax Design speaks to all these issues, including issues of political economy and administration. It sets out the latest theoretical and empirical research in nearly all the key areas of tax policy and design. Its insights have already inspired much new research. We know it has been heavily used by policymakers seeking a deeper understanding of the rationale for, and impact of, tax policy design. It deserves to be read and used for many years to come.

Paul Johnson
Director
Institute for Fiscal Studies

Preface

Thirty years ago the Institute for Fiscal Studies published a seminal review of the UK tax system, the fruits of a commission chaired by the Nobel Laureate Professor James Meade. Explaining the motivation for the review, Dick Taverne, then Director of the IFS, lamented: 'For too long, tax reforms have been approached *ad hoc*, without regard to their effects on the evolution of the tax structure as a whole. As a result many parts of the system seem to lack a rational base. Conflicting objectives are pursued at random; and even particular objectives are pursued in contradictory ways.'

Unfortunately, this critique still holds true today. In some important respects the tax system has evolved in the way that the Meade Report recommended, but it remains the product of often incoherent piecemeal changes rather than strategic design. The tax system has also struggled to adapt to profound changes in the economic, social, and institutional environment in which it operates. And tax design has not benefited as much as it could from advances in theoretical and empirical understanding of the way features of the system influence people's behaviour.

For all of these reasons, we felt that the time was ripe once again to ask an expert commission to take a hard look at the tax system: to try to identify the characteristics that would make for a good tax system in an open economy in the twenty-first century; and to suggest how the British tax system in particular might be reformed to move closer to that ideal. This volume and the companion volume of the Review's final conclusions, *Tax by Design*, are the result.

In thinking of a worthy successor to James Meade as chair of the Review, there was one obvious choice: the Nobel Laureate and founder of the modern theory of optimal taxation, Professor Sir James Mirrlees, of Cambridge University and the Chinese University of Hong Kong. We are very grateful to him and to the other directors of the Review's work: Professor Tim Besley of the Bank of England and the London School of Economics; Professor Richard Blundell of the IFS and University College London; Malcolm Gammie QC of One Essex Court and the IFS Tax Law Review Committee; and Professor James Poterba, President of the National Bureau of Economic Research in the US. They have been joined in editing this volume and writing *Tax By Design* by Stuart Adam of the IFS; Professor Stephen Bond of Oxford University; Paul

Johnson of the IFS and Frontier Economics; Professor Gareth Myles of Exeter University; and me.

The Meade Report confined its attention largely to direct taxes in the UK, whereas we wanted the Mirrlees Review to examine the tax system more broadly and from a global perspective as well as a British one. To provide a foundation upon which our final conclusions could be built, we therefore began by asking small teams of experts from the IFS and around the world to address a number of key themes in tax design, with equally distinguished experts to comment on their work. These authors and commentators were not constrained by the views of the core review team, and neither was the core review team constrained to agree with all or any of their conclusions. We are enormously grateful to them all for their analyses, which are of considerable interest and value in their own right, above and beyond any inspiration they have provided for the final report. They are published in full in this volume, while the conclusions of the core team are to be found in *Tax by Design*.

From the outset, the intention of the review was to take a 'big picture' view of tax design, asking what society wants the tax system to achieve and how best it might be structured to accomplish that. In the final report we have tried both to set out an overarching vision for the tax system and to suggest some desirable incremental reforms. The starting point has been to look at the economics of the tax system, although we have received a great deal of useful input from tax lawyers, advisers, and practitioners, as well as those currently and in the past involved with the practicalities of tax design and implementation. Inevitably, some of those who spend most of their time thinking about tax design and implementation from these perspectives might have identified different priorities and have taken different approaches if they were to have undertaken this Review themselves. Economists cannot claim to have all the answers to good tax design—and some of our answers will pose new questions. But thinking hard about the economics of the tax system is essential if it is to work effectively.

In addition to administrative practicality and the difficulty of turning economic intentions into robust legislative language, proposals for tax reform are of course constrained by politics—not least the unfortunate observation that those who lose from tax reforms tend be vengeful while those who gain from them tend to be ungrateful. But there is no point in a Review of this sort confining itself only to recommendations that we could confidently expect to receive immediate and enthusiastic support across the political spectrum—it would be a very short report if it did. In the final report we have tried to take explicit account of the political economy of tax reform in setting out a possible path to a better system, but there will always be a tension to some extent between what is economically desirable and what is politically practical.

One of the most important and well-known lessons from economics is that there is no such thing as a free lunch. We must therefore express our heartfelt thanks to those who have paid for this one: the Nuffield Foundation and the Economic and Social Research Council. Both have long been much valued supporters of IFS and we hope that they will think their investment in this project worthwhile. It just remains for me to echo Dick Taverne's words on the launch of the Meade Report: 'We hope and believe that this Report will be a rich quarry for tax reformers and a valuable reference point for students of taxation for decades to come.'

Robert Chote
Former Director
Institute for Fiscal Studies

The Nuffield Foundation is a charitable trust with the aim of advancing social well-being. It funds research and innovation, predominantly in social policy and education. It has supported this project, but the views expressed are those of the authors and not necessarily those of the Foundation. More information is available at www.nuffieldfoundation.org.

The Economic and Social Research Council (ESRC) funds research and training in social and economic issues. It is an independent organisation, established by Royal Charter, receiving most of its funding through the Department for Business, Innovation and Skills.

Nuffield Foundation

E·S·R·C
ECONOMIC & SOCIAL RESEARCH COUNCIL

About the Editors

Sir James Mirrlees is a Fellow of Trinity College and Emeritus Professor of Political Economy at the University of Cambridge, Laureate Professor at the University of Melbourne, and Distinguished Professor-at-large at the Chinese University of Hong Kong. He is a Fellow of the British Academy and past President of the Econometric Society, the Royal Economic Society, and the European Economic Association, and has been awarded numerous honorary degrees. Working primarily on the economics of incentives and asymmetric information, he founded the modern theory of optimal taxation, and was the joint winner of the Nobel Prize for Economics in 1996. He was knighted in 1997 for contributions to economic science.

Stuart Adam is a Senior Research Economist at the IFS. His research focuses on the design of the tax and benefit system, and he has written about many aspects of UK tax and benefit policy, including income tax and National Insurance, capital gains tax, tax credits, incapacity benefit, work incentives and redistribution, support for families with children, and local government finance.

Timothy Besley is Kuwait Professor of Economics and Political Science at the LSE, a Research Fellow at the IFS, and from 2006 to 2009 an external member of the Bank of England Monetary Policy Committee. His work has been mainly in the fields of development economics, public economics, and political economy. He is a former co-editor of the *American Economic Review*, Fellow of the Econometric Society and of the British Academy, and is President-elect of the European Economic Association. He was a 2005 recipient of the Yrjö Jahnsson Prize.

Richard Blundell CBE is Research Director of the IFS, where he is also Director of the ESRC Centre for the Microeconomic Analysis of Public Policy. He holds the David Ricardo Chair of Political Economy at UCL. His research has been mainly in the fields of microeconometrics, household behaviour, and tax policy evaluation. He is a Fellow of the British Academy, honorary Fellow of the Institute of Actuaries, President-elect of the Royal Economic Society, past President of the European Economic Association and of the Econometric Society, and former co-editor of *Econometrica*. A winner of the Yrjö Jahnsson Prize and the Frisch Medal, he was awarded the CBE in 2006 for services to economics and social science.

Stephen Bond is a Senior Research Fellow at Nuffield College, Oxford, a programme director at the Oxford University Centre for Business Taxation, and a research fellow at the IFS. His main interests are in corporate tax policy and the effects of corporate taxation on the behaviour of firms. Other interests include empirical research on company investment and financial behaviour, and the development of econometric methods for the analysis of panel data.

Robert Chote was appointed Director of the IFS in October 2002. He was formerly an adviser and speechwriter to the First Deputy Managing Director of the IMF. He was Economics Editor of the *Financial Times* between 1995 and 1999, and previously served as Economics Correspondent of *The Independent* and a columnist on the *Independent on Sunday*, where he was named Young Financial Journalist of the Year by the Wincott Foundation. He is a governor of the National Institute of Economic and Social Research and a member of the Advisory Board of the UK Centre for the Measurement of Government Activity at the Office for National Statistics.

Malcolm Gammie CBE QC is a barrister at One Essex Court. He has been associated with the IFS for almost thirty years, and is currently Research Director of its Tax Law Review Committee. He was a senior tax partner at the City law firm of Linklaters until moving to the Bar in 1997, becoming a QC in 2002. He was named Tax Lawyer of the Year 2008 at the LexisNexis Taxation Awards. A past president of the Chartered Institute of Taxation, he teaches at universities in Australia, the Netherlands, and the UK. He has advised governments of several countries, the European Commission, and the OECD on tax policy issues and was awarded the CBE in 2005 for services to taxation policy.

Paul Johnson is a Research Fellow at the IFS and an associate of Frontier Economics. From 2004 to 2007 he was Director of the Public Services and Growth Directorate and Chief Microeconomist at HM Treasury, as well as Deputy Head of the Government Economic Service. He previously worked in senior posts at the Department for Education and Skills and the Financial Services Authority. Until 1998 he was a full-time researcher at the IFS, eventually taking on the roles of Deputy Director and Head of the Personal Sector Research Programme.

Gareth Myles is Professor of Economics at the University of Exeter and a research fellow at the IFS. He is a Fellow of the Royal Society of Arts and has been a Professorial Fellow at the Australian School of Taxation. He is a managing editor of *Fiscal Studies* and an associate editor of the *Journal of Public Economic Theory*. His main research areas are public economics, labour economics, and microeconomics. His publications include numerous research papers on taxation with imperfect competition, international taxation, and public goods. He has also written the textbooks *Public Economics* (1995) and *Intermediate Public Economics* (2006).

James Poterba is Mitsui Professor of Economics at MIT, President of the National Bureau of Economic Research, and President of the National Tax Association. He is also a Fellow of the American Academy of Arts and Sciences and of the Econometric Society. His research focuses on how taxation affects the economic decisions of households and firms. He served as a member of the US President's bi-partisan Advisory Panel on Federal Tax Reform in 2005, and is a past editor of the *Journal of Public Economics*. He studied economics as an undergraduate at Harvard University, and received his doctorate in economics from the University of Oxford.

1

Taxation in the UK

*Stuart Adam, James Browne, and Christopher Heady**

Stuart Adam is a Senior Research Economist at the IFS. His research focuses on the design of the tax and benefit system, and he has written about many aspects of UK tax and benefit policy, including income tax and National Insurance, capital gains tax, tax credits, incapacity benefit, work incentives and redistribution, support for families with children, and local government finance.

James Browne is a Research Economist at the IFS. His research focuses on various aspects of the tax and benefit system. In particular, he has looked at the effect of various potential policy reforms on poverty rates among children and pensioners, the effects of welfare-to-work programmes, changes to the level of support for families with children over time, and the effect of tax and benefit changes on work incentives and the distribution of income.

Christopher Heady is Head of the Tax Policy and Statistics Division at the OECD. He has published widely on the economics of public policy, including tax policy issues in both developed and developing countries. He was previously Assistant Professor at Yale, Lecturer then Reader at UCL, and Professor of Applied Economics at the University of Bath. His books include *Poverty and Social Exclusion in Europe, Fiscal Management and Economic Reform in the People's Republic of China*, and *Tax Policy: Theory and Practice in OECD Countries.*

* This chapter draws heavily on the IFS's *Survey of the UK Tax System* <http://www.ifs.org.uk/bns/bn09.pdf>, which is updated annually and was itself originally based on the UK chapter by A. Dilnot and G. Stears in K. Messere (ed.), *The Tax System in Industrialized Countries*, Oxford University Press, 1998. The authors thank Richard Blundell, Steve Bond, Mike Brewer, Michael Devereux, Carl Emmerson, Andrew Leicester, Cormac O'Dea, Jonathan Shaw, and Matthew Wakefield for comments, advice, and help with data and calculations. Any errors and omissions are the responsibility of the authors. Family Resources Survey data are produced by the Department for Work and Pensions and available from the UK Data Archive; Family Expenditure Survey and Expenditure and Food Survey data are collected by the Office for National Statistics and distributed by the Economic and Social Data Service. Crown copyright material is reproduced with the permission of the Controller of HMSO and the Queen's Printer for Scotland. None of these bodies bears any responsibility for the analysis or interpretation presented herein.

Stuart Adam, James Browne, and Christopher Heady

EXECUTIVE SUMMARY

n 2008 the UK government forecast that its total revenue in 2008–d be 37.3% of national income. This is a lower share than in 1978–ecting a fall in non-tax receipts (such as surpluses of nationalized industries): taxes alone were forecast to raise 35.3% of GDP, a larger share than thirty years ago.

Most other developed countries have also seen a rise in tax as a share of GDP since 1978. In 2006 (the latest year for which comparative data are available) the share of national income taken in tax in the UK was around the average for developed countries: lower than most of the EU15 countries (such as France, Italy, and the Scandinavian countries), but higher than in most of the new EU countries of eastern Europe and higher than in the USA, Japan, and Australia.

Most of the key developments in UK taxation over the last thirty years have been very much in line with those seen internationally:

- The share of revenue provided by VAT has greatly increased, while the share provided by taxes on specific goods has fallen by a similar amount.
- Basic and higher rates of income tax have been cut, and the number of rates reduced.
- Income tax has moved towards taxing members of couples independently.
- Tax credits have brought support for low-income workers within the tax system.
- Statutory rates of corporation tax have been cut, and the tax base broadened by reducing the value of allowances for capital investment.
- Shareholder taxation has been reformed to give less credit for corporation tax already paid on profits.
- New environmental taxes have been introduced.

However, in some respects the UK is unusual:

- An unusually small share of UK tax revenue comes from social security (National Insurance) contributions, and an unusually large share comes from recurrent taxes on buildings (council tax and business rates).
- The UK applies a zero rate of VAT to many more goods than most other countries.
- The UK is unusual in having abolished tax relief for mortgage interest.

- Tax raising in the UK is exceptionally centralized, with only 5% of revenues raised locally; and it has become more centralized over time, notably with the move of business rates from local to central control.

The tax and benefit system as a whole redistributes significantly from rich to poor. But whether tax and benefit reforms have contributed to or counteracted the sharp increase in income inequality seen in the UK over the last thirty years is hard to determine definitively, in part because it depends on what is meant by 'reform'. The tax and benefit system in 2008 does more to reduce inequality than if the system of thirty years ago had remained in place with tax thresholds and (more importantly) benefit rates increased in line with inflation, but does less to reduce inequality than if the rates and thresholds of the 1978 system had kept pace with GDP per capita. Within this period, though, Labour's reforms have been clearly more progressive than the Conservatives': Labour's reforms since 1997 have had a similar effect on overall inequality as increasing benefit rates in line with GDP, while the Conservatives' reforms were roughly equivalent to increasing them in line with inflation.

On the other hand, reforms under the Conservatives did more to strengthen financial work incentives than those under Labour. The Conservatives' tax and benefit reforms unambiguously strengthened average incentives for people to be in work and for those in work to increase their earnings. Reforms since 1997, however, have had much less impact on incentives to be in work—on average, they are now slightly stronger than they would have been if Labour had increased the benefit rates they inherited in line with growth in the economy, and much the same as if they had increased benefit rates in line with inflation—and Labour's reforms have weakened average incentives for those in work to increase their earnings. All of these broad trends, however, hide substantial variations across the population.

The tax system influences the amount that people save and the form in which they do so. Owner-occupied housing and Individual Saving Accounts (ISAs) are not subject to personal income taxes; pensions are effectively subsidized by the provision of a 25% tax-free lump sum and by the exemption of employer pension contributions from National Insurance contributions (although deferral of tax from the point at which earnings are paid into a pension fund to the point at which they are withdrawn from the fund means that the attractiveness of saving in a pension depends a great deal on whether an individual's marginal tax rate is different at those two points). Pensions, ISAs, and housing cover the significant saving activity of the bulk of the population, but other forms of saving are discouraged by income tax and capital gains tax—and to a markedly greater extent than the statutory tax rates might suggest, because no allowance is given for inflation. The decline of inflation from the very high rates prevalent thirty years ago has been a major factor reducing the extent to which the tax system biases the choice between different saving vehicles. Policy reforms have also reduced these distortions by reducing the highest income tax rates, introducing tax-free saving vehicles such as ISAs, and abolishing the subsidies offered through tax relief for life assurance and mortgage interest. The result of all this is that saving is now less likely to be heavily taxed, and less likely to be subsidized, than in the past.

Like different forms of personal saving, different forms of business investment are treated differently by the tax system. In the UK, as around the world, debt-financed investment is treated more favourably than equity-financed investment, and investment in plant and machinery is treated more favourably than investment in industrial buildings. Both of these distortions have been reduced since 1979.

1.1. INTRODUCTION

This chapter provides a description and assessment of the UK tax system, placing it in historical, international, and theoretical contexts. We begin in Section 1.2 by outlining the evolution of the size and composition of tax revenues in the UK since 1978 and comparing this to developments in other OECD countries. Section 1.3 describes what has happened to the design of major taxes over the same period and compares this to worldwide trends in tax reform. The economic analysis of these developments is taken up in Section 1.4, which assesses their effects on the income distribution and incentives to work, save, and invest. Section 1.5 concludes with a summary of the main issues raised. An appendix describes each of the main taxes in 2008–09.

1.2. THE LEVEL AND COMPOSITION OF REVENUES

Total UK government receipts are forecast to be £545.5 billion in 2008–09, or 37.3% of UK GDP.[1] This is equivalent to roughly £10,900 for every

[1] All 2008–09 revenue figures in this chapter are 2008 Pre-Budget Report forecasts.

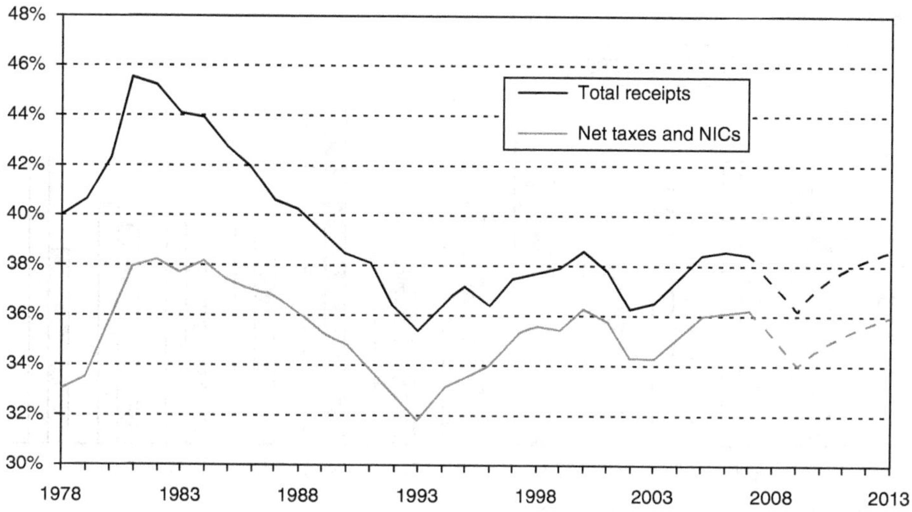

Notes: Years are fiscal years, so 2008 means 2008–09.

Sources: HM Treasury, Public Finances Databank (27 January 2009 version), <http://www.hm-treasury.gov.uk/psf_statistics.htm>.

Figure 1.1. The tax burden, % of GDP

adult in the UK, or £8,900 per person. Not all of this comes from taxes (or National Insurance (social security) contributions): net taxes and National Insurance contributions are forecast to raise £516.6 billion in 2008–09, with the remainder provided by surpluses of public-sector industries, rent from state-owned properties, and so on.

Figure 1.1 shows the development of total government revenues and tax revenues since 1978–79. Receipts rose sharply as a proportion of GDP from 1978–79 to 1981–82, fell steadily from the early 1980s until the mid-1990s, but have risen again since then, with a dip during the current recession forecast to be only temporary. The share of non-tax revenues fell substantially over the 1980s and 1990s as many public-sector industries were privatized, so that, although total receipts are now slightly lower than in 1978–79 as share of GDP, tax revenues are higher.

Figure 1.2 places this increase in tax revenue in an international context. Between 1978 and 2006, most other OECD countries also experienced an increase in their tax-to-GDP ratios, and the UK's increase was smaller than most. In 1978 the UK's tax-to-GDP ratio was about two percentage points higher than the OECD (unweighted) average while in 2006 it was about one point higher. The share of national income taken in tax in the UK in 2006 was below the EU15 (unweighted) average, but higher than in most of the

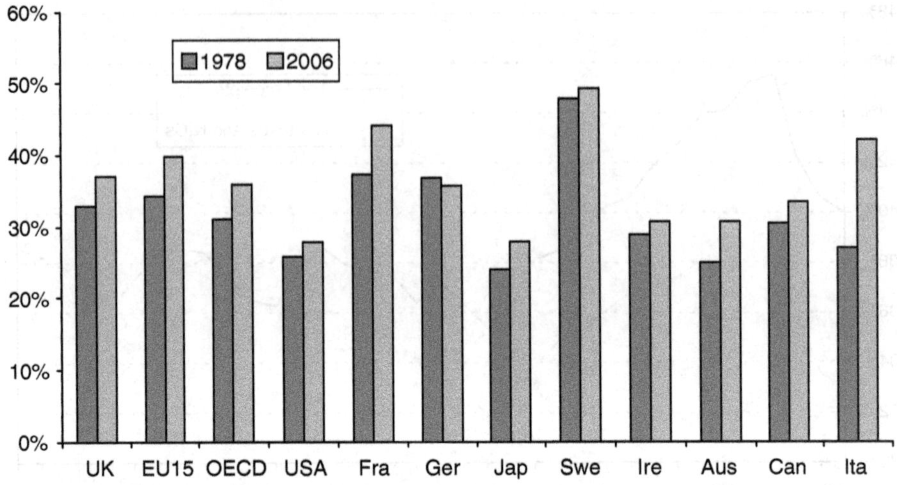

Notes: All taxes and compulsory social security contributions.
Sources: OECD (2008a).

Figure 1.2. Tax revenues as a share of GDP

new EU countries of eastern Europe and higher than in the USA, Japan, and Australia.[2]

Table 1.1 shows the composition of UK government revenue. Income tax, National Insurance contributions, and VAT are easily the largest sources of revenue for the government, together accounting for almost two-thirds of total tax revenue. Figure 1.3 summarizes how the composition of tax revenue has changed over the last thirty years. The biggest change has been a doubling of the share of tax revenue provided by VAT, with a reduction of similar size in the share of other indirect taxes (mainly excise duties). This follows a worldwide trend of moving from taxes on specific goods to general consumption taxes. Corporation tax revenues are highly cyclical but have increased overall as a proportion of the total, as have revenues from other capital taxes (principally stamp duties). Reliance on personal income

[2] All international averages in this chapter are unweighted unless otherwise stated. The EU15 countries are members of the EU prior to the 2004 expansion, namely Austria (abbreviated as Aut), Belgium (Bel), Denmark (Den), Finland (Fin), France (Fra), Germany (Ger), Greece (Gre), Ireland (Ire), Italy (Ita), Luxembourg (Lux), the Netherlands (Neth), Portugal (Por), Spain (Spa), Sweden (Swe), and the UK. The OECD countries included vary over time because OECD membership changed and figures are not always available for all countries. Other country abbreviations used are for Australia (Aus), New Zealand (NZ), Japan (Jap), the United States of America (USA), and Canada (Can).

Table 1.1. Sources of government revenue, 2008–09 forecasts

Source of revenue	Revenue (£ bn)	Proportion of tax revenue (%)
Income tax (gross of tax credits)	156.7	30.3
Tax credits counted as negative income tax by HM Treasury[a]	(−5.5)	(−1.1)
National Insurance contributions	97.7	18.9
Value added tax[b]	82.6	16.0
Other indirect taxes		
Fuel duties	25.1	4.9
Tobacco duties	8.2	1.6
Alcohol duties	8.5	1.6
Betting and gaming duties	1.5	0.3
Vehicle excise duty	5.8	1.1
Air passenger duty	1.9	0.4
Insurance premium tax	2.3	0.4
Landfill tax	0.9	0.2
Climate change levy	0.7	0.1
Aggregates levy	0.4	0.1
Customs duties and levies	2.6	0.5
Capital taxes		
Capital gains tax	4.9	0.9
Inheritance tax	3.1	0.6
Stamp duties	8.3	1.6
Company taxes		
Corporation tax	44.9	8.7
Petroleum revenue tax	2.6	0.5
Business rates	23.5	4.5
Council tax (net of council tax benefit)	24.6	4.8
Other taxes and royalties	15.7	3.0
Net taxes and National Insurance contributions	**516.6**	**100.0**
Interest and dividends	7.7	n/a
Gross operating surplus, rent, other receipts, and adjustments	21.1	n/a
Current receipts	**545.5**	**n/a**

[a] Most of the cost of tax credits is counted as government spending rather than a reduction in income tax revenue. See Appendix for details.

[b] Net of (i.e. after deducting) VAT refunds paid to other parts of central and local government: these are included in 'Other taxes and royalties'.

Note: Figures may not sum exactly to totals because of rounding.

Source: HM Treasury, Pre-Budget Report, 2008 <http://www.hm-treasury.gov.uk/d/pbr08_annexb_262.pdf>.

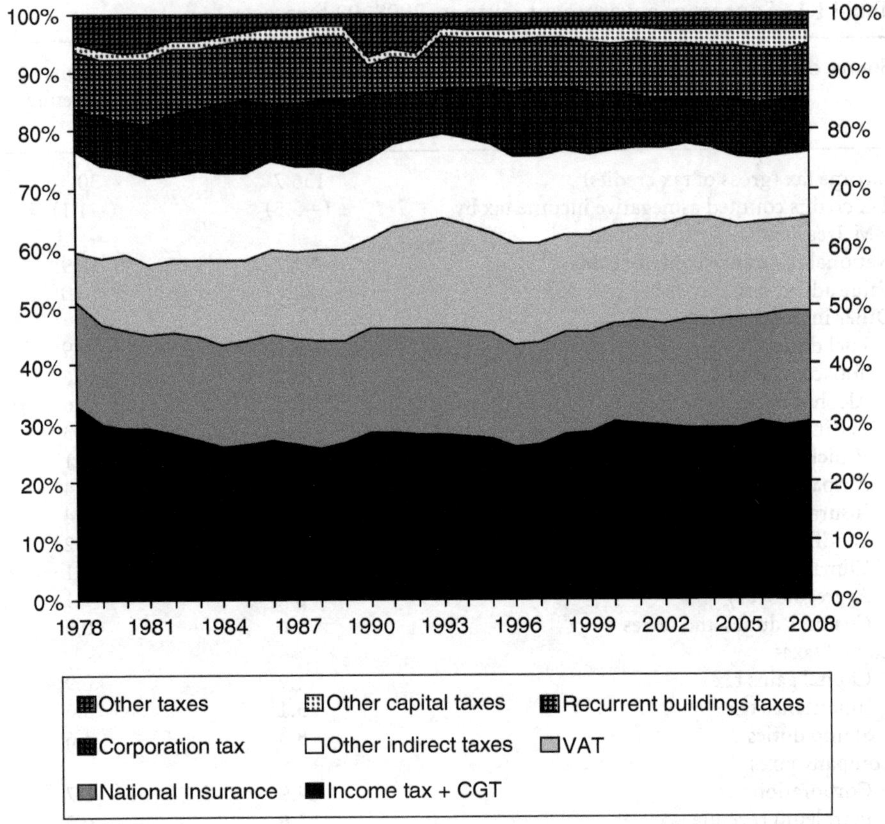

Notes: Net taxes and National Insurance contributions. Years are fiscal years, so 2008 means 2008–09. CGT = capital gains tax. 'National Insurance' excludes NI surcharge when it existed, and 'VAT' is net of refunds paid to other parts of central and local government: these are both included in 'other taxes'. 'Other indirect taxes' are excise duties, environmental taxes, and customs duties. 'Corporation tax' includes petroleum revenue tax, supplementary petroleum duty, and the 1997–98 windfall tax. 'Other capital taxes' are inheritance tax (and its predecessors) and stamp duties. Recurrent buildings taxes are council tax and (business and domestic) rates; the community charge is included in 'other taxes'.

Sources: HM Treasury: see <http://www.ifs.org.uk/ff/revenue_composition.xls>.

Figure 1.3. The composition of UK tax revenues, 1978–79 to 2008–09

taxes fell sharply in the late 1970s and early 1980s but they have since recovered their share. The replacement of domestic rates by the community charge (poll tax) dramatically reduced revenues from property taxes, but then the replacement in turn of the poll tax by council tax restored property's share.

Figure 1.4 compares the structure of tax revenues in the UK with that in other OECD countries. The UK particularly stands out with its relatively

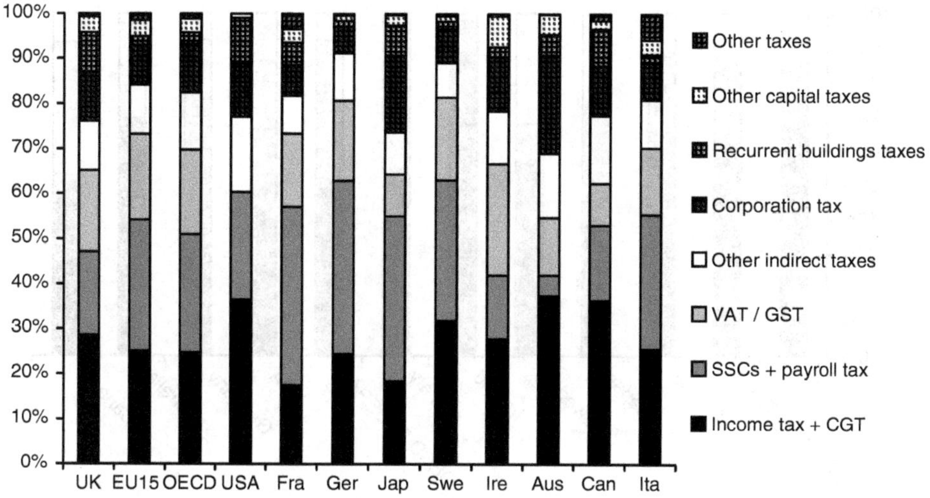

Notes: All taxes and social security contributions (SSCs). GST = General Sales Tax.
Sources: OECD (2008a).

Figure 1.4. The composition of tax revenues, 2006

low (but not lowest) share of social security contributions[3] and its relatively high share of recurrent taxes on buildings (although these are also relatively high in the USA, Japan, and Canada). It is also somewhat above average in the share of personal income tax, but several countries have even higher shares.

Figure 1.5 compares the distribution of revenues by levels of government in the UK to the averages of OECD unitary countries and OECD federal countries, and a selection of individual unitary and federal countries.[4] This comparison shows that the UK has a particularly large share of revenue going to central government, a share that is exceeded only by Ireland. This is reflected in the fact that UK local authorities are particularly dependent on grants from central government rather than tax revenues of their own.

[3] This category also includes payroll taxes (which do not give entitlement to contributory benefits) for those few countries that have them. The most significant example in this set of countries is Australia, which does not have social security contributions but does levy payroll taxes.

[4] This figure attributes revenue to levels of government on the basis of their legal entitlement to the revenue rather than their control over the tax rate (or base). Thus the state level of government in both Germany and Australia receives a substantial part of their revenues from taxes whose rates are set at national level (although in consultation with state governments). In contrast, UK business rates are not classed as local because central government has complete discretion as to how the revenue is allocated.

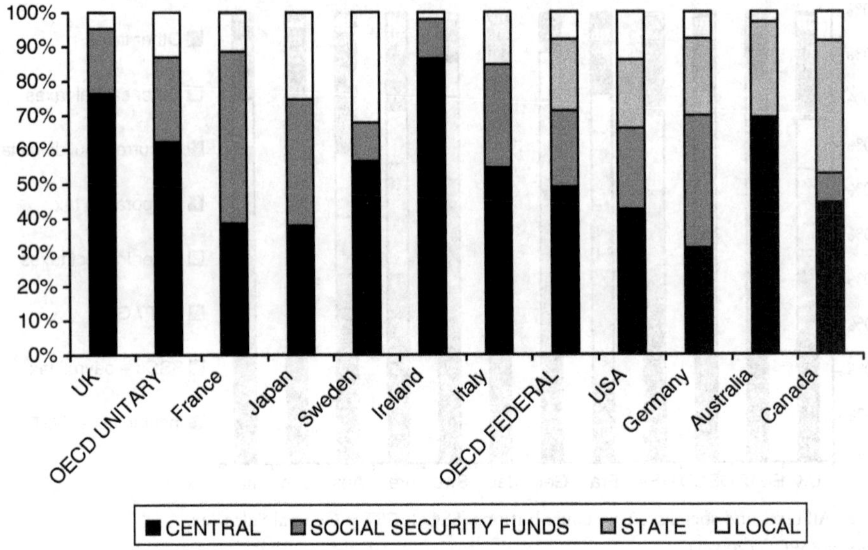

Sources: OECD (2008a).

Figure 1.5. Tax revenues by level of government, 2006

1.3. DEVELOPMENT OF THE MAJOR TAXES SINCE 1978

Table 1.2 lists some of the most important changes in the UK tax system seen since 1978.[5] It is clear that the tax system is now very different from the one that existed then. The income tax rate structure has been transformed, the taxation of saving has been repeatedly adjusted, the National Insurance contributions system has been overhauled, the main VAT rate has more than doubled, some excise duty rates have risen sharply while others have fallen, the corporate income tax system has been subject to numerous reforms, and local taxation is unrecognizable. Figure 1.3 and the associated discussion in Section 1.2 show how these changes have been reflected in the composition of aggregate government revenue (although there have been other factors that have played a part, such as the effect of property and stock markets on stamp duty revenues).

[5] For a timeline of the main tax changes announced in each Budget and Pre-Budget Report since 1979, see <http://www.ifs.org.uk/ff/budget_measures.xls>.

Table 1.2. Summary of main reforms, 1978–2008

Income tax	Basic rate cut from 33% to 20% Top rate 98% (unearned income), 83% (earnings) cut to 40% Starting rate abolished, re-introduced and abolished again Independent taxation introduced Married couple's allowance abolished Children's tax credit and working families' tax credit introduced, then abolished Child tax credit and working tax credit introduced Mortgage interest tax relief abolished Life assurance premium relief abolished PEP, TESSA, and ISA introduced*
National Insurance	Employee contribution rate increased from 6.5% to 11% Ceiling abolished for employer contributions Ceiling for employees raised and contributions extended beyond it 'Entry rate' abolished and floor aligned with income tax allowance Imposition of NI on benefits in kind
VAT	Higher rate of 12.5% abolished Standard rate increased from 8% to 17.5% Reduced rate introduced for domestic fuel and a few other goods
Other indirect taxes	Large real increase in duties on road fuels and tobacco Real decrease in duties on wine and spirits, little change for beer Air passenger duty, landfill tax, climate change levy, and aggregates levy introduced
Capital taxes	Introduction and abolition of indexation allowance and then taper relief for capital gains Capital gains tax rates aligned with income tax rates then returned to flat rate Capital transfer tax replaced by inheritance tax Graduated rates of stamp duty on properties abolished then reintroduced Stamp duty on shares and bonds cut from 2% to 0.5%
Corporation tax	Main rate cut from 52% to 28% Small companies' rate cut from 42% to 21% Lower rate introduced, cut to 0%, then abolished R&D tax credits introduced 100% first-year allowance replaced by 20% writing-down allowance Advance corporation tax and refundable dividend tax credit abolished
Local taxes	Domestic rates replaced by council tax (via poll tax) Locally varying business rates replaced by national business rates

* PEP = Personal Equity Plan; TESSA = Tax-Exempt Special Savings Account; ISA = Individual Savings Account.

1.3.1. Personal income taxes

There are two principal personal income taxes in the UK: income tax and National Insurance contributions. Capital gains tax, which has existed as a tax separate from income tax since 1965, can also be thought of as a tax on personal income, but it supplies very little revenue compared with income tax or National Insurance.

Income tax rate structure

The most dramatic change to income tax has been the reform of the rate structure, as illustrated in Table 1.3. In 1978–79 there was a starting rate of 25%, a basic rate of 33%, and higher rates ranging from 40% to 83%. In addition, an investment income surcharge of 15% was applied to those with very high investment income, resulting in a maximum income tax rate of 98%. In its first Budget, in 1979, the Conservative government reduced the

Table 1.3. Income tax rates on earned income, 1978–79 to 2008–09

Year	Starting rate	Basic rate	Higher rates
1978–79	25	33	40–83
1979–80	25	30	40–60
1980–81 to 1985–86	—	30	40–60
1986–87	—	29	40–60
1987–88	—	27	40–60
1988–89 to 1991–92	—	25	40
1992–93 to 1995–96	20	25	40
1996–97	20	24	40
1997–98 to 1998–99	20	23	40
1999–2000	10	23	40
2000–01 to 2007–08	10	22	40
2008–09	—	20	40

Notes: Prior to 1984–85, an investment income surcharge of 15% applied to unearned income over £2,250 (1978–79), £5,000 (1979–80), £5,500 (1980–82), £6,250 (1982–83), and £7,100 (1983–84). Different tax rates have applied to dividends since 1993–94 and to savings income since 1996–97. The basic rate of tax on savings income has been 20% since 1996–97, and the 10% starting rate which was largely abolished in 2008–09 continues to apply to savings income that falls into the first £2,320 of taxable income. The basic rate of tax on dividends was 20% from 1993–94 to 1998–99 and has been 10% since 1999–2000, when the higher rate of tax on dividends became 32.5%. However, an offsetting dividend tax credit means that the effective tax rates on dividends have been constant at zero (basic rate) and 25% (higher rate) since 1993–94. When calculating which tax band different income sources fall into, dividend income is treated as the top slice of income, followed by savings income, followed by other income.

Sources: *Tolley's Income Tax*, various years.

basic rate of income tax to 30% and the top rate on earnings to 60%. In 1980 the starting rate was abolished; in 1984 the investment income surcharge was abolished; and through the mid-1980s, the basic rate of tax was reduced. In 1988 the top rate of tax was cut to 40% and the basic rate to 25%, producing a very simple regime with three effective rates—zero up to the personal allowance, 25% over a range that covered almost 95% of taxpayers, and 40% for a small group of those with high incomes. The sharp reduction in top rates in 1979 was the start of an international trend, while the continued reductions in the basic rate are also part of an international trend.

This very simple rate structure was complicated by the reintroduction of a 20% starting rate of tax in 1992 (in a pre-election Budget), cut to 10% in 1999 (fulfilling a pre-election promise made by the Labour Party). Budget 2007 announced the abolition again of the starting rate from 2008–09 to pay for a cut in the basic rate, though as a simplification this was limited by the decision to keep the starting rate in place for savings income. The abolition of the starting rate proved highly controversial because many low-income families lost out (although many more potential losers were protected by other reforms announced at the same time). As a result, the government announced in May 2008 that it would increase the tax-free personal allowance by £600, compensating most of those losing from the reform.[6]

The 2008 Pre-Budget Report announced a considerable complication of the income tax rate structure for those on the highest incomes. From 2010–11, the personal allowance will be withdrawn in two stages from those with incomes greater than £100,000, creating two short bands of income in which tax liability will increase by 60 pence for each additional pound of income; and from 2011–12, incomes above £150,000 will be taxed at a rate of 45%.[7]

The income levels to which the various tax rates apply have changed significantly over the period as a whole. The basic-rate limit, beyond which higher-rate tax becomes due, has failed to keep pace with price inflation, while the personal allowance has risen in real terms. The overall effect of rate, allowance and threshold changes on the shape of the income tax schedule is shown in Figure 1.6, with 1978–79 values expressed in 2008 prices for ease of comparison.

Table 1.4 gives the numbers of people affected by the different tax rates. In 2008–09, out of an adult population in the UK of almost 50 million, an

[6] The basic-rate limit was correspondingly reduced to eliminate any gain from the increased personal allowance for higher-rate taxpayers. The personal allowance was increased only for under-65s: an increase in the allowances for those aged 65 and over was part of the original package announced in Budget 2007. For analysis of these reforms, see Adam et al. (2008).

[7] Browne (2009) discusses these proposals.

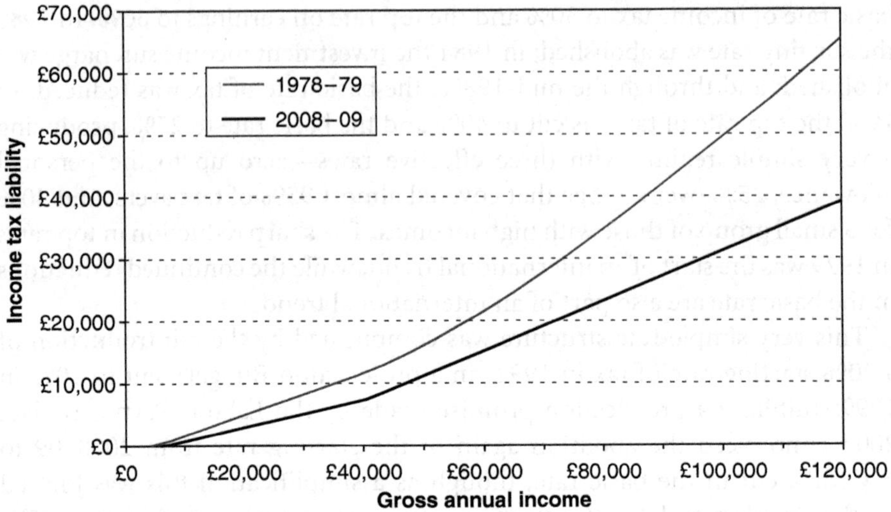

Notes: 1978–79 thresholds have been uprated to April 2008 prices using the Retail Prices Index. Assumes individual is aged under 65, unmarried, and without children.

Sources: HM Treasury, *Financial Statement and Budget Report*, various years; *Tolley's Income Tax*, various years; National Statistics, <http://www.statistics.gov.uk>.

Figure 1.6. Income tax schedule for earned income, 1978–79 and 2008–09

Table 1.4. Numbers liable for income tax (thousands)

Year	Number of individuals paying tax	Number of starting-rate taxpayers	Number of basic-rate taxpayers[a]	Number of higher-rate taxpayers
1978–79	25,900	—[b]	25,137[b]	763
1990–91	26,100	—	24,400	1,700
2000–01	29,300	2,820	23,610	2,880
2007–08[c]	31,900	3,190	24,860	3,870
2008–09[c]	30,600	348[d]	26,710	3,640

[a] Includes those whose only income above the starting-rate limit is from either savings or dividends.

[b] Basic-rate figure for 1979–80 covers both starting-rate and basic-rate taxpayers.

[c] Projected.

[d] From 2008–09 the starting rate applies only to savings income that is below the starting-rate limit when counted as the top slice of taxable income (except dividends).

Sources: HM Revenue and Customs, <http://www.hmrc.gov.uk/stats/income_tax/table2-1.pdf> and table 2.1 of *Inland Revenue Statistics 1994*.

Table 1.5. Shares of total income tax liability (%)

Year	Top 1% of income taxpayers	Top 10% of income taxpayers	Top 50% of income taxpayers
1978–79	11	35	82
1990–91	15	42	85
2000–01	22	52	89
2007–08[a]	23	53	90
2008–09[a]	23	53	89

[a] Projected.

Sources: HMRC Statistics <http://www.hmrc.gov.uk/stats/income_tax/table2-4.pdf> and table 2.3 of *Inland Revenue Statistics 1994*.

estimated 30.6 million individuals are liable for income tax. This is a reminder that attempts to use income tax reductions to help the poorest in the country are likely to fail, since less than two-thirds of the adult population have high enough incomes to pay income tax at all.[8] The total number of income taxpayers has increased slowly over the years, while the number of higher-rate taxpayers has grown much more quickly, from around 3% of taxpayers in 1978–79 to around 12% in 2008–09. Some of this growth reflects periods when the threshold above which higher-rate tax is due has not been raised in line with price inflation, some reflects the fact that incomes on average have grown more quickly than prices, and some the fact that the dispersion of incomes has grown, with especially rapid increases in the incomes of those already towards the top of the income distribution, pushing more of them into higher-rate income tax liability.

Although only 12% of income taxpayers face the higher rate, that group is expected to contribute 56% of total income tax revenue in 2008–09.[9] Table 1.5 shows that the top 10% of income taxpayers now pay over half of all the income tax paid, and the top 1% pay 23% of all that is paid. These shares have risen substantially since 1978–79, despite reductions in the higher rates.

Figure 1.7 shows the 2007 income tax burden on single workers at 67%, 100%, and 167% of average full-time earnings in the UK in comparison with other OECD countries. This shows that the UK imposed a relatively high income tax burden on low-paid workers, substantially higher than both the EU15 and OECD averages. The progressivity of the income tax system—as

[8] We might be more interested in the proportion of adults that live in a family containing a taxpayer. Authors' calculations using the IFS tax and benefit model, TAXBEN, run on data from the Family Resources Survey, suggest that this figure stood at 76% for the UK in 2006–07 (the latest year for which data are available): most non-taxpaying adults do not have a taxpayer in the family.

[9] Source: HM Revenue and Customs Statistics Table 2.5 <http://www.hmrc.gov.uk/stats/income_tax/table2_5.pdf>.

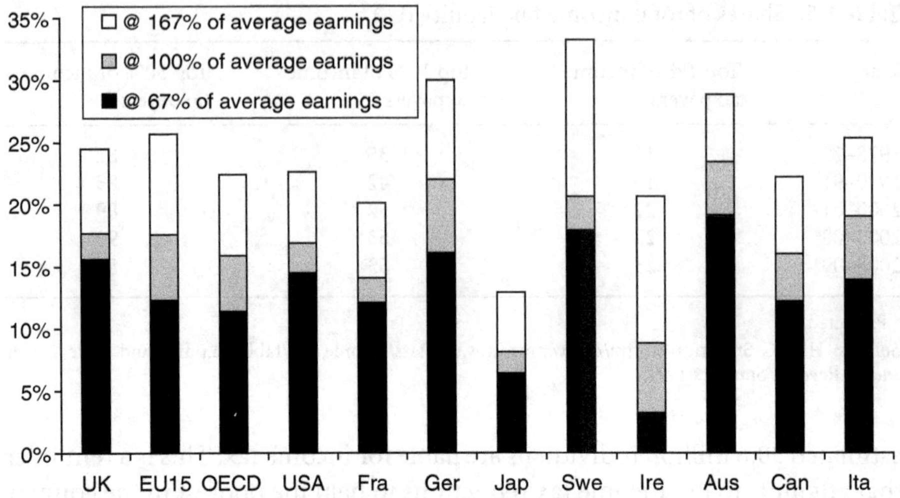

Notes: Income tax due is calculated for a single worker without dependents and expressed as a percentage of earnings. 'Average earnings' are the mean earnings of full-time workers in industries C to K of the International Standard Industrial Classification. For more detail, see OECD (2008b).

Sources: OECD (2008b).

Figure 1.7. The income tax burden for a single worker, 2007

shown by the extra burden on average and above-average earners—was less than average for the OECD and, especially, for the EU15.

The treatment of families

Prior to 1990, married couples were treated as a single unit for income tax purposes. The 1970 Income and Corporation Taxes Act (in)famously announced that, for the purposes of income tax, 'a woman's income chargeable to tax shall . . . be deemed to be her husband's income and not her income'. Reflecting the 'responsibilities' taken on at marriage, the tax system also included a married man's allowance (MMA). The system was widely felt to be unpalatable and a consensus emerged that a new system, neutral in its treatment of men and women, should be introduced. The new system introduced in 1990 was based on the principle of independent taxation of husbands and wives, but included a married couple's allowance (MCA), which was available to either husband or wife. This established equal treatment of men and women, but not of married and unmarried people. In fact, married and unmarried people with children had been treated equally since 1973 through the additional personal allowance (APA), an allowance for unmarried people with children which was set equal to the

MMA and then the MCA; but unequal treatment persisted for those without children.

Between 1993 and 2000, the MCA and APA were reduced in value, and they were eventually abolished in April 2000 (except the MCA for people aged 65 or over at that date). A year later, children's tax credit was introduced, reducing the tax liability of those with children by a flat-rate amount (gradually withdrawn from higher-rate taxpayers) but making no distinction between married and unmarried people. Meanwhile, in-work support for low-paid families with children was brought within the tax system when working families' tax credit (WFTC) replaced family credit from October 1999.[10] Children's tax credit and WFTC (along with parts of some state benefits) were replaced in April 2003 by child tax credit and working tax credit. Child tax credit provides support for low-income families with children irrespective of work status, while working tax credit provides support for low-income families in work whether or not they have children; but neither depends on marriage. In short, over the past twenty years, the UK income tax has moved away from providing support for marriage and towards providing support for children.

National Insurance contributions

National Insurance (social security) contributions (NICs) originated as (typically) weekly lump-sum payments by employers and employees to cover the cost of certain social security benefits—in particular, the flat-rate pension, unemployment benefits, and sickness benefits. Since 1961, however, National Insurance has steadily moved towards being simply another income tax. The link between the amount contributed and benefit entitlement, which was once close, has now almost entirely gone, and substantial progress has been made in aligning the NICs rate structure and tax base with those of income tax. Most of this has occurred in the last twenty-five years.

Figure 1.8 shows the structure of combined employee and employer NICs in 1978–79 and 2008–09, all expressed in 2008 prices.

In 1978–79, no NICs were due for those earning less than the lower earnings limit (LEL). For those earning at least this amount, employees paid contributions of 6.5% and employers 12% of total employee earnings, including earnings below the LEL. This meant a jump in contributions at the LEL (the 'entry rate'), and it is not surprising that this discontinuity led to significant

[10] For more information on these two programmes, see Dilnot and McCrae (1999).

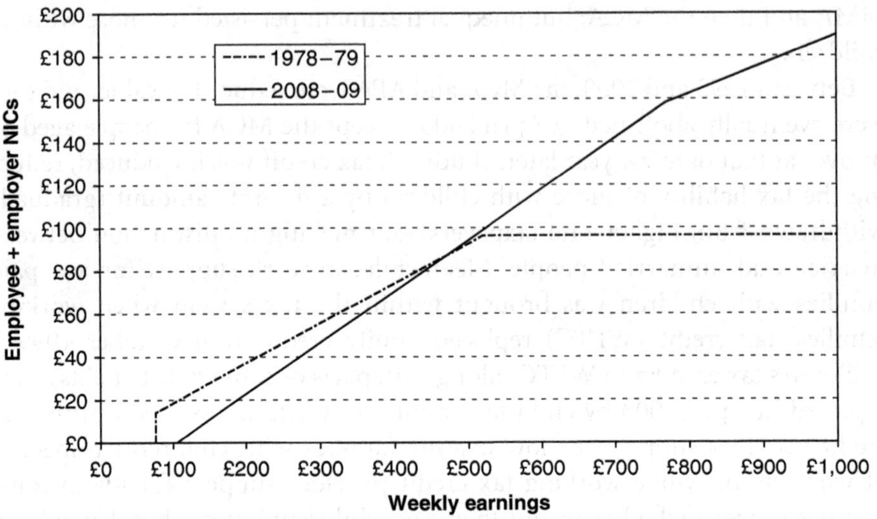

Notes: 1978–79 thresholds have been uprated to April 2008 prices using the Retail Prices Index. Assumes employee contracted into State Earnings-Related Pension Scheme (SERPS) or State Second Pension (S2P). The 1978–79 schedule includes National Insurance surcharge at a rate of 2%, the rate that applied from April to October 1978.

Sources: *Tolley's National Insurance Contributions*, 1989–90 and 2008–09; National Statistics, <http://www.statistics.gov.uk>.

Figure 1.8. National Insurance contributions schedule, 1978–79 and 2008–09

bunching of earnings just below the LEL. No NICs were payable on earnings above the upper earnings limit (UEL).

This rate schedule was substantially changed in 1985: the UEL was abolished for employers, and the single large jump in NICs at the LEL was replaced with a number of graduated steps instead. Subsequent reforms have continued in the same direction. The UEL is still in place for employees, but no longer acts as a complete cap on contributions: a one percentage point rise in NIC rates in April 2003 extended employee NICs to earnings above the UEL. The entry rate was phased out altogether and the graduated steps removed, so that since April 1999 the earnings threshold in NICs has operated in a similar way to the income tax personal allowance, essentially being discounted from taxable income. Furthermore, the earnings threshold for employers (from 1999) and employees (from 2001) were aligned with the income tax personal allowance, and the 2007 Budget announced that the UEL would be aligned with the higher-rate income tax threshold from April 2009.[11]

[11] The increase in the personal allowance announced in May 2008 (see p. 13) decoupled it from the NI earnings threshold. The earnings threshold for employees is due to be realigned with the

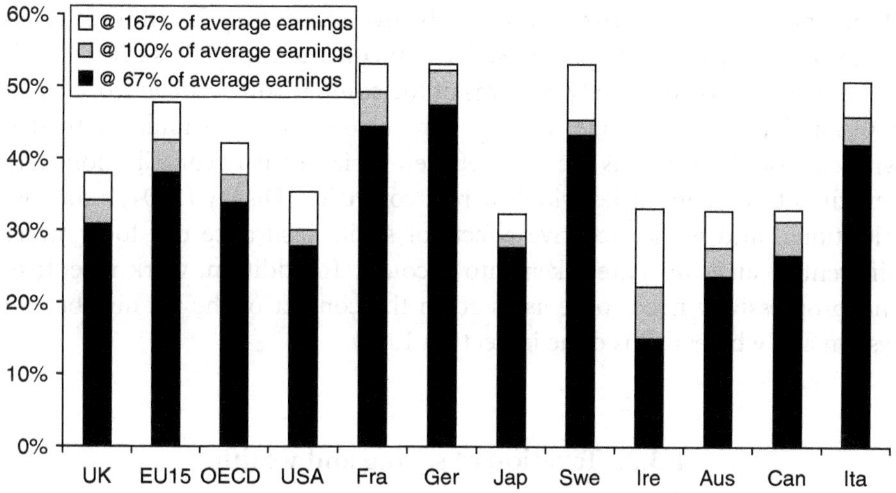

Notes: Income tax plus employee and employer social security contributions due are calculated for a single worker without dependents and expressed as a percentage of earnings plus employer social security contributions. 'Average earnings' are the mean earnings of full-time workers in industries C to K of the International Standard Industrial Classification. For more detail, see OECD (2008b).

Sources: OECD (2008b).

Figure 1.9. The burden of income tax and SSCs for a single worker, 2007

The abolition of the entry rate, the alignment of thresholds with those for income tax and the abolition of the cap on contributions have made NI look more like income tax. Important differences remain: in particular, the self-employed face a very different, and much less onerous, National Insurance system (see the Appendix). NICs are also charged on a different base: it is a tax on earnings only, whereas income tax is levied on a broader definition of income. However, the NICs base has expanded to match the income tax base more closely; this can be seen, for example, in the extension of NICs to cover benefits in kind.

Economically, there is little rationale for having separate income tax and NI systems in the UK given how weak the link is between the amount contributed and the benefits received. There is a strong argument for either merging income tax and National Insurance into a single system (as in Australia and New Zealand) or strengthening the link between contributions and benefits.

Figure 1.9 shows that the addition of employee and employer social security contributions to income taxes has a considerable effect on the UK's relative tax burden on labour. In contrast to Figure 1.7, which showed income tax

personal allowance from 2011–12, although as yet there are no equivalent plans for the employers' earnings threshold. For more on this, see Browne (2009).

alone, the UK now appears as a relatively low tax country for all three levels of earnings. However, the progressivity of income tax and NICs combined is still unusually low, especially in terms of the comparison between workers on 100% and 167% of average earnings. These comparisons should be treated with caution, however, as the link between social security contributions and benefit entitlements varies widely across countries (Disney (2004)): the distributional and work incentive effects of social insurance can look rather different if such links are taken into account. In addition, work incentives and progressivity need to be assessed in the context of the tax and benefit system as a whole: this is done in Section 1.4.

1.3.2. Taxation of saving and wealth

The income tax treatment of saving has changed significantly over the last thirty years. The radical reforms to the rate structure of income tax, reducing the top marginal rate on savings income from 98% to 40%, are discussed above. But there have also been major changes to the tax treatment of different savings vehicles, with some forms of savings becoming more generously treated and some less so.

The two most significant changes widening the base of income tax have been the abolition of life assurance premium relief in 1984, which had given income tax relief on saving in the form of life assurance, and the steady reduction and final abolition of mortgage interest tax relief (MITR). Until 1974, MITR had been available on any size of loan, but in that year a ceiling of £25,000 was imposed. In 1983, this ceiling was increased to £30,000, which was not enough to account for general price inflation and much too little to account for house price inflation. From 1983, the ceiling remained constant, steadily reducing its real value. From 1991, this erosion of the real value of MITR was accelerated by restricting the tax rate at which relief could be claimed, to the basic rate of tax in 1991 (25%), 20% in 1994, 15% in 1995, and 10% in 1998, with the eventual abolition of the relief in April 2000.

The main extension of relatively tax-favoured saving came in 1988 with the introduction of personal pensions, which allowed the same tax treatment for individual-based pensions as had been available for employer-based occupational pensions (tax relief on contributions, no tax on fund income, tax on withdrawals apart from a lump sum not exceeding 25% of the accumulated fund). The other main extensions were the Personal Equity Plan (PEP) and the Tax-Exempt Special Savings Account (TESSA), introduced in 1987 and 1991 respectively. The PEP was originally a vehicle for direct holding of equities, but it was reformed to allow holdings of pooled investments such as unit trusts. The TESSA was a vehicle for holding interest-bearing savings accounts. Both PEP and TESSA benefited from almost the reverse tax treatment to that of pensions: saving into a PEP or TESSA was not given any tax relief, there was no tax on income or gains within the fund and there was no tax on withdrawals. The PEP and TESSA have now been superseded by the Individual Savings Account (ISA), which is similar in most important respects.

For those (very few) who can and wish to save more than £7,200 per annum (the current ISA limit) in addition to any housing or pension saving, capital gains tax (CGT) is potentially relevant. Prior to 1982, CGT was charged at a flat rate of 30% on capital gains taking no account of inflation. Indexation for inflation was introduced in 1982 and amended in 1985, and then in 1988 the flat rate of tax of 30% was replaced by the individual's marginal income tax rate. The 1998 Budget reformed the CGT system, removing indexation for future years and introducing a taper system which reduced the taxable gain for longer-held assets by up to 75%, depending on the type of asset. The taper system created predictable distortions and complexity, and the 2007 Pre-Budget Report announced the abolition of both tapering and indexation from April 2008 and a return to a system like that before 1982, in which gains are taxed at a flat rate, now 18%, with no allowance for inflation.[12]

Capital is taxed not only directly by taxes levied on investment income and capital gains, but also by stamp duty on transactions of securities and properties, and by inheritance tax on bequests.[13] The current form of inheritance tax was introduced in 1986 to replace capital transfer tax. When capital transfer tax had replaced estate duty eleven years earlier, gifts made during the donor's lifetime had become taxable in the same way as bequests. But differences in treatment were soon introduced and then widened, until finally the new inheritance tax once again exempted lifetime gifts except in the seven years before death, for which a sliding scale was introduced (see Appendix) in an attempt to prevent people avoiding the tax by giving away their assets shortly before death.

With all of these capital taxes, the 1980s saw moves to reduce the number of rates and/or align them with income tax rates. Thus in 1978 capital transfer tax had no fewer than fourteen separate rates; since 1988 its successor,

[12] The announcement in the 2007 Pre-Budget Report met with an angry reaction from business organizations, and entrepreneurs' relief (described in the Appendix) was introduced as a concession. These reforms are discussed in Adam (2008).

[13] Corporation tax is also relevant for capital invested in companies, and council tax or business rates for capital invested in property. These taxes are discussed in Sections 1.3.3 and 1.3.5 respectively.

inheritance tax, has been charged (above a tax-free threshold) at a single 40% rate, equal to the higher rate of income tax. As mentioned above, capital gains tax was charged at the individual's marginal income tax rate from 1988. Four rates of stamp duty on properties were replaced by a single 1% rate in 1984. Stamp duty on shares and bonds was almost abolished entirely: the rate fell from 2% to 0.5% during the 1980s, and in 1990 the then Chancellor, John Major, announced that stamp duty on shares and bonds would be abolished in 1991–92 when the London Stock Exchange introduced a paperless dealing system known as TAURUS. However, this system was never introduced and stamp duty on shares and bonds remained.

Labour's first Budget following their election in 1997 announced the reintroduction of graduated rates of stamp duty on properties, and these rates were increased in the next three Budgets so that the rates of stamp duty land tax (as it has been known since 2003) are now 1%, 3%, and 4%. However, what did most to bring stamp duty land tax, along with inheritance tax, to public attention was rapid growth in house prices. From 1997 to 2005, house price inflation averaged more than 10% a year, far outstripping both the inheritance tax threshold (which has typically increased in line with general price inflation) and the stamp duty zero-rate threshold (which has typically been frozen in cash terms).

Table 1.6 illustrates the implications of this. When Labour came to power in 1997, around half of property transactions attracted stamp duty; over the following six years this rose to almost three-quarters as house prices doubled while the stamp duty threshold was unchanged. The link between house prices and inheritance tax is less direct, but since housing makes up about half of total household wealth, house prices are clearly an important determinant of how many estates are affected by inheritance tax. A widely reported concern was that rising house prices were making inheritance tax into a tax on 'ordinary people' instead of only on the very wealthy. However, although the proportion of death estates liable for inheritance tax more than doubled in a decade—increasing from 2.3% of the total in 1996–97 to 5.9% in 2006–07—it remained small. And recently two factors have counteracted the spread of stamp duty and inheritance tax. One is policy reforms: in April 2005 the stamp duty land tax threshold was doubled (then increased by a further £50,000 for one year only from 3 September 2008), and in October 2007 unused inheritance tax nil-rate bands became transferable to a surviving spouse or civil partner, reducing the number of estates liable to tax by a third and removing the threat of future inheritance tax for many couples. The other is that property prices have fallen substantially from their autumn 2007 peak.

Table 1.6. Stamp duty, inheritance tax and house prices

Year[a]	Average house price[b] (£)	Inheritance tax threshold (£)	Stamp duty (land tax) zero-rate threshold[c] (£)	Death estates liable for inheritance tax (%)	Property transactions liable for stamp duty[d] (%)
1993	62,333	140,000	60,000	2.7	42
1994	64,787	150,000	60,000	3.0	43
1995	65,644	154,000	60,000	3.1	43
1996	70,626	200,000	60,000	2.3	45
1997	76,103	215,000	60,000	2.6	49
1998	81,774	223,000	60,000	2.8	53
1999	92,521	231,000	60,000	3.2	58
2000	101,550	234,000	60,000	3.7	62
2001	112,835	242,000	60,000	3.8	69
2002	128,265	250,000	60,000	4.5	73
2003	155,627	255,000	60,000	4.9	73
2004	180,248	263,000	60,000	5.4	71
2005	190,760	275,000	120,000	5.7	55
2006	204,813	285,000	125,000	5.9	59
2007	223,405	300,000	125,000	4.9	61

[a] Years are fiscal years (so 1993 means 1993–94) except average house prices, which are for calendar years.

[b] Simple average, not mix-adjusted, so changes reflect changes in the types of property bought as well as changes in the price of a given type of property.

[c] Threshold for residential properties not in disadvantaged areas.

[d] Excludes Scotland. Other columns are UK-wide.

Sources: Average house prices from Communities and Local Government Housing Statistics Table 503 <http://www.communities.gov.uk/housing/housingresearch/housingstatistics/housingstatisticsby/housingmarket/livetables/>; thresholds and numbers of taxpayers from HMRC Statistics Tables A.8, A.9, 1.4, and 16.5 <http://www.hmrc.gov.uk/stats/>; total number of registered deaths from Monthly Digest of Statistics Table 2.4 <http://www.statistics.gov.uk>.

1.3.3. Taxation of company profits

Figure 1.10 charts the evolution of statutory rates of corporation tax in the UK, showing a pattern of decline that is common amongst OECD countries.

In the eighteen years of Conservative government prior to 1997, the biggest reform to corporation tax was the 1984 Budget. This announced a series of cuts in the main corporation tax rate, taking it from 52% to 35% (further reduced to 33% by 1991–92), and a very generous system of deductions for capital investment (100% of investment in plant and machinery could be deducted from taxable profits in the year the investment was made) was replaced by a less generous one (25% of the remaining value each year for plant and machinery). The 1984 reform was intended to be broadly revenue-neutral.

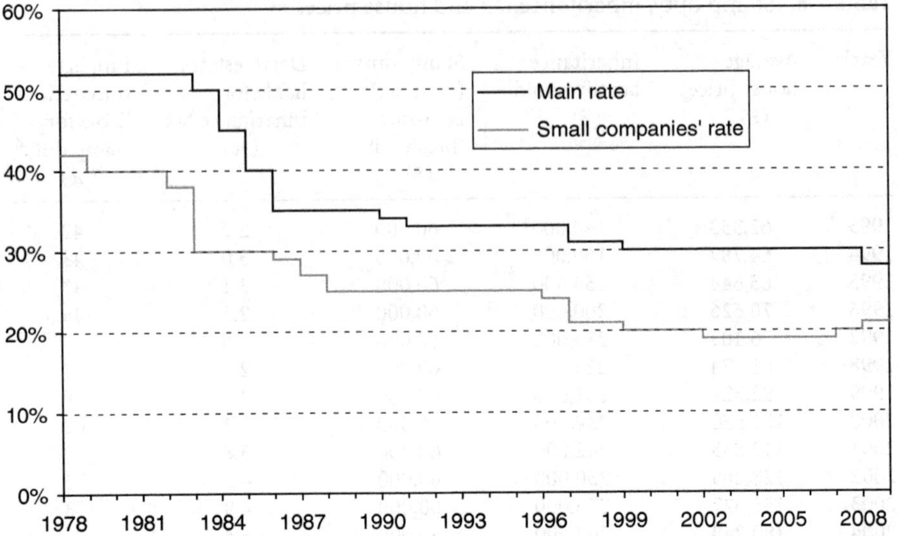

Notes: Years are fiscal years, so 2008 means 2008–09. Small companies' rate applies to companies with profits below a certain threshold, currently £300,000, with a system of relief (described in the Appendix) between that and a higher threshold, currently £1,500,000, above which the main rate applies. From 2000–01 to 2005–06 a lower rate applied to companies with profits below £10,000, as described in the text.

Sources: HMRC, <http://www.hmrc.gov.uk/stats/corporate_tax/rates-of-tax.pdf>.

Figure 1.10. Corporation tax rates

The taxation of company profits changed significantly after 1997. The incoming Labour government changed the way that dividend income was taxed: dividend tax credits, a deduction from income tax given to reflect the corporation tax already paid on the profits being distributed, ceased to be payable to certain shareholders (notably pension funds) that were already exempt from income tax. This was followed in 1999 with a reform of the payments system for corporation tax (see Appendix). In its first five years in office, the Labour government also cut the main corporation tax rate from 33% to 30% and the small companies' rate from 24% to 19%.[14] The 2007 Budget cut the main rate further to 28% and reduced capital allowances for most plant and machinery from 25% to 20%; but at the same time it departed from the previous trend by announcing that the small companies' rate would rise in stages from 19% to 22% and that the first £50,000 per year of investment in plant and machinery would be immediately deductible from profits. Figure 1.11 provides a comparison of the rates of corporate and

[14] Despite its name, the small companies' rate applies not to companies that are small in a conventional sense, but to those with profits below a particular threshold. The threshold has been set at £300,000 since 1994–95, up from £60,000 in 1978–79.

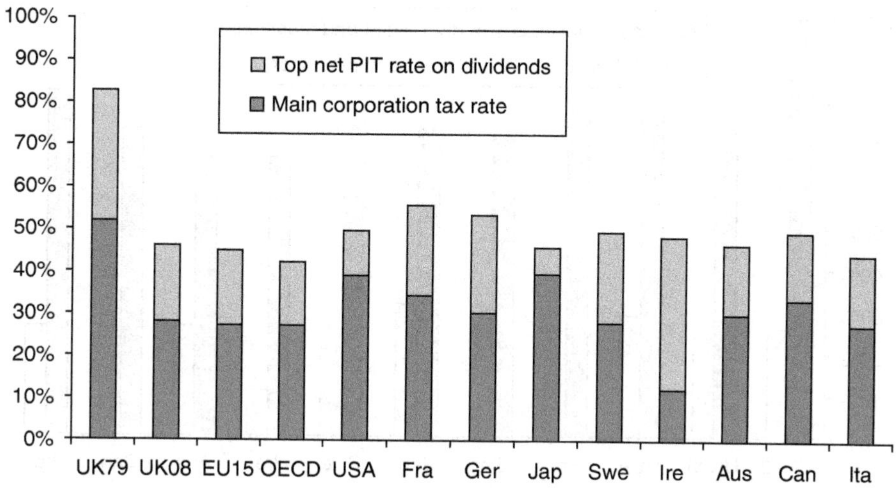

Notes: The calculation is made for dividends paid by a resident company to a resident personal shareholder who is subject to the top marginal income tax rate. It includes the corporation tax paid on the underlying profits and the personal income tax on the dividends, taking account of dividend tax credits or equivalent relief.

Sources: OECD Tax Database: <http://www.oecd.org/ctp/taxdatabase>.

Figure 1.11. Taxation of companies and shareholders, 2008

shareholder taxes in the UK with those in other OECD countries, as well as showing the cuts in the UK since 1979. The bottom part of each bar shows the main corporation tax rate, while the top part shows the additional tax (net of dividend tax credit or equivalent relief) paid by a shareholder resident in the same country who pays the top rate of personal income tax. The UK reduction since 1979 is dramatic, reflecting both the cut in corporation tax rates and the very substantial cuts in the top rate of personal income tax.[15] The UK corporation tax rate is slightly above the OECD and EU15 averages but below the rates in the other G7 countries except Italy. This comparison remains true when shareholder taxes are added, except that the UK's rate is then higher than Japan's.

Of course, corporation tax revenue depends on the base as well as the rate. Figure 1.12 shows the present discounted value[16] of capital allowances for depreciation, the principal deduction from the corporate tax base. It also reports the effective average tax rate (EATR), which combines statutory rates of corporation tax with the deductions from the tax base to estimate (under certain assumptions) the proportion of profits (net of assumed true economic

[15] The fall would be even more dramatic if the comparison were made with 1978, as the personal income tax on dividends was even higher then than in 1979.

[16] This is the sum of future amounts, but reduced to take account of the fact that income in future years is less valuable than current income, as reflected in the interest rate that saved income earns.

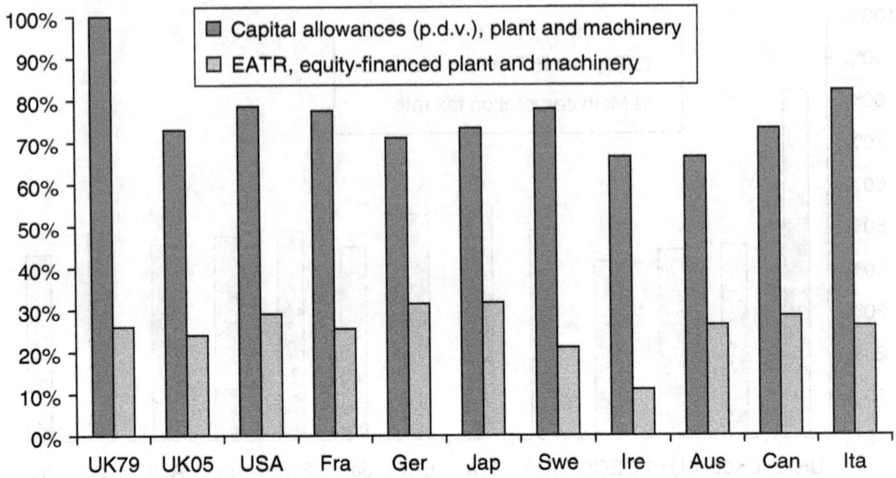

Notes: Corporation tax only. Assumes economic depreciation rate of 12.25%, inflation of 3.5%, real interest rate of 10%, and expected rate of economic profit of 10% (implying a financial return of 20%).

Sources: Tables A2 and A9 of IFS corporate tax rate data <http://www.ifs.org.uk/publications.php?publication_id=3210>.

Figure 1.12. Capital allowances and effective average tax rates, 2005

depreciation) that a company can expect to pay in corporate taxes. This shows the substantial cut in UK capital allowances from 1979 to 2005, but also shows that the cut in the headline rate was sufficient to outweigh this and reduce the EATR. Looking across countries, it is clear that the UK's capital allowances are fairly similar to those in the other countries shown, and so it is not surprising that its EATR is (like its statutory corporate tax rate) lower than in the other G7 countries.[17]

In April 2000, a tax credit for R&D was introduced (see Appendix for details). At the same time, a 10% lower rate was introduced for companies with less than £10,000 of taxable profits, and this lower rate was cut to zero in April 2002. This last tax cut came as a surprise, with potentially large costs if self-employed individuals registered as companies to reduce their tax liabilities.[18] Having apparently failed to anticipate the scale of this effect, the government swiftly reversed the reform. In April 2004, the zero rate was abolished for distributed profits, removing much of the tax advantage but at a cost of greater complexity; and so in December 2005, the zero rate was abolished for retained profits as well. This takes us back to where we were before April 2000, with the standard small companies' rate applying to all firms with profits up to £300,000, regardless of whether the profits are paid

[17] Data for OECD and EU15 averages are not available for the measures used in Figure 1.12.

[18] See Blow et al. (2002) for a view at the time.

out as dividends or retained by the firm. In the meantime, there has been unnecessary upheaval in the tax system, and thousands of individuals have incurred effort and expense to establish legally incorporated businesses that they would not otherwise have set up. This episode provides a clear illustration of how not to make tax policy.[19]

1.3.4. Indirect taxes

Value added tax

As noted earlier, the most dramatic shift in revenue-raising over the last thirty years has been the growth in VAT, which has doubled its share of total tax revenue. The bulk of this change occurred in 1979 when the incoming Conservative government raised the standard rate of VAT from 8% to 15% to pay for reductions in the basic rate and higher rates of income tax. The rate was further increased from 15% to 17.5% in 1991, to pay for a reduction in the community charge (poll tax), although it has been temporarily returned to 15% for a 13-month period from December 2008 as part of a package to stimulate the economy.

There have been a number of (mostly minor) extensions to the base of VAT over the years. Perhaps the most significant was the extension of VAT to cover domestic fuel and power from April 1994, then at a reduced rate of 8%. The original intention was to increase this to the full 17.5% rate a year later, but this second stage of reform was abandoned in the face of fierce political opposition, and in fact the reduced rate was cut from 8% to 5% in 1997, fulfilling a pre-election promise by the Labour Party. The reduced rate has since been extended to cover a few other goods which were previously subject to VAT at the standard rate.

The EU is a major player in VAT policy—indeed, the UK adopted a VAT in 1973 largely because it was a precondition for entry to what was then the European Economic Community. As well as setting out standardized definitions and rules, the EU mandates a minimum standard rate of 15%, restricts the use of reduced rates, forbids the extension of zero-rating to new items, and insists on various exemptions (where, in contrast to zero-rating, VAT paid on inputs is not refunded).

The UK in fact makes less use of reduced VAT rates than many other EU countries, while generally conforming to EU norms on exemptions. However, far more goods are subject to no VAT at all in the UK than in almost any other

[19] See Crawford and Freedman, Chapter 11, and Bond (2006) for more discussion.

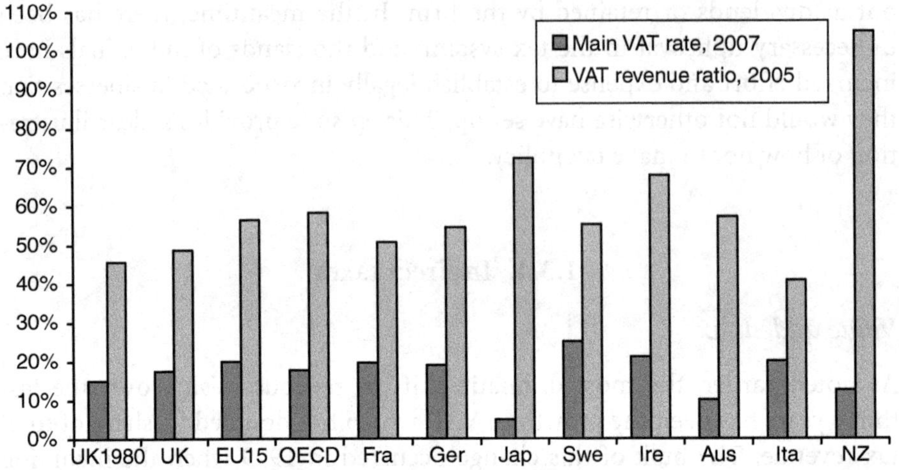

Notes: VAT Revenue Ratio is revenue / (main rate × national consumption), where national consumption is final consumption expenditure as measured in national accounts less VAT revenue. The United States does not have a VAT and is excluded from the data. It is possible for the VAT Revenue Ratio to exceed 100% when VAT is levied on items that are not recorded as consumption in the national accounts, such as new houses in New Zealand.

Sources: OECD (2008c).

Figure 1.13. VAT rates and bases

country: for example, the UK and Ireland are the only EU countries to apply a zero rate to most food, water, books, or children's clothes. Cost estimates of the various VAT reliefs are provided in the Appendix. Figure 1.13 provides an international comparison of VAT rates and bases. It shows the increase in both the VAT rate and the base (measured by VAT revenue as a percentage of what it would be if the main rate were applied to all consumption) since 1980, but also shows that many countries—and especially New Zealand—have found it possible to apply their standard rate of VAT to a much wider range of goods and services.

Excisable goods

Alcohol, tobacco, and road fuels are subject to significant excise duties as well as VAT. Figure 1.14 shows how the levels of these excise duties have evolved relative to general price inflation, while Table 1.7 shows how much of the price of these commodities is made up of indirect tax (VAT and excise duty). Between 1978 and 2000, taxes on cigarettes and road fuels increased rapidly, especially during the 1990s, when both these commodity groups were covered by government commitments to substantial annual real increases in

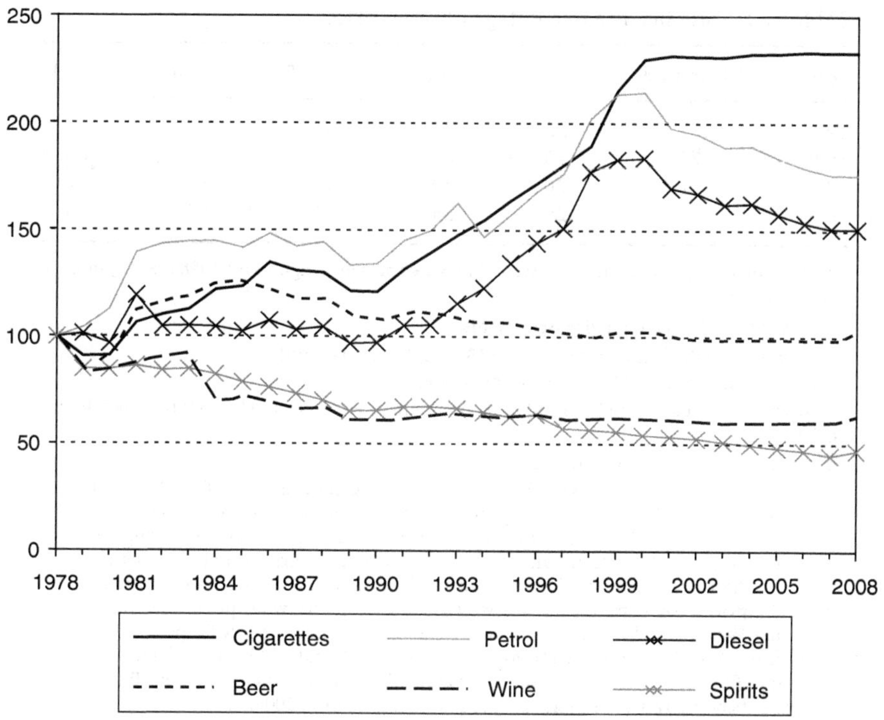

Notes: Assumes beer at 3.9% abv, wine not exceeding 15% abv, and spirits at 40% abv; petrol is leaded (4*) up to 1993, premium unleaded from 1994 to 2000, and ultra-low sulphur from 2001 onwards; diesel is ultra-low sulphur from 1999 onwards. Calculations are for April of each year, except that wine and spirits are for January from 1995 to 1999.

Sources: Duty rates from HMRC website <http://www.hmrc.gov.uk/>, HM Treasury (2002) and various HMRC / HM Customs and Excise *Annual Reports*; Retail Prices Index from National Statistics <http://www.statistics.gov.uk>.

Figure 1.14. Real levels of excise duties (1978 = 100)

excise duty. Since 2000, however, duty on cigarettes has barely kept pace with inflation, while fuel duties have fallen by more than a fifth in real terms. Nevertheless, real duty rates on cigarettes and fuel remain substantially higher than thirty years ago, in addition to the increase in VAT from 8% to 17.5%—although the pre-tax price of cigarettes has also increased sharply, so tax as a percentage of price has not increased as much as might be expected.

The pattern for alcoholic drink is very different. The tax rate on beer has changed little, while the real level of duty on spirits has fallen steadily and is now only half what it was in 1978. Duty on wine fell in real terms through the 1980s and has changed little since; but since the pre-tax price of wine has fallen sharply over time and VAT has risen, tax makes up more of the price of a bottle now than it did thirty years ago. As shown in Table 1.8, implied duty

Table 1.7. Total tax as a percentage of retail price

Year[a]	Cigarettes[b]	Beer[c]	Wine[d]	Spirits[e]	Petrol[f]	Diesel[g]
1978	72	30	45	78	47	49
1988	77	35	48	69	68	63
1998	81	30	50	63	82	82
2008	79	29	55	60	62	58

[a] Figures are for April of each year, except that wine and spirits figures for 1998 are for January.
[b] Packet of 20.
[c] Pint of bitter (3.9% abv) in licensed premises.
[d] 75 cl bottle of table wine (not exceeding 15% abv) in a retail outlet.
[e] 70 cl bottle of whisky (40% abv) in a retail outlet.
[f] Litre of fuel: leaded (4*) in 1978 and 1988, premium unleaded in 1998, and ultra-low sulphur in 2008.
[g] Litre of fuel: ultra-low sulphur in 2008.
Sources: Duty (and VAT) rates as for Figure 1.14. Prices: cigarettes and beer from National Statistics, *Consumer Price Indices* <http://www.statistics.gov.uk>, except that the 1978 prices are estimated by downrating the *Consumer Price Indices* prices for 1987 using the relevant sub-indices of the Retail Prices Index (RPI); wine and spirits from UK TradeInfo 2008 Factsheet <http://www.uktradeinfo.co.uk/index.cfm?task=factalcohol>, except that 1978 prices come from HM Treasury (2002), with the wine price downrated from the 1979 price by the wine and spirits sub-index of the RPI; petrol and diesel from HM Treasury (2002) for 1978 and 1988 and Table 4.1 of Department for Business, Enterprise and Regulatory Reform Quarterly Energy Prices <http://stats.berr.gov.uk/energystats/qep411.xls> for 1998 and 2008.

Table 1.8. Implied duty rates per litre of pure alcohol (April 2008 prices)

Item	1978	1988	1998	2008
Beer	£14.61	£17.25	£14.66	£14.96
Wine[a]	£25.85	£17.26	£15.86	£16.19
Spirits	£45.29	£31.90	£25.74	£21.35

[a] Wine of strength 12% abv.
Source: Authors' calculations from duty rates sourced as for Figure 1.14.

rates per litre of pure alcohol are now much closer together than they were in 1978, but substantial variation persists. This may seem puzzling since a natural starting point for a tax regime for alcoholic drink would be to impose the same level of tax per unit of alcohol, regardless of the form in which it is consumed. Variation in tax rates might be justified if one form of alcohol were more likely to lead to anti-social behaviour, for example, but such arguments are rarely made. The truth appears to be that the current system is more a product of history than of a coherent rationale, and there is obvious merit in reviewing it. Budget 2008 increased all alcohol duties by 6% above inflation and announced further real increases of 2% a year until 2013, but did not change the relativities between different forms of alcohol.

The EU mandates minimum levels of excise duties for its members, but in fact UK duties on cigarettes and petrol are the highest in the EU, and those on alcohol among the highest.[20] The existence of relatively high tax rates in the UK on some easily portable commodities could lead to loss of revenue through cross-border shopping. While it is possible that the UK tax rates are so high that reductions in those rates would encourage enough additional UK purchases to produce a net increase in revenue, the available evidence for alcohol suggests that this is unlikely.[21] Only in the case of spirits is it likely that the current tax rate is high enough for a reduction to have little or no revenue cost, which might help explain why duty on spirits had been consistently cut in real terms until recently.

Environmental taxes

Environmental taxes are difficult to define precisely, since all taxes affect economic activity and almost all economic activity has some environmental impact. However, a classification is attempted in the ONS's *Environmental Accounts*; on that basis environmental taxes are forecast to raise £39.2 billion in 2008–09, some 7.6% of total tax revenue or 2.7% of GDP. This is somewhat reduced from a peak in the late 1990s, and (as most recently measured) similar to the EU average but above the OECD average.[22] More than three-quarters of this revenue is accounted for by fuel tax (duty plus VAT on the duty), and the other sizeable chunk is vehicle excise duty, a licence fee for road vehicles. Thus taxes on motoring account for more than 90% of environmental tax revenues. Since 1994, several new environmental taxes have been introduced, including air passenger duty (1994), landfill tax (1996), climate change levy (2001), and aggregates levy (2002). These are described in the

[20] See UKTradeInfo Factsheets <http://www.uktradeinfo.co.uk/index.cfm?task=factsheets> and European Commission Excise Duty Tables <http://ec.europa.eu/taxation_customs/taxation/excise_duties/gen_overview/index_en.htm>.

[21] See Crawford et al. (1999) and Walker and Huang (2003).

[22] As a share of GDP, environmental taxes in the UK were marginally below both the EU27 and EU15 weighted averages in 2006 (authors' calculations using data from Eurostat, *Environmental Accounts*, <http://epp.eurostat.ec.europa.eu/portal/page?_pageid=1996,45323734&_dad=portal&_schema=PORTAL&screen=welcomeref&open=/data/envir/env/env_acc&language=en&product=EU_MAIN_TREE&root=EU_MAIN_TREE&scrollto=0>). In contrast, it was substantially above the OECD weighted average and slightly above the unweighted average in 2004 (data from the OECD/EEA database on instruments used for environmental policy and natural resources management, <http://www2.oecd.org/ecoinst/queries/index.htm>).

Appendix, but even air passenger duty, by far the largest of them, is forecast to raise only £1.9 billion in 2008–09.

The amount of revenue raised is rather limited as an indicator of the environmental impact of a tax. The more successful the tax is in changing behaviour, the less it will raise. It also matters how well the tax targets environmentally damaging behaviour rather than some broader activity. For example, differential fuel duty rates have been used extensively to encourage a switch to cleaner fuels. Vehicle excise duty changed in 1999 from a flat rate charge to one dependent on engine size, and then in 2001 to one based on vehicle emissions; since then the differential between high-emission and low-emission vehicles has repeatedly been widened. Similarly, from November 2009 rates of air passenger duty are to depend directly on distance travelled rather than on whether the destination is within the EU. Such reforms can be designed either to increase or to reduce revenues while encouraging less environmentally harmful activities. Nevertheless, it remains fair to say that environmental taxation in the UK is dominated by taxes on motoring.

1.3.5. Local taxation

Thirty years ago, local taxes in the UK consisted of domestic rates (on residential property) and business rates (on business property). However, this changed dramatically in 1990 when business rates (described in the Appendix) were taken from local to national control and domestic rates were replaced by the community charge (poll tax), a flat-rate per-person levy.[23] The poll tax was introduced in April 1990 in England and Wales after a one-year trial in Scotland, but was so unpopular that the government quickly announced that it would be replaced. The tax was based on the fact that an individual lived in a particular local authority, rather than on the value of the property occupied or the individual's ability to pay (subject to some exemptions and reliefs). In the 1991 Budget, the government increased VAT from 15% to 17.5% to pay for a large reduction in the poll tax, with a corresponding rise in the level of central government grant to local authorities. The poll tax was abolished in 1993 to be replaced by the council tax, which is based mainly on the value of the property occupied, with some exemptions and reliefs (outlined in the Appendix).

The result of these changes, and particularly the centralization of business rates, is that local services are now largely financed by central government,

[23] These reforms were not introduced in Northern Ireland, which retained a system of locally varying business and domestic rates.

with the only significant local tax left—the council tax—financing only around one-sixth of total local spending (although councils also raise a larger amount from non-tax sources such as user charges). As shown in Figure 1.5, this leaves UK taxation unusually centralized, with only 5% of tax revenues raised locally. At the margin, spending an extra pound locally requires the raising of an extra pound locally, giving local authorities appropriate incentives overall. But this extra money must come entirely from council tax, which bears particularly heavily on those groups (such as pensioners) with high property values relative to their incomes and hence limits local authorities' willingness to increase expenditure. Furthermore, while universal capping of local authority spending ended in 1999–2000, strengthened selective capping powers were retained, and have been used in a few cases since 2004–05. The threat and practice of capping are another limitation on local authorities' financial autonomy.

1.4. ECONOMIC ASPECTS OF THE UK TAX AND BENEFIT SYSTEM

This section assesses some key features of the UK tax system as a whole and how these have changed over the last thirty years. Tax systems can be assessed in terms of their revenue-raising power, their effects on efficiency and equity, and their complexity and compliance costs. Section 1.2 described the revenue effects of the tax system and this is not pursued further here. Also, despite its undoubted importance, the complexity of the tax system and the compliance burden that it places on taxpayers is not examined here because of the lack of robust statistical measures that allow comparisons across time and countries.[24] The focus of this section will, therefore, be on the traditional economic analysis of the tax system on efficiency and equity, examining its effects on the income distribution and on incentives to work, save, and invest.

The division between taxes and benefits seems rather artificial in this context: it is the overall distributional and incentive effects created by all different taxes and benefits together that matters, and we would not wish to change our analysis according to whether tax credits were counted as deductions from tax

[24] But see Shaw, Slemrod, and Whiting (Chapter 12) and Evans (Commentary to this chapter) for discussion.

or additions to benefits, for example. In this section we therefore consider the tax and benefit system as a whole.[25]

1.4.1. The distribution of income

The UK tax and benefit system transfers money from high-income to low-income households. Figure 1.15 shows that the tax and benefit system overall increases the average incomes of the poorest three-tenths of households, while the richest three-fifths make a net contribution on average.

Income inequality is therefore clearly lower after taxes and benefits than before. Figure 1.16 shows the Gini coefficient, a standard measure of inequality that can take values between zero (everyone has equal income) and one (one person has all the income in the economy), before and after personal direct taxes and benefits in the UK and the other EU15 countries in 2003, the latest year available.[26] In that year, personal direct taxes and benefits reduced

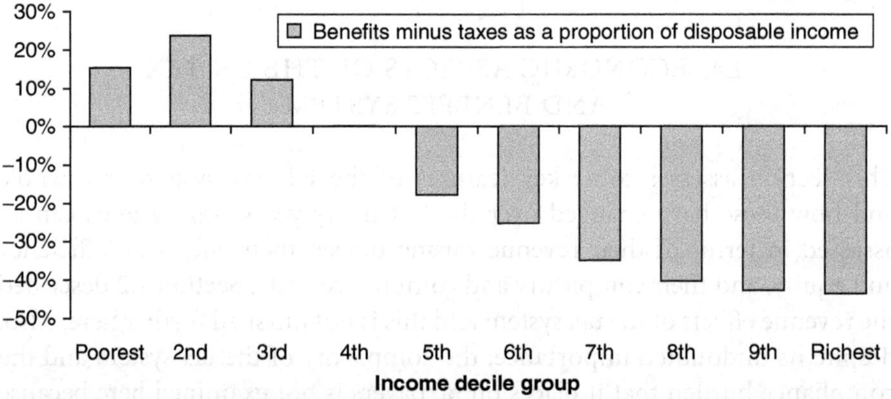

Notes: Excludes corporation tax, inheritance tax, stamp duty on securities, and some smaller taxes. Income decile groups are derived by dividing all households into ten equal-sized groups according to disposable income (i.e. after direct taxes and benefits but before indirect taxes) adjusted for family size using the McClements equivalence scale.

Sources: Authors' calculations from Jones (2008).

Figure 1.15. Distributional impact of the UK tax and benefit system in 2006–07

[25] Laws passed and public services provided can also have distributional and incentive effects. Ideally these too would be taken into account, but in this chapter we restrict our scope to financial transfers. We treat National Insurance contributions purely as a tax, ignoring any link to future benefit entitlements that might change their distributional and incentive effects. We do not believe that this materially affects the analysis for the UK.

[26] The Gini coefficient is half of the average income gap between all pairs of individuals as a fraction of average income. See, for example, Barr (2004) for an introduction and Sen (1973, 1992) for fuller discussion.

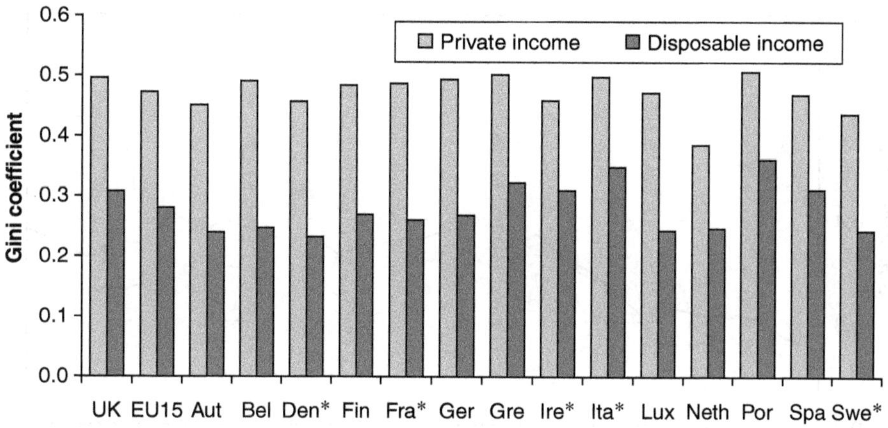

Notes: Difference between 'private' and 'disposable' income represents direct personal taxes and benefits: the calculations exclude indirect taxes, most 'business taxes' (notably corporation tax and business rates, though not employer National Insurance contributions) and most capital taxes (notably inheritance tax, stamp duties, and capital gains tax). Countries indicated with * use figures for 2001, the latest available. The EU15 (unweighted) average uses the most recent figure available for each country.

Sources: EUROMOD statistics on Distribution and Decomposition of Disposable Income, accessed at <http://www.iser.essex.ac.uk/msu/emod/statistics/> using EUROMOD version no. D1 (June 2007).

Figure 1.16. Effect of tax and benefit system on inequality in the EU15, 2003

the Gini coefficient by 0.19 in the UK, very similar to the EU15 average, but this reduction was from a slightly higher starting level of private income inequality.

The UK has seen an exceptionally large rise in income inequality since 1978. Figure 1.17 shows how the Gini coefficient for different measures of income, corresponding to different stages of the redistributive process, has changed since 1978. The Gini coefficient has fluctuated around 0.14 higher for private incomes than for incomes after all taxes and benefits.[27] It is clear from the figure that the benefit system is responsible for the bulk of this reduction in inequality, with direct taxes also reducing inequality slightly and indirect taxes appearing to increase inequality slightly. This last point requires some qualification, however.

Indirect taxes bear heavily on those with high expenditures, and will clearly target those with high incomes in any particular year less precisely than, say, an income tax does. But much low income observed at a point in time is temporary and need not reflect low lifetime living standards: while some people are persistently poor, many have volatile earnings, are temporarily

[27] This is a smaller reduction than that shown in the UK bars of Figure 1.16, largely because Figure 1.16 excludes indirect taxes, which increase the measured Gini coefficient. The effect of including indirect taxes is shown in Figure 1.17.

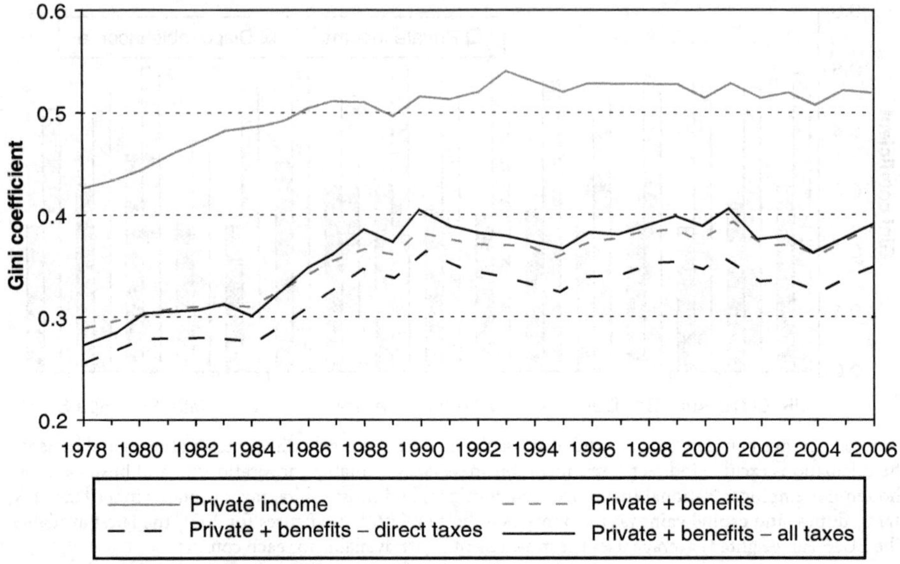

Notes: Excludes corporation tax, inheritance tax, stamp duty on securities, and some smaller taxes. Years are fiscal years from 1993 onwards (so 2006 means 2006–07) and calendar years before that.
Sources: Annan et al. (2008).

Figure 1.17. Inequality of incomes at different stages of the redistributive process

unemployed, are studying, are taking a break from the labour market to raise children, are retired with hefty savings, and so on. People's ability to borrow and save means that those with low current incomes will typically have high expenditure relative to their income, and many of those who in a particular year have low income but pay a lot in indirect taxes are people we would not ordinarily think of as 'poor'. Over a lifetime, income and expenditure must be equal (apart from inheritances), and indeed annual expenditure is arguably better than annual income as a guide to lifetime living standards.[28] If we were to look at the effect of the tax and benefit system on lifetime income inequality, the contrast between 'progressive' direct taxes and 'regressive' indirect taxes would appear much less stark. This is not to say that indirect taxes are progressive relative to lifetime income—that depends on whether goods consumed disproportionately by the lifetime-poor are taxed more heavily (via tobacco duty, for example) or less heavily (as with VAT zero-rating of most food) than other goods—but certainly their effect on the distribution of annual income gives only a partial, and arguably misleading, impression of their overall effect.

[28] Studies that have examined the use of expenditure rather than income for looking at distributional outcomes include Goodman et al. (1997), Blundell and Preston (1998), Meyer and Sullivan (2003, 2004), Goodman and Oldfield (2004), and Brewer et al. (2006).

If we look at the changes over time shown in Figure 1.17, the amount by which taxes and benefits reduce the Gini coefficient (for annual income) is little different at the end of the period from in 1997 or indeed 1978. This does not mean, however, that the tax and benefit systems in place at the start and end of the period were equally progressive. The amount of redistribution that a given tax and benefit system achieves depends on the economy to which it is applied, and there have been major changes in the UK economy since 1978—not least the sharp increase in private income inequality shown in the figure. Other things being equal, a progressive tax and benefit system will redistribute more if applied to a more unequal income distribution, so the fact that the 1978–79 and 2006–07 tax and benefit systems reduce the Gini coefficient by the same amount suggests that reforms to the tax and benefit system may have been regressive, offsetting the tendency for the tax and benefit system to redistribute more as inequality rose.

To measure the effect of policy reforms on inequality more precisely, we use a tax and benefit micro-simulation model to look at how different the Gini coefficient would have been if previous years' tax and benefit systems had been kept unreformed.[29] However, doing this raises the question of exactly what is meant by 'unreformed': would 'no change' mean tax thresholds and benefit rates keeping pace with price inflation, or with growth in average earnings, GDP, or something else? We consider three scenarios for a 'no change' baseline: one in which all taxes and benefits are uprated in line with the Retail Prices Index (RPI) so that there is no real-terms change in rates and thresholds, a second in which they are increased in line with growth in GDP per capita, and a third in which tax thresholds (and rates of excise duties and council tax) are uprated in line with the RPI and benefits (and tax credits) in line with per-capita GDP growth.[30] The rationale for this third scenario is twofold: first, it corresponds reasonably closely to the government's standard uprating practice prior to 1978; and second, reforms since 1978 have had relatively little impact on the overall budgetary position if measured relative to this baseline (much less than relative to universal price-uprating or universal GDP-uprating), which seems like a relatively 'neutral' counterfactual to choose.[31]

[29] The methodology here follows Clark and Leicester (2004): the analysis here updates that work, incorporates local taxes, and adds a third baseline. More information on the methodology and results can be found in Adam and Browne (forthcoming).

[30] For brevity, the rest of this section refers to uprating in line with GDP rather than GDP per capita.

[31] Government borrowing in 2008–09 would be £47.3 billion lower if a price-uprated 1978 tax and benefit system were in place and £39.7 billion higher under a GDP-uprated system, but only £10.2 billion higher in our third scenario. Note again that these estimates, like Figure 1.18, ignore

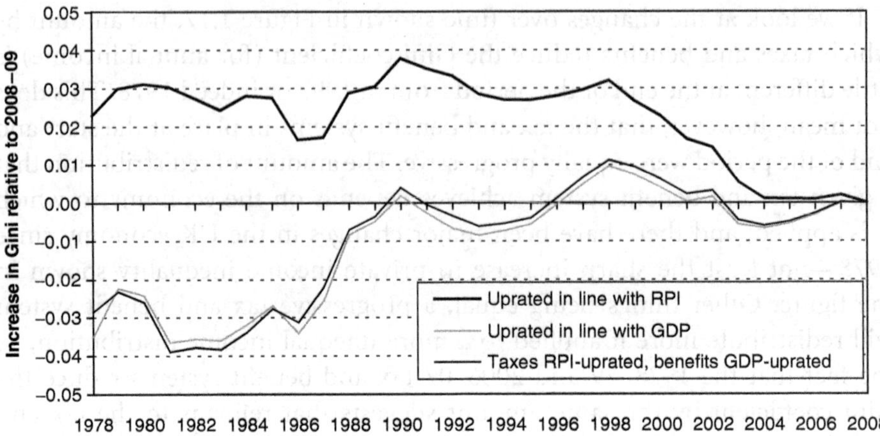

Notes: Gini coefficients are for post-tax income, after direct and indirect personal taxes and benefits: excludes most 'business taxes' (notably corporation tax and business rates, though not employer National Insurance contributions) and capital taxes (notably inheritance tax, stamp duties, and capital gains tax). Taxes and benefits are those applying in April of the year shown; the 2008 regime is that originally in place in April 2008, ignoring later announcements that were backdated to apply as from April.

Sources: Authors' calculations using the IFS tax and benefit micro-simulation model, TAXBEN, run on uprated data from the 2005–06 Expenditure and Food Survey.

Figure 1.18. Effect on the Gini coefficient of replacing the 2008–09 tax and benefit system with those from previous years

Figure 1.18 shows how different the Gini coefficient in 2008 would be if previous tax and benefit systems had been left in place and uprated according to these three baseline scenarios.[32] It shows, for example, that the Gini coefficient would be about 0.03 higher if an RPI-indexed 1998 tax and benefit system were now in place and therefore that reforms relative to RPI-indexation since 1998 acted to reduce the Gini coefficient by 0.03.[33] It is clear that the choice of baseline is of crucial importance. The 2008 tax and benefit system reduces inequality considerably more than the 1978 system would have done if it had been price-indexed, but by much less than if benefits had been GDP-indexed after 1978. (Whether tax thresholds are increased in line with prices or GDP does not significantly alter this conclusion.) Indeed,

changes to most 'business taxes' (notably corporation tax and business rates) and capital taxes (notably inheritance tax, stamp duties, and capital gains tax).

[32] Throughout this section, the 2008 tax and benefit system with which past systems are compared is the one originally in place in April 2008, ignoring later reforms even if they were backdated to apply as from April.

[33] All the tax and benefit systems are applied to a simulated 2008 population (actually a surveyed 2005–06 population with monetary values appropriately adjusted: earnings uprated in line with average earnings, rents with average rents, etc). Clark and Leicester (2004) show that the effect of reforms looks very similar whichever year's population is used.

relative to a GDP-uprated baseline, tax and benefit reforms from 1978 to 2008 acted to increase the Gini coefficient by about 0.035, and accounted for around a third of the total increase in disposable income inequality up to 2006. What is clear, however, is that Labour's reforms have been more progressive than the Conservatives'. Labour's reforms since 1997 have had a similar effect on overall inequality as increasing benefit rates in line with GDP, while the Conservatives' reforms were roughly equivalent to increasing them in line with inflation.

One caveat to these findings is needed. In calculating what would have happened to inequality as the economy evolved if the tax and benefit system had not changed, we assume that tax and benefit reforms did not themselves affect the evolution of the economy. But individuals and firms respond to the incentives created by the tax and benefit system, so this assumption is unlikely to be accurate in practice. The true effect of tax and benefit reforms on inequality, therefore, depends not only on their direct redistributive effects, but also on how they affected people's decisions to work, save, and so on. These indirect effects depend partly on how far individuals respond to such incentives, which is difficult to estimate; but we can more easily estimate how the incentives themselves have been changed by tax and benefit reforms, and it is to this question that we now turn.

1.4.2. Work incentives

Commentators often express concern about the effect of high income tax rates on work incentives, although such complaints faded somewhat as rates were reduced during the 1980s. But means-tested benefits and tax credits, which have expanded significantly in recent years, can be just as important: the prospect of losing such support as income rises can be a crucial factor in the work decisions of low-income families. And indirect taxes can be as important as direct taxes: if the attractiveness of working is determined by the amount of goods and services that can be bought with the wage earned, a tax that reduces all earnings and a tax that increases all prices will clearly have very similar effects.[34] Looking at financial work incentives is not just a matter of inspecting the income tax schedule: the whole tax and benefit system must be taken into account.

[34] In what follows, we incorporate indirect taxes by estimating, for each individual, the average tax rate paid on their household's spending. We can therefore allow for how large the 'wedge' between income and the value of consumption is for that person's household; but this will not quite be an accurate measure of how indirect taxes affect work incentives unless the average tax rate on what additional income is spent on is the same as that on existing purchases.

We should also distinguish between the incentive to be in work at all as opposed to not working—which can be measured by the participation tax rate (PTR), the proportion of total earnings taken in tax and withdrawn benefits—and the incentive for those already in work to increase their earnings slightly, whether by working more hours, seeking promotion or getting a better-paid job—which can be measured by the effective marginal tax rate (EMTR), the proportion of a small increase in earnings taken in tax and withdrawn benefits. High PTRs among non-workers are often referred to as the unemployment trap; high EMTRs among low-income families are known as the poverty trap.[35]

Figure 1.19 shows the distribution of PTRs among working-age people in 2008–09.[36] Reading across, we can see that around 20% of people have a PTR below 40% (a strong incentive to be in work), and around 30% have a PTR above 60% (a weak incentive to be in work). The remaining half of the working-age population have PTRs between these values, with the steepest part of the curve representing the highest concentration of people. The median PTR is 50.7%, and the mean 52.5%. However, almost a tenth of the working-age population—nearly 3 million individuals—have a PTR above 80%, meaning that what they earn (or would earn if they worked) is worth to them less than a fifth of what it costs (or would cost) to employ them. Faced with losing such a large proportion of their earnings, working is clearly a less attractive proposition, and indeed only a million of this group are actually in work. Most of those facing such high PTRs are people who earn (or would earn) little: although they (would) lose little in tax, the loss of benefits is extremely important relative to these low earnings.

The distribution of EMTRs for those in work, shown in Figure 1.20, is much more concentrated: three-quarters of workers face an EMTR of between 40% and 60%, so that a small increase in their earnings is worth to

[35] The analysis that follows updates that in Adam et al. (2006a, 2006b) and incorporates employer NICs and indirect taxes. Adam (2005) incorporated these taxes but did not separate out the effect of tax and benefit reforms from other changes in the economy. See Adam and Browne (forthcoming) for more detail on methodology and results. Brewer, Saez, and Shephard (Chapter 2), show how average PTRs and EMTRs vary with earnings for different family types in 2008–09 but excluding indirect taxes.

[36] In order to calculate participation tax rates for non-workers, we must estimate what they would earn if they worked. To do this, we use their observed characteristics (age, sex, years of education, marriage and cohabitation status, number of children, age of youngest child, ethnicity, and housing tenure) to predict their earnings conditional on being in each of four different hours bands (1–15, 16–23, 24–29, and 30+) using an ordinary least squares regression. We then use the same characteristics to estimate (using a multinomial logit model) the likelihood of each individual being in each of these hours bands were they to work, and weight the participation tax rates associated with each earnings/hours band combination accordingly. Non-workers tend to have characteristics associated with low earnings, and we therefore estimate that they face relatively high participation tax rates as the loss of out-of-work benefits is large relative to what they could earn.

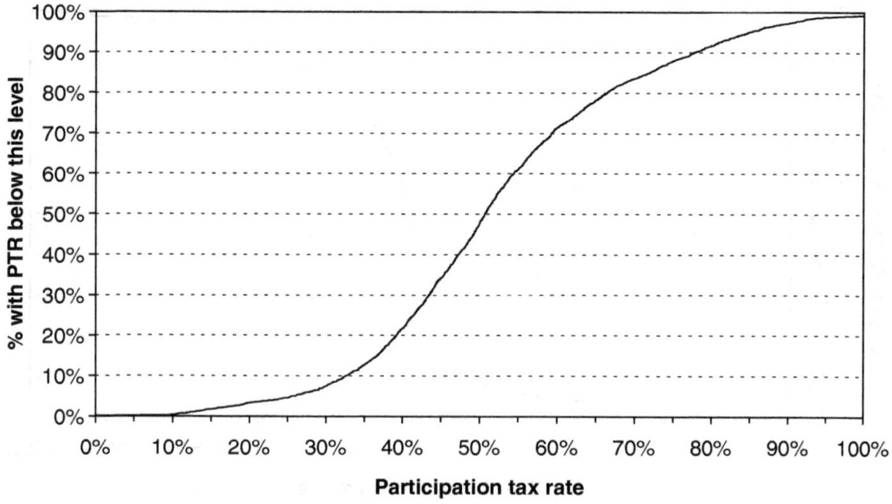

Notes: Calculations for direct and indirect personal taxes and benefits only: excludes most 'business taxes' (notably corporation tax and business rates, though not employer National Insurance contributions) and capital taxes (notably inheritance tax, stamp duties, and capital gains tax). In-work income for non-workers estimated as described in footnote 36. Excludes those over state pension age. Taxes and benefits are those originally in place in April 2008, ignoring later announcements that were backdated to apply as from April.

Sources: Authors' calculations using the IFS tax and benefit micro-simulation model, TAXBEN, run on uprated data from the 2005–06 Expenditure and Food Survey.

Figure 1.19. Cumulative distribution of participation tax rates 2008–09

them around half of what it costs their employer. The median EMTR amongst workers is 49.9%, and the mean is 52.1%. But Figure 1.20 shows that there is also a substantial group of people—around 8% of workers, a little under 2 million individuals—with EMTRs of between 75% and 80%. These people have such high EMTRs because they face steep withdrawal of tax credits or housing benefit if they increase their earnings a little.

Figure 1.21 shows what the average (mean) PTR would be if other tax and benefit systems from the past thirty years were now in place—uprated, as in the previous subsection, in one of three different ways. It therefore shows the impact of tax and benefit reforms since 1978 on financial incentives to be in work, abstracting from other changes (such as demographic shifts and changes in wages, rent levels, and working patterns) which also affect work incentives.

After initially increasing the average PTR (weakening financial incentives to be in work), reforms under the Conservative governments up to 1997 considerably strengthened incentives to be in work. Labour's reforms have had much less impact: on average, financial incentives to be in work are slightly

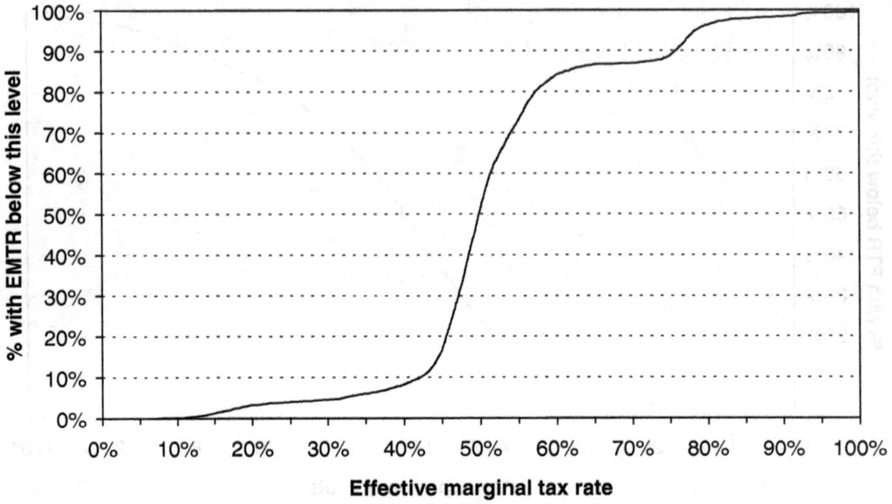

Notes: Calculations for direct and indirect personal taxes and benefits only: excludes most 'business taxes' (notably corporation tax and business rates, though not employer National Insurance contributions) and capital taxes (notably inheritance tax, stamp duties, and capital gains tax). Excludes those over state pension age. Taxes and benefits are those originally in place in April 2008, ignoring later announcements that were backdated to apply as from April.

Sources: Authors' calculations using the IFS tax and benefit micro-simulation model, TAXBEN, run on uprated data from the 2005–06 Expenditure and Food Survey.

Figure 1.20. Cumulative distribution of effective marginal tax rates among workers, 2008–09

stronger than they would have been if the benefit rates Labour inherited had simply been increased in line with growth in the economy, and much the same as they would have been if benefit rates had increased in line with inflation.[37]

A similar analysis for the average EMTR amongst workers is presented in Figure 1.22. Reforms under the Conservatives acted to reduce the average EMTR (strengthen financial incentives to increase earnings) overall, while those under Labour have acted to increase it. But perhaps what is most striking is how stable the average EMTR has been: for all the myriad reforms that have happened over the past thirty years, none of the tax and benefit

[37] It might seem surprising that increasing tax thresholds in line with the RPI but benefits in line with GDP leads to weaker work incentives than either increasing both in line with the RPI or increasing both in line with GDP. This pattern is evident for both PTRs and EMTRs. It arises because more rapid indexation of benefit rates tends to weaken work incentives, raising out-of-work incomes relative to in-work incomes and increasing the number of people facing benefit withdrawal, whereas more rapid indexation of tax thresholds tends to strengthen them, applying higher rates of income tax to fewer people.

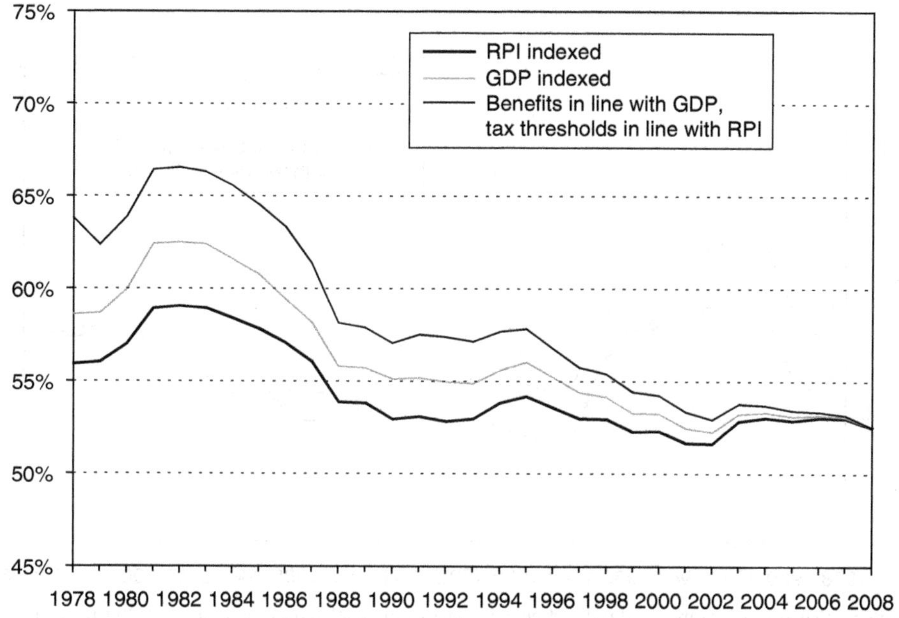

Notes: Calculations for direct and indirect personal taxes and benefits only: excludes most 'business taxes' (notably corporation tax and business rates, though not employer National Insurance contributions) and capital taxes (notably inheritance tax, stamp duties, and capital gains tax). In-work incomes for non-workers estimated as described in footnote 36. Excludes those over state pension age. Taxes and benefits are those applying in April of the year shown; the 2008 regime is that originally in place in April 2008, ignoring later announcements that were backdated to apply as from April.

Sources: Authors' calculations using the IFS tax and benefit micro-simulation model, TAXBEN, run on uprated data from the 2005–06 Expenditure and Food Survey.

Figure 1.21. Average participation tax rates that would be created by tax and benefit systems from 1978 to 2008

systems seen would leave the average EMTR more than 5 percentage points different from its current level of 52.1%.

Trends in the average PTR and EMTR hide variations across the population, of course: the trends shown have not been universal. For example, Labour's reforms have strengthened financial work incentives for some of those previously facing the weakest incentives (and particularly lone parents), and have weakened work incentives for many others who have been brought into means-testing.

Recent data for international comparisons are not available, but in 2003 the UK's average EMTR was slightly lower than the EU15 average, while in 1998, the UK's average PTR was considerably lower than the EU15 average, and indeed lower than that of any other EU15 country except Greece.[38]

[38] 1998 PTR data from Immervol et al. (2005). 2003 EMTR data from EUROMOD statistics on Distribution and Decomposition of Disposable Income, accessed at <http://www.iser.

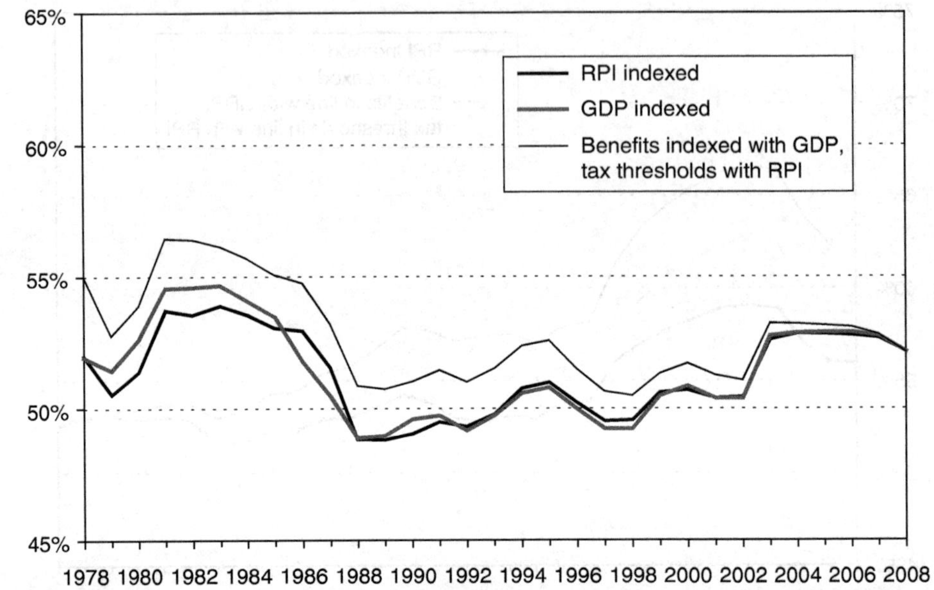

Notes: Calculations for direct and indirect personal taxes and benefits only: excludes most 'business taxes' (notably corporation tax and business rates, though not employer National Insurance contributions) and capital taxes (notably inheritance tax, stamp duties, and capital gains tax). Excludes those over state pension age. Taxes and benefits are those applying in April of the year shown; the 2008 regime is that originally in place in April 2008, ignoring later announcements that were backdated to apply as from April.

Sources: Authors' calculations using the IFS tax and benefit micro-simulation model, TAXBEN, run on uprated data from the 2005–06 Expenditure and Food Survey.

Figure 1.22. Average effective marginal tax rates amongst workers that would be created by tax and benefit systems from 1978 to 2008

1.4.3. Incentives to save and invest

The UK imposes a number of taxes on capital: income tax on savings and dividend income, corporation tax, capital gains tax, stamp duties on properties and securities, council tax, business rates, and inheritance tax. The significance of the revenues from these taxes can be gauged to some extent by looking at Table 1.1 and Figures 1.3 and 1.4. Corporation tax and stamp duties have grown as a proportion of total tax revenue since 1978; but it is the substantial revenue raised from council tax and business rates that stands out internationally.

essex.ac.uk/msu/emod/statistics/> using EUROMOD version no. D1 (June 2007). For a few countries where 2003 estimates are not available, 2001 estimates are used in constructing the EU15 average.

Unfortunately, income tax data do not separate savings income from wage income, so it is not possible to come to clear conclusions on how overall revenues from capital taxes have changed over time or compare to other countries. But it is not only the overall revenue from capital taxation that is of interest. Not all capital taxes have the same effect on incentives to save and invest, and differential treatment of different forms of saving and investment, distorting the form that such activities take, can be equally important. In the rest of this subsection we focus on quantifying how different taxes on capital affect incentives for individuals to save and for businesses to invest.

We can distinguish between taxes that discourage UK residents from saving and taxes that discourage businesses from investing in the UK. To see this distinction, think of the UK as a small country in a vast, liquid international capital market. Savers (in the UK and elsewhere) can invest anywhere in the world, so in order to raise funds, businesses investing in the UK must offer an after-tax return as high as that available on investments elsewhere. A tax on UK investments will therefore not reduce the return that savers receive; but to provide this same after-tax return, UK investments must yield a higher pre-tax return, and less profitable investments will not be undertaken.

Conversely, UK residents subject to a tax on the return to their saving cannot demand a higher pre-tax return to compensate, because businesses can raise capital from savers anywhere in the world (or indeed from tax-exempt institutions such as pension funds in the UK) that are not subject to the tax. Thus the yield required on investments (in the UK and elsewhere) will be unaffected and investment will not be deterred; but UK residents will receive a lower rate of return after tax, discouraging them from saving.[39]

This is, of course, a highly simplified representation of the world. Capital cannot really flow costlessly across borders. Small companies in particular are often reliant on equity capital provided by a single owner-manager (or a small number of closely linked people), which means that personal taxes on those individuals' returns might discourage investment in the company.

Nevertheless, we can broadly characterize income tax, capital gains tax, and inheritance tax as taxing saving by UK residents, and corporation tax as taxing investment in the UK. Stamp duty on shares is also primarily a tax on UK investment rather than on residents' saving. It must be paid on transactions of shares in UK companies, regardless of who buys or sells them, so people will be willing to pay less for shares in UK companies: specifically,

[39] This analysis is for changes to UK taxes in isolation, assuming other countries' tax systems do not change. A change to UK taxes as part of an internationally co-ordinated move would have different effects, since a co-ordinated move would affect the return available to residents of all countries for investment in all countries.

the price of shares will be reduced by the value of the expected stream of stamp duty on all transactions in those shares. A saver buying a share will find that the lower share price offsets the stamp duty that must be paid, making saving in equities as attractive as it would be in the absence of a tax;[40] but a company seeking to issue new equity to raise capital for investment will find that the share issue raises less money than it would in the absence of the tax, so investment will be discouraged.[41]

The distinction between taxes on UK saving and on UK investment is most difficult for property. To some extent similar arguments can be made—stamp duty land tax applies to all UK property whoever buys it, whereas UK income tax on rental income, as on other savings income, applies only to UK taxpayers wherever the property is located—but the notion of a large liquid market in UK property amongst non-UK taxpayers is clearly less plausible than for many financial assets. More importantly, property taxes such as council tax and business rates might affect the rental price of occupation as well as the capital value of the property: they could potentially discourage not only saving in property or investment in property development, but also use of property. However, it is usually argued that the demand for property is more responsive to property prices than the supply of property: as property becomes more expensive, businesses can occupy smaller premises and people live in smaller houses (or, for example, leave the family home at an older age), whereas land is in fixed supply and new construction is severely constrained by planning regulations.[42] Insofar as that is the case, the need to pay council tax or business rates simply makes the same properties worth less to those occupying them, reducing rents and property prices.[43] This is more complicated in the case of income tax on rental income, which applies only to the rental sector (the size of which might be responsive to taxation) and only to UK-taxpaying landlords.[44] In this chapter, we assume

40 Whether the reduced share price more or less than exactly offsets the stamp duty liability for any individual saver depends on how long the saver holds the share. The reduced share price means that a given sum can be used to buy more shares and thus a larger stream of dividends; the longer the shares are held, the more likely it is that this larger dividend stream will outweigh the stamp duty paid on purchase. The two effects will balance for savers holding a share for the average holding period expected by the market.

41 See Hawkins and McCrae (2002) and Bond, Klemm, and Hawkins (2005) for further discussion and empirical evidence that stamp duty on shares is indeed reflected in share prices.

42 Evidence on the extremely low responsiveness of housing supply to house prices in the UK is reviewed in chapter 2 of Barker (2003), for example.

43 Bond et al. (1996) provide empirical evidence that business rates are reflected in lower rents.

44 Council tax is not entirely uniform either: council tax benefit covers the bills of those on low incomes, so that rises in council tax do not increase recipients' net liability. In such cases, council tax might not be reflected in lower property prices to the extent that a property can be sold to a council tax benefit recipient who would pay as much for it as in the absence of the tax.

that income tax on rental income has no effect on rents or property prices, simply reducing the incentive to buy and let out property, but that council tax, business rates, and stamp duty land tax are reflected in lower property prices, so that the incentive to buy (and occupy) property is little affected by the taxes, but property development is discouraged because the taxes mean that the property will sell for less.

We now look in turn at incentives to save and to invest.

Incentives to save

Table 1.9 summarizes the treatment of different assets for income tax, NICs and capital gains tax. For owner-occupied housing and for cash and shares held in ISAs, saving is out of taxed income and there is no tax on returns and no tax on withdrawals (the proceeds of sale in the case of housing). Tax exemption is provided in a different way for pensions: saving is out of untaxed income, fund income is untaxed but withdrawals are taxed. This regime for pensions would produce the same effective tax rate of zero on the normal return to saving;[45] but the 25% lump sum that can be withdrawn from pension funds as a tax-free lump sum means that pension saving is in effect subsidized. In addition, employers' pension contributions are particularly tax-favoured since they are not subject to employer or employee NICs either at the point of contribution or at the point of withdrawal.

Pensions, ISAs, and housing cover the significant saving activity of the bulk of the population. But saving in other forms is discouraged by the tax system. The returns to second or let properties and to cash or shares held outside ISAs are all subject to the combination of income tax and CGT in slightly different ways.

Under certain assumptions, we can calculate the effective tax rate (ETR) on saving in each of the different asset types: the percentage reduction in the annual real rate of return caused by tax.[46] Table 1.10 illustrates ETRs

[45] Assuming that the individual faces the same marginal tax rate in retirement as when making the contribution—the implications of relaxing this assumption are discussed below. Taxing withdrawals from funds instead of the income paid into funds does have significantly different implications, however: by foregoing the up-front revenue on the income saved and taking a share of the returns instead, the government is implicitly investing in the same assets as the individual, changing its investment portfolio as well as the timing of revenue. This is particularly important if the government would not otherwise have access to these assets, or if the investment cannot easily be scaled up to accommodate the government's share without reducing the individual's share by the same amount.

[46] The calculation of ETRs here broadly follows that of IFS Capital Taxes Group (1989). For more detail of methodology and results, see Wakefield (forthcoming).

Table 1.9. Tax treatment of different assets

Asset	Income tax and NICs on contributions	Returns		Income tax and NICs on withdrawals
		Income tax on interest/dividends	Capital gains tax	
Pension (employee contribution)	Exempt from income tax, not exempt from employer and employee NICs	Exempt	Exempt	Taxed except for a 25% lump sum, no NICs
Pension (employer contribution)	Exempt from income tax, employer and employee NICs	Exempt	Exempt	Taxed except for a 25% lump sum, no NICs
ISA	Taxed	Exempt	Exempt	Exempt
Interest-bearing account	Taxed	Taxed at 10%, 20%, or 40%	n/a	Exempt
Direct equity holdings	Taxed	Taxed at 10% or 32.5%, but offsetting dividend tax credit means effective rates are 0% and 25%	Taxed	Exempt
Housing (main or only house)	Taxed	Exempt[a]	Exempt	Exempt
Housing (second or subsequent house)	Taxed	Rental income taxed	Taxed	Exempt

[a] Dividends are effectively the imputed value of income from owner-occupation—this was taxed on the basis of the notional rental value of the property until 1963. Note that income tax is payable on income received from letting out part of a main residence while the owner resides there, although the first £4,250 per year is tax-free.

for basic- and higher-rate taxpayers if all assets earn a 3% real rate of return before tax and inflation is 2%.

Note that the ETR on an interest-bearing account is 33% for a basic-rate taxpayer, not the statutory income tax rate of 20%, because tax is charged on the nominal return, not the real return. With a 3% real return and 2%

Table 1.10. Effective tax rates on saving in different assets

Asset		Effective tax rate (%) for:	
		Basic-rate taxpayer	Higher-rate taxpayer
ISA		0	0
Interest-bearing account		33	67
Pension (employee contribution)	(invested 10 years)	−21	−53
	(invested 25 years)	−8	−21
Pension (employer contribution)	(invested 10 years)	−115	−102
	(invested 25 years)	−45	−40
Housing (main or only house)		0	0
Rental housing	(invested 10 years)	30	50
	(invested 25 years)	28	48
Direct equity holdings	(invested 10 years)	10	35
	(invested 25 years)	7	33

Notes: Assumes 3% annual real rate of return and 2% inflation. Calculations for rental housing and direct equity holdings assume that real returns accrue as rental income or dividends while capital gains match price inflation and are realized at the end of the period in question. Rental housing assumed to be owned outright, with no outstanding mortgages. Calculations for employer pension contribution assume that the employee is contracted into the state second pension. Saver is assumed to be a basic- or higher-rate taxpayer throughout the period in question, to have exhausted the CGT exempt amount where appropriate, and to have no entitlement to means-tested benefits or tax credits.

Source: Wakefield (forthcoming).

inflation, £100 of saving yields nominal interest of about £5; 20% tax on this, £1, represents 33% of the £3 increase in the real purchasing power of the deposit. Inflation does not, however, affect ETRs on pensions, ISAs, and owner-occupied housing, where the return is tax-exempt.

ISAs and owner-occupied housing have ETRs of zero: they are the archetypal tax-free saving vehicles against which we measure ETRs on other assets. Pension saving has a negative ETR because of the tax-free lump sum and because of the NICs exemption for employer contributions. Both of these subsidies are a percentage of total contributions or final fund size; since investment returns make up a larger proportion of the fund the longer it is held, the ETR (which is measured as a percentage of the real return) is therefore less negative for longer investment periods.

The ETRs on direct equity holdings and on rental housing represent a combination of income tax and capital gains tax: for simplicity, we assume that asset price inflation matches general inflation and real returns are received as dividends or rental income. The ETRs are lower for longer holding periods because CGT is levied when an asset is sold rather than when the rise in value

Table 1.11. Final wealth generated by saving in different assets as a percentage of that generated by an untaxed asset

Asset		% of tax-free final wealth generated for:	
		Basic-rate taxpayer	Higher-rate taxpayer
ISA		100	100
Interest-bearing account	(invested 10 years)	91	82
	(invested 25 years)	79	61
Pension (employee contribution)		106	117
Pension (employer contribution)		139	134
Owner-occupied housing		100	100
Rental housing	(invested 10 years)	92	86
	(invested 25 years)	82	70
Stocks and shares	(invested 10 years)	97	90
	(invested 25 years)	95	79

Notes and Sources: As for Table 1.10.

occurs: this interest-free deferral of the latent tax liability is worth more the longer the asset is held, reducing the ETR over time and creating an incentive (known as the 'lock-in effect') for people to hold onto assets for longer than they would in the absence of the tax.

The ETRs in Table 1.10 illustrate the effect of tax on annual rates of return, but the phenomenon of compound interest complicates the calculation of how these translate into the final wealth generated by saving. Table 1.11 shows, under the same assumptions, how tax affects the final worth of the assets. Taxes on the return to saving compound over time: thus a basic rate taxpayer putting money into a bank account would find that, after ten years, she had 91% of what she would have had if the interest was untaxed (or if she had put the money into an ISA instead), but after twenty-five years her savings would be worth only 79% of what they would have been worth untaxed.[47] Taxes on initial contributions or final withdrawals do not have this property, so the net tax subsidies for pensions imply the same percentage increase in the value of the fund (relative to ISA-style treatment) regardless of the duration of saving.

The tax implications of saving in different forms might seem to be radically different. But the last thirty years have in fact seen a significant reduction

[47] This measure is equivalent to looking at how much would have to be saved in a taxed asset to yield the same final wealth as saving £1 in an untaxed asset: the latter can be calculated as 100 divided by the number in Table 1.11.

both in the extent to which the tax system penalizes saving overall and in the extent to which it distorts the return on different savings vehicles. There are three reasons for this. First, inflation rates have declined. As shown above, even modest inflation rates can significantly increase ETRs on assets where the returns are taxed. But at the levels of inflation prevalent in the 1970s and 1980s, this effect can be immense. With the same 3% real return assumed above but inflation at 10% rather than 2%, a basic-rate taxpayer would face an ETR of 89% on an interest-bearing account, while for a higher-rate taxpayer the ETR would be 177%, implying a negative real return: after tax, the savings would be worth less than when they were deposited. Inflation at the rates seen in the last fifteen years is a far less severe problem.

Second, the dispersion of income tax rates has narrowed. If a particular form of saving attracted tax relief at, say, 83%, its underlying performance could be quite poor and yet it could still provide an attractive return. As the number of tax bands has fallen and the highest rates have come down, the distortion caused by the taxation of different forms of saving has also fallen.

Third, there have been a series of reforms that have reduced the tax advantage of previously highly tax-privileged saving, and others that have removed tax disadvantages of other forms of saving, leading to a general levelling of the tax treatment of saving. Tax relief on life assurance and on mortgage interest provided significant net subsidies to saving in these forms, but have now been abolished; meanwhile, the introduction of personal pensions, PEPs, TESSAs, and ISAs greatly extended the range of tax-free saving vehicles available. Over the last three decades we have moved from an incoherent tax regime for saving to one that seems more satisfactory. It has rarely been the case that a clear strategy has been evident, but the power of the practical arguments for similar tax treatment of all saving seems to have been great. There is still some way to go to reach a tax system that is neutral in its effects, but we are far closer to it now than we were thirty years ago.

Income tax, NICs, and CGT are not the only parts of the tax and benefit system that might affect people's saving decisions. Individuals who expect their estates to be worth more than £312,000 (or twice that for married couples) might be discouraged from further saving by the prospect of inheritance tax on their bequests if they are not foresighted or lucky enough to dispose of their assets more than seven years before they die—although inheritance tax does at least treat all major assets equally.

At the other end of the wealth scale, analysis of saving incentives must take account of benefits as well as taxes: if savings reduce entitlement to means-tested benefits and tax credits then this adds to the effective tax on saving. Tax credit entitlement is assessed on the same measure of income as income tax; so saving in ISAs, pensions, and owner-occupied housing is not discouraged by tax credit withdrawal, while other forms of savings income are counted for the means test and reduce tax credit entitlement. Means-tested benefits treat assets in a completely different way. Owner-occupied housing is disregarded, as for income tax and tax credits; pension income is counted, but unlike for income tax and tax credits, only half of pension contributions are deducted from income. For other savings—ISAs receive no special treatment—the actual income generated is disregarded; however, if the total value of these assets is above £6,000, every £250 (£500 for those aged 60 or over) of savings above this level is assumed to give an income of £1 per week for the purposes of the means test, and those with assets of more than £16,000 are not eligible for means-tested benefits at all.[48] These rules, combined with the high withdrawal rates of means-tested benefits, create a very strong disincentive for those who are on means-tested benefits, or consider themselves likely to be eligible for them in the future, to build up financial assets worth more than £6,000.

Finally, it should be noted that means-testing magnifies what was already a significant complication in the taxation of pensions. Putting earnings into a pension fund in effect defers the tax on those earnings until they are withdrawn from the fund. The ETR calculations above assume that an individual faces the same marginal tax rate at these times; but in practice, the tax rate at which an individual receives relief on their pension contributions may be very different from the rate they face in retirement, so the deferral of tax on the earnings saved can make a dramatic difference to the amount of tax actually paid. The possibility of facing withdrawal of means-tested support at either time (or both) increases the spread of possible outcomes.

Table 1.12 shows the ETRs on 25-year pension saving for some common combinations of marginal rates. A basic rate taxpayer receiving 20% tax relief on their contributions may be eligible for pension credit in retirement and see their pension income effectively taxed at 40%, giving an ETR of 18%: the tax and benefit system discourages rather than encourages pension saving for such a person. Conversely, someone contributing to a pension while facing tax credit withdrawal at 39% along with 20% basic rate income tax receives 59% relief on their contributions; if in retirement they are still a basic rate taxpayer but no longer face withdrawal of tax credits, they will pay only 20% tax on the proceeds, giving an ETR of −102%: the tax and benefit system more than doubles the rate of return on their pension saving. The ETR can

[48] This upper limit does not apply to those aged 60 or over.

Table 1.12. Effective tax rates on 25-year pension saving, for different tax and benefit positions in work and in retirement

Tax rate in work	Tax rate in retirement	Effective tax rate (%) for:	
		Employee contribution	Employer contribution
Basic rate (20%)	Basic rate (20%)	−8	−45
Higher rate (40%)	Higher rate (40%)	−21	−40
Higher rate (40%)	Basic rate (20%)	−48	−67
Basic rate (20%)	Pension Credit taper (40%)	18	−19
Tax credit taper (59%)	Basic rate (20%)	−102	−163
Tax credit taper (59%)	Pension Credit taper (40%)	−74	−136

Notes: Assumes 3% annual real rate of return and 2% inflation. 'Tax credit taper' calculations assume that the person is also paying basic-rate income tax. 'Pension credit taper' calculations assume that the person is not liable for income tax. Calculations for employer pension contribution assume that the employee is contracted into the state second pension.

Source: As for Table 1.10.

easily be outside the range shown in Table 1.12 for individuals who face withdrawal of housing benefit or council tax benefit.[49]

Such differentials can make saving in a pension appear hugely attractive or unattractive according to how individuals expect their tax and benefit position to evolve over their life-cycle, and also provides large incentives for people to concentrate their pension contributions at times when their marginal rate is highest: to make contributions at times in their life when they are either higher-rate taxpayers or facing tax credit withdrawal, rather than when they are simply paying basic rate tax. The reduced dispersion of income tax rates has reduced the magnitude of these effects to some degree: the difference between the basic and top rates of income tax is now much less than in 1978, when contributions relieved at 83% could finance pensions taxed at 33%. On the other hand, recent years have seen significant increases in both the number of people paying higher-rate income tax and the number of people subject to means tests, meaning that such considerations now affect many more people than in the past. Furthermore, annual limits on tax-relieved pension contributions were made much more generous from April 2006, increasing the scope for people to manipulate the timing of their contributions.

[49] The marginal tax rate faced by an individual can also vary over time simply because of policy changes: a pensioner currently pays basic rate tax at 20% on their pension income, but contributions he made in 1979—when also a basic rate taxpayer—received relief at 33%.

Incentives to invest

Income tax, capital gains tax, inheritance tax, and withdrawal of means-tested benefits and tax credits affect UK residents' incentives to save, with the (dis)incentive depending on the individual's tax position and the tax treatment of the savings vehicle in question. Insofar as businesses can raise funds from non-UK taxpayers such as pension funds and foreigners, these taxes have little effect on incentives for businesses to invest in the UK. As discussed above, the other main capital taxes—corporation tax, council tax, business rates, and stamp duties on property and securities—can be thought of as primarily taxing investment rather than saving: the stream of taxes to be paid is likely to be reflected largely in lower share or property prices, so that savers do no worse investing in these assets than elsewhere.

The tax system does not discourage all investment to the same degree. House-building, for example, is particularly discouraged by council tax and stamp duty land tax insofar as they reduce the amount that people will pay for the houses built—although other aspects of the tax system (such as the VAT zero-rating of new build) and the planning system are also important in determining the level of house-building in the UK.

We focus here on corporation tax, much the biggest tax on UK investment. Even if we restrict attention to corporation tax, the effective rate at which investments are taxed is not merely the statutory rate, but varies according to a wide range of factors: the form of the company's investment (plant and machinery, industrial buildings, R&D, etc.), whether it is financed by equity or by taking on debt,[50] the depreciation rate of the asset, interest rates, the rate of inflation, and so on.

Figure 1.12 showed the effective average corporation tax rate (EATR) that a firm might expect to pay on all its profits from equity-financed investment in plant and machinery, combining statutory rates and capital allowances, while making assumptions about the profitability of investment, real interest rates, depreciation rates, and inflation. This is a measure of firms' incentive to undertake such investment at all, and so is useful for comparing the relative tax-attractiveness of different countries for inbound foreign direct investment.

For firms already operating in a particular country and deciding whether or not to invest a little more, a more relevant measure is the effective marginal tax rate (EMTR). This looks at a small (marginal) investment that

[50] By equity finance we mean either issuing new shares or retaining profits (paying out lower dividends than the company otherwise would). These two sources of finance have the same treatment for corporation tax, although the personal tax implications are different.

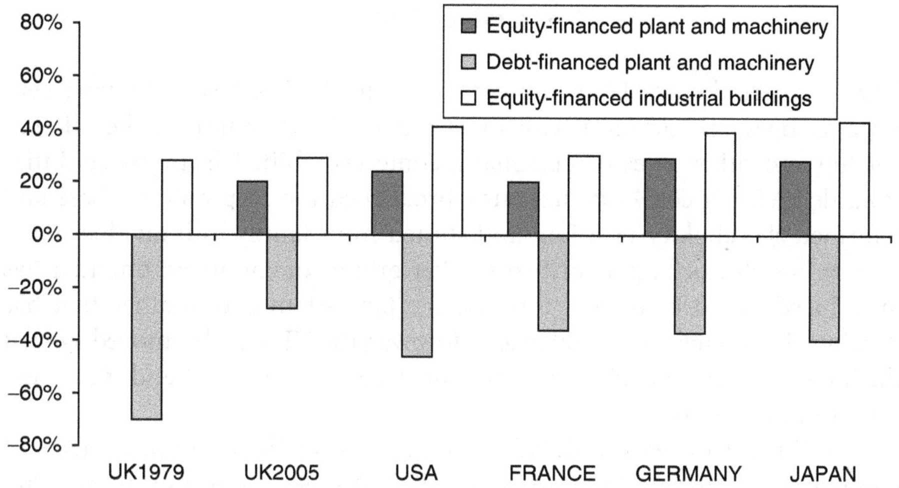

Notes: Assumes economic depreciation rates of 12.25% for plant and machinery and 3.61% for industrial buildings, inflation of 3.5%, and a real interest rate of 10%.

Sources: Tables A5, A6, and A7 of IFS corporate tax rate data <http://www.ifs.org.uk/publications.php?publication_id= 3210>.

Figure 1.23. Effective marginal corporation tax rates on different investments

is only just worthwhile for the firm to make and estimates the proportion of the additional profits it generates that would be paid in corporation tax.

EMTRs (and indeed EATRs) vary widely according to the type of asset invested in and how the investment is financed. Figure 1.23 shows the EMTRs created by corporation tax for three different investments: equity-financed plant and machinery, debt-financed plant and machinery, and equity-financed industrial buildings. All the countries shown treat investment in plant and machinery more favourably than investment in industrial buildings, and all countries treat debt-financed investment more favourably than equity-financed investment.[51] Both of these distortions have been reduced in the UK since 1979, although the removal of 100% capital allowances for plant and machinery (see Figure 1.12) has meant that equity-financed plant and machinery—easily the biggest form of investment—has seen an increase in its EMTR.

[51] Indeed, corporation tax regimes generally give substantial net subsidies to debt-financed investment. This arises because nominal (rather than real) debt interest payments are deductible from taxable profits, and because investment expenditure may often be deducted more quickly than the assets really depreciate.

1.5. CONCLUSION

Over the period since 1978, the tax system in the UK has undergone very large changes. In common with most other OECD countries, the UK has cut top and other rates of personal income tax; shifted from excise duties towards VAT; cut corporate tax rates, broadened the corporate tax base and reformed shareholder taxation; and shifted from family to individual taxation. It has also been part of two smaller groups of countries: one that has introduced in-work support through the tax system and another that has developed new environmental taxes. However, the UK has also moved against the international trends by removing mortgage interest relief and increasing centralization of tax revenues.

It is difficult to reach a definitive assessment of the economic effects of these changes, in part because of the difficulty of establishing what a 'no change' scenario would have involved. However, it is clear that Labour's tax and benefit reforms since 1997 have done more to reduce inequality directly than the Conservatives' earlier reforms, while the Conservatives' reforms did more to strengthen work incentives. There is now less distortion than thirty years ago between different savings vehicles and between different methods of financing investment.

APPENDIX

The UK tax system in 2008–09

1A.1. Income tax

The tax base

Income tax in the UK is forecast to raise £156.7 billion in 2008–09, but not all income is subject to tax. The primary forms of taxable income are earnings from employment, income from self-employment and unincorporated businesses, job-seeker's allowance, retirement pensions, income from property, bank and building society interest, and dividends on shares. Incomes from most means-tested social security benefits are not liable to income tax. Many non-means-tested benefits are taxable (e.g. the basic state pension), but some (notably child benefit) are not. Gifts to registered charities can be deducted from income for tax purposes, as can employer and employee pension contributions, although employee social security (National Insurance) contributions are not deducted. Income tax is also not paid on income from certain savings products, such as National Savings Certificates and Individual Savings Accounts.

Allowances, bands, and rates

Income tax in the UK operates through a system of allowances and bands of income. Each individual has a personal allowance, which is deducted from total income before tax to give *taxable* income. Taxpayers under 65 years old receive a personal allowance of £6,035, while older people are entitled to higher personal allowances (Table 1A.1).

In the past, married couples were also entitled to a married couple's allowance (MCA). This was abolished in April 2000, except for those already aged 65 or over at that date (i.e. born before April 1935). For these remaining claimants, the MCA no longer acts to increase the personal allowance; instead, it simply reduces final tax liability, by £653.50 in 2008–09 (£662.50 for those aged 75 or over). Couples may choose which of them claims the MCA, or they can claim half each.

If income for those aged 65 or over exceeds a certain limit (£21,800 in 2008–09), then first the higher personal allowance and then (where appropriate) the MCA are gradually reduced. The personal allowance is reduced by 50 pence for every pound of income above the £21,800 threshold, gradually reducing it to a minimum level equal to the allowance for the under-65s for those with incomes above £27,790 (£28,090 for those aged 75 or over). Above this latter threshold, those entitled to MCA have it reduced by 5 pence for every additional pound of income until it reaches a minimum level of £254.00 for those with incomes above £35,780 (£36,260 for those aged 75 or over).

The government has announced that, from 2010–11, the personal allowance will be reduced by 50 pence for every pound of income above £100,000 until half has been withdrawn, and the remaining half of the allowance will be withdrawn (at the same rate) once income exceeds £140,000.

Taxable income is subject to different tax rates depending upon the band within which it falls. The first £34,800 of taxable income (i.e. income above the personal allowance) is subject to the basic rate of 20%. Taxable income above the basic-rate limit of £34,800 is subject to the higher rate of 40%. Higher-rate tax is therefore

Table 1A.1 Personal allowances, 2008–09

Type of allowance	Allowance (£ per year)
Aged under 65	6,035
Aged 65–74	9,030[a]
Aged 75 or over	9,180[a]

[a] For higher-income individuals, these are gradually reduced to the level of the under-65s' allowance, as described in the text.

Source: HM Revenue and Customs, <http://www.hmrc.gov.uk/rates/it.htm>.

payable on income above £40,835. A new 45% rate will apply to incomes above £150,000 from 2011–12.

Savings and dividend income are subject to slightly different rates of tax. Savings income is taxed at 20% in the basic-rate band and 40% in the higher-rate band, like other income, except that savings income that falls into the first £2,320 of taxable income is subject to a lower tax rate of 10%. Dividend income is taxed at 10% up to the basic-rate limit and 32.5% above that. However, this is offset by a dividend tax credit, which reduces the effective rates to 0% and 25% respectively. This means that, for basic-rate taxpayers, company profits paid out as dividends are taxed once (via corporation tax on the company profits) rather than twice (via both corporation tax and income tax). When calculating which tax band different income sources fall into, dividend income is treated as the top slice of income, followed by savings income, followed by other income.

Bands and allowances are increased at the start (in April) of every tax year in line with statutory indexation provisions, unless Parliament intervenes. Their increase is announced at the time of the annual Budget, and is in line with the percentage increase in the Retail Prices Index (RPI) in the year to the previous September. Increases in personal allowances are rounded up to the next multiple of £10. The increase in the basic-rate limit is rounded up to the next multiple of £100.

Payments system

Most income tax is deducted at source: by employers through the Pay-As-You-Earn (PAYE) system, or by banks etc. for any interest payments. The UK income tax system is cumulative in the sense that total tax payable for a particular financial year depends upon total income in that year. Thus, when calculating tax due each week or month, the employer considers income not simply for the period in question but for the whole of the tax year to date. Tax due on total cumulative income is calculated and tax paid thus far is deducted, giving a figure for tax due this week or month. For those with stable incomes, this system will be little different from a non-cumulative system (in which only income in the current period is considered). For those with volatile incomes, however, the cumulative system means that, at the end of the tax year, the correct amount of tax should have been deducted, whereas under a non-cumulative system, an end-of-year adjustment might be necessary. To enable employers to deduct the right amount of tax, HM Revenue and Customs supplies them with a 'tax code' for each employee, which describes the allowances to which the employee is entitled. If individual circumstances change (starting to receive a pension, for example), the Revenue issues a new tax code for that individual.

Most people need do nothing more: for those with relatively simple affairs, the cumulative system means that no end-of-year adjustment to the amount of tax paid is necessary. Those with more complicated affairs, however, such as the self-employed, those with very high incomes, company directors, and landlords, must fill in a self-assessment tax return, setting down their incomes from different sources and any tax-privileged spending such as pension contributions or gifts to charity; HM Revenue and Customs will calculate the tax owed, given this information. Tax returns must be filed by 31 October if completed on paper, or 31 January if completed online; 31 January is also the deadline for payment of the tax. Fixed penalties and surcharges operate for those failing to make their returns by the deadlines and for underpayment of tax.

Tax credits

The last ten years have seen a move towards the use of tax credits to provide support that would previously have been delivered through the benefit system. Since April 2003, there have been two tax credits in operation: child tax credit and working tax credit. Both are based on family circumstances (apart from the married couple's allowance, the rest of the income tax system operates at the individual level) and both are refundable tax credits, meaning that a family's entitlement is payable even if it exceeds the family's tax liabilities.

Child tax credit (CTC) provides means-tested support for families with children as a single integrated credit paid on top of universal child benefit. Families are eligible for CTC if they have at least one child aged under 16, or aged 16–18 and in full-time education. CTC is made up of a number of elements: a family element of £545 per year (doubled for families with a child under the age of 1), a child element of £2,085 per child per year, a disabled child element worth £2,540 per child per year, and a severely disabled child element worth £1,020 per child per year. Entitlement to CTC does not depend on employment status—both out-of-work families and lower-paid working parents are eligible for it—and it is paid directly to the main carer in the family (nominated by the family itself).

Working tax credit (WTC) provides in-work support for low-paid working adults with or without children. It consists of a basic element worth £1,800 per year, with an extra £1,770 for couples and lone parents (i.e. everyone except single people without children) and an extra £735 for those working at least 30 hours a week (30 hours in total for couples). Families with children and workers with a disability are eligible for WTC provided at least one adult works 16 or more hours per week; for those without children or a disability, at least one adult must be aged 25 or over and working at least 30 hours per week to be eligible. All childless claimants without a disability will therefore be entitled to the 30-hour premium. There are supplementary payments for disability and for those over 50 returning to work. In addition, for families in which all adults work 16 hours or more per week, there is a childcare credit, worth 80% of eligible childcare expenditure of up to £175 for families with one child, or £300 for families with two or more children (i.e. worth up to £140 or £240). The childcare credit is paid directly to the main carer in the family. The rest of WTC is paid to a full-time worker (two-earner couples can choose who receives it); originally this was done through the pay packet where possible, but this proved rather burdensome for employers, and so since April 2006 all WTC has been paid directly to claimants.

A means test applies to child tax credit and working tax credit together. Families with pre-tax family income below £6,420 per year (£15,575 for families eligible only for child tax credit) are entitled to the full CTC and WTC payments appropriate for their circumstances. Once family income exceeds this level, the tax credit award is reduced by 39p for every £1 of family income above this level. The main WTC entitlement is withdrawn first, then the childcare element of WTC, and finally the child elements of the child tax credit. The family element of the child tax credit, however, is not withdrawn unless family income exceeds £50,000 per year; above that level, it is reduced by £1 for every additional £15 of income.

HM Revenue and Customs estimates that the total entitlement of claimants in 2006–07 was £20.3 billion, of which £14.9 billion was CTC and £5.4 billion WTC. These figures include £2.1 billion that is technically paid as out-of-work benefits rather than tax credits, so the amount formally classified as tax credits was £18.2 billion.[52] However, many families are paid more (and some less) than their true entitlement over the year, mostly because of administrative errors or because family circumstances changed to reduce their entitlement (e.g. spending on childcare fell) and HM Revenue and Customs did not find out early enough (or did not respond quickly enough) to make the necessary reduction in payments for the rest of the year. The scale of this problem has been reduced since the first two years of operation of CTC and WTC, but HMRC still overpaid £1 billion (and underpaid £0.5 billion) in 2006–07.[53] Primarily because of this, the total amount of tax credits actually paid out in 2006–07 was higher than entitlements, at £18.7 billion, of which £4.6 billion is counted as negative taxation in the National Accounts, with the remaining £14.1 billion classified as public expenditure. As at April 2008, 6.0 million families were receiving tax credits (or the equivalent amount in out-of-work benefits): 4.0 million receiving just child tax credit, 0.4 million receiving just working tax credit, and 1.7 million receiving both.

1A.2. National Insurance contributions

National Insurance contributions (NICs) act like a tax on earnings, but their payment entitles individuals to certain ('contributory') social security benefits.[54] In practice, however, contributions paid and benefits received bear little relation to each other for any individual contributor, and the link has weakened over time.

[52] CTC was intended to replace, amongst other things, child additions to several social security benefits. However, families that have been claiming income support or jobseeker's allowance with these child additions since before April 2004 still receive these additions unless they apply for child tax credit instead. This is purely for administrative reasons: the amount received is the same whether paid through child tax credit or additions to out-of-work benefits.

[53] For more on the operational problems with tax credits and attempts to solve them, see Brewer (2006).

[54] For details of contributory benefits, see O'Dea et al. (2007).

Table 1A.2 National Insurance contribution (NIC) rates, 2008–09 (%)

Band of weekly earnings (£)	Employee NICs		Employer NICs	
	Standard rate	Contracted-out rate	Standard rate	Contracted-out rate
0–105 (ET)	0	0	0	0
105–770 (UEL)	11	9.4	12.8	9.1
Above 770	1	1	12.8	12.8

Notes: Rates shown are marginal rates, and thus apply to the amount of weekly earnings within each band. Contracted-out rate applies to defined benefit pension schemes, i.e. contracted-out salary-related schemes (COSRSs). The rates applying to defined contribution pension schemes—i.e. contracted-out money-purchase schemes (COMPSs)—vary according to age.

Source: HM Revenue and Customs, <http://www.hmrc.gov.uk/rates/nic.htm>.

In 2008–09, National Insurance contributions are forecast to raise £97.7 billion, the vast majority of which will be Class 1 contributions. Two groups pay Class 1 contributions: employees as a tax on their earnings and employers as a tax on those they employ. Employees pay NICs at a rate of 11% on any earnings (including employee, but not employer, pension contributions) between the earnings threshold (ET, £105 per week in 2008–09) and the upper earnings limit (UEL, £770 in 2008–09), and at 1% on earnings above the UEL. Employers pay NICs for each employee who earns over the ET, at a rate of 12.8% of all earnings above this level. The 2008 Pre-Budget Report announced that these rates will all increase by 0.5 percentage points—to 11.5%, 1.5%, and 13.3% respectively—from 2011–12.

NICs are lower for those who have contracted out of the State Second Pension (formerly the State Earnings-Related Pension Scheme, SERPS) and instead belong to a recognized private pension scheme. The reduction depends on the type of pension scheme that an individual has joined. For defined benefit pensions, the percentage levied on earnings between the ET and the UEL is currently reduced by 1.6 percentage points for employee contributions and by 3.7 percentage points for employer contributions. The equivalent rebates for those who have opted out into a defined contribution pension scheme depend on age. Table 1A.2 summarizes the Class 1 contribution structure for 2008–09.

Class 1 contributions are remitted to HMRC by employers along with income tax. But unlike for income tax, NICs liabilities are calculated for each pay period (typically a week, fortnight, or month) separately, without reference to earnings in the rest of the year.

The self-employed pay two different classes of NI contributions—Class 2 and Class 4. Class 2 contributions are paid at a flat rate (£2.30 per week for 2008–09) by those whose earnings (i.e. profits, since these people are self-employed) exceed the small earnings exception, currently £4,825 per year. Class 4 contributions are currently paid at 8% on any profits between the lower profits limit (£5,435 per year for 2008–09) and the upper profits limit (£40,040 per year for 2008–09), and at 1% on profits above the upper profits limit; as for Class 1 contributions, these rates are due to increase by 0.5 percentage points from 2011–12. This regime for the self-employed is much more generous than the Class 1 regime, and the self-employed typically pay far less than would be paid by employee and employer combined.

Class 3 NI contributions are voluntary and are usually made by UK citizens living abroad in order to maintain their entitlement to benefits when they return. Class 3 contributions are £8.10 per week for 2008–09.

1A.3. Value added tax (VAT)

VAT is a proportional tax paid on all sales to UK purchasers. Before passing the revenue on to HM Revenue and Customs, however, firms may deduct any VAT they paid on inputs into their products; hence it is a tax on the *value added* at each stage of the production process, not simply on all expenditure. The standard rate of VAT is 17.5%, but this has been reduced to 15% from 1 December 2008 until 31 December 2009 as part of an economic stimulus package. Domestic fuel and power and a few other goods are taxed at a reduced rate of 5%. A number of major items are either zero-rated or exempt. Zero-rated goods have no VAT levied upon the final sale, and firms can reclaim any VAT paid on inputs as usual. Exempt goods have no VAT levied on the final good sold to the consumer, but firms cannot reclaim VAT paid on inputs; thus exempt goods are effectively liable to lower rates of VAT (typically between about 4% and 7%, depending upon the firm's cost structure and suppliers). Table 1A.3 lists the main categories of goods that are zero-rated, reduced-rated, and exempt, together with estimates of the revenue foregone by not taxing them at the standard rate.

Only firms whose sales of non-exempt goods and services exceed the VAT registration threshold (£67,000 in 2008–09) need to pay VAT. Since April 2002, small firms (defined as those with total sales below £187,500, including VAT, and non-exempt sales below £150,000, excluding VAT, in 2008–09) have had the option of using a simplified flat-rate VAT scheme. Under the flat-rate scheme, firms pay VAT at a single rate on their total sales and give up the right to reclaim VAT on inputs. The flat rate varies between industries as it is intended to reflect the average VAT rate in each industry, taking into account recovery of VAT on inputs, zero-rating, and so on. The rates for most industries were reduced in December 2008 when the main VAT rate was temporarily cut to 15%, and currently range from 2% to 12%.

VAT is expected to raise £82.6 billion in 2008–09.

1A.4. Other indirect taxes

Excise duties

Excise duties are levied on three major categories of goods: alcoholic drinks, tobacco, and road fuels. They are levied at a flat rate (per pint, per litre, per packet, etc.);

Table 1A.3 Estimated costs of zero-rating, reduced-rating, and exempting goods and services for VAT revenues, 2008–09

	Estimated cost (£m)
Zero-rated:	
Most food	11,950
Construction of new dwellings[a]	7,650
Domestic passenger transport	2,650
International passenger transport[a]	200
Books, newspapers, and magazines	1,750
Children's clothing	1,300
Water and sewerage services	1,350
Drugs and medicines on prescription	1,500
Supplies to charities[a]	200
Ships and aircraft above a certain size	700
Vehicles and other supplies to people with disabilities	400
Cycle helmets[a]	15
Reduced-rated:	
Domestic fuel and power	3,250
Women's sanitary products	50
Contraceptives	10
Children's car seats	5
Smoking cessation products	10
Energy-saving materials	50
Residential conversions and renovations	150
Exempt:	
Rent on domestic dwellings[a]	3,800
Rent on commercial properties[a]	200
Private education[a]	50
Health services[a]	900
Postal services[a]	200
Burial and cremation	100
Finance and insurance[a]	4,600
Betting, gaming, and lottery[a]	1,250
Cultural admissions charges[a]	30
Businesses below registration threshold[a]	1,650
Total	46,020

[a] Figures for these categories are subject to a wide margin of error.

Note: Costs are relative to taxation at the standard 17.5% rate, not the temporary 15% rate.

Sources: HMRC Statistics Tables 1.5 and B.1<http://www.hmrc.gov.uk/stats/tax_expenditures/ptmenu.htm>.

tobacco products are subject to an additional *ad valorem* tax of 24% of the total retail price (including the flat-rate duty, VAT, and the *ad valorem* duty itself). Since flat-rate duties are expressed in cash terms, they must be revalorized (i.e. increased in line with inflation) each year in order to maintain their real value. Table 1A.4 shows the rates of duties as of April 2008. All of these duty rates were increased in the November 2008 Pre-Budget Report (offsetting the cut in VAT, although duty

Table 1A.4 Excise duties, April 2008

Good	Duty (pence)	Total duty as a percentage of price	Total tax as a percentage of price[a]
Packet of 20 cigarettes:			
specific duty	224.1	63.9	78.8
ad valorem (22% of retail price)[b]	117.7		
Pint of beer	33.2	13.8	28.7
Wine (75 cl bottle)	145.7	40.5	55.4
Spirits (70 cl bottle)	597.8	44.7	59.6
Ultra-low sulphur petrol (litre)	50.4	46.8	61.7
Ultra-low sulphur diesel (litre)	50.4	43.2	58.1

[a] Includes VAT.

[b] 22% was the *ad valorem* rate in effect in April 2008; it rose to the 24% mentioned in the text as part of the duty increases announced in the 2008 Pre-Budget Report.

Notes: Assumes beer (bitter) at 3.9% abv, still wine not exceeding 15% abv, and spirits (whisky) at 40% abv.

Sources: Duty and VAT rates from HMRC website <http://www.hmrc.gov.uk>. Prices: cigarettes and beer from National Statistics, *Consumer Price Indices* <http://www.statistics.gov.uk>; wine and spirits from UKTradeInfo 2008 Factsheet <http://www.uktradeinfo.co.uk/index.cfm?task=factalcohol>; petrol and diesel from Table 4.1 of Department for Business, Enterprise and Regulatory Reform Quarterly Energy Prices <http://stats.berr.gov.uk/energystats/qep411.xls>.

rates will not fall back when the VAT rate returns to 17.5%), and the government had already announced that alcohol duties will increase by a further 2% above inflation every year until 2013. Excise duties are forecast to raise £41.8 billion in 2008–09.

Vehicle excise duty

In addition to VAT and excise duties, revenue is raised through a system of licences. The main licence is vehicle excise duty (VED), levied annually on road vehicles. For cars and vans registered before 1 March 2001, there are two bands. VED is £120 per vehicle for vehicles with engines smaller than 1550 cc; above this size, VED is £185. Cars and vans registered on or after 1 March 2001 are subject to a different VED system based primarily on carbon dioxide emissions. For petrol cars or vans, VED ranges from zero for vehicles emitting less than 100 g of carbon dioxide per kilometre to £210 for vehicles emitting more than 186 g of carbon dioxide per kilometre. Vehicles registered since March 2006 that emit more than 223 g of carbon dioxide per kilometre are liable for an even higher rate, £400. The government has announced changes to the VED regime for cars registered on or after 1 March 2001, with finer gradations of emissions bands to be introduced from 1 April 2009 and different VED rates for the first year of ownership to be introduced from 1 April 2010. These reforms will further increase VED rates for high-emission cars and reduce them for low-emission cars. Different rates apply for alternative fuel vehicles and for other types of vehicles, such as motorbikes, caravans, and heavy goods vehicles. In 2008–09, VED is forecast to raise £5.8 billion.

Insurance premium tax

Insurance premium tax (IPT) came into effect in October 1994 as a tax on general insurance premiums. It is designed to act as a proxy for VAT, which is not levied on financial services because of difficulties in implementation. IPT is payable on most types of insurance where the risk insured is located in the UK (e.g. motor, household, medical, and income replacement insurance) and on foreign travel insurance if the policy lasts for less than four months. Long-term insurance (such as life insurance) is exempt. Since 1 July 1999, IPT has been levied at a standard rate of 5% of the gross premium. If, however, the policy is sold as an add-on to another product (e.g. travel insurance sold with a holiday, or breakdown insurance sold with vehicles or domestic appliances), then IPT is charged at a higher rate of 17.5%. This prevents insurance providers from being able to reduce their tax liability by increasing the price of the insurance (which would otherwise be subject to insurance premium tax at 5%) and reducing, by an equal amount, the price of the good or service (subject to VAT at 17.5%). Insurance premium tax is forecast to raise £2.3 billion in 2008–09.

Air passenger duty

On 1 November 1994, an excise duty on air travel from UK airports came into effect (flights from the Scottish Highlands and Islands are exempt). Currently, the air passenger duty rate on economy flights is £10 for destinations in the EU and £40 for other destinations. The rates for those travelling first or club class are £20 within the EU and £80 elsewhere. In 2008–09, air passenger duty is forecast to raise £1.9 billion. In order to make tax liability more closely related to carbon dioxide emissions, the government has announced that the distinction between EU and non-EU destinations, will be replaced by a distinction between four distance bands from November 2009.

Landfill tax

Landfill tax was introduced on 1 October 1996. It is currently levied at two rates: a lower rate of £2.50 per tonne for disposal to landfill of inactive waste (waste that does not decay or contaminate land) and a standard rate of £32 per tonne for all other waste. The government has announced that the standard rate will increase by £8 per tonne every year until at least 2010–11.[55] The tax is forecast to raise £0.9 billion in 2008–09.

Climate change levy

The climate change levy came into effect on 1 April 2001. It is charged on industrial and commercial use of electricity, coal, natural gas, and liquefied petroleum gas, with the tax rate varying according to the type of fuel used. The levy is designed to help the UK move towards the government's domestic goal of a 20% reduction in carbon dioxide emissions between 1990 and 2010. In 2008–09, the rates are 0.456 pence per kilowatt-hour for electricity, 0.159 pence per kilowatt-hour for natural gas, 1.018 pence per kilogram for liquefied petroleum gas, and 1.242 pence per kilogram for coal. The tax does not apply to fuels used in the transport sector or for electricity generation. Energy-intensive sectors that have concluded climate change agreements that meet the government's criteria are charged a reduced rate equal to 20% of the standard climate change levy. The levy is forecast to raise £0.7 billion in 2008–09.

Aggregates levy

Aggregates levy is a tax on the commercial exploitation of rock, sand, and gravel (e.g. their removal from the originating site or their use in construction). The levy was introduced in April 2002 to reduce the environmental costs associated with quarrying. In 2008–09 it is charged at a rate of £1.95 per tonne and is forecast to raise £0.4 billion.

Betting and gaming duties

Until relatively recently, most gambling was taxed as a percentage of the stakes laid. Since October 2001, however, general betting duty (and pool betting duty for pool betting) has been charged at 15% of gross profits for all bookmakers and the Horserace Totalisator Board (the Tote), except for spread betting, where a rate of 3% for financial bets and 10% for other bets is applied. Pool betting duty (since April 2002) and bingo duty (since October 2003) are also charged at 15% of gross profits on those activities. In all cases, 'gross profits' means total stakes (and any participation fees for bingo) minus winnings paid.

Gaming duty, which replaced gaming licence (premises) duty on 1 October 1997, is based on the 'gross gaming yield' for each establishment where dutiable gaming takes place. The gross gaming yield is money gambled minus winnings paid: this consists of the total value of the stakes, minus players' winnings, on games in which the house is the banker, and participation charges, or 'table money', exclusive of VAT, on games

[55] HM Treasury (2007).

in which the bank is shared by players. Gaming duty is levied at marginal rates of between 15% and 50% according to the amount of gross gaming yield.

Duties on betting and gaming are forecast to raise £1.5 billion in 2008–09.

1A.5. Capital taxes

Capital gains tax

Capital gains tax (CGT) was introduced in 1965 and is levied on gains arising from the disposal of assets by individuals and trustees. Capital gains made by companies are subject to corporation tax. The total capital gain is defined as the value of the asset when it is sold (or given away etc.) minus its value when originally bought (or inherited etc.). As with income tax, there is an annual threshold below which capital gains tax does not have to be paid. In 2008–09, this 'exempt amount' is £9,600 for individuals and £4,800 for trusts. This is subtracted from total capital gains to give taxable capital gains. Taxable capital gains are subject to a flat rate of 18%, subject to certain exemptions and reliefs outlined below.

The key exemption from CGT is gains arising from the sale of a main home. Private cars and certain types of investment (notably those within pension funds or Individual Savings Accounts) are also exempt. Transfers to a spouse or civil partner and gifts to charity do not trigger a CGT liability: in effect, the recipient is treated as having acquired the asset at the original purchase price. Gains made by charities themselves are generally exempt. CGT is 'forgiven' completely at death: the deceased's estate is not liable for tax on any increase in the value of assets prior to death, and those inheriting the assets are deemed to acquire them at their market value at the date of death. This is partly because estates may instead be subject to inheritance tax (see below).

Entrepreneurs' relief reduces the rate of CGT to 10% on the first £1 m of otherwise taxable gains realized over an individual's lifetime on the sale after April 2008 of certain eligible assets. These eligible assets are shares owned by employees or directors of firms who have at least 5% of the shares and voting rights, unincorporated businesses and business assets sold after the closure of a business.

It is estimated that in 2008–09, capital gains tax will raise £4.9 billion. Although this represents only a small proportion of total government receipts, capital gains tax is potentially important as an anti-avoidance measure, as it discourages wealthier individuals from converting a large part of their income into capital gains in order to reduce their tax liability. In 2008–09, approximately 350,000 individuals and trusts will pay capital gains tax.

Inheritance tax

Inheritance tax was introduced in 1986 as a replacement for capital transfer tax. The tax is applied to transfers of wealth on or shortly before death that exceed a minimum threshold. The threshold is set at £312,000 in 2008–09, and the government has

Table 1A.5 Inheritance tax reductions for transfers before death, 2008–09

Years between transfer and death	Reduction in tax rate (%)	Actual tax rate (%)
0–3	0	40
3–4	20	32
4–5	40	24
5–6	60	16
6–7	80	8
7+	100	0

Source: HM Revenue and Customs, <http://www.hmrc.gov.uk/cto/customerguide/page13-1.htm>.

announced that it will increase to £325,000 in 2009–10 and £350,000 in 2010–11. Inheritance tax is charged on the part of the transfers above this threshold at a single rate of 40% for transfers made on death or during the previous three years, and is normally payable out of estate funds. Transfers made between three and seven years before death attract a reduced tax rate, while transfers made seven or more years before death are not normally subject to inheritance tax. This is set out in Table 1A.5. Gifts to companies or discretionary trusts that exceed the threshold attract inheritance tax immediately at a rate of 20%, for which the donor is liable; if the donor then dies within seven years, these gifts are taxed again as usual but any inheritance tax already paid is deducted.

Some types of assets, particularly those associated with farms and small businesses, are eligible for relief, which reduces the value of the asset for tax purposes by 50% or 100% depending on the type of property transferred. All gifts and bequests to charities and to political parties are exempt from inheritance tax. Most importantly, transfers of wealth between spouses and civil partners are also exempt. In addition to this, since October 2007 the inheritance tax threshold is increased by any unused proportion of a deceased spouse or civil partner's nil-rate band (even if the first partner died before October 2007). This means that married couples and civil partners can collectively bequeath double the inheritance threshold tax-free even if the first to die leaves their entire estate to the surviving partner.

The number of taxpaying death estates is forecast to be 17,000 in 2008–09, equivalent to around 3% of all deaths. The estimated yield from inheritance tax in 2008–09 is £3.1 billion.

Stamp duties

The main stamp duties are levied on security (share and bond) transactions and on conveyances and transfers of land and property. They are so named because,

Table 1A.6 Rates of stamp duties, 2008–09

Transaction	Rate (%)
Land and buildings:	
Up to and including £175,000[a]	0
Above £175,000 but not exceeding £250,000[a]	1
Above £250,000 but not exceeding £500,000	3
Above £500,000	4
Shares and bonds	0.5

[a] The £175,000 threshold applies only to residential properties from 3 September 2008 to 2 September 2009; outside this window it is £125,000, or £150,000 for residential properties in certain designated disadvantaged areas. The threshold for non-residential properties is £150,000 throughout.

Source: HM Revenue and Customs, <http://www.hmrc.gov.uk/so/rates/index.htm>, <http://www.hmrc.gov.uk/so/rates/sdrtrates.htm>.

historically, stamps on documents, following their presentation to the Stamp Office, indicated their payment. Nowadays, most transactions do not require a document to be stamped and are not technically subject to stamp duty: since 1986, securities transactions for which there is no deed of transfer (e.g. electronic transactions) have instead been subject to stamp duty reserve tax (SDRT), and since 2003, land and property transactions have been subject to stamp duty land tax (SDLT). This is essentially a matter of terminology, however: the rates are the same and the term 'stamp duty' is still widely used to encompass SDRT and SDLT as well. The buyer is responsible for paying the tax.

Table 1A.6 gives stamp duty rates as they stand currently. For land and property transactions, there is a threshold below which no stamp duty is paid. The threshold is £150,000 for non-residential properties; for residential properties, the threshold started 2008–09 at £125,000 (or £150,000 in certain designated disadvantaged areas) but the government later announced an increase to £175,000 for one year only from 3 September 2008. For land and property above this exemption threshold, a range of duty rates apply, depending on the purchase price. The appropriate rate of duty applies to the whole purchase price, including the part below the relevant threshold. As a result, a small difference in the purchase price can lead to a large change in tax liability if it moves the transaction across a threshold; this structure creates unnecessary distortions in the property market and is long overdue for reform. For shares and bonds, there is no threshold and stamp duty is levied at 0.5% of the purchase price.

Stamp duties are forecast to raise £8.3 billion in 2008–09. In recent years around 70% of stamp duty revenue has come from sales of land and property and the remainder from sales of securities, but these shares are likely to be strongly affected by ongoing upheaval in housing and stock markets.

1A.6. Corporation tax

Corporation tax is charged on the global profits of UK-resident companies, public corporations, and unincorporated associations. Firms not resident in the UK pay corporation tax only on their UK profits. The profit on which corporation tax is charged comprises income from trading, investment, and capital gains, less various deductions described below. Trading losses may be carried back for one year to be set against profits earned in that period or carried forward indefinitely.[56]

The standard rate of corporation tax in 2008–09 is 28%, with a reduced rate of 21% on profits under £300,000. For firms with profits between £300,000 and £1,500,000, a system of relief operates, such that an effective marginal rate of 29.75% is levied on profits in excess of £300,000. This acts to increase the average tax rate gradually until it reaches 28%. The tax rate on the first £300,000 of profits is due to rise to 22% in 2010–11, with corresponding changes to the system of marginal relief.

In broad terms, current expenditure (such as wages, raw materials, and interest payments) is deductible from taxable profits, while capital expenditure (such as buildings and machinery) is not. To allow for the depreciation of capital assets, however, firms can claim capital allowances, which reduce taxable profits over several years by a proportion of capital expenditure. Capital allowances may be claimed in the year that they accrue, set against future profits, or carried back for up to three years. Different classes of capital expenditure attract different capital allowances:

- Expenditure on plant and machinery is 'written down' on a 20% declining-balance basis.[57] But from 2008–09, the first £50,000 per year of plant and machinery investment can be written off against taxable profits immediately.

Table 1A.7 Rates of corporation tax, 2008–09

Profits (£ p.a.)	Marginal tax rate (%)	Average tax rate (%)
0–300,000	21	21
300,001–1,500,000	29.75	21–28
1,500,000 or more	28	28

Sources: HM Revenue and Customs, <http://www.hmrc.gov.uk/rates/corp.htm>.

56 The 2008 Pre-Budget Report announced that, for one year only, up to £50,000 of losses can be carried back for three years instead of the usual one year. The rules for offsetting trading losses, investment losses, and capital losses are complicated. More information can be found in Klemm and McCrae (2002) and full details in *Tolley's* Corporation Tax.

57 The declining-balance method means that for each £100 of investment, taxable profits are reduced by £20 in the first year (20% of £100), £16 in the second year (20% of the remaining balance of £80), and so on. The straight-line method with a 3% rate simply reduces profits by £3 per year for 33 years for each £100 of investment.

- Expenditure on commercial buildings may not be written down at all. Capital allowances for industrial buildings and hotels are being phased out between 2008–09 and 2010–11. In 2008–09, expenditure is written down on a 3% straight-line basis; this will fall to 2% in 2009–10 and 1% in 2010–11 before the allowance is abolished in 2011–12. However, fixtures that are integral to a building are now separately identified and can be written down on a 10% straight-line basis.
- Intangible assets expenditure is written down on a straight-line basis at either the accounting depreciation rate or a rate of 4%, whichever the company prefers.
- Capital expenditure on plant, machinery, and buildings for research and development (R&D) is treated more generously: under the R&D allowance, it can all be written off against taxable profits immediately.

Current expenditure on R&D, like current expenditure generally, is fully deductible from taxable profits. However, there is now additional tax relief available for current R&D expenditure. For small and medium-sized companies, there is a two-part tax credit, introduced in April 2000. The first part is called R&D tax relief and applies at a rate of 75% (allowing companies to deduct a total of 175% of qualifying expenditure from taxable profits, since R&D expenditure is already fully deductible). The second part is a refundable tax credit that is only available to loss-making firms. Firms can give up the right to offset losses equivalent to 175% of their R&D expenditure (or to offset their total losses, if these are smaller) against future profits, in return for a cash payment of 16% of the losses given up (up to a certain limit). An R&D tax credit for large companies was introduced in April 2002. This credit applies at a rate of 30%, allowing 130% of qualifying expenditure to be deducted from taxable profits.

In all cases, to claim R&D tax credit, companies must incur eligible current R&D expenditure of at least £10,000 in a 12-month accounting period; but the tax credit is then payable on all eligible expenditure, not just the amount above the £10,000 threshold.

Before April 1999, all companies paid their total tax bill nine months after the end of the accounting year unless profits had been distributed to shareholders in the form of dividends. In that case, firms had to pay advance corporation tax (ACT), which could then, in most cases, be deducted from the total due nine months after the end of the accounting year. In April 1999, ACT was abolished apart from certain transitional arrangements. Large companies are now required to pay corporation tax in four equal quarterly instalments on the basis of their anticipated liabilities for the accounting year, making the first payment six months into the accounting year. Small and medium-sized companies still pay their total tax bill nine months after the end of the accounting year.

Corporation tax will raise approximately £45.5 billion in 2008–09.

1A.7. Taxation of North Sea production

The current North Sea tax regime has three layers of tax: petroleum revenue tax (PRT), corporation tax, and a supplementary charge.[58] All of these taxes are levied on measures of profit, but there are some differences in allowances and permissible deductions.

Corporation tax on North Sea production is ring-fenced, so that losses on the mainland cannot be offset against profits from continental-shelf fields. Until recently, corporation tax was otherwise the same as on the mainland, but important corporation tax reforms announced in the 2007 Budget do not apply to ring-fenced activities: the rate of corporation tax on these activities remains at 30% (or 19% if profits are below £300,000) while capital allowances are more generous than on the mainland.

The supplementary charge is levied on broadly the same base as corporation tax, except that certain financing expenditure is disallowed. It was introduced in the 2002 Budget, and is currently set at a rate of 20%.

PRT is only payable on oil fields approved before March 1993. It is assessed every six months for each separate oil and gas field and then charged at a rate of 50% on the profits (less various allowances) arising in each chargeable period. PRT is forecast to raise £2.6 billion in 2008–09. It is treated as a deductible expense for both the corporation tax and the additional charge.

1A.8. Council tax

On 1 April 1993, the community charge system of local taxation (the 'poll tax', levied per individual) was replaced by council tax, a largely property-based tax. Domestic residences are banded according to an assessment of their market value; individual local authorities determine the overall level of council tax, while the ratio between rates for different bands is set by central government (and has not changed since council tax was introduced).[59]

Table 1A.8 shows the eight value bands and the proportion of dwellings in England in each band. The council tax rates set by local authorities are usually expressed as rates for a Band D property, with rates for properties in other bands calculated as a proportion of this as shown in the table. But since most properties are below Band D, most households pay less than the Band D rate: thus in England and Wales the average Band D rate for 2008–09 is £1,354, but the average rate for all households is only £1,132.

Property bandings in England and Scotland are still based on assessed market values as at 1 April 1991: there has been no revaluation since council tax was introduced.

[58] Until January 2003, some oil fields were also subject to licence royalties, a revenue-based tax.

[59] Northern Ireland operates a different system: the community charge was never introduced there, and the system of domestic rates that preceded it in the rest of the UK remained largely unchanged—still based on 1976 rental values assessed using evidence from the late 1960s—until April 2007, when a major reform took effect. Domestic rates are now levied as a percentage of the estimated capital value of properties (up to a £500,000 cap) as on 1 January 2005, with the Northern Ireland Executive levying a 'regional rate' (0.36% in 2008–09) across the whole province and each district council levying a 'district rate' (ranging from 0.19% to 0.36% in 2008–09). Reliefs

Table 1A.8 Value bands for England, September 2008

Band	Tax rate relative to band D	Property valuation as of 1 April 1991	Distribution of dwellings by band (%)
A	$\frac{2}{3}$	Up to £40,000	25.0
B	$\frac{7}{9}$	£40,001 to £52,000	19.5
C	$\frac{8}{9}$	£52,001 to £68,000	21.7
D	1	£68,001 to £88,000	15.3
E	$1\frac{2}{9}$	£88,001 to £120,000	9.5
F	$1\frac{4}{9}$	£120,001 to £160,000	5.0
G	$1\frac{2}{3}$	£160,001 to £320,000	3.5
H	2	Above £320,000	0.6

Note: Percentages may not sum exactly because of rounding.
Source: Table 2 of Communities and Local Government, *Council Taxbase 2008* <http://www.local.communities.gov.uk/finance/stats/lgfs/2008/data/ctbdwell2008.pdf>.

In Wales, a revaluation took effect in April 2005 based on April 2003 property values, and a ninth band paying $2\frac{1}{3}$ times the Band D rate was introduced.

There are a range of exemptions and reliefs from council tax, including a 25% reduction for properties with only one resident adult and a 50% reduction if the property is empty or a second home.[60] Properties that are exempt from council tax include student halls of residence and armed forces barracks. Low-income families can have their council tax bill reduced or eliminated by claiming council tax benefit.[61] Council tax, net of council tax benefit, is expected to raise £24.6 billion in 2008–09.

1A.9. Business rates

National non-domestic rates, or business rates, are a tax levied on non-residential properties, including shops, offices, warehouses, and factories. Firms pay a proportion of the officially estimated market rent ('rateable value') of properties they occupy. In 2008–09, this proportion is set at 46.2% in England and Scotland and 44.6% in Wales,[62] with reduced rates for businesses with a low rateable value:

are available for those with low incomes, those with disabilities, those aged 70 or over living alone, and full-time students, among others.

[60] Since 2003, however, councils have had the power to charge second homes up to 90% of council tax and empty homes 100%. Some empty properties are entirely exempt from council tax, e.g. those left empty by patients in hospitals and care homes.

[61] For details of council tax benefit, see O'Dea et al. (2007).

[62] Northern Ireland operates a slightly different system of regional rates (set at 29.9% in 2008–09) and locally varying district rates (ranging from 15.7% to 28.8% in 2008–09).

- In England, businesses with a rateable value below £15,000 (£21,500 in London) are charged a reduced rate of 45.8%. This is further reduced on a sliding scale for rateable values below £10,000, with the liability halved for businesses with a rateable value below £5,000.
- In Scotland, a reduced rate of 45.8% applies to businesses with a rateable value below £29,000. This is reduced by a further 20% for businesses with a rateable value between £10,000 and £15,000, 40% for rateable values between £8,000 and £10,000, and 80% for rateable values of £ 8,000 or less.
- In Wales, business rates are reduced by 25% for businesses with a rateable value between £2,000 and £5,000 and by 50% for businesses with a rateable value of £2,000 or less.

Various other reductions and exemptions exist, including for charities, small rural shops, agricultural land and buildings, and unoccupied buildings (for an initial three-month period, longer in some cases).

Properties are revalued every five years. The latest revaluation took effect in April 2005, based on April 2003 rental values. Major changes in business rates bills caused by revaluation are phased in through a transitional relief scheme.

Business rates were transferred from local to national control in 1990. Rates are set by central government (or devolved administrations in Scotland and Wales), with local authorities collecting the revenue and paying it into a central pool. Formally, this revenue is then redistributed back to local authorities; but since this amount is simply deducted from the grant that central government makes to local authorities, local authorities' income need not bear any relation to the amount that business rates bring in. However, from 2010–11 the government proposes to allow English local authorities to levy (subject to certain restrictions) a supplementary business rate of up to 2% on properties with a rateable value above £50,000 to pay for economic development projects.

Business rates are expected to raise £23.5 billion in 2008–09.

REFERENCES

Adam, S. (2005), 'Measuring the Marginal Efficiency Cost of Redistribution in the UK', IFS Working Paper W05/14, <http://www.ifs.org.uk/wps/wp0514.pdf>.

—— (2008), 'Capital Gains Tax', in Chote, R., Emmerson, C., Miles, D., and Shaw, J. (eds.), *The IFS Green Budget: January 2008*, London: Institute for Fiscal Studies, <http://www.ifs.org.uk/budgets/gb2008/08chap10.pdf>.

—— Brewer, M., and Chote, R. (2008), *The 10% Tax Rate: Where Next?*, Briefing Note 77, London: Institute for Fiscal Studies, <http://www.ifs.org.uk/bn77.pdf>.

—— —— and Shephard, A. (2006a), *The Poverty Trade-Off: Work Incentives and Income Redistribution in Britain*, Bristol: The Policy Press.

——— ——— (2006b), 'Financial Work Incentives in Britain: Comparisons Over Time and Between Family Types', IFS Working Paper W06/20, <http://www.ifs.org.uk/wps/wp0620.pdf>.

—— and Browne, J. (2009), *Redistribution, Work Incentives and Thirty Years of UK Tax and Benefit Reform*, forthcoming.

Annan, D., Jones, F., and Shah, S. (2008), 'The Redistribution of Household Income: 1977 to 2006/07', *Economic and Labour Market Review*, **3**, 31–43, London: Office for National Statistics, <http://www.statistics.gov.uk/elmr/01_09/downloads/ELMR_Jan09_Jones.pdf>.

Barker, K. (2003), *Review of Housing Supply: Interim Report—Analysis*, London: HMSO, <http://www.hm-treasury.gov.uk/consultations_and_legislation/barker/consult_barker_background.cfm>.

Barr, N. (2004), *Economics of the Welfare State*, 4th edn, Oxford: Oxford University Press.

Blow, L., Hawkins, M., Klemm, A., and McCrae, J. (2002), *Budget 2002: Business Tax Changes*, Briefing Note 24, London: Institute for Fiscal Studies, <http://www.ifs.org.uk/bns/bn24.pdf>.

Blundell, R., and Preston, I. (1998), 'Consumption Inequality and Income Uncertainty', *The Quarterly Journal of Economics*, **113**, 603–40.

Bond, S. (2006), 'Company Taxation', in Chote, R., Emmerson, C., Harrison, R., and Miles, D. (eds.), *The IFS Green Budget: January 2006*, London: Institute for Fiscal Studies, <http://www.ifs.org.uk/budgets/gb2006/06chap9.pdf>.

—— Denny, K., Hall, J., and McClusky, W. (1996), 'Who Pays Business Rates?', *Fiscal Studies*, **17**, 19–35, London: Institute for Fiscal Studies.

—— Klemm, A., and Hawkins, M. (2005), 'Stamp Duty on Shares and its Effect on Share Prices', *Finanzarchiv*, **61**, 275–97.

Brewer, M. (2006), 'Tax Credits: Fixed or Beyond Repair?', in Chote, R., Emmerson, C., Harrison, R., and Miles, D. (eds.), *The IFS Green Budget: January 2006*, London: Institute for Fiscal Studies, <http://www.ifs.org.uk/budgets/gb2006/06chap7.pdf>.

—— Goodman, A., and Leicester, A. (2006), *Household Spending in Britain: What Can It Teach Us About Poverty?*, Bristol: The Policy Press.

Browne, J. (2009), 'Income Tax and National Insurance', in Chote, R., Emmerson, C., Miles, D., and Shaw, J. (eds.), *The IFS Green Budget: January 2009*, London: Institute for Fiscal Studies, <http://www.ifs.org.uk/budgets/gb2009/09chap11.pdf>.

Clark, T., and Leicester, A. (2004), 'Inequality and Two Decades of British Tax and Benefit Reform', *Fiscal Studies*, **25**, 129–58, London: Institute for Fiscal Studies.

Crawford, I., Smith, Z., and Tanner, S. (1999), 'Alcohol Taxes, Tax Revenues and the Single European Market', *Fiscal Studies*, **20**, 287–304, London: Institute for Fiscal Studies, <http://www.ifs.org.uk/fs/articles/0009a.pdf>.

Dilnot, A., and McCrae, J. (1999), 'Family Credit and the Working Families' Tax Credit', Briefing Note 3, London: Institute for Fiscal Studies, <http://www.ifs.org.uk/bns/bn3.pdf>.

Disney, R. (2004), 'Are Contributions to Public Pension Programmes a Tax on Employment?', *Economic Policy*, **19**, 267–311.

Etheridge, B., and Leicester, A. (2007), 'Environmental Taxation' in Chote, R., Emmerson, C., Leicester, A., and Miles, D. (eds.), *The IFS Green Budget: January 2007*, London: Institute for Fiscal Studies, <http://www.ifs.org.uk/budgets/gb2007/07chap11.pdf>.

Goodman, A., Johnson, P., and Webb, S. (1997), *Inequality in the UK*, Oxford: Oxford University Press.

——and Oldfield, Z. (2004), *Permanent Differences? Income and Expenditure Inequality in the 1990s and 2000s*, Report Series 66, London: Institute for Fiscal Studies, <http://www.ifs.org.uk/comms/r66.pdf>.

Hawkins, M., and McCrae, J. (2002), *Stamp Duty on Share Transactions: Is there a Case for Change?*, Commentary 89, London: Institute for Fiscal Studies, <http://www.ifs.org.uk/comms/comm89.pdf>.

HM Treasury (2002), 'Tax Benefit Reference Manual 2002–03 Edition'.

HM Treasury (2007), *Financial Statement and Budget Report* <http://www.hm-treasury.gov.uk/media/D/0/bud07-chapter_235.pdf>.

IFS Capital Taxes Group (1989), *Neutrality in the Taxation of Savings: An Extended Role for PEPs*, Commentary 17, London: Institute for Fiscal Studies.

Immervol, H., Kleven, H. J., Kreiner, C. T., and Saez, E. (2005), 'Welfare Reform in European Countries', *OECD Social Employment and Migration Working Papers*, No. 28, OECD publishing.

Jones, F. (2008), 'The Effects of Taxes and Benefits on Household Income, 2006/07', *Economic and Labour Market Review*, **2**, 37–47, London: Office for National Statistics, <http://www.statistics.gov.uk/elmr/07_08/downloads/ELMR_Jul08_Jones.pdf>.

Klemm, A., and McCrae, J. (2002), 'Reform of Corporation Tax: A Response to the Government's Consultation Document', Briefing Note 30, London: Institute for Fiscal Studies, <http://www.ifs.org.uk/bns/bn30.pdf>.

Meyer, B., and Sullivan, J. (2003), 'Measuring the Well-Being of the Poor Using Income and Consumption', *Journal of Human Resources*, **38** (Supplement), 1180–220.

————(2004), 'The Effects of Welfare and Tax Reform: The Material Well-Being of Single Mothers in the 1980s and 1990s', *Journal of Public Economics*, **88**, 7–8, 1387–420.

O'Dea, C., Phillips, D., and Vink, A. (2007), *A Survey of the UK Benefit System*, Briefing Note 13, London: Institute for Fiscal Studies, <http://www.ifs.org.uk/bns/bn13.pdf>.

OECD (2008a), *Revenue Statistics 1965–2007*, Paris: OECD.

—— (2008b), *Taxing Wages 2006–2007*, Paris: OECD.
—— (2008c), *Consumption Tax Trends*, Paris: OECD.
Sen, A. (1973), *On Economic Inequality*, Oxford: Oxford University Press.
—— (1992), *Inequality Re-examined*, Oxford: Oxford University Press.
Wakefield, M. (2009), *How Much Do We Tax the Return to Saving?*, Briefing Note 82, London: Institute for Fiscal Studies, <http://www.ifs.org.uk/bns/bn82.pdf>.
Walker, C., and Huang, C-D. (2003), *Alcohol Taxation and Revenue Maximisation: The Case of Spirits Duty*, HM Customs and Excise Forecasting Team Technical Note Series A no. 10, <http://customs.hmrc.gov.uk/channelsPortalWebApp/downloadFile?contentID=HMCE_PROD_008438>.

Commentary by Chris Evans

Chris Evans is Professor of Taxation in the Australian School of Taxation (ATAX) at the University of New South Wales and an International Research Fellow at the Oxford University Centre for Business Taxation. He specializes in tax law and administration, capital gains taxation, tax policy, and tax reform. He is General Editor of *Australian Tax Review* and has served on a number of governmental and professional body committees and working parties, including the standing advisory panel of the Australian Board of Taxation. Before moving to Australia, he worked successively as a tax inspector, a tax consultant, and an academic in the UK.

1. INTRODUCTION

The tax system in any one country is, as Sandford (2000, p. 3) reminds us, the product of an eclectic and sometimes even fortuitous amalgam of factors. 'Historical circumstance, constitutions and legislative procedures, customs and cultures, lethargy and the costs of change, the effects of pressure groups, the influence of other countries and international groupings and agencies', and even 'the whim of a finance minister', all play their part in shaping a country's tax system as much as the identification and application of any supposedly sound economic policy drivers. The UK's tax system is no exception.

In the light of this observation, commenting on an entire tax system will always be a daunting task, and even more so when it is accompanied by the existence of temporal and geographical filters. My direct and local exposure to the UK tax system was in the 1970s and 1980s, initially as one of Her Majesty's Inspectors of Taxes, later as a tax adviser in Central London, and finally as a tax academic. I am conscious that the practice of tax—if not always the theory—may be very different in the UK now compared to then. I am equally conscious that the tyranny of distance since migrating to Australia can also act as a barrier to full or proper understanding of the intricacies of the operation of the UK tax system in later years.

But I am heartened by the view that distances in time and space can also provide a useful counterbalance to the problems of being too close to the detail of a tax system—they can provide the observer with the capacity to see the wood from the trees. And also—fortunately—this chapter on taxation in the UK by Adam, Browne, and Heady provides a more than useful contextual starting point for this commentary on the UK tax system.

Tax systems are rarely static. It is therefore not entirely surprising that taxation in the UK has moved on in the thirty years since Meade (1978). Adam et al. highlight major changes, identifying a number of the key themes, from historical, international and theoretical perspectives, that are evident in the current UK tax system. They provide a detailed analysis of many of the significant developments in the UK tax system since Meade, including essential material on the tax burden, the tax base and mix, and the tax rates and structure before going on to consider some important economic features of the UK tax system as a whole: its effects on income distribution and on incentives to work, save, and invest.

There are two features, however, that do not receive as much attention in this chapter as other aspects, but which may be more readily apparent to the external observer of the UK tax system. Both merit additional comment. The first is something of a paradox: despite the many changes that have occurred since Meade, it is somewhat surprising that so much remains the same in the UK tax system thirty years on. The second feature is the manner in which the UK tax system has become yet more complex over time in spite of many attempts at simplification. This second observation relates not just to developments in tax law design but also to the manner in which the tax system is operationalized and administered in the UK.

Each of these features is considered in more detail in the following sections.

2. THE MORE THINGS CHANGE THE MORE THEY STAY THE SAME

Reviewing the changes that have occurred in the UK tax system since Meade, there is certainly a sense in which there has been an abundance of activity. There have, for example, been myriad changes to the tax rates and structures of the major taxes.

The rate of VAT has more than doubled over the period, and there have been virtually annual changes to the tax rates and tax brackets relating to the personal income tax. As a result the personal tax schedule is broader and flatter now than it was in the late 1970s, and many of the allowances and concessions (for example, married couples' allowances, life assurance relief, mortgage interest relief) have been allowed to wither on the vine and thus have been ultimately consigned to the scrap heap of history. In the meantime a variety of concessions to encourage savings and investments (such as PEPs, TESSAs, and ISAs) have been introduced. The tax unit has shifted from the family to the individual, with the introduction of independent taxation, despite the tensions this causes alongside a tax-transfer system that operates at the level of the family. The National Insurance contribution, still a separate head of tax despite the lack of any semblance of hypothecation, has, over the period, been more closely aligned with the personal income tax structure, removing some[1] of the anomalies and arbitrage opportunities that hitherto existed.

There have also been significant changes to both the rate and the structure of the corporation tax, and the capital gains tax (CGT) has undergone major changes in the period as a result of re-basing in 1982, rate changes and the introduction and then removal of, initially, indexation and, more latterly, taper relief. Capital transfer tax has been replaced by inheritance tax, and local taxation today, with its focus on the council tax, is barely recognizable from the domestic rates system that Thatcher so fatally and unsuccessfully sought to replace with the poll tax.

And yet, despite these obvious changes to rates and structures, it is surprising how similar aspects of the contemporary taxation system in the UK are to the model that prevailed in the late 1970s. Whilst plentiful changes have taken place affecting tax rates and structure, the tax burden and the broad tax mix and tax base have remained essentially unaltered over the period. Less surprising, perhaps, is how 'comfortably' the UK system fits within the broad family of taxation systems in the developed world in the context of tax burden and tax mix.

As a percentage of GDP, total government revenues in the UK have fluctuated from just over 40% in 1979, down to about 36% in the early 1990s, and back to just over 40% today.[2] Tax receipts were by far the largest portion of those government revenues.

The UK tax burden in 2005 was very close to the OECD unweighted average of tax receipts to GDP, as shown in Table 1.

[1] But not all—witness the debate surrounding the introduction of intermediaries legislation (IR35: working through an intermediary such as a service company) in the early 2000s, designed to eliminate the avoidance of income tax and National Insurance contributions; and the general on-going tension between employment and self-employment status in the UK context.

[2] See Figure 1.1 'The tax burden, % of GDP' in this chapter.

Table 1. Ratio of tax receipts to GDP for selected comparable countries (2005)

Country	Percent of GDP
Sweden	50.7
France	44.1
Italy	41.0
Netherlands	39.1
New Zealand	37.8
United Kingdom	36.5
OECD average (unweighted)	*36.2*
Germany	34.8
Canada	33.4
Australia	30.9
Ireland	30.6
Japan	27.4
United States	27.3

Source: OECD Revenue Statistics 17 October 2007, cited in Smith (2007), p. 5.

Thus the tax burden in the UK in 2005 is not dissimilar to that of 1979, and is very close to the average of OECD countries. In similar vein, the contemporary UK tax mix, in terms of composition of revenues, is not significantly different from that which prevailed in the late 1970s.[3] Nor is it significantly different in recent years from the OECD average.[4] Overall there remains a continued reliance on the personal income tax as the principal source of revenues (roughly 28%), supplemented to a significant degree by National Insurance contributions (roughly 17%). The take from the UK VAT has increased significantly in the period 1978–79 to 2008–09, but that increase has been matched by a corresponding fall in the revenue from other indirect taxes (primarily excise duties), with the result that the revenue collected from all indirect taxes in the UK is similar now to that at the time of the Meade Report, and also similar to the current OECD unweighted average.

This analysis inevitably suggests that, despite the regular and frequent rearranging (and occasional replacement) of the furniture of the UK tax system, the fundamental architecture of the building is still in place. Rebuilding and renovations (in the sense of significant tax reform) may have taken place in other comparable jurisdictions,[5] but that has not been the case in the UK in the period since Meade.

[3] See Figure 1.3 'The composition of UK tax revenues'.

[4] See Figure 1.4 'The composition of tax revenues, 2006'.

[5] For example, in Australia significant and fundamental reform took place in 1985 and again in the late 1990s.

3. 'COMPLIFICATION'

The second striking feature of the UK tax system over the past thirty years is the extent to which its principal stakeholders have been committed to the goal of simplification, combined with their failure to achieve any such simplification over the period. Indeed, many of the initiatives designed to simplify have only served to make that system, at its technical, operational, and administrative levels, yet more complicated. This 'complification' is certainly not unique to the UK—most developed economies continue to struggle in this regard. The Australian 'Simplified Tax System' for small businesses which operated from 2001 to 2007 (Woellner et al. (2008), p. 831) stands out as an obvious example of a system that was anything but 'simplified'.

Surrey and Brannon have noted that 'simplification is the most widely quoted but least widely observed of the goals of tax policy' (1968, p. 915). It has been used (and abused) as a primary justification for tax reform over the last century, and typically it is seen as 'a good thing'—'to say that one is in favour of tax simplification is tantamount to stating that one is in favour of good as opposed to evil' Cohen, Stikeman, and Brown (1975), p. 7. McCaffery (1990, p. 1267) has noted that 'people have long sought, or said they have sought, simpler tax laws'. And yet there would be general agreement that modern tax laws are anything but simple.

A number of factors have been at work to cause the complexity. In the Australian context, Krever (2000, p. 86) identifies 'judicial misapplication [primarily of doctrines from the UK which have little or no relevance to Australia], aggressive manipulation by advisers, poor drafting by wordsmiths and narrow advice by Treasury officials' as factors contributing to complexity in the income tax law, but notes that 'in almost all cases these factors are symptomatic of or derivative from more fundamental causes of complexity'.

The more fundamental causes of complexity that Krever (2000) identifies (p. 86) are the increasing use of the tax system by modern governments to achieve social and political goals ('abuse of tax law as a spending vehicle'), and the 'many legal distinctions used throughout the law to differentiate taxpayers, transactions, investments and entities that are similar in economic effect but different in legal form, and, on the basis of the legal distinction, are subject to significantly different tax burdens'. A third factor, not mentioned by Krever, is the greater complexity of commercial and other transactions in the modern world.

McCaffery (1990) identifies three types, or layers, of complexity: 'technical'; 'structural'; and 'compliance'. All are evident in the context of the UK tax system. Technical complexity relates to the level of understanding or comprehensibility of a particular legislative provision in isolation. Structural complexity (sometimes referred to as transactional complexity), relates to the way in which laws are interpreted and applied, and which can affect the certainty and manipulability of legislative provisions. And finally compliance complexity relates to the variety of record-keeping and form-completing tasks a taxpayer must perform to comply with the tax laws. The introduction of self assessment in the UK in the 1990s, together with the changes to tax schedules and rates already noted, will certainly have considerably added to the compliance complexity. As Smith (2007, p. 24) has noted: 'a broader tax base and lower rates most often involve greater transaction numbers and recording requirements than narrower bases.'

Evidence to support the contention that the UK tax system has become more complicated at all of these levels is not difficult to find. One barometer of complexity, not always entirely convincing, is provided by reference to the volume of primary legislation in a jurisdiction. In the UK context, Broke (2000, p. 19) has noted that in the period from 1945 to 1964 the average number of pages in the annual Finance Act was about 74. Between 1965 and 1986 the average was 189 pages. Since then the average has been 289 pages. More recently a report compiled for the World Bank by Pricewaterhouse-Coopers (2007, p. 16) has suggested that in 2006 Britain had the second largest volume of tax law in the world (behind India);[6] and that the number of pages had more than doubled over the past ten years, from approximately 3,700 to 8,300 (p. 17).

Of course, a simple measure of the volume of primary tax legislation may not be an appropriate measure of the complexity of that legislation. Quantity should not be confused with quality or with impact. For example, the UK experience is undoubtedly distorted by the impact that its Tax Law Rewrite project has had on the volume of tax legislation in the last ten years. Thus far the Rewrite project has considered and redrafted a number of areas of direct taxation, including capital allowances, savings income, employment income, general income and losses, trusts, and avoidance. Relatively early in the process, Lord Howe, the chairman of the Steering Committee, had noted that the project 'can now be seen to be delivering a product that is indisputably an improvement on the previous chaos' (Howe (2001), pp. 113–14). This claim appears to be substantiated by more impartial commentators, including Broke (2000, p. 24), who states that 'there is no doubt that the final result [of the work of the Rewrite teams] is an immense improvement in terms of comprehension'.

[6] Measured by the number of pages of primary tax legislation. The figure for Britain was 8,300 compared to 9,000 pages in India (which ranked first).

A simple count of pages of primary tax legislation also misses the very significant impact that supporting regulations can have on the complexity of a tax system. The USA, for example, ranks only fifth in terms of volume in the World Bank survey (2007, p. 16), reflecting its relatively compact primary code. Once supporting regulations are taken into account, however, many commentators would argue that it has a more complex tax system than the UK.

But even if volume is not necessarily the sole criterion of complexity, it is certainly a reasonable indicator of that complexity. Another indicator of the degree of complexity in a tax system is the extent to which its taxpayers use intermediaries—tax agents—in their fiscal dealings with the revenue authority. Studies by Sandford *et al.* in the 1980s suggest that 10.5% of the personal income taxpaying population (employees and self employed) used paid tax agents in 1983–84 (Sandford et al. (1989), p. 68). Twenty years later the proportion of personal taxpayers required to submit tax returns who used paid tax agents had increased five-fold and was 53% (OECD (2005), p. 59). Although the comparable figures for corporate taxpayers are not available, in 2004, 85% of corporate tax returns were prepared with the assistance of tax professionals (OECD (2005), p. 59). This figure is almost certainly higher than it was twenty years earlier.

Perhaps one of the more reliable or convincing indicators of the complexity of a tax system is the level of its operating costs: compliance costs for taxpayers in dealing with their tax affairs and administrative costs for revenue authorities.[7] The evidence suggests (Evans (2008)) that such costs have been increasing over time in most countries, and recent UK-specific studies (Green (1994); Collard et al. (1998); Hasseldine and Hansford (2002); Evans (2003)) tend to confirm that this is certainly the case in the UK. For example, in 2002, 93% of UK tax practitioners who responded to a survey about the compliance costs of the CGT agreed or strongly agreed with the statement that 'the CGT legislation is more complex now than it was five years ago' (Evans (2003), p. 158). Practitioners identified the complexity of the legislation, and the frequency with which that legislation changed, as the two principal drivers of the high compliance costs in the CGT field (p. 163).

Frequent change in legislation, or the introduction of new legislation, can significantly impact upon the compliance burden, and it does not matter whether that change is as a result of the introduction of a relieving provision or the introduction of an integrity measure designed to protect the revenue

[7] Slemrod (1984) has argued that the total cost of collection is a useful, though flawed, index of the complexity of a tax system. It is flawed, he argues, because it does not distinguish purely compliance costs from planning costs, or between costs of administration and costs of enforcement.

base. Change has the capacity to interfere with the smooth operation of the tax administrative machinery that facilitates the interactions that necessarily occur between taxpayer and revenue authority, and which takes time to settle down to cope with change.

Moreover, if tax change is needed, it is imperative that as much consultation with affected parties as is possible and practical should be undertaken. Taxpayers, representatives from tax professional bodies, and tax practitioners as well as tax administrators all have a very real knowledge of the temporary and recurrent compliance and administrative costs that are likely to occur as a result of change, and can help to ensure that tax change is introduced in a manner that minimizes the expected burden.

Attempts at measuring the administrative burden[8] in the UK by way of a 'total tax contribution' framework[9] are at an early stage of development, but they also tend to confirm that the administrative burden in the UK is high relative to many other countries and also higher than would have been the case in earlier times (World Bank/PricewaterhouseCoopers (2007)).

In short, therefore, the fundamental architecture of the UK tax system may not have needed significant capital works in the past thirty years, but ever higher maintenance costs have been involved in managing the complexity[10] of that system that has steadily increased in that period.

4. CONCLUSIONS AND FUTURE CHALLENGES

At the outset of this commentary, reference was made to the wide range of factors that help to shape a tax system. Overall, the forces that have been at work in shaping the UK tax system have produced one that is robust and which has stood the test of time. Change has taken place, but that change

[8] Administrative burden is a somewhat different concept from operating costs. It is defined by the UK National Audit Office (in OECD (2008), p. 3) as 'the cost to business of carrying out administrative activities that they would not carry out in the absence of regulation, but that they have to undertake in order to comply with it'. It is therefore closer to, but not synonymous with, compliance costs.

[9] The total tax contribution that a corporation makes comprises information from five areas collated to establish a complete appreciation of a company's overall economic contribution. These five areas are: the business taxes borne; the business taxes collected; tax compliance costs; other payments to and from government; and indirect economic impacts. The framework has been developed by PricewaterhouseCoopers, who sought to identify a methodology which would enable companies in different tax jurisdictions to collect and report total tax information in a consistent manner (World Bank/PricewaterhouseCoopers (2007), p. 31).

[10] Both Surrey ((1969), p. 673) and Grbich ((1990), p. 266) explore the notion that the focus needs to be upon 'managing complexity' rather than upon 'simplification'.

has been incremental and has not been as dramatic as might at first be supposed. The system has had to adapt (and has generally adapted well) to new circumstances and realities, including the challenges of globalization and the shift to a much more open economy than was the case thirty years ago. The system is certainly far more complex now, and that complexity exacts a high price in terms of compliance and the burdens it imposes.

There are a number of current and impending challenges—environmental, economic, political, institutional, legal, social, and administrative—that will compel the system to continue to adapt in the future, and will also impose further costs. These factors are worthy of some further, albeit brief, consideration.

The UK tax system currently raises, as Adam, Browne, and Heady note, some 7 or 8% of total tax revenue from what can loosely be called environmental taxes, with the bulk of that coming from various motoring taxes. There is little doubt that environmental considerations—particularly shaped by the climate change debate—will play a greater role in the UK tax system in future years. Various existing taxes can expect to be adapted to serve environmental imperatives better, and new taxes are also likely. Carbon taxes may not ultimately prevail, but the tax implications of their obvious alternative—carbon emissions trading schemes—will nonetheless ensure that environmental factors will take a more central role in shaping the tax system as it moves forward.

An obvious economic factor that will continue to have an impact upon the shape of the UK tax system is globalization. The legislation underpinning the UK tax system in the last thirty years has ensured that London has been able to attain, and subsequently retain, its status as one of the leading financial centres or hubs of the world. But capital is highly mobile, and so too are certain high wealth individuals. Changes to tax rules can have an immediate and potentially devastating impact upon that status, as is evident from the current implications of the change to the legislation relating to the tax status of resident but non-domiciled individuals in the UK.

Tax is politics with a dollar sign in front, and political and institutional factors will always help to shape the future direction of the UK tax system. The hysteria (and subsequent reform by the Labour government) generated by the mass media after the Conservative Party proposals to increase the inheritance tax threshold were aired in 2007 is testament to the force of simple politics in the UK tax system. Such pressures will re-emerge in this and other areas.

Future political and institutional challenges will also include the supranational pressure that will come from the European Union in the direct tax field, matching earlier encroachments on national fiscal sovereignty in indirect taxation. There will be real questions in the future, some of which are already being debated around the issue of a common consolidated corporate tax base, about how much room will be left for national tax policy formulation by member states of the European Union.

Debate about the size of the tax gap and shadow economy, together with the unabated growth of what revenue authorities often term aggressive tax planning, will ensure that legal and social responses relating to tax evasion and tax avoidance will continue to be powerful forces in shaping the tax system of the future, in the UK as well as elsewhere. These responses against what Tanzi (2000) and Braithwaite (2005) have respectively called 'fiscal' and 'moral' termites will continue to include a host of compliance activities as well as the development of specific anti-avoidance rules and further disclosure regimes.

There is now recognition that tax simplification is not always possible, and that managing complexity is all that can be hoped for. This places a strong onus on getting the administration of the tax system right—if tax is inevitably complex at the technical and structural levels, at least ensure that the compliance complexity is as well managed and administered as possible. It also entails appropriate consultation, and getting it right first time whenever possible, in order to avoid the problems associated with frequent tax change. Failure to consult, as the UK's 2006 proposals on the bringing forward of dates for filing of annual returns has shown, can be disastrous. In that case some seemingly sensible recommendations by Lord Carter, made without any meaningful input from affected parties, had to be withdrawn when it became obvious that they were not capable of sensible implementation and would not be happily accepted by tax practitioners because of the compliance cost implications. Earlier and more appropriate consultation would have averted an otherwise embarrassing situation.

The OECD (2008, pp. 5–6) has already identified a number of key policy and administrative strategies that are taking place which can help to contain the administrative burden that the tax system imposes. These include re-engineering government processes for the collection of data and revenue; implementing citizen and business centric approaches to tax administration; leveraging advances in technology; and redesigning compliance interventions. Administrative initiatives such as these will inevitably help to shape the future UK tax system.

It will certainly be interesting to see just what impact these administrative factors, along with the various other factors mentioned above, will have on the shape of the UK tax system in the next thirty years.

REFERENCES

Braithwaite, J. (2005), *Markets in Vice: Markets in Virtue*, Leichardt: Federation Press.

Broke, A. (2000), 'Simplification of Tax or I Wouldn't Start from Here', *British Tax Review*, no. 1, 18–26.

Cohen, M., Stikeman, H., and Brown, R. (1975), *Tax Simplification*, p. 7. 27th Tax Conference of the Canadian Tax Foundation, Quebec (November).

Collard, D., Green, S., Godwin, M., and Maskell, L. (1998), *The Tax Compliance Costs for Employers of PAYE and National Insurance in 1995–96*, London: Inland Revenue Economics papers, no. 3.

Evans, C. (2003), *Taxing Personal Capital Gains: Operating Cost Implications*, 158, Sydney: Australian Tax Research Foundation.

—— (2008), 'Taxation Compliance and Administrative Costs: An Overview', in Lang, M., Obermair, C., Schuch, J., Staringer, C., and Weninger, P. (eds.), *Tax Compliance Costs for Companies in an Enlarged European Community*, Vienna: Linde Verlag; and London: Kluwer Law International.

Grbich, Y. (1990), 'Operational Strategies for Improving Australian Tax Legislation', *Federal Law Review*, **19**, 266.

Green, S. (1994), *Compliance Costs and Direct Taxation*, London: The Institute of Chartered Accountants in England and Wales.

Hasseldine, J., and Hansford, A. (2002), 'The Compliance Burden of the VAT: Further Evidence from the UK', *Australian Tax Forum*, **17**, 369–88.

Howe Lord, G. of Aberavon (2001), 'Simplicity and Stability: the Politics of Tax Policy', *British Tax Review*, no. 2, 113–23.

Krever, R. (2000), 'Simplicity and Complexity in Australian Income Tax', in Petersen, H., and Gallagher, P. (eds.), *Tax and Transfer Reform in Australia and Germany* p. 86. Berlin: Berliner Debatte Wissenschaftsverlag.

McCaffery, E. (1990), 'The Holy Grail of Tax Simplification', *Wisconsin Law Review*, 1267–322.

Meade, J. (1978), *The Structure and Reform of Direct Taxation: Report of a Committee chaired by Professor J. E. Meade for the Institute for Fiscal Studies*, London: George Allen & Unwin. http://www.ifs.org.uk/publications/3433.

OECD (2005), *Survey of Trends in Taxpayer Service Delivery Using New Technologies*, p. 59. Paris: Centre for Tax Policy and Administration.

—— (2008), *Programs to Reduce the Administrative Burden of Tax Regulations in Selected Countries*, Paris: Centre for Tax Policy and Administration.

Sandford, C. (2000), *Why Tax Systems Differ: A Comparative Study of the Political Economy of Taxation*, p. 3, Bath: Fiscal Publications.

—— Godwin, M., and Hardwick, P. (1989), *Administrative and Compliance Costs of Taxation*, p. 68, Bath: Fiscal Publications.

Slemrod, J. (1984), *Optimal Tax Simplification: Toward a Framework for Analysis*, USA: Proceedings of the 76th Annual Conference of the National Tax Association.

Smith, G. (2007), *Australia's Aggregate Tax Burden: Measurement, Interpretation and Prospects*, p. 24. Sydney: Australian Tax Research Foundation.

Surrey, S. (1969), 'Complexity and the Internal Revenue Code: the Problem of the Management of Tax Detail', *Law and Contemporary Problems*, **34**, 673.

—— and Brannon, G. (1968), 'Simplification and Equity as Goals of Tax Policy', *William and Mary Law Review*, **9**, 915.

Tanzi, V. (2000), *Globalisation Technological Developments and the Work of Fiscal Termites*, Washington, DC: International Monetary Fund WP/00/181.

Woellner, R., Barkoczy, S., Murphy, S., and Evans, C. (2008), *Australian Taxation Law*, 831. Sydney: CCH (18th edn).

World Bank/PricewaterhouseCoopers (2007), *Paying Taxes: The Global Picture*, pp. 16–17. Washington, DC: The World Bank.

2

Means-testing and Tax Rates on Earnings

*Mike Brewer, Emmanuel Saez, and Andrew Shephard**

Mike Brewer is Director of the Direct Tax and Welfare Research Programme at the IFS and a Research Affiliate of the National Poverty Center at the University of Michigan. His main research interests are in the impact of welfare reform and the personal tax and benefit system on families with children. He has evaluated the labour market impact of the working families' tax credit, and the impact of a time-limited in-work programme for lone parents in the UK. He has written widely about the current UK government's ambition to eradicate child poverty.

Emmanuel Saez is a Professor of Economics at the University of California, Berkeley, and a Research Associate at the National Bureau of Economic Research. He received his PhD in Economics from MIT in 1999. He is currently Editor of the *Journal of Public Economics.* His main areas of research are taxation, redistribution, and income and wealth inequality. In the field of optimal income taxation, he has notably published 'Using Elasticities to Derive Optimal Income Tax Rates' in the *Review of Economic Studies* and 'Optimal Income Transfer Programs' in the *Quarterly Journal of Economics.*

Andrew Shephard is a PhD scholar at the IFS, where he was previously a Research Economist. His main research interests are in structural models of the labour market, the application of these models in evaluating policy reforms, and the implication of these models for tax design.

* We thank Stuart Adam, Tony Atkinson, Kate Bell, Richard Blundell, Hilary Hoynes, Paul Johnson, Guy Laroque, Costas Meghir, James Mirrlees, Robert Moffitt, James Poterba, and numerous conference participants for helpful comments and discussions. Saez acknowledges financial support from the National Science Foundation grant SES-0134946. The Survey of Personal Incomes, the Labour Force Survey, and Family Expenditure Survey, the Family Resources Survey and the General Household Survey datasets are crown copyright material, and are reproduced with the permission of the Controller of HMSO and the Queen's Printer for Scotland. The SPI, LFS, and GHS datasets were obtained from the UK Data Archive, FRS from the Department for Work and Pensions, and the FES from the Office for National Statistics. None of these government departments nor the UK Data Archive bears any responsibility for their further analysis or interpretation.

EXECUTIVE SUMMARY

The setting of income tax rates and the generosity and structure of income support programmes generate substantial controversy among policy-makers and economists. At the centre is a trade-off between the goals of equity and efficiency: governments want to transfer resources from the rich to the poor; on the other hand, such transfers reduce people's incentive to work.

The key insight from the standard 'optimal income tax model' developed by James Mirrlees is that marginal rates of tax and benefit withdrawal should be higher when people's choices of how much to work are relatively unresponsive to them and when the government is relatively keen to redistribute resources from rich to poor. Furthermore, the government should apply high marginal rates at points in the earnings distribution where there are few taxpayers relative to the number of taxpayers who have earnings exceeding this amount. Using data on the UK earnings distribution, we show that the optimal structure of marginal rates in this simplified model has a U-shaped pattern, with high marginal rates imposed on high and low earners and lower marginal rates on those in the middle. We show how this structure changes as both the assumed responsiveness of hours of work and the government's assumed preferences for redistribution vary.

The way that incomes have responded to the large changes in top marginal tax rates over the past forty years suggests that if the richest 1% see a 1% fall in the proportion of each additional pound of earnings that is left after tax, then the income they report will rise by less than half that—only 0.46%. Although a tentative estimate, this suggests that the government would maximize the revenue it collects by imposing an overall marginal rate on the highest earners of 56.6%, very close to the 52.7% currently charged in the UK (including income tax, National Insurance contributions, and indirect taxes). So there does not seem a powerful case for increasing the income tax rate on the very highest earners, even on redistributive grounds—it would not generate much, if any, extra revenue to transfer to the less well off.

When the optimal tax model is enriched by allowing individuals to respond to taxes and benefits by deciding whether or not to work, as well as how hard, then the optimal structure of marginal rates changes dramatically. In particular, when the decision whether to work becomes relatively more important than the decision about how much to work, then marginal rates and the proportion of gross income taken in tax and withdrawn benefits when people enter work should be set low (and perhaps even negative) for potential low earners rather than set high as the standard model suggests.

We also discuss how the design of taxes and benefits affecting an individual should be affected by the presence of a co-resident partner or dependent children, although it is difficult to reach definitive conclusions. We argue that the practical operation of benefits and tax credits for low-income families is important and that they would be of greatest help to beneficiaries if they were assessed over short periods and paid promptly without retrospective adjustment.

These insights from optimal tax theory are contrasted with the work incentives inherent in the current UK tax and benefit system. Four key deficiencies are identified:

1. The amount of gross income taken in tax and withdrawn benefits when people enter work at low earnings is too high: for most groups it is close to 100% before individuals are entitled to the working tax credit, and they remain high even with it.
2. The marginal rate of 73.4% that many low to moderate earners face when having tax credits withdrawn is likely to be above the optimal rate even if people's decision to work a little harder is relatively unresponsive.
3. Housing Benefit, the main means-tested programme through which the government helps people on relatively low incomes with their housing costs has an extremely high withdrawal rate. This exacerbates the problem of undesirably high marginal rates. It is also hard to administer and is not claimed by many working families entitled to it.
4. While the system for administering income tax and national insurance contributions in the UK is simple and efficient, tax credits, housing benefit, and council tax benefit are all burdensome to claim, relatively expensive for the government to administer, and prone to significant fraud and error.

Given this diagnosis, we suggest a set of changes to the existing tax and benefit structure that could be made immediately based on the lessons from our analysis. Our package of 'immediate reforms' involves:

- Increasing the amount people can earn before they have means-tested benefits withdrawn. This would increase the financial gain on entering work at low earnings.
- Increasing the amount that second earners can earn before a family's tax credits are withdrawn. This would improve the financial incentive for a second earner to enter work, especially if they have children.

- Reducing the rate at which child and working tax credits are withdrawn with every extra pound earned.
- Targeting increases in working tax credit on groups other than lone parents.

This would cost around £9 billion per year. If it had to be financed from within the income tax and benefit system, the money could be raised by cutting child benefit and/or increasing the basic rate of income tax. Neither would undo the objectives of the reform package to improve work incentives, although both would pose big political challenges.

We also suggest a more radical and comprehensive plan for reforming the UK household tax and benefit system that attempts to deal not only with these work incentive issues, but also the administrative failings that we identify. Our plan replaces the existing piecemeal benefits for low-income families (income support, working and child tax credits, housing benefit, and council tax benefit) with a single Integrated Family Support (IFS) programme which provides stronger and simpler incentives for work at the bottom, reduces compliance costs for families, and is means-tested by employers' withholding from earnings in the same way as for National Insurance contributions. We show how, after including an assessment of the behavioural responses, the IFS manages to redistribute more income with minimal impact on total earnings and total net tax revenue, by targeting net tax cuts where incentives to work are currently at their weakest.

2.1. INTRODUCTION

The setting of income tax rates, and the generosity and structure of income support (or transfer) programmes generate substantial controversy among policy-makers and economists. At the centre is an equity–efficiency trade-off. On the one hand, governments value redistribution, and so want to transfer resources from the rich to the poor, usually by taxing the incomes of the rich and subsidizing the incomes of the poor. On the other hand, this redistribution is generally costly in terms of economic efficiency because of the disincentive effects of taxes and transfers (we explain this in more detail in Section 2.2). The costs arise for two reasons: first, raising income taxes may weaken the labour supply and entrepreneurship incentives of middle- and high-income individuals who face the taxes. Second, income transfer programmes may weaken the labour supply incentives of their recipients.

These two responses can substantially raise the cost of improving the living standards of low income families.

The goal of this chapter is to provide an overview of the way economists think about the design of taxes and benefits affecting households, and to apply the lessons from this literature to the design of the UK tax and benefit system.

In economics research, the problem of designing taxes and benefits is tackled in two steps. The first step is a positive analysis, where economists develop models of individual behaviour to understand how individuals' work decisions respond to taxes and benefits. The central part of the positive analysis is the empirical estimation of models of individual behaviour, and there is a very broad literature that tries to estimate the size of the behavioural responses to taxes and benefits.[1]

The second step is the normative analysis, or optimal policy analysis. Using models developed in the positive analysis, the normative analysis investigates what structure and size of the tax and benefit system would best meet a given set of policy goals; following Mirrlees (1971), economists call this line of research 'optimal tax theory'. Despite its name, optimal tax theory concerns itself just as much with the design of benefits as it does the setting of income tax rates: one of the key concepts of optimal tax theory is that of a net tax function, whereby people with high incomes pay some of that income in positive taxes to the government, and people with a low income receive money from the government (by paying negative taxes); no conceptual distinction is made between net recipients from and net contributors to the state's finances.[2]

At its heart, optimal tax theory says that the two desirable features of a tax and benefit system are that it be fair, and that it minimize disincentive effects.[3] But the problem of having two desirable features is that one has to know how much weight to give to each. For example, a poll tax (under which all individuals have to pay the same level of tax) might have no disincentive effects, but is rather unfair to those on low incomes. As Heady (1993, p. 17) says, 'the approach of the optimal tax literature is to use economic analysis to combine these criteria into one'. It does this by saying that the objective

[1] The way that these models are estimated, and the key insights, are summarized in Meghir and Phillips, Chapter 3.

[2] One difference between the tax system and the transfer system is that the former is usually cheaper to administer, and these distinctions can be reflected in more complicated optimal tax models.

[3] More complicated models can allow for other desirable features: one might be that a tax and transfer system is cheap to administer; Shaw, Slemrod, and Whiting, Chapter 12, consider how this alters optimal tax models.

of the government when designing the tax and benefit system should be to maximize social welfare (subject to a need to raise a certain amount of revenue). Precisely how social welfare is expressed is not relevant at this stage, but the idea is that it reflects in a single index (or number) the desire both to have the economy as large as possible (because this directly increases people's well-being) but also to have the income distributed as equally as possible. The expression for social welfare precisely quantifies the trade-off between these two desiderata: returning to the previous example of an economy with only a poll tax, replacing that with an income tax which raised the same amount of money would give a more equal distribution of income, but—if there are any disincentive effects to taxation—a smaller economy.

The normative analysis is crucial for policy-making because it shows how taxes and benefits should be designed in order best to attain the goals of the policy-maker. In particular, the normative analysis allows one to assess separately how changes in the redistributive criterion of the government, and changes in the size of the behavioural responses to taxes and transfers, affect the optimal tax and benefit programme. Conversely, the normative analysis makes it explicit that one cannot hope to say how best to design taxes and transfers both without knowing how individuals will respond, and without specifying what one is trying to achieve overall. Often, these two elements are confused in policy debates: right-of-centre policy-makers rarely state explicitly that they have little taste for redistribution, but instead justify their lack of taste for redistribution because they believe that the adverse behavioural responses to high taxes or generous benefits are large. Conversely, left-of-centre policy-makers emphasize the redistributive virtues of benefits and assume that adverse behavioural responses to these and the high tax rates needed to fund them are negligible.

We provide this overview as follows: Section 2.2 introduces the standard optimal tax model developed in Mirrlees (1971). This shows directly how the optimal tax and benefit system is determined by both the social welfare criterion used by the government and the size of behavioural responses to taxation. Despite the simplifications inherent in the model, we can use it to analyse the optimal tax rate that should apply to top incomes, where we present new, albeit tentative, evidence on the response of top incomes to the large changes in top marginal tax rates that have taken place in the UK over the last forty years. Section 2.3 extends the optimal tax model to allow for labour supply participation effects, and shows that allowing for such responses can drastically change the optimal tax system affecting low-income individuals: instead of traditional welfare programmes with high withdrawal rates, large in-work benefits such as Working Tax Credit in the UK or the Earned Income Tax Credit from the US, which can have very low or negative withdrawal rates, can be optimal.[4] We also discuss the issue of migration and tax design, which can be dealt with in optimal tax models in a similar manner to the issue of labour market participation. Throughout Sections 2.4 and 2.5, we make use of the summary of the literature on the behavioural response to taxation provided in Meghir and Phillips, Chapter 3.

In Section 2.4, we discuss how the family should be taxed: the models considered in Sections 2.2 and 2.3 abstract from family issues, but a majority of adults in reality live in couples, and so can be assumed to pool income to some extent. We also discuss how the presence of children should be reflected in the optimal tax design. Section 2.5 discusses conditionality, the contributory principle and administrative and operational issues concerning benefit systems.[5] Section 2.6 describes how the main elements of the current UK personal tax and benefit system affect incentives to work and earn more and, in Section 2.7, we provide a critique of the UK tax and benefit system, and set out the direction of reform suggested by the insights from optimal tax theory, and the latest evidence on the behavioural response to taxation. To crystallize ideas, we propose specific changes that could be implemented in the short run. But most optimal tax theory uses simplified models which leave aside a number of important practical issues such as administrative burden for the government and employers, and ease of use for families.[6] Those issues have always been important in practice, and the recent 'behavioural economics' literature is starting to incorporate them in the analysis. Therefore, we go further and propose a longer-term reform that builds on the short-run changes to incentives by addressing the main practical issues with the current benefits in the UK. Our plan replaces the piecemeal benefits for low-income families (income support, working and child tax credits, housing benefit, and council tax benefit) into a single *Integrated Family Support* programme which provides stronger and simpler incentives for work at the bottom, reduces compliance costs for families, and is provided 'as-you-earn' and administered in the same way as social contributions through the PAYE withholding system.We show how this can be done in a revenue-neutral fashion, and estimate the behavioural responses to such a reform.

[4] To anticipate our discussion in Section 2.5, the WTC can lead to negative PTRs, but not negative METRs, whereas the EITC can lead to negative METRs as well.

[5] Shaw, Slemrod, and Whiting, Chapter 12, discuss administrative and operational issues affecting tax design.

[6] A number of those issues are discussed in more detail in Chapter 12 by Shaw, Slemrod, and Whiting.

2.2. THE STANDARD OPTIMAL INCOME TAX MODEL WITH INTENSIVE RESPONSES

This section presents the standard model of optimal income tax, based on Mirrlees (1971), in which individuals respond to the tax and benefit system by choosing only how much to work. We then give two applications of the model to the UK:

- First, we can derive an expression for the optimal top marginal tax rate (i.e., the marginal tax rate facing the highest income individuals), and we go on to calculate this using new, albeit tentative, evidence on the responsiveness of top incomes in the UK to changes in top marginal tax rates over the last forty years.
- Second, we simulate the entire optimal tax system for the UK given some various highly simplifying assumptions in order to show how the optimal tax system is determined by both the social welfare criterion used by the government, and the size of behavioural responses to taxation.

Before that, though, Section 2.2.1 sets out some of the key terms which will occur throughout this chapter.

2.2.1. Key concepts

The budget constraint, PTRs and METRs

A useful tool to investigate the disincentive effects of taxes and transfers is the budget constraint.[7] This shows the relationship between gross earnings (or hours of work) and net income after taxes and transfers, and an example is given in Figure 2.1A (the example is for a lone parent with two children, and we discuss this figure in more detail and look at other family types in Section 2.6).

The budget constraint contains all the information we need to know about how taxes and transfers affect financial incentives to work, but in this chapter we frequently refer to some summary measures of work incentives:

- The participation tax rate (PTR) is defined as 1 minus the financial gain to work as a proportion of gross earnings. It measures how the tax and benefit system affects the financial gain to work. If someone who did not work had an income from a benefit programme of £60 a week, and would earn £250 in gross earnings, but pay £40 of that in income tax if

[7] This draws on Chapter 2 of Adam et al. (2006).

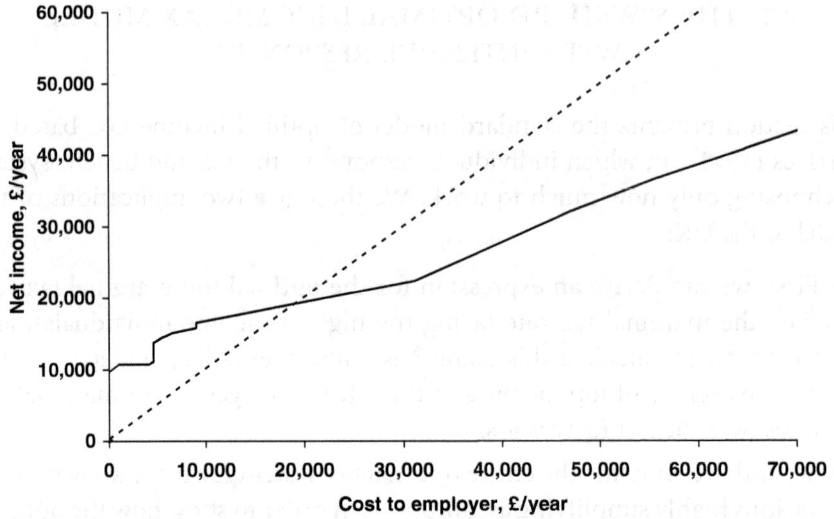

Notes: Assumes a lone parent with two children, paying £80 per week in rent, no childcare costs, average Band C council tax, and with a wage of £5.52 per hour. Incomes are calculated under the April 2008 tax and benefit system with announced changes to the higher-rate threshold and UEL, but without the £600 rise in the income tax personal allowance.

Figure 2.1A. Example budget constraint, lone parent

they were to work, then the PTR is given by 1−(210–60)/250, or 40%. The higher the number, the more the tax and benefit system reduces the financial gain to work. A PTR in excess of 1 means the individual would be worse off in work than not working; a PTR equal to 1 means that there is no financial reward to work; a PTR of zero means that the financial reward to work is equal to gross earnings; negative PTRs are possible where benefits are conditional on being in work or having positive earnings.

- The marginal effective tax rate (METR) measures how much of a small rise in gross earnings is lost to payments of tax and reduced entitlements to benefits. It is equal to the slope of the budget constraint at any particular point. The higher the number, the more the tax and benefit system reduces the gain to earning a bit more: a METR in excess of 1 means that an individual would be worse off if they earned a bit more; a METR of 1 means that an individual would be unaffected by any small change in earnings; a METR of zero means that the individual is keeping all of any small rise in earnings; and a negative METR means that an individual's net income increases by more than a small change in earnings (this can arise where benefits act as a proportional subsidy on

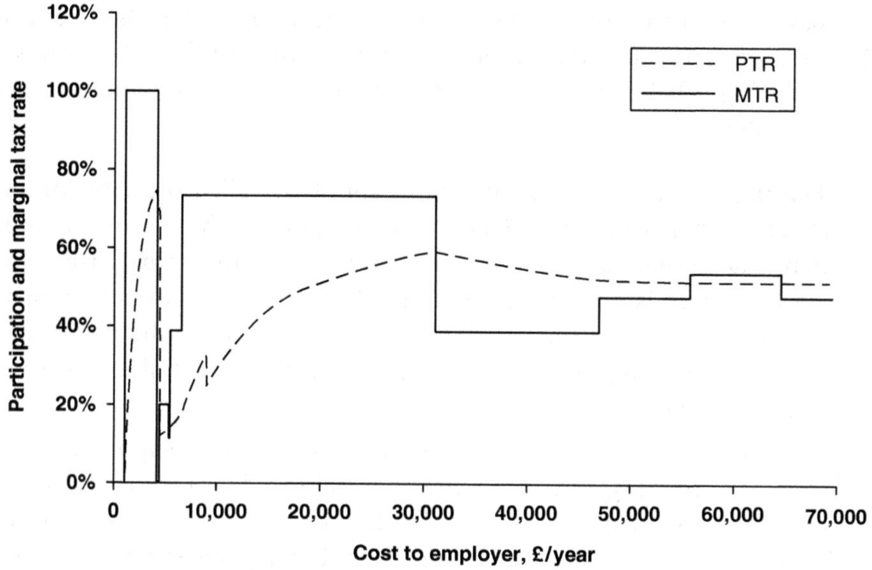

Notes: As for Figure 2.1A.

Figure 2.1B. Participation and marginal tax rates, lone parent

earnings, such as the phase-in portion of the earned income tax credit in the US).

- It is sometimes more useful to consider the net-of-tax rate, or one minus the METR: this measures how much work pays at the margin.

Figure 2.1B shows the schedule of PTRs and METRs for the example budget constraint in Figure 2.1A; we discuss the particular features of this budget constraint in Section 2.6.

Labour supply responses to taxation

Economists think about the disincentive effects of the tax and benefit system using a labour supply model.[8] A basic labour supply model assumes that, when deciding whether and how much to work, people trade off the financial reward to working (plus any intrinsic benefits from working) with the loss of leisure time (by 'work' we mean 'participate in the labour market', rather than doing unpaid work at home or elsewhere).

As we discussed above, taxes and transfers affect labour supply because they alter the financial reward to working, both by making the net wage lower than

[8] See Meghir and Phillips, Chapter 3, and references therein, for more detail.

the gross wage (most taxes, some transfers) and by reducing the financial gain from working compared to not working (most transfers). Economists usually distinguish between two ways that financial considerations affect labour supply:[9]

1. The impact of the METR on labour supply is called the substitution effect, as increasing the METR (thereby reducing the net-of-tax rate) may lead individuals to work less, or to substitute some leisure for work. Economists often measure this effect using the elasticity of earnings with respect to the net-of-tax rate: this measures the percentage increase in earnings following a one percent increase in the net-of-tax rate (Box 2.1).
2. In addition, taxes and transfers may also affect labour supply through income effects: higher taxes or cuts in benefits reduce the income available to individuals, and so may induce individuals to work more in order to increase their standard of living. Equally, lower taxes or more generous benefits increase income, and hence may induce individuals to work less. Because the derivation of optimal income tax models is much simpler when there are no income effects (Diamond (1998) and Saez (2001)), we will assume no income effects in the analysis below, and discuss later informally how the main results change when there are income effects.

Box 2.1. The elasticity of earnings

We denote the marginal effective tax rate by τ so that the net-of-tax rate is given by $1 - \tau$. The elasticity of earnings z with respect to the net-of-tax rate $1 - \tau$ is defined as:

$$e = \frac{1-\tau}{z}\frac{\partial z}{\partial(1-\tau)}.$$

This elasticity e is always positive. The higher is e, the more responsive are earnings to the net-of-tax rate.

To give an example of its use, if e is 0.2, and the net-of-tax rate changes from 20% to 25% (i.e., the METR falls from 80% to 75%), then earnings will rise by $0.2 \times \frac{5\%}{20\%} = 5\%$. If the net of tax rate changes from 80% to 75% (i.e., the METR rise from 20% to 25%), then earnings will fall by $0.2 \times \frac{5\%}{80\%} = 1.25\%$.

[9] Meghir and Phillips, Chapter 3, shows the different impacts graphically.

2.2.2. The Mirrlees model

In the Mirrlees model of optimal taxes, the government is trying to design a tax and benefit system that will maximize social welfare and raise a given amount of revenue. Mirrlees (1971) allowed the tax and benefit system to be non-linear, which means that METRs at a particular point of the earnings distribution can be set to any value without altering METRs at other points. The model assumes that people vary in their earnings potential (or what they would earn if there were no taxes or transfers), and that everyone always works, but chooses how much effort to supply ('effort' can be thought of as hours of work, with a given hourly wage for each individual, but there are other interpretations, as we discuss later).

Before discussing how this model can be used to determine the optimal METR at any point in the income distribution, we first show how it can be used to derive the optimal METR for high-income individuals, a simpler task.

The optimal top marginal tax rate

To determine the optimal top METR, we will consider the different ways in which a small increase in the top METR affects social welfare. Some of these effects will be positive, and others negative, but at the optimum they must be exactly offsetting, so that no small change in the tax rate can better achieve the goals of the government.

We assume that this top METR applies to earnings above a given level, and we will refer to this level as the top bracket.[10] There are three impacts on social welfare:

1. With no behavioural response, increasing the top METR will increase government revenue. This is the mechanical effect on tax revenue, and this is a benefit to society, as the revenue can be used for government spending or higher transfers.
2. However, increasing the top METR may also induce top bracket taxpayers to reduce their earnings (but not below the top bracket, because the budget constraint has not changed below this point) because of the substitution effect described above. This is known as the behavioural response on tax revenue, and it is a cost to society as tax revenues will fall.

[10] The top rate of income tax in the UK is 40% and applies to annual earnings greater than £41,435 (in 2008–09). When National Insurance contributions are included, the marginal effective tax rate is 47.7% on top earnings.

3. Finally, any increase in the top METR will reduce the welfare of top bracket taxpayers. This is the welfare effect, and it is a loss to society. How large is this loss depends on the redistributive tastes of the government: if the government values redistribution, then, for incomes above a certain level, it will consider that the marginal value of income for top-bracket tax-payers is small relative to that of the average person in the economy. In the limit, the welfare effect will be negligible relative to the mechanical effect on tax revenue.

An optimal top METR is one where the marginal costs and benefits of increasing it further are balanced. If the welfare effect is negligible, then the government should increase the top METR up to the point where the mechanical increase in tax revenue is equal to the loss in tax revenue from the behavioural response. This effectively amounts to setting the top METR so as to maximize the tax revenue collected from top bracket taxpayers; this can therefore be considered as an upper bound to the top METR above which no government should ever go.[11]

A precise formula for this optimal top METR is provided in Box 2.2. The more responsive are earnings to the net-of-tax rate, and the thinner is the income distribution at the top (we formalize this concept in Box 2.4), then the lower should be the top METR. Later in this section, we provide estimates for both these parameters for the UK.

Box 2.2. Determining the top rate of income tax

Here we present the optimal marginal tax rate τ for high earners that maximizes tax revenue. We denote by z the *average* income reported by taxpayers in the top bracket (incomes above $\bar{z}$). By balancing the mechanical and behavioural effects, the optimal rate τ^* can be shown to be given by:

$$\tau^* = \frac{1}{1 + a \cdot e}$$

where a denotes the ratio $z/(z - \bar{z})$ and is a measure of the thinness of the top of the income distribution. The optimal rate is decreasing in both the elasticity e and the shape parameter a. See Appendix for derivation.

[11] It is straightforward to extend the theory to the case where the government has less redistributive tastes and hence the welfare effect is not negligible. See, e.g., Saez (2001).

Optimal marginal tax schedule

Using a similar technique to how we derived the optimal METR in the top bracket, we can also derive the optimal METR at any point of the income distribution. As before, the optimal METR at any point is set so as to balance the costs and benefits from changing the METR by a very small amount.

As before, an increase in the METR over a very small band of income has three effects on government tax receipts and welfare:

1. First, the reform increases taxes paid by every taxpayer with incomes above the small band (the mechanical effect).
2. Second, the rise in the METR will reduce earnings for taxpayers in the very small band through the substitution effect, and so generates a loss in tax revenue.
3. Third, the extra taxes paid by every taxpayer with incomes above the small band generates a welfare cost whose size will depend upon the extent to which the government values redistribution.

For an optimal METR, these effects must exactly offset, so that no change in the tax schedule can increase social welfare. An exact expression is presented in Box 2.3.

The key differences with this analysis and that in the previous section that looks at the optimal top rate are:

- changing the METR at any point affects not just those facing that METR, but also all those with higher earnings
- the welfare cost of extra taxes paid is no longer negligible.

Box 2.3. Determining the optimal marginal tax schedule

We assume that the government imposes a tax schedule $T(z)$ that depends on earnings z. As shown in Figures 2.1A and 2.1B, the slope of this schedule, $T'(z)$, gives the METR when earnings are z. Let $H(z)$ denote the fraction of taxpayers with income less than z (i.e., cumulative distribution of individuals), and let $h(z)$ denote the density of taxpayers. The optimal tax system is characterized by a grant to those with no earnings (equal to $-T(0)$) combined with a schedule of marginal tax rates $T'(z)$ which define first how the grant should be reduced as earnings increase, and then how additional earnings should be taxed once the grant has been fully tapered away. The government's preferences for redistribution are given by $G(z)$ which measures the social

(cont.)

Box 2.3. *(cont.)*

marginal value of consumption for individuals with earnings above z (this should be decreasing in z if the government values redistribution). The optimal marginal tax rate $T'(z)$ is set so as to balance costs and benefits at the margin, and is given by the following formula:

$$\frac{T'(z)}{1 - T'(z)} = \frac{1}{e} \cdot \frac{1 - H(z)}{zh(z)} \cdot (1 - G(z))$$

The optimal tax rate $T'(z)$ is decreasing with the elasticity e, and decreasing in $G(z)$, and increasing in the income distribution ratio $(1 - H(z))/(zh(z))$ which measures the thinness of the earnings distribution. See Appendix for more details.

The formula in Box 2.3 shows how the optimal METR depends upon the size of the behavioural response to taxation, the government's preferences for redistribution, and the underlying shape of the (potential) earnings distribution. In particular, METRs should be higher:

- the less responsive are individuals to the net-of-tax rate;
- the more value is placed on redistribution;
- at points in the earnings distribution where the number of individuals is small relative to the number of taxpayers with earnings exceeding this amount (this is because the revenue gained from increasing METRs at a given earnings level will be proportional to the number of individuals who have earnings greater than this level; the precise way that we summarize this shape of the income distribution is discussed in Box 2.4).

Box 2.4. Summarizing the shape of the income distribution

The shape of the income distribution is an important determinant of the optimal structure of METRs. We summarize this shape by the income distribution ratio:

$$\frac{1 - H(z)}{zh(z)}$$

which appeared in the optimal taxation formula presented in Box 2.3 (where we say that it measures the thinness of the income distribution). The optimal formula shows that the government should apply high marginal tax rates at levels where the density of tax payers, measured by $h(z)$, is low compared to the number of taxpayers with higher income, measured by $1 - H(z)$.

To anticipate the discussion in Section 2.3, it is worth noting that negative METRs are never optimal: if the METR were negative in some range, then increasing it a little bit in that range would raise revenue (and lower the earnings of taxpayers in that range), but the behavioural response (which would be to work less) would also be to raise revenue, because the marginal tax rate is *negative* in that range. Therefore, this small tax reform would unambiguously increase social welfare.

Saez (2001) shows how the analysis changes when income effects are introduced. Income effects encourage work for middle- and upper-income earners because taxes reduce disposable income, but income effects discourage work for low-income earners, because transfers increase disposable income. Hence income effects make taxing less costly, but make transfers more costly. Therefore, if other things are held constant, income effects lead to higher METRs at the upper end, allowing the government to redistribute more, but make redistribution at the low end more costly, and so the net effect on the level of transfers is ambiguous. If income effects are concentrated at the bottom, then they are likely to reduce the size of the optimal transfers at the bottom. If income effects are spread evenly throughout the distribution, then numerical simulations by Saez (2001) show that income effects allow the government to increase the level of transfers paid for by higher METRs across the distribution.

2.2.3. Empirical evidence on intensive elasticities, and applications to the UK

This section presents two applications of the results shown earlier to the UK tax system. We first derive the optimal top METR, using new, albeit tentative, evidence on the responsiveness of top incomes in the UK to changes in tax rates, based on the response of top incomes to the large changes in METRs applying to top incomes that have taken place in the UK over the last forty years. We then derive the entire optimal tax schedule in the standard intensive-responsive Mirrlees model, given assumptions for the labour supply elasticity and the government's preferences for redistribution.

Top incomes and the optimal top tax rate in the UK

Although there is a large literature analysing the effects of changes in METRs on reported incomes using tax return data in the US (see e.g., Saez (2004) for a recent survey; some are cited in Meghir and Phillips, Chapter 3), there has been little study of the British case. This is especially surprising, given that the UK experienced a dramatic drop in top METRs. Up to 1978, the top METR on earnings was 83%.[12] Under the Thatcher administrations, the top rate dropped to 60% in 1979, and then dropped further to 40% in 1988.[13]

In this section, we propose a very preliminary analysis of the link between top METRs and top incomes, using and extending the top income share series constructed by Atkinson (2007). Those series estimate the share of total personal income accruing to various upper income groups such as the top decile group (the top 10%), or the top percentile group (the top 1%), and so they measure how top incomes evolve relative to the average.[14] We have computed the average METR faced by various upper income groups from 1962 to the present (in fact, there are two METR series, one including income tax and employer and employee National Insurance contributions, and one that also includes the impact of consumption taxes, such as VAT and excise duties).[15]

Figure 2.2A displays the METRs (excluding and including consumption taxes) on earnings faced by the top 1% (on the left axis), and the top 1% income share (on the right axis) from 1962 to 2003. It shows an increase in

[12] The top rate on capital income was even higher and reached the extraordinary level of 98% from 1974 to 1978, although very few individuals had taxable incomes high enough to face this rate.

[13] Dilnot and Kell (1988) try to analyse this issue, but have only access to a single year of micro-tax returns, and rely on aggregate numbers for their time-series analysis. More recently, Blow and Preston (2002) have used micro-tax data for 1985 and 1995 to analyse responses to tax rates, but they focus exclusively on the self-employed, and do not look specifically at top incomes. Atkinson and Leigh (2004) have analysed the link between top income shares and the top statutory marginal tax rate in five English-speaking countries including the UK but their study does not estimate effective marginal tax rates and does not focus specifically on the UK case.

[14] The definition of income used by Atkinson (2007, p. 89) (and therefore by us in this section) is close to the broad income definition used in Gruber and Saez (2002), as it excludes capital gains and certain renumeration in kind. However, there are some inconsistencies over time: the most important is that the data represents families before 1990 and individuals after 1990, and we make an adjustment to the pre-1990 data to correct for that (see online appendix at http://www.ifs.org.uk/mirrleesreview/reports/rates_app.pdf for details). Atkinson (2007) also says that the series omits employees' superannuation contributions before 1985, and before 1975–76, the series is net of retirement annuity premiums, alimony and maintenance payments, and allowable interest payments.

[15] The consumption tax rate is assumed to be uniform, and estimated using total consumption tax receipts. These and other computations are described in the online appendix. The METR is an average of the METR on earned and unearned income weighted by the share of earned and unearned income in each group. Our METRs are also weighted by income within each group, as larger incomes have a proportionately larger contribution to the total behavioural response of the income group (indeed, in the optimal top tax rate formula (1), one needs to use the elasticity weighted by income).

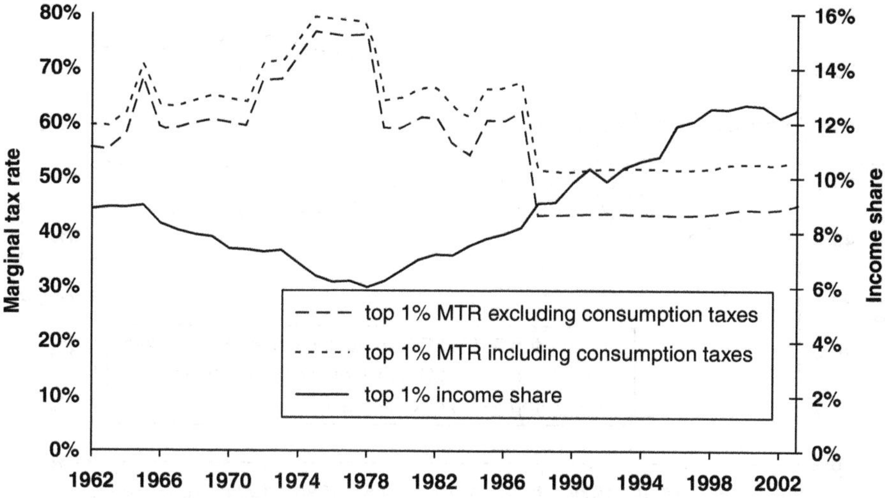

Notes: Income shares from Atkinson but 1962–89 are adjusted up by 5% (factor 1.05) for continuity from 1989 to 1990 when filing shifts from couples to individual. Shares since 2000 calculated by authors from SPI. Tax rates calculated by authors.

Figure 2.2A. Top 1% Income share and marginal tax rate

the METR from 1962 to 1978 followed by a dramatic decline in the two key income tax reforms of 1979 and 1988. The top income share series shows an erosion of the top 1% income share up to 1978, followed by sharp upturn starting exactly when the top METR was reduced in 1979, suggesting that top income shares did respond to the lower METR. From a long-term perspective, the top 1% income share doubled from 6% in 1978 to 12.6% in 2003 while the net-of-tax rate (one minus the METR) doubled from $1 - 0.79 = 21\%$ in 1978 to $1 - 0.53 = 47\%$ in 2003 (using the rates including consumption taxes). If all the increase in top incomes (relative to the average) can be attributed to the reduction in the METR, this would imply a substantial elasticity almost equal to one.[16]

Figure 2.2B displays the METR and income share of the next 4% (income earners between the 95th and the 99th percentile). In contrast to that for the top 1%, the METR in 1978 is virtually identical to the current METR: this illustrates that the Thatcher tax reforms cut the progressivity of the income tax within the top 1%, but had relatively small effects on those with slightly lower incomes. However, the income share of the next 4% also shows a break in 1979: the income share is roughly constant at around 12% before 1979,

[16] These elasticities are calculated by computing $\hat{e} = (\log S_1 - \log S_0)/(\log(1 - \tau_1) - \log(1 - \tau_0))$ where S_0 the top 1% income share before the reform, S_1 the share before the reform, τ_0 the marginal tax rate of the top 1% before the reform, and τ_1 the rate after the reform. In this case, the elasticity is estimated as: $\log(12.6/6.0)/\log((1 - 0.79)/(1 - 0.53)) = .93$.

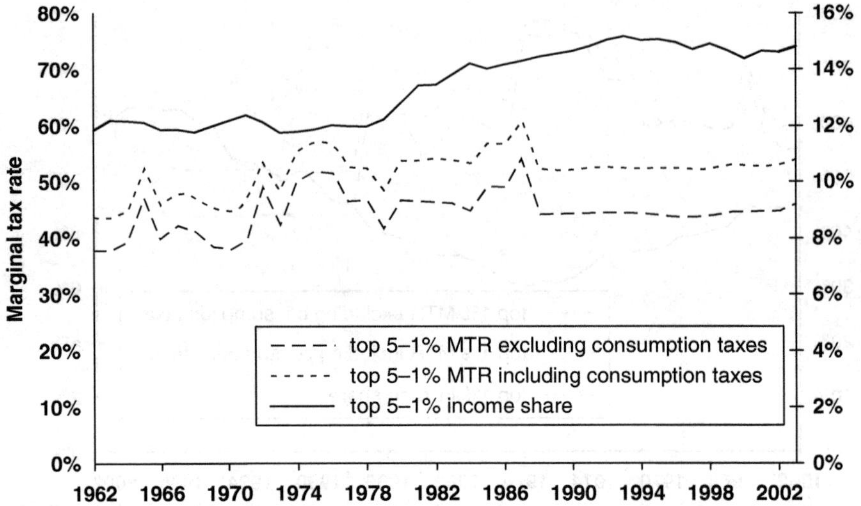

Notes: Income shares from Atkinson but 1962–89 are adjusted up by 5% (factor 1.05) for continuity from 1989 to 1990 when filing shifts from couples to individual. Shares since 2000 calculated by authors from SPI. Tax rates calculated by authors.

Figure 2.2B. Top 5–1% Income share and marginal tax rate

and then increases steadily from 12% to 15% from 1979 to 2003 despite there being little change in the METR.

Two interpretations of this are possible. First, it could be argued that the change in high incomes was not entirely due to the cuts in the METR, and may have been caused by other reforms enacted by the Thatcher administration that were favourable to high incomes. In that case, our previous estimate of 0.93 is biased upward. Second, it is conceivable that income earners in the next 4% group were also motivated to work harder by the prospect of facing much lower rates should they succeed in getting promoted and become part of the top 1% in coming years.[17] In that case, if a cut in the METR facing the top 1% stimulated incomes below the top 1%, our estimate of 0.93 would understate the overall effect on government revenues.

We show more systematically in Table 2.1 how this data can be used to estimate the elasticity of broad income with respect to the net-of-tax rate. The first two rows of Table 2.1 focus on the two key tax cuts of 1979 and 1988, and compare 1978 with 1981 and 1986 with 1989, respectively.[18] Column (1) estimates the elasticity of the top 1% incomes by calculating how the

[17] Gentry and Hubbard (2004) have tried to estimate such effects in a model of entrepreneurship with US data.

[18] We do not use 1990 because of the change from couple to individual tax filing which creates a small discontinuity in the Atkinson series.

Table 2.1. Elasticity estimates for top income earners

	Simple difference (1)	Simple difference (excluding consumption tax from MTR) (2)	DD using top 5-1% as control (3)
1978 vs. 1981	0.34	0.32	0.08
1986 vs. 1989	0.37	0.38	0.41
1978 vs. 1962	0.61	0.63	0.86
2003 vs. 1978	0.93	0.89	0.64
Full time-series regression	0.73	0.69	0.46
(s.e. in brackets)	(0.13)	(0.12)	(0.13)

Note: Authors' calculations using data underlying Figures 2.2A and 2.2B.

share of income received by the richest 1% of individuals changes relative to the change in the METR that this group was subject to. It shows positive, but not very large, elasticities of 0.34 and 0.26. However, as we discussed above, the longer-run perspective suggests higher elasticities. Indeed, the third and fourth rows compare years 1962 to 1978 (when METRs for the top 1% increased) and years 1978 to 2003 (as we discussed above), and these comparisons imply substantially higher elasticities of 0.61 and 0.93. Finally, the bottom row presents the coefficient of a simple time-series regression of the income share of the top 1% on the METR. Rather than just comparing the changes between two different years, this approach uses data over the entire 1978 to 2003 period, and suggests an elasticity of 0.73 (which is statistically significant). In column (2) we again calculate the elasticity estimates of top earners, but we exclude consumption taxes from our measure of METR: this hardly changes the elasticity estimates (because average consumption tax rates have changed by much less than the marginal rate of income tax applying to top incomes).

The elasticities reported in columns (1) and (2) are unbiased estimates only if, absent the tax change, the top 1% income share would have remained constant. As we explained above, this assumption seems contradicted by the fact that the top 5-1% income share increased from 1978 to 2003 in spite of no change in METRs. If we assume that, absent the tax change, the top 1% share would have increased as much as the top 5-1% share, we can calculate what is referred to as a *difference-in-differences* estimate, which is presented in column (3) of the table.[19] These difference-in-differences (DiD) estimates are

[19] Those elasticity estimates are $\hat{e} = (\log S_1/S_1^c - \log S_0/S_1^c)/(\log(1-\tau_1)/(1-\tau_1^c) - \log(1-\tau_0)/(1-\tau_0^c))$ where S^c and τ^c are the income share and marginal tax rate for the 'control group', top 5–1%.

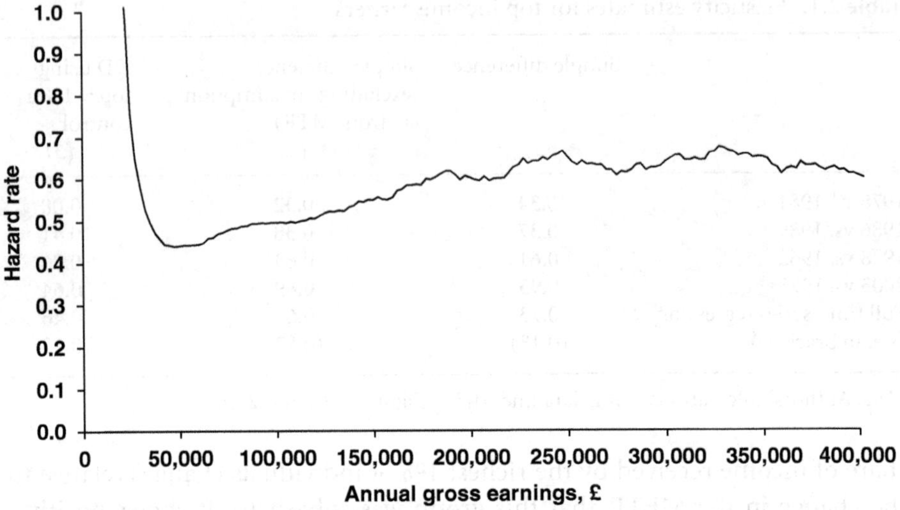

Note: Authors' calculation using FRS 2003–04 and SPI 2003–04.

Figure 2.3. Hazard rate in the UK, 2003–04

smaller for the long-term 1978–2003 comparison, and for the full time-series regression, although they remain substantial at 0.64 and 0.46 respectively. It is conceivable that, absent the tax change, the top 1% share would still have increased more than the top 5-1% share, perhaps because the Thatcher administration implemented other policy changes favourable to top incomes, or because of structural changes in the labour market and changes in the returns to human capital.

The second parameter in formula (1) is a, the measure of the thinness of the income distribution at the top (Box 2.4). Figure 2.3 shows how our measure of the shape of the income distribution (discussed in Box 2.4 above) varies with earnings in the UK: the hazard ratio is very high at the bottom, falls as income increases, and then rises slightly until it becomes flat around 0.6, implying a value of a of $1/0.6 = 1.67$.

What do these estimates mean for the optimal top rate in the UK? We gave an expression for the optimal top rate in Box 2.2 of $\tau^* = \frac{1}{1+a\cdot e}$. With $a = 1.67$ and an estimate of $e = 0.46$, the revenue-maximizing top rate is 56.6%, only a little higher than the actual total top METR in 2008–09 (52.7% including consumption taxes).[20] But we would stress that, as our estimate of the elasticity is tentative, so is the estimated optimal top rate. Taking values of the elasticity 1 standard deviation either side of the central estimate gives

[20] The revenue-maximizing top rate is the optimal top rate if the government places no cost on the top 1% having less income as a result of the tax rise.

a range for the optimal top rate of 50.4% to 64.5%. But our analysis is also consistent with the current top METR being too high: using the value of the elasticity from the simple difference over the period 1978–2003 would give an optimal top rate of 40.2%, and using the difference-in-difference estimate of the elasticity from the same period would imply an optimal top rate of 49.4%, slightly lower than the actual top rate. Indeed, both these estimates imply that cuts in the METR facing the richest 1% in the UK would actually increase tax revenues (although see Box 2.5 for a discussion of the difference between taxable income and broad income elasticities).[21]

Box 2.5. Taxable income and broad income

Note that to estimate the revenue implications of raising the METR that applies to the top 1% of earners in the UK given all other aspects of the current UK tax regime, one would want to use a taxable income elasticity (which measures how income that is subject to income tax changes when the net-of-tax rate changes). But the income measure used in our analysis was close to a broad income measure, rather than taxable income (so it includes some sources of income not subject to income tax). For optimal tax design, the right concept to use is a broad income elasticity, because the difference between broad income and taxable income is a function of the tax system and enforcement efforts, and therefore depends entirely on the choices made by governments. For the same reason, the taxable income elasticity is unlikely to be constant across income tax regimes. For example, we might expect the taxable income elasticity to be higher in the US, than in the UK, because there are more opportunities to reduce taxable income in the US tax code than in the UK. In the UK, the main ways in which one can reduce taxable income would be through higher contributions to private pensions (which to some extent represent only deferred taxation because eventual pension income is taxable), and through charitable giving (to which there may be externalities).

This first-pass analysis shows that identifying the elasticity of top incomes, a key ingredient in the optimal tax rate formulas derived above, is not simple. The evidence is consistent with significant behavioural responses by top taxpayers to METRs, certainly suggesting that the key elasticity is not zero. As the formula (1) shows that the upper bound on METRs depends critically on the level of this elasticity, it would be very valuable to explore this issue in more detail using the rich UK tax return micro-data (the Survey of Personal Incomes) that have now become available to researchers. Unfortunately, there

[21] In 2004–05, the richest 1% of adults, or 470,000 individuals, had incomes in excess of £100,000, with a mean of £156,000: see Brewer et al. (2008a).

has been no large change in METRs since 1988; and without such a change it is extremely difficult to estimate this elasticity. It is conceivable that these behavioural responses change over time; see, for example, the discussion of migration effects below.

Note also that these calculations have only derived the optimal rate for the richest 1% of the population. For many years, the highest rate of income tax in the UK has applied to a much greater proportion: in 1991–92, 3.5% of adults paid income tax at the highest rate, and this has risen to 6.8% in 2004–05, and almost 8% by 2007–08.[22] This means that the conclusions in this section should not be seen as implying that the existing higher rate of income tax with its existing thresholds should be changed: as the section below shows, the optimal METR that applies to, say, people in the top 6% of income earners but outside the top 1% could be lower or higher than the optimal METR at the top.

Simulations of the whole optimal tax system in the UK

Having estimated the optimal top METR, we below simulate the whole optimal tax structure using the Mirrlees model set out in the previous section, and based on the actual UK earnings distribution, and various assumptions about the intensive labour supply elasticity (full details are in the Appendix). The simulations attempt to show the optimal tax schedule which provides total net tax revenues equal to the current tax system, including revenue from individual income tax, NICs, and consumption taxes, net of spending on existing transfers for families with children or those with disabilities.[23] To focus specifically on income tax, we have computed the optimal income tax schedule when we keep consumption taxes (VAT and excise taxes) at their current level (around 17% on average), which we assume to be constant as income varies. The simulations assume that the tax and benefit system is at an individual level.

Figure 2.4A shows the optimal income tax schedule, exclusive of consumption tax, assuming a constant elasticity of 0.25 and with the government valuing redistribution (we define this more precisely in Box 2.6). It shows that for very low levels of earnings, individuals face a METR of around 70%; the METR then decreases relatively quickly with income, reaching 36% as

[22] See HMRC (2007c).

[23] We assume total transfers are equal to the amount spent on Jobseekers Allowance, income tax credits and reliefs, child benefit, housing benefit, council tax benefit, and income support.

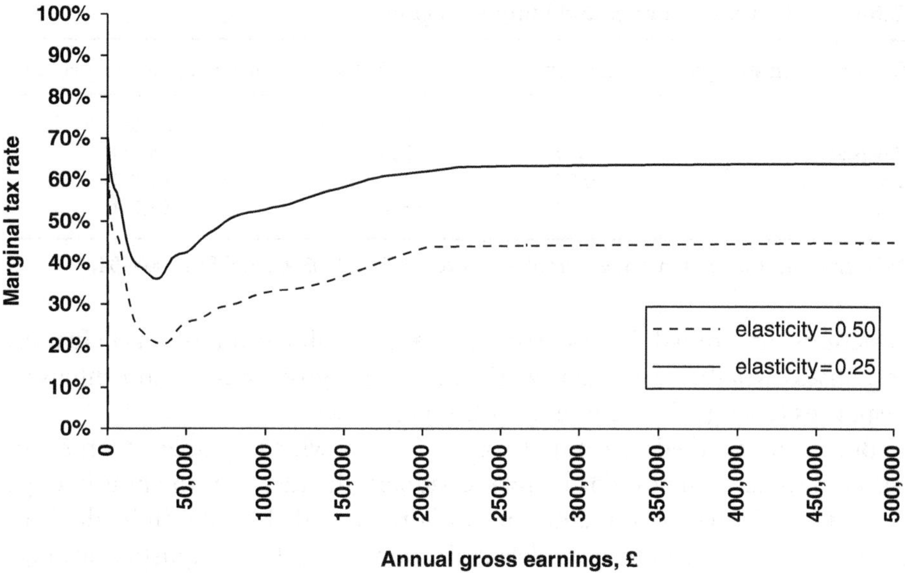

Notes: Authors' calculation using formulae in text and FRS 2003–04 and SPI 2003–04.

Figure 2.4A. Optimal tax sensitivity, labour elasticity

incomes approach £30,000 per year. As incomes increase further, so too does the METR, eventually settling at around 64% for incomes above £200,000.[24]

The U-shape pattern of optimal marginal tax rates is not surprising in light of our theoretical discussion: it is driven by the U-shape of the hazard ratio $(1 - H)/(zh)$ (see Box 2.4; this describes the thinness of the income distribution), as well as the decreasing shape for $1 - G(z)$, the government's preferences for redistribution, both combined with the assumption that the elasticity does not vary with earnings.

We now consider how our views regarding the optimal schedule depend on the labour supply elasticity. Meghir and Phillips (Chapter 3) survey the elasticity of hours worked with respect to the wage. For men, they say that 'although one can start discussing the relative merits of the approaches taken, existing research will lead to the conclusion that the wage elasticity is zero'. For women, they conclude that the elasticity of weekly hours worked is 'in the range of approximately 0.0 to 0.3'. Their preferred estimate is a value of 0.13 for all married women except those with young children (for those with children aged 3–4, the value is 0.37). They also say that 'the results of annual labour supply show greater responsiveness to wages', probably because

[24] These marginal rates will increase once we consider the impact of consumption taxation: for example, consumption taxes act effectively to raise the marginal rate of high incomes from 64% to 70%.

Table 2.2. Optimal tax rates and lump-sum grants

Redistribution strength	Elasticity	Average MTR	Lump-sum grant (per year)
$\gamma = 1$	0.25	45%	£5,580
Rawlsian	0.25	73%	£8,150
$\gamma = 1$	0.50	31%	£4,270
Rawlsian	0.50	58%	£6,760

Note: Authors' calculation using formulae in text and FRS 2003–04 and SPI 2003–04.

variations in annual hours worked are a combination of participation responses (whether a woman works at all in a given week), and intensive responses (changes in the hours worked per week).

But hours worked are not the only way in which taxable income can respond to tax changes. For many individuals, the idea that the hourly wage cannot be affected by the amount of effort expended by the individual (as assumed in the theoretical models in Section 2.3) is too simplistic; earnings could respond to tax changes through changes in the hourly wage (whether through bonuses, tips, job changes, or even by workers on piece rates working faster) as well as hours worked. Taxable income reported to the revenue authorities, though, is not the same as gross earnings, and can vary in response to tax changes through changes in the form of compensation, the response of non-labour income, and changes in the amount of income reported to the tax authorities, whether through avoidance or evasion. Saez (2002) argues that 'elasticities of earnings with respect to the tax rate [at the bottom end] are ... perhaps around 0.25', and that: 'there is little consensus about the magnitude of intensive elasticities of earnings for middle income earners, although this elasticity is likely to be of modest size for middle income earners and higher for high income earners. Gruber and Saez (2002) summarize this literature and display empirical estimates between 0.25 and 0.5 for middle and high income earners' (Saez (2002), p. 1057), although most of this is focused on the US.

Figure 2.4A also displays an optimal schedule in the case where individual labour supply is more responsive to changes in income (an elasticity of 0.5). The figure demonstrates that this would produce lower METRs across the earnings distribution, falling as low as 20%, with a top rate of 45% (slightly below the existing rate). The intuition for the difference here is simple: when individuals are more responsive to tax changes, they will react more to a given METR (reducing their labour supply by more), and this places a limit on how high METRs can go. Correspondingly, and as shown in Table 2.2, the benefit programme is less generous when the elasticity is higher.

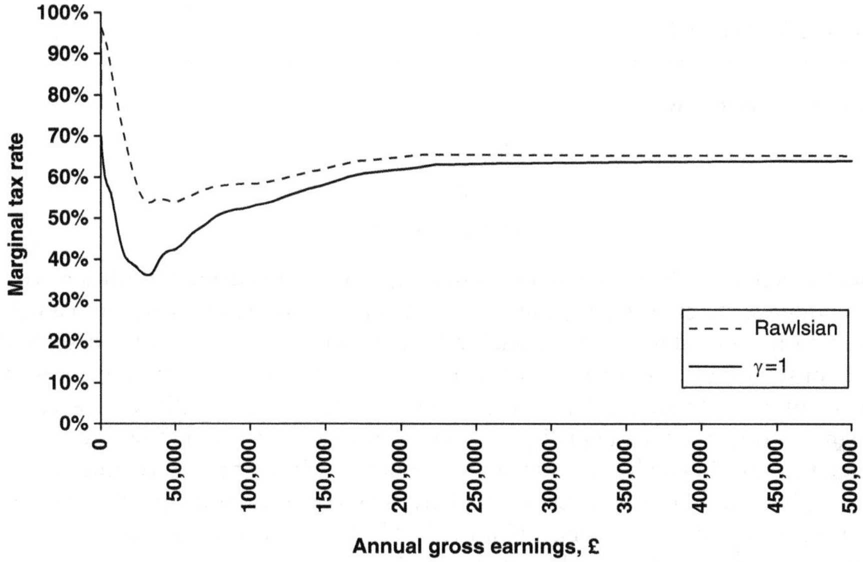

Note: Authors' calculation using formulae in text and FRS 2003–04 and SPI 2003–04.

Figure 2.4B. Optimal tax sensitivity, redistribution preference

Finally, we consider how the government's preferences for redistribution affect the optimal schedule (see Box 2.6 and the online appendix (see footnote 14) for more detail). An interesting case to consider is known as the Rawlsian case, which seeks to maximize the welfare of the least well-off member of society.[25] As Figure 2.4B and Table 2.2 show, under this criterion, we would have a higher lump-sum grant and higher METRs across the entire distribution of earnings. Hence, rates are higher at the bottom, and are the same as the utilitarian case at the top. Therefore, with a Rawlsian criterion, the optimal shape becomes closer to an L- than U-shape.

Box 2.6. Expressing the preference for redistribution

In calculating social welfare, we first transform (money metric) utilities so that we allow for the possibility that the government attaches more weight to the welfare gains of individuals whose level of utility is initially low. A convenient and simple way of capturing this concern for inequality is to transform original

(cont.)

[25] The Rawlsian criterion can therefore be seen as a bound on the maximum level of redistribution that the government wishes to do; note that in the optimal tax model, even the Rawlsian government has to raise revenue for some reason, and this places a limit on the size of the transfer to the poorest in society.

Box 2.6. (*cont.*)

utilities u as follows:

$$\frac{u^{1-\gamma}}{1-\gamma} \quad \text{if } \gamma \neq 1$$

$$\log(u) \quad \text{if } \gamma = 1$$

Social welfare is then obtained by summing these transformed utilities across individuals. Whenever γ is positive, any increase in utility translates into a less than proportional increase in social welfare. When $\gamma = 1$, which is the case that we consider here, the government is placing twice as much weight on the utility gains of an individual relative to another individual whose utility is twice as high. If concerns for inequality were even stronger, represented by say $\gamma = 2$, then they would be placing four times as much weight on the utility gains of the less well-off individual. When $\gamma = 0$, there is no concern for inequality; when γ gets very large, only the worst-off individual in society determines social welfare (the Rawlsian case discussed further below).

The form of individuals' utility function is given in the online appendix (see footnote 14), but note that it is quasi-linear in income, and so it does not display diminishing marginal utility of income, which can by itself provide a motive for redistribution even if a government has a strictly utilitarian social welfare function.

2.3. OPTIMAL TAXES AND TRANSFERS WHEN THERE ARE PARTICIPATION EFFECTS

The model described in the previous section assumes that individuals respond to the tax and benefit system only by varying their earnings as a function of the net-of-tax rate they face (known as the intensive margin/response). However, changes in whether people participate in the labour market at all (known as participation or extensive responses) are poorly captured within such a framework (see Blundell and MaCurdy (1999)). Indeed, following a small increase in the net gain of work, people tend to enter employment at, say, twenty or forty hours a week, rather than one or two hours. Such extensive labour supply responses are particularly important at the bottom of the income distribution, and can be incorporated into a model of labour supply using fixed costs of work (Heim and Meyer (2004)).

Participation effects are important: accounting for them radically modifies the structure of optimal taxes for low income families from the one obtained above (Diamond (1980), Saez (2002)). In this section, we outline the key theoretical results, and then discuss recent applications using UK data.

2.3.1. Theory

We continue to work with a simple labour supply model, but this time individuals only choose whether or not to work, and this decision depends on the relative rewards to working and not working (including the costs of work). The responsiveness of this decision to the financial rewards can be summarized in the elasticity of participation with respect to the net return to work, similar to the elasticity defined in Box 2.1. If individuals do work, their earnings are fixed.

If the government implements a tax and benefit schedule that determines the disposable income of individuals both in and out of work, then an individual chooses to work if the net return to work exceeds her cost of working.[26] Consider the impact of a small rise in the PTR at a given level of earnings. This reform affects only individuals with this earnings potential, because there are no intensive responses. As in Section 2.2.1, this reform has three effects on government tax receipts and welfare:

1. The reform increases the taxes paid by every taxpayer at the given level of earnings who works, increasing government revenues.
2. Those extra taxes reduce the welfare of the workers who pay this extra tax, with the value that the government places upon this dependent upon its redistributive preferences.
3. The tax rise induces some of the workers at this earnings level to drop out of work, and this has a cost.

At the optimal, these effects must balance. In the Appendix, we derive formally what this means for the optimal tax schedule, with the result presented in Box 2.7.

[26] Since individuals of a given ability level may differ in their costs of working, for any given tax system some of these individuals may choose to work and others not.

Box 2.7. Optimal tax rates with participation responses

Let $g(z)$ denote the value the government places on increasing income of individuals with income z. If the government values redistribution, then $g(z)$ will fall as z rises.

Defining the participation tax rate as $t(z) = (T(z) - T(0))/z$, we can derive the optimal tax rate as:

$$\frac{t(z)}{1 - t(z)} = \frac{1}{\eta} \cdot (1 - g(z))$$

This formula is a simple inverse elasticity tax rule for the participation tax rate on work. The PTR decreases with the elasticity η and with $g(z)$, the social value of marginal consumption for individuals earning z.

As Box 2.7 shows, the optimal average tax rate at any given earnings level will be lower:

1. The more highly the government values income at that earnings level.
2. The higher is the participation elasticity (since it is not desirable to tax individuals who adversely respond to reductions in their incomes).

A striking implication is that, if the government values redistribution—so that $1 - g(z)$ is negative—then the participation tax rate should be *negative* for low earnings—in other words, low income workers should receive an earnings subsidy. Hence, in sharp contrast to the intensive model, the extensive model implies that earnings subsidies or work-contingent credits (such as the earned income tax credit or the working tax credit) should be part of an optimal tax system.[27]

The intuition for this result can be understood as follows. Starting from a tax and benefit system with a positive participation tax rate for low-skilled workers, and suppose the government contemplates strengthening work incentives for low-skilled individuals by reducing the taxes that they would pay when working. This has the following effects:

- The cut in taxes means that tax revenues fall, and this is a cost.
- But the associated increase in income of low-skilled workers is viewed positively by a government that values redistribution, because it would prefer these individuals to have income more than the average individual. By our assumption that we are considering low income individuals (for whom $g(z)$ exceeds 1), this benefit effect has to outweigh the costs of reduced revenue.

[27] This result is robust to introducing income effects, as formula (3) remains valid with income effects: see Saez (2002a).

- The behavioural response from cutting the PTR is to induce some low-skilled individuals to start working, and this increases government revenue (because the individuals who move into work pay positive net taxes).

Hence, this reform is unambiguously desirable, and the implication is that positive PTRs for low-income workers cannot be optimal.

These arguments were true for a model where the only response is along the extensive margin. A more realistic model which allows for both intensive and extensive effects is presented in Saez (2002a). To summarize the implications of such a model, consider the situation outlined above, where the government lowers taxes (which are currently greater than zero) for low-skilled workers. If there are both intensive responses and extensive responses, then cutting taxes here would induce some higher skilled workers to reduce their labour supply, as well as inducing some non-workers to work. Although the latter response is a benefit to society, the former is a cost, and so cutting taxes has ambiguous effects on labour supply and therefore overall social welfare. A government contemplating strengthening incentives by cutting taxes facing low-income workers must therefore weigh precisely the positive participation effect and the negative intensive labour supply effect, and the model in Saez (2002) gives a precise formula for that trade-off.

Interpreting the participation response

The extension of the optimal tax model to allow for non-participation has other applications. Two of those are tax evasion and migration.

To apply the model to tax evasion, our earlier concept of 'earnings' could be interpreted as 'earnings reported to the government agency administering taxes and transfers'. Suppose that low-income earners can decide to work either in the formal sector, where we assume full compliance with the tax and benefit rules, or in the informal sector, where we assume full non-compliance. In that case, the decision to work or not work can be replaced by the decision to work and report earnings, or to work informally and not report earnings. In that case, for a given level of tax enforcement efforts, our earlier analysis (and the formula presented in Box 2.7) remains valid. However, in such a model, the government might recognize that some of all individuals reporting no earnings are in reality working informally, and so might actually be better off than low-income workers in the formal sector. This may lead the government to place a lower value on the consumption of individuals with no reported earnings than they do on workers with low reported earnings (i.e., $g(0) < g(z)$ for some z), and this would make subsidies for work even more likely to be optimal.[28]

Second, taxes and transfers might affect migration in or out of the country. For example, high tax rates on skilled workers in continental Europe might induce some of them to move to the UK or the US where the burden of tax on high-income individuals may be lower, and generous benefits for lower-income individuals in certain countries might encourage migration of low-skilled workers toward those countries.[29] In the online appendix (see footnote 14), we discuss how the migration decision can be incorporated into optimal taxation models.

2.3.2. Evidence on extensive elasticities and empirical applications

Meghir and Phillips (Chapter 3) show that there is a wide range of participation elasticities for women in the literature: 'Aaberge et al. (1999), Arrufat and Zabalza (1986) and Pencavel (1986) find results of 0.65, 1.41 and 0.77–0.89 respectively using cross-sectional data-sets from Italy, the UK and the US, and using significantly different modelling and estimation strategies. . . . Devereux (2004), however, finds a lower degree of responsiveness with the elasticity at the median family income equal to 0.17.' There is consensus, though, that participation is more elastic amongst women from poorer families so that 'participation is likely to be the key margin of adjustment for poorer women'.

For men, the two studies of static labour supply cited by Meghir and Phillips (Chapter 3) suggest an elasticity close to zero, but they highlight that a separate literature on the effect of unemployment benefits on the duration of unemployment has consistently found that higher benefits lead to a longer period out of work. Even including these effects, though, they suggest the overall participation elasticity for men is very close to zero, at 0.04. A dynamic model for young men in Germany (Adda et al. (2006)) gives a similarly low participation elasticity (0.06). But Meghir and Phillips also provide their own, new empirical evidence. This very clearly shows the heterogeneity of responses: for highly educated men, it is hard to reject the idea that the

[28] However, subsidies for low-income individuals might induce individuals to over-report self-employment income. In the US, Saez (2002b) shows that the self-employed are much more likely than wage earners to report income which makes them entitled to the maximum EITC payments, strongly suggesting that self-employed individuals manipulate their reported earnings to take advantage of the EITC, making use of a flexibility not available to wage earners.

[29] Clearly, governments can use other tools to affect immigration, and such policies are taken here as given. In the EU, emigration and immigration across EU countries is almost completely deregulated, and so our analysis is particularly relevant in this context.

participation elasticity is zero, but the estimate for men with low educational qualifications is 0.23 for single men, and 0.43 for men in couples.

There are very few empirical studies of optimal tax systems that incorporate intensive and extensive responses: Saez (2002) is an example for the US. Of course, one approach to the second goal of this chapter—where we seek to apply the lessons from optimal tax theory to make recommendations for the UK tax and benefit system—would have been to use an optimal tax model that allowed for intensive and extensive responses to solve for the optimal schedule. We have not taken this approach, though, primarily because we needed to reflect that the current tax system in the UK has different tax schedules for single people and couples, and schedules that vary by the number of children, but also because we also consider the impact of the tax and benefit system on family formation and fertility, and administrative issues, and it is to these we turn in the next section.

2.4. HOW SHOULD TAXES AND BENEFITS TREAT 'THE FAMILY'?

The models we have considered thus far were based on individuals and so abstracted from family issues. In reality, a majority of adults live in couples, and can be assumed to share income to some extent. In this section, we discuss how the family should be taxed, and how the presence of children should affect taxes and benefits. See Boxes 2.8 and 2.9 for a discussion of how these issues are currently treated in the UK.

Under a pure individual-based taxation, tax liability is assessed separately for each family member and is therefore independent of the presence or income of other individuals living in the family or household. At the other extreme, in a system of fully joint taxation of couples, tax liability is assessed at the family level, and depends on total family income (this is how income tax works in the US, for example). Over the past three decades, there has been an international trend from joint to individual taxation of husbands and wives, and today the majority of OECD countries use the individual as the basic unit of taxation (income tax in the UK moved from being family-based to individual-based in April 1990). But tax credits and transfers for low-income families in the UK are based on total family income, as are the equivalent welfare benefits in most other OECD countries, and there has been much less impetus to move to an individual-based system for assessing transfers. Of course, there are many other ways of designing a tax and benefits schedule for individuals that varies with the presence of a partner than a fully joint tax and benefit system, and many EU countries with individual tax systems have some form of recognition of marriage or the presence of a partner (see Di Tommaso et al. (1999)).

In general, there are several important points to be considered when designing taxes and benefits for individuals who can live either alone or in a couple:

1. If there is any sharing of resources within a family, a person with a low income living with a high-income spouse is better off than an otherwise-equivalent person living with a low-income spouse. Therefore, if the government values redistribution, two adults earning the same ought not to be taxed the same if their partners' incomes are very different. This redistributive principle is achieved to a limited extent by having a progressive income tax system based on family income, since it imposes higher average tax rates on adults with high-income spouses than on otherwise-identical people with low-income spouses. By contrast, an individual-based income tax does not meet this redistributive criterion: it imposes the same tax burden on individuals irrespective of their partner's earnings.
2. If there are economies of scale in households, so that two adults living apart could achieve the same standard of living with less income if they lived together, then this arguably provides a reason for the tax system to take account of whether individuals are in a couple or not, presumably by taxing individuals more when they are living as a couple than when they are living alone.
3. Family-based income tax and benefit systems are highly likely to create a marriage (or cohabitiation) subsidy or penalty, as the net tax liability of the two adults might change if they decide to cohabit or marry. This is well-documented in the US, where the income tax system is family-based for married couples, but not for cohabiting couples. Because the US tax system is progressive—in other words, the tax burden rises as income rises—couples with very unequal incomes (such as single-earner couples) benefit from a marriage subsidy, while couples with similar incomes (such as two-earner couples) face a marriage penalty. Although the marriage penalty/subsidy attracts substantial public attention, it becomes relevant for optimal taxation only if the decision to marry is sensitive to those fiscal incentives. Hoynes (commentary on this chapter) concludes that 'overall, the research [mostly

using US data] finds tax effects on marriage that are consistent with the theoretical predictions but are small in size' (these studies are cited in Eissa and Hoynes (2004)); a related literature finds that marriage is also sensitive to the financial incentives inherent in welfare systems (almost always anti-marriage incentives), but that the elasticities are small (see Hoynes (1997)). Overall, then, Hoynes concludes that 'the estimated elasticities with respect to the tax-induced financial incentives to marry (and divorce) are small'. However, even if marriage or partnership decisions are relatively insensitive to fiscal consequences, we might expect that how individuals report their family circumstances to the government authorities would be affected by sufficiently large cohabitation penalties or subsidies.[30]

4. The empirical literature has shown that the labour supply of secondary earners is more responsive to taxes than that of primary earners (see Meghir and Phillips, Chapter 3, or Blundell and MaCurdy (1999)). Therefore, the earnings of secondary earners should be taxed at a lower rate than the earnings of primary earners for efficiency reasons.[31] This goal is achieved to some extent by a progressive individual-based income tax, since primary earners have higher incomes and hence tend to face higher METRs than secondary earners. By contrast, a family-based tax and benefit system generates identical METRs across members of the same family, and thus does not meet this efficiency principle.
5. Any tax and benefit system other than a fully joint system will give individuals in a couple a tax incentive to equalize their asset holdings or income streams. While this might be a deliberate policy intention, a consequence is that it gives couples an opportunity to reduce their tax burden by transferring assets from an adult with the higher METR to the lower METR.

Deriving general optimal tax results for couples is, in general, extremely complicated. Kleven et al. (2006) consider a simple optimal tax model for

[30] In the UK, Her Majesty's Revenue and Customs and the Department for Work and Pensions both estimate the extent of money lost to such fraud or error relating to the presence of a partner: these estimate that £67 million was overpaid in income support, jobseekers allowance and the pension credit, £30 million in housing benefit (both in 2005–06) and £320 million overpaid in tax credits (in 2004–05) (DWP (2007a) and HMRC (2007b)). Powerful circumstantial evidence that such fraud exists comes from the fact that the UK government is paying child-contingent support to between 5 and 10% more lone parent families than are thought to live in the UK (Brewer et al. (2008b); Brewer and Shaw (2006)).

[31] This is in line with the traditional Ramsey principle of optimal taxation that commodities with relatively more elastic demands should have relatively lower tax rates. See also Boskin and Sheshinski (1983) and Alesina and Ichino (2007).

couples where the primary earner chooses only how much to work (as in the models outlined in Section 2.2) and the secondary earner chooses only whether or not to work (as in the models outlined in Section 2.3). In contrast to the separable and linear tax system in Boskin and Sheshinski (1983), they consider a fully general joint taxation system. Naive intuition suggests that, for redistributive reasons, the participation tax rate on the secondary earner should be higher when the earnings of the primary earner are larger, as the contribution of the secondary earner's income to the family's well-being is minimal. However, the authors show that the reverse is true: the participation tax rate on the secondary earner should be decreasing with the earnings of the primary earner and, symmetrically, the primary earner should face a lower METR if his or her spouse works.

The correct intuition is the following: conditional on the earnings of the primary earner, two-earner couples are always better off than one-earner couples. Hence, the government would like to redistribute from two-earner couples to one-earner couples. The value of such redistribution is larger for couples with low primary earnings because the contribution of the secondary earner to household utility is then more important. Therefore, the redistributive virtue of taxing secondary earnings is actually higher at the bottom of the primary earnings distribution, explaining why the tax rate on a secondary earner is decreasing with the primary earner income. If the tax schedule for two-earner couples is seen as the base schedule, the optimal schedule for one-earner couples is obtained from that base schedule by introducing a tax allowance for non-working spouses that is larger for couples with low primary earnings than for couples with high primary earnings. This shrinking tax allowance generates an implicit tax on secondary earners which decreases with primary earnings.

This result suggests that a progressive joint income tax system goes in the wrong direction, and that neutral individual taxation is closer to the optimum. However, it is important to note that, in practice, benefits for low-income families are almost always based on joint family income, and the phasing-out of those programmes creates implicit taxes on secondary earners which are decreasing with primary earnings. For example, a secondary earner in the UK with modest earnings would face a relatively high (average and marginal) tax rate when his or her partner's earnings are low, because the second adult's earnings reduce the family's tax credit entitlement as well as being subject to income tax and National Insurance contributions, and would face a relatively low (average and marginal) tax if their partner's earnings are high, because the secondary earnings are subject only to the individual income tax and NICs. Hence, the results in Kleven et al. (2006) suggest that the broad way in which tax and benefit systems of many OECD countries treat the incomes of a couple, including that of the UK, are consistent with optimal tax results.

Box 2.8. Marriage and cohabitation penalties in the UK tax and transfer system.

As we discuss in Section 2.6, the UK has individual assessment for income tax, but welfare programmes and the child and working tax credit are assessed against the joint income of co-resident couples, where legally married or not. There are currently very few tax-induced marriage penalties or subsidies in the UK.[a] However, there are substantial so-called cohabitation or couple penalties or subsidies in the UK: these arise because welfare benefits and tax credits are assessed against the joint income of cohabiting couples, whether legally married or not.[b] The same structural features that lead to such cohabitation penalties also give differences between the incentives to work facing the first and second earner in a couple. Typically, the PTR of the second earner will be considerably lower than that of the first earner (see also Figure 2.6A), but the direction of recent reforms has tended to increase PTRs of second earners as entitlement to tax credits has risen in real terms (see Brewer (2007)).

[a] See Bowler (2007); some groups have argued that there should be more subsidies: see Social Justice Policy Group (2007).

[b] Such couple penalties or subsidies are usually shown either by calculating the change in net transfers from the state that two adults would experience if they were to cohabit—a complicated calculation that requires assumptions on how housing costs and labour supply would change upon cohabitation—or by calculating the change in net transfers that a cohabiting couple would experience if they (fraudently) claimed to be living apart. See Anderberg et al. (2008); see also Kirby (2005) and Draper (2007).

2.4.1. Collective labour supply model

How disposable income is allocated among family members raises interesting issues. Empirical findings by Lundberg et al. (1997) show that giving an allowance for children directly to the mother instead of giving it to the main earner through a reduction in taxes increased spending on children significantly. This shows that families do not fit what is called the 'unitary model', whereby a family acts as if all the adults in it care about the same things. Many other models of behaviour of couples are possible, and Chiappori (1988, 1992) developed a model where consumption is allocated within family members in an efficient way (so that it is not possible to make one member in the family better off without making another worse off), but that the power each family member has in the decision-making process depends on their relative incomes or on who is entitled to the government transfers (this is known as a collective labour supply model).

How does this affect our analysis? Suppose, for example, that husbands have too much power within a couple, and get too much control over how income is used relative to their spouses, and suppose that the government would like to achieve a fairer distribution of consumption within families. If the government wants to increase parents' spending on children, Blundell, Chiappori, and Meghir (2005) show that what matters is how the *marginal* willingness to spend on children differs across parents. If mothers have a higher *marginal* willingness to spend, then it is valuable to transfer resources from husband to wife. The empirical analysis of Lundberg et al. (1997) suggests that this can be done at no fiscal cost simply by switching who is the nominal recipient of the benefit in the family (and without altering the total disposable income of the family). Therefore, in sharp contrast to the previous models we have considered so far, this within-family redistribution does not create any efficiency costs (as long as the within-family bargaining is efficient, as assumed in Chiappori (1988, 1992).

These results suggest that within-family distributional issues could be addressed by transfers from wallet to purse, but leaving unchanged the total level of transfers going to low-income families. The issue of transferring between high- and low-income families is not fundamentally affected by bargaining issues within the family.

2.4.2. The treatment of children

In Box 2.9 we briefly discuss actual child-contingent transfers in the UK. There are various arguments why the optimal tax schedule should depend upon the presence of children:[32]

1. The presence of children could be used as a tag (Akerlof (1978)), if the presence of children in a family is correlated with the parents' ability to pay taxes, or because it is correlated with the labour supply elasticity (we cited evidence in support of the latter in Section 2.2).[33]
2. To the extent that children represent a cost to their families, so that a family with children needs more disposable income than one without

[32] Similar arguments can be made for matters such as old age, or long-term sickness or disabilities, but we do not explore these here.

[33] Note that this argument does not say whether, for a given level of income, a family with children should face a lower average tax burden or METR than a family without in an optimal tax system, merely that they could be different.

to reach a given standard of well-being, then there is an argument that this should be reflected in the optimal tax schedule, so that for a given family income level, the presence of children should reduce the family's tax liability or increase the transfers received. But this is not a universally held viewpoint: certainly children do cost money, but given that there is a degree of choice in having children, there must be some benefits to families too, it can be questioned why society should compensate families for a particular lifestyle choice;[34] given the benefits that arise from having children, compensating families for the extra cost of having children cannot be justified as easily as compensating families for the extra costs imposed by long-term sickness or disability, for example.

3. A society may feel a responsibility for children's well-being directly because they are unable to affect their parents' income, and there is therefore an argument for an optimal tax system to provide a means of insuring children against growing up in a household with a low income (this argument is strengthened if there are costs to society as a whole from having children grow up in a household with low income).

However, it is also possible that decisions on whether to have children (and if so, how many) are affected by the generosity of child-contingent transfers. If so, this introduces another aspect of behaviour which can be distorted by the design of the tax system, potentially leading to efficiency costs.[35] Surveying recent evidence, Brewer et al. (2007b) conclude that fertility can be responsive to financial considerations, but the implied elasticity is low.[36] If fertility does respond to financial incentives, then this introduces another dimension to the optimal tax problem.

[34] This argument was made forcibly by Dilnot et al. (1984).

[35] Clearly if there are benefits (or costs) to society as a whole from the presence of children which parents do not take account of when making fertility decisions, and if fertility decisions are affected by the generosity of the tax and transfer system, then this may provide a rationale for using the tax system to subsidize (or tax) children (this is a standard argument for using the tax system to correct for externalities: see Fullerton, Leicester, and Smith, Chapter 5).

[36] In the US, there is little conclusive evidence that welfare benefits or the EITC have any effect on fertility (see Hoynes (1997) and Baughman and Dickert-Conlin (2007)) but studies of specific programmes in other countries have shown there to be small responses of fertility to child-contingent transfers (see Laroque and Salanié (2005) and Milligan (2005)).

Box 2.9. Child-contingent transfers in the UK

The UK tax and benefit system varies markedly with the presence of and number of children. At the time of the Meade Report (Meade, 1978), the UK government was replacing child tax allowances and a programme known as family allowances with child benefit: a non-means-tested cash payment for all children almost always paid direct to the child's mother. But child benefit is no longer the most expensive programme for supporting children thanks to the growth, since 1997, of means-tested tax credits conditional on the presence of children.[a] Overall, then, child-contingent transfers in the UK are now more means-tested than universal, and are higher for the first child than subsequent children (both these features have been accentuated since 1997).

Because there have been large increases in entitlements to welfare benefits and tax credits for families with dependent children but none for those without, the size of net transfers that is conditional on having children has risen substantially since 1997: the real value of child-contingent transfers per child grew by around 50% between 1997 and 2003, more than it had risen by in the previous twenty-two years, and Brewer, Ratcliffe, and Smith (2007) provide new evidence suggesting this increase has led to a rise in fertility amongst couples likely to be eligible for such programmes.

[a] See Adam and Brewer (2004) and Adam et al. (2007). These changes have come about because the current UK government is particularly concerned about the high (by international and historical) levels of relative child poverty, and this concern—and the tough quantified targets that accompanied it—has led to very large real increases in entitlements to welfare benefits and tax credits for families with dependent children since 1998 (see Brewer et al. (2008b)).

2.5. ADMINISTRATIVE AND OPERATIONAL CONCERNS IN OPTIMAL TAX DESIGN

In this section, we discuss whether and how a benefit system for low-income individuals should be complemented by requirements (backed up with sanctions) for failing to accept suitable jobs and/or work a sufficient number of hours, and other administrative and operational issues concerning benefits or in-work credits.

2.5.1. The role of conditionality and active labour market policies

A general trend throughout many OECD countries in the 1990s was the adoption of active labour market policies in order to encourage work among welfare recipients and the unemployed. Such policies range from training programmes, assistance in finding jobs, or requirements, backed up with sanctions, for welfare recipients to look for work and to accept reasonable job offers.[37]

If participation tax rates for low-skilled workers are high, then the tax and benefit system discourages low-skilled work. In that context, it would be socially desirable to induce those who are just indifferent between working and not working to start working, since doing so would raise revenue (a gain to society), and the cost to the individuals of having to work is negligible. Obviously, strengthening financial incentives is one way to achieve this goal, as we discussed in Section 2.3. However, conditionality or active labour market policies can provide alternative tools that the government can use to induce work. If the direct cost of providing ALMPs or enforcing job-search requirements plus the welfare cost of forcing individuals to do things they would not have chosen otherwise is smaller than the fiscal savings obtained from having more people work, then such policies are socially desirable.[38] The general principle follows the theory of quotas and rationing developed by Guesnerie and Roberts (1984): goods that are subsidized by the optimal tax system should be rationed. In a system where participation tax rates for low-skilled workers are high, then being out of work is effectively subsidized, and should be rationed.

Two points should be noted. First, in reality, the welfare costs of forcing some individuals to work is higher than it is for others, and it might be difficult for the government to target precisely the individuals who do face low costs of working (and therefore for whom requirements to seek and accept job offers are most likely to be welfare-improving for society), and those active labour market policies might generate substantial welfare costs if, for example, they require beneficiaries with very high costs of working to start working. A crude but common way to achieve such targeting is to use family and disability status.[39]

Second, if the optimal tax system is such that the participation tax rate among low-skilled individuals is low (and even more so if it is negative as our

[37] A very large empirical literature analyses such programmes, and Kluve et al. (2007) provides a comprehensive survey of this literature and meta-analysis for policies in European countries.

[38] HC 32 (2007–08) compares the direct cost of providing different New Deal programmes in the UK in 2005–06 with the net tax savings from getting participants into work, and finds that most of the UK's active labour market programmes are not worthwhile (the calculation takes only a short-run view of the fiscal savings, but on the other hand, it does value the costs of making individuals work when they would have preferred not to).

[39] For example, after the 1996 welfare reform in the US, welfare recipients were required to enrol in training programmes or work part-time unless they had very young children. In the UK, the conditions that apply to claimants of out-of-work benefits are different for lone parents, those who have a long-term sickness or a disability, and other individuals (although the current government has proposed changes to reduce these differences). See Cm 7290 (2006–07) for the UK government's current strategy.

previous analysis suggested), then the desirability of using such active labour market policies is weakened as the tax savings from inducing people to work are small (or even negative, if the PTR is negative). In the optimal tax model developed in Section 2.2.2, it is desirable to induce out-of-work high-skilled individuals to start working, but in reality, active labour market policies rarely target high-skilled individuals.

This discussion (like previous sections) assumes the government maximizes a social welfare function that depends only on individual utilities; the approach to optimal taxation pioneered by Mirrlees is considered 'welfarist' in the sense that it disregards any information not related to individuals' well-being or welfare. In such a model, if individuals make a well-informed decision not to work given the tax schedule facing them, then that decision should be respected by the government. In contrast, a non-welfarist approach to optimal taxation allows for the government to use a criterion for evaluating social welfare that is different from the preferences of the individuals. Clearly, departures from the welfarist approach to optimal non-linear income taxation may lead to very different implications for taxation design. For example, Kanbur, Keen, and Tuomala (1994) consider an optimal tax problem where the objective of the government is to reduce poverty defined using a standard income-based poverty index.[40] Moffitt (2006) argues that the history of redistributional policy in the US suggests that the government values work per se and given this, considers an optimal taxation problem where the government has a direct objective to maximize the number of individuals in work (the same conclusion would almost certainly be drawn about recent UK governments). In this setting, earnings subsidies are often optimal, and work requirements emerge as an instrument for improving the government's view of social welfare (see the commentary by Robert Moffitt).

Box 2.10 discusses the extent to which transfers in the UK can be viewed as conditional, rather than unconditional, transfers.

Box 2.10. Conditionality in the main transfer programmes

The shape of the budget constraint for those with no or very low earnings (and hence PTRs for all workers) in practice depends on whether the benefits are conditional or unconditional.

Of the benefits mentioned above, HB/CTB and CTC are paid to all who are income-eligible, and the WTC is paid to all who are income-eligible and where

[40] By contrast, a welfarist government might be deeply concerned about, for example, poverty measured by a standard income-based poverty index, but only as an intermediate objective.

one person in the family works some minimum number of hours a week: for these programmes, claimants are not required to do any other activities as a condition of receiving benefit. However, conditions do apply to those claiming IS or JSA (which are two identically structured programmes for people who are out of work and on a low income). Claimants of JSA have to be available for work, actively seeking work, and have agreed a jobseeker's agreement with Jobcentre Plus; furthermore, people may be unable to claim JSA if they left their previous job voluntarily, or were sacked for misconduct. In principle, this means that people who do not make sufficient effort to look for work, or who turn down reasonable offers of work, can lose their entitlement to benefit for between 1 and 26 weeks (with exceptions made for vulnerable groups). Claimants of IS may have to attend periodic meetings at a Jobcentre Plus office, but do not have to look for work as a condition of receiving benefit; however, only some groups are allowed to claim IS, the main ones being people who are sick or disabled, people who are caring for a sick or disabled individual, and lone parents whose children are all aged under 7.[a]

Adults who are incapable of work through sickness or disability may receive incapacity benefits (incapacity benefit and income support on the grounds of disability), continued receipt of which is conditional only on attending periodic meetings at a Jobcentre Plus office. New claimants from April 2008 must instead claim the Employment and Support Allowance, which has requirements on claimants, backed up with sanctions for non-compliance.

[a] At the time of writing in 2008, lone parents could claim IS until their youngest child reached 16, but this will fall to age 7 by October 2010. See Cm 7290 (2006–07).

2.5.2. The assessment period and timing of taxes and transfers

In most countries, individual income taxes are assessed on annual income, and transfers often assessed on a monthly basis (in the UK, weekly). Standard economic models predict that families should budget over long time periods, by borrowing (or using credit) and saving. If families have fluctuating incomes but are able to smooth consumption over time by borrowing and saving, then income assessed over a longer period of time is a better measure of economic welfare or well-being than income assessed over a short period of time.

In reality, costs of using financial services and other credit market failures, low levels of literacy, numeracy and financial education, and self-control problems with savings all create significant departures from the standard model. These departures are likely to be more prevalent amongst low-income families, and tend to lead to such families budgeting consumption over short periods of time, such as a month or a fortnight. It therefore seems desirable to operate transfers for low-income families on a high-frequency basis, and operate taxes on higher incomes on a lower frequency, such as annual.

Another important aspect is the timing of tax payment or benefit receipt relative to the period of earnings assessment. Because of imperfect credit markets and some families' imperfect ability to budget (as described above), many families would be unable to pay a significant level of tax if it is not withheld at the time they receive the earnings: this is why setting up tax withholding systems operated by employers is key to implementing broad-based taxes (or social insurance contributions) on earnings.[41] In this way, income tax can be withheld throughout the year at levels which are approximately correct, and a small adjustment made once a year if the amount withheld does not correspond to the actual tax liability. A similar argument applies to the design of benefits: the closer is the timing of payment to the period of assessment, the better targeted is the benefit; paying credits through a single annual payment (as almost always happens with the EITC) can be very inefficient if families are credit constrained.[42]

One way of aligning the timing of payment to the timing of assessment is to administer benefits for workers through the income tax system; such a scheme can also have lower administrative and compliance costs relative to traditional welfare programmes and relative to the child and working tax credits in the UK, discussed further below. For example, a (refundable) tax credit could be administered through a system of 'negative withholding', where the revenue authorities fund employers to top up earnings instead of withholding taxes. Having an automatic system of benefit payments may also reduce stigma costs for recipients.[43]

However, the experience of the first two years of the working and child tax credits in the UK (see Box 2.11), the Advance EITC in the US, or Prime à l'Emploi in France, all show that such a system will cause difficulties if there is

41 We use 'withholding' in the same sense as Shaw, Slemrod, and Whiting, Chapter 12.

42 It is possible that the prospect of a large annual lumpsum tax refund induces families to borrow against the forthcoming tax refund with high interest costs. Indeed, surveys show that US tax refunds received by low- and moderate-income families are used primarily for paying down debts. Alternatively, one-off tax refunds can be seen as forced savings devices which allow low-income families with self-control problems to save for purchasing consumer durables or investing in human capital. Empirical work has not yet been able to distinguish those two scenarios. It is striking to note, however, that there is little demand for such forced savings devices in the UK where transfers are paid monthly or fortnightly.

43 Exactly as taxpayers disliked interactions with the tax collector in past centuries, welfare recipients today dislike the close scrutiny required to qualify for such transfers.

a significant risk that families incur an overpayment which they have to repay to the government. This fear leads the vast majority of EITC recipients in the US to opt to receive it annually in arrears, and the UK government changed the way tax credits depend on income in 2005 so that they are predominantly based on the previous tax year's income (except where income falls), meaning that most rises in income should not lead to over-payments (although this change was predicted to reduce the number of over-payments by just a third). But such a design makes tax credits rather like a retrospective benefit scheme based on annual income, and this means the credits are then not as well targeted as they could be.[44]

Box 2.11. The administration and operation of tax credits in the UK

In-work programmes increased in importance during the early to mid-1990s, partly as a response to the growing prevalence of lone parent families. But their importance changed beyond recognition between 1999 and 2003. The working tax credit now supports working families with or without children with a low income, and the child tax credit is now received by around 90% of all families with children. These tax credits are administered by Her Majesty's Revenue and Customs (HMRC), but they have many elements which feel much more like traditional welfare programmes: they are jointly assessed, paid regularly and directly to recipients' bank accounts, and do not reduce income tax liabilities.

The administration of tax credits has been extensively criticized, with a cross-party group of Members of Parliament concluding in early 2008 that 'there is little evidence that [HMRC] has the scheme under control. Many claimants continue to struggle to understand tax credits and why they are overpaid. There have been many complaints about the process of recovering overpayments and the Ombudsman continues to receive and uphold a large number of complaints.'[a]

These administrative problems mostly derive from policy choices, so it is worth discussing these briefly. One of the predecessors of the child and working tax credit was Working Families' Tax Credit (WFTC). WFTC awards were retrospective, so entitlement to WFTC, having been determined, was paid for 6 months regardless of any changes in the family's circumstances; any changes in circumstances were reflected in the next award if the family re-applied after 6 months. Because awards were based on verified information, there was no need to re-assess awards.

(cont.)

[44] Many of these issues were discussed in detail when the UK government proposed merging working families' tax credit (a 6-monthly retrospective transfer programme) and the children's tax credit (an annual transfer implemented through PAYE) to form the child and working tax credit: see Brewer et al. (2001) and Whiteford et al. (2003) for more discussion. See also Brewer (2006).

Box 2.11. (*cont.*)

But the retrospective nature, combined with the 6-month gap between assessments, meant that payments need not have reflected current circumstances, and these, plus the perceived compliance costs to families of providing verified earnings details twice a year, were the main motivations behind the introduction of the child and working tax credits. Their design reflects an attempt to reconcile these tensions. The principle of the child and working tax credits is that they should depend on current family circumstances, and income in the current year. But the tax authorities do not know the details on which tax credit entitlements depend (the earnings of all adults in the family, the number of children, whether any adult is working for 16 or 30 or more hours a week, and how much is being spent on childcare) so tax credits rely on two things: first, there is a responsibility on claimants to tell HMRC when there is a change in their circumstances—such as whether they are living with a partner, how many children they have, and also what they are spending on childcare—within a month of its happening. Second, tax credits are likely to be based on the claimant's previous year's annual income: claimants whose income is lower than last year's can have tax credits assessed on their best estimate of their current income, but claimants whose income is higher than the previous year can have tax credits assessed on the previous year's income, provided that is within £25,000 of their current annual income.

[a] HC 300 2006–07. See also Brewer (2006) and references therein.

2.6. THE CURRENT HOUSEHOLD TAX AND BENEFIT SYSTEM IN THE UK

This section describes the inherent work incentives for working-age adults in the UK tax and benefit system that arise from income tax, employer and employee National Insurance contributions (the payroll tax), the working and child tax credits, and other benefits.[45] Box 2.12 summarizes the key changes since Meade (see also Adam, Browne, and Heady, Chapter 1, and references therein).[46]

[45] There is more detail on individual taxes in Adam, Browne, and Heady (Chapter 1) and on individual transfer programmes in O'Dea et al. (2007). We do not show the schedule affecting those over the state pension age, nor do we discuss health- or disability-related transfers: the main differences for those above state pension age are: there is no payroll tax on earned income, there are higher personal allowances for income tax, welfare programmes are more generous, and health-related transfers are more important.

[46] Adam et al. (2006) shows the distribution of key work incentive measures has changed over time; their measures of work incentives exclude employer NI, however. Adam, Browne, and Heady, Chapter 1, show how tax and transfer changes have affected key work incentive measures.

Box 2.12. The main changes to the UK tax and transfer system since the Meade Report

Much has changed in the personal tax and benefit system in the UK since the Meade Report in 1978, but we would highlight three particularly important developments:

First, statutory rates of tax have fallen at the top, but marginal effective tax rates (METRs) have not necessarily fallen. In 1978, the highest marginal income tax rate on earned income was 83%; a decade later, it had fallen to 40% (with extensions of National Insurance contributions over this period, the overall marginal tax rate on top earnings, before considering the impact of consumption taxes, is now 47.6%). But this tells us only about the change in the marginal tax rate facing the very richest in the UK: between 1974 and 1978, the mean income of the richest 1% of adults in the UK was not high enough for the highest marginal rate to be applicable, but the mean income in the top 0.1% was. In fact, across the whole population, statutory income tax rates are generally lower than in 1978, but METRs across the whole distribution are not necessarily lower now than in 1978, partly because of the expansion of income-related in-work programmes, and partly because tax allowances have not kept pace with growth in earnings (a phenomenon known as fiscal drag) (see Adam, Browne, and Heady, Chapter 1, and Adam et al. (2006)).

Second, income tax is assessed at the individual level, rather than jointly, but many married or cohabiting couples in the UK still face some form of joint assessment of their incomes, thanks to the expansion of income-related in-work programmes, and of means-tested benefits for those aged 60 or more. Income tax became individualized in 1990, and there have been few political pressures to reverse this reform. Instead, there has been a trend of increasing use of means-tested benefits that depend upon the joint income of a co-resident couple, whether legally married or not (see the commentary by Hoynes for further discussion).

There has been an expansion of in-work programmes or refundable tax credits conditional on work. In fact, the UK has had a programme to support low-income working families since 1972, but the importance of benefits to families who are working is much greater now than at the time of the Meade Report.

Figure 2.5A-1 shows how the annual net income of a lone parent with two children varies with the annual employer cost (ie, annual earnings plus employer NICs).[47] While this is not intended to be a typical family, it does

[47] Throughout this section we assume that there are no childcare costs. Owing to the hours rules in the tax system, the actual budget constraint will depend upon the wage received. We assume

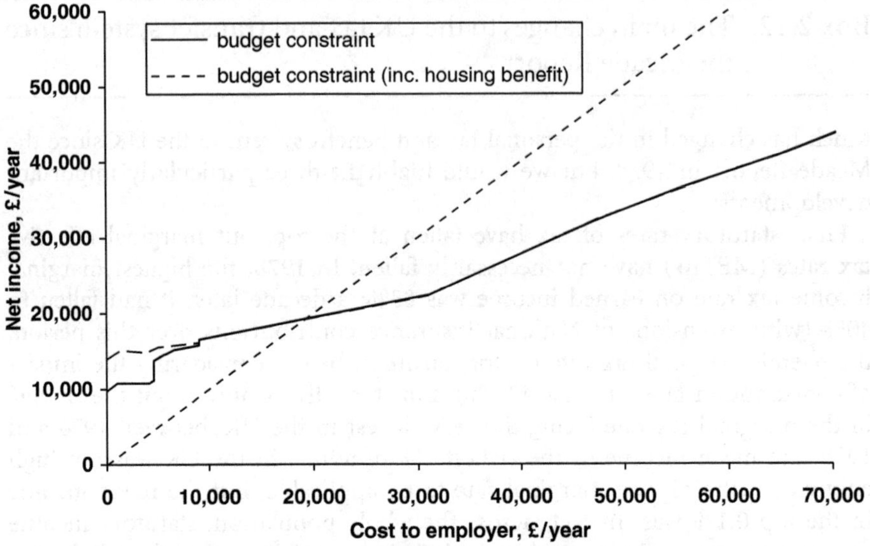

Notes: Assumes a lone parent with two children, paying £80 per week in rent, no childcare costs, average Band C council tax, and with a wage of £5.52 per hour. Incomes are calculated under the April 2008 tax and benefit system with announced changes to the higher-rate threshold and UEL, but without the £600 rise in the income tax personal allowance.

Figure 2.5A-1. Budget constraint, lone parent

illustrate some of the key features of the UK tax and benefit system (Box 2.13 discusses how the tax and benefit system varies across different family types).

Figures 2.5B-1 and 2.5C-1 show how the associated participation tax rate (PTR) and METR vary with earnings for the same specimen family type. They also show the empirical relationship between PTRs and METRs and the employer cost for all working lone parents, given the underlying demographic structure, employment patterns, and distribution of earnings in the UK (the main reason why the empirical distribution differs from the hypothetical relationship is that, on average, lone parent families have fewer than two children, and children serve to raise PTRs and extend the range of income over which a high METR applies).

that the wage rate is equal to the minimum wage (as of October 2007) of £5.52 per hour. The benefits system works on a weekly basis, and the tax system on an annual basis, but the figures have assumed both work on an annual basis. The figures show the 2008–09 tax system before the £600 rise in the income tax personal allowance, and with the small changes to the Upper Earnings Limit for employee NICs and the income tax higher-rate threshold scheduled for April 2009.

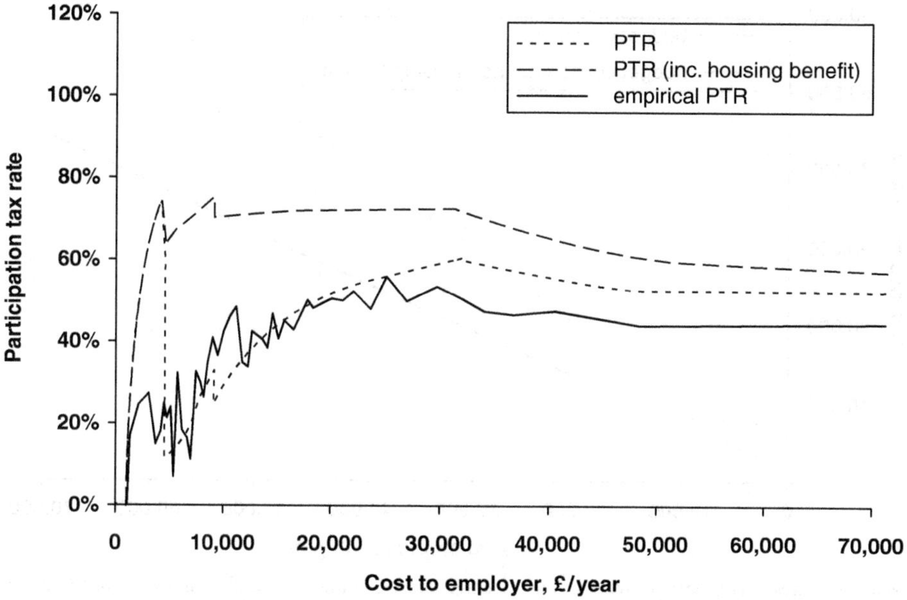

Notes: Example PTRs as for Figure 2.1A. Empirical PTRs based on all workers in families where no adult is aged 60 or over in FRS 2004–05 with net incomes calculated using TAXBEN.

Figure 2.5B-1. Participation tax rate, lone parent

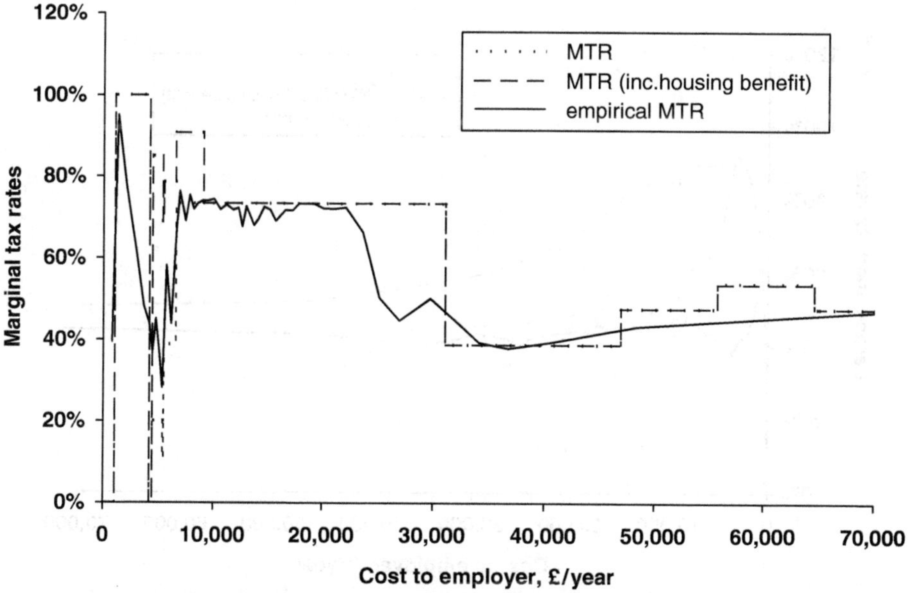

Notes: Example PTRs as for Figure 2.1A. Empirical PTRs based on all workers in families where no adult is aged 60 or over in FRS 2004–05 with net incomes calculated using TAXBEN.

Figure 2.5C-1. Marginal tax rates, lone parent

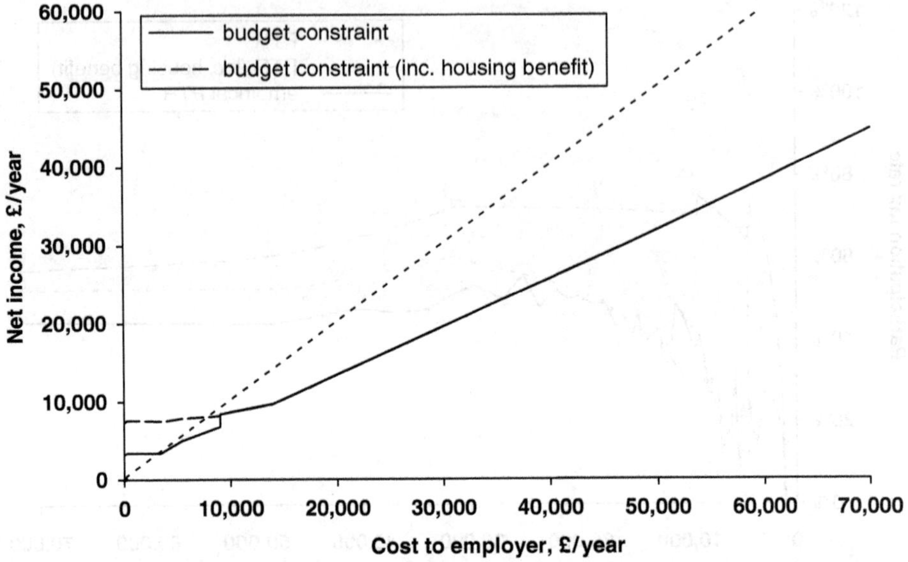

Notes: Assumes paying £80 per week in rent, average Band C council tax, and with a wage of £5.52 per hour. Incomes are calculated under the April 2008 tax and benefit system with announced changes to the higher-rate threshold and UEL, but without the £600 rise in the income tax personal allowance.

Figure 2.5A-2. Budget constraint, single no children

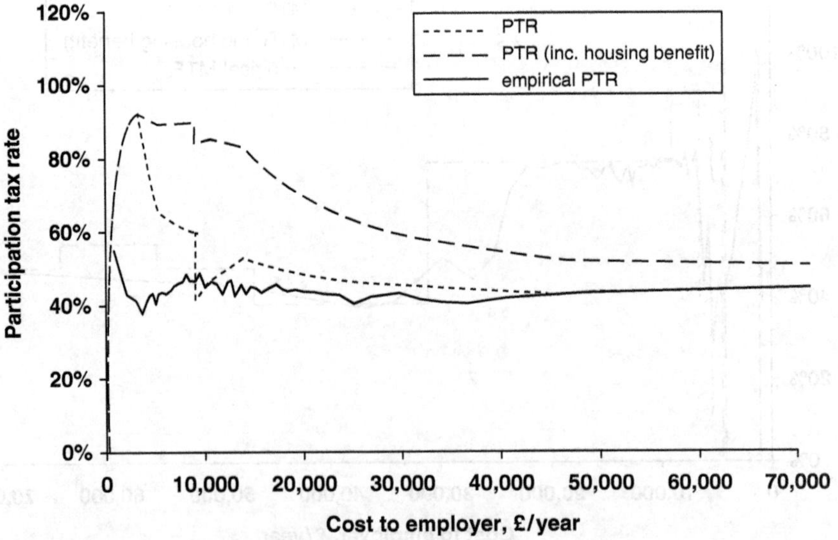

Notes: Example PTRs as for Figure 2.1A. Empirical PTRs based on all workers in families where no adult is aged 60 or over in FRS 2004–05 with net incomes calculated using TAXBEN.

Figure 2.5B-2. Participation tax rate, single no children

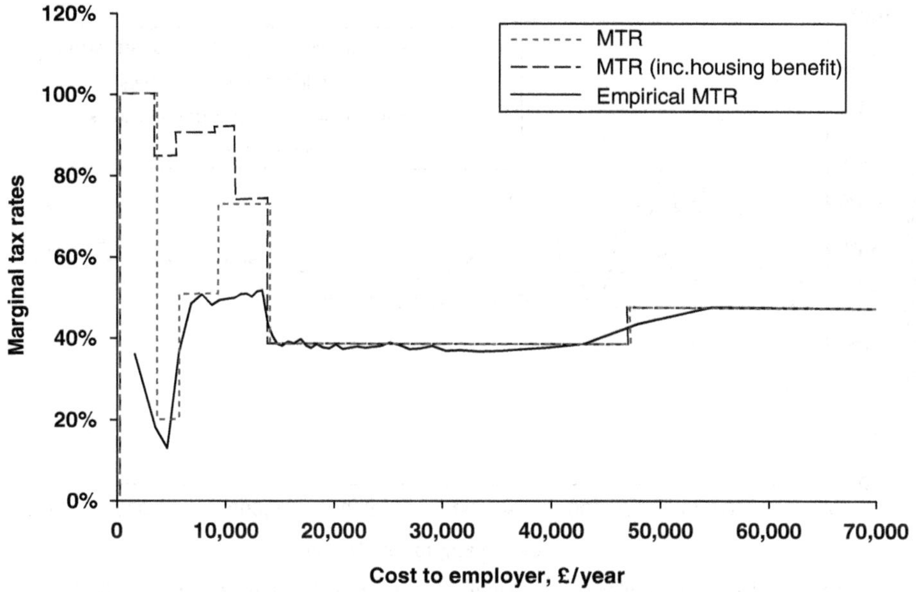

Note: Example PTRs as for Figure 2.1A. Empirical PTRs based on all workers in families where no adult is aged 60 or over in FRS 2004–05 with net incomes calculated using TAXBEN.

Figure 2.5C-2. Marginal tax rates, single no children

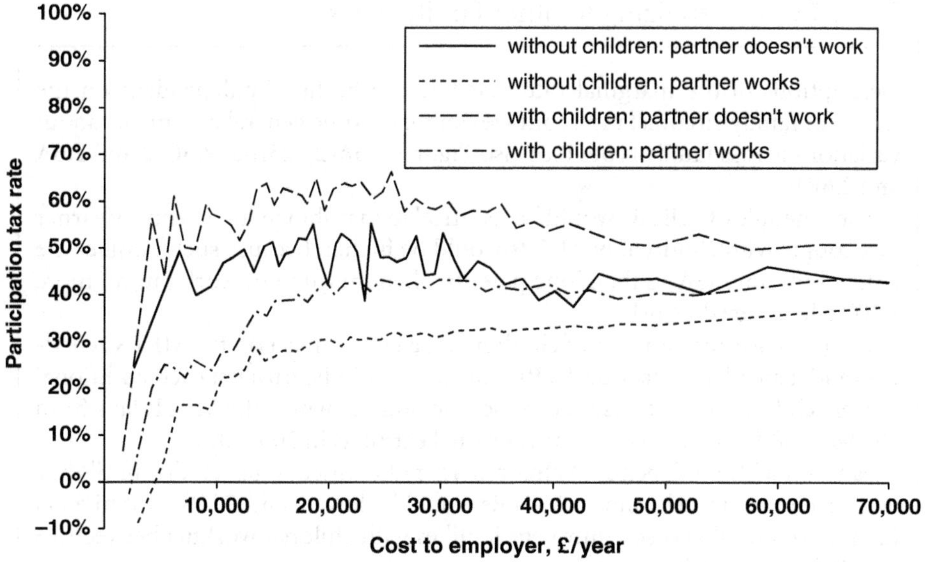

Note: Empirical PTRs based on all workers in families where no adult is aged 60 or over in FRS 2004–05 with net incomes calculated using TAXBEN. Assumes tax system as described in notes to Figure 2.1A.

Figure 2.6A. Empirical Participation tax rates, couples with and without children

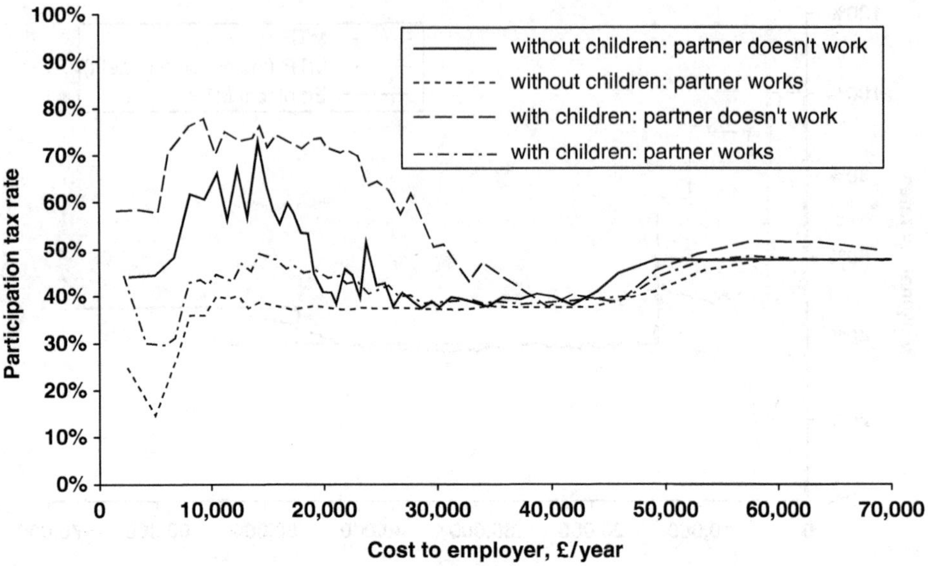

Note: Empirical PTRs based on all workers in families where no adult is aged 60 or over in FRS 2004–05 with net incomes calculated using TAXBEN. Assumes tax system as described in notes to Figure 2.1A.

Figure 2.6B. Empirical Marginal tax rates, couples with and without children

Box 2.13. Generalizing to other family types

Descriptions of the marginal rate schedule can be heavily dependent on the choice of family circumstances, but we can make some general comments about variations across family types (see also Figures 2.5A-2, 2.5B-2, 2.5C-2 and 2.6A and 2.6B):

The schedule of METRs would be identical to that shown for a primary earner in a couple with children, but PTRs would be higher, because such families are entitled to more JSA/IS than lone parents when they do not work but no more WTC when they do work.

The presence and number of children has a large impact on the METR schedule (and a smaller impact on PTRs) for low to middle earners: each additional (fewer) child would increase (decrease) the point at which the METR falls from 73.4% to 38.8% by £5,346 a year (personal earnings in 2008–09).

Families without dependent children are not entitled to tax credits until they work 30 hours a week, and so METRs would be lower (and PTRs a lot higher) than those for otherwise-equivalent families with children working between 16 and 29 hours a week.

Because of the various hours rules in the UK tax and benefit system, assuming higher hourly wages given a value of employer cost measured weekly would change the pattern of METRs and PTRs at the bottom of the earnings distribution, but not at the top, where income tax, National Insurance contributions, and tax credits depend only on weekly or annual earnings.

Generalizing across other forms of income is harder: unearned income is treated differently from earned income in IS/JSA, and by National Insurance contributions, but treated similarly to earned income by income tax and tax credits; self-employment profits are treated differently from earnings from employment by National Insurance contributions, but not by income tax or benefits.

They illustrate the following features of the UK tax and benefit system:

1. The PTR is 0% for very low earnings and then increases rapidly. This reflects the structure of the main means-tested benefits for families with no earnings and who work no more than 15 hours a week (Jobseekers' Allowance (JSA) and/or Income Support (IS)[48]). For families on JSA/IS, a 100% METR applies after a small earnings disregard (£5 a week for single adults, £10 a week for couples, £20 a week for lone parents): families therefore face no direct financial incentive to increase their earnings above the very low disregard unless they earn enough to exhaust fully entitlement to IS/JSA, or they work a sufficiently high number of hours to qualify for the working tax credit. In April 2008, a single adult aged 25 or over would receive £60.50 a week in JSA. Receipt of these benefits also confers entitlement to various benefit-in-kind programmes, the most important of which is entitlement to free school meals.[49]
2. Hours rules are an extremely important part of the benefit system in the UK:[50] the most important ones are that individuals working 16 or more hours may not claim JSA/IS, and individuals with (without) children working 16 (30) or more hours may instead claim working tax credit.[51] Figures 2.5B-1 and 2.5B-2 show that these hours rules lead to

[48] There is also a short-term non-means-tested jobseekers' allowance for those who have paid sufficient National Insurance contributions, but a minority of JSA recipients qualify for this.

[49] The loss of these benefits-in-kind can substantially increase PTRs; the difficulty is modelling their value to individual families. For a qualitative study, see Community Links et al. (2007).

[50] In principle, making the working tax credit means-tested against weekly earnings and conditional on working 16 or more hours a week means it is more closely focused on low-wage workers than would be the case if it were conditional solely on having positive earnings. In practice, there may be very few high wage workers who would wish to work small numbers of hours if there were an earnings-based in-work credit, and so there may be little efficiency gain from having an hours rule. Furthermore, under the current rules for the WTC, hours of work are self-reported (although potentially verifiable if HMRC consults with employers).

[51] The take-up rate for the WTC for those without children is extremely low, at 20% (25% by value; see HMRC (2007a)).

a striking discontinuity in the PTR schedule: after reaching a maximum at the point just before entitlement to JSA/IS is exhausted, the PTR falls substantially at 16 hours work a week (there is a further discontinuity at 30 hours a week—annual earnings of £8,611 for a minimum wage worker—when an additional credit in the WTC is payable).

3. Families with dependent children receive child-contingent support through a non-means-tested child benefit, and most receive more through a means-tested fully refundable child tax credit.[52] In 2008–09, a lone parent and two children with no private income would receive £183 a week from income support, child benefit, and child tax credit combined, three times as much as the single adult with no children.
4. The shape of the budget constraint for low to middle earners varies considerably by whether a family is entitled to the means-tested benefits known as housing benefit and council tax benefit (together, HB/CTB) (Box 2.14). Families who are receiving JSA/IS are automatically entitled to the full amount of HB/CTB, but once JSA/IS has been exhausted, HB/CTB are withdrawn at a rapid rate. This can dramatically reduce the gain to work: in Figure 2.5A-1, for example, net income increases by over £2,626/year when the earner works 16 hours a week, but with housing costs of £4,160 / year, this is reduced to £312/year.[53]
5. For most people, METRs are determined by the rates of income tax and National Insurance contributions. Income tax (20%) and employee NICs (11%) are both liable when annual earnings reach £5,435 a year (£104.52 a week) to give a METR of 31% (plus 12.8% on the employer, or 38.3% overall).[54] This increases to 47.7% (41% plus 12.8% on the employer) when earnings are sufficiently high for the higher rate of income tax to be liable (from April 2008, this will be £41,435 a year, but the government has already announced a real rise in this

[52] In the rest of this section, we use children to mean dependent children, which is currently defined as children under 16, or aged 19 or under in full-time education or approved training schemes.

[53] The 2008 Budget—which took place as this chapter was being finalized—announced that earnings disregards in housing benefit and council tax benefit would effectively be increased substantially for families with children from October 2009. This is not reflected in Figures 2.5–2.6.

[54] If an employer pays £1 in notional gross earnings, then the employer actually pays out 112.8p, and the individual actually receives 69p, with the government receiving 43.8p. The overall METR is therefore 43.8/112.8 or 38.3%.

threshold from April 2009 which we allow for in our reform proposals in Section 2.7).[55]

6. But METRs are considerably higher for families entitled to tax credits or HB/CTB. Once annual earnings have reached £6,420, entitlement to tax credits begins to fall, and this increases the METR by 39 percentage points (ppts) to 70% (with the 12.8% on the employer, this reaches 73.4% overall). For a family with two children and a full-time earner, the 70% (or 73.4%) METR falls back to 31% (or 38.3%) once gross annual earnings reached £28,150. But what complicates—and raises—METRs even further is the way this combined income tax–NI–tax credit METR interacts with HB/CTB: to give an example, someone facing a combined income tax–NI–tax credit METR of 70% and entitled to HB/CTB would face an METR of 95.5% (plus 12.8% on the employer side, or 96% overall): see Box 2.14.

Box 2.14. Housing benefit and council tax benefit

Housing benefit is a rental subsidy programme which can potentially cover the full cost of renting (subject to locally determined rent ceilings), but where actual entitlement depends upon family income and household composition.[a] Council tax benefit is a very similarly structured programme that provides a (potentially 100%) rebate on council tax payments. Hereafter we refer to these programmes together as HB/CTB.

The withdrawal rate in HB is 65%, and in CTB, 20%; these are cumulative, but they apply to net income, not gross income, and so the 20%/65%/85% withdrawal rate of CTB/HB/both combined is not added to the combined income tax–NI–tax credit METR, but instead applied to whatever earnings are left. For example, someone facing a combined income tax–employee NICs–tax credit METR of 70% and on the taper of both HB and CTB would lose 85% of the remaining 30%, giving a total MTR of 95.5% (plus 12.8% on the employer side, or 96% overall). Someone with a combined income tax–employee NICs METR of 31% and on the taper of CTB would lose 20% of the remaining 69%, giving a total MTR of 44.8% (51% with employer NI).

[a] In the private rental sector, the rules for HB changed in April 2008 so that the maximum entitlement depends on household size and composition (and locality), and not on the actual rent paid.

[55] When joint family earnings are between £50,000 and £57,783, the family element of the child tax credit is withdrawn at a rate of 6.7%, giving a slightly higher METR of 47.7% plus 12.8% on employer, or 53.6% over this range.

Table 2.3. Distribution of participation tax rates amongst workers, 2008–09 tax and benefit system

	Centile of distribution of PTRs					
	10th	25th	50th	75th	90th	Mean
Single, no children	0.31	0.40	0.42	0.47	0.63	0.44
Couple, no children						
Partner not working	0.28	0.35	0.45	0.55	0.67	0.45
Partner working	0.18	0.25	0.30	0.35	0.41	0.29
Lone Parent	0.01	0.25	0.44	0.55	0.66	0.36
Couple with children						
Partner not working	0.40	0.48	0.56	0.64	0.78	0.55
Partner working	0.15	0.29	0.39	0.50	0.57	0.37

Notes and sources: Authors' calculations based on FRS 2004–05 with net incomes calculated using TAXBEN. Sample is all workers. Adults in families with anyone aged 60+ are excluded. Assumes tax system as described in notes to Figure 2.1A.

Table 2.3 shows the distribution of work incentives measures for various family types (and see also Figures 2.5B-1, 2.5B-2, 2.5C-1, 2.5C-2 and 2.6A and 2.6B). It shows that:

- METRs and PTRs are generally higher for families with children than those without with identical incomes.[56]
- PTRs are generally lower for adults whose partner is in work than for the sole earner in a couple.

2.7. A PLAN FOR REFORMING TAXES AND TRANSFERS IN THE UK

In this final section, we first suggest a set of changes to the existing tax and benefit structure that could be made immediately and that address problems we identify with the work incentives inherent in the current system. We then set out a more radical and comprehensive set of structural changes to the tax and benefit system that attempt to deal not only with the work incentive issues, but also with the administrative failings that we identify. None of

[56] One slight exception is that low-earning lone parents can face lower PTRs than low-earning single adults without children: this is because WTC requires fewer hours of work for lone parents than low-earning single adults without children, and because the interaction of child maintenance payments with IS/JSA and WTC means that lone parents receiving child maintenance payments can face very low or negative PTRs if they do not receive HB/CTB.

the reforms described below would apply to those aged 60 or over, nor do we propose specific changes for those with long-term sickness or disabilities, nor do we address how conditionality should be applied to out-of-work benefits nor how welfare to work policies should be designed.

As we discussed earlier, one direct way to arrive at an optimal tax and benefit schedule for the UK would be to use an optimal tax model for the UK that reflected extensive and intensive responses. But such a model would most likely miss out on some of the considerable heterogeneity between different sorts of families in the tax and benefit schedules (as the schedule differs by the number of adults and the number of children), and it would be even more complicated to allow for responses other than to taxable income (for example, to reflect that household formation may be sensitive to tax incentives) and to allow for concerns over administrative and compliance costs. Instead, we have sought in this section to apply the lessons from optimal tax theory combined with the best available evidence on the scale of behavioural responses, and our knowledge of the incentives inherent in the existing UK tax and benefit system.

In formulating these suggested reforms, we have been guided by the following points or principles, discussed earlier in this chapter:

- For certain groups, such as second earners and individuals with low levels of education, extensive responses are likely to be more important than intensive responses (see Section 2.3.2).
- The responsiveness of hours worked to the tax system is very low for most groups, and perhaps zero. The responsiveness of taxable earnings is greater, with an elasticity of perhaps 0.25 for low- and middle-income earners, rising for high-income earners (see Section 2.2.3).
- There may be little or no scope for raising METRs applying to top earners in the UK. The current tax system in the UK has METRs from income and NICs that rise modestly: the combined tax rate on earned income rises from 31% to 41% (from 40.6% to 47.7% including employer NI) when earnings reach £41,435 (April 2008). Section 2.2.3 showed that, with reasonable preferences for redistribution, METRs should rise in the upper part of the earnings distribution if the elasticity of taxable income with respect to tax rates is constant across income groups. Our numerical simulations (Figures 2.4A and 2.4B) showed that, if elasticities were constant and modest in size—our numerical example used an elasticity of 0.25—then increasing tax progressivity of the current UK tax system by adding yet an additional higher tax rate for the richest 1% would be desirable. However, our empirical analysis reported in Table 2.1 suggests

that the relevant elasticity of the richest 1% might exceed 0.25, in which case it is undesirable to increase top METRs because doing so would reduce government revenues. We therefore do not propose changes to the METR affecting top incomes.

- We take it for granted that the income tax system will remain individual, reflecting the extremely strong current political consensus in support of individualized income tax, and we conclude that the redistributive benefit of jointly assessed transfers for lower-income families outweighs any efficiency losses (see Section 2.4).

The present UK tax and benefit system described in Section 2.5 suffers from four important defects:

- Participation tax rates for low levels of earnings are high: for most groups, they are close to 100% before individuals are entitled to the working tax credit, and they remain high even with the working tax credit. These PTRs appear much too high in a context where optimal tax theory suggests that the participation tax rate should be low, possibly even negative, at low levels of earnings, so as to encourage people to move into work. And PTRs for families potentially entitled to HB/CTB remain extremely high (over 70%) even at medium and high incomes.
- The phasing-out of the working and child tax credit, which operates on top of income tax and NICs, generates METRs of 73.4% including employer NICs (higher if also entitled to HB/CTB) for a large number of low to moderate earners; such a high METR is highly likely to be above the optimal rate even with modest behavioural responses.
- The main means-tested programme to help with housing (housing benefit) has an extremely high withdrawal rate, administrative difficulties, and problems of misperception which deter low-income working families from claiming it (Turley and Thomas (2006)), and, by its design, predominately affects a minority group in society—tenants of social housing—who we might expect to have low earnings capabilities and a weak labour market attachment, and therefore relatively high labour supply elasticities.
- While the system for administering income tax and NICs in the UK is simple and efficient, the systems for administering child and working tax credits, and those for housing benefit and council tax benefit, are administratively burdensome for claimants, relatively expensive for the government, and prone to large amounts of fraud and error: all mean

that neither is as well-targeted on the economic situation of beneficiaries as it could be.[57]

We set out reforms that could address these shortcomings in the following two sections.

2.7.1. Immediate changes to household taxes and transfers

There are a number of straightforward steps that could be taken within the current system in order to address the key work disincentives.[58]

- Increase the level of earnings disregards (the amount of earnings a person is allowed to earn before benefits are withdrawn) in all of the means-tested benefits (in order of priority, HB/CTB then JSA/IS) to reduce PTRs on earnings of less than £90 a week for all, and on higher earnings for individuals receiving HB/CTB: these groups currently face very weak incentives to work at all.[59] An increase of HB/CTB disregards to £50/week would cost £1.7 billion a year, to the value of 16 times the minimum wage would cost £4.3 billion. Duplicating this in JSA/IS would cost an extra £0.3 billion or £0.6 billion respectively. This policy should lead to an increase in employment, but it would also extend eligibility to HB/CTB to many more working families, and so this measure should be considered only alongside measures dramatically to speed up processing times for HB/CTB claims, or a move to fixed or retrospective HB/CTB awards (to eliminate the problem of overpayments). Hopefully such measures, plus the clear signal sent by a large disregard, would themselves do much to increase the take-up rate of HB/CTB amongst eligible working families. Higher disregards in IS/JSA would also increase the number of people eligible for such benefits both through its immediate effects

[57] Tax credits are expensive to administer (HMRC spent £587 million in 2006–07 to administer net spending of £18.7 billion, a ratio of 3.13%, compared to a ratio of 2.12% to administer WFTC, its much smaller predecessor (see Cm 6983 2006–07 and HC 626 2006–07) tax credits have the highest rates of fraud and error in central government (£1 billion to £1.3 billion in 2004–05 out of total spending of around £16 billion; HMRC, (2007b)), they can often serve to increase (rather than cut) volatility of income (Hills et al. (2006)), and there remain concerns about their impact on recipients (see HC 1010 (2006–07)).

[58] These are not all novel proposals: Bell et al. (2007) analyse large increases in the earnings disregards in transfer programmes affecting lone parents, and HC 42-I (2007–08) recommends them for all family types; Adam et al. (2007) analyse increases in the working tax credit; Brewer (2007) analyses an extra credit for second earners in the working tax credit, as proposed by CM 6951 (2006–07) and Cooke and Lawton (2008).

[59] As this chapter was being finalized, Budget 2008 announced an effective rise in the earnings disregard for families with children of £20 a week for those with one child, and more for larger families. This clearly reduces the cost (and impact) of our proposal.

(because it extends eligibility up the income distribution), and after considering the behavioural response (because it makes working fewer than 16 hours and claiming IS/JSA relatively more appealing than working 16 or more hours and not claiming IS/JSA). Higher disregards in IS/JSA might be less appealing, then, if a government had a direct objective to get people off IS/JSA, which it might do if it had a non-welfarist objective function (see earlier section), or if the cost of administering IS/JSA were much higher than the cost of administering transfers for low-income families in work.

- Introduce an additional earnings disregard in tax credits for second earners (or an additional credit in the working tax credit for families with two earners). This would reduce PTRs for secondary earners, particularly those with children. Giving each individual their own earnings disregard of £6,200 in tax credits would cost £1.3 billion before any behavioural change. The downside of this policy would be that it merely shifts upwards the range of income over which second earners can expect to face a very high METR through the withdrawal of tax credits alongside payment of income tax and National Insurance. However, this seems justifiable given the strong evidence that participation elasticities are relatively high for second earners in couples with children, and that the extensive response is more important than the intensive response.
- Reduce the withdrawal rate in child and working tax credits. This would reduce METRs and PTRs for individuals receiving the working or child tax credits, most of whom will be earning more than £90 a week. A cut from 39% to 34% would cost £1.4 billion before any behavioural response. It would increase the number of individuals who face high METRs through a withdrawal of tax credits on top of income tax and NICs, but our assessment is this is acceptable if it permits the combined tax credit–income tax–NICs withdrawal rate to fall from its current high level of 73.4% (including employer NI), and it if acts to lower PTRs for low-earning families.[60]

[60] In the UK, most high METRs occur when income tax and NICs are liable at the same time as tax credits are withdrawn. One way of solving this problem is to introduce large tax allowances, so that income tax is not deducted until tax credits are fully withdrawn; this change could be accompanied by a rise in the tax credit withdrawal rate. This reform is appealing because it allows well-off families to receive support through tax cuts administered automatically through PAYE, whilst focusing the part of the programme that pays out cash on the families with the lowest incomes. Compared to the current system, though, such a change is expensive, because it effectively grants tax allowances to families previously too rich to receive much or any tax credits, and it would only be possible if the system of tax allowances were based on family, not individual, circumstances.

- Increase the working tax credit for groups other than lone parents (the level of the working tax credit for low-earning lone parents currently exceeds entitlement to IS/JSA if they did not work, leading to low or negative PTRs at low earnings; no increase is needed here on efficiency grounds). This would lower PTRs for low-earning individuals eligible for WTC. Equalizing WTC rates with JSA/IS rates would cost £3.2 billion; halving the gap would cost £1.6 billion. Two downsides of this policy are that it would increase the number of individuals who face a withdrawal of tax credits on top of income tax and NICs, and that it would reduce the gain to work for some second earners in couples (so directly offsetting the impact of the additional earnings disregard in tax credits proposed above). However, the rationale for recommending this policy is that these downsides would be outweighed by the increase in the number of adults working, as participation tax rates are cut for eligible families.

Of course, all of these changes would mean the government paying out considerably more in transfers or tax credits.[61] We do not at this stage propose offsetting changes to increase tax revenue or reduce spending on transfers elsewhere. However, we have suggested these reforms on efficiency (rather than equity) grounds, and so it follows that any widespread tax rise (such as a rise in VAT, income tax, or National Insurance) to fund these tax cuts should still lead to a reform package that is desirable on efficiency grounds (in other words, it should be possible to find a revenue neutral set of tax and benefit changes that leads to a overall increase in aggregate earnings).[62]

These reforms have suggested themselves on efficiency grounds, not because we are seeking to redistribute to particular groups. But whether these proposals seem sensible to the government will obviously depend on their own priorities for redistribution, so Tables 2.4A and 2.4B show the distributional impact of these policies, and the average gain for different family types, assuming no change in behaviour, and ignoring the impact of any revenue-raising measures to pay for them (which could be chosen to have any desired distributional effect).

[61] Note that all the costs have been estimated assuming no behavioural change, and that only one reform at a time is implemented. However, the reforms, and therefore their costs, interact: a £50 disregard in all means-tested benefits plus the three tax credit changes would cost just over £8.8 billion).

[62] Furthermore, it might be appropriate to reduce spending on child benefit (or the family element of the child tax credit) in order to pay for at least some of these reforms, given that families with children tend to benefit more than families without, and given that these reforms suggested themselves on efficiency grounds, and not from a desire to redistribute more to particular groups.

Table 2.4A. Distributional impact of reforms (% gain in net income)

Income Decile Group	Reform: Increase earnings disregards	Raise WTC entitlements	Cut tax credits taper	2nd adult disregard in tax credits	All reforms
Poorest	2.88	0.26	0.00	0.00	3.13
2	2.90	1.69	0.24	0.10	4.55
3	2.08	3.41	1.27	1.05	7.01
4	0.85	3.39	1.61	1.65	7.84
5	0.36	1.13	0.58	0.69	4.46
6	0.15	0.19	0.19	0.09	1.70
7	0.10	0.07	0.06	0.01	0.36
8	0.06	0.03	0.02	0.00	0.12
9	0.02	0.01	0.01	0.00	0.04
Richest	0.00	0.00	0.00	0.00	0.00

Notes: Authors' calculations based on FRS 2004–05 data and the TAXBEN micro-simulation model. Pre-reform tax system as described in notes to Figure 2.1A.

Table 2.4B. Distributional impact of reforms by family type (% gain in net income)

Family Type	Reform: Increase earnings disregards	Raise WTC entitlements	Cut tax credits taper	2nd adult disregard in tax credits	All reforms
Singles, no children	0.45	0.66	0.08	0.00	1.32
Couples, no children	0.17	0.20	0.05	0.00	0.45
Couples, with children	0.51	1.06	0.52	0.67	3.21
Singles, with children	0.58	0.00	0.69	0.00	1.26

Notes: Authors' calculations based on FRS 2004–05 data and the TAXBEN micro-simulation model. Pre-reform tax system as described in notes to Figure 2.1A.

2.7.2. Radical reform: the Integrated Family Support

The radical reform plan we propose goes one step further. It is designed not only to be targeting net tax cuts where incentives to work are currently at their weakest but also to simplify administration and enforcement for the government, and to reduce the compliance costs of employers and claimants.

The centrepiece of our new tax and benefit system is a new programme, called the Integrated Family Support (IFS), which acts as a replacement for child and working tax credit, income support/JSA, child benefit, housing benefit, and council tax benefit.

The key features are as follows (there are more details on how it would work in the online appendix (see footnote 14), but at this stage, we do not claim that we have identified or resolved all the operational and administrative difficulties):

- Integrating most of the current benefits means that claimants can feel more secure about continuing to receive transfers when their circumstances change, and also removes the problems that can occur when the benefits interact (this particularly applies to the current interaction between tax credits and HB/CTB); these should reduce the compliance costs of claimants. It should also mean fewer opportunities for fraud and simplify administration and enforcement for the government.
- The maximum entitlement to the IFS would be *family* based, and would be the sum of a family component (different for single adults and couples), a child component (depending on the presence and number of dependent children), and a housing component (depending on whether the family rents or owns, and on the local rental and council tax levels). This structure broadly reflects the current set of maximum entitlements provided through transfers and tax credits.
- The IFS allowance would be means-tested based on *family* income, but there would be an *individual* earnings disregard of £90, or just over 16 hours work at the current minimum wage.[63] This disregard would apply to each adult in the family, so each of the two adults in a couple could earn up to £90 and still keep the maximum IFS allowance. The aim of this, which echoes our suggested immediate reforms, is to lower PTRs—potentially to zero for low-earnings work—in order to encourage labour market participation amongst those currently not working.
- The IFS would be paid directly by the government to eligible low- and moderate-income families, but the withdrawing of the IFS would be achieved, for the vast majority of families, through the existing (and augmented) system of income tax and NI withholding.[64] The IFS would not be an annual system, but instead be operated on a non-cumulative basis, with a weekly or monthly periodicity, so maximum entitlements

[63] We describe the reform in 2008–09 prices (i.e., as if it were an alternative to the April 2008 tax and transfer system), although we include in the base system for costing the reform the small change to the Upper Earnings Limit for employee NICs and the income tax higher-rate threshold due in April 2009. However, this chapter was written before the £600 rise in the income tax personal allowance for 2008–09 was announced in May 2008.

[64] We use the word 'withholding' in the same sense as in Shaw, Slemrod, and Whiting, Chapter 12.

would be determined weekly or monthly, and the withdrawal would depend on the earnings in each pay period. The aim is to ensure that the IFS is more transparent and provides more certainty than child and working tax credits.[65]

- There will be two taper rates for the IFS: 30%, if the family is receiving only the child and family elements, or 45% if the family is receiving the housing element. These imply a lower overall METR than currently applies to families entitled to tax credits and/or HB/CTB. This is in line with our earlier conclusion that METRs for low to middle earners are far too high, even if behavioural responses are modest.
- This system does not do away with under- or over-payments, but their incidence should be much reduced compared to the current systems. Similarly, end-of-year reconciliations will still be needed, although these ought to be combined with the self-assessment process for income tax (as they would only be needed for relatively well-off families receiving the IFS). If, for various reasons, a family is under-withheld, the government would not ask for an immediate repayment, but could gradually reduce the balance over time through reasonable reductions in future IFS payments.

Financing the IFS, and its effect on household incomes

The substantial increase in the earnings disregard of the IFS relative to the current system for IS/JSA, HB/CTB and in the working tax credit for second earners, the effective cut in the withdrawal rates of HB/CTB and tax credits, and the extension of the IFS to groups currently eligible for neither IS/JSA nor tax credits all cost a significant amount.

For the reform to be revenue neutral before behavioural responses, there need to be net tax rises elsewhere. In this proposal, this has been achieved by:

1. Subsuming child benefit and the family element of the child tax credit within the IFS, and thereby removing both from better-off families through a means test.[66]

65 It would clearly be much simpler if the IFS was an annual, retrospective scheme, because then it could be aligned fully with income tax. But doing this would mean that IFS payments could be weakly related to families' circumstances, and this is significantly at odds with the principles of transfer programmes in the UK.

66 There would then be no difference in the net taxes paid by well-off families with children and those without children, which makes sense if children are not seen as imposing extra costs: see the discussion in Section 2.4. A version that retains child benefit would cost an extra £3.3 billion, and therefore it would be necessary to increase the basic rate of income tax by around 1 ppt to be revenue-neutral.

Table 2.5. Parameters of the IFS reforms

Single adult	£50
Couple	£80
Amount per child	£50
Supplement for first child	
Lone parent family	£30
Couple family	£20
Earnings disregard (for each adult)	£90
Withdrawal rates†	
IFS	30%
HB/CTB	15%
Income tax and National Insurance thresholds	
Personal allowance/primary threshold	£4,680/yr (£90/wk)

§ Weekly values unless stated otherwise.

† Rates applied to gross income in excess of disregard.

2. Lowering the income tax personal allowance and the point at which NICs start to be due to the IFS disregard of £90 a week.
3. Increasing the basic rate of income tax by 1 ppt.
4. Setting family and child entitlements to the IFS that are below the current rates of JSA/IS and child tax credit, but higher than the current rates of working tax credit.[67]

The key parameters are shown in Table 2.5.[68]

The effect of the IFS on household incomes

Figures 2.7A–2.7D show how the budget constraint for some specimen families would change under the IFS. The main implication of the IFS is that it starts withdrawing means-tested support at higher income levels than the present system, and then withdraws it more slowly. This strengthens the very weak work incentives currently created by aggressive means-testing, but it

[67] The last of these changes leads to losses for some low-income families with no private income. A version of the IFS where the family and child elements of the IFS are set at the existing rates of IS/JSA and child tax credits (so as to produce no change in net transfers to families with no private income) would cost an extra £6 billion a year, and would imply considerable gains for low-earning adults without children, and all but the richest couples with children. To make this revenue-neutral would require increasing the basic rate of income tax by nearly 2 ppts (after considering the behavioural responses).

[68] Estimates of the cost of the IFS have been made assuming no behavioural change, and that all benefits and tax credits are taken up. The second of these assumptions may understate the cost of the IFS; if the IFS succeeds in having a lower compliance burden for families, then some currently not claiming tax credits or HB/CTB when in work may be induced to do so.

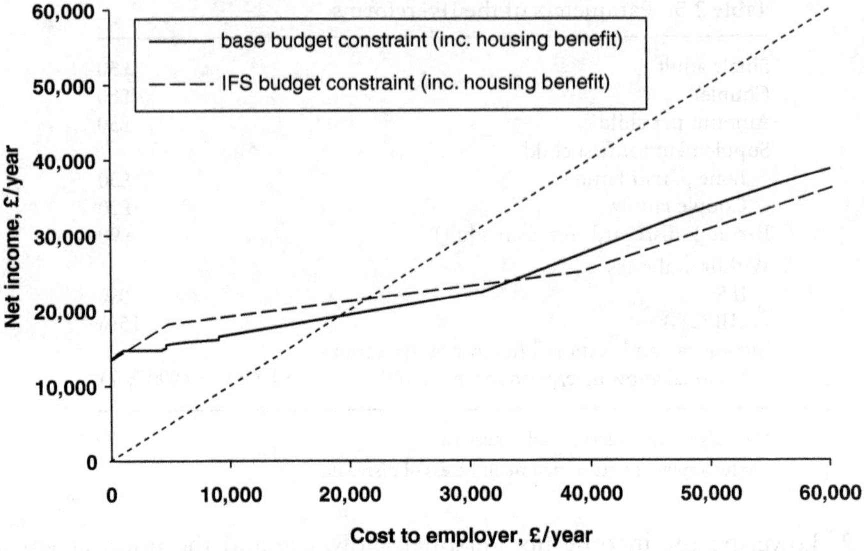

Notes: 'Base budget constraint' based on tax system as described in notes to Figure 2.1A. 'IFS budget constraint' based on tax system as described in text.

Figure 2.7A. IFS Reform, budget constraint, lone parents

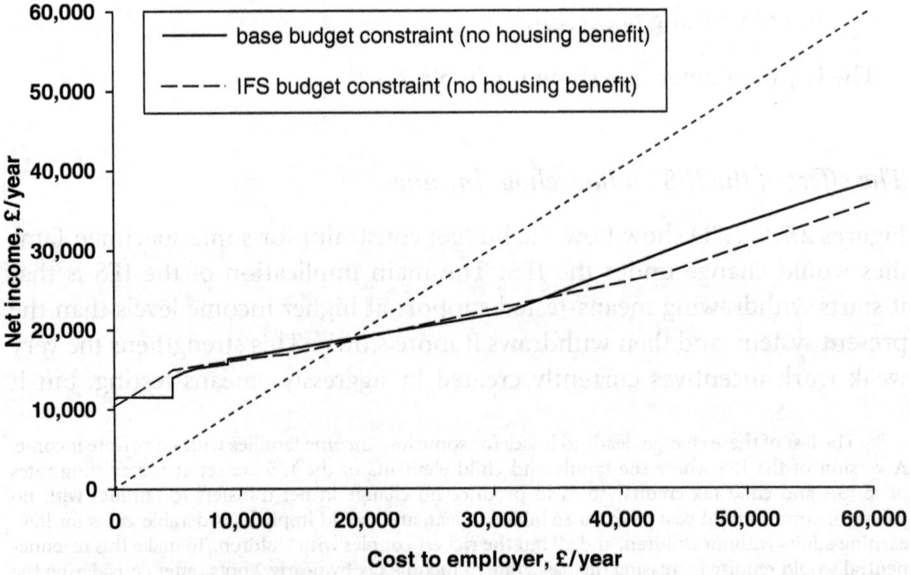

Notes: 'Base budget constraint' based on tax system as described in notes to Figure 2.1A. 'IFS budget constraint' based on tax system as described in text.

Figure 2.7B. IFS Reform, budget constraint, one earner couple with children

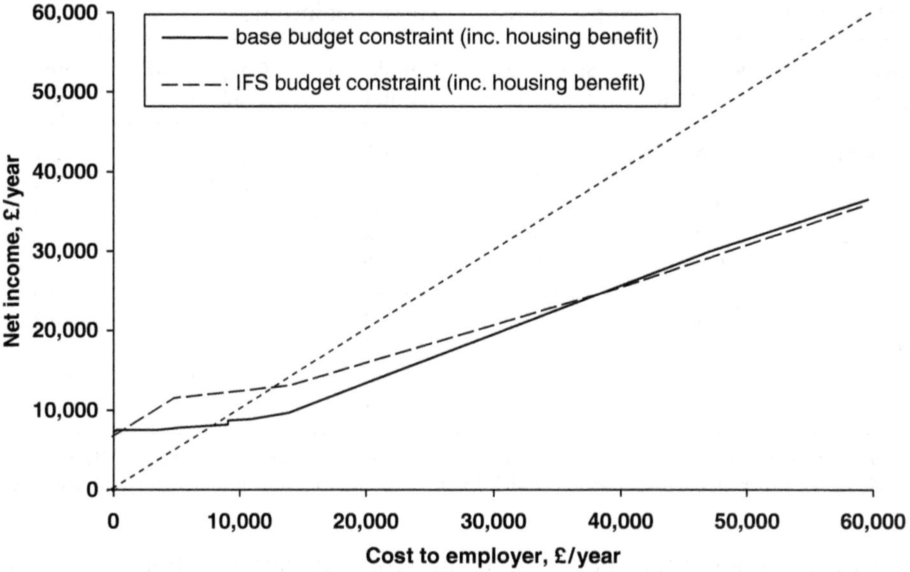

Notes: 'Base budget constraint' based on tax system as described in notes to Figure 2.1A. 'IFS budget constraint' based on tax system as described in text.

Figure 2.7C. IFS Reform, budget constraint, single no children

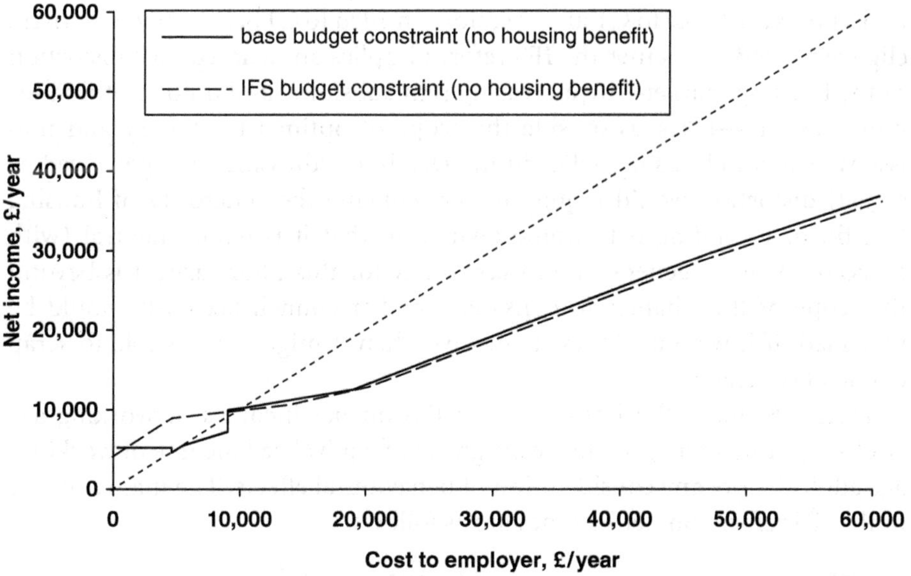

Notes: 'Base budget constraint' based on tax system as described in notes to Figure 2.1A. 'IFS budget constraint' based on tax system as described in text.

Figure 2.7D. IFS Reform, budget constraint, one earner couple without children

Table 2.6. Distributional impact of IFS (% gain in net income)

Decile group	Overall population	Singles no children	Couples no children	Couples with children	Lone parents
Poorest	4.6	4.1	11.8	1.4	3.7
2	4.3	6.2	6.7	3.6	2.4
3	4.8	2.4	5.4	6.1	4.1
4	4.0	3.0	3.8	5.1	2.7
5	0.9	2.1	0.9	0.1	1.2
6	−1.7	1.3	−0.1	−4.6	0.3
7	−2.4	0.5	−0.4	−6.2	−0.2
8	−2.2	1.4	−1.2	−5.4	−2.5
9	−1.6	0.9	−1.2	−3.9	−3.2
Richest	−1.2	−0.4	−1.1	−2.1	−1.5

Note: Based on uprated data from the Family Resources Survey 2004–05 and the Institute for Fiscal Studies' tax and benefit micro-simulation model, TAXBEN. Tax systems described in notes to Figure 2.7A.

does bring many more people into the scope of means-testing on top of income tax and NICs.

Given the focus on strengthening the very weak work incentives for those on HB and CTB, there is a substantial shift in resources between those not entitled to HB and CTB to those who are (in practice, the vast majority of households are liable to CT and therefore entitled to CTB, but only renters are eligible for HB). Whether the IFS reform implies an unacceptable distortion to the housing market—by increasing rent subsidies, and doing nothing for home-owners—takes us outside the scope of optimal tax theory and into issues related to housing policy in the UK, but addressing this (perceived or actual) distortion would require either reducing the generosity of housing benefit, or extending it to home-owners so that it is tenure-neutral (with an accompanying general rise in tax to pay for this). Similarly, it is beyond the scope of this chapter to consider whether council tax itself should be reformed; if it were made less regressive, then it might be possible to scrap council tax benefit.

Table 2.6 shows the impact of the IFS on net incomes of working-age adults, by family type, and by decile group of equivalized income of working-age adults before any consideration of behavioural effects. The main impacts of the IFS reform on net incomes are as follows.

- The maximum entitlements to the IFS are a little higher than current tax credit entitlements but lower than current IS/JSA rates (except for lone parents), and this leads to losses for IS/JSA recipients with no other sources of income. However, the fact that the IFS is made available without any hours rules means that some low-income individuals (particularly single adults aged 25 or over with no children and working under 30 hours a week) currently entitled to neither IS/JSA nor tax credits gain substantially.

- Low-income families entitled to HB/CTB tend to gain because the equivalent support is withdrawn more slowly under the IFS.
- Better-off families with children tend to lose as support currently provided through the non-means-tested child benefit is now tapered away as part of the IFS.
- All taxpayers lose slightly as the income tax personal allowance and the NICs primary threshold has been cut slightly.
- All taxpayers lose as the main rate of income tax is increased.

Across the whole population, the bottom half of the income distribution tend to be better off, and the top half to be worse off, but the changes are not entirely progressive: the largest gains are in the middle of the bottom half of the distribution, and the largest losses are in the middle of the top half.[69]

Figures 2.8A to 2.8H show the impact of the IFS on (mean) PTRs and METRs by earnings for the same four family types.[70] In general, PTRs are lowered for all adults with low earnings, reflecting the universal £90 earnings disregard, and the lower out-of-work safety net for some. For some adults in families with children, the IFS increases PTRs on higher earnings, reflecting that support currently provided through the non-means-tested child benefit would be withdrawn as part of the IFS.

The impact on METRs is more complex. All family types see a fall in METRs on earnings below £90, reflecting that the £90 earnings disregard in the IFS is much higher than in current means-tested benefits. Above this, there are different patterns for the different family types. Lone parents and primary earners in couples with children tend to see METRs fall slightly at low earnings (that are above £90) but rise at higher earnings: this directly reflects that the IFS taper is lower than the current tax credit taper, and that currently the IFS taper extends further up the earnings distribution than the tax credit taper does. However, the other family types tend to see

[69] Another statistic summarizing the impact on the income distribution is the impact on relative poverty rates. If the poverty line is calibrated so that 21% of children are in relative poverty (the rate in 2004–05, where poverty is defined as living in a household with less than 60% of median equivalized income), child poverty falls by 1.4 ppts, or just under 200,000 children before allowing for behavioural responses but allowing the IFS reform to shift the median.

[70] These figures are based on estimates of the METR and PTR of each working adult in the 2004–05 FRS made using TAXBEN. All figures plot individual earnings on the horizontal axis.

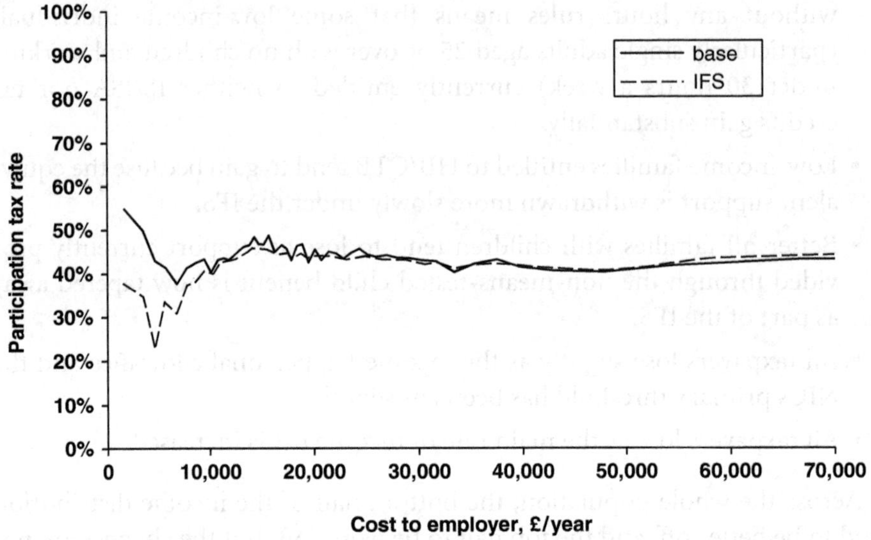

Notes: Based on uprated data from the Family Resources Survey 2004–05 and the Institute for Fiscal Studies' tax and benefit micro-simulation model, TAXBEN. Tax systems described in notes to Figure 2.7A.

Figure 2.8A. Participation tax role—Singles no children, impact of reform

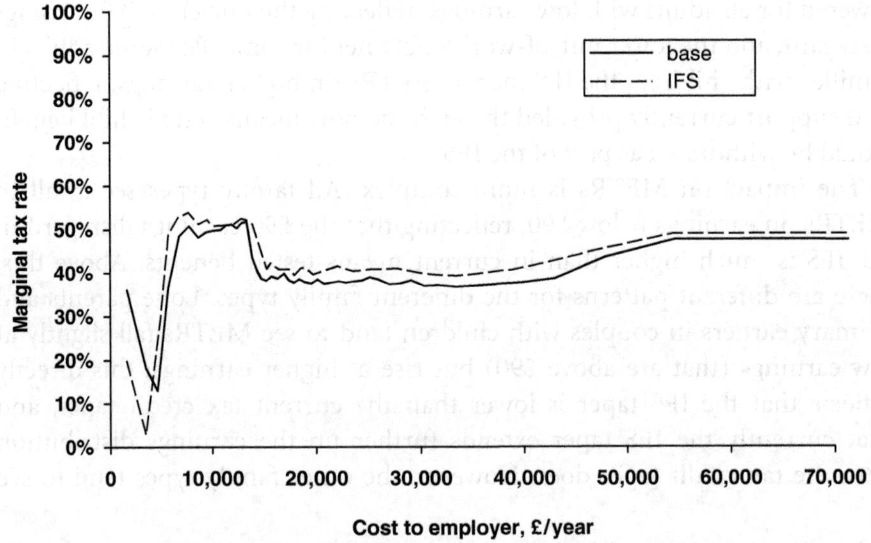

Notes: Based on uprated data from the Family Resources Survey 2004–05 and the Institute for Fiscal Studies' tax and benefit micro-simulation model, TAXBEN. Tax systems described in notes to Figure 2.7A.

Figure 2.8B. Marginal tax rate—Singles no children, impact of reform

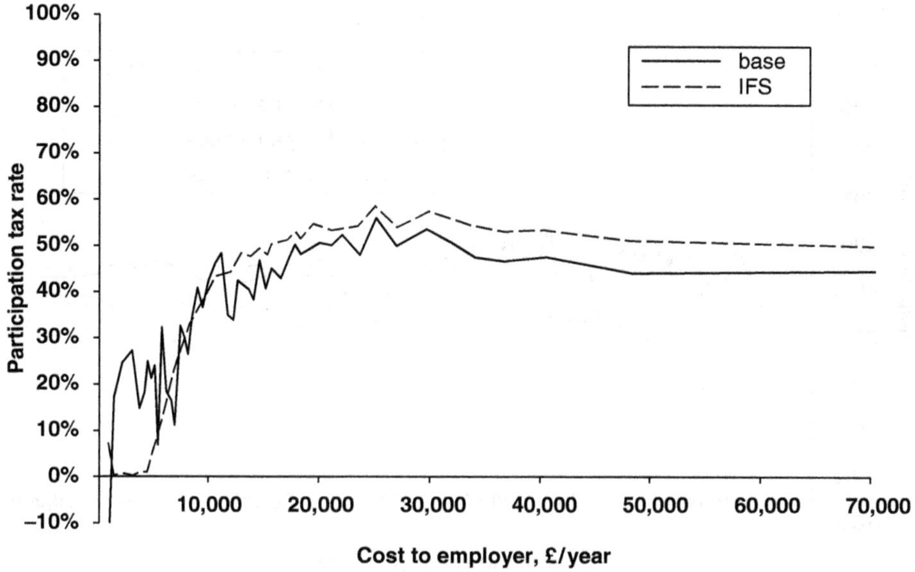

Notes: Based on uprated data from the Family Resources Survey 2004–05 and the Institute for Fiscal Studies' tax and benefit micro-simulation model, TAXBEN. Tax systems described in notes to Figure 2.7A.

Figure 2.8C. Participation tax rate—Lone parents, impact of reform

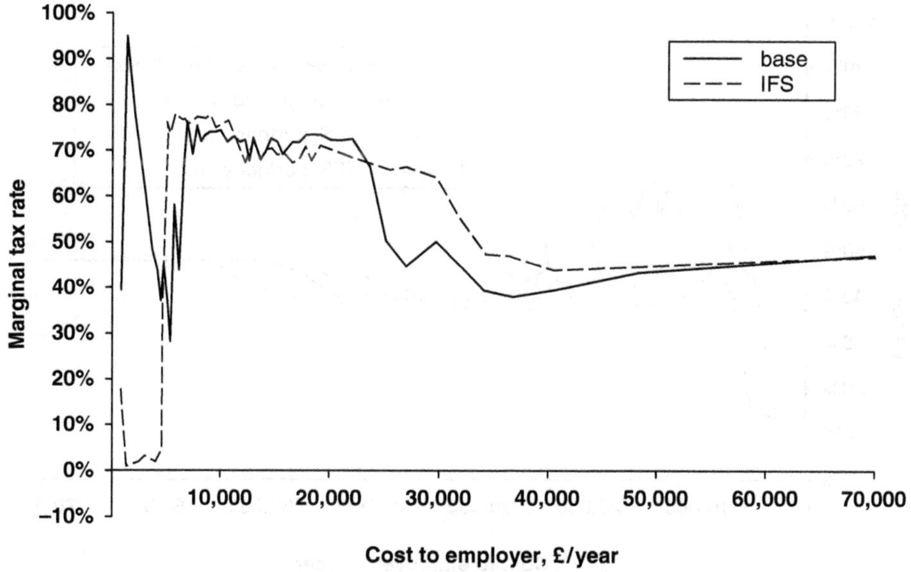

Notes: Based on uprated data from the Family Resources Survey 2004–05 and the Institute for Fiscal Studies' tax and benefit micro-simulation model, TAXBEN. Tax systems described in notes to Figure 2.7A.

Figure 2.8D. Marginal tax rate—lone parents, impact of reform

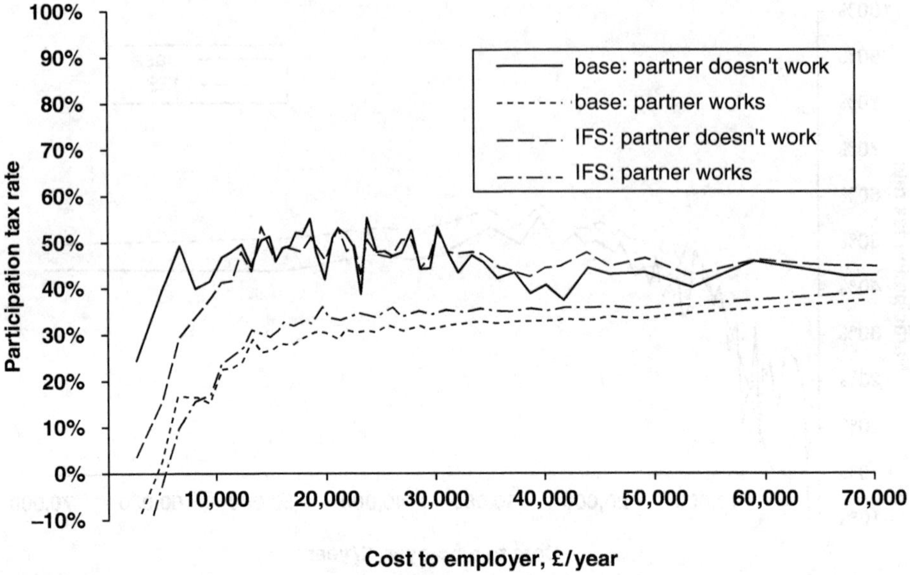

Notes: Based on uprated data from the Family Resources Survey 2004–05 and the Institute for Fiscal Studies' tax and benefit micro-simulation model, TAXBEN. Tax systems described in notes to Figure 2.7A.

Figure 2.8E. Participation tax rate—Couples no children, impact of reform

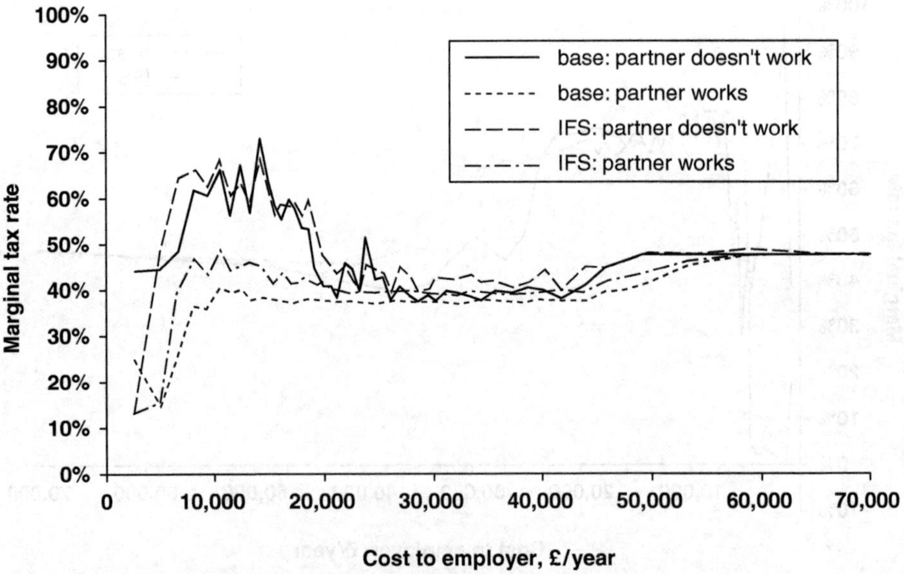

Notes: Based on uprated data from the Family Resources Survey 2004–05 and the Institute for Fiscal Studies' tax and benefit micro-simulation model, TAXBEN. Tax systems described in notes to Figure 2.7A.

Figure 2.8F. Marginal tax rate—Couples no children, impact of reform

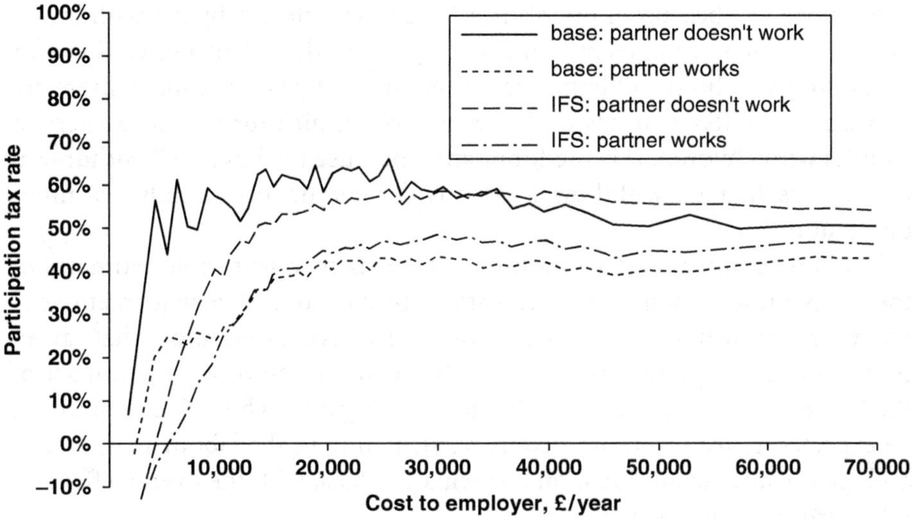

Notes: Based on uprated data from the Family Resources Survey 2004–05 and the Institute for Fiscal Studies' tax and benefit micro-simulation model, TAXBEN. Tax systems described in notes to Figure 2.7A.

Figure 2.8G. Participation tax rate—Couples with children, impact of reform

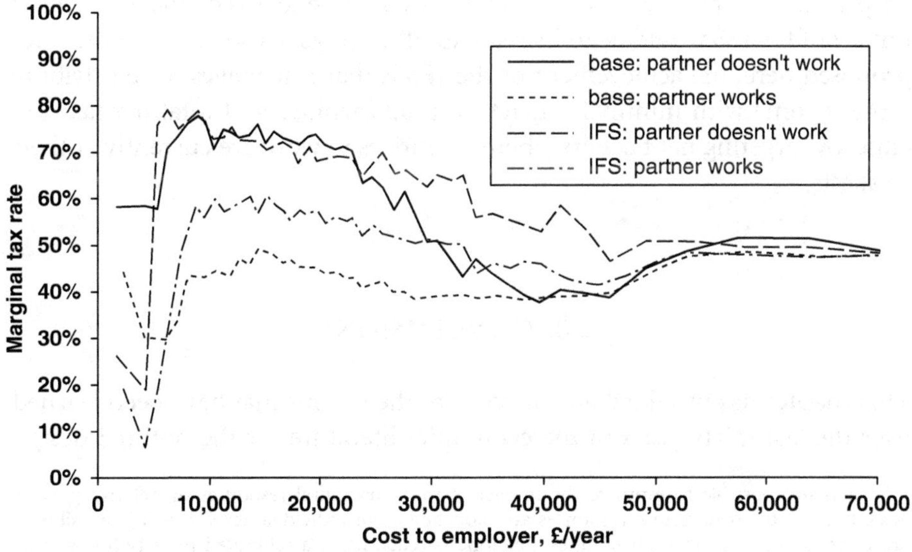

Notes: Based on uprated data from the Family Resources Survey 2004–05 and the Institute for Fiscal Studies' tax and benefit micro-simulation model, TAXBEN. Tax systems described in notes to Figure 2.7A.

Figure 2.8H. Marginal tax rate—Couples with children, impact of reform

rises in METRs because more of these adults are affected by the withdrawal of the IFS than are currently affected by a withdrawal of tax credits (for single adults without children, this is predominantly because many more are entitled to the IFS as it has no hours of work limits; for second earners in couples with children, it is predominantly because the lower IFS withdrawal rate means that its withdrawal extends further up the (family) earnings distribution).

The online appendix (see footnote 14) explains how simple estimates of the behavioural response to the IFS affect the cost to the Exchequer, employment, and total hours worked (or total earnings). These show that, given reasonable assumptions on the size of behavioural responses, the impact of the IFS reform on the Exchequer is small but negative. The IFS reform would be expected to lead to more people participating in the labour market, but average earnings conditional on participation falls, with the overall effect on total earnings being negative.[71]

Part of the reason for this negative behavioural response is that we have tried to reduce the generosity of the system for those with no private income by relatively small amounts, and we have made no cuts at all in the generosity of HB/CTB. If those programmes were made less generous to those with no private income, then income tax rates could be lowered, and the overall impact of the IFS would be to increase total earnings. However, with the rates proposed here, the achievement of the IFS is that it manages to redistribute more income with minimal impact on total earnings and total net tax revenue, by targeting net tax cuts where incentives to work are currently at their weakest.

2.8. CONCLUSION

This chapter has provided an overview of the lessons that have been learned over the last thirty years in the economics literature for the optimal design

[71] It is not possible to estimate the impact of the behavioural responses on relative poverty rates, because the behavioural responses are modelled at an individual level. But it is possible to say something for single adult families. For lone parents, using a calibrated poverty line so that 21% of children were in relative poverty in the base system, 41% of children with lone parents were in poverty. Before behavioural responses, this falls to 40% (70% for children with a workless lone parent, 7% for children with a working lone parent, with 48% of children having a working lone parent). The estimated impact of behavioural responses is to increase the number of children with a working lone parent by 3.4 ppts, and to cut the poverty rate of children with working lone parents to 5%. Together, this makes the poverty rate for all children in lone parent families equal to 38%.

of household tax and benefits, and an application to the UK. We derived formulae for the optimal tax rates using the simple Mirrlees model, and showed the result of simulations of the whole tax system based on the UK earnings distribution and empirically estimated labour supply elasticities. We investigated the link between top incomes and top marginal income tax rates since the 1960s. We discussed how the optimal tax system is affected by allowing for participation responses, migration, and how families and children should be treated.

These insights from optimal tax theory were contrasted with the work incentives inherent in the current UK tax and benefit system, and it is worth repeating our conclusions.

First, participation tax rates at low earnings are high: for most groups, they are close to 100% for jobs of too few hours to grant individuals entitlement to the working tax credit, and they remain high even with it. Secondly, the phasing-out of the working and child tax credits, which operates on top of National Insurance and income tax, generates METRs of 73.4% (including employer NICs) for a large number of low to moderate earners which is likely to be above the optimal rate even with modest behavioural responses. Third, the main means-tested programme to help with housing (housing benefit) has an extremely high withdrawal rate (further increasing METRs), administrative difficulties, and problems of misperception which deter low-income working families from claiming it. Finally, while the system for administering income tax and NICs in the UK is simple and efficient, the systems for administering child and working tax credits, and for housing benefit and council tax benefit, are administratively burdensome for claimants, relatively expensive for the government, and prone to large amounts of fraud and error: all mean that neither are as well-targeted on the economic situation of beneficiaries as they could be.

Given this, we suggest a set of changes to the existing tax and benefit structure that could be made immediately based on the lessons from our analysis. Our package of 'immediate reforms' is costly, and involves increasing the level of earnings disregards in all of the means-tested benefits to reduce PTRs on low earnings and introducing an additional earnings disregard in tax credits for second earners to reduce PTRs for secondary earners, particularly those with children. Work incentives can be further improved by reductions in the withdrawal rate in child and working tax credits, and by targeting increases in the working tax credit on groups other than lone parents.

We also provide a more radical and comprehensive plan for reforming the UK household tax and benefit system that attempts to deal not only with these work incentive issues, but also the administrative failings that we identify. Our plan replaces the piecemeal benefits for low-income families (income support, working and child tax credits, housing benefit, and council tax benefit) into a single *Integrated Family Support* programme which provides stronger and simpler incentives for work at the bottom, reduces compliance costs for families, and is provided 'as-you-earn' and administered in the same way as NICs through the PAYE withholding system. We show how this can be done in a revenue-neutral fashion, including an assessment of the behavioural responses. The key achievement of the IFS is that it manages to redistribute income with minimal impact on total earnings and total net tax revenue, by targeting net tax cuts which work with the grain, rather than against the grain, of individuals' work incentives.

We have used the framework of optimal tax theory to guide our discussion throughout this chapter. We argued that one attractive feature of this theory is that it makes explicit that one cannot hope to say how best to design taxes and transfers without specifying what one is trying to achieve overall. This, of course, may prove to be our ultimate downfall. Without knowing the government's preferences for redistribution or other objectives, we cannot hope to predict whether our reform will appeal.

APPENDIX

This appendix provides a more formal discussion of the derivation of optimal income tax rates. We first show how to determine the optimal marginal tax rate for high earners, and then how to derive optimal tax rates for taxpayers more generally.

2A.1. Determining the top rate of income tax

Consider a reform that changes the top tax rate τ by a small amount $d\tau$ (with no change in the tax schedule for incomes below the top bracket $\bar{z}$). Here, let us denote by z the *average* income reported by taxpayers in the top bracket and let us assume that there are N taxpayers in the top bracket. As mentioned in the main text, this small tax reform has the following effects on tax revenue:

1. There is a mechanical increase in tax revenue because taxpayers face a higher MTR on incomes above $\bar{z}$. Hence, the total mechanical effect is $dM = N[z - \bar{z}]d\tau > 0$. This mechanical effect is the projected increase in tax revenue if there were no behavioural response.

2. The increase in the tax rate triggers a behavioural response which reduces the average reported income in the top bracket by $dz = -e \cdot z \cdot d\tau/(1-\tau)$ on average (by definition of the elasticity e—see Box 2.1 in Section 2.2) and hence produces a loss in tax revenue equal to $dB = -N \cdot e \cdot z \cdot d\tau \cdot \tau/(1-\tau) < 0$.

Rather than necessarily assuming that the marginal value of consumption for top taxpayers is negligible relative to that of the average person in the economy, let us assume that the government values giving one additional pound to the average top bracket taxpayer at g. If the government values redistribution, g will be strictly less than one, and will be zero if the government has strong redistributive tastes (the case considered in the main text). Hence, the small tax reform also creates a social welfare cost equal to $dW = -g \cdot N[z - \overline{z}]\, d\tau < 0$.

Summing the mechanical and the behavioural tax revenue effect and the welfare effect, we obtain the net effect of the reform from the government perspective:

$$dM + dB + dW = Nd\tau(z - \overline{z}) \cdot \left[1 - g - e \cdot \frac{z}{z - \overline{z}} \cdot \frac{\tau}{1 - \tau}\right]$$

At the optimum, this expression must be zero. As before, let us denote by a the ratio $z/(z - \overline{z})$, which measures the thinness of the top of the income distribution. Note that $a \geqslant 1$. The optimal τ can then be expressed as:

$$\tau^* = \frac{1 - g}{1 - g + a \cdot e}. \qquad (1)$$

Unsurprisingly, the optimal tax rate is decreasing in g (the value that the government sets on the marginal consumption of high incomes), decreasing in the elasticity e of behavioural responses, and decreasing in a, the parameter which measures the thinness of the top of the income distribution. Note that this expression is identical to that presented in Box 2.2 when $g = 0$. This important case gives an upper bound on the optimal top rate equal to $1/(1 + a \cdot e)$. This corresponds to the tax rate maximizing tax revenue from top bracket taxpayers: the so-called Laffer rate. Finally, we note that it is well known that top tails of income distributions are closely approximated by Pareto distributions,[72] in which case the parameter a does not vary with $\overline{z}$ and is exactly equal to the Pareto parameter.[73]

[72] A Pareto distribution has a density function of the form $f(z) = C/z^{1+\alpha}$ where C and α are constant parameters. α is called the Pareto parameter.

[73] When $\overline{z}$ reaches the level of the very highest income earner, $z = \overline{z}$ and a is infinite and the optimal tax rate is zero, which is the famous Sadka–Seade zero top result. However, this zero top result is a very misleading result for practical tax policy as the empirical a does not go to infinity except for the very highest income earner.

2A.2. Determining the optimal marginal tax schedules

We can extend the above analysis to consider how the optimal tax rate varies more generally across the income distribution. Here, we let $T(z)$ denote the (possibly non-linear) tax schedule that the government imposes, where z denotes a given level of earnings. This tax schedule incorporates both transfers (when $T(z)$ is negative) and taxes (when $T(z)$ is positive). Let us denote by $H(z)$ the cumulative distribution of individuals (fraction of taxpayers with income less than z) and by $h(z)$ the density distribution of taxpayers. The optimal tax system is characterized by a lump-sum grant received by those with no earnings (equal to $-T(0)$) combined with a schedule of marginal tax rates $T'(z)$ which define how the lump-sum grant should be reduced as earnings increase and how additional earnings should be taxed once the lump-sum grant is fully tapered out. Again, the optimal marginal tax rate $T'(z)$ is set so as to balance costs and benefits at the margin.

Suppose that the government increases the marginal tax rate $T'(z)$ by $d\tau$ in a small band of income $(z, z + dz)$. As above, this reform has three effects on government tax receipts and welfare:

1. The reform increases taxes by $d\tau dz$ for every taxpayer above the small band, and hence collects extra taxes $dM = (1 - H(z))d\tau dz$.
2. Those extra taxes generate a welfare cost to taxpayers. If we denote by $G(z)$ the average social value for the government of distributing £1 uniformly among taxpayers with income above z, the welfare cost is simply $dW = dM \cdot G(z)$.[74] If the government values redistribution, $G(z)$ will be decreasing in z. As we have assumed away income effects, $G(0) = 1$,[75] and we assumed above that $G(z)$ goes to zero when z is large (i.e. in the top tax bracket). The more redistributive the tastes of the government, the smaller $G(z)$.
3. The marginal tax rate increase $d\tau$ in the small band reduces earnings by $-e \cdot z \cdot d\tau/(1 - T'(z))$ for taxpayers in the small band due to the substitution effect. There are $h(z)dz$ such taxpayers in the small band, and so this produces a loss in tax revenue equal to $dB = -e \cdot z \cdot \left[T'(z)/(1 - T'(z))\right] d\tau \cdot h(z)dz$.

At the optimum, $dM + dW + dB = 0$, which generates the following optimal tax rate formula:[76]

$$\frac{T'(z)}{1 - T'(z)} = \frac{1}{e} \cdot \frac{1 - H(z)}{zh(z)} \cdot (1 - G(z)).$$

[74] This is a consequence of the envelope theorem as each individual maximizes utility.

[75] Distributing £1 uniformly among all individuals does not generate behavioural responses and hence has a cost of exactly £1 for the government.

[76] This formula is not exactly accurate but very close for discussion and intuition purposes. In the exact formula, $h(z)$ should be replaced with the 'virtual' density $h^*(z)$, which is the density of earnings at z that would arise if the tax system were replaced by the linearized tax system at z. See Saez (2001) for complete details.

The optimal tax rate $T'(z)$ is decreasing with the elasticity e. It is also decreasing in $G(z)$ which measures the social marginal value of consumption for individuals with earnings above z, and decreasing in the hazard ratio $(1 - H(z))/(zh(z))$ which measures the thinness of the distribution.

2A.3. Optimal tax rates with participation responses

Here, an individual with skill z who decides to work will get $z - T(z)$ in disposable income. If the individual decides not to work, she will get $-T(0)$ in disposable income. We assume that individual utility is simply $u = c - q$ where c is disposable income and q are costs of work. Hence, the individual will work if the net return to work $z - T(z) + T(0)$ exceeds her costs of working q. If we assume that costs of work q are distributed with a (cumulative) distribution $P(q|z)$ among individuals with skill z, the number of individuals of skill z who work is simply $P(z - T(z) + T(0)|z)$. We can define the elasticity of participation with respect to the net return to work as:

$$\eta(z) = \frac{z - T(z) + T(0)}{P} \cdot \frac{\partial P}{\partial q}. \tag{2}$$

To derive an optimal tax formula, let us consider a small increase in dT in $T(z)$ but only at skill level z. As there are only extensive responses, this reform affects only individuals with skill z. As above, this reform has three effects on government tax receipts and welfare:

1. The reform increases taxes by dT for every taxpayer with skill z who works and hence collects extra taxes $dM = P(q|z)dT$.
2. The extra taxes that are now collected generate a welfare cost to workers with skill z. If we denote by $g(z)$ the social value for the government of distributing £1 among taxpayers with income z, the welfare cost is simply $dW = dM \cdot g(z) = P(q|z)g(z)dT$. If the government values redistribution, $g(z)$ will be decreasing in z. The 'no income effect' assumption implies that the average $g(z)$ across the population is equal to one. Note that the $g(z)$ of this section and the $G(z)$ of the previous section are related by the formula $G(z)(1 - H(z)) = \int_z^{\infty} g(z)h(z)dz$.
3. The tax increase dT at income level z induces some of the workers at z to drop out of work. All those with fixed cost of work q between $z - T(z) + T(0) - dT$ and $z - T(z) + T(0)$ drop out. There are $dT\partial P/\partial q = dT\eta P/(z - T(z) + T(0))$ such workers. The fiscal cost of this behavioural response is $dB = [(T(z) - T(0))/(z - T(z) + T(0))] \cdot \eta \cdot P(q|z)dT$.[77]

[77] Note that those dropping out of the labour force are indifferent (within dT) between working and not working and there is only an infinitesimal number of switchers. Hence the welfare effect on movers is second order relative to the welfare effect on those who work and can be neglected. This is directly equivalent to the situation from Section 2.2 where behavioural responses do not create a first-order welfare effect.

To proceed, define the participation tax rate, a measure of the extent to which the tax and benefit system weakens the reward from working, as $t(z) = (T(z) - T(0))/z$. As discussed above, $1 - t(z)$ measures the increase in disposable income (relative to earnings) when an individual decides to work. Using this definition, and noting that at the optimum we again must have $dM + dW + dB = 0$, we generate the following optimal tax rate formula:

$$\frac{t(z)}{1 - t(z)} = \frac{1}{\eta} \cdot (1 - g(z)). \tag{3}$$

This formula is a simple inverse elasticity tax rule for the average tax rate on work. The average tax rate decreases with the elasticity η and also decreases with $g(z)$, the social value of marginal consumption for individuals earning z.

REFERENCES

Aaberge, R., Colombino, U., and Strøm, S. (1999), 'Labor Supply in Italy: An Empirical Analysis of Joint Household Decisions, with Taxes and Quantity Constraints', *Journal of Applied Econometrics*, **14**, 403–22.

Adam, S. (2005), 'Measuring the Marginal Efficiency Cost of Redistribution in the UK', IFS Working Paper, W05/14.

—— and Brewer, M. (2004), *Supporting Families: The Financial Costs and Benefits of Children since 1975*, Bristol: The Policy Press.

—— —— and Shephard, A. (2006), *The Poverty Trade-off: Work Incentives and Income Redistribution in Britain*, Bristol: The Policy Press.

—— —— Browne, J., and Phillips, D. (2007), 'Government Financial Support for Children across the United Kingdom: How does Northern Ireland Compare?', Belfast: NICCY.

—— Emmerson, C., and Kenley, A. (2007), 'A Survey of UK Local Government Finance', IFS Briefing Note 74, http://www.ifs.org.uk/bns/bn74.pdf.

Adda, J., Dustmann, C., Meghir, C., and Robin, J-M. (2006), 'Career Progression and Formal versus On-the-Job Training', IZA Discussion Papers 2260, Institute for the Study of Labor (IZA).

Akerlof, G. A. (1978), 'The Economics of "Tagging" as Applied to the Optimal Income Tax, Welfare Programs, and Manpower Planning', *The American Economic Review*, **68**, 8–19.

Alesina, A., and Ichino, A. (2007), 'Gender based taxation', Harvard University Working Paper, April.

Anderberg, D., Kondylis, F., and Walker, I. (2008), 'Partnership Penalties and Bonuses Created by UK Welfare Programs', *CESifo Economic Studies*, **54**, 1–21.

Arrufat, J., and Zabalza, A. (1986), 'Female Labor Supply with Taxation, Random Preferences, and Optimization Errors', *Econometrica*, **54**, 47–64.

Atkinson, A. (2007), 'Top Incomes in the United Kingdom over the Twentieth Century', in Atkinson, A. and Piketty, T. eds., *Top Incomes from a Historical and International Perspective*, **89**, Oxford: Oxford University Press.

—— and Leigh, A. (2004), 'Understanding the Distribution of Top Incomes in Anglo-Saxon Countries over the Twentieth Century', Department of Economics, Australian National University. http://cepr.anu.edu.au/~aleigh/pdf/TopIncomesAnglo.pdf.

Baughman, R., and Dickert-Conlin, S. (2003), 'Did Expanding the EITC Promote Motherhood?', *American Economic Review*, American Economic Association, **93**, May, 247–51.

Bell, K., Brewer, M., and Phillips, D. (2007), 'Lone Parents and Mini Jobs', York: YPS.

Blow, L., and Preston, I. (2002), 'Deadweight Loss and Taxation of Earned Income: Evidence from Tax Records of the UK Self-Employed', IFS Working Paper No. 02/15.

Blundell, R., Chiappori, P.-A., and C. Meghir, (2005), 'Collective Labor Supply with Children', *Journal of Political Economy*, **113**, 1277–306.

—— and MaCurdy, T. (1999), 'Labour Supply: A Review of Alternative Approaches', in Ashenfelter, O., and Card, D. (eds.), *Handbook of Labour Economics*, vol. 3A, Amsterdam: North-Holland.

—— and Shephard, A. (2008), 'Employment, Hours of Work and the Optimal Design of Earned Income Tax Credits', IFS Working Paper W08/01.

Boskin, M., and Eytan, S. (1983), 'Optimal Tax Treatment of the Family: Married Couples', *Journal of Public Economics*, **20**, 281–97.

Bowler, T. (2007), 'Taxation of the Family', TLRC Discussion Paper 6, http://www.ifs.org.uk/comms/dp6.pdf, London: IFS.

Brewer, M. (2006), 'Tax Credits Fixed or Beyond Repair?', in Chote, R. Emmerson, C. Harrison, R., and Miles, D. eds., *The IFS Green Budget 2006*, London: IFS.

—— (2007), 'Supporting Couples with Children Through the Tax System', in Chote, R., Emmerson, C., Leicester, A., and Miles, D., eds., *The IFS Green Budget 2007*, London: IFS.

—— Browne, J., Emmerson, C., Goodman, A., Muriel, A., and Tetlow, G. (2007a), *Pensioner Poverty Over the Next Decade: What Role for Tax and Benefit Reform?*, Commentary 103, London: IFS.

—— Clark, T., and Myck, M. (2001), 'Credit where it's Due? An Assessment of the New Tax Credits', IFS Commentary 86, London: IFS. doi: 10.1920/co.ifs.2001.0086.

—— Duncan, A., Shephard, A., and Suarez, M. J. (2006), 'Did Working Families' Tax Credit Work? The Impact of In-work Support on Labour Supply in Great Britain', *Labour Economics*, **13**, 699–720.

—— Muriel, A., Phillips, D., and Sibieta, L. (2008b), 'Poverty and Inequality in the UK: 2008', IFS Commentary 105, London. IFS: doi: 10.1920/co.ifs.2008.0105.

Brewer, M., Ratcliffe, A., and Smith, S. (2007b), 'Does Welfare Reform Affect Fertility? Evidence from the UK', CMPO Working Paper 07/177.

—— and Shaw, J. (2006), 'How Many Lone Parents are Receiving Tax Credits?', Institute for Fiscal Studies Briefing Note 70.

—— Sibieta, L., and Wren-Lewis, L. (2008a), 'Racing Away? Income Inequality and the Evolution of High Incomes', IFS Briefing Notes, BN76, doi: 10.1920/bn.ifs.2008.0076.

Chiappori, P.-A. (1988), 'Rational Household Labour Supply', *Econometrica*, **56**, 63–90.

—— (1992), 'Collective Labour Supply and Welfare', *Journal of Political Economy*, **100**, 437–67.

Cm 6951 (2006–07), (2006), *Delivering on Child Poverty: What Would it Take?*, A report for the Department for Work and Pensions, Cm 6951, November 2006.

Cm 6983, (2006–07), *HM Revenue and Customs Annual Report 2005–06*, London: The Stationery Office.

Cm 7130 (2006–07), *In Work, Better Off*, London: TSO.

Cm 7290 (2006–07), *Ready for Work: Full Employment in our Generation*, London: TSO.

Community Links, Low Incomes Tax Reform Group and Child Poverty Action Group (2007), 'Interact: Benefits, Tax Credits and Moving into Work', London: Community Links, Low Incomes Tax Reform Group and Child Poverty Action Group.

Cooke, G., and Lawton, K. (2008) 'Working out of Poverty: A Study of the Low Paid and the "Working Poor"', <http://www.ippr.org/publicationsandreports/publication.asp?id=581>.

DWP (2007a), 'Fraud and Error in the Benefit System April 2005 to March 2006', <http://www.dwp.gov.uk/asd/asd2/fem/fem_apr05_mar06.pdf>.

Devereux, P. J. (2004), 'Changes in Relative Wages and Family Labor Supply', *Journal of Human Resources*, **39**, 696–722.

Di Tommaso, M. L., Dex, S., and Rowthorn, R. E. (1999), 'Women's Labour Supply Decisions in the Light of Possible Fiscal Reforms', Research Paper WP36/99, University of Cambridge: Judge Institute of Management.

Diamond, P. (1980), 'Income Taxation with Fixed Hours of Work,' *Journal of Public Economics*, **13**, 101–10.

—— (1998), 'Optimal Income Taxation: An Example with a U-Shaped Pattern of Optimal Marginal Tax Rates', *American Economic Review*, **88**, 83–95.

Dilnot, A., Kay, J., and Morris, N. (1984), *The Reform of Social Security*, Oxford: Clarendon Press.

—— and Kell, M. (1988), 'Top-Rate Tax Cuts and Incentives: Some Empirical Evidence', *Fiscal Studies*, **9**, 70–92.

Draper, D. (2007), 'Families Compared 2006/7', CARE Research Paper, <http://www.care.org.uk/Publisher/File.aspx?ID=13022>.

Eissa, N., and Hognes, H. (2000), 'Explaining the Fall and Rise in the Tax Cost of Marriage: The Effect of Tax Laws and Demographic Trends, 1984–1997'. *National Tax Journal*, **53**, 683–711.

—— —— (2004), 'Taxes and the Labor Market Participation of Married Couples: The Earned Income Tax Credit', *Journal of Public Economics*, **88**, 1931–58.

Gentry, W. R., and Hubbard, R. G. (2004), 'Success Taxes, Entrepreneurial Entry, and Innovation', NBER Working Paper No. 10551.

Griffith, R., and Klemm, A. (2004), 'What has been the Tax Competition Experience of the last 20 Years?', *Tax Notes International*, **34**, 1299–316.

Gruber, J., and Saez, E., (2002), 'The Elasticity of Taxable Income: Evidence and Implications', *Journal of Public Economics*, **84**, 1–32.

Guesnerie, R. and Roberts, K. (1984), 'Effective Policy Tools and Quantity Controls', *Econometrica*, **52**, 59–86.

Heim, B. T. and Meyer, B. (2004), 'Work Costs and Nonconvex Preferences in the Estimation of Labour Supply Models', *Journal of Public Economics*, **88**, 2323–38.

Hills, J., McKnight, A., and Smithies, R. (2006), 'Tracking Income: How Working Families' Incomes Vary Through the Year', CASE report 32, London: CASE/LSE.

HC 32 (2007–08), 'Sustainable Employment: Supporting People to Stay in Work and Advance', London: TSO.

HC 42-I (2007–08), 'The Best Start in Life? Alleviating Deprivation, Improving Social Mobility and Eradicating Child Poverty', London: TSO.

HC 609 (2006–07), 'Helping People from Workless Households into Work', London: TSO.

HC 626 (2006–07), 'HM Revenue and Customs 2006–07 Accounts: The Comptroller and Auditor General's Standard Report', London: TSO.

HC 1010 (2006–07), 'Tax Credits: Getting it Wrong', London: TSO.

HMRC (2007), 'Child Tax Credit and Working Tax Credit Take-up rates 2004–05', <http://www.hmrc.gov.uk/stats/personal-tax-credits/takeup-rates2004-05.pdf>.

HMRC (2007b), 'Child and Working Tax Credits: Error and Fraud statistics, 2004–05', <http://www.hmrc.gov.uk/stats/personal-tax-credits/cwtc-error0405.pdf>.

HMRC (2007c), 'Number of Individual Income Taxpayers', <http://www.hmrc.gov.uk/stats/income_tax/table2-1.pdf>.

Hotz, V. J., and Scholz, J. K. (2003), 'The Earned Income Tax Credit', in Moffitt, R., ed., *Means-Tested Transfer programmes in the U.S.*, Chicago: University of Chicago Press.

Hoynes, H. (1997), 'Work, Welfare and Family Structure', in Auerbach, A. (ed.), *Fiscal Policy: Lessons from Economic Research.*

Immervoll, H., Kleven, H., Kreiner, C., and Saez, E. (2007), 'Welfare Reform in European Countries: Microsimulation Analysis', *Economic Journal*, **117**,1–44.

Kanbur, R., Keen, M., and Tuomala, M. (1994), 'Optimal Non-linear Income Taxation for the Alleviation of Income-Poverty', *European Economic Review*, **38**, 1613–32.

Kirby, J. (2005), *The Price of Parenthood*, London: Centre for Policy Studies.

Kleven, H., Kreiner, C., and Saez, E. (2006), 'The Optimal Taxation of Couples', NBER Working Paper No. 12685.

Kluve, J., Card, D., Fertig, M., Góra, M., Jacobi, L., Jensen, P., Leetmaa, R., Nima, L., Patacchini, E., Schaffner, S., Schmidt, C. M., van der Klaauw, B., and Weber, A. (2007), *Active Labor Market Policy in Europe: Performance and Perspectives*, Berlin et al.: Springer.

Laroque, G., and Salanié, B. (2005), 'Fertility and Financial Incentives in France', *CESIfo Economic Studies*, **50**, 423–50.

Lundberg, S. J., Pollak, R. A., and Wales, T. J. (1997), 'Do Husbands and Wives Pool Their Resources: Evidence from the United Kingdom Child Tax Credit', *Journal of Human Resources*, **32**, 463–80.

Meade, J. (1978), *The Structure and Reform of Direct Taxation: Report of a Committee chaired by Professor J. E. Meade for the Institute for Fiscal Studies*, London: George Allen & Unwin. http://www.ifs.org.uk/publications/3433.

Milligan, K. (2005), 'Subsidizing the Stork: New Evidence on Tax Incentives and Fertility', *Review of Economics and Statistics*, **87**, 539–55.

Mirrlees, J. (1971), 'An Exploration in the Theory of Optimal Income Taxation', *Review of Economic Studies*, **38**, 175–208.

—— (1982), 'Migration and Optimal Income Taxes', *Journal of Public Economics*, **18**, 319–41.

Moffitt, R. (2006), 'Welfare Work Requirements with Paternalistic Government Preferences', *Economic Journal*, **116**, F441–F458.

O'Dea, C., Phillips, D., and Vink, A. (2007), 'A Survey of the UK Benefit System', Institute for Fiscal Studies Briefing Note 13.

Pencavel, J. (1986), 'Labor Supply of Men: A Survey', in Ashenfelter, O., and Layard, R. (eds.), *Handbook of Labor Economics*, **1**, 3–102. Amsterdam: North-Holland.

Piketty, T., and Saez, E. (2007), 'How Progressive is the U.S. Federal Tax System? A Historical and International Perspective', *Journal of Economic Perspectives*, **21**, 3–24.

Saez, E. (2001), 'Using Elasticities to Derive Optimal Income Tax Rates', *Review of Economic Studies*, **68**, 205–29.

—— (2002a), 'Optimal Income Transfer programmes: Intensive Versus Extensive labour Supply Responses', *Quarterly Journal of Economics*, **117**, 1039–73.

—— (2002b), 'Do Taxpayers Bunch at Kink Points?', NBER Working Paper No. 7366.

—— (2004), 'Reported Incomes and Marginal Tax Rates, 1960–2000: Evidence and Policy Implications', in Poterba, J. (ed.), *Tax Policy and the Economy*, **18**, 117–74.

Simula, L. and Trannoy, A. (2006), 'Optimal Non-Linear Income Tax when Agents Vote with their Feet', *Finanzarchiv*, **62**, 393–415.

Social Justice Policy Group (2007), *Breakthrough Britain*, London: Social Justice Policy Group.

Turley, C., and Thomas, A. (2006), *Housing Benefit and Council Tax Benefit as In-work Benefits; Claimants' and Advisors' Knowledge, Attitudes and Experiences*, DWP Research Report **383**, Leeds: CDS.

Whiteford, P., Mendelson, M., and Millar, J. (2003), *Timing it Right? Tax Credits and how to Respond to Income Changes*, York: JRF.

Commentary by Hilary Hoynes*

Hilary Hoynes is a Professor in the Department of Economics at the University of California, Davis. Her work has mainly been in the area of household behaviour, poverty, inequality, and tax and benefit policy. She has particular interests in the impact of government tax and transfer policies on the labour supply and demographic behaviour of low-income families. She is currently a co-editor of the *American Economic Journal: Economic Policy*.

1. INTRODUCTION AND SUMMARY

The chapter by Brewer, Saez, and Shephard examines the optimal design of income tax systems. Their work addresses the substantive policy issues while simultaneously making important contributions to the literature; it will be well cited and influential. They begin by providing an overview of the income tax system in the UK and reviewing the impacts on labour supply. In so doing, they provide new empirical estimates of the effects of top marginal tax rates on taxable income. They present the optimal tax analysis and perform simulations using data from the UK and elasticities from the literature. They conclude by providing a proposal for reforming the UK tax system based on the lessons from their work.

The focus in this commentary is 'taxing the family'. Brewer, Saez, and Shephard consider optimal taxation in a model with a single decision maker and an individual taxation system. Yet economic models typically consider two potential decision makers—for example the husband and wife in the case of married couples—and some features of the UK tax system apply to

* I wish to thank Andrew Shephard for tabulations of the UK data and Alan Barreca for tabulations of the US data. Family Resources Survey data are produced by the Department for Work and Pensions and available from the UK Data Archive; Family Expenditure Survey and Expenditure and Food Survey data are collected by the Office for National Statistics and distributed by the Economic and Social Data Service. Crown copyright material is reproduced with the permission of the Controller of HMSO and the Queen's Printer for Scotland. None of these bodies bears any responsibility for the analysis or interpretation presented herein.

joint rather than individual incomes. I will explore the issues that arise in the optimal tax framework when accounting for issues around taxing the family such as the impact of tax policy on labour supply when labour supply decisions are 'joint' (depend on husband and wife's preferences), and the impact of taxation on family structure decisions such as the decision to marry, cohabit, and have children.

I begin with a conceptual discussion of individual versus joint taxation and implications for equity and efficiency of the tax system. Here I contrast the primarily individual based tax system in the UK with the pure joint tax system in the US. I then go on to provide an empirical setting for the importance of taxing the family showing that there are substantial differences in labour supply by family type and the magnitude of tax-based penalties and subsidies to marriage. Finally, I summarize what is known about the likely efficiency costs of individual versus joint taxation, focusing on the distortions to marriage and secondary earner labour supply.

2. TAXING THE FAMILY: CONCEPTUAL DISCUSSION

Tax systems across countries vary in many ways. One important way they vary is whether they are individual or joint. A system of individual taxation is one where the tax basis and the tax schedule are individual based. In that case, a worker would owe the same taxes regardless of the earnings of their partner (married or otherwise). A system of joint taxation is one where the tax basis and tax schedules are applied to joint income. In that case, married couples are taxed jointly on their total income.

The tax system in the UK, while typically characterized as individual based, is actually a hybrid of the joint and individual systems. The assignment of the tax schedule and tax rates is individual based, but tax credits (importantly the WFTC/WTC) are assessed based on family income and earnings. In addition, in the UK and most other countries, income conditioned transfers are family based. In contrast, the US has a 'pure' joint system. The assignment of the tax schedule and tax rates is joint, as are all tax credits (importantly the EITC) and income conditioned transfer programmes.

The choice between an individual and joint tax system reflects preferences over appropriate notions of equity and concerns over efficiency consequences of taxation. All tax systems strive for fairness or equity—with commonly stated goals of treating equal individuals equally (horizontal equity) and expecting those with a greater ability to pay to bear greater tax burdens (vertical equity). Yet notions of 'equals' and consequent implementation of horizontal equity can vary from one country to the next. Individual based tax systems embody horizontal equity at the individual level—one's tax burden should depend on one's own income and not the income of one's spouse. Joint tax systems reflect beliefs that the ability to pay is a family concept and therefore horizontal equity should be applied to joint tax units.

There are also efficiency costs to consider in the choice between individual and joint tax systems. In a joint tax system, a family's total tax burden will (typically) differ depending on whether they are married or not. This creates a possible distortion to family structure decisions, generating an adverse efficiency cost of taxation. In addition, with joint taxation and progressive marginal tax rates, tax rates on secondary earners are necessarily higher than on primary earners, which can generate important efficiency costs.

It is well known that a tax system can not simultaneously achieve progressivity, horizontal equity based on family income, and marriage neutrality (Rosen (1977)). By marriage neutrality, it is meant that the total tax burden for a couple with the same total income should not change upon marriage. In the UK, the tax system is progressive and is marriage neutral but does not satisfy notions of horizontal equity based on family income. In the US, the tax code is progressive, and maintains horizontal equity based on family income but is not marriage neutral.

3. FAMILY LABOUR SUPPLY AND MARRIAGE TAX PENALTIES

To illustrate the importance of taxing the family, and in particular to understand the potential connections between family structure, labour supply, and tax systems, here I present some basic statistics on family labour supply and the tax penalties of marriage.

3.1. Descriptive statistics on labour supply

Table 1 presents employment rates by marital status, gender, and presence of children. The first two columns present statistics for the UK based on the sample of men and women aged 19 to 54 in the 2005–06 Family Resources Survey.[1] The first column presents the employment rate and the second

[1] The Family Resources Survey is an annual demographic file of approximately 24,000 households. Respondents are asked a wide range of questions about their current circumstances. These

Table 1. Employment rates by marital status, gender and presence of children

	UK, 2005–06 FRS		US, March CPS 2006	
Definition of employment:	*Current employment*		*Employed this week*	
	Employment Rate	Percentage of total Families	Employment Rate	Percentage of total Families
Single, no children				
Women	0.775	21.6	0.709	20.7
Men	0.752	30.6	0.742	31.2
Single, children				
Women	0.576	12.1	0.710	11.2
Men	0.817	4.6	0.810	2.9
Married couples, no children				
Women	0.833	11.3	0.781	8.2
Men	0.907		0.886	
Neither work	0.044		0.047	
Married couples, children				
Women	0.683	19.8	0.675	25.7
Men	0.911		0.929	
Neither work	0.055		0.025	

Source: Tabulations of 2006 March CPS and 2005–06 FRS.

column presents the percentage of 'families' (from the universe of single men, single women, and married couples who are between the ages of 19 and 54) accounted for by this gender–marital status–presence of children subgroup. The table illustrates the considerable variation in labour supply across demographic groups. Overall employment rates are lower for women, and especially for women with children. Employment rates for women vary from 0.58 for single women with children, 0.68 for married women with children, to 0.78 for single women without children, and 0.83 for married women without children. There is less variation for men with employment rates varying from 0.75 for single men without children and 0.82 for single men with children, to 0.91 for married men.

The remaining columns of Table 1 provide similar tabulations for the US. The statistics for the US are based on the sample of men and women ages

include occupation and employment, together with highly detailed measures of income and state support received. Throughout our analysis, we restrict our sample to include persons between the ages of 19 and 54. We restrict the sample in this way because we do not want to address issues of early retirement and exit from the labour market. We use reported current employment status as our measure of work. This measure captures both employees and the self-employed, and includes individuals who are temporarily away from work but who have a job.

19 to 54 in the 2006 March Current Population Survey.[2] If the labour supply variables across the US and UK are compared, the striking difference is the much higher employment rates among single mothers with children in the US (0.71) compared to their counterparts in the UK (0.58). This difference is likely to be attributable to US policies which increased the incentives to work due to welfare reform and the expansion in the Earned Income Tax Credit (Eissa and Hoynes (2006)). In fact, between 1992 and 1999 alone the employment rate of single women with children in the US increased by about 15 percentage points. In the UK, the expansion of the WFTC was offset somewhat by the coincident expansions in the welfare system (Blundell and Hoynes (2004)). It is also notable that married women with children have higher employment rates in the UK, while a larger fraction of married couples with children have neither parent working compared to their counterparts in the US. In terms of the relative size of these family types, single parents with children make up a larger share of families in the UK, while married couples with children make up a larger share in the US.

Figure 1 shows trends in the employment rates for women by marital status and presence of children in the UK over the period 1978 to 2005.[3] This shows that there is little change over time in the employment rates of women without children. There is a steady increase in employment rates for married women with children starting in the early 1980s, while the increase for single women with children is more muted and does not begin until the mid 1990s. Figure 2 shows the trend in the percentage of married couples with children where neither adult is employed. These 'workless couples' increased between 1978 and 1987 peaking at about 10% of couples with children. It has steadily declined since the late 1980s, and now represents about 6% of married couples with children.

There are many reasons for the variation in labour supply across these groups and over time—reflecting differences in labour market opportunities, tax and transfer policies, and preferences and fixed costs for work. Further, there are likely to be many explanations for the differences between the UK and the US. For the purposes of this discussion, however, it is important to

[2] The March Current Population Survey is an annual demographic file of between 50,000 and 62,000 households. For each individual in the household, the survey contains information on labour market status last week as well as detailed labour market information for the previous calendar year. We use a sample of persons between the ages of 19 and 54 and the labour market measure is work status last week.

[3] The results we present here use the Family Expenditure Survey from 1978 to 1994, and the Family Resources Survey (FRS) from 1995–06 to 2004–05. The Family Expenditure Survey (FES) has about 6,500 respondents each year and is used for years when the FRS was not available.

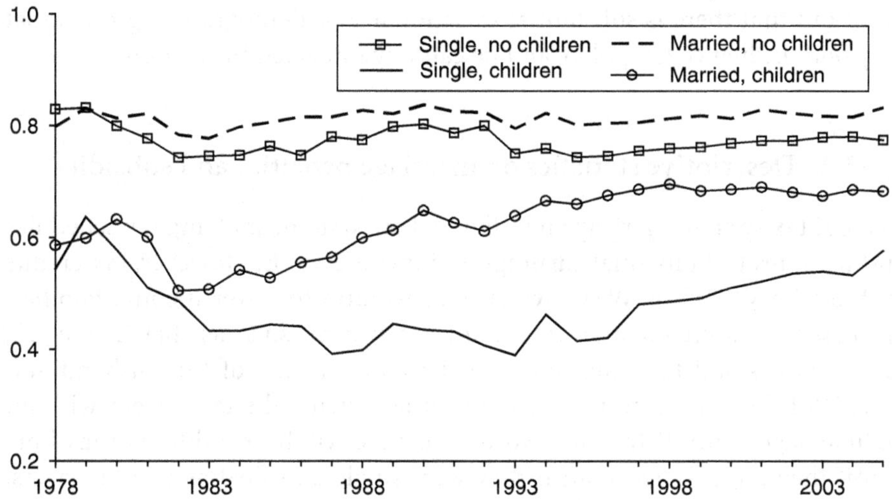

Sources: Tabulations of FES and FRS.

Figure 1. Female employment rates by marital status and presence of children UK, 2005–06 Family Resources Survey

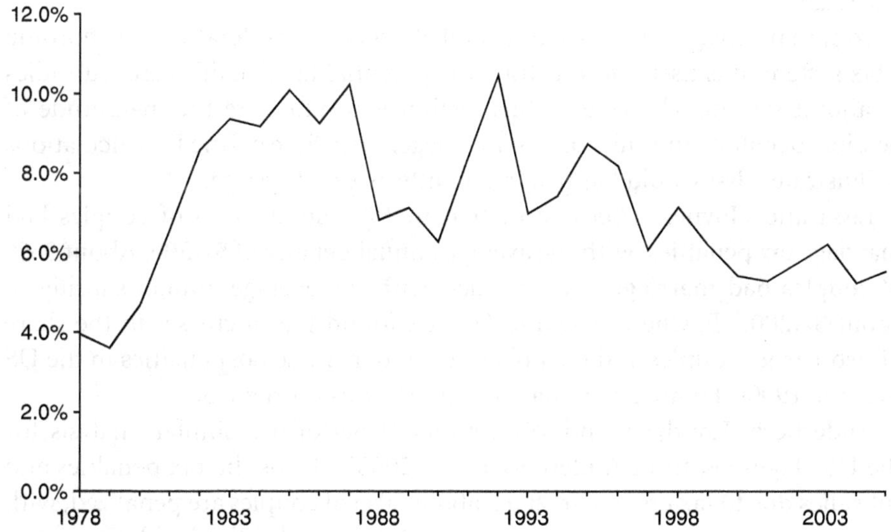

Sources: Tabulations of FES and FRS.

Figure 2. Percentage of married couples with children with no working parent UK, 2005–06 Family Resources Survey

point out that there is substantial variation across demographic groups that may both influence tax policy and be causally impacted by tax policy.

3.2. Descriptive statistics on marriage penalties and subsidies

The UK tax system is largely an individual tax system, applying tax schedules and tax rates to individual earnings and income levels. However, tax credits such as the WFTC or WTC, which redistributes to lower-income families, are based on joint income. In a joint tax system, such as that in the US, tax schedules and tax rates apply to the joint income of the husband and wife. With joint income taxation and progressivity, the tax system will not be 'marriage neutral'. In other words, a couple will have a different tax burden if they are married than if they were single and filed as two taxpayers. While this is often referred to as a 'marriage penalty'—in practice a joint tax system creates marriage tax *subsidies* for some and marriage tax *penalties* for others. Importantly, as discussed in Eissa and Hoynes (2000), two-earner couples generally experience tax penalties (tax-induced costs to marriage) while single-earner couples experience tax subsidies (tax-induced gains to marriage).

To gain perspective on the equity and efficiency considerations in choosing a tax system, it is useful to illustrate the potential tax penalties and subsidies in a joint system. The goal of this section is to illustrate the magnitude of possible penalties and subsidies to marriage. I rely here on the US calculations to illustrate what would happen in a jointly assessed system.

Eissa and Hoynes (2000) show that in 1997 about 55% of couples had marriage tax penalties, with the average annual penalty of $1,300. About 35% of couples had marriage tax subsidies, with the average annual subsidy of about $2,200.[4] Further, Eissa and Hoynes found that increases in the share of two-earner couples and tax policy acted to increase tax penalties in the US over the 1990s. Figure 3 summarizes these trends for the US.

Anderberg, Kondylis, and Walker (2008) perform a similar analysis for the UK. Figure 4, from Anderberg et al. (2008), shows the tax penalties and subsidies due to tax credits. In 2004, about 70% of couples are penalized, with an average penalty of £55 per week. About 25% are subsidized with an average weekly subsidy of £30 per week.

[4] To calculate the marriage tax cost, Eissa and Hoynes simulate a 'separation' of the couple. In particular they assume that the children will reside with the mother, the husband and wife each keep their earned income (which is assumed to be unchanged with separation), and unearned income is shared equally between the two persons. These same assumptions are used in the UK calculations, from Anderberg et al. (2008).

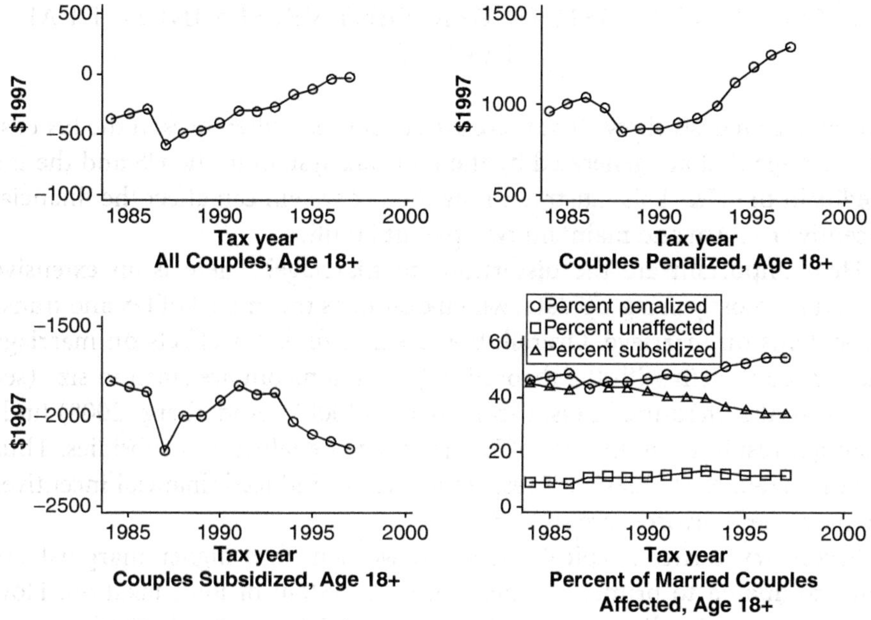

Sources: Eissa and Hoynes (2000), Figure 1.

Figure 3. Average marriage tax cost: married couples 1984–1997 US, March Current Population Survey

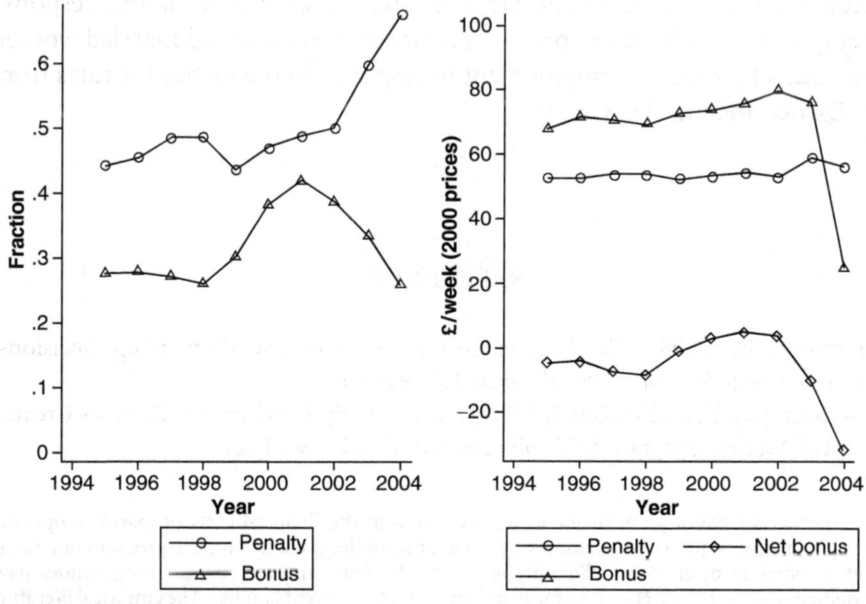

Sources: Anderberg et al. (2008), Figure 4.

Figure 4. Average marriage tax cost: couples with children, 1994–2004 UK, Family Resources Survey

4. EFFICIENCY COSTS UNDER JOINT VERSUS INDIVIDUAL TAXATION

The above analysis shows that there are substantial differences in the tax cost of marriage that are generated by the joint tax system in the US and the tax credits in the UK. This illustrates how the tax system can affect the financial incentive to form and maintain two-parent families.

How important are the distortions to marriage? There is an extensive literature, mostly using US data, which examines the impact of tax and transfer systems on marriage. Overall, the research finds tax effects on marriage that are consistent with the theoretical predictions but are small in size (see review of the literature in Eissa and Hoynes (2008)). Anderberg (2008) finds a similar result in his analysis of UK marriage penalties and subsidies. Thus the estimated elasticities with respect to the tax-induced financial incentives to marry (and divorce) are small.[5]

Secondary earners, typically married women, face higher marginal tax rates compared to primary earners under a system of joint taxation. How important are the distortions to labour supply? Here, the elasticities, especially on the participation or employment margin, tend to be quite large. For example, Eissa (1995) finds that married women increased employment substantially in response to the reduction in marginal tax rates with the Tax Reform Act of 1986. Eissa and Hoynes (2004) also find substantial response to employment with tax reform—in their case low educated married women responded by reducing employment in response to the higher tax rates from the Earned Income Tax Credit.

REFERENCES

Anderberg, D. (2008), 'Tax Credits, Income Support and Partnership Decisions', *International Tax and Public Finance*, **15**, 499–526.

—— Kondylis, F., and Walker, I. (2008), 'Partnership Penalties and Bonuses Created by UK Welfare Programs', *CESifo Economic Studies*, **54**, 1–21.

[5] Another source of government-induced changes in the financial costs of marriage operates through income support programmes. Almost universally, income support programmes assess joint incomes in determining eligibility and benefits. Thus, income support programmes have unambiguous negative incentives to form and maintain two-parent families. The empirical literature examining this issue also finds small elasticities of marriage with respect to these financial factors (e.g. see Hoynes (1997) for a review).

Blundell, R., and Hoynes, H. (2004), 'Has In-Work Benefit Reform Helped the Labour Market?', in *Seeking a Premier Economy: The Economic Effects of British Economic Reforms, 1980–2000*, edited by Card, D., Blundell, R., and Freeman, R., Chicago: University of Chicago Press.

Eissa, N. (1995), 'Taxation and Labor Supply of Married Women: The Tax Reform Act of 1986 as a Natural Experiment', NBER Working Paper, 5023.

—— and Hoynes, H. (2000), 'Explaining the Fall and Rise in the Tax Cost of Marriage: The Effect of Tax Laws and Demographic Trends, 1984–1997', *National Tax Journal*, **53**, 683–711.

—— —— 'Good News for Low Income Families? Tax-Transfer Schemes and Marriage', mimeo.

—— —— (2004), 'Taxes and the Labor Market Participation of Married Couples: The Earned Income Tax Credit', *Journal of Public Economics*, **88**, 1931–58.

—— —— (2006), 'Behavioral Responses to Taxes: Lessons from the EITC and Labor Supply', *Tax Policy and the Economy*, MIT Press, **20**, 74–110.

Hoynes, H. (1997), 'Work, Welfare, and Family Structure: What Have We Learned?', in *Fiscal Policy: Lessons from Economic Research*, Auerbach, A. (ed.), 101–46. Cambridge, Mass: MIT Press. 101–46.

Rosen, H. (1977), 'Is it Time to Abandon Joint Filing?', *National Tax Journal*, **30**, 423–28.

Commentary by Guy Laroque*

Guy Laroque is Head of the Macroeconomic Unit at INSEE-CREST and Professor of Economics at UCL. He has spent most of his career at the French statistical institute INSEE, alternating between administrative positions, such as responsibility for issuing the national accounts, and research or teaching assignments. He has been an Editor of *Econometrica* and a President of the Econometric Society. He has worked on a wide range of subjects, from macroeconomics, money, and finance, to econometric methods, with application to commodity prices. In recent years, his main interest has been in taxation issues.

Brewer, Saez, and Shephard have produced a very interesting chapter which covers a lot of ground. The chapter begins with a brief description of the essential features of the UK tax system. It follows with a pedagogical presentation of the main results of the theory of optimal taxation, with extensions to account for migrations, and the treatment of families. Finally, the authors use the empirical evidence which is available on labour supply elasticities to implement empirically the theory of optimal taxation and as a consequence provide both theoretical and empirical foundations for a wide-ranging tax reform. This last part of the chapter is particularly innovative. The application of optimal tax theory, developed more than thirty years ago by James Mirrlees, has been made difficult by a number of unpleasant properties, in particular the result that, under Mirrlees's original assumptions, there should be a zero marginal tax rate on the highest-earning individual. As far as I know, this chapter is the first to bring together the theory and the empirical knowledge of the labour economists to back the proposal of an income tax reform. This is path-breaking work.

I shall divide my comments into two parts. The first part is devoted to the chapter itself, which studies a static model of labour supply, and focuses on family issues. I am in broad agreement with the analysis proposed by the authors, but I am unsure whether I would back their precise proposal.

* I benefited from many discussions with James Banks, Richard Blundell, Anne Laferrère, and the authors and from detailed comments of Stuart Adam.

The second part of my comments takes a broader view, and presents some thoughts on the long-run evolution of the tax system with the next thirty years of the UK tax system in mind.

1. THE CHAPTER ITSELF

Income tax in the UK, seen from France, is notable for its simplicity and transparency. There are only three brackets for earned income and most taxpayers, those with an annual taxable income between £7,455 and £39,825,[1] face a marginal rate of 20% (fiscal year 2007–08). The marginal rate on higher incomes is 40%. National Insurance contributions (NIC) are a bit more involved. The employee rate is 11% up to an upper earning limit, where it becomes 1%, but the current plan to align this upper limit with the higher-rate income tax threshold will make things simpler.

The administrative side of income tax, the Pay-As-You-Earn (PAYE) scheme, is particularly impressive: of 31.6 million taxpayers, fewer than 9 million were required to complete a return.[2]

Of course benefits and tax credits are more complex: they depend on details of the household size and structure, on top of individual incomes. The authors rightly focus their attention at the boundary between taxes and benefits where the UK welfare state may leave room for improvement.

As already mentioned, the chapter matches the conditions for the optimality of a tax schedule with the available evidence on labour supply elasticities. Both the decision to participate or not in the labour force (extensive margin) and the number of hours worked in case of participation (intensive margin) are duly taken into account.

The authors discuss at length the behaviour of the wage earners at the top of the wage distribution and put forward some (controversial) tentative estimates of the labour supply elasticities of the high income tax payers. At the other end of the income distribution, a lot of econometric work is available in the UK on the behaviour of lone parents and is described in detail here. Comparatively, not much is said on the behaviour of married mothers, nor on men.

[1] The lower bound is the sum of the tax personal allowance, £5,225, and of the starting rate limit £2,230. The upper bound is the sum of the tax personal allowance and of the basic rate limit, £34,600.

[2] It seems that the 22.6 million tax payers who do not file a return do not always have a clear idea of how much tax they pay.

With this partial information in hand, the authors offer a proposal in two parts. The first part consists of 'immediate changes' intended to reduce the level of participation tax rates at the bottom of the income distribution. This is made through tax reductions, which are not financed at this stage. The second part of the proposal is a wide-ranging reform, the *Integrated Family Support* (IFS), which integrates family benefits and housing benefits into the income tax schedule. The main aim of IFS is to simplify the distribution of family benefits, to make it more transparent and better adapted to the current situation of the families. This reform is financed largely through redistribution among low and middle income groups, lowering the income tax personal allowance, and reducing benefits for better-off families. The authors' proposals are thought-provoking and stimulating. I have a couple of remarks:

1. A motivation for the suggested 'immediate changes' lies in possible inefficiencies of the current system. Adam (2005) finds the effective marginal tax rates facing lone parents to be beyond the Laffer bound for most of the period since 1979 (though this does not seem to be true any more). According to Blundell and Shephard (2008) this inefficiency is likely to hold more specifically for lone parents with children of school age: lone parents with very young children are much less responsive to financial incentives to work. There is no doubt that, for any overtaxed segment of the population, including the lone parents with children of school age, reducing the participation tax rate should be a priority, indeed a self-financing measure.

   On the other hand, the authors' suggestions are not limited to lone parents, but concern most low earners, on the grounds that they face very large participation tax rates. But large participation tax rates, including tax rates above 100% (i.e. benefits when out of work exceeding net income when working, which typically may happen for people with very low earning capacity), are not a symptom of inefficiency (see Laroque (2005)). The proposed change may very well be worthwhile if one favours redistribution towards low earners but it does not follow directly from theory: it reflects the preferences of the authors.

2. As the authors mention, more studies are needed to make precise the details of the *Integrated Family Support* before implementation. Two issues in particular seem worth investigating:

   (a) Most of the description of the reform implicitly supposes a relative permanence of the couples. It would be nice to spell out how it would fare in case of separations, formation of new couples, divorces, and in particular whether there should be some formal links with judiciary decisions to assess periods of rights. Should one expect behavioural changes in family formation?

(b) To achieve simplification and transparency, the proposed reform does not go in the direction of more decentralization. It is sometimes said that a close knowledge of the beneficiaries could make the welfare state more efficient. This presumably would involve leaving more decision power at the local level. Some discussion of this issue, which is likely to be important for housing and council tax benefits, would be welcome.

2. INSURANCE AND INTERTEMPORAL SMOOTHING

The reform suggested by the authors is certainly to be commended in that it looks at the overall impact of the tax and benefit system. But it keeps a static viewpoint. I would like to suggest some directions for changes linked to the passing of time. The following remarks are highly tentative, if only because empirical knowledge is scarce on these issues.

The typical life cycle profile involves financing education at an early age, a fluctuating wage rate that generally increases over time, at least up to mid age, with possibly episodes of unemployment, sickness or maternity leave (involving perhaps changes in the preference for leisure or work at home instead of in the market), followed by a period of decreasing wages into retirement. Any optimal tax and benefit system involves some mutualization of risks, as indeed we see through students' loans, unemployment benefits, and pensions. The limits to insurance and redistribution come from the limited knowledge of governments, which leaves room for opportunistic behaviour (such as the reaction of labour supply to tax rates), which is the object of study of optimal tax theory.

My aim here is *not* to come back to the lessons of optimal tax theory, which are detailed by Banks and Diamond in Chapter 6. I simply want to sketch some possible directions of integration of these intertemporal or insurance aspects into the welfare system. Such an integration may take a long time to achieve, but is likely to be a fact of life thirty years from now when the next generation of economists at the IFS discusses a follow up to the Mirrlees Review!

2.1. Return on capital

By definition, the intertemporal aspects of the welfare state imply transfers over time, and the beneficiaries are bound to compare the returns on these transfers to the cost of credit or the (after tax) returns on savings that prevail in the market. A prerequisite is therefore briefly to review how the market works in the UK (see Banks and Diamond (Chapter 6) for a thorough study of the issues bearing on the taxation of capital).

The current state of affairs

The Meade Report (Meade, 1978) recommended not taxing capital, in large part on grounds of neutrality of the tax system towards diverse investments. From a consumer perspective, while progress in this direction has been made since the publication of the Meade Report, there are still some differences in the tax treatment of the three main savings vehicles of the British households: housing, financial instruments, and pension contributions.

Owner-occupied homes do enjoy a near absence of taxation. The services brought by the occupation of the home are not recorded as income and therefore left untaxed.[3] Furthermore, capital gains when selling the main home are not subject to tax either.

On the other hand, savings through financial channels are subject to taxes. The most glaring of those taxes is the corporate tax on profits, which creates a premium for debt versus equity finance of firms.[4] Of financial capital income accruing to the households, currently basic savings in Individual Savings Accounts (up to the annual ceiling of £7,000 of accrual to deposits) are treated like housing: they are exempted of all taxes on interest income, dividends, or capital gains. Pension contributions are deductible from current taxable income, but the pensions themselves (and therefore the returns on the pension contributions) are subject to income tax at retirement time. I am not aware of a convincing justification for this difference of treatment, which possibly pushes higher-rate tax payers to save for their pensions in the expectation that they will be basic-rate tax payers when retired.

[3] The council tax is collected from the person that occupies the home. Its burden, the part of the tax that exceeds the value of the local public services, such as garbage collection, provided by the city, is likely to fall on the owner.

[4] One rationale for corporate taxes is that they may be a way to track the income of entrepreneurs who otherwise would easily evade other forms of taxation.

Intertemporal equity and the rate of return on capital

Idiosyncratic returns to capital in themselves create some of the most glaring inequalities: the founder of Microsoft is one of the richest persons in the world; more prosaically, the owner of a well-located house can be much better off than someone who puts his savings in government bonds. A government which wants to reduce the inequalities in people's lifetime utilities should tax some of these very high returns on capital.

On the other hand, to maintain incentives to put capital to its most productive use, the incomes of entrepreneurs must reflect the profits that they generate. For the discussion to come, I assume that there is a normal macroeconomic rate of return, often referred to as the safe rate, that is left untaxed. The tax treatment of returns above this normal rate is immaterial for the remainder of the discussion.

2.2. Towards a closer intertemporal integration of taxes and benefits?

A history-dependent tax and benefit scheme could be experimented with along the following lines. Aside from private wealth or debts, any resident would hold an account with the government, retracing her/his cumulative debts or claims towards her/his fellow citizens. To fix ideas, let D_t be the balance of this *social account* at the end of year t, that is the nominal debt that the person has contracted towards society. Typically, D_t would start at zero at birth. It would decrease when the person contributes by paying high rate taxes, contributing to a public pension fund. It would increase when drawing on health and welfare benefits or receiving a pension. For instance, D_t might evolve over time through the relationship

$$D_{t+1} = (1 + \rho_t)D_t + B_t,$$

where ρ_t is the normal interest rate discussed above which would be used to update the account balance from one year to the next, and the term B_t represents private benefits obtained from society during the year t depending on circumstances, such as:

- when the government finances one's education, the cost of the studies and of the possibly associated scholarship increases B_t;
- a worker who pays taxes and National Insurance contributions sees a fraction of his payments accounted for in a reduction of B_t; levies on

educated workers might be designed so that they reimburse the education subsidies which they received earlier in life;

- unemployment benefits would increase B_t;
- a retired person with a negative D, linked to contributions to a public pension fund, may draw on her/his accumulated capital.

In my opinion, the aim of such an accounting scheme would *not* be to get a precise description of all the costs and benefits of a private individual towards society. Indeed, pure public services (such as police and defence, etc.) or infrastructures, by their very nature, cannot be easily measured. But it would be useful to keep track of the publicly provided *private* services, such as education, welfare contributions and benefits, and pensions, if only to make sure that the various benefit schemes, which are often independently designed, be evaluated with a global perspective.

The tracking over time of the social debt D_t would allow the government to make the tax and benefit rules dependent on the value of D_t. Both equity and behavioural elasticities would probably play an important role on the actual design of the rules that could be implemented. For instance, one might think of modifying at the margin the simple current income tax scheme, by having brackets and rates vary with D_t: following the above examples, this would simultaneously make students refund some of their scholarships in taxes, reduce the benefits of people who spent too long on out-of-work benefits, or mimic aspects of a minimum pension.

The main advantage of such a time dependent tax and benefit scheme is to allow people to plan the timing of their work life better, bypassing some of the credit constraints. The costs of education would be supported by the students at the time where they would be able to afford them and, if appropriately discounted as in the above formula, the normal interest rate would be the benchmark return on investments in human capital. The scheduling of breaks to rear children or take care of old parents would be easier and tailored to circumstances. If the accounting were extended to pensions, it also might allow for more flexibility in the age of retirement and/or working part-time at an old age. This type of development is made possible by the information society and the low cost of computerization. One difficulty is that for such an extended welfare state to work, the rules have to be kept stable and predictable: there must exist a long-run commitment of the population to the benefits of such a renovated welfare state, so that it binds successive governments independently of political changes.

REFERENCES

Adam, S. (2005), 'Measuring the Marginal Efficiency Cost of Redistribution in the UK', Working Paper 05/14, London: IFS.

Blundell, R., and Shephard, A. (2008), 'Employment, Hours of Work and the Optimal Design of Earned Income Tax Credits', Working Paper 08/01, London: IFS.

Laroque, G. (2005), 'Income Maintenance and Labor Force Participation', *Econometrica*, **73**, 341–76.

Meade, J. (1978), *The Structure and Reform of Direct Taxation: Report of a Committee chaired by Professor J. E. Meade for the Institute for Fiscal Studies*, London: George Allen & Unwin. http://www./ifs.org.uk/publications/3433.

Commentary by Robert A. Moffitt

Robert Moffitt is the Krieger–Eisenhower Professor of Economics at Johns Hopkins University. His research is in the area of labour supply, taxation, and the economics and design of social assistance programmes. He has published papers on these topics in the *American Economic Review*, *Econometrica*, and the *Journal of Political Economy*. He is Chief Editor of the *American Economic Review* and past Editor of the *Review of Economics and Statistics* and the *Journal of Human Resources*.

The optimal income tax model developed by Mirrlees (1971) and refined and extended in the economics research literature since that time is a great intellectual achievement and also one with enormous practical usefulness. Although economists, and some policy-makers, were quite cognizant prior to 1971 of the trade-off between redistribution through the tax system and work incentives, the formulation proposed by Mirrlees and later extended by many others provides a formal means by which that trade-off can be assessed. More important, it is capable of quantification, thereby providing a basis for substantive policy recommendations by economists based on the numerical specification of the trade-offs involved. The model is also quite capable of extension, both by relaxing its various assumptions and positing alternative channels through which taxation can affect incentives (human capital, tax evasion, etc.).

The heart of the model is its emphasis on the incentive effects of taxation, and this is, arguably, the main contribution of economists to tax policy. Many policy-makers focus more heavily on other issues concerning the choice of tax policy: revenues raised, distributional effects, and administrative efficiency and practicability, for example. Economists tend to describe the estimates of tax reforms made by such tax experts as 'before-behavioural-response' estimates. Economists, on the other hand, emphasize the 'after-behavioural-response' effects—those which occur after taking into account the fact that individuals and households may change their behaviour, especially their levels of work effort, in response to a change in the tax system. Thus the optimal tax model rightly focuses on the issue that economists have a comparative advantage in studying.

At the same time, it should be emphasized that the optimal tax model is mostly a shell, or framework, which cannot deliver policy recommendations for tax reforms without some assumption on societal, or governmental, preferences for who should be the winners and losers as a result of a reform, and what, more generally, the optimal distribution of income (or, more precisely, well-being) should be. The model can only make recommendations conditional on an assumption of such societal preferences, and therefore economists require input from policy-makers on those preferences prior to making concrete recommendations. But given such input, the model is the best vehicle for assessing the magnitude of behavioural responses and the implications of those responses for the distribution of well-being.

The Brewer, Saez, and Shephard chapter (henceforth BSS) is an excellent exposition of the optimal tax model, described in simple intuitive terms and in as transparent a way as possible. The essay also notes the important extension of the model (Diamond and Saez) to consider the case of optimal taxation when individuals in the population choose between working and not working (i.e. the extensive margin) and show that this leads to much lower marginal tax rates (MTRs) at the bottom of the income distribution. BSS also show some MTRs and average tax rates (ATRs, which they call the participation tax rate) in the existing UK income tax system, the results suggesting very high MTRs and ATRs at the bottom of the distribution. Although the BSS chapter pays some attention to top earners—even providing a crude calculation of their behavioural response elasticities to changes in income tax rates—the focus of the chapter is mostly on the bottom of the distribution. Finally, they are courageous enough actually to propose a tax reform with a fair amount of specificity detailing MTRs and ATRs for different groups and at different points in the income distribution. Following their previous work in the chapter, the main feature of the reform is that they propose that tax rates at the bottom be reduced. However, they also, admirably, attempt to address several practical and administrative issues with their proposed reform.

In my Commentary, I will focus on the proposed tax reform in BSS. I will (1) compare the reform to the classic negative income tax model; (2) address the issue of what societal preferences are and how that affects the design of tax reform; and (3) discuss some alternative motivations for tax reform that have been suggested elsewhere by economists.

1. THE BSS REFORM AND THE NEGATIVE INCOME TAX

If many of the details of the BSS reform proposal are ignored, it is basically a proposal for a negative income tax (NIT). An NIT was first discussed by Friedman (1962) and Tobin (1966), who were concerned, as BSS are, with high MTRs in the then-existing transfer programmes in the US. The fear of significant work disincentives from those high MTRs pre-dated the development of the optimal income tax model, it should be noted, and was based on a simple perception of the nature of work disincentives when MTRs are very high.

On a simple prima facie basis, and even without the optimal tax machinery employed in this chapter, a reduction in MTRs at the bottom in the UK would certainly seem warranted. From a US perspective, the UK and many other European countries have long been characterized, roughly speaking, by social welfare systems with a high G and high *t*—where G (the 'guarantee') is roughly the amount of income that nonworking families are given and t (the MTR) is the rate at which benefits are withdrawn as income rises. In the UK, when the many different transfer systems are added together, especially the relatively generous housing benefit, G is quite high. But, as BSS emphasize, so is t. Both the high G and the high t tend to discourage work. In the US and some other countries, on the other hand, transfer systems are more characterized by low G and low t, which each have their own effects in encouraging work.

Traditionally, the problem with lowering the MTR in systems with a high G is that it extends subsidies higher up into the income distribution. In a simple NIT, the breakeven point—the highest income where benefits are still paid—equals G/t. Therefore, a given reduction in t has a greater effect on the breakeven point in a system with a high G than one with a low G because the relationship is multiplicative. This has three effects. One is that programme costs rise more in systems with a high G, which means that more revenue must be raised from some other source to finance the reduction in the MTR. A second is that there will be work disincentives generated higher up in the income distribution, often where the distribution of workers is quite dense, because the MTR on the groups made newly eligible for subsidies rises rather than falls. A third is that the number of families receiving a subsidy necessarily rises and, again, if the population density in the relevant region where eligibility is newly established is high, this raises the number of families who are on benefit. In the conventional optimal tax model, this third effect is irrelevant because the number of families on benefit is immaterial apart from its effects on their work effort and income. But it could matter if some voters care about the fraction of the population that is on benefit per se.

The high cost of reducing the MTR as called for in an NIT is the reason that BSS do not propose a negative tax rate (i.e. an earnings subsidy) for any but very low income groups even though their optimal tax calculations suggest such tax rates would be desirable. They also do not propose any significant lowering of G which would release funds for extension of negative tax rates higher up into the distribution. Nevertheless, BSS propose significant reductions in the MTR at the bottom (i.e. those with no other income) for many groups (their Figures 2.8A–2.8H). For lone mothers, the MTR is reduced from around 70% to less than 10% for low ranges of earnings, although this is primarily because of a moderately generous exemption level BSS provide for in their plan (i.e. before the real NIT kicks in). The MTR for very low-income one-earner couples with children is reduced from the 60–70% range down to the 20–40% range, another major reduction and with an earnings subsidy (negative ATR) at the very bottom.

The cost of these reductions is borne by increasing MTRs in the middle range of incomes in the BSS proposal. BSS explicitly propose not financing the NIT by increasing the MTR on the highest income groups but instead hasten the withdrawal rate of benefits in some programmes for some demographic groups, which primarily affects those in the middle or lower-middle of the distribution. Among couples with children, for example, the MTR for one-earner couples rises from the 40–50% range to a 50–65% range for middle incomes (Figure 2.8H) and this results in their largest pre-response income losses coming in the 7th income decile group (Table 2.6). For the population as a whole, the largest percentage income reductions also occur in the 7th decile group.

This method of financing reinforces the work-decreasing effects inherent in the NIT mentioned previously, which arise because the MTR reduction at the bottom increases MTRs for those made newly eligible for benefits. This occurs even when the NIT is not revenue neutral; when it is made revenue neutral, as BSS properly make it, MTRs must be increased above and beyond this, and their increase in the middle range of earnings is where the NIT-inducing MTRs were also rising. For most groups in the population, the reform causes the MTR to fall for those below approximately £5,000 of equivalized annual earnings and causes it to rise beyond that level.

It is worth emphasizing that distributional considerations necessarily play a major role in the decisions of where to place the decreases and increases in the

MTR. By definition, any revenue-neutral policy will have to increase MTRs for some groups and ranges and decrease MTRs for other groups or ranges. In the US, estimates and simulations of a (non-revenue-neutral) NIT show that, for many groups—husbands and wives, for example—average labour supply is essentially unchanged by an NIT because the increases in work effort arising from MTR reductions at the bottom are mostly cancelled out by work-effort reductions higher up. Indeed, for wives, simulations of these types of programmes (including the phase-out region of earnings subsidies) often show work-effort reductions because more women face higher MTRs than lower MTRs (Hotz and Scholz (2003)). This would presumably occur in the BSS plan because MTRs for the second earner in married couple households with children rise beyond about £100 of weekly earnings. For lone mothers in the US, the effect of an NIT depends on how responsive such families are to MTR changes, but for some responsiveness assumptions, there again appears to be no change in average labour supply arising from the NIT (Moffitt (1992)). Some empirical studies of actual MTR reductions in US welfare programmes for lone mothers likewise show no effects on average labour supply (Levy (1979)).

This does not mean that an NIT is not optimal because average labour supply is not the factor determining rates in optimal tax models. Increases in income at the bottom are more highly valued than decreases higher up, and work-effort increases at the bottom could conceivably be more highly valued than work-effort reductions higher up (more generally, it is the marginal increase in well-being that drives the optimal tax model, not labour supply per se). However, the argument has had force in the US. President Ronald Reagan, an otherwise forceful advocate for reduction in MTRs in the income tax, actually increased MTRs in US welfare programmes back to 100% after taking office in the early 1980s, arguing that he did not want to reduce work incentives for families higher up in the income distribution and did not want to subsidize them. Making sense of this kind of policy change may require thinking about different societal preferences than those embodied in the usual optimal tax model.

Making judgements about the effects of different ranges of MTR increases and decreases may also be assisted by the magnitudes of the work-effort effects involved. Traditionally, for example, the research literature on the work effort of prime-age males has suggested that such men have rather low response elasticities to tax rates and returns to work in general. This is consistent with evidence suggesting that the US earned income tax credit has had very modest, if any, effect on the work effort of married men. Lone mothers, on the other hand, are usually considered to be much more responsive to changes in the reward to work and hence these work-effort-distributional considerations could be much more important.

A related issue is how important the work incentive effects of tax reforms are, in general, relative to their distributional impact ignoring any behavioural response. An NIT is often proposed because society wishes to provide additional income support to those somewhat higher up in the income distribution, who work at least a modest number of hours. Most earnings subsidies like the WFTC are also partly designed to provide support to a perceived needy group (low-wage workers). For the WFTC, about 76% of expenditures on married couples go to families who have at least one worker in the absence of the WFTC; that is, those who have positive work effort to begin with (Brewer, Duncan, and Shephard (2006)). A lower percentage, but still over half (55%) of WFTC expenditures go to lone mothers who would have worked in the absence of the programme. The same would surely be true of the IFS programme proposed by BSS.

This simply reinforces the fundamental importance of redistributional preferences in driving tax reform proposals. Therefore the basic question of whom society, and voters, want to help cannot be avoided. Do they want to put more funds into those who are able to work significant numbers of hours or to those slightly lower in the income distribution?

Some economists have suggested that modifications in the standard optimal tax model could have different implications for where in the income distribution society prefers to put its money. For example, Boadway et al. (2002) and Cuff (2000) have demonstrated that if workers differ in their work-effort intensities (in their terms, individuals are heterogeneous in their preferences for leisure), society may not wish to subsidize those at the very bottom because they are disproportionately composed of individuals who are not working or who are working very little voluntarily. Their well-being (utility) is relatively high and hence government subsidies to them would be unwarranted. This leads to a positive preference to concentrate government subsidies to those slightly higher up in the distribution (see also Choné and Laroque (2009)). This is contrary to the standard assumption that society would always prefer to concentrate funds on those at the very bottom. Alternatively, Beaudry and Blackorby (2004) show that if one introduces a value for 'non-market' work—e.g. the value of raising children—whose value differs across families, then, once again, those at the bottom of the distribution may be those who are voluntarily pursuing other preferred activities and hence are not particularly low in well-being. This also can lead to a preference to provide subsidies slightly higher up in the income distribution. None of this is inconsistent with the actual NIT reform proposed by BSS, but instead could be thought of as an alternative rationale. However, these other considerations could suggest a different pattern of MTRs (not to mention G's) from the specific ones they propose.

2. OTHER FEATURES OF THE BSS REFORM PROGRAMME

Two other features of the BSS reform programme are worth noting because they suggest alternative approaches to the problem. One is that BSS propose a monthly accounting system and integration with PAYE. The economic rationale for a monthly, rather than annual, accounting system is that low-income individuals and households have a difficult time smoothing fluctuations in income. I find it interesting, however, that in the US the major work-incentive transfer programme, the Earned Income Tax Credit, operates mostly on an annual accounting frame—almost all households receive a lump-sum tax refund in April of each year—and the recipient households are, by most available evidence, quite happy with that arrangement. The reason is that households use the lump-sum refund to pay off debt and to purchase consumer durables. Although they could equally do so if the subsidy had been received monthly during the previous year, that would have required them to make conscious savings decisions. The annual accounting frame thereby provides a forced savings mechanism which households seemingly prefer. Such a result is consistent with much of the 'behavioural economics' literature that has developed in the last several years.

A second is that BSS propose to fold six existing programmes—the child tax credit, the working tax credit, income support, child benefit, housing benefit, and council tax benefit—into their new, integrated programme. This would rationalize the MTR schedule and achieve savings in administrative cost. Once again, this is quite reminiscent of the proposal for an NIT by Milton Friedman, who also wished it to replace all existing transfer programmes. While integration of different transfer programmes is a long-time ideal of academic economists, it has not fared well in the US (Moffitt (2003)) and my perception is that most other European countries likewise have not made many attempts at integration. My view is that most governments see different programmes as serving different needy groups and as providing different types of in-kind subsidies. For these reasons, they prefer a variety of programmes. This does not mean that one should not address the cumulative impact of multiple programmes on the total MTR, only that one has to recognize that integration may actually not be desirable to some.

3. OTHER MODELS OF OPTIMAL TAXATION AT THE BOTTOM

It may be useful to note two alternative models of optimal taxation that would generate somewhat different proposed reforms from that recommended by BSS.

One is the proposal by Akerlof (1978) for categorical programmes—that is, programmes that provide different tax schedules to different groups as a function of some observable characteristic like marital status or family composition. Akerlof noted that the optimal tax model of Mirrlees and its many extensions assume that the government observes household income but does not observe hours of work and hourly wage rates separately. If the government could observe the wage rate, it could base redistribution on that alone and achieve a superior result. However, if the government does observe a variable which is correlated with the unobserved wage rate, it might be able to do better by separating the population into those groups and offering them different schedules. Single mothers who have been out of the labour force are likely to have low wage rates and might deserve a greater lump-sum payment for not working, for example; and prime-age males with a great deal of work experience might have high wages and might be deserving of very little government support. Categorical systems of this type have the disadvantage of giving individuals an incentive to change their category, but adding that to the model just turns it into a conventional benefit–cost calculation which would suggest categorization up to the point where the marginal social benefit equals the marginal social cost in terms of distortions in decisions of what group to belong in.

In practice, the BSS proposal is not inconsistent with this notion because different schedules are proposed for different family types, although not for the reasons posited by Akerlof. However, the Akerlof model goes a long way towards explaining why so many countries do, in fact, make distinctions between different groups that do not seem to be solely based on differences in income distribution and work-effort responsiveness. The force of the Akerlof model is to work against non-categorical programmes like the NIT which make as few distinctions between family types as possible to be able to get as close as possible to the universal ideal.

A second strand of research on optimal income taxation drops the 'welfarist' assumption of the standard model, which assumes that society only cares about how individuals perceive their own well-being and wishes to redistribute to households if that redistribution makes individuals feel better off, even if it means reducing hours of work or quitting work altogether. An example of a non-welfarist assumption is the model of Besley and Coate (1992), who assume that society wishes to raise the incomes of the poor, preferably to reach some minimum income target, even if it means a loss of leisure that might be valued more by the individual than by the society. Another example is the model proposed by Moffitt (2006), who suggests that society might care about work per se quite independently of well-being as perceived by the individual. If society values work per se, it may also wish to subsidize work to a greater degree than individuals prefer. Both of these 'paternalistic' assumptions on societal preferences—paternalistic because society has its own views of what is best for recipient families and does not wish to be a passive observer of the preferences of the poor for work and nonwork—lead to greater emphases on work than would ordinarily be the case.

In addition, these views on societal preferences often lead to programmes with minimum hours restrictions (both the Besley–Coate and Moffitt models lead to this). Programmes with minimum hours restrictions are not infrequently observed in different countries, including the UK with its 16-hour requirement in the working tax credit. BSS propose dropping that requirement, which presumably follows because the conventional optimal tax model does not generate such requirements as optimal (or at least not without considerable difficulty). However, such hours restrictions could be socially optimal if society has different preferences from those assumed by BSS.

REFERENCES

Akerlof, G. (1978), 'The Economics of "Tagging" as Applied to the Optimal Income Tax, Welfare Programmes, and Manpower Training', *American Economic Review*, **68**, 8–19.

Beaudry, P., and Blackorby, C. (2004), 'Taxes and Employment Subsidies in Optimal Redistribution Programs', mimeo?.

Besley, T., and Coate, S. (1992), 'Workfare vs Welfare: Incentive Arguments for Work Requirements in Poverty-Alleviation Programs', *American Economic Review*, **82**, 249–61.

Boadway, R., Marchand, M., Pestieau, P., and del Mar Racionero, M. (2002), 'Optimal Redistribution with Heterogeneous Preferences for Leisure', *Journal of Public Economic Theory*, **4**, 475–98.

Brewer, M., Duncan, A., and Shephard, A. (2006), 'Did Working Families' Tax Credit Work? The Impact of In-Work Support on Labour Supply in Great Britain', *Labour Economics*, **13**, 699–720.

Choné, P., and Laroque, G. (2009), 'Negative Marginal Tax Rates and Heterogeneity', IFS Working Paper W09/12, April 2009.

Cuff, K. (2000), 'Optimality of Workfare with Heterogeneous Preferences', *Canadian Journal of Economics*, **33**, 149–74.

Friedman, M. (1962), *Capitalism and Freedom*, Chicago: University of Chicago Press.

Hotz, V. J., and Scholz, J. K. (2003), 'The Earned Income Tax Credit', in *Means-Tested Transfer Programs in the United States*, ed. Moffitt, R., Chicago: University of Chicago Press.

Levy, F. (1979), 'The Labor Supply of Female Heads, or AFDC Work Incentives Don't Work Too Well', *Journal of Human Resources*, **14**, 76–97.

Mirrlees, J. M. (1971), 'An Exploration in the Theory of Optimum Income Taxation', *Review of Economic Studies*, **38**, 175–208.

Moffitt, R. (1992), 'Incentive Effects of the U.S. Welfare System: A Review', *Journal of Economic Literature*, **30**, 1–61.

—— (2003), 'The Negative Income Tax and the Evolution of U.S. Welfare Policy', *Journal of Economic Perspectives*, **17**, 119–40.

—— (2006), 'Welfare Work Requirements with Paternalistic Government Preferences', *Economic Journal*, **116**, F441–F458.

Tobin, J. (1966), 'On the Economic Status of the Negro', *Daedalus*, **94**, 878–98.

3

Labour Supply and Taxes

*Costas Meghir and David Phillips**

Costas Meghir is Professor of Economics at UCL and Co-Director of the ESRC Centre for the Microeconomic Analysis of Public Policy at the IFS. He is a Fellow of the British Academy and of the Econometric Society. He has been co-editor of *Econometrica* and joint managing editor of the *Economic Journal.* His research interests lie in empirical microeconomics and microeconometrics and their relationship to public policy, with special interest in labour supply and wage determination, the economics of education, development economics, and firm investment. He was awarded the Frisch Medal in 2000.

David Phillips is a Research Economist at the IFS. His work focuses upon analysis of poverty and inequality, labour supply, and the impact of tax and benefit reforms on households. Other aspects of his work include social capital, consumption and education decisions in developing economies.

* **Acknowledgements.** We would like to thank the contributors to this volume and in particular Stuart Adam, Richard Blundell, Mike Brewer, Eric French, and Guy Laroque for their comments. Financial support by the ESRC is gratefully acknowledged. Costas Meghir has been financed under the ESRC Professorial fellowship scheme. The Family Resources Survey is crown copyright material, produced by the Department for Work and Pensions and available from the UK Data Archive. Crown copyright material is reproduced with the permission of the Controller of HMSO and the Queen's Printer for Scotland. The Department for Work and Pensions and the UK Data Archive bear no responsibility for the analysis or interpretation presented herein.

EXECUTIVE SUMMARY

This chapter provides an overview of the voluminous literature relating tax and the supply of effort that has developed since the Meade Report (Meade, 1978) on the UK tax system thirty years ago, with a focus on the empirical consensus on how taxes and benefits affect incentives.

Our starting point is the traditional view of labour supply, where hours of work and participation in work are the key measures of effort supplied by individuals. We discuss the way that economists think about labour supply conceptually. We begin by imagining a simple world in which individuals have completely free choice over their hours of work. We then take into account important real-world features of the labour supply choice, including fixed costs associated with working, the complications created by the benefits system, how labour supply choices evolve over time and how decisions take place in the context of the family. We discuss what such thought experiments tell us about the effects of tax reform on work behaviour.

We then discuss the 'New Tax Responsiveness' literature which takes a more general view of effort and does not assume that it can be perfectly measured by hours of work supplied. Here the focus is on how people's taxable income responds to the marginal tax rate they pay on every extra pound earned. This approach recognizes that hours worked are not a very good measure of effort for people with high levels of autonomy on the job and who already work long hours, such as the self employed or senior executives. This literature typically uses a 'difference-in-differences' approach, which compares the taxable income of groups affected and not affected by a particular change in the tax system, before and after the change takes place. This leads to several problems because of the impact of temporary changes in income, long-term trends in the income distribution, and the interrelationship between tax changes and pre-tax wages. Unfortunately, it is not clear whether these complicating factors mean that the extent to which labour supply responds to tax changes is overstated or understated. Efforts to take account of these factors are important, but because the specifics of each tax change are different, it is difficult to generalize from any one of them. This can be seen by applying a consistent methodology across the full range of tax reforms in the twentieth century.

Finally, we discuss the impact that taxes and benefits can have on longer-run outcomes which affect standards of living, such as education and training choices. These effects should be taken into account in analysing or designing any tax and benefit system.

After discussing the theory, we summarize the relevant empirical estimates and the methodology underlying the studies. We use this work to formulate an overall view of the responsiveness of labour supply, and place by far the greatest weight on work that avoids relying on unrealistic assumptions about how the world works, but that tries to develop an explicit understanding of the underlying processes at work so that the conclusions can be applied to different circumstances. We consider labour supply as measured by hours worked, the decision to take a job at all, and taxable income.

Our conclusion is that hours of work do not respond particularly strongly to the financial incentives created by tax changes for men, but they are a little more responsive for married women and lone mothers. On the other hand, the decision whether or not to take paid work at all is quite sensitive to taxation and benefits for women and mothers in particular. Within this chapter we present new estimates for both married and single men based on the numerous reforms over the past two decades in the UK. We find that the decision whether or not to work by low education men is somewhat more responsive to incentives than previously thought. For men with high levels of education, the work decision is very unresponsive. The amount of taxable income they earn does seem to be responsive, but more because they shift their income and spending into non-taxable forms than because they reduce their work effort. This is economically costly.

3.1. INTRODUCTION

Since the Meade Report (Meade, 1978) and indeed for sometime before then, there has been an intensive research programme focused on the way labour supply responds to incentives.[1] The impact of taxation on work effort is one of the main sources of inefficiency of a distortionary tax system. The magnitude of the inefficiency depends on how effort reacts to incentives as well as how the tax and transfer system changes the incentives to work and earn. More broadly, if one is to design a tax and benefit system with some element of optimality one needs to know how individuals react to taxes and benefits. This implies knowledge of how sensitive effort is to incentives for different education groups and for both men and women. This chapter reviews the main issues that have arisen in this voluminous research agenda

[1] Heckman (1974), Burtless and Hausman (1978), Hausman (1985), Mroz (1987), MaCurdy, Green, and Paarsch (1990), Blundell and Walker (1986), Blundell, Meghir, Symons, and Walker (1988), Blundell, Duncan, and Meghir (1998) to mention but a few.

and offers what we view as the central empirical conclusions about the impact of incentives on the supply of effort.

In the first part of the chapter we describe the modelling approaches to labour supply, and we discuss the main implications of these theoretical contributions. We explain how these are relevant to modelling and understanding the incentive effects of taxation and welfare benefits and demonstrate that policy analysis requires one to consider the incentives implied by the entire tax and benefit system as an integrated whole.

The key issue is how effort reacts to incentives. However, effort can be adjusted on many different margins: people can change their hours of work per week or per year, whether they work at all or not[2] and the amount of effort they put into working. Some may also be able to change the way they earn income (salary, dividends, capital gains) or how they consume so as to change the tax liability. For many people hours worked is quite a good approximation to effort and the study of the incentive effects of taxation is a study of how hours worked are affected by taxes and transfers. However, for some higher skill individuals in particular, hours worked is not a good measure of effort. They can adjust effort by working harder at ideas and being more creative within a particular time period. In addition, given the way the tax systems are designed, taxation may provide an incentive to over-consume items that are tax-deductible or to shift earnings to tax-favoured forms. Thus the tax incentives of the wealthy have other dimensions than hours of work and these can be an important source of distortions in the tax system. We explain the empirical issues relating to estimating the incentive effects on the various margins of labour/effort supply providing a critical review of the various empirical approaches.

In the second part of the chapter we review empirical results and offer a unified view of the consensus that has emerged. We base our description on elasticities, which reflect the sensitivity of labour supply to small changes in incentives. These measures are not necessarily sufficient for understanding the impact of reforms (as we explain in the chapter) but they do offer a way of providing coherent comparisons across models.[3]

[2] We refer to this as participation or labour force participation. The way we use the term should not be confused with whether someone is in the labour force (searching for work or working). For us a participant is someone actually in work.

[3] An elasticity of hours of work with respect to the wage, say, is the proportional change in hours of work caused by a proportional change in the wage. So an elasticity of 1 means that a 10% increase in the wage will lead to a 10% increase in hours. So suppose for the sake of argument that someone is facing a 20% tax rate and that his wage elasticity is 0.5. Suppose the tax rate is raised to 22%. This represents a 2.5% reduction in the after tax wage; with the 0.5 elasticity, this would imply a 1.25% reduction in hours worked. In Appendix 3A we define several terms that we will use many times throughout this chapter.

The review of the literature yields a very interesting picture. Incentives certainly matter, but the relevant margin differs by demographic and education group. For some groups, such as women with young children, taxes and benefits can affect whether to work or not as well as how many hours they work. For low education men, tax and benefit incentives are also important, but only for the participation decision; their hours of work are insensitive to changes in taxes and benefits. These men either do not work at all (and up to 25% do not) or work full time—this margin is quite sensitive to how the tax and benefit system is structured. Among full-time workers there is quite a dispersion of hours worked, but taxes and benefits have never been able to explain this effectively. For highly educated and wealthy men, taxes do not affect whether they work or not and how many hours they put in a week or even a year. Taxes do, however, affect their total as well as their taxable income; they respond both by reorganizing their affairs to benefit from the way different sources of income are taxed and by shifting consumption to deductible sources. They can also adjust the amount of effort they put into their work. Empirical approaches differ and data sets differ; however, we believe there is a broad consensus in these issues, if not at the detail or the precise numbers, definitely for the overall picture.

3.1.1. Taxes, benefits, and labour supply

We start by considering the basic labour supply model which is at the heart of the large literature on the incentive effect of taxation. Labour supply models express the trade-off between market work and leisure.[4] Under suitable conditions on preferences, the labour supply function depends on a measure of non-labour (or 'unearned') income denoted by μ and the marginal wage rate ω, which represents the amount earned in real terms for an extra hour of work. Non-labour income may include any source of income that is unrelated to the work decision of the person in question. Thus it cannot include means-tested transfers, but it can include universal benefits such as the UK's child benefit. Labour supply can also depend on a collection of background and family characteristics which affect one's tastes for work and which we summarize as Z. Thus the Z variables can include the number and ages of children, education level, and so on. The relationship expressed is just a reflection of the way individuals are willing to trade off leisure for pay at a given period of time. Now we need to see how the effects of taxes

[4] A better and more accurate term for leisure might be non-market time. However, we use these terms interchangeably.

are incorporated within this framework. We will then discuss the role of fixed costs of work and dynamics or intertemporal trade-offs, making the framework richer for policy analysis.[5]

Progressive taxes and tax reform with continuous hours of work

Taxes and means-tested transfers affect the returns to work, often in complicated ways. A key purpose of a labour supply model is to provide a framework for understanding and measuring the way that tax and welfare systems affect incentives. In the simplest possible proportional tax system, the marginal tax rate is a constant; in most cases this will lead to less work, but when the income effect dominates the substitution effect at high hours of work it may increase effort. From an empirical/econometric point of view, ignoring taxes will lead to biased estimates of labour supply effects because we will have mismeasured the returns to work; from a policy point of view we will have no framework for understanding how taxes affect behaviour.

However, suppose instead that individuals face a tax on earnings (E) of the following form: no tax is paid up until earnings A_1, earnings between A_1 and A_2 are taxed at a rate of τ_1, earnings above A_2 but below A_3 are taxed at a rate τ_2 and earnings above A_3 are taxed at a rate τ_3 (and perhaps there are further tax brackets). With this structure and with the tax rates increasing

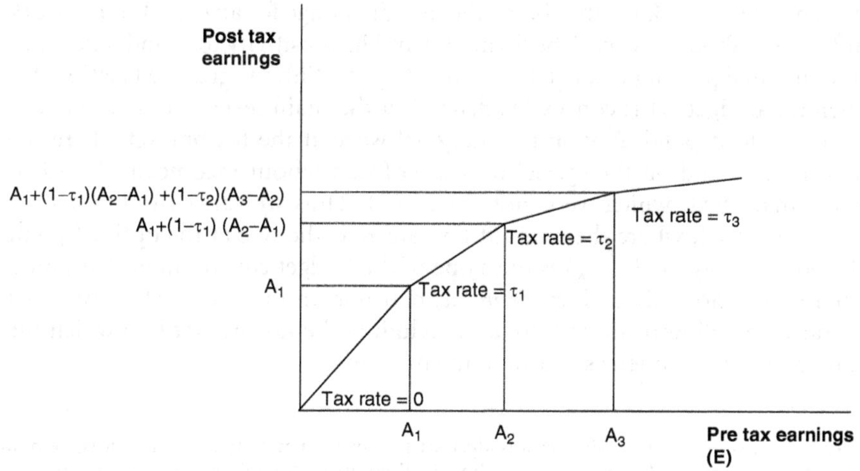

Figure 3.1. A progressive (convex) tax schedule

[5] A comprehensive analysis of the issues relating to estimating labour supply models with taxes can be found in Blunell, MaCurdy, and Meghir (2007).

we say that the budget set is *convex*.[6] Figure 3.1 shows how pre and post tax earnings relate under this standard tax system.

In this special case the labour supply decision can be expressed *as if* the tax system were proportional (not progressive) with the applicable tax rate being the actual marginal tax rate that the individual faces (τ_1, τ_2, τ_3, etc.) and a suitable adjusted non-labour income, which we call $m_k(\mu)$ where k denotes the tax bracket to which the person belongs. The value of this adjusted non-labour income depends on all the tax rates up until the one facing the individual as well as on the thresholds (A_1, A_2, etc.). Thus if the individual is facing a zero marginal tax rate she behaves as if her relevant non-labour income is $m_0(\mu) = \mu$. If she is facing tax rate τ_1 she behaves as if her non-labour income is $m_1(\mu) = \mu + \tau_1 A_1$; if she is facing tax rate τ_2 her adjusted non-labour income is $m_2(\mu) = \mu + \tau_1 A_1 + (\tau_2 - \tau_1) A_2$. Thus behaviour along the convex budget set (progressive tax system) can be characterized by increasing marginal rates *and* increasing non-labour income.[7] As we explain below this structure of the tax system implies that changing marginal tax rates have stronger impacts than they would in a simple proportional tax system.

Box 3.1. Modelling labour supply with convex budget sets—a technical digression

More formally, suppose the hours of work someone is willing to supply can be written as $h(\omega,\ \mu \mid Z)$ with ω being the marginal wage for an extra hour of work and μ non-labour income. The form of h and its sensitivity to ω and μ depends on individual preferences, partly explained by Z. With progressive taxation, i.e. when the budget set is convex (as defined in the main text) labour supply can be shown to depend only on the marginal wage at the tax bracket where she is positioned and on the special measure of non-labour income, as described in the main text, which we denote by $m_k(\mu)$. Thus we can write $h = h((1 - \tau_k)w, m_k(\mu)|Z)$, where the relevant tax rate τ_k is the one at the optimal point of labour supply; $w(1 - \tau_k)$ is the slope of the budget constraint at that point. The relevant non-labour income $m_k(\mu)$ depends on the entire set of marginal tax rates and allowances up until and including the tax bracket k in which the individual is positioned as shown in the main text.

[6] There is a simple test of whether a budget set is convex or not. Take any two feasible hours income combinations and join them with a line; if all points on the joining line are also attainable then the budget set is convex. Otherwise it is non-convex and the underlying tax system is not progressive everywhere.

[7] Individuals may not always end up at the part of the tax schedule they planned to be. So the observed tax position may not be the desired one. The implication of this measurement or misclassification error, originally discussed by Burtless and Hausman (1978) is not discussed in this chapter.

The behaviour of one group of individuals is not described by the approach above: these are individuals who chose hours of work exactly on the kink where the marginal tax rate changes. The reason this happens is because these individuals wish to work more than the tax threshold when facing the lower tax rate and less than the tax threshold when facing the higher tax rate; the only feasible point is then the kink. In principle there is a mass of individuals at these points and they cannot be ignored when carrying out policy analysis. In practice, individuals are rarely found on such convex kinks, but the reason for this is not clear; it may be because people make small errors, or they cannot find precisely the job they wish, or perhaps we measure their hours with error.

Within this simple framework there are a number of econometric and policy issues to deal with. We will discuss the econometric issues later. For now we take the labour supply function as known, which is akin to saying that we know preferences (i.e. the utility function) and consider the implications for policy analysis. In particular take a decrease in the marginal tax rate at different points in the system. We can distinguish the following simple cases:[8]

- The tax rate being changed relates to earnings higher than those earned by the individual. In this case the tax rate change has no impact on her optimal hours of work (Figure 3.2).
- The tax rate being changed is precisely the one faced by the individual. In this case the effect on labour supply comes about because both the marginal wage and the effective non-labour income changes: the decrease in the tax rate increases the slope of the budget constraint (the incentive effect of the wage rate) and reduces its intercept, as if the individual had less non-labour income. Hence, the effects of reduction in taxation above the non-taxable allowance in the context of a non-linear tax system can be understood as having the combined effect of increasing the after tax wage rate and taking away some of the persons 'non-labour' income. Now suppose that increasing the after tax wage increases hours of work.[9] The effect of the tax decrease is going to be reinforced by the virtual decline in non-labour income which acts to encourage work. Figure 3.3 shows this. Thus it seems that a tax rate reduction above a threshold has a larger impact than the same tax rate reduction if it is applied to all income

[8] In this discussion we will abstract from the possibility that income effects dominate and counteract substitution effects, leading to negative effects of wages on hours of work. Empirically this has not proved to be an important issue.

[9] This means that the standard substitution effect of improved incentives (that make one wish to work more) dominates the standard income effect of increased net earnings (which would make one want to work less provided leisure is a normal good, i.e. one that you consume more as income rises).

(for the same person). The intuition for this is as follows: the reduction in taxes causes a substitution in favour of work, because of improved incentives. It also leads to an increase in overall resources leading to a tendency to reduce work. However, a reduction in the tax rate that applies only above a certain point involves a smaller rise in net earnings than if that tax rate applied to all income. Hence, the magnitude of the income effect that counteracts the substitution effect will be smaller than in the case of a simple proportional tax. The tax cut would therefore imply a larger rise in labour supply than if the reduction in the tax rate applied to all income.

- The tax rate being changed corresponds to a lower income bracket than the one in which our individual is positioned. In this case there is only an income effect—individuals receive a windfall increase in net earnings but without a change in their marginal wage. In this case a decrease in the tax rate unambiguously decreases labour supply if leisure is a normal good.
- Changes in the thresholds of taxation (A_k) will have pure income effects for individuals earning above that threshold, but whose marginal tax rate remains unchanged. However, for some individuals the change in thresholds will lead to changes in the tax rates faced and the effect on labour supply will again be ambiguous, but will be more likely to involve an increase in labour supply than under a simple proportional tax system.

Thus, even in this simple framework it becomes apparent that the policy implications of tax reform cannot easily be summarized by one elasticity. In the simple world of a tax system with increasing marginal tax rates the implications of tax reform will depend on both income effects and wage effects, as well as on the way individuals are distributed over the entire budget constraint.

In Figures 3.2–3.4 we show what happens to optimal hours of work when the tax rate changes. In these graphs the straight lines show how after tax income changes when hours increase and thus in work income increases. This part is just as in Figure 3.1, except that the horizontal axis depicts hours of work instead of pre-tax earnings and we have shifted the graph upwards by the amount of non-labour income μ. Thus, as hours (and hence pre-tax earnings) increase, take home pay increases. When the individual earns above the tax exempt threshold the gradient of the budget line declines by the amount implied by the tax rate in force. The curved lines are the *indifference curves* and represent the rate at which the individual needs to be compensated to accept to work more. These curves underlie the labour supply functions we estimate from the data. In Figure 3.2 a tax rate is changed for individuals earning more

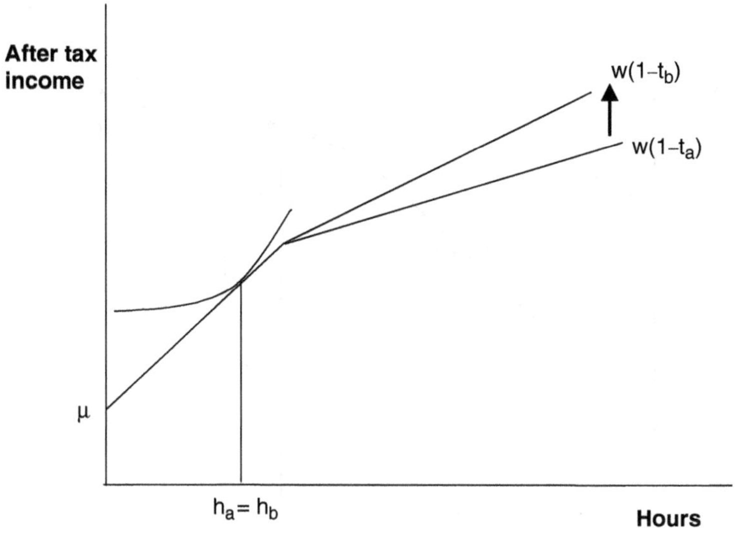

Figure 3.2. A decrease in the marginal tax rate above current earnings

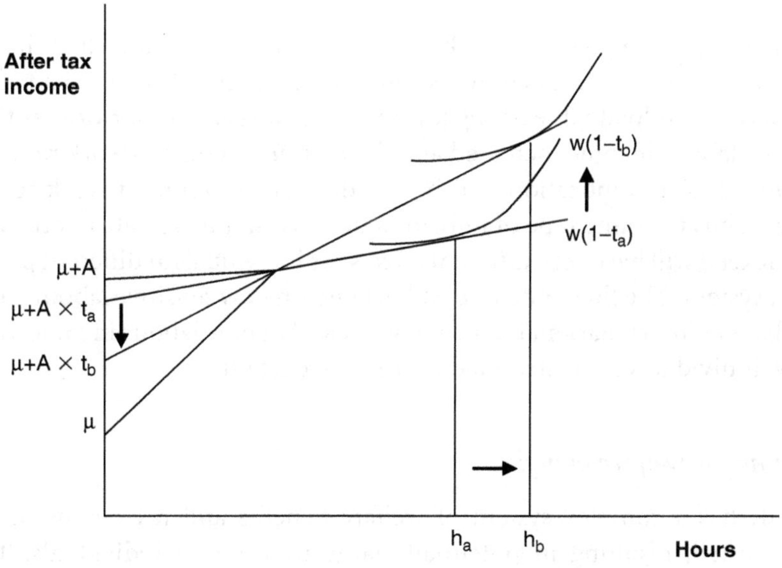

Figure 3.3. A decrease in the marginal tax rate currently faced

than our worker. She has no incentive to change her work-plans. In Figure 3.3 the tax rate is decreased above the allowance A from t_a to t_b. In effect this can be interpreted as an increase in the marginal wage (the return to an extra hour of work) from $w(1 - t_a)$ to $w(1 - t_b)$ and a *decline* in non-labour income

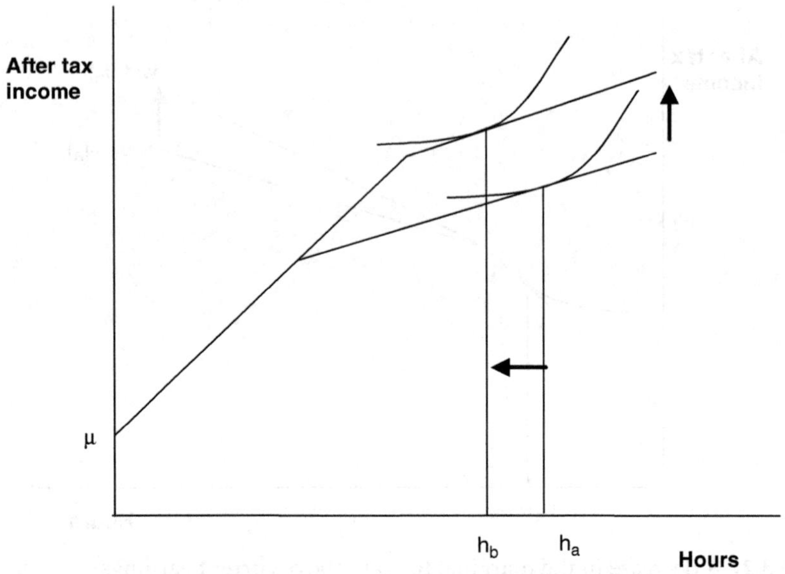

Figure 3.4. A decrease in the marginal tax rate below current earnings

from $\mu + A \times t_a$ to $\mu + A \times t_b$. Given the current empirical results this will lead to an increase in hours of work. Finally, in Figure 3.4 (case C) a tax rate is reduced for individuals earning less than our worker. For our worker this is as if non-labour income increased and the marginal return to work remained unchanged. The implication will be a reduction in hours of work for our worker. Thus the same type of reform (a decrease in the tax rate in one of the tax brackets) will have very different effects for individuals at different parts of the tax system. The final outcome will depend on how sensitive labour supply is to changes in the marginal return to work and in non-labour income as well as how individuals are distributed over the budget set.

Allowing for welfare benefits

The UK has a complex system of welfare benefits and tax credits, mostly means-tested, resulting in potentially large transfers to individuals. Their aim is to provide a safety net against poverty and sometimes to provide work incentives at the same time, such as the working tax credit programme in the UK (and the Earned Income Tax Credit in the US). At the margin, welfare benefits may act as taxes on individuals, because in many cases the levels of entitlement vary with earnings or income; whilst this serves to limit the eligible population to a targeted group it also implies a marginal tax rate on earnings as benefits are withdrawn. Suppose an individual receives a

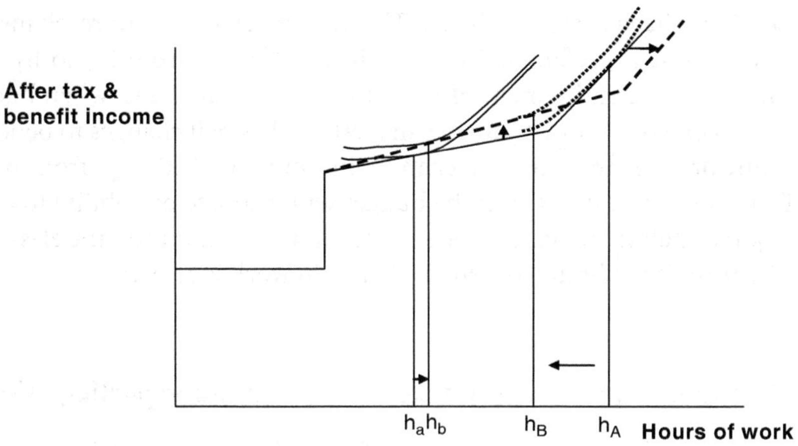

Figure 3.5. The working tax credit

means-tested transfer. When earnings increase, some of the transfer will be taken away. This is equivalent to an additional tax on these earnings on top of any regular income tax they pay. In some cases welfare benefits are associated with a subsidy over a range of earnings. This is the case in the US tax credit scheme, where an increase in earnings is associated with an increase in the benefit for very low earnings. In the UK tax credits offer a maximum benefit for those working above 16 hours of work with a means-tested amount tapered at 39% for each extra pound earned. Thus understanding the effect of means-testing is equivalent to understanding how welfare benefits change the budget constraint and how changes to the latter affect labour supply behaviour.

The UK (as well as the US) system leads to a non-convex budget set as demonstrated in Figure 3.5.[10] The jump up represents eligibility for the tax credit at 16 hours. The magnitude of the jump reflects the amount of the benefit. The gradient following that point reflects the taper rate. The budget constraint becomes steeper when all the benefit has been withdrawn and earnings increase at the rate of the actual hourly wage rate.

On the same figure we also show how a change in the taper rate from 39% to say 29%, may affect an individual originally in the system and receiving tax credits (continuous curve) and an individual originally earning too much to obtain tax credits (dotted curve). The budget set changes in the direction of the arrows to the dashed line. The person originally receiving the tax credit now has an incentive to increase hours of work from h_a to h_b, very much like

[10] The nature of the US system is completely different and has no condition attached to hours of work. The non-convexity arises there only at the point where all the benefit has been withdrawn through the taper and earnings start increasing at a rate equal to the wage rate.

the case where the tax rate is reduced. The person originally not receiving tax credits now finds it preferable to *reduce* hours of work from h_A to h_B and enjoy the increased entitlement of the reformed system. Thus, when budget sets are not convex it is quite possible that relatively small changes to benefits, tax credits, or taxes lead to large changes in hours worked (e.g. from h_A to h_B). Thus the *non-convexities* in the budget set invalidate our ability to carry out marginal analysis of tax and benefit reforms based simply on the elasticity, or local sensitivity of hours to a small change in work incentives.

3.1.2. Family labour supply, taxes, and programme participation

We now turn to describing an approach for modelling family labour supply and the take-up of welfare benefits. This approach addresses the complexities that arise in trying to model the incentive effects of taxation and welfare in a two-person household and offers an insight in how models can simulate policy in this context.

Observing the distribution of weekly hours one gets the impression that hours of work are discrete with a number of focal points where people bunch together. While we are not able to explain why people bunch at certain points, the discrete labour supply approach at least allows us to recognize the existence of the phenomenon. And it is certainly convenient because we can use the apparatus of the so-called *discrete choice* literature where the individual chooses among a number of specific alternatives. In this case each choice is a bundle of hours for each household member and the resulting income.

On the basis of this idea, we outline a model of labour supply for a couple. Our model is going to be of the *unitary* type, i.e. where there is a single household utility function and we ignore the issues relating to intrahousehold allocations of income. However, we will also address one important policy concern, namely the take-up of means-tested benefits; while taxation is compulsory, taking up benefits is usually not, making the entire shape of the budget constraint that an individual is facing a choice of the individual: individuals who do not take up a benefit, will not face the same budget constraint as those who do. Understanding the determinants of take-up is important for properly targeting benefits and for budgetary planning.

Suppose individuals derive satisfaction (utility) from leisure, disposable income, and programme participation P; the latter entails dissatisfaction because the process of applying for benefits and receiving them may carry stigma or other indirect/psychic costs. By allowing for this in the model we are able to model the decision to take up benefits and how this will depend on programme characteristics. It thus offers a mechanism for simulating tax reform, allowing for the effects on take-up.[11]

The budget constraint defines household disposable income Y depending on the combination of hours chosen by the male and the female and on the tax and benefit system and its take-up. The budget constraint may also depend on household characteristics such as the number and ages of children and the type of housing occupied, because of the way the tax and benefit code is defined.

Now simplify the problem by assuming that individuals can work certain specific hours of work, say $(0, h^1, h^2, \ldots, h^k)$ where 0 allows for non-work, and suppose for illustrative purposes that there is just one means-tested programme. Given a particular pair of hourly wage rates for the woman and her partner there are then $(k + 1)^2$ possible values of income Y with welfare programme participation and another $(k + 1)^2$ without (although some of the income points would overlap because not all hour–income combinations would be affected by the programme). The household chooses hours of work and programme participation by trading off income against the disutility of effort (hours of work) and monetary or psychological costs of programme participation; in other words, it chooses the combination that maximizes utility.

Apparently identical households facing identical options often make different decisions. As a result there is some chance (probability) of observing any feasible hours–income–programme participation combination for any individual with certain observable characteristics. The typical way that this is accounted for in empirical economic models is to allow for preferences to vary randomly in the population. The econometric problem of measuring preferences and stigma costs consists of choosing the parameters that will make the probabilities predicted by the model equal (or as close as possible) to frequencies of hours–income–programme participation combinations we see in the data. From an empirical point of view, identification (i.e. the ability to recover the actual parameters of the model) will depend on the existence of variations in the budget constraint and in the costs of programme participation, shifting the opportunities available to the households in a way that is unrelated to the unobserved taste components in the data. It is increasingly popular to use the differential impact of policy reforms across the population as such a source of variation.

To simulate alternative policy options we need to predict what the probabilities of each alternative hours–programme participation combination

[11] See Keane and Moffitt (1998).

will be with the new tax parameters. Once we have parameter estimates, this involves recomputing the $2(k+1)^2$ income possibilities and finding the best combination for each type of household. We then need to aggregate these outcomes using as weights the frequency with which each type occurs in the population. These weights and the types of household are themselves an outcome of the estimation process mentioned above. This illustrates that the information required to understand the impact of tax reform is quite complex. Experience from observing what happened around one reform will typically not be useful for predicting the effects of another. We really need to understand the entire structure of preferences for work over a broad range of hours and incomes.

One of the key issues in family labour supply is understanding how intra-household allocations of time and consumption actually take place. The models used typically, including the one described above, work on the basis that the household is a unit with well-defined preferences (hence the term unitary model). But this brushes the issue under the carpet and more importantly does not allow us to understand how policies affect within-household allocations. Indeed, one of the sources of inequality is within-household and one would wish to know how policies target individual members. Beyond the couple the issue extends to resource allocations for children. Tax and welfare policy may well be designed with the aim of targeting children. But without knowing how different tax and benefit structures affect resource allocations within the household it is not possible to know whether the policies are going to be effective. The empirical issue relates to the fact that we do not typically observe allocations of consumption within a household; we just observe total expenditures. So one needs to understand how much we can learn about intrahousehold allocations based on what is actually observed or at least observable with better data. Chiappori (1988, 1992) explored the possibilities using the Collective model, which assumes that whatever outcomes are observed are efficient; in other words, any change in allocations would have to imply that improving one member's position can only be achieved at the expense of the other. In this context Chiappori (1988, 1992), followed by Blundell, Chiappori, Magnac, and Meghir (2007), derived conditions under which observing individual labour supply and total household consumption would reveal the entire intrahousehold decision mechanism. Blundell, Chiappori, and Meghir (2005) extended the original Chiappori framework to one where the household spends on public goods (such as children).[12]

[12] There has been a growing literature in this field. The papers of Thomas (1990) and Browning et al. (1996) showed the empirical relevance of considering the household as a group of individuals, rather than one unit.

Once the mechanism has been estimated, one can ask questions relating to how taxes and benefits affect not only labour supply but also children's consumption and within-household inequality. This literature is currently better developed theoretically than empirically. Blundell et al. (2007) do provide possibly the only structural model of labour supply in a collective model. However, their households do not include children. Moreover, they have not allowed for taxes and benefits. This is very much an active and important research area that needs further development before we can be confident that we understand intrahousehold allocations and how they interact with policy.

3.1.3. Intertemporal labour supply decisions and taxes

Continuous hours of work

The majority of work that has taken place on labour supply and taxes has been static. Introducing dynamics poses a number of interesting questions and allows us to extend the scope of the analysis to the impact of taxes on other important life-cycle decisions. Moreover, if we are to address the question of optimality of tax systems over time, we need to study how labour supply varies over the life-cycle and how this is affected by tax incentives and this involves considering people's saving decisions as well. Here our aim is, of course, much more circumscribed: we wish to discuss some of the empirical issues that arise when we view labour supply decisions in an intertemporal context.

What does the basic labour supply model look like when we allow for savings? To consider this, suppose preferences are separable over time, meaning that past choices do not affect current preferences or the budget constraint, and that within each period preferences just depend on current consumption and hours of work. Then the labour supply model takes exactly the same form as in the static case with an important difference in the interpretation of non-labour income μ.[13] This is now defined by $\mu = c - wh$ where c is the value of consumption in the current period, which itself is a result of an intertemporal optimization problem. The problem can be described by the following *two-stage budgeting* procedure first discussed by Gorman (1959). Individuals first allocate consumption to a particular time period, and given this choice, they then decide what should be the optimal hours of work.[14] Adding taxation

[13] See MaCurdy (1983), Blundell and Walker (1986), and Arellano and Meghir (1992).

[14] More precisely the first stage takes place in the knowledge that the second stage will be optimal. There are a number of conditions under which optimal consumer decisions can be thus broken down, but this is beyond the scope of this chapter.

when the budget set is convex is in principle simple and the labour supply model does not change in form from the one described earlier. In other words, we simply replace the wage with the appropriate after tax wage rate and unearned income for the tax adjusted one, starting with μ defined above as the basis. Although the form of the relationship does not change, in that labour supply can still be expressed as depending upon the marginal wage and some measure of non-labour income, substantively, things do change because consumption, which determines the relevant measure of non-labour income, will now depend on current taxes and *future expectations of the tax system.*

Thus the simplicity of the problem does not carry over when one wants to allow for intertemporal substitution. First a change in any aspect of the tax system will affect the optimal amount of saving, in general. This means that simulating a tax reform with a fixed μ will be insufficient for evaluating the behavioural impact of a reform. The change in the saving decision will reflect possible shifts in labour supply to future periods where tax liabilities are expected to be lower. For example, suppose the higher rate of tax is to be increased, and that one's wage rate is expected to decline with age. An increase in the current tax rate will make the difference between the current and the future after tax wage rate bigger, implying that work effort now could decrease relative to that in the future, if we ignore income effects at least. In this simple model this will be reflected as an increase in the current value of μ induced by a decision to increase current consumption (remember $\mu = c - wh$) and a consequent decline in hours worked, over and above what would be implied by the static model. This also implies that to estimate the incentive effects of reforms in a reliable way we need to use consumption data to compute μ and estimate a model consistent with intertemporal optimization.

In the case of convex budget sets the difficulties caused by intertemporal considerations are confined to simulation. The labour supply model can be estimated in a straightforward way, by using the suitable definition of μ, as given above. However, the situation is not as simple when the budget set is non-convex. In this case estimation as well as the evaluation of tax reform require simulation of the impact of taxation on savings and hence μ.[15]

These issues may be very important for understanding labour supply effects. However, to our knowledge little or no work has been done in this direction, at least from the perspective of simulating tax reforms. Apart from the computational difficulties involved, the requirements for high quality data (particularly assets) has been an inhibiting factor in estimating complex

[15] In order to evaluate the likelihood function we need to compare the utility achieved at different parts of the budget constraint. This involves solving the labour supply model in counterfactual situations, such as not-working.

intertemporal models that allow for the complete structure of the tax system.[16] An exception is the work of French (2005) who estimates a life-cycle model of labour supply, savings, and retirement, accounting for key aspects of the US tax code including important non-convexities.

Which is the correct elasticity concept?

Often, labour supply sensitivity to incentives is summarized by elasticities. Indeed, we use them to summarize empirical results. However, there are several wage elasticity concepts, depending on what is being kept constant. In a static labour supply context we can define the wage elasticity that keeps utility constant (the substitution effect or compensated wage elasticity), the wage elasticity that keeps non-labour income constant, and the one that keeps full income constant (total potential earnings plus non-labour income). Once we introduce intertemporal concerns there are a number of additional elasticities we could consider as well as modifications of the concepts already defined. In an intertemporal context, the direct analogy to the static wage elasticity, which holds constant non-labour income, is the one that keeps consumption based unearned income (μ) constant. Although useful for characterizing the properties of the estimated labour supply function, this is clearly not the correct measure for understanding the effects of policy, when adjustments to savings are to be expected.

We can straightforwardly define at least three additional elasticity concepts in the intertemporal context, each with a different interpretation. First, we have a notion of compensated wage elasticity. However, in an intertemporal context this does not keep life-cycle welfare constant but only within-period utility constant. Hence it does not have a direct welfare interpretation as the one we get in the static context. Nevertheless this elasticity is always positive. One can in principle define a lifetime utility constant elasticity, but this is not usually done. Second, we have the Frisch elasticity, which keeps the marginal utility of wealth constant. This elasticity reflects the impact of *anticipated* marginal changes in wages on hours of work. Thus it reflects how people plan to allocate their work effort between different periods of the life-cycle, depending on the return to work at each point. As such it is clearly not the elasticity of interest when considering changes in tax policy: considering the effects of tax policy would require one to compare two alternative tax regimes.

[16] It is possible to simplify the problem by effectively ignoring savings and either assuming that consumption equals income or by assuming that individual utilities depend linearly on income. In this case individuals do not care when the income will arise. However, once taxes are introduced, which depends very much on when income arises, the simplicity provided by this last assumption is partly lost.

However, this elasticity is an upper bound to the wage elasticity which keeps within-period unearned income (μ) constant. Finally, we can also define an hours elasticity with respect to an unanticipated change in wages. This will combine the effects of an anticipated change and the wealth effect of the change in the wage profile. Quite clearly, the magnitude of the effect will depend on whether the change in wages is perceived to be permanent and if not on the speed with which wages will revert to the original profile. This is probably the best elasticity for understanding the overall effects of a tax change perceived to be permanent.

Generally, to understand how labour supply will change as a result of a permanent tax reform, we need to understand how savings will change as well as how sensitive labour supply is given savings.

Taxes and human capital

Taxes and welfare benefits affect more than labour supply. Of course, this is well understood and it may be thought that in addressing this issue we are going beyond the scope of this chapter. However, the reason we wish to consider this issue now is because these decisions are intimately linked with labour supply and labour market behaviour more generally. In particular, we have in mind choices relating to education and human capital investment.

Appropriate models along these lines should include decisions on education and labour supply, as well as wage formation. The seminal paper addressing the latter two is Eckstein and Wolpin (1989) who model employment and wages of women when wages depend on experience. Since then these models have been developed to greater levels of sophistication and now include other decision margins, such as occupational choice as in Keane and Wolpin (1997) and education and job mobility as in Adda et al. (2006). We use the latter as an illustration of some of the issues involved.

Adda et al. (2006) focus on population who, having completed formal schooling, face the choice of following formal vocational training (which offers on-the-job and classroom training in return for a reduced wage) or entering the labour market directly (and receiving no formal training but a higher initial wage).[17] In taking this decision they trade off current earnings of a non-apprentice with working as an apprentice at a lower wage, while obtaining formal training and then obtaining an improved career path.

[17] Utility is linear in earnings making risk and the timing of consumption irrelevant for decision making, thus bypassing the need to model savings.

Once the education choice has been made the individual starts his career (whether qualified through training or directly without a formal training component). All individuals receive job offers at some rate, which may differ depending on whether the worker is employed or not. Associated with an offer are fringe benefits and a wage which defines the initial pay level in a firm given the person's skills and experience as well as how well they fit in the firm. While the worker remains on the job, pay may evolve due to random unaccounted factors. When out of work the individual has a stream of transfer income depending on the way unemployment insurance works. Individual choices include moving between jobs when the opportunity arises and between work and unemployment, as well as the initial education choice.

This model, estimated on long-run administrative data following individuals from the end of their schooling to mid-career, offers an empirical framework for considering the impact of taxes on life-cycle decisions: a tax or benefit may affect the decision to train, because future returns are changed. It could affect job mobility, because the benefits from moving job are, in effect, taxable. Finally, it can also affect the incentive to work in any given period. But, more interestingly, the overall employment effect will be different when we allow for the other effects, from when we condition on education and do not consider job mobility. This allows for a clear distinction between short-run effects of taxes and benefits and long-run ones, which can be very different. The latter certainly need a complex intertemporal model to analyse them and cannot be measured on the basis of simple experiments or by static labour supply studies. The empirical work mentioned above demonstrates that this can be an important issue.

3.1.4. Taxable and total income elasticities

For many individuals, particularly the self-employed and the high earners, hours of work is just one dimension of work effort. Take, for example, the executive who spends most of the week in the office and takes work home at the weekend. She does not have much margin of adjustment for her hours of work. However, with the right incentives, she may put in more thinking effort during these long hours, surf less on the Internet, or find ways to become more creative. In these cases the output of an hour of work (or better an hour *at* work) may differ and hence hours supplied are not necessarily a good measure of effort. In some cases it is also difficult to measure hours of work in the first place, such as for the self-employed or individuals whose work may well be hard to distinguish from leisure time. In these cases the sensitivity of hours of work to changes in wages or taxes is only a part of the story; indeed, it may be a small part only. In terms of work incentives the *total income elasticity* with respect to taxes is probably more relevant. However, in terms of revenue and possibly also in terms of welfare the *taxable income elasticity* would also be required. Both together would give a more complete picture as to how individuals change effort and rearrange their income and expenditure in response to taxes.

Key papers in this field, constituting, *the new tax responsiveness literature*, have been written by Feldstein (1995, 1999). He stresses the importance of considering taxable income for a number of reasons: taxation can distort not only effort but also the way one organizes the sources of income and consumption to reduce tax liability. Such reallocations of income from one source to another (e.g. employee earnings to self-employment) or of consumption from one type to another that is tax deductible (e.g. from non-housing to housing in the US) affects government revenue and welfare. The latter is true because individuals are not indifferent to the type of consumption or even to the way that their income is generated. Thus, tax exempt consumption may not be a perfect substitute for ordinary consumption. The tax system may encourage individuals to consume more housing, say, than they intended when interest payments are tax deductible (as in the US) causing a welfare loss as behaviour is thus distorted. Hence, particularly for higher income individuals—who, plausibly, have more opportunity to shift income and consumption to tax favoured forms and whose main labour supply response is not measured directly through hours of work—a good way of summarizing the behavioural effects of taxation is through its effects on taxable income.

However, measuring these effects is fraught with problems, some of which we discuss now. Perhaps the key difficulty which prevents a structural economic modelling of these important dimensions is that we do not observe effort. If we cannot measure effort, we cannot measure the price of effort (termed the effective wage rate). As this is likely to differ across the various skill group of workers the unobservability of effort and its effective wage rate can become a very important confounding factor when measuring incentives. This does pose a challenge for policy analysis and evaluation.

The most common estimation approach for the taxable income and total income elasticities has been *difference-in-differences*, comparing outcomes before and after reforms. To see how this works and to illustrate some important problems, consider a single period model where utility depends on income and effort.[18] For simplicity suppose we are interested in measuring the effect of taxes on earnings, the latter being the product of (unobserved) effort and the price per unit of effort. Conceptually the model is identical to the labour supply one, with effort substituted for hours. The appropriate wage rate is the after-tax marginal return to effort and the appropriate measure of non-labour income is the adjusted other income measure exactly as in the hours discussion earlier. This adjusted measure does not depend separately on the price of effort—so the relevant measure of other or non-labour income is observed. However, the price of effort is not observed. The standard approach has taken a simplified model, where the price of effort is treated as an aggregate time effect, common across individuals (like a trend, which is the same for all) and where the income effect is ignored. The effect of taxes is estimated by considering what happens to different groups of individuals, depending on their marginal tax rates, following a reform. To fix ideas, suppose a higher rate of tax is reduced by a reform. Individuals are split up depending on whether in the period before the reform their marginal tax rate was the one to be reduced or not. In other words, they are split up by past income. The approach to estimating the taxable income elasticity[19] is then to compare the growth of earnings for the group that was subject to the tax reform on the basis of their pre-reform income (say the very high earners) to a group with earnings just below the level at which the tax cut took effect. The approach reports the proportional change in earnings due to a proportional change in the share of income retained after tax: the so-called taxable income elasticity.[20]

This approach is sensitive to three sources of bias. The first is due to 'mean reversion': the income of individuals is subject to temporary random changes. Following a large negative shock we can usually expect income to grow again towards its previous level. Thus among people selected because they have lower income, some have incomes that are only temporarily low and we can expect some positive income growth as this temporary negative shock works its way out. Among those with higher income we can expect negative income growth as those who had only temporarily high income experience a similar reversion to their typical income. Both these movements would happen anyway, irrespective of the tax reform. In our empirical experiment this mean reversion will be attributed to the tax reform and will lead to an

[18] For further critical analysis of the difference-in-differences method and for examples of use and extensions see Blundell, Duncan, and Meghir (1998), Blundell and MaCurdy (1999), and Moffitt and Wilhelm (2000).

[19] See Feldstein (1995, 1999) for example.

[20] Note that this is not the same as (minus) the elasticity of earnings with respect to the tax rate. The latter is $-\beta\frac{t}{1-t}$.

underestimate of the effect of lowering taxes. This source of bias is discussed at length by Gruber and Saez (2000).[21] The second source of bias relates to the possibility that growth in income can be different at different parts of the income distribution. This is particularly the case for some of the studies carried out using data from the 1980s when inequality was growing rapidly. This means that the incomes of those higher up in the distribution are growing faster than those lower down for reasons that may not be related to the tax reform directly and this will bias upwards the effect we wish to estimate. The final source of bias relates to the effect that a tax reform may have on skill prices and hence on earnings. In general one can show that a tax reform reducing higher tax rates will lead to a relative reduction in the skill price of those facing these rates. For example, cutting marginal tax rates of high skill individuals may increase their hours and effort, which may push down the price of their labour. This is called the general equillibrium (GE) effect. This will bias the effect downwards. Thus these three sources of bias do not all go in the same direction, creating some ambiguity on the credibility of the results. In Appendix 3B we consider this issue in greater detail.

The above difficulties are compounded by the fact that reforms rarely involve the change of just one tax rate and, moreover, the impact of the change may depend on adjusted non-labour income, which is typically ignored by this approach. Thus, the results obtained, even if unbiased for a particular reform, are unlikely to have much external validity and are more of a description of what happened in one specific instance. This was illustrated clearly by Goolsbee (1999) who applied such a method to all major tax reforms in the twentieth century for which data was available and demonstrated that the results differed widely from one reform to another. In order to derive more general conclusions we need an approach that allows for the issues discussed above as well as for income effects and other complexities of the tax system. A credible structural model is imperative in this as in many other areas of empirical economics.[22]

Moffitt and Wilhelm (2000), Gruber and Saez (2000), and Blow and Preston (2002) make the most serious attempt to overcome the numerous problems we have listed above. In particular they discuss many of the issues we raise here and they try to account for them, including allowing for income effects, taking into account differential trends where possible, controlling for the mean reversion, etc. In addition, Gruber and Saez (2000) use information

[21] Note that Feldstein categorizes people on the basis of the pre-reform marginal tax rate. This is a function of the pre-reform income. Hence although more complicated this is in effect a categorization by initial income and the same arguments apply.

[22] See also the discussion of Goolsbee (1999) by Hall and Katz, which follows the article.

from many tax reforms taking into account the complexity of the changes. Thus their approach is closest to a structural approach whilst at the same time using actual reforms to estimate the effects. They cannot, however, get round the issue of changing effort prices for different skill groups. Finally, they use two income measures; a broad income measure which reflects mainly changes in effort and a more narrow measure of taxable income, which also captures the effects of avoidance. Their estimates are probably the most credible available. Blow and Preston who consider the self-employed in the UK, also control for income effects and for mean reversion by grouping individuals by occupation and region. The key issue is whether their grouping is correlated with tax liability and it clearly is. We next review the results of this and other papers.

3.2. A REVIEW OF SOME EMPIRICAL RESULTS ON LABOUR SUPPLY

Much of the empirical analysis on labour supply focuses on estimating wage elasticities. Some take account explicitly of taxes. Only a few are directly designed to ask specific policy questions, such as the effect of benefits. The aim of this brief review of empirical results is to provide a picture of how sensitive labour supply is to changes in work incentives and to see if we can provide a sense of consensus on what is currently known about labour supply. Our aim is not a formal meta-analysis or even an exhaustive survey. However, we hope that by providing information on the methods and a way of assessing reliability we can allow readers to decide for themselves, whilst providing our own guidance and the results of some 'representative' studies.

Individuals who value leisure less and thus work longer hours than others are also likely to command higher hourly wage rates[23] and, abstracting from those with incomes low enough to be in receipt of means-tested benefits, are likely to face higher marginal tax rates than those who work fewer hours (precisely because they like to work more and thus earn more). This creates a circularity between incentives and effort and constitutes the classic endogeneity (or reverse causality) problem that plagues our attempts to estimate the impact of incentives on hours of work. We will illustrate these issues with some examples.

[23] They probably invested in education more when they were younger.

Take someone who has a low preference for work and therefore works for few hours. This person is also likely to have invested less in human capital accumulation and is thus likely to have a low pre-tax (gross) wage. This causes a spurious positive correlation between hours and wages leading to an impression that incentives and hence taxes may matter more than they actually do; this is the problem of *endogeneity* of the gross wage. On the other hand, the progressive tax system will lead us to underestimate incentive effects if we do not take into account its presence: individuals with a stronger preference for work will face higher tax rates and hence, all else equal, will have lower after tax wages. This will cause a negative correlation between hours and marginal after tax wages, which if not accounted for may lead to a downward bias in wage elasticities and even reversal in signs, implying negative incentive effects. The picture is further complicated by the fact that some persons do not work. Typically those not working will have higher reservation wages. Workers are thus drawn from the group of individuals who have a lower dislike for work. More to the point this selection will generate a spurious correlation between preferences for work and wages or unearned income (μ in our earlier notation): if we observe someone working at a particularly low wage they will have a high preference for work and vice versa. This illustrates at least three confounding factors working in opposing directions and obscuring the genuine incentive effects we need to estimate. While formal econometric techniques abound for dealing with these issues, they do not offer magical instant solutions: their effectiveness will depend on the credibility of the assumptions used when implementing them.

The above examples illustrate the difficulty of estimating wage effects for labour supply and emphasize that the direction of bias is not known *a priori* and cannot be inferred. A number of early labour supply studies[24] emphasized the issues of endogeneity of taxes and solved the problem by explicitly taking into account how work preferences affect the decision process that leads individuals to choose to work while facing a specific marginal tax rate. In other words, they modelled the dependence of tax rates on individual unobserved preferences components. The most elaborate of these studies allow for measurement or optimization errors—where the individual is observed working a number of hours that differs from those planned—as well as preference heterogeneity. Issues that have not been addressed by this generation of models include unobserved fixed costs of work (other than those implied by the tax system) and the endogeneity of the pre-tax (gross)

[24] e.g. Heckman (1974), Burtless and Hausman (1978), Hausman (1985), Moffitt (1984), MaCurdy, Green, and Paarsch (1990).

wage rate. Ignoring these issues is likely to overstate the incentive effects. A further issue, which is equally important but a bit more esoteric in nature has been raised by MaCurdy, Green, and Paarsch (1990): the combination of estimation methods that impose theoretical consistency of the labour supply model everywhere in the sample, with restrictive functional forms that do not allow enough curvature of the relationship between hours, wages, and unearned income, can lead again to an overstatement of incentives.

Estimating incentive effects in a convincing way thus requires us to find solutions to all these problems at the same time. This calls for a sufficiently flexible approach, that allows for fixed costs of work, does not impose theory *a priori* everywhere in the sample (thus in a sense increasing model flexibility), uses exogenous changes to work incentives to identify their effect, and allows for taxes and benefits. This is of course a large set of requirements, but all have been shown to be important empirically; in our review of empirical results we will use these criteria to judge the value of the estimates. However, there will always be trade-offs in the way the model is implemented empirically. For example, Blundell, Duncan, and Meghir (1998), rather than solving for the full solution to taxes, simplify the problem substantially by exploiting the fact that most working women would find themselves paying a single basic rate of tax, *once one conditions upon having a working husband*. This approximation allowed them to treat the marginal wage as a single endogenous variable; the cost of their approach is that the sample they use is selected and this has to be allowed for. They then exploit the change in the UK wage structure and the numerous tax reforms that have occurred to control for the endogeneity of wages and taxes. Their approach uses the *differential* time series variation in after tax wages for different cohorts and different education groups. Their identifying assumption is that while preferences for work may be different between education groups and cohorts, these differences are permanent. Hence differential changes in the labour supply of these groups can be attributed to differential changes in the incentives they face. Thus, the argument goes, given permanent differences in the work behaviour of higher and lower education groups, a change in the relative wage between the two groups (say because of changes in the tax structure following a reform) will reflect a pure change in the incentives faced by the two groups and cause a change in their relative labour supplies. This illustrates the kind of reasoning and 'experiments' that one needs to find in the data to argue that the effects of incentive have been uncovered. In our view using changes in incentives that can be credibly considered as exogenous (i.e. unrelated to observed aspects of preferences for work) and controlling suitably for aggregate changes in hours of work (time shocks) is the most convincing way of controlling for unobserved heterogeneity in this context. The relative merits of treating taxation with a full solution approach or with approximations are less clear. Here there is a trade-off between putting more structure (and thus making more assumptions) on the labour supply problem and accurately taking into account all the details of the tax system.

3.2.1. Empirical results on female labour supply

There have been a large number of studies focusing on female hours of work in the US, the UK, and many other developed economies. Research has focused on women for a number of reasons. First, in many countries they work fewer hours and participate less in the labour market than men; hence if they were to be drawn into the labour market this could lead to substantial economic growth. In addition, their hours of work tend to be more dispersed and there is a belief that they are more responsive to incentives, which implies that they respond more to tax rate changes this being an important source of distortions due to the tax system.

Table 3C.1 (see pp. 257–9) presents some of the estimates of elasticities for married women. It becomes immediately obvious that the range of estimates is very wide indeed. Very few estimates are, however, larger than 1 and all are positive. However, those estimates (except Cogan (1981)) that rely on annual hours of work tend to be higher and clustered close to 1. Those based on weekly hours tend to be much smaller. This is to be expected because on an annual basis individuals have more margins of adjustment, such as weeks per year as well as hours per week, than they do on a weekly basis.

Key empirical issues are the treatment of censoring (that arises as a result of some women not working), endogenous wages, and the treatment of taxes. One of the first studies of female labour supply allowing for endogenous wages and recognizing the effect on estimation of the fact that some women do not work is by Heckman (1974, 1974a). In the 1974a study he finds an annual hours elasticity of 0.8 at 2,000 hours of work and more at lower hours. He also reports an effect on weeks worked per year, which implies an elasticity of 1. This study is based on a single cross-section and some of the identification assumptions may not be used now: he assumes that education and experience affect wages but not preferences, which may be biasing the elasticities upwards.

A further important distinguishing feature of the studies is whether they allow for fixed costs of work. Ignoring fixed costs tends to increase the labour supply elasticities. The first study to allow for fixed costs of work is that of Cogan (1981).[25] His annual hours of work elasticity at 1,400 hours is 0.864 which, adjusting for hours, is lower than that of Heckman; other than fixed costs he uses similar assumptions.

Arellano and Meghir (1992), allow for fixed costs, endogeneity of taxes and pre-tax wages and non-labour income and they find elasticities for weekly hours of work in the range of 0.3–0.7, depending on the demographic group. However, their identification strategy, based on a single cross-sectional dataset, relies on education not having an independent effect on hours of work as in the studies mentioned above.

Many of the early results are reviewed by Mroz (1987) who in addition applies the various methods that had been used up to then to a dataset he drew from the Michigan Panel Study of Income Dynamics (PSID). He thus illustrates how sensitive the results can be to different approaches. Of the estimates that are not rejected by statistical tests the highest wage elasticities are about 0.12, while the unearned income effect is zero. His estimates, as well as those he reviews, are based on cross-sectional comparisons, meaning that differences in incentives can usually be attributed to differences in education levels or other similar characteristics, that we now believe also affect preferences. Interestingly in all cases where Mroz allows for taxes, the incentive effects turn out to be negative. We believe this is because the endogeneity of taxes is not allowed for and the reverse causality effects we discussed earlier are in effect.

Several more recent studies are based on some time-series variation and relax many of the assumptions imposed in the earlier studies. For instance, Blundell, Duncan, and Meghir (1998) use long time-series variation and allow for the endogeneity of pre- and post-tax wages as well as for fixed costs, without using the assumption that all education groups have the same work preferences. In this study the highest elasticity observed for weekly hours of work is found for those women who have young children. For all other married women the wage elasticity is around 0.13, which implies a very low responsiveness of hours to small changes in work incentives.

[25] In the presence of fixed costs of work the individual needs to decide whether to work at all or not. If she decides to work she works a sufficient number of hours to make it worth her while. Cogan (1981) termed this *reservation hours*. Thus wage fluctuations can lead to large jumps from zero hours to some large positive number, e.g. 20 hours. The same wage fluctuation for workers may lead to just a small hours adjustment. Thus under fixed costs the hours adjustment is driven by different factors from the adjustment of whether one works or not. By ignoring fixed costs one is forcing the model to explain hours and participation changes in the same way, biasing upwards the effect of wages on hours.

The prevailing consensus annual labour supply elasticity for women is close to 1. However, the annual hours results that we report have to be regarded with some caution because they rely almost exclusively on cross-sectional comparisons. Weekly hours, on the other hand, respond much less to changes in wages with elasticities in the range of approximately 0.0–0.30. These results are based on weaker assumptions than those used in the annual hours results.

For the purposes of tax simulation and welfare analysis, income elasticities are also very important both for measuring welfare effects and for obtaining the full behavioural effects of a reform. First, a large income effect will translate a modest wage elasticity to a large compensated wage elasticity, which is the source of deadweight loss. In addition the measure of unearned income will be a function of the tax rate when the tax system is nonlinear as shown earlier. Thus the change in the tax rate will also affect unearned income providing an additional channel for a response to a tax change reinforcing the effects of changes in marginal tax rates. The range of estimates we find in the literature is quite limited ranging from about −0.1 to −0.3 across all studies reported, again implying small behavioural effects.

If all these results are put together the picture is of small elasticities for hours worked per week. For most married women—other than those with pre-school children—working the mean 25 hours per week, it would take a 20% increase in the wage rate to induce an increase of 1 hour in the work week. An elasticity of 0.2 with the income effect at about the same level implies a compensated elasticity of 0.3. Thus if we just consider hours the welfare and incentive effects of wage/tax changes are quite small. As already emphasized, in a non-linear tax system, the impact of a change in the marginal wage would be reinforced by the income effect. However, this is also small. Finally, with non-convex budget sets, such as those induced by tax-credits or other welfare benefits, some individuals may respond to quite small tax changes by a large repositioning in their hours of work decisions. Although low elasticities are likely to imply that the number of these individuals may be small, the final outcome depends very much on the overall shape of the budget constraint and on the distribution of hours of work.

The results on annual labour supply show greater responsiveness to wages. Annual labour supply can be viewed as combining the effect of adjustment across many different margins: These include hours per week, weeks per year, as well as participation, the latter because annual hours of work will vary as the individual takes time off between jobs. So it follows that with similar methods the annual hours adjustments should be more sensitive to wages than any one of these margins, at least if leisure across all these margins is a normal good. However, we believe that more empirical work is needed to establish the responsiveness of annual hours of work to work incentives.

Female participation elasticities

Several studies allow us to look more closely at participation elasticities, and the results of these suggest that this is an important margin of adjustment (and may explain much of the difference between weekly and annual hours results). Table 3C.2 (see p. 260) presents the results of several of the main studies that look separately at participation responsiveness. Aaberge et al. (1999) and Arrufat and Zabalza (1986) find results of 0.65 and 1.41 respectively using cross-sectional datasets from Italy and the UK. Both these studies allow for taxes and their endogeneity but are based on a single cross-section. Possibly the most comprehensive study here is by Pencavel (1998) which covers a long period of time, documenting changes in participation for different schooling groups and estimating participation effects of wages with various approaches and instrument sets. However, Pencavel does not allow for the tax system and uses pre-tax wage rates. He finds a range of elasticities from 0.7 to 1.8 with various approaches. Devereux (2004) (who also ignores taxes) finds a lower degree of responsiveness with the elasticity at the median family income equal to 0.17. As with Aaberge, he finds evidence that participation is more elastic amongst women from poorer families, and together their results suggest that participation is likely to be the key margin of adjustment for poorer women. We look at this issue below when considering lone mothers. Thus the overall consensus (with the exception of the result by Devereux) is that participation elasticities for married women are quite high and that this margin for adjustment is perhaps more important than weekly hours of work.

The labour supply of lone mothers

Lone mothers form a demographic group of special policy interest because they tend to be poor and because they face very high costs of work. Creating the right conditions and incentives for them to work and thus escape poverty has been a central concern of the UK government. The main tool for this purpose has been the Working Families Tax Credit (WFTC) and its successor Working Tax Credit (WTC). From the perspective of understanding how effective such interventions are likely to be, we need to know the extent to which lone mothers are likely to respond to work incentives.

There have been a number of papers estimating directly the effect of in-work benefit programmes on lone mother labour supply as well as more conventional labour supply studies. A collection of some results is presented in Table 3C.3 (see pp. 261–2). Eissa and Liebman (1996) estimate a participation elasticity for lone mothers of 1.16, using directly *difference-in-differences* based on a reform on the Earned Income Tax Credit in the US. Their approach has the advantage of using the variation induced by the reform. However, the control group (single women without children) is sufficiently different from the treatment group and with such high participation rates that this puts into question the ability of the approach to control for overall trends and thus credibly to estimate the effects of the reform. A convincing alternative approach is given by Brewer et al. (2005) who combine the use of a structural model of labour supply with the reform to the UK WFTC system to estimate the impact of the reform to the UK Working Families Tax Credit. Again the implied participation elasticity with respect to in-work income is 1.02. For the US, one of the most comprehensive studies, which is based on a long time series of cross-sections and exploits the numerous reforms in the US over the 1980s and 1990s with cross state variability is that of Meyer and Rosenbaum (2001). From their specification it is difficult to compute an elasticity of participation with respect to wages, because changing these would affect disposable income, not only through after tax earnings when in work, but also through benefit eligibility. However, they conclude that the incentive effects of taxation and benefits are substantial; over the period 1984–96 they attribute about 62% of the change in employment of lone mothers relative to single women to changes in taxation; 25% of the change is attributed to changes in benefits over the same period.

The other participation elasticities presented in the table are similarly quite large. It is reassuring that the ones based on actual reforms lead to similar conclusions as the ones based on comparing individuals facing different wages. Thus there is a strong consensus in the literature that the participation elasticity for lone mothers is among the highest of all demographic groups. This implies that thoughtfully designed policies should be able to attract quite a few into work, thus improving substantially their long-run standard of living.

Finally, Blundell, Duncan, and Meghir (1992) estimate a structural model of lone mother labour supply and provide estimates for the elasticity of *hours* with respect to small changes in the wage rate. Although the credibility of these estimates is undermined by the fact that they rely on a single cross-section, the results are quite similar to what we saw before, with the largest elasticity reported as 0.34, very much like the results on married female labour supply discussed above.

3.2.2. Male labour supply

There has been a consistent effort to measure male labour supply elasticities. One key characteristic of male labour supply in many countries is that men work primarily full time. In the UK, for example, although there is some variability in actual hours of work, there is a clear lack of individuals working below a certain level such as 35 hours, as shown in Figure 3.6. In the US one also observes a great concentration of annual hours of work at the full time all year work. This does pose a number of generally unanswered questions relating to why such a concentration exists and how it should be treated in practice. Most studies ignore these issues and attempt to estimate the labour supply curve with continuous hours.

The results obtained generally show low income and wage elasticities for hours of work (see Table 3C.4, pp. 263–4). A variety of methods and datasets have been used and there is a consensus that the sensitivity of hours worked

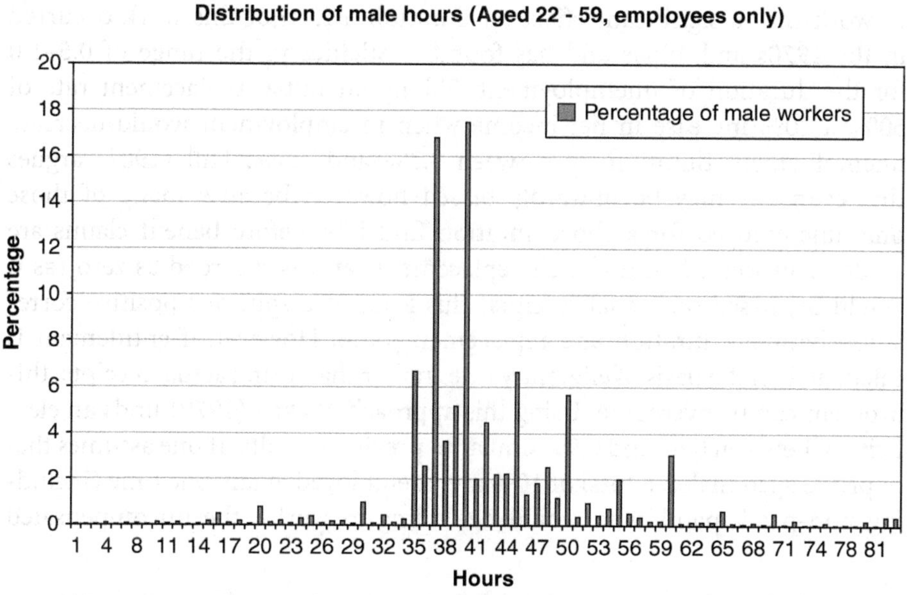

Figure 3.6. Distribution of male hours

is very small. So although one can start discussing the relative merits of the approaches taken, existing research will lead to the conclusion that the wage elasticity of hours of work is close to zero. For example, MaCurdy, Green, and Paarsch (1990), which represents one of the most comprehensive and carefully carried out studies, report an elasticity of zero for the US. Pencavel (2002) reports a number of negative elasticities. At the same time the income elasticities reported are low and also close to zero. As we reported above, some groups of women, particularly those with young children, showed wage elasticities as high as 0.4. *No* male elasticity is reported as high as that. It would be a fair description to say that male hours adjustment to changes in marginal wages is very low indeed and can almost be ignored for welfare purposes. However, this may not be the right margin to consider. We will thus also consider employment elasticities which we will show are quite high for unskilled men, and total income elasticities, which are quite high for high earning/high skill men (Table 3C.5 (see p. 265)).[26]

Owing to historically very high rates of participation for males, most of the empirical literature has abstracted from the participation decision and there are very few estimates of the standard participation elasticity for men. However, Aaberge et al. (1999) produce an estimate of approximately 0.05.

However, an extensive literature has also investigated the impact of unemployment insurance on the duration of employment and this has found significant evidence that a higher replacement rate (i.e. reduced incentives to work) has a significant effect on duration. Much of this work occurred in the 1970s and 1980s and has found elasticities in the range of 0.5–1.0 for the duration of unemployment. Taking an initial replacement rate of 50%, a 10% increase in net income when in employment would decrease unemployment duration by between 2.3% and 4.5%. Hill (1982) argues that estimates may be upwardly biased however, because many of those only unemployed for a short duration find jobs before benefit claims are made or processed, and if their replacement ratio is recorded as zero (as it would be, based on actual receipts) this leads to a spurious positive correlation between duration and replacement ratio. However, if entitlement is calculated on the basis of eligibility rules rather than using actual receipts, this problem can be overcome. Using this approach Nickell (1979) finds an elasticity of between 0.61 and 0.99, similar to previous results. If one assumes that of prime aged males, a total of 10% are unemployed at any one time (including non-participants who would be willing to work), the uncompensated

[26] French (2005) shows that male labour supply at certain ages is very elastic, with intertemporal elasticities as high as 1.2. However, for prime age men the elasticities seem to be consistently lower.

participation elasticity is approximately 0.04. This low estimate should not detract from the sizeable impact out-of-work benefits have on unemployment duration.

We are not convinced that the research on male participation has adequately dealt with the numerous confounding factors. Again most of the estimates are based on simple cross-sectional comparisons and not on exogenous changes in the incentive structure. This is an important omission and we here present our own estimates for the UK based on a long time series of cross-sections and based on the numerous changes in the tax system and the widening of the wage distribution.

3.2.3. Family labour supply—The collective model

Family labour supply is a particularly difficult area for two reasons. First, we need to deal with a joint tax system, which can be very complicated because benefits are often assessed on the basis of family income. As a result, determining the incentive effects of a reform requires solving jointly over both partner's labour supplies in the face of a budget 'plane' which may be non-convex. Second, beyond this we also face the conceptual problem of how to model a household. Should we use the 'unitary' framework where the household is viewed as a unit with a well-defined preference ordering? Should we recognize the individuality of each member of the household, with their own preferences and define/model the way they share resources? And if so should we follow the collective approach, which assumes within-household efficiency or should we admit inefficient outcomes? There has been a recent increase in interest in such models. Blundell, Chiappori, Magnac, and Meghir (2007) estimate a collective model of family labour supply, where the male has the choice of working or not—hours are not modelled and where the female chooses hours and participation. The model does not take into account taxes. The wage elasticity for female labour supply is estimated to be 0.66 and the non-labour income elasticity 0.72. Donni (2003, 2007) allows for taxes in a collective model. More recently Lise and Seitz (2007) use the collective model *with taxes* to account for changes in within-household inequality, when considering overall inequality. The reported elasticity of substitution between consumption and labour supply is over 1, implying strong incentive effects. Although recent developments are encouraging, we believe a lot more needs to be done here before we can be confident that we have a reliable family labour supply model that can be used for public policy analysis. It is a clear case where better data on how families share resources and allocate time to various activities is crucial.

3.2.4. Dynamic models of labour supply

We now turn to models that recognize explicitly intertemporal linkages. In some cases these linkages are due to savings. In this context intertemporal substitution is reflected in the Frisch elasticity, which represents the willingness of individuals to postpone leisure in favour of work during periods of anticipated high wages. As we explained earlier the Frisch (or intertemporal substitution) elasticity does not have a direct policy implication but it is an upper bound for the standard wage elasticity that we have been discussing. In Table 3C.6 (see pp. 266–7) we present some results from the literature. Most of the results are for male hours, although we also present results by Heckman and MaCurdy (1980, 1983) and Blundell, Meghir, and Neves (1993) for women. As we may expect, elasticities are higher than the equivalent within-period ones.

A study that stands out in this literature (because of the type of data used) is that of Pistaferri (2003) using Italian data. He uses subjective expectations data to decompose actual wage changes into anticipated and unanticipated changes. He finds an intertemporal elasticity of substitution for men of 0.7, which is larger than usual. He also estimates the elasticity of a complete shift in the wage profile (i.e. allowing for wealth effects) of 0.5. This is perhaps the most relevant elasticity for tax reform analysis, if we are to assume that individuals perceive this to be permanent. Given the quality of the expectations data the estimate of the intertemporal elasticity of substitution should be quite robust, unless of course the human capital considerations raised by Imai and Keane (2004) are important. However, the Pistaferri approach to estimating the effect of unanticipated changes to the wage profile on hours of work relies on the assumption that any unaccounted changes to preferences for hours of work are not correlated with updates to wage expectations; this may be controversial. Moreover, comparing this to the paper by French (2005), while Pistaferri does allow for taxes, by using the after tax wage, he does explicitly not take into account the implications of non-linearities in the tax code, as French does. Nevertheless, this potential criticism should not detract from the fact that this study uses unique data on expectations and as such adds a new dimension to this literature. His estimate is both reasonable and credible.

Beyond the intertemporal issues relating to savings there is a growing literature that introduces other important dimensions. These models, which include analysis of human capital accumulation, both on the job and during formal education, highlight a number of important points, such as the possible propagation effects of taxation through its impact on job experience and wages.

Two studies have highlighted the importance of dynamics and 'non-separabilities' over time; that is, the case where current choices affect future preferences for work or future wages (or both). Hotz et al. (1988) show convincingly that preferences are likely to be non-separable over time. This means that individuals working a lot today are likely to shift their preferences in the future and towards more work tomorrow. This may imply that incentive effects are reinforced by habits.

A further important example is provided by Imai and Keane (2004). In their paper current work hours enhance individual skills and thus lead to higher wages in the future adding to the work incentives. In their empirical results the intertemporal elasticity of labour supply with respect to wages is 3.82, which is very much larger than anything previously estimated using microeconomic data. Theirs is a joint model of savings and labour supply, where past hours and accumulated human capital affect wages. The economic implication is that the opportunity cost of leisure for young low paid workers is very high. As the importance of training declines with the life-cycle this opportunity cost also declines, but wages increase. Thus despite the sensitivity of labour supply to wages, hours of work do not vary much over the life-cycle. Moreover, for the young the opportunity cost of leisure is so high, due to the loss of future earnings, that it implies that the elasticity for the young is much lower. Indeed, the labour supply elasticity, allowing for the implied effects of human capital accumulation, is lower and depending on age ranges from 0.8 for a 20-year-old to 3 for a 60-year-old. Even with this consideration, hours would probably vary considerably as a response to a permanent shift in the life-cycle profile of wages, such as would be implied by a change in the tax rate, particularly for older individuals where human capital accumulation is less relevant. This analysis demonstrates the potential importance of allowing for dynamics in understanding the impact of policy. However, the specific results may be questionable because the authors do not allow for any persistent unobserved heterogeneity and all shocks are taken to be independent over time. To see why this may be of concern consider that people who work a lot in one period tend to work a lot in following periods and, moreover, they tend to have higher wages in the future. This phenomenon can be attributed to two different causes. First, perhaps some people are productive and therefore both earn a lot and enjoy their work so that they work more; this is the unobserved heterogeneity story. On the other hand, it could be that people work a lot because (as in Imai and Keane (2004)) they realize this will increase their skill and hence their wages.[27] The policy implications of the two cases are quite different and by assuming only the latter effect operates, there is cause for serious doubt on the robustness of this empirical analysis and the credibility of the high elasticities found.

A further example of important policy dimensions, beyond the work incentives, is offered in Adda et al. (2006) who specify a model with human capital accumulation, job mobility (between firms) and labour force participation. The Adda et al. model is estimated using German administrative data, where individuals are observed from the point when they enter the labour market and followed up during their whole career.[28] This model also considers the choice to undertake vocational education and thus includes labour supply, training and job mobility in one integrated framework. This allows us to address directly the importance or otherwise of tax and benefit reforms on longer term training decisions, as well as labour supply.

Adda et al. (2006) report the effects of introducing an EITC programme in Germany. The programme is assumed permanent and they estimate the effects on cohorts who have not yet completed their training decisions. They report that a programme characterized by the same parameters as the US one would increase overall participation by 1%. It would also reduce the proportion trained by about 6 percentage points as the policy reduces the life-cycle returns to training at the bottom of the earnings distribution. This demonstrates that policies designed to support low income individuals may well have other sizeable effects, which may be unwanted and may work against the original purpose of the policy design.

3.2.5. Taxable and total income elasticities

We now present results found in the 'New Tax Responsiveness' literature and which relate to the effects of taxation on taxable income. The elasticities relate either to some broad income measure that includes expenditure on tax deductible items or to taxable income. All elasticities are with respect to the share of income retained (i.e. the effect of a percentage change in $1 - t$ as opposed to a percentage change in t). The distinction matters because away

[27] In the jargon of the literature, all persistence is assumed to be state-dependence. Distinguishing between this and unobserved heterogeneity is the holy grail of empirical labour economics.

[28] To be specific they are dealing with German blue collar workers who have a choice to become qualified with an apprenticeship degree, or not.

from a 50% tax rate a 10% increase in the tax rate will not correspond to a 10% increase in the proportion of income retained.[29] We already discussed the theoretical and practical issues underlying this approach. The results in Table 3C.7 (see pp. 268–9) need to be interpreted carefully and subject to the caveats already discussed.

In his seminal paper Feldstein (1995) uses a two-period (1985 and 1988) panel of married individuals with incomes exceeding $30,000 to analyse the impact of the 1986 tax reform on the taxable incomes of those with middle and high levels of income. Using a simple difference-in-differences methodology, he finds a significant elasticity of taxable income of between 1.1 and 3.05 (depending upon definition), and of broader 'adjusted gross income' of between 0.75 and 1.3. Sillamaa and Veall (2000) use the 1988 Canadian tax reforms as their source of identifying variation, and break down results by source of income. For the whole sample, taxable income from employment has an elasticity of 0.22, whilst self-employment income has an elasticity of 1.12; restricting the sample to those with high incomes increases gross taxable income elasticities considerably, but no separate elasticities by source are given.

Goolsbee (1999) demonstrates the fragility of the difference-in-differences approach. He used the same approach for a number of reforms in the twentieth century. He shows that the elasticity varies considerably from one reform to another. This illustrates precisely the difficulty of the approaches being followed as well as the characterization of the reform as consisting of a single tax rate. First, the aggregate conditions may differ between each reform. If the estimator does not control for aggregate effects the biases will differ each time, sometimes increasing and sometimes decreasing the estimates. Second, reforms rarely affect just one relevant marginal rate; hence the estimates will be a function of other factors changing. Third, the constant elasticity assumption is likely to be invalid. Fourth, the GE effects we mentioned may be quite different each time, depending on which groups are being compared, for example.

As we already mentioned, three papers attempt to address the numerous issues raised above and allow for the economic structure of the problem. Interestingly all three papers support quite high elasticities of total or taxable income, although not all as high as one. Moffitt and Wilhelm (2000) using the Survey of Consumer Finances and based on the 1986 tax reform obtain an

[29] Hall and Katz, in their discussion of Goolsbee (1999), emphasize this point: To get to a tax elasticity and hence to a Laffer type result one needs to multiply the elasticities presented here by $t/(1-t)$. For marginal tax rates less than 50% this implies that the tax elasticity is lower than the elasticity with respect to the share of earnings retained.

adjusted gross income elasticity (AGI) for the US of about 2, close to the Feldstein results when using a similar methodology. They then proceed to control for mean reversion of income by classifying people based on the pre-reform value of their house (which is unlikely to be subject to mean reversion in the short run). They also control for other characteristics; with these adjustments they obtain even higher elasticities of about 2.5, indeed as we would predict from our analysis of the *difference-in-differences* estimator. However, none of these approaches can control for the rising inequality, which could be driving part of the increase of the incomes for the richer versus the poorer individuals. Interestingly they find an annual hours elasticity of 0.2 for middle income individuals but zero for the 'rich', which is consistent with all the studies we have been reporting.[30]

Gruber and Saez (2000) have presented probably the most comprehensive study in this literature. There are certain important differences with the Moffitt and Wilhelm (2000) paper, although not all represent improvements: first Gruber and Saez pool information from a large number of reforms using more information. Second, they match individuals on past income as a way of getting round the mean reversion problem and they predict the tax position based on past income; this is an interesting approach to the problem, but not necessarily better than grouping individuals on the basis of constant or slow-moving characteristics that are correlated with income as Moffitt and Wilhelm do. Finally, they allow for income effects and take a more structural and theoretically coherent modelling approach. Probably as a result of pooling information from many reforms, they obtain a more modest taxable income elasticity of 0.4 overall. For those on incomes in excess of $100,000 the elasticity is 0.57 which is quite high but well below 1. They also consider a 'broad-income' definition with an estimated elasticity of 0.12 for the whole sample. Both numbers are of course important, first and foremost because as Feldstein stressed reallocating income and consumption to avoid tax has welfare consequences. Indeed, these numbers show that the largest of these effects is the income reallocation effect and not effort; this is consistent with the low hours elasticities we have reported. It is noteworthy that the elasticity for those with high income is as high as 0.57 showing that the revenue to be

[30] 'Adjusted gross income' (AGI) is a US tax term for an amount used in the calculation of an individual's income tax liability. AGI includes all gross income adjusted by certain allowed deductions, and is an important benchmark determining certain other allowed benefits. Gross income includes wages, interest income, dividend income, income from certain retirement accounts, capital gains alimony received, rental income, royalty income, farm income, unemployment compensation, and certain other kinds of income.' Source: Wikepedia <http://en.wikipedia.org/wiki/Adjusted_Gross_Income>.

gained by high marginal tax rates for the 'rich' are not very large, at least in the US, and the welfare consequences may be high.[31]

Finally, Blow and Preston (2002) use tax returns of the self-employed in the UK. They use grouped data by region and occupation to construct a pseudo-panel over a period that includes major tax changes. By grouping the data in this way they get round the mean reversion problem and at the same time create groups that differ in their sensitivity to tax, simply because some occupations tend to be remunerated better than others. Their model is again inspired by the standard labour supply model and also allows for income effects. They find a range of elasticities depending on the group considered. These are mostly well over 1 implying that the taxable income of the self-employed is very sensitive to the tax rate and indeed increases in tax rates may lead to reductions in the revenue raised from this group. This group has most scope of reallocating income in the UK tax code. Unfortunately, their specification forces the elasticity to decline with income, which does go against the main intuition in this literature, namely that elasticities are higher at high income levels. The Blow and Preston results for the UK are not necessarily inconsistent with those of Gruber and Saez. The former consider the self-employed; the latter consider the entire population, which will have less opportunity to reallocate income to non-taxable activities.

In Table 3C.7 we present numerous elasticities that have been estimated on the basis of a number of different reforms. They present quite a diversity of results, consistent with the Goolsbee study. Our view is that the Gruber and Saez study presents the most reliable set of estimates. In addition Brewer, Saez, and Shephard (Chapter 2) provide taxable income elasticities for the top 1% of UK earners, likely the group with the greatest potential for avoidance. They find a range of estimates with the lowest one being 0.46 and the highest close to 1. This set of numbers is consistent with the American literature discussed in more detail in this chapter.

3.3. REVISITING MALE LABOUR SUPPLY

In reviewing the literature on male participation it became apparent to us that there was no clear consensus of robust results. This led us to estimate a model of male labour force participation using the best methods available and relying on policy reforms to identify the effects. We thus combine the

[31] Note that Gruber and Saez (2000) find very low income effects, which implies that these elasticities can be taken as compensated ones.

approaches of Blundell, Duncan, and Meghir (1998) and Blundell, Reed, and Stoker (2003) to identify the effect of wages, taxes, and benefits on the male work decision.[32]

3.3.1. The model

We specify a model of the probability that someone works. This depends on total income measures in and out of work. In deciding whether to work or not he considers what total income he would have if he did decide to work; this leads to some level of satisfaction while in work. He compares this to the satisfaction obtained if he decides not to work and obtains whatever income benefits and other sources will provide. This is a combination of various means-tested welfare benefits, including the Job Seeker's Allowance and Housing Benefit. The latter consists of payments towards rent and on certain occasions mortgage payments. The total amount of out-of-work income to which an individual is eligible will depend on housing costs and on family composition.

The in-work utility/satisfaction is complicated by the fact that, whether out of choice or chance, individuals can work a number of different hours of work. In this study we assume that individuals work a random number of hours and that the only decision they make is whether to work or not. We then evaluate in-work utility at the expected in-work income. The determination of actual hours of work will be disregarded here.[33] In-work income is thus constructed as follows. We split hours in intervals 0–60+ and we assign a probability for each interval consistent with what is actually observed in the data. We then evaluate income at the average hours of each interval depending on pre-tax earnings at that point and taking into account all taxes and benefits (including tax-credits) for which the individual would be eligible if he were to work that many hours. The measure of in-work income is then the weighted average of post-tax and benefit income at all these points. It should be noted that where the individual has a spouse, both the in-work and out-of-work measures of income take account of the spouse's actual earnings, without considering the possibility that she may change her decision as a result of what he does.

[32] The approach we use is similar in spirit to that used by Meyer and Rosenbaum (2001) for lone mothers in the US. However, they use as explanatory variables predicted taxes and benefits if the person works and predicted benefits if the person does not, all as separate variables. We use total income in work and total income out of work as explanatory variables.

[33] Formally, the correct model would be to compute the in-work probability as the average probability of working all possible hours. For the purpose of this study we simplified matters by computing one probability of working evaluated at the expected in-work income.

Now consider the impact of a reform. If this reform changes earnings at a point where there is a high probability of observing a worker it will have a much larger impact on in-work income than if it changes them at a point with low probability. While this is realistic, it does not allow for the impact of a change in hours in response to a reform of taxes or benefits. Nevertheless, this may be less of a restriction than it sounds at least for reasonably small-scale reforms, because the overall consensus is that hours are in fact quite insensitive, particularly for men.

Box 3.2. Estimating a model of male employment

Here we discuss the more technical issue of identifying and estimating the effects of incentives of the work probability. We start by defining the utility from working to be

$$U^P = a^P + b^P Y^P + c^{P'} X$$

and similarly the utility from not working

$$U^{NP} = a^{NP} + b^{NP} Y^{NP} + c^{NP'} X + e$$

where Y^P are Y^{NP} are measures of total after tax income including any benefits when in work and out of work respectively. The X variables are taste-shifters which affect individual welfare differently when the individual works and when he does not. These include year dummies, to reflect changing preferences over time, education, and age, as well as region. Similarly, income has a different impact on utility depending on whether it is received in work or out of work; this reflects the fact that income may be valued differently when working and when out of work. Finally, e is an unobserved term expressing the relative preference for work *vis-à-vis* non-work and which differs across individuals—this is the usual econometric 'error term'. We will assume for simplicity that it is normally distributed. The work decision compares these two utilities allowing for the different incomes in and out of work as well as how they are valued:

$$\text{work if } e < \left(a^P - a^{NP}\right) + b^P Y^P - b^{NP} Y^{NP} + \left(c^P - c^{NP}\right)' X.$$

Implementing the estimation of the work probability and identifying the effects of income in and out of work requires us to observe wages for the entire sample. Moreover, we wish to allow for the possibility that pre-tax wages are correlated with (unobserved) preferences for work (endogenous pre-tax wages). This is addressed by using *predicted* rather than actual wages for both workers and non-workers.

(cont.)

Box 3.2. (*cont.*)

We specify a wage equation of the form

$$\ln w_{it} = d_t^{ed} + \beta_t^{ed'} A_{it} + \gamma^{ed} Region + u_{it} \qquad (1)$$

where A_{it} is age effects and *Region* is a set of region dummies and the superscript *ed* signifies a parameter which varies according to which education group a person belongs to. Thus the wage equation is specific to each education group and all coefficients vary with time. The main conceptual difficulty with estimating this equation here is the fact that wages are observed for workers only. To correct for selection we use the well-known Heckman (1979) two-step estimator. The key assumption that allows us to do this is that the income that one would gain when out of work can be taken as random once we take as given family composition, housing tenure, and region. The randomness comes partly from government policy changes and the way that changes in the housing market conditions affect the level of benefits to be received. More formally the *instrument* for correcting for this selectivity bias is defined by

$$Z_{it} = Y^{NP} - G'_{it}\gamma$$

where we have defined $E(Y^{NP}|\textit{Family composition, tenure, region, time}) = G'_{it}\gamma$, with G_{it} representing the variables in brackets and where the time dummies enter additively with no interactions with the other variables. By taking the residual rather than the level of non-work income we avoid the endogeneity problem arising from the potential correlation of family composition and region with wages. Thus we start by estimating a reduced form probit equation for participation including time effects interacted with region and education and the instrument Z_{it} defined above. On the basis of this reduced form probit we construct the inverse Mills ratio, which we then include in the wage equation. Using the estimated wage equation (1) we predict wages for all individuals, whether they work or not.

We will use these wages to construct in-work income for each individual. Each person is assigned a predicted wage. Then for each person we evaluate income, whether working or not, allowing for all benefits and taxes (depending on personal circumstances) and based on this predicted wage for hours 0, 23, 37, 41, 46, 51, 63. Note that actual income earned based on actual hours for workers is disregarded, making the measure comparable for workers and non-workers.

Following the computation of the two measures of income, in-work and out-of-work we can estimate the participation probability using a probit model. However, there is still one important difficulty here. We cannot take these measures as exogenous for the participation equation, even if they are based on predicted wages: higher preferences for work due to unobservables will tend to be related to higher marginal tax rates; this is but one example of reverse causality. We thus use a 'two stage least squares' approach, where the two measures of income are predicted using appropriate instruments. To motivate the instruments we need to explain the policy context and the reforms of the 1980s that subsequently affected the evolution of transfer income right through the period of our investigation (1994 to 2004).

Where does the variability of income come from?

To estimate the effects of taxes and benefits credibly we need to argue that these incomes vary across time and individuals for reasons that are unrelated to work preferences. Over the sample period of our data numerous reforms took place changing the levels of benefits and taxes at various points in time. In itself this is not sufficient because the effects of the policy reforms could be confounded with aggregate shifts in hours of work. However, these reforms have affected different groups of individuals differently as argued in Blundell, Duncan, and Meghir (1998). One such reform is crucial to identification and has been used in particular by Blundell, Reed, and Stoker (2003). In the 1980s public housing rents started growing at the market rate following a reform by the then government. The implication is that housing benefit, which compensates one for rents, started rising in line with these increases. As the housing market moved in different ways across different parts of the country this meant that out-of-work income would change in differential ways across the country too. Once we control for aggregate time effects and region we rely on this residual variation (i.e. region–time interactions) to identify the impact of out-of-work income on labour supply. The same set of reforms will also help identify the effect of in-work income, which also depends on housing benefit. However, further reforms, including tax credits and changes in the tax rates will induce further variability in this measure, which will affect individuals in different cohorts differently.

Given the above discussion, there will be substantial *differential* effects on benefit entitlement due to the reforms in different parts of the country. Thus instead of using the actual in-work and out-of-work income measures, which depend on actual housing costs which may be endogenous (in the sense that they relate to household preferences and past choices), we predict these and thus average them over different types of households; we only use the variation over time for different regions and education groups. Moreover, we never use actual in-work income; rather we use in-work income derived by using predicted wages and taking averages over all possible hours intervals, with weights for the observed distribution of hours. The participation equation excludes time–region and time–education interactions, allowing only for constant region and education effects in labour supply as well as additive time effects. This assumes that preferences for work do not exhibit different trends across groups. Although levels may differ across groups.

The data

Our data source is the Family Resources Survey (FRS). This is an annual cross-sectional survey of approximately 23,000 households in Great Britain and has been designed specifically for socio-economic research with a focus on income, expenditures and employment. We use eleven annual waves of the FRS from 1994 to 2004 and choose a sample of men, either single or living with partners and aged between 22 and 59 inclusive. We exclude the self-employed, those in full-time education, and those entitled to disability benefits as well as those living in Northern Ireland. This leaves us with a sample of 31,461 single males (with an average age of 35), and a sample of 91,372 men with partners (with an average age of 41).

The in-work and out-of-work net incomes are calculated using the IFS tax and benefit model (TAXBEN) and are derived using the full set of determinants of taxes and benefits as observed in the FRS. This model combined with the FRS is remarkably accurate at predicting tax revenues and benefit expenditures.

Results

In Table 3.1 we present the 'marginal effects' of increasing the two income measures on the probability of participation by education group and marital status of the man.[34] Thus each number

probability of work as a result of a percentage increase in out-of-work or in-work income respectively. First, note that dealing with endogeneity of in-work income in particular is very important and indeed the bias is the direction one would expect: the positive correlation between the tax rate faced and the propensity to work means that everything else equal, those most favourable to working for reasons of preference also end up with lower

[34] These are changes in probability of work corresponding to a unit increase in log income measure. Each person has two income measures: one is the predicted income were he to work (in-work income) and one is the predicted income were he not to work (out-of-work income). The combination of these two measures together with their coefficients reflects the return to work for each individual. The participation probability does not depend on the difference in incomes, but on the income measures individually with separate weights: each income measure has a different weight because income is valued differently when in work than when out of work.

Table 3.1. Marginal effects of in-work and out-of-work income on male participation (UK)

	Income exogenous		Income endogenous	
	Log out-of-work income	Log in-work income	Log out-of-work income	Log in-work income
		Single Men		
Low Education	−0.1837	−0.0243	−0.2517	0.1683
	(0.0079)	(0.0302)	(0.0509)	(0.0936)
Medium Education	−0.0583	−0.1359	−0.1411	0.3081
	(0.0086)	(0.0325)	(0.0418)	(0.0770)
High Education	−0.0300	−0.1402	−0.0061	0.0732
	(0.0061)	(0.0276)	(0.0304)	(0.0469)
		Married or Cohabiting Men		
Low Education	−0.2220	0.3636	−0.1698	0.3182
	(0.0041)	(0.0066)	(0.0348)	(0.0644)
Medium Education	−0.1039	0.1526	−0.1246	0.1267
	(0.0052)	(0.0092)	(0.0274)	(0.0480)
High Education	−0.0608	0.1152	−0.0515	0.0341
	(0.0039)	(0.0081)	(0.0292)	(0.0413)

Standard errors in parentheses.

after tax in-work income (because of taxation), causing a negative bias. This is clearly the case for single men where the results in the first two columns, that do not allow for endogeneity, give negative incentive effects. Once we deal with this issue the incentive effects of higher in-work income become apparent (last column).

The results in the last two columns are sensible. First, income incentives matter most for the lower educated individuals. The participation probability of higher educated persons responds less to both changes in out-of-work and in in-work income. Indeed, for those with college education the effects are not significant at conventional levels and the point estimates are very small. However, for those with statutory education the marginal effects are large. At a participation rate of 60%, which is about the number for the unskilled, the elasticity of participation with respect to in-work income is 0.27 for single men and about 0.53 for married men. The out-of-work income elasticities for the two groups are 0.42 and 0.60 respectively. These are quite high numbers and imply that welfare benefits can have substantial effects on the work behaviour of unskilled men and even for men with high school education. However, as we argued earlier simple elasticities like that can be quite misleading as far as evaluating specific reforms. Moreover, reforms we are likely to consider in practice may affect incomes at many parts of the budget constraint and there may be interactions with other welfare benefits. In the next section we undertake a simple illustrative exercise and we use our model to predict the impact of a couple of simple reforms to give an idea of what these results imply.

Simulating reforms

The model we have estimated ignores the hours dimension, taking hours to be drawn randomly from the observed distribution. In other ways, however, the model is more sophisticated than many in the literature in that it allows for the complete structure of the tax and welfare-benefit system, whilst at the same time allowing for the endogeneity of both hourly wages and post tax incomes. It achieves this by using the information from a number of tax reforms over time and the different way they have affected different types of individual living in different parts of the country.

Within the context of this model, simulating a tax reform implies changing the required parameters of the tax and welfare-system and then computing how this will change the out-of-work and expected in-work income of each individual and the resulting work probability. The purpose of this section is to illustrate what a model such as this has to say about tax reform. It also emphasizes the fact that knowing the elasticity alone is not sufficient to predict what the effects will be. If anything, the reform will typically change the in-work and out-of-work incomes of different types of individuals in different ways: making tax credits more generous will affect low wage individuals but not higher wage ones for instance.

The baseline British tax system which we will 'reform' can be described as follows: there is a non-taxable earnings allowance (£4,745 at the time) beyond this (in 2004) there is a 10%, a 22%, and a 40% tax bracket. In addition to these taxes individuals contribute to National Insurance, a tax which is justified as funding pensions. The employees' National Insurance (NI) rate is 11% and declines to 1% beyond a particular level of earnings called the Upper Earnings Limit (UEL). This means that effectively the marginal tax rates were 21%, 33%, and 41%, abstracting from employers' National Insurance contributions. Both National Insurance (NI) and income tax payments are assessed on individual income and there are no deductions allowed for consumption or mortgages. In addition there are a number of welfare benefits, including housing benefit and tax credits which are assessed on the basis of family income. In particular the Working Tax Credit (WTC) is a means-tested tax credit for those working a qualifying number of hours per week, whilst the Child Tax Credit (CTC) provides means-tested support

Table 3.2. Details of simulated reform

Flat Tax Reform: Integrated Income Tax National Insurance and Tax Credits	
Flat-rate income tax of 31% (36.65% for married men) on all income exceeding increased personal allowance. Removal of UEL on National Insurance contributions. Tax Credit not tapered away at additional rate.	
Single Men Overall **42%** marginal tax rate	Cohabiting Men Overall **47.65%** marginal tax rate

to families with incomes up to approximately £57,000. For more information on the UK tax and benefit system see Adam, Browne, and Heady (Chapter 1) and O'Dea, Phillips, and Vink (2007).

To illustrate the implications of the estimates we will carry out a relatively sweeping reform where the system described above will be replaced by a flat tax. We consider two sets of tax parameters: one is revenue neutral for single men and the other for married/cohabiting men. The employment behaviour of the female partner is taken as fixed here. Table 3.2 provides the details of the reform, while Figures 3.7 and 3.8 show graphically how the reform affects single and married men.[35]

The flat tax has distinctly different impacts upon the net-income of the single man and the cohabiting man (with one child); this is because of the differing entitlements to tax credits which are fully integrated and tapered away as part of standard income tax payments in this reformed system. The single man, eligible only for working tax credit (when working at least 30 hours per week), faces a higher tax rate implying lower net income at hours less than 30 as well as above 55 when the working tax credit has been 'tapered away'.

For the cohabiting man, on the other hand, the new system involves higher transfer income in the form of the more generous working tax credit for couples and the child tax credit. Below 35 hours, the marginal tax rate is lower because tax credits are no longer being tapered away at their pre-reform 37% rate. Despite a 47.65% marginal tax rate, 'universal tax credits' ensure that with a £10 hourly wage, income is considerably higher in the reform system even at 70 hours per week. The reform is financed by individuals with higher wages. Figures 3.7 and 3.8 illustrate the impact of the reform on the budget constraint of a single and a cohabiting man with one child respectively.

[35] In these figures the man is assumed to earn £10 per hour. The spouse (if there is one) works 20 hours at £6 per hour; their child is aged 10.

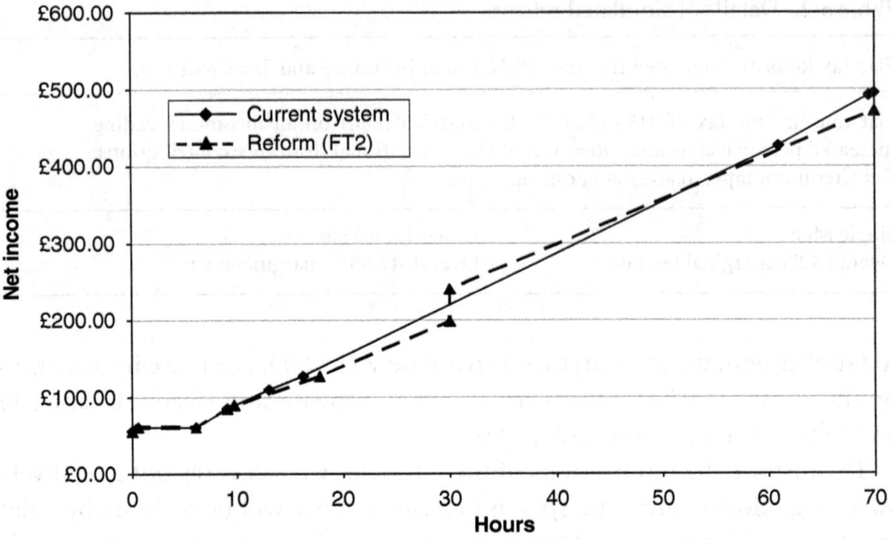

Figure 3.7. Single men

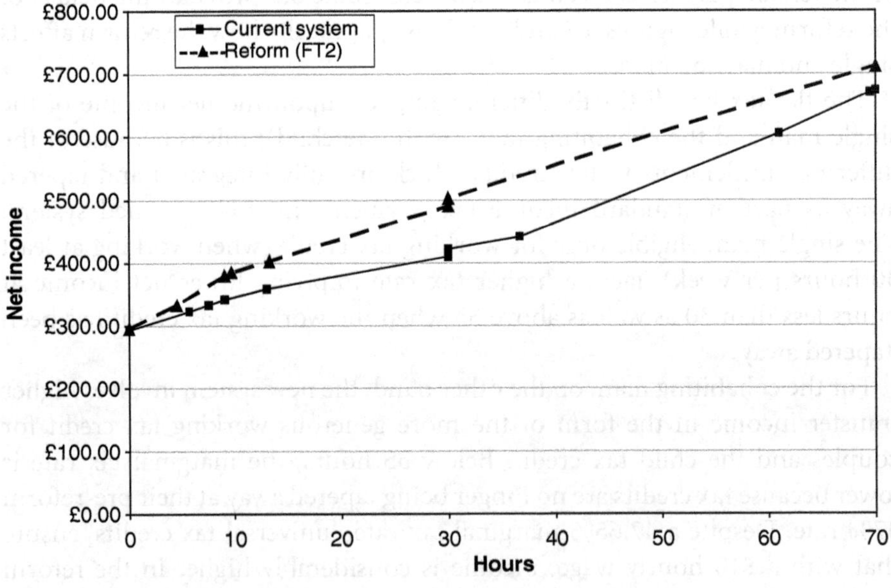

Figure 3.8. Cohabiting men

Overall the reforms reduce the income of those not entitled to tax credits and increases the incomes of those eligible, particularly those in couples with children. Table 3.3 shows the estimated effect of the reform, separately for single and cohabiting men. This uses the actual FRS data and consequently

Table 3.3. Probit results for male participation – marginal effects

Group	Estimated Overall Impact %
Single Men	
Lowest Quartile	−0.20
Quartile 2	0.65
Quartile 3	0.66
Highest Quartile	0.08
Overall	0.31
Cohabiting Men	
Lowest Quartile	2.02
Quartile 2	0.68
Quartile 3	−0.02
Highest Quartile	−0.25
	0.61

the results are representative of the population and include all observed demographic groups with their frequencies as found in the data. The results are broken down by quartile of wages.

The reform has a modest positive impact on the employment probability, with this being more notable for men with partners. For single men the small positive employment effects are observed for those with wages in the second and third quartiles. However, the reform predicts a substantial positive employment effect for low wage cohabiting men, with some small negative employment effects for higher wage individuals. The reform does not discourage participation for those paying for the reform basically because their work probability is so high. So it looks as if this reform has the important advantage of encouraging work for the lowest wage individuals but has little cost in terms of lost employment by those who pay for it. The conclusion, however, may be misleading because our model is incomplete in at least two important dimensions. First, we do not allow hours to change. Second, we do not allow non-hours effort to change. Finally, a reform such as this is likely to have longer-term effects on investment in human capital as well as possible General Equilibrium effects. These would need to be evaluated carefully if such a reform is to be considered seriously. Nevertheless, our aim was not so much to discuss the merits of such a reform, but to illustrate the implications of our estimates for the sensitivity of participation to a major reform and to show what the magnitude of the parameters would mean for a major change to the tax system.

3.4. CONCLUSIONS

The study of labour supply is key to understanding the welfare and revenue effects of taxation. However, there are many dimensions to labour supply and each seems to be most relevant for a different group of persons. We have thus considered hours of work per week and per year, labour force participation, and total taxable income. The picture that emerges is very interesting. Incentives matter and taxation can generate important distortions.

Male hours of work are almost completely irresponsive to changes in work incentives; however, male participation, particularly for those with low or medium levels of education can be responsive. The number of people working among the low skilled can be sensitive to the design of welfare benefits and tax credits as operated in the UK with an hours condition, for instance. Hours of work and labour force participation for women with young children and particularly for lone mothers are also quite sensitive to tax and benefit incentives. Participation elasticities (work/non-work) are positive and demonstrate quite a lot of sensitivity to incentives for the decision to work or not. For highly educated individuals the sensitivity of both hours of work and participation to work incentives are almost zero. However, for higher income and higher skill individuals the total income elasticity is substantial, but probably less than one. Thus for low skill men the structure of the benefit system is likely to affect their work probability. For high skill men higher rates of taxes are likely to discourage effort and creativity quite substantially to imply important efficiency effects of taxation.

In our chapter we have also tried to give a flavour of the complexity of estimating the effects of tax and benefit reforms, particularly when the system has elements of regressivity. The size of the elasticity is not sufficient to give us a complete view of the labour supply effects of tax and benefit reforms. The magnitude of the responses will also depend on the whole structure of the budget constraint. Non-convexities, such as those induced by the tax credit system, can induce large behavioural responses, even if the elasticities are quite small. So a complete analysis of the effort/hours responses of reforms requires simulation taking into account the whole structure of the tax and transfer system.

Finally, it is important to remember that taxes and welfare benefits affect more than just work effort. They can change other decisions, including most importantly the decision to accumulate human capital. We have presented some evidence that such a margin of adjustment may be important. However, this adjustment is 'hidden' because its impact is much longer term which, likewise, makes it more difficult to estimate due to the difficulties in disentangling the impact of tax reforms from secular trends. Genuine policy analysis has to address the longer-term issues, which could prove to be the most important for behavioural and welfare effects. A well-designed tax and benefit system will need to recognize that all groups in the population can be quite sensitive to taxes and benefits in many different dimensions.

APPENDIX 3A

Some technical terms explained

- Budget set: in this context, a relationship between hours worked and the amount of income this provides.
- Utility function: a utility function is the economists' way of representing individual preferences over different goods; for given quantities of each good a utility function implies a rate that the individual is willing to trade one good for another (consumption for leisure in our case)—the marginal rate of substitution. Individuals choose a point on their budget set so as to maximize their utility. The size of the marginal rate of substitution is directly related to the impact of incentives on the supply of effort.
- Marginal tax rate: the tax rate that would be paid on a small additional amount of income (i.e. at the margin). This may be higher or lower than the average tax rate which is the total amount of tax paid at a given income divided by that income.
- Income and substitution effects: suppose the tax rate is increased. The income effect is the effect of the reduction in net income implied by higher taxes. It implies one would work more because one is poorer. The substitution effect, on the other hand, causes one to work less because the trade-off between work and leisure (i.e. the net wage) has been made less favourable. In this case, the two effects work in opposite directions but this is not always so.
- Elasticity: this is the 'proportional change in X, given a "1%" change in Y'. In this context, the labour supply elasticity with respect to the wage is the 'proportional change in labour supply, given a "1%" increase in the (net hourly) wage rate'. An elasticity of 1 means labour supply increases by 1% for a 1% rise in the net wage; an elasticity of 0.1 means a 0.1% rise for a 1% increase in the net wage.

The size of the elasticity is determined by the income and substitution effects detailed above.

Further concepts and terms are defined in the relevant sections of the chapter.

APPENDIX 3B

The difference-in-differences estimator and the taxable income elasticity

In this appendix we look in some detail at the difference-in-differences estimator that has been used to estimate the impact of reducing higher marginal tax rates. When we refer to the treatment group we refer to individuals who benefit from a tax reduction (or more generally change). The control group is the group to whom these are compared. Specifically what is frequently estimated is some version of the following double log specification

$$\log E_{is} = \alpha_0 + \beta \log p_s + \beta \log(1 - t_{is}) + u_{is} \quad (1)$$

where E_{is} stands for earnings for individual i in period s, p_t is the unit price of effort in period s, and t_{is} is the tax rate faced by the individual.[37] The last term u_{is} is unobserved and constitutes the *random income shock*. The nature of this shock plays an important role in our attempts to understand incentive effects. In this simplified framework, the effect we wish to estimate is β, namely the proportionate effect on earnings (or taxable income in other contexts) of a percentage change in the proportion of earnings retained after tax.[38] The approach to estimating β followed in the literature[39] is to compare the growth of earnings for a group that was subject to a tax reform (say the very high earners) to a group with earnings just below the level at which the tax cut took effect. This approach ignores the fact we do not observe the price of effort p and treats it as a common factor affecting every group in the same way; hence it drops out when we compare across groups of individuals.

To see how this works, suppose we have two populations operating in the same labour market, but one consisting of individuals who earn less initially so that they face lower tax rates than the members of the other group. Suppose a policy reform is introduced whereby the tax rate of the higher earners is reduced. The lower-earnings group with incomes not targeted by the reform will constitute the *control*

[37] Notice that by the properties of logs the log of the after tax price of effort is $\log((1-t)p) = \log p + \log(1-t)$.

[38] Note that this is not the same as (minus) the elasticity of earnings with respect to the tax rate. The latter is $-\beta\frac{t}{1-t}$.

[39] See Feldstein (1995, 1999) for example.

group. It is assumed that we observe the same set of individuals before and after the reform; the classification in treatment (those affected by the reform) and control group (those not affected) is based on their original income. We ignore observed unearned income, which in practice we can control for. The difference in these two groups will be reflected in differences in the mean of u in the pre-reform period (i.e. the mean of u_{i0}); the method indeed needs to assume that this mean affects outcomes in both periods in exactly the same way. In technical jargon this means that any changes in income are permanent. The *difference-in-differences* estimator for the effect of the tax reduction is based upon the *difference* in the change (Δ) in log earnings in the treatment group ($\log E_1$) from that of the control group, i.e. $\Delta \log E_1 - \Delta \log E_0$. This is then scaled by the percentage change in the proportion of earnings taken home $(1-t)$, or more accurately the change in $\log(1-t)$. This calculation aims at obtaining an estimate of β. However, there are three important difficulties with the interpretation of the results: (a) income shocks are unlikely to be permanent; (b) the price of effort may change differently for each of the groups; and (c) aggregate economic trends may differ across lower and higher earning individuals. The approach described has to assume all these issues away. The expression below summarizes the problems by including three different confounding components. To do this in a simple way we have expressed the way the income shocks persist from one period to the next as $u_{i1} = \rho u_{i0} + \varepsilon_{i1}$. This means that in period 1 (after the reform) a proportion ρ of the income shock that occurred in period 0 continues to affect the observed level of income. The approach assumes that this proportion is 1, i.e. that the shock is permanent. Suppose there is a tax reform and call D the percentage change in the proportion of earnings that the person in the *High* income group can keep minus the same for the *Low* income group.[40] Formally, $D = \Delta \log(1-t)^H - \Delta \log(1-t)^L$. Thus what the method really estimates is

$$\frac{\Delta \log E^H - \Delta \log E^L}{D} = \beta + (\rho - 1)\frac{\left(u_0^H - u_0^L\right)}{D} + \frac{(g^H - g^L)}{D} + \frac{\Delta \log(p^H/p^L)}{D} \tag{2}$$

where a superscript H denotes those with a higher income in the first period and L those with a lower one. u_0^H is the average first period random income 'shock' for those classified as high income in the first period (the treatment group) and similarly u_0^H for the low income individuals. So for example $\Delta \log E^H$ is the earnings growth of those classified as 'high income' in the pre-reform period. In what follows we will suppose that the reform reduced the tax rate faced by the higher income individuals relative to that of the low income individuals; thus $D > 0$.

The first term in (2) reflects mean reversion of incomes. Unless all shocks are permanent ($\rho = 1$) we expect this term to be negative and will bias downward the effect β we are seeking to estimate. This is the bias caused by mean reversion and is discussed

[40] The *High* and *Low* categories are defined by the income position before the reform took place.

at length by Gruber and Saez (2000).[41] The second term reflects the aggregate growth rate of individuals in different parts of the initial income distribution. So during periods of increasing inequality, such as the 1980s in the US and the UK, this term will be positive; this means that the incomes of those higher up in the distribution are growing faster than those lower down for reasons that may not be related to the tax reform directly and this will bias upwards the effect we wish to estimate. The final term has to do with whether individuals at a lower part of the income distribution offer a different type of skill to those at a higher part. In the extreme, all these individuals just offer the same type of skill, more or less effectively, and then the adjustment $\Delta \log \frac{p1}{p0}$ will be zero because the price for a unit of effort across the two groups grows in the same way. However, under reasonable assumptions $\Delta \log \frac{p1}{p0}$ will be negative when the tax rate relating to the higher earning individuals is cut.[42] This can occur because the decrease in tax for the higher income group will increase their supply of labour and will lead to a shift in the demand for labour from the lower skill to the higher skill group. In equilibrium one can show that $\Delta \log \frac{p1}{p0}$ is then negative. The result is a downward bias for the estimated earnings elasticity. Thus accounting for such *general equilibrium* effects would lead to larger elasticities (β) than those implied by the *difference-in-differences* framework. The approach we described above is thus fraught with problems: mean reversion in income and general equilibrium effects bias downward the elasticity, while aggregate trends can go either way. For the specific case of the reforms analysed in the US (the 1986 reform in particular) the increase in inequality would bias the elasticity upwards.

APPENDIX 3C

Supplementary tables

[41] Note that Feldstein categorizes people on the basis of the pre-reform marginal tax rate. This is a function of the pre-reform income. Hence although more complicated this is in effect a categorization by initial income and the same arguments apply.

[42] To show this we have taken a CES production function with two types of labour. The labour supply elasticities of the two groups can differ.

Table 3C.1. Married female labour supply (continuous hours elasticities)

Study	Data/Sample	Variables Used	Labour Supply Model	Uncomp. Wage Elasticity	Income Elasticity
Arellano & Meghir (1992)	UK Family Expenditure Survey and Labour Force Survey 1983 Age 20–59 **married,** 11,535 employed, 13,200 non-employed	H: Weekly hours Y: Consumption based other income measure W: Marginal wage rate	Semi-log labour supply with fixed costs and job search costs; Budget set assumed convex and piecewise linear; allows endogenous wages and unearned income using IV approach	0.29 to 0.71 Depending on age of children and woman. At sample means: 0.37	−0.13 to −0.40 −0.13
Blomquist & Hansson-Brusewitz (1990)	Swedish Level of Living Survey 1981: sample size 795, 640 employed Age 25–55 **married**	H: Annual hours W: Wage, SS Y: Spouse's net income plus benefits and capital income	Linear & Quadratic labour supply; Convex and Non-convex piecewise linear budgets; some specifications control for taxes and benefits, others do not; predicted wages, both Heckman corrected and full information maximum likelihood (FIML); fixed and random preferences	Evaluated at Means Heckman Fixed: 0.386 FIML Fixed: 0.79 Heckman, quadratic, Fixed: 0.58 Heckman, Random: 0.77	 −0.03 −0.243 −0.05 −0.06
Blundell, Duncan, & Meghir (1998)	UK Family Expenditure Survey 1978–92: sample size 16,781 employed 7,845 non-employed, aged 20–50 **married or cohabiting**	H: Usual weekly hours & overtime W: after tax Usual pay and overtime over H Y: Non-durable weekly consumption minus earnings	Semi-log linear labour supply; includes controls for children, education and cohort; accounts for taxes and benefits; grouping estimator (based on education and cohort) to overcome simultaneity	No children: 0.14 Youngest child 0–2: 0.21 Youngest child 2–5: 0.37 Youngest child 5–10: 0.13 Youngest child 11+: 0.13	0 −0.19 −0.17 −0.10 −0.06

(*cont.*)

Table 3C.1. (*cont.*)

Study	Data/Sample	Variables Used	Labour Supply Model	Uncomp. Wage Elasticity	Income Elasticity
Bourguignon & Magnac (1990)	French Labour Force Survey 1985: sample size 1,175 employed, 817 non-employed aged 18–60 **married**	H: Normal weekly hours W: Hourly net wage and SS Y: Spouses net income and benefits	Linear labour supply; convex piecewise linear budget constraint; accounts for taxation but ignores non-convexities induced by benefits; random preferences; can include fixed costs; exogenous wage	Tobit: 0.3 Hausman-style: 1 Fixed costs: 0.05	−0.2 −0.3 −0.2
Cogan (1981)	US National Longitudinal Study of Mature Women 1967: **Married women** aged 30–35. 898 workers and 939 non-workers	H: Annual hours of work W: Hourly wage Y: Husband's earnings	Semi-log labour supply (linear in hours); wages predicted using selection correction; and labour supply subject to reservation hours to account for fixed costs; does not account for taxes or benefit payments	Elasticity at mean 1,400 hours per year 0.864 No fixed costs 2.4	At $10,000 0.16 0.66
Hausman (1981)	US Panel of Income Dynamics 1975: sample size 575 participants, 510 non-participants **married**	H: Annual hours of work W: Hourly wage, SS Y: Transfer and asset income evaluated at 8% return	Linear labour supply. Convex (piecewise linear) and Non-convex (fixed costs) budget set	0.995 0.906	−0.121 −0.13
Heckman (1974a)	National Longitudinal Survey of Work Experience 1967 for Women 2,100 white women—married spouse present	H: Annual hours W: Hourly wage Y: Husbands earnings and non-labour income	Maximum likelihood estimation of wage and reservation wage function Non-separable male labour supply No taxes or benefits accounted for	Hours worked at 2,000 hours per year 0.8 Weeks worked per year (at 50 weeks) 1	Income effect given male wage 0.0

Ashenfelter & Heckman (1974)	US 1960 Census of Population **Married Women** aged 25–54	H: Participations W: Hourly wage Y: Unearned income	Labour supply linear in differentials, proxying differentials by differences from mean values; exogenous wages; does not account for taxes or benefits; unitary family framework	Evaluated at Means: 0.912 (−0.075 cross elasticity) Imposing unitary assumptions 1.15 (0.12 cross elasticity)	N/A N/A
Kaiser et al. (1992)	German Socio-Economic Panel 1983: sample size 1,076 employed, 2,284 non-employed, non-retired **married**	H: Annual hours W: Hourly wage, SS Y: Income from rents, benefits, and capital	Linear Labour Supply Convex piecewise linear budget set	1.04	−0.18
Mroz (1987)	US PSID 1976 753 married white women between the ages of 30 and 60 in 1975, with 428 working	H: Annual hours W: Hourly wage Y: Non-wife household income	Semilog linear labour supply. Sensitivity analysis using many different methods, including allowing for fixed costs and endogenous wages and non-labour income	Max wage elasticity in acceptable model (at 1,300 hours of work) 0.12	0.0
Triest (1990)	US Panel Study of Income Dynamics 1983 sample size: 715 employed, 263 non-employed aged 25–55 **married**	H: Yearly hours, all jobs W: Average hourly wage, SS Y: Income from rents, dividends, etc	Linear labour supply; convex and piecewise linear budget set; accounts for taxes and benefits; uses actual wages and imputed wages separately; other income exogenous	IV: 0.03 ML 0.26 to 0.28 (Depends on error terms)	−0.19 −0.15 to −0.17

Note: H: Hours/Work measure used, W: Wage measure used, Y: Income measure used. SS Net wage includes social security deductions

Table 3C.2. Female labour supply—participation elasticities

Study	Data/Sample	Variables Used	Labour Supply Model	Uncomp. Wage Elasticity	Income Elasticity
Aaberge et al. (1999)	Italian Survey of Household Income and Wealth 1987 Families aged 20–70, self-employment income <20%	H: Not given W: Net wages Y: Other income	Family labour supply, not subject to unitary restrictions; non-linear labour supply; non-convex budget constraint; accounts for taxes and benefits; hours and supply constraints (demand/institutions); exogenous wages and unearned income	Mean of sample: 0.654 10th income percentile 2.837 11th–89th percentiles 0.742 90th income percentile 0.031	−0.014 −7.00 0.096 −0.051
Arrufat & Zabalza (1986)	UK: 1974 General Household Survey 3,495 married women aged less than 60 with husbands less than 65	H: Weekly hours / Participation W: Gross wages Y: Adjusted unearned income plus husband	CES utility function convex budget constraint; optimization errors and preference heterogeneity; accounts for taxes but not benefits	Mean of sample: 1.41	−0.14
Blundell, Ham, & Meghir (1987)	UK FES Survey 1981. 2,011 married women 1,076 employed, 935 zero hours Aged 16–60 married to men 16–65	H: Participation W: Marginal net wages Y: Consumption-based other income	Non-linear labour supply model with unemployment (relaxation of Tobit); accounts for both taxes and benefits; predicted wages for non-participants	Tobit: 0.04 Double Hurdle 0.08	
Pencavel (1998)	US March CPS 1975–94 Sample selection: women aged 25–60	H: Participation W: Hourly wage Y: Non-labour income	Log-linear labour supply; controls for age and cohort (each cohort has own wage profile); education allowed to vary and indirect wage effect via education; does not account for taxes or benefits; wages treated as both exogenous and endogenous; not selection-corrected	WLS, corrected for selection 0.77–0.839 IV—US trade balance and education, corrected for selection. 0.791–0.892 IV—as above with control for education 1.826	

Note: H: Hours/Work measure used, W: Wage measure used, Y: Income measure used. FES: UK Family Expenditure Survey. CPS: US Current Population Survey. CES: Constant Elasticity of Substitution.

Table 3C.3. Lone mothers' labour supply

Study	Data/Sample	Variables Used	Labour Supply Model	Uncompensated. Wage Elasticity
Blundell, Duncan, & Meghir (1992)	UK: Family Expenditure Survey 1981–1986: sample size 1,654. Lone mothers no self-employed	H: Usual weekly hours W: Hourly wage Y: Consumption based	Marginal rate of substitution function; accounts for taxation but not benefits; wages and income endogenous, and wages selection-corrected	Basic rate taxpayers: 0.16 All lone mothers: 0.34 Excluding hours 'bunches' 0.14
Brewer, Duncan, Shephard, & Suarez (2005)	UK: Family Resources Survey 1995–2002: 13,458 lone mothers aged < 60, not self-employed and not disabled	H: Usual weekly hours W: Hourly wage Y: Net income evaluated at discrete hours	Discrete choice over 5 positive hours; fixed costs, heterogeneous tastes and joint choice over programme participation; accounts for taxes and benefits; endogenous childcare use	Net income Participation Elasticity: 1.02
Dickert, Houser, and Scholz (1995)	USA SIPP 1990. Single women with children. Exclude those with high assets	H: Participation W: Gross hourly wage Y: Net income evaluated at discrete hours	Discrete choice over non-participation and 2 positive hours points; taxes and benefits accounted for; IV—return to work instrumented by whether state has high or low benefits	Participation Elasticity from EITC: 0.85 From returns to work: 0.35
Eissa & Liebman (1996)	USA CPS 1985–87 and 1989–91. Single women with children	H: Participation W: Hourly wage Y: Net income evaluated at discrete hours	No explicit structural labour supply model. Difference-in-difference estimator comparing those with children and those without following US TRA86 reform	Participation Elasticity: 1.16
Ermisch & Wright (1991)	UK: 1973–82 General Household survey: 2,062 lone mothers with 966 employed.	H: Work or not W: Net hourly wage Y: Net income evaluated at different points	Discrete choice of work and not-work; accounts for taxes and benefits in a simplified manner; includes fixed costs of work; predicted wages, Heckman selection-corrected; includes demand-side controls (regional unemployment)	Participation Elasticity: 1.7 Eligible for FIS: 1.8 Ineligible for FIS: 1.2 (Both net wages)

(cont.)

Table 3C.3. (*cont.*)

Study	Data/Sample	Variables Used	Labour Supply Model	Uncompensated. Wage Elasticity
Jenkins (1992)	UK: 1989 Lone Parents Survey: 1,235 lone mothers, with 519 in employment	H: Full or part time W: Gross hourly wage Y: Net income evaluated in and out of work	Discrete choice over two positive hours points; double hurdle model (participation and employment); includes fixed costs; accounts for benefits but not taxes; predicted wages for non-participants, selection-corrected	Participation Elasticity: 1.80 Full-time work Elasticity: 1.44 (Both gross wages)
Keane and Moffitt (1998)	USA: 1994 SIPP Single women with children Exclude those with high assets	H: Full or part time W: Gross hourly wage Y: Net income evaluated in and out of work	Discrete choice over two positive hours points; joint model decision of labour supply and welfare programme participation; accounts for benefits but not taxes; predicted wages for non-workers; identification of cross-state variation in programme generosity	Participation Elasticity: 0.96 Total Elasticities: 1.82 1.47–1.97
Walker (1990)	UK: 1979–84 Family Expenditure Survey with 1,729 lone mothers	H: Work or not W: Gross hourly wage Y: Net income evaluated in and out of work	Discrete choice of work and not-work; accounts for benefits; predicted wages used, not selection corrected	Participation Elasticity: 0.7 (net income)

Note: FIS: Family Income Supplement, an early name for the UK in work benefit System. EITC: the US Earned Income Tax Credit. H: Hours/Work Measure used, W: Wage measure used, Y: Income measure used. SIPP: US Survey of Income and Programme Participation, FES: UK Family Expenditure Survey, GHS: UK General Household Survey, PSID: US Panel Study of Income Dynamics. TRA86 the US tax reform of 1986

Table 3C.4. Male labour supply (continuous hours elasticities)

Study	Data/Sample	Variables Used	Labour Supply Model	Uncomp. Wage Elasticity	Income Elasticity
Ashenfelter & Heckman (1974)	US 1960 Census of Population; **married** men aged 25–54	H: Annual hours W: Hourly wage Y: Unearned income	Labour supply linear in differentials, proxying differentials by differences from mean values; exogenous wages; does not account for taxes or benefits; unitary family framework	Evaluated at means: 0.06	−0.11
Blomquist & Newey (2002)	Swedish Level of Living Survey 1973, 1980, 1990; **married** aged 20–60; 2,321 across 3 waves	H: Annual hours of Work Y: Other income W: Calculated hourly wage	Non-parametric labour supply; convex budget constraint with allowance for 'small' non-convexities; estimated non-parametrically over the budget set; actual wages used	0.06–0.08	(Parametric model) −0.02
Bourgiugnon & Magnac (1990)	French Labour Force Survey 1985; all employed **married** aged 18–60; sample size is 1,992	H: Normal weekly hours Y: Family allowances W: Hourly net wage	Linear Labour Supply; Convex (Piecewise Linear) Budget Constraint; accounts for taxation but ignores non-convexities induced by benefits; random preferences; can include fixed costs; exogenous wage	Evaluated at means: 0.1	−0.07
Flood & MaCurdy (1992)	Swedish Household Market and Non-Market Survey 1984 all employed, **married** men 25–65; sample of 492	H: Annual hours of work Y: Asset income and benefit income W: Calculated hourly wage	Linear and semi-logarithmic convex (piecewise linear and differentiable); allows for benefits and taxation; uses calculated (actual) wage with no selection-correction	−0.25 to 0.21	0.04 to −0.1

(*cont.*)

Table 3C.4. (*cont.*)

Study	Data/Sample	Variables Used	Labour Supply Model	Uncomp. Wage Elasticity	Income Elasticity
Kaiser et al. (1992)	German Socioeconomic Panel 1983, **married,** non-retired; sample of 2,382 employed, 939 not	H: Annual hours of work Y: Rents, capital income, and transfer payments W: Calculated hourly wage	Convex and non-convex (piecewise linear)	Evaluated at means: −0.04	−0.28
MaCurdy, Green, & Paarsch (1990)	USA Panel Study of Income Dynamics 1975: sample size 1,017, all employed, **married** aged 25–55	H: Annual hours of work Y: Rent, interest, dividends, spouses income, etc. W: Calculated hourly wage	Linear labour supply; piecewise linear and differentiable budget set; non-convex portions 'convexified'; accounts for taxes and tax credits	Evaluated at means: −0.24–0.032	−0.01
Pencavel (2002)	USA Current Population Survey 1968–1999 **All** employed males Sample size not given	H: Annual hours of work Y: Current non-wage income (for standard uncomp. wage elasticity). W: Calculated hourly wage	Log-linear labour supply; linear budget constraint; no explicit treatment of tax and benefit system; actual wages; includes controls for demographic characteristics; same IV approach as Pencavel (1998), table A1	Labour Supply Function (A) White: −0.14 Black: −0.12 (B) White: 0.25 Black: 0.12 First Differenced (A) White: −0.02 Black: −0.17 (B) White: −0.18 Black: 0.10	

Note: H: Hours/Work measure used, W: Wage measure used, Y: Income measure used.

Table 3C.5. Male labour supply (participation elasticities)

Study	Data/Sample	Variables Used	Labour Supply Model	Uncomp. Wage Elasticity	Income Elasticity
Aaberge et al. (1999)	Italian Survey of Household Income and Wealth 1987 Families aged 20–70, self-employment income <20%	H: Not given W: Net wages Y: Other income	Family labour supply, not subject to unitary restrictions; non-linear labour supply; non-convex budget constraint; accounts for taxes and benefits; hours and supply constraints (demand / institutions); exogenous wages and unearned income	Mean: 0.046 10th income percentile 0.053 11th–89th percentiles 0.051 90th income percentile −0.01	−0.003 −0.01 −0.04 0.014

Note: H: Hours/Work measure used, W: Wage measure used, Y: Income measure used.

Table 3C.6. Intertemporal labour supply elasticities (male and female)

Study	Data / Sample	Variables Used	Labour Supply Model	Inter-temp (Frisch) Wage Elasticity
Ackum-Agell & Meghir (1995)	Swedish Engineering Employers Confederation Survey of Employment. 1970–87 **All men**	W: Calculated hourly wage H: Quarterly hours of work (including overtime) Y: Not observed	Log linear labour supply with first difference specification; life-cycle labour supply and within period; does not account for taxes or benefits	Evaluated at means: 0.14
Altonji (1986)	USA PSID 1968–81 **Married men** aged no less than 25 in 1968 or older than 60 in 1979	W: Hourly wage profile H: Annual hours of work Y: Assets instrumented by consumption	Double log Frisch labour supply function	Varies by estimation approach 0.00–0.35
Blundell, Meghir, & Neves (1993)	Pseudo-panel constructed from UK FES 1970–84 **Married women**	W: Hourly wage H: Weekly hours	Flexible specification of preferences allowing for corner solutions and uncertainty; fixed costs Marginal after tax wages	No children 0.58 With children 0.80–1.22
Domeij & Floden (2006)	USA PSID **male household heads** with sample based on 1984, 1989, and 1994	W: Hourly wage (calculated for salaried workers) H: Annual hours Y: Asset stocks (focus on total but suggests liquid may be more appropriate)	Borrowing Constraints; Log-linearization of the Euler Equation; includes specifications with separable and non-separable utility; does not account for taxes	Full sample 0.16 Low liquid assets 0.33–0.49 Low total assets 0.19–0.49 Exclude Borrowing Constrained 0.55
French (2004)	USA PSID and Validation data **Males, head of households** 1980–86	W: Hourly wage (as reported) and employer provided 'true hours' H: Annual hours—same as above	Log linear Frisch labour supply; does not account for taxes or benefits; wages exogenous; IV approach that controls for non-classical measurement error	Controlling for measurement error −0.03–0.16 (insignificant)

French (2005)	USA PSID between 1968 and 1997	W: Hourly wage H: Annual hours and participation Y: Asset profile	Accounts for key aspects of the US tax code and for private and state pension entitlements; wages selection corrected; considers tied wage/hours packages	Age 40: Standard model: 0.37 Wage/hours packages: 0.19 Age 60: Standard model: 1.33 Wage/hours packages: 1.04
Heckman & MaCurdy (1980, 1983)	USA PSID 1968–75 Continuously **married women** aged 30–65 White. 672	W: Hourly wage profile H: Annual hours and participation Y: Asset profile	Log-linear Frisch labour supply model allowing for corner solutions; Linear budget constraint; does not account for taxes or benefits	Evaluated at means: 1.8
Imai & Keane (2004)	USA NLSLME 1979–95 **White Men** aged 20+ with 6 years of continuous data, no periods of unemployment	W: Hourly wage H: Annual hours Y: Asset stock	Dynamic structural model with past hours of work affecting current wages through human capital accumulation. All persistence is attributed to state dependence	Evaluated at means: 3.82 Allowing for incentives through human capital accumulation Age range 20–60 0.8–3
Lee (2001)	USA PSID 1967–76 balanced **All men** 5,787 1967–90 unbalanced **All men** 29,405	W: Hourly wage (calculated for salaried workers) H: Annual hours	Log-linear labour supply, first differenced; correction for finite sample bias; actual wages; does not account for taxes or benefits	Evaluated at means: 0.50
MaCurdy (1981)	PSID prime age, white, **married men** 1967–76 Age 25–46 years in 1967	W: Average annual earnings H: Annual hours	Double log Frisch labour supply (CES utility function). IV on wage using family background, education, age, and time dummies	0.10–0.23
Pistaferri (2003)	Panel section of the Bank of Italy SHIW 1989–93 **Married men**, age 26–59	W: Hourly wage H: Weekly hours	Log-linearized Euler equation Uses after tax marginal wages Decomposes changes in wages to anticipated and unanticipated components based on subjective expectations	Intertemporal Frisch elasticity 0.70 Unanticipated wage change 0.51

Note: H: Hours/Work measure used, W: Wage measure used, Y: Income measure used. FES: UK Family Expenditure Survey, PSID: US Panel Study of Income Dynamics. NLSLME: US National Longitudinal Study of Labor Market Experience.

Table 3C.7. Taxable and total income elasticities

Author (Date)	Data (Years)	Tax Change	Sample	Controls for Income Distribution and Mean Reversion	Definition of Income	Elasticity Results
Lindsey (1987)	Repeated Tax Cross-Sections 1980–84	ERTA 81	AGI > $5k	None	Taxable income	1.05–2.75 Central: 1.6
Feldstein (1995)	NBER Tax Panel 1985 and 1988	TRA 86	Married, non-aged non-S corp Income > $30k	None	AGI Taxable income	0.75–1.3 1.1 ('lower income') to 3.05 ('higher income')
Navratil (1995)	NBER Tax Panel 1980 and 1983	ERTA 81	Married Income > $25k	Average income	Taxable income	0.8
Feldstein & Feenberg (1996)	IRS published data 1992 and 1993	OBRA 93	High income	None	Taxable income	1
Auten-Caroll (1997)	Treasury Tax Panel 1985 and 1989	TRA 86	Age 25–55, non-S corp. Income > $15k	Include log income in base year	Gross income Taxable income	0.57 0.57
Sammartino & Weiner (1997)	Treasury Tax Panel 1985 to 1994	OBRA 93	Age < 62	None	AGI	Zero long-run response
Goolsbee (2000)	Panel of Corp. Exec 1991 to 1994	OBRA 93	Corporate Execs 95% income > $150k	Average income	Wages, bonuses and stock options	Short run: 1 Long run: 0.1–0.33
Caroll (1998)	Treasury Tax Panel 1985 and 1989	OBRA 93	Married aged 25–55 Income > $50k	Average income	Taxable income	0.5
Goolsbee et al. (1999)	Tax Statistics (agg.) 1922–89	Various reforms	Income > $30k	None	Taxable income	−1.3 to 2 depending on the reform

Saez (1999)	NBER Tax Panel 1985 and 1988	Fiscal Drag	Married and singles	Include log income and polynomials of income	AGI Taxable Income	0.25 0.4
Moffitt & Wilhelm (2000)	SCF Panel 1983 and 1989	TRA 86	Oversampling of high incomes	Use various sets of instruments	AGI	2 Hours worked 0.2
Gruber & Saez (2000)	NBER Tax Panel 1979 to 1990	ERTA 81 and TRA 86	Same marital status in paired-years	Include log income, trend effects and a 10-piece spline	'Broad income' Taxable income	0.12 0.4 0.57 (high income) 0.18 (low income)
Sillamaa & Veall (2000)	Canadian Longitudinal Admin Survey 1986 to 1989	Canadian TRA 88	Federal Tax paid > $625 (Can) Aged 25–64 65+	Include log income in base year. Instrumental variables approach	Gross income Taxable income Employment income S/E income High-income GI	0.25 0.14 0.22 1.12 1.30
Saez (2003)	NBER Tax Panel 1978 to 1983	Fiscal Drag	Married and singles	Include log income and polynomials of income	AGI Taxable income Wage income	0.4 0.4 0
Kopczuk (2005)	University of Michigan Tax Panel 1979 to 1990	ERTA 81 and TRA 86	Same marital status in paid-years Other criteria	Include current income, non-linear controls for income	Taxable income	0.2–0.57
Eissa & Giertz (2006)	Treasury Tax Panel 1992–2003 and Execucomp 1992 to 2004	OBRA 93, TRA 97, EGTRRA	Executives of S&P 500 companies and top 1% of Tax Panel.	Includes current and future after-tax rates. No controls for mean reversion etc.	Earned income AGI 1993: long run (SR) 2001: long run (SR)	 0.19 (0.82) −0.7 (0.00)

Note: ERTA 81: Economic Recovery Tax Act (1981), TRA 86: Tax Reform Act (1986), OBRA 93: Omnibus Reconciliation Act (1993), TRA 97: Taxpayer Relief Act (1997), EGTRRA: Economic Growth and Tax Relief Reconciliation Act (2001). (A)GI: (Adjusted) Gross Income. NBER: National Bureau of Economic Research. IRS: Internal Revenue Service.

REFERENCES

Aaberge, R., Colombino, U., and Strom, S. (1999), 'Labour Supply in Italy: An Empirical Analysis of Joint Household Decisions, with Taxes and Quantity Constraints', *Journal of Applied Econometrics*, **14**, 403–22.

Ackum-Agell, S., and Meghir, C. (1995), 'Male Labour Supply in Sweden: Are Incentives Important?', *Swedish Economic Policy Review*, **2**, 391–418.

Adda, J., Dustmann, C., Meghir, C., and Robin, J-M. (2006), 'Career Progression and Formal versus On-the-Job Training', IZA working Paper.

Altonji, J. G. (1986), 'Intertemporal Substitution in Labour Supply: Evidence from Micro Data', *Journal of Political Economy*, **94**, S176–S215.

Arellano, M., and Meghir, C. (1992), 'Female Labour Supply and On-the-Job Search: An Empirical Model Estimated Using Complimentary Datasets', *Review of Economic Studies*, **59**, 537–59.

Arrufat, J. L., and Zabalza, A. (1986), 'Female Labour Supply with Taxation, Random Preferences and Optimization Errors', *Econometrica*, **54**, 47–63.

Ashenfelter, O., and Heckman, J. (1974), 'The Estimation of Income and Substitution Effects in a Model of Family Labor Supply', *Econometrica*, **42**, 73–85.

Auten, G., and Carroll, R. (1999), 'The Effect of Taxes on Household Income', *Review of Economics and Statistics*, **81**, 681–93.

Blomquist, S., and Hansson-Brusewitz, U. (1990), 'The Effect of Taxes and Male and Female Labor Supply in Sweden', *Journal of Human Resources*, **25**, 317–57.

—— and Newey, W. (2002), 'Nonparametric Estimation with Nonlinear Budget Constraints', *Econometrica*, **70**, 2455–80.

Blow, L., and Preston, I. (2002), 'Deadweight Loss and Taxation of Earned Income: Evidence from Tax Records of the UK Self Employed', Institute for Fiscal Studies Working Paper WP02/15.

Blundell, R., Chiappori, P., Magnac, T., and Meghir, C. (2007), 'Collective Labour Supply: Heterogeneity and Nonparticipation', *Review of Economic Studies*, **74**, 417–45.

—— —— and Meghir, C. (2005), 'Collective Labour Supply with Children', IFS Working Paper, WP02/08.

—— Duncan, A., and Meghir, C. (1992), 'Taxation in Empirical Labour Supply Models: Lone Mothers in the UK', *Economic Journal*, **102**, 265–78.

—— —— —— (1998), 'Estimating Labor Supply Responses Using Tax Reforms', *Econometrica*, **66**, 827–61.

—— Ham, J., and Meghir, C. (1987), 'Unemployment and Female Labour Supply', *Economic Journal*, **97**, supplement, 44–64.

—— and MaCurdy, T. (1999), 'Labor Supply: A Review of Alternative Approaches', in *Handbook of Labor Economics*, Ashenfelter and Card (eds), **3A**.

—— —— and Meghir, C. (2007), 'Labour Supply Models: Unobserved Heterogeneity, Nonparticipation and Dynamics', forthcoming, *Handbook of Econometrics*, Heckman and Leamer (eds).

—— Meghir, C., and Neves, P. (1993), 'Labour Supply and Intertemporal Substitution', *Journal of Econometrics*, **53**, 137–60.

—— —— Symons, E., and Walker, I. (1988), 'Labour Supply Specification and the Evaluation of Tax Reforms', *Journal of Public Economics*, **36**, 23–52.

—— Reed, H., and Stoker, T. (2003), 'Interpreting Aggregate Wage Growth: The Role of Labor Market Participation', *American Economic Review*, **93**, 1114–31.

—— and Walker, I. (1986), 'A Life Cycle Consistent Empirical Model of Family Labour Supply Using Cross Section Data', *Review of Economic Studies*, **53**, 539–58.

Bourguignon, F., and Magnac, T. (1990), 'Labor Supply and Taxation in France', *Journal of Human Resources*, **25**, 358–89.

Brewer, M., and Browne, J. (2006), 'The Effect of the Working Families' Tax Credit on Labour Market Participation', IFS Briefing Notes, No. 69.

—— Duncan, A., Shephard, A., and Suarez, M. (2005), 'Did Working Families' Tax Credit work? The final evaluation of the impact of in-work support on parents' labour supply and take-up behaviour in the UK', IFS report for HMRC.

Browning, M., Bourguignon, F., Chiappori, P.-A., and Lechene, V. (1996), 'Incomes and Outcomes: A Structural Model and Some Evidence from French Data', *Journal of Political Economy*, **102**, 1067–96.

Burtless, G., and Hausman, J. (1978), 'The Effect of Taxation on Labor Supply: Evaluating the Gary Negative Income Tax Experiment', *Journal of Political Economy*, **86**, 1103–30.

Chiappori, P.-A. (1988), 'Rational Household Labor Supply', *Econometrica*, **56**, 63–89.

—— (1992), 'Collective Labor Supply and Welfare', *Journal of Political Economy*, **100**, 437–67.

Cogan, J. (1981), 'Fixed Costs and Labor Supply', *Econometrica*, **49**, 945–63.

Devereux, P. J. (2004), 'Changes in Relative Wages and Family Labor Supply', *Journal of Human Resources*, **39**, 696–722.

Dickert, S., Houser, S., and Scholz, J. (1995), 'The Earned Income Tax Credit and Transfer Programs: A Study of Labor Market and Program Participation', in Poterba, J. (ed), *Tax Policy and the Economy*, NBER and MIT Press.

Domeij, D., and Floden, M. (2006), 'The Labor-Supply Elasticity and Borrowing Constraints: Why Estimates are Biased', *Review of Economic Dynamic*, **9**, 242–62.

Donni, O. (2003), 'Collective Household Labor Supply: Nonparticipation and Income Taxation', *Journal of Public Economics*, **87**, 1179–98.

—— (2007), 'Collective Female Labour Supply: Theory and Application', *Economic Journal*, **117**, 94–119.

Eckstein, Z., and Wolpin, K. (1989), 'Dynamic Labour Force Participation of Married Women and Endogenous Work Experience', *Review of Economic Studies*, **56** (3).

Eissa, N., and Giertz, S. (2006), 'Trends in High Incomes and Behavioural Responses to Taxation: Evidence from Executive Compensation and Statistics of Income Data', Congressional Budget Office Working Papers, No. 2006–14.

Eissa, N., and Liebman, J. (1996), 'Labor Supply Response to the Earned Income Tax Credit', *Quarterly Journal of Economics*, **111**, 605–37.

Ermisch, J., and Wright, R. (1991), 'Welfare Benefits and Lone Parents' Employment in Great Britain', *Journal of Human Resources*, **26**, 424–56.

Feldstein, M. (1995), 'The Effects of Marginal Tax Rates on Taxable Income: A Panel Study of the 1986 Tax Reform Act', *Journal of Political Economy*, **103**, 551–72.

—— (1999), 'Tax Avoidance and the Deadweight Loss of the Income Tax', *Review of Economics and Statistics*, **81** (4).

—— and Feenberg, D. (1995), 'The Effects of Increased Tax Rates on Taxable Income and Economic Efficiency: A Preliminary Analysis of the 1993 Tax Rate Increases', NBER Working Paper Series, No. W5370.

Flood, L., and MaCurdy, T. (1992), 'Work Disincentive Effects of Taxes: An Empirical Study of Swedish Men', Carnegie-Rochester Conference Series on Public Policy.

French, E. (2004), 'The Labor Supply Response to (Mismeasured but) Predictable Wage Changes', *Review of Economics and Statistics*, **86**, 602–13.

—— (2005), 'The Effects of Health, Wealth, and Wages on Labour Supply and Retirement Behaviour', *Review of Economic Studies*, 72, 395–427.

Goolsbee, A. (1999), 'Evidence on the High-Income Laffer Curve from Six Decades of Tax Reform', *Brookings Papers on Economic Activity*, **1999**, 1–64.

—— (2000), 'What Happens when you Tax the Rich? Evidence from Executive Compensation', *Journal of Political Economy*, **108**, 352–78.

Gorman, W. (1959), 'Separable Utility and Aggregation', *Econometrica*, **27**, 469–81.

Gruber, J., and Saez, E. (2000), 'The Elasticity of Taxable Income: Evidence and Implications', NBER Working Paper Series, No. 7512.

Hausman, J. (1981), 'Labour Supply: How Taxes affect Economic Behaviour', *Tax and Economy*, The Brookings Institution.

—— (1985), 'The Econometrics of Nonlinear Budget Sets', *Econometrica*, **53**, 1255–82.

Heckman, J. (1974), 'Effects of Childcare Programs on Women's Work Effort', *Journal of Political Economy*, **82**, S136–S163.

—— (1974a), 'Shadow Prices, Market Wages and Labor Supply', *Econometrica*, **42**, 679–94.

—— (1979), 'Sample Selection Bias as a Specification Error', *Econometrica*, **47**, 153–61.

—— and MaCurdy, T. (1980), 'A Lifecycle Model of Female Labor Supply', *Review of Economic Studies*, **47**, 47–74.

—— —— (1983), 'Corrigendum on A Life Cycle Model of Female Labour Supply', *Review of Economic Studies*, **49**, (Oct., 1982), 659–60.

Hill, S. (1982), 'Estimating the Relationship Between Unemployment Compensation and Duration of Unemployment: The Problem of Non-Filers', *Journal of Human Resources*, **17**, 460–70.

Hotz, V. J., Kydland, F. E., and Sedlacek, Guilherme, L. (1988), 'Intertemporal Preferences and Labor Supply', *Econometrica*, **56**, 335–60.

Imai, S., and Keane, M. (2004), 'Intertemporal Labor Supply and Human Capital Accumulation', *International Economic Review*, **45**, 601–41.

Jenkins, S. (1992), 'Lone Mothers' Employment and Full Time Work Probabilities', *Economic Journal*, **102**, 310–20.

Kaiser, H., Spahn, P., and van Essen, U. (1992), 'Income Taxation and the Supply of Labour in West Germany', *Jahrbücher für Nationalökonomie und Statistik*.

Keane, M., and Moffitt, R. (1998), 'A Structural Model Multiple Welfare Participation and Labor Supply', *International Economic Review*, **39**, 553–89.

—— and Wolpin, K. (1997), 'The Career Decisions of Young Men', *Journal of Political Economy*, **105**, 473–522.

Kopczuk, W. (2005), 'Tax Bases, Tax Rates and the Elasticity of Taxable Income', *Journal of Public Economics*, **89**, 2093–119.

Lee Chul-In (2001), 'Finite Sample Bias in IV Estimation of Intertemporal Labor Supply Models: Is the Intertemporal Substitution Elasticity Really Small?', *Review of Economics and Statistics*, **83**, 638–46.

Lindsey, L. (1987), 'Individual Taxpayer Response to Tax Cuts: 1982–1984, with Implications for the Revenue Maximizing Tax Rate', *Journal of Public Economics*, **33**, 173–206.

Lise, J., and Seitz, S. (2007), 'Consumption Inequality and Intra-household Allocations', IFS Working Papers, W09/07, Institute for Fiscal Studies.

MaCurdy, T. (1981), 'An Empirical Model of Labor Supply in a Life-Cycle Setting', *Journal of Political Economy*, **89**, 1059–85.

—— (1983), 'A Simple Scheme for Estimating an Intertemporal Model of Labor Supply and Consumption in the Presence of Taxes and Uncertainty', *International Economic Review*, **24**, 265–89.

—— Green, D., and Paarsch, H. (1990), 'Assessing Empirical Approaches for Analyzing Taxes and Labor Supply', *Journal of Human Resources*, **25**, 415–90.

Meade, J. (1978), *The Structure and Reform of Direct Taxation: Report of a Committee chaired by Professor J. E. Meade for the Institute for Fiscal Studies*, London: George Allen & Unwin. http://www.ifs.org.uk/publication/3433

Meyer, Bruce, Rosenbaum, D., and Dan, T. (2001), 'Welfare, the Earned Income Tax Credit, and the Labor Supply of Single Mothers', *Quarterly Journal of Economics*, **116**, 1063–114.

Moffit, R. (1984), 'The Estimation of a Joint Wage-Hours Labor Supply Model', *Journal of Labor Economics*, **2**, 550–66.

—— (1984), 'Profiles of Fertility, Labor Supply and Wages of Married Women: A Complete Life Cycle Model', *Review of Economic Studies*, **51**, 263–78.

—— and Wilhelm, M. (2000), 'Taxation and the Labor Supply Decisions of the Affluent' in Slemrod, J. (ed.), *Does Atlas Shrug? The Economic Consequences of Taxing the Rich*, Cambridge: Cambridge University Press.

Mroz, T. (1987), 'The Sensitivity of an Empirical Model of Married Women's Hours of Work to Economic and Statistical Assumptions', *Econometrica*, **55**, 765–99.

Navratil, J. (1995), 'The Economic Recovery Tax Act of 1981: Evidence on Individual Taxpayer Behavior from Panel Tax Return Data', Unpublished Harvard Thesis (see Gruber and Saez (2000) for discussion).

Nickell, S. (1979), 'The Effect of Unemployment and Related Benefits on the Duration of Unemployment', *Economic Journal*, **89**, 34–49.

O'Dea, C., Phillips, D., and Vink, A. (2007), 'A Survey of the UK Benefit System', Institute for Fiscal Studies.

Pencavel, J. (1998), 'The Market Work Behaviour and Wages of Women: 1975–94', *Journal of Human Resources*, **33**, 771–804.

—— (2002), 'A Cohort Analysis of the Association between Work Hours and Wages among Men', *Journal of Human Resources*, **37**, 251–74.

Pistaferri, L. (2003), 'Anticipated and Unanticipated Wage Changes, Wage Risk, and Intertemporal Labor Supply', *Journal of Labor Economics, 2003*, **21**, No. 3.

Saez, E. (1999), 'The Effect of Marginal Tax Rates on Income: A Panel Study of "Bracket Creep"', NBER Working Paper 7367.

—— (2003), 'The Effect of Marginal Tax Rates on Income: A Panel Study of "Bracket Creep"', *Journal of Public Economics*, **85**, 1231–58.

Sammartino, F., and Weiner, D. (1997), 'Recent Evidence on Taxpayers' Response to the Rate Increases in the 1990's', *National Tax Journal*, **50**, 683–705.

Sillamaa, M., and Veall, M. (2000), 'The Effect of Marginal Tax Rates on Taxable Income: A Panel Study of the 1988 Tax Flattening in Canada', QSEP Research Report, No. 354.

Thomas, D. (1990), 'Intra-Household Resource Allocation: An Inferential Approach', *Journal of Human Resources*, **25**, 635–64.

Triest, R. (1990), 'The Effect of Income Taxation on Labor Supply in the United States', *Journal of Human Resources*, **25** (Special Issue), 491–516.

Walker, I. (1990), 'The Effect of Income Support Measures on the Labour Market Behaviour of Lone Mothers', *Fiscal Studies*, **11**, 55–74.

Ziliak, J., and Kniesner, T. (1999), 'Estimating Life Cycle Labor Supply Tax Effects', *Journal of Political Economy*, **107**, 326–59.

4

Value Added Tax and Excises

*Ian Crawford, Michael Keen, and Stephen Smith**

Ian Crawford is a Reader in Economics at the University of Oxford, a Fellow of New College, and a Research Fellow at the IFS. His main areas of research are applied microeconomics, consumer theory, and index numbers. In the past he has written about taxation of alcohol, road transport, and domestic energy. Current interests include the analysis of habit formation and the tricky business of unobserved heterogeneity in microeconomic data.

Michael Keen is an Assistant Director of the Fiscal Affairs Department of the IMF, where he was until recently head of Tax Policy. Previously Professor of Economics at the University of Essex, he was President of the International Institute of Public Finance from 2003 to 2006, is currently a member of the Board of the National Tax Association, and has served various journals, including as an early editor of *Fiscal Studies*. He has published on a wide range of public finance issues and is a co-author of the book *The Modern VAT*.

Stephen Smith is Professor of Economics and Executive Dean of the Faculty of Social and Historical Sciences at UCL and a Research Fellow at the IFS. His research covers various topics in the economics of tax policy—especially VAT and excises—and environmental economics. Before joining UCL he worked at the Department of Trade and Industry (1977–85) and at the IFS (1985–97), where he was Deputy Director from 1990 to 1997. He has acted as a consultant to HM Treasury, DEFRA, the UK Environment Agency, the OECD, the European Commission, and the IMF.

* We are grateful to Richard Blundell and Stuart Adam for their editorial input and advice, to Mike Brewer and James Browne for their contribution to the reform simulation discussed in the chapter, to the commentators Richard Bird, Sijbren Cnossen, Ian Dickson, Jon Gruber, and David White, and to participants at the Mirrlees Review conferences in London and Cambridge for vigorous and constructive discussion of earlier drafts of the chapter. Views expressed here should not be attributed to the International Monetary Fund, its Executive Board, or its management. Expenditure and Food Survey data are collected by the Office for National Statistics and distributed by the Economic and Social Data Service.

EXECUTIVE SUMMARY

The thirty years since the Meade Report (Meade, 1978) have seen a remarkable shift in the balance of taxation in the UK towards the Value Added Tax (VAT), which now accounts for around one sixth of all tax revenue. Reliance on alcohol and tobacco excises, in contrast, has fallen. This chapter considers the strategic design issues that we believe should shape the future course of UK policy on VAT and these excises. Given the strength of EU restrictions on indirect tax policy, this also means, to some degree, considering their future in Europe more widely.

The chapter is in four parts. The first considers theoretical insights into the role and optimal structure of indirect taxes. The second focuses on the VAT, and the third on alcohol and tobacco excises. The fourth considers the increasingly important international issues bearing on the design and implementation of these taxes.

The appropriate balance between direct and indirect taxation—between income taxes and taxes on goods and services—is one of the oldest issues in public finance, but still imperfectly understood. It is clear, however, that the differences between the two types of tax are less sharp than once thought. In particular, the close equivalence between a uniform tax on consumption and a uniform tax on wage and profit income means that—as long as people take price levels properly into account—the two taxes should have broadly equivalent effects on the labour market. So shifting the balance of taxation towards VAT cannot be expected to have a great impact on work incentives or levels of employment. Indeed, the appropriate mix of direct and indirect taxes may be primarily a matter of administration and compliance. Running a broad-based consumption tax in parallel with taxes on income reduces the risk of revenue losses by spreading taxation across a number of sources, each of which is to some degree independently enforced.

Indirect taxes offer scope, not available with an income tax, for taxing different components of consumption at different rates. One group of reasons for taxing some goods more heavily is to deal with pollution (considered in Fullerton, Leicester, and Smith, Chapter 5) and other external costs. The external costs of alcohol and tobacco consumption are frequently seen as the principal economic justification for continuing to levy high excise duties on them, so policy needs to be informed by a clear appreciation of the nature and scale of these external costs. Nevertheless, conventional externalities may not be the only grounds for high taxation of tobacco and alcohol. Recent economic literature argues that people's lack of consistency and self-control may justify higher taxes than would be warranted if consumption choices were being made by wholly rational, well-informed consumers.

Whether the opportunity to charge different tax rates on different commodities should be exploited more generally depends on the range of other tax instruments available, and the characteristics of people's demands for those commodities. Lower tax rates on items such as childcare costs, travel costs to work and labour-saving food items (such as ready meals), and higher tax rates on items like leisure-time consumption and DIY inputs, could help to offset the disincentives to work created by the tax system. But it is far from clear how much differentiation would be justified on these grounds, or which commodities should be taxed more and less heavily. There are also plenty of practical obstacles to the complex pattern of tax rates that might be required, and these need to be weighed against any potential labour market gains.

One clear implication of this line of analysis, however, is that the case for using preferential rates of VAT to help the less well-off is weak: there are better redistributive instruments available to the UK government than fine-tuning rates of commodity taxation. The chapter shows that ending all current zero and reduced rates (except for housing and exports) while increasing all means-tested benefit and tax credit rates by 15% would leave the poorest 30% of the population better off, on average, and raise £11 billion that could be used to help them further or for some other purpose. The essence of this result is nothing new. Finding the political will to implement such a change needs to begin with a recognition of the fundamental unfairness—and wastefulness—of the existing rate structure.

Still new at the time of the Meade Report, the VAT systems of EU countries are now starting to look outdated by comparison with more recently designed systems, both in terms of the rate structure and in aspects of basic design. Two issues stand out:

First, are the widespread exemptions—for public agencies and health, education, medical services, and financial services, in particular—which break the chain of VAT paid on sales and reclaimed on purchases of inputs, creating inefficiencies of unknown magnitude. Recent international experience—including that of New Zealand—shows that many of these exemptions are unnecessary, and demonstrates the potential for a base-broadening reform of the VAT. The case for considering alternatives to exemption is especially clear in relation to financial services, though comprehensive solutions are difficult. One possibility meriting close attention is cash flow treatment of financial services—treating all cash inflows to providers of such services (including deposits) as reflecting VAT-able sales to customers and treating all cash outflows (including loans made) as purchases of inputs—but zero-rating financial transactions with registered businesses. While there are many practical issues that require further attention, movement to such a system would not only remove distortions but likely entail a substantial net revenue gain.

The second key structural issue is the VAT treatment of trade between EU member states. We argue that while the goal of a systematic destination principle VAT treatment of internationally traded goods and services remains desirable, the current mechanisms by which this is achieved need reconsideration. In particular, zero-rating of exported goods exposes the VAT system to significant risks of fraud and evasion—exploited by recent high-profile instances of 'carousel fraud', as well as by more mundane evasion. We argue that while the extent of these problems should not be over-stated, a reform of the VAT treatment of intra-EU trade, in which goods would be exported bearing VAT, would reduce the vulnerability of the VAT system to frauds and evasion surrounding international transactions.

4.1. INTRODUCTION

The Meade Report was confined to direct taxation: it was initially intended to review the whole tax system, but time constraints led the committee to exclude indirect taxes.[1] One reason for this prioritization, perhaps, was that the UK had then only recently implemented a major indirect tax reform, introducing a value added tax (VAT) to replace the 'purchase tax' (a single-stage sales tax) as a requirement of entry into the European Community. It may have seemed that there would be little appetite for further reforms to the UK's indirect tax system for some time to come. As it turned out, however, developments in indirect taxation, and particularly the rise of the VAT, have been amongst the most marked changes in the UK tax system since the publication of the Meade Report, and one of those most consistent with the central thrust of the Meade Report—its advocacy of expenditure taxation.

Indirect taxes evidently merit closer attention than the Meade Report was able to provide. Moreover, there have been significant developments in the area since, conceptually and practically:

- Theoretical developments since the Meade Report have considerably altered our understanding of the contribution that can and cannot be made by indirect taxes—both VAT and excises—to raising revenue and pursuing distributional and other social objectives.

[1] The only substantive discussion of indirect taxes is in the context of one of the more radical reform options, the ITVAT, under which existing income taxes would be transformed into a tax on expenditure using a VAT-type mechanism.

- Having been in place for some thirty-five years the UK VAT, like that of many EU members, is now beginning to show its age, and a fundamental review, in the light of experience with more modern VATs, is overdue.
- The elimination of internal frontiers in the EU has brought new and challenging issues of administration, enforcement, and tax competition in relation to the VAT and excises, undreamt of thirty years ago and as yet still unresolved.
- Indirect tax policy in the UK is more explicitly constrained by international agreements than is any other area of tax policy (with the sole exception of tariff design). To a large degree, assessing indirect tax policy in the UK requires assessing it in the EU more widely, a key question being whether EU constraints have been a help or a hindrance.
- Recent developments—notably the growth of trade in international services and e-commerce, and high profile VAT fraud—have raised challenges that question basic design features of the VAT, to a degree that causes some to doubt its future.

The focus of this chapter, for the most part, is on the strategic design issues that we expect and/or hope will shape the development of indirect tax policy in the UK, and the EU, in the coming years.

The chapter is in four main parts. The first considers economic theory and empirical evidence on the optimal structure of commodity taxes.[2] What, in particular, do taxes on goods and services contribute to an efficient tax structure that cannot be achieved equally or more efficiently by other available tax instruments? We then consider in turn the two principal categories of indirect tax in the UK: the VAT, applied to a considerable proportion of spending, and the excise duties levied at high rates on a limited number of goods. We compare the strengths and weaknesses of the VAT with alternative broad-based taxes on goods and services, in particular the single-stage retail sales taxes common in the US, and discuss issues concerning VAT rates, base, the treatment of small firms, financial services, and compliance. Turning to the excises we discuss externality arguments for levying high excise duties on alcohol and tobacco (those on fuel being considered in a separate chapter), and issues concerning the choice of tax base. The fourth main part outlines

[2] One key issue not addressed here is the incidence of these taxes. This is only partly for brevity, there also being little hard evidence to draw on (especially for broad-based commodity taxes). It is simply assumed that the incidence is fully on consumers, which such evidence as there is suggests is not unreasonable, at least for the longer run. (See, for example, Carbonnier (2007) and the references therein.)

and assesses international issues in indirect taxation. Conclusions are drawn in Section 4.6.

4.2. THE ROLE AND DESIGN OF INDIRECT TAXES

The years since the Meade Report have seen a significant change in the pattern of indirect taxation in the UK. Over the period as a whole, reliance on indirect taxes has increased only moderately, from around 23% of total tax revenue (including National Insurance) in 1978–79 to about 25% in 2007–08.[3] There has, however, been a marked change in the way in which this revenue is raised, with a substantial increase in reliance on the VAT (from about 9 to 16% of total tax revenue[4]) and a reduction in that on the excises on alcohol and tobacco (each falling from around 4% of the total to about 1.5%).[5] These developments have not occurred evenly or even monotonically over this period. The rise of the VAT began with the dramatic first budget of the Thatcher government in 1979, which raised the standard rate of VAT from 8 to 15% (while reducing income tax rates sharply), and continued with the increase in the standard rate of VAT to 17.5%—its level at the time of writing[6]—in 1991.[7] Since the early 1990s, when it reached more than 18%, the share of the VAT in total tax revenue has actually decreased. Most of the reduced reliance on excises also dates from around then (though receipts from those on alcohol and tobacco have declined throughout the period), so that the overall share of indirect taxes has also fallen since the early 1990s by about 5 percentage points. The shift towards indirect taxation has thus, to a large extent, come and gone, leaving the compositional change—the shift from excises to VAT—as the most striking structural development.[8]

[3] Revenue statistics in this paragraph come from HM Treasury: see <http://www.ifs.org.uk/ff/revenue_composition.xls>.

[4] HMRC reports VAT revenues net of refunds paid to various public bodies but includes those amounts refunded in total tax revenue, so that the implied VAT shares need to be interpreted with caution.

[5] For the period as a whole, revenue from fuel excises and other indirect taxes (such as the former car tax and more recent climate change levy) have both been broadly unchanged, at something under 5% and 2% respectively.

[6] This chapter was finalized before the temporary reduction in the standard rate of VAT, until the end of 2009, from 17.5 to 15%.

[7] A reduced rate of 8%, mainly for domestic energy use but subsequently extended to other items, was introduced in 1994, and reduced to 5% in 1997.

[8] The OECD *Revenue Statistics*, which include in VAT revenue amounts refunded to public bodies, do not show the same peak in VAT revenues as do the HMRC figures used here. They do, however, also show a peak in reliance on indirect taxes in the early 1990s.

These developments highlight two key questions for tax policy: what is the appropriate balance between direct and indirect taxation, and what is the best structure of indirect taxes?

4.2.1. Equivalences and the balance between direct and indirect taxation

The appropriate mix between direct and indirect taxes is one of the oldest issues in public finance: it was a key issue, for example, in mid-Victorian politics, when the future—indeed survival—of the income tax remained in doubt.[9] More recent and formal theory has brought relatively few additional insights. The most important, perhaps, is a recognition that, in principle at least, the balance is to some degree arbitrary, there being a close similarity in terms of their impact on individuals' budget constraints—and hence, in the absence of some form of fiscal illusion, on their behaviour—between a uniform tax on consumption and a uniform tax on wage and profit income. This is immediately clear for a consumer who lives only one period and receives income only from these sources: for them, a tax of 20% on all the income they receive is equivalent to a 25% tax on everything they spend.[10] In such a world, the balance between commodity and wage taxation would be immaterial.

For a consumer who lives for several periods, consumption over the lifetime (and any bequest given at the end of it) has to be financed from the initial stock of savings, wage earnings, and receipts of profit and transfer income. The equivalence is then somewhat more subtle: a uniform consumption tax, levied at an unchanging rate over time,[11] is equivalent to a proportional tax on wage, transfer, and profit income, also at an unchanging rate, combined with a tax on initial assets and subsidy to bequests at the same rate.

Such equivalences point to the potential fallacy, for example, in arguing that relatively heavy reliance on commodity rather than wage taxation (whether through the personal income tax or social security contributions)

[9] See, for example, Matthew (1979), who notes that in his famous comparison of direct and indirect taxes to 'two attractive sisters' to both of whom he felt it allowable to pay his addresses, Gladstone carefully did not in fact say he felt obliged to pay them equal attention.

[10] The only reason these numbers differ is that income tax rates are conventionally described in tax-inclusive form (including the tax itself in the base) and VAT rates in tax-exclusive form (excluding it).

[11] If its rate is expected to change over time (to increase, say), then a uniform consumption tax affects (reduces) the return on savings and so is in part equivalent to a (positive) tax on capital income.

is 'good for employment': absent other sources and uses of funds, such a shift has no real impact on labour supply. Other distortions may mean that there is some effect on labour market equilibrium: with a binding minimum for the wage before tax and employee's social contributions, for example, a reduction in the employer's social contribution may reduce gross wage costs and so increase employment. But dealing with such distortions is a matter more for labour market than tax policy. Absent such considerations, such a shift has effects only through its impacts on the real value of other sources and uses of funds. Labour market outcomes may be affected, for instance, if such a shift somehow moves the real burden of taxation to those out of the labour market, for example by reducing the real value of unemployment benefit. In practice, however, this can be hard to do: pressures to raise benefit levels in the face of commodity tax increases, for example, can be hard to resist. Most simulations find that the likely employment effects of such tax shifts are relatively minor: see, for example, the recent analysis of such proposals for France in Besson (2007). There is some evidence, however, that relatively heavy reliance on commodity rather than income taxation has been associated with faster growth (Kneller, Bleaney, and Gemmell (1999)).

These equivalences also imply that the choice across alternative tax mixes can be driven largely by considerations of administration and compliance. And these can plausibly point towards the simultaneous deployment of taxes that would be entirely equivalent if their enforcement were costless, as a means of diversifying enforcement risk. It may be optimal, for example, to deploy both a sales tax and a uniform wage tax levied by withholding: withholding is likely to be a good way of capturing a large part of taxpayers' wage income before they receive it, but perhaps relatively ineffective in reaching the self-employed; sales taxation may be a good way to capture a large part of taxpayers' incomes, including that of the hard-to-reach self-employed, when they spend it. This point is stressed by Boadway, Marchand, and Pestieau (1994), who show that when some income escapes tax it may be helpful to deploy a uniform commodity tax even when there would be no other reason to do so. (Such practical considerations also have implications for the form in which indirect taxes should be levied, notably for the relative merits of the VAT and retail sales taxes, to which we return later.)

Beyond these fairly general observations, the appropriate balance between direct and indirect taxation has received relatively little formal attention. Slemrod and Yitzhaki (1996) provide a conceptual framework for determining the appropriate tax mix when enforcement is imperfect, requiring that the marginal social cost incurred by raising an additional £1 by some tax instrument, defined to include both administration and compliance costs as well as those from the implied distortion of economic activity, be the same for all such instruments. But it remains unclear, in practice, whether the balance currently struck in the UK is in any sense broadly appropriate.

4.2.2. The structure of indirect taxes

There are broadly two aspects of this issue: the way in which commodities (by which we mean both goods and services) should be taxed, and the rates at which they should be taxed.

How should commodities be taxed?

The starting point is the Diamond–Mirrlees (1971) production efficiency theorem: in the absence of externalities and non-competitive behaviour, and in the absence of restrictions on the distorting tax instruments that can be deployed or the ability to levy firm-specific taxes on pure profits,[12] a necessary feature of an optimal tax system—in the strong (Pareto) sense that if this were not the case then one could find a tax reform from which everyone would benefit—is that production decisions are left undistorted. Put simply, business transactions should not be taxed. The intuition is simply that any distortion of production decisions reduces aggregate output, which cannot be wise so long as there is some useful purpose to which that output could be put.

Strictly, these conditions are unlikely to be met in practice. Externalities are the most obvious (and conceptually easiest) source of failure: commodities generating external effects should on this account be taxed at the same rate whether used as intermediate goods or as final consumption (the damage done by CO_2 emissions being the same, for instance, whether fuelling industry or private travel). The other requirements of the Diamond–Mirrlees theorem are also inherently implausible as descriptions of reality, but—with this one exception—the precise consequences of their failure appear to be sufficiently circumstance-specific, and the political risks from allowing special treatment sufficiently troubling, for production efficiency to remain the best guiding principle for practical tax design.

[12] Pareto efficiency from a worldwide perspective may also involve production inefficiency in the allocation of resources across countries if there are constraints on the effective ability to make international lump sum transfers (Keen and Wildasin (2004)). But this generally calls for the use of trade taxes and so does not bear directly on the domestic indirect tax design on which we focus here.

The requirement of production efficiency proves to be a powerful one. As will be seen, it is both a key reason for the use of the VAT (or, equivalently—in principle—a retail sales tax) in preference to taxes that impact intermediate goods transactions, and also has strong implications for the improvement of the VAT both in the UK and in the EU more generally.

What structure for commodity tax rates?

Turning to the second aspect, the key theoretical question—given the equivalences noted above between a uniform proportionate tax on all elements on final consumption and the combination of a proportionate tax on wage income and other items—is that of whether it is desirable to tax some goods or services more heavily than others.[13]

The optimal design of such commodity tax structures has received substantial attention, from Ramsey (1927) on. One key insight—from the results of Besley and Jewitt (1990), Deaton and Stern (1986), and Atkinson and Stiglitz (1976)—is that the case for such rate differentiation is weaker the greater is the government's ability to pursue its distributional objectives by other means, including, but not only, by taxing (or subsidizing) income.[14] The central point here is that differential commodity taxation is a very blunt instrument for the pursuit of equity objectives, with the zero-rating of food and children's clothing in the UK being a classic example.

Take food, for example. It is, indeed, the case that the less well-off spend a higher *proportion* of their income on food than do the better off. But this is not in itself a good reason—even on distributional grounds, leaving the need to raise revenue aside—for subjecting it to a differentially low rate of tax. This is for two reasons.

First, looking only at a snapshot of spending and income patterns in the population at any moment may be misleading given the variability of income

[13] Here we confine our discussion to linear commodity taxes of the type that characterize the UK VAT and excises: charges that are simply proportional to purchases. It is possible to envisage more complex non-linear tax structures, as in Mirrlees (1978). Commodity taxes might, for example, vary more or less than proportionately with the quantity consumed. While this may be feasible in some cases—some countries levy non-linear charges on domestic electricity use, for instance—the possibilities of resale or splitting purchases commonly rule it out. Alternatively the tax paid might in principle depend on the history of consumption, or such characteristics as age: this could in principle be helpful in dealing with addiction problems that can arise with alcohol and tobacco (indeed regulatory restrictions on under-age drinking, for example, effectively implement an infinite tax rate).

[14] More precisely, these results imply that the preference restrictions under which commodity taxation is unnecessary become weaker the more flexible is the instrument by which wage income can be taxed.

over a lifetime: those with low incomes now may be the young or elderly who will be, or have been, amongst the high income groups at other times. Put differently, a commodity tax looks regressive when assessed relative to current incomes in part because those with high incomes tend to have high savings, and so appear to escape the tax—but they will face it when they come to spend those savings. One way to address these issues is to relate food spending not to income in any period but to total spending, since the latter may be a better reflection of households' perceptions of their own long-run spending ability. Doing so, as Kay and Davis (1985) show for items zero-rated in the UK—and as subsequent studies have shown for a range of taxes on particular commodities[15]—tends greatly to dampen the apparent distributional case for tailoring commodity taxation to consumption patterns.

The second reason—perhaps potentially more persuasive to non-economists—is that even if the better off spend a smaller *proportion* of their current income on such items as food than do the less well-off, they are unlikely to spend a smaller *absolute* amount on them. If there were no other way of transferring resources to the poorest, setting a low tax rate on these items might be sensible policy. But it is unlikely to be so when, as in the UK, there are a range of other instruments—not only the income tax, but tax credits and benefits—that could be targeted more directly upon them. Kay and Davis (1985) and Hemming and Kay (1981) provided early illustrations of this point for the UK, the latter showing, for example, that the distributional impact of eliminating zero-rating could be very largely offset by cutting the standard rate of income tax and increasing the tax threshold. We revisit this simple but crucial insight, using more recent data, in Section 4.3.2—and show that it has lost no force over the years.

With sufficiently rich possibilities for income-related payments, the potential case for differential commodity taxation thus rests primarily on efficiency considerations. This is often taken to mean that tax rates should be especially high on commodities with especially low own-price elasticities of demand (meaning that demand for them is relatively insensitive to their price), the intuition behind this 'inverse-elasticity rule' being that in such cases a relatively high tax rate does little to reduce demand, and so causes little distortion of behaviour, while providing a robust revenue source. This prescription can prove dangerously misleading, however. One evident limitation is that it ignores the effect that increasing the tax on one commodity may have on the

[15] See Poterba (1989) on alcohol and tobacco, and Hassett, Mathur, and Metcalf (2007) for a recent analysis of petrol/fuel taxes.

demands for—and hence distortions associated with, and revenue collected from—other commodities. Unless all cross-price elasticities are zero (so that the demand for each commodity is unaffected by the price of any other), it is quite possible that increasing the tax on some good with a low price elasticity, while increasing revenue from that item, may actually reduce total tax revenue and/or lead to more distortion rather than less. And tempting though it may be to ignore cross-price elasticities, doing so evidently becomes inherently less plausible at degrees of disaggregation over commodities sufficiently fine to make tax differentiation meaningful. A tax on beer, for instance, may have little effect on the generality of spending on other commodities but quite powerful effects on the demand for spirits, wine, or tobacco.

There is an even deeper sense, however, in which the inverse-elasticity rule is misleading. For the fundamental determinant of the case for a differentially high tax on some commodity is the way in which taxing it affects market labour supply. As a general principle, commodity taxes should be heaviest—all else equal—on those items that are most complementary with (or least substitutable for) leisure (by which is meant time not spent in the formal labour markets).[16] Thus season tickets to watch football games should be taxed more heavily, for example, than season tickets to commute to work. Intuitively, taxing either particular commodities or income in general unavoidably discourages labour supply—recall the similarity between a uniform commodity tax and a tax on wage income noted earlier—and the only useful purpose that taxing different commodities can serve is in mitigating this distortion by making leisure less attractive than it otherwise would be: which means taxing most heavily those goods whose consumption tends to be associated with that of leisure. Conversely, if all commodities are equally complementary with leisure—a condition referred to as 'weak separability'—then all should be taxed at the same (proportionate) rate. This result, due to Atkinson and Stiglitz (1976), is a central insight from the modern theory of indirect taxation.[17] The inverse-elasticity rule is simply a special case

[16] The relevant sense of 'complementarity' differs according to the capacity of the government to tax wage income: see for instance Atkinson and Stiglitz (1980). The situation in mind here, as seems most relevant in the UK, is that in which there are no restrictions on the shape of the tax schedule applied to such income.

[17] Atkinson and Stiglitz (1976) derive the optimality of uniform—or, equivalently (since such a tax can be absorbed in the wage tax), no—commodity taxation for an atemporal world in which all individuals have the same preferences and an optimal, potentially non-linear wage tax is deployed. Kaplow (2006) and Laroque (2005) show that the conclusion continues to apply even if the wage tax is not optimal, while Boadway and Pestieau (2003) consider its robustness to various forms of heterogeneity. In a genuinely dynamic context, with earnings evolving stochastically and the possibility of conditioning tax payments on all observable actions, Golosov, Kocherlakota, and Tsyvinski (2003) show that weak separability continues to imply the optimality of uniform taxation.

of these more general observations, applicable in the further special case in which wage income is in itself untaxed (and, even more interesting, all individuals are the same): if, for example, an increase in the price of some good had little effect on the demand for it, and none on demand for other commodities, then taxing it more heavily would mean an increase in total expenditure that could only be paid for by working harder—and so that good must in a broad sense be a complement with leisure. But it is the link with labour supply, not the own-price elasticity, that is the fundamental concern.

Further perspectives on the structure of optimal commodity tax structures are provided by recent contributions which have stressed that what is regarded simply as 'leisure' in the standard optimal tax framework described above—time not spent in paid work—may also be put to productive use in household production. In such settings, Kleven, Richter, and Sørensen (2000) and Piggott and Whalley (2001) show, a case emerges for relatively low taxation of commodities that are close substitutes for such self-supply—which generally means such services as home improvement and repair—as a means of mitigating the unavoidable discouragement of market labour. If hiring a gardener is cheap, people might work overtime instead of mowing the lawn themselves. Thus Piggott and Whalley (2001), for example, report calculations suggesting that extension of the Canadian VAT to include such services may have been welfare-reducing. In somewhat similar spirit, a series of papers[18] consider tax design when consuming commodities takes time (such as doing the laundry, or watching a DVD). Boadway and Gahvari (2006) show that it may then be optimal to tax less heavily those commodities for which time spent in consumption is pleasurable (being more like leisure in the everyday sense of relaxing) and tax more heavily those for which it is not (being more like work); and amongst the latter, those that require a lot of time to consume should be taxed more heavily than those that do not (again pointing to relatively light taxation of services that can readily be replicated at home). Thus DVDs should be taxed less heavily than ironing boards, which (since ironing is not only dull but time consuming) should be taxed more heavily than dishwashers (dull to fill, but quick to use). Intuitively, such a structure serves the same broad purpose of counteracting tax-induced disincentives to undertaking paid work, while also recognizing that it is better that any given amount of time not spent in paid work be passed doing pleasant

Though by no means of universal applicability, the result has thus survived as a benchmark for thinking on the uniformity issue.

[18] Christiansen (1984) considers the issue briefly, Gahvari and Yang (1993) and Kleven (2004) do so in detail.

rather than unpleasant things (it making no direct difference for tax revenue, in particular, how that time is spent).

These models, it should be noted, are perfectly consistent with the standard framework described above, which simply takes the enjoyment of time not in paid work and the consumption of marketed commodities to be the objects of choice: one can conceive of individuals as having already decided how to use their time not in paid work before applying that framework. What these models do is add detail—relating for instance to the time intensity of consumption—on the relationship between time spent outside paid work and the household's final well-being, and show how that detail is reflected in the structure of commodity demands and labour supply, and hence in optimal tax rates. Quite how informative for policy design a focus on this additional structure will prove remains to be seen: we know relatively little, for instance, on whether time spent consuming particular goods is enjoyable or not (shopping is a pleasure for some, a chore for others), and, as stressed by Gahvari (2007), these approaches do not obviate the need to know price elasticities in order to calculate optimal tax rates. The important point for present purposes, however, is that the principles of optimal tax design set out above continue to apply. In particular, weak separability between market consumption goods and time in paid work remains sufficient—given the atemporal context and other ancillary assumptions—for uniform commodity taxation to be optimal.

Is it then the case that preferences do, in practice, appear to be weakly separable? The only detailed study of this key issue of which we are aware is that of Browning and Meghir (1991), who are able to reject weak separability with great confidence. Revisiting this issue with more recent UK data (Crawford, Keen, and Smith (2008)), we have arrived at the same conclusion. This finding needs to be interpreted with caution. It is possible, for instance, that commodity demands are linked with hours worked in the data not because of properties of tastes but as reflections of intertemporal considerations that are not modelled within the estimation framework used. Nevertheless, there emerges no clear presumption that one can simply tax all commodities at the same rate—and, by the same token, some presumption that well-designed commodity taxes have—in principle—some role to play.

The question then arises as to precisely what form such rate differentiation should take. Table 4.1 reports estimates from Crawford, Keen, and Smith (2008) of the complementarity of commodity demands with leisure for twenty broad groups of spending by UK households. Commodities found to be complements with leisure (in the sense of time not in paid work)—and so candidates for relatively heavy taxation or, more precisely,

Table 4.1. Estimates of commodity demand complementarities with leisure (Crawford, Keen, and Smith (2008))

	Impact on budget percentage share of an additional hour worked (t statistics in brackets)	
Bread and cereals	−0.024	(64.3)
Meat and fish	−0.060	(−49.2)
Dairy products	−0.045	(−66.6)
Tea and coffee	−0.008	(−29.5)
Fruit and vegetables	−0.037	(−52.8)
Other zero-rated foods	−0.020	(−28.1)
Standard-rated foods	−0.027	(−40.0)
Food eaten out	0.054	(38.5)
Beer	0.020	(13.3)
Wine and spirits	0.020	(21.2)
Tobacco	−0.026	(−16.6)
Domestic fuels	−0.049	(−30.6)
Household goods and services	0.064	(24.2)
Adult clothing	0.000	(−0.0)
Childrens' clothing	−0.006	(−8.7)
Petrol and diesel	0.046	(35.9)
Public transport	−0.006	(−6.2)
Leisure goods	0.019	(9.4)
Books and newspapers	−0.001	(−2.0)
Leisure services	0.086	(28.1)

Note: Results from demand system estimates reported by Crawford, Keen, and Smith (2008), based on household micro-data from 22 years of the UK Family Expenditure Survey (1978–99). The table shows the impact of an additional hour worked on the budget (percentage) share of each commodity group in household spending. Thus, for example, an additional hour worked reduces the (average) percentage of households' spending devoted to bread and cereals by 0.024 points. Commodities for which the coefficient is negative are leisure complements, and those for which the coefficient is positive are leisure substitutes. All coefficients except that on adult clothing are significantly different from zero, implying that weak separability is firmly rejected.

whose consumption should be most strongly discouraged by the indirect tax system—include most foodstuffs, domestic fuels, tobacco, children's clothing, and, perhaps surprisingly, public transport. This list includes some commodities which we might also wish to tax more heavily on externality grounds, but here we are considering only the implications of non-separability with labour supply. Complements with work, on the other hand—commodities whose consumption should be less discouraged by taxation—include alcoholic drink, food eaten out of the home, motor fuels, and leisure items (the last of these perhaps reflecting the use of such goods as substitutes for time in producing relaxation, in line with household production considerations discussed above). Again, the list of commodities includes some associated with pollution and other externalities, which might have implications for tax rates tempering those arising from the issues of preference structure addressed here.

What this implies for the level and even sign of the various tax rates themselves is less clear-cut, however, since that depends not only on the sign but also on the magnitude of demand responses, and, moreover, also depends on patterns of cross-price effects. In Crawford, Keen, and Smith (2008) we demonstrate the significance of this observation; the pattern of relative tax rates that should be applied to different groups of goods differs quite markedly from the pattern of complementarity and substitutability shown by the estimated coefficients on hours worked in the commodity demand equations. For example, while domestic energy appears as a leisure complement—according perhaps with the intuition that those working less will spend more time at home and incur higher costs of heating and lighting—it appears to be a commodity that, on efficiency grounds, should actually be taxed less than others, once the cross-price effects are taken into account. Likewise, the estimated coefficients on the broad categories of 'leisure goods' and 'household goods and services' are both positive, indicating that both are leisure substitutes, but taking account of cross-price effects suggests that we would want to tax the former more heavily than other goods and services, and the latter at lower rates. This work is still some way from being able to provide a definitive answer to the question of the pattern of optimal commodity tax rates for the UK. Nevertheless, the significant role played by the pattern of cross-price effects does serve to stress that conventional wisdom and crude intuition can be unreliable guides in thinking about indirect tax design.

It is unclear, however, whether the social gain from moving to an optimally differentiated rate structure would be large. Since the effects on commodity demands of hours worked reported by Crawford, Keen, and Smith (2008) are small, there is reason to suppose that—even assuming we knew the optimal structure—it would not be. And that is important because against any such benefits must be set the evident practical costs of implementing differential rate structures. Applying the very large number of distinct rates to which theory might point would require ensuring, for instance, that commodities are not to an unacceptable degree misrepresented as liable to a lower rate than intended. Issues thus arise concerning the number of distinct rates to apply, and which commodities to combine for identical tax treatment.[19] Further and distinct practical difficulties arise under the VAT, since multiple rates

[19] The optimal partitioning of commodities into a fixed number of rate categories is analysed by Gordon (1989).

increase the reporting burden on traders (there being evidence that this effect is substantial)[20] and, even if honestly applied in themselves, multiple rates exacerbate control problems by increasing the likelihood that some traders (producing lightly taxed outputs from highly taxed inputs) will be entitled to refunds, an aspect of VAT implementation that all tax administrations have difficulty with (see, for instance, Harrison and Krelove (2005)). This is especially likely to be the case when—as with domestic zero-rating in the UK—the reduced rate is applied largely to final products. And in a wider context the potential effectiveness, in terms of both targeting and ease of implementation, of alternative spending measures would need to be weighed against any case for rate differentiation: if child care is a strong substitute for leisure, for instance, application of a reduced VAT rate may be inferior to public support for provision.

4.3. THE VALUE ADDED TAX

The rise of the VAT has been one of the central developments in UK tax policy since the Meade Report. This chapter reviews key aspects of the design of the VAT and associated implementation issues. As background, Box 4.1 provides a quick primer on the main features of the VAT, and distinctive terminology.

Box 4.1. A VAT Primer

Value added tax (VAT) is levied on the sale of goods and services by registered businesses (those with annual turnover above some threshold level—the choice of which is discussed in Section 4.3.2—or who choose to register voluntarily). It applies to all sales, whether to private consumers or other businesses (in contrast to the retail sales taxes levied in the US, for example, which aim to tax sales to final consumers only).

Under the 'invoice-credit' form of the VAT—and all national level VATs are of this form, except that in Japan[21]—registered businesses offset the VAT they

(cont.)

[20] Cnossen (2003) reports that firms in the UK subject to more than one output VAT rate have more than twice the compliance costs of those subject only to one.

[21] The VAT in Japan retains elements of being levied on a 'subtraction basis': that is, on the book difference between total sales inputs. There also exist a number of subnational VATs levied on other than an invoice-credit basis. The Italian IRAP (*imposta regionala sulle attività produttive*), for instance, is an origin-based (no remission for exports, or taxation of imports) subtraction method VAT, while both Michigan and New Jersey have implemented what are essentially VATs levied on origin additions basis (that is, applied to the sum of wages and profits). Bird (2000) makes a general case for such taxes as a suitable source of subnational revenue, an issue not considered here.

Box 4.1. (*cont.*)

have been charged on their purchases ('input VAT') against the liability ('output VAT') on their sales, remitting only the net amount due. The result, if this chain of output tax and input credit remains unbroken, is that no net revenue is collected from the taxation of intermediate goods sales (business-to-business or 'B2B' sales), so that the ultimate base of the tax is final consumption (in the sense, more precisely, of sales other than to registered businesses).

For example, consider a simple chain of production consisting of two firms. Firm F makes sales of £30,000 to final consumers and no B2B sales. In the course of production, it uses inputs purchased from Firm Y at a cost of £10,000 plus VAT. Firm Y makes no sales to consumers and uses no taxed inputs; its entire £10,000 output is sold to firm F.

If the sales of both firms are subject to VAT at the (tax-exclusive) rate of 17.5% Firm Y will be liable for £1,750 (= 17.5% of £10,000) in VAT on its sales to F. Firm F will be liable for output VAT of £5,250 (= 17.5% of £30,000) on its sales of £30,000, but can offset against this the £1,750 tax paid on its own purchases, giving a net VAT liability of £3,500. Total VAT remitted by the two firms taken together is £1,750 + £3,500 = £5,250, which is equivalent to 17.5% of the (tax-exclusive) value of the sales made to final consumers.

'Zero-rating' means that the seller charges a VAT rate of zero on its sales but is still entitled to credit for the input VAT paid, so that no VAT remains: the Australian term 'VAT-free' is perhaps more descriptive. So long as some input VAT has been paid, the business will on this account be due a refund.

For example, if the sales of Firm F in the above example are zero-rated while Firm Y's remain standard rated, Firm F would charge no VAT on its sales and would be due a refund of the £1,750 VAT paid on its purchased inputs. Total VAT collected is zero.

The universal practice is to zero-rate exports and fully subject all imports to the VAT. This is as a way—though, as discussed later, not the only one—of ensuring that the VAT applies only to domestic consumption, consistent with the 'destination principle' discussed, and contrasted with the origin principle (of taxation by place of production), in Section 4.5.1. Quite where the place of consumption is, however—and so what 'export' and 'import' mean—is generally fairly clear-cut for goods. But it is much less so for services, so that 'place of supply' rules, determining where tax should be charged, are especially problematic in that context: this issue is discussed in Section 4.5.3.

'Exemption' means that sales are not subject to VAT but, in contrast to zero-rating, the firm does not have the right to reclaim the VAT paid on its inputs: the Australian term 'input-taxed' is more telling. The input VAT thus 'sticks', and the VAT acquires elements of a tax on production rather than consumption.

If Firm F in the example is selling VAT-exempt goods, it would charge no VAT on its sales but would not be able to reclaim the £1,750 VAT paid on the inputs purchased from Firm Y. Firm F's sales would thus indirectly bear some VAT, in the form of the VAT charged earlier on the inputs purchased from Firm Y. Revenue is lower than it would be if F were taxed, by the amount of the tax due on its own value added.

If instead it is Firm Y, selling the intermediate good, that is exempt, there is no effect on total revenue: Firm Y itself then charges no output VAT (and by assumption, pays no input VAT either) so that F simply has no input VAT to credit against its output VAT of £5,250. This is the self-correcting feature of the VAT noted in the text. Revenue would be affected, however, if Firm Y had paid some tax on its inputs: exemption means it would not be able to recover that VAT, and since the output VAT charged by Firm F would be unchanged—or, if anything, increased, as Y increases the price it charges F in order to meet its increased input costs—the total revenue collected would actually increase.

4.3.1. The nature and strengths of the VAT

The VAT has now been adopted by more than 130 countries, including all members of the OECD other than the US. While each country had its own reason for adoption, the main reason in the UK was simple: it was (and is) a precondition for entry into the EU. And the central reason for the EU's insistence on the VAT is to provide a transparent means of ensuring that exports are relieved of indirect taxation (or subsidy) and imports brought into tax on an even footing.[22] A well-functioning VAT—with unbroken chain of crediting and refund—is also consistent with the theoretical preference, described above, for taxing commodities (other than those generating production externalities) only on their final sale to consumers, so as to preserve production efficiency. But, as we see shortly, there are other ways of achieving the same effect. What then is the particular merit of the VAT?

This question is of more than historical interest. Somewhat ironically, the zero-rating of exports under the VAT that has proved so effective in facilitating trade between member states by removing indirect tax as commodities pass between them has also proved highly problematic when the later stage of economic integration—the removal of fiscal frontiers—was reached. And these difficulties have called into question fundamental design features of

[22] Södersten (1999) provides an interesting historical account of the adoption of the VAT in Europe.

(and even the wisdom of retaining) the VAT, as discussed in Sections 4.3.3 and 4.5.2.

One way of pursuing production efficiency and the taxation only of domestic consumption is by exploiting the equivalence between the VAT and other combinations of instruments. For instance, a destination-based VAT, levied on the difference between the domestic sales S of every firm and its purchases of material inputs (the latter comprising investment spending I and other material purchases P) is equivalent to a tax on the firm's wage bill W combined with another on cash flow earnings $S - W - I - P$. (More precisely, the final part of this equivalence is with a destination-based, R-form cash flow tax: see Auerbach, Devereux, and Simpson in Chapter 9.)[23] Thus a VAT would be unnecessary if there were no constraints on the ability to tax labour income or destination-based cash flow profit. Conversely, such a cash flow tax might not be needed if a reasonably functioning VAT and wage taxation were available. It may nevertheless be optimal to deploy all instruments, including both a VAT and a cash flow profit tax, if—in similar spirit to the analysis of Boadway, Marchand, and Pestieau (1994) mentioned above—evasion possibilities differ between them (Gordon and Nielson (1997)).

The second way of pursuing these same two objectives would be deploying a retail sales tax (RST), which levies tax only at the point of final sale. (In the first example of Box 4.1, for instance, the same final effect could be achieved by taxing, at the same rate of 17.5%, only the sales of Firm Y.)

Since a VAT and RST are economically equivalent when both function perfectly, the choice between them must rest on the differential challenges for administration and compliance that they imply, and in the opportunities and incentives for evasion that they create. And here the key difference[24] lies in the 'fractional' nature of the VAT, with tax in principle collected at each stage of production, compared with the single-stage nature of the RST.[25] Put simply, if the final sale of some commodity escapes tax, no revenue is collected

[23] Or to an origin-based cash flow—in turn equivalent in present value, if the tax rate is unchanging, to a tax on pure profits combined with a levy on the initial capital stock (hence the notion of consumption taxation as bearing on 'old' capital)—and a subsidy to inflows from abroad. The flat tax of Hall and Rabushka (1983) is equivalent to an origin-based VAT, collected by the subtraction method, supplemented by the application of a single marginal rate to labour income (with a non-refundable tax credit).

[24] There are also likely to be differences in the number of firms that need to be subject to the tax, but it is not clear a priori whether this will be greater or less under the VAT: it will be greater in that all types of businesses, not just retailers, are brought into the tax, but less to the extent that the fractional nature of the VAT means that many small firms can be excluded from the system, by means of a registration threshold, without major revenue losses (a point explored further).

[25] This does not mean that revenue accrues to the government sooner under the VAT, since—if the system is working as intended—the same tax that is collected from the seller of some item used as an intermediate input is also (and quite possibly simultaneously) credited to the buyer.

under an RST; under the VAT, on the other hand, all that is lost is the tax on value added at that final stage, since tax (in principle) will have been collected on the final seller's purchases. This means, of course, that in such circumstances the VAT does indeed tax intermediate transactions, which runs foul of the presumption for production efficiency created by the Diamond–Mirrlees theorem discussed above. Recall, however, that this result presumes that all final sales can be taxed. When they cannot, then, as noted by Newbery (1986), it is generally desirable to tax inputs as a surrogate for the missing output tax. And it is here that the VAT may do a particularly good job, since the unrelieved input tax is likely to arise precisely where, for some reason, output tax is not charged.

This distinctive fractional nature of the VAT is a feature stressed by its advocates, and a prime consideration in arguing, along the pragmatic lines above, for substantial reliance on the VAT within the tax mix. But while influential in practice, the strength of this case for the VAT has received little analytical or empirical attention. Nor has the possibility of exploiting it still further. Keen (2008) notes, for example, that a uniform VAT taxes informal sector purchases from VAT-compliant firms at the same rate as formal sector final sales, when one might in principle want to tax the former more heavily—which could be done by the use of some creditable withholding tax or other supplement on sales likely to be to informal sector operators. Such taxes are indeed quite common in emerging market and developing countries, but less so in developed. That is surprising, in that they are more likely to be able to implement the crediting needed to prevent such taxes becoming an additional burden on legitimate traders, but presumably reflects a lesser concern with informality issues. Indeed, the trend in the EU (though not in the UK, as noted later) has been to set low output tax rates on items potentially subject to informality, not high input rates. This aspect of indirect tax policy, in any event, is pursued no further here.

Building on the fractional nature of the VAT, some suggest that—in its invoice-credit form—the VAT is 'self-enforcing' in the sense that each trader has an incentive to ensure that their suppliers have themselves properly paid output VAT, in order that they themselves can then claim an appropriate credit.[26] There is an element of truth in this. Certainly businesses registered

[26] At the opposite extreme, it is also sometimes claimed that the ability to cross-check invoices—verifying that every credit claim is matched by some payment of output tax—can make the VAT especially abuse-proof. While there is again an element of truth in this—invoices do indeed provide a useful trail for VAT auditors—this too can be overstated. Even with the developments in information technology in recent years, complete cross-checking of invoices remains, at least for the present, effectively impossible.

for VAT can gain nothing (beyond perhaps some cash flow advantage) by purchasing inputs on an untaxed basis, since they are in any event able to claim credit or refund for any tax so paid. Indeed, there is a strict advantage in purchasing from VAT-registered businesses, since unregistered businesses will be unable to reclaim the VAT they themselves have been charged on their inputs, and so may charge a higher output price. Thus traders selling to other businesses may indeed wish to register to charge the VAT even if their annual turnover is below the threshold at which VAT registration is mandatory, and arrangements for such voluntary registration are a key part of any well-designed VAT. There is also a sense in which the VAT is self-correcting: if for some reason output VAT is not charged at some intermediate stage of production, proper payment by a trader later in the chain will replace that missed tax (since they then charge the proper output tax themselves, with their input tax credit reduced by precisely the amount of the output VAT that their suppliers should have charged but did not).

But the strength of these intrinsic features of the VAT should not be over-stated. It remains the case that those selling to private individuals and businesses not registered for VAT have similar incentives to sell without tax as under an RST, although muted to the extent that they have paid VAT on their own purchases. That is, while the VAT contains incentives for the formation of 'good' chains of compliant traders, it also contains incentives for 'bad' chains of non-compliance: de Paula and Scheinkman (2006) argue that the latter has been an important feature in Brazil, for example. Moreover, while registered traders have an incentive to ensure that their suppliers provide them with an invoice that the authorities will accept as establishing their right to refund or credit of input VAT, they have no incentive—unless specific requirements are imposed—to ensure that this tax has actually been remitted to the tax authorities. Furthermore, the credit and refund mechanism of the VAT creates its own opportunities for fraud, as we also discuss later.

Whether the VAT has proved to be a particularly effective form of taxation is, or should be, ultimately to some degree an empirical matter. But the question has received little attention. Such evidence as there is on the performance of the VAT (in Keen and Lockwood (2006, 2008)) suggests that it has indeed proved an effective form of tax: countries with a VAT, especially higher income countries, tend to have higher tax ratios—modestly, but significantly so—than those without, which is as one would expect if the VAT has had the effect of reducing the marginal distortionary and other costs of mobilizing tax revenue.

4.3.2. Key design features of the UK VAT

The design of a VAT requires a wide range of decisions as to its rates and coverage. This section reviews the central choices made in the UK. Those choices are constrained by a variety of EU rules on the common VAT: some key features of these, mostly as they relate to rate structure, are summarized in Box 4.2, and others will be set out and discussed below.

Box 4.2. EU rules on the value added tax

The common VAT rules, with the 1977 Sixth VAT Directive at their core and recently consolidated in directive 2006/112/EC, establish broad commonality in definitions on such core matters as taxable person, taxable event, and place of supply. Beyond this, particular rules apply to permissible rates and exemptions.

Rates

With the adoption of the internal market in 1992, and fear that the removal of internal fiscal controls would put downward pressure on VAT rates, member states agreed not to set their standard VAT rate lower than 15% (a provision recently extended to 2010). Member states may set no more than two reduced rates: at no less than 5% on a positive listing of ('Annex III') items and, on condition that competition is not distorted—in effect restricting the application to final sales—on use of electricity, natural gas, and district heating.

As transitional provisions—until the adoption of a 'definitive' regime for the taxation of intra-Community trade, for which no date is set—member states are allowed to retain a variety of otherwise prohibited measures that were in place at the start of 1991: 'super-reduced' (including zero) rates applied for social reasons—by which means the domestic zero-rating in the UK survives—rates of less than 5% on Annex III items, and a reduced rate of no less than 12% (the 'parking rate') on Non-Annex III items. Many of the new EU members, of course, did not have a VAT in place at this date, and so are unable to benefit from this provision: they are required to be fully compliant by 2010 at the latest: Malta, for example, must by then remove its zero-rating of foodstuffs and pharmaceuticals, though there is no similarly unconditional obligation on the UK.

Member states may also apply (until the end of 2010) a reduced rate to no more than three specified labour-intensive services (such as hairdressing, domestic service, and the renovation and repair of private dwellings).

(cont.)

Box 4.2. (*cont.*)

Exemptions

EU rules mandate several exemptions, including for medical care, education, social welfare and cultural activities, financial services, and the letting of immovable property (with member states allowed, in the last two cases to provide taxpayers an option to be taxed—which the UK currently does for letting but not for financial services). Supplies by public bodies are also exempt (strictly, are outside the scope of the VAT) so long as this does not distort competition; a few member states provide for the refund of input VAT to such bodies in some cases, as the UK does automatically for local authorities, the government of Northern Ireland, and some other named bodies, and on a discretionary basis for others.

By way of background, Table 4.2 provides comparative information on key design characteristics for all OECD countries (other than the US, which of course does not have a VAT).

Rate structure

At 17.5%, the standard rate is around the OECD average and comfortably above the EU minimum of 15%. Indeed, that minimum is currently binding for only one member state, Luxembourg. It is theoretically conceivable that a lower rate in Luxembourg would have induced the UK to set a lower rate (perhaps because other and larger countries might have been induced to do so), but this seems unlikely: certainly the most direct form of interaction between national indirect tax systems—smuggling and cross-border shopping—seems to be fairly limited in relation to the VAT.[27] Nor, by the same token, is there any evidence that the UK is constrained from further increasing the standard rate in a way that further increasing the EU minimum would ease.

More striking than the level of the standard rate is that the UK VAT is marked by very substantial rate differentiation: domestic zero-rating is extensive (including notably most foodstuffs, children's clothing, and residential construction), and a reduced rate of 5% is also applied to domestic power and energy, and a range of other items (such as contraceptives, certain

[27] The main exception to this appears to be that between Germany and Denmark, with a differential in the standard rate that was 9 percentage points until the 2007 increase in Germany. Gordon and Nielson (1997) estimate that this caused the former to lose only around 0.8% of its VAT revenue from cross-border shopping, though this was before the removal of fiscal frontiers and may have increased since.

Table 4.2. VAT rates, revenues and C-efficiency in the OECD[1]

	Standard rate (percent)	Reduced rates[2] (percent)	Threshold[3] (in USD)	C-efficiency[4] (percent, 2005)
Australia	10	Zero	35,500	57
Austria	20	10, 12	34,400	60
Belgium	21	Zero, 6, 12	6,400	50
Canada	6	Zero	25,000	52
Czech Republic	19	Zero, 5	70,000	59
Denmark	25	Zero	5,800	62
Finland	22	Zero, 8, 17	9,700	61
France	19.6	2.1, 5.5	87,500	51
Germany	19	7	20,000	54
Greece	19	4.5, 9.0	11,500	46
Hungary	20	5	30,800	49
Iceland	24.5	Zero, 7	4,800	62
Ireland	21	Zero, 4.8, 13.5	63,000	68
Italy	20	Zero, 4, 10	8,000	41
Japan	5	–	80,600	72
Korea	10	Zero	None	71
Luxembourg	15	3, 6, 12	11,500	81
Mexico	15	Zero	None	33
Netherlands	19	6	2,200	61
New Zealand	12	Zero	26,300	105
Norway	25	Zero, 8, 14	5,600	58
Poland	22	Zero, 7	20,900	48
Portugal	21	5, 12	11,500	48
Slovak Republic	19	–	86,700	53
Spain	16	4, 7	None	56
Sweden	25	Zero, 6, 12	None	55
Switzerland	7.6	Zero, 2.4, 3.6	44,100	76
Turkey	18	1,8	None[5]	53
United Kingdom	17.5	Zero, 5	93,600	49
Unweighted Average	17.7			58

[1] As at 1 January 2007 except for C-efficiency.
[2] 'Zero' indicates zero-rating of some domestic sales.
[3] This is the general threshold. Some countries apply a lower threshold to services.
[4] VAT revenue divided by the product of the standard rate and final consumption expenditure less VAT revenue.
[5] Small retailers and taxpayers taxed on a lump sum basis or exempt from personal income tax, and farmers, are not required to register. Personal income tax thresholds and conditions apply to VAT.
Source: OECD (2008). Rates applying only in particular regions—such as the reduced rate applied in border regions by Mexico, and to overseas departments by France—are excluded.

energy-saving products, and children's car seats). HMRC put the revenue cost in 2007–08—the additional VAT that would be raised if tax were instead charged at the standard rate (ignoring any behavioural response)—at around £29 billion for domestic zero-rating (around 40% of this being from food, and around 30% from new dwellings) and £3 billion for the reduced rate (almost all of this being for domestic fuel and power). Exemptions are reckoned to cost another £12 billion (the largest item, accounting for over one-third of this, being financial services).[28] This compares to total VAT revenue of around £80 billion. It all means that C-efficiency in the UK—the ratio of VAT revenues to the product of the standard rate and private consumption, which would be 100% for a textbook VAT levied at a uniform rate on all consumption (and comes close to that in New Zealand)[29]—is very low by OECD standards.[30]

It has been recognized for more than twenty years that the policy rationale for the zero-rating of food and children's clothing is extremely weak. Theoretical and empirical developments over the last twenty years, as reviewed above, have only confirmed these doubts. Our own empirical results, reported in Table 4.1 above, do not provide any suggestion that differentially low rates on these items—or indeed any others—is warranted, given the availability of fairly flexible earnings-related instruments: most foodstuffs appear to be complements with leisure. The survival of zero-rating of food and children's clothing appears simply to reflect politicians' doubts of their ability to explain why a package involving its removal need not have a regressive impact: as discussed by Alt, Preston, and Sibieta in Chapter 13, the commitment to this zero-rating appears to have become a signal of commitment to at least a moderately pro-poor policy.

The rationale for the reduced rate is also far from clear: to the extent that its original purpose is to mitigate 'fuel poverty', such measures as the additional winter allowance for pensioners provide reasonably well-targeted relief (though a strong case could be made for an element of income-relation). Indeed, there is some perversity in applying the reduced rate to both energy use and purchases of some energy-saving materials. The deeper issue here is the proper design of energy taxes, and similar mechanisms, such as cap-and-trade systems along the lines of the EU Emissions Trading Scheme, to address environmental and other non-revenue concerns such as supply security (see Fullerton, Leicester, and Smith in Chapter 5). With these in place, there would be little case for differential treatment of final energy use; and without them, as at present, it is hard to make a case for rates on final use that are actually lower. Experience with this lower rate, into which an increasing and

[28] Table 1.5 at <http://www.hmrc.gov.uk/stats/tax_expenditures/menu.htm>.

[29] The use and limitations of C-efficiency measures are discussed in Ebrill et al. (2001) and OECD (2008), which relabels it the 'VAT revenue ratio'.

[30] The OECD calculations reflect a figure for VAT revenue substantially above that reported by HMRC: £83 billion for 2005 compared to £73 billion, the difference largely reflecting the treatment of refunding of VAT to public bodies.

diverse number of items have been moved, also illustrates the further general experience that preferential treatment, once granted, tends to spread, and that in its doing so the wider coherence of the tax system suffers. Quite why parents should pay no VAT when they buy clothes for their children but 5% when they buy them a car seat is by no means clear.

Indeed, in a broader sense the extensive rate differentiation still found in the VATs of EU members is coming to look increasingly quaint. Most new VATs adopted in recent years have a single rate: not only in Australia and New Zealand, but also in developing countries, where the case for a single rate is actually weaker (because of a lesser ability to deal with the distributional implications through other instruments). Others, it seems, have learnt lessons from the EU experience that EU members themselves have not.

Experience also shows, however, that moving towards a uniform VAT rate structure is not easy once differentiation has been admitted (though there are some success stories: the Slovak Republic, for instance, unified its two distinct VAT rates in 2004[31]). What will evidently be needed, to overcome distributional concerns, is the packaging of movement to uniformity with other reforms intended to neutralize the equity impact (just as in the Slovak Republic the VAT reform was part of a much wider package, including increased generosity of in-work support).

What might such a reform package for the UK look like? By way of illustration, consider applying the current standard rate of 17.5% to all commodities except housing and items currently exempt from VAT[32]—eliminating, that is, the current reduced and zero-rate—and combining this with a 15% increase in all income support, income-based jobseeker's allowance and tax credit rates, and in the associated housing benefit and council tax benefit thresholds.[33]

Figure 4.1 shows the implied change in VAT payments across the income distribution. As one would expect, the largest absolute financial losses (solid line, left scale) are found amongst richer households simply because they spend more, on average, on reduced- and zero-rated goods than do less well-off households. However, the increased VAT payments are a larger proportion of disposable income (right-hand scale) at lower income levels, since the less

[31] But, it must be admitted, also reintroduced a reduced rate in 2007.

[32] This is in order to respect exemptions currently required under EU rules (though simulations not reported here show that these too could be removed as part of a rate-unifying reform with the same features as that in the text, protecting the poorest and increasing total revenue). The Insurance Premium Tax is kept at its current rate of 5%.

[33] It is assumed that the incidence of the VAT reform is fully on retail prices and that of the compensating measures fully on net incomes.

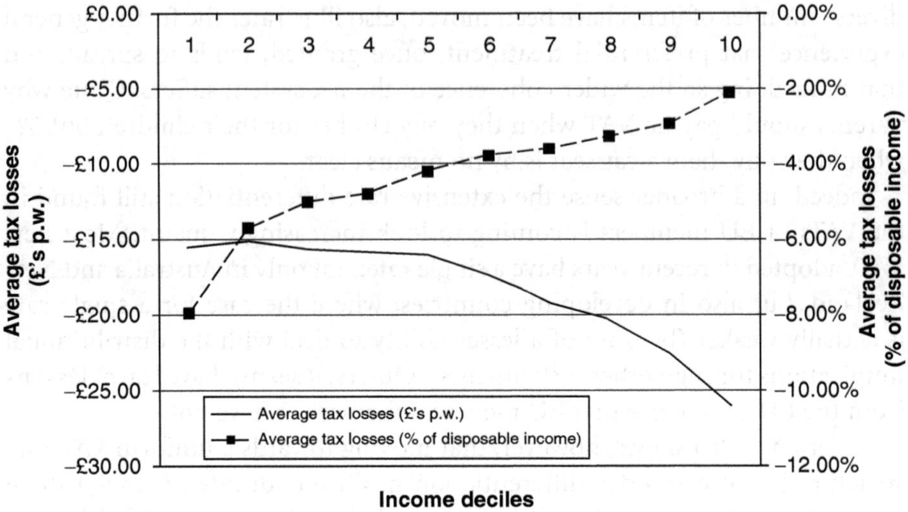

Note: Income decile groups (1=poorest, 10=richest) are derived by dividing all households into ten equal-sized groups according to disposable income adjusted for household size and composition using the McClements equivalence scale.

Source: IFS calculations using the IFS tax and benefit microsimulation model, TAXBEN, run on uprated data from the 2005–06 Expenditure and Food Survey.

Figure 4.1. Distributional impact of unifying VAT rates at 17.5%

well-off spend a greater proportion of their incomes on food and other items currently taxed preferentially.

When the compensating measures are combined with the VAT reform, however, the net impact across the income distribution is quite different, as shown in Figure 4.2. Households in the lowest income decile group, for example, gain on average about £2.50 per week whereas those at the top lose around £25 per week. It is not quite the case that those on lower incomes always gain more than those on higher—those in the second decile group gain more than those in the first—but the broad distributional impact is clear-cut: the poorest three-tenths gain on average while those on higher incomes tend to lose.

Importantly, the package implies a net increase in tax revenue: the VAT reform raises around £23 billion while the compensating package costs only about £12 billion. If so desired, this £11 billion saving could be used to finance further pro-poor measures.

This package is intended to be essentially illustrative. Behind the aggregate effects shown in the figures are effects that vary across household type. The component of the package relating to child tax credit, for example, means that those with children tend to gain more than those without. There are

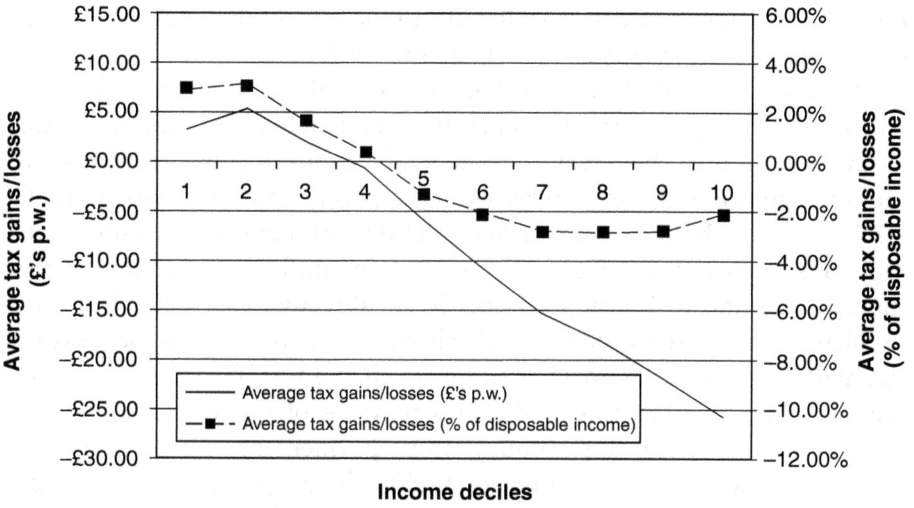

Note: Income decile groups (1=poorest, 10=richest) are derived by dividing all households into ten equal-sized groups according to disposable income adjusted for household size and composition using the McClements equivalence scale. Uniform VAT rate excludes housing and non-insurance financial services: see text for details of the reform.

Source: IFS calculations using the IFS tax and benefit microsimulation model, TAXBEN, run on uprated data from the 2005–06 Expenditure and Food Survey.

Figure 4.2. Distributional impact of the reform package

also potential impacts on labour supply that are not included in the modelling here but would need to be considered in developing a fully formulated proposal. The key point, however, is that it is not difficult to find ways of compensating the losers from VAT rate unification, arriving at a package of reforms that improve both the progressivity and efficiency (including in terms of administration and compliance) of the overall tax system—and in the process provide revenue that could finance further desirable reforms.[34]

Two other aspects of the VAT rate structure merit comment. First, the UK has notably not taken up the option under current EU rules (until 2010) to apply reduced rates to specified labour-intensive activities. Such rate reductions can be defended in principle on optimal tax grounds in terms of the arguments cited above for relatively low taxation of services readily self-supplied by consumers. Against this, of course, they carry the administration and compliance burden associated with increasing the extent of rate differentiation. And an assessment by the Commission of the European Communities (2003) is sceptical as to the effectiveness of such provisions in increasing

[34] This reform would increase the Retail Prices Index by around 3.5%. Note that this is a one-off jump in the price level, not a permanent change in the rate of inflation.

formal sector employment. It is difficult to make a compelling case that the UK has made a mistake in not taking up this option.

The second striking feature is that the UK is alone among OECD countries in zero-rating construction and sale of residential properties (residential letting is exempt). This creates a potentially significant distortion towards the consumption of housing services, and especially owner-occupation, of a kind that the UK, to its credit, has carefully counteracted by eliminating mortgage interest deductibility. The underlying difficulty, of course, is that the consumption of housing services is not directly observable. The same problem arises to some degree with all durable goods, of course, and the standard if imperfect approach is simply to charge VAT at the first sale: since the price of a durable reflects the present value of the stream of services it is expected to yield, this amounts to prepayment of VAT on those services. The same approach can be adopted for housing, fully taxing the first sale of residential properties (as is already done in the UK for commercial properties).[35] Doing so in the UK would be permissible under EU rules, and is already done in Belgium and France, for example. The increase in (VAT-inclusive) house prices this would imply would create difficulties: first-time buyers would suffer, while owners of existing properties would enjoy a windfall gain. The former could be addressed by providing a (perhaps temporary) subsidy to new buyers, as Australia did when introducing its VAT in 2000. The latter would be eliminated (and tax receipts increased) if the tax were instead levied on all house sales after some implementation date (since the same prepayment logic applies to the sale of old but previously untaxed houses).

The political resistance to moving away from the present extensive domestic zero-rating has proved formidable, to such an extent that it is hardly on the policy agenda. Moving instead to exemption might seem a tempting compromise. This is not only untransparent, however, but may not even reduce implementation costs (given the difficulties faced and posed by partially exempt traders). Moreover, as argued next, strengthening the UK VAT requires less exempting, not more. More appealing would be to tax these items at below the standard rate (for some period), perhaps moving them to the present reduced rate. Consideration could also be given to earmarking the proceeds, to pay not only for the compensation but some other popular items (including tax reductions or social security increases). Presenting VAT increases in this way has been considered in France and Japan, for instance,

[35] Commercial letting is exempt, but with an option to tax. Thus arrangements for commercial property properly allow for the full operation of the VAT chain.

and recently done with success in Ghana (where resistance to the VAT has historically been particularly high). Against any political advantage of doing so must be weighed, however, the implied inflexibility in the use of funds—the absence of earmarking is one of the wider (if often unremarked) merits of the current UK tax system that should not be taken lightly.

Exemptions

Exemptions under the UK VAT are extensive, reflecting the EU law summarized in Box 4.2 above and including most of what the OECD (2004) calls 'standard' exemptions.[36]

Any exemption is anathema to the logic of the VAT, since it inherently breaks the chain of credit and refund, leading to an element of production taxation. The consequent distortions can take a number of forms. These include an incentive to self-supply (banks providing security services in-house, for example, so as to avoid unrecovered VAT if hiring the services from others), distortions of competition (as financial institutions across the EU face different input costs as a consequence of being charged different rates on their inputs, this effect also cascading into the costs of business using those services; and as exempt public services compete with taxable ones provided by the private sector), and a bias towards imports (since these will have been freed of VAT in the country of export). They also create additional administration and compliance burdens (and opportunities for tax planning) through the need to allocate input VAT between taxable and exempt outputs (credit being available for the former but not the latter) for producers selling both. As Bird and Gendron (2007) note, there is little firm evidence on the quantitative importance of these distortions. The rebating of input VAT to local authorities and similar bodies in the UK may limit those from the exemption of public bodies (the revenue impact of which may also be fairly modest, since full taxation means one part of government paying taxes to another). There is though every sign that these are a serious concern in the financial sector, and certainly its sheer (and increasing) size—Zee (2006) reports that it accounts for 30% of GDP—suggests that the risk of distortion deserves serious attention.

These standard exemptions are to a large degree the hallmark of 'old' VATs—such as that laid down for the EU has become. They reflect outdated

[36] These include postal services; hospital and medical care; dental care; charitable work; education; non-commercial activities of non-profit making organizations; sporting services; cultural services (except radio and television broadcasting); insurance and reinsurance; letting of immovable property; financial services; betting, lotteries, and gambling; supply of land and buildings; and certain fund-raising events.

presumptions on the arrangement of economic activity—a vision of a large public sector largely insulated from competition with private operators—and, to a large degree, a failure to recognize that the logic of the VAT can be applied to these items. Aujean, Jenkins, and Poddar (1999), for instance, explain how the public sector can be brought fully into the VAT system, and New Zealand in particular now largely does this (even charging VAT on public subsidies used to provide goods and services without charge). There is a very strong case, as argued by Cnossen (2003 and Commentary on this chapter) for eliminating many of these exemptions. These are not matters, however, on which the UK can act unilaterally (or on which we have much to add), so we simply refer the reader to the cited sources, and the general treatments in Ebrill et al. (2001) and Bird and Gendron (2007), for discussion of how the common rules might usefully be restructured.

There is though one aspect of such importance, for reasons noted above, and so central to this wider review of the tax system, as to require some comment. This is the VAT treatment of financial services.[37] Those charged for in the form of a fee raise no conceptual difficulty—they can and should be fully taxed, though in practice it seems few do so as a general principle (South Africa being an exception).[38] The difficulty arises for those charged for as a margin, between bank's borrowing and lending rates, for example. The choice of exemption in the EU[39] to a large degree reflected an inability to see how (continuing with that example) that margin could be broken down into value provided to depositor and borrower, as appeared to be necessary if only that part accruing to any households involved in the transaction is to be taxed. Following Poddar and English (1997), however, it is now understood that such transactions can be properly brought into an invoice-credit VAT by treating all cash inflows to those providing financial services (including principal amounts) as reflecting VAT-able sales to customers, and treating all cash outflows (including loans made) as the purchase of inputs carrying

[37] Some have argued that financial services should not be taxed on the grounds that they do not represent consumption since they do not enter the direct utility function. This now seems largely discredited: no one knows what the arguments of final utility are. Boadway and Keen (2003) review the theoretical arguments in this area.

[38] One reason for this, as noted by Zee (2006), may be concern that different approaches to the taxation of financial services paid for by fee and those paid for implicitly in a spread is the risk of financial institutions arbitraging between the two. McCann and Edgar (2003) argue that the scope for this is likely to be limited in practice, though the issue remains open.

[39] Many other approaches have been adopted: see for instance Bird and Gendron (2007) and Zee (2006). Some—notably using fixed coefficients to simplify the allocation of inputs to taxed and exempt activities (as, in somewhat different ways, do Australia and Singapore)—seem likely to be superior to exemption. Other than outright zero-rating, however (which to large degree gives up on the basic objective of taxing financial services entering final consumption), only the cash flow method about to be described fits within an invoice-credit VAT.

creditable VAT. Intuitively, this ensures that all flows involving registered traders are subject to a tax that is fully credited; the revenue that remains thus derives from transactions involving households.

This approach operates straightforwardly for some financial transactions, not only those charged for as an explicit fee but also term insurance (see for instance Box 8.1 in Ebrill et al. (2001)), and is in such cases already applied in some of the more modern VATs, such as those of Australia, New Zealand, and Singapore. The literature has struggled, however, to find simple ways of administering such a system for other intermediation services. One possibility, suggested by Huizinga (2002) and Poddar (2003), is to zero rate all transactions with registered businesses—as is now done in New Zealand—while providing cash flow treatment of transactions with households, so that responsibility for remittance falls on the financial institution. While this would require financial institutions to distinguish between registered and non-registered customers, that is a distinction which is not only already made in many cases but is also inherent in a wider approach to VAT redesign, the 'VIVAT', that we shall argue later has appeal on quite different grounds. The essence of the VIVAT, as it might operate in the EU, is that all sales to registered traders would be taxed at a common EU rate, while other sales are taxed at the final rate specified by each member state. The arrangement just described fits well into such a system: all that is needed is to apply a common intermediate rate of zero on financial services transactions involving unregistered traders and to tax provision to non-registered traders, at the final rate specified by each country, and on a cash flow basis. Box 4.3 illustrates how this would work.

Box 4.3. Cash flow treatment of banking with zero-rating of transactions with businesses

Consider first the case of a bank that deals only with households. In period 1, one household deposits £1,000 and another borrows the same amount. In period 2, the latter repays the loan with interest at 15% and the former withdraws the principal with interest at 5%. The VAT rate is 10%.

The VAT consequences in period 1 are that the bank remits £100 in respect of the deposit (10% of £1,000), this being treated as a taxable sale, but receives a credit of £100 in respect of the funds it loans out, treated as a taxed purchase. In period 2, repayment of the loan creates a VAT liability of £115 (10% of principal and interest of £1,150) while withdrawal of the interest-augmented deposit gives a credit of £105 (10% of £1,050). The only net VAT collected, all in period 2,

(cont.)

Box 4.3. (*cont.*)

is thus £10. This is equal to the product of the VAT rate and the entire value of the bank's spread (£100)—which is as it should be, since in this case the entire value of the intermediation service provided by the bank accrues to final households.

Now suppose that the borrower is a registered trader. With transactions involving the borrower then zero-rated, and so triggering no tax payment, all that remains is the payment of £100 in period 1 and credit of £105 in period 2.[40] Denoting by R the interest rate available to the government, the net revenue effectively collected, in period 2 equivalent, is 10% of $(R - 0.05) \times$£1,000. In effect, the intermediation services enjoyed by the depositor are valued, and taxed, at the excess of the government's discount rate over the deposit rate.

In terms of equivalences of the kind discussed in Section 4.3.1, such a VIVAT form of cash flow tax would be closely related to the R + F destination-based cash flow tax discussed by Auerbach, Devereux, and Simpson in Chapter 9. It would not quite be equivalent, at firm level, to such a tax (combined with a wage tax), since it would exclude cash flows related to financial services purchased by registered businesses. Summed across firms, however, these flows net to zero, so that such an equivalence would apply at an aggregate level.

There are evidently many challenging practical issues to address before a scheme of this kind could be firmly recommended. But the potential benefits appear significant, not only in terms of easing distortions but also in simple revenue terms. A priori, it is not clear whether such a system (or any form of cash flow treatment) would lead to an increase in VAT revenue (since the unrecovered tax on financial sector inputs under the present exemption system, amplified by further cascading into the taxable value of other commodities, could exceed that due on the value enjoyed by final consumers). In practice, however, it seems likely that it would. For the EU as a whole, Huizinga (2002) estimates, such a scheme would raise an additional

[40] This simplifies, in that payment of the tax on deposit leaves only £900 available for loan. But this is inessential: taking account of the absence in this case of any tax on the repayment of the loan, it is readily verified that, given the credit on the depositors' withdrawal of £1,050, the bank earns £1,150. Alternatively, arrangements might be put in place (along the lines of the Tax Calculation Account (TCA) of Poddar and Morley English (1997)) to defer (with interest payable) remittance of tax on inflows from households until the credit in respect of withdrawal becomes available. Note too that zero-rating transactions with registrants eliminates any need for TCAs by or on behalf of registered businesses, which has been seen as a major compliance obstacle to cash flow taxation.

€12 billion, while for Germany alone Genser and Winker (1997) estimate a net increase of DM 10 billion (€5 billion).

The threshold

One particular form of exemption is that, de facto, of businesses falling below the VAT threshold (unless, as discussed above, they choose to register voluntarily). At £61,000, the threshold in the UK is the highest in the OECD (Table 4.2). But there is also evidently massive variation in VAT thresholds, some countries having none at all. The natural question is whether the UK has set it too high.

Since any threshold distorts competition between those above and below it, the only rationale for excluding smaller businesses from the tax is to save administration costs to the authorities and compliance costs to the taxpayer. Against this, of course, must be weighed the revenue foregone[41] by excluding those businesses from tax. Box 4.4 sets out a simple framework for thinking systematically about these trade-offs. It shows too that if plausible parameter values (for implementation costs and the social value of tax revenue) are inserted, a threshold at the UK level is not hard to rationalize.

Box 4.4. Setting the VAT threshold

For a benchmark case in which these administration and compliance costs, A and C respectively, are independent of firm size, Keen (2004) show that trading off the implementation costs saved and the revenue foregone by excluding some firms from the VAT implies an optimal VAT threshold of:[42]

$$Z^* = \frac{\delta A + C}{(\delta - 1)\tau N} \qquad (1)$$

where δ denotes the marginal cost of public funds, τ the rate of VAT, and υ the ratio of value added to turnover. None of these parameters is known with great certainty. But supposing, for illustrative purposes, that the marginal cost

(*cont.*)

[41] Although exemptions may in general increase rather than reduce revenue, small traders in the middle of the chain will generally find it advantageous to register voluntarily. The expectation is thus that a threshold will lose revenue.

[42] The underlying intuition is simple. The social benefit from slightly increasing the threshold from some initial level of Z is the saving in compliance costs C and the administration costs A, with the latter, since it is financed from distorting tax revenue, being weighted by the marginal cost of public funds, all multiplied by the number of taxpayers $f(Z)$ taken out of the VAT. The social cost is the revenue foregone, τN, multiplied by the excess of the marginal cost of public funds over unity (the reduction in revenue being a private gain) and, once more, that number of affected taxpayers. Equating these marginal social costs and benefits to characterize an optimal threshold Z^* gives the result in (1).

Box 4.4. (*cont.*)

of public funds is 1.2, administration and compliance costs £120 and £600 respectively,[43] then with a VAT rate of 17.5% and a ratio of value added to sales of 30%, the implied VAT threshold is about £71,000—rather higher than at present, but a similar order of magnitude. While this suggests that the UK value is well within the bounds of the plausibly optimal, it should be noted that the value implied by (1) is quite sensitive to parameter values: changing the marginal cost of public funds to 2.0, for example, reduces the optimal threshold to around £16,000.

The simple rule set out in the box ignores many potentially important considerations. Implementation costs are likely to vary with firm size, for example, and account must also be taken of the inefficiencies created by distorting competition between firms of different size and potentially inducing artificial splitting to remain below, or simply discouraging expanding firm size above, the threshold.[44] This raises important questions, as Bird (commentary on this chapter) points out, as to whether some simple 'replacement' for the VAT should apply to those below the threshold (which may itself affect where that threshold should be).[45] These considerations significantly complicate the analysis, with the distribution of firm size, for example, playing an important (and theoretically ambiguous) role. Simulations by Keen and Mintz (2004), however, tend to point to thresholds optimally higher than that implied by (1); the somewhat different model of the determinants of firm size in Zee (2005), on the other hand, points in the opposite direction.[46] Further considerations, awaiting closer analysis—such as the propagation of beneficial VAT chains of the kind described above—may point to lower thresholds. But others, such as the need to control registration as a defence against

[43] A recent study of tax compliance costs in the UK by KPMG (2006) implies an average VAT compliance burden per registrant of £562 (combining figures in table 3 and in section 3.3.4). Another for New Zealand (Colmar Brunton (2005)) implies a cost in terms of internal time alone (so neglecting bought-in advice and equipment) of around £660 (though varying fairly substantially, if not entirely systematically, with firm size). It seems unlikely that it is cheaper to comply with the relatively complex UK than with the simpler one in New Zealand, so that £600 seems a reasonable order of magnitude. Earlier estimates by Cnossen (1994) suggest administrative costs of around 20% of compliance costs: hence the £120 figure.

[44] KPMG (2006, annex C p. 4) report that some firms interviewed indicated a deliberate decision to keep their size below the VAT threshold.

[45] For discussion of this, and more generally of the potential importance of the VAT threshold in anchoring the tax treatment of SMEs, see International Tax Dialogue (2007).

[46] Both Keen (2004) and Zee (2005) have firms differing in underlying productivity, the former have them producing a homogeneous product whereas the latter has them producing Dixit–Stiglitz substitutes. Dharmapala, Slemrod, and Wilson (2007) explore the same issue in a model with endogenous entry and exit; the likely quantitative implications for the optimal threshold, however, remain to be analysed.

carousel and other fraud (as discussed below) point to higher. There is good reason to suppose that the relatively high threshold should be counted as a strength of the UK VAT.

4.3.3. VAT enforcement and compliance issues

Like all taxes, the VAT is subject to evasion. For example, traders large enough to be liable to register may fail to do so, they may under-report sales, or, where different commodities are subject to tax at different rates, they may misclassify sales into the category subject to a lower rate of tax. As discussed above, the fractional nature of the VAT in some respects reduces its exposure compared with other systems of sales taxation.

In other respects, however, VAT offers distinctive opportunities for evasion and fraud, especially through abuse of the credit and refund mechanism. Revenue may be lost through exaggerated claims for credit for VAT paid on inputs. Moreover, the opportunity exists for outright fraud through the construction of business activities with the sole purpose of defrauding the exchequer, because some categories of business can be entitled to net refunds of VAT from the revenue authorities. These include firms selling predominantly zero-rated goods that are due refunds of input VAT. The extensive domestic zero-rating means that refunds are particularly extensive in the UK, at around 40% of gross VAT receipts (Harrison and Krelove (2005)). Little is known about the extent to which domestic zero-rating gives rise to fraud problems. The zero-rating of exports, however, has clearly become a significant source of difficulty.

Particular attention has come to be paid to 'Missing trader intra-community' (MTIC) frauds, which abuse the refunding of VAT to exporters by means of a series of contrived transactions. Figure 4.3 provides a simple example of a 'carousel fraud', the best-known example.

The two key features of the VAT that this exploits are the zero-rating of exports and the system of 'deferred payment' for VAT on imports from other EU member states, adopted in the EU since the removal of fiscal frontiers in 1992.[47] Under deferred payment, VAT on imports from one member state into another is levied not at the border but at the time of the importer's next periodic VAT return. As a result, there may be a considerable time lag between the date at which the importing firm (Company B in the example) brings the goods into the UK and the time at which the VAT authorities seek payment of the VAT due. In the meantime, the goods are sold on, via complicit—or

[47] There are indications that the general level of VAT revenue losses rose by about one-third by the mid-1990s compared with pre-1992 levels (see table 2.1 of HM Customs and Excise, *Measuring Indirect Tax Losses*, 2002, <http://www.hm-treasury.gov.uk/media/389/E5/admeas02-297kb.pdf>).

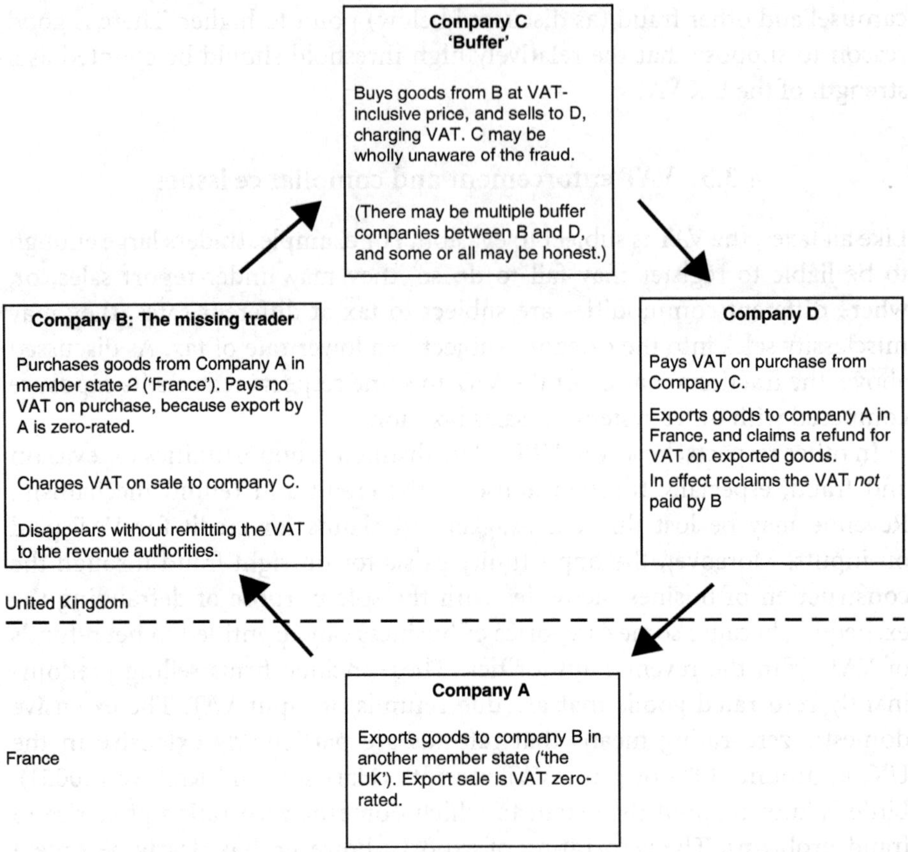

Figure 4.3. Carousel fraud: A simple example

perhaps unwitting—'buffer' companies in the UK, to Company D, which exports the goods, claiming a refund of the VAT paid when it purchased the goods from Company C. In the basic carousel illustrated, the exported goods are then re-imported by Company B—or more likely a new firm, B having gone missing—and so on, following a cycle in which VAT refunds are claimed repeatedly whenever the goods are exported, while the corresponding import VAT liability accumulates but is never paid. This example is extremely simple. In practice, the basic structure of the fraud may be obscured by the use of buffer companies that may or may not be complicit. Moreover, innovation has been a constant feature of these forms of fraud, as those perpetrating them seek to stay one step ahead of the authorities' ability to detect fraudulent transactions.

Key design features of the VAT system influence the extent to which it is exposed to systematic missing trader frauds. These include the ease with which the system allows intending missing traders (such as Company B in

Figure 4.3) to register for VAT, and the relative timing of VAT payments and receipts. *Ex post* audit and investigation, while important, is unlikely to forestall considerable loss of revenue, because the essence of the fraud is that money is made quickly, in the time gap before the missing trader is required to remit the VAT it has supposedly charged on its sales. Once the money has disappeared into the complex web of transactions, tracing and recovering unjustified VAT refunds becomes time-consuming and costly.

Other than more vigorous investigation, two broad approaches may be taken to designing-out the opportunities for fraud based on current treatment of trade between EU member states. One is essentially administrative, in the sense that it retains the zero-rating of intra-community supplies. The other, more fundamental to the structure of the tax itself, removes export zero-rating altogether.

Administrative measures that could be taken while maintaining the current VAT design include, for example: tighter checks on firms seeking to register for VAT (for example, with an on-site visit) and requiring guarantees in dubious cases; slowing down the payment of VAT refunds relative to the collection of VAT due (although this can impose severe cash flow burdens on legitimate businesses); adopting or strengthening joint and several liability rules by which traders can be held responsible for fraud elsewhere in the chain that they might reasonably have been expected to be aware of; and establishing better and quicker information exchange between national tax authorities (so that the country of import can become promptly aware that exports to it that have been reported in another member state have not shown up in its own VAT system). However, while measures of this sort may reduce the risk of VAT fraud, they clearly have undesirable side-effects. More bureaucratic VAT registration procedures and slower payment of VAT refunds might harm legitimate businesses as well as discouraging fraud, for example, and these effects may outweigh the enforcement gains. The authorities have a difficult balance to strike, between ensuring that VAT administration does not impose excessive burdens on business in general and ensuring that it is not unduly exposed to fraud. Some level of VAT evasion has to be tolerated in the wider business interest.

More radical measures within the context of a system that preserves zero-rating of intra-community exports include:[48]

- The use of 'reverse charging', by which liability in a business-to-business (B2B) transaction is placed on the buyer rather than the seller. This

[48] There are others not discussed here, such as the 'prepayment VAT' (PVAT) of Poddar and Hutton (2001), under which goods would not be shipped without adequate guarantee of payment of import VAT. Ainsworth (2007) attempts an exhaustive listing.

would close the carousel fraud in Figure 4.3 by making the VAT due on the sale by B (the missing trader) the responsibility of the buyer, C. In turn, the tax due on the sale from C to D would be the responsibility of D. The zero-rating of the subsequent export sale would then offset D's tax liability on its purchases from C, reducing the tax payment by D but not requiring outright refunds. The opportunity to make fraudulent gains by claiming refunds of tax that have not in fact been paid would thereby be eliminated. The UK recently received EU approval to apply reverse charging for mobile phones and computer chips, both having proved popular instruments for carousel fraud. More radically still, Austria and Germany have proposed allowing reverse charging for all B2B transactions above a certain size (€10,000 in the case of the Austrian proposal and €5,000 in the German proposal). The proposals differ in terms of the scale of the reporting obligations placed on firms and their customers: the German proposal would require both parties to a B2B transaction to report it to the tax authorities, and electronic cross-checking of this information, while the Austrian proposal would place fewer reporting burdens on firms.

The difficulty of reverse charging limited to certain products—as proposed by the UK—is that MTIC frauds may simply move on to other goods, not covered by reverse charging. There would also be new enforcement issues, at the 'boundary' between commodities subject to reverse charging and those subject to 'normal' VAT. Universal reverse charging, as proposed by Austria and Germany, avoids these difficulties. But it also, in effect, turns the VAT into something closely akin to a single-stage retail sales tax, with tax payments suspended until goods are sold to final consumers (albeit with the possibility of cumbersome reporting procedures for B2B transactions). The danger of this is obvious: it undermines the fractional nature of the VAT and instead collects all VAT revenue at the final sale, so exposing the system to substantially greater risks of revenue loss through unreported sales to final consumers. In effect, the VAT would be converted into an RST. Extensive reverse charging might help to stem losses from MTIC frauds, but would also expose the VAT to other risks of revenue loss through more mundane forms of evasion.

- 'Reverse withholding' schemes would tackle VAT frauds in a broadly similar way to reverse charging, by requiring the purchaser in a B2B transaction to make a direct payment to the authorities of part or all of the VAT due on its purchase. The difference is that the seller would remain liable for output VAT, receiving a credit for the amount withheld by the purchaser. Depending on the proportion of the VAT that the purchaser is required to withhold, this would diminish or even eliminate the scope to generate revenues through fraudulent refund claims, since exporting firms will themselves have paid part or all of the VAT on their purchases that they subsequently reclaim on export. The principal drawback of reverse withholding (which is quite common in Latin America but untried in Europe) would be its administrative complexity (which arises because of the need to ensure that the seller is given credit for withholding only when this has actually taken place) and the increased likelihood that traders will be due a refund (because of the reduced output tax they pay).

- Adoption of a system of 'VAT accounts', under which traders would be required to open a distinct bank account into which they would transfer the amount of VAT charged to their customers. VAT refunds would only be paid if the authorities were able to verify that the corresponding VAT payment had been made. This has been proposed by Sinn, Gebauer, and Parsche (2004) as a solution to the problem of VAT fraud, and a system of this sort has been tried in Bulgaria. The key feature is that it requires the VAT payment to be made *earlier* than in the present system, so that when refunds are paid, they can be checked against past payments made. Apart from this matter of timing, however, it does not fundamentally alter the situation. It is not clear that cross-checking refund claims against past payments to a bank account would be any easier, or more reliable, than checking that past payments have been remitted to the revenue authorities themselves. The scheme also eliminates the cash flow benefit that firms enjoy (providing some offset to their compliance costs) by retaining VAT collected until the next periodic payment becomes due. Reflecting these difficulties, Bulgaria has decided to remove its VAT account system.
- The compulsory use of a third party to guarantee VAT payments, either in general or for particular sectors, as set out by Ainsworth (2006). In the example set out in Figure 4.3, Company B, the future missing trader, would be required to obtain a guarantee that its VAT payments would be made. The principal difficulty with this is the cost involved; it is far from clear that banks or other potential guarantors would be any better placed than the revenue authorities to prevent firms disappearing with outstanding VAT liabilities, and the premium required to cover this risk would place substantial burdens on honest firms operating in the sectors most subject to VAT fraud.

These various administrative solutions all have weaknesses, either in creating other opportunities for fraud and/or in increasing taxpayers' compliance costs. A more durable solution to the problem of missing trader fraud requires a fundamental redesign of the VAT treatment of international transactions. The opportunity to claim fraudulent VAT refunds arises principally because of the break in the VAT chain that occurs as a result of the zero-rating of exports; and the break occurs at an especially vulnerable point in the chain, where control passes from one national tax administration to another. Export zero-rating requires substantial amounts of VAT receipts to be paid back as refunds, and a system that requires refunds on such a large scale creates opportunities for correspondingly large-scale revenue fraud. Ending VAT zero-rating for trade between EU member states would sharply reduce the scale of refunds and eliminate some of the most tempting opportunities for missing trader frauds. We discuss ways in which this could be done in Section 4.5.2.

4.4. EXCISE TAXES ON ALCOHOL AND TOBACCO

The UK, in common with all EU countries, applies excise taxes,[49] as well as VAT,[50] to three principal groups of goods: motor fuels, tobacco products, and alcoholic drinks. The scale of these taxes varies widely across the EU (Table 4.3). In the case of all three, UK excise rates are at the top end of the range, and their revenue contribution is significant: some £40 billion in 2006–07 (8.2% of total revenues), of which more than half (some £24 billion) was from motor fuel taxes, with £8 billion each from tobacco and alcoholic drinks. As noted earlier, however, the period since the Meade Report has seen a substantial reduction in the importance of the excises as a source of revenue. Intellectually, too, they have—until recent years—been out of fashion. What role, if any, remains for excises, and on what basis should they be levied?

[49] By an 'excise' we mean a single-stage sales tax applied to a limited group of commodities. The UK excises on alcoholic drinks and tobacco products discussed here are levied at the wholesale stage, with production and movements of these goods before the excise is levied subject to close monitoring and control by the revenue authorities. The UK also levies single-stage sales taxes on a number of other goods and services, including gambling, insurance premiums, and airline tickets, which for practical or historical reasons are not covered by VAT, and also levies some environmental taxes which are basically single-stage excises on certain goods and services including landfill use and quarried aggregates such as gravel. EU rules govern the structure and, to some extent, the rates of the three principal excises—on alcohol, tobacco, and mineral oils—and also discourage proliferation of additional new excises. Nevertheless, some EU members, notably Denmark, have historically levied excises on a much wider range of goods and services, and continue to do so.

[50] VAT is levied on the price of the product, including the excise. This sequencing makes no difference when excises are ad valorem, but when they are specific it preserves the (potential) role of the VAT as a generalized tax on consumption in the sense that a uniform change in the VAT rate applied to all commodities then leaves their relative consumer prices unchanged.

Table 4.3. Excise duty rates in the UK and the EU, July 2007 (in euros)

Member state	Cigarette excise per pack of 20	Specific excise as % of total tax	Beer per litre, at 12.5 degrees Plato	Still wine per 75 cl bottle	Spirits per 70 cl, 40%
Belgium	2.29	11	0.21	0.47	4.91
Bulgaria	0.70	7	0.10	0	1.57
Czech Rep.	1.16	42	0.11	0	2.62
Denmark	2.29	54	0.34	0.82	5.63
Germany	2.81	46	0.10	0	3.65
Estonia	0.70	39	0.19	0.66	2.72
Greece	1.61	5	0.14	0	3.05
Spain	1.53	9	0.11	0	2.32
France	3.20	8	0.13	0.03	4.06
Ireland	4.28	55	0.99	2.73	10.99
Italy	1.99	5	0.29	0	2.24
Cyprus	1.69	20	0.24	0	1.70
Latvia	0.52	43	0.09	0.43	2.53
Lithuania	0.55	54	0.10	0.43	2.60
Luxembourg	1.76	15	0.10	0	2.91
Hungary	1.00	45	0.25	0	2.40
Malta	2.20	12	0.09	0	6.52
Netherlands	2.28	50	0.25	0.59	4.21
Austria	2.00	21	0.25	0	2.80
Poland	0.91	35	0.22	0.34	3.21
Portugal	1.86	49	0.17	0	2.68
Romania	0.83	39	0.09	0	2.10
Slovenia	1.28	20	0.34	0	1.95
Slovakia	0.91	52	0.17	0	2.12
Finland	2.40	10	0.97	2.12	7.91
Sweden	2.45	18	0.79	2.37	15.04
UK	4.97	52	1.01	2.63	8.08

Source: Authors' calculations from data in *European Commission Excise Duty Tables* ref 1.025 (July 2007), downloaded from <http://ec.europa.eu/taxation_customs/index_en.htm#>.

This section focuses on alcoholic drinks and cigarettes: the taxation of motor fuels is discussed in Fullerton, Leicester, and Smith, Chapter 5 on environmental taxation.

The case for higher taxation of alcohol and tobacco does not immediately entail the use of completely separate additional taxes for these commodities. Why not, instead, implement such differential taxes by differential VAT rates? There are three main reasons. First, excises are a natural way of correcting for damages that arise from the use of the commodity in production as well as in final consumption; by contrast, higher VAT on production inputs would do little to alter the behaviour of VAT-registered producers. Second, in so far as there is a strong case for taxing some commodity on a specific rather than ad valorem basis, this can be implemented more easily with a separate excise. Third, very high tax rates create particular enforcement risks that call for physical controls beyond the book-based enforcement on which the VAT is based.

4.4.1. Revenue-raising efficiency in the taxation of tobacco and alcohol

Leaving externality arguments aside for the moment, are the characteristics of demand for these commodities such as to call for above-average taxation on standard optimal tax grounds? The question is often posed in terms of the 'inverse-elasticity rule': the presumption that commodities with low own-price elasticities of demand provide a relatively efficient revenue source. But, as discussed in Section 4.2.2, the key demand characteristic relevant to revenue-raising efficiency is not the own-price elasticity of demand but rather the degree of complementarity/substitutability with leisure. Is there any reason to believe that cigarettes and/or alcoholic drinks are particularly (relatively) complementary with leisure (in the sense, more precisely, that, conditional on a given level of total expenditure, those who supply more market labour will smoke or drink less)?

It is unclear, a priori, whether cigarette consumption is likely to be a complement with leisure or a substitute. For some people smoking may be a leisure-time pursuit; for others, it may help with the stresses and social interactions involved in working; for some it may be both. The overall relationship between cigarette consumption and labour supply cannot be resolved on the basis of a priori reasoning. Systematic empirical evidence is sparse. Parry (2003) notes that, while some studies have suggested a slightly negative income elasticity of demand for cigarettes, it is difficult to infer much about complementarity or substitutability with labour supply from this; he suggests that workplace smoking restrictions might be a reason to believe that smoking and working may not be complementary. A similar conclusion emerges from the results from Crawford, Keen, and Smith (2008) reported in Table 4.1 above, which suggest that labour supply and tobacco spending are modest substitutes, with an effect that is statistically significant, but relatively small.

Overall, the evidence is far from overwhelming, and its reliability is greatly compromised by the sharp socio-economic differences in smoking patterns which have emerged in most countries in recent years. In the current state of knowledge it is unlikely that cigarette consumption is sufficiently complementary with leisure to warrant high taxation on these grounds alone, though as Parry (2003) finds, different values for the relative substitution between cigarettes and leisure, within a relatively moderate range, can make a considerable difference to the estimated optimal tax on cigarettes.

The relationship between alcohol and the labour/leisure choice is also likely to be complex. More leisure means more time to consume alcohol and also reduces the risk that the consequences of over-consumption (hangovers and so on) will negatively affect work performance. On the other hand, some level of alcohol consumption may be complementary with time spent working (and hence a leisure substitute), either because drinking helps workers unwind after a stressful day or because of social drinking and networking with colleagues. The balance between these two effects may vary with individual alcohol consumption. At low consumption levels, alcohol may be complementary with work, but at higher levels it may be complementary with leisure. The results from Crawford, Keen, and Smith (2008) reported earlier for two categories of alcoholic drinks, 'beer' and 'wines and spirits', show a positive and significant relationship between their budget shares and hours worked, suggesting that both are, on average, leisure substitutes rather than complements. This result should, however, be viewed with some caution, as it is well known that alcohol expenditure is under-reported in UK household budget surveys, particularly because of under-representation of high consumers. If the relationship between alcohol consumption and labour supply is very different among heavier drinkers than the rest of the population, then the estimates will be biased by the omission of heavy consumers. Nevertheless, and as with cigarettes, the evidence does not create a compelling case for taxing alcohol more heavily than other goods on grounds of revenue-raising efficiency alone.

4.4.2. Consumption externalities and commodity taxation

The excises on alcohol and tobacco might alternatively be justified in terms of their role in discouraging consumption that has consequences beyond the immediate pleasure of the consumer themself.

Even if we put aside any paternalist inclinations and regard individual consumers as best placed to judge the costs and benefits of consumption to themselves, externality-correcting taxes may be needed to ensure that costs imposed on others are properly considered. The case for using taxes to discourage *socially* harmful activities was set out by Pigou (1920) and has been developed subsequently in the context, primarily, of environmental policy. In an otherwise first-best context—with prices undistorted by taxation, imperfections of competition or other factors—the tax should be set equal to the marginal external cost of each unit consumed. In more realistic contexts, this conceptually simple policy prescription becomes nuanced. When taxes also serve a revenue-raising purpose, for instance, Sandmo (1976) and Pirttilä and Tuomala (1997)—dealing with the cases in which direct taxes may and may not be imposed—show that optimal commodity tax rules take an additive form in which a Ramsey-type component is supplemented by one related to the marginal external damage, but potentially somewhat lower to reflect any intensification of the distortions from pre-existing taxes. Understanding the nature and extent of external damage is thus key to proper tax design.

The external costs of tobacco and alcohol consumption include direct externalities experienced by other individuals, such as the harm that drunken drivers cause to others, and collectively borne resource costs such as the cost of publicly funded medical treatment for smoking- and alcohol-related conditions. In both cases, individual consumption decisions will not reflect the full social costs of consumption, because the individual consumer does not bear the marginal costs of medical treatment or of direct externalities that follow from their smoking or alcohol consumption decisions. Excise taxes may provide a way of confronting the consumer with these costs.

Frequently, the discussion of whether alcohol consumption and smoking are socially harmful also includes discussion of the consequences for the individual consumer's own health, employment prospects, accident risks, and so on. Such costs to the individual consumer are not, however, externalities. Arguments that they might warrant higher taxation to discourage consumption involve an element of paternalism, perhaps reflecting a concern that individuals may be poorly informed about some of the consequences for themselves of consumption. Viscusi (1995), for example, discusses whether individuals accurately perceive the health risks of cigarette smoking. However, unless there are grounds to believe that consumers are poorly informed about some of the consequences of consumption, paternalist arguments tend to meet with scepticism among economists.

Nevertheless, with tobacco and alcohol, the case for discouraging consumption, in the individual's own interest, should not be dismissed too lightly. Some of the individual costs of smoking and drinking arise as a result of the addictive nature of consumption, and this adds a further dimension to the problem. Current consumption may increase the risk of future addiction.

A well-informed and rational consumer would presumably be less willing to start smoking than if there were no risk of future addiction (Becker and Murphy (1988); Chaloupka (1991)). However, it is unrealistic to assume that all individual users of tobacco and alcohol fully grasp the addictive risks associated with each unit of consumption (Orphanides and Zervos (1995)). In addition (except in an empty and tautological sense), it is unrealistic to assume that all consumption decisions—particularly of alcohol—are based on a rational calculus of the costs and benefits of each unit consumed.

These departures from standard norms of rational behaviour have been emphasized by some authors—notably Gruber (2001) and Gruber and Köszegi (2001, 2004). What is central to these arguments, which are reviewed at greater length in Gruber's commentary on this chapter, is not simply the addictive properties of cigarettes and alcohol, but rather that individuals may show a basic time inconsistency in their behaviour: wanting to quit in the future, for example, but when the time comes preferring not to. They may then welcome devices that help to commit their future behaviour, with high current prices, for example, inducing a reduction in present consumption that will make it easier to amend their future behaviour (Gruber and Mullainathan (2005)). Various ways have been suggested of thinking about this kind of behaviour: Gruber refers to this as an 'internality', while Viscusi (1995) discusses the concept of an 'externality to one's future self'. This can lead, as Gruber points out, to fairly high levels of cigarette taxes—though not ones far out of line with those currently levied in the UK. Quite how persuasive these ideas are remains as yet unclear. One implication, for example, is that smokers would vote for a cigarette tax increase.

To the extent that such behaviour may undermine the case for setting tobacco and alcohol taxes based on the level of traditional externalities, the key consideration in public decision-making becomes the effectiveness of taxes in modifying the behaviour of those most likely to make ill-informed choices and face commitment difficulties. For this reason, the impact of taxes on the smoking and drinking behaviour of children and young adults becomes a major focus. The balance of evidence suggests that higher taxes are more effective in restraining consumption by this group than for the population in general (Lewit et al. (1981); Lewit and Coate (1982); Chaloupka and Wechsler (1997)).

External costs and tobacco taxes

What level of cigarette taxation would be required to reflect the marginal external costs (as traditionally defined) of smoking? These costs fall into three broad categories. The first consists of direct externalities experienced by other individuals, including the annoyance and adverse health effects from passive smoking. These people may include work colleagues and wholly unrelated individuals (other patrons of a bar or restaurant, for instance), but a high proportion will be friends and family members. The second comprises collectively borne costs, such as those of publicly funded medical treatment for smoking-related conditions. The third category of externalities arise through the tax system. Smoking may have consequences for the individual consumer's income and expenditure, especially through a higher rate of sickness absence. While these effects would be wholly internal in a 'first-best' world without distortionary taxes, the presence of income taxes and spending taxes gives rise to what is, in effect, a tax revenue externality. Given the efficiency cost of raising public revenues through distortionary taxation, induced changes in revenues have a clear social significance.

There is an extensive literature on the social costs of smoking. Much of this is not directly relevant to the estimation of corrective taxes, however, because an insufficiently clear distinction is drawn between costs experienced and internalized by the individual consumer and external costs experienced by others.

The most widely quoted US estimates of tobacco consumption externalities, appropriately defined, are those of Manning et al. (1989). These distinguish between the gross costs of smoking (higher costs of medical treatment, and so on, as a result of conditions caused by smoking), and the net costs, which offset against the gross costs a range of cost savings (mainly public expenditure effects) arising from the premature death of smokers. Gross costs were estimated at 42 cents per pack, discounting future costs at 5%, while net costs were 15 cents per pack, on the same basis. Adding amounts to reflect the costs of passive smoking and smoking-related fires raises the net costs to 38 cents per pack—very close to the 37 cents per pack average tax on cigarettes in the US at the time.

These estimates were subsequently updated by Viscusi (1995), with adjustments to reflect the lower tar levels of cigarettes smoked by more recent generations of smokers, and to reflect the lag profile with which this change in tar content feeds through into health effects after consumption. Table 4.4 summarizes some of the key components in the estimates presented by Viscusi, again with total external costs expressed in terms of the externality per pack. The effects of Viscusi's tar and lag adjustments in the example shown are relatively modest, but such adjustments have been controversial in the light of some evidence suggesting that smokers may smoke lower-tar cigarettes more intensively (Evans and Farrelly (1998)).

Table 4.4. Expected external costs of cigarettes for the United States, in cents per pack

	External cost, raw data	External cost, tar adjustment based on 20-year moving average
Medical care before 65	0.326	0.302
Medical care after 65	0.172	0.153
Total medical care	0.498	0.455
Sick leave	0.012	0.011
Group life insurance	0.126	0.114
Nursing home care	−0.221	−0.197
Retirement pension	−1.099	−1.000
Fires	0.016	0.016
Taxes on earnings	0.351	0.326
Total net external costs	−0.317	−0.274

Source: Viscusi (1995); based on 3% discount rate.

The picture in Table 4.4 may be partial. No estimates are included for the direct externalities of passive smoking, in terms of either annoyance, or the substantial items that could arise from the health effects of passive smoking, especially on children and other family members. Evidence on these effects has been accumulating rapidly in recent years, and is reviewed in Adams et al. (1999). Viscusi (1995) argues that passive smoking effects are insufficiently precisely determined to permit point estimates, but shows a range of possible values, leading to a bottom line which varies from a net saving to a larger net cost, among which he suggests the median estimate of zero net external costs may be regarded as a plausible upper bound.

Taking account of public expenditure offsets arising from the premature death of smokers has been controversial in the public debate. It nevertheless seems wholly correct. If these items were private costs (for example, if individuals were responsible for paying actuarially differentiated private insurance premiums to cover future costs arising from their consumption decisions), then a rational consumer would experience the additional health costs and reduced future social care costs in the same way, and there is no reason to believe that they would treat the two insurance premiums differently. Since the purpose of externality taxation is to confront the individual decision-maker with the external costs of their decision, on the same basis as if they were private costs, consistency would require that both additional costs and cost reductions be treated in the same way.

One reason that public expenditure offsets arising from premature mortality have been controversial is their size. On Viscusi's unadjusted figures, additional medical care costs for smokers are approximately 50 cents per pack, while savings on nursing home care and retirement pensions are equivalent to about $1.30 per pack. But there is even controversy about the sign of the health care cost component. In a study for the Netherlands, Barendregt et al. (1997) found that the long-term effect of smoking cessation was to increase health care costs. In the short term, they estimated health care costs would fall, as ex-smokers cease to suffer the illnesses caused by smoking, but this 'conventional' effect on the costs of treating smoking-related diseases would then be offset by longer-term costs, as ex-smokers survive long enough to suffer the very costly medical conditions of old age. By contrast, Rasmussen et al. (2004) use a similar approach, but find that the overall lifetime effects of smoking cessation on health care costs are beneficial.

The externality case for cigarette taxes requires clear identification and measurement of the external costs of smoking. Nevertheless, attempts to draw a clear boundary between internalized and external costs are not straightforward, and a number of areas of conceptual and practical difficulty can be identified.

- *Effects on family members*. One controversial area is the treatment of costs borne by family members. Family members of a smoker may experience considerable costs, including ill-health, and pain and distress as a result of the illness and premature death of the smoker. Many of the consequences of smoking during pregnancy, including severe damage to the lifetime health of the child, also come under this heading. There are, in addition, further important costs for the healthcare system in treating these conditions. Whether, and to what extent, costs experienced by other family members should count as externalities has been controversial. As Viscusi (1995) notes, it turns, in principle, on whether the welfare of other members enters into the utility function of the smoker, and, in other areas of policy, it is often assumed that family members are assumed to care for each other's welfare to the extent that the welfare of the household can be considered as a single entity. In the case of smoking, however, this seems an extreme position, and at least some of the harm inflicted on family members and unborn children would seem best treated as externalities.
- *Healthcare Finance and External Costs*. How far are the costs of medical treatment and healthcare internalized when tobacco consumption decisions are made, and how far should they be counted as an externality? In the case of publicly funded, tax-financed systems such as the UK National Health Service, the answer is straightforward: the treatment costs of illnesses resulting from individual consumption decisions are collectively

financed. The same may largely be true of other collectively financed systems, such as employer-financed healthcare. By contrast, a system of private insurance capable of appropriate differentiation of insurance premiums might be able to internalize a large part of the healthcare costs associated with smoking.

- *Effects on wages and productivity*. A large part of the total social cost of smoking estimated by Manning et al. (1989) and Viscusi (1995) consists of foregone tax revenues on earnings, due to the shorter and less-productive working lives of smokers. This seems fairly uncontroversial. Whether more of the income or output loss from sickness absence and other smoking-related productivity effects should be counted as an externality depends primarily on how far the effects of smoking on worker productivity are reflected in wages. If workers are paid their actual marginal product, then there is no externality: smokers who are less productive receive correspondingly lower wages. However, employers may not always be able to differentiate the wages paid to smokers and non-smokers: Employment protection and sick pay legislation may, for example, compel an employer to continue making payments to a worker who has fallen sick as a result of smoking. In this case, the lower productivity of smokers generates externalities of two forms. First, the employer paying a smoker wages that exceed the worker's marginal product will experience a real income externality. Secondly, since the overall marginal product has fallen and the employer is unable to differentiate the wages paid to different workers, both smokers and non-smokers will receive lower wages as a result of the lower productivity of smokers.

External costs and alcohol taxes

The external costs of alcohol consumption, like those of smoking, include (i) direct externalities experienced by other individuals, including the victims of accidents, property damage, and violence caused by other people's drinking, (ii) collectively borne costs, such as the cost of public order policing and publicly funded medical treatment for alcohol-related conditions, and (iii) tax revenue externalities. The most widely quoted US estimates of alcohol consumption externalities, appropriately defined, are those of Manning et al. (1989), who estimate that net external costs are equivalent in value to about 35% of the producer price of alcohol. A very large proportion of these are from alcohol-related traffic fatalities. Parry (2003) notes that there are fewer such accidents in the UK, so that marginal external costs are consequently also likely to be lower.

Estimates of external costs of alcohol consumption for the UK by Maynard, Godfrey, and Hardman (1994) included various categories of direct externality (such as the damage caused in road traffic accidents) and also the cost of defensive measures (such as policing costs and the costs of research on alcohol problems). The costs of collectively funded medical treatment in the UK National Health Service of alcohol-related illnesses are also included. But the largest items are under the heading 'costs to industry', including the substantial costs of sickness absence and unemployment. Quite how far these should count as external costs depends on what is assumed about the effects of alcohol-induced productivity effects on individual wages, an issue discussed above for smoking. Overall, Maynard et al. (1994) calculate the total externalities associated with alcohol consumption in the UK to be around £2.7 billion, equivalent to some 17% of pre-tax alcohol expenditure.

Translating such estimates into appropriate rates of Pigouvian taxation on alcoholic drinks is complicated by the fact that most are of total costs, not marginal. Unlike cigarette externalities, which may well be almost constant across each unit consumed, the externalities from alcohol consumption largely relate to abusive consumption, and the marginal external cost of consumption may well differ sharply from the average. Excessive consumption, leading to serious drunkenness in individual episodes or alcoholism over time, is the prime source of the externalities, and the external costs associated with moderate consumption may be close to zero. While the results of Maynard et al. (1994) suggest that the average external cost from alcohol consumption in the UK might be of the order of 17% of the pre-tax price of alcohol, the marginal external cost may be quite different—and higher.

Diamond (1973) considers the design of corrective taxation when all individuals causing externalities must be taxed at the same rate, but where the externalities from some are more damaging than those from others. Where there is separability between the externality and consumption, the optimal tax is simply the weighted average of the marginal contributions to the externality, across different individuals, where the weights are given by the sensitivities of demand for the externality-generating good. If the primary reason for differences in the external costs of alcohol arises from differences between individuals, rather than between units of drink consumed by a particular individual, then this result may provide some support for regarding the average external costs as a rough-and-ready indicator of the optimal externality tax. But if the external damage caused by alcohol consumption varies across units consumed by each individual (for example, if the 'last drink' causes all the problems), then the appropriate externality tax would be considerably higher.

Pogue and Sgontz (1989) investigate further the implications for optimal alcohol taxation of the requirement that the alcohol sold to abusive and non-abusive drinkers be taxed at the same rate. Their analysis is directed at quantifying the trade-off between the reduction in welfare of non-abusive drinkers and the social benefits from the reduction in consumption by abusive drinkers. The balance will depend on the size of marginal social costs from abusive consumption, the size of the welfare loss from distorted non-abusive consumption, the relative numbers of abusive and non-abusive consumers, and the price elasticities of the two groups. (There is also the difficult issue of principle of whether alcohol-dependent consumers of alcohol should be treated as deriving utility from their abusive consumption, or not.)

4.4.3. Distributional aspects of alcohol and tobacco excises

As argued earlier, the availability of a sophisticated income tax and direct transfer system effectively undercuts any distributional rationale for differential commodity taxation, and any reason to have particular concern about the distributional characteristics of taxes on most commodities. As a general rule, the distributional incidence of individual components of the tax system is of less concern than the overall distributional incidence of all taxes (or, indeed, all government fiscal interventions) taken together. The fact that a particular regressively distributed component of the tax system may bear disproportionately heavily on poorer households may be unimportant if it is counterbalanced by distributional progressivity in other taxes.

Nevertheless, where, as with tobacco taxes, taxes are distributed extremely unevenly across households at similar income levels, there may be reason to look at the separate distributional incidence of the tax, since any adjustment to other taxes can only offset on average the distributional impact of the excise tax on tobacco. The distributional incidence of taxation on heavy smokers will be more heavily influenced by the distributional characteristics of the tobacco tax; and for non-smokers, the incidence of the tobacco tax will be an irrelevance.

Studies for the US have found that alcohol and tobacco taxes appear substantially less regressive when a longer time frame is used for analysis than when analysed on the basis of current income. Poterba (1989) shows that the regressivity in relation to current (annual) income of alcohol and tobacco excises in the US is diminished sharply if distributional incidence is assessed in relation to household expenditures, a measure arguably more consistent with life-cycle analysis. Lyon and Schwab (1995) use data from

Table 4.5. Income and expenditure shares of tobacco and alcohol, United Kingdom, 2003

Quintile group	Current income quintiles, and tobacco spending as % of total current income	Expenditure quintiles, and tobacco spending as % of total current expenditures
1 = poorest	2.37	1.60
2	2.04	1.95
3	1.53	1.69
4	0.99	1.32
5 = richest	0.56	0.92
Quintile group	**Current income quintiles, and spending on alcoholic drinks as % of total current income**	**Expenditure quintiles, and spending on alcoholic drinks as % of total current expenditures**
1 = poorest	6.09	2.53
2	4.28	4.16
3	3.84	4.86
4	3.88	4.94
5 = richest	3.10	4.72

the US Panel Survey of Income Dynamics (PSID) to compare the effects of analysing distribution based on incomes over different periods. Both alcohol and tobacco taxes appear more regressive when analysed using income data for a single year than five-year data, and a further reduction in regressivity is found if the analysis is based on lifetime, rather than five-year, income.

Table 4.5 shows a similar analysis, using more recent data for the UK. Analysed on the basis of current income, tobacco taxes look massively regressive, because household tobacco spending as a percentage of income for the poorest income quintile is some four times that for the richest quintile. On the other hand, analysed on the basis of household spending quintiles, tobacco taxes still look significantly regressive, but much less so than when based on current income. The average tobacco budget share for the lowest-spending quintile is less than double that for the highest-spending quintile. Likewise with spending on alcoholic drinks, a distributional analysis based on current income would suggest that alcohol taxes would be significantly regressive, with spending as a percentage of income by the poorest income quintile twice that of the richest. Analysed on the basis of household spending quintiles, however, alcohol taxes do not look regressive, and indeed appear somewhat progressive across the first four quintiles.

4.4.4. Specific versus ad valorem taxes

Unlike VAT, which simply taxes commodities in proportion to their selling price at one of a limited number of percentage tax rates, the separate excises for alcohol and tobacco offer—in principle at least—a wider menu of possibilities for the precise specification of the tax base. These are constrained by EU rules. For cigarettes, member states must levy an excise comprising both ad valorem (price-related) and specific (per 1,000 cigarettes) components, and the specific element should be between 5 and 55% of the total tax (including VAT) levied on the 'Most Popular Price Category' of cigarette in the member state concerned. In 2008–09, the UK tobacco excise (in conformity with EU rules) includes both ad valorem and specific components: cigarettes bear a specific excise of £112.07 per 1,000 cigarettes, and an ad valorem excise of 22% of the retail selling price. The UK alcohol excises, by contrast, are wholly specific taxes, based—as in all EU member states—on product volume and/or alcohol content.

Issues arising in the choice between specific and ad valorem taxes are surveyed in Keen (1998). The latter have a distinctive 'multiplier effect', in the sense that actions which change the producer price by some given amount will have a larger effect on the price charged to the consumer. As a result, ad valorem taxes will tend to discourage costly improvements in product quality and to promote more vigorous price competition between producers. Specific taxes, on the other hand, will tend to have an upgrading effect on product quality. The overall implications for consumer welfare and tax revenue of the choice between specific and ad valorem taxation will vary, depending on the structure of preferences and on market structure.[51] Ad valorem taxation of goods will also tend to be more attractive where producers exert a degree of monopoly power and where there is little product differentiation. Specific taxes would be preferred where there are reasons to want to maintain product quality or where taxation is partly intended to affect an externality that is broadly related to the quantity of the product rather than to its value. Other considerations include the potential distributional advantage of ad valorem taxation in retaining relatively low price variants (though again this is unlikely to be a powerful concern, given the range of distribution-sensitive instruments available in the UK), the perhaps greater ease of administering specific

[51] Delipalla and Keen (2006) show that, in competitive circumstances, the mix should be such as to have minimal effects on product quality, in the sense that, at an optimum, uniform intensification of both taxes would leave quality unchanged. Recognition that ad valorem taxation leads to a lower consumer price than does specific, for a given level of revenue, in circumstances of imperfect competition, dates back to Musgrave and Suits (1953), and is explored further in Delipalla and Keen (1992).

taxes (which require physical checks rather than valuation), and the differing responsiveness of revenues to variations in the underlying producer price (being more stable under specific taxation, for example, when the demand elasticity is low—but not a concern if tax rates can be adjusted frequently relative to these underlying price movements).

For tobacco products, the importance of potential differences in product quality—the wide variation in prices across bands suggests that product differentiation in this market is not simply horizontal—point to substantial reliance on specific taxation. The most plausible argument for ad valorem taxation is likely to lie in market dominance concerns, but the objective of maintaining a low price for the final product does not sit easily with the corrective arguments for tobacco taxation. As for the form of the specific element of the tax base, EU rules require this to be based on the number of cigarettes, in contrast to earlier UK excises based on weight of tobacco (a shift which led to considerable changes in the pattern of competition within the industry). It is sometimes suggested that there might be merit in targeting more precisely the active or harmful content within cigarettes (taxing in proportion to nicotine or tar content), but the case for this is somewhat undermined by evidence that smokers can compensate for changes in strength by smoking weaker cigarettes more intensively (Evans and Farrelly (1998)).

In the case of the alcohol excises, one particular issue frequently raised (and where there is scope for UK reform, despite the current EU constraints on the definition of the excise tax base) is the role of alcohol content in defining the tax payable, both within a single category of drink (beer, wine, or spirits) and across the three principal categories of drink.

Spirits are currently taxed much more heavily per unit of alcohol than beer and wine. More uniform taxation of alcohol content across the three principal categories of drink has been advocated persuasively by Crooks (1989) among others. It would avoid distortion between competing drinks. It would also seem a natural way to structure the Pigouvian taxation of alcohol, in that it would appear to target the externality tax precisely to the underlying source of the externalities. Nevertheless, the issue is not straightforward, because different drinks may differ in their propensity to generate external costs per unit of alcohol content. Arguably, spirits offer the greatest potential to get very drunk very quickly, which may exacerbate some of the externality problems. If uniform taxation of alcohol content would make low-cost industrially produced spirits the cheapest form of alcohol, the shift of abusers to spirits consumption might then not be a matter of social indifference.

4.5. INTERNATIONAL ISSUES

International considerations in the setting of indirect taxes have come to be far more pressing than they were at the time of Meade (as in other areas of tax policy too), with the increased cross-border mobility of commodities, fostered within the EU by the elimination of internal fiscal frontiers, posing new and potentially profound challenges for both the VAT and excises. These concern the fundamental basis on which commodities are taxed, the difficulties created by zero-rating exports under the VAT, the treatment of border-crossing services—an issue that has required little attention until recent years—and interactions in tax-setting.

4.5.1. Origin or destination taxation?

The international norm is for commodities to be taxed where they are consumed: the destination principle. As seen above, however, implementing this—particularly with the zero-rating of exports under the VAT—has become problematic. One broad solution that might suggest itself, and is also consistent with a long-standing EU objective of allowing traders to treat sales anywhere within the union in the same way, is to shift to taxation in the place of production: an origin principle. This has brought back to the fore a long-running debate on the comparison between destination and origin taxation.

It is important first to be clearer on terminology than much of the policy discussion has been. With consumption and production occurring in different jurisdictions, there are a wide variety of ways in which commodities entering international trade might be taxed, differing in which jurisdiction (including, potentially, a supranational one) sets the applicable tax base and rate(s), which collects the revenue, and which ultimately benefits from the revenue (Messere (1994)). The current international rule, WTO-approved, is that the country in which consumption occurs does all three of these things. But such a dichotomy cannot do full justice to the range of possibilities. The point is of some importance, since, as will be seen, some of the schemes proposed to overcome present difficulties disassociate the three aspects, having, for instance, one country collecting tax but transferring the proceeds to another. For definiteness, we here take the destination (respectively, origin) principle to refer to a situation in which the applicable tax rate is set by the country of consumption (production), though as will be seen, even this needs further elaboration for the VAT.

Implementing the destination principle requires some mechanism for border tax adjustment, taking commodities out of tax in the exporting country and bringing them into tax in the importing country. Conceptually straightforward for the excises, this is achieved under the VAT by zero-rating exports and bringing imports fully into tax.[52] This means that purchasers, whether final consumers or registered businesses, have no tax reason to prefer domestic products over imports or vice versa. This procedure typically uses border controls to monitor exports and imports, but as noted in Section 4.3.3 this is implemented in the EU in the course of traders' normal periodic returns.[53] These arrangements are explicitly regarded as transitional, the ultimate objective being movement to 'origin taxation' which (an example of the potential for linguistic confusion in this area) in this context simply seems to refer to the collection of tax by the country of export.

Under the origin principle, no border tax adjustment is needed for excises. Matters are not so straightforward, however, for the VAT. While an origin-based VAT (in the general sense above) could take a number of forms, the most natural is that in which the value added in the production of any commodity is taxed at the rate of the country in which it is added. This requires that VAT be charged on exports at the rate of the exporting country, but credit then given in the importing country not for the export VAT actually paid but the hypothetical amount that would have been paid had VAT been charged at the rate of the country of import.[54] This is referred to as the 'stage of processing method' by Grossman (1980) and the 'notional credit method' by Genser et al. (1995).

These then are quite different methods of taxing commodities entering international trade. The destination principle is well established as the international norm. Nevertheless, the transitional nature of current arrangements within the EU, and more generally the difficulties that federal countries experience in operating destination-based invoice-credit VATs levied by

[52] Unregistered businesses and cross-border shopping final consumers are currently taxed on an origin basis in that sense (for the former, within limits of reasonable personal use). Mail order firms and other distance sellers are required to register for VAT in countries to which they sell once their sales exceed threshold levels.

[53] A second-order distortion this creates is the possible cash flow advantage which may arise as a result of the tax treatment of intra-Community transactions. In the present system this favours importing goods from a supplier in another member state over purchases from a domestic supplier, although the effect is small, and depends on the timing of VAT payments and recovery. Vanistendael (1995) gives greater weight to this issue.

[54] Suppose for example that a good with producer price €100 is exported from a country with a VAT rate of 10% to another where the VAT rate is 25%: the tax-inclusive price to the importer will then be €110 and the available credit (€110/1.25)0.25 = €22. This ensures that the part of the value that is added in the country of export is taxed at 10% and sets the stage for taxing further value added beyond that at 25%.

lower-level governments (which in turn arise from the same problems of zero rating exports in the absence of border controls as now faced in the EU) suggest that, as international integration deepens, so the case for applying VAT on a destination basis—or at least the way it is currently implemented—requires reconsideration.

Conditions for equivalence

At first sight, origin taxation seems to run counter to the whole thrust of EU policy to eliminate impediments and distortions to intra-EU trade: it would mean that a British firm purchasing goods from other member states would no longer treat the VAT rates of other member states as a matter of indifference. In comparing possible suppliers in Denmark and Germany, for example, it would need to take into account the respective VAT rates there (currently 25% and 17.5% respectively), since these would affect the input tax credit available. It might seem that such a system would involve massive, and costly, tax-induced distortions of business purchasing decisions, unless severe restrictions were placed on member states' powers to determine their own VAT rates.

It is certainly likely that the system would be *perceived* as one in which tax differences between member states are much more likely to distort business purchases than under the 'level playing field' provided by the destination principle. Cnossen and Shoup (1987), in reviewing the relative merits of origin and destination principles for VAT, see this as a key obstacle to adoption of an origin-basis VAT and it is hard to disagree. Nevertheless, they and many others have noted that there are circumstances in which origin and destination principles are equivalent in the sense that they lead to exactly the same patterns of trade and economic welfare. Despite appearances, the playing field is then no more level under one principle than under the other.

The most general statement of such results is in Lockwood, de Meza, and Myles (1994a), but the gist is easily stated. Start with the simple case of a world lasting for a single period and comprising two countries, each of which taxes all commodities at a uniform proportionate rate (which may differ between the two countries). It is then easily seen that the shift from destination to origin principles need have no effect on the real allocation of resources, with no need even for compensating international transfers. All that is required to restore the initial allocation of resources is either a devaluation by, or a reduction in the general price level of, the country with the higher tax rate: this will ensure, for instance, that the change of basis has no effect on the foreign currency price of its exports. There are then neither substitution effects through changes in relative prices nor income effects through tax revenues. The intuition is straightforward. A uniform tax levied on a destination basis is a tax on the value of aggregate consumption, while a uniform tax levied on an origin basis is a tax on the value of aggregate production; and with balanced trade, these are the same thing.

Recent work has shown the equivalence between destination and origin taxation to hold in rather more general circumstances too. It continues to hold, for example, under imperfect competition, and in intertemporal trade models which have the feature that trade must be balanced in present value.[55] Striking as these equivalence results are, however, their practical applicability is likely to be limited:

- *Problems with partial application.* A 'restricted origin' regime—in which the origin principle applies to trade between some subset of countries (such as the EU member states) while trade with the rest of the world remains subject to the destination principle—raises two sets of difficulties (Shibata (1967)). First, it opens up the possibility of trade deflection: traders operating in a high tax member state, for example, would have an incentive to export to a low tax member via the rest of the world (so incurring the lower tax rate of the country of final consumption)[56] rather than directly (incurring the high rate of their own jurisdiction). Second, since trade flows between the countries adopting the origin system need not be balanced, a change in tax basis generally redistributes revenue between them (with net exporters on trade within the group being the winners); this latter is less of a concern in pure efficiency terms, since it could in principle be undone by a simple lump sum transfer between countries. As Lockwood, de Meza, and Myles (1994b) observe, both problems can be avoided if member states adopt the origin principle not only with regard to each other but also with regard to the rest of the world: a 'non-reciprocal restricted origin system'. This provides a clear analytical solution, but it is equally clear that it would be hard to persuade practitioners and policy-makers of the neutrality of a scheme in which exports from the EU are taxed twice (once in the EU, once in the country of destination) while imports into it are not taxed at all.
- *Intergenerational redistribution.* A change of tax basis can have complex and potentially powerful intergenerational effects (Bovenberg (1994)). A shift from destination to origin taxation, for example—somewhat akin to a shift from taxing consumption to taxing wages, as discussed in

[55] Genser, Haufler, and Sorensen (1995).

[56] The story is complicated, but not fundamentally overturned, by the possible existence of tariffs.

Section 4.2—would tend to benefit the relatively wealthy and old (financing high consumption levels from past earnings) at the expense of the relatively young and poor (saving a high proportion of their factor incomes), with potentially adverse effects on capital accumulation.

- *Non-uniform taxation.* Unless all commodities are taxed at the same proportionate rate in each country—or a somewhat weaker similarity of tax structures holds[57]—adjustment of the exchange rate or general level of internal prices alone cannot offset the effects of a change in tax basis. In practice, of course, indirect tax systems are far from uniform, reflecting not only multiple rates of VAT but also the excises. There appears to be little evidence, however, on whether the non-equivalence that this implies is in practice likely to be quantitatively substantial.
- *Altered incentives in tax-setting.* Still more fundamentally, the equivalence results presume that tax rates remain unchanged with a shift from one basis to another. National incentives in setting those tax rates, however, are likely to be quite different in the two cases, a point returned to shortly.

When equivalence fails, which is better?

Since origin and destination bases are thus not in general equivalent, the question arises: which is to be preferred? Three groups of issues are relevant.

A first set concerns that comparison if taxes are set cooperatively. Attention then focuses on the quite different arbitrage conditions they imply. Under the destination principle, residents in any country pay the same tax on both imports and domestically produced items, and are thus led to equate producer prices across countries. With perfect competition, this in turn implies that relative marginal costs prices are equated across countries: which means an efficient pattern of production. Under the origin principle in contrast, consumer prices will tend to be equalized across countries, leading to exchange efficiency (that is, an efficient allocation of consumption across countries). The choice thus resolves to one between production and exchange efficiency. It might then seem that, under conditions outlined there, the Diamond–Mirrlees (1971) theorem discussed in Section 4.2 applies, so that production efficiency has priority. As Keen and Wildasin (2004) point out, however, the Diamond–Mirrlees theorem is not directly applicable in international settings when distinct governments face distinct revenue constraints.

[57] When tax rates vary across commodities, devaluation or general price movements can neutralize the real effects of a change in basis if for every commodity the tax factor (unity plus the ad valorem tax rate) in one country is the same multiple of the tax factor in the other. Uniform taxation within each country is sufficient for this, but not necessary.

In the absence of international transfers, Pareto-efficient tax design may then require deploying taxes on trade or other instruments that drive a wedge between producer prices in different countries. Given the ability to transfer resources across members of the EU, however—effectively consolidating, to some degree, their governments' budget constraints—their results suggest a presumption for production efficiency within the union.

Even with cooperative taxation, however, any presumption for destination taxation becomes less clear-cut under conditions of imperfect competition. The destination principle no longer implies production efficiency, because equalizing after-tax prices across producers does not necessarily equalize marginal costs (Keen and Lahiri (1998)); in addition, taxing intermediate transactions could in principle be desirable (in the absence of more directly targeted measures) to offset monopolistic output distortions.

Second, important distinctions arise if taxes are set non-cooperatively. The incentives for strategic tax-setting are fundamentally dissimilar between the two: towards base-stealing and (pushing in the opposite direction) tax exportation under the origin principle; towards taxation of importables (to induce favourable movements in the terms of trade and to some degree capturing profits otherwise accruing to foreign producers) under the destination principle. Not surprising, the two regimes cannot in general be unambiguously ranked (Lockwood (1993); Keen and Lahiri (1998)).

Third, there is a major practical difference between the two: under an origin-based VAT, producers would have an incentive—not present under the destination principle—to transfer price value-added into jurisdictions characterized by relatively low effective rates on value-added (Genser and Schulze (1997)). Given the considerable difficulties faced in monitoring transfer pricing devices driven by corporate taxation, this is a potentially major drawback.

Implications

Is there then a case for shifting from the destination to the origin principle? One advantage is that it would resolve the present asymmetry between the tax treatment of cross-frontier purchases of goods by individuals and by businesses. Under the current VAT system, differences in tax rates between countries are sustainable only to the extent that there are significant transport costs or other impediments to individual purchasing. If the pressure on the current system from individual cross-border shopping intensifies greatly (as anticipated by Sinn (1990)), movement to the origin principle could be the best (or only) option available. It is also the case that recent results have placed the origin principle in a less-unfavourable light than before. But it remains hard to make a strong case for clear gains from moving to its wholesale adoption, at least for the foreseeable future. Doing so would throw away the potentially useful ability to tailor national tax systems to national preferences, and risks inducing unwelcome production inefficiencies. It would fundamentally change strategic incentives in tax-setting, with unclear consequences. And it would open up potentially powerful possibilities for transfer pricing. Abandoning the destination principle in favour of a full-blown origin system seems unlikely to offer sufficient gains to offset these various costs and risks.

4.5.2. Alternative VAT mechanisms for intra-EU trade

There are therefore good reasons to retain the destination principle as the underlying basis for the treatment of international trade. In relation to the VAT, however, there remain a range of important issues about the practical mechanism, export zero-rating, which currently implements it. For it is important to recognize that although both the zero-rating of exports and the adherence to the destination principle are effectively universal, the former is not a necessary condition for the latter. Indeed, export zero-rating has two significant drawbacks. One, discussed in Section 4.3.3, is that it creates problems for VAT enforcement. It breaks the chain of VAT revenue cumulation whenever the chain of production and distribution crosses national boundaries, a point of particular enforcement vulnerability. Goods supposedly exported, and therefore zero-rated, may be diverted to the domestic market bearing no tax. And the refund of VAT to exporters coupled with the deferred payment of VAT on imports gives scope for profitable criminal exploitation through large-scale 'carousel frauds' and similar schemes.

The second drawback, highlighted in the European Commission's 1987 proposals for an alternative VAT mechanism to accompany the elimination of intra-EU border formalities at the end of 1992, is the sharp difference in VAT procedures applied to domestic sales and exports when exports are zero-rated. As a consequence, businesses' VAT compliance costs are increased by the need to treat differently domestic sales and exports to other EU member states. Views differ on the importance of removing such differential treatment, and achieving what Keen and Smith (1996) call 'compliance symmetry': it is not achieved, for example, within the US, given different treatment of inter- and intra-state sales. Nevertheless, it has played a significant role in the EU debate, where removing impediments to intra-union trade, not least by smaller and medium-sized enterprises (most of them likely to be within the VAT system, even with a threshold as high as in the UK).

Much of the '1992' programme of measures to complete the internal market of the Community was motivated by a concern that border formalities could increase the costs to a firm of doing business in other member states. Indeed, there was a concern that on occasion member states may have employed frontier bureaucracy as a form of trade protection against products from other member states. In order to remove the opportunities for such non-tariff barriers to arise, the 1992 programme abolished internal fiscal frontier formalities. In addition, in its original proposals, the Commission sought (but failed) to put in place after 1992 a VAT mechanism for cross-frontier transactions which enabled registered traders to treat sales to all member states, including their own, identically so as to ease closer integration within the internal market. In practice, however, the measures adopted, which continue to apply, treat trade within and between member states very differently; and the new procedures then introduced to prevent VAT evasion on international transactions in the absence of frontier controls may well have magnified tax compliance costs on export transactions (Verwaal and Cnossen (2002)).

Several VAT mechanisms have been proposed that would achieve economic outcomes conforming to the destination principle but without zero-rating exports:

Exporter rating

Export rating, advocated by Cnossen (1983) and adopted as the initial proposal of the Commission (1987) for the post-1992 world, means taxing intra-EU exports at the rate of the country from which the goods were exported, with credit then being available in the country of import and some clearing house mechanism put in place to ensure that revenue ultimately accrues, as at present, to the country in which consumption takes place. Exports and domestic sales would thus be taxed identically, which may be an advantage, since it reduces the danger that firms may be deterred from exporting by the need to deal with an unfamiliar export tax regime.

The central problems with this scheme relate to the operation of clearing. Under the initial proposal this was to have been done on the basis of individual transactions, necessitating complicated (and permanent) arrangements for measuring the required clearing flows. This would suffer, moreover, from the fundamental flaw of undermining the incentive for member states to check the validity of claims for VAT credit on imported goods: the cost of giving this credit would be underwritten by the Clearing House, and there would be little incentive for member states to spend resources in reducing fraudulent claims (Lee, Pearson, and Smith (1988)). An alternative would be a one-off compensation settlement (perhaps involving agreed annual revenue flows), reflecting the scale of the anticipated revenue changes. But while this would restore the incentive for member states to detect fraudulent claims for VAT credit on imports, it would introduce a new problem, giving rise to undesirable incentives for member states to raise their VAT rates so as to increase revenues from the taxation of exports. Since the importing member states would be required to give credit for whatever rate of tax was applied to exports, there would be no competitive restraint on this; the only limit would be the willingness of domestic customers to accept the higher VAT rates that would also apply to domestic sales.[58]

Uniform rating

Under the uniform rating scheme, intra-EU exports would continue to be zero-rated for the national VAT in the country of export but would then be subject to a uniform VAT rate, determined by the Community. This fixes, to the extent of that uniform VAT rate, the break in the VAT chain on intra-union exports, though compliance symmetry is not achieved, since exports and domestic sales are subject to different tax treatments. Such uniform rating can in turn be achieved in a number of ways.

CVAT

In the CVAT regime advocated by Varsano (2000) for Brazil (which faces similar problems subnationally) and McLure (1999, 2000) more generally, this special tax rate for exports is operated as a separate tax, by a single tax authority operating across all the jurisdictions concerned. Since the additional tax on intra-EU exports (the 'compensating VAT') would be collected by the same authority that then gives credit for the input tax paid on imported goods, and since these amounts in principle cancel out—except that revenue would be raised to the extent of imports by other than registered traders—this system avoids any revenue redistribution between member states without any need for clearing between them. But it does so by establishing a parallel VAT operation and bureaucracy (for the taxation of intra-EU trade) that generates little net revenue—which seems likely to be a hard political sell.

[58] While Article 90 of the Treaty of Rome proscribes the use of domestic taxes to provide indirect protection, it is not clear that the use of domestic taxation as a tax exporting device is similarly prohibited (just as WTO rules do not prohibit export taxes). Experience with Article 90 suggests, in any event, that it is effective only against the most egregious uses of domestic taxes to such trade-related ends.

Quite how large the administrative and compliance costs would be in this parallel VAT administration is unclear, and it may be able to draw heavily on VAT information already gathered in national systems. But unlike exporter rating there is a clear danger of asymmetry in VAT compliance costs between exports and domestic sales.

One of the two options recently proposed by the Commission for dealing with VAT fraud—the other (with many hesitations) being reverse charging, as discussed in Section 4.3.3—applies essentially the CVAT logic, in applying a uniform common VAT, at 15%, on trade between member states (Commission (2008)). Implementation, however, would remain wholly with national tax agencies, with proceeds from export VAT being reallocated to the country of import. This has the substantial appeal (in contrast to reverse charging) of strengthening the VAT chain. But by opting against separate administration of the CVAT—no doubt for understandable political reasons—it effectively dissipates the key advantage of the CVAT in avoiding any need for revenue reallocation. And it does nothing to simplify VAT compliance or render it more symmetric.

Dual VAT

Some similar properties are exhibited by the dual VAT regime proposed by Bird and Gendron (1998), who draw on the Canadian experience from the combination of a federal VAT and the provincial VAT levied in Quebec. This envisages the continuation of national VAT systems, including the zero-rating of intra-union exports, but run in parallel with a new Community VAT, set at a uniform rate EU-wide, and operated without regard to national boundaries. This Community VAT generates revenues for the Community, and at the same time ensures that intra-EU exports, although zero-rated by the member state VATs, do move between member states bearing at least some tax. An EU-wide VAT has some appeal as a source of own resources for the Union (being more transparent, for instance, than the current use of a notional VAT base to determine, in part, national contributions). The political prospects do not currently appear bright, however, and the revenue need would readily be met by a VAT rate so low—in the order of 2–3% would suffice to finance all the Unions' activities—that the impact on fraud is likely to be limited. Compliance symmetry would also not be achieved.

VIVAT

The main feature of the VIVAT, proposed by Keen and Smith (1996, 2000), is that a uniform Community-wide rate of VAT would be applied to transactions between all VAT-registered traders in the EU (perhaps with a rate of zero applied to financial services as part of the cash flow approach described in Section 4.3.2), while member states would retain the power to determine the rate of VAT on sales by traders to final consumers. This would achieve compliance symmetry, fix the break in the VAT chain between member states (with a firmness that depends, of course, on the level of the intermediate rate), and avoid some of the 'incentive' defects of the other main schemes, in terms of both enforcement and rate-setting incentives, noted above. And it does so without altering in any way the current ability of member states to choose the rate applied to final sales, and hence—since it is that, not the rate applied to intermediate transactions, which determines it—the total revenue finally raised (at least in so far as the crediting mechanism works properly). There is thus, in that sense, no real loss of national sovereignty. While some form of clearing would be needed to ensure that all revenue continues to accrue to countries of final consumption, the VIVAT lends itself more readily than does exporter-rating to some form of macro-related settlement—so ensuring adequate incentive, for instance, to control claims for credit of intermediate tax on imports—since the commonality of the intermediate rate removes scope for game-playing.

A further attraction of VIVAT is that it could ease some of the difficulties created by the current VAT exemptions, discussed in Section 4.3.2. The application of different national rates currently distorts competition (reflecting the cascading effects of differing degrees of unrecovered VAT implicit in prices paid for financial services, for instance) and requires complex (almost unworkable) rules for hospitals, universities, local governments, and others to declare their purchases in other member states so as to negate the incentive to buy abroad purely for tax reasons by ensuring that the appropriate VAT adjustments are made (by the revenue authorities of the importing country). A VIVAT would enable these distortions to be removed simply by enabling those producing exempt items to purchase at the intermediate rate, removing both the competitive distortion and the need to adjust tax on purchases from other member states. This would not remove the distortions that the widespread exemptions in the EU create, so the case for reforming them out of the system, stressed in Section 4.3.2, would remain. But it would ease them.

The principal disadvantage of VIVAT, beyond the need to arrange revenue transfers between member states, is that it requires an 'end user' distinction to be made—and enforced—between the sales which a business makes to other VAT-registered businesses and those sales it makes to final consumers: between, that is, B2B and B2C transactions. These would be taxed differently under VIVAT, and there would be additional compliance costs to businesses and extra administration costs for the tax authorities in accounting separately for the two categories and in handling difficult borderline cases. Assuming that the VAT rate on intermediate sales was never higher than the rate on final sales (the uniform Community-wide rate on intermediate sales might be 15%, say, with rates on final sales ranging as at present from 15% to 25%), the central risk is of sales to final consumers being disguised as sales to registered traders. This would of course rely heavily on the use of VAT registration numbers, as at present, to identify VAT status. But it would be possible to apply the rules rather more stringently than at present, without serious damage to the firms concerned. If a firm failed to substantiate a claim to be allowed to apply the intermediate rate, it would have to apply the final goods rate, which in some countries would be very little higher. (It might also be possible to credit input VAT claims at that rate where it could be shown that the final consumer rate had been wrongly applied to an intermediate goods transaction.) And it may even be that the opportunity to charge an inappropriately low rate would in some cases reduce VAT evasion on final sales: instead of entirely concealing transactions and remitting no VAT, the better bet for those so inclined could be to offer to charge and remit the intermediate rate.

More fundamentally, however, the central distinction needed to operate a VIVAT, between B2B and B2C transactions, is one that is in any event likely to become increasingly important in the operation of the VAT, and is indeed at the core of recent initiatives in connection with the VAT treatment of international services.

4.5.3. VAT and internationally traded services

International trade in services has grown much more rapidly than trade in goods in recent decades, placing increasing strain on some aspects of current consumption tax legislation and procedures, in the EU and elsewhere. The EU's VAT rules and procedures were primarily developed to handle goods trade, for which the notion of a trade transaction can be defined clearly in terms of the physical movement of the taxed commodities. For services, no such physical movement exists, making it much less straightforward to define transactions to which the tax provisions relating to international trade should apply. The main concern is that some transactions might end up untaxed or taxed twice, and that loopholes may be extensively exploited in the organization of international services businesses. Similar anxieties arise about the continuing viability of consumption tax systems in the face of the rapid growth of e-commerce. This has undermined national regulation and taxation in certain areas (such as gambling services), and turned some readily taxed goods (records and video-tapes, for instance) into hard-to-tax quasi-services (digital downloads).

Many of the problems in the VAT treatment of traded services can be traced to the 'absence of internationally agreed principles to determine where taxation should take place' (OECD (2004)): in other words, to the lack of a systematic and uniformly applied definition of the 'place of supply'. Current EU rules provide ad hoc treatment for particular categories of service. Some are taxed on the basis of the place of the supplier, others on the basis of the place of consumption; further complexity arises through the use of proxies (such as the place of establishment, or the place of performance) to define the place of either production or consumption of certain services.

The consequences of alternative approaches to the taxation of international services vary considerably across different types of transaction:

B2B transactions between VAT-registered traders

Which side of the transaction applies VAT is in this case unimportant in terms of economic efficiency because the tax rate has no ultimate impact: any tax paid is recovered later through the natural mechanism of the VAT (assuming, as current EU rules seek to ensure, that recovery operates effectively across any borders that the transaction spans), and there is no advantage (apart from second-order cash flow considerations) to purchasing from a lower-taxed source. Having the seller charge tax—by deeming the place of supply to be that in which they are located—has the merit of securing revenue by maintaining a chain of VAT payments, but requires some mechanism for reallocating revenue if it is to accrue to the country in which final consumption occurs. Instead having the buyer reverse charge themselves tax on such purchases—deeming the place of supply to be where they are located—avoids any need for revenue reallocation, but at the cost of breaking the VAT chain.

Sales to exempt traders

Since VAT paid on inputs then 'sticks', the VAT treatment (in particular, the tax rate at which supply is taxed) matters for efficiency. The problems here mirror similar problems in the taxation of domestic sales of services to exempt firms, and again point to the importance of scaling back exemptions as discussed in Section 4.3.2. These difficulties are exacerbated to the extent that domestic and cross-border sales of services might be taxed differently: for example, if the former is subject to normal VAT, and the latter zero-rated.

B2C sales

Distortions arise if some final consumers face different tax rates for similar products. For goods, these problems arise primarily through cross-border shopping, because the country of purchase may differ from the country of consumption, or of residence of the final consumer. Distance selling (mail order) raises similar issues of distortion, mitigated by the special regime applied to such trades. For services, distortions would arise through the equivalent of cross-border shopping or distance selling: in other words, the possibility that a consumer might be able to obtain equivalent services from suppliers located in different member states, and these might, under some definitions of the place of supply, be taxed differently.

Key issues

The key efficiency issues in defining the Place of Supply for services thus primarily concern cross-border sales of services to final consumers and entities not registered for VAT, and are broadly analogous to the issues of cross-border shopping or distance selling for goods.

As with cross-border shopping for goods, the practical significance of the problem, in terms of the risk of significant economic distortion, will vary considerably between products. At one extreme there are services which are effectively different if they are performed in different locations. Examples include passenger transport (a tram journey in Brussels is no use to the Manchester commuter trying to get to work), service performed on fixed property (by a plumber, for example), and various entertainment services (a cinema ticket in Stockholm is not a close substitute for a ticket for the identical film in Rome). At the other extreme there are services (including most e-services) where the location of the supplier is irrelevant to the performance of the service, and where a private customer could, in principle, purchase the service from a supplier in another member state without any penalty in terms of cost, inconvenience, or quality as compared with the equivalent domestic supply.

For the first group of services, the location of the customer coincides with the location of the supplier when the service is performed, and defining the place of supply as either would have an equivalent effect on economic efficiency. Problems of distortion in purchasers' decisions only arise if the place of supply is defined in terms of the location of the supplier, and if this can differ from the place where the service is performed. For the second group of services the definition of the place of supply is an issue of much greater significance for economic efficiency. For these services, distortion in sales to final consumers and B2B sales to exempt traders can be avoided only by taxing where the customer is located.

There is no simple way, however, of implementing this outcome.

- If the supplier remains liable for the tax, a small-volume EU supplier with customers spread thinly across all member states would have to deal with twenty-seven separate tax authorities. A potential solution to this would be some form of 'one-stop shop', allowing a supplier to deal with a single agency in respect of all EU-wide sales. There are various ways in which this could be organized, but the key idea is that the agency would charge VAT at the rate appropriate to each country, and remit the tax collected, and information about the transaction, to the VAT authorities in all member states to which sales were made.
- In some specific cases, such as digital downloads, the supplier may have no idea of the location of the customer, and so be unable to apply tax on the basis of the customer's location. This suggests that some EU-wide regime (a common rate of tax on all exports of digital services, or even on all sales of digital services within the EU) would be the most appropriate solution.
- If the supplier is located outside the EU, enforcement poses evident difficulties.

And while the alternative of making the customer liable for the tax on purchases of services is in principle a complete solution to the problem of ensuring economic efficiency, there are considerable practical difficulties. For B2B transactions, such reverse charging breaks the VAT chain. And for final consumers, it is evidently unworkable—the experience of the use tax in the US, which in principle requires taxpayers to declare out of state purchases but in practice is almost entirely ignored, illustrates the point.

The approach recently adopted by the EU (with effect from 2010), which follows OECD guidelines, is to tax B2B service purchases in the place where the customer is located, but B2C purchases where the supplier is located (at the rate applicable to the country of the consumer).[59] The former opts for

[59] Council Directive 2008/8/EC of 12 February 2008 amending Directive 2006/112/EC as regards place of supply of services. Application to telecoms is from 2015, and a range of special treatments apply.

avoiding revenue allocation. This is clearly a more coherent approach than at present, albeit one with risks: of ensuring that the break in the VAT chain for B2B trade is not exploited, and of identifying the proper rate at which to charge final consumers and implementing a transactions-based reallocation of revenues. Interestingly, it is built on precisely the distinction between sales to registered and to non-registered traders that is at the heart of the VIVAT, but without securing the full advantages that it offers in maintaining the VAT chain and ensuring compliance symmetry. A more thoroughgoing application of the VIVAT logic would not avoid all the difficulties in this area—such as, in some cases, identifying the location of final consumers—but could provide a more coherent framework for addressing these as other issues.

4.5.4. Excise tax competition and cross-border shopping

Tax-induced cross-border shopping and smuggling pose significant policy challenges for the EU. Not only do they cause a direct revenue loss—or perhaps gain to low tax countries—but they are likely to lead to tax rates being set lower than they otherwise would be.

The extent and impact of cross-border shopping

The problem of revenue losses from legal cross-border shopping by individuals has come into prominence as a result of the abolition of border controls between EU member states at the end of 1992. Before this, most member states applied restrictive travellers' allowances on personal imports of tax-paid goods from other EU countries, as well as from the rest of the world, and this kept legal cross-border shopping within tightly constrained bounds. As a result of the abolition of border controls, individuals can purchase goods in another member state and bring them home without restriction or fiscal adjustment, so long as the goods are for their personal use and not for resale.

The scale of revenue losses from both legal and illegal cross-border movements of alcohol is controversial. HM Customs and Excise estimated the UK revenue loss from *legitimate* cross-Channel shopping for alcohol in 1998 at £285 million, about 5% of total UK alcohol duty revenues. Some part of this revenue loss would have arisen as a result of duty-free purchases, rather than tax-paid purchases in other member states, though it is a reasonable guess that a significant part of the alcohol purchased duty-free would have been purchased outside the UK in the absence of the opportunity to make duty-free purchases (Christiansen and Smith (2004)).[60] HM Customs and Excise estimated that *illegal* cross-Channel smuggling of alcohol in 1998 involved a revenue loss to the UK of some £230 million, around 4% of total alcohol excise revenue.

For individual member states in this position, alcohol tax policy needs to take account of the potential revenue losses through legal and illegal cross-border activities. Crawford and Tanner (1995) and Crawford, Smith, and Tanner (1999) consider whether the revenue losses through cross-border shopping induced by duty differentials are sufficiently large that UK revenues could be increased by cutting the rates of UK excise duties. They observe that the post-1992 abolition of border controls acts so as to increase the price elasticity of demand for UK-bought alcohol: as the price is increased, some consumers reduce their consumption of alcohol altogether (the normal effect, in the absence of cross-border shopping opportunities), but in addition others may now switch to buying abroad. The higher elasticity for UK-bought alcohol might suggest that UK tax rates on alcohol should be reduced. Indeed, if the increase in elasticity is sufficiently large, it is possible that the existing rates of duty might exceed the revenue-maximizing duty rates.

Using data from the UK Family Expenditure Survey for the years spanning completion of the Single Market, Crawford, Smith, and Tanner (1999) find, however, no evidence of a significant change in elasticities. Whether a reduction in duty rates on the various categories of alcoholic drinks would increase or reduce UK tax revenues depends on the own- and cross-price elasticities of demand for the various categories of alcoholic drinks. Crawford et al. find that the UK tax rates on beer and wine are still lower than revenue-maximizing tax rates, meaning that a cut in duty on these drinks would reduce total revenues (even though it would repatriate a certain amount of cross-border shopping). On the other hand, they cannot reject the hypothesis that the current UK tax rate on spirits is at around the revenue-maximizing rate. This suggests that the duty on spirits may be closer to the level at which a cut might reduce cross-border shopping by enough to compensate for the revenue lost on each unit.

[60] In 1999 the EU countries abolished duty-free sales on intra-EU travel. Christiansen and Smith (2004) note that the global welfare gains from abolition of duty-free may be asymmetrically distributed between countries, and that high-tax countries may have relatively less to gain from its abolition than lower-tax countries; in particular it may deny them an opportunity to appropriate rents from sales to foreign travellers that would not otherwise be made. Christiansen and Smith (2008) discuss the implications of duty-free sales for the optimal structure of commodity taxes.

Policy problems and responses

The question for policy is what, if anything, should be done about the implications of such potential tax-induced cross-border purchases, legal and otherwise. In assessing this, it is important to remember, the extent of the problem cannot be inferred simply from the extent of observed cross-border shopping. Observing zero cross-border shopping could mean that there is simply no inclination to exploit tax differentials, as would be the case with literally non-tradable goods. But cross-border shopping would also be zero in equilibrium if intense tax competition drives all countries to charge the same excise tax rates, with all standing to benefit from setting a collectively higher rate.

In response to EU proposals to require member states to set VAT rates within specified bands, Lee, Pearson, and Smith (1988) argued that fiscal externalities arising from cross-border shopping between member states could warrant some level of EU tax coordination. However, since these negative fiscal externalities primarily arise where member states cut their rates below those of neighbours, this would indicate an EU-wide floor to excise duty (and VAT) levels, but no corresponding need to place an upper limit on member states' tax rates.[61]

The subsequent formal literature on tax policy in the presence of cross-border shopping has explored in more detail the potential impact of cross-border shopping (including for this purpose smuggling of tax-paid goods) and the tax competition it can lead to, and the appropriate policy responses. Using a stylized two-country model in which governments set their tax rates non-cooperatively, each concerned only to maximize its own tax revenue, Kanbur and Keen (1993) show that[62] imposing a minimum tax rate (a tax floor) leads both countries to gain relative to the non-cooperative outcome: even the low tax country benefits despite being forced to raise its tax rate, because this enhances the ability of the other country to increase its rate. Simply imposing a common rate, on the other hand, must cause the low tax country to lose, unless the common rate is set at a sufficiently high level.

[61] A ceiling on tax rates could be justified where countries have a degree of monopoly power, which would otherwise permit tax exporting.

[62] In the Kanbur–Keen (1993) framework it is the smaller country that sets the lower tax rate in equilibrium (since in setting a lower rate than the other it has more to gain by attracting the large tax base from abroad than it has to lose from reducing revenue from its own domestic tax base). Location may also matter for tax-setting incentives: Ohsawa (1999) shows that with three otherwise identical countries ordered on a line, that in the middle tends to set the lower tax rate as it has more borders to attract tax base across. Keen (2002) reviews the literature on cross-border shopping.

Some argue, however, that unrestricted tax competition may be a useful mechanism to control the tendency of governments to excessive growth. The case for the EU imposing some form of duty coordination—and indeed potentially coordinating in other areas of tax policy too—thus to some degree turns on fundamental differences of philosophy about the nature and value of governments. Those who view governments as choosing tax and spending policies to maximize social welfare may regard tax coordination as a way to ease what would otherwise be an undesirable constraint on their choices, while those who believe that there is a natural tendency towards excessive growth in government spending may view tax coordination in a less positive light. Even in this latter case, however, some degree of coordination may be desirable if—as seems plausible—policy-makers are not simply Leviathans having no selfless concerns and facing no electoral constraints.[63]

These considerations suggest to us a strong case for the agreement of minimum excise tax rates. And this is indeed the strategy that the EU has followed since the advent of the single market. The key issue is not the wisdom of the approach, but the low level—zero, in some cases—at which these minima are set. Raising them to more appropriate rates has, however, proved difficult, and this is unlikely to change.

4.6. CONCLUSIONS

One of the most remarkable developments in UK tax policy in the thirty years since Meade has been the shift towards indirect taxation, with the VAT—still new at the time of the report—coming to acquire a pivotal role in the overall tax system. Some aspects of this development, and of indirect tax design more generally, remain less than fully understood. In particular, the proper broad balance between direct and indirect taxes turns on relative efficiency and implementation costs about which little is known. And while much has been learnt about the theoretical case for some degree of differentiation in the rates of indirect taxation across commodities, limitations of empirical knowledge and understanding of implementation costs still leave some disconnect between these results and their practical application. What does seem clear, nevertheless, is the potential for building on the inherent strengths of the VAT to improve its effectiveness within the wider UK tax system, and the need for clearer thinking of the role of the traditional excises.

[63] On this wider political economy issue, see Edwards and Keen (1996) and Besley and Smart (2007).

4.6.1. Rate differentiation

Theory, much of it having come to prominence since Meade, suggests that when—as in the UK—government has at its disposal a fairly sophisticated range of instruments for redistribution, the potential contribution of commodity taxes to efficient revenue-raising is likely to be limited. Certainly there are grounds to tax at particularly high rates goods and services associated with external costs in either production or consumption, an issue explored at more length in Fullerton, Leicester, and Smith, Chapter 5, on environmental taxes, and relevant also to the case for the excises on alcoholic drinks and tobacco in the UK. But, except where externalities are involved, theory indicates that differential commodity taxation is unnecessary if patterns of commodity demand are independent of labour market status (the 'weak separability' condition). In this situation, patterns of spending convey no information that cannot be better exploited by more directly targeted redistribution, and taxes which vary with patterns of spending—the additional sophistication in the tax structure which commodity taxes offer—achieve nothing that cannot be achieved by other tax instruments. Nevertheless, the available empirical evidence firmly rejects weak separability, implying that appropriate rate differentiation could reduce the overall distortionary costs of taxation.

Precisely what kind of differentiation would be helpful, however, is much harder to say. In principle, tax rates should be chosen so as to reduce most the demand for goods that are, in an appropriate sense, complements for leisure (meaning time not spent in market work). In this way, unavoidable distortions against market work can be mitigated. The empirical work reported in Crawford, Keen, and Smith (2008) suggests that on these grounds we might think of taxing the broad category of 'leisure goods' more heavily than other goods and services, and domestic fuels and 'household goods and services' at lower rates. But the limitations and uncertainties of both the theory and the empirical work are such that, at least as yet, they provide little firm basis for policy prescription. The finding that the departures from weak separability, while significant, are quantitatively small suggests too that the gains from differentiation may not be large, though this requires more thorough investigation. And the administrative and compliance costs of rate differentiation would certainly need to be weighed against any advantage to be had in exploiting features of commodity demands. There is some evidence, and much anecdotal wisdom, that implementing such rate differentiation through the VAT would be quite costly (in terms, for example, of the likely increased need for refunds—to those selling lightly taxed items using more heavily taxed inputs—and to monitor borderline issues). Experience suggests that implementation of multiple stand-alone excises is likely to be even more problematic. And, not least, departures from uniformity may make it harder to resist simple lobbying for preferential treatment.[64] Externality issues aside, there is thus a strong case, albeit a largely pragmatic one, for uniformity in commodity taxation, and this is indeed the path that has been taken in most of the more modern VATs that have been introduced in recent years.

Since the VAT is at present marked by significant rate differentiation, the implications of this for the UK are substantial. The present domestic zero-rating and the reduced rate serve little purpose that could not be better achieved by other means. We have shown here that eliminating both would provide enough revenue to reconfigure tax credit and income support systems so as to ensure that most poorer households gained from the reform and still leave an additional £11 billion, all with only a modest one-off impact on the price level. Similar remarks apply to the present zero-rating of residential construction. Though not explicitly analysed above, here too there is evident scope for eliminating distortions by following others in including new sales fully into the VAT while putting in place measures to compensate the losers.

The essence of this has been known for many years, at least in relation to the zero-rating of food and children's clothing. What has been lacking is political will, a first step towards forming which is likely to be better public understanding of the inherent unfairness of the current rate structure. There may even be a case for some appearance of earmarking the proceeds from such a VAT reform.

4.6.2. Exemptions, international trade, and the VAT

New at the time of Meade, the VAT is now starting to look old, and imperfectly adapted to the changed international circumstances in which the UK finds itself. This is true not only of the rate structure, but more deeply too of aspects of its fundamental structure. Two issues stand out, with the EU in each case playing a key role. The proper response, in each case, is not to compromise but rather to build on the underlying logic of the VAT.

First are the widespread exemptions that are enjoined by current EU rules, notably in relation to public agencies and health, education, medical services, and financial services. In breaking the chain of tax and credit, these violate

[64] As argued in the context of tariff formation by Panagariya and Rodrik (1993).

the logic of the VAT in a way that rate differentiation does not. There is little quantitative evidence on the costliness of the inefficiencies this creates—including the incentive to self-supply and other distortions to production decisions, increased implementation costs for partially exempt traders, the bias towards imports—but good reason to suppose they are not trivial, and greater now (as a consequence of privatization and increased financial sophistication) than they were thirty years ago. And at a technical level it is now much better understood—and illustrated by experience in New Zealand, discussed in the commentary by Dickson and White—that these exemptions are not inescapable.

The case for considering alternatives to exemption is especially clear in relation to financial services, though this is one area in which no country has implemented a full solution. One possibility discussed above is to apply a cash flow treatment to financial services—treating all inflows as VAT-able purchases and outflows as sales—while zero-rating transactions with registered businesses. Movement to such a system would not only remove distortions but likely to enable a substantial net revenue gain. And while much closer examination is clearly required, it could fit neatly within the VIVAT form of VAT that we believe has other attractions too.

Eliminating these exemptions would require, however, a change in EU rules, which in turn requires unanimity among the twenty-seven member states. It is not hard to imagine change in the VAT treatment of the financial sector, in particular, being vetoed. This raises wider questions as to the appropriateness of EU provisions that may impede member states' adopting measures that may improve the operation of their domestic VAT systems without having any obvious adverse spillover effects. The first step, in this as perhaps in other areas, may be to allow some degree of experimentation by member states.

The second key structural issue is the VAT treatment of trade between EU member states. Ironically, while the VAT proved well-suited to the early stages of integration, as a means of limiting hidden protection and export subsidies, it has proved problematic (as seen in Section 4.3.3 above) at the later stage in which internal fiscal controls are removed. It is important not to over-react to much-publicized missing trader frauds exploiting current arrangements: they are but one part of an overall level of VAT abuse that may be broadly comparable to that under the personal income tax. Nevertheless, action is clearly needed to strengthen the integrity of the VAT.

Part of this response must of course be improved administrative cooperation, but the greatest assurance in addressing the underlying structural problem—the break in the VAT chain from the zero-rating of intra-union exports—is likely to come from a structural solution. For this it is not necessary to move towards a genuine origin principle for commodity taxation, and indeed doing so would be unwise (not least because it would introduce transfer pricing problems into the domain of the VAT). The most promising approach is to strengthen the implementation of destination-based taxation by building on the fractional nature of the VAT, which is its fundamental strength—not to undermine it (as would be done, for example, by further reverse charging, whether for selected commodities or for all B2B transactions). And in the absence of an over-arching EU-wide VAT, the two most appealing ways to do so are by adopting either a CVAT (which maintains domestic zero-rating of exports but imposes an EU-wide VAT on inter-union trade) or a VIVAT (which taxes all B2B transactions, throughout the Union, at a common rate while maintaining national discretion in rates applied to final sales). Each has its own advantages and disadvantages. One criticism of the VIVAT, for instance, is that it requires traders to treat differently sales to registered traders and to final consumers. This, however, is a distinction that seems likely in any event to become increasingly important: it is already made in respect of intra-union sales, and is at the heart of the Commission's recent proposals for the treatment of international services. Either CVAT or VIVAT, in any event, offers scope for significant improvement over the current (and explicitly transitional) arrangements.

4.6.3. Excises on alcohol and tobacco

The UK levies excises on alcohol and tobacco which are substantially higher than in many other EU member states. In terms of their demand characteristics, these goods are not markedly different from many others. The estimates in Crawford, Keen, and Smith (2008) suggest that beer and wine and spirits may be moderately complementary with hours worked, while tobacco products appear to have moderate substitutability with labour time. In neither case, however, do considerations of revenue-raising efficiency alone seem likely to justify taxing these goods so much more heavily than the generality of consumer spending. The externalities associated with consumption of these commodities are, however, appreciable, and justify taxing these goods at higher rates than the general VAT. Nevertheless, policy towards these goods needs to be informed by a clearer appreciation of the nature and size of the externalities associated with their consumption.

In the case of tobacco taxes, the evidence is highly controversial. Given that smokers die early, saving the rest of society a significant burden in pension and old-age case costs, it is far from clear that the existing level of tobacco taxes can be justified solely on the basis of smoking externalities. Behavioural issues of time inconsistency and lack of self-control in consumption decisions, as discussed in the commentary by Gruber, may be particularly important in this area, and may justify higher taxes than would be warranted if decisions were being made by wholly rational, well-informed consumers.

Using alcohol taxes to reduce the externalities associated with alcohol consumption (and, especially, abusive over-consumption) involves targeting the incentive somewhat imprecisely to the underlying externality, since alcohol externalities are not proportional to alcohol consumption but are largely confined to abusive over-consumption by a subset of all consumers. Externality taxation of alcohol thus involves a compromise between the potential gains from reducing external costs of abusive consumption and the welfare costs of discouraging non-abusive consumption.

The external costs of tobacco and alcohol consumption are likely to be heavily affected both by the institutional arrangements for financing healthcare, pensions, and so on, and by the cultural context in which alcohol is consumed. It is therefore unlikely that estimates from the US can be carried over without modification to the European context, or that externalities will be uniform throughout Europe. Because of the likely differences across European countries in external costs of smoking and alcohol consumption, it is unlikely that the optimal tax treatment of tobacco products and alcoholic drinks will be identical in all members of the EU. Imposing greater uniformity on the very diverse pattern of EU excises may thus involve some economic inefficiency. Experience has confirmed, however, that for these items there is significant risk of revenue erosion—and hence pressures towards setting tax rates lower than would be collectively desirable—from the legal cross-border shopping and the various forms of illegal smuggling and tax evasion that are encouraged by significant tax differences. The EU-wide floors to alcohol and tobacco excises have the potential to play an important role, both in preventing the various forms of smuggling and evasion which exploit the massive duty differentials between member states, and also in ensuring the sustainability of these duties at levels which properly reflect the external costs of consumption of these goods. The levels at which these excise floors are currently set, however, put little constraint on tax rate decisions in member states, and so make little practical contribution to preventing inefficient downward pressure on duty rates. Raising them—though clearly desirable—has, however, proved difficult, and will no doubt remain so.

REFERENCES

Adams, E. K., Melvin, C., Merritt, R., and Worrall, B. (1999), 'The Costs of Environmental Tobacco Smoke (ETS): An International Review. Background paper', prepared for World Health Organization Framework Convention on Tobacco Control (FCTC), International Consultation on Environmental Tobacco Smoke (ETS) and Child Health. Available at: <http://www.who.int/tobacco/framework/consultation/ets2/en/>. Accessed 4 September 2007.

Ainsworth, R. T. (2006), 'Carousel Fraud in the EU: A Digital VAT Solution', *Tax Notes International*, May, 443–8.

—— (2007), 'Tackling VAT Fraud: Thirteen Ways Forward', *International Tax Notes*, 1205.

Atkinson, A. B., and Stiglitz, J. E. (1976), 'The Design of Tax Structure: Direct versus Indirect Taxation', *Journal of Public Economics*, **6**, 55–75.

—— (1980), *Lectures on Public Economics*, London: McGraw Hill.

Aujean, M., Jenkins, P., and Poddar, S. (1999), 'A New Approach to Public Sector Bodies', *International VAT Monitor*, **10**, 144–9.

Barendregt, J. J., Bonneux, L., and van der Maas, P. J. (1997), 'The Health Care Costs of Smoking', *New England Journal of Medicine*, **337**, 1052–7.

Becker, G. S., and Murphy, K. M. (1988), 'A Theory of Rational Addiction', *Journal of Political Economy*, **96**, 675–700.

Besley, T., and Jewitt, I. (1990), 'Optimal Uniform Taxation and the Structure of Consumer Preferences', pp. 131–56 in Myles, G. D. (ed.), *Measurement and Modelling in Economics*, Amsterdam: North Holland.

—— and Smart, M. (2007), 'Fiscal Restraints and Voter Welfare', *Journal of Public Economics*, **91**, 755–73.

Besson, E. (2007), 'TVA sociale', Ministry of Economy, Finance, and Industry, Secrétariat d'état chargé de la prospective et de l'évaluation des politiques publiques, Report, September 2007 <http://www.premier-ministre.gouv.fr/IMG/pdf/TVA_sociale_rapport_remis_par_Eric_Besson.pdf>.

Bird, R. (2000), 'Subnational Revenues: Realities and Prospects', Mimeo: World Bank Institute.

—— and Gendron, P.-P. (1998), 'Dual VATs and Cross-border Trade: Two Problems, One Solution?', *International Tax and Public Finance*, **5**, 429–42.

Bird, R., and Gendron, P.-P. (2007), *The VAT in Developing and Transitional Countries*, Cambridge: Cambridge University Press.

Boadway, R., and Gahvari, F. (2006), 'Optimal Taxation with Consumption Time as a Leisure or Labor Substitute', *Journal of Public Economics*, **90**, 1851–78.

—— and Keen, M. (2003), 'Theoretical Perspectives on the Taxation of Capital Income and Financial Services', 31–80 in Honahan, P. (ed.), *The Taxation of Financial Intermediation*, World Bank and Oxford University Press.

Boadway, R., Marchand, M., and Pestieau, P. (1994), 'Towards a Theory of the Direct–Indirect Tax Mix', *Journal of Public Economics*, **55**, 71–88.

—— and Pestieau, P. (2003), 'Indirect Taxation and Redistribution: The Scope of the Atkinson–Stiglitz Theorem', 387–403 in Arnott, R., Greenwald, B., Kanbur, R., and Nalebuff, B. (eds.), *Economics for an Imperfect World: Essays in Honor of Joseph E. Stiglitz* Cambridge, Mass: MIT Press.

Bovenberg, L. (1994), 'Destination- and Origin-based Taxation under International Capital Mobility', *International Tax and Public Finance*, **1**, 247–73.

Browning, M., and Meghir, C. (1991), 'The Effects of Male and Female Labour Supply on Commodity Demands', *Econometrica*, **59**, 925–51.

Carbonnier, C. (2007), 'Who Pays Sales Taxes? Evidence from the French VAT Reforms, 1987–1999', *Journal of Public Economics*, **91**, 1219–29.

Chaloupka, F. J. (1991), 'Rational Addictive Behavior and Cigarette Smoking', *Journal of Political Economy*, **99**, 722–42.

—— and Wechsler, H. (1997), 'Price, Tobacco Control Policies and Smoking Among Young Adults', *Journal of Health Economics*, **16**, 359–73.

Christiansen, V. (1984), 'Which Commodity Taxes Should Supplement the Income Tax?' *Journal of Public Economics*, **24**, 195–220.

—— and Smith, S. (2004), 'National Policy Interests in the Duty-free Market', *CESifo Economic Studies*, **50**, 351–75.

—— —— (2008), 'Optimal Commodity Taxation with Duty-free Shopping', *International Tax and Public Finance*, **15**, 274–96.

Cnossen, S. (1983), 'Harmonization of Indirect Taxes in the EEC', in McLure, C. E., Jr. (ed), *Tax Assignment in Federal Countries*, 150–71. Centre for Research on Federal Financial Relations. Canberra: ANU Press.

—— (1994), 'Administrative and Compliance Costs of the VAT: A Review of the Evidence', *Tax Notes*, **63**, 1609–26.

—— (2003), 'Is the VAT's Sixth Directive Becoming an Anachronism?', *European Taxation*, 434–42.

—— and Shoup, C. S. (1987), 'Coordination of Value-Added Taxes', in Cnossen, S. (ed.), *Tax Coordination in the European Community*, Kluwer: Deventer.

Colmar Brunton (2005), *Measuring the Tax Compliance Costs of Small and Medium-Sized Businesses—A Benchmark Survey*, Wellington: Colmar Brunton.

Commission of the European Communities (1987), 'Commission Communication on Completion of the Internal Market: Approximation of Indirect Tax Rates and Harmonization of Indirect Tax Structures', COM (87), 320.

—— (2003), 'Evaluation Report on the Experimental Evaluation of a Reduced Rate of VAT to Certain Labor-intensive Services', Working Paper SEC(2003) 622.

—— (2008), 'Communication from the Commission to the Council and the European Parliament on Measures to Change the VAT System to Fight Fraud', SEC(2008) 249.

Crawford, I., Keen, M., and Smith, S. (2008), 'Preference Structures and Optimal Commodity Taxation', Institute for Fiscal Studies, Working Paper.

—— Smith, Z., and Tanner, S. (1999), 'Alcohol Taxes, Tax Revenues and the Single European Market', *Fiscal Studies*, **20**, 287–304.

—— and Tanner, S. (1995), 'Bringing it all back Home: Alcohol Taxation and Cross-border Shopping', *Fiscal Studies*, **16**, 94–114.

Crooks, E. (1989), *Alcohol Consumption and Taxation*, Report Series 34, London: Institute for Fiscal Studies.

de Paula, Á., and Scheinkman, J. A. (2006), 'The Informal Sector', mimeo, Princeton University.

Deaton, A., and Stern, N. (1986), 'Optimally Uniform Commodity Taxes, Taste Differences and Lump Sum Grants,' *Economics Letters*, **20**, 263–6.

Delipalla, S., and Keen, M. (1992), 'The Comparison Between ad valorem and Specific Taxation under Imperfect Competition', *Journal of Public Economics*, **49**, 351–67.

—— —— (2006), 'Product Quality and the Optimal Structure of Commodity Taxes', *Journal of Public Economic Theory*, **8**, 547–54.

Dharmapala, D., Slemrod, J., and Wilson, J. D. (2007), 'Optimal Tax Remittance with Firm-level Administrative Costs', mimeo, Michigan State University.

Diamond, P. (1973), 'Consumption Externalities and Imperfect Corrective Pricing', *Bell Journal of Economics*, **4**, 526–38.

—— and Mirrlees, J. A. (1971), 'Optimal Taxation and Public Production I: Production Efficiency, II Tax Rules', *American Economic Review*, **61**, 8–27 and 261–78.

Ebrill, L. P., Keen, M., Bodin, J.-P., and Summers, V. (2001), *The Modern VAT*, Washington DC: International Monetary Fund.

Edwards, J., and Keen, M. (1996), 'Tax Competition and Leviathan', *European Economic Review*, **40**, 113–34.

Evans, W. N., and Farrelly, M. (1998), 'The Compensating Behaviour of Smokers: Taxes, Tar and Nicotine', *RAND Journal of Economics*, **29**, 578–95.

Gahvari, F. (2007), 'On Optimal Commodity Taxation when Consumption is Time-consuming', *Journal of Public Economic Theory*, **9**, 1–27.

—— and Yang, C. C. (1993), 'Optimal Commodity Taxation and Household Consumption Activities', *Public Finance Quarterly*, **21**, 479–87.

Genser, B. (1996), 'A Generalised Equivalence Property of Mixed International VAT Regimes', *Scandinavian Journal of Economics*, **98**, 253–62.

—— and Haufler, A. (1996), 'Tax Competition, Tax Coordination and Tax Harmonization: The Effects of EMU', in Holzmann, R. (ed), *Maastricht: Monetary Constitution without a Fiscal Constitution*, Baden-Baden: Nomos Verlagsgesellschaft.

—— Haufler, A., and Sørensen, P. B. (1995), 'Indirect Taxation in an Integrated Market: Is there a way of Avoiding Trade Distortions without Sacrificing National Autonomy?' *Journal of Economic Integration*, **10**, 178–205.

—— and Schulze, G. G. (1997), 'Transfer Pricing under an Origin-based VAT System', *Finanzarchiv*, **54**, 51–67.

Genser, B. and Winker, P. (1997), 'Measuring the Fiscal Revenue Loss of VAT Exemption in Commercial Banking', *Finanzarchiv*, **54**, 565–85.

Golosov, M., Kocherlakota, N., and Tsyvinski, A. (2003), 'Optimal Indirect and Capital Taxation', *Review of Economic Studies*, **70**, 569–87.

Gordon, J. (1989), 'Tax Reform via Commodity Grouping', *Journal of Public Economics*, **39**, 67–81.

Gordon, R., and Nielsen, S. B. (1997), 'Tax Evasion in an Open Economy: Value-added Taxes vs Income Tax', *Journal of Public Economics*, **66**, 173–97.

Grossman, G. M. (1980), 'Border Tax Adjustments: Do they Distort Trade?', *Journal of International Economics*, **10**, 117–28.

Gruber, J. (2001), 'Tobacco at the Crossroads: The Past and Future of Smoking Regulation in the United States', *Journal of Economic Perspectives*, **15**, 193–212.

—— and Köszegi, B. (2001), 'Is Addiction "Rational"? Theory and Evidence', *Quarterly Journal of Economics*, **116**, 1261–303.

—— —— (2004), 'Tax Incidence when Individuals are Time-inconsistent: The Case of Cigarette Excise Taxes', *Journal of Public Economics*, **88**, 1959–87.

—— and Mullainathan, S. (2005), 'Do Cigarette Taxes make Smokers Happy?' *Advances in Economic Analysis and Policy*, **5**, 1–43.

Hall, R. E., and Rabushka, A. (1983), *Low Tax, Simple Tax, Flat Tax*, New York: McGraw-Hill.

Harrison, G., and Krelove, R. (2005), 'VAT Refunds: A Review of Country Experience', International Monetary Fund Working Paper WP/05/218 <http://www.imf.org/external/pubs/ft/wp/2005/wp05218.pdf>.

Hassett, K., Mathur, A., and Metcalf, G. (2007), 'The Incidence of a U.S. Carbon Tax: A Lifetime and Regional Analysis', NBER Working Paper 13554.

Hemming, R., and Kay, J. A. (1981), 'The United Kingdom', 75–89 in Aaron, H. J. (ed.), *The Value-Added Tax: Lessons from Europe*, Washington, DC: Brookings Institution.

Huizinga, H. (2002), 'Financial Services VAT', *Economic Policy*, **17**, 499–534.

International Tax Dialogue (2007), 'The Tax Treatment of Small and Medium Enterprises', available at <http://www.itdweb.org>.

Kanbur, R., and Keen, M. (1993), 'Jeux sans frontières: Tax Competition and Tax Coordination when Countries Differ in Size', *American Economic Review*, **83**, 877–92.

Kaplow, L. (2006), 'On the Undesirability of Commodity Taxation even when Income Taxation is not Optimal', *Journal of Public Economics*, **90**, 1235–50.

Kay, J. A., and Davis, E. (1985), 'Extending the VAT Base', *Fiscal Studies*, **6**, 1–16.

Keen, M. (1998), 'The Balance Between Specific and ad valorem Taxation', *Fiscal Studies*, **19**, 1–37.

—— (2002), 'Some International Issues in Commodity Taxation', *Swedish Economic Policy Review*, **9**, 11–45.

——(2008), 'VAT, Tariffs and Withholding', *Journal of Public Economics*, **92**, 1892–906.
——and Lahiri, S. (1998), 'The Comparison Between Destination and Origin Principles under Imperfect Competition', *Journal of International Economics*, **45**, 323–50.
——and Lockwood, B. (2006), 'Is the VAT a Money Machine?', *National Tax Journal*, **LIX**, 905–28.
————(2008), 'The Value Added Tax: Its Causes and Consequences', forthcoming in the *Journal of Development Economics*.
——and Mintz, J. (2004), 'The Optimal Threshold for a Value-Added Tax', *Journal of Public Economics*, **88**, 559–76.
——and Smith, S. (1996), 'The Future of Value-Added Tax in the European Union', *Economic Policy*, **23**, 375–411 and 419–20.
————(2000), 'Viva VIVAT!' *International Tax and Public Finance*, **7**, 741–51.
————(2006), 'VAT Fraud and Evasion: What do we Know and What can be Done?' *National Tax Journal*, **59**, 861–87.
——and Wildasin, D. (2004), 'Pareto Efficient International Taxation', *American Economic Review*, **94**, 259–75.
Kleven, H. J. (2004), 'Optimum Taxation and the Allocation of Time', *Journal of Public Economics*, **88**, 545–57.
——Wolfram, R., and Sørensen, P. B. (2000), 'Optimal Taxation with Household Production', *Oxford Economic Papers*, **52**, 584–94.
Kneller, R., Bleaney, M. F., and Gemmell, N. (1999), 'Fiscal Policy and Growth: Evidence from OECD countries', *Journal of Public Economics*, **74**, 171–90.
KPMG (2006), *Administrative Burdens: HMRC Measurement Project* (KPMG LLP).
Laroque, G. (2005), 'Indirect Taxation is Superfluous under Separability and Taste Homogeneity: A Simple Proof', *Economics Letters*, **87**, 141–4.
Lee, C., Pearson, M., and Smith, S. (1988), *Fiscal Harmonisation: An Analysis of the Commission's Proposals*, Report Series 28, London: Institute for Fiscal Studies.
Lewit, E. M., and Coate, D. (1982), 'The Potential for Using Excise Taxes to Reduce Smoking', *Journal of Health Economics*, **1**, 121–45.
————and Grossman, M. (1981), 'The Effects of Government Regulation on Teenage Smoking', *Journal of Law and Economics*, **24**, 545–69.
Lockwood, B. (1993), 'Commodity Tax Competition under Destination and Origin Principles', *Journal of Public Economics*, **52**, 141–62.
——de Meza, D., and Myles, G. (1994a), 'When are Destination and Origin Regimes Equivalent?', *International Tax and Public Finance*, **1**, 5–24.
——————(1994b), 'The Equivalence Between Destination and Non-reciprocal Restricted Origin Regimes', *Scandinavian Journal of Economics*, **96**, 311–28.
Lyon, A. B., and Schwab, R. M. (1995), 'Consumption Taxes in a Life-cycle Framework: Are Sin Taxes Regressive?', *Review of Economics and Statistics*, 77, 389–406.

McCann, E., and Edgar, T. (2003), 'VAT Treatment of Interest and Financial Services with Competitive Banking and Insurance Sectors', *Tax Notes International*, **26**, 791–808.

McLure, C. E. (1999), 'Protecting Dual VATs from Evasion on Cross-border Trade: An Addendum to Bird and Gendron', mimeo, Hoover Institution.

—— (2000), 'Implementing Subnational VATs on Internal Trade: The Compensating VAT (CVAT)', *International Tax and Public Finance*, 7, 723–40.

Manning, W. G., Keeler, E. B., Newhouse, J. P., Sloss, E., and Wasserman, J. (1989), 'The Taxes of Sin: Do Smokers and Drinkers Pay Their Way?', *Journal of the American Medical Association*, **261**, 1604–9.

Matthew, H. C. G. (1979), 'Disraeli, Gladstone and the Politics of Mid-Victorian Budgets', *The Historical Journal*, 22, 615–43.

Maynard, A., Godfrey, C., and Hardman, G. (1994), 'Conceptual Issues in Estimating the Social Costs of Alcohol', paper prepared for an international symposium on the economic costs of substance abuse, Banff, Canada, 11–13 May. Available at <http://www.ccsa.ca/Costs/maynard.htm>.

Meade, J. (1978), *The Structure and Reform of Direct Taxation: Report of a Committee chaired by Professor J. E. Meade for the Institute for Fiscal Studies*, London: George Allen & Unwin. http://www.ifs.org.uk/publications/3433

Messere, K. (1994), 'Consumption Tax Rules', *Bulletin for International Fiscal Documentation*, **48**, 665–81.

Mirrlees, J. A. (1976), 'Optimal Tax Theory: A Synthesis', *Journal of Public Economics*, **6**, 327–58.

Musgrave, R. A., and Suits, D. B. (1953), 'Ad valorem and Unit Taxes Compared', *Quarterly Journal of Economics*, **67**, 598–604.

Newbery, D. M. (1986), 'On the Desirability of Input Taxes', *Economics Letters*, **20**, 267–70.

Ohsawa, Y. (1999), 'Cross-border Shopping and Commodity Tax Competition among Governments', *Regional Science and Urban Economics*, **29**, 33–51.

Organisation for Economic Cooperation and Development (2004), *The Application of Consumption Taxes to the Trade in International Services and Intangibles*. Report. Centre for Tax Policy and Administration, Paris: OECD.

—— (2007), *Revenue Statistics 1965–2006*, Paris: OECD.

—— (2008), *Consumption Tax Trends, 2008 Edition* (Paris: OECD).

Orphanides, A., and Zervos, D. (1995), 'Rational Addiction with Learning and Regret', *Journal of Political Economy*, **103**, 739–58.

Panagariya, A., and Rodrik, D. (1993), 'Political-economy Arguments for a Uniform Tariff', *International Economic Review*, **34**, 685–703.

Parry, I. W. H. (2003), 'On the Costs of Excise Taxes and Income Taxes in the UK', *International Tax and Public Finance*, **10**, 281–304.

Piggott, J., and Whalley, J. (2001), 'VAT Base Broadening, Self Supply, and the Informal Sector', *American Economic Review*, **91**, 1084–94.

Pigou, A. C. (1920), *The Economics of Welfare*, London: Macmillan.

Pirtillä, J., and Tuomala, M. (1997), 'Income Tax, Commodity Tax and Environmental Policy', *International Tax and Public Finance*, **4**, 379–93.

Poddar, S. (2003), 'Consumption Taxes: The Role of the Value-Added Tax', 354–80 in Honohan, P. (ed.), *Taxation of Financial Intermediation: Theory and Practice for Emerging Economies*, Washington, DC: World Bank.

—— and English, M. (1997), 'Taxation of Financial Services under a Value-Added Tax: Applying the Cash-flow Method', *National Tax Journal*, **50**, 89–111.

—— and Hutton, E. (2001), 'Zero-rating of Interstate Sales under a Sub-national VAT', *National Tax Association Proceedings: Ninety Fourth Annual Conference*, 200–7.

Pogue, T. F., and Sgontz, L. G. (1989), 'Taxing to Control Social Costs: The Case of Alcohol', *American Economic Review*, **79**, 235–43.

Poterba, J. M. (1989), 'Lifetime Incidence and the Distributional Burden of Excise Taxes', *American Economic Review*, **79**, 325–30.

Ramsey, F. (1927), 'A Contribution to the Theory of Taxation', *Economic Journal*, **37**, 47–61.

Rasmussen, S. R., Prescott, E., Sørensen, T. I. A., and Søgaard, J. (2004), 'The Total Lifetime Health Cost Savings of Smoking Cessation to Society', *European Journal of Public Health*, **15**, 601–6.

Sandmo, A. (1976), 'Direct versus Indirect Pigovian Taxation', *European Economic Review*, **7**, 337–49.

Shibata, H. (1967), 'The Theory of Economic Unions: A Comparative Analysis of Customs Unions, Free Trade Areas and Tax Unions', in Shoup, C. S. (ed.), *Fiscal Harmonisation in Common Markets*, New York: Columbia University Press.

Sinn, H.-W. (1990), 'Tax Harmonization and Tax Competition in Europe', *European Economic Review*, **34**, 489–504.

—— Gebauer, A., and Parsche, R. (2004), 'The Ifo Institute's Model for Reducing VAT Fraud: Payment First, Refund Later', *CESifo Forum*, **2**, 30–4.

Slemrod, J., and Yitzhaki, S. (1996), 'The Cost of Taxation and the Marginal Efficiency Cost of Funds', *IMF Staff Papers*, **43**, 172–98.

Smith, S. (2005), 'Economic Issues in Alcohol Taxation', in Cnossen, S. (ed.), *Theory and Practice of Excise Taxation*, Oxford: Oxford University Press.

Södersten, J. (1999), 'Why Europe Adopted the Value Added Tax', Mimeo, Uppsala University.

Vanistendael, F. (1995), 'A Proposal for a Definitive VAT System: Taxation in the Country of Origin at the Rate of the Country of Destination, Without Clearing', *EC Tax Review*, No. 1995/1, 45–53.

Varsano, R. (2000). 'Sub-national Taxation and Treatment of Interstate Trade in Brazil: Problems and a Proposed Solution', 339–55 in Burki, S. J., and Perry, G. (eds.), *Decentralization and Accountability of the Public Sector*, Proceedings of the Annual Bank Conference on Development in Latin America and the Caribbean, Washington DC: The World Bank.

Verwaal, E., and Cnossen, S. (2002), 'Europe's New Border Taxes', *Journal of Common Market Studies*, **40**, 309–30.

Viscusi, W. K. (1995), 'Cigarette Taxation and the Social Consequences of Smoking', *Tax Policy and the Economy*, **9**, 51–101.

Zee, H. (2005), 'Simple Analytics of Setting the Optimal VAT Exemption Threshold', *The Economist*, **143**, 461–71.

—— (2006), 'VAT Treatment of Financial Services: A Primer on Conceptual Issues and Country Practices', *Intertax*, **34**, 458–74.

Commentary by Richard M. Bird

Richard Bird is Professor Emeritus of Economics at the University of Toronto, an Associate of the Institute for International Business of the Rotman School of Management, and Senior Fellow of the Institute for Municipal Finance and Governance of the Munk Centre for International Studies. A Fellow of the Royal Society of Canada, he has taught in the US, the Netherlands, and Australia among other countries and has frequently worked for the International Monetary Fund and other international organizations. His main interests are tax policy, tax administration, and fiscal decentralization issues in developing countries.

The value-added tax (VAT) was unquestionably the most successful fiscal innovation of the last half-century. No other significant tax, not even the income tax, spread so rapidly and quickly around the world to the point where VATs currently exist in over 150 countries, including of course all member states of the EU. Why was the VAT so successful? Essentially, because virtually every country—apart from the always exceptional United States and a few small islands and oil-rich countries—needs some form of mass consumption tax to support state activities, and experience has shown that the VAT is not only the least distorting such tax but also the one that can, despite some problems, be administered most effectively in most countries. Of course, not all VATs are the same, and none is perfect (Bird and Gendron (2007)).

In general, as Crawford, Keen, and Smith (hereafter CKS) show, in principle the VAT approach to imposing a consumption tax is perhaps the most economically efficient way in which countries can raise significant tax revenues. The marginal cost of raising funds for public purposes through VAT is generally lower than it would be if other taxes were employed. This economic advantage may cut two ways politically, however. By lowering the cost of taxation, VAT makes it relatively cheaper to expand the level of state activity—an outcome that some may consider good and others bad. On the other hand, given any level of state activity, VAT does less damage to economic incentives than would equally productive alternative taxes. What more could one ask of a tax?

Picking up this theme, CKS suggest that the apparent increase in tax ratios associated with VAT in developed countries such as the UK reflects the reduced marginal cost of public funds. However, other factors are at work here than simply the lesser distortionary costs of VATs. Canada recently reduced its national VAT (the GST, in Canada) rate from 7% to 5%.[1] Most Canadian economists did not like this move, but it was certainly politically popular in large part because Canada's VAT is much more visible than in those found in other countries. In Canada, the GST is not included in product prices but is added on separately at the time of purchase: it is thus highly visible every time anyone buys anything. Everyone is aware of it every day, and, unsurprisingly, no one likes it. In economic terms, VAT in Canada as in most countries has the lowest Marginal Cost of Public Funds (MCPF) of any significant tax (Baylor and Beausejour (2004)). In political terms, however, matters are very different owing to the high visibility of the VAT. Some may argue that, since income taxes carry high political as well as economic costs and consumption taxes are lower on both metrics, a hidden VAT may yield a better revenue portfolio not just in enforcement terms but also in terms of bringing more closely together the marginal economic and political costs of raising public funds. On the other hand, it is hard to believe that it is a good thing for government revenues to grow more than they otherwise would simply because people do not understand how much tax they are paying. Little is known about these deep and murky waters.[2] Perhaps, however, it is more than time for those concerned with establishing sound tax policy to pay more careful attention to what may perhaps be called the reality of perception in shaping the design of tax instruments.

The scholarly literature on VAT that is so well summarized and reviewed by CKS provides surprisingly little useful guidance to those responsible for VAT policy and administration. Much of this literature concerns matters that have already been decided in practice—for the most part, fairly satisfactorily—and are hence unlikely to be worth reconsidering in practice. Further discussion here of the essential policy irrelevance of such matters as the direct–indirect 'tax mix' or 'tax balance' question, the origin versus destination issue, and the relative merits of VAT and retail sales taxes would thus serve no point. Only after clearing a good deal of such relatively unproductive theoretical underbrush do CKS get to the more salient policy issues with respect to

[1] As Bird, Mintz, and Wilson (2006) show, Canada is unusual in that it also has significant subnational consumption taxes some of which are VATs. On average, the level of consumption taxation even after the federal tax cut is about 13%.

[2] For a promising initial empirical foray, see Chetty, Looney, and Kroft (2007).

VAT—rates, exemptions, thresholds, enforcement, compliance, fraud, and the international setting.

What do we really know about these issues? Consider the summary picture of VATs in the OECD depicted in Table 4.2 of the chapter. About the only conclusion one can derive from the information in this table is that countries, it seems, can do almost anything they want with respect to rates, thresholds, coverage, and enforcement (C-efficiency combines these two factors), subject only to a mild EU constraint in the case of EU countries. Since practice provides so little guidance, CKS understandably turn once more to theory for answers. As it turns out, however, apart from the issue of the threshold, where what seems to be an unanswerable case is made that the UK should certainly not lower it, there seem to be no very substantial answers with respect to the flesh and bones of any VAT—rates, zero-rating, and exemptions.

In practice no VAT is quite as good as it might be for a number of reasons: less than general coverage, less than optimal rate structure, and less than perfect administration. In the EU, for example, there are three major components of the base where coverage is arguably less than ideal—real property, the PNC (public, non-profit, charitable) sector, and the financial sector. CKS discuss the last of these sectors in some detail and provide an excellent overview of the relevant literature.[3] But they do not provide any clear guidance as to just what, if anything, the UK, the EU, or anyone else should do with respect to the treatment of the financial sector—or for that matter the other two troublesome sectors mentioned above. The reader is, perhaps unintentionally, left with the feeling that it is all just too difficult to find an acceptable solution and we should perhaps just give up.

Of course, this characterization is not entirely fair. With respect to the financial sector, for example, CKS clearly do think that something should be done, perhaps along Australian lines. However, we are left up in the air as to exactly what should be done and what the costs and consequences of changing the present treatment might be. Similarly, with respect to real property, while an offset to first-time buyers is suggested, again the eager reader is left in the dark with respect to the critical details. Finally, when it comes to the equally troublesome issue of the public and non-profit sectors, neither any discussion of the nature of the problem nor even a hint of a possible solution is to be found. Even after decades of experience around the world with a variety of approaches, there is much more that we do not know than we know about the relevant parameters and behavioural responses determining such matters. These are the sorts of issues that consume the time

[3] For a similar overview of the PNC question, see Gendron (2005).

and efforts of VAT policy designers everywhere. The absence of any solid theoretical or empirical framework within which to make such decisions is presumably why CKS do not discuss such issues more fully. Still, it is striking that when they come to the concluding section of the chapter not a word is said about any domestic aspect of VAT.

A more positive approach might have been to note that the EU model in general (and perhaps the UK version in particular) is very much a 'first-generation' VAT. Since a second-generation VAT demonstrating that it is both possible and desirable to have much more comprehensive coverage has been on display in Australia and especially New Zealand for some years, it would have been interesting to consider more systematically the pros and cons (if any) of moving closer to this model in the UK. Such an exercise might also have made clearer the extent if any to which such improvements in the UK VAT are or may be restricted by EU rules. Finally, since New Zealand is not the last word when it comes to VAT, it would also have been interesting if the authors had set out their view of the structure of an 'ideal' (third-generation?) VAT or at least reviewed more systematically how EU rules might need to be altered to enable member states to improve their national VATs.

The analytical discussion in the chapter of some other issues such as the distributional aspects of VAT and the treatment of cross-border transactions seems more directly relevant to VAT policy and administration in the UK and more widely. However, the discussion of these issues also leaves a number of important questions unanswered—and in some cases even unasked.

One such question relates to VAT rate structure. Neither the inconclusive optimal tax literature nor the interesting empirical estimates provided by CKS (which reject, though not strongly, weak separability) provide particularly useful guidance on this point. In the end, the rule implicitly suggested for policy-makers, at least in developed countries like the UK, appears to amount to little more than the old rule of thumb that a uniform rate is likely to be as good, if not better, than any 'scientific' differentiation—let alone the politically driven differention that actually prevails in the UK, as in most countries. As CKS demonstrate, there is little case for differential rates on distributional or incidence grounds. Moreover, although CKS do not stress this point, there is considerable experience (though apparently no solid evidence) suggesting that multiple rates increase compliance and administrative costs and perhaps facilitate evasion.

If both theory and practice suggest that rate differentiation (like domestic zero-rating for consumer goods) seems to make little sense, why are these features so pervasive in VATs around the world? The answer may lie deep in the murky waters of perception, electoral psychology, and the political economy of taxation and hence be well beyond the scope of this chapter. Still, given the existence of such differentiation in the UK VAT, it would have been useful to see, for example, a discussion of whether it makes any difference how 'reduced' (compared to the standard rate) the 'reduced' rate is. For example, if the lower rate is 'too low' it may, like zero rating, generate both excessive refunds and an attractive opportunity for evasion. In principle, presumably the optimal reduced rate for VAT—admitting that, however deplorable it may be, most countries seem to end up with such a rate—should be susceptible to the same kind of analysis as the optimal threshold.

Recently, increasing attention is being paid to some of the important relatively unexplored implications of the way in which VAT is commonly administered through the so-called invoice-credit system. Since input VAT cannot be credited by those not registered as VAT taxpayers, to the extent that taxed inputs—for example, imports—are purchased by 'informal' enterprises, VAT offers a simple and effective way to tax the informal sector. Silver linings seldom come without accompanying clouds, however. Viewed from another perspective, the effective imposition of VAT on enterprises outside the VAT system, like the relatively high compliance costs imposed on small firms within the system, creates a barrier to the growth of the important—and often politically favoured—sector of 'small business'. Unfortunately, although the treatment of small businesses, both within and outside the VAT system, is a matter of increasing interest in many countries, including the UK, the issue is not discussed in this chapter. In response to these conflicting concerns, a growing number of countries in Europe and elsewhere seem to be introducing gross receipts taxes on small business sometimes within the framework of the VAT and sometimes as a separate 'simplified' levy. Such composite transactions taxes deserve closer attention than they appear to have received to date anywhere.[4] Similarly, the costs and benefits of the various special schemes for small business found in many VATs, including that in the UK, also need closer examination.

Instead of going into such knotty and largely unresolved issues in VAT design, CKS devote a substantial fraction of the chapter to a particular form of VAT fraud currently giving rise to concern in the EU and more generally to the related question of how best to apply VAT to cross-border transactions. Since the UK has much more extensive zero rating than almost any other

[4] A related issue is how VAT on real property interacts with other taxes that impact the sector in differential ways such as local property taxes, capital gains taxes, inheritance taxes, and, in many countries, special transfer taxes imposed on real property sales. Once again, important policy decisions are being made about an important economic sector with little guidance from either theory or empirical analysis.

developed country it is surprising that the possible linkage between this feature of the UK VAT and the much discussed problem of 'carousel fraud' is not even mentioned. However, the exposition of the evasion game is clear, and the discussion of possible solutions good. CKS find all the solutions currently on offer—such as reverse charging—to be wanting and end by throwing the issue into the more general VIVAT hat discussed next.

On the whole, the chapter is careful not simply to restate the case for the particular alternative mechanism for cross-border trade that some of the authors have argued at length in earlier works (Keen and Smith (2000)). As an EU outsider, however, I still find it difficult to understand the emphasis on 'symmetry' in most EU discussions of these matters, including this chapter. In reality, there must always be some 'asymmetry' in any VAT since any VAT 'includes' some and 'excludes' others involved in transactions. Those within the system are treated differently from those outside. The relevant question in the EU, from the perspective of any member state, is whether those in other member states are 'in' or 'out'. (Those outside the EU are always 'out' of course.) It is true, as CKS note, that 'in' may have importantly different manifestations—whose rate applies, who administers what—but no matter where the lines are drawn with respect to either the basic in/out or the degree of 'in-ness' there is always a line and hence always arbitrage possibilities, and marginal costs and benefits of being on one side or the other. Much of the problem in discussing these matters sensibly in the EU (or anywhere else) is that what is best—and for whom—depends on relationships between various empirical characteristics about which we know little or nothing.

In the end, CKS conclude, perhaps unsurprisingly, that the best solution at least for the UK and the EU is the VIVAT approach. Indeed, it appears that the central idea of this approach, a uniform 'intermediate' rate, is becoming more widely accepted in Europe. Nonetheless there remain many important unanswered questions about the system: the appropriate level of the intermediate rate, the politically significant issue of compensation for 'losing' member states, the increased weight this approach places on the distinction between the characteristics of end-users and the related apparent need for an accessible real-time EU VAT registration base. In tax design as in tax implementation, the devil is always in the details, and there remain many details about which there is a high degree of uncertainty with respect to this issue.

To conclude, CKS provide on the whole an excellent review of the current state of the theoretical and the (considerably less impressive) empirical literature on the VAT. Like the literature on which it draws, however, the chapter does not provide either clear answers to many of the critical questions facing those concerned with designing and implementing VATs in the UK and around the world or much guidance to where they might look to find such answers. For better or worse, VAT practice is way ahead of VAT theory in the sense that practitioners are daily facing and dealing with problems with little or no theoretical or empirical guidance. Both practitioners and scholars have much to learn from each other with respect to VAT: they need to talk to each other more, both to learn what the relevant questions are and to obtain the information that may in the long run enable either VAT reality to come closer to the ideal VAT of theory or VAT theory to come closer to dealing with the problems confronting VAT in reality. There is much to be done, and this chapter provides an excellent starting point from which to begin doing it.

REFERENCES

Baylor, M., and Beausejour, L. (2004), 'Taxation and Economic Efficiency: Results from a Canadian CGE Model', Working paper, Department of Finance, Ottawa.

Bird, R. M., and Gendron, P.-P. (2007), *The VAT in Developing and Transitional Countries*, Cambridge: Cambridge University Press.

—— Mintz, J. M., and Wilson, T. A. (2006), 'Coordinating Federal and Provincial Sales Taxes: Lessons from the Canadian Experience', *National Tax Journal*, **49**, 889–903.

Chetty, R., Looney, A., and Kroft, K. (2007), 'Salience and Taxation: Theory and Evidence', NBER Working Paper, National Bureau of Economic Research, Cambridge MA, September.

Gendron, P.-P., (2005), 'Value-Added Tax Treatment of Public Bodies and Non-Profit Organizations', *Bulletin for International Fiscal Documentation*, **59**, 514–26.

Keen, M., and Smith, S. (2000), 'Viva VIVAT!', *International Tax and Public Finance*, **7**, 741–51.

Commentary by Sijbren Cnossen*

Sijbren Cnossen is an Advisor at CPB Netherlands Bureau for Economic Policy Analysis, emeritus Professor of Economics at the University of Maastricht and emeritus Professor of Tax Law at Erasmus University, Rotterdam. He has been a consultant to the IMF, OECD, World Bank, European Commission, US-AID, and Harvard Institute for International Development, in which capacity he advised some thirty countries on the design and implementation of their tax systems. He is a past editor of *De Economist* and *International Tax and Public Finance*, and has published numerous books and articles on the economics of taxation.

1. INTRODUCTION

A large body of research analysing the properties and workings of the value-added tax (VAT) is now available.[1] The best practice that can be distilled from the literature, particularly as it applies to the European Union (EU), strongly indicates that the consumption base of the VAT should be defined as broadly as possible and that all goods and services should be taxed at a uniform rate. This promotes fiscal neutrality and administrative simplicity. On both counts, the VATs of the EU member states leave much to be desired, compared with the new VATs of New Zealand, Canada, Australia, and various other countries. The 'standard exemptions' (sic!) of the harmonized EU-VAT[2] defy the logic and inherent integrity of the VAT, and the differentiated rate structures in most member states are ill-targeted instruments to affect

* The author thanks Richard Bird, Charles McLure, and Ben Terra for their comments on an earlier version of this commentary.

[1] See, for instance, Bird and Gendron (2007) and Ebrill et al. (2001), and the literature cited therein.

[2] It should be noted that the 2006 VAT Directive on the Common System of Value Added Tax (Council Directive 2006/112/EC) merely recasts the 1977 VAT Sixth Directive (Council Directive 77/388/EEC), incorporating a previous directive and various subsequent amendments. The new date is misleading to the extent it suggests that substantive design changes have been made.

the VAT burden distribution, yet increase administrative complexity and compliance costs.

Another, perhaps more topical, point of discussion concerns the most appropriate treatment of intra-community trade. It is widely agreed that VAT revenue should be allocated among member states in line with consumption, that is, on the basis of the destination principle,[3] but there is no consensus on how this principle should be applied in the EU. Currently, intra-community supplies (exports) are zero-rated and intra-community acquisitions (imports) are subject to VAT in the state of importation. This is called the 'transitional regime', because the European Commission believes that it should be replaced by a definitive regime based on exporter rating, that is, the taxation of intra-community exports by exporting member states and the use of the revenue thus collected to finance equivalent tax credits provided in importing states.

Crawford, Keen, and Smith (this chapter) also believe that the EU should change over to exporter rating. In their view (p. 337) zero rating at export breaks 'the chain of VAT revenue cumulation', which invites fraudulent practices. These practices are documented in Keen and Smith (2006), who conclude (p. 39) that 'a fundamental redesign of the VAT treatment of intra-community trade may be required', preferably in the form of a viable integrated VAT (VIVAT) (Keen and Smith (1996)). VIVAT envisages an EU-wide, harmonized single VAT rate on all pre-retail (intermediate) transactions by registered firms within and between member states (with credit for VAT in importing member states), supplemented by a surtax at retail (in fact a retail sales tax (RST)) if governments wish to exploit the VAT base more intensely.

This commentary argues that the current system deserves another hearing. While zero rating and exporter rating are identical in terms of revenue allocation, VIVAT involves substantial additional administrative complexity and may violate tax autonomy (subsidiarity), because it requires some form of central involvement in settling net VAT balances. More importantly, the commentary argues that it is not the break in the VAT-collection chain at intra-community borders that is a matter of concern, but rather the break in the VAT-audit trail, broadly defined as the jurisdictional reach of each VAT administration's ability to control compliance. Accordingly, VAT coordination efforts should focus on improving information exchange between member states and on establishing bilateral and multilateral VAT audit and

[3] By contrast, under the origin principle, VAT accrues to the state of production. Accordingly, value added up to the export stage is taxed in the state of production, while imports are not taxed.

investigation units to monitor compliance with VAT obligations regarding intra-community transactions.

Against this background, the commentary is organized as follows. Section 2 dwells briefly on the history and current treatment of intra-community transactions in the EU, essential in understanding and evaluating the current regime against the various reform proposals. Subsequently, Section 3 highlights the proposals that the European Commission has made to replace the transitional regime by some form of exporter rating. Next, Section 4 does the same for the exporter rating proposals made in the tax literature. Whatever proposal is ultimately adopted, the proper treatment of intra-community transactions would be facilitated by various VAT base broadening measures, as argued in Section 5. Section 6 concludes.

In passing, the commentary notes that VAT does not cumulate throughout the production process.[4] Just as under a retail sales tax (RST), no net VAT is collected within the ring of registered firms, provided, quite plausibly, that the average length of time required for remitting tax and for processing any refunds is the same as the average length of time required for settling accounts receivable and payable.[5] Net VAT is collected only after the consumer (or unregistered trader) has been invoiced for the full amount of VAT on his purchases. Subsequently, this amount is collected fractionally throughout the production process. In essence, suppliers are made tax collectors on behalf of the government for the consumer's VAT on the rationale that retailers (and other firms) are less likely to default on tax invoiced by their suppliers than on tax payable directly to the tax office (Cnossen (1987)).

2. VAT AND INTRA-COMMUNITY TRANSACTIONS

In discussing the VAT treatment of intra-community transactions (and the full implications of the transitional and various definitive regimes), it is

[4] Accordingly, in this sense, there is no break in the VAT-collection chain at export. An exporter would still be entitled to a refund for the VAT he has paid to his suppliers if in any VAT return period he would not export the goods he holds in inventory. However, there is a break in the VAT-chargeability chain: no tax is invoiced to foreign buyers.

[5] To be sure, cash flow benefits (or costs) do arise if a registered firm's collection period (the period during which the tax is collected before being handed over to the tax office) does not coincide with the grace period (the period after the collection period but before the latest day designated for handing over the tax). This will happen under RST if sales are made against cash but the tax is remitted, say, every three months, or if accounts receivable are settled earlier than tax is remitted to the tax office. If the tax payment conditions are similar, the effect also arises under VAT, but part of the tax-induced cash flow benefit may be spread upstream if retail purchases, including VAT, are also made against cash.

useful to make a distinction, generally overlooked in the economics literature, between the cross-border VAT treatment of goods and that of services.

2.1. Cross-border transactions in goods

Prior to 1993 (the year in which intra-community border controls were abolished in the EU), most member states included imported goods in the domestic VAT base by taxing them at their borders under the supervision of customs authorities, while a credit for the VAT was provided when the goods entered the domestic production process. Similarly, the VAT on exports was refunded at the export stage and border controls could be used to check whether the goods had actually left the country. These 'border tax adjustments' (BTAs) ensure that the VAT is levied on the destination principle, while border controls can be viewed as a helpful backstop for enforcement and verification (in lieu of the audit trail).

From 1993 onward, physical controls for VAT at interstate borders have been replaced by accounting controls at the first inland stage of the production process. Registered firms of taxable imported goods have to include these goods (intra-community acquisitions are deemed to be a separate chargeable event) in the return due for the period in which the goods are imported. The VAT is self-assessed, as it were, and a credit is provided at the same time. Accordingly, no net VAT is due and payable, unless the acquisition is made by an exempt firm. This arrangement is called 'deferred payment' (Cnossen (1983), p. 156), because the VAT does not have to be paid upfront at the border.[6] In 1982, the European Commission proposed the EU-wide introduction of deferred payment (Draft Fourteenth VAT Directive),[7] but changed its position three years later (European Commission (1985)) in favour of exporter rating. The member states, however, insisted on deferred payment, which had proven its feasibility in Benelux, ever since Belgium, Luxembourg,

[6] Although correct if looked at from the border VAT point of view, deferred payment is a misnomer when viewed in the domestic context, because it treats imported goods exactly on a par with domestic goods (the right to a tax credit arises at the same time that the VAT on supplies is accounted for). Particularly, it eliminates the previous cash flow disadvantage, i.e. the interest foregone by the importing firm on the VAT paid at import before this VAT was credited (or refunded) against the domestic VAT payable on sales. Some member states used to neutralize this cash flow disadvantage by allowing importing firms a grace period of, say, 6 weeks, before the import VAT had to be paid.

[7] Without abolishing border controls. Importers of VAT-liable goods still had to hand over VAT documentation to customs authorities at the point of importation without actually being assessed for VAT at that point.

and the Netherlands introduced their VATs in the late 1960s and early 1970s.[8]

Deferred payment places the charge to VAT on the purchaser of imported goods rather than the supplier: the charge to VAT is reversed, as it were. Reverse charging, generally applied, is believed to take care of the 'missing trader', that is, the trader who charges VAT on his supplies but then disappears, while his customer takes credit for VAT that has not been accounted for. The missing trader may be an importer, but can also be a domestic trader. Essentially, contrived insolvency has the same effect; it was practised long before 1992.

Reverse charging, applied throughout the domestic production–distribution process, would nullify the fractional collection nature of the VAT, under which the tax office has a lien, as it were, on suppliers for the tax payable by their customers (ultimately the retailers that collect the VAT from consumers). Austria and Germany have requested permission to apply reverse charging to transactions above €10,000 and €5,000, respectively, but the European Commission (2006) has denied the requests on the ground that reverse charging would increase compliance control problems at the lower end of the production chain where most small businesses can be found.[9] This commentator believes that comprehensive reverse charging would throw the baby out with the bathwater.

At the time the transitional regime was introduced, customs controls were replaced by a functionally equivalent, if perhaps less certain, VAT information exchange system (VIES) (Council Regulation 1798/2003/EC).[10] VIES requires registered firms to report their intra-community supplies (exports) to registered firms in other member states (indicating their VAT identification numbers preceded by a country code) on a quarterly or monthly basis (listing requirement) to the VAT office. Similarly, the purchaser has to report the total of his intra-community acquisitions. The information is fed into a central data bank and enables the various VAT administrations in the EU to match total intra-community acquisitions per trader against individually reported supplies. VIES imposes differentially higher

[8] Prior to 1993, deferred payment was also practised for some time in Ireland and the UK where it was called postponed accounting.

[9] For Germany, see the proposals in Dziadkowski et al. (2002) as well as Gebauer et al. (2007). The European Council (Decision 2007/250/EC), however, has permitted the UK to apply reverse charging to supplies of mobile phones, computer chips, and some other goods.

[10] Furthermore, a statistical data collection system, referred to as the Intrastat system, was set up to collect trade data on goods and (later) services between member states (Council Regulation 638/2004/EC). Recently, the Intrastat obligations have been simplified (COM(2008) 58 final).

compliance costs on interstate traders—a source of discrimination and trade distortion.[11]

2.2. Cross-border transactions in services

Although services are economically equivalent to goods, their VAT border-crossing treatment differs. Prior to 1993, arrangements for BTAs on goods through border controls could not deal effectively with (non-tangible) services whose location of supply or purchase is difficult to ascertain. Obviously, interstate differences in VAT rates would generate distortions if the liability to tax was determined by the state in which the service was supplied. But if the purchasing firm's state would be the taxing locus, it would be difficult to tax purchases by final consumers.[12]

Article 43 of the 2006 VAT Directive (previously Article 9 of the 1977 Sixth VAT Directive) provides a workable solution to the issue by taxing services, in principle, in the state where they are performed. Highly significant exceptions, however, are made in Article 56 for services rendered by banks, insurance companies, professional firms, advertising agencies, and various other services (nearly all B2B transactions). Upon export, these services are exempt, although the exporter retains the right to a credit for the VAT in respect of any inputs used in performing the services. In the importing state, furthermore, the taxable users of services are liable to VAT on them under Article 196 of the 2006 VAT Directive (previously Article 21 of the 1977 Directive). In essence, prior to 1993, the current transitional regime for goods was already being applied to services.

Initially, there was no need to have separate rules for the acquisition of out-of-state services similar to the rules for goods bought by exempt entities, those sold by mail order firms or for individually imported means of transport—which are all taxable in the destination state. Few high-value services were bought out-of-state in low-VAT countries. This changed dramatically, however, with the advance and privatization of telecommunication, radio, television, and electronic services. Firms providing these services sprung up in Luxembourg (which has one of the lowest VAT rates in the EU) to the chagrin

[11] See Verwaal and Cnossen (2002) who point out that most of the differential costs should be attributed to Intrastat obligations (see footnote 10 above), not to VAT obligations.

[12] Note that the much feared wave of cross-border purchases of consumer goods (Sinn (1990)) was already a non-issue for services prior to 1993. In fact, the treatment of border-crossing services, before and after 1993, indicates that the implications of the break-in-the-VAT-chain for goods when border controls were abolished, were not unfamiliar phenomena.

of the member states where the services were consumed and supposed to be taxed.[13]

To remedy this situation and, more generally, to put the VAT treatment of services on a par with the treatment of goods, recently, new rules (which will take effect in 2010) for the place where services are deemed to be rendered have been promulgated with the primary goal of taxing services as much as possible at the place of consumption or use (Council Directive 2008/8/EC of 12 February 2008). In effect, the deferred payment system for goods will be extended to B2B services under an identical reverse charging system. Basically, the exceptions have become the main rule: B2B services will be deemed to be provided where the customer carries on his business. Overriding exceptions are provided for immovable property, cultural services and education, restaurants and catering, transportation of persons, and short-term rentals of vehicles, which are deemed to be provided where the services are actually performed. As is the case with goods, the VAT identification number will play a crucial role in verifying compliance.

The main rule for B2C services, as before, is that they are deemed to be provided at the place where the provider of the services carries on his business. To limit administrative costs, a mini one-stop shop arrangement will be provided for telecommunication, radio, and television services (effective 2015). The tax on these services will be payable in the state where the services are provided. Subsequently, that state distributes the VAT revenue to the member states where the customers are located according to an agreed formula. In fact, this is a mini-form of exporter rating!

2.3. Improving compliance and enforcement symmetry

Basically, the latest directive unifies the VAT treatment of intra-community transactions in goods with similar transactions in services (not, of course, for trade with third countries). Deferred payment/reverse charging (VAT in the destination state) is explicitly applied to goods and B2B services. B2C consumer services are taxed in the state where the services are actually performed, similar to cross-border purchases of goods which are taxed, with minor exceptions, on an origin basis. VIES reporting obligations for goods as well as services potentially extend the verification trail across borders. Compliance symmetry between in-state and out-of-state transactions has been enhanced by requiring in-state suppliers to show their VAT identification number and

13 In addition, complications arose regarding third-country providers of services which had to choose a member state of domicile to discharge their VAT obligations.

that of their customers on invoices, as out-of-state suppliers have to do. What remains to be done is the establishment of tax audit units with EU-wide investigative powers to monitor VAT compliance with intra-community transactions. In other words, verification should be complemented by audit control. For all practical purposes, the new arrangements for services seem to transform the transitional regime into the definitive regime, although, as shown below, the debate on some form of exporter rating instead of deferred payment continues.

3. EXPORTER RATING SYSTEMS PROPOSED BY THE EUROPEAN COMMISSION

Very different, perhaps more exciting if less practical, coordination proposals have been made in the tax literature and by the European Commission, which focus mainly on repairing the supposed break in the VAT collection chain. In the early 1980s, Cnossen (1983), argued that the destination principle[14] could be maintained without border controls if intra-community exports would be taxed at the VAT rate of the exporting member state, invoiced to the importer in the importing member state, and credited by him against his VAT liability on sales. To restore the revenue allocation under the destination principle, the importing state would have to reclaim the importer's credit from the exporting state. In essence, only net balances (VAT collections on exports over VAT credits on imports) would have to be settled between member states. This could be done on an EU-wide basis through what Cnossen (1983) called a clearing house system. The idea was adopted by the European Commission (1985) in a paper known as the Cockfield White Paper,[15] and forms the basis of subsequent exporter rating proposals.

[14] Early on, the origin principle was viewed as the only way of doing away with border controls for VAT (Neumark Committee (1963), pp. 145–9). In fact, the doctrine of the 'restricted origin principle' (applied in the EU but not to trade with third countries; Shibata ((1967), pp. 193–4), became a standard tenet in public finance textbooks; see e.g. Due and Friedlaender ((1975), p. 519), Musgrave and Musgrave ((1980), p. 644), and Shoup ((1969), p. 644). For an analysis in the US setting, which reaches the same conclusion, see McLure ((1980), pp. 127–39). Subsequent writings, however, emphasized that origin taxation violated production efficiency—a more important criterion than exchange efficiency (Diamond and Mirrlees (1971))—and that it involved contentious transfer pricing problems (Cnossen and Shoup ((1987), pp. 72–73). After weighing the theoretical and technical arguments, this chapter (Section 4.5.1) concludes that the destination principle is the best lode star for practical VAT design.

[15] Interestingly, as perceived by the European Commission, exporter rating seemed to be in line with the erstwhile pronouncement on origin taxation in Article 4 of the First VAT Directive (which called for the abolition of 'the imposition of tax on importation and the remission of tax on exportation in trade between member states'), since intra-community supplies were taxed in the

The Commission's arguments, however, failed to persuade the governments of the member states which wanted to retain full control over the VAT administration of imports and exports, and, therefore, opted for the deferred payment system, although they agreed that exporter rating should receive a second hearing before 1997. In the tax literature, moreover, Lee et al. (1988) had criticized the Commission's clearing house proposal, pointing out that it had an adverse impact on enforcement incentives, because importing member states might not be inclined to root out fraudulent claims for import VAT credits (after all these would presumably be paid by exporting states), while exporting states would have little incentive to uncover fraudulent failure to charge VAT on exports. Solving this problem would require uncoupling the clearing house flows from taxes actually paid.

Subsequently, the European Commission (1996) made another attempt to persuade the member states of the benefits of exporter rating. The fresh proposal was called home-state taxation, because firms involved in intra-EU trade would have to deal only with the VAT system of the member state in which they were established.[16] Cross-border sales would be taxed in the same fashion as domestic sales, although cross-border movement of goods within the same business would go untaxed. VAT revenues on intra-community transactions would be allocated between member states on the basis of national accounts statistics of aggregate consumption. Complete uniformity in the scope and definition of VAT would also be necessary, as well as close cooperation and EU supervision of VAT administrations.

In an eloquent commentary, Smith (1997) pointed out that the new proposal would put substantial limitations on member states' autonomy to set rates, require an extensive programme of legislative harmonization, cause difficulties in identifying firms entitled to be taxed in a single member state, and a flight of businesses to least-taxed locations or, if rates were the same, to states where VAT evasion would be less tightly controlled. Also revenue allocation rules would undermine incentives to devote adequate resources to VAT collection and enforcement.

state of origin even though revenue would be allocated on the destination principle. Accordingly, to this day the Commission continues to insist on dubbing exporter rating as origin taxation, confusing principle and method for the sake of an outdated point of view.

[16] Since intra-EU exports were zero rated under deferred payment, the European Commission (1996) noted that more than €700 billion worth of goods circulated VAT-free in the internal market, and observed that due to the break in the VAT-collection chain 'some of that amount may well be diverted to the black economy'. In light of the above discussion, it will be noted that all goods and services, not just intra-community traded products, circulate VAT free within the ring of registered firms.

The proposal did not leave the drawing board, but was briefly resurrected in 2004 as the one-stop shop proposal under which exporters would be able to discharge all their obligations with respect to border-crossing transactions at one place only, that is, their place of establishment.[17] This time clearing would not be necessary because exporters would be required to remit the gross VAT collected by them and calculated at the destination-state rate directly to the state of final destination, an idea which had earlier been proposed by Vanistendael (1995).[18] Few details were provided. In the meantime, the Commission seems to believe that the transitional regime will be around for some time to come: in the 2006 VAT Directive, the transitional measures are no longer grouped together, but integrated with related provisions.

4. SHOULD VIVAT BE LAID TO REST?

In the belief that the supposed break in the VAT-collection chain threatens VAT's integrity, Keen and Smith (1996, 2000) have made an imaginative, high-profile proposal for a viable integrated VAT (VIVAT), which would impose a harmonized dual EU-VAT rate, administered by member states, on all pre-retail (intermediate) transactions by registered firms within and between EU member states, supplemented by a surtax at retail (in fact an RST integrated with a member state's VAT) if governments wish to exploit the VAT base more intensely. Clearing would be provided if the VAT collected on exports exceeded the VAT credits provided for imports.

According to Keen and Smith (1996), as well as the authors of this chapter, VIVAT would bolster the destination principle and hence subsidiarity in taxation. The commonality of the EU single rate would lessen the pressure on the clearing system and enforcement. Traders would be able to report exports and imports in aggregate rather than per member state. The uniform single rate would remove the incentive for strategic rate setting, that is, the incentive member states would have under exporter rating with non-harmonized rates to tax exports higher because the VAT would anyway be creditable in importing states.[19] The hassle of the clearing system could be resolved through a

[17] Some details can be gleaned from IP/04/1331 and MEMO/04/249.

[18] The one-stop shop proposal may receive further scrutiny in the run up to the implementation by 2010 of the Services Directive (Council Directive 2006/123/EC), which calls for 'points of single contact' in each member state where traders can discharge all their obligations in other member states.

[19] It is difficult to view this as an advantage of VIVAT, since any attempt at strategic rate setting would be stopped in its tracks by the European Court of Justice on the ground that it would be a gross violation of the non-discrimination principle.

one-off deal, that is, a system of lump sum transfers between member states, obviating the need for future clearing.

VIVAT, however, would not be without its own problems. Uniform exporter rating may appear to repair the break in the VAT-collection chain, but does nothing to solve the break in the VAT-audit trail. Importing member states would still not be able to audit importers' invoices (received from exporters in other member states) for which they have no authority. This would provide a powerful incentive to produce false import invoices, possibly arranged through third countries, showing VAT eligible for credit instead of no VAT as under the current regime. Keen and Smith's (1996) proposal that the excess of collections on exports over imports should be allocated on the basis of export and import listings by businesses of aggregate rather than individual transactions would undermine enforcement efforts, since it would not be possible, as under VIES, to link individual transactions to monitor compliance for audit purposes.

Furthermore, under VIVAT, member states with a greater than average preference for VAT would have to impose an additional RST. In other words, they would have to incur higher administrative and compliance costs than currently and than member states making do with the revenue collected under the VIVAT rate. Registered traders, moreover, would have to make a distinction between sales made to other registered traders (taxable at the VIVAT rate) and sales made to non-registered persons, that is, individuals and exempt entities (taxed at the RST-inclusive rate)—'not a trivial burden', as Keen and Smith (1996, p. 406) admit. The RST-element would have all the drawbacks of a normal RST, noted in the literature (e.g. Cnossen (1987)).

Beyond that, it is difficult to envisage a uniform VIVAT rate in light of the established, if perhaps misguided, preference for greater rate differentials shown by the member states. Also, reduced rates are levied on a product-specific basis. Their application (with revenue consequences) to intermediate transactions would complicate VIVAT and open up other avenues for fraud, particularly if it is not possible to audit import invoices. Substantial refunds might have to be paid out if the VAT rate on a product applied at retail in the importing state would be lower than the VIVAT rate in the exporting state. Politically, VIVAT would further entrench the (high) VAT rate agreement in the EU, making it more difficult to convert the differentiated rate structures into single uniform rates or to reduce the VAT rates in individual member states at some future date.

Finally, a staff working paper issued by the European Commission (SEC/2008/249) notes that member states would become dependent on each other for, on average, some 10% of total VAT revenues if exporter rating were applied at a uniform rate of 15% (the Netherlands, Germany, Belgium, and Ireland would become large net contributors to the clearing system). The level of mutual trust, therefore, would have to be exceptionally high, particularly in view of the wide variation in VAT fraud levels. Furthermore, mismatches between supply and acquisition listings would arise. In 2006, the excess of reported acquisitions over supplies was €80 billion. At a rate of 15%, the potential amount of VAT involved could be €12 billion. Exporter rating, moreover, would only target missing trader fraud. It would not solve and might even exacerbate VAT losses through the shadow economy, contrived insolvencies, or other domestic fraud.

Other proposals for VAT coordination in the EU have been made by McLure, and Bird and Gendron. McLure (2000), building on a proposal by Varsano (1999) for the Brazilian states, suggests that a separate uniform rate EU-VAT (which he calls 'compensating value added tax' or C-VAT) should be introduced, administered by a central agency (or a consortium of states), on all interstate exports matched by a credit for tax on all interstate imports (accordingly, there would be no need for a clearing mechanism). State VATs would be retained along with the deferred payment system for interstate trade. In essence, C-VAT is functionally equivalent to VIES but involves greater administrative complexity.

Bird and Gendron's (1998) dual VAT (D-VAT), based on the experience in Canada (which has a federal VAT, while Quebec operates a state VAT), envisages a central VAT (next to the state VATs), which would apply to all in-state and interstate sales. Unlike the C-VAT, the D-VAT would raise revenue for the centre. As Keen and Smith (2000) have pointed out both C-VAT and D-VAT currently are not options in the EU if there is to be a central administration. Bird and Gendron ((1998), p. 439), however, do allow for a virtual, functionally equivalent D-VAT in the form of 'some closely coordinated overarching administrative structure which would, for example, facilitate and ensure information exchanges, development of agreed audit plans, and so on', in order to give states the capacity to monitor cross-border transactions. It is this idea that is also central to the gist of this commentary.

It is hard to avoid the impression that VIVAT, C-VAT, and D-VAT are heavily predicated on the assumption that a solution has to be found for the VAT treatment of interstate trade in (physical) goods[20]—so central to the

[20] See, for instance, Keen and Smith ((2000), pp. 743–4) who make their case for VIVAT against the background of the abolition of 'effective border controls'.

EU's 1992 programme—while the practice and experience with (intangible) services is just as or even more important. Bringing services into the equation emphasizes the point that it is the break in the VAT-audit trail that should be the focus of concern. Deferred payment involves fraud, of course, but the answer to fraud, it seems, is audit, investigation, and prosecution, not another system that may be equally susceptible to abuse. Substituting a tried and proven system of deferred payment by some form of exporter rating may turn out to be a costly risk. A simple system of no tax and no valuation of exports would be replaced by a system with a positive tax and perhaps valuation problems. It is quite telling, perhaps, that the Netherlands (which has had deferred payment for nearly forty years!) has the lowest VAT evasion rate (the VAT gap as a percentage of hypothetical revenue) among ten member states for which figures are available (Gebauer and Parsche (2003)), although it is the most open economy of all.

5. VAT BASE BROADENING

One of the contentious issues under deferred payment is the treatment of cross-border acquisitions by exempt entities, which have to self-assess their intra-community acquisitions (which are zero rated in the supplying member state) on a transaction-by-transaction basis. Ad hoc self-assessment with its attendant complexity would not be necessary if the entities were not exempt but registered for VAT purposes like other businesses. More generally, the EU-VAT exemptions violate the logic and functionality of the tax. They distort input choices, harm exports, and complicate administration because the VAT on inputs has to be denied with respect to exempt supplies if performed in combination with taxable transactions. Accordingly, a strong case can be made for repealing most of the 'standard exemptions'.[21]

The case against the exemption of cultural services is particularly strong. Admissions to theatres, concerts, museums, sporting facilities, and the like compete with taxable forms of entertainment, such as travel and reading, and should therefore be taxed. Similarly, public radio and television broadcasts compete with taxable privately financed broadcasts and other forms of communication. This applies also to postal services (which compete with taxable private letter or parcel carriers), newspapers, and periodicals. Since it is difficult to justify these exemptions on externality grounds, withdrawal seems indicated. Various member states, including the UK, are coming around to

[21] This section draws heavily on Cnossen (2003).

the view that cultural services should be taxed, but taxation is by no means universal in the EU.

Even the exemptions for healthcare and for education services hardly stand up to close scrutiny. Admittedly, the externality arguments are stronger than in the case of cultural services, but if health and education services should be provided below cost, then (an increase in) budget subsidies (or a zero rate) would be the appropriate policy response. The exemptions violate production efficiency because the institutions providing healthcare and education services are induced to perform laundry, cleaning, food preparation, and various other services in-house in order to save the payment of VAT on the labour element of these services, which would be payable had they been acquired from outside, taxable establishments. This hampers the contracting-out of these services (privatization) and thus the efficient functioning of the institutions. Exemption also raises the cost for companies wishing to conduct research through hospitals and universities, because they cannot take implicit credit for the VAT on the inputs used by the exempt institutions. These considerations become more important as the private provision of health care and education grows relative to public provision, as is happening in the EU.

Administratively beyond reach so far are financial transactions, because the intermediation charge, which should be taxed, cannot be separated from the pure interest rate, premium or rate of return which should not be taxed. Perhaps the cash flow approach, pioneered by Poddar and English (see Poddar (2003)), deserves further scrutiny. The EU has closely considered their ingenious idea, but doubts remain about its practicability. There is little doubt about the desirability of taxing public bodies more widely, particularly local and provincial governments. Competition is distorted to the extent government services compete with similar services provided by the private sector. As with hospitals, universities, and financial institutions, taxation would obviate the need for delineation between taxable and exempt government activities as well as for ad hoc self-assessment if taxable goods and services are acquired out-of-state.

Another anomaly is the flat rate schemes for the agricultural sector which exempt farmers from the obligation to register for and pay VAT, but compensate them for the tax borne on inputs. The schemes provide only rough justice and, just like the old turnover tax, can be used to subsidize farmers. Best practice would be to make farmers fully liable for VAT, subject to the small-business exemption. Similar comments can be made about the various small-business schemes, which add greatly to administrative and compliance costs without contributing much to revenue. Experience in new VAT countries indicates that the simplest small-business scheme is a fairly generous exemption without any strings attached. Indeed, this is also the outcome of the formula discussed in this chapter.

6. CONCLUSIONS

This commentary has argued that exporter rating does not seem to have obvious advantages over deferred payment for the VAT treatment of intra-community transactions and may complicate VAT administration. Instead, the search should be for a workable system that extends the VAT audit trail by setting up cross-border tax audit and investigation units to monitor intra-community transactions. Precedents for this can be found in police and judicial units with cross-border pursuing and investigative powers. If this is done, the current transitional regime can be retained. Furthermore, explicit reverse charging should remain the exception rather than become the rule.

Last but not least, the 2006 VAT Directive, which is based on its 1977 predecessor (long before the wall came down), has not stood the test of time. Efficiency in production and tax collection is not served by the large number of so-called standard exemptions. Admittedly, improvements to the 2006 VAT Directive require the consent of twenty-seven member states, which is hard to come by.[22] If the member states are not to be locked into outmoded VATs, perhaps they should be permitted to have better VATs than provided by the 2006 VAT Directive. The time has come to support this chapter's call for allowing more experimentation than has hitherto been the case.

REFERENCES

Bird, R. M., and Gendron, P.-P., (1998), 'Dual VATs and Cross-Border Trade: Two Problems, One Solution?', *International Tax and Public Finance*, 3, 429–42.

——(2007), *The VAT in Developing and Transition Countries*, Cambridge, Cambridge University Press.

Cnossen, S. (1983), 'Harmonization of Indirect Taxes in the EEC', chapter 7 in McLure, C. E. Jr. (ed.), *Tax Assignment in Federal Countries*, 150–68. Canberra: ANU Press.

22 This chapter argues that a common VAT base is helpful in determining the VAT-contribution to the EU's 'own resources', but this contribution is calculated by statistical agencies on the basis of national accounts, divorced from actual VATs. In other words, the actual VAT base does not have to coincide with the agreed VAT-contribution base.

——(1987), 'VAT and RST: A Comparison', *Canadian Tax Journal*, **35**, 559–615.

——and Shoup, C.S. (1987), 'Coordination of Value-Added Taxes', chapter 2 in Cnossen, S. (ed.), *Tax Coordination in the European Community*, 59–84, Deventer, the Netherlands: Kluwer Law and Taxation Publishers.

——(2003), 'Is the VAT's Sixth Directive Becoming an Anachronism?', *European Taxation*, **43**, 434–42.

Diamond, P. A., and Mirrlees, J. A. (1971), 'Optimal Taxation and Public Production: I Production Efficiency, II Tax Rules', *American Economic Review*, **61**, 8–27.

Due, J. F. and Friedlaender, A. F. (1975), *Government Finance: Economics of the Public Sector*, 6th edn., Homewood, Ill.: Irwin.

Dziadkowski, D., Gebauer, A., Lohse, W. C, Nam, C. W., and Parsche, R. (2002), 'Entwicklung des Umsatzsteueraufkommens und finanzielle Auswirkungen neuerer Modelle bei der Umsatzbesteuerung', *Ifo Forschungsberichte* **13**, Munich.

Ebrill, L., Keen, M., Bodin, J-P., and Summers, V. (2001), *The Modern VAT*, Washington DC: International Monetary Fund.

European Commission (1985), *Completing the Internal Market*, White Paper from the Commission to the European Council ('Cockfield' White Paper), COM(85) 310 final, Brussels.

——(1996), *A Common System of VAT: A Programme for the Single Market*, COM 328(96), final, Brussels.

——(2006), *Communication from the Commission to the Council in Accordance with Article 27(3) of Directive 77/388/EEC*, COM(2006) 404 final, Brussels.

Gebauer, A., and Parsche, R. (2003), 'Evasion of Value-Added Taxes in Europe: IFO Approach to Estimating the Evasion of Value-Added Taxes on the Basis of National Accounts Data (NAD)', *CESifo DICE Report*, **2**, 40–4.

——Nam, C. W., and Parsche, R. (2007), 'Can Reform Models of Value Added Taxation Stop the VAT Evasion and Revenue Shortfalls in the EU?', *Journal of Economic Policy Reform*, **10**, 1–13.

Keen, M., and Smith, S. (1996), 'The Future of Value-Added Tax in the European Union', *Economic Policy*, **11**, 373–411 and 419–20.

————(2000), 'Viva VIVAT!', *International Tax and Public Finance*, **7**, 741–51.

——(2006), 'VAT Fraud and Evasion: What Do We Know and What Can Be Done?', *National Tax Journal*, **59**, 861–87.

Lee, C., Pearson, M., and Smith, S. (1988), *Fiscal Harmonisation: An Analysis of the Commission's Proposals*, IFS Report Series 28, London: Institute for Fiscal Studies.

McLure, C. E., Jr. (1980), 'State and Federal Relations in the Taxation of Value Added', *The Journal of Corporation Law*, **6**, 127–39.

——(2000), 'Implementing Sub-National VATs on Internal Trade: The Compensating VAT (CVAT)', *International Tax and Public Finance*, **7**, 723–40.

Musgrave, R. A., and Musgrave, P. B. (1980), *Public Finance in Theory and Practice*, 3rd edition, New York: McGraw-Hill.

Neumark Committee (1963), Report of the Fiscal and Financial Committee, in *The EEC Reports on Tax Harmonization*, Amsterdam: International Bureau of Fiscal Documentation.

Poddar, S. (2003), 'Consumption Taxes: The Role of the Value-Added Tax', chapter 12 in Honohan, P. (ed.), *Taxation of Financial Intermediation: Theory and Practice for Emerging Economies*, New York: Published for the World Bank by Oxford University Press, 345–80.

Shibata, H. (1967), 'The Theory of Economic Unions: A Comparative Analysis of Customs Unions, Free Trade Areas and Tax Unions', in Shoup, C. S. (ed.), *Fiscal Harmonization in Common Markets, vols. 1 and 2*, New York: Columbia University Press.

Shoup, C. S. (1969), *Public Finance*, Chicago: Aldine Publishing Company.

Sinn, H-W. (1990), 'Tax Harmonisation and Tax Competition in Europe', *European Economic Review*, **34**, 489–504.

Smith, S. (1997), *The Definitive Regime for VAT*, Commentary 63, London: Institute for Fiscal Studies.

Vanistendael, F. (1995), 'A Proposal for a Definitive VAT System. Taxation in the Country of Origin at the Rate of the Country of Destination without Clearing', *EC Tax Review* **1**, 45–53.

Varsano, R. (1999), 'Subnational Taxation and Treatment of Interstate Trade in Brazil: Problems and a Proposed Solution, in Burki, S. J., and Perry, G. (eds.), *Proceedings of the Annual Bank Conference on Development in Latin America and the Caribbean*, 339–55. Washington, DC: The World Bank.

Verwaal, E., and Cnossen, S. (2002), 'Europe's New Border Taxes', *Journal of Common Market Studies*, **40**, 309–30.

Commentary by Ian Dickson and David White*

Ian Dickson is a shareholder and director in Burleigh Evatt Consulting, a New Zealand professional services firm. Ian began his career in the New Zealand Treasury, where he was involved in the introduction of the Goods and Services Tax in 1986. Since leaving the Treasury he has been involved in investment banking, corporate finance, and strategy consulting. Recently he has been an adviser contributing to the revenue reform programme in the Kingdom of Tonga. The Kingdom introduced a VAT called 'Consumption Tax' in 2005.

David White has been responsible for the tax research agenda of the Centre for Accounting, Governance and Taxation Research at Victoria University of Wellington, New Zealand, since the Centre was set up in 2001. His research focuses on tax policy and tax policy process design, especially in relation to the Goods and Services Tax and international income taxation. He worked in the New Zealand Treasury tax policy branch 1987–2000. He studied law at Victoria University of Wellington and the London School of Economics and received his doctorate in law from the University of Sydney.

1. INTRODUCTION

The editors of the Mirrlees Review asked us to evaluate the UK VAT and the European Union VAT Directive and compare them to the New Zealand VAT model, which is called GST (Goods and Services Tax). At first sight, this brief might seem strange. After all, the VAT is a European invention that has swept the world, now applying in around 150 countries while GST is merely a more recent, modified European VAT.

Yet, for the whole life of the New Zealand GST, international VAT experts, including from Europe, have made favourable comparisons between the old

* We are grateful to two anonymous reviewers for their helpful comments on the manuscript.

European VAT model and the GST model.[1] In many cases, these comparisons have concluded that the changes that New Zealand made when introducing its VAT in the mid-1980s were improvements on the European model—a case of same wine, new bottle. Countries seeking to introduce VAT have often been advised to consider New Zealand's approach, and many countries have done so.

Surprisingly, there has been little research on GST, particularly of an empirical nature, to test objectively the merits of the innovations and the international experts' advice.[2] The recent twentieth anniversary of the New Zealand GST, however, did provide an opportunity to begin rectifying that omission and to develop a research agenda.[3] A multidisciplinary team of twenty-nine experts from eight countries analysed and discussed the New Zealand GST experience, the influence of the New Zealand model around the world, and current issues for VAT tax systems everywhere. This commentary draws on the work of that team,[4] our experience as tax policy-makers, and our research.

New Zealand's GST is different from the UK VAT in the important respect that it is applied comprehensively at a single domestic rate. There are no reduced or super-reduced rates, exemptions, or zero rates—other than those necessary to define the appropriate base of the tax.[5] Food, children's clothing, medical care, education services, publications, energy, and other necessities of life are taxed at 12½% like all other goods and services. This was a deliberate policy choice made at the time of introduction and maintained intact over the intervening years. Applying the most widely used indicator of VAT performance, the C-efficiency ratio,[6] the New Zealand GST scores twice as highly as the UK VAT.[7] Indeed, the GST is apparently a huge 43.5 percentage points above the OECD average for C-efficiency.[8] It is this long-standing, comprehensive application of GST that provides insights for formulation of indirect tax policy for the UK. The commentary will also briefly consider aspects of how the New Zealand GST applies to services and organizations that in Europe are often considered too hard to tax.

[1] See, for example, Cnossen's (2003) recent call for a comprehensive overhaul of the EU VAT Directive.

[2] Early analysis by New Zealand Institute of Economic Research staff is summarized and discussed in Bollard (1992).

[3] White (2007a) especially at 372–4. A shorter version of this article also appeared in (2007b).

[4] Krever and White (eds.) (2007).

[5] In the category of 'base-defining' exemptions and zero rates, we include exports, provision of labour services, and investment capital.

[6] C-efficiency is the ratio of VAT revenue to consumption expenditure, divided by the standard tax rate, expressed as a percentage.

[7] OECD (2006) at 53.

[8] If 'departmental GST' is excluded from the calculation (since it results in no net revenue

2. UNITED KINGDOM AND NEW ZEALAND: COMMONALITIES AND DIFFERENCES

Before analysing the New Zealand GST model, we need to examine the contextual similarities and differences between New Zealand and the UK. The similarities are easiest. Both countries are islands of roughly the same area. New Zealand is a former colony of the UK and is English-speaking. The two countries have a great many cultural similarities and historical ties, including a common legal heritage, political institutions, and experience of geopolitical conflict. Naturally, the development of many areas of government policy in New Zealand has over time followed the lead of policy in the UK—although the development of indirect tax policy in the last twenty years is a notable exception. Britain's policy choices, such as to enter the Common Market in 1973, have also affected aspects of social, economic, and foreign policy and the sense of national identity in its remote former colony. Both countries have modern information technology systems in both the private and public sectors (including, in the customs and revenue authorities).

New Zealand and the UK also employ broadly similar tax types, with some variation. New Zealand has neither separate capital taxes nor National Insurance contributions (pensions are funded from general revenue on a pay-as-you-go basis). New Zealand relies a little more heavily on its VAT as a source of taxation than the UK while the UK relies a little more heavily on its excise duties on specific goods and services, like motor fuels, alcohol beverages, and tobacco products (Table 1).

Both countries have extensive social welfare systems and both provide income tax credits for families with insufficient market income to provide an acceptable living standard. New Zealand's tax-funded universal pension is available at the age of 65 years to all who meet residential requirements. The level of payment is reviewed each year and is adjusted to take account of increases in inflation and wages. When wages increase, New Zealand

to government), the New Zealand C-efficiency ratio reduces by about one-third, as shown in the following table.

Years ended 30 June	1999	2000	2001	2002	2003	2004	2005
C-efficiency ratio	105.9	107.6	106.3	88.3	90.9	94.9	93.1
C-efficiency ratio adjusted for departmental GST	78.2	79.4	78.4	65.2	67.1	70.1	68.7

Sources: Statistics New Zealand's Consolidated Accounts of the Nation; Financial Statements of the Government of New Zealand (Annual).

Table 1. Comparison of VAT and Excises in the United Kingdom and New Zealand

	United Kingdom	New Zealand
Year VAT introduced	1973	1986
Standard VAT rate	17.5	12.5
General threshold (US$)	93,700	26,846
VAT revenues as % of total taxation (2003)	19.8	26.1
C-efficiency ratio for VAT (2003)[9]	46.4	96.4
Tax on general consumption as % of GDP[10]	7.0	9.1
Tax on general consumption as % of total taxation	19.5	25.6
Tax on specific goods and services as % of GDP	4.0	2.3
Tax on specific goods and services as % of total taxation	11.2	6.5

Source: OECD (2006), 25–8, 30, 32, 52–3.

Superannuation is adjusted so that it is between 65% and 72.5% of average ordinary time earnings after tax.

The settings of the respective countries, however, are very different. New Zealand is a nation of 4.5 million individuals separated from its nearest neighbour, Australia, by 2,000 kilometres of sea, so that New Zealand has no proximate borders with any other countries. While New Zealand has economic integration agreements with Australia, and a growing number of trade agreements with countries in the Asia–Pacific region that generally have VATs of their own, it is not a member of any multilateral relationship that compares with the UK's membership of the European Union in limiting domestic policy flexibility. Consequently, VAT administration issues that arose for the UK with the elimination of internal frontiers in the European Union, and the potential tax competition, have not been ones for New Zealand.

3. A COMPREHENSIVE BASE AND SINGLE RATE: LESSONS FROM NEW ZEALAND

The Meade Report[11] had an immense influence on the development of tax policy thinking in New Zealand in the years following its publication. It

[9] See note 6 above for the definition of the C-efficiency ratio. Also, in note 8 above, we suggested an adjustment to the C-efficiency ratio for New Zealand in order to exclude departmental GST. Using official New Zealand statistics, we calculate the C-efficiency ratio adjusted for departmental GST in 2003 at 67.1.

[10] These last four tax ratios use 2004 data.

[11] Meade (1978).

was much pored over, studied, debated, and quoted at length in officials' reports to New Zealand ministers. It provided guidance about how problems relating to the taxation of individuals and businesses, and wealth, should be addressed. Under Meade's influence, the formulation of tax policy advice became systematic and principles-based.

By the early 1980s, New Zealand was lumbered with an awful wholesale tax that omitted around 67% of the potential indirect tax base, and the country relied significantly upon international trade taxes. Other horrors abounded in the tax, regulation, and subsidization of industry, as well as the conduct of economic management generally. The ad hoc grab bag of taxes could not fund existing expenditure demands, let alone shoulder the burden of a switch towards a greater reliance on indirect taxation that was government policy. Meade could give New Zealand policymakers no direct guidance on how to address this problem, nor on the pressing question of the day, 'which is better, VAT or retail sales tax?' Meade, however, inspired an investigative approach to these problems that eventually resolved these questions.

There are still many questions about the directions for indirect taxation in the twenty-first century. There are two central questions where the evidence from New Zealand can provide insights for the authors' proposed reforms of the UK VAT, which imposes reduced rates on more total consumption expenditure than the VAT in any other EU-15 Member State:[12]

- Are the alleged administration and compliance benefits of a comprehensive single-rate VAT[13] borne out by the New Zealand experience?
- What is the evidence on the ability to alleviate the distributional impacts of a comprehensive single-rate GST on the poor and lowest paid?

Embodied in these two questions are the essential contrasts between the European-style and New Zealand-style VATs. This section first considers the New Zealand debate on comprehensiveness prior to introduction of GST in 1986, secondly, administration, compliance, and public acceptance issues, and, finally, the evidence on distributional impacts.

[12] Cnossen (2003).

[13] Cnossen (1994). Cnossen concludes this review by arguing that overall compliance costs and administrative costs can be reduced by, among other things, broadening the VAT base, imposing a single rate, and increasing the threshold for registration.

3.1. The New Zealand debate on GST base comprehensiveness: 1981–86[14]

New Zealand policymakers were fortunate in having a dry run at indirect tax reform issues and arguments in 1981–82, several years before the successful campaign to introduce a GST in 1984–86. A task force that reviewed the tax system had proposed that the wholesale sales tax should be converted to a credit-offset basis, the indirect tax base should be broadened and supplies of services should be taxed separately.[15] The then New Zealand Prime Minister adopted much of the task force's advice in 1982 but not their indirect tax proposal.

New Zealand policymakers learnt from the 1981–82 experience that maintaining a comprehensive tax base would be one of the most difficult issues, particularly in relation to food and clothing. They developed arguments for taxing food and other necessities on equity and economic efficiency grounds. They realized, moreover, that they would need to run public relations, consultation, and education campaigns on a scale previously not carried out and fully involving both the public and private sectors.[16] This was a high-risk strategy since it focused on the very things the public would be most sensitive about paying tax on. If that debate were won, the strategy suggested, other people seeking exemptions would find it much harder to get public acceptance of their claim and there was a better chance of enacting a comprehensive indirect tax.

The argument conceded that taxing food was regressive. Evidence available at the time suggested that while the bottom 20% of households allocated between 23 and 29% of their budgets to food, the top two deciles spent between 7 and 10% of weekly expenditure on food. However, the answer to the question 'who spends the most on food?' was that upper-income households spend twice as much as low-income households. Of every $100 spent on food in New Zealand, the least well off spent $6.50, whereas the most well off spent $12. Taxing all food thus made revenue available to redistribute and supplement the income of the poor. This argument, presented by a government with credibility, was broadly accepted and GST went ahead with a comprehensive base and single domestic rate.

[14] This section draws on the historical and policy perspective in Dickson (2007).

[15] McCaw (1982).

[16] See the following chapters in Krever and White (eds.) (2007): Douglas (2007); Green (2007); Todd (2007); Dickson (2007).

3.2. Administration costs, compliance costs, and public acceptance

The first question under this heading is whether the alleged administration benefits of the comprehensive single-rate VAT are borne out by the New Zealand experience. Unfortunately, the administrative costs of operating GST are not separately identified because GST-related work is often not separate from other tax-gathering functions.

It is possible, however, to identify areas of considerable administrative cost saving in the GST system. GST does not require hundreds of pages of classifications of goods, services, and providers and the associated interpretations and rulings. It does not, to take one recent UK example, require officials to distinguish a 'biscuit' from a 'cake', and, if they make a mistake, to consider whether the refund should be for the total amount wrongly charged or whether this would constitute 'unjust enrichment' of the taxpayer.[17] It also does not require officials to identify the public organizations that shall, and shall not, be subject to GST. GST remains quietly agnostic on such questions: the general rules apply.

It is also possible to identify areas of administrative cost and risk in the GST system.[18] First, a comprehensive tax applied in an island country without near neighbours is still a 'cash refund' tax that carries the attendant risks of refunds. Even with the taxation of imports, some missing trader fraud occurs and a particular problem area has been property developers. Secondly, GST requires regular legislative maintenance, in one recent case blocking GST refunds with an estimated revenue cost of up to NZ$200 million.[19] Thirdly, in contrast to the UK, New Zealand still has separate agencies administering the border and inland collection of GST. The fragmented administration in New Zealand requires agency-to-agency information exchanges to audit the deduction for GST collected at the border and this may be more costly. The New Zealand Customs Service increasingly focuses on border security rather than revenue collection, so differing agency priorities are a risk issue.

[17] The Marks & Spencer teacake case, concerning the misclassification of their chocolate teacakes as standard-rated biscuits rather than zero-rated cakes from 1973 to 1994, is still not settled after 10 years of argument. Marks & Spencer claim repayment of £3.5 million but the Commissioners of Customs & Excise refuse to refund more than 10% of the overpaid VAT.

[18] The consideration of revenue risk draws, in part, on Snell (2007) in Kever and White (eds.) (2007).

[19] The Taxation (Annual Rates, Taxpayer Assessment and Miscellaneous Provisions) Bill 2001 retrospectively blocked some GST refunds affecting inbound tour operators and educational institutes. See officials' letter to the Finance and Expenditure Committee of the New Zealand Parliament dated 31 July 2001, attached as Annex A in R. Oliver, 'Taking a Fixed Tax Position in a Changing World—A Personal Perspective', 19–25, available at <http://taxpolicy.ird.govt.nz/publications/files/icanz2003.pdf> (as at 26 February 2008).

While administrative costs of GST may be difficult to ascertain, policy administration costs are demonstrably low. In twenty years, GST has had one major policy review, which produced no recommended structural change. The Inland Revenue Department, responsible for most of the legislative work on GST, has the time of around around $1\text{–}1\frac{1}{2}$ professional policy staff dedicated to GST out of a total tax policy complement of 45. The key point is that GST has been a 'low maintenance tax' from a policy administration cost perspective[20] and this is generally attributed to the twin policy pillars of comprehensive coverage and a single domestic rate.

The second question is whether the alleged compliance benefits of the comprehensive single-rate VAT are borne out by the New Zealand experience. Here the evidence is less conclusive so this question cannot receive a short answer. There are five main observations that we would like to make. First, as international experts argue, VAT compliance costs are difficult to measure and interpret correctly[21] and 'international comparisons of administrative and compliance costs should be regarded as tools to raise questions rather than providing immediate answers'.[22] Therefore, care is needed in interpreting and drawing conclusions from the various surveys.

Secondly, two major New Zealand surveys in the last fifteen years have attempted to quantify GST compliance costs:

- In 1991–92, a benchmark survey by Sandford and Hasseldine[23] concluded that total compliance costs of the GST were large (7.3% of GST net revenue) and that mean annual compliance costs were regressive ($1,066 or 1.6% of turnover for firms with $30,000–$100,000 turnover; $3,521 or 0.2% of turnover for firms with $1 million–$2 million turnover; $9,615 or 0.005% of turnover for firms with more than $50 million turnover). The overall value of the cash flow benefit from the delayed payment of GST reduced these compliance costs figures by around 39%, providing greatest benefit to larger firms. Substantial offsetting managerial benefits from improved accounting practices were reported, mostly by smaller firms. At the time, only 23% of respondents used computers for their GST accounting.

[20] This label was used to describe the perspective of another key tax policy advising agency in New Zealand, the Treasury. See Snell (2007).

[21] Cnossen (1994), at 1665.

[22] Sandford (2000).

[23] Sandford and Hasseldine (1992). All figures in New Zealand dollars.

- In 2004, a survey of SMEs[24] to provide a baseline for evaluating the effectiveness of future policy and administrative initiatives was conducted by an independent research organization for the Inland Revenue.[25] On average, respondents reported mean annual compliance costs of $2,471 for income tax and $1,553 for GST. GST compliance costs are regressive ($1,285 for firms with $40,000–$99,000 turnover; $2,646 for firms with more than $1.3 million turnover). Fifty-three per cent used computers for their GST accounting. The survey revealed that levels of stress in meeting tax compliance requirements and finding the money to pay the tax were higher for GST (3.8%) and provisional income tax (3.7%) than for pay-as-you-earn income tax (3.2%) and fringe benefit tax (3.2%).

The results of both surveys are consistent with what is known about the relatively fixed nature of costs associated with administrative tasks in small businesses. They show that GST compliance costs are very regressive. The 2004 SME study says, for example, that the irreducible cost of GST compliance is around £40 per month.

Thirdly, a difficult issue concerns the marginal cost of GST compliance (that is, the amount that would be saved if the GST did not exist). There are two aspects to this issue. First, compliance costs must be attributed between tax types (in particular, the income tax and the GST). Secondly, compliance costs must be attributed between tax and core accounting costs. We believe that marginal GST compliance costs may not be as high as the New Zealand surveys suggest. A New Zealand case study that required participants to record tax and accounting functions in a weekly diary over 12 months, supplemented by regular interviews, provides an interesting insight. It concluded that the high proportion of tax compliance costs allocated to GST rather than to income tax in earlier New Zealand studies (the main one being Sandford and Hasseldine (1992)) may well be explained by the fact that GST reporting is more frequent (monthly, bimonthly, or six monthly) and that small-business people perceive income tax as the by-product of accounting first prepared for GST returns.[26] This suggests it may be fraught to attempt a meaningful attribution of tax compliance costs by tax type. The potential overlap between core external and internal accounting costs and GST compliance costs is even more problematic.[27] A strong possibility

[24] Firms that employed fifty or more staff and had an annual turnover of more than NZ$10 million were excluded.

[25] Colmar Brunton (2005). All figures in New Zealand dollars.

[26] Ritchie (2001), in Evans, Pope, and Hasseldine (2001), at 312.

[27] For a discussion of the considerable efforts made to improve the compliance cost estimates in the 2004 survey and some of the outstanding issues, see: Oxley, Turner, and Sullivan (2005); and Oxley and Elwela (2006).

remains that the costs of basic business record keeping are represented as GST compliance, since merchants commonly refer to 'doing their GST' as shorthand for such activities.

Reinforcing this argument is the point that if GST compliance costs were an unreasonable burden on smaller businesses there would have been much more adverse comment than has occurred. Compliance costs with tax, regulatory, health and safety, and statistical obligations have been an on-going complaint from business advocacy groups, but the focus has been on other areas of fiscal encroachment on day-to-day business affairs rather than GST. This speaks to us of a GST system that nevertheless finds acceptance amongst the business community that collects the tax. Compliance with the huge volume of income tax changes, with fringe benefit tax and provisional income tax, where there is an element of uncertainty about establishing liability (as there would be in a VAT system with extensive exemptions), and with requirements that do not mirror ordinary day-to-day business activities (in the way that issuing and receiving invoices do), have attracted more comment and criticism.[28]

Fourthly, further corroborating evidence on the level of compliance costs of GST may come from the tax advisory (as opposed to the tax compliance) profession. Until recently, the tax teams of all large law and accounting professional firms in New Zealand, with one exception, did not include a specialist GST partner. It was only in 2006 that a small number of other large professional firms considered that giving GST advice justified appointing a specialist GST partner.

Fifthly, a 15-year-old New Zealand and UK compliance cost comparison is available. The two studies had one author in common (Sandford) and used the same methodology. The comparison shows UK VAT compliance costs were lower at low turnovers (US$0–500,000) and higher at high turnovers (above US$500,000) than in New Zealand. For example, for turnover under US$50,000, UK VAT compliance costs as a percentage of taxable turnover were 1.49 compared to 2.06 in New Zealand, for turnover of US$50,000–100,000, 0.70 compared to 0.91, for turnover of US$100,000–200,000, 0.50 compared to 0.67, and for turnover of US$200,000–500,000, 0.44 compared

[28] From 2003 onwards, an annual private-sector survey of tax compliance costs for all sizes of enterprise has reported very high tax compliance costs (in 2007, annual total average internal and external compliance costs for all types of tax advice was $11,592 and the average total cost per full-time equivalent staff was $402). This survey does not break down tax compliance costs by size of enterprise or tax type. The marked changes in the respondents each year mean that year-on-year comparisons are difficult. Business New Zealand–KPMG Compliance Cost Survey, October 2007, 35–9. See <http://www.businessnz.org.nz/surveys/504> (as at 26 February 2008).

to 0.47. On the other hand, for turnover of US$500,000–1 million UK VAT compliance costs as a percentage of taxable turnover were 0.34 compared to 0.28 in New Zealand and for turnover of US$1 million–10 million, 0.07 compared to 0.04.[29]

A common author of these studies suggests the following explanation of the higher New Zealand GST compliance costs for smaller businesses: 'Because compliance cost[s] as a percentage of turnover are negatively correlated with size, the overwhelming reason for the difference will be the much lower registration level for the New Zealand tax (about one-third of the UK threshold of 1986–87) and its wider coverage and the pressure put on small operators in New Zealand to register voluntarily.'[30] Another factor may be the different tax return periods most commonly used in the two countries (in most cases, two months for New Zealand and three months for the UK).

We are inclined to put most weight on the threshold, voluntary registration and the tax return period factors. Cnossen would add the registration of non-profits in New Zealand. After preparing the table comparing the 15-year-old UK VAT and the New Zealand GST compliance costs surveys, Cnossen still concludes that broadening the VAT base is one of three ways of reducing overall compliance costs.[31] We agree with Cnossen and with the conclusion that Sandford earlier reached with his co-author Hasseldine that, 'the wider base of the New Zealand tax . . . could be expected to reduce compliance costs compared with the UK. Only a much more detailed comparison than is currently possible would reveal the areas of significant difference in compliance costs.'[32] That work has still not been done.

The final question under this heading concerns public acceptance of the twin pillars policy. Acceptance of GST by the business community, in particular, was aided by extensive consultation and adaptation prior to enactment of legislation. This was the first time that the New Zealand public had been consulted on tax policy and legislation. Moreover, submitters could see the results of expressing their views as the draft legislation contained in the *White Paper* (1985) was completely rewritten before enactment. An extensive public relations programme aimed at educating taxpayers was also undertaken under the auspices of the GST Coordinating Office.

[29] Sandford (2000), 132, reporting the comparison and conversion into US dollars made by Cnossen (1994), 1665–7.

[30] Sandford (1994), 137. Cf. Sandford and Hasseldine (1992), 112.

[31] Cnossen (1994).

[32] Sandford and Hasseldine (1992), 112–13.

A comprehensive single-rate VAT has found such acceptance in the New Zealand social, political, and economic context that the concept has gone virtually unchallenged for two decades. There have been no serious attempts to challenge the model.[33] In 1987, the year after GST's introduction, the main opposition National Party proposed an 'Extax' that would have introduced exemptions and suspended the credit-offset mechanism. Following their defeat in the general election, the National Party dropped Extax. Later, after the change of government at the 1990 general election, National's Minister of Finance described the introduction of GST as 'a model of tax reform'.[34]

To what extent does this public acceptance result from unique circumstances in New Zealand not replicable in the UK? One set of circumstances might be the broad national consensus in New Zealand in 1984 that reform was desperately needed. This swept the Fourth Labour government to power and returned the same administration three years later, despite its 'root and branch' reform policies. There is a sense that in a national emergency, such as New Zealand faced in 1984, the public will temporarily accept the 'unacceptable'. By the mid-1990s the emergency had ended, yet acceptance of, indeed popular support for, a comprehensive single-rate VAT system now appears to be as strong as ever. Some other economic reforms of the Fourth Labour government, including the move towards a more comprehensive income tax, may have been partly or wholly reversed in the last twenty years but the twin pillars of the GST model remain standing. This suggests that the public is able to be convinced of the merits of such an approach when the arguments are presented and provides support for the authors' illustrative proposal of a more comprehensive 17.5% VAT applied to all commodities except housing and items currently exempt from VAT for the UK.

3.3. Evidence on distributional impacts

The position of two groups in society is of particular concern when examining the distributional impacts of a proposal to extend VAT to food, clothing, and the other necessities of life:

- pensioners;
- low-paid workers and social security beneficiaries.[35]

[33] The application of GST to local authority property rates and to tourist expenditure have been continuing issues that successive governments have declined to change.

[34] Quoted in Todd (2007).

[35] This section draws, in part, on Stephens (2007) especially 77–87.

Distributional impacts for pensioners arising from the introduction of GST were dealt with adequately with a one-off benefit adjustment that reflected the estimated consumer price effect of the reform.[36] It should be noted, moreover, that under the universal New Zealand Superannuation scheme (a pay-as-you-go scheme) the pension is explicitly linked to average after-tax wages. Pensioners therefore participate in the higher after-tax incomes of working age individuals and are protected, at least as far as their state-funded pensions are concerned, from the inter-generation equity implications of a direct-to-indirect tax shift. Obviously, no such protection is available in respect of savings and non-indexed private pensions.

Low-paid workers and social security[37] beneficiaries present different issues. At GST's introduction there were one-off adjustments to social security benefits as occurred for pensions. The low-paid were recipients of targeted relief through income tax credits. However, the income tax credits were confined to families with dependent children, meaning that low-paid individuals and couples not on a benefit received nothing other than small tax cuts. This decision reflected the results of official studies of the incidence when a 10% GST was substituted for the wholesale sales tax.[38] These studies, based on data gathered from household income and expenditure surveys, showed that the vertical incidence of the increase in the indirect tax burden[39] would be regressive by income level for each family type, but manageably so within the scope of the available compensatory measures. Three interesting results clearly stood out and influenced the shape of the compensation package:

- The incidence of indirect taxes is regressive, with a much higher average impact on households in low-income deciles[40] compared to higher-income deciles.[41] For example, the incidence on the second decile was 25% compared to 15% for top income earners.

36 The official estimate of the price impact of GST's introduction was a one-off increase in the general level of prices of 5.5%. Other estimates ranged between 5 and 7%. The actual increase in consumer prices measured in the December quarter 1986 was 8.9% up from 3.3% in the September quarter. The March 1987 quarter recorded a 2.4% increase in consumer prices.

37 Income tested benefits paid to individuals reflecting unemployment, sickness, widowhood, or being a solo parent.

38 New Zealand Planning Council (1990). See also the following unofficial studies: Scott, C. Goss, P. and Davis, H. (1985); Broad and Bacica (1985).

39 The average household burden from indirect taxes rose from 11.4% to 18.4% between 1985–86 (the year before GST's introduction) and 1987–88.

40 A decile divides sorted data into ten equal parts, so that each part represents $\frac{1}{10}$th of the population. The 1st decile cuts off the lowest 10% of data at the 10th percentile and the 9th decile cuts off the lowest 90% of data at the 90th percentile.

41 As Stephens notes, the incidence for the first decile needs to be treated cautiously as self-employed people comprise a large part of that decile and they can declare income tax losses while spending freely. Stephens (2007), in Keever and White (eds.) (2007), at 79.

- The presence of dependent children within a family type magnified the effect of taxing food and other necessities. This result strongly associated with the number of dependent children in the family unit. In the third decile, for example, it was estimated that the impact of GST would reduce household disposable income for families of 2 adults and 1 child by 6.1% and reduce household disposable income for families of 2 adults and 3 children by 9.5%. The net impact for the top decile for these family types would be just 4.5%.
- The impact on pensioners was less than for a typical household due to their relatively low food consumption.

The identified above-average impacts were addressed through compensatory income supplementation. The compensatory approach is an available and workable alternative to preferring food and other necessities in the VAT. However, it relies on a social bargain between the government and low-paid workers and beneficiaries that the supplementation will keep up with costs. There were periods in the 1990s and the early 2000s when social assistance lagged behind costs.

Stephens[42] makes an observation that may be important in assessing the ability to translate the New Zealand GST experience to the UK. He argues that a prime reason that mid-1980s New Zealand tax and economic reforms have endured was the attention given to the issue of horizontal equity. Horizontal equity—like treatment of people in similar circumstances—seems to underpin the notion of fair play in the New Zealand context to a greater degree than redistribution.

4. THE HARD-TO-TAX: LESSONS FROM NEW ZEALAND

In this section, we identify aspects of the New Zealand experience that may be relevant in addressing the problem of hard-to-tax services and organizations. We make comments in Table 2 on the following subjects and issues:

- financial services (intermediation and for-fee);
- residential dwellings;
- threshold;
- government services (including health and education);
- overseas travel.

[42] Ibid. 78.

Table 2. The hard-to-tax: Lessons from New Zealand

Subject	Issue	Lessons from New Zealand
Intermediation financial services	Financial services that are remunerated by a margin or spread are not able to be integrated with the general invoice system of VAT. There is no feasible, conceptually correct, solution. Is it not time to put the search for a 'solution' to intermediation financial services into the category of a quest that has no practical value? The choices are to zero-rate, exempt (without credit), or a hybrid of both.	In an attempt to reduce the cascading effects of exemption for businesses, New Zealand has applied a hybrid system since 2005. To date, the fiscal impact of the new zero-rating for business-to-business financial services and reverse charge rules has been as officials forecast but it is too early to judge whether the new rules have opened up tax planning opportunities.[43]
For-fees financial services	New Zealand has successfully taxed for-fee financial services, such as fire and general insurance, giving credit for a notional tax content of claims.	This is a potentially useful expansion of the UK VAT tax base.[44]
Real property	Taxing supplies of real property causes compliance problems analogous to the missing trader fraud discussed by the authors in Section 4.3.3 at 311–16.	The problem essentially arises from the delay between claiming VAT during the construction phase and the completion tax point. The possible solutions replicate the authors' suggestions in relation to missing traders in Section 4.3.3 at 311–16.[45] Fiscal risks can also arise from deferred settlement schemes that take advantage of differing accounting bases (accruals, cash, or hybrid).
Residential dwellings	New Zealand taxes residential construction activities and the first sale of new dwellings while the UK does not. The issue noted by the authors in Section 4.3.2 at 304 appears to be increasing house prices to new buyers (housing affordability) and the windfall gain to existing owners.	The authors correctly make the comment that taxing new construction would give a windfall to existing homeowners. Direct compensation is one approach. However, other factors affecting housing

(*cont.*)

43 Pallot (2007) especially at 169–70.

44 For a discussion of the merits of the New Zealand and Australian regimes for taxing fire and general insurance, see Edgar (2007) at 156–61.

45 See also the discussion and solutions suggested in Harley (2007) especially at 234–41. See also Snell (2007) especially at 424 and 429.

Table 2. (*cont.*)

Subject	Issue	Lessons from New Zealand
	Landlords and owner-occupiers face the same GST treatment. All purchases, insurance, local authority rates, maintenance charges as well as construction costs—the inputs to the provision of shelter—are taxable, but the value added in the provision of shelter is not subject to the tax.	affordability should also be considered before dismissing an application of tax to repairs, improvements, and new dwelling construction. New Zealand made no special arrangements in this regard. Australia did.
Threshold	While it is an elegant exposition, we are not convinced that the Keen and Mintz optimal threshold formula[46] is a sufficient basis for the conclusion that a high threshold is justified for the UK. It seems to rely on key assumptions about the variability of administration and compliance costs with firm size, and does not capture the potential distortions of trade from unregistered input-taxed suppliers competing with registered firms, especially where services are being provided with high labour and low goods content.	The New Zealand solution is a low threshold[47] combined with a choice of three return periods[48] and simplified accounting requirements for micro and small businesses. Complaints about competition from unregistered suppliers are rare. However, the evidence would suggest that a disproportionately higher compliance cost burden on the smallest firms is a negative consequence of the New Zealand approach.
Government services (including health and education services)	The conventional European treatment of government-provided services excludes them from the VAT base. This means that services such as education, medical care, and services to residents by local authorities are outside the VAT base. This is an erosion of the potential VAT base and may exacerbate problems of competition between public and private suppliers.[49]	New Zealand taxes all government-provided services, including the notional outputs of policy and administrative agencies. Government-provided services, such as healthcare and education, are also taxed, as are such services in the private sector. The cost of this approach is that it may be more

[46] Keen and Mintz (2004).

[47] The New Zealand Government is currently seeking submissions on increasing the current GST threshold from NZ$40,000 to NZ$50,000. It observes that the New Zealand registration threshold is low by international standards but that about 40% of the taxpayers currently registered for GST are voluntary registrants with an annual turnover of less than NZ$40,000. The estimated cost of allowing about 24,000 taxpayers to exit the GST base is about NZ$15 million a year. Cullen and Dunne (2007).

[48] The standard return period is two months, which is shorter than in many other jurisdictions. Micro businesses may apply to use a six-monthly return period. There is also a one-month return option.

[49] The case for the VAT in the EU fully taxing all public sector bodies (and non-profit organizations) is well argued in Aujean, Jenkins, and Poddar (1999).

Table 2. (*cont.*)

Subject	Issue	Lessons from New Zealand
		administratively complicated than exempting agencies, but not more complicated than zero-rating. It also inflates the size of GST receipts and expenditures by corresponding amounts (subject to timing mismatch). The advantage is that it makes agencies indifferent between charging and appropriations, and so preserves a competitive position between the state and private sectors.
	The New Zealand model goes further and treats the policy and administration services supplied by government departments as taxable activities regardless of whether their funding is appropriated by Parliament or sourced from fees and changes.	
Overseas travel	Tourist expenditure is by convention taxed in the country of destination, but expenditure on travel between countries generally falls outside any countries' tax net. Overseas travel is a significant (and growing) item of household consumption and worthy of attention by tax policymakers.	Very few countries impose VAT on overseas travel. New Zealand does not. Indirect taxation of overseas travel might require an arrangement analogous to postal revenue sharing between nations on either a regional or multilateral basis. Indirect tax reform is worthwhile contemplating.[50]

5. CONCLUDING COMMENTS

The authors have identified a compelling case for reforming the UK VAT supported by empirical evidence on the small potential gains from rate differentiation. Moreover, they have identified an illustrative reform package of a uniform standard rate of 17.5% applied to all non-housing consumption goods and items currently exempt from VAT, which, while not completely

[50] For a broad consideration of the indirect tax issues and an optimal policy proposal for fuel and ticket taxes, see Keen and Strand (2007).

removing the distortions of the current UK VAT scheme, can be introduced without waiting for the EU ground rules for VAT to be renegotiated.

This commentary has sought to provide insights from the New Zealand GST model for UK indirect tax policy and the authors' proposals on the following three issues:

- Are the alleged administration and compliance benefits of the comprehensive single-rate VAT borne out by the New Zealand GST experience?
- What have been the distributional impacts of a comprehensive single-rate GST on the poor and lowest paid in New Zealand?
- What lessons arise from how New Zealand GST applies to services and organizations that in Europe are often considered too hard to tax?

The broad conclusion from two decades of the New Zealand GST is that the alleged benefits of maintaining a comprehensive base with a single domestic rate are, on balance, borne out by experience. While VAT/GST compliance costs are undoubtedly regressive in relation to turnover, we consider that the New Zealand surveys may overstate marginal GST compliance costs, in part because the regular reporting of VAT/GST on a one-, two-, or six-monthly basis means that GST is the first tax return for which a business must complete accounts each year. The wider base of the GST is likely to have reduced compliance costs compared with the UK VAT but this has not been empirically tested.

We have argued that the public is able to be convinced of the merits of a comprehensive single-rate VAT and that this provides contextual support for the authors' illustrative proposal of a 17.5% VAT applied to all non-housing consumption goods and items currently exempt from VAT for the UK.

To the extent that taxing the basic necessities of life will affect the economic position of the poor, relief can be provided using more effective support tools than GST exemptions. However, it relies on a social bargain between the government and low-paid workers and beneficiaries that the income supplementation will keep up with costs. In New Zealand, the political consensus has been to apply compensating assistance via the income tax and social welfare systems, with an emphasis on supporting working families with children. Critics may point out that, as a result, New Zealand has an army of bureaucrats administering its social welfare and income tax credit systems instead of an army of revenue officers administering the boundaries between rates and exemptions. If the former army is taken as a given in a modern developed country, the absence of the latter is clearly a cost saving to be added to the reduced deadweight costs of the New Zealand style of GST.

REFERENCES

Aujean, M., Jenkins, P., and Poddar, S. (1999), 'A New Approach to Public Sector Bodies', *International VAT Monitor*, **10**, 144–9.

Bollard, A. E. (1992), 'New Zealand's Experience with Consumption Tax', *Australian Tax Forum*, 473–93.

Broad, A., and Bacica, I. (1985), *The Incidence of Indirect Taxes, Vol. 2*, Wellington: Institute of Policy Studies.

Colmar Brunton (2005), *Measuring the Tax Compliance Costs of Small and Medium-Sized Businesses—A Benchmark Survey*, 95–103, Wellington: Colmar Brunton.

Cnossen, S. (1994), 'Administrative and Compliance Costs of the VAT: A Review of the Evidence', *Tax Notes International*, **8**, 1649–68.

——(2003), 'Is the VAT's Sixth Directive Becoming an Anachronism?', *European Taxation*, **43**, 434–42.

Cullen, M., and Dunne. P. (2007), *Reducing Tax Compliance Costs for Small and Medium-Sized Enterprises*, **13–14**, Wellington: Policy Advice Division of Inland Revenue.

Dickson, I. (2007), 'The New Zealand GST Policy Choice: An Historical and Policy Perspective', in Krever, R., and White, D. I. (eds.), *GST in Retrospect and Prospect*, 45–63, Wellington: Brookers Ltd.

Douglas, R. (2007), 'The New Zealand GST Policy Choice and its Political Implications', in Krever, R., and White, D. I. (eds.), *GST in Retrospect and Prospect*, 3–11, Wellington: Brookers Ltd.

Edgar, T. (2007), 'The Search for Alternatives to the Exempt Treatment of Financial Service under a Value Added Tax', in Krever, R., and White, D. I. (eds.), *GST in Retrospect and Prospect*, 131–61, Wellington: Brookers Ltd.

Evans, C., Pope, J., and Hasseldine, J. (eds.) (2001), *Taxation Compliance Costs: A Festschrift for Cedric Sandford*, Sydney: Prospect Media.

Green, R. (2007), 'Consulting the Public in Developing a GST', in Krever, R., and White, D. I. (eds.), *GST in Retrospect and Prospect*, 13–25. (2007), Wellington: Brookers Ltd.

Harley, G. (2007), 'Dilemmas for GST Tax Policy Designers—Land Transactions', in Krever, R., and White, D. I. (eds.), *GST in Retrospect and Prospect*, 213–41, Wellington: Brookers Ltd.

Keen, M., and Mintz, J. (2004), 'The Optimal Threshold for a Value-Added Tax', *Journal of Public Economics*, **88**, 559–76.

——and Strand, J. (2007), 'Indirect Taxes on International Aviation', *Fiscal Studies*, **28**, 1–41.

Krever, R., and White, D. I. (eds.) (2007), *GST in Retrospect and Prospect*, Wellington: Brookers Ltd.

McCaw, P.M. (1982), *Report of the Task Force on Tax Reform*, Wellington: Government Printer.

Meade, J. (1978), *The Structure and Reform of Direct Taxation: Report of a Committee chaired by Professor J. E. Meade for the Institute for Fiscal Studies*, London: George Allen & Unwin. http://www.ifs.org.uk/publications/3433.

New Zealand Planning Council (1990), *Who Gets What? The Distribution of Income and Wealth in New Zealand*, Wellington: New Zealand Planning Council.

OECD (2006), *Consumption Tax Trends*, Paris: OECD.

Oxley, P., and Elwela, D. (2006), 'Tax Compliance Costs of New Zealand Small Businesses, 2004: Designing the Survey for its Policy Purpose', paper presented at the Seventh International Conference on Tax Administration held in Sydney on 20–21 April 2006.

—— Turner, S., and Sullivan, C. (2005), 'Tax Compliance Costs of Small Businesses 2004: Improving the Estimates', paper presented at the 2005 IRS Research Conference held in Washington, DC on 7 June 2005, <http://www.irs.gov/pub/irs-soi/05oxley.pdf>.

Pallot, M. (2007), 'GST and Financial Services—Rating Zero Rating', in Krever, R., and White, D. I. (eds.), *GST in Retrospect and Prospect*, 163–78, Wellington: Brookers Ltd.

Ritchie, K. (2001), 'The Tax Compliance Costs of Small Businesses in New Zealand', in Evans, C., Pope, J., and Hasseldine, J. (eds.), *Taxation Compliance Costs: A Festschrift for Cedric Sandford*, 297–31, Sydney: Prospect Media.

Sandford, C. (2000), *Why Tax Systems Differ: A Comparative Study of the Political Economy of Taxation*, **137**, Bath: Fiscal Publications.

—— and Hasseldine, J. (1992), *The Compliance Costs of Business Taxes in New Zealand*, 57–79, Wellington: Institute of Policy Studies, Victoria University of Wellington.

Scott, C., Goss, P., and Davis, H. (1985), *The Incidence of Indirect Taxes, Vol. 1*, Wellington: Institute of Policy Studies.

Snell, D. (2007), 'GST—Revenue and Business Risk', in Krever, R., and White, D. I. (eds.), *GST in Retrospect and Prospect*, 423–30, Wellington: Brookers Ltd.

Stephens, R. (2007), 'The Economic and Equity Effects of GST in New Zealand', in Krever, R., and White, D. I. (eds.), *GST in Retrospect and Prospect*, 65–87, Wellington: Brookers Ltd.

Todd, J. (2007) 'Implementing GST—Information, Education, Co-ordination', in Krever, R., and White, D. I. (eds.), *GST in Retrospect and Prospect*, 27–43, Wellington: Brookers Ltd.

White, D. I. (2007a), 'Twenty Years of GST: The Best Path Forward', *New Zealand Journal of Taxation Law and Policy*, **13**, 357–80.

—— (2007b), *International VAT Monitor*, **18**, 343–51.

White Paper on Goods and Services Tax: Proposals for the Administration of the Goods and Services Tax (March 1985), Wellington: New Zealand Government.

Commentary by Jonathan Gruber

Jonathan Gruber is Professor of Economics at MIT and Director of the Program on Children at the National Bureau of Economic Research. He is a co-editor of the *Journal of Public Economics* and an Associate Editor of the *Journal of Health Economics*. He has written broadly on public policy, with a focus on health insurance coverage and on retirement, consumption decisions, and labour supply. Dr Gruber was elected to the Institute of Medicine in 2005, and in 2006 he received the American Society of Health Economists' Inaugural Medal for the nation's best health economist aged 40 or under. In 2006 he was appointed to the board of the Massachusetts Insurance Connector, the main implementing body for the state's ambitious health care reform effort.

Public policy makers have long been fascinated with the notion of taxing sinful consumption. The notion that the government could encourage proper behaviour, and, in the process, raise revenues to spend on other beneficial causes, is a powerful one. And developed nations have a long history of specific excise taxes on sin goods like tobacco and alcohol. In the United States, in 1960, 12.8% of government revenues were raised by specific excise taxes. By 2005, however, this had fallen to 3.2% (Gruber (2007)).

While sin taxes may make good politics, however, economists have often claimed that they make bad policy. The traditional economics argument towards sin taxes is straightforward. If sinful consumption levels are chosen by rational and fully informed agents, and those activities cause no harm to others, then the government has no more right to tax these activities than any other activities that are non-externality producing. By revealed preference arguments individuals are pursuing the optimal level of such activities and there is no need for 'correction' through taxation. The only particular role for excise taxation is to correct the externalities that sinful consumption may cause, in addition to their usual role in the optimal system of commodity taxation.

Section 4.4 of the chapter by Crawford, Keen, and Smith provides a very careful discussion of the role of excise taxation on smoking and drinking.

The authors make four important points. First, they integrate these specific commodity taxes into the larger optimal commodity taxation argument developed earlier in the chapter. They conclude, I think rightly, that the evidence is sufficiently unclear to motivate specific excise taxes on these particular goods (relative to the standard VAT rate) solely from elasticity-type arguments.

Second, they raise the well-known equity concerns around such taxes. Since lower income groups spend a much larger share of their income on 'sinful' consumption such as smoking or drinking, then these taxes are typically viewed as more regressive than the general VAT, which would offset any efficiency argument for higher taxes. Third, they review estimates of externalities due to alcohol and tobacco consumption and their implications for optimal taxation, highlighting the difficulties of translating externalities to tax policy when damage is highly non-linear (as is the case with alcohol). Finally, they discuss the same issues in the appropriate structure of excise taxation, particularly the equality of taxation across types of alcohol.

In this commentary, I will take issue with the baseline model that underlies the analysis of the chapter. On the basis of existing evidence and recent developments in behavioural economics, the standard economics model of 'sinful' consumption appears woefully inadequate. When sensible alternatives are applied, traditional conclusions such as those drawn here can be turned on their heads. My discussion will focus on the cases of smoking and alcohol, as discussed in this chapter; I will also include a discussion of perhaps the most important externality of all in the US context, obesity. I will leave aside the issue of proper taxation of motor fuel, which is discussed extensively in recent work by Don Fullerton and co-authors (e.g. Fullerton and Gan (2005)).

1. THE STANDARD MODEL OF SINFUL CONSUMPTION AND IMPLICATIONS FOR GOVERNMENT POLICY

In the standard economics model, there is nothing special about consumption of sinful goods as opposed to standard goods. Individuals optimize a well-defined utility function over a bundle of goods, some of which are sinful and some of which are not. If there are no external effects on others from the sinful consumption, then there is no call for government intervention.

For years, an informal claim was that the addictive nature of some sinful consumption (e.g. cigarette smoking) would justify government intervention even if there were no externalities. This claim was rejected in a pathbreaking article by Becker and Murphy (1988). In the Becker and Murphy model, individuals recognize the addictive nature of choices that they make, but may still make them because the gains from the activity exceed any costs through future addiction. In this 'rational addiction' framework, individuals recognize the full price of addictive consumption goods: both the current monetary price, and the cost in terms of future addiction.

Becker and Murphy model the act of addictive consumption (such as smoking) as the building of an addiction stock. The more cigarettes smoked today, the greater the addiction capital tomorrow. High addiction capital lowers *average* utility but raises the *marginal* utility of smoking. In this way, smoking lowers future utility but also increases the craving for another cigarette. The key feature of any addiction model is on how people deal with this intertemporal problem. In the original Becker–Murphy formulation individuals discounted the future *exponentially*, meaning that they discount k-periods forward by δ^k, where δ is the per-period time discount factor. This assumption has turned out to be central, as will be discussed further below.

Rational addiction subsequently became the standard approach to modeling consumption of goods such as cigarettes. The key normative implication of this approach is that the optimal regulatory role for government related to smoking is solely a function of the interpersonal externalities induced by smoking. Since smoking, like all other consumption decisions, is governed by rational choice, the fact that smokers impose enormous costs on themselves is irrelevant; it is only the costs they impose on others that gives rise to a mandate for government action.

The conclusions of this traditional economics literature create a central policy importance for the measurement of externalities associated with sinful activities. Over the past twenty years, a sizeable literature has been devoted to the measurement of these externalities. This chapter provides a nice review of externality estimates. While there are a number of interesting details, the bottom line is that the estimated externalities from smoking are quite small, while those from drinking are large. This is because most of the damage done by smoking is *internal* (through shorter lives), not external. Indeed, the limited external damage done by smoking (through higher system wide health costs) is largely offset by the savings through reduced pension payments due to earlier death of smokers (the so-called 'death benefit'). On the other hand, most of the damage from drinking is *external*, in the form primarily of drunk driving and induced criminal activity (the latter being a platform where it is much harder to measure the causal impacts of alcohol per se).

It is important to recognize some controversy in these estimates, however. The most important source of controversy is the relevance of external costs imposed on family members, such as through secondhand smoke or alcohol abuse. If smokers are maximizing a family utility function, rather than simply considering individual utility, then these costs should not be considered externalities. That is, if maximizing family utility, the smoker or drinker will take into account any damage done to others in the family in trading off the costs and benefits of smoking. Available evidence, however, suggests that family utility maximization is far from complete. For example, Lundberg, Pollak, and Wales (1997) show that, in contrast to the family utility maximization model (where everyone cares equally about all the family members), shifting the control of household financial resources from husbands to wives significantly increases the expenditures made on behalf of children.

2. PROBLEMS WITH THE STANDARD MODEL

A major problem with the perspective just outlined is that it is not consistent with observed excise tax policy in developed nations. Taxes on tobacco are typically many multiples of the externality estimates, particularly in European countries, while taxes on alcohol are much lower than the externality estimates. One explanation for this inconsistency is a lack of faith in the standard model among policy makers—and, implicitly, among the public as well.

2.1. The irrationality of youth

This lack of faith may reflect two realities about sinful behaviours that are not reflected in the standard model. This first is that engagement in such behaviours often begins at a young age. Of all US adults who smoke, more than 75% begin smoking before their nineteenth birthday (Gruber and Zinman (2001)). One-quarter of the estimated number of illegal drug addicts in the US are under the age of 17 (Pacula et al. (2001)). Despite the illegality of sales to, and consumption of, alcohol by minors in the US, 88% of 15-year-olds report having had a drink, one-quarter report drinking at least weekly, and one-third report having been drunk twice or more in their life. On this last count, in fact, the US appears to have much less child usage than other nations; the US ranks tenth in developed nations, for example, in the share of 15-year-olds who have been drunk twice or more in their life (Cook and Moore (2001)).

While models such as Becker and Murphy's presume a 'homo economicus' who is making rational and forward-looking decisions, most would admit that such a model does not fit the teenagers who are making potentially addictive decisions.

Indeed, there is some evidence that this monumental decision may not be made in the forward-looking fashion required by rational addiction models. A survey asked high school seniors who smoked a pack a day or more whether they would be smoking in five years and then followed the seniors up five years later. Among those who had said they would be smoking in five years, the smoking rate was 72%—but among those who said they would *not* be smoking in five years, the smoking rate was 74%! This result suggests that teens who smoke may not account for the long-run implications of addiction.

So how do young persons make decisions about whether to smoke, drink, overeat, or use drugs? In fact, we know remarkably little about this question. The state of knowledge is reviewed in the papers in Gruber (2001), and is summarized in the introduction to that volume. There are three key lessons from the analyses that underlie that volume. First, the actions taken by children along a variety of such 'sinful' behaviours have important implications for their behaviour as adults. For example, Gruber and Zinman (2001) document a strong intertemporal correlation between youth smoking and adult smoking; the causal link is established by exploiting variation in the taxation of cigarettes faced by individuals as youths (those who face higher taxes as youths smoke less both as youths *and* as adults). And Cook and Moore (2001) show that individuals who grew up in states and years with higher drinking ages are less likely to engage in binge drinking later in life.

Second, we know that these youth behaviours do respond to economic incentives. Most of the papers in the Gruber (2001) volume show that youth risky behaviours do respond rationally to incentives: youths smoke less, drink less, and use fewer illicit drugs when prices are higher; youths use fewer illicit drugs and drive more safely when the criminal penalties for not doing so are higher; youths stay in school and avoid unprotected sex when the labour market returns to completing education are higher; and so on. Finally, unfortunately, we know that economic incentives and other standard socio-economic controls can only explain a small part of the behaviours of youth over time. There are enormous time trends in smoking, drinking, drug use, crime, and youth fertility that are not readily explained by our economics models.

As a result, it is extremely unlikely that the complicated mechanics underlying the Becker and Murphy (1988) model can do much to explain the decision of youth to pursue addictive behaviours. This may be a well-earned source of scepticism among policy makers as they seek to apply these conclusions to policy making.

2.2. The inconsistency of adults

The other type of evidence, or at least introspection, that may deter policy makers from applying the standard model is the inconsistency in adult decision making over sinful activities. There is an enormous body of evidence that adults are *time inconsistent* in their behaviour towards such activities: the problem isn't their rational ability to make plans, the problem is that they lack the self-control to carry out those plans.

The term 'rational addiction' obscures the fact that the Becker and Murphy model imposes two assumptions on consumer behaviour. The first is that of forward-looking decision-making, which is a centrepiece of most welfare analysis in economics. Becker and Murphy also assume, however, that individuals *can not only optimize their utility function, but that they can then carry out those optimal plans.* There is much evidence from psychology, however, that contradicts this assumption: individuals are often unable to carry out long-term plans that involve self-control when there are short-term costs to doing so. An excellent example of this is smoking, where there is a short-term cost of quitting (in terms of physical discomfort and perhaps mental distress), but a long-term health benefit. Perhaps as a result, eight in ten US smokers express the desire to quit smoking, but many fewer than that actually do quit. Other examples include retirement savings (short-term cost in terms of foregone consumption today, but long-term benefits in terms of a higher standard of living in retirement), or whether to diet and/or exercise (short-term costs in terms of less food or more work today, but long-term benefits in terms of a longer life). In many arenas, individuals appear unable to control their short-term desires for their own longer-term well-being.

There are three types of evidence for the existence of self-control problems. The first is from laboratory experiments in psychology. In laboratory settings, individuals consistently reveal that they are willing to be patient in the future, but are impatient today, the defining characteristics of self-control problems. A person with self-control problems has the right long-run intentions (he rationally optimizes his utility function given his budget constraint), but he just can't carry them out. For example, in one experiment, most people preferred a cheque for $100 they could cash today over a cheque for $200 they could cash two years from now. Yet the same people prefer a $200 cheque eight years from now to a $100 cheque six years from now, even though this is the *same choice*—it's just six years in the future (Ainslie and Haslam (1992)). This is indicative of self-control problems: individuals are willing to be patient in the future, but not today when faced with the same choice.

The second type of evidence for self-control problems is the demand for *commitment devices*. If individuals have self-control problems and are aware of those problems, they will demand some type of device that helps them fight these problems. And the search for such commitment devices is the hallmark of most recommended strategies for quitting smoking: people regularly set up systems to refrain from smoking by betting with others, telling others about the decision, and otherwise making it embarrassing to smoke. These practices help individuals combat their self-control problems by raising the short-run costs of smoking to offset the short-run benefits of smoking. The use of self-control devices is widespread in other arenas as well: individuals set up 'Christmas Clubs' at their banks to make sure they have enough money to buy Christmas presents, and they buy memberships at sports clubs to commit themselves to work out when it would generally be cheaper to just pay each time they go.

The final type of evidence is patterns of data that are inconsistent with the standard model. For example, Angeletos et al. (2001) calibrate a model of the savings decision which shows that asset holding patterns in the US, with many individuals holding savings in illiquid forms but no savings (and often debt at high interest rates) in liquid forms, is inconsistent with the standard model but arises naturally in a model with self-control problems (since illiquid savings provides a commitment device).

Gruber and Mullainathan (2005) provide a test in the context of cigarette smoking. They note that an important distinction between the Becker–Murphy model and models with time inconsistency is the welfare impact of taxation. In the Becker–Murphy model, since an exponential individual makes a time-consistent choice to smoke, a rise in taxes can only *lower* discounted utility today. If it were to raise it, then the rational addict could raise utility by simply reducing smoking by the amount that the tax does, that is, by emulating the tax. So cigarette taxes should reduce the welfare of time-consistent rational addicts. Yet Gruber and Mullainathan find that higher cigarette taxes lead to *higher* levels of reported well-being among smokers. This is inconsistent with the standard model but, as explained below, could be due to the welfare gains of government provision of a commitment device in the self-control model.

It is equally important to clarify that there is a host of evidence on addictive behaviours that *does not* distinguish time inconsistency. The fact that consumers, even youths, are price sensitive in their consumption decisions of goods such as cigarettes, alcohol, and illegal drugs does not mean that they are time consistent, simply that they are rational (which is true in most alternative models discussed below). Particularly misleading is the sizeable literature growing out of Becker, Grossman, and Murphy (1994) that shows that addictive consumption responds to future prices as well as current prices. This finding has been taken to support the Becker–Murphy model *in toto*, but this is not the case. As highlighted by Gruber and Koszegi (2001), this evidence simply serves to prove that individuals are rational and forward-looking, not that they are time consistent.

3. POLICY IMPLICATIONS OF AN ALTERNATIVE MODEL: THE CASE OF SMOKING

There is by now broad agreement among many economists on the failures of the Becker–Murphy model appropriately to capture sinful behaviours such as smoking. Over the past seven years, several alternatives have been developed. While these alternatives differ, sometimes dramatically, in detail, they all have at their core the same concept: problems of self-control in the face of temptation. In this section I discuss in detail one such model, the quasi-hyperbolic discounting model of Gruber and Koszegi (2001, 2004). Since much of the literature is focused on the case of smoking, I will consider that case here as well; below I will expand the discussion to encompass other 'sinful' activities.

3.1. The quasi-hyperbolic discounting model and its implications

A major alternative approach to Becker and Murphy's (1988) model uses the *quasi-hyperbolic discounting* model developed by Laibson (1997) and O'Donoghue and Rabin (1999). In contrast to the exponential discounting used by Becker and Murphy, in this quasi-hyperbolic formulation, the next period is discounted by $\beta\delta$, the following period by $\beta\delta^2$, and k periods in the future by $\beta\delta^k$, where $\beta < 1$ is an extra discount factor that changes the discounting of this period relative to the entire future. The key feature of such a hyperbolic model is that individuals will have self-control problems. Specifically, a sophisticated hyperbolic individual (one who knows that he discounts hyperbolically) would like to smoke less in the future than he actually can. The problem arises because he is patient about the future (the relative discount rate between future periods is δ), but impatient about the present (the relative discount rate between today and tomorrow is $\beta\delta < \delta$). This means that when the future arrives he will end up making more impatient choices (i.e. smoke more) than he would like to from today's vantage point.

An alternative formulation of time inconsistency is the *I* case, where individuals do not recognize their own self-control problems (O'Donoghue and Rabin (1999)). One feature that distinguishes time-consistent agents from time-inconsistent agents is an inability to realize desired future levels of smoking. As noted above, unrealized intentions to quit at some future date are a common feature of stated smoker preferences.

Gruber and Koszegi (2001, 2004) augment the Becker–Murphy model by applying such quasi-hyperbolic preferences. This simple change has a radical implication: the discounted utility of a sophisticated hyperbolic consumer can rise if a tax is imposed. The reason is that the tax serves as a self-commitment device, which the private sector cannot perfectly supply.[1] As Gruber and Koszegi (2001) highlight, 'The argument that people act in their best interests so . . . the government should leave them alone, is immediately invalidated in our setting. Therefore . . . a benevolent social planner would want to intervene in this economy.'

That self-control problems could overturn the externalities-only motivation for taxation in the standard model is not very surprising. More striking is the implications of this alternative model for levels of optimal taxation. Gruber and Koszegi (2002) undertake a detailed calibration exercise based on their quasi-hyperbolic formulation to account not only for the externalities but also the *internalities* of smoking—that is, to value the cost to the individual themselves. They do so just for the mortality effects of smoking, ignoring other personal costs such as non-fatal illness and personal discomfort.

For this calibration exercise, they use consensus estimates of the value of a life from Viscusi (1993), and account for the fact that the years lost from smoking are at the end of life and so should be discounted to the present. Their results suggest that the internality from smoking a pack of cigarettes

[1] Gruber and Koszegi rule out perfect private sector commitment devices by assumption. As they discuss, any voluntary commitment device can readily be undercut by a voluntary 'de-commitment' device, and non-binding contracts for long-term commitment cannot be readily enforced. At the same time, they recognize that there are limits on government taxation, such as smuggling. So while they refer to the calibrations discussed below as optimal taxation, they recognize that they really refer to the optimal combination of private commitment and enforceable government policies.

is *over $35 per pack*. This is an enormous figure which is of the order of 100 times as large as the externalities associated with smoking. This large figure is driven by the large damage that smoking does to health and the high implied value of life from Viscusi's work.

Gruber and Koszegi (2002) present a range of estimates for the implied optimal tax based on this internality (which would be in addition to any externality-based effects discussed earlier). The optimal tax level depends on a number of parameters in the model, most importantly the shape of the discount rate (determined by the quasi-hyperbolic parameter β) and the level of the discount rate δ. As individuals are more hyperbolic in their decision making, the optimal tax rises; but as they are less patient, the optimal tax falls, since they care less about the damage done at the end of life. The optimal tax is estimated to be about $1 for individuals who are impatient (10% discount rate) and close to time consistent ($\beta = 0.9$), rising to over $9 for individuals who are patient (3% discount rate) and far from time consistent ($\beta = 0.6$); the lower level of β is much more consistent with available laboratory and calibration evidence. Thus, this alternative model rationalizes the higher levels of cigarette taxation that we see in developed countries.

This model also has a number of other important implications. First, the optimal level of taxes rises with the stock of addiction; individuals with more past exposure to the addictive behaviour should face higher taxes, since the internalities to them are largest from continued participation in the activity. This implies, for example, that the optimal pattern of taxation of such goods is to have a high tax initially that declines as habits are broken. This is the opposite of the traditional prescription of rising taxes over time, which are usually supported on distributional grounds; but I question such distributional motivations below.

Second, a key underlying feature of the Becker–Murphy model is intertemporal complementarities in smoking decisions. Thus, raising the tax in one period can lower consumption in all periods. This implies that if there are barriers to raising taxes at some stage in life (e.g. on adults), it would motivate higher taxes at a different stage (e.g. on children). Moreover, if one extends this point to space rather than time, it suggests a novel justification for smoking bans in restaurants or at work. Since we cannot effectively regulate smoking in the home, if smoking is complementary across locations, we may want to regulate it more severely in observable locations. That is, since we are undertaxing in one location, we want to overtax in another, so that clean air regulations are not only protecting non-smokers, but potentially the smoker themselves as well.

Third, these conclusions also hold for naive time-inconsistent consumers, but there is an important distinction. In this case the tax corrects not just a self-control problem but a misperception problem as well. Unlike the sophisticated case, therefore, it is possible in the naive case that the appropriate policy prescription is a complete ban rather than just corrective taxation. Thus, if we think that young smokers are 'irrational' naive consumers, then a ban on youth smoking with a tax on adults could be the optimal policy prescription.

Finally, contrary to popular perception, taxes on goods such as cigarettes are *not* regressive. Since sinful goods such as cigarettes and alcohol consume a larger share of budgets for lower income households, such taxes are typically viewed as regressive. But the goal of tax incidence analysis is not simply to measure who consumes more of a good, but rather who is 'hurt' by taxation of the good. The two are typically viewed as equivalent for incremental taxes by the envelope theorem. But the envelope theorem does not hold for quasi-hyperbolic consumers. In that case, measuring the burden of taxation implies measuring both the burden due to current consumption and the self-control benefits from taxation.

Gruber and Koszegi (2004) develop a 'self-control adjustment' to account for this point. This adjustment is rising in the price sensitivity of smoking decisions; the more price sensitive are consumers, the larger is the self-control value of taxation. It is also rising in the degree of time inconsistency, but falling in the discount rate (for reasons discussed above) and falling in the value of life. They undertake a number of calibrations which account most importantly for the fact that lower income groups are much more price sensitive in their smoking decisions than are higher income groups. As a result, for a broad range of parameters, they find that cigarette taxes are *not* very regressive, and may actually be progressive. This contradicts the presumption made towards regressivity in this chapter by Crawford, Keen, and Smith.

4. POLICY IMPLICATIONS FOR TAXING ALCOHOL AND OBESITY

Determining the optimal taxation of cigarettes is hard in one sense, which is the weight to put on internalities. But in other senses it is quite simple, because cigarettes have the nice feature that damage is monotonic and essentially linear: every cigarette is bad for you, and each additional cigarette is worse by a roughly equal amount (at least as far as science can tell today). This is not true for other important sources of 'sinful' consumption.

4.1. Alcohol

These problems are easily illustrated for alcohol. Much, if not most, alcohol consumption is likely done by those who will exert little external impact on others. Indeed, when Manning et al. (1991) measure the externalities due to alcohol, they focus on 'heavy drinkers' who report having more than two drinks per day (and likely have many more given under-reporting of consumption); consumption by such drinkers is less than half of total alcohol consumption. It is infeasible, however, to tax only heavy drinkers and not others. This non-linearity in external damage may, in fact, explain the low taxation of alcohol relative to its external damage: the typical drinker is not responsible for such damage and so would view as highly unfair taxation to compensate for it.

As noted in this chapter, this issue was initially addressed by Diamond (1973), who discusses externality taxation in a context where all individuals causing externalities must be taxed at the same rate, but where the externalities from some are more damaging than those from others. Diamond shows that if the externality function is linear, then the corrective tax should be a weighted average of the marginal externalities, where the weights are the elasticities of demand for the good. If the externality function is non-linear, however, then the corrective tax is related to the total cost of the externality divided by the number of consumers, which can be much *higher* than the weighted average marginal externality.

A behavioural perspective on this question is taken by O'Donoghue and Rabin (2006). They use a model with self-control problems to investigate the importance of population heterogeneity in driving the optimal tax. They find that even if only a small share of individuals have self-control problems, if internalities are large, the optimal tax on the full population can be large (when revenues are lump sum rebated). Thus, under both the standard model and this alternative, broad-based taxation of alcohol can be justified.

Of course, this may not be enough to sway public opinion! It is therefore worth considering whether more targeted tax policies towards alcohol are merited. One is to move to a purely alcohol-content based tax, rather than the rough approximations (taxes on beer vs. wine vs. spirits) used in most nations. This is a difficult issue, as noted in this chapter, because different alcohol 'delivery devices' have different potential for damage. For example, spirits have about eight times as much alcohol per unit volume as does beer. Yet individuals who so desired could consume more than six times as much alcohol in a short period of time drinking spirits than they could drinking beer. Technically, the appropriate basis for alcohol taxation might be something like blood alcohol content per unit time of concentrated drinking.

That said, within type of alcohol, there is clear scope for differential taxation by alcoholic content. For example, all US states have only one tax on beer despite alcoholic content that varies from 4% (light beer) to 8% (dark beer). They also typically have just one tax rate on spirits despite alcoholic content that varies from liqueurs like Amaretto (28% alcohol) to grain alcohol (up to 95% alcohol).

A second approach is to consider differential taxation of alcohol in settings where it is differentially harmful. In the US, for example, it seems reasonable to conjecture that much of the damage due to drunk driving involves individuals leaving drinking establishments rather than drinking at home. This might suggest differentially high taxes on alcohol served in establishments. To overcome political opposition from bar owners, the revenue could be redistributed to them through a one-time tax credit to overcome their loss in asset value.

4.2. Obesity

Given the enormous growth in obesity in the US, it is rapidly becoming this nation's most important health problem. In principle, this issue could also be addressed with corrective taxation. But this is an even more challenging case than alcohol, and certainly more challenging than cigarettes, for three reasons.

First, damage from poor eating habits is not only non-linear—it is non-monotonic. Any food is unambiguously good for individuals who would otherwise starve, and it is only past a certain point that we would worry about the damage caused by overeating. Second, there remains considerable uncertainty in the science linking consumption of particular goods to the ultimate externalities and internalities of obesity. Finally, there remains uncertainty about the substitution patterns across inputs that might impact the shape of tax policy. If individuals, for example, substitute from fats to sugars when the former is taxed, is that obviously health-improving?

For all of these reasons, addressing obesity issues through taxes on inputs is very difficult. But the problem of obesity at least raises concerns about a common pattern of consumption taxation world-wide: excluding food from consumption taxes. For example, in the UK, most foodstuffs for home consumption are exempt from tax; similarly, in the US food for home consumption is often excluded from state sales taxes. These exclusions can be clearly justified on distributional grounds, using a distribution-weighted approach to optimal commodity taxation.

Yet if there are obesity externalities from overeating, this provides a further rationale (along with relative inelasticity) against tax favouring foodstuffs. The UK VAT tries to address the obesity issue by standard-rating some food stuffs, such as ice cream. Yet other obesity-causing foodstuffs, such as cakes or chocolate chip cookies from a bakery, are zero-rated; potato-chips are standard-rated, yet tortilla chips are zero-rated. The difficulty of assigning obesity externalities to particular types of foodstuffs suggests that this is an extremely difficult approach to addressing them.

A better approach might be to follow the approach of a number of US states, which is to include food at the standard sales tax rate, but to provide rebates to low-income families to approximate the burden of food taxation (Johnson and Lav (1998)). Since these rebates would not depend directly on food spending, this system does not provide a marginal subsidy to food consumption, while in theory preserving the redistributional properties of a food exemption. In practice, however, a problem with this approach is that the rebate typically falls below the taxation of food expenditures for low income families, as politicians do not sufficiently inflate the rebate to match the rise in food expenditures (Johnson and Lav (1998)).

Unlike the case with smoking (where you can't tax those with lung cancer) or driving (where you can't sufficiently tax those who kill others through drink driving), there is a feasible output based taxation mechanism here: taxing body fat. If direct scientific evidence shows a strong link between certain measures of body fat and health costs, then the tax system could include body weight taxes. Of course, such a system is more easily proposed than implemented. Proxies for body fat, such as Body Mass Index (BMI), are only indirect; for example, African-Americans have a much higher BMI for any given level of body fat. And gathering data on even such proxies would be daunting.

REFERENCES

Ainslie, G., and Haslam, N. (1992), 'Hyperbolic Discounting', in Loewenstein, G. and Elster, J. eds, *Choice Over Time*, New York: Russell Sage Foundation.

Angeletos, G. M., Laibson, D., Tobacman, J., Weinberg, S., and Repetto, A. (2001), 'The Hyperbolic Buffer Stock Model: Calibration, Simulation and Empirical Evaluation', *Journal of Economic Perspectivies*, **15**, 47–68.

Becker, G. S., and Murphy, K. M. (1988), 'A Theory of Rational Addiction', *Journal of Political Economy*, **96**, 675–700.

—— M. G., and Murphy, K. (1994), 'An Empirical Analysis of Cigarette Addiction', *American Economic Review*, **84**, 396–418.

Cook, P., and Moore, M. (2001), 'Environment and Persistence in Youthful Drinking Patterns', in Gruber, J. (ed.), *Risky Behavior Among Youths: An Economic Analysis*, Chicago: University of Chicago Press.

Diamond, P. (1973), 'Consumption Externalities and Imperfect Corrective Pricing', *The Bell Journal of Economics and Management Science*, **4**, 526–38.

Fullerton, D. and Gan, L. (2005), 'Cost Effective Policies to Reduce Vehicle Emissions', NBER Working Paper No. 11174, March.

Gruber, J. (2001), *Risky Behavior Among Youths: An Economic Analysis*, Chicago: University of Chicago Press.

—— (2007), *Public Finance and Public Policy, 2nd Edn*. New York: Worth Publishers.

—— and Koszegi, B. (2001), 'Is Addiction "Rational"? Theory and Evidence', *Quarterly Journal of Economics*, **116**, 1261–303.

—— —— (2002), 'A Theory of Government Regulation of Addictive Bads: Optimal Tax Levels and Tax Incidence for Cigarette Excise Taxation', NBER Working Paper No 8777, February.

—— —— (2004), 'Tax Incidence when Individuals are Time Inconsistent: The Case of Cigarette Excise Taxes', *Journal of Public Economics*, **88**, August, 1959–88.

—— and Mullainathan, S. (2005), 'Do Cigarette Taxes Make Smokers Happier?', *Advances in Economic Analysis and Policy Advances in Economic Analysis and Policy*, **5**, art. 4 (2005). Available at <http://www.bepress.com/bejeap/advances/vol5/iss1/art4>.

—— and Zinman, J. (2001), 'Youth Smoking in the U.S.: Evidence and Implications', in Gruber, J., ed., *Risky Behavior Among Youth: An Economic Analysis*, Chicago: University of Chicago Press, 69–120.

Johnson, N., and Lav, I. (1998), *Should States Tax Food?*, Washington, DC: Center on Budget and Policy Priorities. Available at <http://www.cbpp.org/stfdtax98.pdf>.

Laibson, D. (1997), 'Golden Eggs and Hyperbolic Discounting', *Quarterly Journal of Economics*, **112**, 443–77.

Lundberg, S. J., Pollak, R. A., and Wales, T. J. (1997), 'Do Husbands and Wives Pool Their Resources? Evidence from the United Kingdom Child Benefit', *Journal of Human Resources*, **32**, 463–80.

Manning, W. G., Keeler, E. B., Newhouse, J. P., Sloss, E. M., and Wasserman, J. (1991), *The Costs of Poor Health Habits*, Cambridge, MA: Harvard University Press.

O'Donoghue, T., and Rabin, M. (1999), 'Doing it Now or Later', *American Economic Review*, **89**, 103–24.

—— —— (2006), 'Optimal Sin Taxes', *Journal of Public Economics*, **90**, 1825–49.

Pacula, R. L., Grossman, M., Chaloupka, F. J., O'Malley, P. M., Johnston, L. D., and Farrelly, M. C. (2001), 'Marijuana and Youth', in Gruber, J., ed., *Risky Behavior Among Youths: An Economic Analysis*, Chicago: University of Chicago Press.

Viscusi, W. K. (1993), 'The Value of Risks to Life and Health', *Journal of Economic Literature*, **31**, 1912–46.

5

Environmental Taxes

*Don Fullerton, Andrew Leicester, and Stephen Smith**

Don Fullerton is Gutsgell Professor at the University of Illinois, in the Finance Department and the Institute for Government and Public Affairs. He is Program Director for Environmental and Energy Economics at the National Bureau of Economic Research. He is also Editor of the *B.E. Journal of Economic Analysis and Policy.* He has taught at Princeton, Virginia, Carnegie Mellon, and Texas, and served as Deputy Assistant Secretary for Tax Analysis in the US Treasury. His research has included topics in taxation, social security, and environmental policy.

Andrew Leicester is a Senior Research Economist at the IFS. His research looks at factors affecting consumer behaviour, such as prices, incomes, and indirect taxes. He has also examined the use of household expenditures as a guide to economic well-being. He has written several pieces on UK environmental taxes, including fuel taxes, congestion charging, aviation taxes, and green tax revenues.

Stephen Smith is Professor of Economics and Executive Dean of the Faculty of Social and Historical Sciences at UCL and a Research Fellow at the IFS. His research covers various topics in the economics of tax policy—especially VAT and excises—and environmental economics. Before joining UCL he worked at the Department of Trade and Industry (1977–85) and at the IFS (1985–97), where he was Deputy Director from 1990 to 1997. He is a member of the Department for Environment, Food and Rural Affairs' Academic Panel on Environmental Economics and of the High-Level Economics Group of the European Environment Agency, and has acted as a consultant to HM Treasury, DEFRA, the UK Environment Agency, the OECD, the European Commission and the IMF.

* The authors are grateful for helpful suggestions from the editors of this volume, from Paul Johnson and Nick Stern, and from all participants at the conferences where this work was presented and discussed. We are particularly grateful to Agnar Sandmo, the discussant at the 2007 conference in Cambridge. Any views expressed here are solely those of the authors, however, and we are responsible for any remaining errors. Family Expenditure Survey and Expenditure and Food Survey data are collected by the Office for National Statistics and distributed by the Economic and Social Data Service. Crown copyright material is reproduced with the permission of the Controller of HMSO and the Queen's Printer for Scotland.

EXECUTIVE SUMMARY

The case for using taxes, charges, and emissions trading schemes (rather than regulation) to help achieve environmental goals is primarily a matter of cost-efficiency. Economic instruments may be able to achieve a given level of environmental protection at lower cost by providing incentives for polluters to choose the most cost-effective abatement mechanisms and by encouraging the greatest abatement effort from those polluters for whom it is least expensive. Economic instruments also provide ongoing incentives for innovation in pollution control. They may also be less prone to influence by polluters themselves than regulations negotiated case-by-case with individual firms. However, they are not a panacea. They can encourage costly avoidance activities, such as illegal waste dumping, and in some cases they may have significant distributional consequences, placing heavy burdens on the poor. They are most useful when wide-ranging changes in behaviour are needed across a large number of polluters—the costs of regulation in such cases are large, and the efficiency benefits of economic instruments are likely to be greater. Little will be gained, however, by making the tax structure too sophisticated when the environmental costs are low.

The choice and design of the instrument is crucial. One broad choice is between taxes and emissions trading schemes. In a world in which the costs of pollution abatement are certain, the two are virtually indistinguishable, but when there is uncertainty about these costs trade-offs do occur. When the need to reduce emissions below a set threshold is urgent, the cap on the quantity of pollution implied by auctioning a fixed number of permits may be preferable. But under a trading scheme the costs of pollution abatement are uncertain, and excessive costs could be incurred. Better policy might use some combination of taxes and trading that implies both a ceiling and a floor on the costs of pollution abatement. Where trading is involved, it is imperative that the market for pollution permits be competitive and that the case be made strongly for up-front auctioning of allowances.

In environmental tax design, a direct tax on the quantity of emissions generated is ideal but often infeasible because emissions cannot be directly measured at reasonable cost. Where close proxies for emissions exist that are measurable and already subject to market transactions, green taxes can be successful. Fuel combustion is directly related to carbon emissions, and so a fuel tax closely resembles a carbon tax, for example. Where such links do not exist, a combination of taxes may generate better targeted environmental incentives than any one isolated instrument.

The potential for revenue generation from environmentally related taxes has led to calls for a 'green switch' in the tax base, with higher environmental taxes and commensurate reductions in other taxes. The rhetoric recalls the idea of a 'double dividend'—using green tax receipts to pay for reductions in distorting taxes like income tax can achieve not only environmental benefits but also a more efficient tax system. The economic argument is, however, far from clear. Environmental taxes create their own distortions, raising the price of goods, which may or may not be offset by reduced distortions elsewhere in the tax system. The case for environmental tax reform should appeal first and foremost to the potential environmental gains.

It is not obvious that environmental taxes have significant revenue-raising potential. Existing large-scale taxes such as excises on motor fuel are already near the upper limit of what can be justified by the environmental costs involved. Taxes on waste management represent an interesting case for reform but are unlikely to raise much additional revenue. Only, perhaps, in the case of a widely applied carbon or energy tax might we get large extra revenues. Even then, political pressures to exclude households or energy-intensive industry could limit the revenue potential.

Empirical evidence on the scale of the environmental damage is crucial for good policymaking. Moves towards a carbon tax need to consider the right rate to set. However, the damage from carbon is extremely uncertain and hard to value—partly because the effects of emissions are spread over a long period and affect future generations. Given the global nature of climate change, and the insignificant impact that could be made by unilateral action, coordinated international action is essential. Barriers to implementing a domestic carbon tax could also come from concerns over international competitiveness and distribution. It would be undesirable for production to move abroad as a result of a unilateral carbon tax, reducing any net environmental gain, and widespread sectoral exemptions from any tax would significantly blunt its environmental impact. In addition, compensating low-income households for the burden of a domestic carbon tax is likely to be complicated and imprecise.

In terms of transport policy, significant gains could be made by a more precisely targeted structure of economic instruments. By far the largest external cost of motoring comes from congestion, yet existing taxes are targeted almost entirely on fuel purchases. While fuel is relevant for carbon emissions, it has little relationship to congestion. On the other hand, the development of a national system of road pricing that could accurately target the costs of congestion faces formidable implementation and political barriers. In addition, any congestion pricing system would almost certainly have to be accompanied by substantial reductions in fuel taxes. Targeting the environmental externality more precisely is difficult—direct exhaust emissions measurement is impractical. However, combinations of taxes and regulatory instruments can provide gains that are similar to those available from direct emissions taxation. A similar multi-instrument approach may be desirable for aviation where severe constraints limit the range of possible instruments that can be used: the best available package would include fuel taxes and ticket excise taxes on domestic flights coupled with suitably varying taxes on international departures based on the characteristics of the flight.

Decisions over waste management need to take into account the environmental impact of the various options—such as landfill, incineration, or recycling. One of the first explicit environmental taxes introduced in the UK was a Landfill Tax, initially set at rates reflecting best estimates of the costs involved. However, subsequent large increases in the rate, and the introduction of the Landfill Allowance Trading Scheme, appear designed to ensure compliance with EU targets on landfill reduction. These targets look too stringent to be justified by the environmental costs.

Reforms to waste taxes may see unit charges for waste collection introduced for households. International experience suggests that unit charges may have some impact on the amount of waste generated, although the possible gains could be small and charges may lead to avoidance activities like waste dumping. A more complex multi-instrument scheme might include taxes, subsidies, and regulation. An artful combination may achieve more desirable outcomes, such as promoting efficiencies in packaging at the producer level and encouraging efficient levels of recycling and reuse.

5.1. INTRODUCTION

Growing concern about climate change has brought environmental issues to the forefront of the policy agenda in many European countries. In addition to the substantial scientific literature assembled under the auspices of the Intergovernmental Panel on Climate Change, the October 2006 Stern Review of the Economics of Climate Change argued strongly for immediate and urgent action to mitigate the potential costs of global climate change. Taxes, charges, tradable permits, and other economic instruments can play an important role in achieving cost-effective control of greenhouse gas emissions, but their potential scale and revenue contribution raise many wider economic and fiscal policy implications. A number of European countries introduced carbon taxes during the 1990s, though a proposal for an EU-wide carbon-energy tax was ultimately unsuccessful. More recently, attention has shifted to emissions trading, and the EU Emissions Trading Scheme, introduced in 2005, is the most substantial application to date of this approach.

In the UK, a number of tax measures have been implemented primarily with environmental objectives in mind.[1] They have included three new national environmental taxes: on landfill, industrial energy use (the climate change levy), and the extraction of aggregates (quarry products). Taxes on motor fuels and the annual vehicle excise duty have both been restructured, with differential rates reflecting the different environmental attributes of fuels and vehicles. In London, the transport authority has introduced a congestion charge for vehicle use in the central area. In addition to these explicitly environmental tax measures, a wider range of areas of tax policy-making routinely include some discussion of environmental issues.

The increasing use of environmental taxes, emissions trading and other economic instruments has been partly driven by a recognition of the limitations of conventional environmental regulation. To make any serious impact on some of the major environmental problems now facing policy-makers—acid rain, global warming, traffic congestion—environmental policy cannot be approached purely as a technical issue, to be resolved merely by requiring the use of specified abatement technologies and setting emissions limits on large firms. Extensive and far-reaching changes to existing patterns of production and consumption will be needed, and these changes will inevitably entail substantial economic costs. The search for instruments capable of minimizing these costs, and of achieving behavioural changes across all sectors, has led policy-makers to pay much closer attention to the potential for incentive-based environmental regulation, that is, through economic instruments.

This approach to environmental policy has the potential to generate additional government revenues—in the form of environmental tax receipts, or the proceeds of auctioned emissions trading allowances. This calls for a much closer interaction between environmental policy and tax policy than in the past. At one level, the new government revenues that could be generated may provide an opportunity for tax reform. At a deeper level is an issue about how far the availability of environmental taxes alters the constraints and costs of current tax policy, in terms of the distortionary impact of existing

[1] See Chapter 1 for a brief description of UK environmental taxes. More detail is given in the online appendix to this chapter at <http://www.ifs.org.uk/mirrleesreview/reports/environment_app.pdf>.

taxes on labour and capital markets. Here, the issues are more complex. 'Packaging' environmental tax reform with offsetting reductions in taxes on labour income or the payroll taxes paid by employers may have political attractions, but the fiscal benefits of this type of tax substitution are much more contentious.

This chapter provides an overview of key economic issues in the use of taxation as environmental policy. Following this introduction, the chapter has two main parts. First, Sections 5.2 to 5.4 discuss the economic principles of environmental taxation, reviewing the arguments for using taxes and other market mechanisms in environmental policy, the efficient design of environmental taxes, and the fiscal value of the revenue contribution from environmental taxes. In what sense—if at all—would an environmental tax reform provide a 'double dividend', in the form of a less distortionary fiscal system as well as a cleaner environment? Second, Sections 5.5 to 5.8 apply these principles to four specific environmental tax areas—energy, road transport, aviation, and household waste. The first two of these—general taxes on energy and taxes on road transport—perhaps have the greatest revenue potential, but in all four areas taxes or other similar instruments could make a significant contribution to efficiency in environmental policy.

Before embarking on the main analysis of the chapter, we have some preliminary observations of a general nature about this field of tax policy, and about the approach we have adopted:

First, the focus of the chapter is primarily on the economic aspects of environmental taxes. In addition to economic considerations, however, both politics and public opinion will play a crucial role in determining the scale of action needed, and the range of acceptable measures. This is a fast-changing landscape, and we have tried, as far as possible, to avoid constraining the analysis by our own personal speculations about what measures would be publicly or politically acceptable in current circumstances.

Secondly, technology is developing rapidly, and is a key issue in determining the types of environmental taxes that are practicable. For example, technological advances that make it easier and cheaper to measure emissions directly may open up new possibilities for direct, targeted emissions taxes, based on measured emissions. Also, as viable technologies are developed for large-scale carbon capture and storage, it may be necessary to replace straightforward taxes on energy use with more complex and targeted taxes that provide appropriate incentives for the use of carbon capture.

Thirdly, environmental policy choices depend on some key value judgements as well as objective data. For example, a central issue in deciding whether the costs of action to curb greenhouse gas emissions are justified by the environmental benefits is the weight to be given to the interests of future generations. The Stern Review's conclusions on the scale of the damages from global warming, which are much higher than many earlier economic estimates, reflect not only the accumulating scientific evidence about the severity of climate change, but also a judgement that the interests of future generations should be weighted more heavily than in much of the literature.

Finally, while the primary focus of the chapter is on national tax policy, a key international dimension to some major areas of environmental policy-making cannot be neglected. For energy and carbon, in particular, the relevant externalities are global in their impact—all greenhouse gases emitted in any country have similar global effects. This means that effective policy cannot be implemented by a single country, and that national policies have to be formulated in the context of wider international policy developments.

PRINCIPLES

5.2. ENVIRONMENTAL REGULATION: INSTRUMENT CHOICE

From the perspective of environmental policy, the case for using environmental taxes, emissions trading, and other economic instruments is primarily a matter of efficiency.[2] In comparison with 'conventional' regulatory policies based on technology mandates or emissions standards, economic instruments may be able to reduce the costs of achieving a given level of environmental protection (or, alternatively, can achieve a greater environmental impact for a given economic cost). Not all environmental problems, however, are best tackled in this way, and other approaches, including various forms of command-and-control (CAC) regulation, may be preferable in some cases.[3] Likewise, different economic instruments have various advantages and disadvantages, and the balance between these will vary from case to case.

[2] The potential use of environmental taxes is assessed by, among others, Smith (1992), OECD (1993, 1996), Bovenberg and Cnossen (1995), Fullerton (2001), Bovenberg and Goulder (2002), Stavins (2003), and Newell and Stavins (2003). The seminal work is Pigou (1920).

[3] Bohm and Russell (1985) and Fullerton (2001) also review the goals and objectives of environmental policy, and they discuss how the trade-offs among these goals might imply when to use incentives, direct regulation, or other policies.

5.2.1. Advantages of environmental taxes and other economic instruments

'Static' efficiency gains through reallocation of abatement

Where the costs of pollution abatement vary across firms or individuals, economic instruments such as environmental taxes and emissions trading have the potential to minimize costs, as discussed in Box 5.1, for two reasons. First, other policy instruments cannot fully differentiate between polluters with different marginal costs of abatement, and thus may require some to undertake abatement with high costs. Economic instruments provide each polluter with incentive to abate in all of the least-expensive ways, thereby achieving a given level of abatement at lower total abatement cost. Second, economic instruments can side-step the need for the regulatory authority to acquire detailed information on individual sources' abatement costs, which lowers the authority's administrative costs. Newell and Stavins (2003) find that the cost of abatement using command-and-control regulation can be several times the minimum cost achieved by using an emissions tax.

Box 5.1. The static efficiency gain from the least-cost pattern of abatement compared with uniform abatement when two types of polluter differ in abatement costs

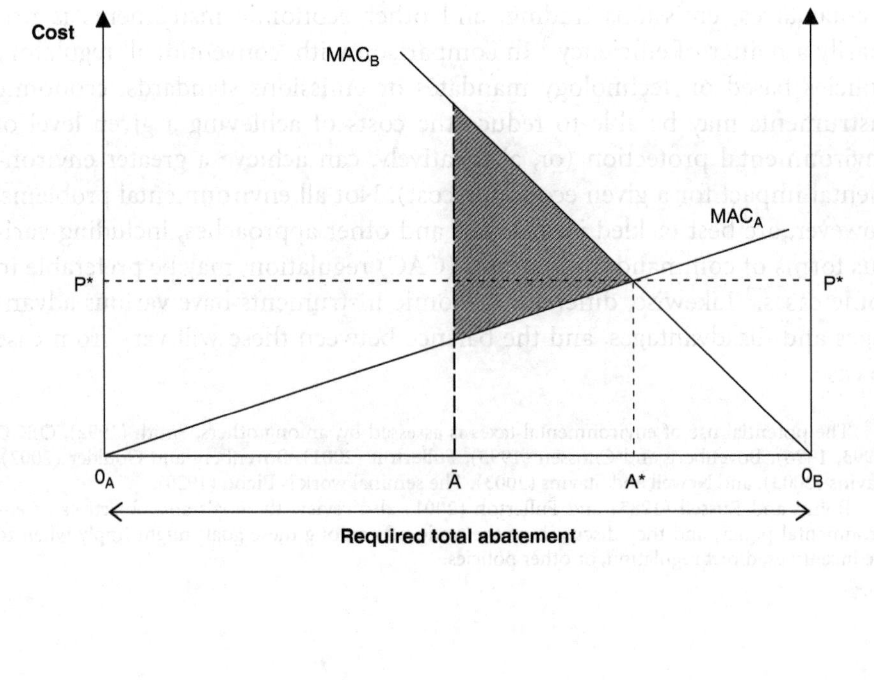

Point A* represents the least-cost division of a given total abatement requirement between two groups of polluters with different marginal abatement costs, represented by the schedules MAC_A and MAC_B, measured from the origins 0_A and 0_B respectively. The pollutant is assumed to be 'uniformly mixed', so that the environmental benefits are a function only of the total abatement achieved, and not of how this is divided between the sources. Economic instruments such as taxes or trading should achieve point A* (e.g. through emissions trading in a competitive market, with equilibrium allowance price equal to P*, or through an emissions tax set at a rate P* per unit of emissions). If, instead the informational limitations of command-and-control regulation compel the regulator to give the two types of polluter equal abatement requirements (point $\bar{A}$ in the diagram), higher total abatement costs will be incurred, shown by the shaded area.

A large number of empirical studies have used data on marginal abatement costs for a range of different sources to compare the costs of achieving a given abatement outcome using uniform and least-cost regulation. The cost savings are a function of differences in marginal abatement costs between sources. Where these are large, the efficiency saving from the least-cost pattern of abatement is correspondingly large (Tietenberg (1991); Newell and Stavins (2003)).

Dynamic innovation incentive

Regulatory policies which stipulate that polluters must use particular technologies or maintain emissions below a specified limit may achieve compliance but do not encourage polluters to make further reductions below this specified limit. Indeed, where regulations are negotiated on a case-by-case basis, polluters may fear that any willingness to exceed requirements may simply lead the regulator to assign the firm a tougher limit in future. By contrast, environmental taxes provide an ongoing incentive for polluters to seek to reduce emissions, even below the current cost-effective level, since the tax applies to each unit of residual emissions, creating an incentive to develop new technologies that have marginal cost below the tax rate (see e.g. Fischer et al. (2003)).

Robustness to negotiated erosion ('regulatory capture')

Efficient implementation of regulations requires firm-by-firm negotiation of individual abatement or technology requirements. CAC regulatory policies should require different amounts of pollution abatement from different firms to minimize total abatement costs. The regulator is dependent on the regulated firms for information about their abatement costs, however, and is liable to be drawn into dialogue and negotiation with the firms. The regulated firms, in turn, then control a key element in the process by which regulatory policies are set, and may be able to extract a price from the regulator for their cooperation, in the form of less stringent abatement targets, or other changes that work to their advantage.

In contrast, uniform environmental taxes achieve a cost-effective distribution of abatement, taking account of the different abatement costs of individual firms, while taking a robust, non-negotiated form. All firms face the same pollution tax rate. The regulator has no need to consider the circumstances of individual firms, and thus individual polluters have little scope to negotiate more favourable terms. The risk is thus substantially reduced that this process of negotiation would erode the environmental effectiveness of the policy.

Revenue potential

Environmental taxes and auctioned tradable permits raise revenues, as a result of the payments made on each unit of residual emissions. The extent to which these revenues should really count as a further *benefit* of the use of environmental taxes or emissions trading has been controversial, and we defer discussion of this so-called 'double dividend' to Section 5.4.

From a fiscal policy perspective concerns are also sometimes raised about the stability and predictability of environmental tax revenues, and, in particular, their erosion as a result of the behavioural responses of polluters. We suspect this problem has been greatly overstated. The revenue from all taxes is affected by behavioural responses, and environmental taxes based on inelastically demanded commodities such as energy might well be less affected by behavioural responses than other tax bases.

5.2.2. Disadvantages of environmental taxes and other economic instruments

Economic instruments such as environmental taxes have, however, a number of identifiable drawbacks and limitations that may be sufficiently important to rule out their use in particular applications.

Geographically varying damage

If pollution damage varies with the source of emissions, then a uniform pollution tax is liable to result in inefficiency, and source-by-source regulation may be needed to achieve a more efficient outcome (see, e.g. Helfand et al. (2003)). In principle an environmental tax need not be constrained to apply the same rate to all sources, and could thus achieve the efficient outcome through appropriately differentiated tax rates. However, once the tax rate has to be set individually for each source, the tax may become exposed to lobbying influence from the regulated firms. Also, some forms of environmental tax may have to apply at uniform rates, even where damage is known to differ between locations. Thus, for example, environmental taxes on pollution-related inputs may be unable to differentiate between sources, because of the difficulty of preventing resale of inputs to firms with more-damaging emissions.

Incompatibility with firm decision-making structures

Except in very small firms, many business decisions may be efficiently decentralized. Specialized divisions of the firm may be given responsibility for decisions requiring particular expertise or detailed information, subject only to general instructions or guidelines from the centre. This decentralization represents an efficient division of labour, but it implies that all aspects of the firm's operations are not necessarily taken into account. The internal organization of the firm needs to be designed so that related decisions are grouped together, while unrelated decisions are separated.

For environmental taxes to induce efficient polluter responses, firms must draw together information on both technology choice and tax payments. Firms considering whether to undertake more pollution abatement need to balance the marginal tax savings against the marginal costs of abatement. This type of interaction may not otherwise be a high priority in the internal organization of the firm, and may require significant changes to the decision-making structure of the firm so that tax and pollution-control technology decisions are taken together. Restructuring the firm so that such interactions can take place may be costly, and may well not be worth doing if the tax at stake is small. Firms may not, therefore, respond at all to 'small' environmental taxes, and conventional regulatory measures may be more effective in terms of both abatement costs and decision-making costs.

Damaging avoidance activities

Sometimes the consequences of an environmental tax may be adverse if those subject to the tax respond in a way that is more damaging to the environment than the taxed emissions. For example, a tax on toxic waste may provide a powerful incentive to reduce waste, but it may also induce illegal dumping or burning.[4] Even if the overall amount of such dumping is 'small', any amounts of toxic waste may be dangerous. Per unit, this waste can have much higher social costs when dumped than when taken to a proper disposal facility, and the net environmental effect of a policy that reduces total waste but leads to some dumping may be negative. In Section 5.3 we discuss alternative incentive-based methods, such as a 'two-part instrument', that may be able to avoid these undesirable side effects.

Distributional effects

As described throughout this chapter, environmental taxes may apply to transport, carbon content of fuels, or energy generally. Yet a high fraction of low-income household budgets are spent on electricity, heating fuel, and transportation. Thus environmental taxes are often regressive. To make matters worse, the gains from environmental protection may accrue to high-income households who have the most 'willingness to pay' for that public protection. A clean environment may be a luxury good. Environmental policy reforms must be careful to use a package of changes that account for and offset these distributional effects. However, this distributional problem is not specific to environmental taxes; the same problem arises with mandates that require generators to add expensive scrubbers, or car manufacturers to add expensive pollution control equipment.

Concerns about international competitiveness

Taxes on industrial inputs increase the costs of production. Where domestic output competes with products of foreign producers not subject to similar environmental taxes, the impact on the competitive position of domestic firms may be a concern. These issues have been particularly prominent in discussions of taxes on industrial energy inputs, as discussed in Section 5.5.

[4] Government monitoring and enforcement activity is quite low. For instance, the US EPA fined only 200 firms in 1995. Estimates of firm compliance vary widely: Magat and Viscusi (1990) find that, despite low enforcement activity, pulp and paper mills complied with environmental regulations about 75% of the time between 1982 and 1985. The US General Accounting Office (1990) finds that only 200 of 921 polluters thought to be in compliance actually were (Cohen (1999)).

5.2.3. Other relevant considerations in instrument choice

Administration and enforcement costs

Both environmental taxes and conventional regulations require mechanisms for administration and enforcement. The relative costs of these arrangements should be taken into account in choosing between the different instruments (Bovenberg and Goulder (2002)). Generalizations are difficult, but a few points are worth noting.

First, a pollution tax may require counting tons of emissions whereas a design standard simply requires authorities to confirm the use of a particular kind of pollution control equipment. Government inspectors can easily check that the plant has a working scrubber but, for some kinds of emissions, they may have much difficulty trying to confirm the exact number of tons to be able to collect a tax or permit price. In some cases, the goal of monitoring and enforcement might be met more easily by some kinds of CAC regulations.

Second, a general principle of taxation is that a tax can readily be imposed upon any market transaction such as the sale of a final good or service, because the invoice can be verified by the other party to the transaction. Similarly, eligibility for a subsidy can be verified for clean market inputs such as the use of labour, capital, or legal disposal, or the purchase of forest-conserving technologies or abatement technologies. Problems arise with an environmental tax because the producer enters no market transaction for deforestation, dumping, or emissions. Trees can be cut without any record that they ever existed. Illegal waste can be dumped at midnight. Emissions are self-reported. Without expensive audits, they are relatively easy to hide.

Third, however, excise taxes on inputs may be an inexpensive way of regulating polluting processes that use these inputs. Unlike other forms of environmental regulation, input taxes do not require direct contact between the regulator and polluters. The number of polluting sources does not, therefore, affect the costs of administration and enforcement. The incentive is transmitted through the excise tax levied on the production or sale of the input. With few producers this tax will be comparatively cheap to operate. The excise duties levied on mineral oils are a case in point; the number of petrol companies is small, and their activities are tightly controlled and well documented.

Effect on attitudes and perceptions

Environmental taxes may have effects on individuals' attitudes and perceptions that may affect the environmental outcome either positively or negatively. For example, it is sometimes suggested that imposing an environmental tax may have a particularly large effect on taxpayer behaviour because it 'signals' and encourages 'green' behaviour. On the other hand, the effect of a small environmental tax could be adverse if taxpayers believe that paying the tax legitimizes their polluting behaviour.

5.2.4. Environmental taxes versus emissions trading

Under conditions of certainty, the economic properties of emissions taxes and tradable emissions permits are very similar, and from a broad fiscal policy perspective the two instruments are largely equivalent. If an environmental tax set at rate per unit of emissions T leads to an emissions level Q, then alternatively regulating the same problem by issuing a quantity Q of tradable emissions permits will lead to a permit price per unit of emissions T, if the permit market is competitive. The level and pattern of pollution abatement will be the same under the two instruments, and the abatement cost incurred by firms will be the same.

These equivalences hold regardless of whether the permits are distributed free, or sold (for example through an auction). In either case, the value of the last permit used is given by the abatement cost that would otherwise be incurred, and this is given by the marginal abatement cost at emission level Q, which is T per unit. The value of tradable emissions permits, therefore, is independent of the way in which the permits are distributed, again so long as the permit market is competitive. In addition, where permits are sold in a competitive auction, the revenue yield will be the same as the tax revenue that would be collected from the equivalent environmental tax.

The implication of the above discussion is that, under conditions of certainty, emissions taxes and tradable emissions permits are close substitutes as policy instruments. They have broadly the same environmental and fiscal properties, and the policy choice between the two instruments can be made on the basis of other considerations, such as the administrative cost of the two forms of regulation or the competitiveness of the permit market.

This equivalence does not, however, hold where the regulator faces uncertainty about polluters' abatement costs and has to determine the tax rate or the quantity of permits to be issued, without accurate knowledge of the abatement costs. Neither instrument is unambiguously superior in this situation. Taxes that set a price for emissions and trading schemes that set a quantity have opposing strengths and weaknesses.

An environmental tax cannot guarantee a particular environmental impact; polluters' behavioural responses may be less, or more, than expected. In cases where the precise achievement of an environmental target is a high priority, this may be an important drawback of environmental taxes, and quantity instruments such as emissions trading may be preferred. For example, some pollution problems may exhibit a threshold beyond which environmental damage per unit of emissions rises sharply. On the other hand, while emissions trading guarantees that emissions will not exceed the quantity cap, it does so at uncertain abatement cost. Some abatement measures might be much more costly than the resulting environmental benefits. In such cases, environmental taxes can insulate polluters from the risk of excessive abatement costs. The tax rate per unit of emissions places an upper limit on the unit abatement cost to be incurred, and if abatement turns out to be more costly per unit than the tax, firms can simply pollute and pay the tax rather than paying for costly abatement. For this reason, Pizer (2002) finds that a carbon tax might be preferred to quantity regulation of carbon emissions.

Weitzman (1974) compares the relative merits of 'price' and 'quantity' regulation under uncertainty, and concludes that the one likely to perform better will depend on the relative slopes of the marginal abatement cost and marginal damage cost schedules (i.e. the rates at which marginal abatement costs and marginal pollution damage change when emissions differ from the optimum). This is an empirical matter, and will vary from case to case. Emissions taxes (or other instruments that involve the authorities setting a price for emissions) will on average get closer to the optimal outcome if marginal abatement costs increase with extra abatement more rapidly than marginal damage costs increase with extra emissions. Quantity instruments such as emissions trading will perform better if the reverse is true (i.e. if marginal damage costs are more steeply rising than the marginal costs of pollution abatement).

Developing this line of argument further, Roberts and Spence (1976) observe that a combination of price and quantity regulation may perform better under uncertainty than reliance solely on one or other approach. An emissions trading system with upper and lower 'safety valves' (setting a high price at which the authorities would be willing to issue additional permits and a low price at which the authorities would buy back permits) might perform better than a single fixed quantity cap on emissions. This could be implemented in various ways, and one possibility is that a (small) emissions tax could be used to set a floor to the marginal incentive for abatement.

Market efficiency

Where markets are created (as with emissions trading), these need to be low-cost and competitive. If pollution abatement is to be allocated efficiently between firms, all should face the same marginal incentive for abatement. If transactions costs or monopoly power in allowance markets drive a wedge between the marginal abatement cost of allowance buyers and sellers, some potential efficiency gains will be foregone.

Allowance allocation

The allocation of emissions trading permits may appear to offer an attractive degree of flexibility in policy implementation. In broad terms, the choice is between free distribution of allowances to firms, based typically on their past output or emissions levels (referred to as 'grandfathering') or some form of sale or auction. In formal terms, this issue is equivalent to the choice between two ways in which the revenue from an environmental tax could be employed—either returned to polluters on a basis unrelated to their current emissions (which may be seen as equivalent to a form of grandfathering), or used as revenue contributions to the general exchequer (corresponding to the auction case). In practice, emissions trading systems have generally involved grandfathering, and have made little use of the potential for auctioning, despite the economic case for doing so (see Section 5.4.2). By contrast, governments appear to have been able to use environmental tax revenues flexibly. Only in certain examples such as the NOx tax in Sweden have tax revenues been returned to firms in a way very similar to grandfathering.

Price versus quantity regulation of exhaustible resource depletion

A further consideration in choosing between environmental taxes and emissions trading arises in the case of climate change policies. It has long been recognized that using price-based instruments to regulate environmental problems resulting from the use of an exhaustible resource (e.g. fossil fuels) involves complications arising from the interaction between the regulation and the time profile of the price for the resource itself. Energy tax policy may, for example, accelerate the depletion of fossil fuel energy resources if it raises expected future energy prices by more than current prices (Sinclair (1992)). Revenue-maximizing owners of the resource may wish to exploit the resource sooner rather than later, if the tax reduces the future net revenue. As Sinn (2007) has recently argued, these effects on resource pricing may operate distinctly differently if regulation takes the form of emissions trading instead of taxes. Emissions trading could be used to place quantity constraints on the use of the resource in each period, so that the inter-temporal shift in energy consumption is avoided.

5.2.5. The balance between costs and benefits of using environmental taxes

The considerations above imply that environmental taxes are likely to be particularly valuable where wide-ranging changes in behaviour are needed across a large number of production and consumption activities. The costs of direct regulation in these cases are large, and in some cases prohibitive. In addition, where the activities to be regulated are highly diverse, society may gain substantially from changing these damaging activities in the most cost-effective manner.

In other areas, market instruments may work less well. In the next section we discuss the high costs that may sometimes be incurred in operating well-targeted environmental taxes. In other cases, an outright ban might be substantially easier to implement and enforce than a tax rate that requires fine measurement, or where avoidance activities are costly or dangerous.

Little can be gained from over-sophistication in the tax structure through the introduction of finely graded tax differentials to reflect the environmental characteristics of commodities with little environmental significance. Complex tax structures are liable to be costly to operate, and the tax 'boundaries' between products subject to higher and lower rates of tax are always open to socially wasteful litigation, and consequent erosion. Moreover, insufficiently large tax incentives may achieve little change in behaviour. As argued above, firms may not take account of tax incentives when making environmental technology decisions if the tax incentives are too small to justify the costs of changing established decision-making structures. It is perhaps an over-generalization to suggest that environmental taxes should be large, or not be imposed at all. However, the costs of complexity and the risk that minor environmental taxes will simply be ignored should both caution against too much environmental fine-tuning of the fiscal system.

5.3. DESIGNING ENVIRONMENTAL TAXES

The key to achieving the potential gains from environmental taxes does not lie in the indiscriminate introduction of taxes with a vaguely defined environmental justification. Rather, it lies in the effective targeting of incentives to the pollution or other environmental problems that policy seeks to influence. Poorly targeted environmental taxes may increase the economic costs of taxation, while offering little in the way of environmental gains.

This issue is highlighted by the contrast between different types of environmental tax:

- *Taxes on measured emissions* Practical examples of such taxes include Sweden's tax on nitrogen oxides emissions (Millock and Sterner (2004)), and emission charges for water pollution in the Netherlands (Bressers and Lulofs (2004)). Environmental taxes based directly on measured emissions can, in principle, be very precisely targeted to the policy's environmental objectives. When polluting emissions rise, the polluter's tax base rises, and the polluter pays additional tax directly in proportion to the rise in emissions. Likewise, any actions the polluter can take to reduce their tax liability also reduce emissions. The costs of measuring individual emissions may deter widespread use of environmental taxes of this form,[5] except where small numbers of emissions sources are involved, or where it is important to relate the incentive precisely to the amount of pollution emitted rather than basing the tax on some more easily assessed proxy for emissions.
- *Tax on a market good that is related to emissions* An alternative to direct taxation of emissions is to set or modify a rate of indirect tax (excise duty, sales tax, or value-added tax), or to introduce an environmental tax based on the sale of polluting goods or production inputs. Goods and services associated with environmental damage in production or consumption may be taxed more heavily (e.g. tax on batteries and fertilizers). Goods believed to benefit the environment may be taxed less heavily than their substitutes, as with reduced tax on lead-free petrol (Hammar and Löfgren (2004)). Environmental taxes of this sort may have lower administrative costs than taxes based on measured emissions. In some cases it may be possible to use existing taxes (for example by differentiating VAT), and this may be less costly than wholly new administrative apparatus and procedures.[6] Even where this is not possible, a separate environmental tax levied on transaction values may have lower administrative cost than one levied on measured emissions,

[5] The existence of administrative costs may affect the optimal structure and level of environmental taxes (Polinsky and Shavell (1982); Cremer and Gahvari (2002)).

[6] 'Piggy-backing' environmental taxes onto existing tax systems such as VAT is unlikely to be wholly costless, however. As Crawford, Keen, and Smith (Chapter 4) discuss, the administrative complexity of multiple-rate VAT systems is a strong reason to minimize the extent of VAT rate differentiation.

especially if it can be operated in a way compatible with existing definitions of the tax base. The drawback of such taxes is that they are less-precisely targeted to emissions than measured-emissions taxes, and they may therefore encourage an inefficient pattern of polluter responses (Sandmo (1976)). Some of the responses of polluters to the tax may seek to reduce tax payments in ways that do not lead to any environmental benefit.

- *Multi-part instrument* Using a tax on a proxy for emissions can thus economize on the administrative costs of directly measuring emissions, but risks behavioural responses that do not always achieve the most efficient patterns of pollution abatement. In some cases, a more efficiently targeted environmental incentive can be created through artful *combination* of indirect taxes—a 'multi-part instrument'—to approximate more closely the effects of a tax on measured emissions. An excise tax on the sale of a commodity plus a subsidy for clean technology together can provide the desired substitution and output effects, and may be better than either on its own. A tax directly based on motor vehicle emissions may not be feasible, but it may be approximated by the combination of instruments such as a tax on petrol, a subsidy to new car purchases, or tax on older cars, and a tax on cars with low fuel-efficiency or high emission rates (Fullerton and West (2002)). Likewise, efficient incentives to reduce consumption of waste-intensive products and to dispose of waste properly, approximating the effects of an otherwise infeasible Pigouvian tax on waste disposal, may be achieved by a combination of an 'advance disposal fee' (an excise tax on sales, based on the product's waste content) and a subsidy for proper disposal (Fullerton and Wolverton (1999)). One example of this is a simple deposit on glass bottles with a refund for recycling, but the idea can be applied much more widely. It can even apply to industrial pollutants. A targeted tax on emissions may be difficult if the emissions cannot be measured, especially since the tax does not apply to a market transaction. But the same effects can be achieved by the combination of a tax on the output of the firm and a subsidy to the purchase of pollution abatement technology. Since both the sale of output and the purchase of clean inputs are market transactions, these two instruments together may cost less to administer than the single ideal tax on emissions.

Each such form of environmental tax may be appropriate in particular circumstances. The choice among them needs to take account both of the administrative costs of different tax options and the extent to which different tax designs can achieve effective targeting of the environmental incentive.

The institutional assignment of responsibility for tax-setting and the allocation of the revenues may also affect the efficiency of the outcome.

A particularly severe problem of linkage arises for indirect environmental taxes on inputs when pollution abatement can efficiently be achieved through effluent 'cleaning' at the end of the production process. This would significantly limit the scope to regulate sulphur dioxide emissions from power stations by taxing the sulphur content of input fuels, since end-of-pipe effluent cleaning technologies in the form of flue gas desulphurization (FGD) equipment are one of the principal abatement options; a tax on input fuels would encourage abatement through fuel switching, but would not ensure an efficient balance between fuel switching and FGDs.[7] By contrast, a tax on the carbon content of fuels would lead to efficient abatement of carbon dioxide emissions, where effluent cleaning is not currently a commercially viable option. In a dynamic context, however, it would provide no incentive to develop new end-of-pipe technologies, unlike a direct tax on carbon dioxide emissions; and as such technologies (e.g. for carbon capture and storage) are developed it would require increasing adaptation, to ensure efficient incentives for their use. The acceptability of a carbon tax on fuel inputs rather than on measured carbon emissions therefore depends on the likely speed of these technological developments and on the extent that their development might be inhibited by the choice of a tax on inputs rather than on measured emissions.

Many of the so-called 'environmental taxes' introduced in practice have been used primarily for revenue-raising (Opschoor and Vos (1989)), sometimes to raise earmarked revenues for particular public expenditures related to environmental protection. 'Environmental taxes' of this sort have been used to recover the costs of administering environmental regulation, to pay for public or private expenditures on pollution abatement, and, in the US, to pay for Superfund clean-up of contaminated waste sites. The environmental effects of these taxes themselves may be limited. In some cases, their link to the environment is solely through the use of their revenues.

5.4. REVENUE ASPECTS OF ENVIRONMENTAL TAXES: A 'DOUBLE DIVIDEND'?

Some commentators such as Pearce (1991) and Oates (1991) have drawn attention to a potential 'double dividend' from environmental taxes—the

7 A fuel tax based on sulphur content can be combined with a subsidy for installing FGD, which is an example of a two-part instrument.

possibility that an environmental tax might both improve the environment *and* provide revenue that can be used to reduce other distorting taxes on labour supply, investment, or consumption. This argument[8] has a number of implications for two important kinds of policy decisions. First, in the tax policy choice about how to raise a given revenue, some have argued for a switch from conventional distorting taxes to environmental taxes. Second, for the environmental policy choice about how to control pollution, some have argued for a switch from non-revenue-raising instruments (quotas or grandfathered permits) to revenue-raising instruments (environmental taxes or auctioned permits). We look at each such choice in turn.

5.4.1. Tax policy choice: the switch from distorting taxes to environmental taxes

Most taxes induce undesirable behavioural adjustments that reduce labour supply or investment. These adjustments create 'excess burden', meaning that they reduce individual welfare by more than the actual tax payment. Raising the rate of conventional taxes typically increases these distortionary costs, by an amount called 'marginal excess burden'. For existing taxes, empirical estimates suggest these marginal distortionary costs are appreciable. Bovenberg and Goulder (2002) review several estimates (such as in Ballard et al. (1985)), and they find that marginal excess burden is 20–50 cents for each extra dollar of tax revenue. However, environmental taxes induce desirable behavioural adjustments that reduce emissions. In these circumstances, making use of environmental taxes would appear distinctly preferable to relying on conventional taxes. Isn't it better to raise revenues from taxes that correct distortions rather than from taxes that create distortions?

This case for environmental taxation is very important, but ambiguous, so some simple analytics are worthwhile. To understand the pros and cons most clearly, start with the market for a polluting good on the left-hand side of Figure 5.1, and suppose that the original equilibrium has no policy to control pollution. The normal downward-sloping demand curve reflects marginal benefits to consumers; it crosses the flat private marginal cost (PMC) curve at the original quantity (Z^o) and at the original low price (P^o). However, the social marginal cost (SMC) is higher than the cost faced by firms and consumers, because pollution imposes costs on others. In this diagram, an ideal Pigouvian tax at rate τ would raise the private marginal costs enough for the consumers to face a new price (P'), so that they reduce purchases to

[8] A recent review is in Bovenberg and Goulder (2002).

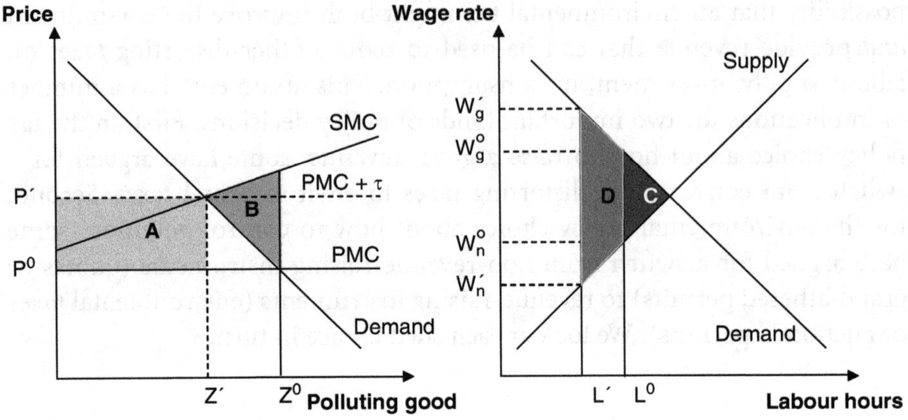

Figure 5.1. Tax on a polluting good, with revenue used to cut the labour tax rate

Z'. At the new equilibrium, revenue from the tax is area A. In addition, the welfare gain from controlling pollution is area B—the extent to which the social costs exceed the marginal benefits to consumers for all those purchases from Z' to Z^o.

To show the value of collecting revenue in that way, consider the supply and demand for labour in the right-hand side of Figure 5.1. In this diagram, a pre-existing tax on wage income means that the old net wage $\left(W_n^o\right)$ is less than the old gross wage $\left(W_g^o\right)$. Since the old quantity of labour is L^o, the excess burden is area C. If the government needed more revenue and increased the tax rate, this excess burden could increase to include both area C and area D. Thus D is marginal excess burden.

The simplest form of the double dividend hypothesis is the claim that the addition of the environmental tax would provide two benefits: it would provide the welfare gain B by fixing the pollution problem, and its revenue would allow the government to reduce the wage tax, which would raise the net wage, raise labour supply, and reduce the welfare cost C.

An extensive academic literature has focused on the general validity of this proposition. Most importantly, Bovenberg and de Mooij (1994) and Parry (1995) have shown that the analysis above is missing one key element: the environmental tax has its own distorting effects on labour supply and therefore can have more or less excess burden than the labour tax itself! The second dividend might not arise.

This new point can also be seen in Figure 5.1, again by using both diagrams. First, on the left-hand side, note that the environmental tax raises the price of the polluting good (from P^o to P'). Since this polluting good is one of the goods in the basket of consumer goods, this tax also raises the overall price of consumption goods (relative to the wage rate). This effect *reduces* the *real* net wage (the bundle of goods that can be purchased with an hour of labour). Bovenberg and de Mooij (1994) remind us that labour supply depends on this *real* net wage. If the higher price P' reduces the real net wage (to W_n'), it might *reduce* labour supply, adding to excess burden. However, if the environmental tax revenue is used to cut the labour tax rate, this would *raise* the real net wage and *raise* labour supply, reducing excess burden. Either effect might dominate, and so the real net wage might rise or fall. The second dividend is positive if labour supply rises, but it is negative if labour supply falls. In other words, the environmental tax by itself might have welfare gain area B, but it has ambiguous effects on the real net wage, labour supply, and excess burden area C.[9]

Another way to see this ambiguity is to remember that the first dividend from the environmental gain must be set aside in order to consider the second dividend from improving the tax system. Aside from environmental considerations, a given amount of revenue may be raised most efficiently with a particular 'optimal' set of tax rates on different goods. If one such good is taxed at less than its optimal rate, *and* this good is associated with uncontrolled pollution, then indeed, an increase in that rate may provide two dividends—an environmental gain and a more efficient tax system. If the good is taxed at exactly its optimal rate already, however, then an increase in that rate may provide only the environmental dividend. If the pollutant is already controlled in some other way such as through command-and-control regulation, then an increase in the tax on this good may not even provide an environmental dividend. Finally, if the good is already taxed at a rate that is higher than optimal, an increase in the environmental tax may reduce welfare. Clearly, the possibility of a 'double dividend' cannot be ruled in or out; it must depend on the circumstances.

In summary, starting from a position in which the system of taxes has been designed to minimize excess burden without any concern for the environmental implications of the tax structure, usually welfare would indeed improve by shifting the balance of revenue-raising towards greater reliance on environmental taxes—from the environmental dividend alone. In this sense, the tax system is more efficient if environmental taxes are used than if they are neglected. Yet this improvement could only hold up to a certain point. As the

[9] This definition of 'excess burden' ignores any environmental gain. Environmental taxes could be said to have negative excess burden if the definition of excess burden were to include environmental benefits, but this definition would risk double counting (if one were to say that the tax has negative excess burden in addition to environmental benefits).

environmental tax rate is increased, the excess burden costs of behavioural changes rise more than proportionately, eventually overtaking the additional environmental benefits.

5.4.2. Environmental policy choice: The switch from quotas to revenue-raising taxes or permits

A second strand in the 'double dividend' literature concerns the choice of environmental policy instrument. If policy employs a revenue-raising environmental policy instrument, such as an environmental tax or auctioned tradable permits, do the revenues collected as a 'by-product' of its environmental effects provide a more efficient fiscal policy, compared with the use of an equivalent non-revenue-raising instrument?

This point is important but ambiguous, so we turn again to some simple analytics. On the left-hand side of Figure 5.1, the 'optimal' quantity of the polluting good is Z', where marginal benefits to consumers are exactly offset by the social marginal costs of production. Policy-makers have several ways to achieve this quantity (all of which are equivalent in this simple model):[10]

(a) Impose a tax at rate τ, which raises the price to P' and reduces purchases to Z'. This policy raises revenue, area A in the figure.

(b) Impose Z' as a simple legal limit on the total quantity of production. This mandate or non-tradable quota is a type of command-and-control (CAC) policy that does not raise revenue.

(c) Set a fixed number Z' of tradable permits and hand them out for free to existing firms. These permits are 'grandfathered' in the sense that each firm is given permits in proportion to their emissions in some prior period. This policy does not raise revenue.

(d) Set a fixed number Z' of tradable permits and sell them at auction. This policy raises revenue.

The number of permits is the same for either (c) or (d), so the permits are equally valuable. Since consumers are willing to pay P' for that limited output, and production costs are only P^o, firms are willing to pay the difference $(P' - P^o)$ as the price to buy a permit. Because the number of permits is limited, this value is called a 'scarcity rent'. As can be seen in the figure, this

[10] In particular, this model assumes constant costs, competitive markets, no uncertainty, and a fixed amount of pollution per unit of output. These assumptions can be relaxed without changing the basic intuition of this section, but the model would become unnecessarily complicated.

price of a permit is exactly equal to the tax rate τ. Thus, the total 'scarcity rent' is exactly the rectangle, area A.

All four policies can be viewed in the left-hand side of Figure 5.1: all raise the consumer's price to P' and reduce purchases to Z', so all reduce pollution and achieve the environmental gain (area B). All four policies make output scarcer, and thus generate scarcity rents. The key difference is that the tax and auctioned permits ((a) and (d)) allow the government to 'capture' the scarcity rents as revenue, while the quotas and grandfathered permits ((b) and (c)) allow *firms* to capture the rents. Thus the grandfathered case is equivalent to the case where permits are auctioned, but with the revenues transferred back to firms through lump-sum transfers.[11]

Even though firms are competitive in this model, they make pure profits! How can competitive firms make pure profits? Normally, antitrust authorities do not let firms collude, act like a monopoly, restrict output, raise prices, and make profits. With quotas or grandfathered permits, however, the environmental authority essentially *requires* firms to restrict output! The policy erects an 'entry barrier', because new firms would have to buy permits to sell their product in this market.

In contrast, the tax and the auctioned permits capture the scarcity rents, as revenue. In this simple competitive model, the policy has no long-run effect on firms: they had zero profits before the policy, and they still have zero profits after the tax or auctioned permit policy. Output shrinks, as is necessary to reduce pollution. If this industry is not too large, and if labour and capital are mobile, then these factors can be re-employed elsewhere—at the same wage or rate of return they earned before. If not, then clearly the industry may suffer some transition costs such as temporary unemployment. Yet all four policies above shrink the industry the same amount, and they thus have similar transition costs.

If the government captures the scarcity rents, then it can use the revenue to reduce other distorting taxes, such as the labour tax on the right-hand side of Figure 5.1 It *might* even be able to raise the net wage and reduce excess burden (area C). But remember the problem above: the environmental policy itself raises the price of the polluting good (to P'). That effect *reduces* the real net wage. Thus labour supply may rise or fall, so the excess burden from labour taxes may rise or fall.

[11] In a one-time, unanticipated, permit allocation, the transfers are lump-sum in the sense that they cannot be influenced by any current decision of the firms. In a repeated, or anticipated, allocation, firms may realize that their current decisions could influence future permit allocations, and grandfathering could be distortionary rather than equivalent to a lump-sum transfer.

Now we are in a position to restate the importance of raising revenue. It is not that the revenue allows the government to reduce excess burden from labour taxes. Rather, the environmental policy inherently raises the cost of production and exacerbates labour tax distortions, *unless* the government captures the scarcity rents and uses this revenue to offset that effect by cutting the labour tax rate.

This point has clear and important implications for environmental policy choices. Handout of permits may be a way for government to 'buy' the co-operation and agreement of industry to enact the new environmental policy, but those firms are indeed paid for their acquiescence. That payment is delivered to firms in the form of being able to charge higher prices. If these higher prices reduce the real net wage enough, the exacerbation of labour supply distortions (extra area 'D') could completely offset the environmental gain (Goulder et al. (1997) and Fullerton and Metcalf (2001)).

Coordinating tax and environmental policy can be treacherous. Even starting with an uncorrected pollution problem, the introduction of a pollution quota or grandfathered permits may raise prices, reduce the real net wage, and exacerbate labour supply distortions—enough to exceed the environmental gain and provide a net negative effect on welfare.

5.4.3. Is the double dividend weak, strong—or irrelevant?

The environmental gain is the first dividend from any of the environmental policies listed above. When does the second dividend arise? In his discussion of the double-dividend debate, Goulder (1995) defines a 'weak' double dividend as the case with a positive welfare gain from using the environmental tax revenues to reduce distortionary taxes instead of returning those tax revenues to taxpayers through lump-sum payments. This weak double dividend also arises by using auctioned permits, rather than grandfathered permits, if the auction revenue is used to cut distorting labour taxes. He points out that the existence of this weak double dividend is uncontroversial, because 'the idea that swapping a distortionary tax for a lump-sum tax has a positive welfare cost is part of the usual definition of distortionary' (Goulder (1995), p. 160). Note that this weak double dividend is related to our earlier discussion of the environmental policy choice between quotas or grandfathered permits on the one hand, versus an environmental tax or auctioned permits (with revenue that can be used to cut distorting taxes).

The claim of a double dividend in this form is undramatic, but not without policy significance. In making a choice between environmental policy instruments, it implies that—other things being equal—a substantial premium should be placed on selecting instruments that do not create scarcity rents and leave them in the hands of private parties. If scarcity rents are captured, through taxes or the auction of a fixed number of permits, then the scarcity rents can be used by government to reduce the rates of existing distortionary taxes. Significant costs are incurred if the potential revenues from environmental taxes or permit auctions are dissipated or foregone.

In a more demanding sense of the term, Goulder (1995) defines a 'strong' double dividend as the case where raising an environmental tax and reducing a distorting tax has not only the environmental gain (first dividend), but also reduces the overall distortionary costs of taxation. If a strong double dividend does arise, it means that the environmental tax reform has negative 'gross costs' (defined to include all the welfare costs of behavioural changes from the tax switch, but to exclude environmental benefits). A tax reform with a strong double dividend is an attractive policy because it has 'no regrets'; even if the changes in energy use turn out to have no environmental benefit (no area B), it has been costless because the overall fiscal costs of the tax change are negative (a reduction in excess burden area C). The environmental tax itself distorts labour supply decisions, however, because it reduces the real net wage. This effect could outweigh the reduction in the labour tax. Thus, the 'strong' double dividend may be attractive, but it is far from guaranteed.

The double dividend debate points to the importance of thinking about tax and environmental policy simultaneously (Bovenberg and Goulder (2002)). The number of dividends, however, is not relevant in itself. Once we integrate tax and environmental policy reforms properly, all that really matters is whether the net effect is positive or negative on overall welfare.

APPLICATIONS[12]

5.5. ENVIRONMENTAL TAXES ON ENERGY

5.5.1. The policy context

At the Earth Summit in Rio in June 1992, more than 150 countries signed the UN Framework Convention on Climate Change, making a collective commitment to action to avert dangerous man-made effects on the global climate.

[12] Tax rates and revenues mentioned in this part of the chapter are correct as at fiscal year 2007–08 (or forecasts at that time) unless otherwise stated.

This commitment responded to the accumulating scientific evidence from the Intergovernmental Panel on Climate Change (IPCC) that the increasing concentration of greenhouse gases in the atmosphere, arising from human activity, was causing discernible and pervasive changes in global climate. Subsequent negotiations led to the Kyoto Protocol, agreed in 1997, under which a number of industrial countries took on binding commitments to reduce their emissions of a basket of the principal greenhouse gases.

Under the Kyoto Protocol the EU is committed to reduce greenhouse gas emissions by 8% by 2008–12, measured against a baseline of the 1990 emissions level. Within this overall EU target, the UK is required to achieve a 12.5% emissions reduction. In addition, however, the UK has unilaterally stated a policy goal of reducing emissions of carbon dioxide, the principal greenhouse gas, to 20% below 1990 levels by 2010. The 2003 Energy White Paper stated a further ambition to achieve a 60% cut in CO_2 emissions by 2050, 'with significant progress by 2020'.

Current international discussions are considering the form of a further agreement, to follow the Kyoto commitments. These discussions have been given added impetus by the increasing strength of the IPCC's concern about climate change, and, in the UK, by the publication in 2006 of the Stern Review of the Economics of Climate Change. This Review analysed the economic and environmental costs of climate change, and the costs and benefits of policy action. It makes a strong economic case for urgent and significant action to reduce greenhouse gas emissions, to stabilize the concentration of greenhouse gases in the atmosphere, with the aim of limiting the rise in global temperatures, and reducing the risks of catastrophic changes to the global climate.

Given the global nature of the climate change problem, effective policy needs to involve international coordination. The impact that an individual country can make on climate change through independent action is negligible, while this action incurs appreciable domestic costs of abatement. Sufficient international cooperation will not be straightforward to achieve,[13] and UK policy-making will be influenced by the nature of whatever international policy framework can be concluded. However, it is difficult to imagine that any substantial reduction in the UK's emissions can be achieved without according a significant role to energy pricing measures, in some form, whether through taxes or emissions trading. The extensive and

[13] An extensive economic literature involves achieving efficient bargains for the control of international environmental problems, including the distribution of the costs of CO_2 control and the achievement of a stable coalition of signatories to an international agreement. See, for example, Barrett (2003).

far-reaching changes that would be needed to existing patterns of production and consumption across a wide range of economic activities can be stimulated by general price signals more efficiently than by detailed regulatory intervention. Equally, it is unlikely to be possible to tackle the problem using simple pricing instruments alone, because of the range of both real and perceived obstacles to setting pricing instruments at first-best levels.

In this section we discuss how tax instruments, and the closely related approach based on emissions trading, could be used to establish price signals to encourage reduced emissions of carbon dioxide. In Section 5.5.2 we begin with some observations on the scale of the carbon price that would be justified by current evidence on the costs and risks of climate change. We then consider in Section 5.5.3 the range of available pricing instruments, including existing taxes on energy, carbon pricing through EU emissions trading, and possible new taxes on carbon-based fuels. In Section 5.5.4 we note the potential scale of the revenues that could be raised from these instruments, and emphasize the significant opportunity cost if these revenues are foregone by distributing emissions trading allowances without charge to incumbent firms ('grandfathering'). Finally, in Section 5.5.5, we look at the difficulties that would be encountered in setting carbon prices at first-best levels, especially in terms of perceived effects on industrial competitiveness and distribution, and set out strategies to overcome these obstacles.

5.5.2. How high should the carbon price be?

A carbon tax or emissions trading would aim to set a price on the use of fossil fuels (and more generally on activities that generate greenhouse gas emissions) that would reflect the otherwise-unpriced social costs of their use. The 'price of carbon' at which policy should aim—in other words, the appropriate rate of carbon tax, or the emissions trading price from a chosen quantity constraint on emissions—should in principle reflect an assessment of the climate change consequences of the marginal tonne of carbon dioxide emitted, at the socially optimal level of abatement. As with any other externality tax, the aim would be to ensure that private decisions that result—directly or indirectly—in additional greenhouse gas emissions take account of the costs imposed on the global climate. These costs will be spread over a considerable period of time, and will include costs of adapting to sea-level rise and changed temperature and weather patterns, changes in agricultural productivity, health effects, damage caused by a greater frequency of extreme climate events such as storms and floods, and—with more severe climate change—the costs of population displacement and conflict caused by rapid changes in climate and living conditions in different parts of the world.

Two broad approaches could be taken to assessing the carbon price at which policy should aim. The first is to build up a picture of the economic costs of climate change from models reflecting the various effects, including both 'predictable' effects such as regional changes in agricultural productivity resulting from changes in mean temperature and rainfall, and also, where possible, assigning values for 'unpredictable' catastrophes and irreversible changes. The resulting estimates could then, in principle, be used to describe a marginal damage cost function, and compared with the corresponding marginal abatement costs for reduced CO_2 emissions. The level of abatement at which policy should aim, and the carbon price or Pigouvian carbon tax needed to achieve this outcome, would then be identified by the point where marginal climate change damage equals the marginal cost of reducing CO_2 emissions.

The difficulties in such an approach are formidable. Any assessment of the economic effects of climate change must begin from scientific assessments of the underlying physical/environmental processes which are in themselves surrounded by considerable uncertainty and enormous margins for error. The science relating to the risks of major threshold effects (such as the reversal of deep ocean currents) and the consequences of greenhouse gas accumulation at higher concentrations is uncertain, and cannot be modelled in terms of precise trajectories with clearly defined probabilities. Nevertheless, this has to form the starting point for economic assessments, with further uncertainties—and plenty of scope for disagreement—in translating the scientific projections into economic values.

The difficulties in assessing the value of changes in CO_2 emissions are complicated by the unprecedented length of time over which the effects of emissions are felt. Since the rate of decay of any addition to the stock of atmospheric CO_2 is slow, current emissions have an effect that extends into many future periods. Likewise, policy measures taken now potentially confer benefits to future generations as well as to the current ones. Given the length of the time horizon involved, balancing the interests of present and future generations in climate change policy raises unusually difficult philosophical issues (Broome (1992)). These issues concern the treatment of large gains and losses in the distant future, which conventional discount rates could render of negligible current value.

An approach of this sort underlies many estimates of the 'social cost of carbon'—the monetary value of worldwide damage caused by marginal emissions in the current year. Pearce (2005) exemplifies this approach, reviewing the evidence on the appropriate value for the social cost of carbon to be used in UK policy appraisal. His conclusions suggest a range for the social cost of carbon of £0.82–£1.64 per tonne of carbon dioxide (/tCO_2), assuming a 3% discount rate. Incorporating equity weighting and time-varying discount rates could increase the range to £1.09–£7.36/tCO_2. Both ranges lie well below the UK government's central estimate of the marginal social cost of carbon of £19/tCO_2 (Clarkson and Deyes (2002)).[14] These figures are likely to overstate the corresponding optimal carbon price, to the extent that marginal damage costs rise with emissions, because the optimal carbon price will be lower than marginal damage costs at unconstrained emissions.

The 2006 Stern Review of the Economics of Climate Change bases its principal recommendations for emission-reduction targets on a different approach altogether, but supports this approach with estimates of the marginal damage cost based on model simulations similar to the above, albeit with some critical differences in assumptions and methodology.

The key policy recommendations of the Stern Review are based on its assessment of the target that should be adopted for stabilization of the concentration of greenhouse gases in the atmosphere. The Review argues that policy should aim at stabilizing this concentration at a maximum of 550 parts per million of carbon dioxide equivalent (ppm CO_2e). A higher concentration would involve substantial risk of temperature rises above 5°C, which the Review argues could involve dangerous and potentially disastrous changes to the planet. Even stabilization at 550 ppm CO_2e involves a 7% chance of temperatures rising by more than 5 °C, and a 24% chance of more than 4 °C. The Review argues that a path stabilizing at 550 ppm CO_2e would require global emissions to reach their peak within twenty years, and reductions in emissions against business as usual of around 30% by 2050 compared with 2000. Drawing on data on the costs of emissions abatement, Stern (2008) argues that this implies a global CO_2 price of around \$30/tCO_2 (roughly £75/tC).

In its modelling of the economic effects of emissions trends and policy intervention, the Review argues that 'business as usual' would generate a 50–50 chance of warming by around 5 °C relative to pre-industrial temperatures.[15] A key feature of the Review's approach has been explicit modelling of

[14] Equivalent to £70 per tonne of carbon. As with the other figures quoted from Pearce (2005) the estimates in the text are shown in terms of £ per tonne of CO_2, to assist comparison with EU ETS prices which are quoted on this basis. A price of £1 per tonne of CO_2 is equivalent to a price of £3.67 per tonne of carbon.

[15] The Review's estimates of the external cost of carbon emissions reflect particular assumptions about the relative weighting of the interests of present and future generations which have attracted some criticism (e.g. Dasgupta (2006); Nordhaus (2007)). These estimates reflect a low value of 0.1%

the risks and their associated costs, rather than simply focusing on an average trajectory across the range of possible outcomes. Incorporating the risk of very high costs into its estimates, the Review finds that the costs of unchecked climate change are around 5–20% of global output, and estimates the current social cost of carbon at \$85/tCO2e (about \$300/tC). But if emissions were restricted to a level consistent with long-term stabilization of greenhouse gas concentrations of 550 ppm CO_2e, the stabilization goal recommended by the Review, the efficient carbon price would fall to \$30/tCO_2.

5.5.3. Energy taxes and emissions trading

Existing energy taxes in the UK

The current tax treatment of energy in the UK has three main components. In quantitative terms the most significant taxes levied on energy in the UK are the excise taxes on mineral oils, in particular motor fuels, which raise some £25 billion in revenue. Petrol and diesel are currently subject to an excise of 50.35 pence per litre.[16] Lower rates of duty are applied to some alternative fuels such as LPG and biofuels.

Domestic energy is subject to VAT at a rate of 5%. Before 1994 domestic energy had been zero-rated (i.e. untaxed) in the UK's VAT system. In 1993 the government proposed extending standard-rate VAT to domestic energy, primarily for revenue reasons, but also recognizing the growing environmental concerns about fossil fuel use. The measure proved highly controversial, and the planned two-stage transition to the standard rate stalled at the first stage, with the rate at 8%. This rate was subsequently reduced to 5% by the incoming Labour government in 1997. Compared with uniform

for the rate of 'pure time preference' (δ), a parameter reflecting the extent to which well-being in future periods should be discounted relative to today, and justifies this low value on the grounds that the only ethical reason to weight differently the interests of people living at different times is the small probability of future planetary annihilation, some small risk that future generations will not exist. Secondly, the elasticity of the marginal utility of consumption (η), which describes how to value income of the rich compared to income of the poor (regardless of when they may exist) is set equal to 1. Higher values imply that an extra pound of income is valued much less for someone with high income than low income; if future generations are richer than the present, this reduces the weight given to future effects. The Review's conclusions are relatively sensitive to the choices of these two parameters, both of which imply much lower discounting of future costs and benefits than in most earlier research in this field. The central conclusion that the cost of 'business as usual' emissions amounts to about 5% of global output is reduced to 2.9% if η is increased from 1 to 1.5, and to 2.3% if δ is increased from 0.1% to 1%.

[16] VAT is also levied on motor fuels, charged at the standard VAT rate of 17.5%. However, we regard VAT as a general tax on consumption, and the VAT charged on motor fuels should not be counted in any comparison of the level of motor fuel externalities and taxes.

taxation of all consumption at the standard VAT rate, the UK effectively subsidizes domestic energy at 12.5%, at an annual revenue cost of almost £3 billion.

The third element of the current energy tax regime is the climate change levy (CCL), a single-stage excise tax imposed since 2001 on industrial and commercial energy use. The full rates of the levy are 0.154p/kWh on gas, 0.441p/kWh on electricity, and 1.201p/kg on coal; the tax is not applied to renewables. Firms in some forty-five energy-intensive sectors that have concluded 'climate change agreements' with the government, making commitments to legally binding targets for reduced energy use or reduced emissions, are entitled to an 80% reduction in the rate of the levy, which raises around £0.7 billion annually.

The CCL has been criticized, by Helm et al. (2005) amongst others, for its failure to tax fuels in proportion to carbon content. To the extent that electricity is taxed at a single rate, regardless of the fuel mix in generation, the tax simply raises the cost of energy to users, and provides no incentive to switch the fuel mix in generation to lower-carbon inputs. Also, if the rates of the levy are expressed as an implicit tax per tonne of CO_2, the tax on coal is considerably less (£4.30 per tonne of CO_2) than on electricity and gas (both approx £8.10 per tonne of CO_2). The lower tax on coal appears to have reflected an explicit political decision to avoid adverse effects on the mining industry, but its unfortunate impact is to penalize switching from coal to lower-carbon fuels.

In addition to taxes on energy, some of the regulatory obligations placed on the power sector and the introduction of the EU emissions trading scheme (ETS) for CO_2 both have some quasi-fiscal effects.

Power generators are subject to a Renewables Obligation, obliging them to obtain a given proportion of their electricity from renewable sources. Compliance with these obligations is verified by Renewables Obligation Certificates (ROCs), which are tradable, allowing flexibility in compliance. The cost of meeting the targets is, however, significant, and will result in higher electricity prices to consumers.

The EU ETS covers the power sector and CO_2-intensive industries (such as iron and steel, cement, pulp and paper), a total of around 1,000 plants in the UK. It began operation in 2005, for a first three-year trading phase (2005–07). Phase two (2008–12) covers the Kyoto commitment period, and is now underway. Allowances can be traded within phases, but not between phases, and the cost of allowances thus reflects the cap on emissions set in each phase. For phase one the allowance cap is widely regarded as having been too permissive, and out-turn CO_2 emissions were well within the cap such that the allowance price dropped to zero. The phase two cap, however, is more restrictive, and the market price of phase two allowances is currently around €20(£14)/tCO_2. Although allowances have been distributed free to existing firms in phase one, and only some 7% of allowances are scheduled to be auctioned by the UK in phase two, the allowance price has much the same effect on abatement incentives and on marginal costs as a tax.

Design of a carbon tax

Ideally, a tax to control atmospheric emissions of CO_2 would be levied directly on the individuals or firms who are responsible for the emissions, and based directly on the amounts of CO_2 emitted. In practice, sources of emissions are too numerous and varied for direct measurement of emissions. Carbon taxes therefore normally take the form of a tax on the carbon content of fuels, intended to proxy for the carbon emissions that result from combustion. The relationship between carbon content and eventual carbon emissions is very close, because no viable end-of-pipe emissions cleaning technologies are generally available. And while technologies for carbon capture and storage are developing rapidly, they generally will be implemented on a scale sufficiently large that appropriate credit for these activities could be given—for example, by refunding carbon tax—without extensive and costly administrative complications.

Nevertheless, some practical issues about the structure and administration of an energy tax could affect how efficiently it reduces CO_2 emissions. Some of these issues have a counterpart in the design of emissions trading arrangements for carbon dioxide.

In the European countries that have actually introduced carbon taxes (Sweden, Norway, Finland, the Netherlands, and Denmark), these taxes take the form of extended systems of fuel excises. Rates of tax are defined separately for each fuel, and relative tax levels on different fuels are set so as to equate the implicit rate of tax per unit of carbon. This requirement is not, however, always observed; in Denmark and Norway, for example, some fuels are not subject to the carbon tax. Also, the tax can vary across types of energy user; in Sweden and the Netherlands, much lower rates of tax apply to industrial energy users than to private households. Most of the carbon taxes actually implemented in these countries have provisions exempting firms or sectors that are particularly exposed to international competition.

The presumption that a carbon tax should naturally be implemented as an extension of existing fuel excises has been questioned by Pearson and Smith (1991). A 'primary' carbon tax, levied on primary fuels where they are mined, extracted, or imported (e.g. crude oil, coal, and gas) would have some advantages compared to excises levied on final fuel products sold to industrial users or households (such as coke, anthracite, and petrol). It would involve fewer payers of tax than would a 'final' tax, and it would have no need for fiscal supervision of the energy chain beyond the first point; administrative costs would be expected to be low, and tight supervision could prevent evasion.

Applying the tax at an earlier stage in the production chain does not necessarily imply any difference in the economic incidence of the tax or its environmental effects. The prices paid by industry and consumers would be much the same as with an equivalent set of excises. However, the primary carbon tax, because it taxes carbon at the earliest possible stage, accurately reflects the carbon emissions during processing as well as in the final product, and encourages lower processing emissions, as well as the use of fuel products containing less carbon. An exact equivalence could only be achieved with fuel excises if these could somehow be differentiated according to the carbon emissions associated with the processing of each product—its carbon 'history'—as well as its actual carbon content. Where different processing technologies are used, with different emissions during processing, a final carbon tax levied on the basis of average carbon emissions during processing is liable to lead to inefficient technology choices, providing poorer incentives to adopt low-emissions processes. In principle, therefore, a primary carbon tax might be more efficient, in both static and dynamic terms, although the quantitative significance of this issue remains unclear. It may be more significant with greater variation in intermediate emissions across different fuel-processing technologies.

A somewhat similar issue is discussed by Poterba and Rotemberg (1995) who consider the case with joint production of final fuel products, where the output mix is a choice variable. In other words, they consider the case where a single primary fuel is processed into more than one final fuel product, and where the mix of final fuels produced can be varied. They show that no objective basis can be used to estimate the intermediate carbon emissions associated with the production of particular final fuels.

One implication of these arguments is that environmental and economic efficiency is unlikely to be fully attainable with a carbon tax levied on final fuel products (such as an excise tax). Broadly similar issues apply in defining the point at which an emissions trading system should operate. In practical terms, the most significant choice has been whether to apply emissions trading to power station input fuels or electricity outputs. The EU emissions trading scheme has chosen to take the former route and provides better incentives to reduce carbon 'wastage' in the course of generation than would permits or taxes applied (like the UK's climate change levy) to electricity outputs.

Carbon tax in parallel with EU emissions trading

Given the establishment of the EU ETS in 2005, the context for policy-making is one in which a substantial part of carbon emissions are already priced. Taxes on carbon or energy may have a role to play in regulating the energy use of activities outside the scope of the EU ETS. But does taxation play a role in sectors already covered by the EU ETS?

Since emissions taxes and emissions trading have such similar economic properties, the market prices of emissions allowances will be directly affected by environmental taxes applied to the same emissions or to closely related transactions. In the case where the same emissions regulated by emissions trading are also subject to an emissions tax, the effect of a tax will generally be to reduce the value of emissions allowances by the amount of the tax. The allowance price is determined by the value of the marginal allowance at the constraint—the 'cap'—set by the ETS, and in the absence of an emissions tax, holding this allowance has a value given by the marginal abatement cost that would otherwise have to be incurred. With an emissions tax, however, the value of an allowance is lower, because the saving that can be made by holding an allowance is now the difference between the marginal abatement cost and the tax per unit of emissions.

Where the tax is less than the allowance price in the absence of tax, the tax would reduce the allowance price pound for pound, but would have no effect on the level of emissions. If the tax is set higher than the no-tax allowance price, emissions will fall below the cap, and the permit price will fall to zero. In effect, the emissions cap no longer binds, and allowances have no value. What determines the level of emissions is simply polluter responses to the tax, and the ETS is superfluous.

It is well known that where abatement costs are uncertain, a better outcome can be achieved by a mixture of price and quantity regulation than by reliance on tradable permits or an emissions tax alone (Roberts and Spence (1976)). Price 'safety valves' could be set to limit the range of feasible variation in allowance prices, avoiding the costs and inefficiency of the extreme outcomes that could arise if policy was based solely on a fixed emissions cap. An emissions tax, set at a lowish level, might be a way of instituting a welfare-improving floor to the price incentive for abatement. If the emissions tax applies to all firms in the emissions trading system, it will reduce the allowance price by the amount of the tax; the lower threshold thus comes into play when the allowance price reaches zero.

Less clear-cut relationships between taxes and emissions trading arise where some, but not all, of the emissions covered by a trading scheme are also subject to an environmental tax. An example would be a national carbon tax, covering activities already regulated by EU emissions trading; the tax would only apply to the emissions in the country concerned, and not to all emissions covered by the ETS. In this case, if the tax rate is low, and the proportion of EU-wide emissions covered by the tax is small, the tax will have a correspondingly small effect on permit prices (though perhaps not wholly negligible in the case of a significant carbon tax imposed by one of the larger EU countries). Its principal effect would be to induce an inefficient pattern of abatement across countries, since the abatement incentive in the country imposing the tax would be higher than elsewhere.

As discussed below, one of the effects of free distribution of EU ETS allowances has been to confer windfall profits on the firms to which allowances are allocated, since their selling prices are expected to rise to reflect the impact of allowances on the marginal cost of production. The effect of a carbon tax on allowance values suggests that it would be possible to recover some of the excess profits given to firms through allowance grandfathering by introducing an emissions tax on a base that closely proxies the use of allowances. Then the value of allowances will fall by the amount of the tax. However, except where the tax is imposed by all countries in concert, it would lead to abatement inefficiency as well as recovering windfall profits. And if all countries could act in concert to impose a tax, a similar outcome could have been achieved more directly by auctioning the allowances.

5.5.4. Revenues from energy taxes and emissions trading

The scale of potential revenues

Total UK emissions of the six groups of greenhouse gases regulated by the Kyoto Protocol were 652 million tonnes CO_2e in 2006.[17] If all UK greenhouse gas emissions were to be taxed (or covered by auctioned tradable permits)

[17] Some 85% of these emissions were of carbon dioxide (of which 40% was emitted by the power sector, 17% by other industry and business, 22% by road transport, and 15% by the residential sector), 7.5% methane (principally from landfill decomposition and agriculture), and 6% nitrogen oxides (largely from agriculture). See <http://www.defra.gov.uk/environment/statistics/globatmos/index.htm> for latest UK emissions data.

at the price of carbon implied by the Stern Review (€30/tCO_2, or roughly £20), then the aggregate revenue would be about £13 billion, equivalent to some 2.6% of total receipts from taxes and National Insurance contributions. However, this represents an upper bound to the net revenue potential of carbon taxes or emissions trading, and assumes systematic taxation of all emissions sources. If some sectors are exempted, or if some energy users receive grandfathered allowances, revenues would be reduced. For example, exemption of residential sector energy use would reduce the revenue potential by about £1.7 billion. Also, at least some existing taxes on energy should probably be deducted from this sum, including the £0.7 billion currently raised from the climate change levy. Rather more significantly, existing taxes on road transport fuels might arguably already be justified partly as a tax on greenhouse gas emissions, in which case the £2.4 billion that would be raised by carbon tax on road transport should be offset by a corresponding reduction in motor fuel tax.

The case for auctioning ETS allowances

Auctioning tradable emissions allowances has significant economic advantages over 'grandfathering' free allowances to existing polluters. Moreover, as Hepburn et al. (2006) describe, plenty of practical experience has been gathered in regular auctions of government securities, which provide a model on which allowance auctions can draw. So far, however, auctioning of EU ETS emissions allowances has been very limited, and initially confined to the 'new entrant reserve' in some member states; the rules of the ETS restrict member states to auctioning no more than 10% of allowances in Phase II. The free allocation of EU ETS allowances has mainly been a reaction to concerns about adverse effects of auctioned allowances on competitiveness, and we argue below that this response is misplaced.

The economic case for auctioning emissions trading allowances is argued clearly by Fullerton and Metcalf (2001), Cramton and Kerr (2002), and Hepburn et al. (2006). The arguments fall into three principal groups—those concerning the auction revenues, those concerning the windfall gains that grandfathering typically confers on polluters, and those concerning the better dynamic properties of an industry where new firms and existing firms are treated on an equal basis.

The principal argument for auctioning is the value of the revenues. These can be used to reduce other taxes, with consequent gains in the overall efficiency of the economy compared with non-revenue-raising forms of allowance allocation. This efficiency argument is the well-established and uncontroversial 'weak' double dividend hypothesis discussed in Section 5.4, which asserts that an efficiency gain is achieved if environmental tax revenues are used to reduce the rates of distortionary taxes in the economy, rather than being returned on a lump-sum basis (Goulder, 1995). In the emissions trading context this means that an efficiency gain is made by auctioning and using the auction revenues to reduce the rates of distortionary taxes in the economy, rather than foregoing the revenue through free distribution (the counterpart to taxing with lump-sum return of the revenues).

The aggregate asset value created by the EU ETS is substantial. Allowances have been issued for each year corresponding to 2 billion tonnes of CO_2 EU-wide, with an aggregate annual value of some €40 billion. Within this total, the allowances allocated within the UK (245 million tonnes) have an aggregate annual value of some €5 billion (£3.3 billion). The market value of these allowances should not be affected by the method of distribution—whether auctioned or grandfathered—because the price of allowances in a competitive market is determined by the marginal abatement cost at the emissions constraint set by the quantity issued. Full, competitive, auctioning of allowances in the ETS would therefore have generated annual revenues broadly equivalent to these asset values.

Equivalently, grandfathering foregoes the potential to raise these revenues. If the marginal excess burden of raising tax revenue is assumed to be of the order of 20–50 pence per pound raised (the range of US estimates surveyed by Bovenberg and Goulder (2002)), then as a first approximation, the aggregate economic cost to the UK economy of *not* auctioning £3.3 billion of EU ETS allowances is some £0.7 billion to £1.7 billion.

Parry presents some comparative simulations of the net benefits of policies to achieve a reduction in US greenhouse gas emissions by 150 million tonnes, based on an assumption of a \$20 per tonne environmental benefit from reducing carbon dioxide emissions. If the fiscal consequences of raising the price of carbon are ignored, such a policy would generate benefits of \$3 billion, and net benefits (after abatement costs) of \$1.5 billion per year. Taking into account the fiscal interactions between policy measures that raise the price of carbon and the distortionary cost of the existing tax system, Parry calculates that the net benefit from implementing this policy using a carbon tax (or, equivalently, auctioned permits) would be \$1.13 billion per year. By contrast, implementing the policy using grandfathered permits incurs a welfare loss of \$6 billion. In other words, the choice between auctioning and grandfathering makes a difference of over \$7 billion to the net benefit of controlling emissions, a huge figure compared with the gross environmental gain ($3 billion) or the abatement costs incurred by polluters ($1.5 billion). The comparison between the benefit of auctioning and the other costs and benefits of environmental policy interventions depends on the particular policy measures being studied, and is not always as dramatic as in the calculation described. Nonetheless, the point remains that the choice of grandfathering over auctioning entails substantial economic costs in an economy where existing taxes are high.

The counterpart to the foregone revenues if allowances are grandfathered rather than auctioned is that substantial and arbitrary windfall profits are conferred on polluters receiving free allowance allocations. Free allowance allocations do not simply compensate firms for the costs of an emissions trading system. Instead, an emissions trading system acts to raise the marginal costs of output, because additional output requires additional costly allowances, which have to be bought, or, if already held, could otherwise have been sold. The effect is to raise product prices, so that allowance costs are passed on to customers, regardless of whether allowances were auctioned or distributed free.[18] The windfall gains made by polluters are essentially an arbitrary redistribution within the economy. Auctioning would avoid this redistribution, and, to the extent that firms or industries do experience adverse effects from emissions trading, the revenues gained by auctioning can be partly deployed in targeted measures to offset undesired distributional effects.

The windfall profits conferred by grandfathering can generate costly political lobbying and 'baseline inflation' to influence the pattern of free distribution. A further advantage of auctioning is that it avoids giving rise to these potentially wasteful activities.

Auctioning allowances also has better effects on industry dynamics, promoting a more efficient long-term evolution of the regulated industries, avoiding the adverse effects on new entry and exit that can arise when allowances are grandfathered to existing firms. Auctioning ensures that existing firms and new entrants are treated the same, obtaining allowances in the same way, facing the same allowance cost per unit of emissions. Regular auctioning will also tend to increase market liquidity, ensuring that potential purchasers have the opportunity to buy; new entrants cannot be excluded by the unwillingness of incumbent firms to release allowances for sale. Likewise, auctioning tends to promote efficient decisions about whether to cease production and leave the industry. Firms will choose to do this if, when the full

[18] These product price effects are not confined to emissions trading, or to economic instruments; they arise with many other environmental policy measures including some forms of command-and-control regulation, as noted by Fullerton and Metcalf (2001).

costs of their pollution are taken into account, they cannot earn profits. Exit in these circumstances is one of the ways of achieving cost-effective pollution reductions. Allowance grandfathering can tend to inhibit exit, especially if 'use it or lose it' allocation rules are applied, so firms that leave the industry forego their allowance allocation.

If auctioning ETS allowances has such substantial economic benefits, what explains the choice of grandfathering, not only of EU ETS allowances, but also of allowances in the large-scale US Acid Rain Programme, and in nearly all other emissions trading applications? Grubb et al. (2005) discuss two main arguments for grandfathering emissions trading allowances, in terms of compensation and competition respectively.

In many areas, environmental policy-makers are reluctant to impose regulation on existing plants as stringent as that applied to new facilities. Regulation is frequently 'vintage differentiated' (Stavins (2005)), to avoid imposing unforeseen regulatory costs on the owners of sunk assets. Grandfathering can be seen as an alternative approach to this issue, compensating holders of existing assets for the effects of environmental regulation that was not foreseen at the time of the initial investment. This argument does not necessarily entail grandfathering all allowances; nor does it justify grandfathering in perpetuity. To the extent that a case can be made for compensation, it should presumably be transitional, for the foreseeable lifetime of existing assets; moreover, it is clear that any free distribution should not apply to new entrants. Johnston (2006) assesses the legal issues, and contends that any compensation made through grandfathering needs to be proportionate to the profit foregone as a result of the unanticipated additional regulation, if grandfathering is not to be vulnerable to EU state aids legislation. If firms pass forward part of the cost into higher prices, and if they can do substantial abatement at low cost, their additional costs may be very much lower than the benefit they would receive from a completely free distribution of allowances.

Grandfathering is also widely seen as a way of offsetting the impact of competition from foreign producers not subject to similar regulation. Again, the proportion of allowances that need to be grandfathered to offset this effect may be less than 100%. Grubb and Neuhoff (2006) point out that most industries covered by the EU emissions trading system would need to increase prices only a little to cover their net exposure to the costs of emissions trading. In practice, many have increased prices by more than this, passing the opportunity costs of allowances into product prices. This has allowed firms to earn higher profits than in the absence of regulation, even at the costs of sometimes significant reductions in international market share.

5.5.5. Barriers to carbon pricing: competitiveness and distribution

Two widely perceived obstacles to more extensive use of carbon taxes or emissions trading are the effects on international industrial competitiveness and the income distribution. Concerns about the (perceived) additional business costs imposed by carbon taxes or emissions trading, and the effects of these costs on the competitive position of businesses in international markets have been a source of political opposition in many countries. In Sweden, this quickly prompted changes to its carbon tax regime in the early 1990s, sharply reducing the additional tax paid by many firms. The issues are, in principle, most significant where countries introduce a carbon tax unilaterally. It is possible to identify strategies to offset these effects (for example, by using the revenue raised from environmental taxes to reduce other taxes), but concerns remain, especially about the impact of energy taxes on internationally exposed energy-intensive sectors. These concerns explain the widespread use of sectoral exemptions from environmental taxes and free allocation of emissions trading allowances.

Similarly, others are concerned about the regressive distributional impact of environmental taxes or permits, to the extent that they would raise the prices of goods that form a higher proportion of the spending of poorer households (domestic energy in particular). Again, the revenue raised from environmental taxes or permits auctions provides scope for compensating measures to offset these effects, but they are likely to remain an obstacle of considerable political significance in the UK.

Competitiveness

It is important to recognize that the effects of a carbon tax or emissions trading on the international competitiveness of a country's industry are not uniform across all sectors: the overall impact on competitiveness could be offset, on average, by exchange rate movements. Much the same effect could be achieved by returning the revenues from the tax to the industrial sector, through reductions in other taxes (such as corporate profit taxes or payroll taxes). In each case, the net impact of the carbon tax would be to worsen the relative position of carbon-intensive sectors, whilst improving the competitiveness of sectors of industry with low carbon intensity.

In the long run, some contraction of carbon intensive sectors might be one of the desired outcomes from policies to reduce carbon emissions. If other countries do not impose the tax, however, then these sectors may contract too much, relative to the ideal where all countries impose similar carbon taxes. Part of this contraction may represent 'carbon leakage'—international displacement of carbon intensive production. This leakage may impose adjustment costs and loss of profits, without any corresponding environmental gain.

Exemptions were proposed for the six most energy-intensive sectors in the European Commission's 1991 plans for a carbon tax (Commission of the European Communities (1991)). Exemptions have been a feature for most countries introducing carbon taxes, and the 80% reduction in the UK's climate change levy for firms in energy-intensive sectors performs a similar function.[19] These exemptions raise some difficult issues, however. First, they are liable to lead to inefficiency in abatement, because the incentive for abatement differs across sectors. Second, they typically exempt the sectors with the greatest emissions, and hence the greatest scope for abatement; for the same overall effect, more abatement is then required elsewhere in the economy. Third, as with the free allocation of emissions trading allowances, significant resources are likely to be consumed in socially unproductive but privately profitable lobbying. The same processes are likely to make it very difficult to discontinue the arrangements. Trade policy shows many examples of the extraordinary durability of sectoral trade protection measures, even when they were originally introduced on a temporary basis, and the same is likely to apply here.

Border tax adjustments provide an alternative way of neutralizing the competitiveness effects of carbon pricing policies. The effects of a carbon tax or allowance costs on the relative competitive position of producers could, in principle, be neutralized by levying a tax on competing imports and rebating carbon tax or allowance costs on exports. Imports would need to be charged a tax equal to the carbon tax or allowance costs that would be borne by an equivalent domestic producer, while refunds to exports should reflect the costs of tax or allowances incurred during domestic manufacture. The introduction of border tax adjustments has significant legal impediments, as they might not be compatible with WTO rules (OECD (2006)). They also involve difficult practical and economic issues. First, border tax adjustments may erode incentives for cost-effective pollution abatement, because of the rebating of the cost of carbon used in producing exported goods. Second, a decision would have to be made whether border tax adjustments would apply to all imports and exports, or only to trade with countries that did not pursue

[19] As discussed above, the 80% reduction is conditional on reaching a climate change agreement with the government, in which the sector commits to a legally binding target for emissions reductions or improved energy efficiency. All the main energy-intensive sectors have concluded such an agreement.

broadly equivalent environmental policies; the latter case raises considerable difficulties in defining policies of equivalent stringency. Third, it may be impossible to define the appropriate rate of tax adjustment, where domestic firms have a choice of production techniques involving different levels of pollution (Poterba and Rotemberg (1995)). If the border tax adjustments are calculated on the basis of average pollution characteristics, then they will overcompensate some firms and undercompensate others.

Hoel (1996) discusses the relative efficiency of border tax adjustments and sectoral differentiation of carbon tax rates (either in the form of exemptions for some sectors, or differential tax rates). He observes that if countries are not able to levy tariffs on trade with non-signatories to an international agreement to restrain carbon dioxide emissions, then differentiated taxes across sectors may be used to offset the competitive advantage that energy intensive sectors receive in non-signatory countries. However, if countries are able to set tariff rates without restriction, then tariffs should be employed for this purpose, and the optimal pattern of tax rates across sectors is uniform. Wider international agreement on carbon pricing, however, would be preferable to either border tax adjustments or sectoral differentiation, which are only really justifiable as temporary measures while international agreement remains partial.

Within the context of emissions trading, similar issues arise, but have typically been approached differently by distributing allowances for free. While free distribution could, in principle, be confined to internationally exposed sectors (corresponding to exemption of these sectors from a carbon tax), the EU ETS and most other emissions trading systems have distributed free allowances to all existing producers, and not only those exposed to pressure from international competitors not subject to similar regimes. The effect, as already noted, has been to confer considerable windfall profits on those firms—including the power producers—able to raise output prices to reflect the increased opportunity cost of marginal output. Firms in sectors exposed to more intense international price competition do not have the same opportunity to raise prices, but nonetheless experience higher marginal costs of production—regardless of whether they have been granted the allowances for free or have had to pay for them. Free distribution would thus be wholly ineffective in preventing output reductions and closures by marginal firms, unless rules withdraw allowances from firms that close down. The net effect is messy: firms in internationally exposed sectors face higher costs because of the effect of carbon pricing on opportunity costs of marginal output, but some remain in operation only because closure would lead to the forfeit of future allowance allocations. Emissions trading with grandfathering has an advantage over a carbon tax with sectoral exemption in that it preserves a more uniform incentive for carbon abatement across all sectors, but the complex distortions to business decision-making in exposed sectors need to be weighed against this advantage.

Distribution

The distributional impact across household groups of a carbon tax or other measures that raise energy prices will reflect the impact of the carbon tax on the prices of household electricity, motor fuels, and other goods and services (through the higher cost of energy inputs to production).[20] The distributional issues are most acute in the case of the additional tax on domestic energy, which in the UK and some other economies has the character of a necessity, forming a much larger part of the budgets of poor households than of the population as a whole.

Figure 5.2 shows the proportion of non-durable expenditures devoted to domestic fuel for UK households across the (non-housing) expenditure distribution in the mid-1980s, 1990s, and 2000s. In each period, the share of non-durable spending devoted to fuel for the poorest households is around

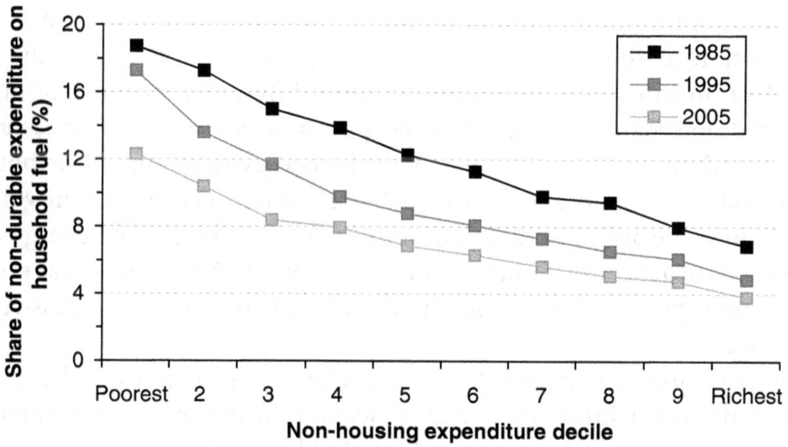

Notes: Deciles are calculated from household expenditures corrected by the OECD equivalence scale. Those spending less than £5 per week on average are excluded, as are households with recorded incomes below £5 per week.

Sources: Authors' calculations from UK Family Expenditure Survey and Expenditure and Food Survey, various years.

Figure 5.2. Share of non-durable expenditure devoted to domestic fuel by expenditure decile

[20] Poterba (1991), Symons, Proops, and Gay (1994), and Cornwell and Creedy (1996).

three times larger than for the richest households. Over time, the non-durable budget share of fuel has fallen for all deciles, but at a similar rate, so the relative differences have remained largely unchanged. By 2005, the lowest spending households devoted around 12% of their budget to fuel, compared to just under 4% for the highest spenders (and 7% across all households).

Taxes on domestic energy thus tend to be regressive, in the sense that extra energy tax payments represent a higher percentage of income (or of total spending) for poorer households than for the better-off. Additional revenues from energy taxation can be used in a revenue-neutral package to provide higher transfers to poorer households, however, and the package can be designed to leave poorer households at least no worse off (OECD (1996); Metcalf (1999); Dresner and Ekins (2006)).

Overall, a wide-ranging carbon tax that does not apply to all emissions may be more or less regressive than a domestic fuel tax alone, depending on the distributional effect of price rises of other products resulting from the tax. Smith (1992) showed that for the UK, a carbon tax would have an overall regressive distributional effect, because the effect of higher taxation of domestic energy outweighs the progressive effect of higher taxes on motor fuels, but that in many other EU countries this might not be the case.

Another issue is the distribution of the burden of reductions in energy consumption in response to higher energy prices. In the case of the UK, the reduction in energy consumption induced by the imposition of higher taxes on domestic energy appears to be greater amongst poorer households; Pearson and Smith (1991) estimate that the energy spending of the bottom quintile falls in response to a $10 per barrel carbon tax by 12% in volume terms, whilst the average reduction in the volume of household energy consumption is around 7%. Similarly for the US, West (2004) finds that greater price responsiveness of poor households generally reduces the regressivity of petrol taxes.

The social and distributional costs of higher energy prices may be exacerbated if market failures in energy efficiency investment are particularly concentrated amongst low-income households or other vulnerable groups (Brechling and Smith (1994)). Thus, for example, income-related market failures such as those in the credit or housing markets may tend to amplify the distributional cost of a carbon tax. Measures to rectify the underlying market failures, such as building regulations, or home energy audits, would then have the twin merits of reducing the aggregate economic cost of achieving energy efficiency, and helping to reduce the social and distributional cost of higher energy taxation.

5.6. ROAD TRANSPORT EXTERNALITIES AND THE TAX SYSTEM

This section examines the use of taxes and economic instruments to correct for the external costs generated by road transport. Many different externalities that may vary by time and location are involved, which makes the situation very complicated. Whilst these costs are not always 'environmental' in a strict sense—most obviously congestion—any green policies on road transport will have to consider how best to take into account the various externalities involved and so it is appropriate to consider the full range of the problem in this section.

We begin with an assessment of the scale of the different externalities involved and then examine the recent history of UK tax policy towards road transport. We consider the options for transport tax reform, starting with a discussion of 'first-best' policies that would separately and accurately price each of the externalities involved. The focus here is on the prospects for an explicit congestion charge introduced at a national level and on the appropriate design of such transport taxes. We then consider how tax policy might look, were such a charge either technologically or politically constrained, and whether existing fuel taxes are set at the right rate. Drawing on evidence from the US, we consider the extent to which multi-part tax and non-tax instruments could be used to approximate the first best outcome.

5.6.1. The external costs of road use

A study by Sansom et al. (2001) identified the key externalities from road use as operating costs, accident costs, air pollution, climate change, noise, and congestion. Their range of estimates for the scale of the marginal externality in each case for the average motorist is presented in Table 5.1.

The total external cost of an extra kilometre travelled is about 11.5–15.5 pence, of which congestion costs are by far the largest element, at around three-quarters of the total. Congestion externalities, however, vary hugely according to time and location—marginal externalities were estimated at around 86p/km for central London peak-time roads but just 3p/km for non-major rural roads. A more recent study by the Department for Transport (2006) estimated the marginal external congestion costs in 2003 across the British road network and again found considerable variation by location: almost 900 roads in and around major conurbations had a cost in excess

Table 5.1. Estimated marginal external road costs (pence/km), 1998 estimates

Externality	Low estimate	High estimate
Operating costs*	0.42	0.54
Accidents	0.82	1.40
Air pollution	0.34	1.70
Noise	0.02	0.05
Climate change	0.15	0.62
Congestion	9.71	11.16

* This mainly refers to road wear and tear costs resulting from a marginal increase in vehicle kilometres.

Source: Sansom et al. (2001).

of 56p/km but almost 6,000 roads in more rural areas had costs of less than 2p/km.

Other components of the external cost also vary with a variety of factors, such as vehicle and fuel type, engine size, location, vehicle maintenance, and driving style. The key question for this section is to consider what policy or range of policies may be best suited to take account of this range of externalities and how far existing policy succeeds in doing so. To pre-empt our conclusions somewhat, the broad story is that whilst in some cases the variation in costs per kilometre are closely proxied by one of the available tax bases—climate change externalities are strongly related to fuel consumption, for example—in other cases, notably congestion, existing taxes are inadequate to reflect the externalities involved. The range of decisions that individuals make need to be appropriately guided by social costs of choices such as whether to own a car, what type of car, when to drive, and where to drive. Thus, fuel taxes need to be supplemented by other measures to reflect externalities that are not closely related to fuel consumption. Congestion charging is the obvious approach, but formidable costs and political constraints may preclude establishing a wide-ranging national scheme at present. Nevertheless, artful combinations of existing tax bases can better approximate an ideal outcome than at present.

5.6.2. Current UK road transport taxes

Motor fuel taxation is a significant source of Exchequer revenues.[21] Duties on hydrocarbon oils are expected to generate receipts of around £24.9 billion in

[21] See section 5 of Leicester (2006) for more details of UK fuel taxation.

2007–08, or 4.5% of total revenue.[22] In the UK tax system, more revenues are raised only by the income tax, National Insurance contributions, VAT, and corporation tax.

Most road fuel sold in the UK is either ultra low sulphur petrol (ULSP) or diesel (ULSD). Both are taxed at a rate of 50.35p/litre (around £1.91 per US gallon), though lower rates apply for vehicles powered by biofuels or LPG. Between 1993 and 1999, real rates of duty were increased as the default option at each Budget—known as the 'fuel duty escalator'. Between 1997 and 1999, the accelerator increased fuel duties by 6% above inflation each year. By mid-1999, real duties were around 55–60p/litre (in 2007 prices). The accelerator was abandoned in the pre-Budget Report of November 1999, and the high price of petrol sparked protests and blockades of oil refineries in Autumn 2000. Nominal duty rates were increased only once between April 2000 and November 2006, leading to a significant real-terms decline in duties, though Budget 2007 pre-announced inflation-linked increases that would be enacted in 2007, 2008, and 2009.[23]

Real duty rates are now around their lowest in almost a decade, as highlighted in Figure 5.3 The duty escalator period of 1993 to 1999 is clearly visible from the 'saw-tooth' pattern of annual real duty rate increases that are gradually eroded by inflation within each year.

This decline in real duties has corresponded with a decline in fuel tax revenues as a share of national income since 2000. This decline has been largely responsible for the falling share of total green tax revenues in GDP, which in 2006 fell to the lowest level since the late 1980s.[24] Figure 5.4 shows the receipts from fuel duty (both including and excluding the VAT charged on top) as a share of national income since the mid-1970s. In 2006, the figure fell to the lowest level since the start of the escalator period.

The decline in revenues relative to national income is also due in part to the significant switch towards diesel fuel that has taken place in recent years as car manufacturers have developed diesel engines for domestic car owners. Diesel engines have a much higher fuel efficiency than petrol engines, and so fuel purchases can be reduced even as total distance driven rises. In 1997–98, 52% of all fuel released for consumption was petrol compared to diesel's 32% share. By 2006–07, it is estimated that the petrol share had fallen to 44%, the same as diesel. This trend looks set to continue.

[22] Estimate from October 2007 Pre-Budget Report.

[23] The real decline in duties since 1999 was justified in part by the higher crude oil prices that raised the pre-tax fuel price. However, we see no real economic justification for taxes to adjust to the pre-tax price: the tax per litre should vary with inflationary increases in monetary *damages* from fuel use, not with increases in fuel prices per se.

[24] See Etheridge and Leicester (2007) for more on total green tax revenues.

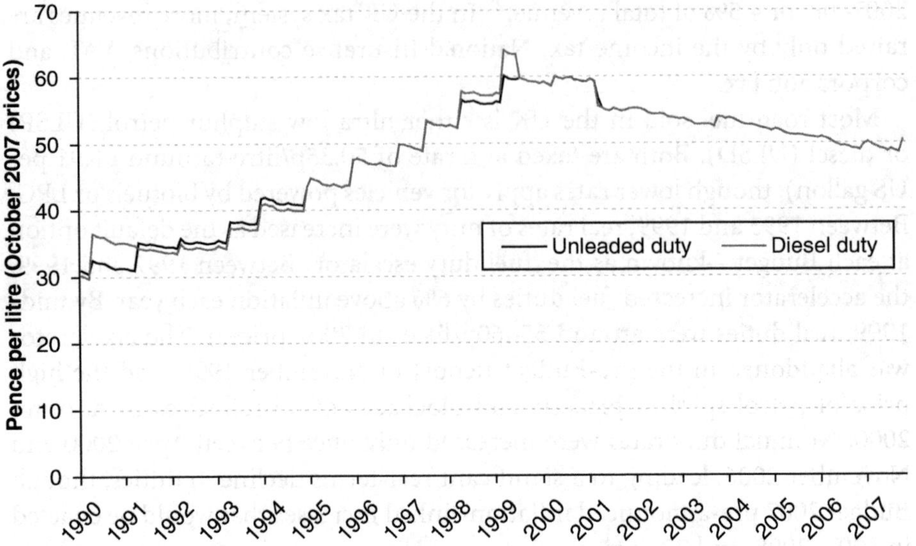

Notes: This figure updates figure 5.5 of Leicester (2006).

Sources: Calculated from DBERR data; duty rates are deflated to October 2007 prices using the all-items RPI index.

Figure 5.3. Real rates of duty for most commonly purchased unleaded and diesel fuels, 1990–2007

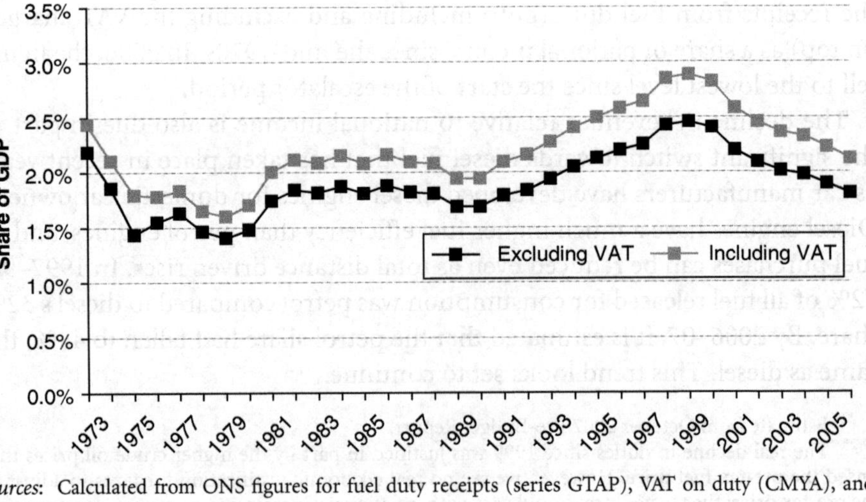

Sources: Calculated from ONS figures for fuel duty receipts (series GTAP), VAT on duty (CMYA), and GDP (YMHA).

Figure 5.4. Fuel duty receipts as a share of national income, 1973–2006

Despite the real decline in fuel duties over the last few years, the UK pump price of petrol and diesel has a higher tax component than any other EU country. Figures from the Department for Business, Enterprise and Regulatory Reform (DBERR, formerly the DTI) for April 2007 show that taxes (including duties and VAT) made up 67% of the pump price of a litre of unleaded fuel in the UK, compared to an (unweighted) EU-25 average of 57% and an (unweighted) EU-15 average of 60%. For diesel, the differences are even greater: the tax component in the UK is 66% compared to EU-25 and EU-15 averages of 51% and 53%, respectively. Interestingly, *pre-tax* fuel prices in the UK are amongst the lowest in the EU, though the variation across the twenty-five member states is relatively small compared to the variation in post-tax prices. Old EU member states (i.e. those that joined before 2004) typically have higher fuel prices than new member states, and this effect is tax-driven, as pre-tax prices are similar across most countries. Importantly, however, the UK is alone in the EU-25 countries in making no tax differential between unleaded and diesel fuels; all other member states have substantially lower taxes on diesel than on unleaded (we discuss this point further in Section 5.6.4).

Aside from fuel duty, the other major road transport tax in the UK is Vehicle Excise Duty (VED), an annual per-vehicle tax that varies according to the type of vehicle, the age of the vehicle, engine size, and (since 2001) the vehicle's CO_2 emissions. For new cars in 2008–09, the top rate payable by the most polluting cars is £400/year, whilst the least polluting vehicles are exempted altogether. In their most recent annual review of the new car market, however, the Society for Motor Manufacturers and Traders (2007) note that fewer than 300 vehicles in the exempted 'A' class for VED were registered in 2006. Nevertheless it appears that the graduation of VED by CO_2 emissions has coincided with a decline in the average emissions of new cars, though the extent to which this is directly attributable to the VED system is unclear. In 2000, around 34% of new cars sold emitted more than 186 g of CO_2/km compared to 21% in 2006; the proportion emitting less than 150 g of CO_2/km rose from 19% to 37% over the same period.

Company car and fuel taxes were also reformed in 2002 and 2003, respectively, to make the liability reflect the emissions rating of the vehicle supplied by the employer. As company car fleet vehicles make up more than half of new vehicles purchased each year, obvious benefits arise from providing incentives to firms to select lower emissions vehicles. An estimated value of the benefit in kind from the vehicle and fuel is derived by multiplying the list price by a percentage that varies from 10 to 35% for petrol cars (13 to 35% for diesel cars), with a lower multiplier for lower emissions cars. The higher multiplier for diesel cars presumably reflects some belief about additional externalities from diesel fuels, as discussed in more detail below, though it is strange that the 'diesel supplement' should be a fixed three percentage points up to a cap of 35%. The result is that a low emissions diesel vehicle with the same list price as a corresponding petrol vehicle will attract an extra 30% tax, whereas a high emissions diesel vehicle will not attract any extra tax. More sensible, perhaps, would be an additional percentage increase for diesel vehicles. It is also not clear why diesel cars would be more heavily taxed, while diesel fuel itself is typically taxed at the same rate as petrol.

5.6.3. A 'first-best' system of road transport taxes

The key feature of a tax system designed to ensure that individual decisions properly take account of external costs is that the taxes should impact on the marginal decisions regarding vehicle purchase and fuel use at a level that reflects the *marginal* externalities generated. It is not that taxes should reflect *average* externalities from motoring or that total tax receipts from road users should cover the total costs.

Clearly the existing system of road transport taxes cannot adequately take account of the range of externalities associated with road use, which may vary by time and location. A litre of fuel is taxed at the same rate no matter where it is purchased, and VED is a lump-sum tax that does not vary at all with distance driven.

Fuel duties *are* effective at capturing the externalities relating to climate change: the cost of a tonne of CO_2 emissions is the same no matter where and when it is released, and emissions are closely related to fuel consumption. Further, variation in fuel duty by fuel type has been successful in influencing consumers and manufacturers to switch to lower-emissions fuel types (for example, unleaded petrol enjoyed a significant tax advantage relative to leaded petrol in the 1980s and 1990s). Current tax reductions for alternative fuels may help further fuel switching in the future, though considerable debate concerns the environmental benefits of alternative fuels (see Section 5.6.4).

VED may help capture the external costs of road damage, and it may also help influence consumers to purchase less polluting vehicles (particularly since its reform is to be based on emissions in 2001).

It is clear, however, that an optimal system of road transport taxes would require taxes that could be precisely targeted against the various externalities involved. In particular, road pricing should charge drivers according to the distance driven, location, and time. If so, then prices would vary to take account of congestion and noise externalities, leaving fuel duties to capture environmental externalities. It is not clear that a restructuring of the road transport tax system along these lines would raise any significant extra revenues, but it would send a much more precise signal to motorists and would significantly affect patterns of traffic and perhaps overall traffic levels. This section considers how such a pricing system could be enacted and possible difficulties in doing so.

Congestion Pricing

In 2006, a report for the Department for Transport headed by Sir Ron Eddington came out strongly in favour of a national system of road pricing where the charge varied by location, time, and distance driven. A scheme would require vehicles to be fitted with on-board units (OBUs) that could monitor their location; drivers would be sent bills over a set period for their driving. Flexibly designed, such a scheme could closely capture the marginal external costs on a road-by-road basis and so in principle induce the most efficient use of the road network and substantially reduce the need to invest in extra capacity. Eddington's projections, drawing on work carried out as part of a feasibility study into road pricing by the Department for Transport (2004), suggested that a complex pricing scheme with seventy-five different pricing levels could reduce congestion by 50% by 2025 relative to a no-charging baseline and generate gross welfare benefits in the order of £25 billion per year. Revenues were estimated at around £8 billion per year.

Of course implementing such a scheme has enormous practical difficulties. Identifying the correct price to charge for each road at each time would be extremely difficult. The marginal externalities in the Sansom et al. and Department for Transport studies highlighted above assume no road pricing; in a world where roads are priced, the congestion externality from an additional kilometre driven would be considerably lower as congestion levels fall. Nash et al. (2004) suggested that model estimates showed that marginal external congestion costs in a post-pricing world could be, on average, just 20% of the costs before pricing. One key problem with identifying the appropriate prices to charge is the lack of practical experience on which to draw, with most estimates coming from traffic models. Estimates of the response to the central London congestion charge proved ultimately too pessimistic—the charge reduced traffic levels and congestion by more than was predicted (and hence the scheme generated lower net revenues than had been forecast).

Another problem would be ensuring that the pricing scheme is transparent and well understood by motorists. With a large number of price bands that vary by time as well as location this would obviously be difficult, with an obvious trade off between simplicity versus precise targeting of the marginal externality. Modelling results in Eddington (2006) and the Department for Transport (2004) study suggest that simpler schemes with fewer pricing bands could still generate substantial benefits and revenues—for example, by having only ten price bands or by targeting the scheme on urban areas where the congestion costs are greatest.

A severe initial obstacle to a complex road pricing scheme would be technological—the costs of implementation and annual running would be extremely high. The Department for Transport feasibility study produced a wide range of estimates for the initial set-up costs of £10–£62 billion. This range reflects huge uncertainties over the scope of the charge (such as the complexity and gradations of the prices by time and location). It also reflects technological costs and 'optimism bias' (the idea that initial cost estimates are almost always revised up). The main costs would be fitting each existing vehicle in the fleet with an on-board unit and the costs to develop and procure the administrative side of the system in the first place. Annual running costs could also be high—Eddington suggested a figure of £2–£5 billion per year (largely for administration and access to telecommunications networks for location monitoring of vehicles). The costs of compliance and enforcement would also need to be considered.

Whilst costs and uncertainties constrain the ability of governments to implement a national road pricing scheme, an additional political problem arises. If the perception is that road pricing would be introduced on top of existing motoring taxes, any such proposal is likely to face substantial opposition (as evident in online petitions that arose in 2006–07 against any such scheme). A key question is therefore to what extent current taxes could be reduced or replaced by a road pricing scheme.

Fuel duty after congestion charging

Assuming a national system of road pricing is established that accurately captures congestion (and possibly noise) externalities, what role would remain for fuel duty? As discussed earlier, fuel taxes are good at capturing the carbon externality from motoring and may be the best current way of capturing other environmental and road damage costs.

Box 5.2. The London Congestion Charge

An explicit congestion charge was introduced in central London in 2003.[25] The initial charging zone covered 21 square kilometres mainly in the City and the City of Westminster. Originally set at £5 per day, the charge rose to £8 per day from July 2005 for any vehicle entering or parking in the zone between 7 am and 6.30 pm on a weekday (the charge now ends at 6 pm). Exemptions are provided for taxis, motorcycles, pedal cycles, buses, emergency service vehicles, those holding a disabled person's badge, and some alternative fuel vehicles. Residents of the zone are also entitled to a 90% discount. From February 2007, the zone was extended towards West London.[26]

The latest impacts monitoring report (Transport for London (2007)) suggests that traffic within the original zone was around 20% lower than pre-charging periods in 2006, and congestion levels were around 8% lower. Earlier reports had suggested much larger falls in congestion in the order of 25–30%; the 2007 report notes that a large increase in roadworks within the zone in 2006 had contributed to a rise in congestion and that the charge was still reducing congestion levels by around 30% relative to a world with no charge. Revenue from the charge for 2006–07 amounted to £123 million net of running costs. These revenues are hypothecated towards funding public transport in London. The congestion charge is also cited as one of the major factors contributing towards reduced emissions from transport in London, by allowing traffic to flow more freely and by reducing time spent idling in traffic queues. Latest estimates suggest the charge has reduced road traffic emissions of CO_2 by around 16% within the charging zone.

Sansom et al. (2001) estimate the external costs from congestion in central London during peak hours at around 86 pence per vehicle kilometre driven. The London charge does not vary according to time spent or distance travelled within the zone, nor with the time at which the vehicle first arrives in the zone; payment of the £8 entitles the driver to full access for the day. Thus, it does not represent an attempt to capture the marginal external costs of congestion directly, but monitoring the distance driven inside the zone would be difficult. In addition, the exemptions and discounts suggest that environmental, political, and social considerations have also been built into the charge, further removing it from an explicit congestion payment.

Currently, fuel duty for most fuel types is 50.35pence per litre. If a 'typical' fuel efficiency is around 40 miles per gallon, a litre of fuel will allow a vehicle

[25] Blow et al. (2003) discuss the workings of the scheme and background to it in depth.

[26] A study by Santos and Fraser (2006) argued that the benefit to cost ratio of the extension would be in the range of around 0.74 to 0.9.

to travel around 14.2 kilometres.[27] Thus 'per kilometre' duty is around 3.5 pence. If we take the estimates from Table 5.1, excluding congestion and noise, the external costs of a marginal kilometre are around 1.7–4.2 pence per kilometre (if we also exclude accident costs the range is around 0.9–2.8 pence per kilometre). This calculation suggests that in a world with a first-best congestion charge, current rates of duty would be towards the upper end of levels that might be justified by other motoring externalities.

Modelling results carried out by the Department for Transport as part of their 2004 feasibility study showed that with a 'revenue neutral' scheme whereby revenues from road pricing were recycled in the form of reduced fuel duty, net total benefits would be around £8 billion per year by 2010, similar to the £10 billion or so from a scheme where revenues were not recycled. The difference arises largely because estimated combined revenues from fuel duty and congestion charges actually fall, by around £2 billion per year, if the revenue recycling occurs.[28] This is due to traffic flowing more efficiently after the charge, improving fuel efficiency and thus depressing fuel purchases relative to a no-charge environment. What seems clear is that the scope for introducing significant revenue-raising reforms to road transport policy through congestion charging is limited, since it would be likely to be accompanied by reductions in existing transport taxes.

5.6.4. 'Second-best' road transport taxation

Given the significant costs, technological and perhaps political constraints that may prevent congestion pricing schemes being established, it is worth considering how policy could develop without it. Specifically, we consider the extent to which existing tax bases can approximate the first-best outcome.

Optimal fuel duties

We start by considering the case where the only available tax the authorities can use is fuel duty, and where duty rates can only vary according to the

[27] Forty miles per gallon = 64.4 kilometres per gallon (1 mile = 1.61 km) = 14.2 km per litre (1 litre = 0.22 UK gallons).

[28] Clearly this implies a distinction between 'revenue neutral' at the time of implementation and how revenues may evolve over time.

type of fuel and not the type of vehicle. VED and local road pricing and toll schemes aside, this case fairly closely approximates the current UK road transport taxation situation. What rate of fuel duty should be set to reflect the external costs of motoring?

Parry and Small (2005) calculate the optimal level of fuel taxes in the UK and in the US based on estimates of the marginal externalities from motoring, allowing for the fact that the fuel duty induces improved fuel efficiency, and allowing for interactions between fuel taxes and other taxes. Under their central modelling assumptions, they derive an optimal fuel tax for the UK of \$1.34/US gallon, which equates to around 18 pence per litre (significantly below the current rate in the UK of 50.35 pence).[29] Their estimate for the fuel-related pollution caused by carbon emissions is less than 1 penny per litre, and for congestion around 8 pence. In calculating their fuel-related pollution costs, however, they choose \$25 for the marginal damage caused by a tonne of carbon emissions, drawing on various estimates from the international literature. The UK Stern Review estimates the damage cost at closer to \$100/tC (and perhaps considerably higher under 'business as usual' emissions). Even at this level, assuming everything else unchanged, the optimal UK tax would rise only by around 3–4 pence per litre. Their central estimate of the marginal external congestion cost is only around 2.2p/km, only around one quarter of the low-end estimate given by Sansom et al. in Table 5.1.[30] Using Stern estimates of climate change costs and much higher marginal congestion costs, the Parry and Small approach could lead to a fuel tax rate much closer to the existing UK figure. Clearly, estimating optimal fuel taxes is extremely complicated and sensitive to parameter estimates.

A key feature of UK policy is differentiation of fuel tax rates to encourage fuel substitution: 'alternative' fuels such as bioethanol are also favoured in their tax treatment, for example, and unleaded petrol is taxed more lightly than leaded petrol (which is now virtually never bought). The major fuels sold for private motoring are Ultra Low Sulphur Petrol (ULSP) and Ultra Low Sulphur Diesel (ULSD), both of which are taxed at the same rate, 50.35p/litre. In the past, petrol and diesel have been taxed differently; typically diesel attracted a lower rate of duty because carbon emissions from diesel are less

[29] We use a market exchange rate of around £1 = \$1.95 and a conversion of 1 litre = 0.2642 US gallons.

[30] The Parry and Small estimates of the marginal congestion cost are derived from an uprated estimate made by Newbery (1990) of costs of around 3.4p/km that are then reduced because of the way the congestion estimates enter into their specification as adjusted by fuel price demand elasticities. Sansom et al. (2001) discuss their congestion estimates relative to Newbery's and argue that the Newbery figures are based on estimates using data from 1985, at which time traffic volumes were considerably lower.

than those from petrol. However, a 1993 report by the Quality of Urban Air Group (QUARG) suggested that diesel cars have higher particulates emissions that affect respiratory illness, with a severe impact on urban air quality. The differential for diesel was subsequently removed.

Other European countries have considerably lower taxes on diesel than on petrol, which may represent an attempt to reduce the tax on fuel for commercial vehicles from a Diamond–Mirrlees efficiency perspective (reducing the tax on an intermediate input). This perspective suggests that diesel fuel duty should be lower if diesel fuel is a proxy for commercial as opposed to residential motor fuel and if fuel taxes exceed the marginal external costs in order to raise revenue. Clearly the growth of diesel engines in non-commercial cars makes diesel fuel an increasingly poor proxy for a commercial input, and we see no *environmental* reason why commercial road use should be tax favoured.

From a purely environmental perspective, having some assessment of the relative damage caused by climate change and through particulates is crucial for estimating appropriate differential tax rates for petrol and diesel. Using Stern estimates of the costs of carbon points to a more favourable tax treatment for diesel, whereas using the lower estimates from other literature may point to the opposite.

A non-trivial issue for diesel fuels relates to 'cross-border' shopping and might explain why diesel duty rates are often lower in other EU countries: commercial enterprises that operate abroad can refuel vehicles in low-duty countries rather than at home. The most obvious examples are commercial vehicles crossing between Northern Ireland and Eire and those using the Channel Tunnel. The marginal additional revenue to be gained from such firms from small changes to diesel duty rates is likely to be close to zero. HMRC estimates for 2006–07 suggested that the non-UK duty paid market share of diesel fuels in Northern Ireland is around 40%, with associated revenue losses of around £200 million. For petrol, the corresponding figures are around 14% and £50 million.[31]

A more recent focus has been on alternative fuels. Particularly in the US, considerable resources are now being devoted to bringing them onto a more commercial footing, especially biofuels. These alternative fuels, either alone or blended with traditional fuels, may emit less greenhouse gases in combustion. Over the lifecycle, however, if emissions associated with biofuel production are taken into account, the environmental impact may be considerably more than that of more traditional fuels. More evidence is urgently

[31] See <http://www.hmrc.gov.uk/pbr2008/mtg-2450.pdf>, tables 3.8 and 3.9.

needed to determine the extent to which such fuels should be tax favoured. At the moment, however, they account for an extremely small share of the UK market: in 2006–07, biodiesel and bioethanol combined made up around 0.6% of fuel consumed. However, the Renewable Transport Fuel Obligation (see below) will require this proportion to rise substantially in the next few years.

A multi-part instrument

Clearly policy-makers face huge difficulties both in implementing an optimal road transport taxation policy and in relying on fuel duty alone as the dominant transport tax. Road transport taxes have enormous technological, cost and political opposition barriers, while fuel duty alone is inadequately differentiated to deal with the range of externalities involved. However, a range of instruments together can approximate the optimal outcome using existing tax bases and technologies.

So far, policy-makers in most nations have addressed vehicle emission problems with a variety of mandates and restrictions. In the UK, passenger cars are required under European legislation to be sold with information about their fuel consumption and CO_2 emissions levels, and the latest 'Euro IV' emissions standards limit the emissions of carbon, nitrogen oxides, and particulates from petrol and diesel engines in passenger cars and commercial vehicles. From 2008, fuel suppliers will be required to ensure that 5% of their sales will be biofuels by 2010 under the Renewable Transport Fuel Obligation. Suppliers will be issued with certificates according to their sales of biofuels. These certificates can be traded. So the plan will have the flavour of a 'cap and trade' scheme.

Such regulations can guarantee vehicle emission reductions, but they do not provide much flexibility or incentives to go beyond them. As an alternative, a direct tax on vehicle emissions would provide these ongoing incentives and would minimize vehicle emissions at least cost, but it would require complex measurement of individual vehicle emissions. Technological advances may make such a tax feasible in the future: Harrington and McConnell (2003) discuss ways in which this might be achieved, though each method has problems.

Alternative incentive instruments that apply to market transactions *rather* than to emissions may therefore be needed. One possibility would be to bring fuel suppliers into the European Emissions Trading Scheme, such that emissions would be priced into the final pump price. This scheme covers carbon emissions only, however, and the existing fuel tax can already be used effectively to cover carbon emissions. Another alternative would be to introduce a general carbon tax that covers all emissions, as discussed in the previous section; this tax would then apply to the carbon content of vehicle fuels, again as a replacement for existing duties. However, the carbon tax does not solve the problem of pricing other transport emissions and externalities.

Recent research considers the availability of alternative instruments. As a benchmark for comparison, consider a world where the emissions tax is perfectly available and enforceable, and use a model to calculate the theoretically ideal set of driving behaviours that would minimize the costs of achieving a given air quality. Then suppose that the ideal emissions tax is *not* available, and consider alternative instruments. In order to take advantage of the cost-reducing characteristics of incentive instruments, policy-makers can consider alternative taxes and subsidies on various market transactions that reflect choices affecting emissions.

Fullerton and West (2002) build a simple theoretical model in which many different consumers buy cars with different characteristics and fuels of different types. They specifically model the consumer's choice of engine size, pollution control equipment, vehicle age, fuel cleanliness, and amount of fuel, capturing the most important determinants of emissions other than driving style. They also capture consumer heterogeneity: individuals differ by income and tastes for engine size and miles. Using this model, they confirm that a single rate of tax on emissions of all different consumers minimizes the total cost of pollution abatement, by inducing each consumer to change their behaviour to a different extent for each method of pollution abatement (such as buying a smaller car, newer car, better pollution control equipment, cleaner petrol, or less petrol).

Given the difficulties of direct emissions taxation, alternatives might be limited to charging the same uniform rate for all consumers—one tax rate per unit of engine size, one tax rate that depends on vehicle age, and one tax rate on each grade of petrol, no matter who buys it. A set of uniform tax rates can use all available information (including how these various vehicle characteristics are correlated). If it is still limited to uniform rates across all consumers, it does not perform as well as the emissions tax, but it outperforms all other *available* incentive-based policies.

In a computational model, Fullerton and West (2000) employ actual data for more than a thousand individual cars and their owners to assess the potential welfare gains of these second-best policies relative to an ideal emissions tax. The main result from this model is that the second-best combination of tax rates on engine size, vehicle age, and fuel type achieves a welfare gain that is 71% of the maximum gain obtained by the ideal-but-unavailable tax on emissions. If only a petrol tax can be employed, the welfare gain is 62% of the gain from the ideal emissions tax. Thus a petrol tax is the key ingredient of any market-based incentive emissions policy where the ideal tax is unavailable.

The focus of existing research has been approximating an optimal emissions tax; less has been said about approximating an optimal congestion charge, though some of the research examined in Section 5.6.3 suggested that simpler congestion schemes targeted on urban areas may still achieve substantial welfare benefits. Another key question concerns policy towards public transport; subsidies here may be a crucial component of any multi-part incentive structure—the London congestion charge has been introduced at the same time as a wide-ranging investment in the capital's bus services. Over the last twenty years, the price of private transport has been constant compared to other prices (and falling over the last five or six years). Yet the price of public transport has risen substantially, in the order of 25%. Clearly public transport cannot be neglected in the consideration of transport tax policy as a whole.

5.6.5. Distributional aspects of road transport taxes

The very poor do not own cars and do not buy petrol, so a tax on petrol does not hurt the poorest families. Using data from the 2005–06 Expenditure and Food Survey (EFS), households are broken into ten decile groups based on their expenditure.[32] Amongst the lowest-spending 10% of households, only 29% are car owners, compared to 77% in the middle of the expenditure distributions, and 93% for the highest spending households. Only 4% of the poorest households own more than one car, compared to 28% of the middle decile and 50% of the richest.

Figure 5.5 shows the impact of a 5% rise in petrol prices across the expenditure distribution. The bars show the average increase in the cost of living that results from the price rise—darker bars represent the increase across the whole population, and the lighter bars the increase across just the population of car-owning households. Over the whole population, the impact is lowest for the very poorest and the richest households, with the biggest impact on those in the middle of the spending distribution. Amongst car-owners only,

[32] We present results based on household expenditure rather than income, though the story is similar for both measures of well-being. Expenditure may better capture household's long-run living standards than does a snapshot measure of current annual income.

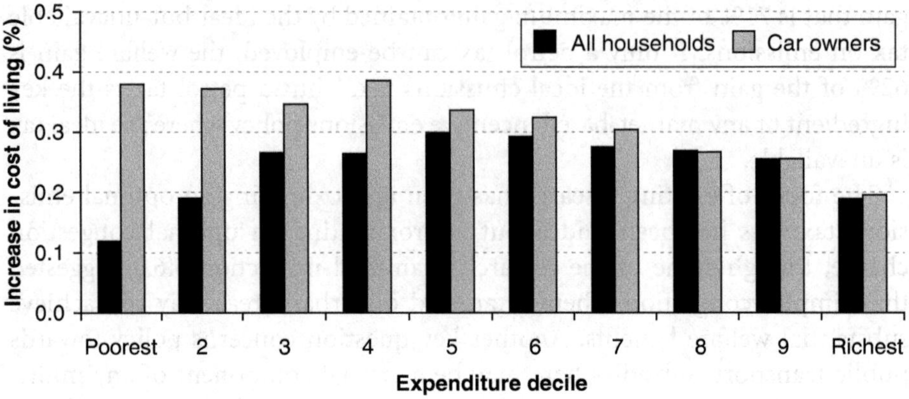

Notes: Assumes no behavioural response to price rise.
Sources: Calculated from Expenditure and Food Survey 2005–06.

Figure 5.5. Distributional impact of 5% petrol price increase, 2005–06

poorer deciles are hit slightly harder than those in the middle, whilst the richest car owners have the smallest increase in the cost of living.

Even if a petrol tax is regressive, the existing tax and benefits system can be used to compensate. Low income drivers cannot in a practical way be exempted from fuel taxes altogether (or from congestion charges). Lower tax rates in rural areas would also have adverse effects, as people drive from urban areas to take advantage of the reduced rates.

A move towards congestion charging would have substantial redistributive effects that would need to be modelled alongside concurrent reforms to other road transport taxes. The most obvious effect is that urban commuters would be negatively affected, whilst rural car owners would benefit substantially.

5.6.6. Conclusions

Conceptually at least, the principles of road transport taxation are quite well understood, and a growing body of evidence covers the extent to which different approaches would have considerable benefits relative to the existing reliance on fuel duties. However, any wholesale reform of the tax structure will depend crucially on public support as well as on technological developments that may reduce the cost of initial investments and ongoing financial commitments. Part of any public concern may be the perception that tax reform would have adverse distributional consequences, though this effect can be modified by offsets. In any event, a move towards congestion charging would be extremely hard to justify without commensurate reductions in fuel duty, which would leave overall revenues unchanged or possibly even slightly reduced.

5.7. AVIATION TAXATION

Aviation represents one of the fastest-growing sources of greenhouse gas emissions in the UK and other developed economies. Total CO_2 emissions from domestic and international aviation have increased from around 7.29 million tonnes (1.0% of the national total) in 1970, to 16.95 million tonnes (2.8% of the total) in 1990, and further to 37.47 million tonnes (6.3% of the total) in 2005.[33]

The 'greenhouse effect' caused by aviation is greater than that caused by carbon alone. Additional effects are attributable to emissions of water vapour, nitric oxide (NO), nitrogen dioxide (NO_2), sulphur oxides (SO_x), and soot (Penner et al. (1999)). The IPPC estimated in 1999 that the total effect that can currently be quantified is between two and four times the effect of carbon dioxide alone. Much of the uncertainty surrounding this estimate has to do with the unknown effect of the formation of aviation-induced cirrus clouds. Sausan et al. (2005) also investigated the relative effects of these gases and came to a qualitatively similar conclusion to that of the IPCC. Taking a broader view of all greenhouse gases, figures from the UK Environmental Accounts suggest that in 2005, air transport accounted for 5.8% of emissions, compared to 2.5% in 1990.[34]

Aviation taxation is enormously complicated by international considerations. International aviation is governed by the International Civil Aviation Organization (ICAO), developed as a result of the 1944 Chicago Convention, whose resolution on the taxation of aviation fuel, for example, states that:

> the fuel, lubricants and other consumable technical supplies contained in the tanks or other receptacles on the aircraft shall be exempt from customs and other duties.[35]

Further, European rules on aviation as well as bilateral Aviation Service Agreements (ASAs) between different countries can act as constraints on government policy towards airlines. For example, Norway introduced a CO_2 fuel tax on all flights in January 1999, but by May that year had to abandon

[33] <http://www.defra.gov.uk/environment/statistics/globatmos/download/xls/gatb05.xls>.

[34] See table 2.3 of <http://www.statistics.gov.uk/downloads/theme_environment/EADec2007.pdf>.

[35] See ICAO (2006).

the tax for international flights because it violated the rules of ASAs between Norway and other countries.[36] In 1999, Sweden had to remove a domestic aviation fuel tax, because it conflicted with the EU Mineral Oil Directive. As a result, new rules were drawn up that allow domestic flights to be subject to fuel taxes and that will allow intra-EU flights to be similarly taxed.

The key instrument for aviation taxation in the UK has been Air Passenger Duty (APD), a tax levied on airlines on a per-passenger basis, introduced in the November 1993 Budget and implemented in November 1994. It was not introduced with explicitly environmental incentives in mind, and it has often been seen as a revenue-raising measure at a time when the government finances were in relatively poor shape. Given that air tickets are exempt from VAT, however, and that airline fuel is exempt from duty, aviation might be relatively under-taxed compared to its increasing contribution to emissions. APD represents one relatively straightforward way in which aviation can be taxed.

APD varies according to the destination and the class of the flight. In broad terms, European destinations are taxed at £10 for standard-class flights and £20 for other classes, whilst those rates for non-European destinations are £40 and £80, respectively. These rates apply from February 2007, having been doubled in the December 2006 Pre-Budget Report. APD raised around £1 billion in 2006–07 before the doubling and are forecast to raise £2 billion in 2007–08 after the doubling of the tax rates.

Pearce and Pearce (2000) estimate the marginal external costs from pollution and noise at Heathrow airport for different models of aircraft, and argue that the per-passenger tax should be £3 on a short-haul flight on a Boeing 747–400, and £15 on a long haul. Even after uprating to current values, these figures are below current APD rates, though APD clearly also has a significant revenue-raising component given the absence of other forms of aviation taxation.

APD can be considered an environmental tax to the extent that it reduces the demand for flights (and that the demand is not instead taken up by more polluting forms of transport). The Department for Transport works on the assumption that a 10% rise in the price of flights reduces demand by 10% (i.e. the own-price elasticity is −1.0). This elasticity could vary according to the purpose of the flight (business flights are much less price elastic than pleasure flights).[37] The rates do not vary, however, according to the emissions of the aircraft or the total distance travelled within Europe or beyond. As a

[36] See ECON Analyse (2005) for more details.
[37] See Gillen, Morrison, and Stewart (2004).

per-passenger tax, it provides no incentives to airlines to ensure that planes depart as fully loaded as possible, and it is not applicable to freight flights. In the October 2007 Pre-Budget Report, the government announced that from 2009, the basis of the tax would change from the passenger to the aircraft, a reform previously advocated by both the Liberal Democrats and the Conservatives. No final details have been announced though an initial consultation document[38] suggested that the tax rate could vary with the maximum take-off weight of the aircraft (which is argued to correlate closely with environmental emissions) and with three distance bands rather than two as at present.

A per-plane tax would encourage fuller flights (as presumably the airlines would have to absorb the tax for unfilled seats). It may be more easily applied to freight flights (though freight-only flights account for only a very small fraction of total departures from UK airports). To the extent that the reformed tax is passed on to passengers, those likely to benefit (relative to APD) will be those flying on fully loaded aircraft, on smaller, less polluting aircraft, and those flying relatively short distances. However, any reforms that set the tax rates finely according to a wide range of aircraft and destination characteristics will make the tax substantially more complex to administer.[39]

An alternative approach to aviation taxation might be to bring aviation into an international system of emissions trading. In principle, such a scheme could be managed at a global level, though in practice regional variants are likely to emerge first. In December 2007, European environmental ministers drew up plans to include aviation in the EU Emissions Trading Scheme (ETS) from 2012,[40] covering all flights departing from or arriving into an EU airport even for non-EU airlines. The number of permits available to airlines will be capped at the average level of EU aviation emissions between 2004 and 2006. Any increases in aviation emissions above this level will have to be matched by emissions reductions elsewhere in the scheme. In the first year of aviation's inclusion, only 10% of allowances are planned to be auctioned with the remaining 90% allocated for free according to the tonnage-kilometres flown by each airline.

To the extent that aviation is included in the ETS, a domestic aviation tax can hardly target CO_2 emissions. However, aviation also produces considerable noise externalities that vary according to airport of departure, as well as other non-CO_2 environmental emissions, and contributes to congestion both

[38] See <http://www.hm-treasury.gov.uk/media/E/2/consult_aviation310108.pdf>.

[39] A full discussion of the issues around this tax reform can be found in Leicester and O'Dea (2008).

[40] See <http://www.consilium.europa.eu/ueDocs/cms_Data/docs/pressData/en/envir/97858.pdf>.

in the skies and around airports. All may provide ongoing justifications for a domestic aviation tax.

A recent paper by Keen and Strand (2007) examines an optimal system of international aviation taxation and summarizes the current practice of domestic aviation taxation in different countries. Many EU nations currently charge VAT on domestic tickets, though only Germany and the Netherlands do so at the full rate. Ireland, Denmark, and the UK are the only countries to zero-rate domestic aviation tickets. The US does not charge a sales tax on domestic aviation tickets, but it does impose a 7.5% ticket tax as a 'security charge'. Trip-based charges are more popular, whether as an 'airport tax' that accrues to the airport authority or as a departure tax that accrues to the government. Keen and Strand estimate that the average international passenger in the UK pays between 27 and 109 US dollars in such charges per trip, compared to $34 for US passengers and around $9–$16 in France. The paper argues that taxation should take the form of a combination of internationally coordinated fuel and ticket taxes that apply as non-refundable excise taxes rather than a VAT: the former would approximate an emissions tax, and the latter could be used both to internalize noise externalities and to raise revenue. Given the constraints imposed by international agreements, however, such a system could be extremely difficult to implement. Fuel excise and ticket taxes on domestic aviation coupled with suitably varying departure taxes for international aviation may be the best feasible policy.

5.8. TAXES AND WASTE MANAGEMENT

Considerable public concern about the environment and the environmental 'sustainability' of current patterns of production and consumption focuses on the generation and disposal of waste. Many households devote time and effort to recycling, and many resist excessive product packaging. One prominent anxiety has been that society is using up the earth's finite, non-renewable, resources of raw materials at an excessive rate, so that 'not enough' will be left for future generations. This concern raises questions of efficient inter-temporal resource pricing that are important, but beyond the environmental-policy focus of this chapter. However, important environmental externalities are associated with waste generation and management that require attention. Moreover, this field has considerable scope for taxes and other incentive mechanisms to be employed as part of an efficient policy package.

The environmental issues concerning waste largely have to do with the environmental consequences of different methods of waste disposal—the pollution and disamenity costs of landfill disposal, incineration, illegal dumping, and so on. Other forms of waste management besides disposal may also involve pollution and amenity costs. The energy used in glass recycling, for example, adds to CO_2 emissions, and bottle banks and other collection methods could impose disamenity costs on some local residents.

The generation of waste involves a series of decision-makers, and interrelated decisions. Product manufacturers determine product design and packaging, both of which influence subsequent waste management costs. Consumers decide which products to purchase, and when and how to dispose of waste. Households also play a key role in initiating recycling in many systems, by separating recyclables from other household wastes. The public authorities or private firms who collect household and industrial waste decide what disposal option to employ—landfill, incineration, or recycling. The environmental problems of waste management arise because at each of these stages the decision-makers concerned do not face costs that reflect the full social costs of the choices they make. In some cases decision-makers face no costs at all—households, for example, face a zero marginal cost for waste disposal in the UK. In other cases, while decision-makers may face some costs such as the charges by operators of landfill sites or incinerators, these costs do not reflect the social and environmental costs of choosing a particular course of action. In short, therefore, price signals may be wrong, or non-existent.

Clearly taxes on various elements of the waste process can be used to correct these faulty price signals, so that decision-makers face the full social costs of their actions. Externality taxes on disposal options can, for example, be used to ensure local authorities and others involved in waste disposal take environmental costs into account in their choice of disposal option. Likewise, unit charging for household waste disposal could encourage households to minimize waste and to increase their use of recycling. We discuss these approaches in Sections 5.8.1 and 5.8.2.

The difficulty for policy, however, is that it is unlikely to be practicable to levy appropriate taxes on all disposal options, or to ensure that the financial incentives link all of the relevant decision-makers. Illegal disposal (such as fly-tipping) remains, by definition, uncharged, and raising the costs of legal disposal options may encourage greater use of illegal routes, which could have significant environmental costs. Transmitting the financial signals back may be difficult, too. Even where charges for the collection of household refuse seek to provide households with an incentive to minimize waste volumes, they rarely distinguish between different categories of waste according to their costs of disposal. Also, if increased household waste disposal costs are to provide an incentive for manufacturers to change the design of products and packaging, this requires not only shifts in consumer demand towards products with lower disposal costs, but also that firms identify correctly the shifts in demand, and their reason. For certain products a different approach may be necessary—for example, advance disposal fees in the form of taxes levied when products are sold, deposit-refund systems (to encourage proper disposal), and other policy interventions to encourage product manufacturers to take end-of-life product disposal costs into account. We discuss these approaches in Sections 5.8.3 to 5.8.5.

5.8.1. Pricing the external costs of landfill disposal

Three main methods can be used for the disposal of waste: landfill, incineration, or recycling. Historically the UK and the US have made extensive use of landfill, a sharp contrast with Japan and some northern European countries including Denmark, Belgium, and the Netherlands, where incineration plays a much greater role. The European Union has actively discouraged landfill disposal in member states, and the 1999 European Landfill Directive commits EU countries to a timetable of demanding quantitative targets for reducing the amount of biodegradable municipal waste sent to landfill by 2020. For the UK the Landfill Directive requires reductions in landfilled biodegradable municipal waste to 75% of the 1995 level by 2010, 50% by 2013, and 35% by 2020.

To begin with, what are the grounds for policy intervention to reduce landfilled waste? In many countries, landfill sites for waste disposal are becoming increasingly scarce, as existing sites are exhausted, and as planning obstacles limit the development of new sites. This trend is forcing many countries to reappraise waste management strategies, to reduce reliance on landfill disposal, and to increase the proportions of waste reused and recovered. However, it does not involve any obvious externality, nor any role for environmental taxation. Where waste management is operated by decentralized agencies of government and by private sector firms paying the full market rate for the landfill facilities they use, the central government has no obvious need for intervention to discourage the use of landfill disposal on grounds of future scarcity. Scarcity of landfill sites will be reflected in higher charges levied for their use by private owners and operators, reflecting the opportunity cost of current landfill use, in terms of the loss of future landfill capacity. In areas where landfill is becoming scarce, market forces should ensure that disposal of waste to landfill is correspondingly expensive.

Government intervention in waste management is, however, needed to regulate the externalities from landfill and other waste disposal options that are not reflected in the charges levied by operators. Three principal externalities may be relevant:

- current environmental externalities from landfill sites, which may include disamenity costs to local residents, emissions of greenhouse gases and 'conventional' air pollutants, leachate seeping into water systems, and environmental costs of transporting waste to the landfill;
- future social costs, which may arise if landfill operators make inadequate provision for the long-run costs of managing landfill sites and are able to avoid liability for these costs through bankruptcy or other means;
- lost social benefits from alternatives to landfill, which may arise if disposal through incineration leads to energy production that substitutes for more-polluting forms of energy supply.

For the UK, studies commissioned in the 1990s by the Department of the Environment provide quantitative evidence on these landfill externalities, for different types of landfill, differentiating between urban and rural locations, and landfill with and without energy recovery. They also estimated externalities from incineration with energy recovery, the most likely long-term possibility for diversion of landfilled wastes. The external costs of landfill were estimated to lie in the range between −£1 and £9 per tonne of waste, depending on the type of landfill, while incineration with energy recovery had a net external benefit of £2–£4 per tonne of waste, reflecting the greenhouse gas and other emissions of the power generation that would be displaced (CSERGE (1993)). The largest external cost element of landfill disposal was the climate change externality from methane emissions from landfill sites, valued at £0.86–£5.40 per tonne; in addition, the climate change impact of carbon dioxide emissions was valued at some £0.08–£1.27 per tonne. The external costs of leaching accidents were estimated at some £0.90 per tonne from existing landfill sites (while the regulatory conditions attached to new sites were assumed to internalize the cost of leaching risks). Transport externalities were estimated to be less than £1 per tonne, and disamenity costs were approximately £2 per tonne (inferred mainly from US evidence). Averaging across the whole waste stream and the various types of landfill shows that the externality was about £5 per tonne, or approximately £7 for 'active' and £2 for 'inactive' waste (where inactive wastes are those that do not biodegrade).

The UK's landfill tax is charged per tonne of commercial, industrial, and municipal (household) waste delivered to landfill sites. Two different components of the waste stream are taxed at different rates. The standard rate applies to 'active' (biodegradable) waste, and a reduced rate applies to 'inert' waste, such as building rubble. When first introduced in 1996, the rates applied were £7 per tonne for standard waste and £2 per tonne for inert waste, in line with the above estimates of the external costs of landfill (Davies and Doble (2004)). On introduction, the projected revenues were used to finance a cut of 0.2% in the rate of employers' National Insurance contributions (a payroll tax), with the declared aim of ensuring that the tax would not lead to a net increase in overall business costs. It was also possible for landfill operators to make contributions to registered environmental trusts in lieu of paying the tax (the 'Landfill Tax Credit Scheme').

Prior to the introduction of the landfill tax, some consideration of the relative merits of weight- or volume-related taxes on the one hand, and ad valorem taxes on the charges levied by landfill operators on the other was made. The initial proposal announced in the 1995 Budget was for an ad valorem tax, which attracted considerable criticism. One relevant consideration was the documentation needed to levy taxes on the different possible bases; since ad valorem taxes are based on the value of transactions, it is likely they would be more straightforward to operate than taxes based on physical attributes requiring measurement. The choice of a weight-related tax requires records to be kept for tax purposes of the weight of deliveries to landfill sites, but the additional costs of this documentation were in most cases believed to be small, as most landfill operators were charging waste disposal authorities by weight and had suitable weighbridges already in place at many sites. A second consideration in the choice between possible bases was how well each related to the various external costs generated by landfill use—including transport-related externalities, local disamenity through noise, dust, and smell, the leaching of dumped materials into groundwater and rivers. While some of these external costs may be broadly proportional to the weight of materials dumped, an ad valorem tariff would charge more for wastes that required more costly management, which could be a better proxy than weight for some of the leaching externalities. However, a strong argument was that ad valorem taxation would tend to penalize the operators of higher-quality facilities, operating to more stringent—and more costly—environmental standards. The choice of a weight-related tariff with two charging categories was seen as a reasonable compromise between differentiation to reflect the external costs of different components of the waste stream, and administrative practicality and cost.

In a review of the tax, HM Customs and Excise (1998) observed that it had led to a significant reduction in the volume of inactive waste sent to landfill (paradoxically the least-taxed component), but that it had negligible impact on landfilling of other wastes. Landfilling of inactive waste fell from 35.4 million tonnes in 1997–98 to 15.8 million tonnes in 2001–02, a 55% reduction, while landfilling of waste subject to the standard rate of tax actually increased slightly over the same period, from 50.4 million tonnes to 50.9 million.

The standard rate of the landfill tax remained unchanged until 1999, when it was raised to £10 per tonne, and a commitment made to an annual £1 increase in the rate over the five years 2000–04, so that the rate reached £15 per tonne in 2004. Noting that the tax had, so far, been ineffective in reducing the amount of non-inert waste landfilled, a Cabinet Office Strategy Unit paper in 2002 concluded that 'a rise to £35 a tonne is required over the medium term'. Accordingly, the annual escalator was then raised to £3 per tonne, with the aim of raising the rate eventually to the £35 per tonne level. By April 2007 the rate had reached £24 per tonne, and rises to £32 per tonne from April 2008 and £40 per tonne from April 2009 have been announced. In contrast to this succession of increases in the standard rate, the lower rate of landfill tax for inert waste has so far remained unchanged from the start of the system, but is scheduled to rise to £2.50 per tonne from April 2008.

Recent trends suggest a substantial decline in active landfill waste volumes, but the decline in inactive landfill waste has slowed down and possibly halted altogether. By 2006–07, inactive waste landfill volumes had fallen only slightly further from their 2001–02 volumes, to 13.1 million tonnes, whilst active waste landfill volumes were down to 40.8 million tonnes, a fall of around 20% since 2001–02.

The steady acceleration in the standard rate of the landfill tax reflects increasing concern about the inability of the UK to reduce its use of landfill as required under the EU Landfill Directive. Failure to meet these mandatory EU targets will subject the UK to substantial penalties for non-compliance. What has driven the acceleration in UK landfill tax rates is not an upward revision in estimates of landfill externalities, but the overriding priority that has been given to attainment of the EU landfill targets. The setting of these targets appears not to have been based on quantitative assessment of landfill externalities, nor on the relative external costs of different disposal options, and measures to achieve these targets therefore imply tax rates well in excess of marginal external costs. Even raising the landfill tax to very high levels cannot, however, guarantee compliance with the quantity targets set by the Landfill Directive. The UK therefore has turned to a tradable permit system, to operate in parallel with the existing landfill tax, as a mechanism intended to achieve a predictable quantity outcome in the target years specified in the Landfill Directive.

The Landfill Allowance Trading Scheme (LATS) is designed to restrict landfill disposal of biodegradable municipal waste (BMW), in order to ensure UK compliance with EU targets (Salmons (2002); Barrow (2003)). The scheme started in April 2005. Permits relate to a particular target year and are allocated without charge to Waste Disposal Authorities (local governments) according to a formula based on current landfilling and total current waste quantities. The first allocation was for the period up to 2010, by which date the UK must reduce its landfilling of BMW to 75% of the 1995 level.

Unsurprisingly, given the purpose of the scheme, the compliance obligations for local waste disposal authorities have a structure that mirrors the timing of the UK's targets under the EU Landfill Directive, for years 2009–10, 2012–13, and 2019–20. Waste Disposal Authorities are required to meet targets in those years, without recourse to borrowing or banking, that sum to the relevant global target (75% of 1995 levels in 2010, 50% in 2012–13, and 35% in 2019–20). For these target years, too, substantial penalties for non-compliance with the scheme will apply: any penalties imposed on the UK by the EU (up to approximately £0.5 million per day) would be passed on to non-compliant authorities. For the years between Landfill Directive targets, local waste disposal authorities are also assigned targets, implying a broadly linear adjustment to each successive EU target year. Greater inter-temporal flexibility is allowed in compliance with these intermediate targets: during the period between each EU target year, waste disposal authorities can bank allowances and can anticipate ('borrow') a small percentage of future allowance allocations (currently limited to 5% of the next year's allocation). This inter-temporal flexibility does not apply in the target years, or across target years, meaning that the trading system effectively consists of six separate sub-periods (the three target years, and the intermediate years before each target).

The interaction between price determination in LATS and the landfill tax should be noted. Since the biodegradable municipal waste regulated by LATS is also covered by the landfill tax, the value of allowances will be given by the marginal cost of diverting biodegradable municipal waste from landfill, at the quantity constraint given by LATS, minus the landfill tax paid on each tonne of waste. The average landfill tax rate applicable over the LATS period prior to 2010 will be £32 per tonne. If LATS allowances are trading at approximately

£20 per tonne, this implies that the marginal cost of achieving the constraint on landfilling set by the first period of LATS is of the order of £20 + £32 = £52 per tonne. Future movements in the LATS allowance price should then reflect changing expectations about the marginal cost of diverting sufficient waste to achieve the aggregate quantity cap set by LATS, and would offset pound for pound any further changes in the rate at which the landfill tax is charged.

As far as BMW is concerned, the introduction of LATS has made the landfill tax effectively redundant in environmental terms, in the sense that it is the quantity constraint under LATS that will determine the use made of landfill, and not the rate at which the landfill tax is charged.[41] The higher rates of landfill tax planned for future years mainly have the effect of depressing the landfill allowance price, pound for pound with the landfill tax rate (although they also act to recover some of the rents distributed to local authorities through free allocation of LATS allowances). Yet some incentive roles remain for the landfill tax. First, it is a floor price, in the event that the LATS targets prove so easy to achieve that the value of LATS allowances falls. Second, it regulates those components of the waste stream, including industrial wastes, not covered by LATS (which only regulates landfilling of BMW).

While this interaction between the LATS price and the landfill tax illustrates the similarity between environmental tax rates and emissions trading prices, the comparison highlights the key difference in terms of abatement outcomes and abatement cost uncertainty. LATS is being employed because of the overriding priority that has been given to achieving quantity targets for reduced landfill use—targets that appear to have been based on no objective assessment of costs, benefits, and risks. The cost of achieving the Landfill Directive targets is unknown, though it will be revealed in due course in the LATS allowance price. Whereas a case can be made in climate change policy for giving high priority to achieving a particular quantity outcome, it is hard to find any corresponding environmental justification for the Landfill Directive's rigid targets. A price-based approach, giving greater weight to environmental taxes than quantity targets, would have been a preferable basis for long-term waste management policy.

The aggregates levy, introduced in April 2002, is intended to reflect the environmental costs associated with quarrying sand, gravel, and rock. The

[41] In economic terms, the quantity constraint on the number of permits is binding, and the permit price is the cost of meeting the constraint. That does not mean the tax is totally irrelevant. It usurps some portion of the value of permits, and so it acts like a windfall profits tax on the value of permits handed to Waste Disposal Authorities. In this respect, it is similar to the US tax on chlorofluorocarbons that took part of the windfall profits associated with quantity constraints of the 1989 Montreal Protocol.

levy is charged at £1.60 per tonne, normally payable by the quarry operator. It further reinforced incentives to avoid landfilling of inert waste, by stimulating demand for recycled materials to replace virgin aggregates in road-building and other applications. Full-year revenues are of the order of £300 million, part of which is used to finance a Sustainability Fund (to promote local environmental benefits in areas affected by quarrying), and the remainder to finance a 0.1 percentage point cut in employer NICs.

5.8.2. Household waste charges

Current arrangements for the collection and disposal of household waste in the UK provide households with no individual financial incentive to change the amount of waste they throw away. Household refuse collection and disposal is provided by local authorities, financed through the council tax. Whilst council tax rates may be affected by the cost of household waste disposal, the tax provides no incentive for individual householders to reduce the amount of waste requiring disposal.

In the UK, as elsewhere, a charge per bag or for volume of waste (a 'unit pricing scheme' or UPS) has been the subject of considerable recent speculation. The possible systems include:

- weighing individual bins;
- 'subscription' programmes, where households pay a monthly fee that depends on their chosen size and/or number of bins;
- revenue stickers, where households purchase stickers that have to be attached to each bag or bin to be emptied.

Many countries now have experience with systems of this sort, and a growing body of research studies their impact on household waste behaviour. The results of a number of studies for various communities in the US are summarized in Box 5.3. The estimated impact on the quantity of household waste varies between studies, and much appears to depend on the design of the UPS, and on parallel policy measures.

In any event, the social benefit of unit charging is not measured by the impact on waste quantities, but the welfare gain from efficient pricing of a service previously supplied at zero marginal cost (Figure 5.6). In this figure, the social marginal cost (SMC) of excess waste includes both operational costs incurred by municipalities and environmental externalities. The social marginal benefit (SMB) is the amount that consumers are willing to pay for

Box 5.3. The effect of unit pricing for household refuse: US evidence

The initial econometric study of unit pricing, Jenkins (1993), gathered monthly data over several years from fourteen US towns (ten with unit pricing). She found inelastic demand for garbage collection; a 1% increase in the user fee leads to a 0.12% decrease in quantity.

Two studies rely on self-reported garbage quantities from households (rather than as reported by municipal governments). Hong et al. (1993) use data from 4,306 households, who indicate whether they recycle and how much they pay for waste collection. Results indicate that a UPS increases the probability that a household recycles, but does not affect the quantity of rubbish produced. Reschovsky and Stone (1994) use data from 1,422 households on recycling behaviour, income, and demographic information. The price of waste disposal alone is estimated to have no significant impact on the probability that a household recycles. When it is combined with a kerbside recycling programme, however, recycling rates increase by 27 to 58%, depending on material type.

Miranda et al. (1994) gather data from twenty-one towns with UPS programmes and compare the quantity of waste and recycling over the year before implementation of unit pricing with the year following it. Results indicate that these towns reduce waste by 17 to 74% and increase recycling by 128%. These large estimates cannot be attributed directly to pricing: in every case, kerbside recycling programmes were implemented during the same year as the unit pricing programme.

Only Fullerton and Kinnaman (1996) use household data that are not based on self-reported surveys. The weight and volume of the waste and recycling of seventy-five households were measured by hand over four weeks before and after implementation of a price-per-bag in Charlottesville, Virginia. A kerbside recycling programme had already been in operation for over a year. Results indicate a slight drop in the weight of rubbish (elasticity of −0.08) but a greater drop in waste volume (elasticity of −0.23). Indeed, the density of waste increased from 15 pounds per bag to just over 20 pounds per bag.

Since collectors and landfills compact the garbage anyway, the compacting by households does not help reduce the actual costs of disposal. Disposal costs are based on the space used in the landfill, and that is not well measured by the number of bags at the kerb, but rather the weight. These results suggest that a price per bag is not very effective at reducing that measure of the space used in the landfill.

Van Houtven and Morris (1999) look at two policy experiments in Marietta, Georgia, including a traditional 'bag or tag' programme and a second programme that requires households to pre-commit or 'subscribe' to

(*cont.*)

Box 5.3. (*cont.*)

the collection of a specific number of containers each week. The household pays for the subscribed number whether these containers are filled with rubbish or not. Direct billing may reduce administrative costs. Yet the subscription programme does not effectively put a positive price on every unit of waste, since the containers may be partially empty most weeks. Indeed, they find that the bag programme reduces waste by 36%, while the subscription programme reduces it by only 14%.

Podolsky and Spiegel (1998) employ a 1992 cross-section of 159 towns clustered in New Jersey, twelve with UPSs. They estimate the largest price elasticity of demand in the literature (−0.39). The authors attribute this estimate to the fact that all towns in their sample had mature recycling programmes in place, and no towns in their sample had implemented subscription programmes. Kinnaman and Fullerton (2000) use a 1991 national cross-section of 959 towns, 114 with user fees. They find that accounting for endogeneity of the policy variables raises the demand elasticity to −0.28, but that is still not very high. They also estimate that subscription programmes have less of an impact than bag/tag programmes on waste and recycling. Other important studies include Hong and Adams (1999) who look at the effect of unit pricing on aggregate disposal and recycling behaviour, and Jenkins et al. (2003) who use household level data to look at recycling behaviour by material. They find that unit pricing has no effect on recycling but that kerbside collection has a big effect on recycling of all materials.

one more unit of disposal. The optimal amount of disposal, Q*, is where SMC = SMB. Any quantities in excess of Q* cause a net loss to the extent that the social costs exceed the marginal social benefits of those units—the grey triangle in Figure 5.6.

Jenkins (1993) and Repetto et al. (1992) use their estimates of price effects on waste demand to estimate this welfare cost to be some $650 million per year in the US, roughly $3 per person per year. Fullerton and Kinnaman (1996) use household data and also estimate the potential benefits of marginal cost pricing to be in the neighbourhood of $3 per person per year.

Even this small welfare gain from unit charging for waste is not necessarily available, however, for a number of reasons:

- First, the administrative costs of implementing the waste-pricing programme may exceed the social benefits. Fullerton and Kinnaman (1996) estimate that the administrative costs of printing, distributing, and

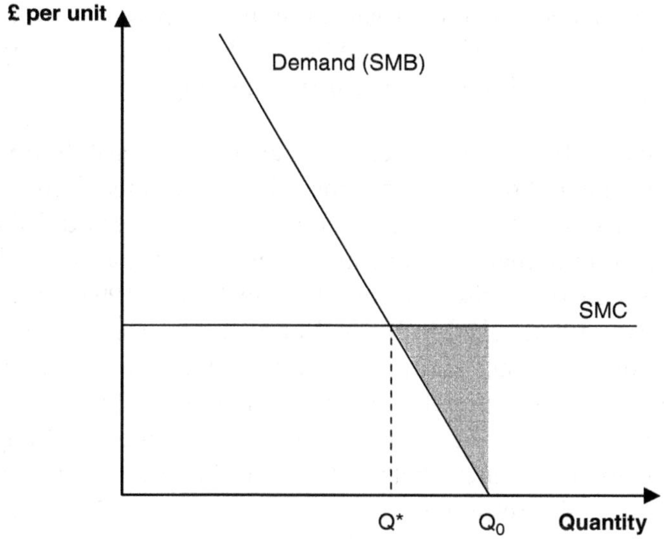

Figure 5.6. The optimal amount of disposal, and the welfare cost of excess waste

accounting for waste stickers in Charlottesville, Virginia, could exceed the $3 per person per year benefits mentioned above.

- Second, some of the available unit charging mechanisms generate only weak incentives to reduce waste; charging per bag, for example, can encourage households to cram as much as possible into a small number of bags—the so-called 'Seattle stomp'—which economizes on bags, but not on disposal costs. Unit charging mechanisms with better incentive properties, such as individual weighing, may be more costly to operate.
- Third, a uniform tax on all types of waste may be inefficient if materials within the waste stream produce different social costs (Dinan (1993)). If the social cost of disposal of batteries is greater than that of old newspapers, for example, then the disposal tax on batteries should exceed that on old newspapers, and unit charging cannot achieve this precise differentiation.
- Fourth, the welfare calculation neglects the costs of any adverse side-effects (possible littering and other avoidance activities). The partial equilibrium method reflected in Figure 5.6 does not consider other disposal methods. It does not convey *why* demand for waste disposal slopes down, that is, what substitutes are available. The welfare gain calculation is correct if recycling is the only alternative, but not if more

costly alternatives such as illegal dumping are possible. In this case, it would be better to offer free rubbish collection than to implement a pricing policy that leads to widespread dumping.

Available data rarely allow for direct comparisons of illegal dumping before and after implementation of unit pricing. Many economists have asked town officials whether they believe illegal dumping has increased following the introduction of unit charging, and many have stated that it has, but many more have stated otherwise. Reschovsky and Stone (1994) and Fullerton and Kinnaman (1996) asked individual households whether they observed any change. In the former study, 51% of respondents reported an increase in dumping. The most popular method was household use of commercial skips. Twenty per cent admitted to burning rubbish, though it was not possible to determine whether this was in response to the charge. Roughly 40% of the respondents to the Fullerton and Kinnaman survey said that they thought illegal dumping had increased in response to pricing. Those authors also use survey responses with direct household waste observations to estimate that 28% of the reduction of waste observed at the kerb was redirected to illicit forms of disposal. Nonetheless, Miranda and Bynum (1999) estimate that more than 4,000 communities use some form of unit pricing in the US.[42] To avoid illegal dumping, some communities have chosen to provide free waste collection for the first bag of garbage, applying unit pricing only to every additional bag. This pricing system leaves some distortion in economic incentives, however, because households have no incentive to reduce their garbage generation below one bag per week.

The great merit of unit charging for household waste is the incentive it gives households to separate wastes for recycling. The problem of dumping and other illegal disposal is a dysfunctional response to the same incentive. Whether unit charging is worthwhile depends on the balance between these effects, which may reflect cultural and social pressures as much as economic incentives. However, unit charging for waste almost certainly needs to be accompanied by additional measures for particular products, tailored to the toxic content of the material for disposal, to the risks and costs of illicit methods of disposal-like dumping, and to reflect monitoring capabilities. The following three sections discuss possible instruments, in the form of product charges, deposit-refund systems, and the assignment of

[42] ISWA (2002) reports that a recent study for Denmark recommended against weight-based charges after finding that municipalities with such charges had more illegal disposal and less recycling than other municipalities.

producer responsibility. Each may help to resolve the inefficiencies generated by excessive reliance on unit charging to control the growth of household waste.

5.8.3. Product charges (advance disposal fees)

In principle, charging households for waste disposal could have effects throughout the chain of production and consumption. If it encourages consumer substitution away from goods with high waste disposal costs, it could provide incentives for manufacturers and retailers to package products so as to minimize the subsequent waste disposal costs on households. However, the impact of waste charges may be insufficient to modify households' purchasing behaviour appreciably. The signal transmitted to producers may be weak and difficult to distinguish from other factors affecting purchasing patterns.

If these signals to manufacturers are too weak, or if new charges on waste disposal would induce too much illegal dumping, then manufacturers may not get the signal to reduce packaging or to make products that can be recycled. In this case, incentives can be introduced at the 'manufacturer' end of the chain, by levying taxes on products and packaging that reflect the costs of their ultimate disposal. The efficient level of the packaging tax on an individual product would be broadly the same as the waste disposal tax that would have been levied on its disposal under unit charging. Higher rates on new products that have higher costs of subsequent disposal provide incentives to switch to products and packaging with lower disposal costs. Thus, the system is compatible with the retention of tax-based financing of household waste disposal, where households face a zero marginal cost for disposal. The fact that households might seek to avoid waste charges by littering and other environmentally damaging practices provides good reasons to collect household waste at zero marginal cost. The downside of the advance disposal fee, however, is that it does not affect household choices about disposal. It is paid by the manufacturer and may affect production decisions, but it is already paid at the time of disposal and provides no incentive or refund for preferred methods of disposal.

Defining efficient product taxes to reflect end-of-life waste disposal costs would be most straightforward and effective where producer choices are flexible and important, and where consumer choices are inflexible or unimportant. If consumers invariably throw batteries in the landfill, for example, then producers could be induced to make the type of batteries that cause less damage once landfilled. On the other hand, if consumers can be induced to recycle batteries at much lower social cost, then a deposit-refund system (see Section 5.8.4) can work much better than advance disposal fees.

Products that are predominantly thrown away by households, ending up in landfill after one use, could be subject to a higher packaging tax than products that get recycled; both might be taxed more heavily than products packaged in reusable containers. Packaging taxes of this form have been introduced for beverage containers and certain types of other packaging in some Scandinavian countries, and have been studied by Brisson (1997) and OECD (1993). Brisson's estimates of the disposal costs of each type of container suggest some surprising conclusions about the relative tax rates that should be applied to drink containers made of different materials. Milk cartons, which are hardly recycled at all, would have low tax rates (about 9 pence per 100 litres in current prices), because their weight and hence disposal costs are low. The corresponding tax rate to be applied to returnable milk bottles would depend on the rates of return achieved. Non-returnable glass bottles without recycling would have tax rates that were some twelve times as high as cartons and plastic containers, but a lower tax rate could be applied to glass bottles used in a context in which reuse is sufficiently substantial and routine. Brisson's figures suggest that returnable milk bottles would need to achieve a 93% rate of reuse for the tax to fall to the same level as the tax on cartons.

The difficulty with an advance disposal fee on products is that it does not provide incentives to encourage reuse, recycling, or other actions that reduce disposal costs. Combining advance disposal fees on products with a subsidy to proper disposal may, however, achieve the efficient outcome. Although neither instrument provides all the right incentives by itself, Fullerton and Wolverton (1999) show conditions under which the combination can match exactly the effects of a Pigouvian tax on waste: incentives to reduce consumption of waste-intensive products *and* to dispose of waste properly.

5.8.4. Deposit-refund systems

Several studies have favoured the use of a deposit-refund system to correct for the external costs of garbage disposal, including Bohm (1981), Dinan (1993), Fullerton and Kinnaman (1995), Palmer and Walls (1997), and Palmer et al. (1997). Worldwide, these programmes have been successful at reducing waste and recovering recyclable materials (OECD (1998)).

To achieve the efficient allocation, the deposit for each good should be set equal to the social marginal cost of dumping the waste, and the refund on return is that deposit minus the marginal external cost of recycling. If the external cost of recycling is zero, then the refund matches the deposit. The deposit could be levied either on the production or on the sale of goods. As long as transaction costs are low, the refund can be given either to households that recycle or to the firms that use the recycled materials. If the refund is given to households, then the supply increase can drive down the price of recycled materials paid by firms. If the refund is given to firms, then firms increase demand for recycled materials and drive up the price received by households. In addition, Fullerton and Wu (1998) find that the refund given under a deposit-refund system can encourage firms optimally to engineer products that are easier to recycle. Households demand such products in order to recycle and thereby to receive the refund. This result is important, since directly encouraging the recyclability of product design can be administratively difficult.[43] If the administrative cost of operating the deposit-refund system is high, then Dinan (1993) suggests that policy-makers could single out products that comprise a large segment of the waste stream (newspapers) or that involve very high social marginal disposal costs (batteries).[44]

Some have suggested that a 'virgin materials tax' might encourage recycling as well as internalize the environmental externalities generated by material extraction (e.g. cutting timber or strip mining). It might increase manufacturers' demand for recycled materials, driving up the price of recycled materials and thus increasing the economic benefits to households that recycle. However, both Fullerton and Kinnaman (1995) and Palmer and Walls (1997) find that as long as other policy options are available, then a tax on virgin materials (such as the UK aggregates levy) is only necessary to correct for external costs associated with extracting the virgin material. The virgin

[43] This result depends on the assumption that recycling markets are complete. Calcott and Walls (2000a, 2000b) argue that imperfections in recycling markets prevent attainment of the first-best. It is costly to collect and transport recyclables, and it is difficult for recyclers to sort products according to their recyclability and pay consumers a price based on that recyclability. If so, then price signals may not be transmitted from consumers and recyclers back upstream to producers.

[44] Deposit-refund systems entail their own administrative costs. Those administrative costs might be quite low if the system is implemented implicitly by the use of a sales tax on all purchased commodities at the same rate, together with a subsidy to all recycling and proper garbage disposal. That practice is currently followed in the US, at least implicitly, since cities do impose local sales taxes, and they do provide free collection of kerbside recycling and garbage. If the recycling subsidy needs to be large, administrative costs can be reduced by providing a subsidy per ton, paid to recyclers, rather than providing an amount for each bottle recycled by each household. But then optimality may require a different tax and subsidy amount for each type of material—a plan that might be very costly to administer. According to <http://www.bottlebill.org>, the eleven states with current bottle bills are California, Connecticut, Delaware, Hawaii, Iowa, Maine, Massachusetts, Michigan, New York, Oregon, and Vermont. In Europe, Austria, Belgium, Denmark, Finland, Germany, the Netherlands, Norway, Sweden, and Switzerland are all listed as having beverage container deposit refund systems. Canada has also had success with their programme.

materials tax is not optimally used to correct for the marginal environmental damages of garbage disposal if a tax is available on garbage disposal.

5.8.5. 'Producer responsibility' for waste costs

One of the most far-reaching policy innovations in waste management in recent years has been the idea of 'Extended Producer Responsibility' (EPR), which makes producers responsible for the end-of-life waste management of their products. This approach was developed in the German legislation on packaging waste, and it resulted in a parallel, industry-run system of waste collection and management for packaging, operated by the industry-financed company DSD (*Duales System Deutschland*). It has underpinned much of the recent direction of EU waste policy, including directives on packaging, end-of-life vehicles, and waste electrical and electronic equipment.

In 'conventional' waste management practices for household wastes, the collection and disposal of end-of-life products is typically the responsibility of local governments, financed through some form of general taxation. In contrast, EPR shifts responsibility for the financing and management of certain categories of wastes to a separate system, run by or financed by producers. EPR schemes vary in how they are organized, but typically include:

- obligations on the producer concerning the collection ('take-back') of product packaging or end-of-life products;
- responsibility for the costs (including environmental costs) of disposal or treatment of the collected products;
- rules or targets governing the methods of waste management of recovered products, for example specifying minimum required rates of reuse or recycling.

Compared with the conventional municipal system of waste management, EPR shifts direct financial responsibility for the costs of waste management 'upstream' to the producer, and away from the municipality and taxpayer. By confronting the producer with the costs of end-of-life disposal of their products, the aim is to provide incentives for the producer to take account of these costs in designing and marketing their products—so-called 'design for environment' innovations. In addition, most EPR schemes set targets for higher rates of recovery and/or recycling than in conventional waste management.

EPR has the merit that it confronts producers directly with the costs of end-of-life waste management for their products, through the payments they have to make to cover the costs of collection, recycling, and disposal. In principle, it thus internalizes all of the costs of production and disposal to a single decision-maker—the firm. It therefore provides the incentive of a product tax or advance disposal fee to make products with less packaging and that can easily be recycled, *and* the incentives of a disposal tax or recycling subsidy to undertake the least costly form of actual subsequent disposal. In other words, as shown by Fullerton and Wu (1998), EPR can in principle provide *all* the optimal incentives inherent in charges for post-consumer waste disposal or an optimal deposit-refund system.

Actual producer responsibility rules differ from an 'optimal' disposal charge in two respects: First, as mentioned above, actual EPR systems may specify quantity targets or particular methods of waste management. Any 'minimum required rate of re-use or recycling' is either redundant with the optimal recycling incentives, or else it takes recycling away from the optimal level. Second, actual EPR systems may be difficult or costly to administer. Bringing the waste back to the responsibility of the producer is an extra step, with extra accounting and linkages, at least compared to direct taxes on each form of consumer disposal if those were feasible.

5.9. CONCLUSIONS

Environmental policy has been transformed over the past decade by the use of environmental taxes, emissions trading, and other economic instruments. These incentives allow stringent environmental protection to be introduced at lower economic cost than with the use of less-flexible forms of conventional regulation that dictate particular abatement technologies. The cost-reducing flexibility of economic instruments will become increasingly important when seeking higher standards of environmental protection.

For example, if the UK and other countries decide to make the drastic cuts in CO_2 emissions advocated by the 2006 Stern Review of the Economics of Climate Change, then taxes or other economic instruments such as emissions trading may need to play a central role in achieving the required extensive changes in energy use of firms and individuals. Energy-pricing measures, either in the form of energy taxes or emissions trading, would provide a common incentive signal to a wide variety of energy users with different abatement costs and opportunities. This pricing can promote cost-effective responses, reducing the cost of achieving any given level of emissions abatement. In addition, the use of taxes instead of regulation can spread the burden of adjustment efficiently across all energy users, rather than concentrating burdens on those subjected to direct regulation.

Despite these efficiency advantages of environmental taxes and other market mechanisms, many areas may still require more conventional regulatory approaches as a major part of the policy mix. In some cases, regulation may be needed to ensure minimum environmental standards, particularly where responses to economic incentives suffer from inertia or where uncertainty over responses means that environmental damages could be significantly larger than anticipated.

In addition to the improved efficiency in environmental policy that could result from greater use of environmental taxes and other market mechanisms, could their use have a significant impact on fiscal policy?

Environmental taxes could make a significant contribution to tax revenues in two particular areas: energy taxes and road transport congestion charges. In both cases, the available tax base is broad, high tax rates may be justified by the environmental externalities, and demand is inelastic (so revenues are not greatly eroded by behavioural responses, particularly in the short term). The potential revenues from these taxes hold out the possibility of tax reform packages that include tax reductions and reforms elsewhere in the fiscal system. The political constituency in support of environmental tax measures could create an opportunity for tax reforms that might not otherwise be politically viable.

In a more fundamental economic sense, however, environmental taxes do not necessarily alter the scope for efficient revenue-raising. A tax reform that introduces new environmental taxes *may* have a 'double dividend' if it provides the dual gain of a cleaner environment and a more efficient tax system, achieved by reducing 'distortionary' taxes that discourage work effort or investment. But that second dividend will not always arise. Environmental taxes raise the costs of production, and hence raise output prices, so they also reduce the net return from each hour worked—just like the taxes being replaced. Hence, a revenue-neutral shift from labour taxes to environmental taxes may or may not reduce the distortionary impact of the tax system.

An implication is that the case for environmental tax reform must be made primarily on the basis of potential environmental gains. The fiscal aspects of environmental tax reforms are still important, however, because the costs of environmental policy can be multiplied by inappropriate use of the revenues or by their unnecessary dissipation. But appeals to beneficial fiscal consequences of environmental tax reforms are unlikely to justify measures that do not pay their own way in purely environmental benefits.

With regard to our discussion of the scope for environmental taxes within each of our main environmental policy applications, these involve three common themes:

1. Empirical evidence is necessary for grounding environmental tax policy on the size of the marginal externalities involved, in order to indicate the level of environmental taxes that might be justified and the potential benefits of policy action.
2. Multi-part instrument combinations can frequently and usefully be employed when available tax instruments do not accurately target the relevant externalities.
3. Environmental taxes may form only part of a portfolio of policy measures. Political and practical constraints may prevent setting environmental taxes at the first-best level, so other measures can then help stimulate the development or use of abatement technologies. The case for such packages may be enhanced by recognizing various market failures in the development or dissemination of new abatement technologies. Thus, well-targeted measures to stimulate research and development or diffusion may enhance efficiency.

5.9.1. Industrial and household use of energy

The Stern Review recommends significant abatement now, to reduce the long-term costs of climate change. A carbon tax would be an appropriate, broadly based incentive measure to achieve the recommended changes in energy use. But the EU is now well advanced along an alternative track, as a carbon tax has been eschewed in favour of a cap on emissions with trading of permits. Similar choices appear in carbon abatement proposals in the northeastern US and California.

The economic properties of carbon taxes and emissions trading are quite similar. Both allow cost-reducing flexibility in polluter responses, a major improvement on conventional regulation. If tradable permits are auctioned, then the similarity between the economic effects of taxes and emissions trading is particularly close; the main economic differences then arise in the case with uncertainty about the costs of reducing emissions. Stern argues that their different properties under uncertainty favour the case for permits over taxes, although Pizer (2002) reaches the opposite conclusion. Most importantly, however, either auctioned permits or carbon taxes would clearly dominate a plan to distribute permits without charge to polluters (as is largely current practice in the EU ETS). Any such policy raises the cost of production and exacerbates labour supply or investment distortions, unless the scarcity rents can be captured and used to reduce existing labour or capital taxes.

If either the UK or EU introduces a carbon policy unilaterally, production may shift abroad in a way that would mute its beneficial environmental impact. An ideal world might have a common global carbon price, but that goal might well be difficult to achieve soon for various political and economic reasons.

With or without global or even national carbon abatement policy, however, a case still can be made for other measures as well to stimulate new abatement technologies. And all such measures are also likely to have distributional consequences that might need to be offset by further supplementary policies. Energy consumption constitutes a relatively high fraction of low-income household budgets, and so any energy policy is likely to be regressive. New energy policy could be combined with other measures to re-establish the desired degree of redistribution within the overall tax system.

5.9.2. Road transport

Road transport is already heavily taxed in the UK, and environmental gains are more likely to be achieved by better targeting of road transport taxes to the externalities involved, rather than further increases in these existing taxes. In other words, for example, petrol taxes might currently account for the combination of externalities from emissions and congestion on average, but some of those petrol taxes could be replaced by charges directly on congestion.

Congestion charges on private motoring could be a major source of tax revenues, if levied at a rate reflecting the congestion externality imposed by each individual motorist. However, separate taxes on congestion externalities weaken the case for high motor fuel excises. Sansom et al. (2001) estimate that the congestion component of motoring externalities constitutes three-quarters of the total externality. If the remaining motoring externalities do not justify retention of the existing high taxes on motor fuels, the net revenue gain from a congestion tax is reduced. The interaction between a well-targeted congestion tax and other externalities requires careful consideration, and so careful modelling is required to establish the right motor fuel taxation policy once a congestion tax is introduced.

Estimates of the relative externalities can be used to make recommendations about the relative taxation of diesel fuel and petrol, though these recommendations would be sensitive to one's view about the appropriate value to place on abatement of CO_2 emissions. Adopting a high value for the social costs of CO_2 emissions would imply a strong preference for diesel, despite its higher emissions of particulates—with adverse health effects in urban areas. Also, biofuels can be promoted through reduced taxation or direct subsidy, but the strict environmental case so far seems weak (depending on further evidence on the size of the various externalities). Finally, a case can be made for policies to stimulate vehicle fuel efficiency, over and above the generalized incentives provided by high taxes on fuels. The UK and EU are considering a set of tradable fuel efficiency targets for manufacturers, and the US experience with CAFE standards is relevant in assessing this proposal.

5.9.3. Aviation

Even without any environmental concerns, a case can be made for reform to aviation taxes. The current UK tax on air travel (air passenger duty) is a rather crudely designed revenue-raising tax, intended to compensate partly for the absence of other aviation taxes, while recognizing the difficulties for a single country in unilaterally taxing international travel. Better revenue-raising taxes on aviation could be designed, although this would require a significant amount of international coordination.

From the environmental point of view, the UK's current taxes are poorly designed, basing the tax on the passenger rather than a closer measure of the environmental impact of each flight. The recently announced reform to air passenger duty may improve matters. Substantial gains could be made by aviation taxes that directly reflected the climate impact, noise, and other environmental effects of individual flights, although international coordination would again be needed for optimal environmental taxation of aviation, without disruptive effects on competition and wasteful diversion and avoidance.

5.9.4. Waste

In the area of waste management, environmental taxes are unlikely to raise major revenues. Still, however, waste taxes can have considerable environmental and economic significance, in ensuring that waste management decisions take account of the environmental consequences of different disposal options—landfill, incineration, recycling, and so on—and encouraging substitution by producers and consumers towards products and packaging that involve less waste, and more efficient recycling.

The UK's first explicit environmental tax was the landfill tax introduced in 1996. When introduced, it was set at a level based on estimates of the external costs of landfill. More recently the tax has been increased sharply, and its effects supplemented with a Landfill Allowance Trading Scheme, both with the aim of ensuring that the UK complies with the targets for a sharp reduction in landfilling of biodegradable municipal waste set in the EU Landfill Directive. The economic case for these changes has not been properly made: it is likely that achieving the directive's targets will require diversion away from landfill, at high and unpredictable cost, probably well in excess of what could be justified in terms of the environmental externalities involved.

A second area of active controversy in waste management concerns the possible use of unit charging for collecting household waste, in place of current arrangements where refuse collection is financed from general local tax revenues. We now have considerable international experience of such systems, and the research evidence suggests that they may make some quantitative impact on the amount of household waste, although the welfare gain from this may be quite modest. One concern, however, is that unit charging may provoke increased dumping and other forms of avoidance.

Alternatives, which may reduce the risk of dumping, include advance disposal fees of products (for example packaging taxes on drinks containers, reflecting their contribution to waste disposal costs), or deposit-refund systems (which may be costly to operate, but which provide explicit incentives for proper waste disposal, reuse, or recycling). In a number of areas, European policies have been built on the notion of 'producer responsibility' for the costs of waste management, typically coupled with tough targets for collection and recycling. While this approach may encourage producers to take end-of-life waste costs into account in product design, it does so at unpredictable cost. The costs of waste management under producer responsibility are less-transparent than with tax-financed municipal collection or unit charging, but ultimately borne by consumers through higher product prices to much the same extent as with conventional waste management.

This area illustrates the complexities of environmental tax policy. Taxing the externalities involved in waste disposal would provide many of the right incentives, including incentives for producers to use designs that facilitate recycling, for firms to sell products with less packaging, for stores to reuse grocery bags, for consumers to buy products with less waste content, for waste processors to recycle, and for landfills to dispose of waste appropriately. Yet this approach would also face many problems of measurement, administration, enforcement, and compliance, risking dumping and other undesirable outcomes. A more complex 'multi-part instrument', combining taxes, subsidies, and various forms of direct regulation may be capable of achieving a better outcome. Each part of this policy can apply to a market transaction, and the appropriate combination of such instruments can reflect the complexities and help provide the right incentives to all parties involved in the generation and disposal of waste: a direct subsidy for use of designs that facilitate recycling, a direct tax on excess packaging, a simple mandate such as for reuse of grocery bags, a tax on the waste-content of goods purchased, and a subsidy for recycling. The multiplicity of instruments might not be simple, but all such instruments together may be more efficient than relying solely on the taxation of waste.

REFERENCES

Balcer, Y. (1980), 'Taxation of Externalities: Direct versus Indirect', *Journal of Public Economics*, **13**, 121–9.

Ballard, C., Shoven, J., and Whalley, J. (1985), 'General Equilibrium Computations of the Marginal Welfare Costs of Taxes in the United States', *American Economic Review*, **75**, 128–38.

Barrat, S. (2003), 'The Theory of International Environmental Agreements', in K.-G. Mäler and J. R. Vincent (eds.), *Handbook of Environmental Economics*, Amsterdam: North Holland.

Barrow, M. (2003), 'An Economic Analysis of the UK Landfill Permits Scheme', *Fiscal Studies*, **24**, 361–81.

Blow, L., Leicester, A., and Smith, Z. (2003), *London's Congestion Charge*, IFS Briefing Note 31, London: IFS.

Bohm, P. (1981), *Deposit-Refund Systems: Theory and Applications to Environmental, Conservation, and Consumer Policy*, Baltimore: Johns Hopkins University Press.

——and Russell, C. F. (1985), 'Comparative Analysis of Alternative Policy Instruments', in Kneese, A. V. and Sweeney, J. L. (eds.), *Handbook of Natural Resource and Energy Economics*, Vol. **1**, New York: Elsevier.

Bovenberg, A. L., and Cnossen, S. (1995), *Public Economics and the Environment in an Imperfect World*, Dordrecht: Kluwer Academic Publishers.

——and Goulder, L. H. (2002), 'Environmental Taxation and Regulation', in Auerbach, A. J. and Feldstein, M. (eds.), *Handbook of Public Economics*, Vol. **3**, Amsterdam: North Holland Elsevier.

——and de Mooij, R. (1994), 'Environmental Levies and Distortionary Taxation', *American Economic Review*, **84**, 1085–9.

Brechling, V., and Smith, S. (1994), 'Household Energy Efficiency in the UK', *Fiscal Studies*, **15**, 45–56.

Bressers, H. T. A., and Lulofs, K. R. D. (2004), 'Industrial Water Pollution in the Netherlands: A Fee-based Approach', in *Choosing Environmental Policy—Comparing Instruments and Outcomes in the United States and Europe*, Washington, DC: Resources for the Future.

Brisson, I. E. (1997), *Assessing the 'Waste Hierarchy': A Social Cost–Benefit Analysis of MSW Management in the European Union*, Samfund, Økonomi, and Miljo (SØM) Publication Number 19, Copenhagen.

Broome, J. (1992), *Counting the Cost of Global Warming*, Cambridge, UK: The White Horse Press.

Calcott, P., and Walls, M. (2000a), 'Can Downstream Waste Disposal Policies Encourage Upstream "Design for Environment"?' *American Economic Review*, **90**, 233–7.

—— —— (2000b), *Policies to Encourage Recycling and 'Design for Environment': What to Do When Markets are Missing*, Resources for the Future discussion paper 00–30, Washington, DC: Resources for the Future.

Centre for Social and Economic Research of the Global Environment (CSERGE, 1993), *Externalities from Landfill and Incineration*, Department of the Environment, London: HMSO.

Clarkson, R., and Deyes, K. (2002), *Estimating the Social Cost of Carbon Emissions*. GES Working Paper 140. London: HM Treasury.

Cohen, M. (1999), 'Monitoring and Enforcement of Environmental Policy', in Tietenberg, T. and Folmer, H. (eds.), *International Yearbook of Environmental and Resource Economics 1999/2000*, Cheltenham: Edward Elgar.

Commission of the European Communities (1991), *A Community Strategy to Limit Carbon Dioxide Emissions and to Improve Energy Efficiency*, Communication from the Commission to the Council SEC(91)1744, 14 October 1991, Brussels.

Convery, F., McDonnell, S., and Ferreira, S. (2007), 'The Most Popular Tax in Europe? Lessons from the Irish Plastic Bags Levy', *Environmental and Resource Economics*, **38**, 1–11.

Cornwell, A., and Creedy, J. (1996), 'Carbon Taxation, Prices and Inequality in Australia', *Fiscal Studies*, **17**, 21–38.

Cramton, P., and Kerr, S. (2002), 'Tradable Carbon Permit Auctions: How and Why to Auction not Grandfather', *Energy Policy*, **30**, 333–45.

Cremer, H., and Gahvari, F. (2002), 'Imperfect Observability of Emissions and Second-best Emission and Output Taxes', *Journal of Public Economics*, **85**, 385–407.

Dasgupta, P. (2006), *Comments on the Stern Review's Economics of Climate Change*, mimeo, <http://www.econ.cam.ac.uk/faculty/dasgupta/STERN.pdf>.

Davies, B., and Doble, M. (2004), 'The Development and Implementation of a Landfill Tax in the UK', in OECD, *Addressing the Economics of Waste*, Paris: Organisation for Economic Cooperation and Development.

Department for Transport (2004), *Feasibility Study of Road Pricing in the UK*, London: DfT.

—— (2006), *Transport Demand to 2025 and the Economic Case for Road Pricing and Investment*, London: DfT.

Dinan, T. M. (1993), 'Economic Efficiency Effects of Alternative Policies for Reducing Waste Disposal', *Journal of Environmental Economics and Management*, **25**, 242–56.

Dresner, S., and Ekins, P. (2006), 'Economic Instruments to Improve UK Home Energy Efficiency Without Negative Social Impacts', *Fiscal Studies*, **27**, 47–74.

ECON Analyse (2005), *The Political Economy of the Norwegian Aviation Fuel Tax*, Paris: OECD.

Eddington, R. (2006), *The Eddington Transport Study*, London: DfT.

Etheridge, B., and Leicester, A. (2007), 'Environmental Taxation', in Chote, R., Emmerson, C., Leicester, A., and Miles, D. (eds.), *The IFS Green Budget*, London: IFS.

Fischer, C., Parry, I., and Pizer, W. (2003), 'Instrument Choice for Environmental Protection when Technological Innovation is Endogenous', *Journal of Environmental Economics and Management*, **45**, 523–45.

Fullerton, D. (2001), 'A Framework to Compare Environmental Policies', *Southern Economic Journal*, **68**, 224–48.

—— and Kinnaman, T. C. (1995), 'Garbage, Recycling, and Illicit Burning or Dumping', *Journal of Environmental Economics and Management*, **29**, 78–91.

—— —— (1996), 'Household Responses to Pricing Garbage by the Bag', *American Economic Review*, **86**, 971–84.

—— and Metcalf, G. E. (2001), 'Environmental Controls, Scarcity Rents, and Pre-existing Distortions', *Journal of Public Economics*, **80**, 249–67.

—— and West, S. (2000), *Tax and Subsidy Combinations for the Control of Vehicle Pollution*, NBER Working Paper No. 7774, Cambridge, MA.: NBER.

—— —— (2002), 'Can Taxes on Vehicles and on Gasoline Mimic an Unavailable Tax on Emissions?', *Journal of Environmental Economics and Management*, **43**, 135–57.

—— and Wolverton, A. (1999), 'The Case for a Two-part Instrument: Presumptive Tax and Environmental Subsidy', in Panagariya, A., Portney, P., and Schwab, R. (eds.), *Environmental and Public Economics: Essays in Honor of Wallace E. Oates*, Cheltenham: Edward Elgar.

—— and Wu, W. (1998), 'Policies for green design', *Journal of Environmental Economics and Management*, **36**, 131–48.

Gillen, D. W., Morrison, W. G., and Stewart, C. (2004), *Air Travel Demand Elasticities: Concepts, Issues and Measurement*, Ottawa: Canadian Department of Finance.

Goulder, L. H. (1995), 'Environmental Taxation and the Double Dividend: A Reader's Guide', *International Tax and Public Finance*, **2**, 157–83.

—— Parry, I. W. H., and Burtraw, D. (1997), 'Revenue-raising versus Other Approaches to Environmental Protection: The Critical Significance of Preexisting Tax Distortions', *RAND Journal of Economics*, **28**, 708–31.

Green, J., and Sheshinski, E. (1976), 'Direct Versus Indirect Remedies for Externalities', *Journal of Political Economy*, **84**, 797–808.

Grubb, M., Azar, C., et al. (2005), 'Allowance Allocation in the European Emissions Trading System: A Commentary', *Climate Policy*, **5**, 127–36.

—— and Neuhoff, K. (2006), 'Allocation and Competitiveness in the EU Emissions Trading Scheme: Policy Overview', Cambridge Working Papers in Economics 0645, Faculty of Economics, University of Cambridge.

Hammar, H., and Löfgren, Å. (2004), 'Leaded Gasoline in Europe: Differences in Timing and Taxes', in *Choosing Environmental Policy—Comparing Instruments and Outcomes in the United States and Europe*, Washington, DC: Resources for the Future.

Harrington, W., and McConnell, V. (2003), 'Motor Vehicles and the Environment', in Folmer, H., and Tietenberg, T. (eds.), *The International Yearbook of Environmental and Resource Economics 2003/2004*, Northampton, MA: Edward Elgar.

Helfand, G., Berck, P., and Maull, T. (2003), 'The Theory of Pollution Policy', in Mäler, K.-G., and Vincent, J. R. (eds.), *Handbook of Environmental Economics*, **1**, Amsterdam: North Holland Elsevier.

Helm, D., Hepburn, C., and Mash, R. (2005), 'Credible Carbon Policy', in Helm, D., (ed.), *Climate Change Policy*, Oxford: Oxford University Press.

Hepburn, C., Grubb, M., Neuhoff, K., Matthes, F., and Tse, M. (2006), 'Auctioning of EU ETS Phase II Allowances: How and Why?', *Climate Policy*, **6**, 137–60.

HM Customs and Excise (1998), *Review of the Landfill Tax: Report*, Newcastle: HM Customs and Excise.

Hoel, M. (1996), 'Should a Carbon Tax be Differentiated Across Sectors?', *Journal of Public Economics*, **59**, 17–32.

Hong, S., and Adams, R. M. (1999), 'Household Responses to Price Incentives for Recycling: Some Further Evidence', *Land Economics*, **75**, 505–14.

—— —— and Love, H. A. (1993), 'An Economic Analysis of Household Recycling of Solid Wastes: The Case of Portland, Oregon', *Journal of Environmental Economics and Management*, **25**, 136–46.

Intergovernmental Panel on Climate Change (IPCC, 2005), *Carbon Dioxide Capture and Storage*, New York: Cambridge University Press.

International Civil Aviation Organisation (ICAO, 2006), *Convention on International Civil Aviation, Ninth Edition*, <http://www.icao.int/icaonet/arch/doc/7300/7300_9ed.pdf>.

International Solid Waste Association (ISWA, 2002), 'Fly-tipping Increases with Weight-based Charging', *Waste Management World*, 2 (March–April).

Jenkins, R. (1993), *The Economics of Solid Waste Reduction*, Hants: Edward Elgar Publishing Limited.

—— Martinez, S. A., Palmer, K., and Podolsky, M. (2003), 'The Determinants of Household Recycling: A Material Specific Analysis of Unit Pricing and Recycling Program Attributes', *Journal of Environmental Economics and Management*, **45**, 294–318.

Johnston, A. (2006), 'Free Allocation of Allowances under the EU Emissions Trading Scheme: Legal Issues', *Climate Policy*, **6**, 115–36.

Keen, M., and Strand, J. (2007), 'Indirect Taxes on International Aviation', *Fiscal Studies*, **28**, 1–41.

Kinnaman, T. C., and Fullerton, D. (2000), 'Garbage and Recycling with Endogenous Local Policy', *Journal of Urban Economics*, **48**, 419–42.

Leicester, A. (2006), *The UK Tax System and the Environment*, IFS Report Series 68, London: IFS.

—— and O'Dea, C. (2008), 'Aviation Taxes', in Chote, R., Emmerson, C., Miles, D., and Shaw, J. (eds.), *IFS Green Budget 2008*, IFS Commentary 104, London: IFS, <http://www.ifs.org.uk/budgets/gb2008/08chap9.pdf>.

Magat, W., and Viscusi, K. (1990), 'Effectiveness of the EPA's Regulatory Enforcement: The Case of Industrial Effluent Standards', *Journal of Law and Economics*, **33**, 331–60.

Marshall, Report (1998), *Economic Instruments and the Business Use of Energy, a Report by Lord Marshall*, London: HM Treasury.

Metcalf, G. E. (1999), 'A Distributional Analysis of Green Tax Reforms', *National Tax Journal*, **52**, 655–81.

Millock, K., and Sterner, T. (2004), 'NOx Emissions in France and Sweden: Advanced Fee Schemes versus Regulation', in *Choosing Environmental Policy—Comparing Instruments and Outcomes in the United States and Europe*, Washington, DC: Resources for the Future.

Miranda, M. L., and Bynum, D. Z. (1999), *Unit Based Pricing in the United States: A Tally of Communities*, Submitted to the US EPA, <http://www.epa.gov/payt/pdf/jan99sum.pdf>.

—— Everett, J. W., Blume, D. I., and Roy, B. A. Jr. (1994), 'Market-based Incentives and Residential Municipal Solid Waste', *Journal of Policy Analysis and Management*, **13**, 681–98.

Nash, C., Mackie, P., Shires, J., and Nellthorp, J. (2004), *The Economic Efficiency Case for Road User Charging*, University of Leeds: Institute for Transport Studies.

Newbery, D. M. (1990), 'Pricing and Congestion: Economic Principles Relevant to Pricing Roads', *Oxford Review of Economic Policy*, **6**, 22–38.

Newell, R. G., and Stavins, R. N. (2003), 'Cost Heterogeneity and the Potential Savings from Market-based Policies', *Journal of Regulatory Economics*, **23**, 43–59.

Nordhaus, W. D. (2007), *The* Stern Review *on the Economics of Climate Change*, mimeo, <http://nordhaus.econ.yale.edu/stern_050307.pdf>.

Oates, W. E. (1991), 'Pollution Charges as a Source of Public Revenues', University of Maryland, Department of Economics Working Paper No. 91-22.

OECD (1993), *Taxation and the Environment: Complementary Policies*, Paris: OECD.

—— (1996), *Implementation Strategies for Environmental Taxes*, Paris: OECD.

—— (1998), *Extended Producer Responsibility: Case Study on the German Packing Ordinance*, Paris: OECD.

—— (2006), *The Political Economy of Environmentally Related Taxes*, Paris: OECD.

Opschoor, J. B., and Vos, H. B. (1989), *Economic Instruments for Environmental Protection*, Paris: OECD.

Palmer, K., Sigman, H., and Walls, M. (1997), 'The Cost of Reducing Municipal Solid Waste', *Journal of Environmental Economics and Management*, **33**, 128–50.

—— and Walls, M. (1997), 'Optimal Policies for Solid Waste Disposal: Taxes, Subsidies, and Standards', *Journal of Public Economics*, **65**, 193–205.

Parry, I. (1995), 'Pollution taxes and revenue recycling', *Journal of Environmental Economics and Management*, **29**, S64–S77.

—— and Small, K. (2005), 'Does Britain or the United States Have the Right Gasoline Tax?' *American Economic Review*, **95**, 1276–89.

Pearce, B., and Pearce, D. (2000), 'Setting Environmental Taxes for Aircraft: A Case Study of the UK', CSERGE Working Paper GEC 2000-26.

Pearce, D. (1991), 'The Role of Carbon Taxes in Adjusting to Global Warming', *The Economic Journal*, **101**, 938–48.

Pearce, D. W. (2005), 'The Social Cost of Carbon', in Helm, D. (ed.), *Climate-Change Policy*, Oxford: Oxford University Press.

Pearson, M., and Smith, S. (1991), *The European Carbon Tax: An Assessment of the European Commission's Proposals*, IFS Report Series 39, London: IFS.

Penner, J. E., Lister, D. H., Griggs, D. J., Dokken, D. J., and McFarland, M. (1999), *Aviation and the Global Atmosphere—a Special Report of IPCC Working Groups I and III*, Cambridge: Cambridge University Press.

Pigou, A. C. (1920), *The Economics of Welfare*, London: Macmillan.

Pizer, W. A. (2002), 'Combining Price and Quantity Controls to Mitigate Global Climate Change', *Journal of Public Economics*, **85**, 409–34.

Podolsky, M. J., and Spiegel, M. (1998), 'Municipal Waste Disposal: Unit-Pricing and Recycling Opportunities', *Public Works Management and Policy*, **3**, 27–39.

Polinsky, A. M., and Shavell, S. (1982), 'Pigouvian Taxation with Administrative Costs', *Journal of Public Economics*, **19**, 385–94.

Poterba, J. M. (1991), 'Tax Policy to Combat Global Warming: On Designing a Carbon Tax', in Dornbusch, R., and Poterba, J. M. (eds.), *Global Warming: Economic Policy Responses*, Cambridge, MA.: The MIT Press.

—— and Rotemberg, J. J. (1995), 'Environmental Taxes on Intermediate and Final Goods When Both can be Imported', *International Tax and Public Finance*, **2**, 221–8.

Quality of Urban Air Review Group (1993), *Diesel Vehicle Emissions and Urban Air Quality*, London: Department of the Environment.

Repetto, R., Dower, R. C., Jenkins, R., and Geoghegan, J. (1992), *Green Fees: How a Tax Shift Can Work for the Environment and the Economy*, Washington, DC: The World Resources Institute.

Reschovsky, J. D., and Stone, S. E. (1994), 'Market Incentives to Encourage Household Waste Recycling: Paying for What you Throw Away', *Journal of Policy Analysis and Management*, **13**, 120–39.

Roberts, M. J., and Spence, M. (1976), 'Effluent Charges and Licenses under Uncertainty', *Journal of Public Economics*, **5**, 193–208.

Salmons, R. (2002), 'New Areas for Application of Tradable Permits—Solid Waste Management', in OECD, *Implementing Domestic Tradable Permits: Recent Developments and Future Challenges*, Paris: OECD.

Sandmo, A. (1976), 'Direct versus Indirect Pigouvian Taxation', *European Economic Review*, **7**, 337–49.

Sansom, T., Nash, C. A., Mackie, P. J., Shires, J., and Watkiss, P. (2001), *Surface Transport Costs and Charges—Great Britain 1998*, University of Leeds: Institute for Transport Studies.

Santos, G., and Fraser, F. (2006), 'Road Pricing: Lessons from London', *Economic Policy*, **21**, 263–310.

Sausan, R., Isaksen, I., Grewe, V., Hauglustaine, D., Lee, D. S., Myhre, G., Köhler, M. O., Pitari, G., Schumann, U., Stordal, F., and Zerefos, C. (2005), 'Aviation Radiative Forcing in 2000: An Update on IPCC (1999)', *Meteorologische Zeitschrift*, **14**, 555–61.

Sinclair, P. (1992), 'High Does Nothing and Rising is Worse: Carbon Taxes Should Keep Declining to cut Harmful Emissions', *The Manchester School*, **60**, 41–52.

Sinn, H.-W. (2007), *Public Policies Against Global Warming*, CESifo Working Paper 2087, Munich: CESifo.

Smith, S. (1992), 'The Distributional Consequences of Taxes on Energy and the Carbon Content of Fuels', *European Economy*, Special Edition No 1/1992 (*The Economics of Limiting CO_2 Emissions*), 241–68.

Society for Motor Manufacturers and Traders (2007), *SMMT Annual CO2 Report, 2006 Market*, <http://smmtlib.findlay.co.uk/articles/sharedfolder/Publications/CO2%20report3.pdf>.

Stavins, R. N. (2003), 'Experience with Market-based Environmental Policy Instruments', in Mäler, K.-G., and Vincent, J. R. (eds.), *Handbook of Environmental Economics*, **1**, Amsterdam: North Holland Elsevier.

——(2005), *Vintage Differentiated Environmental Regulation*, Resources for the Future Discussion Paper 05–59.

Stern, N. (2006), *The Economics of Climate Change*, London: HM Treasury.

Symons, E., Proops, J., and Gay, P. (1994), 'Carbon Taxes, Consumer Demand and Carbon Dioxide Emissions: A Simulation Analysis for the UK', Fiscal Studies, Institute for Fiscal Studies, **15**, 19–43.

Tietenberg, T. H. (1991), 'Economic Instruments for Environmental Regulation', in Helm, D. (ed.), *Economic Policy Towards the Environment*, 86–111, Oxford: Basil Blackwell.

Transport for London (2007), *Central London Congestion Charging: Impacts Monitoring—Fifth Annual Report*, London: TfL.

US General Accounting Office (1990), *Improvements Needed in Detecting and Preventing Violations*, Washington, DC: US GAO.

Van Houtven, G. L., and Morris, G. E. (1999), 'Household Behavior Under Alternative Pay-as-you-throw Systems for Solid Waste Disposal', *Land Economics*, **75**, 515–37.

Weitzman, M. L. (1974), 'Prices versus Quantities', *Review of Economic Studies*, **41**, 477–91.

West, S. (2004), 'Distributional Effects of Alternative Vehicle Pollution Control Policies', *Journal of Public Economics*, **88**, 735–57.

Wijkander, H. (1985), 'Correcting Externalities Through Taxes on subsidies to Related Goods', *Journal of Public Economics*, **28**, 111–25.

Commentary by Paul Johnson and Nick Stern

Paul Johnson is a Research Fellow at the IFS and an Associate of Frontier Economics. From 2004 to 2007 he was Director of the Public Services and Growth Directorate and Chief Microeconomist at HM Treasury, as well as Deputy Head of the Government Economic Service. He previously worked in senior posts at the Department for Education and Skills and the Financial Services Authority. Until 1998 he was a full-time researcher at the IFS, eventually taking on the roles of Deputy Director and Head of the Personal Sector Research Programme.

Lord (Nicholas) Stern is I. G. Patel Chair at the LSE, a Fellow of the British Academy and of the Econometric Society, an Honorary Fellow of the American Academy of Arts and Sciences, and President of the European Economic Association. His research and publications have focused on the economics of climate change, economic development and growth, economic theory, tax reform, public policy and the role of the state, and economies in transition. Among his many economic policy appointments have been those of Chief Economist and Senior Vice President at the World Bank, Second Permanent Secretary to HM Treasury and Head of the Government Economic Service. He headed the *Stern Review on the Economics of Climate Change*, published in 2006. He was knighted for services to economics in 2004, elevated to the peerage in 2007 and sits as a cross-bencher in the House of Lords.

Fullerton, Leicester, and Smith's chapter (henceforth FLS) offers an excellent survey of the theory and practice of environmental taxation. Our purpose in this commentary is not to review either the chapter as a whole or the subject matter as a whole. Rather, it is to expand upon their treatment of climate change.

Responding appropriately to the problem posed by climate change is among the greatest challenges facing policy makers in the UK and internationally. It is important that the response is designed with a clear understanding of the economics. An effective response will require both extremely careful economic analysis and appropriate use of instruments, and very substantial use of the instruments on a global, or near global, scale.

We aim to add to the FLS analysis by taking a slightly different approach to the problem. We hope thereby to complement their analysis without repeating the main elements of it. Our strategy in outlining our view on the role of taxation in dealing with climate change is to start by very briefly reviewing the science, and then the basic economics, demonstrating the unprecedented nature of the climate change problem and the way in which the nature of that problem impacts on the solutions we should be considering. In our view this provides a strong basis on which to conclude that significant action is required. It also provides some strong indication of the economic instruments that are most likely to be effective, in particular given the global and long-term nature of the problem.

The issue of risk is at the centre of our discussion. The scale of the potential problems created by climate change is very large, and the risks associated with atmospheric concentrations of greenhouse gas (GHG) rising above any specified level are both hard to know and potentially very big indeed. Indeed, recent developments both in science and in economics suggest that the scale of these risks and their importance is even bigger than was appreciated at the time the Stern Review was written. This drives us towards conclusions which put mechanisms that limit quantities of emissions at the centre of the policy framework.

We go on to consider some of the options open to the UK and draw some conclusions about the role of pricing generally and of taxation in particular. Pricing the externality imposed by emissions of greenhouse gases is going to be a crucial part of the policy solution, but not the only one. Intelligent regulation and support for technology will also be vitally important. So far as pricing is concerned it is likely to be the case that UK participation in the EU Emissions Trading Scheme (ETS) will be the most effective method for pricing carbon in the UK in the near future. Hence, the role of taxation in the UK response to climate change may be limited to those sectors excluded from the EU ETS. Road transport is the largest such sector and is already subject to very substantial tax levels. So, overall, an *additional* role for the tax system specifically may be quite limited. We stress that this is not necessarily a conclusion that will stand true in all countries where there are particular barriers to trading schemes, nor will it remain true in the UK if the EU ETS does not develop as we hope it will.

1. CLIMATE CHANGE

Before starting on the economics and the policy implications of global warming, it is important to get some of the key scientific issues in perspective.

The economics flows from the science. The four key points about climate change are that:

1. It is global in its origins and effects.
2. It is highly non-marginal (the potential impacts are very big indeed).
3. Risk and uncertainty are pervasive.
4. It is very long term and increases in the flow of greenhouse gases into the atmosphere (near enough) permanently increase the atmospheric stock.

First, and most obviously, this is a global problem. It is global because it matters not a whit where GHGs are emitted—the impact of a tonne of CO_2 emitted in London is the same as that of a tonne emitted in Beijing, Sydney, or Buenos Aires. It is also global because the impacts of climate change will be felt across the globe—differentially to be sure, but globally nonetheless.

Second at plausible, indeed likely, levels of future GHG concentrations and temperature rises, impacts on geography, environment, and therefore economy and social structure of the world are potentially huge. The 2007 Intergovernmental Panel on Climate Change (IPCC) makes this very clear.

The actual scale of climate change, though, is uncertain. Table 1 (using fairly conservative estimates of probabilities from the Hadley Centre) illustrates this uncertainty showing the probabilities of particular temperature increases associated with different greenhouse gas concentrations. Temperature increases of 5 °C, which would be as likely as not with concentrations at 750ppm CO_2e, would be world changing. As Stern (2008) puts it 'the last time temperature was in the region of 5 °C above pre-industrial times was in the Eocene period around 35–55 million years ago. Swampy forests covered much of the world and there were alligators near the North Pole.' We are dealing with the possibility of change on a scale that economists rarely, if ever, have to consider.

Table 1. Likelihood in percent of exceeding a temperature increase at equilibrium

Stabilization level (in ppm CO_2e)	2 °C	3 °C	4 °C	5 °C	6 °C	7 °C
450	78	18	3	1	0	0
500	96	44	11	3	1	0
550	99	69	24	7	2	1
650	100	94	58	24	9	4
750	100	99	82	47	22	9

Concentrations in 2006 were around 430 ppm and are rising at around 2.5 ppm p.a. Given the rapid growth of China, among others, that rate of growth will soon rise above 3 ppm. So, on business as usual, we really could expect to be reaching 750 ppm CO_2e by the end of the current century.

Beyond the uncertainty over the impacts of GHG concentrations on temperature rises there is also uncertainty over the impact of temperature change on a whole range of physical phenomena on which we depend—from the frequency and violence of extreme weather events to the monsoon in Asia and the strength of the North Atlantic thermohaline circulation. And then the actual impact on both natural ecosystems and human society and economy, whilst increasingly well understood, is still subject to much uncertainty.

In addition, it is the stock of GHGs in the atmosphere that matters and once a certain stock level is reached it is, with current and prospective scientific knowledge at least, close to irreversible. In other words, once we reach a certain level of GHG concentration in the atmosphere we will have to live with that level for some time.

2. FROM SCIENCE TO ECONOMICS

From this simple description of the science flows a great deal of economics. First there is the global nature of the problem. The UK emits only about 2% of global annual emissions of GHGs. Any policy action by the UK needs to be seen in a global context. Any analysis of the appropriate policy instruments needs to take account of this. An efficient policy response requires, as near as possible, a global carbon price. There is little point in any one country acting alone.

Importantly there are also major equity considerations. It is both the case that rich countries have created most of the stock of GHGs in the atmosphere, and that poor countries will be hit first and hardest by climate change because of their geography, their low incomes, and their greater reliance on climate sensitive sectors like agriculture. As all international negotiations on these issues make clear, there will be no progress unless these, and other, equity considerations are given full weight. A response to climate change will need to be one in which, through one mechanism or another, developed countries find ways to provide financial support to developing countries.

The economics also needs to address the facts of the non-marginality of the impacts and the associated risks and uncertainties. It is here that the simple-minded approach to pricing for externalities fails us. With uncertainty a price-based policy might involve substantial risks of high emissions. The potential dangers from high emissions are on a scale that requires policies that focus on these risks and thus lead to quantity targets for emissions. We must, of course, check both on the overall costs of implementing such targets in relation to overall benefits in terms of damages avoided and on the marginal costs in relation to marginal benefits. There are, however, great difficulties in calculating the marginal benefits, or social costs of carbon (see below).

This argument on major risks illustrates the importance of the non-marginality of the challenge. Many of the tools of economics, including those usually applied to cost–benefit analysis, have been developed to deal with informing choices over projects or programmes which, in the scheme of things, will have only marginal impacts on overall economic welfare. The choice over whether or not to deal with climate change will have huge effects on welfare of future generations.

Indeed, one issue that the FLS touch on (as have others) is the appropriate weight to attach to future generations. The fact that most of the costs of climate change will be felt by generations yet to come has led some commentators to suggest that action now is hard to justify. There are two possible reasons for believing this to be the case.

The first is just that these are future generations and that their welfare should be of relatively little concern to us. That is the implication of a high pure rate of time preference. If we don't care much about future generations then we won't be willing to do much to protect them from climate change or anything else. If we don't care about the future the problem just disappears. But this hardly seems a sensible basis on which to make policy. It is hard to understand the ethical judgement here—discriminating against someone on the basis of their date of birth does not look attractive.

The second is that since we are poorer than future generations are likely to be, it is inequitable for this generation to spend money on improving the welfare of future generations. This argument might have some force. The conclusions reached in the Stern Review were based on the assumption that the elasticity of the marginal utility of consumption is one. That itself implies a significant ethical judgement in favour of equity—it would imply that we would be happy to transfer income from someone with income of 100 to someone with income of 20, even if 80% of the transfer were 'lost' along the way. Atkinson and Brandolini (2007) point out that most policy, particularly as it affects intra-temporal redistribution, appears to be made on significantly less egalitarian presumptions than that. The argument of Nordhaus (2007), for example, that a much greater egalitarianism is appropriate seems to sit oddly with both observed policy and most intuition. In any case somewhat higher values do not change the conclusion that the discounted benefits of action greatly outweigh the costs. It is additionally important to note that severe climate change could in any case have such an impact that future generations will not be as much better off than us as might otherwise be supposed. We should, of course, note that there will always be pure time discount rates which result in dismissing any future set of damages as negligible.

The fact that the risks and uncertainties associated with different levels of GHG concentrations are substantial is also a reason for action rather than inaction. In the first place the consequences of higher temperature increases than the mean expectation are much more than proportional to the additional increase in temperature. Second, under these circumstances the incomes and welfare of future generations will be lower. In a series of recent papers (Weitzman (2007a, 2007b)) Weitzman has argued that there is a strong case for attaching a lot of weight to the possible extreme outcomes, underlining the centrality of risk in dealing with the economics of climate change.

Importantly, there is also an asymmetry because of the effective irreversibility of GHG levels. If it turns out in the future that the consequences of higher GHG concentration levels are greater than we currently believe we are still stuck with whatever GHG concentration we have at that moment. And a sharp increase in abatement efforts later in response to new information will itself be expensive. On the other hand, if it turns out that the consequences of climate change are less dramatic than we currently believe then it is easy to move on to a less ambitious abatement path. To stabilize at 450 ppm now will be really quite expensive. If we do nothing for twenty years it will by then be very expensive to stabilize at 550 ppm. The Stern Review estimated that, starting now, it would be possible to stabilize below 550 ppm at a cost of 1% of global GDP p.a.

We go through these issues, and we could have developed them further and addressed other issues, because it is important to understand that a reasonable interpretation of the evidence on likely climate change and its likely effects, alongside fairly conservative assumptions regarding how to take account of costs and intergenerational equity, lead to strong conclusions regarding the need to act. In our view it is not the case that the balance of evidence should lead one to take the view that the need for action is uncertain or should be delayed or can be started very gradually. There is a need for swift application of significant economic tools. The issue then becomes which tools, applied how, and in what global context.

3. CHOICE OF MECHANISM

This commentary appears in a volume about tax, yet we have dwelt so far on some basic science and some basic economics regarding the need to respond to climate change. The reason for that is in part to be clear that this does lead to a strong and convincing case for action and in part because the choice of mechanism to deal with climate change depends to a large extent on the basic science and economics.

3.1. Price mechanisms—taxes and trading

The natural starting point is that we are dealing with an externality, and that we would like to internalize that externality by reflecting it in the prices that people and firms face. If we estimate a social cost or shadow price of carbon then we should ensure that that cost is faced by those who emit carbon. We come back to the issue of how to put a price on carbon below.

There are different mechanisms for ensuring this cost is internalized. The obvious alternatives are straight price mechanisms like taxes, and quantity based mechanisms including tradable permits. The standard analysis shows that prices are preferable where the benefits of reductions change less with the level of pollution than do the costs of delivering the reductions. Conversely quantity mechanisms are preferable where benefits of further reductions increase more with the level of pollution than do costs of delivering reductions; in other words, there are large and sharply rising costs associated with a given level of pollution.

This might lead us to prefer taxes in the short run because short-run costs of adjustment might be high and benefits of emission reduction relatively low. And it might point to quantity constrained trading schemes in the longer run as long-run abatement costs are lower and the costs of inadequate total reductions are high.

For an individual country facing an externality this might be a good blueprint for policy. But as we have seen there are many issues specific to climate change, which make it rather different from most externalities. First, as we have discussed, the risks associated with inadequate emission reductions are very significant. Important also is the international nature of the problem and considerations of equity between developed and developing countries. In our view, these create a strong presumption in favour of carbon trading as a primary policy response at an international level. Empirically it seems more likely that international agreements on trading can be reached than international agreement on taxes. There already exists the EU Emissions Trading Scheme, the biggest carbon trading market in the world at present, which has created an active international carbon market within the EU. Active trading schemes also exist, or are being developed, in California, north-eastern states of the USA, and Australia.

Additionally, carbon trading allows significant flows of *private* resources from developed to developing countries. The most important such mechanism at present is the Clean Development Mechanism (CDM), a project-based mechanism created by the Kyoto protocol which allows rich countries to use credits from investments in emissions reductions in poor countries to offset against their own emission reduction commitments. This mechanism as it currently stands is not without significant problems, but it is clear to us that some such mechanism is highly likely to play a key role in global climate policy. It is most readily part of a trading system.

An additional issue that needs to be borne in mind in this context is the fact that CO_2 is produced by burning fossil fuels. Fossil fuels are finite resources and their owners have a choice over if and when to extract them. In the absence of a global cap on emissions, and an expectation that policy will lead to taxes rising over time, there is a risk that the resource owners will respond to a pricing policy designed to limit emissions by raising production and cutting prices in the short run, thereby increasing global emissions.[1] This underlines the need for *global* cap and trading systems to be introduced as soon as possible.

This is not to say that trading schemes are unproblematic either in principle or in practice. To be effective a trading scheme needs to be:

- Credible—if it is deemed likely that direction of policy will change, firms will not invest in the necessary infrastructure.
- Flexible—if the science changes, there must be room to adjust the policy.
- Predictable—the policy framework must allow firms to understand quite clearly when and why policy might change.

If the policy direction is unclear then firms may, rationally, decide on a 'wait and see' approach and delay investment decisions. In the case of power generators, major players in production of CO_2, this can itself create serious security of supply issues. In addition to being credible, flexible, and predictable, trading schemes also need to be deep, liquid, and well designed. Deep in the sense of covering as great a portion of carbon emissions as possible; liquid in that a real shortage needs to be created in the market such that trading

[1] See Sinn (2007) for example.

occurs at prices that are significantly positive and not overly volatile; and well designed in the sense of not creating perverse incentives or market distortions in the way permits are allocated.

Nobody would claim that the first phase of the EU Emissions Trading Scheme met these criteria. Real shortages were not created, allocations were not transparent in the sense that it was not immediately clear that there was no shortage in the market and hence prices were very volatile, settling at a very low level. Crucially, in its own terms, and also by comparison with a tax system, allocations were 'grandfathered' rather than auctioned. In other words, emitting firms were simply given permits on the basis of expected future emissions. As FLS demonstrate quite comprehensively, this is a highly sub-optimal allocation policy.

Since the permits had significant economic value, grandfathering amounted to providing a considerable subsidy to incumbents and, because the marginal cost of power generation was increased by the trading system, in many energy markets prices rose such as to earn 'windfall' or super-normal profits for electricity producers.

Giving away permits also creates a very clear disadvantage for a trading system by comparison to tax—no money is raised for the government.

The important point, however, is that none of these aspects of a trading system is inevitable. Indeed, the EU has clearly learnt from the first phase, has tightened up allocations in the second phase, and has recently indicated a desire to move to 100% auctioning of allowances in the third phase.

3.2. The price level

Whether one uses taxes or trading to set a price on emissions the question, of course, arises of what the appropriate price should be. The way to answer that derives from some of the economics set out earlier in this commentary.

In many circumstances one would look at the marginal cost associated with an additional unit of emission and set the price that needs to be internalized accordingly. The marginal cost in this context is the Social Cost of Carbon (SCC). The SCC measures the full global cost today of an incremental unit of carbon (or other equivalent greenhouse gas) emitted now, summing the full global cost of the damage it imposes over the time it spends in the atmosphere. Obviously the calculation of the SCC will depend on expected damages, discount rates, and so on discussed above.

Using the SCC as a guide to policy is very problematic. Its level depends on a huge array of assumptions concerning model structures over the indefinite future and the value judgements applied. In particular, the SCC itself depends on the future emissions path and long-run stabilization level. Because an extra unit of carbon in the atmosphere does more damage the more GHGs there are in the long run, the SCC associated with a path towards an expected stabilization of 450 ppm CO_2(e) is likely to be considerably less than that associated with a path towards a higher stabilization target of, say, 550 ppm. The SCC associated with a particular path towards stabilization target does not necessarily tell us what price to use: not only do we have to take risk into account, including policy risk in the future, there are all the usual problems of income distribution, market imperfections, and the interactions with other policies.

If we are working in a world with a stabilization target, the appropriate information to use in determining what the appropriate price of carbon should be is the abatement cost associated with the marginal policy required to achieve that change. Enkvist et al. (2007) estimate that 'it would be technically possible to capture 26.7 gigatons of abatement by addressing only measures costing no more than 40 euros a ton'. Stern estimates that by 2030 cuts would need to be in the order of 20 Gt CO_2e for stabilization at 550 ppm, suggesting a CO_2 price of around 30 euros a tonne of CO_2 (or around £80 per tonne of carbon).

This is within the range of the SCC calculated for a 550 ppm stabilization target and seems to us to give a reasonable sense of the appropriate value to use for policy and as such a reasonable price to aim for in a tax or trading system, particularly for tax and trading systems focused on the production side. The approach we are suggesting here has the following logical structure: (1) examine target emission reductions in relation to risk, with an eye on costs of achieving them; (2) infer the related marginal abatement costs (MAC); (3) check these against a relevant range of SCC calculations; (4) check total costs against total benefits; (5) iterate as necessary. This is likely to be a much more transparent and robust process than starting with an SCC with all its attendant problems of calculation. The approach suggested is founded clearly both in the basic scientific and risk structure of the process and in the relevant economics of risk and of public policy.

3.3. Mechanisms other than prices

We have focused so far on the central role of the price mechanism—whether through taxes or trading—as a response to climate change. In the face of an externality this is, for very good reasons, the economist's first port of call. It is, however, worth stressing that we do not believe that the price mechanism is the only available tool, nor indeed is it the only tool that should be used.

A carbon price will, for example, incentivize energy producers to swap from more to less carbon intensive forms of electricity generation if the price is high enough to make the less carbon intensive generation worthwhile. However, it is highly unlikely that a carbon price at a plausible level will be enough to accelerate technological change at a rate which will generate sufficient reduction in emissions. There are in any case significant market failures in the innovation process partly as a result of the public good nature of the benefits and partly because high costs of development with uncertain pay-offs a long time in the future might make the private sector unwilling to take the risk. In addition, in this case there are long-term social returns from innovation which private firms will not take into account in making decisions. There are particular issues in the power generation sector—length of learning process, infrastructure inflexibility, existing market distortions, and low levels of competition—which seem to make returns to, and levels of, R&D low.

Without significant changes in the way that electricity is generated (and in the longer run, in how cars are powered) CO_2 emissions will not fall at anything like the rate required to avoid dangerous climate change. Not least this reflects the availability of large quantities of coal which will be burnt in the developing world if not in the developed world. So, some form of public support for, for example, both research and demonstration of carbon capture and storage technology will be vital.

In different ways non-price instruments are likely to be needed to affect the behaviour of individuals. Energy conservation is an excellent example of an area in which individuals appear to be markedly reluctant to take advantage of clear incentives to reduce energy consumption, and thus expenditure, through straightforward measures like insulation, use of low-energy light bulbs, and purchase of energy efficient goods. This reflects a number of problems including inadequate information, difficulty of monitoring energy consumption, transaction or 'hassle' costs of taking action, possibly lack of access to capital and, for tenants, the lack of incentives for landlords to invest in ways which reduce their tenants' energy bills.

In respect of this set of issues again the price mechanism is unlikely to be the most effective tool. Governments have experimented with a range of measures including building and product regulations, introduction of 'smart meters', direct subsidization of insulation for poorer individuals and provision of information. Many such regulatory and other mechanisms will in fact be economically-optimal responses. Indeed, in those cases like improving energy efficiency, where there appear to be direct benefits to the consumer from acting given current prices, it is immediately clear that responses other than changing the price are likely to be optimal.

The important point about both the need for support for technology and the case for direct regulation or other measures aimed at individuals is that we should not be seduced into believing that either tax or trading mechanisms will be anywhere close to adequate responses by themselves. There is a strong *economic* case for using a variety of instruments including direct regulation. Obviously we are not suggesting carte blanche for policy makers to impose such regulations willy-nilly; there needs to be careful analysis of the costs and benefits of different policies and the market failures they are designed to address, alongside a clear understanding of how they might fit with the central tax or trading mechanism. But the price mechanism must be seen alongside other aspects of the response to global warming, not as the only response.

The fact that multiple tools should be used, though, does create one additional and very important issue for policy makers—how should these additional tools be used and designed in such a way as to fit in with the primary cap and trade policy? This is an issue of immediate and direct relevance in the context of what policies to put alongside the EU ETS in the UK and in Europe. At the most straightforward level, because the ETS creates a cap in affected sectors for a period, additional policies covering that sector will not reduce emissions in that period, though they may still be worthwhile in minimizing costs in a dynamic sense. More complex are large-scale policies like the EU renewables target which sits alongside the trading system and is intended to create an obligation across the EU to produce at least 20% of energy from renewable sources. If implemented there is at least a risk that this will undermine the trading system and result in emissions being cut in a way that is more expensive than would have been the case had the trading system been relied upon by itself.

4. UK CONTEXT

We do not propose to go into much further detail regarding what all this means for the UK. But three points are worth developing somewhat. First, what might this mean for revenues available to the UK government? Second, we mention the role of carbon budgets. Third, we cannot avoid saying a little more about road transport since it lies outside the current trading scheme and is the source of very substantial tax revenue.

4.1. Revenues

To put the discussion of taxation into broad perspective at the UK level one can ask: what level of tax would be raised by applying a carbon tax at a particular level to UK emissions? We broadly agree with the sort of estimates made by FLS. Taking the £80 per tonne of carbon price discussed earlier, and applying a tax at that rate to the 150 million tonnes or so of annual carbon emissions in the UK would raise around £12 billion. This is not a number additional to current receipts. Indeed, it is a lot less than the £25 billion expected to be raised from taxes on hydrocarbon fuels in 2007–08 (reflecting of course the fact that the vast majority of the external costs associated with road transport are congestion costs, not costs associated with carbon emissions). A more useful calculation perhaps is to say that if permits were auctioned at this price for the roughly half of emissions that are covered by the EU ETS some £6 billion might be raised. Applying it to the full 75% or so of emissions that do not emanate from road transport raises that figure to £9 billion.

It is important to add that this ought to be thought of as being additional to extra revenue that would be raised from charging VAT at the full rate on domestic energy consumption. Relative to a neutral system in which all consumption is subject to a value added tax, the reduced rate of VAT on gas and electricity consumption is, in effect, a subsidy on their consumption. It is one of the odder elements of the tax system that it should subsidize this consumption whilst trying elsewhere to reduce energy consumption. As is discussed elsewhere in this volume other, for example distributional, objectives which government might have in mind are best achieved through other elements of the welfare system.

4.2. Carbon budgets

There are numerous other instruments currently in use, including taxes like the Climate Change Levy (and associated climate change agreements) and in addition there are proposals for a new trading system for non-energy-intensive companies—the carbon reduction commitment. We do not propose here to look at them or other elements of the UK context in greater detail. However, there is one innovation which we cannot avoid mentioning. At the time of writing the UK is embarking on a novel and ambitious experiment in policy making with regard to climate change through the introduction of five-year 'carbon budgets' on the way to targeted reductions in emissions in 2020 and 2050. Government will be advised by an independent 'Climate Change Committee' on both the eventual targets and on the path towards the target, defined by the total amount of CO_2 which can be emitted in each five-year period. Following the committee's advice the government will commit itself to particular budgets and targets that will be, in some sense, legally binding. As such the government will be creating an entirely new constraint for the economy—it will be aiming for growth, redistribution, and so on subject to the binding constraint that carbon emissions should be falling along a specified path.

As a way of creating certainty and credibility this type of commitment has some attractions—though the real certainty and credibility needed by investors in particular is around the carbon price and policy in specific sectors. A key question in this context is whether the existence of carbon budgets will alter the attractiveness of tax and trading relative to other instruments or affect the optimality of policy in other ways.

In principle setting targets or budgets should not alter the optimal policy mix. We would draw attention, however, to one potential danger with a system which sets a great deal of political credibility against meeting quite specific budgets over relatively constrained five-year periods. The short-run impacts of taxes might be rather less than their long-run impacts—the short-run price elasticity of demand for petrol, for example, is generally estimated at around −0.25 while the long-run elasticity is about −0.6.[2] This reflects the fact that consumers and manufacturers can take some time to respond to price (tax) changes through manufacture and purchase of more fuel-efficient vehicles, for example. By contrast the immediate effects of some other policies, for example some forms of direct regulation of behaviour or products, might be rather greater. The existence of short-run budgets at least has the potential to distort policy choices.

Cap and trade schemes like the EU ETS might also look more attractive than tax in the context of budgets. By setting tight caps the government can guarantee meeting targets. In principle it should use the ETS sector up to the point at which the marginal abatement costs in that sector are equal to costs elsewhere.

4.3. Road transport

As we have already suggested, and as FLS show, road transport is already very heavily taxed relative to the associated climate change externalities, though most of that tax can be justified by the scale of the congestion externality imposed by drivers. In this sector it is likely that a combination of technology

[2] Goodwin et al. (2003).

support, possible regulation and other policies aimed at changing behaviour will be more effective than further tax increases. The effectiveness of other tax changes, like increased differentiation in favour of biofuels, will depend more on the characteristics of biofuels than what we know to be the effectiveness of tax policy in supporting such behaviour change.

That said we agree strongly with FLS that there is much to be said for congestion charging in the road transport sector. Optimal pricing of congested roads will lead to significant economic efficiencies and reduced demand for road space. We would go further to say that the appropriate pricing of infrastructure in this way should have significant advantages from the point of view of the transparency of a tax system aiming to deal with multiple externalities. It is not helpful to the public debate that there is no sense of the relative importance of congestion, carbon, and other externalities in road fuel duty and certainly it is the implication of many government statements that it is the carbon/pollution externality that is the main determinant of duty levels.

If we are to aspire to a world in which carbon is consistently priced then leaving road transport out of the main pricing mechanism indefinitely is probably not the best long-run solution. It will only be possible to include it if the carbon component is separately identified and dealt with. This is an additional benefit that congestion pricing would facilitate.

5. CONCLUSIONS

We can draw some strong conclusions from this approach. Most importantly, as many economists and policy-makers are coming to understand, the cost of action to deal with climate change is less than the cost of inaction. This view is in contrast to the conclusions drawn in many earlier studies which understated the costs of climate change partly because the science was less well developed, partly because they didn't take full account of the risks, and partly because they did not take account of the range of non-market costs which will clearly be crucial as the physical world changes in the face of climate change. Recent developments in economics and science, even since the publication of the Stern Review, push us further in this direction. In addition an appropriate weighting of future generations generates larger costs associated with inaction.

The second conclusion we draw from the way in which we apply economics to the problem is that there are very powerful reasons for relying on quantity rather than pure price mechanisms.

In the first place the risks associated with greenhouse gas concentrations rising too quickly are very great. We cannot be sure about the effects of a pricing policy (a tax). This is particularly true in a situation where energy markets are oligopolistic and in the face of the fact that we are dealing with extraction of raw materials—without a cap, expectation of rising taxes may incentivize coal and oil producers to produce and sell *more* in the short run, at a lower price. Cap and trade systems allow *quantities* to be constrained in a way which nevertheless allows decisions over how and where to cut emissions to be decentralized through the market system.

Additionally, the international nature of the problem points to cap and trade. Simple experience suggests that such schemes will be easier to introduce on a wide scale than would a large-scale international tax. And trading systems can, if appropriately designed, allow significant flows of funds towards low income countries—flows which will be crucial to get their buy in to, and participation in, a global system.

These conclusions are relevant to the global issue of how to deal with climate change. For the UK, participation in international trading schemes must be at the heart of policy. And swift movement towards auctioning of allowances must be central to that. But that does not answer all the questions about designing the response within the UK. Well-designed regulation can and should bring down costs and provide certainty. But it is crucial to do this in a way which does not undermine the main cap and trade policy and big policy innovations which will interact with the trading system, as the EU renewables targets certainly will, need to be designed with great care to avoid unintended consequences. Technology support, especially for carbon capture and storage must be part of the appropriate policy response. And even for a sector as large and important for this issue as road transport it is not obvious to us that moving it into a cap and trade system is a priority. Taxation of petrol at the point of purchase is straightforward and well established. The greater economic gains may well be accessed by moving first to a system of congestion charging which targets better the major externality associated with road travel—congestion—and associating taxation of petrol more directly with the pollution externalities.

Finally, we concur with FLS. Climate change is a big problem which requires large-scale action and the application of economic tools including taxes and auctioned allowances. But reasonable use of economic tools will not fundamentally alter the balance of taxation in the UK. There is probably not scope for raising even an additional 1% of GDP in additional taxes or auctioned allowances.

REFERENCES

Goodwin, P., Dargay, J., and Hanly, M. (2003), *Elasticities of Road Traffic and Fuel Consumption with Respect to Price and Income: A Review*, ESRC Transport Studies Unit, University College London <http://www.transport.ucl.ac.uk>, commissioned by the UK Department of the Environment, Transport and the Regions (now UK Department for Transport).

Nordhaus, W. D. (2007), *The Stern Review on the Economics of Climate Change*, mimeo, <http://nordhaus.econ.yale.edu/stern_050307.pdf>.

Sinn, H.-W. (2007), *Public Policies Against Global Warming*, National Bureau of Economic Research working paper w13454.

Stern, N. (2007), *The Economics of Climate Change: The Stern Review*, Cambridge: Cambridge University Press.

—— (2008), *The Economics of Climate Change*, Richard T. Ely lecture at American Economic Association meetings, New Orleans.

Weitzman, M. (2007a), *On Modeling and Interpreting the Economics of Catastrophic Climate Change*, mimeo, Harvard University, November.

—— (2007b), 'The Stern review of the economics of climate change', *Journal of Economic Literature*, 45, 703–24.

Commentary by Agnar Sandmo

Agnar Sandmo is emeritus Professor of Economics at the Norwegian School of Economics and Business Administration. He has carried out research on a number of issues in public economics, including analysis of both public expenditure and tax policy. Much of his work has focused on environmental policy; his book *The Public Economics of the Environment* was published by Oxford University Press in 2000. He is a former President of the European Economic Association, a Fellow of the Econometric Society, and elected member of the Norwegian and Swedish Academies of Science and of the Academia Europaea.

Taxes on activities that are harmful to the environment are different from other taxes in one very fundamental respect. Whereas most taxes lead to a less efficient allocation of resources, environmental or Pigouvian[1] taxes have the potential to make the market mechanism work *more* efficiently than would be the case in their absence. Given the environmental problems that we are currently faced with, modern discussions of tax reform therefore have to take account of Pigouvian taxes. Environmental problems move up on the list of research priorities for public finance economists at the same time as they move up on society's agenda for public policy. I will not try to sort out cause and effect here. But it is interesting to note that in 1959, when environmental issues received very little thought and attention, neither from economists nor from policy makers, Musgrave's famous treatise used only a brief paragraph to discuss Pigouvian taxes, and this, curiously, came at the end of a chapter entitled 'The ability-to-pay approach' (Musgrave (1959), pp. 114–15). There can be no doubt that the extensive work that has been carried out in this area of public finance has increased both our awareness of the importance of the environmental problems that confront us as well as our theoretical understanding of the basic issues that arise in the design of policy.

[1] Named after the great Cambridge economist Arthur C. Pigou, who was the first to discuss them in his 1920 book *The Economics of Welfare*.

This interesting and informative survey by Fullerton, Leicester, and Smith of the principles and practice of environmental taxation covers a lot of ground as regards both theory and applications. The following commentary is mostly concerned with theoretical principles. My comments take the form partly of further elaboration and interpretation of the arguments advanced by the authors, partly of points that I feel are in need of greater attention.

1. PRINCIPLES OF POLICY DESIGN

The authors do an excellent job of explaining the case for taxes as instruments of environmental policy, and their exposition should appeal both to economists and to a broader audience. I can actually claim some experience in communicating the economists' way of thinking to the general public, for I published my first article on environmental taxes (in Norwegian) in 1971, and this generated a good deal of discussion. There was, it turned out, much resistance to the idea, particularly from the business community. Some of the arguments advanced against green taxes were such that I first decided that they completely missed the point, while I later came to the conclusion that there was much to learn from them. A good example of this was the objection that this proposal was simply one more attempt by economists to invent new sources of revenue for public sector expansion.[2] This was, of course, not true—I had thought that it could be taken as understood that the size of the public sector should be treated as a separate issue—but I learnt something about the importance of making one's assumptions clear. Other sources of misunderstanding were related to basic economic concepts such as social efficiency and economic incentives. It is my definite impression that the public understanding of these issues has increased considerably during the time which has passed since then, and that it is easier to gain acceptance for the idea that the design of tax incentives is a fruitful approach to environmental policy.

In the literature on this topic a distinction is commonly drawn between so-called command-and-control policies and policies that utilize private incentives. Taxes are the prime example of the latter, but it is important to be aware, as the authors point out, that tradable quotas share many of the properties of the tax solution. Trading quotas in a competitive market will establish a quota

[2] Another reason for the resistance to taxes and the more favourable attitude towards quotas might be that quotas are likely to prevent entry and favour existing firms, a point also made by the present authors.

price which has the same properties as the Pigouvian tax. If the government sells quotas to the polluters, the two cases will be virtually identical both as environmental policies and as sources of government revenue. This equivalence should be kept in mind in reading both the chapter itself and the present commentary, but like the authors I limit my discussion to taxes, leaving the implications for tradable quotas to the reader.

The authors' list of the advantages of taxes is a comprehensive one and also contains at least one point which is usually neglected in the literature, namely the importance of translating firm level incentives into incentives directed towards individual performance; especially for large companies, this point may be of considerable importance and should receive greater attention in the literature. But one of the most general insights that emerges very clearly from the discussion is the importance of the assumption—one that is otherwise usually only made implicitly—that the individuals and firms who respond to environmental policy are what one might call 'tax takers' or, more generally, 'policy takers'.

This may be in need of some elaboration. The point of reference for theoretical discussions of environmental policy is typically the general equilibrium model of the competitive economy, where firms and consumers are 'price takers', meaning that no single agent acting on his own has the power to influence market prices. The analysis of taxes in terms of tax-inclusive prices is also based on the competitive assumption. Agents, being small in relation to the size of the market, take tax rates as beyond their control for exactly the same reason that they take prices as given. This assumption becomes a bit more troublesome when it comes to policy instruments like quotas, for quotas have to be specific for each agent or firm, and in that case it may be profitable for the agent to try to influence the size of the quota by lobbying or even corruption. This would seem to be especially likely when the private agent is a large one who could threaten the government with cutting back on employment or moving its operations abroad unless his emission quota is increased. What is true for quotas would in fact be equally true for taxes in cases where the tax base involves only one or a few agents. This could be the case where the government attempts to achieve a very specific environmental objective, such as the extent of pollution in a particular local community. There is accordingly a trade-off between the degree of targeting of the policy instruments and the extent to which one can rely on the agents to take the policy instruments as fixed by the government, which is the way that we usually model individual behaviour in a mixed economy. The use of Pigouvian taxes to control pollution can, as the authors point out, lead to a cost-efficient reduction of pollution, but this conclusion is crucially dependent on the assumption that agents take tax rates as given. It is because each agent faces the same tax rate on emissions (or factor use or output) that the marginal cost of reducing pollution ends up as being the same for all polluters.

From this point of view I am inclined to put a small question mark in the margin when, in Section 5.2.3, the authors discuss an excise tax on inputs into a polluting production process. The background for their discussion is the point that the amount of emission is the ideal tax base, but, on the other hand, it may be difficult and costly to measure. In order to overcome this problem they consider as a substitute a tax on inputs (e.g. a tax on fuel use instead of a tax on smoke emission) and conclude that 'with few producers, this tax will be comparatively cheap to operate'. If such a tax generates a significant amount of revenue and becomes an important element of cost for the few producers concerned, the likelihood seems high that the producers might join their lobbying efforts against the government in an attempt to bring the tax rate down. If that were to happen, the producers would not be 'tax takers', and haggling over the tax rate could be a costly process. Perhaps future research in environmental economics should devote more attention to this type of situation by investigating the efficiency properties of cases where policy is at least partially determined as a result of a bargaining process between the government and the polluters.

Another aspect of the need to compromise with the principle of targeting emerges in the general discussion of what should be taxed: emissions, input or output volume. The basic principle is that to achieve efficiency the tax should be levied as close as possible to the source of pollution, and this normally calls for taxing emissions. However, as the authors point out, a difficulty about a tax on emissions is that it is not based on a market transaction. The tax collector would then have to establish a relationship with each individual polluter, thereby increasing the role of individual negotiation. Moving from taxes on emissions to taxes on inputs weakens the degree of targeting of the tax system but establishes more of an arm's-length relationship between the polluter and the tax collector. Moving further to taxes on output would in general imply even weaker targeting, but could possibly be justified by the gains from 'tax taking' behaviour.[3]

The attempts by individual agents to influence statutory tax rates or quotas should be clearly distinguished from the case where taxes or quotas are in fact taken as given but where agents engage in evasion activities by

[3] The authors note this point in their discussion of geographically varying damage in Section 5.2.2, but it seems to me that the point is of much more general validity.

under-reporting emissions (or whatever quantity it is that defines the tax base or the quota). The following and somewhat surprising result has been demonstrated in the theoretical literature (e.g. Sandmo (2002)): even if the polluting firm exploits the opportunity to evade the environmental tax by under-reporting emissions, it may still equate the marginal cost of reducing pollution to the tax rate; if all polluters do this, the outcome that emerges is one where the pollution that actually occurs is, indeed, efficiently allocated among the polluters. However, the under-reporting of emissions (or the exaggerated reports of emission reductions) may lead the government to believe that the tax achieves more in the form of pollution reduction than what it really does. This may in turn lead the government to set environmental taxes at inefficiently low levels.

2. THE DOUBLE DIVIDEND

A large number of articles have been written on the subject of the double dividend. The volume and complexity of the literature can to some degree be explained by the numerous different interpretations and definitions of what the double dividend really is. However, the basic intuition is as follows: Pigouvian taxes improve the environment; in addition, they raise revenue. Since they do so, the replacement of ordinary distortionary taxes by green taxes must lead to a reduction of the efficiency cost of raising revenue. Therefore, a tax reform that replaces ordinary by green taxes in the context of constant overall tax revenue must imply a social gain from more efficient revenue-raising in addition to the gain from an improved environment. This is the essence of the double dividend argument.

At this level of generality the proposition that a double dividend exists may seem obvious. However, when one tries to make the proposition more precise, things get rather more complicated. I am in basic agreement with what the authors say about this issue, but let me restate some of their points in a slightly different way.

The theory of optimum taxation is in a way a natural framework to use for an analysis of this issue; after all, the argument is concerned about the efficiency properties of alternative tax systems. On the other hand, it does not make sense to start from a situation where the overall tax system has in fact been optimized. In that case, the government has already achieved an optimal balance between the revenue from distortionary taxes and the environmental gains from green taxes (as shown in Sandmo (1975)). In such a situation a small change in the balance of taxes would not yield any dividend at all, and a large change could only lead to a decline in social welfare. A more realistic analysis must therefore take the perspective of the tax reform literature. In that type of analysis there is no presumption that the tax system is optimal at the point of time of the reform. Instead, one takes as a starting point a state of the tax system that corresponds to the actual situation and then studies the welfare effects of a balanced budget reform that is believed to lead us in the right direction in terms of environmental improvement.

This makes it crucial to specify the initial situation from which the reform starts. A natural case is one where the seriousness of environmental problems increases and Pigouvian taxes—to the extent that they exist at all—are perceived to be too low. It is therefore decided to raise them, and since this generates revenue for the government, the increase must be balanced by a lowering of other taxes.[4] Let us take it for granted that the Pigouvian tax does succeed in reducing environmental pollution. Is there an additional welfare effect via a more efficient system for raising tax revenue? The answer in principle is yes, in the sense that one can distinguish between two separate effects of the reform, one that is related to the environmental benefit and one which concerns the efficiency with which revenue is raised (see Sandmo (2000), chapter 6). On the other hand, starting from some arbitrary initial situation, there is actually no guarantee that the latter effect will be positive, since the introduction of Pigouvian taxes might have as a result that pre-existing distortions become magnified via cross price effects on demand and supply. (An example would be the case where the goods or services that are subject to Pigouvian taxes are complementary with labour, so that the distortions of labour supply that are due to income and payroll taxes are exacerbated by the green taxes.) This argument supports the authors' conclusion: to evaluate double dividend arguments one must be precise both about the policies that are actually in place and about the exact nature of the tax reform.

One version of the double dividend argument that the authors do not mention, but which has in fact received a good deal of attention, is that the second dividend might be a reduction of unemployment (see e.g. Koskela, Schöb, and Sinn (1998), or Bovenberg and van der Ploeg (1996)). My impression is that this version of the double dividend hypothesis has a stronger appeal to political decision makers: in countries where unemployment is high, this secondary effect of green taxes is much easier to understand and

[4] I am assuming that we are not so far from the optimum tax system that tax rates are on the downward-sloping side of their individual Laffer curves; in that case a lower tax rate would increase revenue.

promises to solve a problem of greater urgency than the efficiency loss from distortionary taxes. The reasoning that underlies this particular theory of the double dividend is as follows: If an increase of environmental taxes is accompanied by a reduction of the payroll tax, this will result in a lowering of labour cost to firms and therefore increase their demand for workers. Thus, employment will increase and unemployment will fall. In this case also, the short version of the argument is more convincing than the longer and more elaborate. To explain the existence of unemployment, we have to move away from the assumption of perfectly competitive markets, and the alternative which has been most common in the literature is some version of a model where the wage rate is set by a trade union with firms deciding the amount of employment (as in Oswald (1985)). We then have to consider the incidence of the payroll tax: will a reduced rate lead to a corresponding fall in labour cost, or does the trade union capture some of the gain from the lower rate in the form of higher gross wages? The most likely outcome appears to be that the cut in the payroll tax will lead to some increase of the wage, although not by so much as to undo the direct effect of the lower tax rate. But we also have to take account of the incidence of environmental taxes on the wage claims of the union. If a green tax reform consists of a lower payroll tax in combination with increasing taxes on car use and household energy, it seems likely that the price increases, by increasing the general cost of living, would release claims for wage compensation in a unionized economy. Altogether, it seems likely that the net effect of a green tax reform on labour cost might be considerably less than the immediate effect of a cut in payroll taxes. But there is a variety of models that may be applied to the study of this problem, and the theoretical analyses do not lead to clear-cut hypotheses. In any case, this version of the double dividend theory seems important enough to be mentioned in the present context.

On the whole, I agree with the authors that the main case for green taxes must be their environmental benefits, not their second dividend (however defined). One may wonder why the double dividend argument became so prominent in the policy debate. Of course it raises some interesting analytical problems which are attractive to public finance economists. But one also suspects that the attention given to the double dividend comes from a desire to convince politicians about the merits of green taxes by arguments that economists believe to have a greater appeal to them than the concern for the environment. As a strategy of persuasion this has some risky elements in it, since it makes the case for Pigouvian taxes depend on unstable or uncertain matters like the rate of unemployment and the magnitude of tax effects on labour supply. It would be very unfortunate if, for example, a drop in the unemployment rate were perceived as weakening the case for Pigouvian taxes. The case for environmental policy ultimately rests on much more solid foundations.

3. INTRINSIC AND EXTRINSIC INCENTIVES

The authors allude briefly to the argument that environmental taxes might affect not only the taxpayers' budget constraints but also their attitudes, either by legitimizing behaviour which is detrimental to the environment or by weakening or 'crowding out' intrinsic incentives to environmentally friendly behaviour.[5] In the first case, the argument is that pollution activities may become easier to reconcile with one's social conscience if one is actually being charged for them; in the second case one's incentives to keep the environment clean are weakened by the knowledge that the government is taking charge. I believe that this is an argument that needs to be taken seriously, if only because the neglect of intrinsic incentives is often used as a criticism against the economic approach to environmental problems. Let me briefly consider the crowding out argument. What difference does it make to the standard approach? The assumption is that the individual polluter has an attitude reflecting social responsibility and suffers some individual loss from his own pollution; this makes him pollute less than he 'otherwise' would. The imposition of a tax on pollution lowers the polluter's subjective 'conscience tax', so that the net effect on pollution is less than would be the case with purely self-interested individuals or firms. However, this hypothesis is very hard to test directly. Economists are more interested in elasticities: how does the polluter react to an increased tax on pollution? The exact nature of the preferences underlying the elasticity may, at least for the purpose of descriptive analysis, be of little interest. We are mainly interested in the polluter's reaction to tax incentives, not in the exact nature of the preferences that determine his or her behaviour.

However, this conclusion may be interpreted from a somewhat different angle. The economic emphasis on the need to utilize private economic incentives need not rest on a very narrow view of human motivation. It is perfectly possible to construct models where agents care about the state of the environment and about the effects of their own behaviour, but where taxes

[5] For a general analysis of intrinsic and extrinsic incentives see Bénabou and Tirole (2006).

and other policy instruments still have the potential to change behaviour in desired directions. The reason that we as economists often neglect these more complicated models is that we frequently are able to state our points with simple models. But we should perhaps realize that this kind of simplicity is likely to make us appear unnecessarily narrow-minded to people outside the economics profession.

Although the arguments about intrinsic incentives should be taken seriously, they are unlikely to lead to dramatic changes of the standard policy recommendations in this area. If, for example, one carries the view of taxes as legitimizing pollution to extremes, one might be led to the conclusion that taxation is likely to encourage environmental pollution because elasticities actually have the 'wrong' sign: taxes on car use would lead to more driving, and taxes on household energy would make consumers turn up their room temperature and leave the lights on. But hypotheses like these are so out of touch with empirical evidence that they need hardly be taken seriously.

4. THE IMPORTANCE OF ELASTICITIES

The effects of environmental taxes clearly depend on the magnitude of the relevant elasticities. If the base of a green tax is very price inelastic, the effect on the environment will be very small, and Pigouvian tax enthusiasts will have to face the criticism that this is just another way to raise revenue. Perhaps we ought in general to be more explicit about the time frame that we have in mind when we analyse green tax effects on behaviour. Taxes on cars and car use may be a case in point. In the short run, the effects of taxes on cars and petrol may be small, given the existing stock of cars. But in the somewhat longer run this may change as a result of altered tax incentives. Households may decide not to replace their second car or modify their habits as regards travelling to work. In the even longer run, increased taxes on transportation may reverse the trend in city development that has been so characteristic of the post-war period. Instead of the continuation of urban sprawl, we may come to see a movement towards more compact cities with greater reliance on collective transportation. The classic insight that elasticities are higher in the long run than the short is of crucial importance for environmental policy.

The magnitude of the price elasticities are also likely to depend on other elements of public policy. According to Leape (2006), the success of the London congestion charge in reducing traffic in the central areas of the city was to a large extent due to the presence of a substitute for car use in the form of a well-developed system of public transport. The availability of this substitute was probably also the main reason why the congestion charge could be introduced with only minor effects on local business. Thus, the design of environmental tax policy should be seen in conjunction with that of publicly provided goods and services.

5. INTERNATIONAL ASPECTS OF THE CARBON TAX

Some environmental externalities are global in nature, in particular those that are related to global warming and climate change. These pose particular challenges for environmental policy. Relative to the scale of the problems, each national government becomes a small actor on the world stage. It must bear the cost of its own environmental measures, while the benefits accrue to all nations. There is a potential free rider problem on a global scale, where each individual country has insufficient national incentives to introduce adequate measures to control international pollution. And there is at present no supranational authority that can enforce an international tax policy, in contrast to what is the case in the national jurisdictions.

Fortunately, there are indications that this free-rider problem is perhaps not quite as severe as economic theorists tend to believe. Thus, the UK government has recently presented plans for national reduction of CO_2 emissions that seem to go well beyond what one would expect from calculations based on pure national self-interest. International progress in this area depends on the willingness of some countries to take a lead in introducing carbon taxes and possibly supplementary regulations. An interesting issue is what the ideal policy for the world as a whole should be. What should be the structure of a global carbon tax?

There is a strong efficiency argument in favour of a uniform global tax on carbon emissions; this has recently been strongly recommended in the Stern Review (Stern (2007)). The argument is basically the same as the one that applies to the national economy: By letting all polluters face the same tax on emissions, one ensures that the targeted reduction of global emissions is achieved at the lowest possible cost to the world as a whole. But this is a 'first-best policy'; there are no political or institutional constraints on the choice of policy instruments. We need to ask if there are features of the problem that call for a modification of the ideal policy.

Under ideal conditions, production efficiency is a desirable element of a welfare-maximizing policy. When a given reduction of pollution is achieved at minimum cost to the economy as a whole, one maximizes the total resources available for distribution among the members of society. Potentially, therefore, it becomes possible to give higher income to everyone than under any other policy alternative. However, the appeal of this argument is based on the assumption that society has adequate instruments for redistribution, and for many individual countries this is a reasonable assumption. But is it a reasonable one for the international community? There is admittedly some degree of international redistribution from the rich to the poor countries, but it is still a safe generalization that there is much less redistribution of income internationally than there is within the nation state, particularly as regards the Western welfare states. This provides an argument for designing the carbon tax in such a way that the burden on the poor countries becomes less than it would be under a uniform tax; it is worth giving up some production efficiency if this can result in a more equitable distribution of the costs of environmental improvement (Sandmo (2005)). From this point of view unilateral increases of the carbon tax in the rich countries should be welcomed, even if the poor countries of the world do not follow their lead.

This is not meant to deny that an even better policy would be to combine a global uniform tax with increased international redistribution. But there is an obvious risk involved in letting tax and other policies against global warming wait for a radical improvement of the possibilities for international redistribution.

REFERENCES

Atkinson, A. B., and Brandolini, A. (2010), 'On Analyzing the World Distribution of Income', World Bank Economic Review, forthcoming.

Bénabou, R., and Tirole, J. (2006), 'Incentives and Prosocial Behavior', *American Economic Review*, **96**, 1652–78.

Bénabou, R., and Tirole, J. (2006), 'Incentives and Prosocial Behavior', *American Economic Review*, **96**, 1652–78.

Bovenberg, A. L., and van der Ploeg, F. (1996), 'Optimal Taxation, Public Goods and Environmental Policy with Involuntary Unemployment', *Journal of Public Economics*, **62**, 59–83.

Enkvist, P.-A., Nauclér, T., and Rosander, J. (2007), 'A Cost Curve for Greenhouse Gas Reduction', *The McKinsey Quarterly*, no. 1, 35–45.

Koskela, E., Schöb, R., and Sinn, H.-W. (1998), 'Pollution, Factor Taxes and Unemployment', *International Tax and Public Finance*, **5**, 379–96.

Leape, J. (2006), 'The London Congestion Charge', *Journal of Economic Perspectives*, **20**, 157–76.

Musgrave, R. A. (1959), *The Theory of Public Finance*, New York: McGraw-Hill.

Oswald, A. J. (1985), 'The Economic Theory of Trade Unions: An Introductory Survey', *Scandinavian Journal of Economics*, **87**, 160–93.

Pigou, A. C. (1920), *The Economics of Welfare*, London: Macmillan.

Sandmo, A. (1975), 'Optimal Taxation in the Presence of Externalities', *Swedish Journal of Economics*, 77, 86–98.

—— (2000), *The Public Economics of the Environment*, Oxford: Oxford University Press.

—— (2002), 'Efficient Environmental Policy with Imperfect Compliance', *Environmental and Resource Economics*, **23**, 85–103.

—— (2005), 'Environmental Taxation and Revenue for Development', in Atkinson, A. B. (ed.), *New Sources of Development Finance*, Oxford: Oxford University Press.

Stern, N. (2007), *The Economics of Climate Change: The Stern Review*. Cambridge: Cambridge University Press.

6

The Base for Direct Taxation

*James Banks and Peter Diamond**

James Banks is Professor of Economics at UCL and a Deputy Research Director of the IFS. His research focuses on empirical modelling of individual economic behaviour over the life-cycle, with particular focus on consumption and spending patterns, saving and asset accumulation, housing dynamics, and retirement and pension choices. Recent work looks at broader issues in the economics of ageing such as health, physical and cognitive functioning and their association with labour market status, the dynamics of work disability, and the nature of expectations of retirement, health, and longevity. He is also Co-Principal Investigator of the English Longitudinal Study of Ageing.

Peter Diamond is an Institute Professor and Professor of Economics at MIT, where he has taught since 1966. He has been President of the American Economic Association, of the Econometric Society, and of the National Academy of Social Insurance. He is a Fellow of the American Academy of Arts and Sciences and a Member of the National Academy of Sciences. He has written on behavioural economics, public finance, social insurance, uncertainty and search theories, and macroeconomics. He has just finished *Reforming Pensions: Principles and Policy Choices* (with Nicholas Barr) and is working on a book on taxes, based on the Jahnsson Lectures he delivered in September 2007.

* We wish to thank Henry Aaron, Tony Atkinson, Alan Auerbach, Richard Blundell, Malcolm Gammie, Mike Golosov, Jon Gruber, Bob Hall, Dan Halperin, Ken Judd, Louis Kaplow, Gareth Myles, Jim Poterba, Dick Tresch, Aleh Tsyvinski, Iván Werning, and Eric Zolt for helpful comments, Ben Etheridge, Catarina Reis, Johannes Spinnewijn, and Maisy Wong for research assistance. Financial support from the National Science Foundation under grant SES-0648741 and from the ESRC and Nuffield Foundation through their funding of the Mirrlees Review at IFS is gratefully acknowledged. Data from the British Household Panel Survey (BHPS) and the Survey of Personal Incomes (SPI) were available through the UK Data Archive. The BHPS is copyright Institute for Social and Economic Research; the SPI is crown copyright, reproduced with the permission of the Controller of HMSO and the Queen's Printer for Scotland. None of these institutions bears any responsibility for the analysis or interpretation presented herein.

EXECUTIVE SUMMARY

The study of tax reform is best approached by examining the economic consequences of different tax structures on the levels of lifetime well-being for all people in the economy. Given some view of how the aggregate well-being of society depends on the distribution of well-being among different individuals, this can then become a basis for choosing which tax policy to pursue.

This is the starting point of the 'optimal tax theory' approach to tax policy and it is also the approach taken in this chapter. The traditional debate over the tax base—what it is that we should tax—has been focused on whether to tax total income or total expenditure. We argue that a better question is how to tax income from capital, on the assumption that there will continue to be some annual 'progressive' taxation of earnings in which the share of earnings taken in tax increases as earnings increase.

We focus on three questions:

- How should annual capital income be taxed: not at all, at a flat rate (as in the Nordic dual income tax), at a rate related to the marginal tax rate on earnings, or by taxing all income at the same rates?
- Should net payments into savings vehicles be deductible from earnings for tax purposes?
- Is it worth considering a more complex tax structure, and more particularly tax rates on earnings that depend on the age of the taxpayer? Would greater use of age-dependent rules in capital income taxation also be worthwhile?

Widely recognized optimal tax theory results suggest that capital income should not be taxed, to avoid distorting people's decisions between consuming immediately and saving to finance consumption in the future. But we argue on grounds both of theory and of empirical evidence that there should still be some role for taxing capital income.

Two key findings lie behind this conclusion:

- First, people with high earnings capacity tend to be more willing and more able to smooth consumption over their lifetime by saving than those with low earnings capacity.
- Second, people with different earnings capabilities tend to have different earnings profiles and consumption needs over their life-cycle. Perhaps more importantly, people in early or mid-life are uncertain about their

earnings prospects and the amount of such uncertainty faced most likely differs by earnings capability.

The conclusion that capital income should be taxed does not, however, mean that the tax base should simply be total income, that is, the sum of labour income and capital income. We lean towards relating marginal tax rates on capital and labour incomes to each other in some way (as in the US), as opposed to the Nordic dual income tax where there is a universal flat rate of tax on capital income.

We also argue that age-dependent taxes are attractive for two reasons: first, they take account of the fact that the distribution of people's circumstances differs at different ages, and second, they allow tax policy to target individuals with different expectations of the future. The gains from age-dependent labour income taxes may not be trivial and, in addition, there may be a case for varying by age the amount of capital income people can receive without paying tax. A detailed analysis would, however, be needed to explore how substantial the gains might be, and to assess the transition costs of moving to such a system.

Since the Meade Report (Meade, 1978) there have been developments both in the theoretical debate on optimal taxation and in the availability of empirical evidence on the behaviour of individuals and the economic environments they face. Our chapter reflects these developments and there is no doubt that the evidence available for policy makers is considerably more substantial than it was thirty years ago. But certain issues warrant further research in terms of both the theory of optimal tax design and empirical evidence on the determinants of individuals' lifetime earnings profiles and work, consumption and saving decisions. Other chapters in this volume address the issues of gifts and inheritances and the presence of households and not just individuals who live alone. While related, these are not dealt with in our analysis.

6.1. INTRODUCTION

Chapter 2 of the Meade Report, 'The Characteristics of a Good Tax Structure', is divided into six sections: Incentives and economic efficiency, Distributional effects, International aspects, Simplicity and costs of administration and compliance, Flexibility and stability, and Transitional problems. To consider direct taxation in the UK, the Meade Committee examined each of these issues separately and then combined the insights into a policy recommendation. It seems to us, as it seemed to Alfred Marshall, that this is an appropriate way to proceed.[1] While the capacity of computers to find equilibrium in complex models has grown apace since the Meade Report, the models available for analysis, like much of the underlying theory, are still quite limited and still too far from reality for us to proceed in any other fashion than that followed by the Meade Committee. Whilst citing some simulations, this essay focuses on theoretical findings with regard to the tax base.[2]

The traditional starting place for a study of tax reform, such as the Meade Report, is a definition of an ideal tax base, one that reflects both horizontal equity (treating equals equally) and vertical equity (those with larger ideal tax bases pay larger taxes). This ideal tax base is then adjusted in light of the issues raised by the other five areas of concern identified in chapter 2 of the Report.[3]

Since the mid-1960s, there has been a great deal of analysis that considers both equity and efficiency in a single model, rather than discussing them separately. These studies analyse the maximization of a social welfare function that is defined in terms of individual utilities.[4] Equity issues are incorporated by having a heterogeneous population in the model rather than a single representative agent.[5] After arguing briefly in Section 6.2 (and further in Section 6.8.4) that an initial choice of an ideal tax base drawn from an asserted concept of fairness is not a good starting place for policy analysis, the primary

[1] '... it [is] necessary for man with his limited powers to go step by step; breaking up a complex question, studying one bit at a time, and at last combining his partial solutions into a more or less complete solution of the whole riddle... The more the issue is thus narrowed, the more exactly can it be handled: but also the less closely does it correspond to real life. Each exact and firm handling of a narrow issue, however, helps towards treating broader issues, in which that narrow issue is contained, more exactly than would otherwise have been possible. With each step... exact discussions can be made less abstract, realistic discussions can be made less inexact than was possible at an earlier stage.' Marshall (1948), 366.

[2] For a recent optimal tax calculation and discussion of accomplishments and difficulties, see Judd and Su (2005).

[3] Dedicated taxes for particular expenditures are a common feature of advanced countries (particularly in the context of social insurance) and can play an important political role. And there may be a direct normative gain from doing this in some circumstances. This chapter considers only individual (not corporate) taxation for general revenues.

[4] Some studies consider properties of taxes that result in individual utilities such that it is not possible to make everyone better-off, given the set of allowable taxes. The set of such utilities is referred to as the second-best Pareto frontier.

[5] The standard basic model treats administrative costs of different taxes as zero or (implicitly) infinite and ignores tax evasion. See, for example, the textbooks by Myles (1995); Salanié (2003); Tresch (2002); Tuomala (1990); although there are articles that address administrative costs and evasion. There has not been integration with macro issues incorporating, for example, built-in stabilizers (Auerbach and Feenberg (2000)) nor has the incorporation of international issues (trade, investment, migration) included the macro dimensions of those issues.

purpose of this chapter is to review the optimal taxation literature and draw inferences for policy that sets the tax base.[6]

Section 6.3 considers lessons from the optimal tax literature with regard to the taxation of income from capital in the presence of taxation of earnings. Section 6.4 considers the related issue of the tax treatment of saving. A succession of papers has shown that under certain conditions the optimal tax schedule should not include taxes on capital. This has led some analysts to favour taxing labour income but not capital income or taxing consumption by taxing labour income minus net saving. The analysis discusses both single cohort versions of this result (based on the Atkinson–Stiglitz (1976) theorem) and the infinite horizon result of Chamley (1986) and Judd (1985), the former addressing the problem from the perspective of decisions over the lifetime of a single generation, and the latter looking at an economy of multiple generations. In both cases, however, the required conditions for the optimality of zero taxation of capital income are argued to be too restrictive and the finding of no role for capital taxation is therefore considered not robust enough for policy purposes. Hence there should be some role for including capital income as a part of the tax base. However, the conclusion that capital income should be taxed does not lead to the conclusion that the tax base should be total income, the sum of labour income and capital income. At present, the literature has only a little to say about how to combine the two sources of income to determine taxes.

In Sections 6.3 and 6.4, the rate of return is assumed to be fixed and known. Section 6.5 examines some issues when there are alternative investment opportunities with safe and risky rates of return. Section 6.6 discusses age-dependent taxes (for example, different taxation of earnings for workers of different ages). Section 6.7 examines some implications of recognizing diversity in individual saving behaviour. Section 6.8 touches on a number of issues including a further discussion of the use of a social welfare function (6.8.1), government commitment (6.8.2), some modelling assumptions (6.8.3), and horizontal equity (6.8.4). Section 6.9 presents some empirical underpinnings for two key elements in determining the desirable taxation of capital income—differences in savings propensities and the shape of earnings

[6] In terms of the chapter 2 topics of the Meade Report, we do not consider administrative costs (ignoring them for given tax bases), international aspects (analysing closed-economy models), nor the use of taxes as part of discretionary fiscal policy for macroeconomic stabilization. Oddly, the Meade Report ignores built-in stabilizers, which seem to us to matter. Other chapters in this volume contain discussions of issues not considered here, including tax rates, the presence of families, some administrative issues, and corporate taxation. For some administrative issues in a consumption tax, see Bankman and Schler (2007).

(and uncertainty about earnings) over the lifetime. Section 6.10 sums up and concludes.

This chapter leaves to Chapters 2 and 8, respectively, discussion of the provision for the very poor and concern about inheritances. It also leaves to Chapter 2 discussion of taxation that recognizes the existence of families. And the chapter assumes that annual measurement of wealth is not available and so considers annual capital income taxation instead.[7] While the Meade Report was part of a tradition contrasting taxation of annual income with taxation of annual expenditures, the Report's inclusion of annual taxation of wealth along with taxation of expenditures in its policy recommendation represented a departure from previous debates based on choosing between either income or expenditure taxation. This chapter shares the Meade Report framing of the potential simultaneous use of several tax bases and focuses on three questions:

- If there is annual non-linear (progressive) taxation of earnings, how should annual capital income be taxed—not at all, linearly (flat rate, as in the Nordic dual income tax[8]), by relating the marginal tax rates on capital and labour incomes to each other (as in the US[9]), or by taxing all income the same?
- If there is annual non-linear taxation of earnings, should there be a deduction for net active saving?[10]
- If there is annual non-linear taxation of earnings, is it worth having a more complex tax structure, particularly age-dependent tax rates? Would greater use of age-dependent rules in capital income taxation be worthwhile?

The chapter reaches the conclusions that neither zero taxation of capital income nor taxing all income the same are good policy conclusions. The chapter leans toward relating marginal tax rates on capital and labour

[7] While the values of some types of wealth are readily measurable, others are not. Of course the same is true for accruing capital income. In practice, this is addressed by taxing realized incomes. Such taxation could be, but is not, adjusted to offset the difference between accrual and realization taxation. We are not aware of a literature exploring the relative advantages of wealth and capital income taxation (with the latter supplemented by wealth taxation at death) as part of optimal taxation. Our conjecture is that capital income taxation could do better, but that is just a conjecture awaiting analysis.

[8] On the Nordic dual tax, see Sørensen (2001, 2005).

[9] In the US, the rate of tax on capital gains and dividends, generally 15%, is lowered for individuals whose marginal tax rate is 15% or less. In the past, half of capital gains were included in taxable income, also resulting in a marginal rate that varied with overall taxable income.

[10] Active saving is defined as saving made directly from earnings, i.e. not including 'passive saving'—the increase in account values due to interest, capital gains, or dividend payments. Thus earnings minus net active saving equals income minus net savings.

incomes to each other as opposed to the Nordic dual tax. In parallel, the chapter reaches the conclusion that there should not be a full deduction for all of net saving. And the chapter concludes that age-dependent tax rates seem to offer enough advantages to justify the added complexity, although more research is needed to support this conclusion.

6.2. HORIZONTAL EQUITY AND THE CHOICE OF TAX BASE

Going back at least to Adam Smith, economists have asserted what the base for taxation should be (along with the degree of progressivity, given the chosen tax base).[11, 12] The Meade Report states:

> No doubt, if Mr Smith and Mr Brown have the same 'taxable capacity', they should bear the same tax burden, and if Mr Smith's taxable capacity is greater than Mr Brown's, Mr Smith should bear the greater tax burden. But on examination 'taxable capacity' always turns out to be very difficult to define and to be a matter on which opinions will differ rather widely. [Page 14.]

This is a definition of an ideal tax base, in the sense that it is underpinned by a direct view or argument about what is ideal. But it still relies on a further definition of taxable capacity, and, reflecting the acknowledged difficulty in defining taxable capacity, the Report goes on to ask: 'Is it similarity of opportunity or similarity of outcome which is relevant?' and 'Should differences in needs or tastes be considered in comparing taxable capacities?'[13] Historically, the debate over the appropriate base for annual taxation has

[11] 'The subjects of every state ought to contribute towards the support of the government, as nearly as possible, in proportion to their respective abilities; that is in proportion to the revenue which they respectively enjoy under the protection of the state.' Smith (1937), 777.

[12] Historically there have been two different approaches to an ideal tax base—one drawn from ability to pay and one drawn from the benefits received from government spending. Discussion of the pattern of benefits received from government spending programmes that affect the entire population did not achieve any consensus on its distributional significance and has disappeared from discussion of an ideal tax base. For example, it is hard to see how to allocate the benefit of military spending by income level in a way that is not too arbitrary to be useful. For historical discussion, see Musgrave (1959).

[13] The Meade Report is not the only examination of taxation that concludes that taxable capacity is hard to define in a way to compel wide acceptance, as is needed for the role as an agreed-on normative basis. For example, Vickrey (1947) writes: 'In a strict sense, "ability to pay" is not a quantity susceptible of measurement or even of unequivocal definition. More often than not, ability to pay and the equivalent terms "faculty" and "capacity to pay" have served as catch-phrases, identified by various writers through verbal legerdemain with their own pet concrete measure to the exclusion of other possible measures. Ability to pay thus often becomes a tautological smoke screen behind which the writer conceals his own prejudices' (footnote omitted, pages 3–4).

been an argument between two approaches. One is that total (Haig–Simons) income[14] is the best measure of ability to pay and therefore horizontal equity calls for Haig–Simons income as the tax base. The other, argued particularly in Kaldor (1955), is that annual consumption is the best measure of ability to pay and therefore horizontal equity calls for consumption as the tax base. This latter view is generally supported by the further argument that it is better to tax people on what they take from the economy (consumption) than a measure of what they provide (income).

We agree with the Meade Report that ' "taxable capacity" always turns out to be very difficult to define and to be a matter on which opinions will differ rather widely'. We conclude that the consideration of an ideal tax base lends itself to too many concerns and conflicting answers to be viewed as a good starting point for the consideration of taxation. An alternative start is by examining the economic equilibria that occur with different tax structures.[15] That is, for any tax structure (assuming it generates enough revenue to cover government expenditures), there is an economic equilibrium, and that equilibrium will result in particular levels of lifetime well-being for all the people in the economy. Given a social welfare function relating aggregate benefit to the distribution of individual lifetime utilities, these lifetime utilities can therefore become the basis for evaluating the normative properties of the various alternative equilibria. This is the starting place of an optimal tax approach to tax policy. Thus, optimal tax theory is based on a consequential philosophy. For each tax structure it describes the economic equilibrium, and thus the utility levels of the different economic agents. Then it asks which of these equilibria offers the utility levels judged best by a social welfare function (an increasing function of individual utilities, which thereby incorporates concern about distribution in terms of utilities, not incomes).

With an optimal tax approach, some aspects of horizontal equity can be addressed by viewing horizontal equity arguments as providing limitations on the set of allowable tax policies, as has been argued by Atkinson and Stiglitz (1980). This chapter accepts the view that tax tools should be limited

[14] Haig–Simons income is labour income plus accrued capital income—Haig (1921), Simons (1938). Shaviro (2002) notes that, 'the spirit in which this hypothetical measure [relevant to distributive justice] is discussed (or, rather, deliberately not discussed) was well illustrated by Henry Simons (1938, 31), when he argued that attempts to poke too far behind the supposed objectivity of an income definition "lead directly back into the utter darkness of "ability" or "faculty" or, as it were, into a rambling, uncharted course pointed only by fickle sentiments" '.

[15] Traditionally, economics has been consequentialist in this sense, as shown, for example, by the centrality of the Fundamental Welfare Theorem, examining conditions under which there is equivalence between competitive equilibrium and Pareto optimality. A Pareto optimal allocation is one from which it is not possible to increase the utility of one household without decreasing utility for another.

by such equity considerations and that policies should be restricted to ones that are uniform over their stated tax base, that is, tax systems in which those with equal circumstances in the relevant dimensions are treated equally.[16] Tax tools should also reflect administrative and political feasibility. One would need a great deal of faith in the political process not to want some protections against arbitrary tax assessments under the guise of 'better taxation'. A complication in structuring protections lies in the definition of arbitrary. If one actually can increase social welfare by drawing distinctions between individuals, are the distinctions still arbitrary? A concern with actual and possible motivations in the political process should lie behind restrictions on tax policies, and the concept of horizontal equity is likely to be very helpful in addressing this issue, without necessarily being the starting place for tax analysis.

Although much has been learned about earnings taxation in one-period models since the pioneering work in Mirrlees (1971), one-period models lack an intertemporal dimension suitable for considering the relative tax treatment of capital and labour incomes. When one moves to intertemporal settings a source of concern about the formulation of the objective function individuals are assumed to maximize arises to the extent that some people may not exhibit time consistency in their behaviour.[17] Since this issue is indeed central to the analysis of the relative taxation of capital and labour incomes, the chapter returns to it in Section 6.7, after first exploring implications of models with fully rational agents. For now, the chapter simply proceeds with preferences that are assumed to be fully rational and time-consistent. This approach is based on the idea that a good starting place for policy is the policy for fully rational agents, a policy that can then be adjusted in recognition of the inadequacy of the assumption that all individuals show fully rational behaviour. For example, in considering the taxation of capital income, the chapter first asks how that should be done in an economy with only fully rational agents and then asks (in Section 6.7) about adjustment

[16] The condition of uniform taxation given the base rules out randomized taxation, which, under some circumstances, can raise social welfare. Nevertheless, randomized auditing of returns does not seem unfair to us or, apparently, to the public as long as the probabilities are suitably selected and the audits are not unduly unpleasant.

[17] Time consistency is the property of making the same decision when given the same choices under the same circumstances at different times. Time inconsistency occurs when different choices are made even though the circumstances are the same. Analyses with time-inconsistent quasi-hyperbolic preferences and with the simple assumption that some people do no saving at all do not reach the same conclusions as the usual full rationality model where individuals are consistent in their desire to borrow and save in anticipation of future events. A similar issue of the appropriate objective function for social evaluation arises if the analyst is concerned that individuals discount the future excessively even if they are time-consistent.

in recognition that some fraction of agents do not appear to save enough for their own good and others accumulate vast sums, not aimed at later consumption. Even the first step, with fully rational agents, is complex given the many relevant aspects of the economic environment, which are modelled separately in optimal tax analyses because of the difficulty in making inferences if the model has many complications at the same time.

The focus in this chapter is on the relative taxation of labour and capital incomes, not the relative merits of taxing total (Haig–Simons) income and taxing consumption, as has commonly been the focus of analyses.[18] In the end, the Meade Report effectively did the same—the Report closes with a section entitled 'ULTIMATE OBJECTIVES':

> We believe that the combination of a new Beveridge scheme (to set an acceptable floor to the standard of living of all citizens), of a progressive expenditure tax regime (to combine encouragement to enterprise with the taxation of high levels of personal consumption), and of a system of progressive taxation on wealth with some discrimination against inherited wealth, presents a set of final objectives for the structure of direct taxation in the United Kingdom that might command a wide consensus of political approval and which could be approached by a series of piecemeal tax changes over the coming decade. [Page 518.]

Thus with a tax on expenditures *and* a tax on wealth, the Meade Report did not keep a simple measure of taxable capacity as the basis for taxation, although it argued that wealth and consumption were both relevant for measuring taxable capacity. The chapter discusses equity further in Section 6.8.4.

6.3. OPTIMAL TAXATION OF CAPITAL AND LABOUR INCOME

Optimal tax theory uses simple general models and calculated examples to draw inferences about how taxes should be set in order to strike a balance between equity and efficiency concerns. Different weights on the concern for equity naturally lead to different taxes.[19] So the theory is designed to show a relationship between normative concerns and tax bases and rates. The approach is to consider economic equilibria under different tax structures and to examine which tax structure gives an equilibrium with the highest

[18] See, for example, Aaron, Burman, and Steuerle (2007); Bradford (1986); Pechman (1980).

[19] Formally, differing concerns about equity are incorporated by the choice of a particular cardinalization of ordinal preferences and the degree to which the social evaluation of an individual's utility varies with the individual's level of utility.

social evaluation of the lifetime utilities of the participants in the economy. The specific optimal taxes from any particular model are not meant to be taken literally, but insights from the modelling, when combined with insights from other sources, can help lead to better taxes. That is, just as the Meade Report had multiple concerns beyond its concern with taxable capacity, so too, the optimal tax approach is a starting place, to be combined with concerns that are not in the formal modelling. One additional concern of particular relevance is the complexity of the tax structure. A desire to avoid complexity comes from seeking simplicity in the tasks of taxpayers, tax collectors, and tax-setting legislatures. There are many papers that analyse optimal taxes; and they differ in many ways. This chapter is not a survey of methods and model results, but a selective drawing of some key policy inferences from the literature.

In each year, there are taxpayers with labour income and taxpayers with capital income and taxpayers with both. Apart from previously deferred compensation, labour income comes from time spent working during the year. Earnings are also influenced by earlier decisions about education, on-the-job training, job location, and job history. Capital income within the year comes primarily as a result of the previous accumulation of assets and liabilities on which capital income is earned and paid. Saving and portfolio decisions during the year are influenced by anticipated taxes in future years. Anticipated future taxes have some relevance for earnings as well, with future earnings being a substitute for current earnings in financing lifetime consumption. Focus on taxation in a single year, without consideration of both earlier and later years, is thus incomplete. This incompleteness is more significant for consideration of taxes on capital income than on labour income. This distinction between the roles of the two types of income on a lifetime basis is the basis for consideration of intertemporal models, even when considering taxation levied on an annual basis.[20]

Taking a lifetime perspective, some policy analysts have called for ending the taxation of capital income.[21] This position is based, at least in part, on optimal tax modelling that reaches this conclusion. This chapter presents separately the two arguments for zero taxation of capital income that have been important for the thinking of many economists, and then shows their lack of robustness to changes in the underlying assumptions, changes that are

[20] The analysis in this chapter ignores the existence of a corporate income tax and reasons for having one. The focus is on taxing individuals. The presumption is that the suitable role for a corporate income tax builds on the desired role of taxation of individual capital income, not vice versa.

[21] See, for example, Atkeson, Chari, and Kehoe (1999); Weisbach (2006); and Bankman and Weisbach (2006).

empirically important. The analysis also serves as background for considering the polar opposite policy of basing taxation on total income, the unweighted sum of labour income and capital income. Why this alternative has not received support from optimal tax analyses is discussed briefly below.

6.3.1. A simple two-period model of work and retirement

Our starting place for consideration of the taxation of both labour income and capital income is a model with two periods, with labour supply in the first period and consumption in both the first and second periods.[22] Suppressing a role for taxing initial wealth (discussed briefly in Sections 6.3.3 and 6.8.2), saving from first-period earnings, used to finance second-period consumption, generates capital income that is taxable (in the second period). Since there is only a single period of work, the model can be viewed as shedding light on the taxation of saving for retirement. For an analysis of issues relating to the taxation of early life savings that are intended for possible consumption during mid or late working life one would need a model with two separate labour supplies, representing labour supply at different times or ages. Such models are considered in Section 6.3.2.

A good place to start considering this class of models is the well-known Atkinson–Stiglitz theorem (1976) which states that when the available tax tools include non-linear earnings taxes differential taxation of first- and second-period consumption is not optimal if two key conditions are satisfied: (1) all consumers have preferences that are separable between consumption and labour and (2) all consumers have the same sub-utility function of consumption.[23] The first condition states that the marginal benefit derived from consumption over the lifetime should not depend on labour supply, and the second requires all consumers to be similar in their desire to smooth consumption across their life cycle and across potentially uncertain states of the world. Like the Fundamental Welfare Theorem, this theorem can play two roles—one is to show that limited government action is optimal in an interesting setting, and the second is to provide, through the assumptions that play a key role in the theorem, a route towards understanding the circumstances calling for more government action (in this case distorting taxation of saving

[22] Interpreting the solution from such a model should be in terms of the total taxation that falls on the tax base, not just the particular form of tax used in describing the model.

[23] Separability between labour and the vector of consumptions and the same subutility function for all individuals can be expressed as $U^n[x_1, x_2, z] = \widetilde{U}^n[B[x_1, x_2], z]$, with x_1 and x_2 being consumption in each of the two periods and z being earnings. A special case is the convenient and widely used additive function $U^n[x_1, x_2, z] = u_1[x_1] + u_2[x_2] - v[z/n]$.

and therefore implicitly taxing (or subsidizing) consumption in the second period relative to consumption in the first period). While we present the intuition behind the first use, our focus is on the second use as we identify in differing tastes and uncertainty about future earnings two strong reasons for finding the theorem not a good basis for policy, for finding that some taxation of capital income is part of a good tax system.

The theorem refers to not 'differentially taxing first- and second-period consumptions'. That is, a tax on consumption that is the same in both periods (a VAT or retail sales tax) is equivalent to a tax on earnings since the choice between first- and second-period consumptions financed by net-of-tax earnings does not alter the total taxes paid (on a present discounted value (PDV) basis). It is different tax rates that matter for efficiency by introducing a 'wedge' between the intertemporal marginal rate of substitution (MRS) and the intertemporal marginal rate of transformation (MRT) between consumer goods in different periods.[24] Two ways of having differential taxation of consumption in the two periods are through different tax rates on consumption in the two periods and through taxation of the capital income that is received as part of financing second-period consumption out of first-period earnings. That is, if taxes should not distort the timing of consumption (if the MRS should equal the MRT), then the optimum is not consistent with taxing these consumer goods other than with equal rates, and thus inconsistent with taxing saving at the margin. The theorem extends to having multiple periods of consumption with a single period of labour.

The underlying logic of the theorem extends to additional settings beyond the full optimization of social welfare. Konishi (1995), Laroque (2005), and Kaplow (2006a) consider distortionary taxes in environments with the same preference assumptions, and *any* earned income tax function. They show that one can always move to a system of non-distorting consumer taxes coupled with an appropriate modification of the earned income tax and generate more government revenue whilst leaving every consumer with the same utility and the same labour supply.[25]

The underlying logic behind the Atkinson–Stiglitz result starts with the observation that the incentive to earn comes from the utility achievable from consumption purchases with after-tax earnings. With separable preferences

[24] The intertemporal consumption MRS captures the consumers' valuation of consumption in the second period relative to consumption in the first period. The matching MRT represents the ability of the economy to produce more of the latter by producing less of the former and would be typically reflected in the price of moving consumption between periods. When these ratios are not equal, a change in production can increase utility, if everything else is held constant.

[25] If labour supply is smooth in response to uniform transfers to all consumers (no jumps in labour supply), then this revenue gain can be used to make a Pareto improvement.

and the same subutilities for everyone, differential consumption taxation can not accomplish any distinction among those with different earnings abilities beyond what is already accomplishable by the earnings tax, but would have an added efficiency cost from distorting spending. Thus the use of distorting taxes on consumption (MRS unequal to MRT) is a more costly way of providing the incentives for the 'optimal' earnings pattern in equilibrium.

Of course, an argument that a better policy is available should only be used as an argument against a particular policy proposal if the available alternative is actively pursued. As with the inadequacy of the Hicks–Kaldor–Scitovsky criterion,[26] hypothetical alternatives that would not be adopted are not legitimate arguments against a policy that would increase social welfare. That is, one can argue against a distorting consumption tax that would increase progressivity in taxation by preferring an alternative of increasing the progressivity of the income tax if the increased income tax progressivity is more efficient. However, arguing on the basis of the existence of a dominating proposal is somewhat hypocritical if the dominating proposal is not supported and will not be adopted or pursued for adoption in the future.

The logic behind the Atkinson–Stiglitz theorem gives insight into several changes in assumptions, discussed below, that would no longer lead to the conclusion in the Atkinson–Stiglitz model that there should be no taxation of capital income.[27] Considered first are two changes to preferences—non-separability and then non-uniform separability. Further changes, some of which involve two periods of work are then also analysed.

[26] The Hicks–Kaldor–Scitovsky criterion is that a policy change can be considered worth doing if those made better-off could fully compensate those made worse-off by the policy change. Hence the policy change could lead to a Pareto improvement. The original version was faulted in that a policy change can pass the test but, with the policy having been implemented, cancelling it could also pass the test. The refined criterion is therefore that a policy change can be considered worth doing when a policy passes the test *and* cancelling the policy does not pass the test. The criterion can be faulted for being hypothetical if the compensations do not occur as part of the reform. We agree that hypothetical alternatives do not have the ethical standing needed to support a normative use of the criterion. A similar view is implicit in the condition of the Independence of Irrelevant Alternatives in the Arrow Impossibility Theorem.

[27] The theorem assumes no restriction on the allowable shape of the taxation of earnings. Deaton (1979) notes that if the income tax is constrained to be linear, then the Atkinson–Stiglitz conditions that are sufficient for the non-taxation of capital income with optimal non-linear taxation are no longer sufficient for the result. A further condition is needed when the income tax function must be linear even when preferences are weakly separable between goods and leisure (as in Atkinson–Stiglitz)—that all consumers have parallel linear Engel curves for goods in terms of income. Thus, even with weak separability and uniformity of preferences, different savings rates for different earners because of non-linear or non-parallel Engel curves prevent the general holding of the result. Note that this argument applies as well to each piece of a piecewise linear tax function, with application of the condition to those on a single linear stretch of the tax function. That is, with a linear income tax and differing savings rates, a change in the income tax rate cannot reproduce the tax pattern from taxing savings and without the ability to reproduce a change in the tax rate can not generally be a dominant policy change.

One obvious change would be that preferences do not exhibit separability between consumption and labour. Then the Corlett–Hague (1953) style analysis in a representative agent 3-good model (current work, current consumption, and future consumption) can examine whether a move towards taxing saving or towards subsidizing saving raises welfare.[28] The key issue is the pattern of the cross-elasticities between labour supply and consumptions in the two periods. However, we do not know much about these cross-elasticities and thus do not have clear policy implications. Although the commonly used assumptions of atemporal and intertemporal separability[29] strike us as implausible, that does not lead to a straightforward conclusion about the cross-elasticities. In particular, those in the second period (who are retired) have more time to do home production (and so less reason to value financing from first-period earnings) than those in the first period, but also more time to enjoy consumption opportunities that are time-intensive (and so more reason to value financing from first-period earnings). It is not clear which of these two effects dominates, and hence which cross-elasticity is higher. Consequently, it is not clear whether saving should be taxed or subsidized because of this issue.[30]

Even were separability to be preserved, a second consideration would be that the subutility functions of consumption are not the same for everyone. Saez (2002b) presents an argument against the policy applicability of the Atkinson–Stiglitz theorem based on differences in desired savings rates across individuals with different skills. Saez argues that it is plausible that there is a positive correlation between labour skill level (wage rate) and the savings rate and cites some supporting evidence.[31] (We review some of the

[28] Results in models with a representative agent are not necessarily the same in many-person models with heterogeneous agents. Nevertheless, the results are suggestive that some results will continue to hold, possibly with modified conditions.

[29] For atemporal additivity, utility within a period can be written as a sum of a utility of consumption and a disutility of work. For intertemporal additivity, utility over a lifetime can be written as a sum of utilities in each period.

[30] Recognition of home production is an argument for differential taxation of different goods at a point of time (Kleven, Richter, and Sørenson (2000)), but does not appear to help clarify the issue of intertemporal taxation.

[31] Dynan, Skinner, and Zeldes (2004) report that those with higher lifetime incomes do save more in the US, but that the full pattern of savings requires considerable complexity in the underlying model (including uncertainties about earnings and medical expenses, asset tested programmes, differential availability of savings vehicles, and bequest motives) to be consistent with the different aspects of savings at different ages that they discuss. Thus the higher savings rates are consistent with the behavioural assumption of Saez, but not, by themselves, a basis for necessarily having the discount rate pattern that Saez assumes, since these other factors are also present. From the perspective of this chapter, it seems to us more plausible that there is the assumed correlation in parameters than that it is absent, and so the implication for taxes from this class of models is supportive of positive taxation of capital income, not zero.

evidence on individual saving and wealth holding in Section 6.9.1.) In the Atkinson–Stiglitz two-period certainty setting with additive preferences, this pattern of savings rates is consistent with those with higher earnings abilities discounting future consumption at a lower rate.[32] In terms of the conditions of the Atkinson–Stiglitz theorem, Saez preserves separability in preferences but drops the assumption that the subutility function of consumption is the same for everyone. With the plausible assumption that those with higher earnings abilities discount the future less (and thus save more out of any given income), then taxation of saving helps with the equity–efficiency trade-off by being a source of indirect evidence about who has higher earnings abilities and thus contributes to more efficient redistributive taxation.[33] In the context of this issue, how large the tax on capital income should be and how the marginal capital income tax rates should vary with earnings levels has not been explored in the literature that has been examined. The optimal rate would depend on the magnitude of the differences in savings propensities and on the elasticities that matter for distortions.

Allowing for uncertain earnings

In the Atkinson–Stiglitz model, a worker is assumed to know the return to working before deciding how much to work and, since work is in the first period only, knows full lifetime income before doing any consumption. Uncertainty about earnings from a given labour supply does not influence optimal taxation of saving if the uncertainty is resolved before first-period consumption—the Atkinson–Stiglitz result carries over. But were consumption decisions to be taken before earnings uncertainties are resolved then this would impact the Atkinson–Stiglitz result. This point can be illustrated in a model with a single period of work before turning to the more relevant models with work in successive periods.

[32] Saez works with the utility functions $U^n[x_1, x_2, z] = u_1[x_1] + \delta_n u_2[x_2] - v[z/n]$, with δ_n increasing in n.

[33] Saez derives a condition for the impact of introducing a linear tax on capital income in a setting of optimal taxation of earnings. He shows that this impact is generally non-zero, implying that a zero tax is not optimal. He gives conditions to sign the direction of improvement. In a setting of generally non-linear taxation and two worker types, the optimum involves positive (negative) marginal taxation of capital income when the optimum has positive (negative) marginal taxation of labour income. A parallel condition holds for the introduction of a small linear tax on capital income. Positive taxation is the relevant case.

Within the standard discounting framework there appears to be considerable heterogeneity in the population in discounting of the future. For example, see Hausman (1979) on different discount rates for air conditioner purchasers, or Samwick (2006) on the distribution of discount rates that can rationalize the distribution of retirement saving wealth.

Modifying the model so that earnings occur only in the second period (with probabilities but not exact information as to future earnings known in the first period) would imply that the first-period consumption decision is made before the uncertainty about future earnings is resolved, while second-period consumption occurs after.[34,35] The Atkinson–Stiglitz result no longer holds and second-period consumption should be taxed at the margin relative to first-period consumption (Cremer and Gahvari (1995)). This result holds whether there is general taxation of earnings and saving or only a linear tax on saving with a non-linear tax on earnings.

We can see the underlying logic of this result by comparing it with that of taxing saving when higher earners have smaller discount of the future. To do that, it is useful to consider the problem of welfare maximization in terms of 'incentive compatibility constraints'. A natural starting place for optimizing taxation is to consider alternative tax structures by first determining the equilibrium that happens with each tax structure. Then the social welfare at the different equilibria are compared. In mathematical vocabulary, social welfare is maximized subject to the constraint of the equilibrium that occurs with individual behavioural responses to the chosen tax structure. There is a mathematically equivalent way of setting up the maximization which is helpful for intuition, even though it does not comply with how a government would naturally approach choosing a tax structure.

Consider the mathematical problem of a government deciding how much each person should earn and how much each person should consume in each period (with the relationship among these being an implicit description of the taxation of earnings). The government decision is subject to the resource constraint of the economy. If this is to be mathematically equivalent to the effects of a tax structure, the relationship between consumer spending and earnings (the implicit tax function) cannot be different for individuals with the same earnings. Given that uniformity, the government's consumption and earnings plan will be an economic equilibrium with a tax function if each person is willing to have his earnings and consumption under the government's plan rather than having the earnings and consumption pair

[34] Formally, the skill level, n, is a random variable, with distribution $F[n]$. First-period consumption must be chosen independent of the as-yet unknown skill level, while earnings and second-period consumption depend on the skill level, which becomes known before these decisions are made. With additive preferences expected utility is written as $\int (u_1[x_1] + u_2[x_2[n]] - v[z[n]/n]) dF[n]$, with a separate budget constraint for each value of n and taxes depending only on the realized level of earnings.

[35] With annual taxation, consumption during the year is happening before earnings levels later in the year are known, at least for some workers. This parallels analyses of the demand for medical care with an annual deductible or out-of-pocket cap.

of anyone else. Uniform rules for everyone is referred to as allowing each person to imitate the consumption and earnings of any other person, within the bounds of the individual's feasible earnings levels. The constraint on the government's plan that no one prefers to imitate someone else is referred to as an incentive compatibility constraint. This equivalent formulation allows a discussion of optimal taxes in terms of affecting the ease of imitating someone else. A change in implicit taxes that makes it less attractive for someone with high earnings skills to imitate someone with low earnings skills allows the government optimization to be more effective, that is, improves the equity–efficiency trade-off (weakens the impact of the incentive compatibility constraint).

After that mathematical digression, let us return to comparing the results about taxing saving with random earnings and when higher earners discount the future less. In the latter case a worker choosing to imitate someone with less skill (by earning less than he would otherwise) saves more than that worker with less skill since the discount of future consumption is less for the potential imitator. Thus taxing saving eases the incentive compatibility constraint, having a bigger impact on the would-be higher skill imitator than on the lower earner potentially imitated. That is, it makes such imitation less attractive. In the uncertainty case, a worker planning to earn less than the government planned amount in the event of high opportunities has a higher valuation of saving than if the worker were planning to earn more by following the government plan (assuming normality of consumption). Thus, again, taxing saving eases the incentive compatibility constraint. One example is that retirement tends to be at an earlier age for those with more accumulated savings (earnings opportunities held constant). Thus, discouraging saving encourages later retirement. This logic only holds for workers with optimal savings paths, a point to which we return in Section 6.7.

Next, the chapter considers models with labour supply in both periods. Then, in parallel with this section, with uncertain second-period wages, first-period consumption is occurring after first-period opportunities are realized but before second-period opportunities are known. The same advantage of differential tax treatment of first- and second-period consumptions naturally occurs in this setting.

6.3.2. A two-period model of working life

While the model with a single labour supply decision can shed light on the relative tax treatment of consumption when working and when retired, a model with two labour supply decisions addresses issues about consumption and earnings during a career. It also raises some issues of the sensible degree of complexity of tax structures, that are not present in the single labour supply model.

Consider a setting where individuals work in each of two periods and consume in each of two periods. In the certainty setting with a single period of work discussed above, the starting place was a model where people differed only in their wage per hour of work. To extend the certainty analysis, we now characterize people by a pair of wage rates, representing the wage rates in each of the two periods. As above, we take wage rates to be the only differences across workers in the population. In light of the diversity in age-earnings trajectories, it is natural to assume diversity in the growth of wage rates.[36]

The Atkinson–Stiglitz result, that with separability and uniform subutilities of consumption[37] there should not be a distortion in the intertemporal consumption decision, extends to this case provided that the taxation of earnings over a lifetime depends in a fully general way on earnings in both periods. That is, in the first period of a lifetime, there is taxation of earnings that can be thought of as withholding of taxes while waiting for the determination of lifetime taxes, which will depend on earnings in both periods.[38] With the Atkinson–Stiglitz preference assumptions and an optimal lifetime tax structure, it remains the case that the marginal rate of substitution between first- and second-period consumptions should equal the marginal rate of transformation. This corresponds to an absence of taxation on saving out of after-tax first-period earnings.

As with the analysis of models with a single working period, the result of zero taxation of capital income does not hold if discount factors vary with skill or if there is uncertainty about second-period earnings, both of which seem empirically important. Beyond the theoretical result that there should be positive taxation of capital income in a model with uncertain later-period earnings, we can look at simulation results to see how important and how

[36] We continue to ignore worker decisions that influence future wage rates (investments in human capital).

[37] Separability between labour and the vector of consumptions and the same subutility function for all individuals can be expressed as $U^{n_1,n_2}[x_1, x_2, z_1, z_2] = \widetilde{U}^{n_1,n_2}[B[x_1, x_2], z_1, z_2]$, with x_1 and x_2 being consumption in each of the two periods and z_1 and z_2 being earnings. A special case is the convenient and widely used additive function $U^{n_1,n_2}[x_1, x_2, z_1, z_2] = u_1[x_1] + u_2[x_2] - v_1[z_1/n_1] - v_2[z_2/n_2]$.

[38] Writing lifetime taxes (in present discounted value) as $T[z_1, z_2]$, the budget constraint for a worker is $x_1 + R^{-1}x_2 = z_1 + R^{-1}z_2 - T[z_1, z_2]$, where R is one plus the rate of return on capital. If there was tax collection in the first-period, $T_1[z_1]$, it would still be the case that the tax collected in the second period, $T_2[z_1, z_2]$, would depend on both earnings levels, and the budget constraint would, equivalently, be written as $x_1 + R^{-1}x_2 = z_1 + R^{-1}z_2 - T_1[z_1] - R^{-1}T_2[z_1, z_2]$.

large such a tax might be. Conesa, Kitao, and Krueger (2007) have done a complex simulation of the asymptotic position of an empirically calibrated overlapping generations (OLG) model with uncertain individual wages and lengths of life. They have a three-parameter earnings tax (the same for each age), a 100% estate tax financing poll subsidies, a pay-as-you-go social security system, a linear tax on capital income and no government debt or assets. They choose taxes to optimize the long-run position of the economy and find a capital income tax rate of 36%, while the tax on labour income is nearly linear at 23%.[39] Golosov, Tsyvinski, and Werning (2007) examine a two-period model where there is a wide range of worker productivities in the first period and each worker has a probability of one-half of losing half of first-period productivity in the second period. They allow a fully general tax structure, referred to as a mechanism design optimization.[40] Given the special nature of the economy (with no attempt to resemble an actual economy), the level of implicit marginal taxes (referred to as wedges) are not of direct interest, but the pattern of implicit marginal taxes may have robustness. They find a higher implicit tax on second-period consumption (i.e. on first-period saving) the higher the wage rate of the worker in the first period.[41] While this model is very special, there is little else that casts light on the best pattern of a capital income tax.[42]

Beyond the two arguments detailed above, there is also an issue of the complexity of the tax structure needed for the zero tax result. The extension of the Atkinson–Stiglitz theorem to the setting with two periods of earnings

[39] Optimizing a long-run economic position is different from looking at the long-run position of an optimized economy. Increasing the capital stock has additional costs in a full optimization that are not present when considering only the asymptotic position (Diamond (1980a)). This is similar to the difference between the golden rule and the modified golden rule.

[40] The standard optimal tax analysis begins with a set of allowable tax structures and optimizes the tax rates in the allowable structure. The mechanism design approach only rules out taxes that are assumed to require information that the government does not have. Thus, taxing skills is ruled out by the assumption that skills can not be directly inferred from the available information on earnings (without information on hours worked). Beyond this constraint, there are no further restrictions, allowing complex structures that might be assumed as unavailable for being too complex in an optimal tax setup. That is, individuals choose from the allowable set of complete lifetime consumption and earnings levels. From the marginal utilities at the chosen point, one can infer the wedge, the implicit marginal tax rate.

[41] They assume that there is zero interest rate and zero utility discount rate. Thus we cannot map the implicit marginal tax on second-period consumption (on the savings level), which ranges from 0.01 to 0.05, into a tax on capital income.

[42] These simulation studies and the theoretical results discussed have modelled labour supply with only an intensive margin (with a smooth response of labour supply to taxes) and have been primarily focused on marginal tax rates. In contrast, with an important extensive margin (lumpy decisions whether to work or not), average tax rates matter and results on tax rates differ. See, e.g., Choné and Laroque (2001, 2006); Diamond (1980b); Saez (2002c) for the case of personal incomes, or Griffith and Devereux (1998) for the case of multinational corporations.

(with separability and uniform subutility functions) potentially requires a complex tax structure with the marginal taxes in any year dependent on the full history of earnings levels. For example, in a setting of two periods with two labour supplies, lifetime after-tax consumption spending can depend in a non-linear way on both first-period and second-period earnings including an interaction term.[43] Once one envisions modelling longer lives, this degree of interaction becomes implausible to implement in a general form.[44]

The Atkinson–Stiglitz theorem assumes that individuals are able to solve the complex choice problem of how much to earn in each period and the tax collector and legislature are able to cope with setting up and enforcing such a complex structure. These assumptions are problematic and, in practice, the taxation of labour income in a year is usually dependent only on what happens that year, with some exceptions involving averaging over a relatively short number of years.[45] So it is natural to consider the issue of what happens to the Atkinson–Stiglitz theorem in the context of a limited tax structure that resembles those commonly used. As far as we are aware, this problem has received little attention with a heterogeneous population.[46] Weinzierl (2007)

[43] The theorem needs to allow any function giving the PDV of lifetime taxes as a function of earnings in both periods, $T[z_1, z_2]$. Thus it is not generally the case that this involves simply adding separate tax functions each period, $T[z_1, z_2] \neq T_1[z_1] + R^{-1}T_2[z_2]$. Framing the problem in terms of a PDV of taxes fits with a restriction that everyone has the same safe rate of return on savings. Otherwise we would also track capital income to see the impact of the timing of tax collection on different individuals.

[44] One strand of the literature has explored assumptions under which the optimum can be implemented with tax structures that are not so complex. These findings arise in models that limit worker heterogeneity greatly. Thus they are an interesting starting place for exploring results as the population is made more diverse, but do not seem to lead directly to policy at present. For example, Golosov and Tsyvinski (2006) examine a role for asset testing, which would be interesting to explore in a more diverse model where asset testing can improve the allocation but does not achieve the mechanism design optimum. Asset testing for access to programmes for the poor is widespread even though general taxation of wealth is not. On use of the latter, see Albanesi and Sleet (2006) and Kocherlakota (2005).

[45] It is common in public pension systems to base benefits on a long or full history of earnings records. In contrast to what is needed for mechanism design taxation, basic pension benefit formulas are usually fairly simple, although there is often complexity in special rules.

[46] Erosa and Gervais (2002) have examined the most efficient taxation of a representative consumer (Ramsey taxation) with intertemporally additive preferences in an OLG setting. If the utility discount rate differs from the real discount rate, individuals will choose non-constant age profiles in both consumption and earnings, even if period preferences are additive and the same over time and the wage rate is the same over time. Thus the optimal age-dependent taxes on consumption and earnings are not uniform over time, resulting in non-zero implicit taxation of savings. They also consider optimal taxes that are constrained to be uniform for workers of different ages. It remains the case that the taxation or subsidization of savings is then generally part of such an optimization.

Gaube (2007) examined the difference between general and period tax functions. He did not consider taxing capital income, but showed that the one-period result of a zero marginal tax rate at a finite top of the earnings distribution, which applies to the highest earner with general taxation, has done simulations contrasting labour income taxation that is the same for everyone each period with labour income taxation that can vary with the age of the worker.[47] (The issue of age-dependent earnings taxes is discussed in Section 6.6.) While the chapter only reports results for the case without a capital income tax, it does mention a similar calculation for a capital income tax of 15%. In personal communication, Weinzierl has reported that social welfare is slightly higher with a 15% capital income tax than with a zero tax in both cases—uniform and age-dependent labour income taxation. Weinzierl's model has no physical capital—the benefit of the capital tax in his analysis is that it discourages the use of saving to exploit the redistributive design of the tax system, as discussed above. Thus there is no presumption of the optimality of zero taxation of saving in general, although evidence on the desired structure of taxation with a diverse population and general earnings taxation in each period is very limited.

We have focused on the gap between MRS and MRT for consumption over time, referred to as a wedge, in this case the intertemporal consumption wedge. We have found circumstances in an economy such that this wedge should not be zero, as it is if the Atkinson–Stiglitz theorem holds. There is a similar wedge to consider between earnings in different periods. The presence of non-constant taxation on earnings in the two periods implies that there is a difference between MRS and MRT for earning in period one relative to earning in period two. If the disutility of labour is a power function[48] and everyone has the same age–wage rate profile, then there should not be an intertemporal earnings wedge (Werning (2005)). But if those with higher earnings have steeper age–earnings profiles, as appears to be the case on average, then the marginal taxes on earnings should rise with age and there should be a wedge on the implicit saving done by increasing early earnings and decreasing later ones, consumption held constant (Diamond (2007)). Taxing consumption implies no tax distortion between earnings in different years. While this does not appear to be part of an optimal plan, desirable aspects of this wedge have not received much attention.

The models discussed above had perfect capital markets—no borrowing constraints. But borrowing constraints are relevant for tax policy, providing

does not apply to the two-period model with separate taxation each period when there are income effects on labour supply since additional earnings in one period would lower earnings, and so tax revenues in the other period.

[47] Allowing age-dependent labour income taxation in a two-period OLG model would involve two separate tax functions, $T_1[z_1]$ and $T_2[z_2]$, rather than the same tax function each year, $T[z_1]$ and $T[z_2]$.

[48] A power function is a constant times the variable raised to a power—ax^b.

another reason for positive capital income taxation in the presence of taxes on labour income that do not vary with age (Hubbard and Judd (1986)).

In the models reviewed above, the wage rates in the two periods are parameters for each worker. It is clear that later earnings depend on both education and earlier work decisions. The costs coming from efforts to increase future earnings come from leisure, foregone earnings, and expenditures. Some spending, such as tuition, is clearly linked to education and referred to as verifiable spending (although the mix of consumption and investment in an individual's education experience is not verifiable). Other spending, such as higher living costs while at school, are hard to distinguish from consumption spending and are referred to as non-verifiable spending. With constant tax rates on labour income, there would be no implicit tax on the foregone earnings portion of the investment to increase future earnings. With progressive labour income taxes and a rising age–earnings curve, there would be such an implicit tax. Verifiable spending, such as tuition, could be directly subsidized (and widely is). The optimal degree of subsidy depends on the effects on atemporal choices as well as the intertemporal human capital decision, and so may not be set optimally from the narrow perspective of human capital investment. Non-verifiable spending involves goods that also have consumption uses and so cannot be subsidized without distorting other consumption decisions. The literature has considered models with no subsidy of non-verifiable spending and full subsidy of verifiable spending with a focus on education. Bovenberg and Jacobs (2005b) consider a three-period model of education, work, and retirement. After showing the desirability of taxing capital income despite the preference assumptions of the Atkinson–Stiglitz theorem, they calibrate the model and conclude that the optimal linear capital income tax rate approaches the optimal linear labour income tax rate. While the rejection of the optimality of a zero tax seems likely to be robust, it would be interesting to see a calibrated calculation in a setting with more periods and thus on-the-job training as well as formal education.[49]

6.3.3. Additional issues: Income shifting, taxing total income, general equilibrium effects, initial wealth

Standard modelling assumes perfect observation of capital and labour incomes. This omits issues of tax evasion (Allingham and Sandmo (1972);

[49] Additional studies with two-period models, with education in the first and earnings in the second period, relate optimal incentives to the mix of opportunity costs and out-of-pocket costs (Hamilton (1987) and Bovenberg and Jacobs (2005a)). On the link between the taxation of financial capital income and the return to human capital see Nielsen and Sørensen (1997).

Sandmo (1981, 2005); Slemrod and Yitzhaki (2002)) and the ability of some workers, particularly the self-employed, legally to transform labour income into capital income (and vice versa). Pirttilä and Selin (2007) found significant shifts of labour income to capital income among the self-employed after the 1993 Finnish tax reform to a dual income tax with a lower rate on capital income.[50] On a more widespread basis, labour effort devoted to earning a higher return on savings also represents a shifting from labour income to capital income. Christiansen and Tuomala (2007) examine a model with costly (but legal) conversion of labour income into capital income. Despite preferences that would result in a zero tax on capital income in the absence of the ability to shift income, they find a positive tax on capital income. As noted below, the Chamley–Judd result of zero capital income taxation also does not hold in a model with an inability to distinguish between entrepreneurial labour income and capital income.[51]

Consideration of income shifting supports marginal taxes on capital income that are higher for people facing higher marginal taxes on labour income. Indeed, taxing total income annually would avoid this issue (apart from the greater possibility of tax deferral with capital income). Apart from this consideration, there is no apparent reason why an optimal tax calculation would find an optimum with the same marginal tax rates on capital and labour incomes. The discussion below, accompanying Table 6.1, points out how different the tax wedges are from taxing labour and capital incomes at the same rates. Without extensive analysis of elasticities, one cannot make conclusions about optimal rates in light of this pattern of tax wedges. However, we see no reason to expect that studies would generate results close to uniformity in the relative taxation of the two types of income. This is particularly the case with capital income after retirement, for which the Atkinson–Stiglitz theorem has more relevance because of the absence of relevant uncertainty about earnings abilities. Indeed, we are not aware of any optimal tax study calling for taxing total income.

In addition to uncertainty about future earnings, there is uncertainty about future preferences. There may be uncertainty about how much consumption will be enjoyed when older—either from an inability fully to appreciate future preferences[52] or from shocks that are not fully insured—such as health shocks

[50] Gordon and Slemrod (1998) have argued that a large part of the response observable in US tax returns was due to income shifting between the corporate sector and the individual sector.

[51] Income shifting is also an issue in the conversion of labour income into corporate income, which has received attention in the literature on the corporate tax (e.g. Gordon and MacKie-Mason (1995)).

[52] See, for example, Gilbert (2006).

or spending shocks (medical or legal expenses) or an inheritance.[53] One example of significant uncertainty is in the length of life. Moreover, longer expected lives are positively correlated with earnings abilities (e.g. as proxied by education) for both men and women. Modelling this interaction would need to explore the use of and properties of the annuities market. In the absence of a range of models to draw from, it is not clear what sign to put on the optimal taxation of saving from this consideration.

Following the setup in Mirrlees (1971), the relative wage rates of different workers are exogenous in the Atkinson–Stiglitz theorem, although the absolute wage rates can be endogenous. Naito (1999) has shown that with endogenous relative wage rates of skilled and unskilled workers, the Atkinson–Stiglitz theorem does not hold.[54] If the production of consumption for period one makes different relative uses of skilled and unskilled labour from the production of consumption for period two, then a change in the savings rate alters the relative demands for the two types of labour, changing their relative wages. This is an alternative approach to redistribution, one that is in principle a useful supplement to progressive earnings taxes. That is, there is an aggregate production set involving first-period consumption, second-period consumption, skilled labour and unskilled labour. If, by shifting consumption demand between periods, one can shift relative wages, then the incentive compatibility constraint can be weakened, breaking the dominance of the earnings tax over the non-proportional taxation of consumption. Empirical work supports the finding that increased capital (in the form of equipment) raises skilled relative to unskilled wages (Krusell et al. (2000)), supporting taxation of capital income, although the importance and magnitude of this consideration are unclear.

The models considered above have variation in the population in earnings ability, and sometimes in preferences, but not in wealth at the start of the first period. With variation in initial wealth holdings and an ability to tax initial wealth, the optimum may call for full taxation of initial wealth, particularly when higher wealth is associated with higher earnings abilities. If immediate taxation of initial wealth is ruled out, the presence of capital at the start of the first period, which can earn a return when carried to the second period, can also prevent the optimality of the non-taxation of capital income if there are no fairness issues further limiting the desirability of taxation of initial

[53] Another source of uncertainty comes from uncertain future relative prices. This is present even with savings in real assets based on a price index that is not precisely the right one for a given individual.

[54] This is similar to the failure of the Diamond–Mirrlees (1971) aggregate efficiency theorem with restrictions on the taxation of some commodities, for example, when different commodities must be taxed at the same rates (Diamond (1973)).

wealth. As a modelling issue, one needs to ask where such wealth came from. Presumably gifts and inheritances are a major source. But since these might themselves be taxed and since gifts and bequests might be influenced by future taxation of capital income, a better treatment of this issue would be embedded in an OLG model that incorporates the different ways that people think about bequests.[55] A similar issue arises in tax reform given past savings under a previous tax regime.

6.3.4. Overlapping generations (OLG) models

The analysis above considered the intertemporal dimension of direct taxation for a single cohort. A natural question is the impact of the reality of overlapping generations on such analyses. The OLG literature models choice by successive cohorts of workers, with the basic model having no bequests at all. There are two key aspects of the connection between analysis for a single cohort and OLG analysis. One is the government's role in affecting the lifetime budget constraints of different cohorts (and thus the aggregate capital available to different cohorts). The other is the extent to which taxes can vary with age and so with cohort in a single period.

If the government is free to use public debt and public assets as part of intergenerational redistribution, thereby altering national capital, and if taxes are age-dependent, then a full optimization in the OLG model can be divided to include suboptimizations for each cohort, as above (Diamond (1973)).[56] That is, from the intergenerational optimization there is a constraint on the net contribution to national capital from each cohort. If this net contribution is used as a constraint on optimization of taxes for a cohort, then the type of optimizations we have analysed above hold in the basic case where there is no direct concern about relative prices. The analyses with a concern about relative prices, particularly a concern about relative wages, do not generally have this full separation. Presumably our analysis above remains strongly suggestive. Other links would naturally arise, particularly related to education, since parents look after children.

Thus, with the assumptions on preferences that are sufficient for the Atkinson–Stiglitz theorem for a single cohort, the theorem still holds in

[55] See, for example, Boadway, Marchand, and Pestieau (2000); Cremer, Pestieau, and Rochet (2001). That optimal taxation depends on bequest motivation is brought out in Cremer and Pestieau (2003).

[56] If the government wants to give higher consumption to an early cohort, financed by lower consumption for later cohorts, it can do this in a pay-as-you-go pension system, or by borrowing to finance transfers to the early cohort and financing the debt from taxes on later cohorts.

the setting of overlapping generations with no constraints on government debt policy and on age- (and so cohort-) specific taxes. The reasons for the inapplicability of the theorem discussed above carry over to the OLG setting. A separate issue is whether the government does not adjust debt policies but then uses tax policies to affect capital stocks instead. That is, if the government follows policies, such as too much debt, that reduce capital below optimal levels, then tax policies to increase individual saving may become more attractive as a substitute (third-best) policy (Atkinson and Sandmo (1980)). Such analysis is likely to be sensitive to the way the determination of government debt policy is modelled. It is not clear how best to describe the determinants of UK debt/public capital policy, whether such political behaviour is best thought of as stable over time, and how robust any findings about tax policy would be. There is also a natural suspicion that such third-best arguments can be a cover for other motives.

In practice, taxes do not vary (much) by cohort—that is they are period-specific rather than age-and-period specific. Above, we briefly discussed the issue of taxes for a single cohort that did not vary with age. The same issues arise with period-specific taxes affecting people of different ages. Thus recognition of the OLG setting emphasizes the importance of this consideration and of the possibilities in age-dependent taxes.

6.3.5. Models with infinite horizon agents

These OLG models have an infinite horizon for the economy, but have no direct links across the finite-lived cohorts. Redistribution across cohorts (with its induced change in the capital stock) is then important for capital growth and can be done without having to distort individual saving decisions. Conversely, distorting individual saving decisions can be done without necessarily changing aggregate capital by also redistributing across cohorts. In contrast, if agents optimize over an infinite future, altering the timing of their consumption does require distorting individual saving decisions. That is, a key implication of infinite horizon agents is that a shift of tax collection over time, which would influence capital accumulation when the shift involves different cohorts in an OLG model, is fully offset for infinite horizon agents. Thus the taxation of capital income plays a role in intertemporal allocation that is stronger than in the OLG model because of the lack of effect of this intertemporal redistribution policy tool. Infinitely lived agents are naturally interpreted as doing optimization for a dynasty, and so making bequest decisions. Moreover, recognizing overlapping generations as opposed to sequential ones as part of the infinite horizon planning, the agents are also adjusting incomes of contemporaneous members of a single dynasty.[57]

The central finding in this literature, due to Chamley (1986) and Judd (1985), is the optimality of zero taxation of capital income in the long run. We begin by considering the intuition generally put forth for this result. After discussing its relevance and considering generalizations that imply that optimal taxation of capital income is not zero, we consider a generalization of the basic result in Judd (1999).

Above, we have examined the relationship between the intertemporal consumption MRS and intertemporal MRT that would be optimal in different settings. We start this discussion by noting the relationship between them if there is a constant tax rate on capital income. If we assume an interest rate (marginal product of capital), r, which is constant over time, then a unit of consumption today can be converted into $(1 + r)^T$ units of consumption T periods from now (in period T + 1, if we denote today by period 1). Thus the MRT_{1T+1} is $(1 + r)^T$. If an investor is subject to a tax at rate τ on capital income, then the investor can convert one unit of consumption today into $(1 + (1 - \tau)r)^T$ units of his own consumption after T periods. The ratio between the MRS and MRT between consumption today and consumption T periods from now is $\{(1 + (1 - \tau)r)/(1 + r)\}^T$. This gives the fraction of the available social return that goes to the investor. With a positive rate of tax this expression goes to zero as T goes to infinity. And it gets small for long, finite time spans. Some examples, are given in Table 6.1

Comparing the contents of the table with a tax on labour earnings makes several points. A 30% tax on earnings puts a 30% wedge between contemporaneous earnings and consumption. A 30% tax on capital income puts only a 3% wedge between consumption today and consumption in a year (when the rate of return is 10%). But it puts a 67% wedge between consumption today and consumption in forty years. The difference comes from the shifting relative importance of principal and interest in the financing of future consumption as we look further into the future. Table 6.1 makes clear that the intertemporal consumption tax wedge depends on whether nominal or real incomes are being taxed. This table raises the issue of how far into the future people are thinking when making consumption–saving decisions. It suggests that if people have a long enough horizon, capital

[57] The empirical evidence on the consumption patterns of parents and adult children alive at the same time is strongly contradictory of the idea that people typically behave as if there were a single dynastic utility function being jointly maximized. Moreover, taking this literally and recognizing marriage (which links dynasties to each other) leads to absurdities (Bernheim and Bagwell (1988)).

Table 6.1. Ratio of MRS to MRT: $\{(1 + (1 - \tau)r) / (1 + r)\}^T$

T	r = 0.05, τ = 0.15	r = 0.10, τ = 0.15	r = 0.05, τ = 0.30	r = 0.10, τ = 0.30
1	0.993	0.986	0.985	0.973
10	0.931	0.872	0.866	0.758
20	0.866	0.760	0.750	0.575
40	0.751	0.577	0.562	0.331
60	0.650	0.439	0.422	0.190
80	0.564	0.333	0.316	0.109

income taxation that impacts distant consumption will be inefficient, a suggestion we examine in detail. And it points to potential welfare gains from tax-favoured retirement saving, since that saving tends to be for longer times.

When agents have long horizons, modelling their current decision-making using an infinite horizon model can be mathematically more tractable than a long finite horizon, while doing little violence to conclusions from the analysis that relate to current behaviour. However, when the evolution of an economy over time is being considered, a model with a fixed number of infinitely lived agents behaves very differently from an OLG model, even one with long lives.[58] And that can matter for drawing conclusions about incentives that matter primarily for future behaviours, such as capital income taxes in the distant future.

Let us start with the basic interpretation of the model before turning to detailed modelling assumptions. In the standard OLG model, individuals have no concern for the future after their deaths and leave no bequests. This is empirically inaccurate—most people leave some bequests and we think that some people adjust earnings and/or saving in light of planned gifts and bequests.[59] Results vary in models that extend the basic OLG model for bequests, depending on how bequest decisions are modelled. Models with 'accidental bequests' because of incomplete insurance/annuitization and models with planned bequests arising from motivations that can influence earlier decisions generate different positive and normative tax implications.[60]

[58] Immigration of new dynasties makes a model with infinite-lived agents have some of the properties of a finite-lived OLG model (Weil (1989)).

[59] Part of the debate on the importance of intergenerational links for the evolution of the capital stock relates to the treatment of the financing of education and other gifts that occur well before the time of a parent's expected death. This is ignored in this discussion which focuses on the transfer of financial wealth at death or at a time when remaining life expectancy is small.

[60] The role of saving for bequests appears to be diverse in the population and unclear (Hurd (1987)). As an example of the importance of motivation, if all bequests are accidental from

Empirically, how important bequest considerations are for behaviour is unclear and widely varying in the population. A further complication in interpreting behaviour as dynastic is the sizable tendency to make charitable bequests. Also key to further analysis is how to form a social welfare function since counting both the utility of a donor and the utility of a donee in a social welfare function has implications that can be questioned as being normatively unattractive.

In contrast, the standard infinite horizon agent model is viewed as a dynasty model with incorporation of future utilities in the decision-making of earlier cohorts and a normative evaluation of the utilities of consumption of each generation exactly as they are viewed by the existing generation. This is typically done as if there were only one generation alive at a time and lasting only a single period, rather than the multiple overlapping generations that are actually present. In terms of the normative issue raised above, this can be viewed as counting the utility of the donor and ignoring the utility of the donee, and is one way to approach the concern about overweighting the consequences of concern for others.[61]

It is useful to complement OLG models that unrealistically ignore bequests with models that give bequests a larger role in decision-making than they have in reality—at least until we have better empirics and analytics about bequests. So an evaluation of the role of other assumptions in reaching the Chamley–Judd no-capital-income-taxation conclusion is appropriate. This widely cited result is that when such an economy is in a steady state, there should be no taxation of capital income (with a linked convergence result that the tax rate converges to zero as the economy converges to a steady state). As Chamley (1986) explained: 'The main property of the model which is used in the proof is the equality between the private and social discount rate in the long run' (p. 608) and, in the altruistic dynasty interpretation: 'When the social planner uses the same discount rate for the future life cyclers as the discount rate applied in the altruistic families, the long-run tax rate on capital

incomplete annuitization and also unobservable, then there is a case for capital income taxation when assumed preferences and technology would have a zero tax rate be optimal without the bequests (Boadway, Marchand, and Pestieau (2000)). On the other hand, with the same assumptions, if bequests are given from a utility motivation and if the utility motivation is fully respected in the government objective function, then the optimal tax on capital may be positive or negative (Cremer, Pestieau, and Rochet (2003)).

[61] Farhi and Werning (2007) consider the case of respecting individual dynastic preferences and also giving weight to the dynastic preferences of later generations. As in Kaplow (1995) the thrust of such modelling is to subsidize gifts and bequests since they benefit both the donor and the donee. The results would change if the social welfare function treated dynastic concerns differently from the utility of own-consumption, an issue considered in the context of charitable donations in Diamond (2006).

income is zero. This property... requires that individuals not be constrained at a corner solution for their bequest' (p. 613) or 'This assumes that the social planner and the individuals use the same relative utility weights for intergenerational transfers' (p. 619). Once the weights differ, then the result changes.

As with the Atkinson–Stiglitz result, a key question is how robust the conclusion is to realistic changes in the model. We reach the same conclusion in this case as in the earlier analysis—the finding is not robust for policy purposes.

In the single-cohort model, Naito (1999) has shown that endogeneity of relative wages, together with a uniform earnings tax function, contradicts the optimality of zero capital income taxes when relative wages can be influenced, even with the Atkinson–Stiglitz separability assumptions. Correia (1996) has shown a related result in the infinite horizon model with endogenous relative wages. She assumed two kinds of labour and an inability to tax one kind. The adjustment of capital to offset the absence of taxation of this labour results in a long-run equilibrium with non-zero taxation of capital, with the sign of the tax depending on the details of the technology. A similar result holds if the two types of labour must be taxed the same (and capital affects relative wages). A directly relevant result holds if one of the two types of labour must be taxed the same as capital income is taxed, reflecting an inability to tell apart capital and some labour incomes, which is relevant not only for the self-employed but also in the case of successful corporations with large maintained control by the founders, as with Microsoft or Google. In this case the inability to distinguish between entrepreneurial compensation and the return to capital implies that capital income should be subject to a positive tax (Reis (2007b)).

Also, as in the one-cohort model, uncertainty about the future earnings of those alive and already working as well as about the earnings of those not yet in the labour market or not yet born implies the optimality of positive taxation of capital income (Golosov, Kocherlakota, and Tsyvinski (2003)).[62] Aiyagari (1995) and Chamley (2001) considered borrowing constrained agents in an uncertainty setting. In these models, precautionary saving is high in anticipation of future borrowing constraints, which implies that a positive capital tax is welfare improving in the standard set-up.[63]

[62] Analysis of aggregate uncertainty that affects all earnings possibilities proportionally is quite different. See Golosov, Tsyvinski, and Werning (2007).

[63] Using a different set-up, Chamley (2001) has an example in which randomness is in the timing of future incomes, with the outcome learned ahead of time, giving an advantage to subsidizing capital income rather than taxing it.

Additional considerations arise when there is human capital as well as physical capital in an infinite horizon model. In the presence of both physical and human capital, labour is supplied jointly with human capital, which means that a positive labour tax is also a tax on human capital if its cost is not just foregone earnings and subsidizable spending (such as tuition). In this set-up, it is optimal to converge to zero capital and zero labour taxes (Jones, Manuelli, and Rossi (1997)) unless human capital is observable. If a direct subsidy on human capital is available, then it is optimal to have positive labour taxes in the long run accompanied by a subsidy on human capital and zero taxes on physical capital (Judd (1999)). The result with unobservable human capital suggests that the accumulation of sufficient government resources, relative to expenditures, is a key part of the result on the optimality of asymptotic zero taxation. Thus, at a time of tax reform from a non-optimal tax structure, it is not clear whether the result that long-run taxation of capital should stop is a call for increasing or decreasing the current taxation of capital income. Indeed, the models call for maximal taxation on existing capital since it is inelastically available. Taxation of existing wealth is discussed in Section 6.8.2.

Another source of concern about the results in existing models is that the models assume that the tax on capital income is linear. Saez (2002a) has examined a linear tax with an exemption, as opposed to a tax linear from the origin. Asymptotically no one is paying the capital income tax, as initial wealths above the exemption level decline to the exemption level—with everyone having the same utility discount rate, the before-tax interest rate is driven to the highest discount rate in a steady state, implying a lower after-tax return if there are dynasties with wealth above the exemption level and thus wealth that grows more slowly than the economy. But the tax has served to raise revenue from those with the highest wealth, reducing their wealth to the exemption level—an exemption level that is finite (as opposed to infinite which would be equivalent to no tax) is part of an optimum.

Note that in the long run of the usual models, each period is exactly the same for a dynasty. Recognizing that the dynasties are a collection of successive individuals makes all of the issues considered above for a single cohort relevant in this model as well. For example, earnings are uncertain and the average age–earnings profile is not flat. These observations raise similar issues for capital income taxation as they do in the single-cohort and OLG models. The analysis of Judd (1999) is interesting for addressing this issue. Judd allows greater generality in the evolution of the economy and obtains the result that the average capital income tax tends to zero even if it is not zero in any period.[64] When the model is interpreted as each generation living for a single period, a tax on capital income is equivalent to a tax on bequests. Once individuals live longer than a single period, then one can distinguish between a tax on capital income and a tax on bequests. This point has been made by Chamley (1986, p. 613), 'If a specific tax can be implemented on the interest income of savings used for life-cycle consumption, its rate is in general different from zero.' To preserve a long-run convergence to a zero average tax on capital income while distinguishing between capital income and bequest taxes, if one were taxing capital income during lifetimes, as argued for above, then one would be subsidizing bequests. Such a starting place for analysis focuses attention, appropriately, on the analysis of bequest motives (and their heterogeneity). The relevance of long-run results from this class of models depends critically on the degree of realism of the underlying model of bequest behaviour. Yet, as noted above, how important bequest considerations are for behaviour is unclear and widely varying in the population.[65]

Thus we conclude that the Chamley–Judd result that there should be no taxation of capital income in the long run is not a good basis for policy. Nevertheless the issue remains of the compounding of taxation of capital income resulting in a growing tax wedge the longer the horizon for decision-making—a point also made in models with finite lives of many periods. This is suggestive of a possible role for capital income taxation that varies with the age of the saver and/or with the time lapse between saving and later consumption (as with tax-favoured retirement savings). The role of capital income taxation when earnings are uncertain particularly suggests that rules might well be different for those at ages when workers are mostly retired.

6.4. TAXING CONSUMPTION

Section 6.3 analysed the extent to which capital income should be taxed in the presence of taxation of labour income. While the starting place was the Atkinson–Stiglitz theorem giving conditions under which capital income

[64] For example, assume the period utility functions are the same in all even-numbered years and all odd-numbered years, but different across adjoining years. Then there will be alternating taxes that would show long-run zero taxation across pairs of years (consistent with taxation being zero on average in Judd (1999)).

[65] People give *inter vivos* gifts as well as bequests. Given the tax advantage in the US for *inter vivos* gifts relative to bequests, the dynasty model would imply far more use of *inter vivos* gifts than is the case (Poterba (1998)).

should not be taxed, realistic extensions of the model support the taxation of capital income. There was some support for marginal taxation of capital income at rates that varied with the marginal rate on labour income, as opposed to the linear taxation in the Nordic dual income tax model. Part of the case for the Nordic model is the political argument that base widening is more readily accepted along with lowering the tax rate on capital income—an important point given the efficiency costs of differential taxation of different sources of capital income. Thus, the conclusion of Section 6.3 was that there should be a wedge between the intertemporal consumption MRS and MRT. While not analysed in detail, the models in Section 6.3 did generally also involve a wedge between the intertemporal earnings MRS and MRT.

In this part, we consider the properties of the annual taxation of consumption, rather than the annual taxation of earnings. The recommendation of the Meade Report was for annual progressive taxation of consumption, together with annual taxation of wealth, with particular attention to inheritances.[66] As in Section 6.3, we begin with analysis in a setting of only safe investments—the same rate of return available to everyone. After comparing linear taxation of consumption and earnings, including a discussion of transition, we briefly mention the difference resulting from progressive taxation. Section 6.5 examines issues raised by stochastic returns to investment.

6.4.1. Linear taxation

Consider a worker whose entire life is under the same linear tax on earnings. The PDV of the tax paid is then $t_z \sum_{s=1}^{S} z_s(1+r)^{1-s}$, where t_z is the tax rate on earnings, z_s is earnings in year s and earnings stop after S years. If the worker neither receives nor gives gifts or bequests[67] then lifetime consumption satisfies the lifetime budget constraint, $\sum_{s=1}^{S'} c_s(1+r)^{1-s} = (1-t_z)\sum_{s=1}^{S} z_s(1+r)^{1-s}$, where S' is the length of life. With a tax, t_c on consumption, and no tax on earnings, the lifetime budget constraint is $(1+t_c)\sum_{s=1}^{S'} c_s(1+r)^{1-s} = \sum_{s=1}^{S} z_s(1+r)^{1-s}$, and the

[66] In its discussion of a 'Universal Expenditure Tax' the Meade Report proposed a system of registered and unregistered assets. Only savings and dissavings of registered assets would affect the tax base (with saving in such accounts being deducted from income, and dissaving being added to income, in order to calculate the tax base). The report argued that unregistered assets would be necessary on administrative grounds but also pointed out individuals expecting their marginal rates of income tax to change over time could use unregistered savings and borrowings as a way of averaging their tax liabilities over time.

[67] To incorporate bequests and inheritances we would also want to incorporate estate or inheritance taxes.

taxes paid are $t_c \sum_{s=1}^{S'} c_s(1+r)^{1-s}$. Thus the systems are equivalent on a PDV basis for each member of such a cohort—for each linear earnings tax rate there is a linear consumption tax rate that results in the same budget sets (and so the same earnings and consumption decisions) and same PDV of tax revenues.[68] The matching tax rates satisfy $(1-t_z)(1+t_c)=1$.[69]

In order for equilibrium to be unchanged by this matched change from an earnings tax to a consumption tax, we need government behaviour also to be unchanged. Since the timing of consumption does not match the timing of earnings, the timing of tax revenue changes. While there is some borrowing that permits consumption to exceed earnings for young workers,[70] saving for retirement is the larger element, so that, with consumption taxation, on average individuals would pay taxes later in their lives and so would save more, buying bonds in anticipation of future taxes. In turn, this increased demand for bonds would permit the government to do its financing for unchanged spending as part of equilibrium without altering the interest rate.[71] Whether this is what would actually happen depends on how the government responds to collecting revenue later with a consumption tax rather than earlier with an earnings tax. If government spending changed, so too would the equilibrium.

To see how this plays out over time, consider a change from an earnings tax to a consumption tax in an OLG setting. Assume the transition rules kept taxes the same for cohorts taxed under the old system, so the taxes only involve the new generations and thus do not involve redistribution across generations. Then, after a period with only very young workers taxed, which we ignore, there is a period dominated by saving for retirement, implying a drop in tax revenue as consumption is less than earnings.[72] Once the new steady state is reached, which now includes consumption by retirees, tax revenue exceeds what it would have been under an earnings tax, by an

[68] Below we note the circumstances where equivalence holds with stochastic returns to savings.

[69] If there are binding borrowing constraints limiting consumption to what can be financed by contemporaneous earnings, the equivalence carries over nevertheless. The perfect capital market assumed in this budget constraint ignores differences between borrowing costs and lending returns, which would make the timing of taxes matter to individuals.

[70] Presumably house purchases would not be fully taxed as consumption spending, but rather converted into a flow for later taxation.

[71] Since consumption is larger than earnings because of interest income, the delay in taxes is offset by this source of consumption. In an OLG setting this is combined with differences across cohorts in both size and level of age–earnings trajectories. As long as the rate of interest exceeds the rate of aggregate earnings growth, this difference does not matter on an aggregate PDV basis for all cohorts living fully under one system or the other.

[72] Since workers may borrow early in their careers, this is really referring to a time period with positive savings for retirement consumption. An uncomplicated picture can be seen in a two-period OLG model, with one period of work and two of consumption.

amount matched by the interest cost of government borrowing because of the lower tax revenue in the initial periods. If the government is making its tax and spending decisions based on a long horizon, then the situation is unchanged. However, if the government spends its revenue each period (pay-as-you-go for the full budget), then government spending is lower in the early periods and higher in the later periods as a result of the change to consumption taxation. Adaptation of the economy to this pattern (assuming government spending is consumption, not investment) implies a rise in the aggregate capital stock from having less government consumption earlier, private consumption and output held constant. For private consumption to remain constant generally, government consumption needs to be separable from private consumption in individual preferences. We are also ignoring any change induced by changes in the wage, interest rate, and relative prices of consumer goods.

How does this difference in timing of government consumption matter for evaluation of the tax change? If one were to look only at the new steady state, one would find higher capital with consumption taxation, and so higher output and one might conclude (by erroneous logic) that the change was beneficial, whether it was or not. Proper policy evaluation should look at the entire path of an economy and not just the steady state. Doing that, one would need to evaluate the change in the pattern of government consumption spending (more earlier, less later) as the primary basis for evaluation. The increase in capital from changed timing of government consumption and tax revenue is merely an efficient equilibrium adaptation to the change in the government consumption pattern, not an appropriate source of a positive evaluation.

The political economy of how much borrowing a government does is important and controversial, making it unlikely that some specific model of political outcomes implicit in a particular budget balance constraint will match actual behaviour. Governments generally do not follow such a simple behavioural rule as annual budget balance on average or on the margin. Until we have a better, empirically based understanding of government budgetary practices, an adjustment for government spending behaviour is somewhat speculative. For countries like the UK, the abilities of the government to borrow, to reduce the public debt, and to save; are real. Debt to GDP ratios have varied greatly over time. Examining policy in a setting with a single PDV government budget constraint is in keeping with looking at how governments ought to consider policy.

Note that commenting positively on government policy on the basis of an induced delay in government spending involves saying to the government that since it will otherwise spend relatively too much in the short run (and too little in the long run), the government should choose one tax over another because the choice will lead the government itself to do less spending in the short run (and the reverse later). Legislative process rules that affect political outcomes seem very important. And adjustment of economic advice based on a perception of actual government behaviour, given the advice, also seems important. Yet we are reluctant to base too much on an oversimplified model of the influence of the timing of revenues on spending. Note that this is not a setting of permanently lower revenues but of lower revenues followed by higher revenues. While governments are slow to adapt to perceptions of such a future, anticipatory adjustments in public pension systems that we have observed over the last two or three decades suggest that some degree of forward-looking planning does indeed happen.

A tax on consumption can be collected as a tax directly on consumption, as with a VAT, or by taxing earnings less net active saving (since earnings less net active saving is equal to income minus net saving). The latter permits progressive tax rates, for example by use of annual exemptions.[73] The equivalence for new cohorts between taxing earnings and taxing consumption does not extend from a linear setting to a non-linear annual tax since neither earnings nor consumption are generally constant over time.[74] That is, variations in earnings and in consumption might move above and below break points between marginal rates (for example, above and below the exempt amounts) in different ways. This can happen in certainty models unless the utility discount rate matches the rate of return to saving and can happen with uncertain earnings opportunities.

Note that there is no intertemporal consumption tax wedge *and* no intertemporal earnings tax wedge with linear taxation of either earnings or consumption. With progressive annual consumption taxes there is still no intertemporal earnings wedge. If the age–consumption profile with optimal

[73] This point is drawn out in Hall and Rabushka (2007), which proposes collection through a VAT combined with administrative shift of payment responsibility to the employee. This is a VAT with a rebate equal to earnings up to a ceiling, i.e. a VAT with a zero effective marginal rate below the ceiling.

[74] The equivalence for new cohorts between taxing earnings and taxing consumption extends from a linear setting to a non-linear setting provided that taxation is based on lifetime earnings and lifetime consumption. That is, lifetime taxes might be $T_c[\sum_{s=1}^{S'} c_s(1+r)^{1-s}]$, or $T_z[\sum_{s=1}^{S} z_s(1+r)^{1-s}]$, with annual taxes being withheld toward lifetime taxes. It is not clear how those with different realized lifetimes should be taxed relative to each other. Extending this equivalence to include recognition of bequests and inheritances is complicated by the non-linearity in the tax structure which requires some integration between estate/inheritance and earnings/consumption taxes. We continue to ignore this issue, leaving it for another chapter.

Vickrey (1947) was concerned with the relative treatment by progressive annual taxes of those with constant incomes and those with fluctuating incomes.

taxes is rising more often than falling among workers (as is empirically the case with existing taxes), then they would more often generate a positive intertemporal consumption tax wedge. How these two patterns of wedges (on consumption and on earnings) might relate to a desirable pattern has not appeared in the literature we have seen.

6.4.2. Transition

There is no impact on a generation fully under a new system from a change from a linear earnings tax to the linear consumption tax with the equivalent rate analysed above. However, a change between the two linear systems may matter for older cohorts who live partially under one system and then under the other, depending on the tax treatment of wealth existing at the initiation of the tax regime.[75] Going from an earnings tax to a VAT will increase taxes on people holding wealth (for later consumption) at the time of change, unless there is an offsetting transition adjustment for the implied taxation of consumption from initial wealth. Thus, without a transition adjustment, this change in tax system represents a tax on initial wealth, which is then a non-distorting tax. Indeed, analyses of change to consumption taxation find that a large part of the reported efficiency gain is from the lump sum nature of the taxation of existing wealth (see, e.g., Auerbach, Kotlikoff, and Skinner (1983); Altig, Auerbach, Kotlikoff, Smetters, and Walliser (2001)). Distributionally, the change hurts those with wealth relative to those without at the time of the change. If the tax rates hold the PDV of revenue across all generations constant, then a primary pattern is a higher lifetime tax on those who are older at the time of the tax change, and a lower tax on others, particularly those not yet born. Normative consideration of such a change requires evaluation of this distribution of tax changes as well as consideration of a change from a system that people were relying on and analysis of whether an unanticipated change results in a behavioural response in light of changed expectations of possible future changes. We touch briefly on this issue below in Section 6.8.2.

A different transition issue may arise if the implementation of the tax is through taxing earnings less net active saving. If net active saving is accurately measured then earnings taxation with a savings deduction is equivalent to VAT. However, if net active savings is measured by net deposits into special savings accounts, then accurate measurement of consumption requires

[75] Also relevant is what happens to asset prices, an issue we do not discuss. See, for example, Judd (2001).

measuring net decreases in wealth held outside the accounts insofar as they are used to finance the deposits. With no tracking of outside wealth, transferring initial wealth into the accounts would look like net active saving, resulting in less taxation at the time. Later, withdrawals from the accounts are taxed as consumption (assuming bequests are treated as consumption). Thus consumption from initial wealth is not taxed in PDV terms, preserving the equivalence with earnings taxation and breaking the equivalence with a VAT.

6.5. STOCHASTIC RATES OF RETURN

Many models of optimal taxation assume safe returns to savings. Yet real returns to savings are stochastic. The randomness may be modelled as perfectly correlated across individuals—as would be the case with the risk coming from access to a capital market with stocks and bonds and the same risky portfolio holdings for everyone. However, portfolios vary widely across households. Different people have different beliefs about returns on different assets and access to different information sources and different investment opportunities. And a large fraction of the public holds no stocks at all. Also, not all investments are in market-traded assets.

6.5.1. Marketed risks

Taxing consumption rather than taxing total income has been described as exempting the safe rate of return from taxation, but taxing the difference between the realized risky and the safe rates of return the same (e.g. Gentry and Hubbard (1997); Weisbach (2005)).[76] Similarly, the equivalence between taxing consumption and taxing earnings has been questioned in terms of the taxation of the difference between risky and safe returns (see, e.g., Zodrow (1995)). Evaluation of these issues requires examination of equilibria with different tax structures. Such an evaluation needs to recognize heterogeneity in the population and the behaviour of the government, as noted above.

Lying behind the two equivalence views are the analyses of Gordon (1985) and Kaplow (1994) that linear taxation of the difference between risky and

[76] The bulk of the analysis allows full loss offset, which is not generally the case with income taxes. For discussion of this issue, see Weisbach (2005).

safe returns (with full loss offset) has no effects, with the uses of the revenue that they describe. Before turning to their analyses, let us note the lack of direct impact on an individual with a diversified portfolio and access to market transactions on fixed terms. Without taxation of returns, the individual would realize a return on his portfolio of $\alpha r + (1 - \alpha)\rho = r + (1 - \alpha)(\rho - r)$, where α is the fraction of the portfolio invested in a safe asset paying return r and $1 - \alpha$ is the fraction of the portfolio invested in a risky asset paying return ρ. With a tax, t, on the difference between risky and safe returns (with full loss offset), the realized after-tax return becomes $r + (1 - \alpha')(\rho - r)(1 - t)$. By adjusting the portfolio, assuming no binding limit on borrowing or short selling, the investment in risky assets can be increased so that the after-tax returns from the portfolio match the pre-tax returns when there are no taxes. Thus, the investor can obtain exactly the same returns with and without the tax—$r + (1 - \alpha')(\rho - r)(1 - t) = r + (1 - \alpha)(\rho - r)$ when $(1 - \alpha')(1 - t) = (1 - \alpha)$. In order to analyse equilibria with all investors responding in this way, we need to consider the supply of assets and how the government reacts to the (stochastic) revenue it receives from this taxation.

In showing no effect from a tax on the difference between risky and safe returns, Gordon assumes that the tax revenue from each person is returned to that person in a (stochastic) lump sum way.[77] Kaplow's assumptions are equivalent to having the government sell the stochastic tax yields in the market.[78] In both cases, the imposition of the tax and the government's portfolio or lump sum transfer policy has no effect on equilibrium. That is, the consumers do not change their consumption and earnings plans and the government does not change its real expenditures. When taxing the difference between risky and safe returns has no effect at all, then the tax treatment of this source of income is the same for an income tax, an expenditure tax, and an earnings tax.

Above, we saw that with only safe investments, taxing consumption (linearly) is equivalent to taxing earnings (linearly), provided there is a perfect capital market with only a safe asset and that government behaviour depends on the PDV of tax revenues, not the timing of revenues. There was equivalence in household behaviour for tax rates satisfying $(1 - t_z)(1 + t_c) = 1$. Going from equivalence in household behaviour to equivalence

[77] In this case, the investor does not want to change his portfolio since he is also receiving the risky tax revenues.

[78] Thus, when the investor adjusts his portfolio as above, he purchases precisely the portfolio offered by the government as a consequence of the taxes he is paying. Thus the sale of the government portfolio yields no return. If the investor is indifferent at the margin between stocks and bonds, then the marginal value of the difference between stock and bond returns is zero. The marginal valuation equals the price in equilibrium.

in equilibrium required the government to adjust public debt outstanding to offset the change in the timing of tax revenues. If that is done, then there is no change in equilibrium consumptions and earnings from a change to an equivalent tax (for cohorts fully under the new system; that is, assuming adjustment for transition cohorts).

Examining the household choice problem with safe and risky investment opportunities shows the same equivalence as with only safe investments. In order to have equivalence of equilibrium, the government must adjust in response to the change in the timing of revenues and to the presence of a stochastic pattern of government revenues. As with the safe return case, the government needs to adjust its debt and as with the Gordon and Kaplow analyses, it needs to shift the risk to households in a way that matches the risk they held before the taxation of risky returns. If these are done, then there is equivalence of consumption and earnings taxation, because the taxation of the difference between safe and risky returns has no effect on equilibrium. Similarly taxing total income and taxing earnings differ in the taxation of safe returns, not the taxation of the difference between risky and safe returns.

Key to this result is how the government responds to the change in tax revenues from the taxation of the difference between risky and safe returns. The Gordon and Kaplow assumptions, while informative of the workings of the economic mechanisms, are not similar to actual government practice. That suggests modelling a change in taxes, borrowing, and spending that follows practice more closely, along with a change that makes the workings of the model clear. For example, this suggests a comparison of consumption and earnings taxes without accompanying lump sum transfers or marketing of the risks in future tax revenues. Such modelling would involve two complexities—the description of the menu of risky and safe investments available to the economy and the description of how the government does adapt to a change in the risk characteristics of tax revenues. Discussion of this in the literature has contrasted interpretations with different discount rates for the equivalence in government revenue. But the 'right' discount rate to use for analysis cannot be assumed but needs to be derived from a model of how the government behaves and what the investment options in the economy are. Presumably this can be done along the lines of analysis of the choice of portfolio for a public pension system (see, e.g., Abel (2001); Diamond and Geanakoplos (2003)) and the adjustment of a defined benefit system for different cohorts (see Gollier (2005)). But such analyses have not been done as far as we know. Our presumption is that neither equivalence holds once one recognizes heterogeneity in individual portfolios and government actions that are restricted to issuing safe bonds and adjusting tax rates (on earnings or consumption).[79]

6.5.2. Non-marketed risks

With marketed investments, all those making use of the stock market can share in bearing the risks in return and valuation, and modelling assumes that each investor is small relative to the market. While the government spreads risks from tax revenues differently from how the market would, particularly over time, a comparison of market and government risk allocations involves the entire economy in both cases. Not all investments are marketed through stock markets. Taxation of the returns to non-marketed investments will matter because of the shift in risk from the single investor (or small number of investors) to the economy as a whole through the government's tax and spending policies. Also, non-marketed risks are not likely to have constant returns to scale. Thus the presence of taxation affects the inframarginal opportunities available to entrepreneurs as well as sharing the risks of those opportunities. This has some similarity to the general equilibrium impact of risk sharing through taxation with marketed risks if the government does not return the risks to the economy in an offsetting way. Again, the returns to scale, now on the aggregate level, matter for the impact of taxation.

6.6. AGE-DEPENDENT EARNINGS TAXES

From the perspective of optimal contract theory, any costlessly observable variable correlated with unobserved characteristics or behaviour should influence payoffs, even if it is poorly measured and the correlation is limited.

[79] This framing of the issue is different from that in Gentry and Hubbard (1997). They consider consumption taxation implemented by a wage tax combined with a business cash flow tax. Although they purportedly are addressing distributional implications, their focus is on evaluating the difference in taxation from the perspective of a firm's investment decisions, as opposed to a household's life-cycle labour supply and savings choices. As a consequence, they focus on the marginal value of immediate depreciation of investment to a firm, which they value using the safe rate of interest, supporting the view that consumption taxation exempts the safe rate of interest but not the return to bearing risk or pure rents. Modelling household choice as a base for examining the impact on the distribution of utilities of giving the deferral advantage is more complicated. While stocks and bonds have the same marginal value with portfolio optimization, the impact of deferral on the inframarginal gains from the availability of stocks is relevant for distributional analysis. As a quick example of this issue, for given wealth and Cobb–Douglas preferences the higher the distribution of risky returns, the greater the gain from deferral for a given portfolio mix. Since the optimized portfolios may well be different, a full analysis is more complicated. But this seems the appropriate way to approach the distributional impact.

If this perspective is applied to optimal taxes in an extended Mirrlees model, labour income taxes should depend on all variables correlated with the ability to earn, even those measured poorly. While tax systems have stupefying complexity, it is not from incorporating many such variables.

Primarily, the approach to optimal tax theory in this chapter has been to take as given a set of allowable tax tools (while ignoring the cost of administration), chosen to reflect actual (or plausible potential) use and chosen to enable the inferences from a model to be useful for policy discussions. Some analysts have considered it significant to replace this approach of designated tax tools by assuming that the choice of tax tools is an endogenous part of the optimization, subject only to observability constraints. A common assumption in these formal models is that taxation is based on costlessly, perfectly observed variables while all other variables are not observable at any cost. But this description of observability is not accurate on either side—earnings are costly to measure and are not perfectly observed and there are other (costly, imperfectly) observable variables that could increase social welfare if used optimally. Thus standard assertions about observability, commonly used to 'derive' a tax base rather than assuming it, are not an adequate guide to the choice of a tax base for direct taxation. Complexity of the tax base matters, as do both public reactions and the political economy of a more complex structure, both related in part to views on horizontal equity. We are lacking in analyses that take us very far in considering when additional complexity is a good or bad idea, since issues raised by complexity are not part of the formal modelling. In the absence of extended analyses on which to draw, using complexity concerns to influence policy inferences from formal models is subjective, but seems important. We simply refer to variables as taxable and non-taxable, rather than observable and non-observable, reflecting an *ex ante* judgement call reflecting these multiple dimensions of relevance for choosing a tax base.

To explore the extent to which further complications should enter taxation, we consider three examples of variables that might be used to influence the taxation of earnings—hours worked (and so earnings per hour), height, and age. Only the third is recommended. Two issues are raised by the consideration of additional variables—the ability of (and cost to) governments and taxpayers to deal with greater complexity and perceptions of equity, both by analysts and the public.

Income taxes are based on earnings without an attempt to measure hours worked and so average earnings per hour. Minimum wage rules and requirements for paying higher wages for overtime both require some measurement of hours worked. And the Working and Childcare Tax Credit programmes in the UK base transfers on doing at least a minimum number of hours of work. In the cases of minimum wages and overtime pay rates, the employer and the employee have conflicting interests in the measurement of hours. This makes enforcement easier than enforcement of a tax that depended on hours worked would be, since neither the employer nor the employee has an interest in higher taxation of earnings. While this conflict of interests also does not exist in the tax credit programmes, they follow the common practice of programmes being more intrusive and more measurement focused when applied to poorer people than when applied to the general public. An attempt to incorporate a measure of hours worked into the tax base would plausibly bear considerable correlation with actual hours. For many workers in large firms or government employment, existing financial records would form a good basis for estimating hours worked with reasonable accuracy. Moreover, a requirement for self-declaration of hours, subject to some form of random monitoring, would fit the theoretical category of a correlated, poorly measured, but nevertheless useful basis for further tax distinctions. And it is not as if earnings were measured perfectly either.

Thus, if it did not recognize factors other than observability, optimal tax theory would call for basing taxes in part on estimated earnings per hour. We do not think that using an hours measure in determining taxes would be a good idea, however, and it is useful to consider why not. Basing taxation on inaccurately measured variables leaves more scope for administrative discretion and encourages cynicism about the fairness of the tax system. Both features are likely to add to the difficulty of encouraging voluntary accuracy in reporting and support for the politics of better taxation. This is already a problem resulting from the inaccurate measurement of income. But income (or consumption) is central to distributional concerns and it is hard to see how to have satisfactory taxation without it. Adding to concerns about inaccurate measurement should not be done lightly. The theory of how to use poorly measured variables would not be intuitive to either legislators or the public, again making good tax politics more difficult. In sum, basing taxes in part on hours worked does not seem to be a good idea, although that intuition is not supported by formal analysis as far as we know.[80] As with the Meade Report, concern about multiple aspects of taxation leads to this conclusion, whereas the opposite conclusion would follow from taking optimal tax theory literally and ignoring aspects of taxation not included in the formal modelling.

[80] In the exploration of lessons from the literature, we do not explore the (small) literature using hours worked in determining taxes.

As another example, this one where accuracy of measurement is not at issue, consider the findings of Persico, Postlewaite, and Silverman (2004) and Case and Paxson (2006) that there is a correlation between height and earnings abilities.[81] With standard modelling and different tax structures for adults of different heights (possibly distinguished by gender), one can then have higher social welfare than without such multiple tax structures. While it would be somewhat complicated for tax authorities to have multiple tax structures, there is not much complication for the taxpayer who does not get to choose among tax structures.[82] And by restricting the set of tax functions to a small number of different height intervals, the complexity for legislation would not be enormous. What does seem important is that unlike the example of different tax structures for different ages discussed below, a set of tax functions based on height is a setting of consistently different structures for different (fully grown) individuals rather than individuals passing through the different tax structures as they age.[83] This distinction seems important for political and public acceptability, and possibly for the ethical underpinnings of taxation.

Consider a sequence that starts with extensive research documenting that such differences are real and robust to alternative measurement approaches, explains to the public and tries to convince them that this is the case, and then tries to explain to the public why this is a useful basis for differences in

[81] Mankiw and Weinzierl (2007) also consider relating income taxation to height. They discuss the evidence on the link between height and earnings, present the argument that such an approach would increase social welfare, and do a first pass at the structure of such a tax. The authors' interpretations of the result differ. 'One of us takes from this *reductio ad absurdum* the lesson that the modern approach to optimal taxation, such as the Vickrey–Mirrlees model, poorly matches people's intuitive notions of fairness in taxation and should be reconsidered or replaced. The other sees it as clarifying the scope of the framework, which nevertheless remains valuable for the most important questions it was originally designed to address' (page 2).

We share the second view. As this essay has argued, the insights from optimal tax theory are only part of the considerations relevant for tax policy, but an important part. Indeed, the role of fairness concerns in limiting allowable tax tools was argued by Atkinson and Stiglitz (1980). The methodological error in the 'reconsider or replace' view comes from taking the answer to a formal model as a literal policy recommendation. By their nature, models are a simplification of reality in order to have a sufficiently tractable basis for reaching conclusions within the model. As such, every model has inaccurate assumptions and could be used to derive silly inferences by focusing on the implications of that inaccuracy. At their best, models are good for some questions and not for others. Finding a question for which a model (or modelling approach, as in this case) gives a rejected answer need not detract from the usefulness of the model or modelling approach for the purpose for which it was designed, and does not in this case.

[82] Allowing *ex ante* choice among tax structures may be a source of welfare gains (Luttmer and Zeckhauser (2008)). We do not explore this option—if significant, this added complexity may challenge the ability of many to figure out which tax structure to pick and could be viewed as inequitable as some workers successfully lowered taxes significantly by a good choice while others regretted poor choices.

[83] This ignores the shrinkage that occurs with aging.

taxation. Then picture a legislature considering a half-dozen or so different tax structures on this basis.[84] Presumably the incentive for parents to stunt the growth of their children would be minimal if they also recognized that the factors correlated with height do affect earnings abilities. Does this scenario violate some sense of horizontal equity? If height were irrelevant, it would. But once height is linked to earnings ability, then people of different heights are not identical as far as the government's ability to infer ability is concerned. That is, the government's ability to raise revenue relative to income distribution and efficiency concerns differs by taxpayer height. This is similar to the view that people with different tastes for work are not identical, even if they have the same budget sets. Whether the gain in social welfare were small or large would depend on the magnitude of the correlation and the extent to which different tax structures had an impact on optimized social welfare.

We feel comfortable in rejecting this idea out of hand, as did Mankiw and Weinzierl (2007). What is harder than reaching that conclusion is sorting out its underlying basis. Mankiw and Weinzierl offer several reasons for rejection. One is that this might be the first step in a sequence of taxes that vary with demographics, and while one might be acceptable, the end point of such a process would be unsatisfactory for its administrative burden and invasiveness. They counter this argument with the view that some demographic variables are used already, others are widely unacceptable and this need not be a slippery slope.[85] They note the political risk element—'democratic societies may have an interest in avoiding the taxation of specific groups as a matter of course to counter the majority's temptation to tax minority groups' (p. 13). More generally, there is always concern about politically well-connected groups skewing policy to their advantage, at the expense of some wider measures of the public good. This is an issue here, in part, because height is not the only demographic variable that could be used in this way. We would not like to see an exploration of which variables would be most attractive to the politically more powerful. Mankiw and Weinzierl recognize a possibility of stigma, but do not see that as important. They offer two critiques of utilitarianism—coming from libertarianism and horizontal equity. Unlike libertarians, we are not 'skeptical of the redistribution of income or

[84] Think just about earnings, but it might also be the case that different heights are also correlated with different abilities to invest and so different possible rates of return and different intertemporal discount factors and thus different tendencies to save.

[85] A similar optimal tax argument could be made with regard to gender, given gender differences in life expectancies and the shapes of life-cycle earnings profiles. As with age, gender is not used extensively in tax systems although, again, it has played a large role in public pension system rules in some countries, such as the UK (at present).

wealth because they believe that individuals are entitled to the returns on their justly-acquired endowments' (p. 15).[86] But we do not pursue this issue here. We do share Mankiw and Weinzierl's concern with horizontal equity issues, pursued further in Section 6.8.4. An additional point is that, contrary to the hypothetical above, the public may not be convinced of the equity of such an approach since there is only a stochastic relation between height and earnings abilities. The public's sense of equity, largely formed without deep thought, nevertheless has some relevance in a democratic society. Also relevant is the public's reaction to its sense of equity. This issue is discussed further in Section 6.8.4. Our exploration of this example is to permit distinctions with age-dependent taxes, which involve different issues.[87]

In contrast to height, age is used by actual tax structures, but very little apart from retirement-related rules. In the US there are distinctions for children (who can be dependents and so provide additional deductions) and those over 65, who may receive an additional deduction. In France tax rates depend directly on the number of children through the *quotient familial.* Whilst there are no deductions for dependent children in the UK, the system does include an additional allowance for those aged over 65 and a further additional allowance for those over 75, although for higher income individuals these are both tapered away back to the level of the under-65s allowance.[88] These examples do not provide much variation in taxes across ages, nor do they provide a systematic variation in marginal tax rates. In contrast, age does play a large role in the rules for both public and private pension systems and in some countries in tax-favoured retirement savings opportunities.[89] Eligibility for receiving pension benefits is commonly age-based. Benefits typically increase with the age at which they start and the rates of increase commonly vary with age—for example by only being available for a range of ages, as in the UK, and also by having different percentage

[86] Individuals do have entitlements, but the strength of entitlements and the bases of entitlements do not lead us to scepticism of the appropriateness of redistribution, but to limits in taxation.

[87] An appropriate question to ask is how complicated a tax structure a legislature can use well. Historically legislatures have relied more on their own decision-making in the realm of taxation (and other topics in economics) than in other areas—legislatures vote money for bridges, they don't vote blueprints. Perhaps further addressing of complexity (beyond what is already left to staff) could be allocated to some expert group, as Breyer (1993) has proposed for dealing with health risks. And perhaps the public would accept both the underlying idea and the use of experts.

[88] In addition those over 65 in April 2000 still receive the married couples allowance which was abolished for individuals younger than 65 on that date (i.e. born after April 1935). This allowance is also tapered away as income rises.

[89] In the UK, apart from the tax favouring of partial annuitization and the requirement to annuitize three-quarters of private pension assets by age 75, tax favoured assets are available for withdrawal with no restrictions on age or holding periods and as such are simply tax favoured general savings vehicles, unlike in the US where such assets are retirement saving vehicles (i.e. subject to extra taxation if withdrawn at a younger age).

calculations at different ages, as in the US. In countries that use some form of retirement test, benefit eligibility rules relative to earnings also commonly vary with age. Further complexity often comes with pension reform, with age-related rules being different for people of different birth years. And we note that in Switzerland, the mandatory occupational pension has contribution rates that vary with the age of the worker. Thus, it is natural to explore reducing the large difference in the use of age between pension rules and tax rules.

In the context of a one-period model of income taxation, and with a focus particularly on younger workers, Kremer (2001) called for different tax structures for different ages. Applying the Mirrlees model separately to different age groups, he argues that the distributions of earnings and the labour supply elasticities are so different across ages that the implied pattern of optimal tax rates would vary greatly by age. Borrowing constraints that are prevalent among younger workers may be a further basis for different tax structures.[90]

Let us consider a political process if such an approach were taken. The first step might be to allocate each age to one of a small set of ages, in order to limit the number of tax schedules.[91] Perhaps the set might be under-30, 30–50, 50–65 (or the state pension age), and over-65. For simplicity, there might be a given set of marginal tax rates with only the break points varying as a function of age. This doesn't sound too hard for a legislature to do.[92] And plausibly it could be worked out without undue pressure by the politically better-connected ages. With suitable transition rules, this does not violate horizontal equity concerns that are lifetime based, and presumably would be as publicly acceptable as are age-related pension rules.

As discussed above, formal models do show advantages to age-dependent earnings taxes. Beyond theoretical observations, Weinzierl (2007) has done an optimization calculation to find the advantage from age-varying rules. He compares a single tax regime with a system with three tax regimes for ages 30–39, 40–49, and 50–59. He uses data from the PSID to calibrate a model of wage rates for five representative workers representing different quintiles of

[90] Recent analyses of age-dependent taxes include Blomquist and Micheletto (2003); Erosa and Gervais (2002); Gervais (2003); Fennell and Stark (2005); Lozachmeur (2006); and Weinzierl (2007).

[91] If there are joint returns for couples based on a couple's total incomes, labour income might be taxed on the basis of the age of the earner while capital income might be taxed as if each received half. Or all taxable income could be treated as if half were taxed on the basis of the age schedule of each of the couple.

[92] This assertion may be undercut by the common practice of adjusting public benefit formulae for the age at which they start with a linear formula, when multiplicative or more complex formulae seem to make more sense. Supporting the thought of delegation is the automatic adjustment in Sweden, done on a roughly actuarial basis, although one with rules for the actuaries set by legislation.

lifetime earnings. He uses the mechanism design approach referred to above. With 5 agents and 3 periods, the government sets up to 15 earnings/net-of-tax earnings pairs. Without age-dependent taxes, each period each agent chooses one out of the full 15 pairs for all ages, using the capital market to optimize lifetime utility. With age-dependent taxes, each period each agent chooses one of the (up to 5) offerings available at that age, again using the capital market to optimize lifetime utility. Compared with the optimum with a single tax function (15 choices for each period), he finds that average taxes are lower on young workers and higher on older ones with age-specific taxes (and so only 5 choices each period). He also finds a large welfare gain from the optimal three-age tax function compared with a single tax function, the same for all ages, equivalent to 2% of aggregate consumption. This is two-thirds of the gain from going to the full mechanism design optimum (where individuals are restricted to (up to) five lifetime plans, rather than being free to piece together separate plans each period). While interesting, this is clearly just a start on exploring this issue, so this is really a call for research on an issue that seems to have a good probability of leading to significant policy improvements.

A different approach to taxing earnings over a lifetime looks at current earnings in the context of previous earnings. This could be done in a variety of ways, including a moving average over a fixed number of years or basing lifetime taxes on lifetime earnings, with annual taxes viewed as withholding toward the eventual determination of lifetime taxes.[93] In the discussion of two-period models above, we noted how this might serve social welfare maximization. Now we consider the ability to implement. This certainly is doable, with the government providing historic information along with tax forms. Indeed, we can consider this as parallel to rules that determine public pensions. Defined benefit pensions are based on the history of earnings, possibly a full history (as in Sweden) or a long history (as in the US). In a wage-indexed system for initial benefits (that are then price-indexed), as in the US, the benefit formula relating benefits to earnings varies with date of birth through automatic indexing. Indeed, legislated future ages for receiving full benefits vary with date of birth in the US. In the UK, such a change is already underway with the movement of the state pension age for women from 60 to 65 over the period 2010 to 2020, and further increases in the state pension age for both men and women will follow (from 65 to 66 in 2024, from 66 to 67 in 2034, and from 67 to 68 in 2044), although this can

[93] These would be similar to the approach in Vickrey (1947), who cumulated annual income, not annual earnings and who considered various lengths of time for the cumulation.

also be viewed as different age-dependent rules year-by-year. And Sweden has automatic adjustments that apply to each birth cohort different determinants of initial benefits (for a given earnings history) and of the growth of benefits from a delayed start.

Thus a key question is whether variation in annual tax rates as a function of age is a bad idea because of complexity or a case of theory being ahead of policy, with research on tax design needed, but reform called for. We are inclined to take the latter view for countries that have a good legislative process.

6.7. DIVERSE SAVINGS BEHAVIOUR

The models explored above assumed life-cycle savings. Yet it is clear that this is not a highly accurate model of behaviour for everyone.[94] Alternative modellings of saving behaviour, seemingly relevant for significant portions of the population, include precautionary savings, time-inconsistent behavioural models consistent with too little saving, and utility-of-wealth models which appear to make more sense for those with very high wealth.[95] Moreover, behavioural models and experiments have explored how individuals respond to alternative ways of encouraging additional saving.[96] Behavioural analysis of saving behaviour is highly relevant for the choice of tax base. It is also important for evaluating the role of mandatory programmes that require contributions when working and provide benefits when retired. And these two institutions need to be considered together. A key tax design issue is how to combine concern that some fraction of the population saves too little for an adequate replacement rate in retirement while another fraction saves too much, resulting in their retiring too soon from the perspective of social welfare optimization, as played a role in the models in Section 6.3.

[94] As Bernheim (1997) has written: 'While it would be rash to dismiss the many empirical successes of the LCH [Life Cycle Hypothesis] and discard it unconditionally, it is equally rash (in light of its empirical failures and well-founded skepticism about its underlying premises) to employ this theory as the sole organizing principle for understanding savings incentives.'

[95] On the diversity of savings behaviour, see Carroll (2000); Dynan, Skinner, and Zeldes (2004); and Section 6.9.1.

[96] Behavioural economics has become a major research area for many economists and some of the findings are very exciting (for a survey relative to public finance, see Bernheim and Rangel, 2007). Indeed, analyses of the difference in outcomes with opt-in and opt-out rules for retirement savings plans are already influencing policy makers in both the US and the UK—the introduction of Personal Accounts in the UK, whereby individuals are automatically enrolled in private pensions by their employer unless they choose to opt out was announced in 2007, is being legislated in 2008 and will be introduced in 2012.

Behavioural diversity as well as heterogeneity in life expectancy, intertemporal preferences, and consumption history (in light of realistic links between past consumptions and later marginal utilities of consumption) all call for diversity in individual saving rates, which also played a role in the models in Section 6.3. And alternative modelling of those accumulating very large wealth is relevant for choosing the tax base in light of the great inequality of wealth holdings. This diversity in savings behaviour has not received much attention in tax modelling and would appear to be an important issue for future research. The following conjectures are highly speculative, but seem worth exploring.

The behaviour of those with very large wealth appears to require modelling utility for some people as coming directly from wealth holding, not indirectly from later consumption (Carroll (2000)). This suggests an inelasticity in consumption behaviour that would seem to justify very high taxes on capital income on those with very high wealth.

Concern about too little saving for retirement suggests a programme of tax-favoured retirement saving (to supplement mandatory provision of retirement income if that programme is not extremely large). Recognition of diversity of saving behaviour and the advantage of discouraging too early retirement suggest limiting the extent of access to tax-favoured retirement savings accounts, as well as preserving their character as retirement accounts. But recognition of diversity in the saving behaviour of the population does not appear to call for rejection of the basic conclusions reached above. Instead it suggests modifications of the policy (e.g. tax-favoured retirement savings). And behavioural issues (both mental accounting and self-aware self-control) suggest it may be useful to have additional reform as opposed to just exempting from taxation some level of income from capital. Examples are some form of autoenrolment (see Beshears et al. (2007)) or else some active roles for third parties (e.g. employers and financial institutions) as noted in Bernheim (1997). But this is primarily a call for research and a conjecture about outcomes of such research, not a firm basis for policy.

More research is also warranted on the optimality properties of the different ways of structuring tax-favouring for retirement saving. Options in use for tax treatment of deposits, of accumulations, and of withdrawals include: (1) exempt-exempt-taxable (EET), as in Personal Pensions in the UK or IRAs in the US, (2) taxable-exempt-exempt (TEE), as in Tax Exempt Special Savings Accounts or their successor, Individual Savings Accounts in the UK, or Roth IRAs in the US, (3) having both available, and (4) having partial taxation of accumulation income (as was in Australia). Further research is also warranted relative to proposals and practices that allow tax-favoured saving for other purposes, such as house purchase, medical expenses, and unemployment.

The impact of earnings uncertainty on the desirability of taxing capital income suggests that taxation of capital income might well be different at ages when much of the working population is expected to be retired than at earlier ages. Combining this with the role of tax-favoured treatment of retirement savings and the presence of precautionary balances at all ages suggests there may be an advantage (unexplored in the literature as far as we know) from age varying capital income taxation for capital income outside the retirement accounts. This could be done, for example, by capital income tax exempt amounts that varied with age.

6.8. FURTHER ISSUES

This section touches on a number of issues including a further discussion of the use of a social welfare function (6.8.1), government commitment (6.8.2), some modelling assumptions (6.8.3), and horizontal equity (6.8.4). These sections examine the underpinnings of the approaches to taxation discussed above.

6.8.1. Social welfare function

Based on its use of a social welfare function, the optimal tax approach is often accused of assuming a benevolent government. This criticism has both right and wrong elements. Calculation of what a benevolent government should do is not the same as assuming that there is a benevolent government. Rather it is asking a key question—what policies would one want to see a benevolent government follow? The answer to such a question can help inform a democratic debate about government policies, which is all that academic economic research can hope to accomplish by itself. Moreover, it is hard to see how one gives policy advice without knowing the link between good design of policies and the accomplishment of social ends.[97]

The relevant part of the accusation is that the political tendencies of actual governments are highly relevant for good policy recommendations. Awareness of political tendencies can readily take two separate forms. One is to

[97] As Musgrave wrote: 'Just as homo economicus or a competitive Walrasian system are useful fictions to model an ideal market, so it is helpful to visualize how a correctly functioning public sector would perform... Unless "correct" solutions are established to serve as standards, defects and failures of actual performance cannot even be identified.' Buchanan and Musgrave (1999), p. 35.

extend optimal tax theory to incorporate additional constraints reflecting what governments are likely to do, either in response to current recommendations or in future policies that may be influenced by current legislation. This is a richer, and possibly more relevant, environment than considering a constitutional approach to limits on taxability. The literature on tax policy without government commitment is a form of such analysis, although one that typically does not have a rich, empirically supported theory of government behaviour in a democracy. A second form that awareness of political tendencies can take is through judicious use of the insights from optimal tax results when moving from basic theory to policy recommendations. Recommendations can reflect beliefs about the workings of the political process, based on the current state of politics and political science and projections of political evolution.

The optimal tax literature works simply with a social welfare function. With individual utility depending on both consumption and the disutility of labour, this is not equivalent to attention focused on income distribution, particularly using a social income evaluation function as developed by Atkinson (1970). While we share a concern about income distribution, a social income evaluation function is no substitute for a social welfare function in thinking about tax policy.[98] This approach appears to give too much weight to encouraging work, particularly by low earners, and we do not think that maximizing a social income evaluation function is a useful variant on social welfare function maximization. Nevertheless, one might consider limiting income variation (perhaps because of political implications), which would also imply rejecting possible Pareto gains.

6.8.2. Time frame, commitment, and transition

Support for total annual income as the ideal tax base appears to rely on using a year as the time frame for thinking about individuals when doing normative analysis. In contrast, the optimal tax models that are the basis for this chapter rely on lifetimes (or beyond) as the time frame for normative analysis. Exclusive focus on either of these two time frames seems incomplete. On the one hand, the current position of individuals is a result, in part, of their own past decisions. It does not seem adequate to frame the basis for policy choice in a way that ignores intertemporal aspects of incentives, a normative dimension of responsibility for future consequences of one's current actions,

[98] Nor do we see a case for an objective function that combines both a social welfare function and a social utility function.

and a normative response to the consequences of one's past actions. On the other hand, a lifetime perspective does not adequately allow for individual time-inconsistency and does not contain a normative adjustment for the consequences of decision mistakes. For example, previous high levels of saving do seem to provide some normative support for higher current consumption, while previous low levels do not seem to be sufficient warrant for enforcing some very low levels of consumption. And such concerns need to be tempered by their incentive effects.

In democratic (and non-democratic) societies, further complicating consideration of government policy at a particular time are the inevitable changes in normative evaluations from the bases for past government policies as governments change. Also relevant is the inevitable incompleteness of both government plans for future policies and government understanding of the consequences of chosen policies. That is, normative analysis needs to consider the degree of adjustment that should be made for the implications of past policies. That different models use different time dimensions is part of the reason why it is inappropriate to rely too heavily on any single model's implications.

Commitment

Although tax legislation can have an open-ended horizon, it is expected that taxes will change as circumstances develop and governments change. Moreover, governments do not commit to a complete (contingent) set of future policies. Individuals making decisions that affect their future tax liabilities (such as investments and education) are faced with uncertainty about future circumstances, future governments and their possible tax reforms, and any transition rules the government may include in tax legislation. The Meade Report call for 'a certain stability in taxation in order that persons may be in a position to make reasonably far-sighted plans' (p. 21) also suggests seeking tax instruments that are relatively simple and transparent to aid the formation of appropriate tax expectations by individuals.

In the ongoing process of the adaptation of tax policies to economic and demographic developments as well as to changing normative perceptions and political balance, a set of rules/guidelines for transition issues is important both economically and politically. From this perspective we can appreciate the Meade Report's concern for flexibility and stability:

> A good tax structure must be flexible for two rather distinct purposes... there must be recognition of the need to be able to adjust total tax burdens reasonably rapidly and frequently in the interests of demand management... In a healthy

democratic society there must be broad political consensus—or at least willingness to compromise—over certain basic matters; but there must at the same time be the possibility of changes of emphasis in economic policy as one government succeeds another... But at the same time there is a clear need for a certain stability in taxation in order that persons may be in a position to make reasonably far-sighted plans. Fundamental uncertainty breeds lack of confidence and is a serious impediment to production and prosperity. (Page 21.)

Beyond any possibility of short-run demand management, there are changes in long-run fiscal needs that are likely to occur from trend developments in economic and demographic circumstances, as well as the spreading over the future of short-run changes in fiscal needs (e.g. after a war).[99] A research programme that addresses the need for both adjustment and stability would seek a tax structure that has enough political acceptability to relegate tax changes primarily to parameter changes in a class of parameters anticipated to adjust to circumstances. The tax design would need to recognize that individual expectations about future taxes are endogenous to the policy framework being created. Such modelling would examine a balance between the different effects of changing policies.[100]

In addition, given the difficulty of radical change, the existing basic structure of taxation influences the political process. Indeed, links between the form of public pension design and anticipated future legislation has been part of the debate in the US between defined benefit and defined contribution mandatory public systems.[101] Similarly, implicit in our focus on the tax base, separate from tax rates, is an assumption that tax rates are being optimized for given tax bases, thereby ignoring the political linkage that may well be present between tax base and tax rates. It is incomplete to say that a suitable choice of tax rates can make a different tax base have comparable overall progressivity if that suitable choice will not happen. Recognition of the link between the form of tax institutions and the perceptions and salience that then influence policy making is important.

In light of the expectation of repeated adjustments of taxes, how should we use the findings of the models analysed above, which considered government policy being set for a lifetime or an infinite future? A start of an answer is to say that in thinking about policy, one would like to know what policies

[99] Currently discretionary fiscal policy, while pursued by governments, is not in high favour among academic economists (Auerbach (2002)). But built-in stabilizers, while not getting much active attention, are still viewed positively (Auerbach and Feenberg (2000)). It is odd that there was not discussion of built-in stabilizers in the Meade Report.

[100] Such analysis might parallel for an economy the analysis for individuals in Amador, Werning, and Angeletos (2005).

[101] For example, see Diamond (1999), chapter 3.

would be good if they could be set for a long time. And drawing inferences from a model with committed taxes would recognize the decreased relevance of those parts of the optimization that relied on unrealistic elements of the modelled commitment.

For example, the Chamley and Judd papers have two results. The first, discussed above, is to have no taxation of capital income, either after a finite date or asymptotically (that is taxation can be positive indefinitely, but with a steadily shrinking tax rate). The second is to tax initial wealth as heavily as possible, at least in the representative agent version. In the context of these models with infinitely lived agents, the second finding has had little direct influence on policy recommendations drawing on the literature. Nevertheless, the same perspective, clearly stated, lies behind arguments in OLG models for switching from income taxation to consumption taxation particularly as a way to transfer wealth from older cohorts at the time of tax implementation with little in the way of distorting incentives.[102]

It is appropriate that these two Chamley–Judd results have been viewed so differently. Taxing initial wealth as much as the available tax tools allow (whether as a wealth tax or a capital income tax) strains the relevance of the assumption that the government can commit to a policy that this taxation of wealth will end. Without a genuine commitment technology, confiscatory wealth taxation would adversely affect saving behaviour and have serious efficiency costs (even if the government saves the revenue) because of concern that such taxation will return. A switch from income to consumption taxation (with limited grandfathering of existing wealth) could be interpreted as a move against wealth which has limited implications for future taxation of wealth since the set of politically plausible tax policies has not changed very much—increases in the taxation of consumption are limited because they fall on everyone. On the other hand, some people may recognize that the underlying principle of the efficiency advantage of taxing existing wealth would continue to be present, even if it required a different tax change to implement.

These assertions raise the critical question of how to model the link between tax legislation and expectations about future taxes. One approach in the literature is to model a consistent game-theoretic equilibrium between tax setters, potential alternative tax setters, and taxpayers, with the threatened reactions by the taxpayers limiting the setting of taxes. This literature seems

[102] This basis for a change in taxation is very sensitive to implementation. It works for taxing consumption directly and for taxing consumption as income less savings provided initial wealth is measured, but may not work for taxing consumption as income less savings if initial wealth is not measured.

to rely too heavily on a game-theoretic equilibrium drawn from oligopoly theory with a limited number of sophisticated players for use in a setting of vast numbers of players, many of whom are ill-informed. The literature, now in its early stages, may well develop into something useful, but does not yet seem very informative. Nevertheless, the literature is interesting in making clear the effects of expectations about taxes on economic incentives.[103]

An alternative way to view 'commitment' is in the realm of precedents, paralleling their role in legal decisions (see, e.g., Kaplow (2006b)). Assume the government announces a one-time capital levy. That is a precedent for doing the same again, and so lacks credibility that it really is one time. Perhaps there are special circumstances, such as a war or meteorite impact that is unlikely to recur. Then the precedential cost may be much lower, although there remains the effect of a possible perception of an increased risk of a widening of the precedent. Just as individuals set rules for themselves, with bright-line rules easier to adhere to,[104] so too the government process recognizes that crossing a bright-line rule runs the risk of major backlash—whether it is losing elections, with possible reversals of policies, or street demonstrations, or political backlashes in other realms. Thus one might prefer a small annual wealth tax rather than a large one-time tax, on the grounds that expectations of continuing and possibly slow growth of the annual tax has less of a deterrent effect on saving through perceptions of future policies. Switching from an income tax to a consumption tax has the effect of taxing existing wealth, with possible future increases in the tax rate as then a risk discouraging saving. Again, we would expect less of an impact. This way of approaching the issue of commitment, or its lack, differs from a common game-theoretic approach using trigger strategies in not assuming widespread sophisticated understanding of equilibrium, and in recognizing the limited awareness of politics of some and the multiple motivations affecting voting.

Transition

Transition issues arise in two ways in a discussion of the tax base. First, analysis of the tax base needs to recognize that there will be future tax changes,

[103] We note that the Chamley–Judd finding of asymptotically vanishing taxation of capital income with full commitment has been extended to a setting without commitment (Dominguez (2007); Reis (2007a)). These papers assume a single infinite horizon budget constraint. Zero asymptotic taxation of capital is not optimal when the government faces period-by-period budget constraints. For recent modelling of tax equilibrium with potentially competing governments, rather than a single government, see Acemoglu et al. (2008).

[104] It appears easier to comply with a no-cookies or no-cigarettes rule than trying to allow oneself only a few.

and those changes will involve transition issues. Second, is the set of one-time transition issues if the contents of this chapter (or some other) were to be accepted as the basis for current and future taxation. These issues differ in that current and past expectations are given when considering today's changes, but expectations about future changes are endogenous to the policy framework created today. Both settings can call for giving some degree of respect to legitimate expectations for both incentive and fairness reasons.[105]

Today's changes can influence expectations (and the normative pull of the expectations) by including adjustments for transition reasons and by legislation and statements about future tax changes. Adjustments for transition reasons include grandfathering, delaying implementation, and explicit transition relief.[106] Given the frequency with which taxes change, no one should expect that taxes will never change. Taxes change because circumstances change and because governments change. And sometimes tax legislation has a time limit (a sunset), which gives a date by which taxes are more likely to change again (rather than a commitment to a return to the tax law that would take effect with no further legislation). In their own self-interest people should recognize the possibility of a tax response to changing circumstances. And such recognition can improve social welfare. Modelling with changing taxes (and expectations of changing taxes) in response to changing circumstances is common in the tax literature coming from macroeconomists (e.g. Golosov, Tsyvinski, and Werning (2007)). It may well be useful to take this approach in more complex economic environments (e.g. with human and physical investments of different effective lifetimes) and with explicit transition rules. And it would be good to explore how the basic tax structure may affect tax setting with endogenously changing governments, although it is not clear how to set up a suitable social welfare function.[107]

Beyond standard social welfare analysis in terms of lifetime expected utilities, there may be a further normative concern for limiting the deviations from appropriately held expectations about policies.[108] The presence

[105] For discussion of ongoing changes, see Graetz (1985), and the sources cited there. For discussion of an initial change, see Auerbach (2006), which presents many issues and highlights the importance of transition by contrasting simulations that have the same long-run tax incentive properties but very different transition impacts. Whether ending the taxation of capital income raises or lowers social welfare varies with the transition impact in some simulations.

[106] Use of these tools was raised in Feldstein (1976b).

[107] As noted above, the type of pension system is thought to influence the changes in a pension system in response to changed circumstances (Diamond (1999)). For an example of equilibrium dividend taxation with changing governments, see Korinek and Stiglitz (2008).

[108] This might parallel the same issue in the legal analyses of contracts, where courts attempt to interpret contracts in the light of the expectations of the contract parties. The endogeneity of legitimate expectations to court processes that try to decide in terms of the expectations of the parties has not always received adequate attention.

or absence of an ongoing political discussion should affect the appropriate degree of respect for actions based on expectations. And one would need an evaluation of the political process to allow different normative treatments of changing 'loopholes' that come from less satisfactory aspects of politics and changes of 'appropriate' political outcomes. That is, the degree of respect to past taxes and the expectation of their continuation need to recognize a widely held view that the tax structure is not satisfactory and ought to be reformed (a view that underlies the commissioning of this work).

6.8.3. Modelling assumptions

The optimal tax literature analyses real taxes dependent on real labour and capital incomes. We do not think there is any significant disagreement among economists that to the extent feasible, the relevant basis for taxation should be real capital income, not nominal capital income. A literature has examined how and to what extent this can be done (Aaron (1976)). We have not considered how optimal tax insights should be adapted to the common practice of taxing nominal incomes. Other than pointing out that (with positive inflation) taxing nominal interest and dividends results in taxes on real interest and dividends at rates higher than the stated marginal tax rate, we do not explore the real–nominal distinction. We also do not explore issues related to the realization of income, but note that for equal treatment with other capital income, taxation of deferred realization of incomes, as with capital gains, calls for heavier taxation than non-deferred capital income, not lighter taxation as is common practice (Helliwell (1969); Auerbach (1991); Bradford (1995)). Heavier taxation for longer holding periods can limit the lock-in effect.

Overwhelmingly, optimal tax models assume competitive behaviour by firms. While this is not a genuinely satisfactory assumption, we have not explored the limited literature that considers other market structures.

Typically, the labour market is modelled as if workers can choose the number of hours to work at the wage available to them. Such a simple linear before-tax budget constraint is not realistic for many people, given rules on overtime pay and possibly different earnings per hour on primary and secondary jobs. Also many jobs come with a standard number of hours, although the standard number of hours at an employer is a choice variable that plausibly reflects to some degree the hours that workers would like to work. Some of the literature recognizes the discontinuity in disutility of work at zero hours (e.g. from commuting) that makes withdrawal from the labour force a possible next-best alternative to work with a significant number of hours. The distinction between extensive (labour force participation) and intensive (hours worked) labour supply margins is very important for considerations of tax rates and acknowledging both margins can lead to a greater role for the average tax rate in policy analysis (Saez (2002c)). This issue is particularly important for programmes aimed at encouraging work by low earners. Moreover, since the relative importance of intensive and extensive margins varies widely by age, this is relevant for the case for age-dependent taxes. Since it is most common in the literature, we focus on models with adjustable hours, although the retirement literature often makes use of a zero–one model of employment opportunities.

6.8.4. Horizontal equity

We rejected starting the discussion of tax policy with an ideal tax base based on equity considerations. But we do recognize a role for considerations of horizontal equity, mentioned briefly above. In this section, we elaborate on the reasons for rejecting the centrality of an ideal tax base and then consider some of the literature about horizontal equity.

Ideal tax base

To consider horizontal equity in a simplified setting, let us consider a basic one-period, two-good model. With no saving, consumption and earnings are the same. As indicated in the Meade Report, there is tension between the idea that ability to pay should be based on actual outcomes or on budget sets (potential outcomes).[109] If everyone really does have the same preferences over work and leisure, and preferences have plausible properties,[110] then there is no tension between the actual and potential measures since those with higher potential earnings have higher actual earnings. This convergence of different competing measures of ability to pay could strengthen the case for paying attention to horizontal equity. However, with identical preferences in this two-good model, there is no conflict between this horizontal equity concept and the standard optimal tax calculation since individuals with the same productivities pay the same taxes in equilibrium.[111]

[109] Reflecting the acknowledged difficulty in defining taxable capacity, the Report asks: 'Is it similarity of opportunity or similarity of outcome which is relevant?' and 'Should differences in needs or tastes be considered in comparing taxable capacities?'

[110] It is plausible that preferences are such that those with higher wage rates have higher earnings.

[111] If all workers at each skill level have the same preferences, differences in preferences across skill levels may or may not be a problem for horizontal equity, although the degree of progressivity of an optimal tax is likely to be affected.

In modelling preferences in an optimal tax problem, it is common to use $u[x] - v[z/n]$, where x is consumption, $u[x]$ is the utility of consumption, z is earnings, n represents what varies in the population, and $v[z/n]$ is the disutility of labour. The variable n is normally interpreted as skill. With these preferences, those with higher skill (higher n) earn more. In that case, there is no tension between optimal taxation and a horizontal equity measure based on actual or potential earnings. But, the optimal tax structure is exactly the same if n reflects the extent of dislike of work rather than skill. In this case everyone has the same potential earnings, yet those with less dislike of work earn more and are taxed more heavily.[112] If hours of work were observable, the two cases could be distinguished. If hours are not used in tax determination, does the distinction between interpretations of the variable n matter for the appeal of the calculation? Is there really a good ethical basis for treating ability to earn per hour differently from genuine dislike of working per hour?

Dislike of working may have a variety of sources, involving both physical and mental tolls from working. Reactions to chosen levels of earnings vary with the cause of the difference in earnings. Viewing a worker as lazy (liking leisure) is very different from viewing a worker as having difficulty working, perhaps for physical reasons. And some people choose lower paying jobs because of the characteristics of the jobs, which might reflect simply standard preferences (such as aversion to job stress) or might reflect other concerns, such as a desire to 'do good works' by working in the non-profit sector, or perhaps pursuing a religious calling. That is, the realized relationship between earnings and earnings potential does not seem to be a sufficient statistic for a normative judgement. Should those choosing poverty for religious reasons be taxed on their abilities to earn in the commercial world? Admittedly, the presence of characteristics of jobs that are not subject to taxation (fringe benefits such as the quality of an office) along with taxation based on actual earnings implies a distortion in the choice of jobs. Perhaps these considerations would become less important if the tax code were accompanied by subsidies of certain activities—those viewed as generating externalities or particularly socially worthy in a way not captured by a standard social welfare function.[113] But then we would be choosing a complex solution, not only in taxation but also in government spending, a complexity that may be beyond the capability of the legislature.

[112] Potential earnings are normally interpreted in terms of a budget constraint in hours-consumption space.

[113] One example is the forgiving of student loans for graduates taking particular jobs.

A related issue is the time horizon to be used for considering taxable capacity—annual or lifetime or something in-between? If a lifetime perspective is taken, then the present discounted value of earnings becomes a (partial) measure both of income and consumption on a lifetime basis.[114]

In sum, given the key role played by the definition of ability to pay as the traditional starting place for discussing taxes, we do not find a convincing basis for accepting the budget set (potential outcomes) as an adequate proxy for desired taxation. Nor do we find realized earnings an adequate proxy, for pretty much the same reason viewed in reverse—sometimes the budget set is a better measure. We conclude that we can not see a good argument for adjusting taxes away from an optimal tax calculation (optimizing an evaluation of individual utilities in economic equilibrium) based on concerns drawn from budget sets, which recognize skill differences but not preferences. Nor do we see a strong case for deviating from an optimal tax calculation based on realized income or consumption. As the Meade Report put it: 'But on examination "taxable capacity" always turns out to be very difficult to define and to be a matter on which opinions will differ rather widely.'

Similarly, with many skill levels and diverse preferences at each skill level, different earnings levels are reached by different workers with the same skill but different disutilities, thereby violating a measure of horizontal equity that is based on the workers' budget sets rather than the workers earnings or consumption levels. In other words, satisfying horizontal equity defined as workers with the same budget set should pay the same taxes is impossible in a sensible setting.[115] It is hard to see how to start policy analysis with a measure that is impossible to satisfy. This stance is enhanced by the difficulty of finding a good measure of how much to care about different size deviations from a measure of horizontal equity (Kaplow (1989)).

There may be tensions between tax bases thought to be ideal for horizontal equity definitions and tax bases that optimize social welfare. What if one thinks that the best measure of ability to pay is Haig–Simons income and one also accepts the empirical validity of the conditions under which the social welfare optimum involves no taxation of capital income? What if one thinks that the best measure of ability to pay is consumption expenditures and one also accepts the empirical validity of the conditions under which the social

[114] This discussion ignores inheritances, which need to be considered as well, and are generally taxed separately from the income tax. Inheritance taxes are discussed in Chapter 8.

[115] We focus on earnings since it makes the same point as the one with different discount rates and so different savings rates, which is the more common setting for calling for taxation that does not vary with savings levels since the budget sets are the same. We see no good basis for distinguishing between these cases.

welfare optimum involves positive taxation of capital income? The weight that should be given to a chosen measure of horizontal equity in offsetting the conclusions from social welfare optimization depends on the strength of conviction that one really does have a good (usable, widely accepted) measure of horizontal equity (and sufficient strength in the belief that this consideration matters).[116] Since we do not see a really good usable measure, we do not see a good reason to lower social welfare by using horizontal equity as the starting place for policy analysis.

The end of this discussion is that we reject the Meade Report view, quoted in Section 6.2, that taxes 'should' relate monotonically to some measure of taxable capacity. In addition to finding taxable capacity not well-enough measurable and not sufficiently uniformly evaluated to be usable for this purpose, we also do not see an underlying normative basis for reaching the conclusion that taxes should be related to taxable capacity without full consideration of the equilibrium consequences of following such an approach.[117] That is, we accept the view that the starting place for thinking about taxation should be the impact of taxes on the utilities of people in the economy.

Additional normative concerns

We begin our discussion of additional concerns by recognizing the core argument for concerns beyond a standard social welfare maximization, as stated by Musgrave in Buchanan and Musgrave (1999).

> The state and its public sector thus form an integral part of a multifaceted socioeconomic order . . . That order, I hasten to add, includes not only the Pareto efficient use of resources, important though that is but also other and no less vital dimensions of social coexistence—distributive justice and the balance of individual rights and obligations upon which a meaningful concept of liberty has to be built. A view of fiscal economics, which holds that all is well if only Pareto optimality prevails, bypasses these essential components of social coexistence and fails on both normative

[116] Another concern is that the choice of tax base will influence the degree of progressivity because of political behavioural effects—it is one thing to envision a consistent optimization across interacting dimensions of tax policy and another to recognize that the political process has some sequential elements.

[117] This conclusion is similar to that reached by some earlier economists—that equal marginal sacrifice (minimized sacrifice—equivalent to optimized social welfare) was the appropriate criterion, not equal absolute or equal proportional sacrifices. 'Edgeworth, and later Pigou, held that there was no logical or intuitive choice between the equity principles of equal absolute and equal proportional sacrifice. Arguing on welfare grounds, they considered equal marginal sacrifice the only proper rule, not as a matter of equity, but because it met the welfare objective of least aggregate sacrifice.' Musgrave (1959), p. 98.

and positive grounds. Without allowing for a sense of social justice the good society cannot be defined, and without it democratic society cannot function.

(Pages 31–2.)

It seems useful to distinguish three elements in the 'fair' taxation of individuals. One, reflecting the role of individuals as ends in themselves, and not merely means to increase social welfare, calls for fair treatment of individuals in terms of some ethical basis for fairness. Following Atkinson and Stiglitz (1980), we saw this issue as influencing the allowable tax tools to be used in tax optimization. Second is the extent to which a concept of fair taxation used in tax analyses can influence government behaviour, encouraging both the design of tax institutions and the implementation of policies that better satisfy social objectives. And third is the citizens' perceptions of fairness, which may or may not coincide with some philosophical concept, and which matter for both the political process and individual compliance.

Let us consider these issues in the somewhat analogous, but much starker, setting of punishment for criminal activity. First, severe punishments as deterrents, particularly in the presence of limited apprehensions of those committing crimes, may go too far, violating a sense of the proper treatment of individuals. Indeed, Amendment VIII of the US Bill of Rights states: 'Excessive bail shall not be required, nor excessive fines imposed, nor cruel and unusual punishments inflicted.' Similarly, taxes should not be defined differently for different people in ways that would violate the concept, somewhat slippery in this context, of 'equal protection of the laws'.

Second, reliance on selective enforcement and severe punishments might leave too much power to the discretion of officials deciding which alleged criminal acts are pursued in court. In the tax setting, Adam Smith argued: 'The tax which each individual is bound to pay ought to be certain, and not arbitrary... Where it is otherwise, every person subject to the tax is put more or less in the power of the tax-gatherer' (p. 778).

And third, the perception of excessive punishment may not only violate the extent to which actions of the state should reflect the views of the citizens, but also may be self-defeating if juries are not willing to convict when they view the punishment as too severe. Similarly, taxation perceived as unfair may encourage evasion.

Tax assessments do not affect individuals as sharply as some criminal punishments, as long as tax collections are not too large relative to an individual's ability to pay. Nevertheless the same three elements are present. Consider the situation analysed by Atkinson and Stiglitz (1976) and Stiglitz (1982b), where social welfare maximization calls for different tax treatment of two identical individuals.[118] Total reliance on social welfare function maximization would not be directly concerned by this difference in tax treatment. However, a concern for fairness would strictly prefer a truly random, *ex ante* equal probability mechanism for deciding which individual gets which tax assessment (Diamond (1967)).

But there are several concerns about such an approach. Will the implementation mechanism ensure that the randomization is done properly, avoiding improper assessments? And will individual citizens accept this approach to fairness? These issues arise even if there is sufficient information to conclude that unequal treatment is the right approach, as may or may not be the case, and even if the legislature is sufficiently sophisticated to be willing to accept and vote a suitable implementation. Randomization, as was done for the US military draft during part of the Vietnam War, might be safe from manipulation. But given the complexity and empirical uncertainty of an argument for differential treatment, we have doubts that the citizens would ever accept the underlying argument that it is better than simply levying the same taxes on those in the same circumstances. This is particularly an issue if the tax rate differences are to be long-lasting. Such a concern, assuming it is correct (without any underlying polls or focus groups) lends itself to the idea that some aspects of horizontal equity may best be addressed by viewing them as a limitation on allowable tax tools, as has been argued by Atkinson and Stiglitz (1980). We accept the view that tax tools should be limited by such considerations and that policies should be restricted to ones which are uniform over their stated tax base. And concepts and discussion of horizontal equity may help improve the political process.

Horizontal equity based on hypothetical alternatives[119]

A small literature addressing horizontal equity has followed from Feldstein (1976a, 1976b), which based horizontal equity on utility rankings with and without taxes.[120] This approach is based on comparing outcomes in an existing equilibrium with outcomes in a hypothetical alternative. The

[118] As Atkinson and Stiglitz (1976), p. 355 note: 'If tastes are identical, the equal treatment of equals is still not necessarily implied by welfare maximization ... where the feasible set is non-convex, treating otherwise identical individuals differently may increase social welfare.'

[119] This section draws particularly on Atkinson (1980) and Kaplow (1989).

[120] 'The principle of horizontal equity in tax reform thus requires that any tax change should preserve the utility order, and should imply that if two individuals would have the same utility level if the tax remained unchanged, they should have the same utility level if the tax is altered.' (Feldstein (1976b), p. 124.) Feldstein recognizes that satisfying this definition of horizontal equity is not possible and thus calls for a balance between the degree of horizontal inequity and social welfare maximization.

hypothetical alternative may consider changed behaviour by individuals one-at-a-time or by everyone at once, thereby incorporating general equilibrium responses.[121] The one-at-a-time approach considers what a single individual would do if that individual were exempted from taxation, with prices in equilibrium unchanged. A general equilibrium approach, including changing prices, seems particularly relevant for transition issues. Either way, horizontal equity is approached in terms of the vector of utility levels in the hypothetical alternative and the vector of utility levels in equilibrium.

As an example of this literature, Rosen (1978) considers the pattern of utilities if each person were allowed to maximize utility at equilibrium prices but without taxes. This resembles the measurement of sacrifice in sacrifice-based theories of optimal taxation (Musgrave (1959)). Rosen then looks for utility reversals between this vector of utilities and the vector in the actual equilibrium. We see no reason to give normative consequence to this particular hypothetical alternative, nor have we seen one offered.[122] And we see no reason to be particularly concerned with utility reversals in this comparison or more generally. That is, the hypothetical alternatives depend on the behaviour of both the government (through expenditures) and other individuals (in determining prices). Thus it is not clear why an individual has a particular claim to protection measured from such a position, since the position depends on everyone's behaviour—individuals cannot generally achieve comparable incomes on their own in a world without government expenditures and without trade with others. Indeed, the taxes themselves play a role in the determination of relative prices. Moreover, there are likely to be other hypothetical alternatives that appear as normatively plausible as this one, for example the world with no taxes and no government spending—no police, no regulation of markets, or the like. This would take us back to the benefit approach to taxation, which has suffered from an inability to make useful distributional inferences. And why those best capable of looking after themselves in some such hypothetical setting should be tax protected is not apparent.

[121] This distinction is not as clear as it appears. For example, when considering tax exempt bonds, one can recognize that the bonds would pay higher interest if taxable, relying on an arbitrage interpretation of current equilibrium prices without considering the interest rate changes that would occur in an equilibrium response to removal of the tax exemption (as, for example, in Diamond (1965)).

[122] In referring to Feldstein and the literature pursuing measures of inequity following his approach, Kaplow writes: 'HE [horizontal equity] is now frequently measured and applied even though there has been virtually no exploration of why one should care about the principle in the contexts and in the manner in which it is now being used' (p. 139).

As to giving great importance to rankings—we agree with Kaplow's (1989) criticism of such measures: 'Minute movements leading to order reversals count as full violations of [horizontal equity] while substantial disturbances in the initial distribution that result in no order reversals are ignored' [footnote omitted] (p. 141). More generally, there is no obvious reason why rankings matter at all normatively.

6.9. SOME EMPIRICAL UNDERPINNINGS

The discussions of the previous sections have been predominantly theoretical in nature but they have made clear that theory alone is insufficient for tax policy design. Indeed, in many cases the qualitative policy insights of the dynamic optimal tax approach outlined above depend crucially on the particular nature of some key empirical relationships. In this section we briefly consider the relevant econometric evidence on two of these relationships that crop up as recurring themes throughout our analysis. These are the nature of differences in tastes for saving across types defined by high and low earnings abilities and the degree to which different types face different earnings growth and earnings uncertainty over their lifetimes.[123] Both are areas in which recent econometric evidence, often based on data or methods that have only recently become available, means that substantially more is known about the key empirical relationships than was available to the Meade Committee. This section summarizes some key findings.

To gain insights, theoretical models leave out many aspects of reality. When turning to empirical evidence on the assumptions of such studies, there are two complications. One is that the empirical work can readily incorporate more elements than in the theoretical structure, indeed must do so for plausible results. But, second, the empirical work is also limited, by data availability and complexity, as to the factors that can be included. This section reviews the literatures on differences in saving rates and earnings trajectories and the extent to which one can draw conclusions from the empirical studies. Here we briefly summarize our conclusions.

There is considerable evidence across multiple countries that on average those with higher earnings potential and those with higher earnings levels

[123] Additional empirical evidence might inform not the optimal tax structure itself, but understanding of the nature of gains and losses that would result from movements towards such tax structures given current circumstances. Examples of this might be the life-cycle evolution of the fraction of wealth held in assets with different tax treatments, which is an issue left to others in this volume.

save more and accumulate more wealth during their careers, supporting the relevance of a key theoretical reason for taxing capital income. There is also considerable evidence that those males on higher earnings trajectories have steeper age–earnings profiles that peak at higher ages and after more periods in the labour market. When the amount of uncertainty about future earnings is being considered, a key issue is the nature of information individuals have and how it relates to the information available to the econometricians when estimating earnings models. On a strict cross-section basis, there is considerable variation in earnings in each year and that variation grows with age. Some of this variation is certainly associated with different anticipated earnings tracks, anticipated from an early age, for example, at the time education decisions are made. Indeed, a considerable amount is explainable in this way. But there appears to remain a considerable degree of individual uncertainty beyond this.[124]

6.9.1. Differences in saving propensities across earnings types

Whilst the empirical evidence on differences in savings propensities across individuals of high and low earnings capacities is far from complete there are nevertheless a number of empirical studies that suggest such differences do exist and hence should be taken into account in tax design. But concrete empirical identification of differences in propensity to save across types from economic data alone is often hindered by one (or both) of two factors. First, we do not typically observe preferences directly but instead need to make inferences about preferences from data on saving and wealth outcomes. Second, the true separation of types is not known and must typically be assumed to be proxied by other observed characteristics (such as education group or social class or sometimes current or lifetime income). Typically, caution is therefore required in the interpretation of evidence relating to differences across groups since these proxy characteristics are only imperfect measures of *ex ante* earnings capacity and may indeed be partly dependent on the same intertemporal preference parameters that are under investigation. Nevertheless, in some situations the resulting biases in results can be characterized and qualitative findings may be robust to such biases.[125] Given these issues,

[124] In addition, there is macroeconomic uncertainty about future earnings, which is not fully addressed in the literature exploring individual differences in (past) experiences, and was also not addressed in the theoretical discussion above.

[125] One pertinent example would be if more impatient individuals were less likely to choose to stay in education to older ages and if lower skill groups were on average more impatient. In this case the effects would work in the same direction and qualitative inferences regarding earnings

one useful starting point is to turn to the evidence from cognitive psychology in which recent papers have used experimental methods to examine the relationship between ability, time preference, and willingness to take risks. Such studies typically use experimental designs to reveal preference measures on small groups of subjects in a laboratory environment. Some recent studies have also exploited cognitive load manipulation in the experimental design (essentially distracting subjects whilst they are taking their choices) in order to exploit within-subject variation in 'ability'.[126] Within this literature there seems to be wide acceptance that higher ability individuals are more patient (see, e.g., Parker and Fischhoff (2005); Bettinger and Slonim (2005); and Kirby, Winston, and Santiesteban (2005)). The relationship between risk aversion and cognitive ability is less widely studied, although what evidence there is suggests that higher ability individuals are in fact less risk averse than those of lower ability (e.g. Frederick (2005); Benjamin, Brown, and Shapiro (2006)).

The reason why higher ability may lead to lower risk aversion or more patience is not fully understood, but it seems that cognitive resources are required to make patient, risk-neutral decisions. Frederick (2005) argues that it is not just the ability to calculate expected returns correctly that leads the more intelligent to take a gamble more often. Again, using experimental data he finds that those with higher cognitive ability were more likely to take a gamble than those with lower ability even when the expected return on the gamble was lower than the safe bet.

Consideration of the issue of the extent of cognitive resources employed in decision-making, however, reveals the shortcomings of such empirical evidence for our purposes since the time, effort, and information deployed in making savings decisions in 'real life' situations is itself a choice variable. In contrast, such factors are strictly controlled in a laboratory experiment. As an example, individuals with lower cognitive abilities may spend more (or less) time on their saving and pensions decisions than those with higher ability, or be more likely to use various forms of advice or information in their saving and investment decisions.[127]

Conversely, higher ability (and, particularly, more numerate) individuals may be more able to process information and make complex 'optimal'

capabilities and saving rates could be made from data on education and saving. Other situations may not be as clear cut.

[126] By increasing the cognitive load the 'working memory' capacity of the brain is decreased. Since working memory capacity is almost perfectly correlated with general cognitive function, this manipulation is argued effectively to reduce cognitive ability.

[127] Lusardi (1999), and Ameriks, Caplin, and Leahy (2003) both show an association between financial planning and higher financial wealth but neither study looks at differences by ability.

decisions in a less costly manner. A series of studies has explored how ability to understand and transform probabilities relates to performance on judgement and decision tasks. Peters et al. (2005) summarize their evidence as showing that more numerate individuals were 'more likely to retrieve and use appropriate numerical principles, thus making themselves less susceptible to framing effects'[128] and 'tended to draw different (generally stronger or more precise) affective meaning from numbers and numerical comparisons, and their affective responses were more precise'. Numerical ability appears to matter to complex judgements and decisions in important ways although the extent to which this evidence is relevant depends on the extent to which individuals know their abilities and change their investment planning behaviour accordingly.

Given the complexity of saving and portfolio choices facing individuals in modern financial markets it is not clear that simple preference measures established in somewhat abstract experiments can adequately describe the differences in saving propensities across types that are of interest to economists. Therefore there is still considerable merit in looking at economic data on the distribution of saving and wealth outcomes across abilities, even bearing in mind the empirical difficulties discussed above. Data combining information on economic outcomes and cognitive abilities are now becoming available with which such hypotheses can be investigated. Benjamin, Brown, and Shapiro (2006) use the US National Longitudinal Survey of Youth (NLSY) to look at the relationship between cognitive ability and a very crude measure of asset accumulation and find low cognitive function to be associated with low asset accumulation and financial market participation. Using more detailed data on cognitive abilities and on all components of financial wealth of a large sample of older adults (aged 50–74) in England, Banks and Oldfield (2007) show significant correlations between the level of financial wealth and both a broad measure of cognitive functioning and a narrow measure of numerical ability based on performance in a series of simple calculations. These associations hold when both measures are used simultaneously in a model that also includes measures of education as well as gender and age dummies. Of course, higher cognitive abilities typically result in higher earnings and some of the literature relating to this will be discussed in Section 6.9.2. What is striking, however, is the role of numeracy over and above other dimensions of cognitive abilities. To the extent that human capital is sufficiently controlled for by general measures of cognitive functioning

[128] A framing effect is where the interpretation of a number depends on the way in which it is presented. For example, if meat is presented as being '25% fat' or '75% fat-free'.

and memory in these estimates, the role of numeracy may be thought to be indicating a separate mechanism relating to preferences for saving out of lifetime income. Finally, when it comes to portfolio decisions, Banks and Oldfield show that cognitive ability and numeracy are both associated with a higher likelihood of holding stocks and of having a private pension, even when controlling for the level of financial wealth in addition to the factors mentioned above.[129]

A variety of further evidence is beginning to emerge that relates saving and portfolio choices and outcomes to the psychology of decision-making, and much of that research is motivated by the view that simple preference heterogeneity in the context of a standard intertemporal economic model is not sufficient to explain certain features of observed behaviour or other outcomes. Most important, perhaps, is a rapidly expanding literature broadly relating to people's ability to exercise self-control when choosing between present and future options. Variants of this include experimental evidence on the dynamic inconsistency of choices (e.g. Ainslie (2001)), exploration of the economic implications of quasi-hyperbolic discounting models (e.g. Laibson (1997)), or the modification of the underlying axioms of individuals' economic preferences to allow for temptation (Gul and Pesendorfer (2004)). In each case, important implications for saving, portfolio, and consumption behaviour have been demonstrated and ideally such implications would need to be considered in designing a dynamic optimal tax policy. Empirical evidence suggests that levels of self-control vary substantially within the population and are affected by cognitive load (Shiv and Fedorikhin (1999)). Additionally, those demonstrating higher self-control in early childhood (measured by experimental evaluations of young children's ability to delay gratification) have been shown to have better outcomes in a variety of economic and social dimensions in adolescence and early adulthood (see Eigsti et al. (2006) in particular, or Borghans et al. (2008) for a brief overview of the evidence). This is an area where much more needs to be known, both in terms of theoretical public finance models and relevant empirical evidence, before the full policy prescriptions with regard to the optimal taxation of capital income over the life cycle can be assessed.[130] As such, it represents an important area for future research.

[129] Lusardi and Mitchell (2007) show similar results for a broader measure of financial literacy using data from the US Health and Retirement Study.

[130] Bernheim (1997) discusses the particular problem of implications for tax incentives for retirement saving and Bernheim and Rangel (2007) provide a fine overview of the key issues for broader policy analysis.

The final possibility when looking for evidence in this area is to examine studies looking at direct relationships between economic outcomes, that is, the correlation between levels or rates of saving and levels of education, permanent income or financial wealth. As discussed in 6.3.1, Dynan, Skinner, and Zeldes (2004) show that in a complex economic environment containing income and health uncertainty and means-tested benefits it is still the case that those with higher lifetime incomes save more than those with lower lifetime income. Carroll (2000) shows that differences in saving between the (very) rich and the poor cannot be explained by income differences alone and goes on to argue that if one rules out preference heterogeneity, the observed saving differences cannot be explained by models in which the only purpose of wealth accumulation is to finance future consumption. Evidence relevant to differences further down the wealth distribution can be obtained by looking at differences by education. Lawrence (1991) documents differences in saving rates between education groups that she argues are unexplained by differences in demographic profiles and incomes between groups and suggest a lower savings propensity in the lower education groups.[131] In all these studies, however, the rich are seen to save more than the poor, which is consistent with the preference differences between types identified above.[132]

When it comes to the life-cycle profiles for saving, extensive descriptive evidence on saving profiles by age (and, where possible, age profiles within education and income or wealth groups) is available for the US, UK, Canada, Germany, Japan, and Italy, in a comparative study undertaken as part of an NBER project on comparisons of household saving (see Poterba (1994)). While data limitations are substantial and the studies are far from able to identify all forms of saving, the overall messages that emerge are remarkably consistent across countries. In cross-section, saving rates are higher for those with higher income and education consistent with the studies identified above. Saving rates rise from young to middle age, often by more for high education or high income groups. Following middle age, the data show very little, if any, decline in saving rates which is on the surface somewhat

[131] Of course, these differences may be partly due to the education itself in which case they cannot be taken as direct evidence on differences between types, although the different types will have different educations, sustaining an indirect link that may also matter for optimal taxation. Bernheim, Garrett, and Maki (2001) show that high school financial curriculum mandates have long-term effects on asset accumulation in adulthood.

[132] Patient households will clearly accumulate more wealth than the less patient. Furthermore, reasonable specifications for intertemporal preferences, coupled with the rates of return on risky assets that have been observed in recent years, would lead one to expect individuals with lower degrees of risk aversion to have accumulated more assets over their lifetime.

puzzling.[133] Finally, median saving and financial asset holding is relatively low in all countries, indicating the importance of social security and housing for life-cycle consumption smoothing outcomes for the large majority of individuals.

At any one age, and across ages, saving propensities will ultimately depend on more than pure preference parameters alone and it would be naive to attribute the age or education variation observed in the studies discussed above solely to differences in preferences with age. Additional determinants of saving over the lifetime will be the nature of consumption needs relative to income over the life cycle, life expectancy, access to capital markets, and any possible dependency of the marginal benefit from consumption in one period on factors such as leisure or consumption in other periods, particularly if this dependency changes with age. At the household level, consumption needs show a distinct hump shape over the life cycle due to household formation, marriage, and the presence of children. Other things equal, this will result in the marginal propensity to save out of current income changing systematically with age. Differences in the shape of these demographic profiles also exist for education groups—with less-educated groups having more children and having them, on average, earlier in the life cycle. Such differences, if assumed to be known in advance, lead to differences in the shape of optimal consumption profiles over the lifetime (see, for example, Attanasio, Banks, Meghir, and Weber (1999)) and hence the degree of borrowing and saving for a given income trajectory. These predicted differences are in accordance with the descriptive evidence for the UK by Banks and Blundell (1994) in the previously discussed NBER comparative study, which shows that within age groups saving rates decline with family size.

At younger ages, the possibility for consumption smoothing is also determined by individuals' ability to borrow. Zeldes (1989) shows that, contrary to the predictions of the consumption-smoothing model with no liquidity constraints, consumption paths track predictable changes in income for low wealth groups.

For the other end of the life cycle, substantial empirical evidence is now available on how expenditure changes with age at and after retirement, even if the connection from these results to statements about changing 'needs' is not always totally straightforward. Banks, Blundell, and Tanner (1998) and Bernheim, Garrett, and Maki (2001) show falls in consumption expenditures

[133] The exact interpretation of this in the context of life-cycle accumulation and decumulation depends on the stance one takes on the treatment of pension income and age-related decline in the present discounted value of future pension income schemes which is not explicitly addressed in the Poterba (1994) study.

around the time of retirement and, as briefly discussed above, data from many countries show that saving rates (defined as a ratio of total household income including pensions) remain positive, and often increase, as individuals retire and then move through their retirement. Analysis of expenditure changes for older households have also led to initial investigations into the relationship between consumption expenditures and leisure and how this might change as individuals leave paid work and as they become less healthy. Aguiar and Hurst (2005) show that individuals spend more time shopping for and preparing food after retirement, with the result that consumption of food is smoothed even though expenditure falls. Börsch-Supan and Stahl (1991) argue that a dependency on health of the utility of consumption expenditures can be shown to rationalize the fall in expenditures that is observed as households age post-retirement. Both effects would have implications for tax design to the extent that the dependencies between consumption, health, and leisure are different to those occurring at earlier ages.

One final factor relating to consumption needs is life expectancy, as discussed earlier in Section 6.6. Ideally, for tax-design purposes we would like empirical evidence on how life expectancy (and uncertainty in life expectancy) varies across types defined by high and low earnings capacities. Much as with the debate on preferences above, we can only get an approximate understanding of this from the available data. The UK produces life tables by social class that give some indication of the extent of these effects.[134] While the variation in earnings capacity across individuals will be undoubtedly much greater than that approximated by simple social class differences, the latter will still be strongly correlated with earnings capacity, at least within cohort.

Figure 6.1 shows data on life expectancy by social class in England and Wales in 2004 and displays considerable variation across groups, with the males in the lowest groups having seven years lower life expectancy at birth, and four years at age 65 than those in the highest groups. Differences of similar magnitude are observed for females. If anything, these differences have been increasing over time. Analysis of the same data as that in Figure 6.1 shows that between 1972–76 and 2002–05, both males and females classified to non-manual occupations had a greater increase in life expectancy at birth

[134] Unfortunately similar analyses broken down by either education or wealth are unavailable in the UK although a considerable body of evidence exists in the US (see, e.g., Pappas et al. (1993); or Preston and Elo (1995)). To the extent it has value for our purposes, the use of social class as an indicator of an individual type is probably more appropriate for men than for women given its definitional dependence on occupation. However, microdata linked to mortality records are becoming available so that analyses by education or lifetime wealth could be computed in the future, at least for the case of late-life life expectancy.

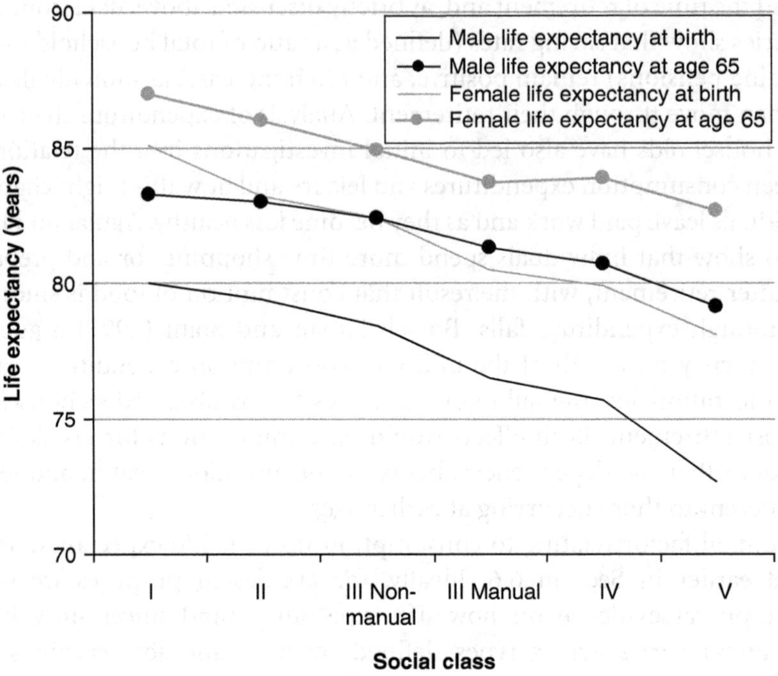

Source: ONS Longitudinal Study (2005).

Figure 6.1. Life-expectancy by social class in England and Wales, 2004

and at age 65 than those classified to manual occupations, although there was some narrowing of the gap in the most recent years from 1997–2001 to 2002–05 (ONS (2007)).

The reduction in life-expectancy differences between types as age increases is presumably due to a healthy-survivor effect whereby those from lower income groups that do live to older ages are a non-randomly selected set with some combination of particularly high resilience, low mortality risk factors, and/or relatively good health behaviours. In contrast, for a given age, such selection is not so acute in the richer groups. The gradual erosion of life-expectancy differentials with age is important for policy design since life expectancy at older ages, not at birth, will determine the consumption and saving behaviour of middle age and older individuals.

Such socio-economic differences in length of life are also apparent when looking at mortality probabilities, where it is possible to look at outcomes by factors other than class. Attanasio and Hoynes (2000) show a strong correlation between mortality and wealth in US data and use their estimates, coupled with further assumptions on wealth mobility, to correct age–saving profiles in cross-sectional data. Examination of the English Longitudinal Study of Ageing also reveals sharp differences in two-year mortality probabilities across the wealth and education distribution for those older than 50. These differences also lessen with age, at least when expressed in relative terms (see Banks et al. (2006)).

Considerable debate exists over the relative importance of the causal mechanisms that might be thought to underlie such differential mortality. In addition to the differences across groups (and differences in any uncertainty surrounding these life expectancies) tax design will also presumably depend on the precise nature of the causal processes underlying these differences. The implications for (age-related) tax systems would be different if we thought that wealth was causally driving longevity outcomes as opposed to being merely a symptom of other omitted factors (such as underlying type or ability, early life factors or even parental income and beginning of life circumstances). There is also the likely possibility that health behaviours leading to subsequent mortality risk are driven by exactly the same underlying variation in intertemporal preferences as the savings outcomes discussed earlier. Whilst much more empirical work needs to be done on the issue, at present what evidence there is suggests that increments to wealth at or after middle age have relatively weak effects on subsequent health and mortality once one controls for initial differences between individuals (see Adams et al. (2003) for a test based on those aged 70 and above, and Smith (2004) for a similar test on those over age 50). In contrast the studies investigating the effects of early life factors on subsequent mortality and morbidity seem to find much stronger results on subsequent trajectories (see, for example, Lleras-Muney (2005) for the effects of education and Van Den Berg, Lindeboom, and Portrait (2006) for the effects of early life economic circumstances).

6.9.2. Life-cycle income profiles and permanent income uncertainty

We have argued above that a second key set of empirical issues in determining optimal tax schedules are those surrounding the nature of differences in lifetime earnings profiles within the population, and the degree to which such differences are correlated with skills and preferences. For our purposes three key features of the data are important: the extent to which the shape of earnings or income profiles over the lifetime differ by types; the extent to which uncertainty about the level of lifetime earnings differs by types; and the extent to which there are systematic age-related patterns in the evolution of earnings uncertainty over the life cycle (and, if there are, whether these age-patterns differ by type). Once again, unravelling the key lessons for the purposes of tax design from the empirical evidence is somewhat difficult, particularly if one wants to move beyond qualitative statements. In addition to the issue, discussed above, that one has to make assumptions to deduce the nature of underlying differences by earnings capacities from data on proxy variables such as education, there are two further problems when looking at earnings profiles. First, the majority of the literature has typically limited its focus to understanding the dynamics of earnings profiles for prime-age males as opposed to for all ages and both sexes. Second, when looking to understand the nature of age profiles, investigators cannot avoid encountering the identification problem that prevents the separation of true age effects from a combination of time and generational effects without further assumptions.[135] Both of these issues need to be borne in mind when considering the available empirical evidence, and each will be referred to below.

With the increasing availability of longitudinal data on individual earnings a gradually growing body of empirical work, using the Panel Study of Income Dynamics in the US but also the British Household Panel Study and various other data sources in the UK, has begun to document earnings processes in some detail. At the crudest level, and in accordance with simple intuition, earnings for more educated households in the US have been shown to rise more steeply in early life and peak at later ages than those for less educated households (see, for one of many examples, Attanasio, Banks, Meghir, and Weber (1999)). Similar calculations from the BHPS data over the period 1991–2004, shown in Figure 6.2, suggest the same is true in Britain, with earnings of full-time workers basically flat for the low education group from age 40 but continuing to rise until age 58 for their high education counterparts.[136] Note that the differences between these two earnings profiles is most pronounced in early and late working life, whereas throughout mid-life (from the late thirties to the mid-fifties) the growth rate of (log) earnings is only slightly steeper for the more educated group than for their less educated counterparts. This is a theme that will be returned to in our reading of the empirical evidence on earnings dynamics below.

[135] Since an individual's age can always be written as the current year minus their date-of-birth this is a fundamental problem that cannot be solved without assuming that the variation observed in data due to (at least) one of these dimensions is either zero, or at least a known function of known factors.

[136] The figure plots wage profiles for full-time workers split by whether they have education up to and including O levels or equivalent—the level of schooling that is compulsory in the UK—and whether they have any more advanced educational qualifications—A levels or their equivalent and above.

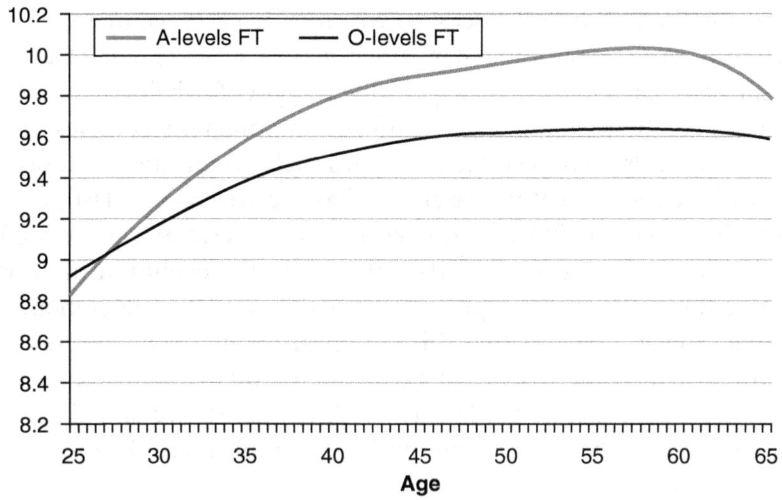

Source: Calculations from 1991–2004 BHPS micro-data.

Figure 6.2. Estimated age profile of log of mean wages (cohort aged 36–38 in 1991)

Given that rather substantial differences emerge even when looking at two very broad skill groups, one might expect the issue to be even more striking if education or skill groups could be disaggregated even further. Ideally, one would need analysis split by a much more diverse set of skills and/or abilities, particularly at the top end where the earnings profiles of successful college graduates will likely differ quite substantially from that of the average profile for those with A levels or equivalent, both in terms of levels, growth and, potentially, variance. Lillard and Weiss (1979) provide evidence on the earnings profiles of American scientists that show considerable heterogeneity within the high skilled group and the same kind of effects appear within this group—the higher earning individuals have profiles that rise more steeply and peak later than the less high earning individuals in the group. In addition, most developed countries have displayed an increasing dispersion of incomes across skill types over the last thirty years. This widening of the returns to education (measured in terms of contemporaneous incomes) has been more acute for younger cohorts than for their older cohorts (see, for example, Card and Lemieux (2001)), suggesting that lifetime income differences across skill groups may well increase further in the future.

It is not just the shape of earnings profiles, but also the uncertainty associated with lifetime earnings, that may differ across abilities. But the empirical understanding of the nature of such uncertainty is considerably more complicated, and depends crucially on what is assumed to be known by individuals about their lifetime earnings profiles and indeed the structure assumed for the nature of 'shocks' to earnings at each age or time-period. In one important strand of the literature, the time series of data observed on log earnings for each individual is typically thought of as being generated by a combination of three components: a known component that evolves with certainty and depends on observable covariates such as education, location, and age, a random component where shocks have relatively long-lasting effects, and a random component where shocks have short-term or transitory effects. Given data on a particular date-of-birth cohort the evolution of variation in each of these random components across time is then documented. As mentioned above, to assert that this variation is due to the effects of time alone would require the absence of a dependence on age, and vice versa. The key early findings come from MaCurdy (1982) and Abowd and Card (1989) who show that the above structure can indeed fit observed data on earnings over the life cycle.

Carroll and Samwick (1997) recover levels of the variance of permanent shocks to earnings of around 0.02–0.03, but do not attempt to draw out life cycle or temporal changes. Hubbard, Skinner, and Zeldes (1995) also report similar numbers and both studies decompose the variance across education groups. In general they find a higher variance for both permanent and transitory shocks among those men without college education than for those with college education. Using the longer time series of data available now in the US, Meghir and Pistaferri (2004) attempt a more detailed investigation of the role of individual differences, both observed and unobserved, in the deterministic earnings growth components and in shocks to earnings. Whilst their estimation does not pin down particularly precise estimates of how the variance of shocks to either earnings or income varies over age, their point estimates at least suggest that the conditional variance of shocks to earnings is U-shaped in age, with a more pronounced pattern for the less educated groups.

Two issues of interpretation arise when considering the results from these and other related studies. The first is that results have predominantly focused on the evolution of uncertainty over time rather than over individuals' life-cycles. Were one instead to focus on age profiles (as in, for example, Deaton and Paxson (1994)), then the dependence of such profiles on the changes happening in the macro-economy would have to be controlled for. In particular, there was a particularly strong rise in the variance of permanent shocks observed in the 1980s, documented in Moffitt and Gottschalk (1994) for the US and Dickens (2000) for the UK, that seemed to hit all cohorts whilst being most pronounced for the young. Through the 1990s this variance seems to have declined and the variance of short-term shocks to earnings has risen.

Thus to ensure that MaCurdy/Abowd and Card type models continue to fit earnings data over this longer period requires allowing the variances of shocks to change over time, a fact which is confirmed by the studies cited below that exploit data on the joint evolution of consumption and earnings. But these secular changes can lead to biases in estimated age profiles for each cohort. Heathcote, Storesletten, and Violante (2004) show that the variance of wages is found to grow considerably less slowly over age if one chooses to control for year effects as opposed to cohort effects.

The key issue of interpretation in these studies of earnings dynamics relates to how differences across individuals are allowed to enter the calculations. Lillard and Weiss (1979) pointed out that if individuals faced differential trends that were not modelled in analysis then measures of the permanent uncertainty faced by individuals would overstate the true level of uncertainty faced. This has been investigated further by Baker (1997), Baker and Solon (2003), and Haider and Solon (2006), where the latter two studies exploit longitudinal income tax records to provide detailed information on the entire lifetime of earnings of large samples of individuals. All three studies point to significant heterogeneity in growth rates which suggests that estimates of the importance of permanent uncertainty and its increase with age may be overstated. In addition, Haider and Solon (2006) show individual differences in trends to be most important in early and late working life which may also suggest that the finding of U-shaped permanent uncertainty may be partially due to the effect of omitted individual differences. Indeed, the nature of earnings profiles in early working life and late working life warrants further investigation more generally, since most studies of earnings dynamics focus on annual earnings of prime age males, precisely to remove any dependence of findings on issues such as the date of leaving higher education, and the timing of retirement (or other labour market withdrawal, such as that due to poor health or disability). Such issues, however, are surely key determinants of individuals' lifetime resources, and will also be characterized by having an element of uncertainty. Hence, for our purposes, we would want to include their effects in an analysis of earnings uncertainty over the lifetime.

Of course, the nature of such assumptions regarding what is known *ex ante* about income processes is much more than a matter of econometric convenience. When assessing lifetime uncertainty one is essentially having to make assumptions about what is known by individuals (of different types) at different stages of the life cycle. With regard to our analysis of previous sections, whether individuals know their type is a key issue. But the nature of uncertainty about the way in which future labour markets will reward the labour supply of different types would also be a constituent factor of uncertainty even if types were perfectly known.[137] When a deterministic component of earnings and/or an average individual effect is assumed to be part of the earnings process, then econometric estimation of that component will typically rely on data across all time-periods and ages of an individual's lifetime. Uncertainty, subsequently measured as deviations around this 'deterministic' component, will be understated to the extent that some of these outcomes were not anticipated by the individual at the time they were making their early-life decisions.

Consideration of this aspect brings in a second broad literature on lifetime earnings processes, which addresses the question of expectations of future lifetime earnings at the time schooling decisions are taken, and looks to estimate the fraction of the returns to education that can be considered known in the sense that it relates permanent and known differences between individuals (i.e. heterogeneity) and the fraction that will ultimately be due to uncertainty or luck. In an early paper on schooling decisions, Keane and Wolpin (1997) estimate that around 90% of the lifetime returns to education are predictable at age 16. Cunha and Heckman (2007a) develop a different approach using test scores to identify types and then look at data on college participation decisions and subsequent earnings profiles to form estimates of the amount of lifetime earnings variance that is forecastable. Their calculations for the US come up with a similar number, suggesting that around 80% of the lifetime variability in returns to schooling can be viewed as forecastable by agents at age 17. Applying this methodology to changes over time, Cunha and Heckman (2007b) calculate that much of the increase in inequality for low skill groups has been due to increases in uncertainty, whereas the vast majority of the increase in inequality for high skill groups has been due to increased variation in the predictable component of earnings. In addition, around one-quarter of the increase in returns to education is calculated to be due to increases in the uncertainty component.[138]

Taken together, compared with viewing individuals as randomly drawing from the distribution of annual earnings, this latter group of studies suggest

[137] Taking a different modelling approach, Guvenen (2007, 2009) chooses to model a process whereby individuals gradually learn about their type and update their expectations as they move through early working life. He finds that learning is slow, and thus initial uncertainty is important throughout the life cycle.

[138] Finally, this literature serves to remind us that schooling decisions are themselves taken in the context of future lifetime income expectations and hence education levels may only be imperfect proxies of *ex-post* earnings capabilities. Cunha, Heckman, and Navarro (2008), for example, use similar calculations to show that, were the future evolution of earnings to be known in advance, one-quarter of high school graduates would have chosen college education and over 30% of college graduates would have left education after high school.

that much of the subsequent evolution of lifetime earnings profiles is known by individuals at the beginning of life and there is a relatively smaller role for uncertainty than that suggested by those studies using the Permanent–Transitory methodology described above. By exactly the same argument as above, however, conclusions are inevitably highly dependent on assumptions of the nature of shocks to earnings. In this case, these studies have only studied environments where shocks are independent and identically distributed across time, which rules out the existence of shocks that have persistent effects and the possibility of earnings processes where the variance of uncertainty changes with age. In both situations, were such factors to be controlled for, the relative importance attributed to uncertainty would increase and the relative importance of known differences across types would decrease.

In short, the empirical literature is at a very early stage in these dimensions and as longer time series of data on larger samples of individuals become available then some of these issues should be resolved. In this respect, further research on tax record data is particularly promising. As an example, whilst the findings of Kopczuk, Saez, and Song (2007) do not directly address the issue of heterogeneity versus persistent uncertainty described above, their related calculations on short-, medium-, and long-run mobility in US earnings processes from 1937 onwards illustrate the potential power of such tax-record data to provide new evidence on these issues.

What is certain, however, is that the outcome of this debate will be important in generating an understanding of individual decision-making over the life cycle, which in turn is at the heart of potential dynamic tax calculations. Some idea of the potential magnitude of the difference between the two alternative scenarios can be seen in the calculations in Scholz, Seshadri and Khitatrakun (2006) who look at the extent to which a particular and somewhat restricted form of the life-cycle model can explain the observed distribution of retirement saving in the US. Under the assumption that the lifetime average of their subsequent income growth rates is known to individuals at the beginning of their life, Scholz et al.'s simulations suggest that the life-cycle model can explain 86% of the variation observed in wealth data in the US. When this assumption is modified, such that individuals are assumed to know only the average of future income growth for people of their broad characteristics (defined by marital status, education, and the number of earners in their household) then the fraction of saving explained by the model falls to 43%.

These latter calculations suggest consideration of an alternative approach to the understanding of lifetime earnings profiles, namely to make indirect inferences about the nature of such profiles from additional data rather than study earnings data in isolation.[139] In particular, since under the standard model of economic decision-making over the lifetime, individuals' expectations of their permanent income should be determinants of their consumption choices, data on income and expenditure have been combined to investigate the importance of permanent and transitory earnings risk. In this case, more sophisticated controls for other factors need to be introduced since consumption will typically depend on many factors other than earnings alone, such as other sources of future household income, expected taxes and transfers, and expected future household circumstances. Deaton and Paxson (1994) document the increasing variance of consumption with age across a wide range of countries and Blundell and Preston (1998) use data on the joint evolution of the variance of consumption and income in the UK to argue that increases in income inequality in the 1980s were predominantly due to increases in permanent uncertainty, and Storesletten, Telmer, and Yaron (2004) show that the increasing consumption and income dispersion is consistent with a standard life-cycle model provided that a substantial fraction (roughly half) of variability in lifetime earnings is accounted for by uncertainty. Finally, for all but low wealth households, Blundell, Pistaferri, and Preston (2008) find such permanent components to be the dominant factor in the evolution of the variance of consumption growth, once demographic change is allowed for. However, accounting for family labour supply behaviour, taxation, and transfers, they find only around 50% of the variance in male earnings growth transmits through to variation in consumption.[140]

Finally, both short- and long-run income mobility, whether anticipated or otherwise, can create substantial movement across marginal rate tax brackets within the population and such mobility is also relevant for our discussions in previous sections. Blundell, Emmerson, and Wakefield (2006) look at such tax rate mobility using BHPS data and show that, for example, 17.3% of non-higher rate income tax payers aged 30 to 39 in 1991 became higher rate income taxpayers at some point in the following 12 years and this proportion

[139] A third alternative would be to measure individuals' income expectations using survey methods. Such measures have been pioneered in a number of dimensions in recent years and have now shown to be feasible and reliable. See, for example, Dominitz and Manski (1996, 1997, 2001) and Guiso, Jappelli, and Terlizzese (1992) for short-run income expectations and uncertainty measures and Betts (1996) or Smith and Powell (1990) for measures of longer-run income expectations. The continued collection and analysis of data on long-run expectations of earnings, or more generally living standards, and in particular on uncertainty surrounding such expectations is an interesting and important avenue for future research.

[140] Once again, such models have predominantly focused on documenting the time-series evolution of uncertainty and any such time-effects, coupled with any changes in the nature of credit markets (as argued by Krueger and Perri (2006)) would need to be accounted for when looking at age profiles.

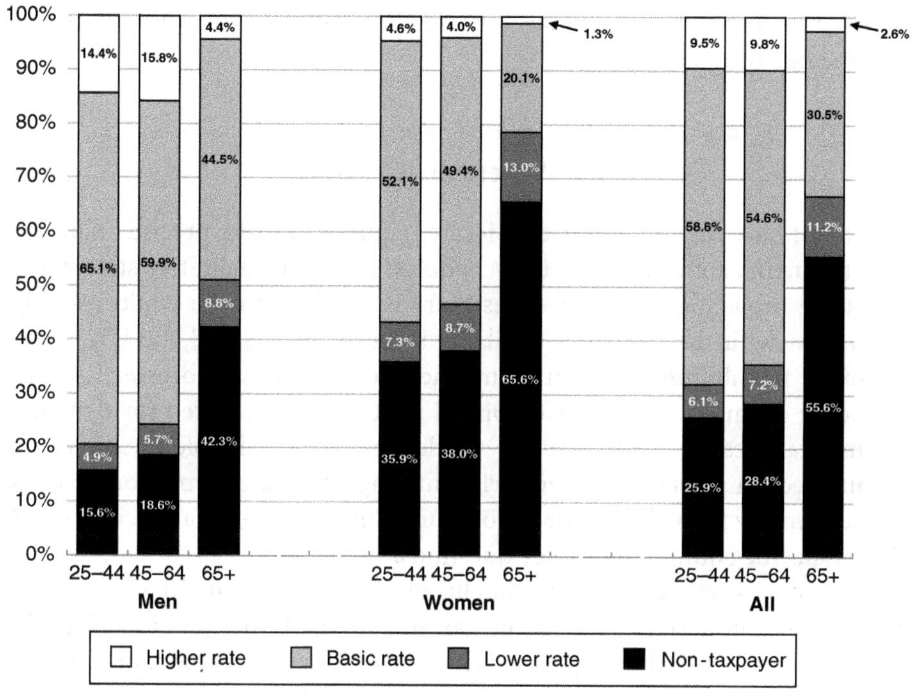

Source: Authors calculations from 2004–05 Survey of Personal Incomes Microdata Additional information on 2004 population by age and sex from ONS Population trends.

Figure 6.3. Distribution of marginal income tax brackets by age and sex, UK 2004–05

was almost one in three (32.5%) if one looked at basic rate taxpayers aged 30 to 39 in 1991. Our own calculations from the Survey of Personal Incomes (the dataset derived from tax returns in the UK) show cross-sectional age variation in the distribution of marginal tax rates (Figure 6.3). The figure shows that whilst 15.8% of men aged 45–64 pay higher rates of income tax, only 4.4% of men aged 65 and over pay that rate.[141] Similarly only 1.3% of women aged 65 and over pay higher rates of tax and there are large fractions of the population moving from basic rates in middle age to lower or non-taxpayer status in old age. Whilst the true cohort profiles are not captured by this age cross-section, the cohort effects in lifetime incomes are unlikely to be sufficient to distort this pattern. And, indeed, differential mortality along the lines discussed earlier—whereby the lifetime rich are more likely to survive to old ages than the lifetime poor—will tend to work in the opposite direction. Consequently, the opportunity for tax-rate smoothing, and the

[141] In reality, due to tapering away of tax allowances and the Pension Credit, the 'true' marginal rates may be higher than those presented in this figure for some income ranges. The marginal tax rates presented in this figure are simply statutory tax rates on income alone.

relative preference for individuals for an EET as opposed to a TEE treatment is immediately apparent.

6.9.3. Where do we stand?

We do not have the full empirical picture required to make precise quantitative statements about optimal tax schedules. Even for qualitative statements about the broad sign of tax wedges there is much more we could usefully know, and with the data now available in both the US and the UK, there are many possibilities for future empirical research that addresses itself to providing estimates of the key empirical relationships required for dynamic optimal tax design. Such research would be hugely valuable and is to be encouraged. At present, what empirical findings there are come from studies whose primary focus is not the set of issues raised here and, as such, are not always specific enough to our key questions.

Nevertheless, some tentative conclusions can be drawn. In short, what matters for the design of dynamic tax policy in the models described in previous sections is the degree to which individuals are able, and willing, to smooth out any variation that they face in 'net' lifetime resources over the lifetime, where by 'net' resources, we mean lifetime earnings adjusted for lifetime needs. To the extent that individuals of higher abilities can be shown to have both higher propensity for saving (lower discount rates and lower risk aversion) and stronger earnings growth over the life cycle, and to the extent that there exist considerable uncertainties in long-run net resources (regardless of differences across ability groups), this combination of factors would lead to a role for an optimal wedge and some taxation of the normal rate of return on capital income. The role of the potential dependency of the benefit of consumption in one period on consumption, leisure, and health in other periods is more complex and we do not know enough about broad empirical patterns to be able to speculate on how such additional considerations would affect optimal wedges.

6.10. CONCLUSION

The long-standing debate on the best base for non-linear (progressive) annual individual taxation has been between total income and total consumption expenditures (with recognition of special treatment for some incomes and/or some expenditures). A more informative debate may be about the relative taxation of different sources of income and, relatedly, the implications for progressive taxation of different uses of income, with the focus here on saving, but plausibly also on medical expenses, education expenses, housing expenses, and taxation by other levels of government. We have proceeded as in the quote from Alfred Marshall at the start of this essay, 'it [is] necessary for man with his limited powers to go step by step; breaking up a complex question, studying one bit at a time, and at last combining his partial solutions into a more or less complete solution of the whole riddle' (Marshall (1948), p. 366). We have seen the implications of a wide variety of individual analyses and asked about policy inferences that seemed appropriate to draw. We do not think we have 'a more or less complete solution of the whole riddle'. But policy making, and so policy recommendations, cannot wait for a complete solution.

As noted at the start, the Meade Report recommends a three-part structure made up 'of a new Beveridge scheme, ... of a progressive expenditure tax regime, ... and of a system of progressive taxation on wealth with some discrimination against inherited wealth'. We have not considered issues being addressed in other chapters, particularly the role of labour force participation (the extensive margin) which is important for policy for those with very low or no earnings and limited wealth. Also, we have not explored models that might shed light on the relative advantages of annual taxation of wealth relative to taxation of capital income, as the models we have examined have mostly been restricted to a single safe asset, available on the same terms to all, leaving the two sources of taxation the same. We have had little discussion of uncertain returns to assets and none to issues related to the realization of income or the value of illiquid assets. And we have not considered bequests.

The Meade Report discussed measuring the ability to pay taxes as part of tax design. It concluded that: 'on examination "taxable capacity" always turns out to be very difficult to define and to be a matter on which opinions will differ rather widely' (p. 14). We see no reason to reach a different conclusion from that in the Report—indeed, we have gone further in dismissing taxable capacity from a central place in tax design.

In considering the Meade Report recommendations in light of thirty years of additional research, experience, and economic development, we explored two questions that shed some light on the Meade Report recommendations:

- If there is an annual earnings tax, how should capital income be taxed?
- If there is an annual earnings tax, should there be a deduction for net active saving, resulting in a tax on consumption?

In addition, we explored an issue not addressed in the Meade Report, the potential advantages, despite increased complexity, of having age-dependent income tax rates. Each of these three issues has both a design dimension and a transition dimension, but we concentrated on the former.

6.10.1. Taxation of capital income with an annual earnings tax

Support by economists and tax lawyers for exempting capital income from direct taxation has been influenced by the well-known Atkinson–Stiglitz and Chamley–Judd analyses. However, we conclude that the policy relevance of the sharp finding of the optimality of no taxation of capital income is thoroughly undercut by the implications of large uncertainty about future earnings and the growing disparity in earnings as a cohort ages. Adding such uncertainty and disparity to the frameworks employed by Atkinson–Stiglitz or Chamley–Judd results in the conclusion that taxation of capital income or of wealth is indeed part of optimal taxation. Furthermore, the full thrust of the Chamley–Judd result depends critically on bequest behaviour, but behaviour assumed in the model is not widespread in the population. In addition, in light of the widely varying individual saving rates in the economy, there is a natural presumption that during working years there is a positive correlation between the tendency to save and earnings potential (although the empirical underpinning is not so clear). This is another reason for taxing capital income as a means of more efficiently taxing those with higher earnings potentials. A further case comes from the difficulties in distinguishing between labour and capital incomes, which gives an advantage to reducing the difference in taxes between them. While we have not explored the literature incorporating human capital investment into tax considerations, with a progressive earnings tax (particularly one that is not age-dependent), the presumption that human capital investment steepens the age–earnings trajectory may call for some taxation of capital income to get closer to even treatment of these two forms of investment.

Should capital income be taxed more or less heavily than labour income? With a thought process that starts with the conditions for zero taxation and then adds some taxation for elements not in the models that imply zero taxation, there is the danger of anchoring towards zero, resulting in a conclusion that capital income taxation should be lighter, without a good basis for reaching that conclusion. There is probably no substitute for extensive calculations using calibrated models, with models that incorporate the elements thought to be most important in determining relative taxation. Some existing calculations show heavier taxation while others show lighter taxation. We did not attempt to evaluate the relevance of different calculations, but point to the need for lots more.

A second issue is the appropriate relationship between the marginal taxation of capital income and the marginal taxation of labour income. The Nordic dual tax has linear taxation of capital income. The tax rate can be set at the highest or lowest positive tax rates or something in between. In the US, recent lower tax rates on dividends do relate that tax rate to the rate on labour income. The old US system that had inclusion of one-half of capital gains in taxable income (for those in lower tax brackets) also had a clear relationship. Apart from the point that trying to discourage conversion of labour income into capital income seems to call for marginal tax rates on the two types of income that relate positively to each other, it is not clear without extensive calibrated calculations how strong the relationship should be. And the choice of tax rate on capital income is plausibly related to the extent of use of tax-favoured retirement savings opportunities. To explore the normative properties of different relationships among marginal tax rates, one would again need extensive calculations. We think such calculations are called for and do not see a way to draw a firm conclusion from the evidence we have examined.

6.10.2. A deduction for active saving with an annual earnings tax

One way to have a consumption tax base is to deduct from earnings the net increase in active savings.[142] In countries such as the UK that already have EET tax-favoured retirement savings accounts, this corresponds to removing limits on deposits in such accounts along with removing limits on withdrawals. Thus, compared with an accrual-based income tax (or an approximation from taxing realized capital gains to adjust for deferral), a consumption tax gives the advantage of deferral on all savings for future consumption. As Judd (1999) has pointed out, this approach does not get incentives right for human capital.

It is worth noting that there are significant differences between exempting capital income from taxation and a consumption tax base. In a model with a single safe rate of interest, the two are the same apart from differences needed in transition rules to match them. However, both different rates of return for

[142] To reiterate, active saving is saving made directly from earnings. Earnings minus net active savings equals income minus net saving.

different investors and uncertain rates of return can make the two approaches different.

6.10.3. Age-dependent taxes

Public pension systems commonly have age-dependent rules for eligibility for claiming benefits, for determination of the size of benefits, and for the implicit taxation of earnings. And Switzerland has contribution rates to the mandatory occupational pension that vary with the age of the worker. Pension systems generally have rules that have a strong reliance on individual histories over a long period in determining benefits. Income taxes make little use of such structures (apart from what is inherent in measuring capital gains). An implicit exception, similar to pension calculations, is tax-favouring of retirement saving, which incorporates explicit tax rules based on age when withdrawing funds as well as different implicit degrees of tax-favouring depending on the age at which funds are put into an account.

Is it worth the administrative complexity and the added political process to extend tax structures to include age-related features? Their presence in existing national pension rules suggests it is feasible, and analyses of optimal pension systems suggests it has value. Support for age-dependent tax rates comes from two separate arguments: differences in the distributions of circumstances across different ages and individual forward-looking calculations when making decisions. Both arguments matter, but the former may be more persuasive than the latter because of ease of measurement and the substantial diversity in individual decision-making.

Because age-dependent taxes can address both of these arguments, we think it is useful for governments to contemplate introducing them in some form and for analysts to explore them in more detail than has happened so far. We reviewed some of the support for age-dependent taxation of labour income, possibly based on setting different break points among marginal tax rates for workers in four age groups—under-30, 30–50, 50–65, and over-65. Analysis of the break points would reflect the distribution of earnings possibilities by age and the intertemporal incentives inherent in facing different break points over time. The latter might reflect uncertainties about future earnings, human capital accumulation, and borrowing constraints. This doesn't sound too hard to model and analyse, nor too hard for a legislature to incorporate in the tax structure. And plausibly this could be legislated without undue pressure by the politically better-connected ages. Obviously, any optimal tax analysis will find a higher-valued optimum from using more policy tools. The literature suggests that the gains from age-dependent labour income taxes may not be trivial and detailed analysis could explore how substantial the gains might be. There may be a case for age-varying exempt amounts of capital income as well.

Any real policy recommendation must address issues of transition. Some transition issues are lost when equity analyses look only at lifetimes of cohorts living under a new system. Others are lost with consideration of the properties of the best steady state rather than the steady state that arises from a full intertemporal optimization.

6.10.4. Concluding remarks

The Meade Report wanted to tax both consumption and wealth annually. We share the view that capital income (or wealth) should be part of the tax base. We do not find any support in optimal tax considerations for the argument that annual capital income should be taxed exactly as annual labour income is taxed—a tax base of Haig–Simons income. We suspect that positively relating marginal tax rates on labour and capital incomes is better than having separate taxation of the two sources of income. We have also argued for the advantages of explicit variation of taxation with age. We have noted repeatedly issues that warrant further research. Pointing out the obvious need for further research is not meant to undercut the relevance of research developments to date for improving tax policy debates, and possibly tax policy.

REFERENCES

Aaron, H. J. (ed.) (1976), *Inflation and the Income Tax*. Washington, DC: Brookings Institution.

——Burman, L., and Steuerle, E. C. (eds.) (2007), *Taxing Capital Income*, Washington, DC: Urban Institute Press.

Abel, A. B. (2001), 'The Effects of Investing Social Security Funds, in the Stock Market when Fixed Costs Prevent Some Households from Holding Stocks', *American Economic Review*, **91**, 128–48.

Abowd, J., and Card, D. (1989), 'On the Covariance Structure of Earnings and Hours Changes', *Econometrica*, **57**, 411–45.

Acemoglu, D., Golosov, M., and Tsyvinski, A. (2008), 'Political Economy of Mechanisms', *Econometrica*, **76**, 619–41.

Adams, P., Hurd, M., McFadden, D., Merrill, A., and Ribeiro, T. (2003), 'Healthy, Wealthy, and Wise?, Tests for Direct Causal Paths between Health and Socioeconomic Status', *Journal of Econometrics*, **112**, 3–56 [pdf].

Aguiar, M., and Hurst, E. (2005), 'Consumption Versus Expenditure', *Journal of Political Economy*, **113**, 919–48.

Ainslie, G. (2001), *The Breakdown of Will*, Cambridge: Cambridge University Press.

Aiyagari, S. R. (1995), 'Optimal Capital Income Taxation with Incomplete Markets, Borrowing Constraints, and Constant Discounting', *Journal of Political Economy*, **103**, 1158–75.

Albanesi, S., and Sleet, C. (2006), 'Dynamic Optimal Taxation with Private Information', *Review of Economic Studies*, **73**, 1–30.

Allingham, M. G., and Sandmo, A. (1972), 'Income Tax Evasion: A Theoretical Analysis', *Journal of Public Economics*, **1**, 323–38.

Altig, D., Auerbach, A. J., Kotlikoff, L. J., Smetters, K. A., and Walliser, J. (2001), 'Simulating Fundamental Tax Reform in the U.S.', *American Economic Review*, **91**, 574–95.

Amador, M., Werning, I., and Angeletos, G.-M. (2005), 'Commitment Versus Flexibility', *Econometrica*, **74**, 365–96.

Ameriks, J., Caplin, A., and Leahy, J. (2003), 'Wealth Accumulation and the Propensity to Plan', *Quarterly Journal of Economics*, **118**, 1007–48.

Atkeson, A., Chari, V. V., and Kehoe, P. J. (1999), 'Taxing Capital Income: A Bad Idea', *Federal Reserve Bank of Minneapolis Quarterly Review*, **23**, 3–17.

Atkinson, A. B. (1970), 'On the Measurement of Inequality', *The Journal of Economic Theory*, **2**, 244–63.

—— (1980), 'Horizontal Equity and the Distribution of the Tax Burden', in Aaron, H. J., and Boskin, M. J. (eds.), *The Economics of Taxation*, Washington, DC: Brookings Institution, 3–18.

—— and Sandmo, A. (1980), 'Welfare Implications of the Taxation of Savings', *Economic Journal*, **90** (September), 529–49.

—— and Stiglitz, J. E. (1976), 'The Design of Tax Structure: Direct Versus Indirect Taxation', *Journal of Public Economics*, **6**, 55–75.

—— —— (1980), *Lectures on Public Economics*, London: McGraw Hill.

Attanasio, O. P., Banks, J., Meghir, C., and Weber, G. (1999), 'Humps and Bumps in Lifetime Consumption', *Journal of Business & Economic Statistics*, American Statistical Association, **17**, 22–35.

—— and Hoynes, H. W. (2000), 'Differential Mortality and Wealth Accumulation', *Journal of Human Resources*, **35**, 1–29.

Auerbach, A. (1991), 'Retrospective Capital Gains Taxation', *American Economic Review*, **81**, 167–78.

—— (2002), 'Is There a Role for Discretionary Fiscal Policy?', in *Rethinking Stabilization Policy: Proceedings of a Symposium Sponsored by the Federal Reserve Bank of Kansas City*, Kansas City: Federal Reserve Bank of Kansas City, 109–50.

——(2006), 'Choice between Income and Consumption Taxes: A Primer', NBER Working Papers No. 12307.
——and Feenberg, D. (2000), 'The Significance of Federal Taxes as Automatic Stabilizers', *Journal of Economic Perspectives*, **14**, 37–56.
——Kotlikoff, L. J., and Skinner, J. (1983), 'The Efficiency Gains from Dynamic Tax Reform', *International Economic Review*, **24**, 81–100.
Baker, M. (1997), 'Growth-rate Heterogeneity and the Covariance Structure of Life-Cycle Earnings', *Journal of Labor Economics*, **15**, 338–75.
——and Solon, G. (2003), 'Earnings Dynamics and Inequality among Canadian Men, 1976–1992: Evidence from Longitudinal Income Tax Records', *Journal of Labor Economics*, **21**.
Bankman, J., and Schler, M. L. (2007), 'Tax Planning under the Flat Tax', in Aaron, H. J., Burman, L. E., and Steuerle, C. E. (eds.), *Taxing Capital Income*, Washington, DC: Urban Institute Press, 245–84.
——and Weisbach, D. (2006), 'The Superiority of an Ideal Consumption Tax over an Ideal Income Tax', **58** *Stanford L. Rev.*, 1413.
Banks, J., and Blundell, R. (1994), 'Household Saving in the UK', in Poterba, J. (ed.), *International Comparisons of Household Saving*, Chicago: Chicago University Press.
————and Tanner, S. (1998), 'Is There a Retirement-Savings Puzzle?', *American Economic Review*, **88**, 769–88.
——Breeze, E., Lessof, C., and Nazroo, J. (2006), *Retirement, Health and Relationships of the Older Population in England: The 2004 English Longitudinal Study of Ageing (Wave 2)*, Institute for Fiscal Studies (July).
——and Oldfield, Z. (2007), 'Understanding Pensions: Cognitive Function, Numerical Ability and Retirement Saving', *Fiscal Studies* **28**, 143–70.
Benjamin, D., Brown, S. A., and Shapiro, J. M. (2006), 'Who is Behavioral? Cognitive Ability and Anomalous Preferences', Available at SSRN: <http://ssrn.com/abstract=675264>.
Bernheim, B. D. (1997), 'Rethinking Savings Incentives', in Auerbach, A. (ed.), *Fiscal Policy: Lessons from Economic Research*, Cambridge, Mass.: MIT Press.
——and Bagwell, K. (1988), 'Is Everything Neutral?', *Journal of Political Economy*, **96**, 308–38.
——Garrett, D. M., and Maki, D. M. (2001), 'Education and Saving: The Long-Term Effects of High School Financial Curriculum Mandates', *Journal of Public Economics*, **80**, 435–65.
——and Rangel, A. (2007), 'Behavioral Public Economics: Welfare and Policy Analysis with Non-Standard Decision-Makers', in Diamond, P., and Vartiainen, H. (eds.), *Behavioral Economics and Its Applications*, NJ: Princeton University Press, 7–84.
——Skinner, J., and Weinberg, S. (2001), 'What Accounts for the Variation in Retirement Wealth among U.S. Households?', *American Economic Review*, **91**, 832–57.

Beshears, J., Choi, J., Laibson, D., and Madrian, B. (2007), 'The Importance of Default Options for Retirement Savings Outcomes: Evidence from the United States', NBER working paper 12009.

Bettinger, E., and Slonim, R. (2005), 'Patience among Children: Evidence from a Field Experiment', Case Western Reserve University Working Paper (May).

Betts, J. R. (1996), 'What Do Students Know about Wages?', *Journal of Human Resources*, **31**, 27–56.

Blomquist, S., and Micheletto, L. (2003), 'Age Related Optimal Income Taxation', Unpublished.

Blundell, R., Pistaferri, L., and Preston, I. (2008), 'Consumption Inequality and Partial Insurance', forthcoming *American Economic Review*.

——and Preston, I. (1998), 'Consumption Inequality and Income Uncertainty', *Quarterly Journal of Economics*, **113**, 603–40.

——Wakefield, M., and Emmerson, C. (2006), 'The Importance of Incentives in Influencing Private Retirement Saving: Known Knowns and Known Unknowns', IFS Working Papers, W06/09, doi: 10.1920/wp.ifs.2006.0609, April, 2006.

Boadway, R., Marchand, M., and Pestieau, P. (2000), 'Redistribution with Unobservable Bequests: A Case for Taxing Capital Income', *Scandinavian Journal of Economics*, **102**, 253–67.

Borghans, L., Duckworth, A., Heckman, J., and ter Weel, B. (2008), 'The Economics and Psychology of Personality Traits', *Journal of Human Resources*, forthcoming.

Börsch-Supan, A., and Stahl, K. (1991), 'Life-Cycle Savings and Consumption Constraints: Theory, Empirical Evidence and Fiscal Implications', *Journal of Population Economics*, **4**, 233–55.

Bovenberg, A. L., and Jacobs, B. (2005a), 'Redistribution and Education Subsidies are Siamese Twins', *Journal of Public Economics*, **89**, 2005–36.

————(2005b), 'Human Capital and Optimal Positive Taxation of Capital Income', Tinbergen Institute Discussion Paper TI 2005-035/3.

Bradford, D. F. (1986), *Untangling the Income Tax*, Cambridge, Mass.: Harvard University Press.

——(1995), 'Fixing Realization Accounting: Symmetry, Consistency and Correctness in the Taxation of Financial Instruments', *Tax Law Review*, **50**, 731–85.

Breyer, S. (1993), *Breaking the Vicious Circle: Toward Effective Risk Regulation*, Cambridge, Mass.: Harvard University Press.

Buchanan, J. M., and Musgrave, R. A. (1999), *Public Finance and Public Choice*, Cambridge, Mass.: MIT Press.

Card, D., and Lemieux, T. (2001), 'Can Falling Supply Explain the Rising Return to College for Younger Men? A Cohort-Based Analysis', *Quarterly Journal of Economics*, **116**, 705–46.

Carroll, C. D. (2000), 'Why Do the Rich Save So Much?', in Slemrod, J. B. (ed.), *Does Atlas Shrug? The Economic Consequences of Taxing the Rich*, Cambridge, Mass.: Harvard University Press, 463–85.

—— and Samwick, A. (1997), 'The Nature of Precautionary Wealth', *Journal of Monetary Economics*, **40**, 41–72.

Case, A., and Paxson, C. (2006), 'Stature and Status: Height, Ability, and Labour Market Outcomes', NBER Working Papers No. 12466.

Chamley, C. (1986), 'Optimal Taxation of Capital Income in General Equilibrium with Infinite Lives', *Econometrica*, **54**, 607–22.

—— (2001), 'Capital Income Taxation, Wealth Distribution and Borrowing Constraints', *Journal of Public Economics*, **79**, 55–69.

Choné, P., and Laroque, G. (2001), 'Optimal Incentives for Labour Force Participation', INSEE Working Paper No. 2001–25.

—— —— (2006), 'Should Low Skilled Work Be Subsidized?', INSEE Working Paper No. 2006–08.

Christiansen, V., and Tuomala, M. (2007), 'On Taxing Capital Income with Income Shifting', unpublished.

Conesa, J. C., Kitao, S., and Krueger, D. (2007), 'Taxing Capital? Not a Bad Idea After All!', NBER Working Paper No. 12880.

Corlett, W. J., and Hague, D. C. (1953–4), 'Complementarity and the Excess Burden of Taxation', *Review of Economic Studies*, **21**, 21–30.

Correia, I. H. (1996), 'Should Capital Income be Taxed in a Steady State?', *Journal of Public Economics*, **60**, 147–51.

Cremer, H., and Gahvari, F. (1995), 'Uncertainty, Optimal Taxation and the Direct Versus Indirect Tax Controversy', *Economic Journal*, **105**, 1165–79.

—— and Pestieau, P. (2003), 'Wealth Transfer Taxation: A Survey', CESifo Working Paper 1061.

—— —— and Rochet, J.-C. (2001), 'Direct Versus Indirect Taxation: The Design of the Tax Structure Revisited', *International Economic Review*, **42**, 781–99.

—— —— —— (2003), 'Capital Income Taxation when Inherited Wealth is not Observable', *Journal of Public Economics*, **87**, 2475–90.

Cunha, F., and Heckman, J. (2007a), 'A New Framework for the Analysis of Inequality', January 2007, IZA Discusssion paper No. 2565, forthcoming in *Macroeconomic Dynamics*.

—— —— (2007b), 'The Evolution of Inequality, Heterogeneity, and Uncertainty in Labor Earnings in the U.S. Economy', October 2007, IZA Discussion paper No. 3115.

—— —— and Navarro, S. (2008), 'Separating Heterogeneity from Uncertainty in Life Cycle Earnings', *Oxford Economic Papers*, **57**, 191–261.

Deaton, A. (1979), 'Optimally Uniform Commodity Taxes', *Economic Letters*, **2**, 357–61.

—— and Paxson, C. (1994), 'Intertemporal Choice and Inequality', *Journal of Political Economy*, **102**, 437–67.

Diamond, P. (1965), 'On the Cost of Tax Exempt Bonds', *Journal of Political Economy*, **73**, 399–403.

Diamond, P. (1967), 'Cardinal Welfare, Individualistic Ethics, and Interpersonal Comparison of Utility: Comment', *Journal of Political Economy*, **75**, 765–6.

—— (1973), 'Taxation and Public Production in a Growth Setting', in Mirrlees, J. A., and Stern, N. H. (eds.), *Models of Economic Growth*, London: Macmillan.

—— (1980a), 'An Alternative to Steady State Comparisons', *Economic Letters*, **5**, 7–9.

—— (1980b), 'Income Taxation with Fixed Hours of Work', *Journal of Public Economics* **13**, 101–10.

—— (ed.) (1999), *Issues in Privatizing Social Security, Report of an Expert Panel of the National Academy of Social Insurance*, Cambridge, Mass.: MIT Press.

—— (2006), 'Optimal Tax Treatment of Private Contributions for Public Goods with and without Warm Glow Preferences', *Journal of Public Economics*, **90**, 897–919.

—— (2007), 'Comment on Mikhail Golosov, Aleh Tsyvinski, Iván Werning, "New Dynamic Public Finance: A User's Guide"', *NBER Macroeconomics Annual 2006*, 365–79.

—— and Geanakoplos, J. (2003), 'Social Security Investment in Equities', *American Economic Review*, **93**, 1047–74.

—— and Mirrlees, J. A. (1971), 'Optimal Taxation and Public Production, I: Production Efficiency', *American Economic Review*, **LXI**, 8–27.

Dickens, R. (2000), 'The Evolution of Individual Male Earnings in Great Britain', *Economic Journal*, **110**, 27–49.

Dominguez, B. (2007), 'Public Debt and Optimal Taxes Without Commitment', *Journal of Economic Theory*, **135**, 159–70.

Dominitz, J., and Manski, C. F. (1996), 'Eliciting Student Expectations of the Returns to Schooling', *Journal of Human Resources*, **31**, 1–26.

—— —— (1997), 'Using Expectations Data to Study Subjective Income Expectations', *Journal of the American Statistical Association*, **92**, 855–67.

—— —— (2001), 'Estimation of Income Expectations Models Using Expectations and Realizations Data', *Journal of Econometrics*, **102**, 165–95.

Dynan, K. E., Skinner, J., and Zeldes, S. P. (2004), 'Do the Rich Save More?', *Journal of Political Economy*, **112**, 397–444.

Eigsti, I., Zayas, V., Mischel, W., Shoda, Y., Ayduk, O., Dadlani, M. B., Davidson, M. C., Aber, J. L., and Casey, B. J. (2006), 'Predictive Cognitive Control from Preschool to Late Adolescence and Young Adulthood', *Psychological Science*, **17**, 478–84.

Elo, I. T., and Preston, S. (1996), 'Educational Differentials in Mortality: United States, 1979–1985', *Social Science and Medicine*, **42**, 47–57.

Erosa, A., and Gervais, M. (2002), 'Optimal Taxation in Life-Cycle Economies', *Journal of Economic Theory*, **105**, 338–69.

Farhi, E., and Werning, I. (2007), 'Inequality and Social Discounting', *Journal of Political Economy*, **115**, 365–402.

Feldstein, M. (1976a), 'On the Theory of Tax Reform', *Journal of Public Economics*, **6**, 77–104.

—— (1976b), 'Compensation in Tax Reform', *National Tax Journal*, **29**, 123–30.

Fennell, L. A., and Stark, K. J. (2005), 'Taxation over Time', UCLA School of Law: Law-Econ Research Paper 05–24.

Frederick, S. (2005), 'Cognitive Reflection and Decision Making', *Journal of Economic Perspectives*, **19**, 25–42.

Gaube, T. (2007), 'Optimum Taxation of Each Year's Income', *Journal of Public Economic Theory*, **9**, 127–50.

Gentry, W. M., and Glenn Hubbard, R. (1997), 'Distributional Implications of Introducing a Broad-Based Consumption Tax', in Poterba, J. M. (ed.), *Tax Policy and the Economy*, **11**, Cambridge, Mass.: MIT Press, 1–48.

Gervais, M. (2003), 'On the Optimality of Age-Dependent Taxes and the Progressive US Tax System', unpublished. <http://aix1.uottawa.ca/~vbarham/PT03.pdf>.

Gilbert, D. (2006), *Stumbling on Happiness*, New York: Alfred A. Knopf.

Gollier, C. (2005), 'Intergenerational Risk Sharing and Risk Taking of a Pension Fund'. No. 391, IDEI Working Papers from Institut d'Économie Industrielle, Toulouse.

Golosov, M., Kocherlakota, N., and Tsyvinski, A. (2003), 'Optimal Indirect and Capital Taxation', *Review of Economic Studies*, **70**, 569–87.

—— and Tsyvinski, A. (2006), 'Designing Optimal Disability Insurance: A Case for Asset Testing', *Journal of Political Economy*, **114**, 257–69.

—— —— and Werning, I. (2007), 'New Dynamic Public Finance: A User's Guide', *NBER Macroeconomics Annual 2006*, 317–63.

Gordon, R. H. (1985), 'Taxation of Corporate Capital Income: Tax Revenues vs. Tax Distortions', *Quarterly Journal of Economics* (February), 1–27.

—— and MacKie-Mason, J. K. (1995), 'Why is There Corporate Taxation in a Small Open Economy?', in Feldstein, M., Hines, J. R. Jr., and Glenn Hubbard, R. (eds.), *The Effects of Taxation on Multinational Corporations*, Chicago: University of Chicago Press.

—— and Slemrod, J. (1998), 'Are "Real" Responses to Taxes Simply Income Shifting between Corporate and Personal Tax Bases?', NBER Working Paper W6576.

Graetz, M. J. (1985), 'Retroactivity Revisited', *Harvard Law Review*, **98**, 1820–41.

Griffith, R., and Devereux, M. P. (1998), 'Taxes and the Location of Production: Evidence from a Panel of US Multinationals', *Journal of Public Economics*, **3**, 335–67.

Guiso, L., Jappelli, T., and Terlizzese, D. (1992), 'Earnings Uncertainty and Precautionary Saving', *Journal of Monetary Economics*, **30**, 307–37.

Gul, F., and Pesendorfer, W. (2004), 'Self-Control and the Theory of Consumption', *Econometrica*, **72**, 119–58.

Guvenen, F. (2007), 'Learning Your Earning: Are Labor Income Shocks Really Very Persistent?', *American Economic Review*, **97**, 687–712.

—— (2009), 'An Empirical Investigation of Labor Income Processes', *Review of Economic Dynamics*, **12**, 58–79.

Haider, S. J. (2001), 'Earnings Instability and Earnings Inequality of Males in the United Sates: 1971–1991', *Journal of Labor Economics*, **19**, 799–836.

Haider, S. J., and Solon, G. (2006), 'Life-Cycle Variation in the Association between Current and Lifetime Earnings', *American Economic Review*, **96**, 1308–20.

Haig, R. M. (1921), *The Federal Income Tax*. New York: Columbia University Press.

Hall, R. E., and Rabushka, A. (2007), *The Flat Tax* (2nd edition). Stanford, CA: Hoover Institution Press.

Hamilton, J. (1987), 'Optimal Wage and Income Taxation with Wage Uncertainty', *International Economic Review*, **28**, 373–88.

Hausman, J. A. (1979), 'Individual Discount Rates and the Purchase and Utilization of Energy-Using Durables', *The Bell Journal of Economics*, **10**, 33–54.

Heathcote, J., Storesletten, K., and Violante, G. (2004), 'The Macroeconomic Implications of Rising Wage Inequality in the United States', Working Paper, New York University (August).

Helliwell, J. (1969), 'The Taxation of Capital Gains', *Canadian Journal of Economics*, **2**, 314–18.

Hubbard, R. G., and Judd, K. L. (1986), 'Liquidity Constraints, Fiscal Policy, and Consumption', *Brookings Papers on Economic Activity* (no. 1), 1–59.

—— Skinner, J., and Zeldes, S. P. (1995), 'Precautionary Saving and Social Insurance', *Journal of Political Economy*, **103**, 360–99.

Hurd, M. D. (1987), 'Savings of the Elderly and Desired Bequests', *American Economic Review*, **77**, 298–312.

Jones, L. E., Manuelli, R. E., and Rossi, P. E. (1997), 'On the Optimal Taxation of Capital Income', *Journal of Economic Theory*, **73**, 93–117.

Judd, K. L. (1985), 'Redistributive Taxation in a Simple Perfect Foresight Model', *Journal of Public Economics*, **28**, 59–83.

—— (1999), 'Optimal Taxation and Spending in General Competitive Growth Models', *Journal of Public Economics*, **71**, 1–26.

—— (2001), 'The Impact of Tax Reform on Modern Dynamic Economies', in Hassett, K. A., and Glenn Hubbard, R. (eds.), *Transition Costs of Fundamental Tax Reform*, Washington: The AEI Press.

—— and Su, C.-L. (2005), 'Optimal Income Taxation with Multidimensional Taxpayer Types', 2006 Working Paper Northwestern University.

Kaldor, N. (1955), *An Expenditure Tax*, London: Allen and Unwin.

Kaplow, L. (1989), 'Horizontal Equity—Measures in Search of a Principle', *National Tax Journal*, **42**, 139–54.

—— (1994), 'Taxation and Risk Taking: A General Equilibrium Perspective', *National Tax Journal*, **47**, 789–98.

—— (1995), 'A Note on Subsidizing Gifts', *Journal of Public Economics*, **58**, 469–78.

—— (2006a), 'On the Undesirability of Commodity Taxation even when Income Taxation is not Optimal', *Journal of Public Economics*, **90**, 1235–50.

—— (2006b), 'Capital Levies and Transition to a Consumption Tax', NBER WP 12259.

Keane, M. P., and Wolpin, K. I. (1997), 'The Career Decisions of Young Men', *Journal of Political Economy*, **105**, 473–522.

Kirby, K., Winston, G. C., and Santiesteban, M. (2005), 'Impatience and Grades: Delay Discount Rates Correlate Negatively with College GPA', *Learning and Individual Differences*, **15**, 213–22.

Kleven, H. J., Richter, W. F., and Sørenson, P. B. (2000), 'Optimal Taxation with Household Production', *Oxford Economic Papers*, **52**, 584–94.

Kocherlakota, N. (2005), 'Zero Expected Wealth Taxes: A Mirrlees Approach to Dynamic Optimal Taxation', *Econometrica*, **73**, 1587–621.

Konishi, H. (1995), 'A Pareto-Improving Commodity Tax Reform under a Smooth Nonlinear Income Tax', *Journal of Public Economics*, **56**, 413–46.

Kopczuk, W., Saez, E., and Song, J. (2007), 'Uncovering the American Dream: Inequality and Mobility in Social Security Earnings Data since 1937', NBER Working Paper 13345.

Korinek, A., and Stiglitz, J. E. (2008), 'Dividend Taxation and Intertemporal Tax Arbitrage', unpublished.

Kremer, M. (2001), 'Should Taxes be Independent of Age?' <http://www.economics.harvard.edu/faculty/kremer/papers.html>.

Krueger, D., and Perri, F. (2006), 'Does Income Inequality Lead to Consumption Inequality? Evidence and Theory', *Review of Economic Studies*, **73**, 163–93.

Krusell, P., Ohanian, L. E., Rios-Rull, J. V., and Violante, G. L. (2000), 'Capital-Skill Complementarity and Inequality: A Macroeconomic Analysis', *Econometrica*, **68**, 1029–53.

Laibson, D. (1997), 'Golden Eggs and Hyperbolic Discounting', *Quarterly Journal of Economics*, **112**, 443–77.

Laroque, G. R. (2005), 'Indirect Taxation is Superfluous under Separability and Taste Homogeneity: A Simple Proof', *Economics Letters*, **87**, 141–4.

Lawrence, E. C. (1991), 'Poverty and the Rate of Time Preference: Evidence from Panel Data', *Journal of Political Economy*, **99**, 54–77.

Lillard, L. A., and Weiss, Y. A. (1979), 'Components of Variation in Panel Earnings Data: American Scientists, 1960–70', *Econometrica*, **47**, 437–54.

—— and Willis, R. J. (1978), 'Dynamic Aspects of Earning Mobility', *Econometrica*, **46**, 985–1012.

Lleras Muney, A. (2005), 'The Relationship Between Education and Adult Mortality in the United States', *Review of Economic Studies*, **72**, 189–221 [pdf].

Lozachmeur, J.-M. (2006), 'Optimal Age-Specific Income Taxation', *Journal of Public Economic Theory*, **8**, 697–711.

Lusardi, A.-M. (1999), 'Information, Expectations and Savings for Retirement', in Aaron, H. J. (ed.), *Behavioural Dimensions of Retirement Economics*, Washington, DC: Brookings Institution Press and Russell Sage Foundation, 81–115.

—— and Mitchell, O. (2007), 'Baby Boomer Retirement Security: The Roles of Planning, Financial Literacy, and Housing Wealth', jointly with Olivia Mitchell (Wharton School, University of Pennsylvania), *Journal of Monetary Economics*, **54**, 205–24.

Luttmer, E. F. P., and Zeckhauser, R. J. (2008), 'Schedule Selection by Agents: from Price Plans to Tax Tables', HKS Faculty Research Working Paper Series RWP08-008 (February).

MaCurdy, T. (1982), 'The Use of Time Series Processes to Model the Error Structure of Earnings in a Longitudinal Data Analysis', *Journal of Econometrics*, **18**, 82–114.

Mankiw, N. G., and Weinzierl, M. (2007), 'The Optimal Taxation of Height: A Case Study of Utilitarian Income Redistribution', unpublished. <http://www.economics.harvard.edu/faculty/mankiw/files/Optimal_Taxation_of_Height.pdf>.

Marshall, A. (1948), *Principles of Economics*, 8th edn., New York: Macmillan.

Mayshar, J. (1977), 'Should Government Subsidize Risky Private Projects?', *American Economic Review*, **67**, 20–28.

Meade, J. (1978), *The Structure and Reform of Direct Taxation: Report of a Committee chaired by Professor J. E. Meade for the Institute for Fiscal Studies*, London: George Allen & Unwin. http//www.ifs.org.uk/publications/3433.

Meghir, C., and Pistaferri, L. (2004), 'Income Variance Dynamics and Heterogeneity', *Econometrica*, **72**, 1–32.

Mirrlees, J. (1971), 'Exploration in the Theory of Optimal Income Taxation', *Review of Economic Studies*, **38**, 205–29.

Moffitt, R., and Gottschalk, P. (1994), 'Trends in the Autocovariance Structure of Earnings in the US: 1969–1987', *Brookings Papers on Economic Activity*, 2.

—— —— (2002), 'Trends in the Transitory Variance of Earnings in the United States', *Economic Journal*, **112**, C68–C73.

Musgrave, R. A. (1959), *The Theory of Public Finance: A Study in Political Economy*, New York: Mcgraw-Hill.

Myles, G. D. (1995), *Public Economics*, Cambridge: Cambridge University Press.

Naito, H. (1999), 'Re-examination of Uniform Commodity Taxes under a Non-Linear Income Tax System and its Implications for Production Efficiency', *Journal of Public Economics*, **71**, 165–88.

Nielsen, S. B., and Sørensen, P. B. (1997), 'On the Optimality of the Nordic System of Dual Income Taxation', *Journal of Public Economics*, **63**, 311–29.

Office for National Statistics (2007), *Health Statistics Quarterly*, **36**, Winter.

Pappas, G., Queen, S., Hadden, W., and Fisher, G. (1993), 'The Increasing Disparity in Mortality between Socioeconomic Groups in the United States, 1960 and 1986', *New England Journal of Medicine*, **329**, 103–109.

Parker, A. M., and Fischhoff, B. (2005), 'Decision-Making Competence: External Validation through an Individual-Differences Approach', *Journal of Behavioral Decision Making*, **18**, 1–27.

Pechman, J. A. (ed.), (1980), *What Should Be Taxed: Income or Expenditure?*, Washington: Brookings Institution.

Persico, N., Postlewaite, A., and Silverman, D. (2004), 'The Effect of Adolescent Experience on Labor Market Outcomes: The Case of Height', *Journal of Political Economy*, **112**, 1019–53.

Peters, E., Vastfjall, D., Slovic, P., Mertz, C. K., Mazzocco, K., and Dickert, S. (2005), 'Numeracy and Decision Making', *Psychological Science*, **17**, 407–13.

Pirttilä, J., and Selin, H. (2007), 'Income Shifting within a Dual Income Tax System: Evidence from the Finnish Tax Reform of 1993', unpublished.

Poterba, J. (ed.) (1994), *International Comparisons of Household Saving*, Chicago: Chicago University Press.

—— (1998), 'Estate Tax Avoidance by High Net Worth Households: Why are There so Few Tax Free Gifts?', *Journal of Private Portfolio Management*, **1**, 1–9.

Preston, S., and Elo, I. T. (1995), 'Are Educational Differentials in Adult Mortality Increasing in the United States?', *Journal of Aging and Health*, **7**, 476–96.

Reis, C. (2007a), 'Taxation Without Commitment', Dissertation chapter, MIT.

—— (2007b), 'Entrepreneurial Labour Taxation', Dissertation chapter, MIT.

Rosen, H. S. (1978), 'An Approach to the Study of Income, Utility, and Horizontal Equity', *Quarterly Journal of Economics*, **92**, 307–22.

Saez, E. (2002a), 'Optimal Progressive Capital Income Taxes in the Infinite Horizon Model', NBER Working Papers No. 9046.

—— (2002b), 'The Desirability of Commodity Taxation under Non-Linear Income Taxation and Heterogeneous Tastes', *Journal of Public Economics*, **83**, 217–30.

—— (2002c), 'Optimal Income Transfer Programs: Intensive Versus Extensive Labour Supply Responses', *Quarterly Journal of Economics*, **117**, 1039–73.

Salanie, B. (2003), *The Economics of Taxation*, Cambridge, Mass.: MIT Press.

Samwick, A. (2006), 'Saving for Retirement: Understanding the Importance of Heterogeneity', *Business Economics*, **41**, 21–7.

Sandmo, A. (1981), 'Tax Evasion, Labour Supply and the Equity–Efficiency Tradeoff', *Journal of Public Economics*, **16**, 265–88.

—— (2005), 'The Theory of Tax Evasion: A Retrospective View', *National Tax Journal*, **58**, 643–63.

Scholz, J. K., Seshadri, A., and Khitatrakun, S. (2006), 'Are Americans Saving "Optimally" for Retirement?', *Journal of Political Economy*, **114**, 607–43.

Shaviro, D. (2002), 'Endowment and Inequality', in Thorndike, J., and Ventry, D. (eds.), *Tax Justice Reconsidered: The Moral and Ethical Bases of Taxation*, Washington, DC: Urban Institute Press.

Shiv, B., and Fedorikhin, A. (1999), 'Heart and Mind in Conflict: The Interplay of Affect and Cognition in Consumer Decision Making', *Journal of Consumer Research*, **26**, 72–89.

Simons, H. (1938), *Personal Income Taxation*, Chicago: University of Chicago Press.

Slemrod, J., and Yitzhaki, S. (2002), 'Tax Avoidance, Evasion, and Administration', in Auerbach, A. J., and Feldstein, M. (eds.), *Handbook of Public Economics*, **3**, 1425–70.

Smith, A. (1937), *Wealth of Nations*, New York: The Modern Library.

Smith, H., and Powell, B. (1990), 'Great Expectations: Variations in Income Expectations among College Seniors', *Sociology of Education*, **63**, 193–207.

Smith, J. P. (2004), 'Unraveling the SES–Health Connection', in Waite, L. (ed), *Population and Development Review Supplement: Aging, Health and Public Policy: Demographic and Economic Perspectives*, **30**, 108–32.

Sørensen, P. B. (2001), 'The Nordic Dual Income Tax—In or Out.' Invited speech delivered at the meeting of Working Party 2 on Fiscal Affairs, OECD 14 June 2001.

—— (2005), 'Dual Income Taxation: Why and How?', CESifo Working Paper 1551.

Stiglitz, J. (1982b), 'Utilitarianism and Horizontal Equity: The Case for Random Taxation', *Journal of Public Economics*, **18**, 1–33.

Storesletten, K., Telmer, C., and Yaron, A. (2004), 'Consumption and Risk Sharing over the Life Cycle', *Journal of Monetary Economics*, **51**, 609–33.

Summers, L. H. (1981), 'Capital Taxation and Accumulation in a Life Cycle Growth Model', *American Economic Review*, **71**, 533–44.

Tarkiainen, R., and Tuomala, M. (1999), 'Optimal Non-Linear Income Taxation with a Two-Dimensional Population: A Computational Approach', *Computational Economics*, **13**, 1–16.

Tresch, R. W. (2002), *Public Finance: A Normative Theory*, 2nd edn., Plano, Texas: Business Publications, Inc.

Tuomala, M. (1990), *Optimal Income Tax and Redistribution*, New York: Oxford University Press.

Van Den Berg, G. J., Lindeboom, M., and Portrait, F. (2006), 'Economic Conditions in Early life and Individual Mortality', *American Economic Review*, **96**, 290–302.

Vickrey, W. (1947), *Agenda for Progressive Taxation*, New York: The Ronald Press Company.

Weil, P. (1989), 'Overlapping Families of Infinitely-Lived Agents', *Journal of Public Economics*, **38**, 183–98.

Weinzierl, M. (2007), 'The Surprising Power of Age-Dependent Taxes', unpublished. <http://www.people.fas.harvard.edu/~weinzier/Age-dependent%20taxes–120407–Weinzierl.pdf>.

Weisbach, D. (2005), 'The (Non)Taxation of Risk', *Tax L. Rev.*, **58**.

—— (2006), 'The Case for a Consumption Tax', *Tax Notes*, **110**, 1357.

Werning, I. (2005), 'Tax Smoothing with Redistribution', Federal Reserve Bank of Minneapolis, Staff Report 365.

Zeldes, S. (1989), 'Consumption and Liquidity Constraints', *Journal of Political Economy*, **97**, 305–46.

Zodrow, G. R. (1995), 'Taxation, Uncertainty and the Choice of a Consumption Tax Base', *Journal of Public Economics*, **58**, 257–65.

Commentary by Robert E. Hall

Robert E. Hall is the McNeil Joint Professor of Economics and Senior Fellow (Hoover Institution) at Stanford University. He will serve as President of the American Economic Association in 2010 and was previously Vice President. He is a Member of the (US) National Academy of Sciences and a Fellow of the American Academy of Arts and Sciences, the Econometric Society, and the Society of Labor Economists. His research interests are in macroeconomics and public finance. He has written throughout his career on consumption taxation, including in *The Flat Tax* (with Alvin Rabushka).

James Banks and Peter Diamond have thought long and deep about the complex issues of designing a tax system. The chapter spans a huge area of modern research. Its main point is to question the view that a tax on consumption at a single rate is the optimal way for the government to raise revenue.

The authors spurn the framework implicit in the title of the chapter in two important ways. First, they reject, quite explicitly, the notion that the relevant question is the definition of a tax base. They frame much of their discussion in terms of the tax rate on capital income, a question whose answer is a real number (contingent on potentially a huge number of variables), not in terms of the inclusion or exclusion of capital income from the tax base, a question whose answer is a binary yes or no. In this respect the authors follow the Meade Report (Meade, 1978), which took the same sensible approach to tax design.

The second departure from the framework suggested by the chapter's title is that the chapter encompasses indirect taxes as well as direct taxes imposed on the incomes or earnings of individuals. This chapter reaches conclusions about a comprehensive tax system, not just the piece labelled direct. Banks and Diamond hardly comment on this departure from the framework of the report. They have my wholehearted support—I do not believe that the distinction between direct and indirect taxation is meaningful or that one should design a direct tax without coordinating with the design of the indirect taxes that are part of the overall tax system. Later I will describe my own approach to tax design, which defies classification into direct or indirect.

The chapter considers an 'Arrow–Debreu' set-up where decisions about behaviour under all possible future contingencies are made prior to the onset of economic activity. The authors are clear that the issue is the variation in tax rates across types of consumption, which may vary by taxpayer characteristics, type of good, time of consumption, and state of the world. Taxation of capital income is a way to achieve higher tax rates for forward consumption. Although it's only a matter of taste, it strikes me that tax rates on different times or types of consumption is the more satisfactory framework for discussing the issues of the chapter. Taxing capital income is a tool for implementing a tax system. Positive tax rates on capital income tax forward consumption at higher rates than current consumption. A related point is that a tax with a uniform positive rate on earnings and a zero rate on capital income achieves equality of implied rates on current and future consumption. The chapter derives the relation between the earnings tax rate and the equivalent consumption tax rate. Consumption-tax systems don't necessarily measure and tax each taxpayer's consumption of goods and services. The Value Added Tax is the leading practical example; a sales tax is another. Towards the end of this comment I will discuss my work with Alvin Rabushka on a simple, progressive way to implement a consumption tax without needing to keep track of each person's consumption. The basic idea is to start with a Value Added Tax and make it progressive through a rebate built into the tax that workers pay.

Many generations of economists have come down in favour of consumption taxation. The traditional line of argument reached that conclusion from the observation that consumption is the best measure of economic well-being. In the days when tax theory was framed in terms of, first, a measure of taxable capacity and, second, equitable distribution of the burden of government across taxpayers with different capacities, a progressive consumption tax seemed to be the answer. After James Mirrlees created the modern theory of mechanism design and applied it to taxation, rationalization of tax proposals took a more sophisticated form. The chapter is firm in rejecting the traditional line of argument in favour of the modern paradigm: define a class of permissible tax functions, determine information limitations and preferences, and choose the tax function that maximizes social welfare within the permissible class.

Two lines of thought within the modern paradigm, thoroughly discussed in the chapter, rationalize the taxation of current and future consumption at the same rate. First is the Atkinson–Stiglitz theorem. Under special but not totally unreasonable assumptions about preferences, as the chapter explains, the optimal tax when the government observes earnings but not work effort is a tax on earnings alone, with zero tax on income from savings. As I noted earlier, a tax on earnings implies equal tax rates on current consumption and future consumption. Thus another interpretation of Atkinson–Stiglitz is that a tax imposed on consumption should have equal current and future rates, under the assumptions of their theorem.

The second line supporting zero capital-income taxation is Chamley and Judd's observation that any positive tax on capital income compounds into a high implicit tax rate on forward consumption. The chapter's Table 6.1 illustrates the resulting distortionary wedges. The distortion becomes overwhelming in an economy with integrated dynastic decision making, but the authors are sceptical on the relevance of that case (I've never been able to make up my mind on this point). The chapter emphasizes the incompleteness of economists' understanding of economic relations between parents and offspring.

The chapter makes it clear that taking consumption as the base for taxation is not a full statement of an optimal tax system. If the consumption tax is progressive and consumption rises over the life-cycle, forward consumption incurs a higher tax and the tax system implies an implicit tax on capital income. Only a linear consumption tax with the same marginal tax rate under all circumstances generates the flat profile of forward rates that is the hallmark of zero tax on capital income. The chapter argues that such a flat profile should not be a focal point of tax design. The pure consumption tax is not the ideal. Rather, the many factors considered in the chapter imply that tax design is a much more complex task, involving many research topics as yet unresolved and in some cases as yet unexplored. Economists should not blindly advocate any tax reform that moves the system towards the flat profile of taxation of forward consumption, in the authors' view. At this stage, they argue, there is reasonable evidence supporting ideas that imply that a rising forward profile of consumption tax rates is probably preferred to the flat profile. Some implicit or explicit taxation of capital income is likely to be part of the optimal tax.

The bias in the chapter towards taxing capital income would make an outsider guess either that Britain had zero tax rates on capital income today or that there was a dangerous probability that a reform was likely that would result in zero rates. In fact, the chapter on the British tax system suggests that the tax rate on capital income is fairly high. My reading of the Banks–Diamond chapter does not convince me that lowering of the British tax on capital income would be an obvious mistake.

The chapter gives the impression that the authors lean in the direction of convincing the reader that taxation of capital income is a better idea than economists generally think. I'm not sure its coverage of ideas pointing in the opposite direction is complete. It omits discussion of Judd's (2002) work on capital taxation with market power, where the optimal rate on capital income is negative.

I have to admit that I'm in favour of work like Chapter 2, by Brewer, Saez, and Shephard, which takes modern theory and modern empirical results, finds the optimal policy design, and then makes a practical reform proposal based on that design. Banks and Diamond take a rather different approach, encompassing a wider variety of issues but not winding up in a policy proposal. How different this chapter would be if the authors had taken the approach of William Nordhaus's (2008) new book on global warming economics. Nordhaus tackles a problem of similar complexity, where research is inconclusive and incomplete, makes assumptions on every point needed, and reaches a definite conclusion about optimal policy (I'm not sure I agree with his conclusion, but I certainly admire the approach). A similar attack on optimal taxation would have wound up with a definite proposal for an integrated income tax system with rates differentiated by age, earnings, and capital income. The Banks–Diamond chapter leaves the reader yearning for some informed guesses about the optimal age profiles, earnings tax schedules, and capital income tax schedules.

There is an interesting point of contact—and divergence—between this chapter and Crawford, Keen, and Smith's Chapter 4 on indirect taxes. These authors discuss a paper of theirs that asks the completely parallel question about equality of tax rates across commodities. The paper estimates a demand system and compares the optimal, differentiated tax rates, to equal rates and concludes that little is lost by equality. One could imagine taking exactly the same approach to equality of rates over time, given that Arrow and Debreu taught us that time is just another way of indexing commodities. Maybe the intertemporal version of Crawford–Keen–Smith would conclude that there is no advantage to differentiating rates by time or age. Or maybe, contrary to my belief, it would conclude that there is no real disadvantage to the steeply inclined profile of forward consumption tax rates implied by the heavy taxation of some forms of capital income in the UK.

By contrast, the Banks–Diamond approach would challenge equality of rates across commodities in the VAT both for the considerations of preferences emphasized by Crawford–Keen–Smith and for more complicated and interesting reasons of the type emphasized in the new public finance based on dynamic mechanism design. In that theory, every commodity conveys information useful to the tax designer trying to make taxes progressive when key information about the taxpayer is hidden.

In my youth, I advocated a consumption tax that went pretty far in removing discrimination in tax rates in every dimension—time, commodity, and state of the world (Hall and Rabushka (1995)). Many people, critics and friends, pointed out that, because the tax exempted lower-consumption families from any taxation, it had two rates, and thus discriminated between consumption at times and in states of the world when a person was in the zero rate bracket relative to the positive rate bracket. I saw that discrimination as an acceptable departure from zero discrimination.

Now that I'm older, I favour greater discrimination, in the form of at least one more bracket to preserve the desirable feature of current taxes that they are paid mainly by the prosperous. The widening of the consumption distribution in Britain, the US, and most other high-income countries seems to call for further discrimination. Still, I find persuasive the Chamley–Judd critique of discrimination by time that reaches extreme rates after a few decades—I'm not ready to endorse any systematic taxation of income from saving. I'm in favour of taxing business income—a feature of my tax reform proposals from the start—because parts of that income are earnings and rents.

The structure of taxation in my original proposal with Rabushka still strikes me as appropriate. It stands halfway between a direct tax and an indirect one. The easiest way to understand it is to start with a comprehensive Value Added Tax covering all of GDP with a deduction for investment and exports and no deduction for imports—the VAT set-up the European Union mandates. Let the rate be the same for all goods and services. Now make a change that is purely administrative—let the part of the VAT previously paid by the employer on labour compensation be paid by the employee instead. Give the business a deduction for compensation and tax the worker on the compensation at the VAT rate. Apart from enforcement issues, the substance of the tax remains unchanged. It is a uniform tax on all consumption. Finally, give each worker an exemption from the tax up to a designated level of, say, £8,000.

This set-up achieves a two-rate consumption tax. Workers whose earnings are below the exemption level face no wedge between consumption and work effort, while those above the exemption level face a wedge defined by the VAT rate. The tax is progressive in the most important way—it removes any burden of taxation from the lowest earners. Its approach to progressivity is way more satisfactory than the method currently in use in the EU of zero-rating products that account for large shares of low-income budgets and small shares of high-income ones.

Because the modified VAT has two rates, it does not achieve complete flattening of the profile of forward consumption-tax rates. Rather, workers who begin their careers with earnings below the exemption level face rising expected consumption tax rates. As we learn from Banks and Diamond, this rising profile may be desirable.

Today, I am inclined to advocate at least one more bracket in the individual compensation tax. Instead of the single positive rate of 19% that Rabushka and I proposed in 1981, rates of say 15 and 30% would come closer to matching the distribution of the burden of the personal and corporate income taxes in the US. This three-rate system would make the profile of forward consumption-tax rates rather steeper.

The recent literature on tax design has explored linkages of tax rates to personal characteristics. The chapter describes this research in detail. The desirability of linking tax rates to age is virtually a consensus in the literature and receives a strong endorsement from Banks and Diamond. In a few more years, we may have a better idea of the age profile of the optimal consumption tax. Height is another matter. The chapter's discussion of this topic is illuminating—in a full mechanism design framework, it's really hard to avoid the conclusion that taxes should depend positively on height, almost certainly adjusted for sex and for heights of parents. For all their enthusiasm for differentiated tax rates, the authors don't make the leap to endorsing taxes based on height. Neither they nor I have a totally coherent framework for explaining why we oppose taxation of height. We talk about simplicity, but even that, as the authors point out, is an elusive concept.

I've started work on the design of a fiscal system that considers the implications of the growth in health spending that will surely occur during the rest of this century. Serious fiscal involvement in health finance is the rule among all high-income countries and it seems likely to grow in the US, where the involvement is currently limited to people over age 65 and to the poor. Because a large fraction of health spending occurs in retirement, because an important fraction of the population seems not to save enough for backloaded spending, because unregulated private insurance markets are not viable, and because the public appears to support more even distribution of health care than of wealth, the governments of high-income countries seem fated to taking in a growing share of output as taxes and distributing the proceeds as insurance payoffs to mostly elderly citizens.

My thinking remains that the revenue needed to accomplish the redistribution towards people with expensive disorders and towards those with low command over resources will and should come from an earnings tax or VAT. As a prediction, this seems to be on reasonably firm ground. Financing of retirement and health programmes from earnings taxes is the rule around the world. As a prescription based on principles of tax design, it is a statement that the profile of forward consumption taxes has approximately the right slope from the progressivity of the earnings tax and does not need to be boosted with any tax on the return to saving.

One of the ways to evaluate the material in this chapter is to ask why I, the most open-minded, middle-of-the-road member of the economics profession, find the arguments in this chapter favouring a moderate tax on capital income unpersuasive.

Notice first that I am not the victim of taking the flat profile of forward consumption taxes as the focal point of tax design. More than ever, I'm in favour of a progressive consumption tax, which implies quite a bit of upward slope to the profile.

One obvious reason that the chapter is unpersuasive is that it makes no attempt to provide a number. Did the US move in the right or wrong direction in 2003 when it cut dividend and capital gains rates? Should Britain have a 10% or a 60% top rate on capital income?

My biggest concern is the Chamley–Judd argument that extreme rates of forward taxation of consumption are surely not the right profile. This argument has its teeth with respect to people who actually hold non-human wealth. It says that we can do a better job of extracting revenue from the wealthy by flattening the forward profile of consumption taxation. The main substantive argument in the chapter against this view is that the wealthy accumulate wealth for its own sake and not just because wealth permits consumption.

I'm hoping that this most interesting chapter will stimulate work that finds the optimal tax design based on empirical research and recognizing the constraints that govern tax design in practice. That's definitely a goal that the authors and I share.

REFERENCES

Hall, R. E., and Rabushka, A. (1995), *The Flat Tax*, 2nd edition, Stanford, CA: Hoover Institution Press.

Judd, K. (2002), 'Capital Income Taxation with Imperfect Competition', *American Economic Review Papers and Proceedings*, **92**, May.

Meade, J. (1978), *The Structure and Reform of Direct Taxation: Report of a Committee chaired by Professor J. E. Meade for the Institute for Fiscal Studies*, London: George Allen & Unwin. http://www.ifs.org.uk/publications/3433.

Nordhaus, W. D. (2008), *A Question of Balance: Weighing the Options on Global Warming Policies*, New Haven, Conn.: Yale University Press.

Commentary by John Kay

John Kay is a Fellow of St John's College, Oxford, a Visiting Professor of Economics at the London School of Economics, a member of the Scottish Government's Council of Economic Advisers, and a director of several public and private companies. He was a member of the Meade Committee, Research Director of the IFS from 1979 to 1981, and its Director from 1981 to 1986. He was Professor of Economics at the London Business School and Professor of Management at the University of Oxford, and set up and sold a highly successful economic consultancy business. The author of books including *The British Tax System* (with Mervyn King) and *The Truth About Markets*, he now writes a weekly column for the *Financial Times*.

The central theme of the Meade Report (Meade, 1978) was a preference for consumption over income taxation. Soon after the Report was published, a thoughtful commentator said to me 'you will never get the name expenditure tax, but you will get everything else'. And so it has proved. Since 1978, the most important developments in the UK tax structure have been

- a rise in the relative significance of general consumption taxes (VAT) and payroll tax (national insurance) relative to income tax;
- the introduction of savings and pension accounts, neutral as between asset categories, providing both TEE and EET reliefs;
- a substantial reduction in the number of income tax rates which established an approximately linear structure above an exemption level.

Britain is now in a transitional period at the end of which, as the Report envisaged, most life-cycle savings will qualify for TEE or EET treatment. The Report envisaged that this change would be accompanied by the introduction of some form of wealth tax (a proposal which, incidentally, was not pursued in the further discussion of the issues by Kay and King (1978)). These wealth tax proposals have not been implemented and have aroused little subsequent interest either amongst academics or policy makers.

The present (Banks and Diamond) chapter revisits the central issue of the main household tax base. It differs from the Meade Report in looking to optimal tax theory for its rationale. Meade did not approach the question in this way but instead focused more on traditional public finance issues of taxable capacity. While much research on optimal taxation has been undertaken since 1978, the basic framework of optimal tax theory was well established by the time of the Meade Report, and the decision by the Meade Committee to tackle the question of the direct base in a different way was a conscious one. In this commentary, I shall give my own perspective on why the Meade Report used that approach and why, broadly speaking, I still take that view.

There are a number of substantial difficulties in using optimal tax theory to model the choice of household tax base. The most fundamental is the use of a utilitarian welfare function. I will begin by mentioning briefly some other issues, and then return to this basic question.

There is always difficulty in achieving correspondence between model variables and operational tax concepts. It is one thing to write down 'let y be household income' and quite another to write a law that defines the calculation of household income. The complexity of the present tax code of all developed countries is in very large part the direct and indirect result of the difficulty of making the economic concept of income an operational tool in a world of uncertainty and financial innovation.

Less obvious, perhaps, is the problem of defining the time period over which income or expenditure is to be measured. Yet this issue is clearly fundamental in considering the basis on which life-cycle savings are to be taxed. The longer the period of assessment, the smaller are life-cycle savings. If income and expenditure are measured over the whole lifetime, the only difference between income and expenditure is bequests. It is conventional to measure income for both tax and accounting purposes on an annual basis. But this choice probably relates to the agricultural cycle, which seems of little current relevance.

If I chose to emphasize that point, it is as a result of experience after the Meade Report, when a number of practitioners attempted to persuade me that the schemes contained in the Report for administering an expenditure tax were not feasible. These practitioners were, as always, ingenious in devising avoidance schemes. Few of their schemes worked: in fact a powerful merit of expenditure taxation and one of the considerations which was influential in persuading the Committee to emphasize expenditure over income is that expenditure taxation is much more robust to avoidance schemes than income taxation.

Expenditure is easier to define than income (there are many fewer VAT avoidance schemes than income tax avoidance schemes and most of these are the result of exemptions within VAT). Most of the avoidance schemes that would have produced tax savings depended on exploiting year-end effects. Matters would have been different if tax liability had been calculated on a daily, or five-yearly, basis. Is what we tax in our model, daily, or annual, or quinquennial income? and why?

The identification of life-cycle savings is closely linked to the treatment of bequests, since it is these two factors, taken together, which make up the difference between income and expenditure. There are two broad perspectives on bequests, as the chapter acknowledges: a purely individual one; or a dynastic one, in which individuals never die but continue to derive welfare indefinitely in the guise of their children (or others) to whom they leave bequests. This is evidently an extension of the questions that arise in deciding whether to take the individual or the household as the taxable unit.

As with the taxable unit, it is evident that neither extreme perspective is acceptable. The case for moving towards a dynastic perspective gains strength from the pressures against inheritance taxes which have built up, since the time of the Meade Report, particularly in Britain and the United States: it is striking that the unpopularity of these taxes is widespread despite their progressive incidence and seems to be felt even among sectors of the population which are most unlikely ever to pay it.

In discussion over Meade, we tended to frame the issue of how bequests should be treated in the form 'did a gift or bequest represent consumption and if so who did it represent consumption by?' While this is a means of beginning debate I do not think it is capable of leading to an answer. In any event, this framework leads away from a utilitarian framework.

Of course, one reason for bequests is that it is impossible (in the absence of perfect annuity markets) to plan to die with exactly zero assets even if that were the goal. This too reflects a larger problem: that the planning of life-cycle savings has to be made within the context, not just of specific risks, but undefined and unqualifiable uncertainties, about both personal and collective futures dealt with in necessarily incomplete markets. It is unlikely that individuals do, or could, make well-considered decisions in these circumstances. Many people demonstrably make bad life-cycle decisions, and, when they do, society is unwilling to respect these decisions. We are not willing to let people die of starvation in old age even if that is the inevitable consequence of apparently free choices they have made. The implied assumption of rational choice in line with the expression of consistent preferences works particularly badly for life-cycle decisions.

The factors I have described above can be modelled, and most have been. But there are many possible models, and the choice between them depends in substantial part on prior decisions about 'fairness'. The model is rarely yielding conclusions, at best helping us to organize the intuitions we already hold.

And even at the time of the Meade Report, it was evident that simple models of the choice of household taxbase yielded no robust results. In a model such as that of Atkinson and Stiglitz (1976), a change in the specification of available tax instruments produced fundamentally different results. If we pose the question 'should income from life-cycle savings be taxed at the same rate as labour income, or should it not be taxed at all?'—which is the appropriate translation of the question 'should income (as conventionally defined) be the main household tax base, or would expenditure be preferable?'—then it is not clear that this kind of modelling can yield a general answer at all.

If it was not these arguments from optimal tax theory of the kind described in the present chapter which led the Meade Committee to favour expenditure taxation, what was the rationale of the Committee's preference? In truth, it was clear from the beginning that the Committee would favour an expenditure tax, and I understood from my very first discussion with the chairman that the task was less to provide objective analysis than to make the case for expenditure tax and to deal with the operational issues that arose. Nevertheless, I personally found the case that was developed convincing and still do.

So why was expenditure tax both the starting point and the conclusion? I think at a visceral level, James Meade believed in the moral case that people should be taxed on what they took out, not on what they put in. This is not really a satisfactory argument, as he knew. But I have no doubt that he, along with most of the Committee, came to the issue from this sort of perspective. The issue of taxable capacity was key. For the Meade Committee, as for most ordinary people, questions of fairness and taxable capacity would seem to be of critical importance—even exclusive importance—in determining the household tax base.

Everyone who has written about public finance knows that taxable capacity is a slippery elusive concept. 'On examination, "taxable capacity" always turns out to be very difficult to define and to be a matter on which opinions will differ rather widely' Meade (1978, p. 14). The Banks and Diamond chapter goes much further:

> We reject the Meade Report view... that taxes 'should' relate monotonically to some measure of taxable capacity. In addition to finding taxable capacity not well-enough measurable and not sufficiently uniformly evaluated to be usable for this purpose, we

also do not see an underlying normative basis for reaching the conclusion that taxes should be related to taxable capacity ... minimized sacrifice—equivalent to optimized social welfare ... [is] the appropriate criterion.

There is sharp, and fundamental, disagreement here. On reading the present chapter, and rereading Meade (or, for that matter, Kay and King), I don't find either discussion satisfactory. I can do no more than raise some issues here.

It is certainly hard to disagree with Meade's statement, echoed by Banks and Diamond, that taxable capacity is difficult to define. But to say that it is hard to define does not necessarily imply that people are not justified in attaching significance to it, or that because it lacks exact meaning it lacks any meaning, or that it is impossible to secure a wide measure of agreement on what taxable capacity is.

We talk of a beautiful face, a kind person, a great work of art or piece of music, without having or being capable of having any quantitative measure of beauty, kindness, or greatness. Yet we are able to identify indicators of beauty, kindness, and greatness and to achieve substantial, though not necessarily complete, consensus on rankings of beauty, kindness, or greatness.

Let me conjecture that most people, asked to describe taxable capacity, would start with income. Let me also conjecture that these people, given examples of people with consumption levels sustainably *above* their income, would agree that their taxable capacity was greater than their income. And let me further conjecture that faced with examples of people with consumption levels substantially *below* their income, most people would feel less inclined to reduce their estimate of taxable capacity. Considerations like these have led me to conclude that average lifetime consumption, plus bequests (with bequests probably valued at less than pound for pound), is probably as good an index of taxable capacity as might be observed. If we must use a single indicator, that should be it. But I am not sure that it is right to use, or seek, a simple indicator. Taxable capacity is a complex concept, probably unobservable, and we must make do with composite instrumental variables. I'll come back to the implications of that.

I think Banks and Diamond are in a weaker position than Meade to stress the difficulty of measuring taxable capacity. If one is to maximize a social welfare function based on an aggregation of individual circumstances, it is necessary to envisage some agreement on what the individual arguments of that social welfare function (call them utilities) would be. I cannot imagine that it would be easier to secure agreement on the definition of utilities than on the definition of taxable capacities: indeed, it is likely that the two definitions would be very similar. I believe it is difficult to argue that it is possible to define utilities but not to define taxable capacities. (Note that saying utility is what a hedonometer or axiomatic system measures simply raises the issue of why society should want to maximize utility in these senses, a debate essentially analogous to whether income equates to taxable capacity.)

And is Meade correct to say that the definition of taxable capacity is 'a matter on which opinions will differ rather widely'? I further conjecture that the subject on which opinions will differ rather widely is not the definition of taxable capacity, on which I would anticipate considerable if not universal agreement. Disagreement would instead focus on the extent to which tax liability should increase with the preferred measure of taxable capacity.

This chapter discusses horizontal equity in terms of maintaining the ranking of pre and post tax utilities, following an idea of Feldstein's, and is rightly sceptical of the available plethora of hypothetical alternatives in the definition of a counterfactual pretax world. But suppose one takes instead the simple criterion that the ranking of direct tax payments should be strongly correlated with the ranking of taxable capacity.

This is a more operational requirement, and probably closer to most intuitive conceptions of equity. It has the obvious weakness of disregarding issues of incidence: taxes are treated, in effect, as lying where they fall. But I am not sure this is truly a weakness. There is a difference between differences in the treatment of largely similar individuals which arise as a result of a deliberate decision to impose differential treatment and differential treatment which is the incidental outcome of decisions made on other, more general grounds. Such a distinction is familiar in the application of anti-discrimination regulation. We prohibit discrimination on racial grounds but do not require that all policies have effects which precisely mirror the racial composition of the population.

There is evidently a close relationship between the measurement of taxable capacity and concern over 'discrimination', and this issue requires elaboration. The person unfamiliar with the implications of models like those of optimal tax theory might be surprised at the notion that there is potential conflict between the objective of welfare maximization and the requirement that the tax burden should be an increasing function of the taxable capacity of individuals. There are several possible reasons but the most likely arises from the issue variously labelled tagging, profiling, or statistical discrimination.

Almost anyone who has stood in an airline security queue will have ruminated that all passengers do not present the same security threat. If the degree of scrutiny were varied according to criteria such as age, gender, and ethnic origin, that scrutiny could be targeted more effectively with results which could reduce queuing time for all passengers—not just those subject to light checks—and improve overall security. As queuing passengers note this, however, they will also have reflected on the compelling reasons why this efficient solution is not adopted. The selection of targets on probabilistic grounds alone is ruled out by other, overriding, social and political considerations.

It needs emphasis that the objection is not to the arbitrary nature of selection. The problem is that such selection is *not* arbitrary: it has a completely rational utilitarian basis (although there is a history of using bogus statistical evidence to disguise simple prejudice). The issue does not hinge on whether the alleged correlation is correctly observed, but on when and whether it is acceptable to use such correlations at all.

And yet it is impossible to operate a tax system, or indeed make many everyday decisions, except by using instrumental variables in this way. We ask whether our doctor has medical qualifications, not because possession of such qualifications is either necessary or sufficient to secure good advice, but because we judge, with good reason, there is a correlation between medical skill and knowledge and a degree in medicine. In a similar way, tax liabilities are based, not on—probably unobservable—taxable capacity, but on variables which we believe to be correlated with taxable capacity. Statistical discrimination is in practice indispensable.

But when is such discrimination justified and when inappropriate? In Table 1 I list some instrumental variables which have been used as part of the household tax base, and make comments on each. I can see no obvious criterion for distinguishing those variables which seem to be found generally acceptable and those which are generally unacceptable: words such as 'arbitrary' and 'inappropriate' simply reiterate intuitive feelings. Moreover, it is plain that social attitudes change over time: measures move in and out of acceptability. This is a more general phenomenon: the 'discrimination' that arouses public concern is mostly discrimination by reference to criteria—such as gender, race, sexual orientation—which were until recently widely used but which are out of line with current social practice.

The present chapter ends with the familiar call for further research. In my view, the further research that is principally required would use focus groups and polls (the possibility is hinted at in this chapter) to elucidate more clearly how people interpret taxable capacity and what criteria are acceptable, and which not, as elements of the household tax base. The chapter cites Atkinson and Stiglitz in support of 'the idea that some aspects of horizontal equity may best be addressed by viewing them as limitations on allowable tax tools' (Atkinson and Stiglitz (1980)). My assessment is that this puts the role of equity and efficiency in the choice of the main household tax base the

Table 1. Components of the tax base

Age	*becoming less acceptable*	**Height**	*not acceptable*
Caring responsibility	*becoming more acceptable*	**Illness**	*probably not acceptable*
Consumption of immoral goods	*becoming less acceptable*	**Income from capital**	*acceptable*
Disability	*becoming more acceptable*	**Intelligence/skill**	*not acceptable*
Earnings	*acceptable*	**Marital status**	*becoming less acceptable*
Educational experience	*not acceptable but becoming so*	**Parental responsibility**	*varying attitudes*
Expenditure	*acceptable*	**Race**	*has become unacceptable*
Expenditure on luxury goods	*becoming less acceptable*	**Relationship status**	*becoming more acceptable (but see marital status)*
Gender	*no longer acceptable*	**Value of property**	*becoming less acceptable*

wrong way round. One should begin by seeking a measure of taxable capacity, with the measurement of taxable capacity constrained by administrative and operational issues and by considerations of efficiency. This was, in essence, the form of reasoning which led the Meade Report to favour a greater role for a progressive consumption tax. I believe that reasoning and its conclusion remain valid today.

REFERENCES

Atkinson, A. B., and Stiglitz, J. E. (1976), 'The Design of Tax Structure: Direct Versus Indirect Taxation', *Journal of Public Economics*, 6: 55–75.

—— —— (1980), *Lectures in Public Economics*, London and New York: McGraw-Hill Economics Handbook Series.

Kay, J., and King, M. A. (1978), *The British Tax System*, 5th edn. 1990, Oxford: Oxford University Press.

Meade, J. (1978), *The Structure and Reform of Direct Taxation: Report of a Committee chaired by Professor J. E. Meade for the Institute for Fiscal Studies*, London: George Allen & Unwin. http://www.ifs.org.uk/publications/3433.

Commentary by Pierre Pestieau*

Pierre Pestieau received his PhD from Yale and is now Professor of Economics at the University of Liège. He is also a Member of the Centre for Operations Research and Econometrics, Louvain-la-Neuve, an Associate Member of the Paris School of Economics, and a Fellow of the Centre for Economic Policy Research and CESifo, Munich. His major interests are pension economics, social insurance, redistributive policies, and tax competition. He is currently Co-Editor of the *Journal of Public Economics* and Associate Editor of *Economica* and the *Journal of Public Economic Theory.*

The chapter by J. Banks and P. Diamond (BD) presents an excellent survey of the existing literature on optimal taxation and discusses a number of lessons that can be drawn from that literature. One of the main lessons on which this chapter focuses concerns the treatment of capital income. The authors argue that the finding that the optimal income tax schedule should not include tax on capital is based on too many restrictions, and is thus not robust for policy purposes. Another lesson is that taxation should vary with age. Not having any quarrel with these two points, I would like in this commentary to discuss a number of points too quickly dealt with or deliberately neglected by BD. They concern the issue of tagging, the problem raised by having more than one unobservable characteristic (besides ability), the issue of myopia and prodigality, the question of equal opportunities, the taxation of couples, and the threat of tax competition.

1. TAGGING

Supplementing optimal income taxation with tagging generally brings more welfare. Yet to qualify such a general statement, one has to distinguish different types of tagging according to whether or not it is costly, it brings stigmatization and it conveys some particular information.

* I am grateful to Robin Boadway and Helmuth Cremer for their helpful suggestions on an earlier draft of these comments.

The tagging BD have in mind when they recommend income taxation varying with age is both costless and neutral. In contrast, characteristics such as height, weight, language, or colour, even though one can show that using them would be welfare improving, can have negative effects that more than offset those positive effects. This would be the case, for example, of tagging Belgian citizens with different tax schedules for Dutch and French speaking along with intergroup transfers.[1]

Boadway and Pestieau (2006) have studied the issue of tagging with optimal income taxation in a two-group-two-skill-level setting. They show that tagging leads to horizontal inequity and more progressivity in the group comprising the higher proportion of unskilled workers.

In general the characteristics considered are given and cannot be changed within a reasonable length of time. When they can be modified, we have an issue of moral hazard and the taxation problem becomes more difficult. One thinks of health status and family size that are important matters in the design of an optimal income tax structure.

When tagging is uncertain and costly, it is not clear that it is worth using. This issue has been extensively studied in work on disability insurance.[2]

Free tagging can convey different types of information. Not only a tagged group has a specific distribution of ability (in the two-type case, the relative number of skilled and unskilled), but also different needs (linked, e.g. to health or family size). Boadway and Pestieau (2003) have studied optimal income taxation when the tag reflects differences in needs, that is, differences in the resource required to achieve a given level of utility. In a two-ability setting, they show that the level of compensation given for needs exceeds the level of needs if a higher proportion of low ability households are needy, and vice versa.

2. MORE THAN ONE CHARACTERISTIC[3]

In the standard model of optimal income taxation, individuals only differ in productivity. This is clearly restrictive as we know that they also differ in other characteristics. When these characteristics are observable and

[1] It is interesting to note that social attitudes towards the acceptability of some tagging (race, gender, ...) vary over time and across countries.

[2] See, e.g., Diamond and Sheshinski (1995).

[3] This section is further developed in the appendix. We make a distinction between the tagging problem which arises when the characteristic just pertains to the distribution of skills and the problem of adding one characteristic which involves utility differences. On this issue see Kaplow (2008).

convey some information on ability, we have the issue of tagging. When they are not observable, we face the analytical difficulty of dealing with a multidimensional principal agent problem. Let us assume that we have as unknown characteristics not only productivity, but also wealth, the rate of time preference or longevity. There is no doubt that these characteristics are not easily observable and also that they are partially correlated with productivity level.

As explained by BD, with these and other characteristics, the Atkinson–Stiglitz proposition does not hold, but furthermore, we have a good case for taxing capital income. The intuition is simple: individuals with low discount rate, high wealth, or high longevity tend to save more than those who are impatient, poor, or have a low life expectancy.

Among the characteristics that can be introduced besides labour productivity, there is the risk of morbidity. As shown by Rochet (1991) (see also Boadway, Leite-Monteiro, Marchand, Pestieau (2003, 2006)), if morbidity risks are negatively related to income so that the poor face higher risks on average, then we have an obvious argument for social insurance. Social insurance combined with a standard distortionary income tax can redistribute more effectively. The reason is that redistributing through social insurance does not involve the same distortion as through income taxation. This result is shown to hold with moral hazard and adverse selection.

3. PREFERENCES FOR LEISURE AND RESPONSIBILITY

The problem of optimal taxation when people have different preferences for leisure raises difficult normative questions. A higher income may be due either to differences in innate productivity and skill levels or to differences in the degree of effort. Progressive taxes can therefore imply redistribution from those with a low preference for leisure to those with a high preference for leisure and from those with high productivity to those with low productivity. The ethical valuation of such redistributions depends on the interpretation given to the preference parameter. One may have ethical objections against redistributing from the hard working to the leisure prone workers. Those objections would, however, disappear for redistribution from the skilled to unskilled. This distinction is linked to the notion of responsibility. One generally feels that people should be compensated for factors that are beyond their control. Innate skills are typical examples of such factors, which have led to the traditional literature on optimal income taxation. In contrast, it is felt that people should be held responsible for factors that are under their control. Typical examples of such factors are preferences for leisure.

Following Roemer (1996) (see also Fleurbaey and Maniquet (2006, 2007)), in a society consisting of individuals with the same productivity but different tastes for leisure, there should be no redistribution. Equality of opportunities would be achieved in such a society.[4]

A further difficulty arises when a low preference for work may mean two different things: taste for leisure and difficulty to work. As BD observe 'viewing a worker as lazy (liking leisure) is very different from viewing a worker as having difficulty working longer, perhaps for physical reasons'. Cremer et al. (2007b) and Marchand et al. (2003) show that when a society consists of those two types of people, disabled and leisure prone, who have the same formal utilities, the only way out in a second-best setting is either to resort to audits or to use indirect taxation given that they most likely don't have the same consumption needs.

4. MYOPIA AND PRODIGALITY

There exists evidence that some households might undersave for two separate reasons: myopia and prodigality. Myopia comes from lacking self-control: individuals try to balance two objectives: instant gratification and retirement planning; quite often they err on the side of using too much of their resources for instant gratification and not enough to plan for retirement. Another source of insufficient saving occurs when individuals know that their government tends to bail out retirees without resources and thus they are tempted to consume all their resources during the active part of their life.

Myopia and prodigality[5] both provide reasons for individuals not to save for retirement, they make a strong case for the government to foster saving through subsidy on retirement saving or even mandatory pensions.

In this particular case, we have an argument not to tax, but to subsidize some types of capital income.

5. NON WELFARISM AND NEW PATERNALISM

We have just mentioned a number of instances where the social planner may be tempted not to follow individual preferences in assessing the social

[4] See also Schokkaert et al. (2004).

[5] See Pestieau and Possen (2008).

desirability of tax policy. There is the case of leisure prone or lazy individuals. The government might be tempted to induce them to work more than the disabled workers, from whom they cannot be distinguished. There is also the case of altruism where laundering out utilities has been advocated by, for example, Hammond (1987).

There is also the whole range of situations where people make decisions against their own good intention. In these situations, individuals might want the government to intervene to induce behaviour that is closer to what individuals wish they were doing. Procrastination, myopia, consumption of sin goods are examples of behaviour that lead to what is called 'new paternalism' and that implies non-welfarist objective functions (see Kanbur et al. (2006)).

Depending on the specific situations, what is called new paternalism is more or less accepted. There is little disagreement on the use of a paternalistic social welfare function for sin goods; for altruism whether or not individual preferences have to be laundered out is more disputed. Finally, the issue of distinguishing characteristics that come from luck and those that come from responsible decisions made by individuals is controversial.

6. THE TAXATION OF COUPLES

For a long time, the implicit picture of the two-person household was clearly one in which there is a complete division of labour between partners, with one specializing entirely in labour supply to the market, the other producing goods and services within the home. With such a picture, the analysis of optimal income taxation by Mirrlees (1971) that took the decision unit as a single individual dividing his time between market work and leisure didn't seem out of place. The spectacular growth in female labour force participation that took place in almost all developed countries called this picture into question and presents a new issue for tax policy. How to tax two-earner couples? The policy choice can be reduced to three alternatives:

- *joint taxation* in which the partners' incomes are added together and taxed at progressive marginal rates as if they had each earned one-half the income. This implies equality of marginal tax rates on partner income, or, that the tax rate on the last dollar of the husband's income was applied to the first dollar of the wife's, as it was at times expressed;

- *individual taxation* in which each partner's income is taxed separately, but according to the same progressive tax schedule;
- *selective taxation* in which secondary earners are taxed on a separate, lower, progressive tax schedule than that of primary earners.

The paper by Boskin and Sheshinski (1983) is generally regarded as having established the conventional rule on this issue, namely that selective, and not joint or individual, taxation is optimal. That is, not only should women be taxed separably from men, but they should be taxed on a lower rate schedule. This model suffers from the limitation that it rests on linear taxation.

Recently a number of papers[6] have been published dealing with this issue in a standard non-linear optimal tax framework without any a priori assumptions on the tax function of the household. Viewing the problem in this way gives arguments for spouses to face different marginal income tax rates, casting doubts on total family income as an appropriate income tax base. It does not, however, vindicate the case for individual taxation. Both the productivity of spouses and the relative position of each have some bearing on the marginal rates faced by both of them.

What is also important is to take a dynamic view. It may happen that the tax structure deemed optimal in a static setting implies that one of the two spouses (traditionally the wife) stops working because of too high marginal tax. This outcome would not remain optimal if the possibility of divorce is taken into account, granted that stopping working strongly decreases the chance of getting a good and well-paid job when needed.

7. CAPITAL INCOME TAXATION AND TAX COMPETITION

The increased integration of the world capital market implies that the supply of capital becomes more elastic and therefore potentially a less efficient base for taxation. It is thus possible that taxing capital income is highly desirable in a closed economy and then becomes difficult in an open economy. This threat of a vanishing tax on capital income has lead some countries to call for some type of cooperation, including the idea of a minimum withholding tax on capital income tax.

[6] Brett (2007), Cremer et al. (2007a), and Kleven et al. (2007).

8. IMPLICATION FOR THE TAX TREATMENT OF CAPITAL INCOME

Some of the points just raised have admittedly little bearing on the gist of BD's chapter, namely the taxation of capital income relative to that of earnings.

One clearly sees the implications of tax competition on capital income taxation. One also understands that introducing additional characteristics such as discount rates or longevity in the optimal tax model can lead to taxing capital income. Finally, the case of myopia and prodigality has clear implication as to the treatment of capital income.

What about the issue of equal opportunities? Let us use the two-period model of optimal income and consumption taxation with two unobservable characteristics: ability and wealth endowment. Assume that wealth endowment can result from either pure luck—unexpected bequest—or assistance to an ailing parent—exchange bequest. According to Roemer's view that there should not be redistribution for characteristics the individuals are responsible for, one can expect the case for capital income taxation to be stronger when bequests are accidental than when they result from family solidarity.

Concerning the taxation of couples, there exists no work addressing the issue of the relative effect of joint versus separate filing on capital income taxation.

APPENDIX

Note on introducing additional features in the optimal income tax

To illustrate the issue at hand, we start with the following two period utility:

$$u(c, d, \ell) = u_1(c, \ell) + \beta u_2(d)$$

where c and d are first- and second-period consumption, ℓ is labour in the first-period, ß is a discount factor (reflecting either time preference or survival probability or both) and u, u_1, and u_2 are utility functions with standard properties.

In a laissez-faire economy, the individual faces the following budget constraint:

$$\omega + w\ell = c + d/R$$

where R is an interest factor, ω is an initial endowment and w, the wage rate or the ability level.

Assume that individuals only differ in their ability. Assume further that the government just observes earnings $y = w\ell$ and neither w or ℓ. For the time being $\omega = 0$.

We want to know what would be the tax system that could lead to maximizing the sum of the utilities of a population with different wage rates. In the case of two types, we have:

$$\sum_{i=1,2} n_i \left[u\left(c_i, d_i, \ell_i\right) - \mu\left(c_i + d_i/R - w_i\ell_i\right)\right]$$

where n_i is the relative number of individuals with ability i, μ is the Lagrangian multiplier, and the optimal package (c_i, d_i, ℓ_i) is subject to the self-selection constraint:

$$u\left(c_2, d_2, \frac{y_2}{w_2}\right) \geqslant u\left(c_1, d_1, \frac{y_1}{w_2}\right)$$

given that we assume $w_2 > w_1$.

The results of this standard problem are well known: an optimal income taxation with zero marginal tax on y_2, and no indirect taxation, here a tax on savings, if there is weak separability between (c_i, d_i) and (ℓ_i). The first result is attributed to Mirrlees (1971) and the second to Atkinson and Stiglitz (1976). In what follows we assume weak separability.

We now modify this setting by introducing some additional features. We consider three that are mutually exclusive by assumption:

(A) differential endowments ω_i,

(B) differential discount factors β_i,

(C) the population can be divided according to a neutral and exogenous characteristic that provides information on the relative number of types. By neutral we mean that the characteristic has no negative connotation (unlike, say, skin colour). By exogenous we mean that it cannot be changed (e.g. weight).

Another distinction one has to consider is the observability of these three features. They can be freely observable, observable at some cost, with or without errors and they are not at all observable. To keep things simple, we consider the two extreme cases: perfect observability or no observability. Table A1 summarizes our six cases.

The questions we want to address for each of these cases are, (i) how the introduction of this additional feature affects the progressivity of income taxation, (ii)

Table A1. Additional features

	Observable	Not observable
Endowment	A1	A2
Discount factor	B1	B2
Tag	C1	C2

whether it has an implication for the Atkinson–Stiglitz proposition, which in this particular setting means zero taxation on capital income.

A1. If one observes those initial endowments, the obvious first step is to redistribute them equally. In addition, if there is any correlation between ω and w, in other words if, for example, individuals with higher endowment tend to be more skilled than those with lower endowment, we go to case C1 with observable tags.

A2. If one does not observe ω but only knows its distribution and its correlation with w, we have the problem dealt with by Cremer et al. (2001) and Boadway et al. (2000). The gist of these papers is that there is a good case for capital income taxation, if the correlation is positive.

B1. There is a big difference between differential endowments and different discount factors (longevity or time preference). In the latter case we deal with different utilities and summing them is questionable. In addition, if one judges that the feature at hand is endogenous—the individual is responsible for it—one might be reluctant to take it into account in the objective function.

If these considerations are kept aside, if the discount factor ß is unrelated to w, there will be some redistribution from those with a lower discount factor to those with a higher discount factor. The Atkinson–Stiglitz proposition will hold. If there is any correlation between ß and w, we have a tagging problem as in C1.

B2. When ß is not observable but is (e.g. positively) correlated with w, the AS proposition does not hold and one expects some taxation of saving on type 1's individuals. Such a taxation relaxes the self-selection constraint preventing type 2's individuals to mimic type 1's individuals.

C1. This is the problem studied by Boadway and Pestieau (2006). It appears clearly that using tags in optimal income taxation is always desirable (provided that the tag is correlated with utility), but generates horizontal inequity. Furthermore, there is more progressivity in the group with a higher proportion of skilled workers than in the group with a lower proportion of skilled workers. The AS proposition holds.

C2. When the 'tags' are not observable, tagging cannot help. We then have a unique tax schedule and the AS proposition holds.

REFERENCES

Apps, P., and Rees, R. (2004), 'The Taxation of Couples', in Cigno, A., Pestieau, P., and Rees, R. (eds.), *Taxation and the Family*, MIT Press.

Atkinson, A., and Stiglitz, J. (1976), 'The Design of Tax Structure: Direct Versus Indirect Taxation', *Journal of Public Economics*, **6**, 55–75.

Boadway, R., and Pestieau, P. (2003), 'Indirect Taxation and Redistribution: The Scope of the Atkinson–Stiglitz Theorem', in Kanbur, R., and Arnott, R. (eds.), *Imperfect Economics: Essays in Honor of Joseph Stiglitz*, Cambridge, Mass.: MIT Press.

——— (2006), 'Optimal taxation with tagging', *Annales d'Economie et de Statistique*, 83–4, 123–50.

—— Marchand, M., and Pestieau, P. (2000), 'Redistribution with Unobservable Bequests. A Case for Taxing Capital Income', *Scandinavian Journal of Economics*, **102**, 253–67.

—— Leite-Monteiro, M., Marchand, M., and Pestieau, P. (2003), 'Social Insurance and Redistribution', in Cnossen, S., and Sinn, H.-W. (eds.), *Public Finance and Public Policy in the New Millenium*, Cambridge, MA: MIT Press 333–58.

————— (2006), 'Social Insurance and Redistribution with Moral Hazard and Adverse Selection', *Scandinavian Journal of Economics*, **108**, 279–98.

—— Marchand, M., Pestieau, P., and Racionero, M. (2002), 'Optimal Redistribution with Heterogeneous Preference for Leisure', *Journal of Public Economic Theory*, **4**, 475–98.

Boskin, M., and Sheshinski, E. (1983), 'Optimal Tax Treatment of the Family: Married Couples', *Journal of Public Economics*, **20**, 281–97.

Brett, C. (2007), 'Optimal Non-linear Taxes for Families', *International Tax and Public Finance*, **4**, 225–63.

Cremer, H., Lozachmeur, J-M., and Pestieau, P. (2007a), 'Income Taxation of Couples and the Tax Unit', CORE DP 2007/14.

———— (2007b), 'Disability Testing and Retirement', *BE Journal of Economic Analysis and Policy*, **7**, issue 1.

—— Pestieau, P., and Rochet, J-Ch. (2001), 'Direct Versus Indirect Taxation. The Design of the Tax Structure Revisited', *International Economic Review*, **42**, 781–99.

Diamond, P., and Sheshinski, E. (1995), 'Economic Aspects of Optimal Disability Benefits', *Journal of Public Economics*, **57**, 1–23.

Fleurbaey, M., and Maniquet, F. (2006), 'Fair Income Tax', *Review of Economic Studies*, **73**, 55–83.

——— (2007), 'Help the Low-skilled or let the Hardworking Thrive? A Study of Fairness in Optimal Income Taxation', *Journal of Public Economic Theory*, **9**, 467–500.

Hammond, P. (1987), 'Altruism', in *The New Palgrave. A Dictionary of Economics*, 85–7, London: Macmillan.

Kanbur, R., Pirttila, J., and Tuomala, M. (2006), 'Non Welfarist Optimal Taxation and Behavioural Public Economics', *Journal of Economic Survey*, **20**, 849–68.

Kaplow, L. (2008), 'Optimal Policy and Heterogeneous Preferences', unpublished.

Kleven, H. J., Kremer, C. T., and Saez, E. (2007), 'The Optimal Income Taxation of Couples', unpublished.

Lozachmeur, J-M. (2006), 'Optimal Age Specific Income Taxation', *Journal of Public Economic Theory*, **8**, 911–22.

Marchand, M., Pestieau, P., and Racionero, M. (2003), 'Optimal Redistribution Programs when Different Workers are Indistinguishable', *Canadian Journal of Economics*, **36**, 911–22.

Mirrlees, J. (1971), 'An exploration in the theory of optimal taxation', *Review of Economics Studies*, **38**, 175–208.

Pestieau, P., and Possen, U. (2008), 'Prodigality and Myopia: Two Rationales for Social Security', Manchester School, **76**, 629–52.

Rochet, J.-Ch. (1991), 'Incentives, Redistribution and Social Insurance', *The Geneva Papers on Risk and Insurance Theory*, **16**, 143–66.

Roemer, J. (1996), *Theories of Distributive Justice*, Cambridge, Mass.: Harvard University Press.

Schokkaert, E., van de Gaer, D., Vandenbrouck, F., and Ivan Luttens, R. (2004), 'Responsibility Sensitive Egalitarianism and Optimal Linear Income Tax', *Mathematical Social Sciences*, **48**, 151–82.

7

The Effects on Consumption and Saving of Taxing Asset Returns

*Orazio P. Attanasio and Matthew Wakefield**

Orazio Attanasio is Professor of Economics at UCL and a Research Fellow at the IFS, where he directs the Centre for the Evaluation of Development Policies (EDePo). A fellow of the Econometric Society and of the British Academy, he works on household consumption and saving over the life cycle, on risk sharing, and on development economics. He was Managing Editor of the *Review of Economic Studies* and he is currently Editor of the *Journal of the European Economic Association.*

Matthew Wakefield is Lecturer in Economics at the University of Bologna and was a Senior Research Economist at the IFS at the time of writing this chapter. He has written extensively about UK public policy interventions—such as Stakeholder Pensions, Individual Savings Accounts, and the 'asset-based' welfare policies of the Child Trust Fund and the Saving Gateway—that have been designed to influence individuals' choices about pensions or other saving. His recent research also focuses on how house purchase decisions interact with the other consumption and saving choices made over the life cycle.

* The authors would like to thank Tim Besley, Carl Emmerson, Paul Johnson, James Poterba, and Guglielmo Weber for detailed comments on an earlier draft; Richard Blundell, Renata Bottazzi, and Ian Preston for helpful discussions; Hamish Low for help with the initial set-up of the simulated life-cycle model used in Section 7.3 of the chapter; and, participants at the first 'Mirrlees Review' conference (at IFS, October 2006) for comments on a presentation of a very preliminary version of the chapter. The usual disclaimer applies.

EXECUTIVE SUMMARY

The aim of this study is to review what we know about how consumption and saving choices respond to tax incentives, and in particular to those taxes that change the interest rate. Whether and how much we should tax the return to saving, and whether different assets should be taxed in the same way, has been a topic of debate for both academics and policy makers. The material that we review provides a useful input to this debate by describing the likely consequences of policies that affect returns on assets.

Understanding whether and how changing the tax regime for savings is likely to alter saving behaviour requires a clear conceptual and theoretical framework. With that in mind we devote the bulk of this chapter to setting out and developing the basic model of saving over the life cycle that is the key tool economists use in thinking about why and how people save. This framework allows the analyst to specify the different incentive effects that alter saving when the return on assets changes, and to describe when the forces that increase saving will outweigh those that reduce it.

There is a large theoretical and empirical literature on the life-cycle model of consumption and saving. This literature has largely been developed separately from empirical investigations of whether changes in taxation of the return to certain assets have affected savings behaviour. A key reason is that modern versions of the life-cycle model, that explicitly incorporate uncertainty, for the most part do not tell us directly how consumption is related to factors such as present and expected levels of income, wealth, and interest rates. Quantifying this relationship is crucial for policy analysts wishing to know *how much* consumption and saving will change in response to a change in the asset return. However, ever-improving numerical techniques now provide the wherewithal to analyse precisely this type of question in increasingly realistic settings. We argue that these techniques therefore have the potential to bridge the gap between the literatures on the life-cycle model and on the observed response of saving to policy changes.

To provide a first step across this gap, in Section 7.2 we outline a specific version of the life-cycle model, which we use to simulate the behaviour of hypothetical individuals faced with different incentives to save (i.e. different interest rates). We consider an increase in the interest rate from 2% to 2.5%, a change which could be brought about by cutting the tax on interest from 40% to 25%, or from 20% to 0. For our baseline version of the model, we show that this increase in the asset return

- raises retirement wealth by almost 20%;
- increases wealth holding over the life cycle such that slightly less than 10% of the extra wealth held over the lifetime is not offset by lost tax revenue, and so can be thought of as new national saving;
- leads to an increase in lifetime welfare equivalent to that delivered by increasing consumption every period by approximately 2.1%; this is somewhat larger than the 1.9% increase in annual consumption that could be funded with the revenue from taxing the return to saving.

These conclusions are shown to be sensitive to some of the assumptions underlying our baseline. Taking account of the way in which changing family needs might shape the profile of consumption over the lifetime, or assuming that people are more reluctant to shift consumption across periods, reduce the change in savings induced by the tax change. On the other hand, a smaller change in savings does *not* necessarily indicate smaller welfare implications; in the case where people are more reluctant to shift their consumption the welfare implications of a *given change in the tax rate* increase as the response of savings gets smaller, although the revenue raised also increases.

A more general summary is that given the basic structure of the model—and the best information we have on people's willingness to shift their consumption and the way their needs and resources change over the life cycle—it is unlikely that changes in interest rates (including those brought about by tax changes) will have a big impact on the level of saving. This is consistent with our (controversial) reading of the literature on how people have responded to past changes in the taxation of assets. That is not to say that there are no behavioural effects coming from such tax changes—the empirical literature has shown that individuals do seem to respond to changes in relative interest rates by altering the mix of assets they hold.

A note of caution is that while we have been as realistic as possible in our analysis, the framework was still relatively stylized. In Section 7.3 of the chapter we outline a set of extensions to the framework that would add to its realism and to its usefulness as a tool for policy analysis. These extensions include allowing people to alter their labour supply; allowing people to hold multiple assets, perhaps including housing, other durable goods and pensions as well as a saving account; and exploring issues of habits, temptation, and procrastination that cannot be captured in the simple view of people's preferences over the life cycle.

In spite of the limitations of our analysis, we believe that our discussion illustrates why the life-cycle model is a useful—indeed, we would say essential—tool for the analyst who wants to know how behaviour and welfare will be affected by changes in the return to saving. We hope that the simulations that we present are a useful early step for understanding how to use the model to analyse these issues.

7.1. INTRODUCTION

There are several possible reasons why policy makers might seek to reduce the taxation of the return to saving. One motivation might be given by the economic theories that, on efficiency grounds, favour an 'expenditure tax' that does not tax income from saving, and indeed the Meade Committee proposed an expenditure tax base (Meade (1978)). Alternatively, the aim might be to encourage more saving, if it is believed that some individuals are not building up adequate resources. Finally, the reduction may apply selectively to certain assets such as private pensions, and the aim may be to make these assets relatively attractive to potential savers.

The assessment of these rationales, and particularly of the first, which is the focus of Banks and Diamond in Chapter 6, is important for the present review of taxation and the UK tax system. While our aim is not as grand as to undertake such a sweeping assessment, the material we will be discussing is useful background to the discussion of whether these rationales are sensible or can be achieved using the policy lever of reducing the tax on the return to saving. Our purpose is to review what we know about how responsive consumption and saving choices are to tax incentives and in particular to interest rate changes.

Changes to the tax regime for saving are frequent and not always consistent. The stated reasons for such changes often refer to the second and third of the arguments mentioned in the opening paragraph. Rather than efficiency, the main motivation for changes to the taxation of interest seems to be that reducing taxes on savings will increase their total amount. Implicit in this argument is that there are good (welfare increasing) reasons for doing so—either because there are sub-optimal allocations across the life cycle or because of a perceived link between savings and investment or indeed a poorly articulated sense that thrift is good.

To understand whether changing the tax regime for savings is indeed likely to alter saving behaviour, and how, requires a clear conceptual and theoretical framework. With that in mind we devote the bulk of this chapter to setting out and developing the basic life-cycle savings model which is a key tool of economists in thinking about savings behaviour. This choice implicitly dispenses with some of the motivations above: we will be assuming that individual households make rational choices and are not myopic or irrational in their behaviour. We justify our choice by referring to some empirical evidence that shows that the model we propose is not a bad representation of available data.

Spelling out a specific conceptual and theoretical framework to analyse the issues at hand is useful because it makes explicit the assumptions and parameters which will determine how changing the return to saving—which is obviously directly affected by the tax rate—will affect levels of saving. In a simple model we are also able to assess the welfare consequences of those changes, crucial for getting to first base in considering the appropriate salience of these issues from a policy point of view. A key point that comes out is that a small change in saving behaviour does not necessarily imply a small welfare impact from *a given change in the interest rate* (i.e. a *given rate of tax* on the return to saving). In particular, as we change the model that we analyse to reflect individuals being more reluctant to shift resources from one period to another, we find that the behavioural response to the given change in the interest rate becomes smaller but the welfare implications of the change increase.[1] On the other hand, the tax revenue raised from the given tax rate also increases.

As we discuss below, even in the simple version of the model that we present in Section 7.2, it will only be possible to quantify the impact that changes in the interest rate has on saving by using numerical simulations of some complexity. These simulations, whose use has become more and more common in the academic research on the life-cycle model, are extremely useful for rigorous policy analysis and, if one accepts a sophisticated version of the life-cycle model as a reasonable representation of reality, an indispensable tool.

A big advantage of the approach we propose is that one can deal with aggregation issues directly, by explicitly allowing for a large amount of heterogeneity across consumers, both in terms of observed determinants of consumption and saving (for instance in needs driven by changing family composition) and, possibly, in unobserved components. Our approach recognizes that heterogeneous individuals are reacting to specific incentives and determine the outcomes policy makers are interested in.

[1] In the formal model this change in preferences is a reduction in the Elasticity of Intertemporal Substitution (see Box 7.1), and the relationship between the behavioural and welfare effects is discussed in more detail in Section 7.2.1, pp. 699–702.

The approach we present is not without limitations, however. There are many important aspects that are left out of our analysis. While in what follows we discuss at some length some extensions to the model we simulate in Section 7.2, here we would like to mention four important issues that are left out of the scope of our discussion, partly to keep the length of this chapter manageable. First, the simulations we report are based on a model that assumes only a single rate of return to saving—equivalently a single asset. In fact all recent changes to the savings tax regime, whilst in general moving towards less heavily taxed status, have been applied to only some of the available savings vehicles. Therefore, these changes do not fit neatly within our exercises. Partly because of this, in Section 7.3 we review some of the empirical literature that has tried to assess the impacts of these reforms. Second, we neglect completely a bequest motive and do not discuss the issue of the taxation of bequests. We do not have a strong justification for this exclusion, which is particularly unfortunate given that there exists a lively debate among policy makers on this specific issue. A detailed and non-superficial consideration of bequests and their taxation would have increased the length of this chapter considerably. Third, we do not discuss the taxation of housing, although real estate constitutes one of the most important assets in household portfolios in the UK and other developed countries. As we explain, incorporating housing into the framework we lay out is complicated because of the transactions costs and credit constraints associated with house purchase. Finally, we do not discuss the issue of penalties to withdrawal of resources from pensions before pensionable age. These restrictions often accompany the tax privileges that are given to private pension schemes in different countries.

As well as being precise about the elements that are left out of our modelling exercises, we should also be clear that our focus is on the role of tax as it can affect the return to saving. As such we do not in general consider other levers such as the provision of information, or increased compulsory saving, that may be used to affect saving decisions (though the former is mentioned in our survey of evidence in Section 7.3). For the sake of space we also do not discuss the role of benefit withdrawal even though this is known to create large changes in the effective return to saving for some individuals:[2] such changes should induce similar incentive effects to those we discuss for a tax change, but limitations of data have made it hard to investigate responses to these incentives as they primarily affect lower-income individuals.

We structure our main discussion in two sections. In Section 7.2, we provide a simple theoretical framework that allows us to organize the discussion

[2] See Wakefield (2008), and section 3.2 of Blundell, Emmerson, and Wakefield (2006).

of the effect of taxation on saving and consumption. To illustrate the insights that this framework can provide, we use it to simulate the behaviour of hypothetical individuals faced with different incentives to save. While the model we use in this section is quite a bit more realistic than the textbook version which is often thought of when referring to the 'life-cycle model', it is necessarily stylized and simplified. Section 7.3 surveys what we know about the empirical relevance of the life-cycle model, with a particular emphasis on its application to considering how consumption and saving respond to changes in the interest rate. We consider both evidence on the validity of the model and estimates of some of its parameters. We then go on to discuss the relevance of more complex versions of the model. While some of these complications are bound to be relevant for our discussion, we will stress that our quantitative knowledge of these extensions is very limited. Therefore, in the last part of the section we also discuss some more direct (and less structural) evidence on the response of savings to changes in its theoretical determinants. Section 7.4 concludes.

7.2. THE LIFE-CYCLE MODEL AND THE RESPONSE OF SAVING TO TAXATION

In this section we provide a simple theoretical framework that allows us to organize the discussion of the effect of taxation on saving and consumption. The behavioural model we use, the so-called life-cycle model of Modigliani and Brumberg (1954), is not meant to be a literal description of reality but can capture some important features of individual households' behaviour. It also constitutes a useful benchmark against which we can contrast the implications of more complex and possibly more realistic models. Before we delve into the specifics of the model, we want to emphasize *why* we think it is important to understand this framework if one wants to analyse the effects on consumption and saving of taxing asset returns.

The life-cycle model is a workhorse of modern macroeconomics and public finance. Proposed by Modigliani and Brumberg (1954) in a seminal contribution, it shares with the Permanent Income Hypothesis of Friedman (1957)[3] the idea that individuals allocate resources over time (and therefore determine current consumption and saving—or, equivalently, present and future consumption) taking into account the resources available over a long

[3] Unlike the permanent income model, which is usually thought of as a model with an infinite horizon, the life-cycle model focuses explicitly on a finite horizon and is therefore particularly useful for studying retirement saving and related issues.

period of time and the possibility of moving them over time. The latter might mean saving to move purchasing power from the present to the future, or borrowing to shift purchasing power from the future to the present. The attractiveness of the life-cycle model and of the permanent income hypothesis is that they treat the allocation of consumption over time (saving) in a manner analogous to that of the allocation of a certain amount of expenditure among several commodities. This powerful intuition is behind some of the optimal taxation results that Banks and Diamond discuss in Chapter 6.

The conceptual framework provided by the life-cycle model makes clear that a change in the interest rate changes the relative price of consumption between time periods. Thus a measure of how much an individual will shift consumption from one time period to another (by saving or borrowing) in response to a change in the relative price of consumption in those two periods becomes crucial for understanding the effects on consumption and saving of a change in the interest rate. Precisely such a measure is provided within the model by a parameter known as the 'elasticity of intertemporal substitution' (EIS—for a fuller discussion see Box 7.1). As this elasticity gets smaller, so the increase in saving when the interest rate increases gets smaller. Indeed, when the EIS is very small saving may actually fall when the interest rate increases (Section 7.2.1, pp. 686–7, discusses the mechanisms through which this may happen). Despite the clear relevance of the EIS, a remarkable feature of the sizeable recent literature on the effect of the preferential taxation of retirement wealth on personal and national saving is that it never refers to the literature that has studied the life-cycle model and estimated preference parameters, including the EIS.

One possible reason for this neglect might be the feeling that the life-cycle model constitutes a poor approximation of reality. An alternative reason for the disjuncture of the two literatures, however, could be that modern versions of the life-cycle model that explicitly incorporate uncertainty, for the most part do not deliver a closed form solution for consumption. That is, one can write down optimality conditions that can be used in the empirical analysis, but cannot use them to solve for an expression for consumption as a function of, say, present and expected future income, current wealth, and the level of current and future (expected) interest rates. This lack of a consumption function that could be used for policy analysis has led public finance economists to neglect the consumption literature. The exercises in this chapter start to fill this gap, and demonstrate the potential for progress in this area through the use of ever-improving computational techniques.

We begin by providing a more specific outline of a simple version of the life-cycle model, which we then use to simulate the behaviour of hypothetical individuals faced with different incentives to save. This exercise will give us the theoretical effect that one would observe in response to changes in the taxation of saving if individuals behave according to the stylized model. We then show that different effects are obtained when additional factors are added to the model. One point we will make is that the life-cycle model is a potentially very rich structure that can encompass and explain different types of behaviour. The issue of which version of the model is relevant is ultimately therefore an empirical question and in Section 7.3 we discuss the available empirical evidence.

Box 7.1. Formalizing the model, the Euler equation and the Elasticity of Intertemporal Substitution

Formalizing the life-cycle model

We interpret the life-cycle model as one in which an individual maximizes lifetime utility derived from consumption using her lifetime resources and taking into account the available inter-temporal trades. Using the assumption that utility is additively separable across periods—i.e. that consumption today does not directly affect the marginal utility from consumption tomorrow—we can write this down as:

$$\max_{\{c_0\}} U(c_0) + E_o \sum_{t=1}^{T} \beta^{-1} U(c_t).$$

Subject to an inter-temporal budget constraint:

$$A_{t+1} = A_t(1+r) + y_t - c_t$$

where $U(\cdot)$ is the within period utility function, c is consumption, β is the subjective discount factor, A is the level of assets, r is the interest rate, y is income, and E is the expectations operator.

The Euler equation

In general, apart from very special assumptions about the utility function and/or the nature of uncertainty, this problem does not have a known closed form solution—that is, there is no known form for the consumption choice as a function of resources.

However, there are certain well-known features of the solution for a more general case. Under certain regularity assumptions for the utility function, and abstracting from factors such as credit constraints, the solution will satisfy the following condition for the evolution of the marginal utility of consumption (the rate of change in utility when there is a small change in consumption).

This is the 'Euler equation':

$$U_{ct} = (1+r)\beta^{-1} E_t\{U_{c(t+1)}\}.$$

(cont.)

Box 7.1. (*cont.*)

Where U_{ci} is the marginal utility of consumption at period i (i.e. the first derivative of the utility function with respect to consumption), and the interest rate and discount factor have been assumed to be certain and fixed.

This condition may be interpreted as saying that consumption will be chosen such that the marginal utility of consumption evolves smoothly over the life cycle. In the case with no uncertainty, the condition says that the marginal utility of consumption will grow at a rate determined by the excess of the interest rate over the rate at which individuals discount the future. With a standard, time-invariant utility function, this will involve consumption declining steadily over the life cycle when the discount rate exceeds the interest rate, or growing steadily when the interest rate is larger than the discount rate.

For more details on the Euler equation and its interpretation see, for example, Attanasio (1999).

The Elasticity of Intertemporal Substitution

We are interested in the responsiveness of consumption and saving choices to a change in the interest rate. A change in the interest rate represents a change in the relative price of consumption at different points in time, and the Elasticity of Intertemporal Substitution (EIS) plays a crucial role in determining the responsiveness of consumption choices to such relative price changes. The larger is the EIS, the larger will be the shift in consumption from one period to another following a change in the relative price of consumption in those two periods, and for a very small EIS consumption will be almost unaffected by such relative price changes.

Formally, the EIS measures the proportional change in the ratio of consumption levels between two periods, divided by the proportional change in ratio of marginal utilities from changing consumption in these periods:

$$EIS = \frac{\partial(c_i/c_j)}{c_i/c_j} \Big/ \frac{\partial(U_{ci}/U_{cj})}{U_{ci}/U_{cj}} = \frac{\partial \ln(c_i/c_j)}{\partial \ln(U_{ci}/U_{cj})}.$$

Where i and j are time periods, and U_c is the marginal utility of consumption. In our simulations we use the constant relative risk aversion utility function:

$$u(c) = (1-\gamma)^{-1}c^{(1-\gamma)} \qquad (*)$$

This functional form implies that the EIS is equal to the inverse of the relative risk aversion parameter, i.e. $EIS = 1/\gamma$.

Using the Euler equation to provide evidence on the EIS

The relationship between the *EIS* and the way consumption changes in response to changes in the interest rate is neatly seen within the Euler equation mentioned above. With the utility function in equation (*), the Euler equation can be written as follows:

$$\Delta \log(c_{t+1}) = k_t + \frac{1}{\gamma} r_{t+1} + \varepsilon_{t+1} \qquad (\dagger)$$

where the left-hand side of the equation is the consumption growth rate, the term k_t represents a variety of observable and unobservable factors, and the term ε_{t+1} is a residual term that represents expectational errors, that is, factors affecting consumption at $t + 1$ that were not known to the consumer at t. The EIS $(1/\gamma)$ is seen directly to capture how much consumption at $t + 1$ changes relative to consumption at t in reaction to a change in the interest rate.

The simplicity of this final representation of the Euler equation makes it a useful basis for empirical analysis aimed at providing evidence on the plausibility of the life-cycle model and/or at estimating the value of the EIS.

7.2.1. A specific life-cycle model

The life-cycle model as we have so far described it is a rather general framework. In order to bring it to bear on reality, we need to make a number of assumptions about the details of the various components of the model. We therefore introduce the version of the model that we use to simulate the behaviour of hypothetical individuals, by discussing some of the key assumptions that we need to make in order to operationalize the model. This discussion highlights why the model is useful, but also awkward to use, for analysing the tax policy and public finance questions we are interested in. The results that we present in this section at pp. 690–702 are intended to provide an accessible introduction to using the model to think about how individuals respond to incentives to save.

Before going into the details of the model it is worth stressing that the model is one of *individual* behaviour. As such it is easy to incorporate various forms of observed and unobserved (by the researcher) heterogeneity in it. This can take the form of heterogeneity in parameters or, more conveniently, heterogeneity in some of the determinants of individual choices, such as needs, income processes, tastes, and so on. As we shall see, once we have the basic model, it is easy to introduce these aspects into the picture.

Features of the model

The basic version of the model that we use corresponds to that formalized in Box 7.1. In the simplest version of the model we consider a single decision unit, that is, an individual whose utility depends on consumption over her life cycle. While we will maintain the assumption of a single and monolithic decision unit that maximizes a single utility function, in a more complicated version of the model that we consider below we consider a household whose composition might change over time as children are born and eventually leave the parental home. In this chapter we do not consider models where different individuals in the households might have different utility functions.

Individuals maximize expected utility, and utility each period is derived from consumption in that period and is not affected by consumption in other periods. Future utility is discounted at a geometric rate.

The resources that individuals use to fund their consumption arrive as an income stream which is exogenous in the sense that we do not model a labour supply choice and so the level of income does not depend on any choice made by the individual. The income process is modelled as being made of a deterministic component, assumed to be known perfectly by the individual, and a stochastic (or risky) component. Our individuals are assumed to be aware of the process that generates it. After a certain age, individuals are assumed to retire and to be entitled to benefits that are a fixed proportion of the last earnings of their working life.

We assume that life has a fixed duration which is known to individuals and that there is no bequest motive. Moreover, individuals are not allowed to die in debt. In terms of the inter-temporal trades available to the individual, we assume that individuals have a single asset that pays a fixed interest rate to move resources in to the future. We also restrict the amount individuals can borrow.[4]

In the simplest version of the model, we assume that the individual/household whose consumption we study has constant consumption needs throughout the life cycle. We then introduce more realistic settings where household size, and therefore the needs households have, vary deterministically with age.

Some of the assumptions we make are very stark and unrealistic. However, many of them can be relaxed in a relatively simple fashion and/or have minimal effect on the main results we obtain concerning consumption choices and how consumption and saving respond to changes in the interest rate. A good example of such an assumption is that of certain life length. One can introduce the possibility that an individual dies with some known probability

[4] Under certain assumptions on preferences, individuals will never want to borrow. This occurs when the marginal utility of consumption goes to infinity at a very low level of consumption. Individuals will not want to borrow if this induces a positive probability of having extremely low levels of consumption.

(possibly increasing in age) without much complication—a probability of not reaching the next period of life essentially has the same effect on current behaviour as an increase in the discount rate.

Other assumptions, however, are crucial for the results we will be discussing and cannot be relaxed without substantially changing the nature of the model[5] and the implied results. One such assumption is that of intertemporal separability, which implies that consumption at a certain date does not affect the marginal utility derived from consumption at different dates. This assumption rules out the existence of durable goods which deliver consumption services for more than one period, and of habit formation whereby current utility is affected by the level of consumption to which the agent has become accustomed. A second such assumption is that labour income arrives without being affected by a labour supply choice. This exogeneity assumption is strong, and the implications for consumption and saving choices will be particularly pronounced if labour supply choices directly affect the utility derived from consumption—because consumption and leisure are either complements or substitutes. We briefly discuss models with labour supply, and models with durable goods or habits, in Section 7.3.2.

Some of the basic insights of the life-cycle model we will be analysing are well known and do not need to be discussed in detail here. Consumption at any point in time depends not only on current income, but also on the total amount of resources available to an individual over her life cycle. Consumption should react to the interest rate, although it is well known that, at least theoretically, the effect on consumption of changes in interest rates is ambiguous. This is because there are several mechanisms by which a change in the interest rate will affect current consumption. We describe these mechanisms considering the case of an increase in the interest rate; the same mechanisms would lead to consumption shifting in the opposite direction following an interest rate decrease. The increase in the interest rate represents a decrease in the price of future consumption relative to current consumption, and this induces a 'substitution effect' of a decrease in current consumption and a commensurate increase in current saving. This would be counteracted by an 'income effect' since with a higher interest rate a given target level of future consumption is achieved with less saving. As noted by Summers (1981), wealth effects concerning the amount that expected future incomes are discounted tend to reinforce substitution effects and also lead to a decrease in consumption or increase in saving when the interest rate goes

[5] When the nature of the model is changed, this can quickly increase computational complexity of the numerical solution.

up. These wealth effects tend to be stronger when the time period that the individual cares about is longer. Ultimately, which of these forces dominates depends on preference parameters and is, therefore, an empirical issue.

The computations we provide have to be obtained by numerical methods. These, however, have become increasingly standard and affordable, both because of the increased power of computers and because of a small literature that, starting with Deaton's (1991) contribution, has looked at the solution of life-cycle models of increasing degree of complexity and realism. Much of the existing literature has been devoted to the plausibility of the standard LC–PI and of slightly different models, such as the so-called buffer-stock model. Here what we do is to simulate some versions of the standard model to show two things. First, we want to see how the responsiveness of savings to the interest rate varies with preference parameters and other features of the model, including the institutional set-up in which the behaviour of our consumers is embedded. Second, we want to compute saving and wealth elasticities to the interest rate implied by parameters estimated from micro data for some realistic versions of the model that is not rejected in an obvious way by the same data.

Details of the model

Having described the key assumptions that we need to make to operationalize the model, we must now be precise about the parameters that we impose when simulating the behaviour that the model predicts. Table 7.1 reports the key parameters of the baseline model and of the alternatives we simulate.[6]

As discussed above, a key preference parameter is the EIS, which is set to 1 for our baseline results.[7] This is at the high end of the range of values that have been estimated for this parameter (see Section 7.3.1, pp. 708–10), and we also conduct analyses for values of 1/2 and 1/4. The discount rate is set at 2.5%, which is equal to the larger of the two real interest rates for which we simulate behaviour.

The process generating income is also important to our results. There is a deterministic component of income which is hump-shaped during working life and assumed to be known perfectly by the individual. The parameters that determine the shape of the profile of this component of income are set to match profiles observed for family incomes in the British Household Panel

[6] We would like to thank Hamish Low for help with the initial set-up of the simulated life-cycle model used here, though we are solely responsible for any errors in the simulations or their interpretation.

[7] The EIS = 1 implies that the utility function has the logarithmic form.

Table 7.1. Model parameters

Parameter	Baseline	Variants
Utility Parameters		
EIS	1	½, ¼
Discount rate	2.5%	
Income process		
Initial income growth rate (expected)	3.4%	
Age at peak expected income	50	
Ratio of peak income to initial income	1.6	
Variance of permanent shock (to log income)	0.030	0, 0.060
Variance of transitory shock (to log income)	0.030	0, 0.060
Replacement rate in retirement	0.5	0.25, 0.75
Retirement age	65	
Others		
Real interest rate	2%	2.5%
Lifespan	60 yrs (21–80)	

Survey (BHPS).[8,9] Income is expected to grow at approximately 3.4% per year at the beginning of the working life, and the expected growth rate then gradually declines until the expected income peak of approximately 1.6 times initial income is reached at age 50. There is also a stochastic component of income and individuals are assumed to be aware of the process that generates this. It is made up of a transitory shock,[10] and a permanent (random walk) component. The variances of the shocks to these components are set approximately to match values estimated by Meghir and Pistaferri (2004),[11] and are similar to the values imposed by Low (2005) in his simulation exercises. Income in retirement is certain, and in our baseline run is equal to half the final income of the working life. As Table 7.1 indicates, we conduct analyses with alternative values of the variances of the income shocks, and of the retirement income replacement rate.

A final factor that we consider in our model is how varying consumption needs affect our results. In the baseline version of the model, we assume that

[8] We use a measure of income that excludes investment income, and data from the years 1991–2002.

[9] Data from the BHPS were made available through the UK Data Archive <http://www.data-archive.ac.uk/>, which is now incorporated within the Institute for Social and Economic Research at the University of Essex. Neither the original collectors of the data nor the Archive bear any responsibility for the analyses or interpretations that are presented here.

[10] The transitory shocks are independently and identically distributed across time and individuals.

[11] Meghir and Pistaferri (2004) use US data, and we take their estimates of the unconditional variance of these shocks. The main discussion of their paper has implications for whether the values of these unconditional variances can be sufficient to characterize the evolution of earnings shocks.

the individual's consumption needs are constant over the life cycle. If, instead of a fictitious individual we consider a household, we can compare this version of the model to one in which consumption needs are increased between the ages of 22 and 58 due to the presence of children in the household. In this version of the model, utility is defined in terms of consumption per adult equivalent, and consumption is scaled down in the utility function during the years when children live in the parental home. The scaling factors are set to match the average number of children of couples of each age in the BHPS in 2002,[12] and family size and consumption needs are assumed to peak in the late 30s.

Model results

(a) Profiles of consumption and asset holding

Probably the best way to introduce our results is to present some pictures of life-cycle profiles for consumption and wealth under different scenarios. For example, in Figure 7.1, we plot the life-cycle profile for consumption in our baseline run. This picture, as the others reported below, is obtained by simulating the life cycle of 10,000 individuals who each receive a particular realization of the assumed income shocks[13] and averaging the relevant variable of interest. The figures report plots of these averages.

The profile for average consumption in Figure 7.1(a) is shaped both by the savings motives that determine individuals' consumption choices and by the ability individuals have to transfer resources over time and, in particular, the presence of credit constraints. In addition, in our specific example, the shape of the consumption profile is also driven by the assumptions made about the stochastic component of income and its variability.[14] To get a clearer picture of the influence of constraints and the motives for saving, in panel (b) of the figure we also plot the mean of log consumption.

The individuals modelled are impatient in the sense that the subjective discount rate on utility received in the future (2.5%) is greater than the

[12] The scaling factor is such that in utility the consumption of a couple with one child is scaled down by a factor of 1.35 relative to that of a couple, for a couple with two children the factor is 1.7, and so on. In order to smooth out the data, we fit a quartic regression through the values of the average number of children at each age, and use the predictions from this regression to compute our scaling factors. We also adjust the equivalence scale equally at all ages so that the discounted value of equivalized income in the model with family needs is equal to the discounted value of income in the baseline version of the model.

[13] The shocks are assumed to be independent across individuals.

[14] Shocks to the permanent component of income are assumed to have a log-normal distribution. The variance of individual income will therefore increase with age. When we average across individuals the *level* of income, Jensen's inequality will imply that the mean of income will also increase.

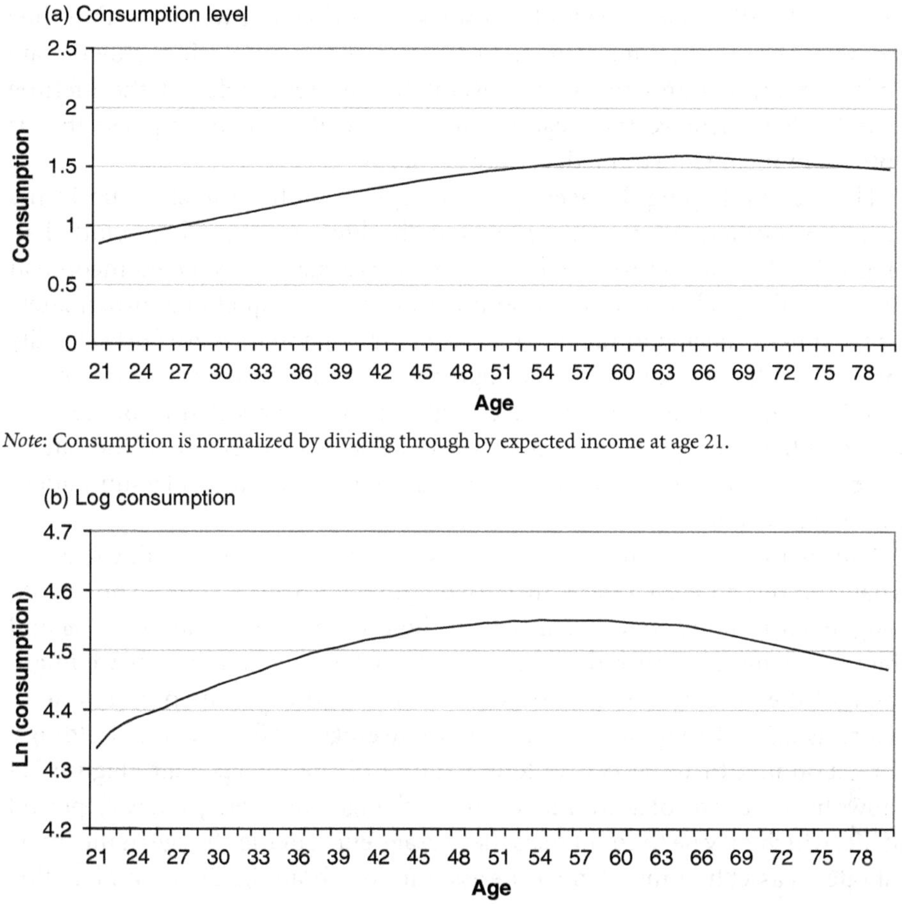

Figure 7.1. Average consumption by age: baseline case

rate of interest (2%). Therefore, as discussed in the section on 'The Euler equation' in Box 7.1, in a certain and unconstrained world these individuals would like consumption to decline steadily throughout the life cycle. This profile is not achieved because of credit constraints and what has been defined 'precautionary saving'. The former prevent the individuals from borrowing to bring consumption forward to the early years of life when income is low relative to expected lifetime resources. Precautionary saving arises because, given the shape of the utility function (technically a convex marginal utility), the presence of uncertainty encourages the holding of assets as a form of insurance against shocks. These factors outweigh the impatience for most of the working life and so the profile for mean log consumption is upward sloping until the late 50s. At the point of retirement (age 65) all uncertainty ceases and individuals have built up stocks of retirement wealth so that they are no longer credit constrained. At this age the consumption growth rate kinks downwards and remains constant for the remainder of the lifetime as individuals achieve the steady downwards drift in consumption that is optimal in the unconstrained, certain scenario.

The factors shaping the average consumption profile also show up in the profile of average asset holdings across the life cycle, which is plotted in Figure 7.2. In this picture, the level of assets is scaled by expected income at age 21, so the peak level of asset holdings at age 65 is equal to approximately eleven times expected initial income. Assets are seen to increase fairly steadily throughout the working life, although most rapidly between the ages of 35 and 50 when income is, on average, high relative to expected resources and so individuals engage in retirement saving. There is a decrease in the rate of increase in assets as retirement approaches and income falls, and a subsequent running down of assets after age 65.

Our main interest is to determine how the profile of asset holding changes when the real interest rate is increased from 2% real to 2.5%. This would roughly correspond to a case in which the pre-tax interest rate is 3.3% and the tax rate on saving is reduced from 40% to 25%, or alternatively we might think of the tax rate being reduced from 20% to 0 when the pre-tax rate of return is 2.5%. In Figure 7.3, we plot two average profiles of asset holdings, corresponding to these two different values of the interest rate. Figure 7.4 shows how the level of accumulated assets changes, on average, in each period of life, which may be thought of as the average effect of the change in the interest rate on asset holdings. Under the assumption about the EIS in our baseline

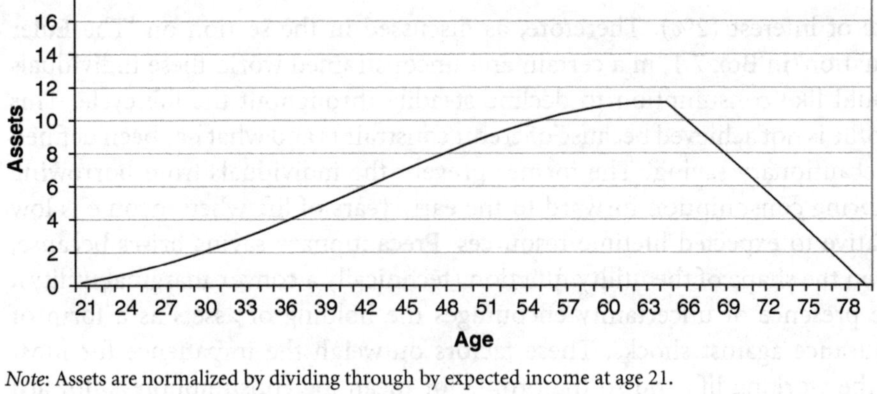

Note: Assets are normalized by dividing through by expected income at age 21.

Figure 7.2. Average asset holdings by age: baseline case

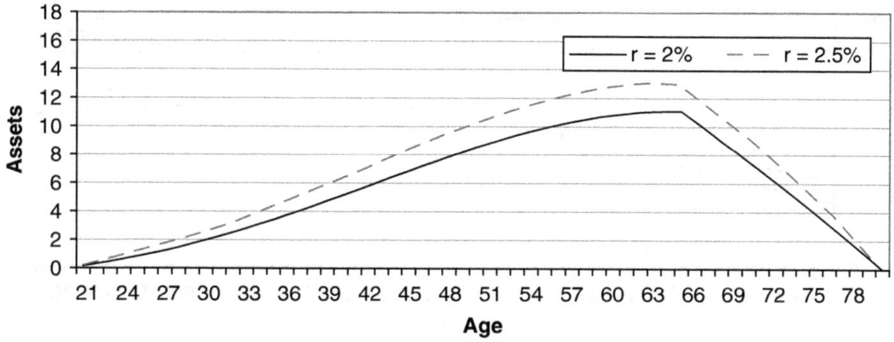

Note: Assets are normalized by dividing through by expected income at age 21.

Figure 7.3. Average asset holdings by age: baseline case, different interest rates

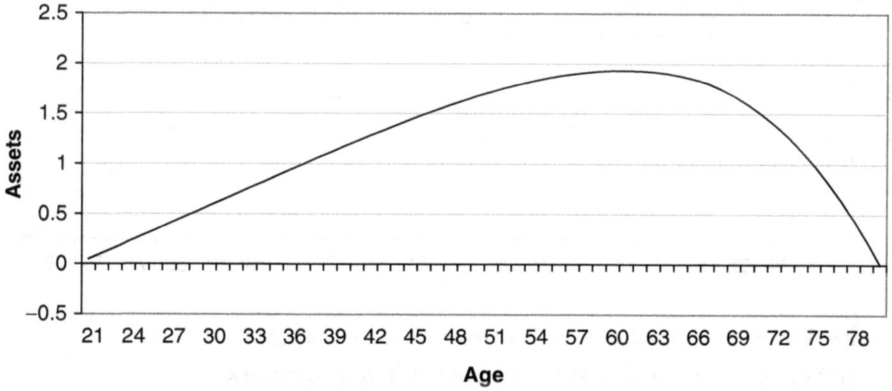

Note: The change in assets is normalized by dividing through by expected income at age 21.

Figure 7.4. Average change in asset holdings by age when r changes: baseline case

run (EIS = 1), the average change in assets induced by the higher interest rate is non-negligible and increases steadily through most of the working life. The average effect on asset holdings is largest around age 61 when assets are increased by approximately 1.9 units (i.e. 1.9 times average initial income), or 18%, in the high interest rate regime compared to the low interest rate regime.

To examine the extent to which the results in Figures 7.1 to 7.4 are driven by the assumptions we have made concerning the level of income risk, in Figures 7.5 to 7.7 we show results for different levels of risk. In order, the figures show average consumption profiles, average asset holdings, and the average change in asset holdings when the interest rate is changed, for three different assumptions about the variance of shocks to income. In each figure,

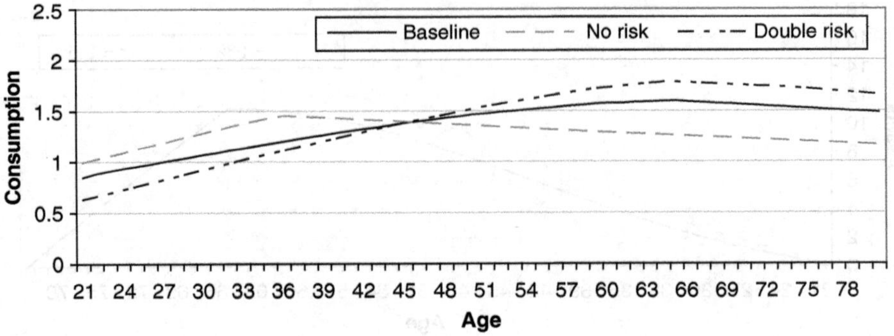

Note: Assets are normalized by dividing through by expected income at age 21.

Figure 7.5. Average consumption by age: different levels of income risk

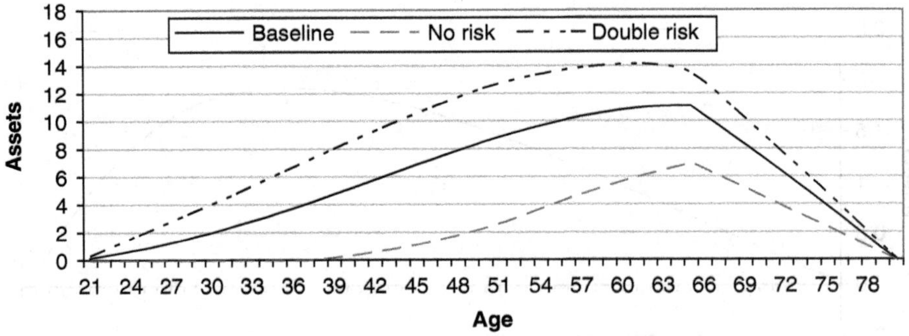

Note: Assets are normalized by dividing through by expected income at age 21.

Figure 7.6. Average assets by age: different levels of income risk

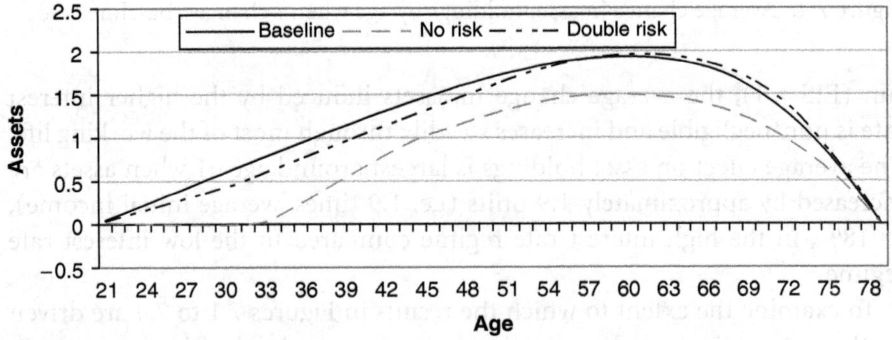

Note: The change in assets is normalized by dividing through by expected income at age 21.

Figure 7.7. Average change in asset holding by age when r changes: different levels of income risk

the continuous line is for the baseline case which we have already discussed, the line made up of alternating dashes and dots is for the case of no income risk,[15] and the dashed line is for a case in which the variances of the shocks to (log) income (both permanent and transitory shocks) are doubled compared to the baseline run.

The plots for the case with no risk are a particularly useful benchmark against which to compare our baseline run, since with no risk in the model the plotted profiles are effectively for a single individual facing a lifetime income profile that is fixed at the mean level in the model. The consumption profile for the individual facing this profile with certainty is initially upward sloping as credit constraints force a consumption profile that tracks income. Once income is sufficiently high that the credit constraint no longer binds, the consumption profile follows the downward sloping path that is preferred by the agent. Figure 7.5 shows that relative to this certain case, average consumption in our baseline case is lower in early life, and higher at later ages, and this pattern is more pronounced when this amount of risk in the economy is increased. The relative shapes of these profiles are reflections of the fact that average saving is higher when there is more uncertainty (Figure 7.6).

When we consider in Figure 7.7 the average change in asset holding induced by the change in the interest rate, we see that the two uncertain cases have rather similar profiles which are higher than the profile for the individual facing certainty. However, as we shall see, this difference between the certain and uncertain cases, is small relative, for example, to those that are due to changing the EIS while holding the level of risk constant.

To see how the EIS affects the results, we repeat the exercise that yielded Figures 7.6 and 7.7 for three different levels of the EIS. We report the graphs corresponding to this exercise in Figures 7.8 and 7.9. In Figure 7.8 we plot the average level of assets corresponding to three different levels of the EIS (1, ½ and ¼), while in Figure 7.9 we report the effect of the change in interest rate corresponding to these same three levels of the EIS. Assets are in general higher for lower levels of the EIS because the lower value of this parameter implies that the individual wants to achieve a smoother path of consumption across the life cycle, and in the set-up we are modelling this requires extra retirement saving. On the other hand, the effect on asset holdings of a change in the interest rate is considerably *smaller* for lower levels of the EIS.[16] For

[15] With no risk in the model the plotted profiles are effectively for a single individual facing a fixed lifetime income profile.

[16] Indeed, in the case with the EIS = ¼, the average change in assets is very slightly negative during the early years of the life cycle. This illustrates how income effects—which tend to reduce saving when the interest rate goes up—become more important relative to substitution effects as the EIS is reduced.

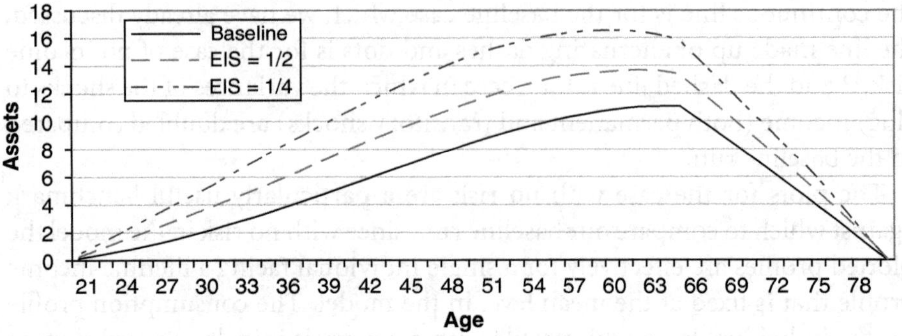

Note: Assets is normalized by dividing through by expected income at age 21.

Figure 7.8. Profile of average asset holdings: baseline case, different preferences

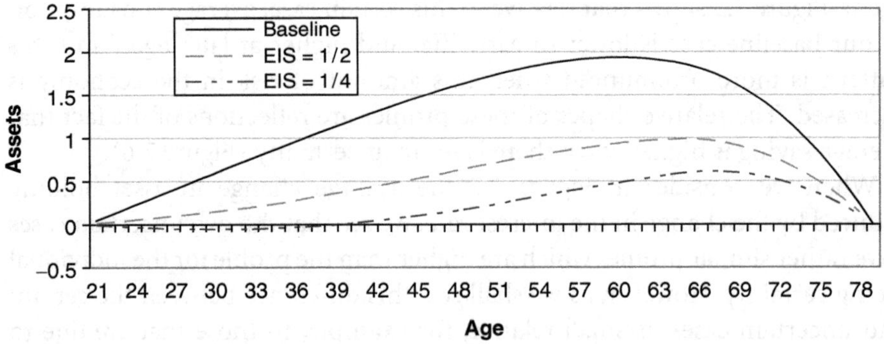

Note: The change in assets is normalized by dividing through by expected income at age 21.

Figure 7.9. Average change in asset holdings when r changes: baseline case, different preferences

instance, halving the EIS from 1 to ½ reduces the peak effect of the interest rate change on asset holdings from about 1.9 units to approximately 1 unit. The decline in this effect clearly illustrates that the EIS is a measure of the responsiveness of consumption choices to relative prices of consumption at different points in time (see Box 7.1): this responsiveness declines as the EIS declines.

The model we have considered so far is unrealistic in that it does not consider changes in consumption needs over the life cycle. Our first extension to the basic model is to introduce such needs. As mentioned at the end of Section 7.2, pp. 689–90, this involves defining utility in terms of consumption per adult equivalent, so that a given level of consumption delivers less utility during the years when children are living in the parental home. Note that

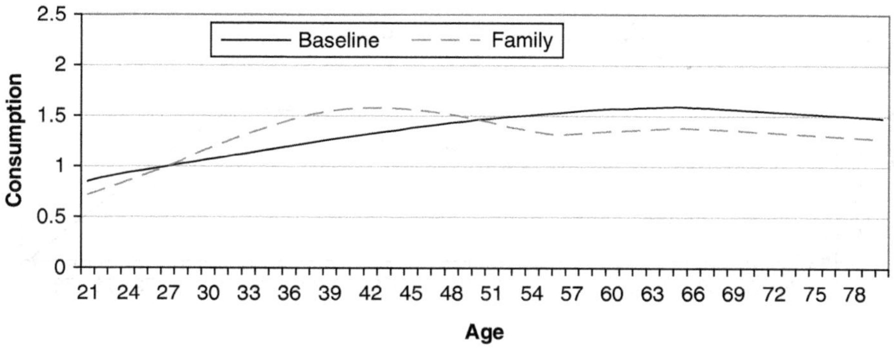

Note: Consumption is normalized by dividing through by expected income at age 21.

Figure 7.10. Profile of average consumption, with and without family

when we introduce family needs, we do this in such a way that the expected present discounted value of equivalized lifetime resources at the start of life is set equal to the present value of lifetime resources when family needs are not modelled.[17] The thought experiment is thus to see how our results changed due solely to the introduction of family needs.

In Figure 7.10, we plot, together with the baseline consumption profile plotted in Figure 7.1, the consumption profile implied by a model with changing consumption needs. As noted in Attanasio and Browning (1995) and Attanasio, Banks, Meghir, and Weber (1999), the explicit consideration of changing family size and composition generates a hump-shaped life-cycle consumption profile. This hump shape follows from the hump-shaped nature of the profile of adult equivalents over the life cycle, and can clearly be seen in Figure 7.10 which contrasts the profile of average consumption when family needs are modelled to that in the baseline run.

In Figure 7.11, for the same two cases, we plot the implied level of assets. In the changing needs model, the level of accumulation for retirement is reduced, a direct consequence of the hump-shaped profile of consumption being closer to the profile for income than was the case when constant consumption needs were assumed. Finally, for the case of changing needs, we also perform the comparative static exercise of increasing the interest rate. As shown in Figure 7.12, the absolute size of the effect of the change in the interest rate is somewhat reduced, at least for the years after the mid-thirties. The peak average effect on asset holdings is now approximately 1.6 units at

[17] This involves dividing the equivalence scale by a factor of 1.2426. In the absence of perfect credit markets to transfer resources across time this is not quite the same as holding expected welfare constant, though in practice it turns out to be very close.

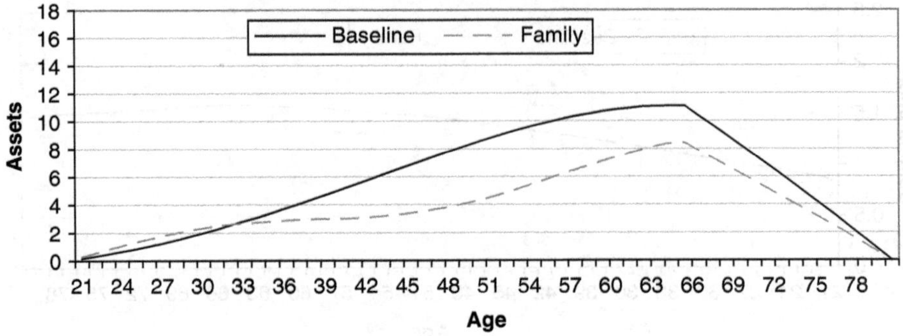

Note: Assets is normalized by dividing through by expected income at age 21.

Figure 7.11. Profile of average asset holding, with and without family

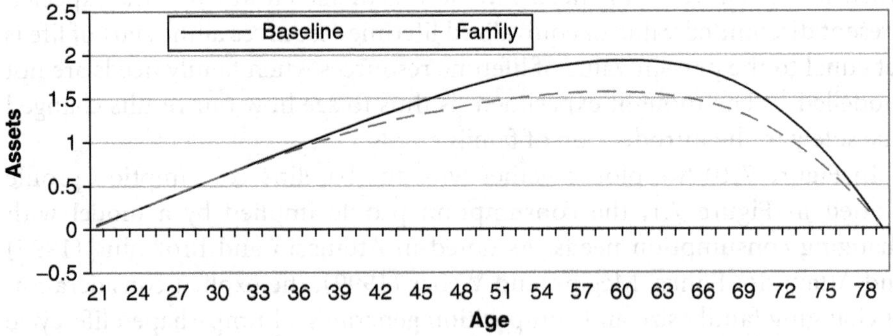

Note: The change in assets is normalized by dividing through by expected income at age 21.

Figure 7.12. Profile of average change in assets, with and without family

age 61, though this still represents approximately 18% of peak average asset holding.

Finally, we consider how our results are affected by the extent to which retirement consumption needs can be funded from 'pension income'. The pension replacement rate is given by the level of pension income relative to the final income received during the working life, where both pension and labour incomes are measured excluding completely interest income. In the base case retirement income is half the final working-age income, and in the comparison cases is set to 25% or 75%. To ensure that this increase (decrease) in retirement income does not represent a direct increase (decrease) in the amount of lifetime resources that can be enjoyed by our individuals, it is accompanied by a commensurate scaling down (up) of lifetime income stream in such a way that the present discounted value of expected lifetime

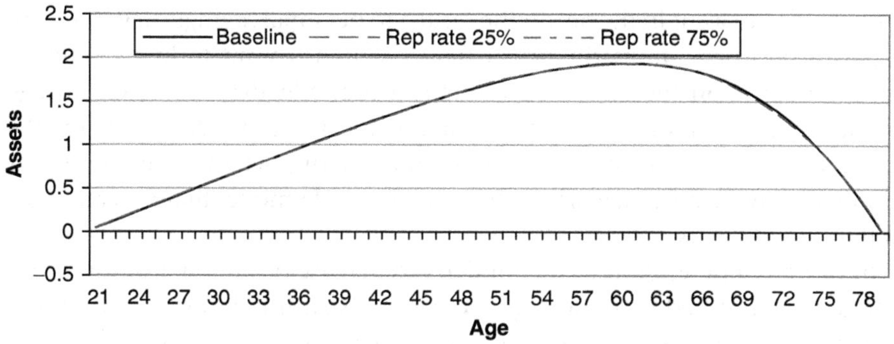

Note: Change in assets is normalized by dividing through by expected income at age 21.

Figure 7.13. Average change in asset holdings due to change in the interest rate from 2% to 2.5%: different replacement rates

resources is held constant.[18] This may be thought of as funding the change in pension payments through a change in proportional payroll tax (or social security contributions).

Given that the wealth-preserving nature of the reform to the pension is effectively increasing or reducing forced saving for retirement, it is unsurprising that individuals almost fully offset this change by adjusting their saving behaviour. That this offset is not exact reflects the fact that moving income away from retirement and towards the working period serves to alleviate credit constraints and allows consumption to be shifted very slightly towards the first years of the working life (the relevant plots of consumption and saving are available from the authors on request). Nonetheless, since the level of saving is affected by changing the pension, it is of interest to check how the changes induced by changing the interest rate are affected by different replacement rates. In Figure 7.13, we plot again the changes in asset holding induced by the higher interest rate for the baseline case, together with the same changes in the two new comparison cases. As can be seen, changes in the replacement rate have almost no effect on the changes in asset holdings that are induced by the change in the interest rate.

(b) Financial implications and welfare consequences of changing the interest rate

We motivated the results presented above on the grounds that the behavioural implications of an increase in the interest rate can be thought of as the

[18] This involves a decrease (increase) in exogenous income each year of 3.6% (3.3%) when the pension is increased (decreased), and the present values are calculated at the low tax interest rate of 2.5%.

implications of a cut in the tax on the return to personal savings. Beyond these behavioural implications the policy maker will also want to know whether cutting the tax on the return on assets is a cost-effective way to encourage saving, and about the implications of the tax for individual welfare. We address these issues in this subsection, and it is important to realize that it is only by having a framework such as the life-cycle model that we can make welfare assessments.

In our baseline version of the model, an increase of the interest rate from 2% to 2.5% resulted in an average increase in wealth holdings at retirement of approximately 18% (see Figure 7.4), and the proportionate increase in wealth holdings was similar (though on a smaller base) when we introduced family needs into the model (Figure 7.12). By contrast, when needs were held constant but the EIS was reduced to 1/4 (Figure 7.9) the proportionate increase in wealth at retirement was approximately 4%.

To think about whether it seems to be cost effective to cut the tax on the return to saving to achieve these increases in wealth, we can compute the tax revenue foregone due to the tax cut, and compare this to the increase in retirement wealth. The cumulative amount of tax revenue foregone up to the retirement age can be computed from the model with behaviour simulated under the lower (2%) interest rate. This is done by taking the sum across ages of the difference between the gross of tax return on savings paid at a 2.5% interest rate, and the amount actually paid to the individual who receives a 2% net of tax interest rate. It turns out that in our baseline version of the model the foregone tax represents around 93% of the expected increase in personal retirement wealth, or, in other words, 7% of the increase in personal wealth is not offset by exchequer cost and so is new national saving.[19,20] In the case with family needs the pattern of saving, and therefore of accumulated tax revenues, is altered and this results in a threefold increase in the proportion of retirement wealth that is new national wealth, to 22%.[21] In these cases, and particularly the latter, the policy change does 'buy' more new personal wealth than it costs in tax revenue foregone. This conclusion is, though, sensitive to the assumptions of the model: if we reduce the EIS to 1/2 then the tax revenue

[19] In calculating the cumulated tax foregone, we assume that a return on tax receipts of 2.5% accrues in the public sector. If we instead ignore any return on tax receipts, then the 7% number would increase to 35%.

[20] Instead of calculating this number for a given age, we could have taken an average across all ages to represent total new saving in an economy in which every generation had been affected by the tax cut: this calculation would have suggested a 10% increase in national wealth.

[21] If returns to public funds are ignored, new national wealth would be approximately half of the extra personal wealth.

Table 7.2. Compensating variation in consumption required to make an agent indifferent between a 2% real interest rate with this compensation, and a 2.5% real interest rate

Case	A: CV (% increase in consumption)	B: % increase in cons available from tax	A–B
Baseline	2.13	1.90	0.23
EIS 1/2	2.95	2.65	0.30
EIS 1/4	4.17	3.44	0.72
No risk	0.70	0.61	0.09
Double risk	3.36	2.87	0.49
Family needs	2.11	1.31	0.80
Replacement rate 0.25	2.46	2.28	0.18
Replacement rate 0.75	1.84	1.56	0.27

foregone by the time of retirement is 2.5 times the amount of extra personal wealth held[22] and this factor increases as the EIS falls.

The preceding analysis suggests that the lower the EIS, the less cost effective is the policy of cutting the tax on the return to saving as a means of encouraging wealth accumulation. On the other hand, we have not so far considered the effect of the interest rate change on the well-being of individuals. To quantify this, we convert the change in expected lifetime utility at the beginning of life that results from the interest rate change, into a 'compensating variation' (CV) consumption value. This is the proportionate increase in consumption each period that would be required to make the individual indifferent between accepting the lower interest rate with this boost to consumption, or accepting the higher interest rate. Column A of Table 7.2 displays such CV values for several of the different examples that are described in the above pictures. Alongside these compensating variation values, column B of the table records the percentage increase in consumption per period that could be funded from the tax raised through taxing interest income. The final column in the table records the difference between columns A and B, which is the excess of the amount of compensation required over the amount that can be funded from the tax revenue.[23]

Column A of Table 7.2 shows that, for most of the cases considered, the change in welfare due to the hypothetical tax cut is equivalent to that deriving

[22] Ignoring returns on public funds reduces this factor to 1.75.

[23] It is unsurprising the CV always exceeds the tax revenue: the interest rate change represents a price distortion that is not corrected by the envisaged proportional adjustment to consumption each period.

from increasing consumption in the low interest rate regime by between 2% and 3% each period. The notable exceptions are the case with no risk, where the welfare change is equivalent to slightly less than 1% of consumption, and the case with a low EIS where a 4% increase in per period consumption is required.

Examples that might be considered practically important modifications of our baseline model are that with changing family circumstances (since these are an important part of many people's lives), and those with a reduced EIS (since, to anticipate Section 7.3.1, empirical evidence suggests this parameter may take a value of slightly less that the level of 1 that we use in our baseline and most of our simulations). As we saw in our analyses above, the reduction of the EIS and the introduction of family needs both reduce the response of savings behaviour to the change in the interest rate, relative to our baseline run (see, respectively Figures 7.9 and 7.12). However, Table 7.2 indicates that smaller behavioural responses do not necessarily reflect smaller welfare consequences of the change in the interest rate. This is particularly clear for the reduced EIS, where the CV increases substantially as the EIS falls, and although the tax raised increases at the same time this increase is not sufficient to fund the extra CV.[24] For the case of family needs, the implications are different: the compensating variation required is almost the same as in the baseline case, but since the presence of a family reduces saving and therefore the tax revenue over the life cycle, less of this payment could be covered from the tax revenue than is the case when family needs are not an issue.

Reflections on model results

We have seen that by using numerical techniques to solve and simulate a life-cycle model, we can analyse how much consumption and saving will respond to a change in the interest rate, and think about the welfare consequences of this change. For example, in the case analysed above that incorporated family needs (Figures 7.10–7.12), we found that increasing the interest rate from 2% to 2.5% raised retirement wealth by almost 20%. Assuming that the increased return had been due to a cut in the tax on interest income, we found that slightly more that 20% of the extra wealth held over the life cycle was not offset by lost tax revenue, and so was new national saving. Additionally, we were able to show that if the tax raised from cutting the asset return had been used to provide extra consumption, this would have provided about 60% of

[24] It is important to realize that this analysis is for a given tax *rate*, and the tax revenue will be changing across different versions of the model. If we had analysed constant tax *revenue*, then the welfare costs of taxing the return to assets would *increase* with the EIS.

the extra consumption required to compensate the family fully for the welfare lost due to taxing the asset return.

We should emphasize that this welfare conclusion is not sufficient to justify a policy of not taxing the return to savings. Given the need to raise revenue to fund public services, we must have distortionary taxes. The framework we have analysed does not provide us with knowledge of whether the welfare consequences of distortions induced by taxing saving are smaller or larger that those induced by other tax instruments (though see Banks and Diamond, Chapter 6).

Nonetheless, knowledge of how consumption and saving would respond to changes in the interest rate is clearly of interest to a policy maker wondering whether changing the rate of return is a good way to encourage saving. To illustrate why analysis of welfare consequences is a useful complement to this for the policy maker, the case of changing the EIS provides a useful example. The analysis suggested that the lower the EIS, the less cost effective is the policy of cutting the tax on the return to saving as a means of encouraging wealth accumulation. On the other hand, the welfare analyses showed that the welfare consequences of taxing saving *at a given rate* are more severe when the EIS is lower, notwithstanding that the response of saving to the change is also smaller. Thus, simply thinking about behavioural responses does not seem to give us sufficient information for evaluating a policy and the potential of our model to facilitate welfare analyses is a clear virtue of the framework in this context.

The potential of numerical techniques to provide specific predictions from a life-cycle model about saving behaviour and welfare is, then, what makes us optimistic about the potential for research to bridge the gap between the literatures that aim to build our knowledge of the life-cycle model, and to analyse whether tax privileges to certain assets achieve discernible increases in saving. The analyses of this section provide an early, small step across this gap. It should be emphasized that our analyses have been for a particular set-up of the life-cycle model, and slight modifications to it. Changes to the set-up could alter the conclusions and so to make analyses of the kind we have conducted relevant for considering actual or proposed policy reforms, it is important that the model is as realistic as possible. This requires accurate knowledge of key parameters such as the EIS and fortunately, as we argue in the next section, we do have quite convincing evidence about this parameter. The next section also surveys ongoing research on extensions such as the addition of labour supply, or of durable goods or habit formation, which are designed to increase the realism of the framework considered here. In considering this research, we will place particular emphasis on what is known about how such extensions modify the conclusions of the stylized model used in this section. A growing understanding of such extended versions of the life-cycle model will only add to its value as a flexible tool for thinking about how tax policy affects saving behaviour, and for interpreting existing evidence on responses to past tax reforms.

7.3. THE LIFE-CYCLE MODEL: WHERE DO WE STAND?

The model that we have used to perform the simple exercises in Section 7.2 is obviously, even in the most complicated version we have used, a fairly simple and to some extent unrealistic framework. Nonetheless we would argue that it constitutes a useful framework to address the issues we have been discussing. Such a stand must be justified on two grounds: first, the model is, at some level, an appropriate conceptualization of individual behaviour; second, the many simplifications we have introduced do not constitute a fundamental drawback of the structure we have used and the latter can provide useful insights. In this section, we will start by discussing the evidence on the plausibility of the life-cycle model. We will first consider structural estimates and tests of the model. We will then move on to consider indirect evidence on the relevance of some implications of the model that can be obtained from the reaction of individuals or groups of individuals to policy reforms. Finally, we will discuss some important aspects that were not included in the model used in Section 7.2 as well as some important alternatives to the life-cycle model.

7.3.1. The evidence on the life-cycle model[25]

In our opinion, since its initial formulation of the 1950s, there have been two important developments in the literature on consumption and the life cycle. First, since the 1970s, economists have learned to introduce uncertainty in a rigorous fashion in the theoretical framework. The assumption of rational expectations has had some important applications in the consumption literature, as we will discuss. While this has made the analytical properties of the model much harder, it has also revealed some important issues. While the precautionary saving motive was discussed already in Dreze and Modigliani

[25] Some of these issues are discussed in Attanasio (1999) and, more recently, in Attanasio and Weber (2009).

(1972), its implications have only been extensively explored much later (see, for instance, Carroll (1997)). Second, household level data have been brought to bear on the empirical relevance of the model and a number of contributions have made a serious attempt at complex specifications of preferences that could be brought to the data. From an empirical point of view, therefore, the first issue to confront is whether it is possible to write a plausible version of the model that is not rejected by individual level data. If the answer to this first question is positive, then one can estimate, using individual level data, the parameters that are crucial for policy analysis. In what follows, we first consider tests of the life-cycle–permanent income model. The aim is to answer the question: is the model we discussed in Section 7.2 at all relevant from an empirical point of view? We then discuss evidence on the size of the parameters that are important from a policy point of view.

Testing the model

Since Hall (1978), Sargent (1978), and Flavin (1981), the empirical analysis of the life-cycle model has taken two main strategies. Some contributions have used the so-called 'Euler equation' for consumption. This equation was discussed in some detail in Box 7.1 and expresses one of the main implications of the model: the consumer will choose consumption and saving so that at the optimum the ratio of expected marginal utilities of consumption at different dates is equal to the ratio of relative prices, that is, the interest rate. Given an assumption about the nature of expectations, the equation incorporates uncertainty in a relatively simple fashion. It is extremely useful for empirical analyses because it implies a relationship among observable variables (notably the interest rate and consumption growth—again see Box 7.1) that can be used to estimate preference parameters and to test the model.

The first focus of this literature, starting with Hall (1978), was on testing the model. In that first paper, the implication tested was that, conditional on current consumption (which under some preferences coincides with marginal utility), other current variables, including income, do not help in predicting future consumption. Subsequent papers (see, for instance, Campbell and Mankiw (1989)) tried to interpret rejection of this strong hypothesis in terms of market failures (liquidity constraints that force some individuals who would like to borrow against future income to consume no more than current income), or rationality failure ('rule of thumb' consumers who consume a fraction of their current income). Most of these papers (an exception being Hall and Miskin (1982)) used aggregate level data and completely neglected aggregation issues.

The life-cycle model is, of course, a theory of *individual* behaviour, and in the late 1980s and in the 1990s, some contributions started to fit the Euler equation to individual level data. Some of the relevant papers were Attanasio and Weber (1989, 1993, 1995), Blundell, Browning, and Meghir (1994), Banks, Blundell, and Preston (1994), Attanasio and Browning (1995). A short and definitely subjective and not unbiased summary of these results is that a rich version of the life-cycle model can fit the available data, especially if one focuses on households headed by prime aged individuals.

The datasets used in this literature contained a large amount of information on household characteristics as well as on consumption expenditure, and this meant that the empirical specification could be rich as well as theory consistent. It could allow, for instance, for a flexible role of demographics and family composition in preferences to reflect changes in needs (our analysis in Section 7.2 indicated how important family composition might be). Flexibility also meant that the specifications adopted in several of these papers were robust to the possibility that labour supply choices directly affect the (marginal) utility derived from consumption, because leisure and consumption are either complements or substitutes. Finally, most of these papers restricted the sample to households headed by prime aged individuals, excluding households headed by very young individuals and households headed by individuals around or past retirement ages.

Formal statistical tests, derived from theory, generally failed to reject versions of the model that were flexible enough and that were estimated on individual level data, and apparent violations of predictions of the model in aggregate data were often no longer evident. For example, with controls for demographics and labour supply, these papers based on individual level data typically found no evidence of 'excess sensitivity' through which, contrary to the predictions of the life-cycle model, consumption responds to predictable changes in income. Attanasio and Weber (1993) also showed that aggregation biases could explain some of the results in the literature based on aggregate data, such as the celebrated Campbell and Mankiw (1989) paper: when 'wrongly' aggregated, the micro data delivered estimates that were very similar to those obtained by Campbell and Mankiw (1989).

The big attraction of the Euler equation approach is that it can deliver an empirically treatable specification without necessarily making very strong assumptions. The approach is robust to the presence of several imperfections in different markets in which the individual acts, it is possible to control for possible interactions between choices concerning leisure and consumption, it can control in a reasonably flexible way for unobserved heterogeneity between individuals and, above all, it is not necessary to specify the whole stochastic environment in which the individual operates. The price one pays for this is that the approach does not deliver a 'consumption function'. It is therefore not possible to establish how consumption or saving will change in reaction to changes in the various variables faced by the individual. This is obviously an important limitation for policy analysis and probably explains the dichotomy mentioned above between the empirical consumption literature and the public finance literature. There are three possibilities to overcome this difficulty. One is to impose enough simplifying structure on the model that a consumption function can be derived; a second is to use numerical methods to obtain consumption functions; the third is to use approximations to the consumption function. We will now briefly discuss the first two.

One of the few cases in which a consumption function can be derived is that in which utility is quadratic and the only uncertainty comes from income. In such a case, Flavin (1981) and subsequently Campbell (1987) and Campbell and Deaton (1989) derived the cross equations restrictions implied by the model on the time series representation of income and consumption. Most of the papers that used this type of approach (including West (1988) and Hansen, Roberds, and Sargent (1991)) used time series aggregate data; one exception that looked at this type of restrictions on micro data is Nalewaik (2006). While the approach can be useful for empirical analysis, the assumptions required still seem difficult to sustain for policy analysis where the focus is on variation in the interest rate as well as fluctuations in income.

These considerations lead us back to the use of numerical methods (or approximations) to address this problem. And, indeed, starting with Deaton (1991), Hubbard, Skinner, and Zeldes (1995), Attanasio, Banks, Meghir, and Weber (1999) and others have developed methods to solve these models. The simulations presented in Section 7.2 are, in effect, an application of this approach.

The big difficulty of this approach, if it wants to be realistic and of policy relevance, is that one needs to specify all of the details of the stochastic environment in which the consumer lives. And, as should be clear from even the simple exercises reported in Section 7.2, some of these details are quantitatively and qualitatively important for the results one obtains. Moreover, even simple modifications of the basic model may introduce considerable complications at the numerical level. This was evident in some of the subsequent papers that have taken this approach, such as Palumbo (1999), who looked at health and consumption, Low (2005), who introduced endogenous labour supply choices, Diaz, Rios-Rull, and Pijoan-Mas (2003), who introduced habits, Gomes and Michaelides (2003), who looked at portfolio choices and habits and, more recently, Attanasio, Bottazzi, Low, Nesheim, and Wakefield (2007), Sanchez-Marcos and Rios-Rull (2006), and Bottazzi, Low, and Wakefield (2007), who introduce endogenous housing choices and, in the case of the last paper, housing and labour supply choices.

These computational difficulties notwithstanding, a remarkable recent paper by Scholz, Seshadri, and Khitatrakun (2006) has demonstrated the potential of the numerical approach. They construct a life-cycle simulation model that they use to predict the saving behaviour of a large set of individuals for whom they have data on earnings over a period of forty years. In the model they try to be as realistic as possible in terms of the institutional factors that might affect saving and consumption choices (taxation, government transfers, medical expenses, uncertainty, and so on), although they do acknowledge that constraints of data and computational feasibility mean that some features of the model, such as the treatment of housing wealth and of bequests and inheritances, remain stylized. They argue that the model 'accounts for more than 80% of the 1992 cross-sectional variation in wealth' and that 'fewer than 20% of households have less wealth than their optimal targets, and the wealth deficit of those who are undersaving is generally small'. While sensitivity to assumptions means that such results must be interpreted with caution, these results do challenge the popular wisdom, and some interpretations of a strand of literature discussed in Section 7.3.3, that many individuals are 'under saving'.

The difficulty in getting numerical solutions of even modestly realistic models implies that this approach can be used only with great difficulty for the estimation of parameters. A possibly more productive approach, which is effectively the one used in Section 7.2 and in the Scholz et al. (2006) paper just discussed, is to obtain estimates for some of the parameters from formal estimation, possibly using robust methods such as Euler equations, and others possibly from matching specific data moments. Key parameters having been retrieved in this way, numerical simulations can then be used to understand the policy implications of the realistically parameterized model.

Estimates of structural parameters: how substitutable is consumption over time? How impatient are consumers?

To simulate a model of the kind sketched in Section 7.2, one needs to specify a utility function and give a value to each of its parameters. As mentioned in the previous subsection, the specification of utility that has been extensively used in the literature that has estimated Euler equations on micro data is of the isoelastic type, with utility defined over consumption per adult equivalent.

Adult equivalent schemes are typically estimated in a flexible fashion and account for the role played by demographic variables in the Euler equation. In this context, the two crucial parameters to determine the size of the effects of changes to the economic environment faced by the agents (such as changes in the interest rate or in expected income) are the elasticity of intertemporal substitution and the discount factor. The former determines by how much consumption shifts between periods when its relative price in those periods changes (see Box 7.1). The latter determines how impatient consumers are and whether, given a certain level of the interest rate, consumption will be increasing or decreasing over time. We now discuss the empirical evidence on the size of these two parameters.

In his famous 1988 paper, Hall argued that, on the basis of aggregate time series data, there are strong reasons to believe that the elasticity of substitution of consumption is close to zero or very small. This is because relatively large (predictable) movements in interest rate do not seem to be associated with movements in (predictable) consumption growth. However, the EIS is a parameter that describes an individual's preferences, and in the late 1980s and 1990s several papers, starting from Attanasio and Weber (1989, 1993), used individual level data to estimate it.[26] These papers typically obtained larger estimates of the EIS than the value of 0.1 suggested by Hall: the values obtained typically ranged from 0.65 to figures slightly above 1. The implications of these much higher estimates for the taxation of saving are obvious, as showed by the simple computations in Section 7.2. And yet these findings have not been consistently used in the public finance literature.

Our choice of different sizes for the EIS in the simulation exercises presented in Section 7.2 should be indicative of what we think are plausible estimates that come out of the empirical literature on the topic. If one wants to fit an isoelastic utility function like the one in equation (*) in Box 7.1, micro data from both the US and the UK indicate that a plausible range of values for the EIS is 0.5 to 1. We would view values of the EIS below 0.4 as very low and values above 1, as too high.

Of course, the assumption of isoelastic preference is analytically and theoretically very convenient. However, there is some evidence that the EIS might change with the level of consumption (see Attanasio and Browning (1995), for instance). Given the discussion in Section 7.2 on the importance of the EIS for the size of the saving response to changes in tax policy, specifications

[26] These are essentially the same set of papers we mentioned at the top of p. 706, when discussing estimation of the Euler equation. As discussed in Box 7.1, a log-linear regression of consumption growth on the interest rate (the form of many empirical Euler equations) identifies the EIS.

of preferences that allow for a non-constant EIS should be an important item on the research agenda.

The second important preference parameter is the discount factor. Its size, relative to the size of the interest rate, defines whether a consumer is 'impatient' in the sense of Carroll (1997). Little evidence exists on the size of this parameter, especially based on micro data. The reasons for this paucity of evidence are many. Probably the most important is the difficulty in identifying such a parameter with any precision. Much of the empirical evidence on Euler equations from micro data comes from log-linearized versions of the equation. In such a situation, the discount factor gets buried into the intercept of the equation and cannot be identified. However, the lack of strong evidence on the size of this parameter might not be too important. As we mentioned above and perhaps not surprisingly, demographic effects have been shown to be very important in explaining variations in consumption over the life cycle. These variables typically enter preferences so that they act as a time varying discount factor. Therefore, possible variations in the level of consumption induced by changes in the discount factor can be dwarfed by changes in demographics and, possibly, the probability of surviving. Whether a consumer shows 'impatience' over the life cycle, consuming at levels close to her current income and saving little, might be driven more by the dynamics of her family size than the relationship between the interest and discount rates.

An indirect piece of evidence on the size of the discount factor and its heterogeneity in the population can be found in Attanasio, Banks, Meghir, and Weber (ABMW) (1999). In that paper, the authors present simulations of a life-cycle model with plausible preference parameters, including the effect of demographics on the utility of consumption, and show that variation in the timing of childbearing can help to explain variation in the shape of the life-cycle profile of consumption of different groups of households, defined in terms of the educational attainment of the household head. The one aspect of the data that the simplest version of the model presented by ABMW does not fit is the fact that consumption profiles peak at different ages for different education groups. A fit to this feature of data is achieved with different discount factors on top of different patterns of family size changes, assuming that less educated individuals are slightly more impatient.

7.3.2. When the simple model does not work

As we have mentioned several times, the model presented in Section 7.2 makes some very stark assumptions. In this subsection we analyse the implications of relaxing some of these assumptions with a focus on the issue of the effects of savings taxation. We start with relaxation of preference assumptions, then move on to assumptions about market structure and availability of intertemporal trades.[27] We conclude this subsection with a brief discussion of preference specifications that might be considered as substantial deviations from the standard model. It is worth noting that with all of these extensions, the factors that we discussed in Section 7.2 as determinants of how consumption and saving will respond to a change in the interest rate will still apply: the shift in the relative strength of income and substitution effects as the EIS changes will, for example, still be pertinent. However, some of the extensions we discuss (such as limits on borrowing that impose constraints on consumption) may restrict the extent to which these previously discussed factors can influence behaviour, while others (such as the modifications of the preference specification that we consider in this section at pp. 716–18) will add a further set of preference effects that must be taken into account.

Labour supply

An important assumption in the simulations we reported was that the income process was exogenous. As we mentioned above, this assumption can be justified with the assumption of 'separability' between leisure and consumption in the utility function, which says that labour supply choices have no direct effect on the (marginal) utility of consumption. Alternatively, the assumption could be justified if one can argue that labour supply is virtually fixed irrespective of the wage so that total income is effectively exogenous. Unfortunately, both these justifications are quite weak. While the second might be justified for men, female labour supply elasticities, both at the intensive (hours) and extensive (participation) margin can be sizeable. Moreover, as measured consumption often includes many items directly related to labour supply behaviour (from transport, to clothing, to home energy consumption), the hypothesis of separability is even conceptually difficult to defend. This has considerable implications for the dynamics of life-cycle consumption and saving, as well as for the response of individual savings to specific incentives.

As we mentioned above, specifications of Euler equations estimated on micro data often found significant labour supply effects, especially for female labour supply and especially at the extensive margin rather than the intensive

[27] Effectively in Section 7.2 we did consider an important deviation from the standard LC model: we did not allow consumers to borrow. Whether this makes a difference to the results we discussed depends on how binding the exogenously given borrowing restriction is, given the income profile and the needs of the individual family.

one (see, for example, Blundell, Browning, and Meghir (1994) and Attanasio and Weber (1993, 1995)). The non-separability of leisure and consumption in the utility function can induce a positive correlation between life-cycle movements in consumption and earnings and 'explain away' the excess sensitivity of income, a point first made by Heckman (1974) in response to a paper by Thurow (1969). Some papers that used aggregate time series data to estimate models with non-separable preferences between consumption and leisure include Mankiw, Rotemberg, and Summers (1985), and Eichenbaum, Hansen, and Richard (1988). The more recent papers mentioned above make the same point empirically within the context of the Euler equation estimated on individual level datasets.

While dealing with these effects with the Euler equation is relatively straightforward, incorporating the non-separability of consumption and leisure in simulation models that obtain numerical solutions for consumption and saving is considerably complex, especially if one considers the extensive margin with fixed costs of going to work. These costs introduce important non-convexities into the life-cycle optimization problem and thus make numerical solution much harder. Moreover, in the presence of tenure effects and the like, the wage process becomes endogenous and the number of state variables one has to keep track of for solving the problem increases. Although some studies now exist that construct life-cycle models with non-separable leisure and consumption and non-convexities,[28] we are not aware of simulations that have directly addressed the issue of the sensitivity of saving to taxation.

A paper that stresses the importance of endogenous labour supply for optimal taxation of capital (and labour) is the recent paper by Conesa, Kitao, and Krueger (CKK) (2007) who consider an overlapping generation model with uninsured idiosyncratic shocks and ability differential. The result that 'taxing capital is not a bad idea after all' and, in particular the high level of the optimal tax rate on capital in this model is in part due to the high elasticity of labour supply and the potential distortion induced in such a context by high labour taxes. It might be interesting to investigate more realistic models of labour supply behaviour (where the elasticity is much lower than that considered by CKK and maybe focused on the intensive margin). It would also be interesting to characterize the interactions between endogenous labour supply and different levels of the elasticity of intertemporal substitution for consumption.

[28] Low (2005), Attanasio, Low, and Sanchez-Marcos (2005, 2008), Bottazzi, Low, and Wakefield (2007) are examples of life-cycle models that incorporate explicitly labour supply with important non-convexities.

Intertemporal non-separabilities: durables and habits

So far we have considered models where preferences are intertemporally separable, that is, consumption in any period does not affect the marginal utility of consumption in subsequent periods. This assumption rules out models of habit formation. Moreover, if the only data on durable commodities are on expenditure (rather than the service flow provided by the stock of durables) and/or if durables are subject to adjustment costs, durable commodities also introduce important intertemporal non-separability in preferences.

Models of habit formation and intertemporal non-separability have a long history. In demand analysis, without uncertainty, the early contributions of Phlips and Spinnewyn (1984) and Spinnewyn (1981) used a dual approach that rewrote the dynamic non-additive problem in terms of an additive utility function that depends on appropriately defined stocks, rather than current consumption. Browning (1991) used a similar idea within a life-cycle model and presents results that allow one to incorporate both durables and habits. Browning (1991) does consider uncertainty but uses point expectations rather than rational expectations. Studies that used macro time series data to analyse intertemporally non-separable models include Eichenbaum and Hansen (1990), Mankiw (1982), Bernanke (1985), and Heaton (1993, 1995). In the 1990s, habits have become very popular as a way to explain certain puzzles concerning asset pricing (see, for instance, Campbell and Cochrane (1999)).

Surprisingly few papers have used micro data to study models with habits. Meghir and Weber (1996) use US Consumer Expenditure Survey (CEX) data to estimate a demand system nested in a life-cycle model which allows for habits, while Dynan (2000) uses the US Panel Study of Income Dynamics (PSID). The remarkable result that Meghir and Weber find is that while the demand system (based on a few commodities) does exhibit persistence, this seems to be entirely explained by non-separability between durables and non-durables, rather than by habits. Padula (1999) presents Euler equation estimates for non-durable consumption that also show strong non-separability between non-durable consumption and the services of the stock of cars, for which he has observations in the CEX.

While the absence of intertemporal separability is likely to have important consequences for the reaction of savings to changes in intertemporal prices, these have not been explored, to the best of our knowledge, in the literature. The only literature that has extensively analysed the implications of different types of intertemporal non-separabilities is the asset pricing literature. As noted by Hansen and Jaganathan (1991), one of the reasons for the empirical failure of some popular asset pricing models is the low variability in the price that individuals are prepared to pay in the light of different information about the future, in order to buy a given amount of consumption in the future. Habits (or other forms of non-separabilities) can substantially improve the fit of these models because they effectively increase the variability that can be exploited. An interesting research agenda would be to check what are the implications of this class of models for the responsiveness of saving to the interest rate and, possibly, for the optimal taxation of capital. To answer such a question, however, one has to be specific both about the nature of the non-separability over time (whether current and present consumption are substitutes or complements would obviously make a difference) and about the magnitude of such intertemporal links.

Intertemporal trades restrictions: liquidity constraints

The basic textbook model assumes that the consumer is able to borrow and save at the same interest rate without limit, except the obligation to repay any debt with certainty. This last constraint, if the utility function implies very high disutility of very low consumption levels, effectively imposes a limit to the amount that an individual will want to borrow. If the income process is not bounded away from zero (that is if zero income is a non-zero probability event), then people will not want to borrow. However, even such potentially tight constraint is sometimes perceived as not tight enough. In particular, many researchers think that although income processes might be bounded away from zero (by some type of safety net, for instance), some individuals might find it difficult to borrow in situations where they would want to. If that is the case, the Euler equation will not hold as an equality, but as an inequality: the current marginal utility of consumption will be higher than the discounted future expected marginal utility as, if they could, individuals would bring resources forward and increase current consumption. It is perceived that this problem is particularly relevant for young consumers who face an upward-sloping income profile and yet might find it difficult to move resources forward. This is one reason why the studies on Euler equations based on micro data typically exclude very young individuals[29] and why in the simulations in Section 7.2 we explicitly considered the case in which individuals could not borrow at all.

[29] When the study is based on time series of cross-sections that are used to construct synthetic cohorts (or pseudo panels) it is thought that at the beginning of the life cycle the composition of households headed by young individuals changes systematically as new households are formed.

The case in which there is a binding and exogenous limit to the amount an individual can borrow is relatively simple to analyse. Such a constraint implies a kink in the intertemporal budget constraint and some households will bunch on that corner. In the period in which the constraint is binding, the individual will consume her income (and run down assets completely). In this respect that period is equivalent to the last period of life: it has been pointed out (see Hayashi (1987)) that a binding liquidity constraint is equivalent to a shortening of the planning horizon and/or to an increase in the discount factor. In such a situation, it is relatively useful to analyse the effect of changes in the interest rate: anything that would lead to an increase in consumption would not have any effect. Consumers at a kink of an intertemporal budget constraint would be less responsive to changes in the interest rate although a sufficiently large increase in the interest rate might induce the consumer to move away from the corner and possibly start to save. However, even in this case, the reaction is likely to be more muted than would be observed in the absence of a constraint.

The presence of liquidity constraints is a symptom of a more general phenomenon which is the incompleteness of insurance markets to allow individuals efficiently to diversify idiosyncratic risk. This type of market incompleteness is central to some of the models, such as that studied by Conesa, Kitao, and Krueger (2006) that imply positive rates of taxation of capital. And yet, the origin of these markets failures is not clear.

Housing and associated market imperfections

Alongside pensions, housing constitutes the largest item in household portfolios, both in the US and in the UK. Moreover, housing is a unique type of asset: it provides a flow of services that consumers enjoy, it is lumpy and can only be transacted and changed by incurring often substantial costs. House prices are often and in many places extremely volatile, and particularly so in the UK (see Banks, Blundell, Oldfield, and Smith (2004)). These fluctuations in the value of houses and the important role they play in household portfolios can generate important wealth effects that have been argued to fuel consumption booms (see, for instance, Muellbauer and Murphy (1990)), although others have argued that an increase in house prices constitutes a disincentive to consumption for households who are net purchasers of housing services (see King (1990); Attanasio and Weber (1994)).

In addition to these considerations, in many countries, including the US and, in the past, the UK, the liabilities associated with housing (such as mortgages) receive special tax treatment relative to other assets and liabilities.

In particular, in the US mortgage interest payments are tax-deductible. In the UK a similar treatment was recently removed. This type of treatment of course adds an attraction to the fact that the housing services enjoyed by home owners are not taxed.[30] Finally, houses can often be used as collateral for borrowing. This means that when house values increase, households might find it easier to borrow for a variety of reasons (see Lustig and Van Nieuwerburgh (2005)).

For all these reasons, housing should play a very important role in every analysis of life-cycle consumption and saving. And yet, very little is known about the interactions of housing and saving/consumption choices. Some papers take a reduced form approach (Attanasio and Weber (1994); Attanasio et al. (2009); Campbell and Cocco (2007); Bottazzi (2004)) although they explicitly use the life-cycle model as a framework to organize the empirical evidence. More recently, some contributions have started to build realistic life-cycle models that include an important role for housing (see Attanasio et al. (2007); Attanasio, Leicester, and Wakefield (2008); Bottazzi, Low, and Wakefield (2007); Li and Yao (2007); and Sanchez-Marcos and Rios-Rull (2006)). The last of these papers even tries to explain the evolution of the house prices. An early attempt at constructing such a model was contained in Ortalo-Magne and Rady (2006).

The papers we cite here constitute only a small first step in the investigation of what we think is an important research agenda. There are still many unanswered questions about the role of housing in life-cycle models, many of which are relevant for the issues discussed in this chapter. We do not have a good equilibrium model and understanding of house prices. We do not fully understand the role of houses and of the fluctuations in their prices in individual wealth accumulation decisions. We do not fully understand the effect of privileged tax treatment of housing on saving behaviour and how this interacts with other forms of wealth taxation.

Hyperbolic discounting and temptations

One of the basic blocks of the intertemporal consumption model described above and extensively used in the literature is that individuals are assumed to discount the future with a constant discount factor. Such a 'geometric discounting' assumption has recently been argued to be implausible. In the past ten years, David Laibson, and Ted O'Donoghue and Matthew Rabin,

[30] Local taxation in the UK is based on property value, but the link to the value of housing services is not very clear for this banded tax and, perhaps more importantly when we are thinking about the taxation of assets, the tax is based on residence rather than ownership.

have been the main promoters of an apparently slight deviation from geometric discounting: hyperbolic or quasi-geometric discounting. This model, that has recently received a considerable amount of attention and originates in the work of Strotz (1956) and Phelps and Pollak (1968), assumes that while the discounting between subsequent dates in the far future is geometric (the ratio of utility at any two future dates $t + k$ and $t + k + 1$ is β) the factor that discounts the immediate future relative to the present is smaller than β so that current utility is weighted more highly than in the geometric case. This model has been deemed to be able to explain several phenomena, such as the tendency to procrastinate over saving decisions and the demand for commitment devices (see Laibson (1994, 1997); Harris and Laibson (2001); and O'Donoghue and Rabin (1999a, 1999b)). Recently, Angeletos et al. (2001) have calibrated such a model using numerical methods similar to those discussed above to construct life-cycle profiles similar to those we presented in Section 7.2, while Laibson, Repetto, and Tobacman (2005) use simulation based estimation methods in an attempt to pin down the discount function. Harris and Laibson (2001) derive an Euler equation relevant for a hyperbolic discounter.[31] Finally, some interesting field experiments (Karlan and Zinman (2008)) have tested for the presence of a demand for commitment devices in saving markets in the Philippines using a randomized trial.

The hyperbolic discounting model, however, is not without drawbacks. The main problem, already noticed by Strotz half a century ago, is that the preferences induced by hyperbolic discounting are time inconsistent. Effectively, instead of one consumer, we have to deal with many selves (the same individual at different points in time) that interact in determining intertemporal choices. This leads to conceptual difficulties with welfare analysis.[32] A second consequence of 'multiple-selves', as noted forcefully by Krusell and Smith (1998) among others, is the presence of multiple equilibria and the consequent difficulty in characterizing intertemporal consumption allocations.

The problems with the hyperbolic discounting model make the recent contributions of Gul and Pesendorfer (2001, 2004) (GP) particularly interesting. These authors build an axiomatic representation of preferences that yield a utility function in which, in addition to the standard terms, a consumer is affected by the temptation of immediate gratification. In particular, utility is assumed to be affected not only by the choice a consumer makes, but also

[31] The empirical applicability of such an Euler equation is doubtful as it requires the evaluation of the derivative of the value function.

[32] Laibson, and O'Donohue and Rabin, have proposed different measures of welfare in these models.

by the choice set from which the choice is made. In this framework, while consuming a certain consumption stream the consumer is also affected by other unchosen streams as they might tempt her and/or force her to exercise costly self-restraint. This structure is captured by two different functions, the first defined as usual over consumption and the second that describes the 'temptation' the consumer might face. The self-control issue induced by this second function generates a utility loss for the consumer.

An advantage of the GP preferences is that they are time consistent while still creating a demand for commitment devices. The GP type specification also evidently generates an extra set of preference effects in responses of consumption and saving to changes in the interest rate, on top of the standard income, substitution, and wealth effects discussed in Section 7.2.1, pp. 686–7. A growing number of studies are now starting to apply these preferences to analyse policy issues: Krusell, Kuruscu, and Smith (2001) embed the GP preferences in a neoclassical growth model to analyse taxation and welfare; Esteban, Miyagawa, and Shum (2007) apply these preferences to derive the optimal selling strategy of a firm facing consumers with self-control problems; Bucciol (2007a) looks at the implications for the design of pension systems while Bucciol (2007b) derives Euler equations that can potentially be taken to data.

7.3.3. The empirical relationship between savings and changes in wealth and intertemporal prices

The evidence on the life-cycle model we discussed in Section 7.3.1 is based on a formal and rigorous approach that takes uncertainty very seriously and exploits the first order conditions of the dynamic problem the consumers are assumed to solve. An alternative and complementary approach is to consider the effects of large reforms that, in a life-cycle framework, should have important implications for consumption and saving plans. Such reforms can be used both to assess the overall validity of the life-cycle model and, in some cases, to measure some of the quantities and elasticities that we have been discussing.

We divide our discussion of the available empirical evidence into two parts. First, we discuss evidence that exploits variation in the value of individual wealth and therefore can change the incentives to save and consume. These changes include changes in pension wealth induced by legislative reforms, changes in house values induced by movement in house prices, and changes in the value of financial wealth induced by movements in stock prices. Second, we discuss evidence on the effects of changes in the return to specific assets, possibly induced by tax incentives designed to stimulate savings.

To anticipate, our discussion points to several broad conclusions. First, when a shock increases wealth in one part of the portfolio, this does (as the life-cycle model would predict) lead to offsetting changes in other parts of the portfolio, although the offset is often found to be somewhat below one-for-one. Second, when the return on a particular asset is increased (perhaps through a tax break), this generally leads to saving in that asset but for at least some groups this saving may be largely due to reshuffling of wealth out of other assets and so not all of the wealth is new personal—let alone new national—saving. These findings are in line with the model presented in Section 7.2 and our best estimates of key parameters as discussed in Section 7.3.1, pp. 708–10. However, the empirical evidence discussed below also points to some heterogeneity in effects across different wealth shocks or policy reforms, and this often seems to be related to the information available to individuals making decisions, and/or the way they form expectations. Thus the provision of information may be an important element of how policy affects consumption and saving.

Changes in wealth

From a theoretical point of view, the relationship between exogenous changes in wealth and savings is fairly clear, as we showed in the simulations reported in Section 7.2. By increasing the generosity of the pension system one reduces the necessity to save for retirement and, in general, savings will be reduced as a consequence. The analysis of the relationship between pension wealth and savings has a long history: Feldstein (1974) tried to use time series variation in the generosity of US social security to analyse such a relationship. King and Dicks-Mireaux (1982) instead studied the cross-sectional variation in financial and pension wealth to estimate the degree of substitutability between the two. Attanasio and Brugiavini (2003) was one of the first papers to use a pension reform (the 1992 reform of the Italian Pay-As-You-Go system) to look at the same issue.

The UK is a particularly interesting case study because of the large number of reforms that, since the 1970s, the public pension system underwent. Attanasio and Rohwedder (2003) use some of these reforms to analyse the effect of the changes they induced in various pension wealth on savings and, indirectly, the degree of substitutability between financial and pension wealth. In particular, they analyse two reforms: the introduction of the State

Earnings-Related Pension Scheme (SERPS) in 1978 and the November 1980 change in the indexation of the Basic State Pension from earnings to prices, which has led to a substantial relative decline over time in its value. Attanasio and Rohwedder (2003) use the fact that these reforms hit different cohorts at different ages, to estimate the degree to which public pensions (in various forms) crowd out private saving at different points in the life cycle. Their evidence suggests that when SERPS was introduced middle-aged households offset around two-thirds of the implied new state pension wealth by adjusting consumption and other forms of saving. The offset was more complete for older households. This evidence suggests that income effects (and not just substitution effects) affect households' decisions on saving for retirement. Attanasio and Rohwedder (2003) interpret this evidence within a simple life-cycle model, which logically would imply that a reduction in the generosity of a pension system would induce an increase in savings. This conclusion, however, should be tempered by the second piece of evidence in the study, which shows that the reduction in generosity, in 1980, of the Basic State Pension, induced by the change in its indexation mechanism, did not lead to a 'crowding in' on financial wealth. One possibility is that the generosity of the introduction of SERPS was more widely understood than the reduction in the generosity implied by changing indexation. This could be related to the amount of publicity surrounding the two reforms or to public perception over how permanent the changes were likely to be—particularly as SERPS was introduced with cross-party support whereas opposition parties have often been in favour of indexing the Basic State Pension in line with earnings.

If individuals do not fully adjust their personal wealth to accommodate social security wealth, then this may show up in consumption patterns later in life, pointing to an important failure of the life-cycle model, which assumes rationality of saving decisions and rational expectations. Banks, Blundell, and Tanner (1998) (BBT) started a small literature examining how consumption changes around the time of retirement. The fact that consumption falls in retirement is well documented. But this does not necessarily mean that individuals had not saved enough—some part of the drop in consumption may be planned and related to changes in work status. Moreover, if one does not use panel data but a time series of cross-sections, the changes in average consumption will be gradual and could also be explained by changes in family composition and other factors that move more slowly, as well as by declines in labour force participation. By modelling individuals' life-time consumption plans, BBT find that around two-thirds of the drop in consumption growth at retirement that occurred for those cohorts retiring in the 1970s, 1980s, and early 1990s can be explained within the context of an optimal consumption plan. The residual third remains a puzzle, with one possible explanation being that at least some individuals had not saved enough. Alternatively, there may be a set of people for whom adverse shocks are important: evidence from panel data (Smith (2006)) suggests that it is those who left the labour market as a result of an employment or health shock who experienced a decline in their food spending and potential indicators of their well-being around the time they left paid employment.

The evidence in BBT for the UK was confirmed for the US by Bernheim Skinner and Weinberg (2001) and by Miniaci, Monfardini, and Weber (2003) for Italy. More recently, however, Aguiar and Hurst (2005) convincingly argue that the drop in food expenditure documented by Bernheim, Skinner, and Weinberg (2001) for the US can be explained by a shift in amount of time spent preparing food and shopping. No similar studies exist for the UK.

The evidence in BBT is important for our discussion because it casts some doubt on the ability of the life-cycle model, at a crucial juncture of the life cycle, to explain savings and consumption. The possibility that the failure of the version of the model is explained by a failure of the rational expectation hypothesis is related to the discussion of the results in Attanasio and Rohwedder (2003) on the failure of individual saving to respond to changes in the value of the Basic State Pension. When individuals respond to the pension system and reforms to it, and indeed when they respond to tax incentives, they will be responding given their own understanding, beliefs, and expectations about the systems and reforms that they are faced with. It may be that those beliefs and expectations do not fully capture the nature of a particular part of the pension system, either because individuals do not fully understand some element of the system or because they believe that some part of the system is not credible or will not endure. If beliefs and expectations do not wholly reflect the current rules of the system, then we cannot expect to observe responses to all elements of the system that would accord with the predictions of an economic theory that is predicated on a full understanding and belief of current rules. An important research agenda, therefore, is one that looks at the information available to individual households when making important saving decisions and at their ability to process it efficiently.

Fortunately, new surveys, such as the Health and Retirement Study (HRS) in the US and the English Longitudinal Study of Ageing (ELSA) in the UK and the Survey of Health Ageing and Retirement in Europe (SHARE) for several European countries, have started to collect data on individuals' expectations that are relevant for their retirement savings decisions.[33] Evidence from ELSA suggests that individuals have quite accurate expectations about some features of their likely retirement, but are less good at predicting other elements. Expectations of being in paid employment at older ages are, on average, similar to the current proportions of older individuals who are in paid work (Banks, Emmerson, Oldfield, and Tetlow (2005)). In addition individuals' expectations of remaining in the labour market at older ages appear to square up with the marginal financial incentives to remain in work: relative to those in SERPS those aged 50 to 54 who are currently in a defined benefit pension on average report that they are less likely, and those who are currently in a defined contribution pension on average report that they are more likely, still to be in paid work five years prior to the State Pension Age (Banks, Blundell, and Emmerson (2005)). On the other hand, on average men and (in particular) women aged 50 and over underestimate their chances of survival to older ages (Banks, Emmerson, and Oldfield (2004)). There is also evidence that, on average, individuals are, if anything, over-optimistic about the amount of private pension income that they can expect to receive (Banks, Emmerson, Oldfield, and Tetlow (2005)).

Good data on expectations of outcomes from pensions is not only interesting in itself, but may also be informative for assessing why individuals respond to the pension system in the way that they do. For example, by using data on retirement expectations and wealth holdings of households in Italy during a recent period of state pension reforms, Bottazzi, Jappelli, and Padula (2006) are able to assess how these reforms affected expectations and then to infer how fully individuals' changes in saving behaviour reflected their new beliefs. They conclude that individuals did not immediately fully internalize the implications of a series of pension reforms in their expectations of retirement outcomes, and that even their expectations about changes in social security wealth were not fully accommodated through changes in private wealth accumulation. Such evidence that inaccurate expectations may be influencing savings decisions is very important since it implies that if different policies are not equally well understood by the affected population then evidence on how saving responds to a particular reform may not be transferable to other episodes even when the same population of savers is involved.

[33] Wave 11 (2001) of the British Household Panel Survey (BHPS) containing a question on individuals self-reported chance of living to age 75 (for those aged under 65) and questions on expected private pension income. The Bank of Italy Survey of Household Income and Wealth, has pioneered questions on replacement rates, expected retirement age, and more generally about income expectations, for some time now.

As we mentioned above, in many countries the largest item in many household portfolios is housing. It is not surprising, therefore, that the relationship between house values and consumption has received a fair amount of attention, especially in a country where house prices have moved considerably, such as the UK. Muellbauer and Murphy (1990), for instance, explain the late 1980s consumption boom as being caused by the increase in house prices over the same period coupled with the development of financial markets that enabled people to borrow against the increased value of their homes. Attanasio and Weber (1994) on the other hand, by looking at micro data, point out that most of the increase in consumption was observed among young consumers, who did not experience large capital gains as ownership rates are lower for that group. Instead, they present simulations of a very simple life-cycle model in which consumers experience an upward revision of future income growth and generate a cross-sectional response (across cohorts) very similar to that observed in the data.[34]

Dynan and Maki (2001) analyse the effect of capital gains in the stock market on consumption in the US. They find sizeable effects on saving and consumption of changes in financial wealth. In particular, they 'estimate that an additional dollar of wealth leads households with moderate securities holdings to increase consumption between 5 cents and 15 cents, with the most likely gain in the lower part of this range'.

Changes in interest rates

There is also a small empirical literature that looks at the effects of changes in interest rates on individual products on savings. Most of these studies look at the changes in the rate of return induced by tax incentives on specific instruments. An early attempt to stimulate household saving by increasing the return on specific assets providing a privileged tax treatment was, in the early 1980s, tried in the US by widening the availability of Individual Retirement Accounts. Subsequently, the focus shifted to the 401k plans that many employers offer in the US. The 401k plans are much more complex than the original IRAs as they often combine the tax exemption with employer's matching contributions and occasionally with financial education (through workshops, newsletters, and so on).

The issue of whether the tax treatment of these assets has increased personal and/or national saving has been hotly debated. One side of the debate

[34] Attanasio et al. (2009) extends the Attanasio and Weber study to more recent years and confirms its basic findings. These contrast with those reported in Campbell and Cocco (2007).

has strongly argued that it has, while another side has argued that most of the large number of contributions to IRAs first and 401ks later have been originated from reshuffling savings that would have occurred regardless. The absence of experimental data has made a definitive answer on this problem difficult to obtain, although many of the papers in this literature[35] have used ingenious methods to assess the counterfactual of what would have been the level of savings of IRA or 401k contributors in the absence of these incentives.

The more recent contributions on the topic have shifted the focus to what is the most common asset, that is 401k accounts. Benjamin (2003), for instance, uses an IV approach to estimate the effect of participation into a 401k programme on net financial assets using 401k eligibility as an instrument and finds a reasonably large effect of 401ks onto private and even national saving. Subsequently, Chernozhukov and Hansen (2004), have used an Instrumental Quantile Regression Analysis to analyse the same data studied by Benjamin and allow for effect heterogeneity. They found that while the effect of the programme on net financial assets seems to be increasing with household wealth, for richer consumers substitution from other sources of wealth seem to be important and it is only for poorer consumers that most of the 401k wealth seems to be 'new' wealth.

If one were to use the life-cycle model and the simulations we performed in Section 7.2, one would conclude that the pure incentive effects of these tax incentives would be, in all likelihood, relatively small. According to the literature we surveyed on the empirical relevance of the life-cycle model, this would not be a completely nonsensical exercise. The Scholz et al. (2006) we cited above, does justify the use of an appropriately detailed version of the model. Moreover, this result would be consistent with the evidence in Attanasio and DeLeire (2002), Gale and Scholz (1994), and Engen, Gale, and Scholz (1996).

The versions of the life-cycle model we considered, however, do not consider explicitly the issue of information and expectation. There is some evidence (see, for instance, Bernheim and Garrett (1995)) that 401k plans might have had an effect on saving by changing the information used by consumers in their investment choices and their financial literacy. This view would also be consistent with the evidence presented in a remarkable new study (see Duflo et al. (2006)) which reports evidence from a randomized trial of saving

[35] A survey article by Bernheim (2002) or the symposium in the *Journal of Economic Perspectives* (1996), with Engen, Gale, and Scholz arguing that the tax incentives had led to little new national saving, Poterba, Venti, and Wise favouring the opposite viewpont, and Hubbard and Skinner adjudicating, provide good introductions to this literature. Some of the key research papers include Venti and Wise (1990); Poterba, Venti, and Wise (1995); Gale and Scholz (1994); Engen, Gale, and Scholz (1996); and Attanasio and DeLeire (2002).

incentives focused on low and middle income families. The authors of that paper conclude that the evidence shows that both incentives and information are important. The focus on the saving behaviour of low and middle income families is particularly relevant for the UK.

As for the case of pensions, the UK provides a very interesting case study, given the variety of new products that have been introduced by the government in an attempt to stimulate the savings, especially of low and middle income families. We have several examples of tax relief on the returns accruing to accessible savings, starting with the introduction of Personal Equity Plans (PEPs) and Tax Exempt Special Savings Accounts (TESSAs), and more recently with the more flexible Individual Savings Accounts (ISAs) (see Adam, Browne, and Heady in Chapter 1 for some discussion of these products, or Attanasio, Banks, and Wakefield (2005) for a fuller discussion).

However, data limitations make it hard to conduct thorough econometric analysis of the UK experience of these accounts, but descriptive evidence is available, again in Attanasio, Banks, and Wakefield (2005). Aggregate evidence on the balances held in TESSAs indicates that these balances tended to jump immediately when new contributions to accounts could be made in a new year, and also that average contributions were often close to the maximum amounts that could be deposited in accounts. This, it is argued, is at least consistent with a pattern of individuals largely reshuffling existing wealth into TESSAs, rather than making substantial new savings during the relatively limited number of years that the accounts operated.

The authors also present microeconomic data on the experience of ISAs which indicate that while the take-up of ISAs was quite high, there is no strong evidence that this had much affect on overall ownership of non-pension financial assets or on levels of saving among those with such assets. However, there was some evidence of an increase in ownership of financial assets among low education groups and the young. This could suggest that ISAs were successful in being more attractive to low-income savers than TESSAs or PEPs had been (chapter 5 of HM Treasury (2000)). On the other hand, this evidence was far from overwhelming and at least one earlier study using micro data had argued that ISAs were little better than TESSAs and PEPs at reaching some low-income groups (Paxton (2003)).

Attanasio, Banks, and Wakefield argue that the UK evidence that they present is consistent with US evidence concerning tax deferred 'Individual Retirement Accounts' (IRAs) that is drawn from Attanasio and DeLeire (2002). Attanasio and DeLeire use short horizon panel data on consumption and argue that while around 40% of contributions to IRAs in the 1980s may have been additional personal saving, once account is taken of the cost of tax relief then less than one dollar in ten of contributions could be considered to be new national saving. Thus, for the cases that they consider, Attanasio, Banks, and Wakefield conclude that 'only relatively small fractions of the funds going into tax-advantaged savings vehicles can be considered to be "new" saving. As such, the best interpretation of the evidence is that such policies are expensive ways of encouraging savings.'

From a conceptual point of view, it should be stressed that the type of tax incentives considered in this literature do not fit neatly within the type of exercise we have been considering in Section 7.2 because in that model we considered only one asset paying *the* interest rate. In this context, instead, we have many assets that form household portfolios and the incentive provided changes the return on *some* but not all assets. A useful simulation, therefore, would also have to consider the portfolio problem and the influence that the incentive has on the portfolio allocation. Within this context one should also consider the role played by pensions that, on the one hand, have important tax advantages, while, on the other, they often involve penalties for early withdrawals. The latter make the numerical simulations like those presented in Section 7.2 considerably harder.

7.4. CONCLUSIONS

In this chapter we have discussed the implications that the life-cycle model has for the effects of the taxation of saving. We started from the fact that even if the life-cycle model is probably one of the best studied and understood models in economics, quantifying the effects that changes to the interest rate might have on the level and pattern of saving is not completely obvious. There are several reasons for this ambiguity.

First, as is well known, within the life-cycle model several competing effects are triggered by a change in the interest rate: substitution effects, income effects, and wealth effects. Moreover, and more importantly for our discussion, how these effects interact with each other depends crucially on the details of the model. The nature of the income process, the evolution of individual needs (such as family size) over the life cycle, the intertemporal trades individuals can access, and pension arrangements all affect in a quantitatively important fashion the responsiveness of the saving to changes in the interest rate and/or the welfare consequences of such changes. To illustrate this point we simulated a reasonably realistic life-cycle model and discussed how this responsiveness changes as features of the model change.

Second, there are reasons to believe that the simplest version of the life-cycle model does not necessarily describe the way individuals act and that realistic deviations from the basic version could have important implications. For this reason, we discussed several deviations from the basic model: we considered the case in which labour supply is non-separable from consumption, the case of intertemporal non-separabilities such as durables or habits, the case of various forms of market imperfections, and the role of housing, amongst other factors. The message that emerges from this discussion is that, unfortunately, there are many issues that are likely to be very important and yet we do not know their quantitative relevance for the issues discussed in this chapter. In our opinion, these constitute important items on the research agenda for the future.

Third, although part of the literature has constructed versions of the life-cycle model that seem to fit some aspects of behaviour, especially for prime aged individuals, there are other aspects that are not captured by the same model or by some of the assumptions typically used in the literature. In particular, it is worth stressing that post-retirement behaviour is particularly difficult to capture and that we do not know much about the early part of the life cycle. Moreover, the assumption of rational expectations sometimes seems a particularly strong one, making a research agenda that looks at the information that people use in making intertemporal decisions (as well as at patterns of evolution of cognitive capabilities) particularly interesting and important.

We have also briefly looked at models that depart substantially from the basic rationality assumption typically used in the life-cycle model. We have mentioned two strands that have been quite visible in the literature: the hyperbolic discounting literature and the temptation literature.

In the last part of Section 7.3, we have considered empirical evidence that, while sometimes using the life-cycle model as a conceptual framework, relies on large policy or other large changes in the economic environment in which individuals operate to identify some of the elasticities that are relevant for the relationship between savings and intertemporal prices. What is remarkable is that this literature (whether testing the degree of separability between pension and financial wealth or testing whether tax incentives can increase savings) has, by and large, been divorced from the formal analysis of the life-cycle model.

What can we conclude from our discussion? We offer some tentative conclusions and propose some themes for future research.

1. The life-cycle model is an extremely useful framework that can be used to conceptualize the analysis of saving and consumption behaviour. However, if one wants to take the model to the data for serious quantitative prediction, it is necessary to work with relatively complex and sophisticated versions of the model that take into account a number of factors that have been proven to be empirically important.
2. Numerical simulations are a very useful instrument to answer the questions posed by the use of complex versions of the basic model. While our ability to deal with more complex models has improved considerably, much work remains to be done to incorporate in workable versions of the model many realistic and important details bound to have first order importance.
3. Given the basic structure of the model it is unlikely that changes in interest rates due to preferential taxation or other movements to interest rates will cause big changes in the level of saving. However, that does *not* necessarily imply that the welfare consequences of taxing asset returns would be small. Furthermore, evidence does indicate that people respond to changes in relative interest rates (possibly induced by tax policy) by adjusting portfolio composition.
4. The quantitative implications of more complicated versions of the life-cycle model that involve endogenous labour supply, durables, housing, and so on need to be explored as we still do not have a good idea of what role these phenomena (which are bound to be of first order importance) play.
5. Models with temptation and with information problems are also worth exploring and developing so that they can be brought to data.

This set of conclusions indicates that there remain several research agendas to pursue to complete our understanding of the life-cycle model and the behavioural and welfare consequences of policies that affect the return on saving.

To make more precise recommendations about *how much* we should tax the return to saving will require embedding the insights of the life-cycle model into a framework that introduces other types of taxation and so can contrast the welfare costs of taxing saving against those from taxing other sources of income, or consumption expenditures. Chapter 6, by Banks and Diamond, considers what is known about such frameworks and so often uses the life-cycle model as an input to address the issue of whether our benchmark for taxing saving should be the tax on other incomes, or the zero taxation proposed in the expenditure tax set-up.

REFERENCES

Aguiar, M., and Hurst, E. (2005), 'Consumption vs. Expenditure', *Journal of Political Economy*, **113**, 919–48.

Angeletos, G., Laibson, D., Repetto, A., Tobacman, J., and Weinberg, S. (2001), 'The Hyperbolic Consumption Model: Calibration, Simulation and Empirical Evaluation', *The Journal of Economic Perspectives*, **15**, 47–68.

Attanasio, O. P. (1999), 'Consumption', in Taylor, J. B., and Woodford, M. (eds.), *Handbook of Macroeconomics*, vol. 1, Elsevier.

—— Banks, J., Meghir, C., and Weber, G. (1999), 'Humps and Bumps in Lifetime Consumption', *Journal of Economic and Business Statistics*, **17**, 22–35.

—— —— and Wakefield, M. (2005), 'Effectiveness of Tax Incentives to Boost (Retirement) Saving', OECD Economic Studies, Special Issue: Tax-favoured retirement saving, No. 39, pp. 145–72.

—— Blow, L., Hamilton, R., and Leicester, A. (2009), 'Booms and Busts: Consumption, Expectations and House Prices in the UK', *Economica*, **76**, 20–50.

—— Bottazzi, R., Low, H. W., Nesheim, L., and Wakefield, M. (2007), *The Demand for Housing Over the Life-cycle*, mimeo: IFS.

—— and Browning, M. (1995), 'Consumption over the Life Cycle and over the Business Cycle', *American Economic Review*, **85**, 1118–35.

—— and Brugiavini, A. (2003), 'Social Security and Households' Saving', *Quarterly Journal of Economics*, **118**, 1075–120.

—— and Deleire, T. (2002), 'The Effect of Individual Retirement Accounts on Household Consumption and National Saving', *The Economic Journal*, **112** (July), 504–38.

—— Leicester, A., and Wakefield, M. (2008), 'Does House Price Growth Drive Consumption Growth in the U.K.?', mimeo: IFS (paper prepared for the National Bureau of Economic Research Summer Institute, Boston, July 2008).

—— Low, H. W., and Sanchez-Marcos, V. (2008), 'Explaining changes in female labor supply in a life-cycle model', *American Economic Review*, **98**, 1517–52.

—— —— —— (2005), 'Female Labor Supply as Insurance Against Idiosyncratic Risk', *Journal of the European Economic Association, Papers and Proceedings*, **3**, 755–64.

—— and Rohwedder, S. (2003), 'Pension Wealth and Household Saving: Evidence from Pension Reforms in the U.K.', *American Economic Review*, **93**, 1499–521.

—— and Weber, G. (2009), 'Consumption and Saving: Models of Intertemporal Allocation and their Implications for Public Policy', mimeo: UCL.

—— —— (1995), 'Is Consumption Growth Consistent with Intertemporal Optimization? Evidence from the Consumer Expenditure Survey', *Journal of Political Economy*, **103**, 1121–57.

—— —— (1994), 'The UK Consumption Boom of the Late 1980s: Aggregate Implications of Microeconomic Evidence', *Economic Journal*, **104**, 1269–302.

Attanasio, O. P., and Weber, G. (1993), 'Consumption, the Interest Rate and Aggregation', *Review of Economic Studies*, **60**, 631–49.

——— (1989), 'Intertemporal Substitution, Risk Aversion and the Euler Equation for Consumption', *Economic Journal*, Conference Papers—Supplement, 59–73.

Banks, J., Blundell, R., and Emmerson, C. (2005), 'The Balance Between Defined Benefit, Defined Contribution and State Provision', *Journal of the European Economics Association (Papers and Proceedings)*, **3**, 466–76.

——— Oldfield, Z., and Smith, J. (2004), *House Price Volatility and Housing Ownership over the Lifecycle*, University College London Economics Discussion Paper 04-09: December 2004 <http://www.econ.ucl.ac.uk/papers/working_paper_series/0409.pdf>.

——— and Preston, I. (1994), 'Life-cycle Expenditure Allocation and the Consumption cost of Children', *European Economic Review*, **38**, 1391–410.

——— and Tanner, S. (1998), 'Is there a Retirement Savings Puzzle?', *American Economic Review*, **88**, 769–88.

—— Emmerson, C., and Oldfield, Z. (2004), 'Not so Brief Lives: Longevity Expectations and Well-being in Retirement', in *Seven Ages of Man and Woman: A Look at Life in Britain in the Second Elizabethan Era*, Economic and Social Research Council. <http://www.ifs.org.uk/publications.php?publication_id=3177>.

————— and Tetlow, G. (2005), *Prepared for Retirement? The Adequacy and Distribution of Retirement Resources in England*, London: Institute for Fiscal Studies.

—— Smith, Z., and Wakefield, M. (2002), *The Distribution of Financial Wealth in the UK: Evidence from 2000 BHPS Data*, IFS working paper WP02/21, <http://www.ifs.org.uk/wps/wp0221.pdf>.

Benjamin, D. J. (2003), 'Does 401(k) Eligibility Increase Saving? Evidence from Propensity Score Subclassification', *Journal of Public Economics*, **87**, 1259–90.

Bernanke, B. S. (1985), 'Adjustment Costs, Durables and Aggregate Consumption', *Journal of Monetary Economics*, **15**, 41–68.

Bernheim, B. D. (2002), 'Taxation and Saving' in Auerbach, A., and Feldstein, M. (eds.), *Handbook of Public Economics*, vol. **3**, Amsterdam: North Holland.

—— and Garrett, D. M. (1995), 'The Determinants and Consequences of Financial Education in the Workplace: Evidence from a Survey of Households', mimeo, Stanford University.

—— Jonathan, S., and Weinberg, S. (2001), 'What Accounts for the Variation in Retirement Wealth among U.S. Households?', *American Economic Review*, **91**, 832–57.

Blundell, R., Browning, M., and Meghir, C. (1994), 'Consumer Demand and the lifecycle Allocation of Household Expenditures', *Review of Economics and Statistics*, **161**, 57–80.

—— Emmerson, C., and Wakefield, M. (2006), *The Importance of Incentives in Influencing Private Retirement Saving: Known Knowns and Known Unknowns*, IFS working paper WP06/09, <http://www.ifs.org.uk/wps/wp0609.pdf>.

Bottazzi, R. (2004), *Labour Market Participation and Mortgage-related Borrowing Constraints*, Institute for Fiscal Studies Working Paper WP04/09 <http://www.ifs.org.uk/wps/wp0409.pdf>.

—— Jappelli, T., and Padula, M. (2006), 'Retirement Expectations, Pension Reforms and their Effect on Private Wealth Accumulation', *Journal of Public Economics*, **90**, 2187–212.

—— Low, H. W., and Wakefield, M. (2007), *Why do Home Owners Work Longer Hours?*, IFS working paper WP10/07 <http://www.ifs.org.uk/wps/wp1007.pdf>.

Browning M. (1991), 'A Simple Nonadditive Preference Structure for Models of Household Behaviour Over Time', *Journal of Political Economy*, **99**, 607–37.

Bucciol, A. (2007a), 'Temptation and Social Security Distortion', Mimeo: University of Padova.

—— (2007b), 'The Role of Temptation in Explaining Individual Behavior', Mimeo: University of Padova.

Campbell, J. Y. (1987), 'Does Saving Anticipate Declining Labor Income? An Alternative Test of the Permanent Income Hypothesis', *Econometrica*, **55**, 1249–73.

—— and Cocco, J. (2007), 'How do House Prices Affect Consumption? Evidence from Microdata', *Journal of Monetary Economics*, **54**, 591–621.

—— and Cochrane, J. H. (1999), 'By Force of Habit: A Consumption Based Explanation of Aggregate Stock Market Behaviour', *Journal of Political Economy*, **107**, 205–51.

—— and Deaton, A. (1989), 'Why is Consumption so Smooth', *Review of Economic Studies*, **56**, 357–74.

—— and Mankiw, N. G. (1989), 'Consumption, Income, and Interest Rates: Reinterpreting the Time Series Evidence', in Olivier, B, and Stanley, F. (eds.), *NBER Macroeconomics Annual*, NBER, Cambridge, 185–245.

Carroll, C. D. (1997), 'Buffer-stock Saving and the Life Cycle/Permanent Income Hypothesis', *Quarterly Journal of Economics*, **112**, 1–55.

Chernozhukov, V., and Hansen, C. B. (2004), 'The Effect of 401k Participation on the Wealth Distribution: An Instrumental Quantile Regression Analysis', *Review of Economics and Statistics*, **86**, 735–51.

Conesa, J-C., Kitao, S., and Krueger, D. (2007), *Taxing Capital? Not a Bad Idea After All!*, NBER Working Papers 12880, National Bureau of Economic Research, Inc.

Deaton, A (1991), 'Saving and Liquidity Constraints', *Econometrica*, **59**, 1221–48.

Department for Work and Pensions (2002), *Simplicity, Security and Choice: Working and Saving for Retirement*, Cm. 5677, London: The Stationery Office <http://www.dwp.gov.uk/consultations/consult/2002/pensions/gp.pdf>.

—— (2006), *Security in Retirement: Towards a New Pensions System*, Cm 6841, London: The Stationery Office, <http://www.dwp.gov.uk/pensionsreform/whitepaper.asp>.

Diaz A., Rios-Rull, J. V., and Pijoan-Mas, J. (2003), 'Precautionary Savings and Wealth Distribution under Habit Formation', *Journal of Monetary Economics*, **50**, 1257–91.

Disney, R., and Emmerson, C. (2005), 'Public Pension Reform in the United Kingdom: What Effect on the Financial Well Being of Current and Future Pensioners?', *Fiscal Studies*, **26**, 55–82.

——— and Tanner, S. (1999), *Partnership in Pensions: A Commentary*, Commentary No. 78, London: Institute for Fiscal Studies.

——— and Wakefield, M. (2007), 'Pension Provision and Retirement Saving: Lessons from the United Kingdom', SEDAP working paper, <http://socserv.mcmaster.ca/sedap/p/sedap176.pdf>.

—— and Whitehouse, E. (1992), *The Personal Pensions Stampede*, London: Institute for Fiscal Studies.

Dreze, J., and Modigliani, F. (1972), 'Consumption Decisions under Uncertainty', *Journal of Economic Theory*, **5**, 305–35.

Duflo, E., Gale, W., Liebman, J., Orszag, P., and Saez, E. (2006), 'Saving Incentives for Low- and Middle-income Families: Evidence from a Field Experiment with H&R Block', *Quarterly Journal of Economics*, **121**, 1311–46.

Dynan, K. E. (2000), 'Habit Formation in Consumer Preferences: Evidence from Panel Data', *American Economic Review*, **90**, 391–406.

—— and Maki, D. M., *Does Stock Market Wealth Matter for Consumption?* (May 2001). FEDS Discussion Paper No. 2001–23.

Eichenbaum M., and Hansen, L. P. (1990), 'Estimating Models with Intertemporal Substitution using Aggregate Time Series Data', *Journal of Business and Economic Statistics*, **8**, 53–69.

——— and Richard, S. F. (1988), *Aggregation, Durable Goods and Nonseparable Preferences in an Equilibrium Asset Pricing Model*, Chicago: Manuscript.

Elmendorf, D. W. (1996), '*The Effect of Interest Rate Changes on Household Saving and Consumption*', mimeo, Washington DC: The Federal Reserve Board.

Emmerson, C., and Tanner, S. (2000), 'A Note on the Tax Treatment of Private Pensions and Individual Savings Accounts', *Fiscal Studies*, **21**, 65–74.

Engen, E., Gale, W. G., and Scholz, J. K. (1996), 'The Illusory Effects of Saving Incentives on Saving', *Journal of Economic Perspectives*, **10**, 113–38.

Esteban, S., Miyagawa, E., and Shum, M. (2007), 'Nonlinear Pricing with Self-control Preferences', *Journal of Economic Theory*, **135**, (July): 206–338.

Feldstein, M. (1974), 'Social Security, Induced Retirement, and Aggregate Capital Accumulation', *Journal of Political Economy*, **82**, 905–26.

Flavin, M. (1981), 'The Adjustment of Consumption to Changing Expectations about Future Income', *Journal of Political Economy*, **89**, 263–86.

Friedman, M. (1957), *A Theory of the Consumption Function*, Princeton: NJ Princeton University Press.

Gale, W. G., and Scholz, J. K. (1994), 'IRAs and Household Saving', *American Economic Review*, **84**, 1233–60.

Gomes, F., and Michaelides, A. (2003), 'Portfolio Choice with Internal Habit Formation: a Life-cycle Model with Uninsurable Labor Income Risk', *Review of Economic Dynamics*, **6**, 729–66.

Gul, F., and Pesendorfer, W. (2001), 'Temptation and Self-control', *Econometrica*, **69**, 1403–35.

—— —— (2004a), 'Self-control and the Theory of Consumption', *Econometrica*, **72**, 119–58.

—— —— (2004b), 'Self-control, Revealed Preference, and Consumption Choice', *Review of Economic Dynamics*, **7**, 243–64.

Hall, R. E. (1988), 'Inter-temporal Substitution and Consumption', *Journal of Political Economy*, **96**, 339–57.

—— (1978), 'The Stochastic Implications of the Life Cycle-Permanent Income Hypothesis: Theory and Evidence', *Journal of Political Economy*, **86**, 971–87.

—— and Miskin, F. S. (1982), 'The Sensitivity of Consumption to Transitory Income: Estimate from panel data on households', *Econometrica*, **50**, 1269–86.

Hansen, L. P., and Jagannathan, R. (1991), 'Implications of Security Market Data for Models of Dynamic Economies', *Journal of Political Economy*, **99**, 225–62.

—— Roberds, W., and Sargent, T. J. (1991), 'Time Series Implications of Present Value Budget Balance and of Martingale Models of Consumption and Taxes', in Hansen, L. P. and Sargent, T. J., *Rational Expectations Econometrics*, Boulder: Westview, 121–61.

Harris, C., and Laibson, D. (2001), 'Dynamic Choices of Hyperbolic Consumers', *Econometrica*, **69**, 935–57.

Harvey, P., Pettigrew, N., Madden, R., Emmerson, C., Tetlow, G., and Wakefield, M. (2007), *Final Evaluation of the Saving Gateway 2 Pilot: Main Report*, <http://www.hm-treasury.gov.uk/media/7/0/savings_gateway_evaluation_report.pdf>.

Hayashi, F. (1987), 'Tests for Liquidity Constraints on Consumption: A Critical Survey and some New Observations', in Bewley, T. F. (ed.), *Advances in Econometrics: Fifth World Congress*, vol II, 91–120.

Heaton, J. C. (1995), 'An Empirical Investigation of Asset Pricing with Temporally Dependent Preference Specifications', *Econometrica*, **63**, 681–717.

—— (1993), 'The Interaction Between Time-nonseparable Preferences and Time Aggregation', *Econometrica*, **61**, 353–85.

Heckman, J. J. (1974), 'Life-cycle Consumption and Labour Supply: An Exploration of the Relationship between Income and Consumption over the Life-cycle', *American Economic Review*, **64**, 188–94.

HM Treasury. (2000), *Helping People to Save*, London: HM Treasury <http://www.hm-treasury.gov.uk./media/8EA/F9/511.pdf>.

Hubbard, R. G., and Skinner, J. S. (1996), 'Assessing the effectiveness of saving incentives', *Journal of Economic Perspectives*, **10**, 73–90.

—— —— and Zeldes, S. P. (1995), 'Precautionary Saving and Social Insurance', *Journal of Political Economy*, **103**, 360–99.

Karlan, D., and Zinman, J. (2008), 'Observing Unobservables: Identifying Information Asymmetries with a Consumer Credit Field Experiment', *Econometrica*, forthcoming.

King, M. A. (1990), 'Discussion' (of Muellbauer and Murphy (1990), 'Is the U.K. Balance of Payments Sustainable?'), *Economic Policy*, **11**, 383–87.

——and Dicks-Mireaux, L.-D. L. (1982), 'Asset Holdings and the Life cycle', *Economic Journal*, **92**, 247–67.

Krusell, P., Kuruscu, B., and Smith, A. A. (2001), 'Temptation and Taxation', Carnegie Mellon University, Tepper School of Business, GSIA Working Paper 2001–12.

——and Smith, A. (1998), 'Income and Wealth Heterogeneity in the Macroeconomy', *Journal of Political Economy*, **106**, 867–96.

Laibson D. (1994), 'Self Control and Saving', Mimeo: MIT.

——(1997), 'Golden Eggs and Hyperbolic Discounting', *Quarterly Journal of Economics*, **112**, 443–77.

——Repetto, A., and Tobacman, J. (2005), *Estimating Discount Functions with Consumption Choices over the Lifecycle*, mimeo: <http://www.economics.harvard.edu/faculty/laibson/papers/EstimatingDiscountFunctions16aug2005.pdf>.

Li, W., and Yao, R. (2007), 'The Life-Cycle Effects of House Price Changes', *Journal of Money, Credit and Banking*, **39**, 1375–409.

Low, H. W. (2005), 'Self-insurance in a Life-cycle Model of Labour Supply and Savings', *Review of Economic Dynamics*, **8**, 945–75.

Lustig, H., and Van Nieuwerburgh, S. (2005), 'Housing Collateral, Consumption Insurance and Risk Premia: An Empirical Perspective', *Journal of Finance*, **60**, 1167–219.

Mankiw, N. G. (1982), 'Hall's Consumption Hypothesis and Durable Goods', *Journal of Monetary Economics*, **10**, 417–25.

——Rotemberg, J. J., and Summers, L. H. (1985), 'Intertemporal Substitution and Macroeconomics', *Quarterly Journal of Economics*, **100**, 225–53.

Meade, J. (1978), *The Structure and Reform of Direct Taxation: Report of a Committee chaired by Professor J. E. mede for the Institute for Fiscal Studies*, London: George Allen & unwin. http://www.ifs.or.uk/publications/3433.

Meghir, C., and Pistaferri, L. (2004), 'Income Variance Dynamics and Heterogeneity', *Econometrica*, **72**, 1–32.

——and Weber, G. (1996), 'Intertemporal Non-separability or Borrowing Restrictions? A Disaggregated Analysis of a U.S. Consumption Panel', *Econometrica*, **64**, 1151–81.

Miniaci, R., Monfardini, C., and Weber, G. (2003), *'Is There a Retirement Consumption Puzzle in Italy?'* IFS Working Paper WP03/14 <http://www.ifs.org.uk/wps/wp0314.pdf>.

Modigliani, F., and Brumberg, R. (1954), 'Utility Analysis and the Consumption Function: An Interpretation of Cross-section Data', in Kurihara, K. K. (ed.), *Post-Keynesian Economics*, New Brunswick, NJ: Rutgers University Press, 128–97.

Muellbauer, J., and Murphy, A. (1990), 'Is the U.K. Balance of Payments Sustainable?', *Economic Policy*, **11**, 345–83.

Nalewaik J. (2006), 'Current Consumption and Future Income Growth: Synthetic Panel Evidence', *Journal of Monetary Economics*, **53**, 2239–66.

O'Donoghue, T., and Rabin, M. (1999a), 'Doing it Now or Later', *American Economic Review*, **89**, 103–24.

—— —— (1999b), 'Procrastination in preparing for retirement', in Aaron, H. (ed.), *Behavioral Dimensions of Retirement Economics*, Washington, DC: Brookings Institution.

Ortalo-Magné, F., and Rady, S. (2006), 'Housing market dynamics: On the contribution of income shocks and credit constraints', *Review of Economic Studies*, **73**, 459–85.

Padula, M. (1999), *Euler Equations and Durable Goods*, CSEF Working Paper No. **30**(December).

Palumbo, M. G. (1999), 'Uncertain medical expenses and precautionary saving near the end of the life cycle', *Review of Economic Studies*, **66**, 395–421.

Paxton, W. (2003), *Tax efficient saving: The effectiveness of ISA*, London: Institute for Public Policy Research (see <http://www.ippr.org.uk/pressreleases/archive.asp?id=688&fID=60>).

Pensions Act 2007: Elizabeth II. Ch. 22. London: HMSO.

Pensions Commission (2004), *Pensions: Challenges and Choices. The First Report of the Pensions Commission*, London: The Stationery Office <http://www.pensionscommission.org.uk/publications/2004/annrep/index.asp>.

—— (2005), *A New Pension Settlement for the Twenty-First Century: The Second Report of the Pensions Commission*, London: The Stationery Office <http://www.pensionscommission.org.uk/publications/2005/annrep/annrep-index.asp>.

Phelps, E. S., and Pollak, R. A. (1968), 'On second-best national saving and game-equilibrium growth', *Review of Economic Studies*, **XXXV**, 185–99.

Phlips, L., and Spinnewyn, F. (1984), 'True indexes and rational habit formation', *European Economic Review*, **24**, 209–23.

Poterba, J. M., Venti, S. F. and Wise, D. A. (1996), 'How retirement saving programs increase saving', *Journal of Economic Perspectives*, **10**, 91–112.

—— —— —— (1995), 'Do 401(k) contributions crowd out other personal saving?', *Journal of Public Economics*, **58**, 1–32.

Rios-Rull, J-V., and Sanchez-Marcos, V. (2008), 'An aggregate economy with different size houses', *Journal of the European Economic Association, Papers and Proceedings*, **6**, 705–14.

Sargent, T. J. (1978), 'Rational expectations, econometric exogeneity and consumption', *Journal of Political Economy*, **86**, 673–700.

Scholz, J. K., Seshadri, A., and Khitatrakun, S. (2006), 'Are Americans saving "optimally" for retirement', *Journal of Political Economy*, **114**, 607–43.

Sefton, J., van de Ven, J., and Weale, M. (2008), 'Means-testing retirement benefits: Fostering equity or discouraging savings?', *Economic Journal*, **118**, 556–90.

Smith, S. (2006), 'The retirement consumption puzzle and involuntary early retirement: Evidence from the British Household Panel Survey', *Economic Journal*, Conference papers, **116**, 130–89.

Spinnewyn, F. (1981), 'Rational habit formation', *European Economic Review*, **15**, 91–109.

Strotz, R. H. (1956), 'Myopia and Inconsistency in Dynamic Utility Maximization', *Review of Economic Studies*, **23**, 165–80.

Summers, L. (1981), 'Capital Taxation and Accumulation in a Life Cycle Growth Model', *American Economic Review*, **71**, 533–44.

Thurow, L. (1969), 'The Optimum Lifetime Distribution of Consumption Expenditures', *American Economic Review*, **59**, 371–96.

Venti, S. F., and Wise, D. A. (1990), 'Have IRAs Increased U.S. Saving? Evidence from Consumer Expenditure Surveys', *Quarterly Journal of Economics*, **105**, 661–98.

Wakefield, M. (2009), 'How Much do we Tax the Return to Saving?', *IFS Briefing Note* (forthcoming).

West, K. D. (1988), 'The Insensitivity of Consumption to News about Income', *Journal of Monetary Economics*, **21**, 17–34.

8

Taxation of Wealth and Wealth Transfers*

Robin Boadway, Emma Chamberlain, and Carl Emmerson

Robin Boadway is David Chadwick Smith Chair in Economics at Queen's University in Canada, a Fellow of the Royal Society of Canada, and an Officer of the Order of Canada. He is President Elect of the International Institute of Public Finance and a past President of the Canadian Economics Association. He is Editor of the *Journal of Public Economics* and former Editor of the *Canadian Journal of Economics*. His work has focused on taxation and redistribution, fiscal federalism, and applied welfare economics. His books include *Welfare Economics*, *Public Sector Economics*, and *Fiscal Federalism* (forthcoming).

Emma Chamberlain is a barrister practising at 5 Stone Buildings, Lincoln's Inn, and a Fellow of the Chartered Institute of Taxation. She specializes in taxation and trust advice for private clients, lectures widely and has written several books on capital taxation, including co-editing *Dymond's Capital Taxes*. She is chair of the CIOT Succession Taxes Committee, in which capacity she works with others to improve draft legislation and HMRC guidance. She was named Private Client Barrister of the Year 2004 by Inbriefs and received the Outstanding Achievement Award at the Society of Trust and Estate Practitioners' Private Client Awards 2006.

Carl Emmerson is a Deputy Director of the IFS and Programme Director of their work on pensions, saving, and public finances. He is an Editor of the annual *IFS Green Budget*. His recent research includes analysis of the UK public finances and public spending, and of the effect of UK pension reform on inequality, retirement behaviour, labour market mobility, and incentives to save. He is also a specialist advisor to the House of Commons Work and Pensions Select Committee.

* The authors thank the Mirrlees Review editorial team and Helmuth Cremer for helpful comments and discussions.

EXECUTIVE SUMMARY

The current system for taxing wealth and wealth transfers in the UK is unpopular. This is unsurprising given that certain features of inheritance tax, capital gains tax, stamp duties, council tax, and business rates are unfair or inefficient or both.

Problems with the current system

1. Inheritance tax is perceived as inequitable because the wealthy are better able to reduce the amount they pay by giving away part of their wealth tax-free during their lifetimes. The moderately wealthy tend to have capital tied up in their house, and anti-avoidance provisions in the tax rules make it hard to 'give away' all or part of the value of a house while you are still living in it.
2. Some assets obtain full relief from inheritance tax, for example, on certain businesses and agricultural land. These reliefs are not always well targeted.
3. Inheritance tax can lead to double taxation, because people may have paid tax on the earnings saved or the gains realized that generate the wealth bequeathed.
4. The single 40% rate of inheritance tax can seem unfair where the deceased was only paying the basic rate of income tax.
5. Inheritance tax is complex, illogical, and sometimes arbitrary in its effects. In some cases neither capital gains tax nor inheritance tax are paid on wealth transfers; in other cases both taxes can be paid.
6. Stamp duties on the transfer of both property and equities raise significant revenue, but distort people's behaviour in an economically costly way, discouraging mutually beneficial transactions and thereby hindering the efficient allocation of assets.
7. Using 1991 house values as the base for council tax in England is difficult to justify.
8. By contrast, business rates are based on up-to-date property values, but the rationale for this tax is not clear.

The rationale for an inheritance tax

The choice of a tax system should be based on sound principles; the fact that a wealth transfer tax involves double taxation must be justified. (However, the current UK inheritance tax system does not always impose double taxation since inheritance tax is often wrongly used as a substitute for capital gains tax.) The standard approach in the theoretical economic literature is to assume that the government chooses a tax structure that maximizes people's welfare, taking account of what makes people happy, how their behaviour is likely to respond, and the need to raise revenue to pay for public services. This approach suggests that intentional wealth transfers, which presumably benefit the donor as well as the recipient, should be taxed more heavily than accidental transfers, which may not. On the other hand, taxing accidental transfers does not distort people's behaviour in a costly way. Unfortunately the motives for, and satisfaction derived from, giving away wealth are not observable. It is sometimes argued that taxing transfers on death differently from lifetime gifts can help to distinguish between intentional and accidental transfers, but in many cases transfers on death are planned.

A better justification for taxing wealth when it is transferred is that this promotes equality of opportunity. On this view an individual should be compensated for disadvantages beyond his control, but not for disadvantages under his control. Therefore, a wealth transfer should be treated as a source of additional opportunity for the recipient that should be taxed, whether or not the donor has already paid income tax or capital gains tax on the assets concerned.

Options

There are a number of different options for the future of inheritance tax. One is wholesale reform with the introduction of a comprehensive donee based tax similar to that operating in Ireland. Under a donee based tax the rate of tax on transfers of wealth is governed not by the value of the donor's estate but by how much wealth the donee has inherited or been given during their lifetime. So each donee pays tax to the extent that transfers of wealth to him from any source exceed a certain limit over his lifetime. One advantage of this approach is that it accords more closely with the equality of opportunity rationale for taxing transfers, because those who have inherited more in the past pay tax at a higher rate on additional receipts. It could therefore be seen as fairer than the current regime. A donee based tax also encourages donors to spread their wealth more widely, which might lead to a more equal distribution of inherited wealth. However, such a system may have higher administrative and compliance costs, in particular the need to keep a record of all lifetime gifts. In the absence of universal tax returns in the UK, a separate system would be needed to record lifetime gifts. In addition some political consensus is needed for this to be implemented successfully. If a government introduced a donee based tax system without Opposition support then many gifts might be delayed in the expectation that the tax would be repealed.

An alternative is to consider limited reform of the existing inheritance tax regime. The government recently introduced a transferable nil rate band, reducing the burden of the tax on many married couples but also its yield. If the current system is retained, other changes could include extending the seven-year limit for lifetime gifts to a longer period and better targeting of both agricultural and business reliefs. The family home should not be exempted, but if certain individuals (such as cohabitees or siblings who do not own other properties) occupy the home then the tax should be deferred until the property is sold. Consideration should also be given to increasing the threshold at which inheritance tax starts being payable or introducing a lower rate band at, for example, 20%.

It is difficult to cost such a package of reforms since the revenue raised from extending the seven-year limit for lifetime gifts is unknown: there are no data on how much wealth is transferred more than seven years before death. If the inheritance tax yield is reduced, retaining it would become harder to justify. If inheritance tax is retained, the case for keeping it needs to be put more forcibly.

Given that the justification for double taxation is arguable and that inheritance tax currently raises less than £4 billion a year, consideration could be given to abolishing it altogether. Regardless of whether or not a tax on wealth transfers is retained, the current rebasing of assets held at death to market value for capital gains tax purposes should be removed. In other words, capital gains should be taxed at death, although payment could be delayed until the assets are sold. This would make the double taxation implied by inheritance tax (if retained) very explicit, but double taxation is a natural feature of any taxation of wealth holdings or wealth transfers and, if justified in its own right, does not provide a rationale for not fully taxing the income (or capital gain) received by donors. Some design issues such as emigration and immigration, gains on business assets, private residences, and so on would need to be resolved if capital gains tax is imposed on death and are discussed in the chapter.

Wealth tax

The chapter does not advocate the introduction of a regular wealth tax. It has been argued in the past that individuals benefit directly from holding wealth (as opposed to just spending it) and that the status and power it brings mean that additional taxation of wealth is appropriate. Even if one accepts this argument, it is debatable whether a tax on all wealth is the right way to tax such benefits. It is costly to administer, might raise little revenue, and could operate unfairly and inefficiently. It is less likely to work well in the current environment where capital is very mobile. Most OECD countries have abolished wealth taxes. One option that could be explored further is an annual tax targeted at very high value residential property with no reduction for debt. Perhaps the easiest way this could be implemented would be through the imposition of an additional council tax which would only affect occupiers of a residential property with a gross value above a large limit and would be paid wherever the occupier was resident or domiciled.

8.1. INTRODUCTION

The current UK system of taxing wealth and wealth transfers has been subject to significant and increasing criticism. Common complaints are that the system is overcomplicated, that the incidence of tax is unfair, that it represents double taxation, and that little revenue is raised. The result is that after twenty years of relative stability, inheritance tax has become the subject of intense political debate in the UK. Suggestions range from its abolition, significantly increasing the threshold, or replacing inheritance tax with a donee based tax based on the total sum of inheritances received by the donee over the course of his lifetime.[1]

Most major economies raise relatively little from inheritance and gift taxes. None of the G7 economies has raised more than 1.0% of national income in revenue from Estate, Inheritance, and Gift Taxes in any one year over the last forty years, as shown in Figure 8.1. Whereas there is marked similarity in

[1] Abolition of inheritance tax, to be financed in part through the introduction of capital gains tax on death was proposed in the Forsyth Report (2006) although they proposed that no capital gains tax would be levied on assets held for more than ten years. The Conservatives proposed a threshold of £1million at their September 2007 party conference. The Labour government has introduced transferable nil rate band allowances between spouses and civil partners with effect from 9 October 2007. The replacement of inheritance tax with a donee based tax was proposed by Patrick and Jacobs (1999). The Liberal Democrats in 2006 favoured an accessions tax but in 2007 proposed increasing the threshold to £500,000 with a 15-year cumulation period.

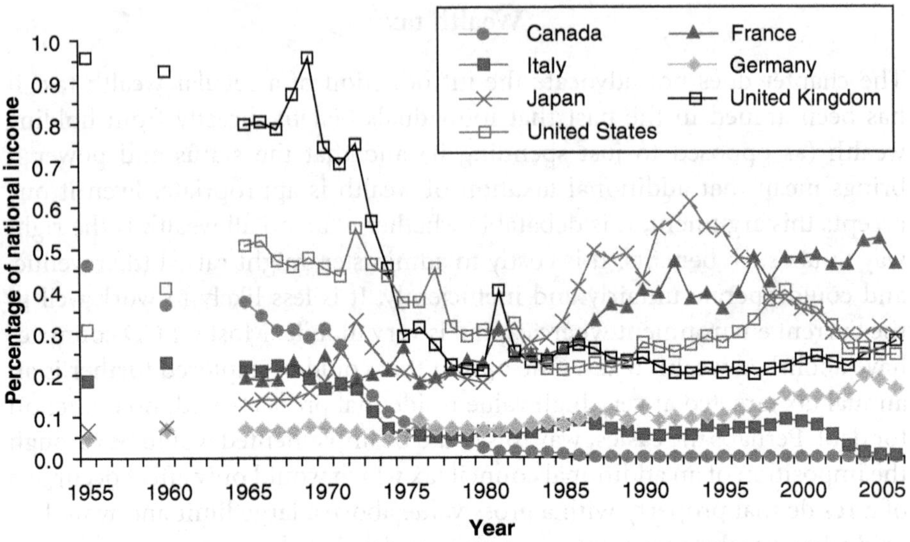

Note: Data on France from 1955 and 1960 not available at time of writing. 'National income' refers to Gross Domestic Product.

Source: OECD, Revenue Statistics.

Figure 8.1. Receipts from estate, inheritance, and gift taxes, as a share of national income 1955 to 2006, across G7 countries

the system for the taxation of income and capital gains across the developed world, there has been no consistent approach taken to how wealth is taxed in the G7 economies.[2] This is partly because wealth and wealth transfer taxation are linked to different succession laws[3] and partly because countries have differing views as to the role and merits of wealth taxation. There is a perceived tension between promoting entrepreneurship and redistributing wealth. A system of taxing wealth has to operate over a person's lifetime, and so is more vulnerable to changes in government. To be effective there must be some political consensus on how wealth is taxed.

This section begins with a brief description of the current taxation of wealth and wealth transfers in the UK before discussing common criticisms

[2] Italy has abolished tax on death albeit retained other gift taxes; Canada imposes only capital gains tax on death; the US has increased the exempt threshold sharply for taxes on death but retained gift tax; France retains wealth, gift, and estate taxes and, unlike the US (since 1999) and Japan (since 1991) where receipts have fallen sharply, receipts in both France and Germany have grown fairly steadily over the last quarter of a century. Receipts in the UK have been relatively stable since the early 1980s although they have been on a slightly rising trend in recent years. For fuller details see appendix B of the additional online material at http://www.ifs.org.uk/mirrleesreview/reports/wealth_transfers_apps.pdf.

[3] Some legal systems have freedom of testamentary succession and others are based around forced heirship.

of inheritance tax. Section 8.2 sets out the principles of tax design in this area, in particular highlighting the lessons from the public economics literature. Section 8.3 discusses the pros and cons of wealth and wealth transfer taxation and the different options for such taxes. Section 8.4 mainly discusses property taxes. Section 8.5 concludes.

In considering the taxation of wealth, we also examine capital gains tax, stamp duty, and property taxes.

8.1.1. Brief description of the current taxation of wealth and wealth transfers in the UK

The main taxes relevant to the taxation of transfers of wealth in the UK are inheritance tax, capital gains tax, and stamp duty/SDLT.[4] There is no wealth tax in the UK, although the idea has been advocated on a number of occasions, for example by Labour in 1975. There are, however, taxes on the occupiers of property, both domestic (council tax in England, Scotland, and Wales and domestic rates in Northern Ireland) and non-domestic (business rates in England, Scotland, and Wales and non-domestic rates in Northern Ireland). These are not strictly wealth taxes as tenants, as well as owner-occupiers, are liable. This section provides a very brief description of the operation of inheritance tax and capital gains tax.[5]

Inheritance tax, despite its name, is a tax on the donor rather than a tax on the inheritance received by the donee. It is levied at a flat rate of 40% on estates above a prescribed threshold, which in 2007–08 was set at £300,000 ('the nil rate band') which is approximately ten times mean annual full-time earnings. Transfers between married or civil partners, whether during lifetime or on death, are generally exempt, as are gifts to charities. Reliefs up to 100% for agricultural property and trading businesses can give full exemption from inheritance tax. All lifetime gifts to individuals (but not to trusts or companies) are exempt provided the donor survives the gift by seven years and gives up all benefit in the gifted asset. Such gifts are called 'potentially exempt transfers', or PETs. If the donor dies within seven years of the gift, the PET is taxed at rates of up to 40% depending on how long the donor survived the gift and whether or not the gift was within the donor's nil rate band.

[4] Although capital gains tax should conceptually be regarded as part of the income tax system, it is often seen as complementary or an alternative to estate tax and similar issues arise in relation to valuation, exemptions, and rates.

[5] For a detailed summary of all of these taxes, along with a brief history of inheritance tax, see appendix A of the additional online material (see footnote 2).

From 9 October 2007, the percentage of any nil rate band which is unused on the death of the first spouse or civil partner can be carried forward and used on the second spouse or civil partner's death. This applies to all married couples and civil partners where the death of the second spouse occurs on or after 9 October 2007 irrespective of when the first death occurred. The government hopes that this measure will reduce the unpopularity of inheritance tax and relieve political pressure on the tax. It does not, of course, apply to unmarried individuals (for example, cohabitees or siblings) living together at death unless the one who dies first has a transferable nil rate band available from a previous marriage or civil partnership. In that event he will be able to pass on (at current rates) £600,000 worth of assets tax free to the surviving cohabitee.

Capital gains tax is a tax charged on disposals of chargeable assets when a gain is realized. Annual realized gains above a certain threshold, set at £9,200 per individual in 2007–08, are subject to the tax. The tax is charged not only on sales but also on gifts since a gift of an asset is deemed to take place at market value. Capital gains tax operates on certain lifetime gifts. By contrast, there is generally no capital gains tax on death—assets are rebased to market value so all unrealized gains are wiped out—and this applies whether or not such assets are liable for inheritance tax. There are various exemptions on lifetime disposals of which the most important is an exemption on the principal private residence. In 1998, taper relief replaced indexation allowance, and taper relief taxed gains on business assets at lower rates than non-business assets. However, from 6 April 2008 taper relief was replaced by a flat 18% rate on all gains irrespective of the nature of the asset or how long it has been held. Entrepreneurs' relief gives additional relief for disposals of trading company shares or business assets on the first £1 million of lifetime gains.[6]

8.1.2. Criticisms of the current UK system—the unpopularity of inheritance tax

The current system of wealth and wealth transfer taxation in the UK is very unpopular. Criticisms are that the system fails to raise any **significant revenue**

[6] Specifically eligible assets are defined as either shares in a trading company (or holding company of a trading group) of which the shareholder has been a full-time employee or director, owned at least 5% of the shares, and had at least 5% of the voting rights, all for at least a year; or an unincorporated business (or share in a business) or business assets sold after the individual stops carrying on the business. Source: <http://www.hmrc.gov.uk/cgt/disposal.htm>.

so could be abolished without serious consequences, is **unfair**, and is overly **complicated.** This section examines whether such criticisms are justified.

Raising revenue

Neither inheritance tax nor capital gains tax currently raises significant sums. Inheritance tax revenues are projected by the Treasury to be £4.0 billion in 2007–08 (0.3% of national income), while receipts of capital gains tax are projected to be £4.6 billion (also 0.3% of national income). Stamp duty is a more significant source of revenue for the government. The Treasury projects a yield of £14.3 billion in 2007–08, with data from recent years suggesting that around 70% of this is likely to be from stamp duty on property transactions with the remaining 30% from stamp duty on share transactions.

Revenues from inheritance tax and its predecessor capital transfer tax have averaged about 0.22% of national income over the period from 1978 to 1979. In 2003–04, the yield reached the highest level seen over this period and, as shown in Figure 8.2 (lighter line and left-hand axis), the overall yield has continued to increase since then. The vast majority of these receipts came

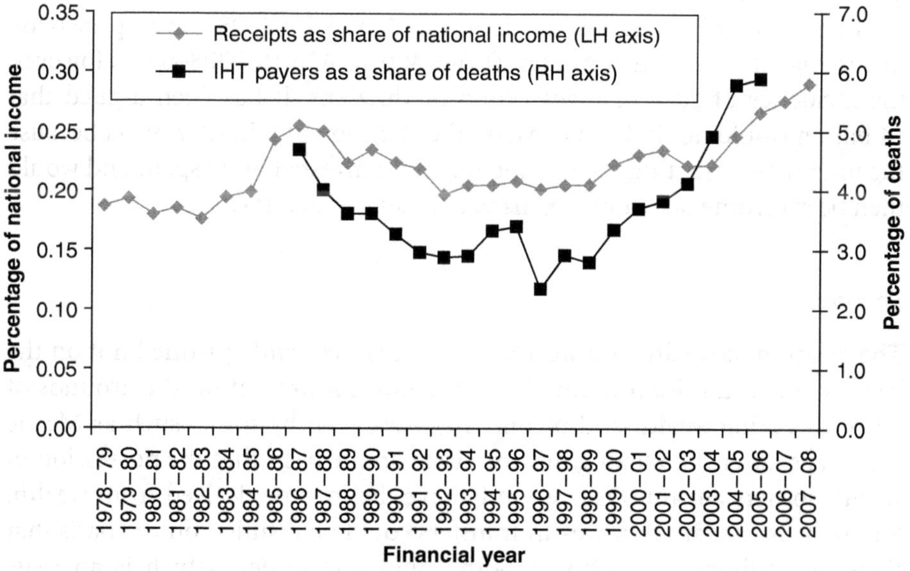

Note: Capital transfer tax was replaced by inheritance tax for transfers on or after 18 March 1986. 'National income' refers to Gross Domestic Product.

Source: Table 1.2 HM Revenue and Customs Statistics http://www.hmrc.gov.uk/stats/tax_receipts/table1-2.xls. Forecast for 2007–08 from Table C8 page 281, of HM Treasury (2007).

Figure 8.2. Inheritance tax and capital transfer tax receipts and percentage of estates liable for tax

from transfers made on death (98% in 2005–06) with very little coming from either trusts or taxes on gifts made in the seven years prior to death. As is also shown in Figure 8.2 (darker line and right-hand axis), only 5.9% of estates paid inheritance tax in 2005–06, although this was the highest level since the tax was introduced in 1986–87 and has increased from 2.3% in 1996–97. In 1996–97, the average inheritance tax paid by taxpaying estates was £90,000, reducing by 2003–04 to £87,000, and has since risen again to £100,000 in 2005–06.[7] Over 70% of taxpaying estates had a net estate of between £200,000 and £500,000 while only 2% had a net estate worth in excess of £2 million. However, the extent to which this reflects the true underlying distribution of wealth, as opposed to the ability of those with high net worth to avoid inheritance tax, for example by making lifetime gifts, is unclear. Although only 6% of estates actually pay inheritance tax, 37% of households now have an estate with a value above the threshold. This partly accounts for the potency of the issue—people feel themselves a potential inheritance taxpayer even if only a few estates will actually pay it.[8]

In summary, one can say that inheritance tax is not an important source of revenue. The revenue raised, £4.0 billion in 2007–08, is less than 1% of total government revenues and could, for example, be covered by a 1p increase in the basic rate of income tax (from 20p to 21p in 2008–09) or a 3p increase in the higher rate of income tax (from 40p to 43p in 2008–09). However, the incidence of such changes would be different. It has been argued that £4 billion would not in fact be lost on the abolition of inheritance tax because the money representing the tax might remain invested or be spent and would then bear income tax/capital gains tax or value added tax.

Fairness issues

The taxation of wealth and wealth transfers is frequently justified not on the basis that it will raise revenue for public expenditure but on the grounds of fairness. Taxing wealth and income has been seen by some, such as Meade (1978), as fairer than taxing income alone on the basis that the possession of wealth confers advantages over and above the income derived from wealth. Similarly, the taxation of wealth transfers could be justified on the basis that these are delivering benefits to both donor and donee, which is an issue explored further in Section 8.2. To the extent that an unequal distribution of receipts of large bequests is a source of inequality of opportunity, the taxation

[7] Source: Hansard question from Michael Gove to Dawn Primarolo 129105, 16 April 2007.

[8] Halifax press release March 2005 estimated that 2.4 million houses were worth more than the inheritance tax threshold.

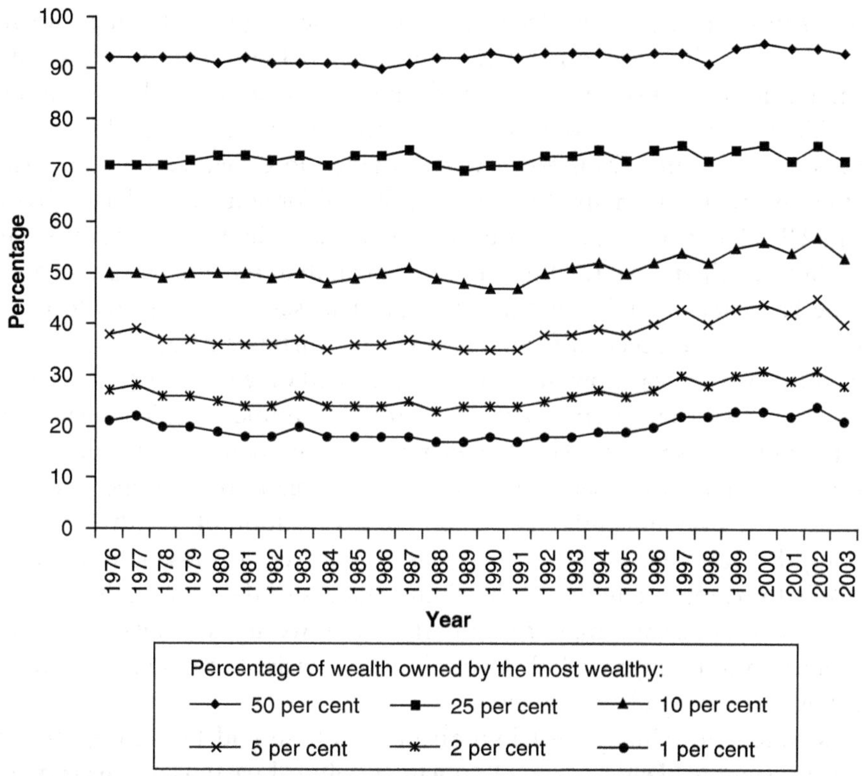

Note: Personal wealth here refers to the value of individuals' marketable assets, such as houses, stocks and shares, and other saleable assets, less any amounts owed due to debts and mortgages. The value of occupational and state pensions is not included since they cannot be immediately realized.

Source: Table 13.5 of HM Revenue and Customs Statistics <http://www.hmrc.gov.uk/stats/personal_wealth/table13_5.xls>.

Figure 8.3. Concentration of personal wealth in the UK

of wealth transfers is sometimes justified on the basis that the government wishes to promote greater equality of opportunity or to redistribute wealth, although these are more controversial aims.

The distribution of marketable wealth appears to have become more unequal in recent years, as shown in Figure 8.3. Using information from inheritance tax records, HMRC estimate that the wealthiest tenth of the population own 52% of the country's total marketable wealth, which is an increase from 49% in 1982. However, these statistics probably do not reflect the true position. First, wealth held in the form of occupational and state pensions is not included, on the basis that these assets cannot immediately be realized. Second, as one might expect, human capital is not included. For many individuals, these assets will form the majority of their overall wealth.

Furthermore, a large guaranteed pension income might enable high wealth individuals to give away other assets during their lifetime in order to avoid paying inheritance tax on death. Third, since the data on the distribution of individual wealth are derived from inheritance tax returns, they do not take into account lifetime transfers of wealth made more than seven years prior to the death, nor in many cases the wealth of foreign domiciliaries living in the UK. These are significant omissions which might mean that the true distribution of personal wealth is more unequal than the official data suggest.

The fact that outright gifts made more than seven years prior to death do not have to be declared for inheritance tax purposes means that it is not straightforward to say how much wealth is passed on each year or determine how much inheritance tax is avoided through lifetime gifts. The new ONS Household Assets Survey (HAS), which will contain detailed information on borrowing, savings, household assets, and saving plans for retirement, should provide much valuable information on the distribution of wealth in the UK among the vast majority of individuals.[9] However, a household survey is unlikely to be representative of the circumstances of the very wealthy due to high non-response among this group. If data on wealth transfers and wealth distribution were improved, this would make it easier to predict the effect or yield of particular policy changes.

The extent to which redistribution of wealth should be an objective of the tax system is likely to depend on which political party is in government. Moreover, even if redistribution of wealth is seen as a desirable aim, people differ on whether different forms of wealth should be taxed differently. There is some behavioural evidence that people may care more about suffering tax on their own inheritance and are less bothered about whether it is fair that their neighbour receives a much greater inheritance tax free. In other words, the negative aspects of the tax outweigh the positive.

However, one of the objections to the current inheritance tax system in the UK is not that it fails to redistribute wealth but that it is inherently unfair in its structure because it falls disproportionately on the middle classes to the benefit of the rich.

The UK's approach to inheritance tax has been to maintain a high rate but to mitigate this through reliefs and exemptions and to allow tax planning through lifetime gifts to reduce the impact of the tax. This approach appears to be failing because rising house prices have brought more and more of the middle classes into the inheritance tax net. Moreover, variations in house

[9] The first wave covers July 2006 to June 2008 and individuals will be re-interviewed every two years. For more information see <http://www.statistics.gov.uk/STATBASE/Source.asp?vlnk=1500&More=Y>.

prices across the country mean that this problem is particularly concentrated in London and the South East where by 2005 31% of houses were worth more than the nil rate band (up from 4% in 1999).[10] Such taxpayers are generally unable to take advantage of many of the tax reliefs because their main asset is the house. While they will be able to benefit from the recent introduction of transferable nil rate bands, the wealthy well-advised taxpayers with business and agricultural assets can also benefit from other exemptions and the ability to make lifetime gifts without affecting their standard of living.

The last Conservative government promised that it would abolish inheritance tax[11] but despite the recommendations of the Forsyth Report of the Conservative Tax Reform Commission[12] which includes abolition as a possible option, the Conservatives did not promise this at their autumn 2007 conference. However, the public support for their proposal to increase the inheritance tax threshold to £1 million demonstrates the unpopularity of inheritance tax.[13]

Even a former Labour government minister advocated the abolition of inheritance tax on 20 August 2006 saying it was 'a penalty on hard work, thrift and enterprise'.[14] (This ignores the fact that the donee has never worked for the money and arguably inherited wealth encourages idleness. All taxes on wealth, income, or spending reduce the reward from work.) In 2001 George Bush repealed estate tax in the US on a phased basis; despite the fact that only 2% of Americans pay it, the repeal lobby was broad-based.[15] Similar 'moral claims' using highly emotive language have been made in the UK.[16] Narrative case studies are used to support abolition such as the Burden sisters case.[17] Those with the least to leave appear to be most in favour of being able to leave their capital to the next generation and therefore most resistant to the possibility that it could be taxed.[18]

[10] Halifax press release 'Inheritance tax revenues to double in 9 years', HBOS, 12 March 2005.

[11] Chancellor of the Exchequer Rt Hon Kenneth Clarke MP Budget speech 26 November 1996 Hansard HC Debs, vol. 286, col. 169.

[12] Tax Matters: Reforming the Tax System 19 October 2006.

[13] The case for the abolition of inheritance tax is forcefully put by Lee (2007).

[14] *Sunday Telegraph*.

[15] For an analysis see Graetz and Shapiro (2005). See also Rowlingson (2007) for comparisons with the UK. Gay men and lesbians who were unable to take advantage of marital tax deductions (unlike in the UK since December 2005) were in favour of complete repeal along with the super-rich; they produced strong narrative case studies as well as moral arguments to bolster the case.

[16] For example, an online petition submitted by a *Daily Express* journalist states, 'inheritance tax is an immoral form of taxation that penalizes hard work and thrift. By raising a 40% levy on earned assets it is also effectively double taxation. This is nothing less than grave robbery.' We outline later why no estate suffers inheritance tax at 40% and why it is not necessarily double taxation. See also the Taxpayers' Alliance comments on their website.

[17] Further details can be found in appendix A of the additional online material (see note 2).

[18] See Rowlingson and McKay (2005).

However, other research has found that attitudes to inheritance tax changed when research participants were given further information and asked to consider broader issues about the tax system as a whole, particularly if abolition was specifically allied to proposals to increase income tax by 1p.[19] The Treasury has tended to respond to attacks on inheritance tax by pointing out that anyone who wants to abolish it needs to explain how the £4 billion revenue is to be raised. However, the recent October 2007 announcement introducing transferable nil rate bands at a cost of £1 billion suggests that the government feels on the back foot with inheritance tax. The pro-inheritance tax lobby has not developed any strong narrative case to increase public support for wealth transfer taxes.[20] Those who favour the retention of some sort of tax on wealth transfers are divided about what system they actually want and the objectives of such a tax so the pro-inheritance tax lobby is weakened.

Double taxation

A commonly stated objection to inheritance tax is that it is **double taxation**, that is, people have already paid income tax or capital gains tax on the income before it is used to purchase an asset which then suffers inheritance tax on their death. President Bush expressed this view in the 2000 election campaign. When asked why he favoured the total abolition of estate tax he replied: 'I just don't think it's fair to tax people's assets twice regardless of your status. It's a fairness issue. It's an issue of principle not politics.'

Multiple taxation is not peculiar to inheritance tax. People pay indirect taxes on goods and services out of their taxed income. However, inheritance tax applies discriminately on some assets (those that are held until death) and not on others. This issue of double taxation will be discussed in more detail in Section 8.2.[21] Moreover, in some cases inheritance tax will be the first time the asset has been taxed. For example, increases in the value of the family home are generally exempt from capital gains tax (and there is no income tax on the imputed rental value). As a result, although the purchase price may well have been paid for out of taxed earnings, any subsequent increases in value—which in recent years have substantially exceeded normal returns—will not have been subject to tax. The current tax system is certainly not logical: at

[19] Lewis and White (2007).

[20] Prabhakar (2008) discusses how much narratives and stories can enhance or diminish public support for inheritance tax.

[21] Prabhakar (2008) also reports that focus group studies participants argued that in the case of VAT they had a choice as to whether to pay it because they could choose not to buy the goods. In the case of inheritance tax they had no choice as to whether to pay it.

present it is possible to avoid both inheritance tax and capital gains tax on lifetime gifts but suffer both taxes in other circumstances.[22] In other words, the double tax objection is not universally valid in that it is not clear that inheritance tax necessarily does involve double taxation.

The double tax objection takes a different flavour if the wealth transfer tax is structured as a donee- rather than donor-based tax. In this case, the tax is paid by the recipient not the donor, so there is no double taxation of the donor. However, now the same asset gives rise to taxation in the hands of both the donor and the donee, which is another form of double taxation.

Equity objections

Proponents of the 'virtue argument' argue that inheritance tax is an unfair tax because it leads to unequal tax burdens on people with equal amounts of wealth but who choose to use their wealth in different ways. So the person who spends his fortune of £1 million prior to death may pay less tax than the person who saves it and leaves it to his heirs on death.

We have already pointed out that the inheritance tax in its current structure is perceived as inequitable because its burden falls disproportionately on the middle classes, not on the very rich who are able to avoid the tax. One could counter this objection by arguing that the inequity should be rectified simply by getting the very rich to pay their share of inheritance tax rather than abolishing the tax altogether. However, to achieve this, the reasons why inheritance tax can currently be minimized by the very rich need to be considered. The two main reasons are the exemption for most lifetime gifts; and the nature of the various exemptions, reliefs, and loopholes that tend to favour the wealthier individual.

Lifetime gift exemption

In contrast to capital transfer tax, inheritance tax does not tax lifetime gifts provided the donor survives seven years and gives up all benefit in the gifted asset. Therefore, the taxman now favours 'the healthy, wealthy and well-advised' as long as they are lucky enough to survive a further seven years.[23] Hence for the very rich who can afford to make large lifetime gifts, it is said that inheritance tax—or at least large payments of inheritance tax—is largely voluntary.[24] This is obviously an exaggeration but has some element of truth in that the middle classes bear a disproportionate burden. For those who are

[22] A worked example is provided in appendix A of the additional online material (see note 2).

[23] Kay and King (1990), p. 107.

[24] Among many others see, for example, Burnett (2007), Patrick and Jacobs (1999), and Sandford (1988).

affluent but not very rich often their home is the main capital asset. Giving the house away tax free effectively is very difficult due to the 'reservation of benefit' rules; these rules mean that no inheritance tax is avoided if he or she continues to live there. While these families will be the main beneficiaries from the recent introduction of a transferable nil-rate band, it is still the case that the rich can more easily give away their assets seven years before death and hence can reduce their inheritance tax bill more effectively.

It seems difficult to argue on grounds of fairness that a person who inherits £1 million on the donor's death, or in the seven years before a donor's death, should be taxed more highly than the person who is given £1 million earlier in the donor's life. As discussed in Section 8.2, if bequests on death represent accidental bequests, it is efficient to tax these more highly since they should not respond as strongly to financial incentives. However, the extent to which bequests on death *do* represent accidental as opposed to intended bequests is not known. Those with less wealth or more illiquid wealth are generally less able to make lifetime gifts and therefore have to give a higher proportion of their wealth on death but the bequests might be no less planned.

Since March 2006 the government has imposed inheritance tax of up to 20% on lifetime gifts into all trusts.[25] But there seems no considered policy on the taxation of wealth transfers behind this change. If the government objected to lifetime gifts in principle, then the natural course would have been to impose inheritance tax on all lifetime gifts, not just gifts into trusts. If the government's target was to prevent individuals holding wealth through trusts, then it is difficult to see why trusts set up on death are still given limited favoured treatment compared with trusts funded by lifetime gifts.

If inheritance tax is to be retained, then it seems clear that the exemption for lifetime gifts needs to be re-examined. A simple reform would be to extend significantly the period of survivorship from seven years. In a number of countries, for example, Germany, USA, Switzerland, and Spain, gift taxes are imposed on lifetime gifts, although (as with the predecessor to inheritance tax namely capital transfer tax) the thresholds operate at different levels from transfers on death. In the UK the Liberal Democrats (2007) proposed an increase in the seven-year lifetime gifts limit to fifteen years.

Exemptions and reliefs

Although the UK's inheritance tax system has a high marginal rate levied at a relatively low level, there are a number of important reliefs, including **spouse**

[25] Further details are provided in appendix A of the additional online material (see note 2).

exemption which was estimated by the Treasury to reduce the potential inheritance tax yield by £2.2 billion for 2006–07 at a time when the actual yield was £3.5 billion.

Business property relief/agricultural property relief Business and agricultural property is often entirely exempt from inheritance tax on the donor's death. These reliefs are justified on the basis that they promote enterprise and provide continuity because they ensure a family business is not sold on death to pay tax. However, the reliefs provide a complete exemption even if the heirs of the deceased subsequently sell the asset immediately after death. Moreover, no capital gains tax is payable. The problem is to ensure that any relief is properly targeted. Business property relief offers a complete exemption to a company which is 51% trading and 49% investment property on death but no exemption if those two figures are reversed.

Both business and agricultural property reliefs are vigorously defended on the basis that they help enterprise and prevent businesses being split up. However, evidence suggests that the retention of medium-size businesses within certain families might, through inferior management practices, actually harm the efficiency of the UK economy (Bloom (2006)). Furthermore, even if tax is payable on businesses, there is also the possibility of claiming instalment relief (in some cases interest free) which enables the tax to be paid over ten years. There are no data on how often a business is sold after death and therefore whether the reliefs do promote continuity or just provide a tax free break for heirs.

Options for reform include varying the value of exemptions by the length of ownership or making the relief conditional on continued ownership of the business for at least some minimum time after the transfer. Both would increase compliance costs and could distort investment decisions. An alternative is to abolish business property relief which would raise £350 million pa and agricultural property relief which would raise £220 million pa. Together these would be sufficient to increase the threshold from £300,000 to £350,000 or could be used to introduce a wider band on which inheritance tax was paid at the same rate as the basic rate of income tax. The inheritance tax bills of smaller businesses and farms could then be made payable over ten years at, for example, a rate of interest equal to standard Bank of England base rate. This proposal is discussed further in Section 8.3.

Foreign domiciliaries Although in theory foreign domiciliaries are liable to inheritance tax on their worldwide estates after seventeen tax years of UK residence, in practice inheritance tax is relatively easy for this group to avoid altogether by use of trusts combined with offshore companies.[26]

The family home In contrast to the reliefs for business and farming property, there is no inheritance tax relief for the family home—the most important asset for the middle class. Much of the debate in the press focuses on the home, not merely because it is many people's main asset and therefore the reason for paying inheritance tax in the first place, but also because of the strong feeling that a parent has the right to pass it to the next generation free of tax. Statistics from HM Revenue and Customs show that 58.5% of property in estates passing on death in 2003–04 comprised real property and the Public Accounts Committee highlighted the fact that house prices have grown more quickly than the tax threshold.[27]

There is no strong case for exempting the family home, not least because doing so would provide a very strong incentive to reduce (or borrow against) chargeable assets in order to invest in a home. Furthermore, exempting the family home could lead to older relatives who should be in sheltered accommodation choosing to stay in their homes because of the tax break.

It is sometimes objected that inheritance tax 'forces' the sale of the majority of family homes. However, the home is usually sold on the last spouse's death not just to pay inheritance tax but because the children do not want to live there: they want the cash from the house. It is true that cohabitees and siblings living together will have no exemption on the first death and therefore may have to sell the house on the first death to pay inheritance tax. Although it is possible to pay the tax in interest bearing instalments over ten years, it may not be easy for the elderly with low income to fund this out of their income or obtain a mortgage to fund the payments and home reversion schemes may not be an attractive alternative.[28] Ireland has a relief that defers payment of tax until the sale of the home when it continues to be occupied by a cohabitee or sibling and something similar could be adopted here to deal with this particular problem.

As noted previously the family home is one of the hardest assets to pass on free of inheritance tax because of the reservation of benefit rules. The

[26] For further details see appendix A of the additional online material (see note 2).

[27] See 29th report of the Committee of Public Accounts Inheritance Tax 2004–05 and also Lee (2007).

[28] See the case of *Burden v Burden* 2007 involving two sisters who live in the family home and will pay inheritance tax on the first death which has attracted widespread sympathy (further details provided in appendix A of the additional online material (see note 2)). It would be possible to deal with the problem of forced sales by introducing a deferment of tax in certain limited circumstances. (See Section 8.3.)

donor cannot simply give away the house and continue living there: the house will still be subject to inheritance tax on his death (and when the house is eventually sold there is also a capital gains tax liability because there is no main residence relief if the owner does not live there; so the donor has made the tax position worse!). By contrast, in the case of gifts of cash and other liquid assets, the reservation of benefit rules are much more easily circumvented.[29] There have been a series of widely publicized schemes to save inheritance tax on the family home whose aim is to avoid the reservation of benefit rules so that the donor can give away his home and continue to live there. The success of such 'cake and eat it' schemes[30] led to anti-avoidance legislation by the government, culminating in the introduction of pre-owned assets income tax (POAT).[31] Unless lifetime gifts are taxed (in which case the anti-avoidance rules such as POAT and reservation of benefit are not needed) such an approach seems necessary if the inheritance tax base is to be maintained in any meaningful way. But it leads to a justified sense of unfairness when contrasted with the possibility of inheritance tax schemes for more liquid assets.[32] Families have a strong desire to pass wealth down to the next generation: to redistribute from the old to the young. Passing on the value of the family home is for many people the most tangible way of achieving this. The current legislation makes this particularly difficult.

Complexity

The current inheritance tax and capital gains tax legislation is very complex, and the reliefs and the interaction between the two taxes often seem arbitrary

[29] e.g. through use of discounted gift schemes and other devices.

[30] e.g. Ingram schemes—stopped in 1999; Eversden schemes stopped in 2003; reversionary lease schemes; home loan schemes now made unattractive by pre-owned asset income tax and SDLT charges.

[31] This was a new approach which abandoned specific targeted anti-avoidance legislation and instead imposed an income tax charge with effect from 6 April 2005 on all such schemes, including all schemes since 1986. Although chattels and certain trusts holding intangibles were also targeted in the legislation, the main practical impact of the legislation has been to stop future inheritance tax schemes on the family home and to encourage the unravelling of past schemes. Although widely criticized, pre-owned assets income tax does appear to be curtailing inheritance tax schemes on the family home.

[32] Even equity release schemes on the family home are problematic. For example, suppose a widow wants to release some equity by selling part of her home. She can go to a commercial provider or she can sell to a relation such as her son who has the money available. She may well prefer to sell to her son at full market value rather than pay the fees of a commercial provider. The son pays SDLT on the purchase price and the widow will be subject to inheritance tax on the unspent cash at her death. Nevertheless if the widow sells say half the house to her son, then since March 2005 she may be subject to an income tax charge on half the rental value.

and illogical. One of the objections often voiced when any change is suggested to the current system is that it would lead to unacceptable complexity.[33] However, there is already great complexity in the wealth taxation system and much of this seems to be arbitrary rather than based on any rational policy considerations. Moving to a system that is equally or nearly as complex cannot in itself be rejected if the complexity achieves a system that is more equitable with fewer unwelcome distortions.[34]

Other criticisms of inheritance tax—rates

Once inheritance tax is payable, the marginal rate is relatively high: a flat rate of 40% on death for taxable assets in excess of £300,000. Of course, the average tax rate is much lower given the high threshold. On an estate worth £½ million, the average tax rate is only 16%; on an estate of £1 million it is 28% and on an estate of £2 million it is still only 34%. However, the top marginal rate is high by international standards and the threshold at which this rate commences is relatively low.[35]

The majority of estates paying inheritance tax are below £500,000 in value. Many such estates only suffer inheritance tax due to the value of the family home and many such deceased individuals have been basic- rather than higher-rate income taxpayers during their working lives. This suggests that a progressive banding structure might be seen as fairer, and would certainly provide a clearer link that inheritance was being treated as windfall income.[36] This could involve a lower rate equal to the basic rate of income tax (20% from 2008 to 2009) and a higher rate set at the higher rate of income tax (40%). It would also be sensible to index the thresholds to nominal growth in the economy, rather than the current approach of inflation increases, since at least over the medium term, this might be sufficient to remove fiscal drag.[37] While all these reforms would reduce the yield of inheritance tax, at least in part they could be paid for through a reduction or restriction in the number of exemptions (such as APR and BPR), and the inclusion of more lifetime transfers would raise revenue. These suggestions are discussed further in Section 8.3.

[33] See, for example, p. 20 of Maxwell (2004): 'collection costs would increase given the greater complexity, compliance costs would increase, due to the demands of record-keeping.'

[34] For worked examples see appendix A of the additional online material (see note 2).

[35] See 'An International Comparison of Death Tax Rates', American Council for Capital Formation, Washington DC, 1999.

[36] See, for example, Maxwell (2004).

[37] The Chancellor announced in the Pre-Budget Report on 9 October 2007 that he would consider linking the threshold to increases in house prices in future.

A related reason why inheritance tax might be disproportionately disliked is the highly visible way that it is paid. It is one of the few taxes where people actually write out a cheque to HMRC. Most people have their income tax on their earnings deducted through PAYE and any income tax on their savings deducted at source; indirect taxes such as VAT and excise duties on alcohol and cigarettes are included in the price of goods in shops. Anecdotal evidence suggests resistance to inheritance tax is increased by the way in which it is paid. The same may also be true of council tax, which is also often paid through one payment per year.[38] There are often additional expenses in paying inheritance tax given that probate cannot be obtained until the tax is paid. In some cases it will not be possible to use the deceased's cash or other liquid assets to pay the inheritance tax due (because until the grant is obtained the assets are effectively frozen) and therefore the personal representatives need to borrow to pay the tax, increasing resentment.

8.1.3. Summary of the current inheritance tax position

Inheritance tax arouses resentment and receives much adverse publicity. The desire of parents to pass wealth on to children is a powerful motivation. Those expecting to receive legacies have come to feel they have a right to inherit. In their survey, the Commission on Taxation and Citizenship commissioned independent research into public attitudes towards taxation. Many respondents of the survey were deeply resistant to the idea of taxing inheritances and half thought that no inheritances should be taxed while only one in ten were prepared to support taxation even in the case of estates of over £1 million. Those aged 65 and over were less likely to say that no inheritances should be taxed, and those most likely to benefit from future inheritances in the younger age group were more opposed to the inheritance tax. People in social classes IV and V were more opposed to inheritance taxes than those in social classes I and II even though they were likely to be least burdened by the inheritance tax system.

Until 2006, inheritance tax remained unaltered in structure for twenty years. Recent political events suggest this stability may not last. Unless the case for a tax on transfers of wealth is put more forcefully, the introduction of a new system of wealth transfer taxation is not likely; abolition now seems a serious possibility.

[38] The Taxpayers' Alliance argues that inheritance tax is regarded as the most unfair tax and council tax the second most unfair tax. See STEP Symposium VI, 27 September 2007.

If it is concluded that inheritance tax should be retained, a number of smaller-scale improvements could be made to the existing system that would improve perceptions of fairness and therefore make it more politically acceptable. This would involve a review of rates, reliefs, and tax on lifetime gifts combined with some simplification of the system. The alternatives include more radical reform or abolition. The options are discussed further in Section 8.3.

Summary of main issues for the policy-maker to consider

The options for the policy-maker which are discussed in Section 8.3 are:

1. to introduce a new system of taxing wealth and wealth transfers;
2. to abandon any attempt to tax wealth transfers;
3. to improve the existing system so that the current inequities are rectified and the burden of the tax ceases to fall disproportionately on the middle classes.

We discuss these options in more detail in Section 8.3. However, before we proceed further, it is worth noting the most commonly discussed options for taxing wealth, which are:

1. Taxing the capital value of assets on a recurrent basis, for example, annually. A wealth tax of this sort has never been introduced in the UK although it was proposed by Meade (1978) and seriously contemplated by Labour in 1975. France, Spain, Norway, and Switzerland have a wealth tax. Most other European countries have repealed their wealth tax.
2. Taxing the capital value of assets when transferred. While Canada, India, and Australia do not have any form of capital transfer tax, most OECD countries do. Some (such as New Zealand) have no tax on death but tax lifetime transfers.
3. Taxing only the increase in value of an asset on a disposal, that is, a capital gains tax. Most countries have capital gains tax on sales but not necessarily on gifts or transfers on death. Canada has a capital gains tax imposed on death and on lifetime gifts. The UK exempts gains on death.

Within these options there are other considerations for the policymaker. In brief they include:

1. Should a tax on transfers of wealth be a donee based or a donor based tax? Should the relationship of the donee to the donor have any effect on the rate of tax—that is, should gifts to immediate family members be taxed more lightly than gifts to other individuals? The UK inheritance tax is misnamed—it does not generally take account of the circumstances of the beneficiary but like estate duty is based on the donor's circumstances at death. No inheritance tax is paid on assets left to a spouse or civil partner.[39] But the same inheritance tax is paid if an estate is shared among three children or if it is only paid to one child. Some have suggested that it is more equitable to consider the circumstances of the donee: the greater the level of previous inheritances received by the donee the greater his tax burden. The arguments for and against a donee based tax are considered later in Section 8.3. Should a tax on wealth transfers be levied only on death or also on lifetime transfers? Is there any justification for a different treatment of lifetime gifts and gifts on death?
2. What is the effect of international tax competition? Some countries such as Australia, Canada, Sweden, India, and Pakistan have abolished inheritance tax. Is it sensible for the UK to continue taxing wealth transfers at all?[40] Given that more people own assets in different countries and are more mobile, should the UK in conjunction with the EU, try to develop greater harmony in how capital is taxed?
3. Who should be chargeable for inheritance taxation? What is the best connecting factor? Should it be linked to the location of the asset and/or the residence of the donor or donee, or the domicile of the donor or donee or his citizenship?[41] This point has become of increasing importance since the 1970s as individual mobility has increased.
4. Overall what rates and thresholds should apply?
5. What reliefs and exemptions should be given? For example, spouse exemption, charity exemption, business property relief, and agricultural property relief. The question of exemptions is also linked to rates. If there are fewer exemptions, rates could be lower and/or thresholds higher. Should certain types of assets such as real property be taxed differently?

[39] Note though that there is a restricted spouse exemption on transfers from a UK domiciled spouse to a foreign domiciled spouse.

[40] Lee (2007) argues for its abolition or substantial reform.

[41] For brief explanations of domicile and residence and a summary of the rules as they affect foreign domiciliaries see appendix A of the additional online material (see note 2).

6. How should inheritance tax interact with capital gains tax? At present, as we have seen, it is possible to pay both taxes on a gift but equally the donor/donee may pay neither tax on a gift or bequest.[42] The results can be quite arbitrary.
7. If one is considering a wealth tax should and could inherited wealth be taxed differently from other wealth?
8. How should trusts be taxed? This relates not only to transfers of capital to trusts compared with gifts to individuals but also to how capital is taxed when held by a trust.

We now turn to a broader consideration of the principles that might inform the design of wealth and wealth transfer taxes as a prelude to considering policy alternatives.

8.2. ECONOMIC PRINCIPLES OF WEALTH AND WEALTH TRANSFER TAXATION

The choice of a tax system should be based on some normative principles. In the case of wealth and wealth transfer taxation, there are a number of difficulties in enunciating and applying such principles. Unlike most other forms of taxation, such as income, commodity, and company taxation, there are few accepted principles and the theoretical (optimal taxation) literature provides relatively little guidance for tax policy. It is therefore not surprising that, as we have mentioned, countries vary widely in how they tax wealth.[43]

In what follows, we first consider the normative criteria that could inform wealth and wealth transfer taxation and briefly summarize what the theoretical tax literature has said about wealth transfer taxation. We then consider the broad implications of these principles for tax design.

8.2.1. Criteria for evaluating a tax system

We begin by outlining the appropriate criteria that could be used to judge any good tax system. How these apply to the taxation of both wealth and wealth transfers will then be considered. Three key constraints in tax design

[42] For example, if the donor dies within seven years of a lifetime gift he may end up paying both capital gains tax and inheritance tax. If the donor dies leaving business property to his heirs, neither inheritance tax nor capital gains tax is payable.

[43] See note 2 above and appendix B of the additional online material cited therein.

stand out. First, **efficiency**, since to the extent that a tax induces an unwanted distortion on decisions to work, to accumulate and dispose of wealth, and so on, that might temper the tax rate. Second, **administrative costs**, which can be considerable in the case of the taxation of wealth and wealth transfers.[44] Some forms of wealth are particularly difficult to measure and some are relatively easy to conceal, for example they can be moved offshore or their legal ownership transferred. Given the inability to tax certain forms of wealth and wealth transfers, the case for taxation of others may be compromised. Third, **political constraints**, since implementing or reforming taxes inevitably creates winners and losers, the latter of whom might be more politically influential than the former. A political consensus to support a coherent tax system on wealth transfers is particularly relevant to both wealth taxation, which has to operate consistently over the lifetime of an individual, and to wealth transfer taxation since otherwise transfers could be timed to take advantage of relatively attractive tax regimes.

Three main criteria underlie tax reform. The first of these is the **welfarist criterion**, which is the standard criterion used in previous tax reform deliberations, including those of Meade (1978). The other two are criteria that have been prominent in more recent literature. We refer to them as **equality of opportunity** and **paternalism**, and these can be especially important in the case of wealth and wealth transfer taxation. The three criteria are not mutually exclusive.

Welfarist criterion

The standard approach taken in the theoretical literature on optimal taxation can be referred to as the welfarist, or utility-based approach. Taxpayer welfare (utility) is taken to depend on the goods and services consumed, including leisure time. It is assumed that welfare increases with consumption but increases at a decreasing rate (that is, marginal utility is diminishing). Since welfare cannot be measured directly it is often summarized by a measure of after tax income or expenditure. The objective of the government is to choose the tax structure that maximizes social welfare (some aggregate of individual utility, such as the sum of utilities), taking account of how individual behaviour will respond to the tax system and the need to raise revenue to finance expenditure on public services. The result is that better-off individuals bear progressively higher tax bills, with the degree of progressivity depending

[44] HMRC Annual Report 2005–06 annex C lists the cost of collection of income tax as 1.27 pence per £ collected, corporation tax 0.71, capital gains tax 0.92, inheritance tax 1.01, stamp taxes 0.20. Moreover, the estate of a deceased taxpayer has to obtain valuations to assess the inheritance tax due.

on the size of behavioural responses (efficiency) as well as the aversion to inequality by the government, as reflected in the rate at which marginal utility of consumption diminishes (equity).[45]

This is the approach that informs much of the tax policy literature, including Meade (1978), the Blueprints for Basic Tax Reform, and the Report of the President's Tax Commission in the USA. In the context of wealth transfer taxation, the welfarist approach has also been dominant (e.g. the recent surveys by Kaplow (2001); and Cremer and Pestieau (2006)). For our purposes, the point is simply that one person's tax liability relative to another person's is directly related to their relative well-being or income. This approach is typically called welfarism in the theoretical literature, a term that refers to the fact that only levels of individual well-being count in determining social welfare.

Following the welfarist approach would lead one to seek as a tax base an indicator of the level of well-being of the taxpayer. The rate structure to apply to the chosen base depends on efficiency and administrative considerations. Our main concern here is with the choice of a base. There are a number of general problems associated with applying the welfarist objective. One is the issue of measurability. An ideal tax base that reflects the well-being of a household contains elements that are difficult to measure, a prime example being leisure or the value of non-market time. The problems with choosing a tax base that takes such things into account are discussed by Banks and Diamond in Chapter 6. Related to the measurability problem is the problem of information. A good tax base, like income or expenditure, may be in principle measurable but not directly observable to the government. The need to rely on self-reporting constrains the scope of the base and the rate structure. There may also be collection and compliance costs arising from the inevitable complexity of any tax system and the incentives that might exist for taxpayers to minimize their tax burdens. The choice of a base and rate structure involves value judgements about both horizontal and vertical equity.[46] In the end, these must reflect some consensus that gets resolved by the political process. A further issue that might constrain the choice of a tax system concerns the fact that policymakers, even if they are perfectly benevolent and respond to what they perceive as social welfare objectives, may not be able to commit to

[45] The marginal utility of consumption should be interpreted here as marginal social utility as judged by government in its notional calculations of social welfare. It should not be interpreted as marginal utility in some objective sense.

[46] Horizontal equity is the principle that individuals who are equally well off should face the same tax burden. Vertical equity is the principle that one person who is better off than another should pay taxes that are appropriately higher reflecting the fact that their marginal social utility of consumption is higher.

tax policies over a reasonably long period of time. Policies that are optimal from a long-term perspective might be time-inconsistent, to use the technical term. Thus, long-run optimal policies will take account of the effect that the tax system has on decisions to save and invest in the future. But, once the future comes around, the savings/investment decision has been made and even a benevolent policymaker would want to tax its proceeds. The consequence is that taxes on capital income and wealth might be excessively high from a long-run perspective, and the policy response might be to attempt to tie the hands of future governments in order to prevent them being able to tax capital income or wealth excessively.

The problems outlined above apply to the design of any tax. However, there are two particular issues in the context of wealth and wealth transfer taxation. The first is whether all sources of individual well-being should 'count' from a social point of view—in particular should the benefits donors obtain from altruistic transfers count as well-being for the purposes of tax policy? If so, a form of double-counting can arise since the same transfers will also yield well-being to the donees. A related issue arises if my well-being is based on my position relative to yours in terms of wealth, income, housing, and so on. If so, increments in wealth have negative effects on others and, by welfarist logic, ought to be taxed. Second, a person might get well-being from holding wealth over and above that obtained when the wealth is used to generate consumption. If one takes the welfarist approach literally (as Kaplow (2001) advocates), all sources of well-being should count regardless of their source. We shall refer to this as the strict welfarist approach. Much of the literature in this area has focused on the taxation of transfers from parents to their children.[47] A number of special problems arise in this context. First, an intergenerational perspective must be taken. Social welfare will need to include, and suitably weight, the well-being of both the parent and the child. Moreover, a transfer from a parent to a child may lead to the child making a larger bequest, and so on down the line. This implies that in order to analyse the consequences of a wealth transfer tax, one must take into account potential impacts into the indefinite future (for example with an overlapping-generations model).

Next, the effect of a given wealth transfer on both equity and efficiency will depend on the motivation for giving it. Four different motives are distinguished in the literature. Even though it is not possible to observe motives and thus to tax on the basis of them, some motives might be more prevalent for some types of transfers (e.g. lifetime vs at death), and this may constitute

[47] A comprehensive survey of the optimal taxation of bequests can be found in Cremer and Pestieau (2006). Our discussion draws heavily on that.

a reason for taxing them differently. First, a transfer of wealth (whether made on death or lifetime) may be made because the donor gets utility simply from the act of giving to his chosen beneficiaries (the utility of bequest motive). Then, utility depends on the amount transferred. Second, it may be given because of altruism of the donor for the donee's utility (the altruistic motive), in which case the utility to the donor depends on how the transfer affects the utility of the donee. Third, it may be given in return for some favour or service, such as personal care (the strategic motive). Finally, it may be given unintentionally as a result of wealth held at death for precautionary or other reasons (the accidental motive). In the first three cases, since the bequest is intentional, it presumably benefits both the donor and the donee. Under the welfarist principle set out above, this could justify the fact that certain types of transfers should be taxed more heavily if they produce utility for both individuals. However, it remains a matter of judgement whether or not such double-counting of utility (i.e. considering the utility of both donor and donee) should be allowed in determining the tax base. One could decide that under both the utility of bequest motive and the altruistic motive it is not appropriate to count the increase in well-being of both the donor and the donee. In the case of strategic bequests, since these are effectively the same as any other transaction between a buyer and a seller, it is clear cut that the increase in well-being of both the donor and the donee should be counted. The transfer reflects a payment for service by the donor and income for the donee just like the purchase of a good. In the case of accidental bequests, since they are not a matter of choice, it is reasonable to think that only the donee benefits and that these transfers should not be double-counted.

A further complication occurs if the donee also cares about the consumption of the donor. In this case the increase in the well-being of the donee from the additional consumption arising from the bequest will be partially offset by the fact that the consumption of the donor is lower as a result of the bequest being made. In this case the welfarist argument for double-counting the bequest (i.e. taxing it more heavily on the basis that it produces greater overall utility) would be reduced.

From an efficiency point of view, only bequests that are a matter of choice—as opposed to those made by accident—could be expected to respond to fiscal incentives. Specifically, higher taxation of wealth transfers would be expected to lead to lower after-tax bequests, although the impact on gross bequests is ambiguous. Among the categories of voluntary bequests, the responsiveness of the bequest to changing fiscal incentives may well vary. In particular, the responsiveness of wealth transfers made for the utility of bequest motive to their tax treatment will depend on whether well-being is derived from the pre-tax or the after-tax size of bequest.

The welfarist argument is that efficiency and equity effects of taxing transfers of wealth should depend on the motive and satisfaction obtained for donor and donee. Thus, it is sometimes argued that since bequests given before death will not have been made by accident while some of those made at death will be, this in itself justifies different tax treatment of lifetime and end-of-life bequests. However, under the welfarist criterion, it is ambiguous which should be taxed higher if the utility of bequests to the donor counts. Efficiency arguments support higher taxes on accidental bequests since such bequests are not responsive to bequest taxes. However, equity arguments suggest lower taxes on accidental bequests since the donor obtains no utility from the bequest.

Unfortunately, the motive for a transfer of wealth is not readily observable. It certainly cannot be the case that all bequests on death are accidental and should therefore be taxed less heavily because they only give satisfaction to the donee or more heavily because they have no disincentive effect. Nor can it be the case that bequests are entirely strategic or altruistic—a donor may be giving during lifetime partly in the hope that his heirs will look after him but also to safeguard their future.

These considerations confirm that even if the bequest motive is known, the theoretical prescriptions for wealth transfer taxation are ambiguous with the policy prescription varying widely with the government's preferences. This is illustrated in Box 8.1 based on the recent survey of optimal bequest taxation by Cremer and Pestieau (2006). The analysis is based on a simple model that has many shortcomings as a basis for making policy conclusions. Most importantly, little headway has been made in analysing the issue of equity, which arguably is the most important dimension of wealth and wealth transfer taxation. Since the focus of the optimal tax approach has been on redistribution across rather than within generations it does not take account of the fact that recipients within the same generation may well receive very unequal inheritances of wealth. A donee who has inherited more in the past will presumably receive lower utility from an additional gift made now. Once heterogeneity of individuals is taken into account, questions about donor- and donee-based taxation become relevant. The government now has a potential interest in addressing inequalities created by inheritances whose distribution affects the utility of donees.

Two lessons emerge from the optimal tax literature. First, the efficiency costs of wealth transfers can vary significantly with the motive for the wealth transfer. Second, the appropriate objective for the government is more difficult to specify when wealth transfers are at stake.

A further serious difficulty with welfarism involves dealing with individuals who have different preferences. This makes it difficult to compare well-being levels in principle, let alone in practice. If otherwise identical individuals have different preferences for leisure, for saving, for family formation, or for uses of their income, they will have different economic outcomes. Should the tax system treat them differently? More to the point, if persons with equal means choose to make different amounts of wealth transfers, should they be treated differently because of these choices?

In conclusion, taking a welfarist approach to wealth transfer taxation leaves some important questions open. What weight should be given to the utility of donors and donees when both may benefit from the same transfer? How should lifetime transfers be treated relative to transfers at death given that different motives might apply to each? How should account be taken of the fact that different individuals have different preferences for saving, making bequests, and so on? We now look at other taxation criteria.

Box 8.1. Lessons from optimal tax literature for bequest tax design

Following the survey by Cremer and Pestieau (2006), a simple approach is to consider an overlapping-generations model, where each generation consists of individuals that live for two periods (working and retirement). There are four 'goods' that individuals can choose: present and future consumption, first-period leisure, and a bequest. They obtain an inheritance from their parent in the previous generation and use it along with earnings to finance current consumption and saving. Saving plus interest is then spent on future consumption and bequests. Population grows at some given rate, with each person having one or more heirs to whom bequests are made.

The government requires a given stream of revenues, and can use proportional taxes on labour income, capital income, and bequests. Given the proportionality of taxes, there is no distinction between a tax on bequests and a tax on inheritances. The government is also assumed to be able to use debt freely, which implies that it can control the level of capital accumulation.

The setting is basically a straightforward extension of the classical Ramsey optimal commodity tax problem with four goods to an overlapping-generations setting in which individuals are linked by parent–heir wealth transfers. Despite this apparent simplicity, the results are agnostic and turn on two key assumptions. The first is which of the four motivations for bequests applies. The second is whether the government gives weight to the utility of bequests to the donor in its social welfare function, which takes the form of a discounted sum of utilities of all present and future generations of individuals.

Cremer and Pestieau report results mainly for the steady state (long run) when all variables have achieved their long-run values. A brief summary is as follows.

Utility of bequests If the government counts the utility of bequests in its social welfare function, the optimal tax may well entail a subsidy on bequests. The government counts not only the utility of bequests to the donor, but also the benefit of the inheritance to the donee. Since the donor does not take account of the latter, bequests are too low from a social point of view on that account.

On the other hand, if the government does not count the utility of the bequest to the donor (to avoid double-counting), taxes on labour, capital income, and bequests depend on compensated elasticities of demand for first- and second-period consumption, leisure, and bequests as in a usual optimal tax problem. The problem is somewhat complicated because the government and the individuals have conflicting preferences: individual bequests are determined by the utility the donor obtains from them, while optimal bequests from society's perspective are determined by the utility generated for donees.

Altruistic bequests When individuals benefit from the utility of their immediate heirs, they will also benefit indirectly from the utility of their heirs' heirs, their heirs' heirs' heirs, and so on (since the utility of their heirs' heirs affects the utility of their heirs). Taking account of this indefinite sequence of utility interdependency, one can represent the utility of a person in the current generation as a dynastic utility function that includes the utility of all subsequent heirs. This leads to the Ricardian equivalence argument that intergenerational transfers will be ineffective. Any attempt to redistribute from, say, the current generation to future generations will be undone by a reduction in bequests so any attempt to tax bequests will be ineffective since bequests will be adjusted to unwind the impact of this redistribution. What weight one should put on these results is not clear. There is no compelling empirical evidence to support the view that government intergenerational transfers are ineffective, and the theoretical underpinnings for the Ricardian hypothesis are very weak in a more realistic setting. (As Bernheim and Bagwell (1988) have shown, the hypothesis falls down once account is taken of the fact that dynastic lines are not linear given the fact that marriage is between two individuals in different families.)

Accidental bequests Accidental bequests occur because, in the absence of perfect annuity markets, individuals have to self-insure against uncertain longevity by holding wealth. When they die, this wealth is passed on to heirs. Since, by assumption, donors obtain no utility from the bequest, the issue of double-counting does not arise. Moreover, taxing it will have no effect on their bequest behaviour. On efficiency grounds, it is therefore optimal to impose as high a tax as possible on accidental bequests.

(*cont.*)

Box 8.1. (*cont.*)

Strategic bequests These bequests are analogous to a sale from one person to another. As such, no issue of double-counting arises if account is taken of the benefits to both the donor and the donee. The actual tax on bequests is complicated by the fact that the bequest is a voluntary exchange involving choice by both parties. Depending on the responsiveness of each, the optimal tax could be relatively high or relatively low.

As noted previously, wealth transfers may well be done from a mixture of these motives.

Non-welfarist criteria: equality of opportunity

In the theoretical redistribution literature, one approach to dealing with the fact that different individuals have different preferences is the so-called equality of opportunity approach, following Roemer (1998) and Fleurbaey and Maniquet (2007). In this approach, a distinction is made between the 'principle of compensation' and the 'principle of responsibility'. Individuals ought to be compensated for disadvantages that they face that are beyond their control, as in the case of differences in innate ability or productivity stressed by the welfarist optimal tax literature. However, they ought not to be compensated for differences arising from things for which they are responsible, an example of which might be their preferences. Applying this distinction in practice is fraught with difficulties—for example if some individuals are innately hard-working or lazy—but one approach that has been fruitful is to equalize opportunities that households have, regardless of how they choose to use them. This might be taken to be an argument for equalizing, say, inherited wealth as an objective of policy. It might also be used to justify not taking special account of altruistic preferences. That is, if personal choice leads some individuals, but not others, to transfer wealth to relatives or to charities, no distinction should be made in the tax system between the two types. On this basis, freely made choices to make transfers should not attract favourable or unfavourable tax treatment in the hands of the donor, although the equality of opportunity argument might suggest that transfers should be differently taxed in the hands of the donee depending on his status. We referred in Section 8.1 to the equity objective—the idea that people should not be taxed more heavily if they choose to save their wealth rather than spend it before their death. Equality of opportunity provides some justification to this objection.

In the case of wealth taxation, as we have seen, the argument is made that wealth confers benefits to individuals over and above its role as a source of income. It might confer status or power, or it might provide opportunities that are otherwise not available to other taxpayers. One has to be wary of double-counting here. To the extent that the benefits of holding wealth ultimately show up as income or expenditure, they will then be subject to direct taxation. For wealth to be a separate base for taxation, one must be persuaded that it does provide benefits over and above the consumption that the wealth finances, or that the benefits that confer utility do not otherwise end up being taxed. (The fact that individuals systematically make wealth transfers at death rather than during life might be prime facie evidence that there is some value to holding wealth, at least for those for whom lifetime transfers are an option.) One example of this is if having a large amount of wealth enables individuals to take a more high risk, high return, approach in their lives. Then, unless these returns are subject to an appropriate amount of tax (and these returns might not necessarily be financial returns and therefore are not taxed), this could be used as a justification for the taxation of wealth. However, it may be that the forms of wealth that do confer extra benefits are those that cannot be easily taxed, such as human capital (i.e. an individual's earning potential, which, among other things, will depend on their talents, education, and health) and other personal attributes.

There is no discernible consensus among experts in tax theory and policy that wealth should be regarded as conferring a benefit on its owners over and above its usefulness as a source of income or expenditure. Despite that, the Meade Report (Meade, 1978) simply assumed it to be the case. Much of the argument for the taxation of wealth—over and above the taxation of wealth transfers—rests on the assertion that wealth itself is a source of benefit.

Non-welfarist criteria: paternalism

Recent literature has stressed various ways in which individual decision-making may lead to outcomes that are not in the long-run interest of the individuals themselves, and the puzzle this poses for government policy (Bernheim and Rangel (2007)). Three general categories of problems have been stressed. Individuals may not be well enough informed to be able to take some types of decisions, such as those involving financial transactions or consumer contracts. To reduce the costliness of such transactions, governments may impose regulations on suppliers or may compel or default individuals into certain types of actions (health care, education, retirement saving, etc.).

Second, individuals might purposely make choices against their own self-interest for reasons of ethics or social norms. Donating to charity might be an example of this. The fact that these actions are against their own self-interest may warrant favourable treatment under the tax system, although it may be impossible to detect the true reason for such donations—for example one could equally argue that large donations to charity can give a donor access to power, media popularity, and possibly non-monetary benefits such as honours. The merits of offering favourable tax treatment will also depend on how the price elasticity of charitable donations compares to the deadweight cost of supporting those donations that would have taken place in the absence of the favourable treatment.

Finally, personal decisions may not always be rational or consistent over time—for example, individuals might make decisions that they subsequently regret—as a result of myopia, self-control problems, or not anticipating the consequences of one's actions. This leads to outcomes such as undersaving for retirement, addictions, excessive gambling, and procrastination. Governments may react to such time-inconsistency problems by second-guessing personal decisions and purporting to correct them so that they align with long-term interests. Such paternalism is very contentious since it contradicts the usual norms of consumer sovereignty. In practice, wealth taxation may discourage saving (although it might have little effect on those not behaving rationally) and providing an incentive to make lifetime gifts (as at present) may lead to donors not retaining sufficient wealth to fund their future needs.

8.2.2. The tax treatment of wealth transfers

The issues surrounding the tax treatment of wealth transfers can best be revealed by considering the simple case in which one person, a donor, makes a voluntary transfer of funds to another person, a donee. We set aside for now the issue of whether there is a particular relationship between the two, focusing instead on the transfer in the abstract. If one takes a strict welfarist approach to tax design (following Kaplow (2001)), one would treat the transfer as yielding welfare to the donor and taxed as such, equivalent to any other spending since it was voluntarily undertaken. By the same token, the transfer constitutes an increase in taxable income to the donee. To evaluate how compelling this strict welfarist argument is, it is useful to consider various caveats that might apply, some of which we have already seen.

The standing of the donor's utility

As we have seen above the strict welfarist approach leads to a form of double-counting in the sense that the transfer is taken to give utility both to the donor and to the donee, and thus calls for taxation in the hands of both. So by way of example if X gave away £1 million to his son Y, then X would receive no tax relief on that donation (even though it had been paid out of after-tax income) and Y would pay tax on it. Whether or not this is appropriate is a matter of judgement. One could equally well depart from strict welfarism and argue that a transfer of funds from one taxpayer to another should be treated like a transfer of the tax base and should only be taxed once.[48] To make this point more forcefully, the same double-counting will occur under strict welfarism even if altruism is not accompanied by a transfer: person A may get utility from person B's consumption without a transfer from A to B. Obviously, the tax system could not take such utility interdependency into account. Is then it appropriate to include the benefit to both the donor and the donee from the same transfer in their respective tax liabilities, even though such common benefits are not included as taxable in the absence of a transfer? So in the above example, if X benefits altruistically from Y's annual consumption of £20,000 financed by Y's own income, that benefit would somehow have to be included in X's taxable income as well as Y's if altruism is to count.

Altruism might not be the only motive for a voluntary transfer. As mentioned, a donor might be motivated by a 'joy of giving' (or a 'warm glow', following Andreoni (1990)) without regard to the benefit to the donee. Or, donors may obtain prestige value from the size of their charitable donations. Alternatively, there might simply be ethical motives involved. Since motives are not observable, it would be impossible to differentiate tax treatment by motive in the case of gifts.

However, there are other arguments in favour of not giving tax relief to donors for transfers. If donations are taken to be the free exercise of one's chosen preferences, the principle of responsibility would say simply that the tax system should treat no differently those who do and do not choose to make donations. By this argument, the only tax consequence of donations would be that they increase the opportunities available to donees and should be taxed as such. So in our above example, the £1 million that X gave to Y would be taxable income for Y but would have no tax consequences for X, albeit he would not receive a tax deduction. Thus, the tax treatment of wealth transfers would be the same under the strict welfarist system and the principle of responsibility, or equality of opportunity: donees should be taxed with no relief for donors. (Note these arguments are quite independent of the case

[48] The Meade Report discounted these arguments out of hand. But, it also seemingly argued against the simple principle of treating a transfer as taxable to both the donor and the donee, and suggested some separate treatment.

for taxing accrued capital gains on death. Since these capital gains represent capital income in the years before death, they should be taxed under an income tax system in any case.)

Transfers on death compared with lifetime transfers

We have already noted that transfers on death may differ from lifetime transfers in two ways. First, they may be involuntary, as in the case of unintended bequests. If donors have held wealth for precautionary purposes solely to self-insure against uncertainty in the length of life, transfers of wealth at death are involuntary in the sense that the wealth was not retained for the purpose of making a transfer. On the other hand, the holding of precautionary wealth does benefit the donor since it presumably yields some value in terms of risk reduction. A clearer case might be that in which the wealth held at death is simply a result of bad planning, myopia, or bounded rationality as has been stressed in the behavioural economics literature. Here it seems clear that there is no benefit for the donor associated with the wealth transferred, so the case for taxing a transfer on death simply on welfarist grounds is weak. On the other hand, the donor may in fact obtain satisfaction from knowing he is providing for his heirs in his will—in other words, many transfers on death are planned and do have a bequest motive. So it seems difficult on welfarist criteria to distinguish precisely between lifetime and death transfers given the difficulty in determining motive.

Second, transfers on death may represent exchanges for services obtained from the donee while the donor is alive. For example, the donor promises the donee a transfer of wealth in return for personal care or attention while alive. This case is no different from any other voluntary exchange where the seller of the service (the donee) is rewarded for the service performed and the donor makes a purchase just like any other consumer purchase although the consideration given for the services provided is less precise. If transfers on death do represent an exchange for past services, there is no double-counting from including the value of the transfer as part of the tax base of both the donor and the donee. This would mean that £1 million that X gave to Y in our example above would be the 'price' paid for services given by Y. To X it would be like any other purchase of a commodity so not tax-deductible, while for Y it would be like income from the supply of the service and therefore taxable.[49]

[49] Of course, this case assumes the donor can commit to a transfer on death. As some UK court cases illustrate, the donee may provide the services but not be given the reward if the donor chooses to leave his assets elsewhere on death or in fact has no property to leave. In fact the court cases illustrate that the services provided by the donee or the detriment he has suffered may well be worth

It has been argued that transfers before death are more likely to be planned than those at death (since any unintended bequests almost certainly occur at death). For this reason lifetime transfers would be taxed differently from those at death. However, it is clear that motives cannot be observed with sufficient certainty so one cannot take them into account in deciding wealth taxation. In addition motive is not a relevant consideration when considering equity and equality of opportunity issues. Moreover, as mentioned in Section 8.1, high-wealth taxpayers are more likely to be able to give assets away during their lifetime yet may have no greater bequest motive than the person who cannot afford to give assets away during his lifetime. Why should they be taxed differently?

Transfers to heirs

Transfers of wealth to heirs, either at death or earlier, constitute a substantial share of wealth transfers. Although there may be no compelling reason for treating intra-family transfers differently from those made outside the family, some conceptual problems with the welfarist approach can be seen at their starkest in this case. Parenting obviously entails providing goods, services, and funds to one's offspring. Does one adopt the welfarist point of view here and treat the act of giving to one's children as yielding benefits to both the parents and the children? Such a position would have significant implications for the tax treatment of the family, implying, for example, a higher tax burden on a single-earner multi-person family than on a single person with the same income. A particularly important form of transfer from parents to children is human capital transfers. If transfers of financial wealth should be taxed because they yield utility to both the donor and the donee, the same should apply to these transfers. Given that it is difficult to do the latter, the question is whether taxation should apply to the former.[50] Many countries (e.g. France) tax a gift to a child more lightly than a gift to a more distant relative but there seems no logic to this unless it is felt that concentration of wealth in the hands of the next generation is to be encouraged. An equality of opportunity approach would suggest the reverse—that wealth should be taxed on the donee more highly where they inherit larger sums.

The case of intra-family transfers also makes the consequences of double-counting transparent. Suppose that as one goes down the line of a family, each

considerably less than any wealth that is inherited. See cases of proprietary estoppel. *Gillett v Holt* [2001] Ch 210; *Crubb v Arun DC* [1976] Ch 179; *Gissing v Gissing* [1971] AC 886.

[50] The consequences of human capital transfers not being taxed are mitigated to some extent by the active role the state plays in the provision of public education.

generation passes on to the next generation on average what they received from the previous generation. (Deviations from the average would occur, for example, if some generation had unusually bad or good luck.) The welfarist logic would imply that the wealth transfer is repeatedly taxed each generation under either an income or an expenditure tax system despite the fact that it had not been dissipated for consumption or allowed to grow. Whether this is reasonable is a matter of judgement, but it is a consequence of the strict welfarist logic. Most countries that have a wealth transfer tax do tax on transfers of the same wealth between each generation and some countries tax transfers which skip a generation more heavily.

More generally, intra-family transfers lead to more profound consequences if one takes the welfarist viewpoint seriously. A transfer from a parent to an offspring could conceivably give utility benefits to several individuals: the donor, the donee, the donor's spouse, the donee's siblings, and so on. There is certainly no practical way of taking these benefits into account in the tax system even if one wanted to do so. The point is simply relying on the strict welfarist principle has severe limitations, principally because it is impossible accurately to assess either motive or quantum of benefits, and leads to seemingly extreme prescriptions.

Externalities

Some forms of wealth transfers can be thought of as generating positive benefits beyond the donor–donee nexus. For example donations to charities and non-profit organizations benefit members of the public who are the object of the charities' help. Rather than subjecting these transfers to additional taxation, some fiscal incentive is usually given. The argument for this treatment arises if other individuals benefit from charitable donations. One might on these grounds argue that because external benefits are being generated by the donation, those benefits should be rewarded by sheltering the transfer from taxation such as through a credit or a deduction. That logic would be fine as far as it goes. However, the third parties who are obtaining the altruistic benefit from the transfers are themselves better off, so their tax liabilities should rise accordingly. Since that is practically impossible to do, the case for subsidizing the initial transfer might be tempered.

A more compelling case for subsidizing transfers to charities and non-profit organizations might be that the alternative for the government is to finance them directly. Given that it is costly for the government to raise revenue because of the distortions its taxes impose, it might be more efficient for the government to subsidize charitable contributions by giving tax relief rather than financing them directly. These arguments do not apply to ordinary wealth transfers since the government typically has no policy interest in facilitating them. However, the evidence cited in Banks and Tanner (1998) for studies in the UK, the USA, and Canada indicate that, at least in the short run, the price elasticity of charitable donations is typically less than one, implying that the tax cost of increasing donations exceeds the size of the donations induced.

Alternative approaches

Alternative approaches are what we call the restricted welfarist approach and the equality of opportunity approach to wealth transfer taxation discussed earlier.

By the restricted welfarist approach, we mean that only benefit of the wealth transfer to the donee is counted. This means that under expenditure or income taxation, donors would receive a tax credit or deduction while donees would treat the transfer as a source of income. So in the above example of X giving £1 million to Y, X would receive a deduction for that gift against his taxable income or gains and Y would be taxed on it as income. In principle, under an income tax system, capital gains should be deemed realized on the gift and treated as taxable income for X since they were accrued in the hands of X.

Apart from possible disagreement in principle with this approach, it also has some drawbacks. For example in the case of transfers on death, the approach is hard to implement since it entails giving a tax deduction to a taxpayer no longer alive although his estate could benefit. Alternatively, one could simply give no credit to the donor and not impose tax on the donee, which if the tax rates are the same is equivalent to not taxing wealth transfers. A further problem is that the argument for not taxing the donor might apply to the case of transfers made out of altruism or joy of giving, but not those that are strategic or unintended. We have seen already the difficulty of varying tax rates by motive.

The equality of opportunity approach would neither penalize nor reward taxpayers according to how they choose to use their income. Those choosing to make wealth transfers would be treated the same as those choosing to spend all their income. At the same time, transfers received by donees would be treated as an advantage (source of opportunity) that should be taxed. Thus, donees would be taxed on transfers while no relief would be given to donors. Nonetheless, transfers would effectively be taxed twice: once in the hands of the donors as they accumulated the wealth and again in the hands of the donees (and multiple times if the same transfer is in turn passed to subsequent heirs). So in our example above, a transfer of £1 million from X to Y would be taxable on Y with no tax relief for X. The equality of opportunity approach ends up in wealth transfers being taxed in the same way as under strict welfarism.

If one accepts the above arguments that wealth transfers constitute a legitimate base for taxation, with the treatment of donors and donees depending on whether one takes a strict welfarist, a restricted welfarist, or an equality of opportunity point of view, there are a number of design issues that must be confronted in implementing such a tax. These are discussed in Section 8.3.

8.2.3. The tax treatment of wealth

Periodic taxes on wealth may perform a different role from taxation of wealth transfers. One is as an alternative to income taxes since, at least for income generating wealth, an annual tax on wealth is roughly analogous to a tax on capital income from that wealth.[51] To the extent that one wants to include capital income in the tax base, wealth taxation may be convenient for some types of assets, particularly those for which measures of asset income are not readily observable. For example, taxes on the value of owner-occupied housing (net of mortgage debt) are a way of taxing its imputed return, given that there is no tax paid on the imputed rental income from owner-occupied housing. In an open economy setting where capital income from abroad is not easily verifiable, a tax on wealth might be a rough-and-ready way of taxing presumed income. Of course, it may be even more practically difficult to measure the value of such wealth than it is to monitor the income it produces.

Wealth taxation may be a supplement to capital income taxation where the latter is constrained by policy design. Thus, in a dual income tax system where capital income is taxed at a uniform rate, wealth taxation may be used as an additional policy instrument to achieve redistributive objectives. These arguments for wealth taxation as a means of enhancing the direct tax system raise no additional conceptual issues that are not already dealt with in the design of a direct tax system. Countries such as the UK which did not introduce wealth tax in the early twentieth century tended to impose an additional tax on capital income. Denis Healey argued for a wealth tax in 1975 partly on the grounds that it would facilitate a reduction in income tax.

[51] Thus, if A is the value of an asset and r is the rate of return on the asset (taking the form of dividends, interest, capital gains, etc.), the capital income on the asset will be rA. Imposing a tax rate t on capital income each year will be equivalent to imposing a tax rate of rt on the asset itself each year.

The more relevant question is whether there are cogent arguments for taxing wealth per se over and above those that inform the choice of a direct tax system. To put it another way, should wealth be subject to double or triple taxation, once when it is created, again when it is transferred, and also in its own right? If one takes a strict welfarist point of view and argues that the proper base for taxation ought to be the consumption of goods and services that generate well-being for the household, one might be led to argue against an additional tax on wealth. However, one can marshal other arguments, some welfarist in nature, to support wealth taxation.

Wealth as a source of utility

As we have already mentioned, and as the Meade Report held, taxpayers might obtain utility from wealth over and above that obtained from its use. Wealth might confer status and power on its owner, at least if held in sufficient and observed amounts. In addition, wealth might have some purely precautionary value as a device for self-insurance against unexpected future needs. To the extent that these things benefit the wealth-owner, it might be argued that they should be subject to additional taxation.

Even if one accepts that wealth bestows some benefit on its owner over and above its use for financing consumption, the issue arises whether that benefit should be taxed. The fact that the benefits of wealth-holding are not measurable would make it difficult for the tax system to take them fully into account in any case. Given these caveats, and given that the usually specified benefits from wealth likely accrue mainly to individuals who hold significant amounts of it, a separate wealth tax based on these arguments would only be justified, if at all, at the upper end of the wealth distribution.

Non-welfarist arguments

Another of the arguments given by the Meade Report for a tax on wealth was equality of opportunity. The objective of equality of opportunity seems to be a widely held one, but there is no consensus about its explicit meaning. The broad interpretation put on it by Roemer (1998), and the one that we drew on in discussing taxation of wealth transfers, is that individuals should be compensated for disadvantages they are endowed with, but should otherwise be free to exercise their choices according to their own preferences. Alternatively, Sen (1985) has stressed that individuals ought to have comparable opportunities to participate in society, both in the market economy and in social interaction, and that these opportunities involve the accessibility not only to purchasing power but also to credit, skills, and so on. Wealth can be seen as an instrument for enhancing one's opportunity in society, and giving one a stake in it or feeling a part of it. Some have even argued that all individuals ought to be given a start-up grant or an ongoing basic income on these grounds, and more generally on the grounds of enhancing the freedom of individuals to participate in society, and reducing the stigma of being dependent (Atkinson (1972); Van Parijs (1995); Ackerman and Alstott (1999); Le Grand (2006)). Others have argued that an 'asset-effect' exists and that this justifies such a policy (Sherraden (1991)). It has also been argued that an observed positive association between asset holding at younger ages and better subsequent life events provides evidence of such an asset effect (Bynner and Paxton (2001)). But this empirical evidence is very weak not least because it is quite possible that some other unobserved characteristic, such as patience, causes both the holding of assets at earlier ages and better subsequent outcomes (Emmerson and Wakefield (2001)). Despite this, the empirical evidence was used to support the introduction of the Child Trust Fund in the UK, which is a lump sum payment to all newborns, with the funds locked away until age 18.

The main point here is that this argument for wealth being a determinant of tax design applies with special force for those towards the bottom of the wealth distribution. A wealth tax itself would do little to reach those with limited wealth to begin with. This might lead one to think of a progressive tax-transfer system for wealth, whereby those at the upper end pay a tax while those with limited or no wealth receive a wealth subsidy.

Arguments for discouraging or encouraging wealth accumulation

The suggestion of a progressive wealth tax might be given further support by the argument that wealth-holding leads to pure status effects whereby one's holding of wealth relative to others is what counts in generating pleasure. According to this argument, not only does an increase in one person's wealth have an adverse effect on other individuals' well-being (which may or may not count from society's perspective), but more important, individuals have an incentive to over-accumulate wealth in a sort of self-defeating rat-race. A progressive wealth tax would blunt this incentive. More generally, there seems to be some evidence that people have not become any happier as average incomes have increased rapidly in recent years (Layard (2005)) which might suggest lower welfare costs of taxing wealth.

At the same time, the behavioural economics literature suggests an opposing consideration. On the basis of psychological and experimental evidence, it has been argued that some individuals are inherently short-sighted and tend to undersave against their own long-run self-interest (Bernheim and Rangel (2007)). This might also lead to them qualifying for more support targeted for low income individuals in retirement and therefore has a cost to other taxpayers. To the extent that this is the case, taxing the accumulation of wealth would be counterproductive. On the other hand, there are other policy instruments in place to deal with undersaving, such as compulsory pension saving. In addition, any 'undersavers' might be expected to respond less strongly to financial incentives, and therefore the presence of a wealth tax might not diminish the amount that they choose to save.

Design issues

If one accepts one or more of these rather weak arguments for a periodic tax on wealth, what problems would there be in implementing a wealth tax? These are discussed in more detail in Section 8.3 but a major problem of principle is that wealth is accumulated for more than one reason. Some wealth exists for purely life-cycle smoothing reasons to reconcile differences in the pattern of consumption spending and income. For example, in a society where all individuals had the same consumption expenditure in all periods, it is far from clear that individuals who received their income early in their life, and therefore who would choose to accumulate assets in order to finance their later life consumption needs, should be taxed more heavily than those individuals whose income profile happened more closely to match their expenditure profile. Presumably one would not want to subject life-cycle wealth to wealth taxation if the purpose of the latter is to tax individuals on the basis of the pure benefits they obtain from holding wealth. In practical terms, the fact that the expected value of defined benefit pensions depends in large part on expected final pensionable earnings and expected final pension tenure means that it is difficult accurately to estimate current wealth since an individual who expected to have a longer pension tenure and a more steeply rising earnings-profile would have more expected pension wealth than an individual who expected to have a shorter pension tenure/less steeply rising earnings-profile. Similarly, if wealth is accumulated largely to make bequests to one's heirs, other wealth-holding benefits might simply be incidental.

A strict welfarist tax designer might therefore want to tax only that wealth annually that was accumulated for reasons other than life-cycle smoothing and bequests, and this would be over and above the tax on the transfer of wealth to one's heirs (or to other donees). Designing a tax system on wealth and wealth transfers that accomplishes this is challenging as Section 8.3 illustrates. To do so perfectly would involve distinguishing between wealth accumulated during one's lifetime according to whether it was intended for life-cycle smoothing or not, something that is extremely difficult. One might also want to be able to distinguish lifetime wealth accumulation that was done primarily for purposes of making a bequest versus wealth-holding per se, which is again impossible. The compromise proposed by the Meade Report was to tax, on a periodic basis, only wealth holdings that were obtained by transfers and not those that were the result of one's own accumulation. This would satisfy the wealth tax motive in part but is rather arbitrary in effect. After all, wealth is not kept separate according to its source. Someone may inherit £1,000 which they invest to start a business which is eventually worth £1 million. Is this £1 million to be subject to an annual wealth tax?

Section 8.3 outlines some of the practical problems with a wealth tax in unmodified form. As noted previously it might therefore be preferable to have an annual wealth tax targeted only at specific assets such as land, with no reduction for debt and set at a relatively high threshold. So, for example, it would only affect individual occupiers of real property with a gross value above a large limit. There would be no exemptions and hence the status of the occupier—whether resident or domiciled here—would be irrelevant. It would be targeted at high net value residential property. This tax then becomes relatively easy to collect since all local councils have a record of properties. This is discussed further in Section 8.4.

A wealth tax does not preclude a separate tax on wealth transfers with no relief granted to the donor and indeed the Meade Report proposed collapsing the wealth tax and the wealth transfer tax into a single tax, the PAWAT, which would be progressive in form. This suggestion is problematic since the two forms of tax are based on different economic principles. The advantage of keeping two systems is that they might differ in their coverage of wealth owners. For example, the wealth tax may affect only high values on specific assets within a relatively small class of individuals who otherwise may be exempt from other taxes.

Wealth tax has also been conceived as a more general mechanism for redistributing wealth along the lines proposed by Le Grand (2006). This sort of wealth tax would involve a fairly progressive rate structure with a negative component at the bottom based on the arguments above that the main direct benefits of holding wealth would accrue to the upper level of the wealth distribution, while the case for a basic wealth capital grant applies at the bottom. An anomaly that might affect this is that, while the argument for a wealth tax implies a periodic (e.g. annual) wealth tax the argument for a basic capital grant may apply only at the start of adulthood. In that case the capital grant would not be part of the general rate structure of the annual wealth tax. Separate decisions should be made over the taxation of wealth and any grant that is paid, since it is highly unlikely to be the case that the appropriate amount of revenue raised through the wealth tax will always be equal to the appropriate amount of expenditure on capital grants.

Similar sorts of incentive problems arise with wealth taxation as with wealth transfer taxation. In the case of wealth taxation, the incentive would be to transfer the wealth early to avoid paying periodic tax. This might not be regarded as a serious problem. Once the wealth is transferred, it no longer yields the alleged benefits attributed to it. Moreover, the donee would—as long as they were resident in the same country—then be subject to wealth taxation, so the tax would not really be avoided. Of course, if the wealth tax is progressive, the donor could mitigate the future liability by dividing it up among donees. Some would regard this as a good thing since it should reduce the concentration of wealth. As the experience of other countries experience indicates, wealth tax has not been particularly successful in breaking up concentrations of wealth or redistributing wealth and has been a particularly inefficient tax to collect. Most countries are moving away from the wealth tax to a simpler model. We do not recommend a wealth tax except in so far as we consider in Section 8.4 whether a higher annual tax on occupiers of high value residential property is an option.

8.3. PRACTICAL AND DESIGN CONSIDERATIONS ARISING OUT OF THE TAXATION OF WEALTH AND TRANSFERS OF WEALTH

In Section 8.1 we highlighted the various points that needed to guide the policymaker when considering the taxation of wealth and wealth transfers. In particular the options for the UK are whether to introduce wholesale structural reform, to abolish inheritance tax, or try to improve the existing capital tax system. In Section 8.2 we considered some of the underlying principles that should be considered in relation to taxes on wealth or wealth transfers. In this section we look at the pros and cons of the various options, starting with a discussion of wealth tax and then looking at wealth transfer tax.

8.3.1. Should the UK have a wealth tax?

Wealth transfer taxes have existed for most of the twentieth century (if not longer) in most countries, whereas wealth taxes (i.e. taxing the **holding** of capital on a recurrent basis) have existed in less than half of OECD countries and were introduced more recently. In fact wealth taxes have failed to live up to expectations and are generally in decline.[52] The UK has never had a wealth tax despite the Meade Report's enthusiasm for one and Labour's Green Paper in 1974[53] which proposed a wealth tax 'to promote greater social and economic equality'. The suggested rates ranged between 1% on net wealth of between £100,000 and £300,000 to 5% on net wealth of over £5 million (for reference average male full-time earnings increased over twelve-fold between April 1974 and April 2006).

The proposals were not introduced. Healey (1989) reflected: 'you should never commit yourself in Opposition to new taxes unless you have a very good idea how they will operate in practice. We had committed ourselves to a Wealth Tax; but in five years I found it impossible to draft one which would yield enough revenue to be worth the administrative cost and the political hassle.' This has been the common problem for most countries with a wealth tax.

Issues to consider in relation to a wealth tax

The 1974 Green Paper is instructive in illustrating the difficulties which need to be addressed. These include the following issues.

The taxable unit

Should individuals be taxed separately or should the unit of taxation be the family which would then include spouses and minor children as one unit?

[52] At the time of writing, France, Spain, Norway, some cantons in Switzerland, Greece, and India impose a wealth tax. France has an annual wealth tax levied at rates of up to 1.8% (as well as an inheritance tax and gift tax) although note that it is limited mainly to real estate when the owner is non-resident and is only charged on the net value of assets, so can be relatively easily circumvented by foreigners charging the asset with debt. Ireland, Austria, Denmark, the Netherlands, and most recently Sweden have all dropped theirs in an attempt to encourage entrepreneurial activity although the Netherlands soon replaced it with a 30% tax on theoretical revenue on capital so wealth tax there stands at 1.3%. In Germany it was ruled unconstitutional on the basis that various types of assets were not given equal treatment and therefore it was inequitable. It was removed in 1997 although there are plans to reintroduce it (see *Financial Times*, 28 March 2007). Their contribution to total government revenue is decreasing and it would appear that the tax did not meet the expectations of the countries that adopted it (see Kessler and Pestieau (1991)). Further details can be found in appendix B of the additional online material (see footnote 2).

[53] In 1974 the then Chancellor of the Exchequer, Denis Healey, presented a Green Paper for a wealth tax on the basis that income was not a sufficient measure of taxable capacity and a tax to redistribute capital could reduce income tax rates. The only exception were one-off levies—one in 1948 called a Special Contribution and the other introduced by Roy Jenkins as a Special Charge in 1968. It is sometimes argued that taxes on immovable property are a type of wealth tax as are stamp duties on registration of deeds to immovable property. However, this tax is typically applied to the gross value of assets without accounting for any liabilities. Property taxes are discussed as a separate subject in Section 8.4.

No firm conclusions were reached in the Green Paper but the issue is even more pertinent now given that family structures are more complicated. The tax credits system demonstrates some of the difficulties involved. Given that the tax system currently treats husband and wife as separate taxable units with independent reliefs and allowances, it is suggested that it is preferable for any wealth tax to follow this model rather than try to aggregate the wealth of husband and wife, civil partners or cohabitees. The wealth held by minor children and derived from the parent donor could be taxed on that parent in the same way as the income is taxed on that parent. Wealth held by minor children derived from other sources, for example from grandparents, would presumably be taxed separately as the minor child's. The Green Paper proposed that the wealth should be allocated to the parent from whose side of the family the wealth derived. But this can lead to sometimes arbitrary results if a grandparent or uncle leaves wealth to a minor and the parent is poor.

Chargeable individuals

Most countries limit wealth tax to assets held by individuals but trusts also need to be considered. Should only UK residents be taxed or should non-residents pay tax on UK situated assets? Should foreign domiciliaries be exempted? Most countries limit the wealth tax on non-residents to real estate and business enterprises actually carried on by the non-resident in the country.

On what assets should the charge be levied?

It is accepted that not all wealth can be taxed and therefore a wealth tax is an imperfect instrument. Human capital, that is, the present value of future earnings that an individual may earn, is not easily measured and is not taxed. Governments do not generally try to tax wealth held in the form of pension rights. Wealth tax can be more easily imposed on all real estate owned directly by the relevant person or indirectly through a company. However, should any reliefs be given for agricultural property or business property? If these assets are not subject to wealth tax then the desired social effects would not be achieved. On the other hand, a wealth tax on capital could prove an unacceptable burden for the owner of illiquid assets since the assets may well not generate sufficient income to enable the owner to pay an annual wealth tax on the capital. Presumably there would be some sort of exemption given for household chattels up to a certain value; if works of art are charged this could well lead to a dispersal of the national heritage. (France exempts works of art and the 1974 Green Paper proposed that assets of pre-eminent national importance should be exempted from wealth tax while made available for public display.) While one could give a conditional exemption for works of art (not merely a deferment) provided the owners continued to meet appropriate conditions about public access there are particular issues of disclosure and valuation for works of art. It is easy to hide a picture. There would be very adverse economic results if wealth tax was imposed on holdings of UK quoted shares by non-residents but if wealth tax is imposed on any commercial enterprises here it is likely to deter foreign investment.

Valuations

A wealth tax requires regular valuations and therefore imposes compliance costs on the taxpayer and increases administrative costs for the revenue. In some cases, for example pictures, unquoted company shares, partnerships, it will not always be easy to value the taxpayer's interest since the underlying assets owned by the business will have to be valued, appropriate discounts for minority shareholdings given, and goodwill is not easily valued. What about hope value on land? Should this be ignored until planning permission is obtained? Valuations may be manipulated; the taxpayer would be entitled to know the extent of their tax liabilities with certainty and without delay and hence to be able to plan their finances. Annual valuations could be avoided by having an annual or biennial tax levied on valuations done every five years. This latter approach has been adopted under pre-owned assets income tax. However, the compliance issues remain considerable since a taxpayer may need to do a valuation of all his assets just to ascertain that he is not subject to the tax.

Deductible liabilities

It would obviously be equitable to charge only net wealth so that liabilities will be deductible from a taxpayer's gross wealth in order to establish the net amount on which he will be liable. On the other hand, this opens up opportunities for avoidance. For example, the foreign resident can charge up his UK property with debt and deposit the borrowed funds which are not taxed abroad. The UK person can charge up his house and invest the borrowed proceeds in an exempt asset such as farmland.

Thresholds

The 1974 Green Paper suggested a threshold of £300,000 which, if uprated in line with average full-time male earnings, would be equivalent to £3½ million–£4 million today.

Trusts

Measures have to be put in place to avoid fragmentation of wealth through trusts. The 1974 Green Paper came up with some crude proposals which highlight the problems. It was suggested that for an interest in possession trust (one in which the person is entitled to the income) the whole capital value should be attributed to the life tenant. But this could be very unfair if the asset produces little income and the interest in possession is revocable. It was suggested that a discretionary trust should be charged by reference to the settlor's circumstances whether or not he can benefit on the basis that 'this will usually be close to the realities of the situation in which the trustees may be expected to follow the settlor's wishes'. But what about trusts set up long before the introduction of the tax or where the settlor is excluded and what about the position where a settlor has died and attribution to the settlor is no longer possible? Alternatively wealth tax for a discretionary trust could be governed by the shares of income distributed to the various beneficiaries in their relevant year and attributed accordingly. However, this can be administratively difficult where income distributions vary each year. The capital position of every beneficiary would have to be examined; they would not necessarily have to make a return of their wealth every year once it was established that they were well below the tax threshold but trustees would still need to go through the process and ascertain each beneficiary's total wealth. Additional rules would be needed where a beneficiary derived income from more than one trust. What about trusts where income was accumulated rather than distributed? The Green Paper suggested that where there is an identified beneficiary for whom income is accumulated contingent on his reaching a specified age the contingency should be disregarded and the capital attributed to him. But a beneficiary may never receive that capital if he fails to satisfy the contingency or the trustees appoint the capital away from him. Similar problems arise with other entities involving 'trust like' relationships.

All these criticisms of the 1974 Green Paper were made by Sandford, Willis, and Ironside (1975) who comment that 'on almost any combination of the main possibilities suggested in the Green Paper, the rich in the UK would be taxed considerably more heavily than in Germany or Sweden. Marginal rates of combined income and wealth tax in excess of 100% would be very likely and carry serious threats to the incentive to save amongst the wealthy and possibly also to incentives to effort and enterprise. No attempt is made in the Green Paper to estimate net yields from a wealth tax or to assess its demand effects.' On the largest wealth holdings they estimated that the tax level in the

UK would be substantially above that of Sweden and some 50% higher than that of Germany. The authors were strongly critical of the particular proposals set out in the Green Paper and concluded that a wealth tax was probably not appropriate anyway for the UK system.

The economic principles for and against a wealth tax were briefly discussed in Section 8.2. Arguments often used by countries in favour of a wealth tax are:

1. Equity: that is, that taxing income itself is an inadequate yardstick for determining ability to pay taxes and does not take into account the benefits from holding capital over and above the income derived from it.
2. That a wealth tax can reduce inequalities.
3. That it can provide useful administrative data which can be cross checked with other information collected by tax authorities (a motive given considerable weight by Norway and Denmark).
4. That it may have a better outreach than other taxes in taxing non-UK residents who own assets here.

Conclusions on wealth tax

However, the experience of many continental countries which have adopted wealth taxes has not been a particularly happy one. As discussed in Section 8.2 the extent to which wealth confers benefits over and above the income it generates is far from clear anyway. In cases where returns are not taxed—such as the imputed rental income from owner-occupied housing or artwork—these do not provide a justification for a broad-based wealth tax that would capture both income generating and non-income generating wealth alike.

Moreover, in practice, wealth tax cannot provide fully comprehensive coverage and precise valuation. The wider the coverage the more fully in theory the tax promotes horizontal equity but the wider the coverage the more difficult it is to prevent evasion by under reporting and to secure uniform valuations. Wealth tax has a higher cost of administration and a higher compliance cost involving regular valuations, with special problems created for agriculture and business and the danger of a new set of inequities between taxpayers of different degrees of honesty. Cost and complexity appear to have been important factors influencing abolition in Austria and the Netherlands.

It is argued that wealth tax would need to be confiscatory in order to bring about any real redistribution while the complexity of wealth tax and its perceived unfairness leads to avoidance.[54] Recent experience suggests that wealth taxes as they now exist have little effect on wealth distribution.[55]

Such a major change in the tax system needs to be justified by a sufficient margin to outweigh the costs of change, and it is far from clear that the advantages of a wealth tax are sufficiently great to justify the risks of such a change. For example, the yield of wealth taxes in countries such as France has not been significant. One of the problems is that, as we have seen already, the UK data on wealth are unsatisfactory and therefore predicting how changes to the taxation of wealth will operate in practice is speculative and therefore risky. The majority of developed countries have abolished wealth taxes. For the UK a risk is that the introduction of a significant wealth tax would be that it gave the perception of being hostile to the creation of wealth which could lead to a flight of capital. The factor that most influenced the Irish and Dutch governments when they decided to do away with wealth taxes was the perceived harmful effect on the country's economic activity, causing productive capital to leave and discouraging foreign investment and entrepreneurship.

If it is to be implemented at all, it should perhaps follow an enhanced council tax, with significantly higher rates of tax for those occupying very high value properties. This is discussed further in Section 8.4.

8.3.2. Wealth transfer taxes

Design issues to consider

The design principles that need to be decided in relation to any wealth transfer tax are summarized below.

Integration

In principle, a wealth transfer tax could be integrated with the broader tax system. The form of integration with the direct tax system would depend on whether income or consumption expenditures were the base. From the perspective of strict welfarism or equality of opportunity, wealth transfers would be treated as income receipts of the donee and as taxable uses of income by the donor. Under both income and expenditure taxation, transfers would be included as taxable income to the donee, while no deduction or credit would be allowed for the donor. In the case of restricted welfarism, a tax credit would be given to the donor for transfers given in either tax system.

54 See Heckly (2004). 55 See McCaffery (1994).

In fact, a substantial proportion of government revenue comes from other taxes, especially the VAT. The VAT is like a proportional expenditure tax and ought to be treated as such from the perspective of the overall tax system. To the extent that one views the transfer of wealth as analogous to expenditure by donors, as strict welfarist and equality of opportunity tax designers would do, it should be treated like any other form of expenditure under the VAT. Thus, donors should be subject to VAT on their transfers over and above the direct tax liabilities they incur. This consideration certainly complicates the tax system, and might lend support to the argument of the Meade Report that wealth transfers be treated separately from the direct tax system.

Rates

Most countries operate a separate system of rates and thresholds for wealth transfers in order to avoid the problem of lumpiness and the taxation of wealth transfers therefore operates as a stand-alone system. Otherwise under an income tax system the size of a transfer in one year could be large relative to the donee's normal annual income and this might lead to unfairness. Under an expenditure tax system, this is less of a problem since the taxpayer can self-average by smoothing expenditure over their lifetime and varying their mix of registered and tax-prepaid assets holdings.

Comprehensiveness of tax

What assets should be exempted? We have already discussed transfers to charitable organizations and transfers of business and agricultural property that currently qualify for special reliefs. Some argue that special preference should be given to transfers of a family house or a family business on social or other grounds. For example, incomplete capital markets make it difficult for UK homeowners to release their housing equity at a fair price. Similarly, access to capital markets, leading to liquidity concerns, may be limited for those who own family businesses. For these assets, even if they are not exempted, it seems sensible to allow taxpayers to smooth their payments over a number of years with interest payable on the outstanding liabilities. This currently occurs under the UK system.

Status of recipient

Special considerations are often given to transfers to a spouse or civil partner given the financial interdependence. So, for example, transfers between spouses are not taxed in the UK whether this takes place during lifetime or on death. However, the old estate duty rules had no spouse exemption for some years and many countries still do not operate a spousal relief. If the concern is that joint occupiers should not be penalized or forced to sell the house on the first death, the Irish proposal could be adopted which defers the tax where there are joint occupiers, irrespective of the relationship of the occupier to the deceased. The taxable status of the donee generally needs to be considered—will tax be payable irrespective of the residence of the donee if the asset is situated in the UK and is the tax avoided if non-UK situated assets are transferred to non-UK resident or domiciled donees by a UK resident or domiciled donor? If tax is imposed on transfers of UK situated assets it is relatively easy for foreign domiciled or non-UK resident donees to avoid this by ensuring the assets are relocated, through use of foreign companies.

Avoidance

The design of wealth transfer taxation must also take account of avoidance possibilities. Since the tax would be triggered every time wealth changes hands, there would be an incentive to minimize the frequency of such transfers. In the case of bequests, one way to do this would be to skip generations or to use trusts. The problems raised by trusts are discussed below. Higher transfer rates can be imposed on transfers that skip a generation (as occurs in the USA).

Efficiency

Like any other tax, wealth taxes affect incentives to work and save. In some countries the system imposes lower rates overall where an estate is split between more donees or where wealth is left to donees with lower incomes or who have received smaller inheritances in the past. This raises the issue about whether to have an estate duty or an inheritance tax? Some countries levy wealth transfer tax by reference to the circumstances of the donor and others by reference to the circumstances of the donee. The pros and cons of such an approach are discussed later in the context of accessions tax.

Interaction with capital gains

How should wealth transfer tax interact with capital gains tax? Should the transfer trigger a deemed realization or not? There are three main options. First, capital gains might be deemed to have been realized when property changes hands through a transfer. In this case, capital gains tax is payable at the time of the transfer, and the tax liability would be that of the donor. Of course, if the transfer takes place on death, the capital gains tax liability would have to be paid out of the estate and would be over and above any wealth transfer tax. The second alternative is not to deem capital gains realization at the time of transfer, but carry forward the accrued capital gains until they are eventually realized by the donee (or his/her heirs). The third alternative is to have only wealth transfer tax on death but all assets are rebased to market value without any capital gains tax payable. This currently occurs in many countries including the UK and US.

Estate duty or inheritance tax?

Some countries apply the wealth transfer tax to the donor and others to the donees. The strict welfarist and equality of opportunity objectives inform this choice. In both cases, the donee should be taxed, and no relief should be given to the donor. This is true whether the tax on wealth transfers is integrated into the income tax or taxed separately. Under restricted welfarism where the benefit to the donor does not count for tax purposes, the tax should still apply to the donor but with no relief being given to the donee. Of course, if the tax rate on wealth transfers were strictly proportional, it would matter little whether donees or donors were taxed. But as soon as some element of progressivity is introduced, either in the rate structure or in the use of exemptions, they would no longer be equivalent.

Harmonization with personal tax reform

Much of our discussion has assumed that the personal tax system used income as its base and applied a single rate structure to that base. Two other personal tax systems are often proposed: a dual income tax and an expenditure tax. Suppose it is decided to tax wealth transfers as part of the personal tax system. No special problems arise under a dual income tax system where a separate rate schedule applies to capital and non-capital income. Wealth transfers should be aggregated with earnings and other transfers as non-capital income. If the personal tax base is expenditures, transfers on death should be treated as expenditure by donors.[56] For the donee, inheritances are simply treated as income received and treated as such for tax purposes.[57]

[56] Specifically if they are made out of registered assets (i.e. those that are financed by tax-deductible saving that become taxable when drawn down), bequeathing ought to involve deemed deregistration. If they are made out of tax-prepaid assets (i.e. those financed out of after-tax savings whose capital income is untaxed under an expenditure tax) no further measures need be taken.

[57] Conceptual problems arise if the tax is not integrated with a direct expenditure tax. The tax on wealth transfers would have to mimic a separate tax on expenditures by both the donor and the donee. For the donors, that can be accomplished by taxing the bequest under the wealth transfer tax, but exempting it from personal expenditure taxation. For the donees, the inheritance should in principle only be taxed to the extent that it is being spent. That entails allowing for the possibility of its being registered separately from other assets. The implication is that deploying a separate wealth transfer tax that respects the principles of expenditure taxation is difficult when it applies alongside direct expenditure taxation.

Lifetime vs death transfers

Related to the issue of rates is whether lifetime gifts should be taxed at the same rate as transfers on death or indeed at all and if so should there be any principle of cumulation with previous transfers? Most countries which tax wealth transfers such as the US and France operate an integrated gift and death tax system. New Zealand is unusual in having gift tax for lifetime gifts but no estate tax; the UK is unusual in having no wealth transfer tax on many lifetime transfers but tax on death transfers.

International considerations[58]

The lack of consistency worldwide in the connecting factors imposing capital taxation can result in double taxation for some individuals. For example, liability to UK inheritance tax other than on UK-situated assets is based on domicile in the UK as a matter of general law or deemed domicile in the UK by virtue of having been resident in the UK for seventeen out of the previous twenty years.[59] The US imposes a federal estate tax on the worldwide assets owned at death by a US citizen or by a US domiciliary; and the Netherlands imposes succession duties on those resident in the Netherlands at the time of their death. Different systems also adopt different approaches to migrating individuals. For UK purposes, an emigrant from the UK will remain within the UK IHT net notwithstanding that they acquire a domicile of choice outside the UK for the first three years outside the UK under the deemed domicile provisions while a person will remain within the scope of the charge to Dutch succession duty if he dies within ten years of leaving the Netherlands and remains a Dutch national.

Not only do the categories of individuals subject to a jurisdiction's capital tax system vary considerably, so do the assets against which those taxes are levied. Some systems such as the UK IHT regime and the US estate duty regime will bite on an individual domiciled in the UK or a US citizen (or domiciliary) respectively in respect of their worldwide assets. In contrast, Singapore estate duty, for example, only applies to moveable and immoveable property in Singapore. It is problematic for countries to devise effective ways of taxing the mobile person. In the UK the insertion of an offshore corporate entity can remove UK situated asset from the capital tax regime. For example, a foreign domiciliary can buy real estate in the UK via an offshore company. The asset will not be within the inheritance tax net until the foreign domiciliary has been resident here for seventeen out of twenty tax years (and even after seventeen years, inheritance tax can be avoided by holding the company shares in a trust).

58 We are grateful to John Riches at Withers LLP for information in this section.

59 S267 IHTA 1984.

While the world is now served with a comprehensive network of double tax treaties in respect of income and corporation taxes, generally now based on the OECD Model Treaty, the number of treaties relating to capital taxes is materially less. The effect of this, unfortunately, is to mean that there is material scope for double taxation or nil taxation in the event of an individual's death. In the UK, by way of example, there are currently eleven capital tax treaties in force as compared with 149 income and corporation tax treaties. Even where double tax treaties are available, there is much scope for double taxation because of the significant differences that exist in the worldwide approach to capital taxation.

What entity should be taxed?

Trusts and foundations are vehicles often favoured in succession planning because the creation of these structures avoids the formalities and expense of probate procedures—no transfer needs to occur on death. But such vehicles pose a conceptual challenge for revenue authorities because there is no identifiable individual in whom property ownership resides. Various responses to the taxation of these wealth holding structures can be identified.

Treat trust as transparent Many taxing regimes have rules providing for assets settled on trust to be included within the taxable estate of the settlor or the trust's beneficiaries on the basis they can simply 'look through' the trust to see them. In the US, for example, a grantor trust is a trust whose settlor is treated as the owner of the trust assets for tax purposes. As a result, distributions of income or capital to beneficiaries are treated as gifts from the settler and not taxable to them as income. If the settlor is a US citizen, he will therefore be fully liable to tax on the income within the trust, whether or not he receives distributions and the trust fund will be included within his estate for US estate tax purposes. The same estate tax issues arise if UK property is owned by a foreign grantor trust.

Attribute ownership of capital to income beneficiary Until March 2006 this was the approach taken by the UK so that the capital interest in a trust fund was attributed to the individual entitled to the life interest.

Create a fictional taxpayer In most jurisdictions, as a matter of general legal principle, neither a trust nor a partnership has legal personality. For tax purposes, however, they are frequently treated as entities and taxed separately according to special rules. Since March 2006, almost all new UK trusts are taxed as separate entities and inheritance tax is levied at a rate of up to 6% every ten years on capital value with exit charges being applied pro rata when property ceases to be held on trust. However, there are no provisions to limit the number of trusts set up by each donor so with care the 6% can be minimized.

Tax an actuarial value ascribed to the life interest/usufruct Under the French inheritance tax regime, a usufruct is, for example, valued on a sliding scale as is the value of the nue properiétaire with the valuations dependent on the age of the donor.[60]

Political consensus

Labour introduced capital transfer tax (CTT) in 1975 which was a cumulative tax on death and on all lifetime gifts, not just those made within a stated period before death. However, Denis Healey acknowledged that four years later when he left office CTT was still raising less revenue than estate duty.[61] This was partly due to a much more generous spouse exemption and a number of other reliefs such as BPR and APR, possibly because some wealthy people had fled the country but also because people delayed making gifts and waited for a change in government.

Donee or donor based tax system?

Taxes on wealth transfers may be broadly categorized as being donor based or donee based: a donor based 'or estate tax' system taxes by reference to the donor (i.e. the deceased). The current UK system is an estate tax system which charges tax on the value of property transferred by the donor, generally on death. It does not take into account the past inheritances received by the donee from any source, the relationship between donor and donee, or the notion that spreading wealth among more donees should be encouraged as a way of reducing the concentration of wealth.

A donee based or 'inheritance tax' system taxes by reference to the donee: the rate of tax on transfers of wealth is governed not by the overall amount held in the donor's estate but by the history of inherited wealth for the donee. So each donee pays tax to the extent that transfers of wealth to him from any source exceed a certain limit over his lifetime. The Capital Acquisitions Tax ('CAT') regime in the Republic of Ireland is an example of a donee based system.[62]

[60] 'An introductory guide to French succession law and French inheritance tax', unpublished, Prettys Solicitors, Ipswich (2004).

[61] See p. 404 of Healey (1989).

[62] A number of European countries such as Switzerland also have a donee based system based on the amount received by the donee and the degree of kinship. See appendix B of the additional online material cited in footnote 2 for further details.

A donor based regime is generally regarded as simpler and easier to administer because it is tied up with the probate process and executors just file a single return. Donee based regimes are more prevalent in civil law systems where forced heirship rules tend to split assets between certain heirs in any event. Countries usually opt for one or other system.[63]

In 1972 the Conservative government published a Green Paper suggesting the possibility of an accessions tax in place of estate duty.[64] The change of government in 1974 prevented any chance of that reform occurring. However, the donee based or accessions tax system was adopted by Ireland[65] in 1976 and has had strong advocates.[66] If adopted, the tax is generally levied not just on bequests but on lifetime gifts received at any time and from any source. The donee based system could look at the cumulative total of all accessions received in the donee's lifetime or over a certain period and so take account of all the recipient's inheritances, whenever received and from whatever source. Patrick and Jacobs (1999) suggested a lower exemption threshold than the current UK system and a more progressive rate structure. Ireland has a lower threshold but a flat rate of 20%.

So an estate left to four children would suffer less tax than an estate left to one assuming the four children had no previous receipts of capital. This is seen to be fairer because four children will necessarily inherit less than one anyway.

In Ireland various exemptions similar to those in the UK are retained: for example, transfers between spouses are entirely exempt; there are reliefs for heritage, business, and agricultural property. The treatment of trusts is relatively straightforward and pragmatic.[67]

Advantages of an accessions tax

Redistribution It is argued that a donee based tax encourages private distribution of wealth and hence is more efficient than a wealth tax in reducing

[63] Tiley, John in Death and Taxes [2007] BTR 300 noted though that for a time the UK had both, since estate duty was donor based but succession duty and legacy duty also applied until 1949 and were both donee based taxes, taxing property by reference to the circumstances of the donee. A widow would pay tax at lower rates than 'a stranger'.

[64] See the Green Paper: 'Taxation of Capital on Death: a possible inheritance tax in place of estate duty', March 1972 Cmnd 4930.

[65] Although cumulation is for periods only rather than over the whole of the donee's lifetime.

[66] See Sandford, Willis, and Ironside, 'An Accessions Tax', and the Fabian Society Report, 'Paying for Progress', 1999. The Liberal Democrats favoured an accessions tax in their 2006 proposals but by 2007 had abandoned this as too complex. See also Robinson (1989).

[67] A one-off discretionary inheritance tax of between 3% and 6% applies to property held in a discretionary trust or becoming subject to a discretionary trust from 25 January 1984. An annual 1% inheritance tax applies to property held in a discretionary trust on 5 April each year commencing with 1986. Further details of the Irish tax system are provided in appendix B of the additional online material (see footnote 2).

inequality or at least constraining the growth in inequality. Donors have an incentive to divide their wealth among more people and moreover to disperse their estates among donees who have not previously received inheritances because the rate of tax on them will be lower. Sandford (1987) argued: 'It is large inheritances not large estates as such which perpetuate inequality and an accessions tax falls heavily on the person who receives most by way of gifts and legacies.' Some encouragement to spread wealth could be provided even under a donor based system by letting the donor give up to a certain amount free of tax to each individual, irrespective of the wealth of the donee but since it cannot take into account the other inheritances received by that donee from other sources it is a cruder method.

Equity It reduces the incentive to make lifetime gifts and removes the lottery of the seven-year rule. If applied over a donee's lifetime there is no difference in tax rates between those who make lifetime gifts and those who keep their wealth until death. The cumulation principle means that a person whose accessions come from one source or in one go is taxed the same as someone receiving the same value of gifts from many sources or at different times.

Flexibility It is more flexible than an estate tax in that it can take account of the particular circumstances of any beneficiary, for example, give a concession to a disabled child. By relating rates of tax to the amounts received by an individual it may be more politically acceptable, although this could come at the cost of greater complexity in the tax system.

Disadvantages of an accessions tax

Reduces incentives It is argued that any increase in inheritance tax or the introduction of a tax on lifetime gifts would reduce saving and provide disincentives to enterprise. Having said that, most lifetime saving is not initially undertaken with the purpose of bequest but simply for security and later consumption. It is also pointed out that a donor prepared to transfer his wealth to a wide range of people pays lower wealth transfer tax. The same arguments about disincentives can be used in respect of any tax on wealth transfers although at present most lifetime gifts are not taxed.

Higher administrative and compliance costs This is often cited as a major problem. All recipients of gifts above the exempt level have to declare them to the tax authorities and keep a lifetime record of gifts received. There are more forms to be processed where tax is related to the shares of the beneficiaries rather than to the total estate. However, the Irish CAT system is quite a complex system with a number of reliefs and different threshold levels according to the relationship of donor and beneficiary[68] but is operated at about the same level of costs per unit of revenue as that of income tax on the self-employed.[69] Costs could be minimized if the rate of duty on the beneficiary is related only to the individual legacy rather than the aggregate received in gifts over his lifetime but this would be open to abuse. It may be sensible to set the initial threshold per donee at a high level above which receipts are taxed on a progressive basis rather than the current flat rate. Most families would then continue to be able to transfer wealth free of tax (although not free of capital gains tax). The existing capital tax system in the UK is complex and relatively expensive to administer. The main additional cost would be the need for each donee to keep a personal record of all lifetime inheritances over a certain limit (assuming all lifetime transfers are to be included) although cumulation could be restricted to ten or fifteen years.

Evasion and avoidance It may be easier to evade than inheritance tax which has to be paid before the grant of probate can be obtained. However, evasion can be cut down by prohibiting the distribution of legacies by executors until the tax liability of the legatees has been calculated. The tax could then either be paid by the legatee before receiving the legacy or by the executors of the legatee receiving the sum net of tax. Gifts of land are registered so presumably information could be sent to the Revenue to chase up on gifts that are not self-declared. On other assets the secondary liability could be placed on the donor if a donee does not pay the tax. Wealth could nominally be spread through a family albeit remain controlled by one person so avoidance provisions need to deal with this.[70]

Rates It is difficult to predict yield because at present the value of lifetime gifts in the UK is not known and, of course, the structure of the tax itself may lead to a different pattern of giving by distributing legacies more widely. The Irish CAT is levied at a flat rate of 20% over the exempt thresholds. However, the Fabian Society 1999 report proposed a nil rate threshold of only £80,000 for the UK and progressive rates thereafter up to 40%.

Failure to redistribute wealth In practice Ireland has for practical reasons modified a pure accessions tax so that gifts between spouses are exempt

[68] In 2007 the threshold above which transfers to children became eligible for tax were €496,824 for transfers to children; €49,682 for transfers to parents, siblings, nieces, nephews, and grandchildren; and €24,841 for transfers to other individuals. A brief description of the Irish CAT system can be found in appendix B of the additional online material (see footnote 2).

[69] The Irish Institute of Taxation website.

[70] For example, the deceased could divide his wealth between his daughter, her partner, their children, and various trusts for these beneficiaries. The daughter's family has increased wealth overall.

and there are different thresholds for different relationships. All of this has increased complexity and lessened the redistributive effects although the tax has not been subject to the same level of criticism as in the UK.

Transitional provisions One would have to consider transitional provisions from the current UK system. Does everyone start at the cumulative total of nil ignoring all previous legacies and gifts? Or will donees have to take account of any capital receipts received in the previous seven years in calculating their tax liability? This again increases complexity.

Political difficulties Since much of the public at present appears to oppose the principle of taxing inheritance at all the introduction of an accessions tax which included lifetime gifts might be seen as politically difficult. Moreover, if one party supports the system and the other does not then donors will simply delay making gifts, as appeared to happen with capital transfer tax.

Conclusions on donee based tax

If the principles of wealth transfer taxation set out in Section 8.2 are taken into account, the donee based system seems more appropriate on fairness grounds than the donor based system. The thresholds could be set at a relatively high level to minimize compliance costs with a lower starting rate of tax, for example, 20% as in Ireland. It would then be clearer that only those who inherit significant sums (i.e. the richer person) will have to pay any tax. So the £1 million estate which is left to four children might suffer no tax under this system because they all inherit less than £300,000 each. Reliefs and exemptions could be similar to the present position or reformed along the lines suggested below.

The main practical difference from the current UK system would be the need for donees to keep records of all inheritances and to accept that lifetime transfers of wealth could end up being subject to inheritance tax depending on the recipient's previous cumulative total. However, there is a very different perception in how the tax operates and this might win a greater degree of acceptance for the principle of a wealth transfer tax. Whether this change is worthwhile unless the yield from any wealth transfer tax were to be more substantial than that raised by the current inheritance tax system is debatable.

Reform of the existing inheritance tax system

Is there a case for keeping the existing system which taxes the estate of the donor but simply improving it so it is perceived as fairer? This seems to be the preferred approach of the government at present. The following reforms could be considered.

Increase the nil rate band threshold

This would take more households out of the inheritance tax net. The threshold could then be raised in line with house prices rather than income or general inflation. The Conservatives proposed an increase to £1 million in October 2007. Labour have now introduced a transferable nil rate band which assists spouses and civil partners although does not actually raise the threshold. The Liberal Democrats have proposed a threshold of £500,000 and cumulation for fifteen rather than just seven years 'to restore the essential character of inheritance tax as a charge on the really wealthy'.[71]

Rates

The 40% rate at which inheritance tax starts being paid is high compared with that in other OECD countries. As noted in Section 8.1, for families where the deceased was always a basic rate taxpayer, the perception that 'their capital' is now being taxed at a marginal rate of 40% is unpopular even though the average rate is much less than this. It might be preferable to have a starting rate of 20% rising to a maximum of 40%. This would result in minimal additional compliance cost given that tax has to be paid anyway, although obviously it would result in a loss of revenue. A more progressive rate structure might make particular sense for a donee based tax—a receipt of capital would initially be taxed at lower rates before the donee moved into higher rates.

An alternative is to have a flat rate but reduce it from 40% to 20% as in Ireland. At the same time, lifetime gifts made over a certain period prior to death, such as fifteen years or potentially longer, could be taxed if above the threshold. The difficulty is in predicting the effect of such changes. Will tax on lifetime gifts compensate for the loss of 20% at death? A tax on lifetime gifts may be more acceptable if it is a donee based tax based on a certain level of inheritances over the prescribed (high) threshold.

Agricultural and business property reliefs

The current reliefs are rather unsatisfactory and arbitrary in effect. These reliefs should be better targeted. For example in Ireland APR is restricted to individuals who are working farmers rather than those who simply own agricultural land (possibly for the tax breaks) but do not intend to pass it on within the family. BPR is available but on a more restricted basis. In both cases there is a clawback of reliefs if the business is sold within six years of death. Such restrictions do not adversely affect family businesses and farmers who

[71] Liberal Democrats (2007).

wish to hand on the enterprise to the next generation but will prevent people buying AIM listed shares or agricultural land simply for the tax breaks. Some consultation and more research in this area would be worthwhile.

Heritage relief

The conditional exemption and douceur arrangements generally work well although anecdotally there have been problems recently in obtaining relief for pre-eminent chattels because museums have not always been able to arrange appropriate security. The maintenance fund regime is generally regarded as too prescriptive and the public access requirements can be rather problematic for smaller houses. Some improvements could be made to provide appropriate public access for smaller houses without their necessarily having to be open for the full 28 days each year. For example more people may visit if open days are run on specific weekends in the year for a number of houses within a particular locality rather than merely having the house open a minimum time each month.

Family home

We do not recommend exempting the family home for the reasons outlined in Section 8.1. However, a carefully targeted relief along the lines given in Ireland (which does not seem to be costly)[72] would deal with the 'hard cases' such as the Burden sisters or cohabitees. Inheritance tax would be deferred for the co-occupant who owned no other property until such time as the property was sold or not replaced.

Foreigners

At present foreign domiciliaries pay inheritance tax on a worldwide basis only if they have been resident in the UK for seventeen years and even then the tax can be avoided by use of offshore trusts. We suggest that their inheritance tax position is re-examined albeit with appropriate transitional provisions and after proper consultation.

Payment of inheritance tax

It was noted in Section 8.1 that payment of inheritance tax can often be problematic because it has to be paid before grant of probate. The Liberal Democrats (2007) proposed ways of improving this and it is suggested that further work should be done in this area.

[72] Further details are provided in appendix B of the additional online material (see note 2).

Recording lifetime gifts

It is difficult to formulate policy when one has little information about the extent of lifetime giving or the distribution and transfer of wealth. Requiring all donors to complete a simple form for lifetime transfers over a minimum annual limit whether or not tax is payable would help bridge this information gap and inform policy making. The form could be one page giving details of the asset, the recipient, his relationship to the deceased as well as values and could be sent to the Inheritance Taxes Office. Alternatively, an extra box could be inserted on the tax return requesting details of lifetime gifts which would at least provide some information from those who have to self-assess.

Abolition of inheritance tax; reintroduction of capital gains tax on death

The objections to inheritance tax were discussed in Section 8.1. In Section 8.2 we could see some case for taxing wealth transfers. However, if the more radical prescription of a donee based tax is not implemented then it might be difficult to justify the retention of either the current inheritance tax, or one that is modified along the lines set out in Section 8.3.2.

Canada, Australia,[73] and Sweden[74] have abolished their estates and gifts taxes. New Zealand abolished its estate duty in 1999 but gift tax remains in place.

As noted in Section 8.1, the lobby group in favour of retaining inheritance tax has been less effective than the group in favour of abolition. One difficulty is in working out what inheritance tax should achieve. Is the aim to redistribute wealth or at least to reduce wealth inequality or one of 'fairness': that is, that someone who inherits £300,000 should not pay zero tax when someone who earns it pays 40%? Supporters of an inheritance tax tend to be divided in what they want: the IPPR called for reform of the current system (Maxwell (2004)) while other organizations such as the Fabian Society (Patrick and Jacobs (1999)) have suggested an accessions tax.

One option is to abolish inheritance tax completely. A way of recouping some of the lost revenue from a similar (but not the same) group would be to reintroduce capital gains tax on death (which was the case in the UK until 1971), along the lines seen in Canada.[75] It is argued that this is simpler[76]

[73] Both federal states where the competition between states and the lack of a comprehensive federal estate tax gradually resulted in abolition.

[74] In 2005 inheritance and gift tax was abolished.

[75] Further details of the Canadian capital tax system see Appendix B of the additional online material (see footnote 2).

[76] The replacement of inheritance tax with capital gains tax was recommended by the Forsyth Commission in October 2006. It was taken up by the Conservatives in Economic Competitiveness

because there are no longer two capital taxes with different conditions and relief and therefore the possibility of double taxation or avoidance is reduced. Moreover, capital gains tax is seen as fairer because only the **gain** arising from the deemed disposal of the asset at death is taxed not the entire value.

However, it is important to note that the two taxes have different rationales and are certainly not mutually exclusive. It is far from clear why assets should be exempt from capital gains at death (as they are at present in the UK) just because they are subject to wealth transfer tax: the aim of capital gains tax is to ensure that capital gains are treated on a par with other forms of income such as dividends and interest which will already have been taxed as they accrue (and are also then subject to a wealth transfer tax). Wealth transfer taxation has different ends. However, removing the exemption from capital gains tax on death but retaining inheritance tax might not be seen as politically acceptable simply because it would make the double taxation more explicit. See pp. 789–90 and p. 809 for further discussion.

Issues to consider in connection with the reintroduction of capital gains tax on death

Should the family home continue to be exempt? This is the asset that currently brings those with moderate wealth into the inheritance tax net. Retaining principal private residence relief on a lifetime transfer of the family home but not on death transfers would be very distorting—people would dispose of their house into trusts or to children while alive to secure the tax free uplift. It might be argued that a principal private residence relief on death would encourage everyone to invest in property. However, it is not thought that distortions would occur in the same way as giving an inheritance tax exemption to the main residence. If the main residence is exempt from inheritance tax then clearly everyone will invest as much money as possible in a large house. The entire proceeds of sale are then tax free. By contrast if capital gains tax is imposed on death and principal private residence relief is maintained there is far less distortion. The incentive is just the gain rather than the proceeds; the gain may not necessarily be greater on a larger house. Moreover, if a person decides to invest more money in a larger house to secure the exemption he will have to sell other assets that do show a gain—and so the capital gains tax is paid earlier. If the money is held in cash there is no capital gains tax to worry about anyway. It might be argued that the elderly person may be forced to stay in his house to ensure a tax free gain rather than move into a nursing home and live off the sale proceeds where future gains could be taxable. However,

Policy Group, 'Free Britain to Compete: Equipping the UK for Globalisation', Submission to the Shadow Cabinet by Rt Hon John Redwood MP and Simon Wolfson, pub. on 17 August 2007.

the investment of such cash will not usually generate sufficient gains over the annual exemption to worry about the difference. The very wealthy may have an incentive to stay in their homes but they can have only one main residence.[77]

Thresholds Should the same capital gains tax exemption operate on death as during lifetime or should there be a higher threshold? (£9,200 for 2007–08).

Reliefs What reliefs should operate for trading businesses and farmland? One option is to allow a rollover provision so that these assets pass on death to the heirs on a no gain no loss basis but capital gains tax is paid at the point of later sale. The extent of the deferral would need to be considered carefully since this could provide an incentive for assets to be retained indefinitely.

International issues If capital gains tax is introduced on death one needs to consider the international context. What is the connecting factor—domicile or residence? Furthermore, would there need to be a revaluation of the assets when the foreigner emigrates from another state and comes to the UK, as occurs in Canada at present? This would rebase the asset and might be regarded as fairer in that gains accruing in the period of non-residence would not then be taxed. Without the former, the tax would be a strong disincentive to immigration of wealthy individuals who would object to paying capital gains tax on assets that had appreciated during a period when they had no connection with the UK. Presumably there would also need to be an exit charge, otherwise older individuals could leave the jurisdiction just before death. However, an exit charge may produce problems under EU law.[78]

Entities How will trusts be taxed given that they do not die and continue for many generations? This is a common problem when considering the capital taxation of trusts and could be solved in one of the ways suggested, for example, charging trusts every ten years or when assets are distributed from the trust or the trust ceases to exist.

In summary, the reintroduction of capital gains tax on death deserves further consideration but the issues would need to be thought through carefully.

[77] Some of the current loopholes which allow people 'to elect' for the relief on residences which are not their main residence as a matter of fact would need to be examined.

[78] See, for example, *De Lasteyrie du Saillant v Ministerie* [2004] 6 ITLR 666—a restriction which deters outward investment or outward movement potentially infringes the freedoms. Exit charges are not therefore generally permissible but a government may retain the right to tax an emigrant's gains insofar as the asset is disposed of within ten years of emigration and the tax is only payable then *N v Inspecteur* (2006) Case c-470/04.

8.4. PROPERTY AND OTHER TAXES—REFORM OPTIONS

So far the focus has been on direct taxes levied on individuals based either on their general wealth holdings or on transfers of wealth to or from other parties. In practice, there are various other taxes on wealth or wealth transfers either levied indirectly or on specific forms of wealth.

8.4.1. Property taxes

Issues to consider

An annual tax on some measure of the value of real property is used by local governments in many countries. The tax can be levied on tenants as well as owner-occupiers as in the UK, or it can be charged only on property-owners as in other countries (US, Canada). When rates are proportional, it will not matter whether the tax is levied on the owner or the occupier since the economic incidence, at least in the long run, should be the same. The tax is regarded as a suitable source of local revenue because the base is relatively immobile and tax liabilities can be related to benefits received from local public spending. Ideally, the tax facilitates local accountability for revenues without compromising efficiency or equity in the national economy. There are a number of issues with respect to its role and design that we briefly mention here. It should be noted though that tax revenues on property in the UK amounting to 4% of GDP are the highest of all the OECD countries and therefore caution should be exercised before taxing property even further.[79]

One particular issue arises when considering the apparent immobility of the tax base. The use of land values rather than property values is preferable when considering taxation since land is relatively more immobile than property.[80] This is because the taxation of land, unlike that of property, does not provide a disincentive for individuals to add to the value of their home through extensions and other such changes. However, while calculating the value of land might be more difficult, and potentially less transparent, than using market property values these problems do not seem insurmountable.

While the benefit tax argument is one rationale for the local use of property taxes, in fact there is no evident one-to-one relationship between property tax

[79] See OECD Economics Department Working Paper No. 301, 2001.

[80] By land values we mean the value of the property less the value of the building.

liabilities and benefits from public services. On the contrary, empirical studies have shown that property taxes and the quality of local schools are capitalized into property values, which would not be the case if higher property taxes were offset by greater benefits from local services. That being the case, the tax can be viewed as one of many tax instruments for raising general revenues, albeit at the local level. The literature on property tax has focused largely on its incidence, arguing that it combines features of a capital tax borne by owners of property more generally with features of an excise tax arising from differences in rates across localities (Wilson (2003)).

From the point of view of tax design, the property tax as it applies to individuals can be considered as a tax on the consumption of housing, or on its imputed return. As such, it undoes, somewhat imperfectly, the sheltering of imputed rents from owner-occupied housing in the personal tax base. Whether this is a good thing or a bad thing depends on one's views of the appropriate personal tax base. However, one aspect of incidence analysis takes on a special importance in the case of real property, especially that part of it consisting of land as opposed to buildings. If the market for property is forward-looking, expected future property taxes should be capitalized into property prices. This implies that initial owners of property effectively bear the burden of all expected future taxes (Feldstein (1977)). To the extent that this is true, it detracts from the value of property taxation as a component of a broader tax system. (Similar arguments might be made about wealth taxes more generally, at least to the extent that they apply to long-lived assets and their prices are not pre-determined as in the case of internationally traded assets.)

Property taxation typically also applies to business property, both commercial and/or industrial. To the extent that the tax does not reflect benefits obtained from the use of the funds, this amounts to a form of wealth tax levied on businesses at source that is not closely related to profitability. As such, it affects business investment decisions and competitiveness with foreign producers in a presumably inefficient way, except to the extent that the tax is simply absorbed into lower land rents. The inefficiency of business property taxes is also mitigated by the existence of residential property taxes. Given these, business property taxes might be justified on second-best grounds as a way of removing the incentive that might otherwise exist to convert residential land into business land. To the extent that concerns over the inefficiency of business property taxes are valid, they have implications for the use of the property tax, and more generally for the manner in which local government is financed. A way of avoiding excessive property taxes is to adjust the size of grants to local governments from higher levels of government, taking care to do so in a way that preserves local accountability and avoids soft budget constraints.

Techniques now exist for tax administrators to maintain reasonably consistent, precise, and up-to-date estimates of property values, and to use those as a basis for annual taxation. There is thus no particular reason why property taxes cannot be based on estimated current property values, as opposed to historic values. Furthermore the use of actual property values, or at least relatively narrow bands of property values, rather than broader and therefore cruder property value bands is desirable. In some countries, property valuation is done by a higher agency, and local governments are given discretion for choosing their own property tax rates. Local choice is important because average property values can vary substantially across jurisdictions for a variety of reasons (demand for housing, amenity values, weather, etc.). Different localities will choose very different tax rates, even if they are providing comparable levels of public services. Indeed, for that reason, revenue-raising autonomy at the local level will typically be accompanied by some form of equalization to compensate for the fact that different localities have different abilities to raise revenues.

The rate structure for property taxes is typically more complicated than simply choosing a tax rate. Different rates may apply to different types or uses of property. Different rates may apply to residential, commercial, and industrial property, although the principles that should inform that choice are by no means clear. Newly developed property may face differential rates to cover part of the cost of infrastructure. And there may be some relief afforded to low-income property owners, such as by a system of credits delivered through the direct tax system or through a separate benefit (which might be important in countries, such as the UK, where the direct tax system operates on an individual basis and the benefit and tax credit system operates on a family basis). This may be particularly important for low-income individuals for whom the house is their main asset, such as retired individuals.

Property taxes in the UK and possible reform options

Since April 1993 the only significant local tax across all of England, Scotland, and Wales has been the council tax (with a different system operating in Northern Ireland).[81] Properties are placed into one of eight broad bands (nine in Wales) based on a measure of their value in 1991 (in England and

[81] The structure of council tax is outlined in more detail in Appendix A of the additional online material (see footnote 2).

Scotland) or 2003 (Wales). It is forecast by the Treasury to raise £22.5 billion in 2006–07 (1.7% of national income), net of the outgoings on council tax benefit.

Business rates—or National Non-Domestic Rates—are levied on the annual rateable value (i.e. market rent) of the property occupied by business. Unlike council tax bandings, rateable values have been updated every five years with transitional arrangements smoothing gains and losses from the old to the new valuations. Some types of property are exempt or qualify for a reduced rate—for example some unoccupied buildings, agricultural land, and rural shops—and a reduced rate applies to businesses with a low rateable value. Charities receive a reduction or exemption in business rates. The Treasury forecasts that in 2006–07 it will raise £21.5 billion (1.6% of national income).

Improvements could be made to both council tax and business rates. Both are currently based (albeit loosely in the case of the council tax) on the value of the property (full or rental for council tax and business rates). It would be preferable if both tax bases could be moved to the taxation of the value of the **land** rather than that of the **property** so as to remove the distortion against making improvements (again, as noted above, while there may be some complications involved in calculating land values these should not be insurmountable).

To the extent to which taxes on business property are retained, careful consideration should be given to whether the reliefs that exist really are well-targeted at a sensible objective. While a lower rate for rural shops might be appropriate on environmental or distributional grounds, reduced rates for empty property, charities, and agricultural land seem harder to justify, and in all these cases it is far from clear that business rates are the best instrument to achieve these objectives. Unlike business rates, the existing council tax does not have regular revaluations and is based on banded rather than continuous valuations. Council tax could also be improved by moving to regular revaluations and the use of actual values rather than banded values (either based on property value, or preferably as discussed above, land value). This is an attractive feature of the system introduced from April 2007 in Northern Ireland and a similar reform in the rest of the UK would be welcome. If the actual value is used, a key decision is whether or not to have a simple linear tax rate. Given that the UK housing stock is valued at around £3,800 billion, an annual tax rate of around 0.56% would raise sufficient funds to cover the £22.5 billion that council tax currently raises (while retaining council tax benefit). Alternatives range from one that is capped (which is also a feature of the Northern Ireland system), to one that is progressive which would be one effective way of taxing high wealth individuals if such an outcome is deemed attractive. So, for example, higher rates of tax could be charged on properties (or land) worth over £500,000, £1 million and £2 million.[82]

Other potential attractions in having a higher rate of council tax include the fact that it is easily observed and likely to be positively correlated with wealth and capital income that may not be easily observed. If the threshold is high, it is a charge that may fall mainly on those living in central London though the threshold like the tax rates could vary by locality. The council tax is also relatively simple to collect since it can be imposed on the occupant of the property irrespective of how it is owned. Switzerland has an accommodation related charge of this kind in relation to foreigners living there. An alternative to this approach would be to have a separate tax on the occupation of high value housing that was not integrated into council tax—for example if it were deemed appropriate that this should not form part of the local tax base.

One important concern with any property based tax is that any such tax is likely to be incident fully on the current owners of these properties. Future residents of these properties would probably not face the incidence of the tax—rather they would be likely to be able to purchase or rent the property at a lower cost that reflects the payment of tax.

8.4.2. Stamp duties

Taxes on specific forms of asset transactions are used in many OECD countries. Many countries, including the UK, impose stamp duties on property transactions. The rate of duty may be related to the value of property. In the UK, stamp duties also apply to sales of shares in UK corporations regardless of where the transaction takes place and who does the transacting. The tax is proportional and based on the value of the transaction. The Treasury estimates that stamp duties will raise £12.7 billion in 2006–07 (1.0% of national income). In 2005–06 two-thirds of the revenue raised came from the sale of land and property and one-third from the sale of shares and bonds.

The argument for stamp duties is not at all clear, apart from a cost efficient revenue-raising motive. One might argue that the tax is a user charge to offset the costs to the state of maintaining ownership records in the case of real

[82] The Liberal Democrats proposed a wealth tax on properties worth more than £1million in 2006. Recent studies on reactions to land taxes suggest that people were concerned about ability to pay—see Prabhakar (2008).

property or regulating the market for shares. However, the revenue raised far outweighs the costs. Presumably asset transactions of all sorts benefit from the general property rights and contracting laws enforced by governments. It is not clear why certain types of asset transactions should be singled out for a tax.

There are a number of drawbacks to stamp duties. Most important, they discourage asset transactions and therefore hinder the efficiency of asset markets. They may also discourage asset owners from investments that increase the value of their assets. In the case of share transactions, the stamp duty particularly hurts firms requiring finance for marginal projects by imposing a charge that is not related to profits. And, if, as in the UK, the duty applies only to shares of locally incorporated firms, it makes takeovers and mergers with non-UK firms more attractive (Hawkins and McCrae (2002)). For these reasons, there is a case for eliminating the stamp duty and making up the revenues from other sources, although it might be argued that this will create a windfall gain for existing asset owners to the extent that expected future taxes are capitalized into asset values. Perhaps this would be more politically palatable if it were done at the same time as reform of the wealth transfer tax to the extent that increases in the latter are seen as affecting roughly the same individuals who would obtain stamp duty relief. In practice this looks difficult to demonstrate since people who move house are not necessarily those who will inherit wealth.

There is currently no stamp duty or SDLT imposed in the UK on transfers of wealth (with a few limited exceptions[83]) since these are by definition gifts. The argument for an additional stamp duty charge on transfers of wealth such as gifts of land (assuming that existing transfers of wealth are taxed) is not at all clear, apart from a revenue-raising motive.

In the UK, stamp duty land tax is set at different rates according to the value and type of the property.[84] If stamp duty is to be retained (and given how much revenue it raises with low cost this seems inevitable) then several of these features could be improved. The fact that the rate applies to the whole value of the property rather than the value above the last band causes distortions to the purchase price of properties. It also means that there is sometimes a very strong incentive for buyers and sellers of properties to collude to arrange a lower price for the property and a corresponding higher separate payment for the fixtures and fittings in order to evade the tax, which leads to the authorities having to engage in costly policing activities. A marginal rate

[83] Such as gifts of land to connected companies, i.e. broadly companies controlled by the donor.

[84] Further details are provided in Appendix A of the additional online material (see note 2).

structure would eliminate this first problem and should reduce the second. Furthermore there is very little justification for differences in the thresholds between different types of properties and, in particular, different parts of the country. Stamp duty land tax does not seem an appropriate instrument for tilting land use towards non-residential rather than residential use; council tax and business rates would seem a more obvious way of doing this, nor is it an appropriate tax to try to carry out redistribution. These features also complicate the tax system unnecessarily. In practice given its yield and the need to raise £14 billion by other means it is unlikely SDLT will be abolished in the near future.

8.4.3. Other taxes at death

At the time of death, other taxes may be triggered. In most tax systems, capital gains are taxed on a realization basis, that is, no tax is due until the asset is sold or otherwise disposed of. Most countries with an estate tax on death do not also charge capital gains tax and some such as the UK and US have an uplift to market value at death so eradicating gains but imposing estate tax on death. It would be possible to impose capital gains tax on death as well as inheritance tax or for the property to change hands on a no gain no loss basis. The transferee then pays the tax when there is a later sale after death (see Section 8.3.2 for options).

At present the UK subjects most lifetime gifts (other than gifts to spouses or civil partners) to capital gains tax since such disposals are deemed to take place at market value, but lifetime gifts are generally free of inheritance tax; transfers on death (other than to spouses and civil partners) are subject to inheritance tax and unrealized gains are wiped out. In other words, the UK seems to regard inheritance tax and capital gains tax as alternative taxes.

Taxing capital gains on death or indeed on lifetime transfers of wealth might be regarded as double taxation if the asset is also subject to an inheritance tax, especially if it is levied on the estate rather on the heir's inheritance. But, from a welfarist point of view, taxing fully the income or gains of donors while also taxing inheritances received by heirs is consistent. The double taxation is a feature of wealth taxation itself, rather than being due to the realization of capital gains. However, imposing capital gains tax on death would highlight the double tax argument, which in practice might make the introduction of capital gains tax on death alongside a retained inheritance tax (or other tax on wealth transfers) unlikely.

8.5. CONCLUSIONS

It is clear that the current system for taxing wealth in the UK cannot be sustained and is justly unpopular. Inheritance tax is complex and inequitable; those who are wealthiest have the greatest ability to avoid the tax. A disproportionate burden appears to fall on those who are moderately wealthy. The current system provides an incentive to make lifetime gifts, but this favours those with abundant non-housing wealth and may not always be in the best interests of the elderly donor who retains insufficient savings.

The current UK inheritance tax raises relatively little revenue compared with other taxes, does not appear to redistribute wealth (itself a controversial aim), and is increasingly inequitable given the current mobility of wealth and labour. It can be avoided by (generally wealthier) individuals who can make lifetime transfers or emigrate permanently to low tax jurisdictions, or those whose domicile remains non-UK. In other words, the negative effects of inheritance tax outweigh the supposed benefits. Administrative and compliance costs are high compared with some other taxes such as corporation tax and stamp taxes.

Proposals tend to range from a reform of the current regime or the introduction of a completely new system of taxing transfers of wealth such as the move to a comprehensive 'donee based' tax which would also tax lifetime gifts. However, the objectives of taxing wealth transfers are often highly political and therefore difficult to agree: should the aim be to promote vertical equity—to redistribute from rich to poor—or to promote horizontal equity—to tax similarly placed individuals in the same way? If there is no political consensus on how to tax wealth then any system that taxes transfers of wealth is unlikely to work as intended since people will simply delay transfers until a change of government (as appeared to occur under the capital transfer tax regime). Hence it is important to obtain some political consensus on how to tax wealth transfers because the system can only work effectively if it operates consistently over the lifetime of an individual. One of the problems with capital transfer tax and inheritance tax is that its effect has been rather arbitrary. Someone dying in 1978 would have paid considerably more inheritance tax on the same wealth in real terms than someone dying in 1989 and would have had far fewer opportunities to pass it on tax free.

We take the view that a wealth tax is not sufficiently justified and dismiss this option apart possibly from a tax on occupation of high net value property which should be considered further. Many of the advantages of a wealth tax can be achieved by the taxation of capital income at appropriate rates within the personal tax system. A wealth transfer tax may have some justification based on the principles set out in Section 8.2 but these depend on a variety of principles which do not conclusively favour one particular system or the retention of a wealth transfer tax at all. If a wealth transfer tax is to be retained then a donee based tax combined with some reform of reliefs and rates, and the reintroduction of capital gains tax on death remains our preferred option particularly if political consensus over such a reform can be achieved. However, it could be that the payment of capital gains tax as well as inheritance tax on death is not politically feasible as it would make the double taxation created by any tax on wealth or wealth transfers very explicit.

If alternatively the current system of inheritance tax is to be retained, then it could certainly be improved. We set out in Section 8.3.2 some points that should be considered as the minimum required for improvement, although these would probably reduce the net yield further. As a result, making even these limited improvements to the current system of inheritance tax may not be preferable to the relatively straightforward reform of abolishing inheritance tax and reintroducing capital gains tax on death (without any wealth transfer taxes).

Therefore if a radical shift to a donee based wealth transfer tax is not deemed appropriate then the imposition of capital gains tax on death imposed only on **gains** not on the entire value should certainly be explored further and wealth transfer tax should be abolished. Now that capital gains tax has been simplified and is at a flat 18% rate, such a change would be relatively easy to implement although a number of issues such as emigration reliefs, and deferral of payment where the asset is illiquid would need to be considered carefully. It is only worthwhile doing this if some political consensus can be obtained but given the recent simplification of capital gains tax this may be inappropriate to consider. It is likely to be more acceptable than inheritance tax in that it is a tax on gains and is not double taxation. The rates are lower (18% compared with 40%), there would be no nil rate band of £300,000 so the yield may not be lower. See Section 8.3.2 for further details.

Finally, reform of the inheritance tax system is not independent of tax reform more generally. For example, the use of an investment income surtax as a surrogate for wealth taxation could not be introduced without regard to taxation of capital income in the rest of Europe. Similarly, the introduction of capital gains tax on death needs to be considered carefully where individuals are much more mobile, particularly within Europe. An exit charge may not be easy to enforce where individuals emigrate to another European country.

REFERENCES

Ackerman, B., and Alstott, A. (1999), *The Stakeholder Society*, New Haven: Yale University Press.

Andreoni, J. (1990), 'Impure Altruism and Donation to Public Goods: A Theory of Warm Glow Giving', *Economic Journal*, **100**, 464–77.

Atkinson, A. B. (1972), *Unequal Shares: Wealth in Britain*, London: Allen Lane.

Banks, J., and Tanner, S. (1998), *Taxing Charitable Giving*, Commentary 89, London: Institute for Fiscal Studies.

Bernheim, B. D., and Bagwell, K. (1988), 'Is Everything Neutral?', *Journal of Political Economy*, **96**, 308–38.

—— and Rangel, A. (2007), 'Behavioral Public Economics: Welfare and Policy Analysis with Non-Standard Decision Makers', in Diamond, P. and Vartiainen, H. (eds.), *Behavioral Economics and its Applications*, New Jersey: Princeton University Press, 7–77.

Bloom, N. (2006), *Inherited Family Firms and Management Practices: The Case for Modernising the UK's Inheritance Tax*, CEP Policy Analysis Paper No. 004, <http://cep.lse.ac.uk/_new/publications/abstract.asp?index=3020>.

Burnett, Lord (2007), 'A New Broom', *Taxation*, 15 March 2007, <http://www.taxation.co.uk/Articles/2007/03/15/51553/A+new+broom.htm>.

Bynner, J., and Paxton, W. (2001), *The Asset-effect*, London: Institute for Public Policy Research.

Cremer, H., and Pestieau, P. (2006), 'Wealth Transfer Taxation: A Survey of the Theoretical Literature', in Gérard-Varet, L-A., Colm, S-C., and Mercier Ythier J. (eds.), *Handbook of the Economics of Giving, Reciprocity and Altruism*, **2** Amsterdam: North-Holland, 1107–34.

Diamond, P. (2006), 'Optimal Tax Treatment of Private Contributions for Public Goods with and without Warm Glow Preferences', *Journal of Public Economics*, **90**, 897–919.

Emmerson, C., and Wakefield, M. (2001), *The Saving Gateway and the Child Trust Fund: Is Asset-Based Welfare 'Well Fare'?*, Commentary 85, London: Institute for Fiscal Studies.

Feldstein, M. S. (1977), 'The Surprising Incidence of a Tax on Pure Rent: A New Answer to an Old Question', *Journal of Political Economy*, **85**, 349–60.

Fleurbaey, M., and Maniquet, F. (forthcoming), 'Compensation and Responsibility', in Arrow, K. J., Sen, A. K., and Suzumura K. (eds.), *Handbook of Social Choice and Welfare*, **2**, Amsterdam: North-Holland.

Forsyth Report (2006), *Conservative Tax Reform Commission: Tax Matters: Reforming the Tax System.*

Graetz, M. J., and Shapiro, I. (2005), *Death by a Thousand Cuts: The Fight over Taxing Inherited Wealth*, New Jersey: Princeton University Press.

Hawkins, M., and McCrae, J. (2002), *Stamp Duty on Share Transactions: Is There a Case for Change?*, Commentary 89, London: Institute for Fiscal Studies.

Healey, D. (1989), *The Time of my Life*, London: Michael Joseph.

Heckly, C. (2004), 'Wealth Tax in Europe: Why the Decline June 2004', excerpt from 'Wealth Tax in Europe: Why the Downturn?' in Taly, M. and Mestrallet, G., *Estate Taxation: Ideas for Reform*, 39–50, Institute Reports, Paris Institut de l'enterprise.

HM Treasury (2007), *Pre-Budget Report*, <http://www.hm-treasury.gov.uk/pbr_csr/pbr_csr07_index.cfm>.

Kaplow, L. (1998), 'Tax Policy and Gifts', *American Economic Review Papers and Proceedings*, **88**, 283–8.

—— (2001), 'A Framework for Assessing Estate and Gift Taxation', in Gale, W. G., Hines, J. R., and Slemrod, J. (eds.), *Rethinking Estate and Gift Taxation*, 164–204, Washington: Brookings Institution.

Kay, J. A., and King, M. A. (1990), *The British Tax System*, Oxford: Oxford University Press.

Kessler, D., and Pestieau, P. (1991), 'The Taxation of Wealth in the EEC: Facts and Trends', *Canadian Public Policy* XVII, 309–21.

Layard, R. (2005), *Happiness: Lessons from a New Science*, London: Penguin.

Lee, N. (2007), 'Inheritance Tax—An Equitable Tax No Longer: Time for Abolition?' *Legal Studies*, **27**, 678–708.

Le Grand, J. (2006), 'Implementing Stakeholder Grants: The British Case', in Wright, E. O. (ed.), *Redesigning Redistribution*, 99–106, New York: Verso.

Lewis, M. and White, S. (2007), 'Inheritance Tax: What Do the People Think? Evidence from Deliberative Workshops', in Paxton, W., White, S., and Maxwell, D. (eds.), *The Citizen's Stake: Exploring the Future of Universal Asset Policies*, London: Institute for Public Policy Research.

Liberal Democrats (2007), *Reducing the Burden*, Policy Paper No. 81, <http://www.libdems.org.uk/media/conference/81%20-%20Reducing%20the%20Burden%20PRINT1.pdf>.

McCaffery, E. J. (1994), 'The Uneasy Case for Wealth Taxation', *Yale Law Journal*, **104**.

Maxwell, D. (2004), *Fair Dues: Towards a More Progressive Inheritance Tax*, London: Institute for Public Policy Research, <http://www.ippr.org.uk/publicationsandreports/publication.asp?id=244>.

Meade, J. (1978), *The Structure and Reform of Direct Taxation: Report of a Committee chaired by Professor J. E. Meade for the Institute for Fiscal Studies*, London: George Allen & Unwin. http://www.ifs.org.uk/publications/3433.

Patrick, R., and Jacobs, M. (1999), *Wealth's Fair Measure: The Reform of Inheritance Tax*, Fabian Society Report.

Prabhakar, R. (2008), 'Wealth Taxes: Stories, Metaphors and Public Attitudes', *Political Quarterly*, **79**, 172–8.

President's Advisory Panel on Tax Reform (2005), *Simple, Fair, and Pro-Growth: Proposals to Fix America's Tax System*, Washington: Government Printing Office.

Robinson, B. (1989), 'Reforming the Taxation of Capital Gains, Gifts and Inheritances', *Fiscal Studies*, **10**, 32–40.

Roemer, J. E. (1998), *Equality of Opportunity*, Cambridge, Mass.: Harvard University Press.

Rowlingson, K. (2007), *Is the Death of Inheritance Tax Inevitable? Lessons from America*, University of Birmingham.

——and McKay, S. (2005), *Attitudes to Inheritance in Britain*, Bristol: The Policy Press.

Sandford, C. (1987), 'Death Duties: Taxing Estates or Inheritances', *Fiscal Studies*, 8, 15–23.

——(1988), 'Towards a Real Inheritance Tax', *Accountancy*, **101**, 110–11.

——Willis, J. R. M., and Ironside, D. J. (1975), *An Annual Wealth Tax*, London: Heinemann Educational.

Sen, A. K. (1985), *Commodities and Capabilities*, Amsterdam: North-Holland.

Sherraden, M. (1991), *Assets and the Poor: A New American Welfare Policy*, New York: M. E. Sharpe, Inc.

Van Parijs, P. (1995), *Real Freedom for All*, New York: Oxford University Press.

Wilson, J. D. (2003), 'The Property Tax: Competing Views and a Hybrid Theory', in Cnossen, S., and Sinn, H-W. (eds.), *Public Finance and Public Policy in the New Century*, Cambridge, Mass.: MIT Press, 217–35.

Yucelik, Z. (1995), 'Taxation of Bequests Inheritances and Gifts', in P. Shome (ed.), *Tax Policy Handbook*, Washington DC: International Monetary Fund.

Commentary by Helmuth Cremer*

Helmuth Cremer is Professor of Economics at the University of Toulouse and a senior member of Institut universitaire de France. He is a Managing Editor of the *German Economic Review* and an Associate Editor of several journals including the *Journal of Public Economic Theory* and the *Journal of Public Economics*. He studies the optimal design of redistributive policies, including taxes, pensions, and education. Another part of his research deals with issues of pricing, competition, and public service in network industries.

1. INTRODUCTION

Taxes are rarely popular, but wealth transfer taxes appear to be particularly and increasingly unpopular. A number of countries are already without an inheritance or an estate tax or, as in the case of France, have dramatically reduced its scope. Some others, including the United States, contemplate to phase it out.

Clearly, death taxation more than any other generates controversy at all levels: political philosophy, economic theory, political debate, and public opinion. Opponents claim that it is unfair and immoral. It adds to the pain suffered by mourning families and it prevents small businesses from passing from generation to generation. Because of many loopholes, people of equivalent wealth pay different amounts of tax depending on their acumen at tax avoidance. It hits families that were surprised by death (and it is therefore sometimes called a tax on sudden death). It penalizes the frugal and the loving parents who pass wealth on to their children, reducing incentive to save and to invest.

Supporters of the tax, in contrast, retort that it is of all taxes the most efficient and the most equitable. They assert that it is highly progressive and a counterweight to existing wealth concentration. They also argue that it has few disincentive effects since it is payable only at death and that it is fair

* I would like to thank Firouz Gahvari and Pierre Pestieau for their helpful comments and suggestions.

since it concerns unearned resources. For a number of social philosophers and classical economists, estate or inheritance taxation is the ideal tax.

The truth probably lies between these two opposite camps. For economists this tax like all taxes should be judged against the two criteria of equity and efficiency to which one could add that of simplicity and compliance. Public economics (and more specifically taxation theory) provides a well-defined and rigorous framework to examine these issues. There exists by now a wide body of literature, some of which goes back to the pioneering age of optimal taxation models, while other contributions are newer and rely on recent developments in economic theory (like the modelling of mulidimensional asymmetric information).

In their chapter Robin Boadway, Emma Chamberlain, and Carl Emmerson (BCE) do mention this literature (which they refer to as the 'welfarist' approach), but only briefly and in a somewhat caricatural way. This is quite in line with their view that 'the results are agnostic'. Instead, they use a different approach both when they discuss the 'economic principles of wealth and wealth transfer taxation' (Section 8.2) and when they consider design and administration issues (Section 8.3). These 'non-utilitarian criteria' include a variety of issues such as paternalism, equality of opportunity, externalities, status (provided by wealth), enforcement, and political support. Summarizing this wide range of arguments in a few paragraphs (or pages) would certainly fail to give them proper credit and I shall abstain from such an exercise. In any event, I am not convinced that a sequence of arguments based on general principles (like vertical and horizontal equity, equal opportunity, the pursuit of efficiency, and the avoidance of administrative cost, etc.) can give us a lot of guidance for the design of tax systems. Consequently, I will elaborate a little further on the optimal tax approach and try to make its results less agnostic. In particular, I will examine what this literature has to say about the main conclusions drawn by BCE and presented in their Section 8.5. My review of the literature draws heavily on a survey by Cremer and Pestieau (2006) which the current version of BCE highlights in Box 8.1.[1]

I am not quite sure how to interpret BCE's recommendations. From what I can see they recommend against wealth taxation which they argue should be abolished. However, it is not entirely clear to me how this relates to the arguments presented in the body of the chapter. As far as wealth *transfer* taxes are concerned they plead either for 'a reform of the current regime or the introduction of a completely new system... such as the move to a comprehensive accessions tax which would also tax lifetime gifts'.

[1] I will provide only a minimal number of references here; detailed references are provided in Cremer and Pestieau (2006).

An important lesson emerging from the literature is that the appropriate tax structure depends on the relevant bequest model. One model states that bequests are simply an accident. People do not know how long they will live and so they keep more money than they turn out to need. If a significant share of bequests are accidental, estate taxation is quite efficient. However, if people are motivated to work and to save by the idea of leaving their families an inheritance, the tax will be distortionary. The impact of the distortion will depend on the bequest motive. If people have a specific amount they wish to leave to their children regardless of their needs and their behaviour, the outcome will be different from what it would be if the amount bequeathed is determined by a concern for the welfare of the heirs. Either way, it turns out that wealth and wealth transfer taxes are useful instruments in most cases. A zero tax is called for only in an extreme case, when individuals are perfectly altruistic (so that they effectively behave as if they were to live for ever). Even then, the result only holds in the steady state. This is true when only efficiency matters but also (and even more so) when redistribution is introduced.

The commentary deliberately adopts a theoretical and normative view. It studies how transfers between generations ought to be taxed along with other tax tools and according to some welfare criterion. The findings have to be qualified by a number of considerations including enforcement and political feasibility and most of the other issues discussed by BCE. From that perspective, BCE's analysis is a useful complement to the traditional optimal tax literature but it cannot replace it.

The rest of this commentary is organized as follows. Section 2 presents a brief overview of alternative bequest motives. Next, Section 3 focuses on efficiency aspects and views wealth and wealth transfer taxes purely as revenue raising devices. I examine the optimal tax structure under alternative models. Section 4 introduces inequality and the redistributive role of wealth transfer taxes.

2. BEQUEST MOTIVES

The role of gifts and estate transfers and their appropriate tax treatment depends on the donor's motives, if any. First of all it is possible that there is no bequests motive at all so that bequests are unplanned or accidental and result from a traditional life-cycle model. Accordingly, people save during their working lives in order to finance consumption when retired. Bequests occur solely because wealth is held in a bequeathable form due to imperfections in annuity markets or the need to have precautionary savings. Either way, with that form of bequest, estate taxes (even at a rate of 100%) should not have any disincentive effect.

With regard to the *planned* bequests, several motives have been suggested in the literature.

2.1. Pure dynastic altruism: altruistic bequest

Parents care about the likely lifetime *utility* of their children and hence about the welfare of their descendants in *all* future generations (because the children in turn care about their children). Pure altruism may give rise to the Ricardian equivalence which occurs when parents compensate any intergenerational redistribution through matching bequests.[2] Observe that this form of altruism is 'non-paternalistic' in the sense that parents respect their children's preference ordering. They care about their children's utility and not (directly) about their consumption, income, leisure, and so on.

2.2. Joy of giving or paternalistic bequest (bequest-as-last-consumption)

Parents here are motivated not by pure altruism but by the direct utility they receive from the act of giving. This phenomenon is also referred to as 'warm glow' giving.[3] It can be explained by some internal feeling of virtue arising from sacrifice in helping one's children or by the desire of controlling their life. In rough terms this amounts to considering bequests as a good 'consumed' by the parents and contributing to their welfare. A crucial element is whether what matters to the donor is the net or the gross of tax amount.[4]

2.3. Exchange-related motives: strategic bequests[5]

Exchange-related models consider children choosing a level of 'attention' to provide to their parents and parents remunerating them in the prospect of bequest. The exchanges can involve all sorts of non-pecuniary services and they can be part of a strategic game between parents and children.

[2] Barro (1974). [3] Andreoni (1990).

[4] One can argue that 'warm glow' and paternalism differ from that perspective. Specifically a warm glow donor can be expected to care about the gross (before tax) gift or estate while this is not necessarily true under paternalistic altruism.

[5] Bernheim et al. (1985).

3. EFFICIENCY

Let us for the time being abstract from issues of redistribution and concentrate on the efficiency aspect. In other words, the different taxes are merely viewed as revenue raising devices. The underlying question is then how to raise a given tax revenue in the 'least costly' way. I follow Cremer and Pestieau (2006) who provide an overview of the taxation of capital income and wealth transfers and show how the answer depends on the underlying bequest motive.

The general result that emerges (except in the steady state under pure altruism) is that taxes on wealth and wealth transfers should not be equal to zero. The highest tax rates emerge under accidental bequests. When individuals do not care about the bequest they may leave and accumulated wealth only to smooth consumption over time or for precautionary motives, a tax on bequest has no impact on savings. Consequently, it is not surprising that accidental bequests should be taxed at a high rate (possibly at 100%).

A similar conclusion emerges when transfers are motived by joy of giving and when the donee only cares about the gross (before tax) bequest. However, when the (paternalistic) donee cares about the after tax transfer, or when bequests arise from exchange (bequest for attention), a more complex picture arises. Tax rates now depend on elasticities according to Ramsey (or rather Atkinson and Sandmo (1980)) type rules. In rough terms, the more responsive a variable is to its price, the less it should be taxed. Bequests may now be subject to a 'double tax': first, the one on savings and then the specific tax on wealth transfers. Interestingly, the specific tax on transfer is, however, not necessarily positive! For instance, in the exchange scenario when demand for attention is more elastic than future consumption we obtain a negative specific tax on bequests. While the exact magnitude of tax rates is to some extent an empirical issue it is clear that the tax rates on planned bequests will not be anywhere near the high rate on accidental bequests. This has interesting implications in practice because it justifies a lower tax on *inter vivos* transfers (which are by their very nature not accidental) than on transfers at death. Similarly, it suggests that any explicitly planned form of transfer at death (like life insurance) should be taxed less heavily than other forms of bequest.

Taxes on capital may also be used to control the level of capital accumulation. This issue is often neglected in the literature by assuming that the government has other instruments to secure the appropriate level of capital accumulation. For instance, it is frequently assumed that public debt can be used to secure the modified golden rule. When this is not the case, the analysis becomes more complicated. But this does not strengthen the case for leaving wealth (or wealth transfers) untaxed. Interestingly, in an overlapping generations model, insufficient capital accumulation does not necessarily call for a reduction in the tax rate on wealth or capital income. This is because saving depends not only on the interest rate but also on earnings.[6]

Finally, when bequests are motived by pure altruism, the Chamley–Judd result implies a zero tax on capital.[7] However, this result relies on strong assumptions and it applies only to the steady state. During the transition period wealth transfers and capital income are subject to taxation.[8]

The literature tends to concentrate on a single bequest motive at a time. In reality, however, we can expect all these motives to coexist. Taxation under mixed bequest motives has received less attention in the literature. However, since each of the coexisting bequest motives (except possibly one) calls for a non-zero tax on capital, one cannot expect that the optimal policy involves a zero tax. The few studies there are confirm this basic intuition. But this point certainly deserves further investigation.

How do these findings compare with BCE's recommendation? First, they do not support the claim that wealth taxes should be dismissed altogether. The theoretical optimal tax literature does not tell us precisely at what level wealth taxes should be set; this is an empirical question. However, what the literature tells us is that instrument of wealth taxation should not be given up altogether. Second, regarding the taxation of wealth transfers, they suggest a more complex structure of tax rates than that advocated by BCE. A bequest is not just 'consumption' or 'income' and wealth transfers should typically be taxed differently from consumption that occurs late in the life cycle. Finally, the analysis shows that to study a wealth transfer tax one cannot leave out the issue of wealth income taxation. The determination of optimal tax rates requires an integrated treatment of the tax mix.

4. EQUITY AND REDISTRIBUTION

Up to now, the discussion has focused on efficiency issues. However, it is clear that aspects of fairness and redistribution are at least potentially important to assess the role of wealth and wealth transfer taxes. To introduce redistributive concerns, one can simply revisit the setting considered in the previous section

6 Atkinson and Sandmo (1980). 7 Chamley (1986), Judd (1985).
8 See e.g. Saez (2002).

and allow for heterogenous individuals. It is then clear that the optimal tax rules will have to be amended. Roughly speaking, we move from simple Ramsey rules to 'many households Ramsey' rule that account for the redistributive properties of the different forms of wealth taxation. However, this exercise does not address the main question namely whether taxes on wealth and/or wealth transfers are the appropriate instruments to be used in the first place. It is by now well known that Ramsey type models which rely on linear (proportional) taxes may artificially create a role for some instruments. This is because they restrict labour income taxes to be linear even though there is no theoretical or practical argument to justify this assumption (except that it makes the model easier to solve). In practice, labour income taxes are levied according to sophisticated non-linear schedules. Atkinson and Stiglitz (1976) have shown that these restrictions on labor income taxes may artificially create a role for differential commodity taxes (and a tax on capital income is from a lifetime perspective a non-uniform consumption tax where future consumption is taxed more heavily).

To understand the implications of this for the subject matter of this commentary, I will consider a simple thought experiment. It is admittedly oversimplified but it allows us to avoid the technicalities of optimal tax models.[9] Consider a world where individuals differ only in their productivity (their wage or more generally their ability to make money by supplying their labour). To make the problem realistic (and interesting) let us assume that productivity is not publicly observable. For the rest, all individuals are identical; they are all born with the same initial wealth (if any) and have the same preferences (including the discount rate), life expectancies, and so on. As individuals grow older their wealth will, of course, differ. However, this heterogeneity is solely due to the accumulation of past labour income. In such a world, a well-designed tax on labour income is sufficient and other taxes are not needed.[10] In particular, taxes on wealth, or wealth income, are redundant. In rough terms, taxing wealth is just an indirect way of taxing past earnings (which have already been taxed) and the observation of wealth does not give us any new information.

The picture changes dramatically when individuals differ in more then one dimension. In other words, individuals differ not only in productivity but also in discount rates, longevity or initial (inherited) wealth. Particularly interesting from our perspective is the case where individuals differ in the

[9] For a more detailed discussion, see Cremer and Pestieau (2006).

[10] See Atkinson and Stiglitz (1976). To get the results some additional technical assumptions are necessary. We neglect them to concentrate on the main issue. The full implication of the Atkinson and Stiglitz result are also discussed by Cremer (2003).

bequest they have received which has been studied by Cremer et al. (2003). Consider first the case where bequests are not observable and thus cannot be taxed. Now, at a given age, individuals with identical productivity will have different levels of wealth. Not surprisingly, it is then no longer true that a tax on labour income is sufficient. The optimal policy now involves taxes on both labour and capital incomes. This is because making taxes dependent on capital income permits a better screening for the unobservable individual characteristics. Cremer et al. (2003) concentrate on the case where transfers are motivated by 'joy of giving' and when there is no correlation between wealth and productivity. In that setting the optimal tax is non-zero. When the joy of giving term is counted in social welfare the tax is necessarily positive. However, when there is laundering a negative tax cannot be ruled out. Interestingly though, the tax is more likely to be positive when we introduce correlation between productivity and wealth. And with perfect correlation it is always positive. To sum up, unobservable bequests introduce the need for wealth taxation especially when there is a positive correlation between wealth and productivity.

On the other hand, if bequests are observable they ought to be taxed. In the specific setting (with correlation) considered by Cremer et al. (2003), the appropriate tax is of 100%. A less extreme solution emerges when bequests are only imperfectly observable or when there are incentive effects. Then the optimal tax mix involves a tax on bequests (of less than 100%) along with taxes on labour and capital income. Intuitively this does not come as a surprise. When inequality is due in part to bequests, wealth (wealth income), and wealth transfers should be taxed.

In reality, the sources of heterogeneity go beyond those discussed by Cremer et al. (2003). Individuals also differ in their longevity, their time preference, and so on. This can only reinforce the role of wealth and wealth transfer taxes in the optimal tax mix. On these issues, the literature remains incomplete and there are plenty of open questions (some of which are discussed in Chapter 6 by Banks and Diamond).

To sum up, heterogeneity in several dimensions along with redistributive concern do provide a rationale for the taxation of wealth and wealth transfers. In a world of asymmetric information, where individuals differ not only on productivity, a tax on labour income (or equivalently a consumption tax) however well designed and sophisticated is not sufficient.

While BCE's analysis deals with a number of related issues (and in particular the issue of equality of opportunity), the optimal tax/multidimensional heterogeneity aspects do not appear to receive a lot of attention. As my discussion suggests, they are not just important to justify the existence of wealth transfer taxes but they are also of crucial importance for their design. Specifically, it does not appear to be possible to disconnect the study of wealth and wealth transfer taxes from that of other taxes (and particularly income taxes). Their design has to be determined as part of an integrated study of the tax mix.

5. CONCLUDING COMMENTS

To sum up, the pure efficiency approach does justify the use of wealth and wealth transfer taxes. This is an empirical question and it depends in particular on demand elasticities (for savings and bequests). We can expect the tax to be the higher the larger the proportion of accidental bequests. When individuals are heterogenous, wealth taxes are a useful instrument as long as individuals differ in more then one dimension. Whether the tax is positive or not depends on the issue of laundering (which may be considered as a technical point) but more interestingly on the degree of correlation between the characteristics. For instance, when individuals differ in productivity and wealth or in productivity and longevity, a positive wealth tax arises when the productive tend to have more wealth (or live longer).

My comments take a normative view and ask if wealth and wealth transfers ought to be taxed in order to maximize social welfare (given the information structure). Even though some issues remain open it seems to me that the literature I have reviewed overall makes a case for a positive answer to this question.

All these results are to a large extent at odds with the fact that wealth transfer taxes are very unpopular. There are, of course, a number of political economy issues I have neglected. For instance, there is the issue of avoidance and enforcement which does lead to a strong departure from horizontal and vertical equity. In addition, there is the phenomenon of tax competition which can put a downward pressure on wealth taxes. BCE do provide a comprehensive and nice discussion of many of these issues but it is not clear how this translates into precise policy recommendations (except maybe when it comes to arguing that wealth taxes ought to be cancelled). In any event, it does not seem to me that the political and enforcement arguments provided here and by BCE are suitable to tell the whole story. How, for instance, can we explain that very rich people are often in favour of estate taxation while many middle classes (whose wealth is below the million dollar benchmark under which the estate is exempted) oppose it? More work is needed on these issues.

REFERENCES

Andreoni, J. (1990), 'Impure Altruism and Donations to Public Goods: A Theory of Warm-glow Giving?', *Economic Journal*, **100**, 464–77.

Atkinson, A. B., and Sandmo, A. (1980), 'Welfare Implications of the Taxation of Savings', *Economic Journal*, **90**, 529–49.

—— and Stiglitz, J. E. (1976), 'The Design of Tax Structure: Direct Versus Indirect Taxation', *Journal of Public Economics*, **6**, 55–75.

Barro, R. (1974), 'Are Government Bonds Net Wealth?', *Journal of Political Economy*, **82**, 1095–117.

Bernheim, B. D., Shleifer, A., and Summers, L. H. (1985), 'The Strategic Bequest Motive', *Journal of Political Economy*, **93**, 1045–76.

Boadway, R., Marchand, M., and Pestieau, P. (2000), 'Redistribution with Unobservable Bequests: A Case for Capital Income Tax', *Scandinavian Journal of Economics*, **102**, 1–15.

Chamley, Ch. (1986), 'Optimal Taxation of Capital Income in General Equilibrium with Infinite Lives', *Economica*, **54**, 607–22.

Cremer, H. (2003), 'Multi-dimensional Heterogeneity and the Design of Tax Policies', *Baltic Journal of Economics*, **4**, 35–45.

—— and Pestieau, P. (2006), 'Wealth Transfer Taxation: A Survey of the Theoretical Literature', in Kolm, S. C., and Mercier Ythier, J. (eds.), *Handbook of the Economics of Giving, Altruism and Reciprocity*, vol. 2.

—— —— and Rochet, J.-C. (2003), 'Capital Income Taxation when Inherited Wealth is not Observable', *Journal of Public Economics*, **87**, 2475–90.

Judd, K. L. (1985), 'Redistributive Taxation in a Simple Perfect Foresight Model', *Journal of Public Economics*, **28**, 59–83.

Michel, Ph., and Pestieau, P. (2002), 'Wealth Transfer Taxation with both Accidental and Desired Bequests', unpublished.

Saez, E. (2002), 'Optimal Progressive Capital Income Taxes in the Infinite Horizon Model', NBER Working Paper No. 9046.

Commentary by Thomas Piketty

Thomas Piketty is Professor of Economics at the Paris School of Economics. He earned his PhD in 1993 at EHESS and LSE (European Doctoral Programme) and taught at MIT from 1993 to 1996 before returning to France. Thomas is Co-editor of the *Journal of Public Economics*, Co-director of CEPR Public Policy Programme, and was the first director of the newly founded Paris School of Economics (2005–07). He recently co-edited (with A. B. Atkinson) *Top Incomes over the 20th Century*.

This commentary offers a personal perspective on wealth taxation in the twenty-first century. Wealth taxation has been the subject of substantial policy action in recent years, with the implementation of large inheritance tax cuts in several OECD countries (e.g. US, Italy, UK, France). More generally, I believe that the issue of wealth and wealth transfer taxation is very likely to play an important role in the public finance debates of the coming decades, for at least two reasons: a theoretical reason, and an empirical/historical reason.

Let me start with the theoretical reason. In spite of the voluminous existing literature, the current state of optimal capital taxation theories is wholly unsatisfactory, and one can (hopefully) expect major developments in the future. Existing theories of optimal labour income taxation, as pioneered by Mirrlees (1971) and recently reformulated by Diamond (1998) and Saez (2001), are in a relatively satisfactory state. They offer formal models and optimal tax formulas that can be calibrated with estimated labour supply elasticities and other parameters (in particular the shape of the labour income distribution) and that can be used to think about the real world and possible tax reforms. These theories are of course imperfect and still need to be improved. But at least they provide normative conclusions about optimal tax rates levels and profiles that are not fully contradictory with what one observes in the real world. For instance, the Diamond–Saez U-shaped optimal profile of marginal rates is observed in most countries (i.e. effective marginal rates tend to be higher for low income and high income groups than for middle income groups), for reasons that are probably to a large extent identical to those captured by the theory (i.e. it is less distortionary to have high average rates but moderate marginal rates on high-density middle income groups). The Diamond–Saez formula for asymptotic marginal rates is also remarkably simple and delivers results that are relatively reasonable.[1] Needless to say, wide disagreements still exist about the level of desirable labour income tax rates—in particular because of persisting disagreements about labour supply elasticities. But at least existing theories of optimal labour income taxation do offer a useful basis for an informed policy discussion.

Nothing close to this exists regarding theories of optimal capital taxation. To put it bluntly, existing models are completely off-the-mark if one tries to use them to think about real world capital taxation. For instance, most models prescribe 100% capital tax rates in the very short run and 0% capital tax rates in the very long run. How can one apply these results to the real world? Is today the short run or the long run? These extreme conclusions reflect inherent difficulties in the modelling of time and the choice of a proper time frame to study these issues. In the short run, capital income is viewed as a pure rent coming from past accumulation, so that the existing capital stock should be taxed at a 100% rate. In the long run, the elasticity of savings with respect to the net-of-tax interest rate is typically infinite,[2] so that even dynasties with zero-capital-stock would suffer enormously from any capital tax rate larger than 0% (i.e. even an infinitely small tax rate would have enormous, devastating effects). Unlike labour supply, capital accumulation is an intrinsically dynamic phenomenon, and economists have not yet found the proper way to develop useful dynamic models of optimal capital taxation, that is, models that can be used for an informed policy discussion.

Another major theoretical difficulty that needs to be addressed has to do with the necessity to distinguish between corporate profits taxation and household capital income taxation. In standard theoretical models both concepts are identical, but in the real world they are not. In order to address this issue, one would need to integrate a proper theory of the firm and retained earnings (as well as a theory of the real estate capital sector) into models of optimal capital taxation. Finally, one needs to introduce new theoretical ingredients in order to distinguish between capital taxation and capital

[1] For example, an uncompensated labour supply elasticity of 0.5, zero income effects and a Pareto parameter of 2 for the distribution of top labour incomes imply an optimal top marginal rate of 50%.

[2] e.g. in standard dynastic models, this follows immediately from the golden rule of capital accumulation, which requires the marginal product of capital to equate to the rate of time preference in the long run.

income taxation. In standard theoretical models, all agents obtain the same rate of return on their capital stock, so that both forms of taxation are fully equivalent. But in the real world they are not. In particular, the central—and fairly reasonable—political argument in favour of capital taxation has always been that taxing the capital stock (rather than the income flow) puts better incentives on capital owners to obtain high return on their assets. In order to address this issue, one would need to develop a model with heterogeneous returns to capital (presumably depending on effort put in by the capital owner, among other things). Capital taxation theory faces major difficulties and is still in its infancy. This is one of the main shortcomings of current economic theory. It seems likely (and highly desirable) that progress will be made in the coming decades.[3]

Second, and maybe more importantly, the issue of wealth taxation is likely to be a big issue in the future simply because wealth is going to be a big issue in the coming decades. In most OECD countries, and especially in Continental Europe, aggregate (household wealth)/(household income) ratios have increased substantially since the 1970s, with an acceleration of the trend since the 1990s. This is certainly a complex phenomenon. To some extent, it is simply due to the rise of asset prices (both property prices and share prices), which in a number of countries were historically low between the 1950s and the 1970s, and have increased enormously since the 1980s–1990s. In countries strongly hit by the twentieth century's World Wars (especially in Continental Europe), the rise of the wealth/income ratio also seems to reflect a long-term recovery effect. For instance, Figure 1 shows that the aggregate (household wealth)/(household income) ratio in France was around 6 at the eve of the First World War, fell as low as 1–1.5 in the aftermath of the Second World War, and then went back up again to around 3 in 1970 and 6 in 2006. Note that there is no strong theoretical reason why the long-term, steady-state wealth/income ratio should be stationary along the development process: it could go either way. However, this kind of long-term picture does suggest that the recent rise of wealth/income ratios is at least in part a structural phenomenon, that is, the capital accumulation patterns of cohorts hit by the wars were severely disrupted, and it took several generations to recover. Capital accumulation takes time.

It would be surprising if the kind of evolution depicted in Figure 1 had no long-term impact on the observed tax mix. On purely a priori grounds, the main impact of such an evolution should be to push the tax mix in the direction of greater reliance on capital taxation (broadly speaking), at least in

[3] This (very) brief review does not do full justice to the extensive recent literature on optimal capital taxation theory (surveyed by Banks and Diamond in Chapter 6). However, it is fair to say that existing models so far do not provide plausible conclusions about optimal capital tax rates.

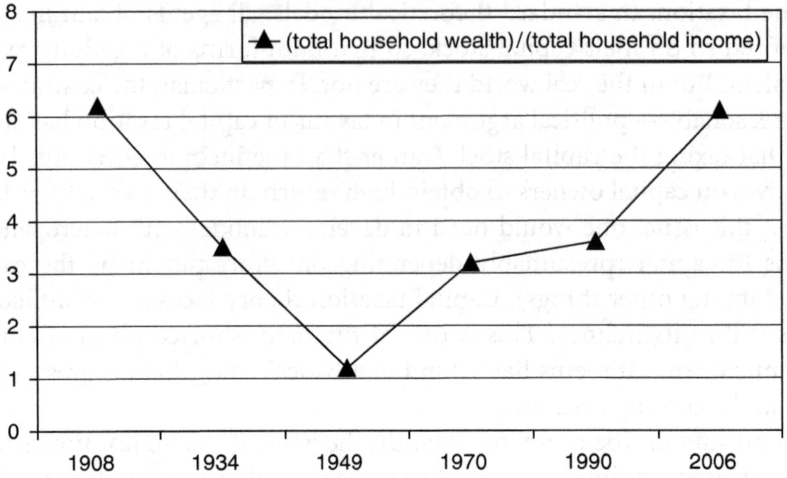

Source: Author's computations based upon Piketty (2003) and National Income and Wealth Accounts (INSEE).

Figure 1. The wealth/income ratio in France, 1908–2006

absolute terms. Other things equal, the share of capital tax revenues in total tax revenues should go up when the aggregate capital/income ratio goes up. It is hard to think of a normative model or a political economy model in which the rise in this ratio would be more than offset by a decline in tax rates on capital relative to other tax bases.

Note, however, that it would be misleading to make predictions about the future tax mix solely on the basis of the aggregate capital/income ratio. Many other effects are at play, for example, the changing distribution of wealth. In most political economy models, a less concentrated distribution of wealth would tend to make the median voter (or whoever is in power) less inclined to tax wealth heavily. If the wealth distribution became less and less concentrated, this could possibly undo the effect of rising capital/income ratios. There is evidence showing that wealth concentration has indeed significantly declined in the long run. For instance, in the case of France, and notwithstanding substantial measurement and time lag issues, the top 1% of estates accounted for over 50% of the total value of estates at the eve of the First World War, and for about 20% during the 1990s (Figure 2).

Whether this long-run decline in wealth concentration is going to continue during the first decades of the twenty-first century is, however, quite uncertain. In particular, it seems plausible that the rise in top income shares observed since the 1970s–1980s—especially in Anglo-Saxon countries, but also, more recently, in other developed countries—will eventually trigger a

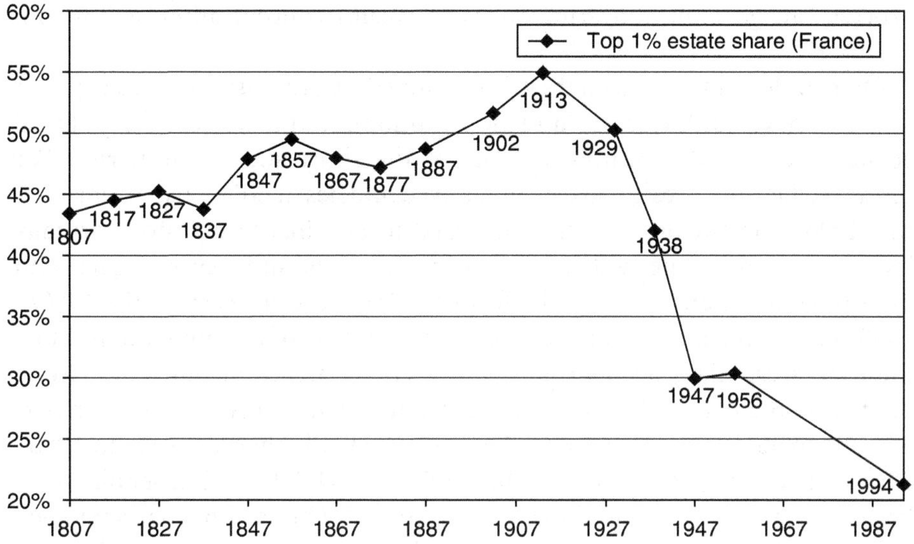

Source: Piketty, Postel-Vinay, and Rosenthal (2006).

Figure 2. Wealth concentration at death in France, 1807–1994

rise in wealth concentration.[4] Other factors, including changes in the income profile of savings behaviour and the age structure of the wealth distribution, might, however, play a key role as well.[5] Note also that there can be some two-way interaction between wealth distribution and wealth taxation. A highly progressive system of wealth and income taxation certainly acts to reduce wealth concentration in the long run. For instance, it seems likely that the highly progressive estate taxes applied in most developed countries since the Second World War have contributed to the long-run decline in wealth concentration.[6] This decline can then reduce political support for wealth taxation. In turn, large cuts in estate tax progressivity—such as the ones recently adopted in the US—are likely to contribute to a rise in wealth concentration a couple of decades down the road, thereby reinforcing the impact of rising top income shares.[7] One can easily see how this kind of

[4] For an international perspective on top incomes shares in the long run (and especially the key role played by top capital incomes), see the country chapters collected by Atkinson and Piketty (2007).

[5] The recent study by Kopczuk and Saez (2004) found no evidence for a rise in US wealth concentration, in spite of the very large rise of top income shares. This might reflect time lag issues as well as complex demographic and asset price effects (e.g. middle wealth and elderly individuals have benefited a lot from the particularly fast rise in real estate prices).

[6] For simple simulation results illustrating the long-run impact of capital tax rates on equilibrium wealth concentration, see Piketty (2003) and Dell (2005).

[7] See Piketty and Saez (2003).

process can generate long-run cycles in wealth concentration and wealth taxation.

Quite independently from these long-run effects, the fast rise in asset prices can also have contradictory and non-monotonic impacts on the political economy of wealth taxation, at least in the short and medium run. For instance, because wealth taxes in many countries tend to use exemption thresholds and tax brackets that are fixed in nominal terms (not normally increased even in line with overall price inflation, and never in line with asset price inflation), the initial effect of rising asset prices since the 1980s–1990s has been a marked increase in the percentage of the population hit by these taxes, especially by inheritance taxes. This clearly contributed to a strong political demand for inheritance tax cuts. For instance, this is certainly in part what happened in the UK: only 2.3% of estates paid inheritance tax in 1986–88; this percentage rose to 5.9% in 2005–06, and 37% of households now have an estate with a value above the threshold.[8] This is also what happened in France: the nominal exemption threshold had not increased since the early 1980s, which largely explained the huge rise in the exemption level that was implemented in 2007.

Finally, historical experience suggests that the political economy of capital taxation involves complex, country-specific and quantitatively important issues. For instance, a recent study has shown that diverging trends in capital tax progressivity (especially estate tax progressivity) largely explain why the US and UK tax systems have become less progressive overall than that of France during the past decades, while they were more progressive than France's until the 1970s.[9] The central conclusion is that the contribution of capital taxation to overall progressivity—both in terms of level and trend—is larger than is commonly assumed. Capital taxation is a key and complex issue and should rank highly in the tax debate and research agenda of the coming decades, from both a normative and a political economy perspective.

REFERENCES

Atkinson, A. B., and Piketty, T. (2007), *Top Incomes over the Twentieth Century : A Contrast between Continental European and English-Speaking Countries*, Oxford: Oxford University Press.

Dell, F. (2005), 'Top Incomes in Germany and Switzerland Over the Twentieth Century', *Journal of the European Economic Association*, 3, 412–21.

[8] See Boadway, Chamberlain, and Emmerson, Chapter 8.

[9] See Piketty and Saez (2007).

Diamond, P. (1998), 'Optimal Income Taxation: An Example with a U-Shaped Pattern of Optimal Marginal Rates', *American Economic Review*, **88**, 83–95.
Kopczuk, W., and Saez, E. (2004), 'Top Wealth Shares in the United States, 1916–2000: Evidence from Estate Tax Returns', *National Tax Journal*, **57**, 445–87.
Mirrlees, J. A. (1971), 'An Exploration in the Theory of Optimum Income Taxation', *Review of Economic Studies*, **38**, 175–208.
Piketty, T. (2003), 'Income Inequality in France, 1901–1998', *Journal of Political Economy*, **111**, 1004–42.
—— Postel-Vinay, G., and Rosenthal, J. L. (2006), 'Wealth Concentration in a Developing Economy: Paris and France, 1807–1994', *American Economic Review*, **96**, 236–56.
—— and Saez, E. (2003), 'Income Inequality in the United States, 1913–1998', *Quarterly Journal of Economics*, **118**, 1–39.
—— —— (2007), 'How Progressive is the U.S. Federal Tax System? A Historical and International Perspective', *Journal of Economic Perspectives*, **21**, 3–24.
Saez, E. (2001), 'Using Elasticities to Derive Optimal Income Tax Rates', *Review of Economic Studies*, **68**, 205–29.

Commentary by Martin Weale

Martin Weale CBE is the Director of the National Institute of Economic and Social Research. He is an applied economist who works on a range of macro- and microeconomic issues. He is also a member of the Board for Actuarial Standards. He holds an ScD in Economics from Cambridge University and an Honorary DSc from City University. He was appointed CBE for services to economics in 1999. His recent work has focused on questions surrounding pension provision, savings adequacy, and means testing of retirement benefits.

Having relied on the interim report of the Meade Committee as a basic public finance text for my finals thirty years ago as well as subsequently working very closely with its lead author, I have a strong affection for that report and also a strong interest in its successor. It is therefore a great pleasure to have the opportunity to write some comments on the chapter by Boadway, Chamberlain, and Emmerson.

Colbert described his aim when collecting taxes as being to pluck as many feathers as he could without the goose squawking. This chapter describes, in some detail, taxes which are currently associated with a great deal of squawking. As the authors point out, taxes which involve the act of making an explicit transfer are much less popular than those which are less visible. On these grounds taxes associated with wealth fail very badly since it is hard to envisage the sort of invisible collection associated with consumption taxes or PAYE income tax. The authors also argue that inheritance tax is expensive to collect, with the cost at 1.01% of revenues, although they do not follow this through to produce a strong argument for expanding stamp taxes with a collection cost of only 0.2%. Various other justifications for taxes are not dismissed as readily as they might be, for example that stamp duty on property covers the cost of maintaining the register. What, one asks, are Land Registry fees for and why was the tax collected on transfers in areas like Cambridge where property was not registered until 1975?

They point to an international drift away from both wealth taxes and inheritance taxes; this is not in itself as convincing as the argument that countries such as Sweden which abolished wealth taxes had found their performance disappointing, in terms of both revenue and perceived impact on the distribution of wealth. Both France and Switzerland are on the list of countries which continue to tax wealth but there is no suggestion that anyone is planning to introduce such a tax.

On the taxation of wealth per se, the main argument produced against the suggestion is that, in the 1970s, the Labour Party was committed to implementing a wealth tax but found itself unable to design the tax sufficiently precisely. The authors do not discuss in much detail the argument that wealth confers advantages on its owners over and above the income it generates. The main economic advantage it offers is insurance against the effects of adverse shocks to human capital and family breakdown. Most other adverse shocks can be insured against, although wealthy people may, for example, choose to self insure a range of risks because (i) they see themselves as lower than average risk, (ii) with constant risk aversion, the ownership of wealth reduces the impact of a given absolute risk, or (iii) insurance markets are not perceived to be efficient. But, apart from the protection offered against uninsurable risks, it is hard to see that these effects can be important.

Are there advantages of wealth over and above the economic advantages associated with its precautionary characteristics? I suspect the authors of the Meade Report (Meade, 1978) thought so. Does ownership of wealth raise future returns by reducing unit costs of managing wealth? Does it offer a means of influence which can be used to raise the returns to human and non-human capital in the future? While both the second and third questions might be answered positively, it could still be argued that, with a tax on investment income, the case for a tax on wealth has not been made. Falling back on the precautionary argument, one might note that, if the main benefit is insurance against shocks to human capital, the tax should presumably fall more heavily on people of working age than on retired people and more on young workers than old workers. Since single people are not at risk of family breakdown, should they pay a reduced rate? Both survey-based findings and simulations suggest that precautionary holdings of wealth are low—with the possible exception of wealth held in old age to finance an uncertain life-span. If this is the case the precautionary argument for a tax on wealth cannot be very strong.

Perhaps the case for a wealth tax is at its strongest when there are other shortcomings of the tax system which do not seem to be properly addressed or when there are other market failures. For example, if income can easily be dressed up as capital gains and the latter cannot be taxed as income, as is perhaps the case current in the UK, then there may, for all its defects, be a case for a wealth tax in addition. Obviously a better solution would be to remedy the primary defect with the tax system and for this reason a wealth tax cannot be considered in isolation from the rest of the tax system. A second strong argument for taxation of wealth or the income from wealth (which is equivalent provided the income is taxable) is that young people are wealth-constrained because credit cannot be easily secured on human capital. Taxes on wealth and income from wealth therefore allow them to defer part of their life-time tax bill to a stage when, to put the point sloppily, they can afford to pay it. In other words, wealth taxes are like a form of credit and, with imperfect private capital markets, the benefit that they offer may offset their deleterious effects in discouraging saving.

There are, however, reasons for thinking that the 1970s arguments might have been presented rather differently in the current circumstances. Income, and therefore presumably also wealth inequality in the UK has risen very sharply since then, and appreciably more so than in other similar countries. In the 1980s and 1990s the rise in inequality was driven by worsening of the low income deciles relative to the mean. In the last ten years or so, it seems to have been driven by a sharp increase in the numbers earning very high incomes and also in the levels of these incomes (Atkinson (2007)). Does this have any impact on the case for a general wealth tax? A general response to this question would probably be positive although at the same time the many practical objections raised by the authors would still be present. But one suspects that the 1970s Labour government would have been put off less easily than they were thirty years ago.

A second, perhaps related reason for seeing things differently is that the amount of wealth is, relative to income, now much greater than at any time since the start of the data series in 1920 (Khoman and Weale (2006)). This wealth has its origins in asset revaluations rather than resulting from past saving. In that sense taxes on wealth and on inheritance are not double taxation. Equally, given the source of the wealth, a more stringent capital gains tax might be more appropriate than a wealth tax.

It is with the discussion of property taxes, which are rightly distinguished from wealth taxes, that the authors come nearer to the dog they have not allowed to bark. They make a good case for a tax on property occupancy with a high threshold, on the grounds (i) that people who live in expensive properties may be missed by other aspects of the tax system, (ii) that they can probably 'afford' to pay more tax, and (iii) that owner-occupied housing is undertaxed relative to other forms of wealth (although their proposal would also apply to tenants). These are all powerful arguments and can be compared with the Council Tax whose threshold system imposes an effective cap. But they do not follow their argument through to the case for a land tax. The argument for taxing land but not other forms of wealth is that the disincentive effects to the accumulation of wealth plainly do not apply to land; the stock is fixed and the tax is non-distortionary. Taxes on land are likely to increase the efficiency with which land is used and particularly so if as in the case of owner-occupation the benefit is currently not taxed. Obviously valuations would be required and they should be kept up to date. The legislation might include the requirement that the government would be obliged to buy any land at its valuation plus a safety margin of say 5% at the request of the owner within three months of the valuation.

Such a tax would depress land values. This objection could be met if it were introduced gradually so as to avoid disturbing the housing market. It, as with other property taxes, would be open to the objection that people who are house (and land) rich but cash poor could not afford to pay it. The authors point out that in the Republic of Ireland inheritance tax due on houses occupied by more than one unmarried person can be deferred until the other occupants die; in the same way the government could extend mortgages to people who did not have the cash to pay the land tax and did not want to move. Whether the tax is collected from the occupier or the owner of the land is probably not very important. At least I am not aware of any analysis of tax incidence which suggests that the burden is affected by the way in which the tax is collected, except perhaps as a result of market rigidities in the very short run—a point which also applies to the artificial distinction the authors make between taxing occupiers and owners of expensive properties.

Welfare would surely be increased if the revenue currently collected by stamp taxes on property transactions were instead collected by a land tax. The main argument against seems to be that the only good taxes are old taxes. Nevertheless, a carefully judged reform in which land tax replaced council tax, inheritance tax on property, and stamp taxes on property might well lead to less squawking than do the current arrangements. Whether a reform commanding bi-partisan support could be designed is less clear. But given the need for gradual introduction, there plainly has to be a consensus about it.

Moving on from these general issues to the more specific issues concerning inheritance taxes, the authors present a helpful account of the momentum against inheritance taxes. There is, however, no discussion of whether taxes, which presumably reduce inheritance through consumption of wealth as well as promoting transfers *inter vivos* mitigate or add to inequality. Tomes (1981) shows that the answer depends on what motivates bequests. The data collected in the new Wealth and Assets Survey may make it possible to answer this question in the UK.

The authors point out that attitudes to inheritance tax are affected by whether people's attention is drawn to the increases in other taxes which would be needed if it were to be abolished. Tax policy is not only about the advantages and disadvantages of any individual tax, but also the overall tax package. I argued above that the case for a land tax might be enhanced by the fact that it could be used to replace an array of unpopular and probably unsatisfactory taxes. The analysis presented here offers wide coverage of the advantages and disadvantages of wealth and property-related taxes. But it ends up suggesting some modest reforms to inheritance tax and a move to a more progressive property tax (although how much more progressive is not clear). Trade-offs between wealth-related taxes and other taxes are, with the minor exception above, not mentioned. The reader who would like a view on the Liberal Democrat proposal in the 2005 General Election to replace council tax with a local income tax will have to look elsewhere for an expert opinion on its desirability. (My own sense is that abolishing existing taxes on property would be a bad idea unless they are replaced by taxes with better structures.) But perhaps radical tax reform is doomed to failure whatever the case to be made so that a chapter of this type is right to focus, for the most part, on practical issues rather than try to offer a root-and-branch redesign of the British tax system.

REFERENCES

Atkinson, A. B. (2007), 'Top Incomes over 100 Years: What can be Learned about the Determinants of Income Distribution'. Presented at the National Institute James Meade Centenary Conference. Bank of England. July.

Khoman, E., and Weale, M. R. (2006), 'The UK Savings Gap', *National Institute Economic Review*, **198**, 97–111.

Meade, J. (1978), *The Structure and Reform of Direct Taxation: Report of a Committee chaired by Professor J. E. Meade for the Institute for Fiscal Studies*, London: George Allen & Unwin. http://www.ifs.org.uk/publications/3433.

Tomes, N. (1981), 'The Family, Inheritance, and the Intergenerational Transmission of Inequality', *Journal of Political Economy*, **89**, 928–58.

9

Taxing Corporate Income

*Alan J. Auerbach, Michael P. Devereux, and Helen Simpson**

Alan Auerbach is Robert D. Burch Professor of Economics and Law and Director of the Burch Center for Tax Policy and Public Finance at the University of California, Berkeley. A Fellow of the American Academy of Arts and Sciences and the Econometric Society, his research focuses on long-run aspects of fiscal policy and behavioural effects of capital income taxation. He was Editor of the *Journal of Economic Perspectives*, is currently Editor of the *American Economic Journal: Economic Policy*, and co-edited the *Handbook of Public Economics*. He received a BA from Yale and a PhD from Harvard.

Michael P. Devereux is Director of the Centre for Business Taxation and Professor of Business Taxation at Oxford University. He is Research Director of the European Tax Policy Forum, and a Research Fellow at the IFS and the Centre for Economic Policy Research. He is Editor-in-Chief of *International Tax and Public Finance* and Associate Editor of *Economics Bulletin*. He has been closely involved in international tax policy issues in Europe and elsewhere, working with the OECD, the European Commission, and the IMF. His current research is mainly concerned with the impact of different forms of taxation on the behaviour of businesses and the impact of such behaviour on economic welfare.

Helen Simpson is a Senior Research Fellow at the Centre for Market and Public Organisation, University of Bristol and a Research Fellow at the IFS. Her research covers the analysis of firm location decisions, productivity, innovation, and foreign direct investment. She is an Academic Associate of the HM Treasury Productivity Team and acts as an Academic Expert for the Research Directorate-General of the European Commission. She was previously Director of the IFS Productivity and Innovation Research Programme and has been an editor of the journal *Fiscal Studies* and of the *IFS Green Budget*.

* The authors would like to thank Stephen Bond, Harry Huizinga, Jack Mintz, other conference participants, and Al Warren and for helpful comments.

EXECUTIVE SUMMARY

This chapter discusses current issues in the design of a corporation tax system and specific reform proposals that have been under recent debate.

We begin by laying out a framework for characterizing different options for taxing corporate income. This has two dimensions. First, the tax base—what do we want to tax? And second, the location of the tax base—where do we want income to be taxed? The first dimension compares a standard corporation tax on the return to equity investment, with a tax on economic rent, and with a tax on the return to all capital. The second dimension is geographic, comparing source-based taxation with taxation based on the location of shareholders or corporate headquarters (residence-based taxation), or on the location of final consumers (destination-based taxation).

As background, we describe the structure of the UK corporation tax system, and outline significant reforms since the Meade Report (Meade, 1978). We set the UK reforms in the context of changes to corporate tax systems in other countries, and present evidence on trends in corporation tax revenues and the industrial composition of revenues, in particular the increased share of the financial sector.

We then discuss developments since the Meade Report that affect the design of a corporate income tax system, and consider how the Meade proposals fare in the light of both economic changes and advances in the research literature. In a world of increased international capital mobility, we highlight how the corporate tax system can affect (i) where firms choose to locate their investment, (ii) how much they invest, and (iii) where they choose to locate their profits. The average tax rate in different countries might influence the first decision, the marginal tax rate the second, and the statutory tax rate the third. Hence the flow-of-funds tax advocated by Meade would distort firms' investment location choices and decisions regarding transfer pricing.

We point out that avoiding inconsistent treatment of debt and equity in the tax system has become an even more important issue since its discussion in the Meade Report, as the boundaries between the two forms of financial instrument have become increasingly blurred. We also consider the relationship between corporate taxes and personal taxes and how the tax system affects a firm's choice of organizational form, emphasizing the potential for different responses depending, for example, on whether a firm is a small domestic concern or a large multinational.

We assess options for reform in the context of the choice of tax base and the choice of where income is taxed. In terms of the tax base, we compare a standard corporation tax, levied on the return to shareholders, with two alternatives: a tax on economic rent such as a flow-of-funds tax or an Allowance for Corporate Equity (ACE), and a tax on the return to all capital, such as under the Comprehensive Business Income Tax and the dual income tax.

We contrast the typical approach of source-based taxation to the alternatives of residence and destination bases. In doing so we raise the question of whether it is possible to isolate *where* profit is generated, when a firm owns subsidiaries engaged in the provision of finance, R&D, production, and marketing in number of countries.

In the context of increased international capital mobility, and in the absence of significant location-specific rent, we highlight the potential for a source-based tax to divert economic activity abroad to locations where the activity would face a lower tax rate. We also note that a flow-of-funds tax or an ACE, which entail a smaller tax base compared to a standard source-based corporation tax, would both require a higher statutory tax rate for a revenue-neutral reform within the corporation tax system, creating greater incentives to shift profit between jurisdictions.

However, we suggest that moving from predominantly source-based corporate taxation to residence-based taxation is not an attractive option. Taxing corporate income in the hands of the parent company is in any case still like source-based taxation, since the location of the parent is not fixed. So true residence-based taxation would have to be at the level of the individual investor; but in a globalized world, this is scarcely feasible, partly because tax authorities have no reliable way to get information about residents' foreign income.

An alternative which we put forward for consideration is a destination-based tax, levied where a sale to a final consumer is made. This takes the form of an extension of the flow-of-funds taxes of Meade. Specifically, we suggest that one might improve on Meade's proposed taxes by adding border adjustments: imports would be taxed, but tax on exports would be refunded. The result is a destination-based cash flow tax, essentially a destination-based VAT, but with labour costs deductible. Such a tax would leave location choices unaffected by the tax, and would also considerably reduce the opportunity for companies to shift profits between countries. We put forward a case for implementing a tax of this type on both real flows and on financial flows, on the grounds that this would also tax the economic rents generated by banks on lending to domestic borrowers.

9.1. INTRODUCTION

The design of corporation income taxes has long raised difficult questions because of the complex structure of corporate operations, the flexibility of corporate decisions, and the need to trace the ultimate influence of taxes on corporations through to their shareholders, customers, and employees and other affected groups. But the nature of these questions has evolved over the past few decades, as advances in economic theory and evidence have resolved some issues and changes in corporate practices and government policies have raised others. This chapter discusses current issues in the design of a corporation tax system and specific reform proposals that have been under recent discussion.

The chapter proceeds as follows. Section 9.2 lays out a framework for characterizing different options for taxing corporate income. It describes the structure of the corporation tax system currently in operation in the UK and outlines significant reforms to the structure of the UK corporate tax system since the Meade Report. Section 9.3 puts these reforms in the context of changes to corporate tax systems in other countries and presents evidence on trends in corporation tax revenues and the industrial composition of revenues. Section 9.4 discusses developments since the Meade Report that affect the design of a corporate income tax system. These include both economic changes and advances in the research literature. We discuss the implications of increased international capital mobility and of the asymmetric treatment of debt and equity and consider how the tax system affects a firm's choice of organizational form. Section 9.5 considers optimal properties of corporation taxes in order to develop criteria against which options for reform can be assessed. In light of this, and the evidence presented in Section 9.4, Section 9.6 considers specific options for corporation tax reform. We offer some concluding comments in Section 9.7.

9.2. CHARACTERIZING A CORPORATE INCOME TAX SYSTEM

To aid comparison of different reforms we begin by briefly laying out a framework for characterizing different options for taxing corporate income. We do so in an open economy setting, where firms' productive activity, sales, profits, and shareholders can be located in different countries. We then place the proposals from the Meade Report and the current UK corporate tax system within this framework.

Table 9.1. Characterizing corporate income tax systems

Location of tax base	Type of income subject to business tax		
	Full return to equity	Full return to capital	Rent
Source country	1. Conventional corporate income tax with exemption of foreign source income	4. Dual income tax 5. Comprehensive Business Income Tax	6. Corporation tax with an Allowance for Corporate Equity 7. Source-based cash flow corporation tax
Residence country (corporate shareholders)	2. Residence-based corporate income tax with a credit for foreign taxes		
Residence country (personal shareholders)	3. Residence-based shareholder tax		
Destination country (final consumption)			8. Full destination-based cash flow tax 9. VAT-type destination-based cash flow tax

Table 9.1 characterizes different ways of taxing corporate income in an open economy along two dimensions—the location of the tax base and the type of income subject to business tax.[1] If the different locations are considered, alternative tax bases are corporate income earned in the country where productive activity takes place (*source-based taxation*), income earned in the residence country of the corporate headquarters or personal shareholders (*residence-based taxation*), or the sales (net of costs) in the destination country where the goods or services are finally consumed (*destination-based taxation*). Alternatives for the type of income included in the tax base are, first, the full return to corporate equity, including the normal return on investment and economic rents over and above the normal return; second, the full return to all capital investment including debt; and finally, only economic rents.

We discuss the specific systems in the table in Section 9.6, but first it is useful to place the options discussed in the Meade Report within this framework.

[1] This framework follows that in Devereux and Sørensen (2005).

Table 9.2. R, R + F, and S bases

	R base	R + F base	S = R + F base
Inflows	Sales of products, services, fixed assets	Sales of products, services, fixed assets Increase in borrowing, interest received	Repurchase of shares, dividend payments
	Minus	*Minus*	*Minus*
Outflows	Purchases of materials, wages, fixed assets	Purchases of materials, wages, fixed assets Repayment of borrowing, interest paid	Increase in own shares issued, dividends received

Meade's alternative tax bases, the real (R base), real and financial (R + F base), and share (S base) were all options for source-based taxation[2] which aimed to tax only economic rent. Taxing only economic rent can be considered desirable since it is non-distortionary, leaving the (normal) return earned by the marginal investment free of tax. Table 9.2 provides a simple outline of the R, R + F, and S bases. Under these bases, taxing only rent is achieved by allowing all expenses to be deducted from taxable profits as they are incurred, essentially taxing positive (inward) and negative (outward) cash flows at the same rate. In practice, as outlined below for the UK system, many corporate tax systems do tax the normal return to capital in addition to economic rent, thus affecting the cost of capital and potentially introducing distortions in firms' choices over different forms of finance.

A further characteristic of a corporate tax system which is of relevance is its relationship with the personal tax system. This can be thought of in two dimensions. First, some businesses have a choice with respect to the system under which they are taxed, for example in the UK whether they incorporate or whether the owner of the business is registered as self-employed and taxed under the personal tax system. Differential tax treatment under these alternatives can potentially affect the choice of organizational form. The second dimension in which the interaction of the corporate and personal tax systems is of relevance is the tax treatment of shareholders in incorporated businesses. Under a classical system dividend income is taxed twice, at the corporate and

[2] In fact in the closed economy setting considered, source, residence, and destination would all be the same location.

at the personal level. Alternatively, an imputation system alleviates double taxation by making an allowance for all or some of the corporate tax already paid when calculating the income tax owed by the dividend recipient. Realized gains on equity investment may also be subject to capital gains tax at the personal level.

9.2.1. The UK corporate tax system

The UK corporate tax system taxes UK-resident companies (i.e. those with UK headquarters) on their global profits (with a credit for tax paid on profits generated abroad), and taxes non-UK resident companies on their profits generated in the UK. Corporation tax is charged on income from trading, investment, and capital gains, less specific deductions. In particular the system allows interest payments to be deducted from taxable profits and can be characterized as taxing the full return to equity, rather than the full return to all capital investment. The UK system therefore comprises a combination of residence-based and source-based systems numbered 1 and 2 in Table 9.1.

In 2007–08 the main rate of corporation tax in the UK stands at 30% with a lower small companies' rate of 20% for firms with taxable profits up to £300,000. Firms with taxable profits between £300,001 and £1,500,000 are subject to marginal relief so that the marginal tax rate they face on their profits above £300,000 is 32.5%, and the average tax rate they face on their total profits rises gradually from 20% to 30% as total taxable profits increase. Table 9.3 summarizes the different rates.[3] In 2004–05 only around 5% of companies paid corporation tax at the main rate, however, they accounted for 75% of total profits chargeable to corporation tax.[4] See Crawford and Freedman in Chapter 11 for further discussion of the taxation of small businesses.

Table 9.3. UK corporation tax rates, 2007–08

Taxable profits (£ per year)	Marginal tax rate (%)	Average tax rate (%)
0–300,000	20	20
300,001–1,500,000	32.5	20–30
1,500,000 plus	30	30

Source: HM Revenue and Customs, <http://www.hmrc.gov.uk/rates/corp.htm>

[3] We do not discuss the separate regime for the taxation of North Sea Oil production. See Adam, Browne, and Heady in Chapter 1 for further details.

[4] <http://www.hmrc.gov.uk/stats/corporate_tax/11-3-corporation-tax.pdf>.

Current expenditure such as wages is deductible from taxable profits and firms can claim capital allowances which allow a deduction for depreciation of capital assets. For example, expenditure on plant and machinery is written down on a 25% declining balance basis, (50% in the first year for small and medium-sized companies), and expenditure on industrial buildings is written down at 4% per year on a straight line basis, although these rates are due to change from 2008–09.

Capital expenditure related to research and development (R&D) receives more generous treatment under the 'R&D allowance' and receives a 100% immediate deduction. Under the R&D tax credit current R&D expenditure also receives more favourable treatment than other forms of current expenditure. In 2007–08 large companies can deduct 125% of eligible R&D expenditure, and small and medium-sized companies can either deduct 150% of eligible expenditure, or if they are loss-making can receive the credit as a cash payment.

Since the early 1980s the UK corporation tax system has moved away from the taxation of economic rent towards taxing the full return to equity through a broadening of the tax base brought about by a reduction in the value of capital allowances. Box 9.1 summarizes some of the main reforms. The main changes occurred during the mid-1980s with the phasing out of 100% first year allowances for plant and machinery and 50% initial allowances for industrial buildings.[5] This broadening of the tax base was accompanied by a substantial fall in the statutory rate (from 52% in 1982–83 to 35% by 1986–87), and this type of restructuring has been mirrored in other countries as discussed in Sections 9.3 and 9.4. Since the mid-1980s there have been a series of further falls in the main rate of corporation tax and in the rate of advanced corporation tax (ACT) (from 30% in 1985–86 to 20% in 1994–95), which was paid by the company at the time it distributed dividends.[6] ACT was then abolished in 1999–2000. The small companies' rate has also been reduced in line with falls in the basic rate of income tax. However, from 1997–98 onwards the small companies' rate has been below the basic rate of income tax, although this situation is now due to be reversed from 2008–09. Indeed, the changes announced in the 2007 budget (summarized in Box 9.1) move towards a broadening of the tax base and lowering of the tax rate for

[5] The first-year allowance was applied in place of the writing down allowance, while an initial allowance was applied on top of the writing down allowance.

[6] The remainder of the corporation tax due, mainstream corporation tax, was paid nine months after the end of a firm's financial year. After ACT was abolished a new quarterly payments system was introduced for large companies.

Box 9.1. UK corporate tax reforms since the Meade Report

In 1978 at the publication of the Meade Report, the main corporation tax (CT) rate was 52% and the small companies' rate 40%. There was a first-year allowance of 100% for plant and machinery and an initial allowance of 50% for industrial buildings. Yearly writing down allowances were 25% for plant and machinery (reducing balance) and 4% for industrial buildings (straight line).

1983: Small companies' rate cut from 40% to 38% from 1982–83.

1984: Announcement of stepwise reduction in CT rates, from 52% in 1982–83 to 35% in 1986–87. First year and initial allowances phased out by 1986–87. Small companies' rate cut in one step to 30% from 1983–84.

1986: Small companies' rate cut from 30% to 29%.

1987: Small companies' rate cut from 29% to 27%.

1988: Small companies' rate cut from 27% to 25%.

1991: CT rate cut from 35% to 34% in 1990–91 and to 33% from 1991–92.

1992: Temporary enhanced capital allowances between November 1992 and October 1993. First-year allowance of 40% on plant and machinery and initial allowance of 20% on industrial buildings.

1995: Small companies' rate cut from 25% to 24%.

1996: Small companies' rate cut from 24% to 23%.

1997: Main CT rate cut from 33% to 31%. Small companies' rate cut from 23% to 21%. Windfall tax imposed on privatized utilities. Repayment of dividend tax credits abolished for pension funds.

1998: Main CT rate cut from 31% to 30%, small companies' rate cut from 21% to 20% from 1999–2000. ACT abolished from 1999–2000. System of quarterly instalment tax payments phased in from 1999–2000. Repayment of dividend tax credits abolished for tax-exempt shareholders and rate of dividend tax credit reduced from 20% to 10% from 1999–2000.

1999: New starting rate for small companies introduced at 10% from 2000–01.

2002: Small companies' rate cut from 20% to 19%. Starting rate cut from 10% to 0%.

2004: Minimum rate of 19% for distributed profits introduced.

2006: 0% starting rate abolished 2006–07.

2007: Small companies' rate increased to 20% in 2007–08. Further increases announced, to 21% in 2008–09 and 22% in 2009–10. Main CT rate to be cut from 30% to 28% in 2008–09. New Annual Investment Allowance introduced from 2008–09 allowing 100% of the first £50,000 of investment in plant and machinery to be offset against taxable profits. From 2008–09 general plant and machinery writing down allowance to be reduced from 25% to 20% and writing down allowances on industrial buildings to be phased out.

larger firms, and for firms paying at the small companies' rate and benefiting from the new Annual Investment Allowance, a narrowing of the tax base and an increase in the tax rate.

9.3. TRENDS IN CORPORATION TAX RATES AND REVENUES

The base-broadening, rate-cutting reforms to the structure of the UK corporation tax in the mid-1980s have also been carried out in other countries. Figures 9.1 and 9.2 show that both statutory corporation tax rates and the present value of depreciation allowances have been falling across the G7 economies. Figure 9.1 shows falling statutory rates, and for this group of countries some evidence of convergence to main rates between 30% and 40%. There are some differences in the timing of cuts in statutory rates across countries. The figure shows the UK and USA making significant cuts to the main rate in the mid-1980s, whereas Italy (having previously raised the main rate), Japan, and Germany only make significant cuts from the late

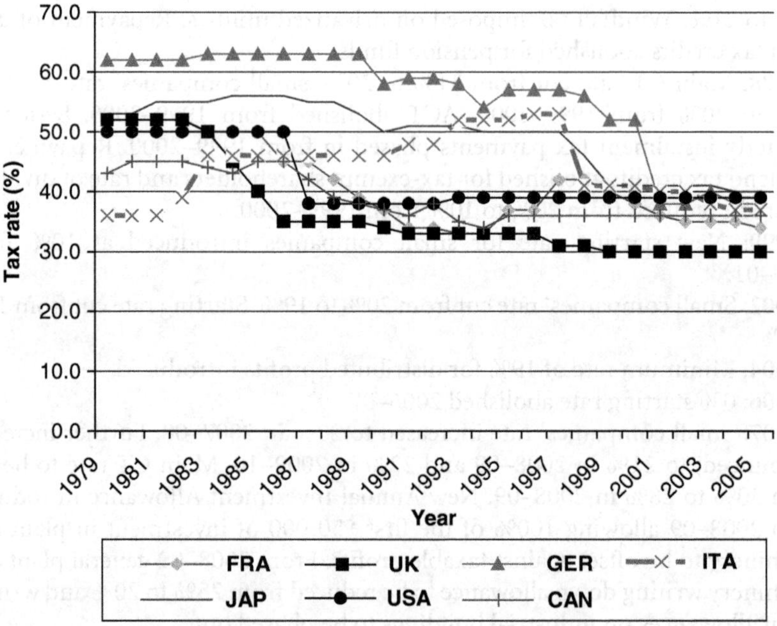

Sources: Devereux, Griffith, and Klemm (2002), updated, table A1. For countries applying different rates the manufacturing rate is used. <http://www.ifs.org.uk/publications.php?publication_id=3210>

Figure 9.1. Statutory corporation tax rates

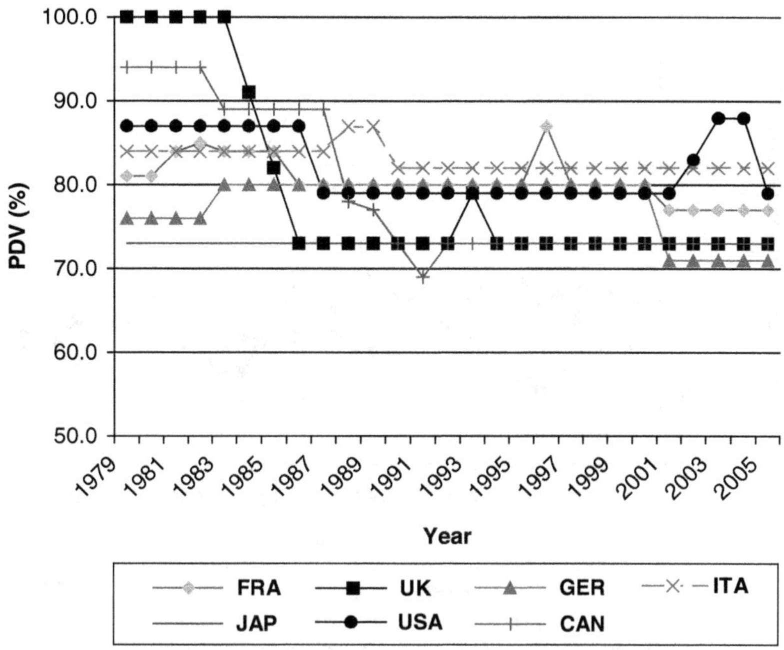

Notes: Definition: The PDV of allowances is calculated for an investment in plant and machinery. Special first year allowances are included if applicable. Where switching between straight-line and reducing balance methods is allowed, such switching is assumed at the optimal point. The assumed real discount rate is 10%, the assumed rate of inflation is 3.5%. For countries applying different rates the manufacturing rate is used.

Sources: Devereux, Griffith, and Klemm (2002), updated, table A2 <http://www.ifs.org.uk/publications.php?publication_id=3210>.

Figure 9.2. Present Discounted Value of depreciation allowances

1990s onwards. Figure 9.2 shows declines in the present discounted value of depreciation allowances; most noticeably the significant base-broadening reform in the UK in the mid-1980s. The implications of these reforms for the effective tax rates faced by companies are discussed further in Section 9.4.

For the UK these reforms have not led to significant changes in the share of corporation tax receipts in total tax revenues, or in corporation tax receipts measured as a share of GDP. Figure 9.3 shows corporation tax revenues as a share of total tax receipts for the G7 over the period 1970 to 2004. Although there is some fluctuation over the period, corporation tax revenues in the UK make up around 8% of total UK tax revenues at the beginning and end of the period. For the remaining G7 countries, other than for Japan there is no evidence of a substantial decline in the share of corporation tax revenues in total tax receipts. Figure 9.4 shows that UK corporation tax revenues comprised

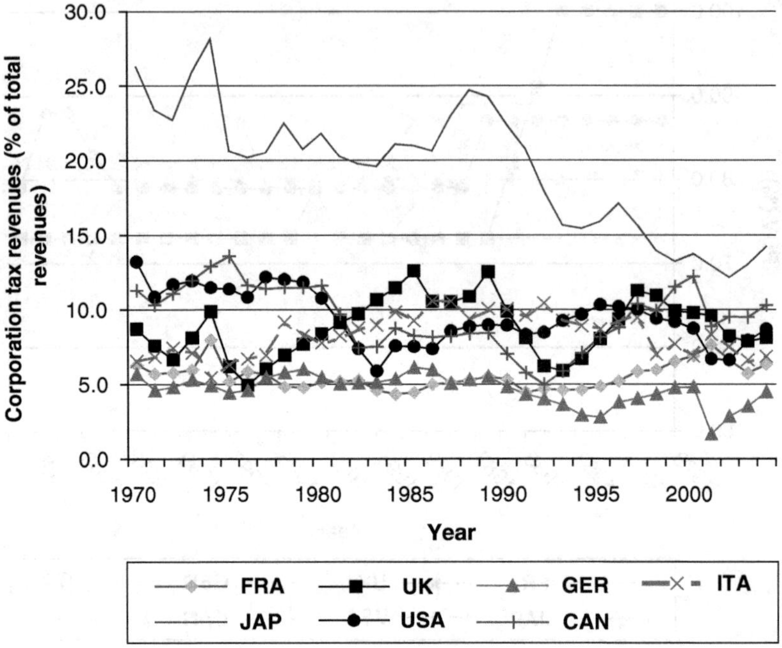

Sources: OECD Revenue Statistics.

Figure 9.3. Corporation tax revenues as a percentage of total tax revenues

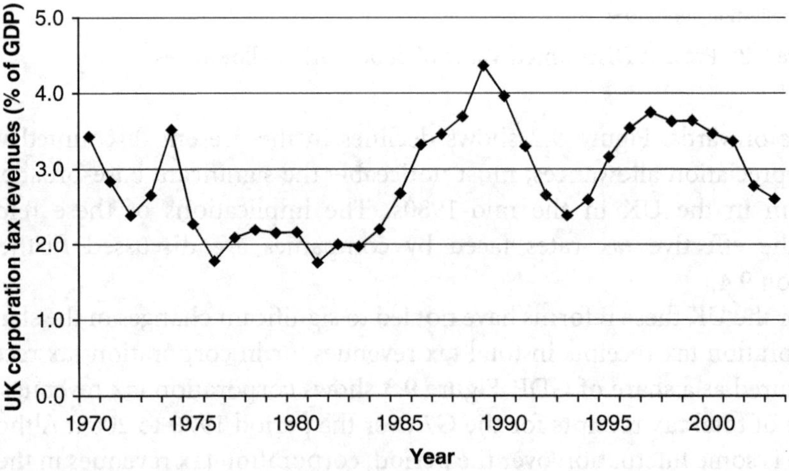

Sources: *Financial Statistics*, Office for National Statistics.

Figure 9.4. UK corporation tax revenues as a percentage of GDP

between 2% and 4% of GDP over the period. Though falls in corporation tax revenues as a proportion of GDP generally coincide with periods of recession, the decline in 2002 and 2003 appears to be an anomaly.

Devereux, Griffith, and Klemm (2004) also consider evidence on the size of the corporate sector and on rates of profitability underlying UK corporate tax revenues. Using data for the non-financial sector they do not find any evidence of a significant change in the rate of profitability for this sector of the economy from 1980 to 2001. They find some evidence of an expansion in the size of the corporate sector (measured by profits as a share of GDP), which, given the evidence on the profitability rates in the non-financial sector, they conclude could be due to some combination of a general expansion or an increase in profitability in the financial sector.

For the UK and the US there is evidence of significant changes in the sectoral composition of revenues, most strikingly in the share of total corporate tax revenues accruing from the financial sector. Since the early 1980s, in the UK there has been a substantial increase in the share of total profits that are chargeable to corporation tax arising in the banking, finance, and insurance sector (and in service sectors more broadly), and a decrease in the manufacturing sector share. Figure 9.5 shows that the increase in the share due to financial corporations is also mirrored in the US. The two countries

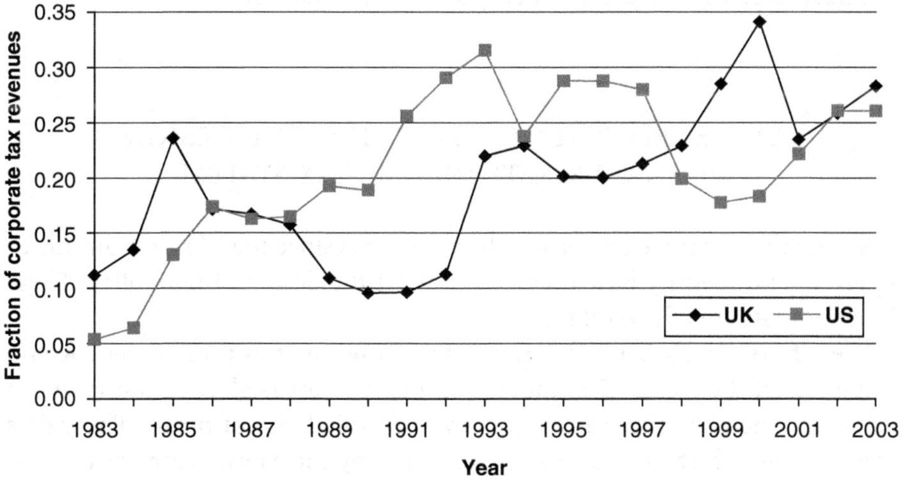

Sources: Internal Revenue Statistics, Statistics of Income; HM Revenue and Customs; Office for National Statistics.

Figure 9.5. Taxes on financial corporations as a share of corporate tax revenues, UK and US

show an increase from around 5% to 10% in the early 1980s to over 25% of corporation tax revenues in 2003. This increased importance of the financial sector demonstrates that discussion of reforms to the corporation tax system should consider implications for both the financial and non-financial sectors.

Finally, Auerbach (2006) presents evidence for the US on a further factor underlying the continued strength of corporation tax revenues—an increase in recent years in the value of losses relative to positive taxable income. Since taxable income and losses are treated asymmetrically under corporation tax systems, (losses do not receive an immediate rebate and firms may have to wait until they earn sufficient taxable profits to offset them, and may also face a delay in claiming capital allowances thus reducing their value), this increase in the value of losses led to an increase in the average tax rate on *net* corporate profits (positive income net of losses). This trend may signal a need to re-examine this asymmetry within corporate tax systems and the extent to which it distorts investment decisions.

In summary the evidence suggests that corporate tax revenues have continued to make a substantial contribution to total tax receipts despite falls in statutory rates. A potential driver of these reductions in corporation tax rates is increased tax competition between countries seeking to attract mobile capital. We consider this issue in more detail in Section 9.4, together with evidence on other economic developments and advances in the academic literature affecting the design of corporation tax systems.

9.4. DEVELOPMENTS AFFECTING THE DESIGN OF A CORPORATE INCOME TAX SYSTEM

In this section we trace important developments since the Meade Committee reported, and identify how they might affect the design of tax policy. These developments are of several forms.

There have clearly been changes in the economic position of the UK and of the rest of the world. The most prominent factor is globalization; and in particular, the rise of international flows of capital and of profit. This raises several issues which were not fully discussed by the Meade Committee. For example, in a globalized world, the owner (typically the supplier of equity finance) of an investment project may be resident in a different jurisdiction from where the project is undertaken; which may be different again from where the consumer of the final product may reside. This raises several important and difficult questions.

First, where is profit generated? And is this actually an appropriate question for taxation—should the international tax system attempt to tax profit where it is located, or on some other basis? To the extent that the international tax system aims to identify the location of profit and tax it where it is located, then there are incentives for multinational companies to manipulate the apparent location of profit (conditional on where real economic activity takes place) in order to place it in a relatively lightly taxed country.

Second, another aspect of this difference in jurisdiction between activity and owner is the role of personal taxes. At the time the Meade Committee reported, many countries—especially in Europe—had some form of integration of corporate and individual taxes. For example, the UK had an imputation system, under which UK shareholders received a tax credit associated with a dividend payment out of UK taxable income; this credit reduced the overall level of tax on UK-sourced corporate profit distributed to UK shareholders. But increasingly the ownership of UK companies has passed to non-UK residents. The relevance of such a tax credit for efficiency or equity purposes is therefore open to question.

A third consequence of globalization is that companies make discrete investment choices: for example, whether to locate an operation in the UK or Ireland. Although there may be many other examples of discrete choices (whether to undertake R&D or not, whether to expand into a new market or not), it is the discrete location choice which has received most attention to date. The influence of tax on a discrete investment choice is rather different from the case analysed by Meade, and the flow-of-funds taxes advocated by Meade would not generally be neutral with respect to discrete choice.

A fourth aspect of increased globalization is tax competition between countries. In order to attract internationally mobile capital into their jurisdiction, governments have to offer a business environment at least comparable to that available elsewhere. The taxation of profits is part of that environment. Consequently, there has been downward pressure on various forms of tax rates, as globalization and other factors have led to lower statutory and effective tax rates.

There have also been developments in the type of economic activity seen in the UK and other major industrialized countries. Manufacturing has played a decreasing role in the economy; services and the financial sector are now very much more important. This suggests that at least one of the traditional aspects of corporation taxes—the rate of depreciation allowed on buildings and plant and machinery—has shrunk in importance. By contrast, investment in intangibles and financial assets has become more important.

Incentives for R&D are common. Also, the taxation of profit in the financial sector is quantitatively more important.

Part of the development of the financial sector has involved innovation in financial products. The traditional distinction between debt and equity is much less clear than it might have appeared to the Meade Committee. The combination of characteristics which apply to traditional debt are that it has a prior claim to income generated, it receives a return which is determined in advance (in the absence of bankruptcy), and that debt-holders typically do not have voting rights. But there is no reason for a single financial instrument to have either all or none of these characteristics. If an instrument has only one or two of these characteristics, it may be difficult to define as debt or equity. This issue becomes still more complex when combined with the effects of globalization, where countries may not take the same view as to whether an instrument qualifies as debt and therefore whether the return should be deductible in the hands of the borrower and taxable in the hands of the lender.

There have also been developments in economic theory. One important development returns to the role of personal taxes. The 'new view' of dividend taxation states that under some circumstances dividend taxes do not affect investment decisions. If at the margin investment is financed by retained earnings and the tax rate on dividend income remains constant, then the net cost to the shareholder is reduced by dividend taxes at exactly the same rate at which the eventual return is taxed. These two effects cancel out to leave the required rate of return unaffected, and hence the effective marginal tax rate equal to zero. In fact this is a very similar effect to that generated by the S-based corporation tax analysed by the Meade Committee, since taxes on net distributions are a form of cash flow tax. The same argument would apply to investment financed by new share issues if a tax credit were associated with the new issue, as would be the case under the S-base.

In the remainder of this section we look in more detail at some of these developments. We begin by considering aspects of globalization: how does international integration affect the manner in which taxes can affect business decisions? We then briefly consider the issue of tax competition among countries. Next we turn to consider how developments in financial markets, and particularly in financial instruments, affect the choice of whether a tax regime should differentiate between debt and equity. Finally, we address issues in personal taxation, and consider whether integration of corporate and personal taxes is a necessary feature of overall taxes on profit.

In each of these cases, we examine in principle how taxes can create distortions. We also briefly summarize evidence on the extent to which business decisions are affected by tax, and investigate the implications for tax design.

9.4.1. Decisions of multinational corporations

A useful way of considering the impact of corporation taxes on flows of capital and profit is first to describe a simple approach to understanding the choices of multinational firms. The model described here is a simple extension of the basic model of horizontal expansion of multinational firms, drawing specifically on Horstman and Markusen (1992). Many extensions are examined by Markusen (2002), but it is not necessary to address them in any detail here.

To understand the effects of tax, it is useful to consider a simple example. Suppose a US company wants to enter the European market. It helps to think of four steps of decision-making. First, a company must make the discrete choice as to whether to enter the market by producing at home and exporting, or by producing abroad. To make this discrete choice, the company must assess the net post-tax income of each strategy. Exporting from the US to Europe will incur transport costs per unit of output transported. Producing in Europe will eliminate, or at least reduce, transport costs, but may incur additional fixed costs of setting up a facility there. The choice therefore depends on the scale of activity, and the size of the various costs. The scale of the activity would depend on the choices made in stages 2 to 4 below.

What is the role of corporation taxes in this decision? If production takes place in the US, then the net income generated would typically be taxed in the US. If production takes place in a European country, then the net income generated will generally be taxed by the government in that country. There may be a further tax charge on the repatriation of any income to the US. Taking all these taxes into account, the company would choose the higher post-tax profit. Conditional on a pre-tax income stream, the role of tax is captured by an average tax rate—essentially the proportion of the pre-tax income which is taken in tax.

If the company chooses to produce abroad, the second step faced by the company is where to locate production. The company must choose a specific location within Europe to produce, for example within the UK or Germany. This is a second discrete choice. The role of tax is similar to that in the first discrete choice, and can be measured by an average tax rate.

The third step represents the traditional investment model in the economics literature, and the one considered by the Meade Committee: conditional on a particular location—say the UK—the firm must choose the scale of its investment. This is a marginal decision. The company should invest up to the point at which the marginal product of capital equals the cost of capital. As such the impact of taxation should be measured by the influence of the tax on the cost of capital—determined by a marginal tax rate. Under a flow-of-funds tax, such as proposed by the Meade Committee, this marginal tax rate is zero; the tax therefore does not affect this third step in decision-making.

In a slightly different model, this third step might play a more important role. Suppose that the multinational firm already has production plants in several locations. If it has unused capacity in existing plants, then it could choose where to generate new output amongst existing plants. The role of tax would again be at the margin, in that the company need not be choosing between alternative discrete options. However, note that this is a different framework: in effect, it implies that the firm has not already optimized investment in each plant up to the point at which the marginal product equalled the cost of capital.

The fourth step in the approach described here is the choice of the location of profit. Having generated taxable income, a company may have the opportunity to choose where it would like to locate the taxable income. Multinationals typically have at least some discretion over where taxable income is declared: profit can be located in a low tax rate jurisdiction in a number of ways. For example, lending by a subsidiary in a low-tax jurisdiction to a subsidiary in a high-tax jurisdiction generates a tax-deductible interest payment in the high-tax jurisdiction and additional taxable income in the low-tax jurisdiction. Hence taxable income is shifted between the two jurisdictions. The transfer price of intermediate goods sold by one subsidiary to the other may also be very difficult to determine, especially if the good is very specific to the firm. Manipulating this price also gives the multinational company an opportunity to ensure that profit is declared in the low-tax jurisdiction rather than the high-tax jurisdiction.

Of course, there are limits to the extent to which multinational companies can engage in such shifting of profit. (If there were no limit, then we should expect to observe all profit arising in a zero-rate tax haven, with no corporation tax collected elsewhere.) Indeed, companies can argue that complications over transfer prices may even work to their disadvantage: if the two tax authorities involved do not agree on a particular price, then it is possible that the same income may be subject to taxation in both jurisdictions.[7]

Broadly, one should expect the location of profit to be determined primarily by the statutory tax rate. It is plausible to suppose that companies take advantage of all tax allowances in any jurisdiction in which they operate.

[7] On the other hand, operating in jurisdictions with different rules regarding the measurement of revenues and deductions also provides multinational companies with scope to structure financial arrangements so that some revenues may not generate tax liability anywhere and some expenses may be deductible in more than one country.

Having done so, their advantage in being able to transfer a pound of profit from a high-tax jurisdiction to a low-tax one depends on differences in the statutory rate.[8] However, many of the complications of corporation tax regimes have been developed precisely to prevent excessive movement of profit; so there are many technical rules which are also important.

There is growing empirical evidence of the influence of taxation on each of the four steps outlined here. For example, Devereux and Griffith (1998) presented evidence that the discrete location decisions of US multinationals within Europe were affected by an effective average tax rate rather than an effective marginal tax rate. Similar evidence has been found by subsequent papers.[9] The estimated size of the effects of taxation on the allocation of capital across countries is typically much larger than the estimated size of the effect of taxation on the scale of investment in a given country.

There is also a large empirical literature that investigates the impact of tax on the location of taxable income. This literature has three broad approaches: a comparison of rates of profit amongst jurisdictions; an examination of the impact of taxes on financial policy, especially the choice of debt and the choice of repatriation of profit; and other indirect approaches have also been taken, including examining the choice of legal form, the pattern of intra-firm trade, and the impact of taxes on transfer prices. Much of the literature has found significant and large effects of tax on these business decisions.

The four-stage problem outlined above involves three different measures of an effective tax rate. The first two discrete choices depend on an effective average tax rate. The third stage depends on an effective marginal tax rate. And the fourth depends on the statutory tax rate. This makes the tax design problem complicated. It is possible to design a tax system which generates a zero effective marginal tax rate, and this is what the Meade Committee proposed. But this clearly does not ensure neutrality with respect to all of the four decisions outlined here. Eliminating tax from having any influence on these decisions could only be achieved if the effective marginal tax rate were zero and the effective average tax rate and the statutory tax rate were the same in all jurisdictions. This would clearly require a degree of international cooperation which is beyond reasonable expectation. However, while achieving complete neutrality with respect to the location of capital and profit would be beneficial from a global viewpoint, as noted above, this may not be true from the view point of any individual country.

[8] It may also depend on withholding taxes and the tax treatment of the parent company.

[9] Earlier papers used measures of average tax rates, but did not do so explicitly with the intention of testing the effect of tax on discrete choices; typically they were used as a proxy for effective marginal tax rates.

9.4.2. Tax competition

Tax competition can clearly result from a situation in which governments do not cooperate with each other. In that case, governments may seek to compete with each other over scarce resources.

The factor most commonly considered as a scarce resource in the academic literature is capital—the funds available for investment. In a small open economy, the post-tax rate of return available to investors is fixed on the world market. Any local tax cannot change the post-tax rate of return to investors, but must raise the required pre-tax rate of return in that country; this would generally be achieved by having lower capital located there. Strategic competition would be introduced in a situation where there were a relatively small number of countries involved in attempting to attract inward investment. In this case the outcome of such competition would depend on the degree to which capital is mobile across countries and the cost to the government of raising revenue from other sources. In line with the discussion above, such competition may be over average tax rates for discrete choices, over marginal tax rates for investment, and over statutory tax rates for the shifting of profits. Overall, governments may be competing over several different aspects of corporation taxes.[10]

Several empirical papers, largely in the political science literature, attempt to explain corporation tax rates with a variety of variables, including political variables, the size of the economy, how open it is, and the income tax rate. Some of these papers start from the premise of competition. However, we know of only two papers which attempt to test whether there is strategic international competition in corporation taxes.[11] These papers find empirical support for the hypothesis that tax rates in one country tend to depend on tax rates in other countries; there is support for the hypothesis that other countries follow the US, but also for more general forms of competition.

What role does competition play in the design of corporation taxes? Essentially it acts as a constraint. In a closed economy, in principle, a flow-of-funds tax could be levied at a statutory rate of 99% and still have no distorting effect on investment; the effective marginal tax rate—which affects investment in such a setting remains zero even with a very high tax rate.[12] However, in open economies, competition would almost certainly rule out a very high

[10] Haufler and Schjelderup (2000) and Devereux et al. (2008) analyse the case of simultaneous competition over the statutory rate and a marginal rate; there have been no studies attempting to model competition also over an average rate.

[11] Altshuler and Goodspeed (2002) and Devereux et al. (2008).

[12] This abstracts, of course, from other domestic activities that might be influenced by a high statutory tax rate, such as managerial effort or the diversion of corporate resources.

statutory rate, and might also constrain the choice of effective marginal and average tax rates. This might affect the design of the tax system. If there were a specific revenue requirement, and an upper limit on the statutory tax rate, for example, the revenue might be achieved only by broadening the tax base—which in turn implies increasing the marginal tax rate and hence distorting investment decisions. This creates a trade-off in competition for capital and competition for profit, although governments can in principle use the two tax instruments of the rate and base to compete for both simultaneously.

9.4.3. Debt versus equity

The Meade Report recognized the differing tax treatment of income accruing to owners of debt and equity as a source of economic distortion, and recommended alternative methods of taxing business returns—utilizing the R, $R + F$, and S bases as discussed earlier in the chapter—aimed at removing the influence of taxation from the debt–equity choice. Under each of these tax bases, the returns to marginal investment financed by debt and equity each would be taxed at an effective rate of zero, so in principle neither the investment decision nor the financial decision would be distorted.

In the years since the Meade Report, several developments have shaped consideration of how to reform the tax treatment of corporate debt and equity. First, empirical research has clarified the strength of the behavioural response of corporate financial decisions to taxation. Second, financial innovation has raised questions about the ability of tax authorities to distinguish debt from equity, highlighting the potential problems of tax systems seeking to distinguish between debt and equity. Indeed, as will be discussed, such problems might arise even under the Meade Report's reformed tax bases in spite of their apparently neutral treatment of debt and equity.

Taxation and the debt–equity decision

With a classical tax system that permits the deduction of interest payments but, until 2003, offered no offsetting tax benefits for the payment of dividends, the US has taxed equity and debt quite differently and therefore offers an opportunity to consider the behavioural response of corporate financial decisions. But uncovering corporate financial responses to this disparate treatment is not straightforward, given that the US corporate tax rate has changed relatively infrequently over time and that essentially all corporations face the same marginal tax rate on corporate income. The major identifying strategy utilized in empirical research in the years since the Meade Report has been based on the asymmetric tax treatment of income and losses, under which income is taxed as it is earned but losses can generate a commensurate refund only to the extent that they can be deducted against the corporation's prior or future years' income. For firms with current losses and without adequate prior income to offset these losses, the need to carry losses forward without interest (and subject eventually to expiration) reduces the tax benefit of additional interest deductions.

Calculations by Altshuler and Auerbach (1990) for the early 1980s suggested that tax asymmetries were quantitatively important for the US corporate sector as a whole and that there was also considerable heterogeneity with respect to the value of interest deductions, depending on a corporation's current and recent tax status. Thus, tax asymmetries did provide a useful source of variation in the tax incentive to borrow. Using a somewhat different methodology, Graham (1996) also found considerable variation across firms in the potential tax benefit of additional interest deductions, and used this variation to assess the influence on corporate decisions, finding a significant response. This confirmed the results of earlier empirical research that used cruder measures of tax status as determinants of borrowing.[13] Related research has found an influence of a company's tax status on its decision to lease equipment rather than borrowing to purchase it, the lease providing a method of shifting the interest and investment-related deductions to a lessor with potentially greater ability to utilize deductions immediately.

The observed reaction of borrowing to tax incentives confirms that the tax treatment of debt and equity influences corporate financial decisions, although it does not show that economic distortion is minimized when debt and equity are treated equally. Another strand of the literature on corporate behaviour, dating from Berle and Means (1932) and revived especially in the years following the Meade Report, emphasizes the distinction between corporate ownership and control and the potential divergence of interests between corporate managers and shareholders. This work suggests that the decisions of executives may not be efficient or in the shareholders' interest. In this setting, tax distortions need not reduce economic efficiency, and this is relevant for the tax treatment of borrowing, given that some, notably Jensen (1986), have argued that the increased commitments to pay interest serve as an incentive to elicit greater efforts from entrenched managers. Thus, while a tax bias in favour of interest appears to encourage borrowing, it is harder to say whether it encourages too much borrowing.

[13] See Auerbach (2002) for a survey of this and related research discussed below.

Financial innovation

The literature provides unfortunately little guidance as to how taxes on financial decisions might be used to offset managerial incentive problems. But recent developments in financial markets cast this issue in a different light. By blurring the debt–equity distinction and potentially transforming the debt–equity decision into one of minor *economic* significance (tax treatment aside), financial innovation may have lessened any potential benefits of encouraging corporate borrowing and moved us more towards a situation in which corporations incur real costs in order to achieve more favourable tax treatment but are otherwise unaffected in their behaviour.

The empirical results mentioned above, showing the sensitivity of leasing to tax incentives, provide one example of how borrowing may be disguised or recharacterized to take advantage of tax provisions. But many more alternatives have gained popularity over the years. The basic thrust has been to narrow the distinction between debt and equity through the use of financial derivatives and hybrid instruments.

Starting with the Black–Scholes (1973) option-pricing model, it has come to be understood how the prices of shares and derivatives based on these shares must be related in a financial market equilibrium in which investors can hold the same underlying claims in different form. Relevant to the debt–equity decision, one can move from a position in shares to a position in debt by selling call options and purchasing put options, with the 'put–call parity theorem' indicating that the two positions, being essentially perfect substitutes, should have the same market value. But when the tax treatment of these equivalent positions differs at the individual and corporate levels, the incentive is to choose the tax-favoured position, a choice that is essentially unrelated to the other activities of the corporation.

Legal restrictions have been attempted but are difficult to implement, given the many alternative methods of using derivatives to construct equivalent positions, methods that have grown in popularity as financial transaction costs have declined.[14] The result has been a growth in the issuance of so-called 'hybrid' securities, based on ordinary debt and structured with enough similarity to debt to qualify for favourable tax treatment but also incorporating derivatives designed to allow the securities to substitute for regular equity. Figure 9.6 shows the volumes in the main categories of US hybrid-security issues for the period 2001–05, along with the volume of common equity issues, confirming that hybrid securities have become a significant source of funds for corporations.

[14] For further discussion, see Warren (2004).

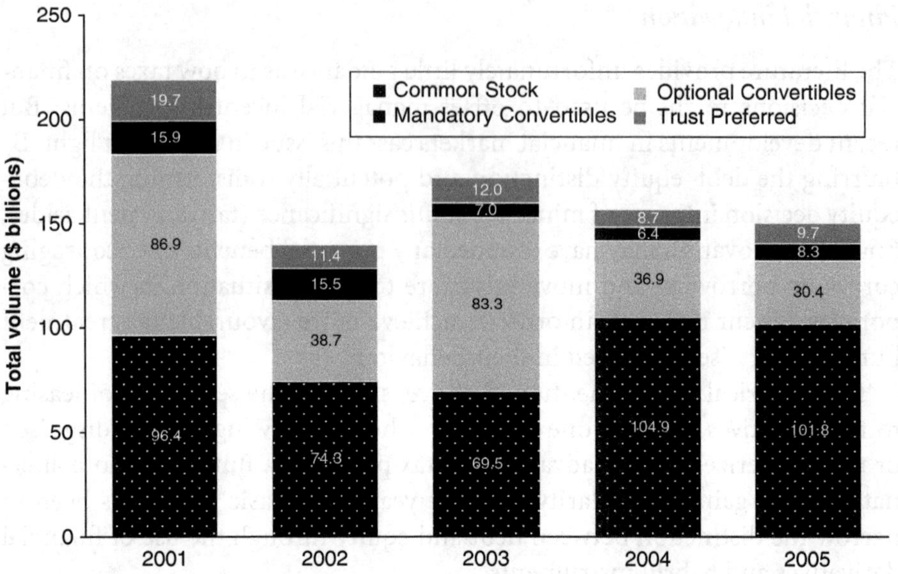

Sources: Goldman Sachs; issues of common stock include primary and combined (primary + secondary) issues but exclude purely secondary issues.

Figure 9.6. Issues of US hybrid securities

Implications for tax reform

In light of financial innovation and the blurring of the distinction between debt and equity, how should one view the Meade Report's recommendations for taxing business activities? Under the *R* base, no distinction is made between debt and equity. Regardless of how funds are raised, there are no taxes on the flows between businesses and their investors. Thus, businesses may choose among debt, equity, and hybrid securities without consideration of the tax consequences. Under the $R + F$ base, however, a timing distinction would remain between debt and equity, with equity being ignored by the tax system and debt being provided an effective marginal tax rate of zero through offsetting taxes on borrowing and interest and principal repayments. Assuming that tax rates are constant over time, the timing distinction is minor for marketable securities issued at arm's length. But related-party transactions could take advantage of the difference by reporting lower payments to equity and higher payments to debt, thereby converting tax-free payments into tax-deductible payments to the same investors. The *R* base would seem a preferable policy to the $R + F$ base from this perspective, but an offsetting factor is the treatment of real and financial flows in product markets, in the interactions not with investors but with customers.

Under the $R + F$ base, real and financial transactions with customers are treated symmetrically, with sales subject to taxation and expenses deductible. Under the R base, financial proceeds and expenses are ignored, so that firms providing the same customers with both real and financial products have an incentive to overstate the profits from financial services and understate the profits from real activities. A related problem concerns financial companies, a sector that, as discussed earlier, has been growing steadily in importance in the UK. The returns that financial companies earn from the spreads generated by financial intermediation are automatically picked up by the $R + F$ base but ignored under the R base.

Innovation in finance thus favours the R-base version of the Meade Report's company tax system, while the growing importance of companies that specialize or engage in providing financial services calls for the $R + F$ base. Which approach is to be preferred is discussed further below, but the benefits of either approach are clear in comparison to a system that attempts to maintain an even greater distinction between debt and equity.

9.4.4. Relationship between corporate and personal income taxes

Traditionally, the corporation income tax has been seen as imposing an extra level of taxation on investment in the corporate sector, thereby discouraging corporate investment activity and shifting capital from the corporate sector to the non-corporate sector. The alternatives offered by the Meade Report were aimed to remove this distortion of investment activity. However, the report devoted relatively little attention to the level at which taxes were imposed—investor or company—or to the choices other than the level of investment or the method of finance (already discussed) that might be distorted by the corporate tax, notably the choice of a company's organizational form. In the years since, theoretical and empirical research has considered how corporate-level and investor-level taxes may vary in their effects on investment, and how corporate taxation influences the choice of organizational form and other corporate decisions. As a result, we have a different perspective on both the priorities and the potential alternatives for corporate tax reform.

Corporate and personal income taxes and the incentive to invest

Dating to the work of Harberger (1962), the corporation tax was viewed as an extra tax imposed on the investment returns generated by the corporate sector, with personal income taxes applied to both corporate and non-corporate investment. From this perspective, reducing the tax burden on corporate source income, either through a reduction in the corporate tax rate or through a reduction in investor-level taxes on corporate source income, would improve the economy-wide allocation of capital. Indeed, policies such as the UK imputation system were structured to reduce the double taxation of corporate-source income.

Since the Meade Report, there have been several challenges to the argument for alleviating double taxation. Miller (1977) hypothesized an equilibrium in which investment financed by corporate equity faced no extra tax when compared to debt-financed investment or non-corporate investment, as a result of the interaction of progressive individual taxation and the favourable tax treatment of equity at the investor level (due to lighter and deferred taxation of capital gains). For individuals in sufficiently high personal tax brackets, Miller argued, the tax gain at the individual level would just offset the extra tax at the corporate level. If only individuals with such a tax preference for equity held shares, then the corporate tax would impose no extra tax on corporate investment, but indeed would reduce the overall tax on the returns of high-bracket investors. Thus, reducing the corporate tax would favour the corporate sector *even more*, as would reducing individual taxes on corporate source income. Although actual shareholding patterns do not follow the market segmentation envisioned by Miller, diversification can be understood as a balancing of tax incentives and portfolio choice that does not fully undercut Miller's argument (Auerbach and King (1983)).

Another line of reasoning, complementary to Miller's, suggests that the tax burden on equity investment is lower than would be implied by simply averaging the tax rates on dividends and capital gains. Following an argument by King (1974), developed further in Auerbach (1979) and Bradford (1981), equity funds acquired through the retention of earnings should, under certain assumptions, have a before-tax cost unaffected by the tax rate on dividends; the logic is that because dividend taxes are avoided when earnings are retained, subsequent dividend taxes are merely deferred payment of the dividend taxes avoided initially, not additional taxes on investment earnings. This logic suggested that reducing taxes on dividends, either directly or, for example, through an imputation system, should have no impact on investment incentives except to the extent that firms issue new equity. While various empirical tests have not definitively resolved its significance in explaining the investment behaviour and valuation of corporations,[15] this 'new view' of equity finance clearly emphasizes the distinction between

[15] See Auerbach (2002) and Auerbach and Hassett (2007) for recent reviews of the relevant literature.

ongoing equity finance through retentions and the initial capitalization of corporate enterprises, a distinction laid out, for example, by Sinn (1991) in a model integrating the capitalization and subsequent growth of a firm subject to taxes on corporate earnings and dividends. We will return to this distinction between capitalization and investment when discussing the choice of organizational form.

A related point is the relevance of corporate cash flow to the investment decision. Among firms facing a lower cost of capital when financing through retentions, there will be a positive relationship between investment and the level of internal funds, for some investments will be worth undertaking only if adequate internal funds are available. This relationship, which has found some support in the empirical literature since the writing of the Meade Report,[16] may also be a consequence of asymmetric information: if managers are unable to reveal their firms' true prospects to capital markets, then the act of seeking external funds may convey a negative signal about a firm and raise its cost of capital. Whatever the reason for its existence, a link between internal funds and investment makes after-tax cash flow relevant to a firm's investment. Thus, traditional calculations of the cost of capital and marginal effective tax rates based on discounted tax provisions may only partially measure the impact of these tax provisions on the incentive to invest—the timing of these provisions will matter, too.

Personal taxes and the multinational enterprise

In a closed economy, savings equals investment and it does not matter on which side of the market for funds taxes are imposed, assuming that the taxes on each side would have the same structural form. The previous arguments have suggested that the *structure* of individual taxes on corporate-source income serves to mitigate the impact of double-taxation. Progressive individual taxes combined with favourable treatment of capital gains plus the taxation of dividends when they are distributed (rather than when corporate earnings accrue) each contribute to a lower tax burden on the income from new corporate investment. But this analysis does not hinge on the fact that the taxes in question are assessed on investors rather than on companies. In an open economy, though, taxes on saving and investment may not have comparable effects, even if they are similar in structure, and as a result there

[16] The paper by Fazzari, Hubbard, and Petersen (1988) is notable here, although some (e.g. Cummins, Hassett, and Oliner (2006)) have argued that cash flow is simply acting as a proxy for firm prospects that are difficult to measure directly.

is an additional reason why investor-level taxes may have little impact on the incentives for investment.

The tax treatment of multinational enterprises is an extremely complex subject, touched on above and treated more fully in Chapter 10 by Griffith, Hines, and Sørensen. However, if one thinks of the taxation of companies as being largely done at source, and the taxation of investors as being based on residence, then the openness of the UK economy to capital flows increases the impact of company-level taxation on domestic investment, for such investment must compete for mobile capital with investment projects in other countries. The taxation of individual UK investors on their portfolio income, on the other hand, should have relatively little impact on UK investment, for UK investors are only one possible source of funds for domestic enterprises and other investors will jump in to take advantage of potentially higher returns should individual tax provisions discourage UK investors.

The strength of this reasoning depends on the extent to which the well-known 'home bias' in the portfolio choice of investors is overcome. If individuals invest primarily in their own countries, regardless of the tax incentives for investing abroad, then such tax incentives can have little impact. Such home bias has certainly been evident historically in the close relationship between domestic saving and investment (e.g. Feldstein and Horioka (1980)) as well as in the weak international diversification of individual portfolios. But such diversification has been on the rise over time. As Figure 9.7 shows, around a third of UK listed shares are now held by foreign investors, compared to around 5% when the Meade Report appeared.

Thus, the rise in international capital flows provides yet another reason why individual taxes may have less influence than once believed on the level of domestic corporate investment. There is a distinction here, though, in that higher taxes on the portfolios of domestic individuals may still have a considerable impact on national saving, depending on how responsive saving is to capital income taxation.

Taxes and the choice of organizational form

As discussed above, it is important to distinguish the effects of taxation on existing companies and new ones. While existing corporations may finance their expansions through retained earnings, new corporations must establish an equity base and may face a higher cost of capital as a result. As a consequence, the decision to start a corporation may be discouraged more than

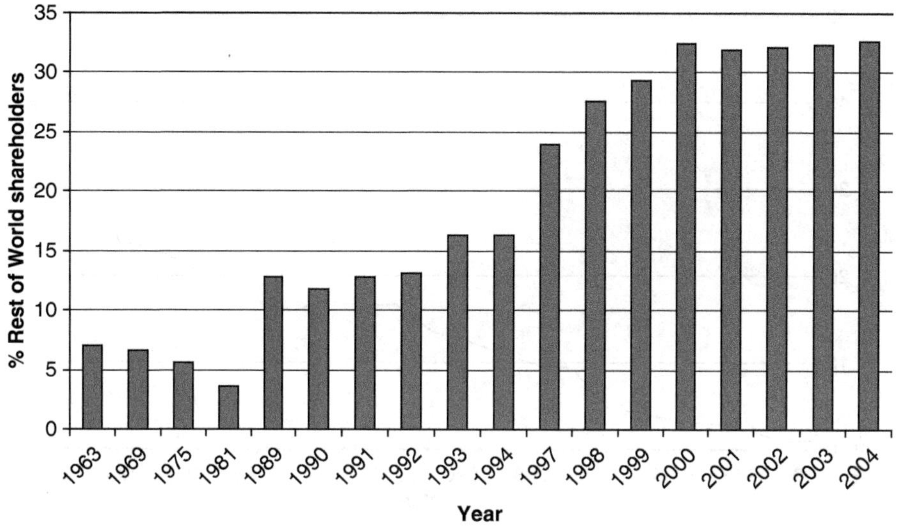

Notes: Figure shows % of UK listed ordinary shares owned by Rest of World. UK offshore islands were reclassified to RoW in 1997.

Sources: ONS, Share Ownership 2004.

Figure 9.7. Ownership of UK listed shares by Rest of the World

the decision to invest, once incorporated. If there is a choice of organizational form, this decision may be affected by corporate taxation.

Put slightly differently, one needs to distinguish how taxation affects the intensive decisions of companies—how much to invest, given their organizational form—and the extensive decisions of companies—which organizational form to adopt. Just as in the case of the international location decision, the choice regarding organizational form depends on more than the treatment of marginal investment projects by existing companies whose locations are already determined.

It is customary to think of the choice of organizational form as one unlikely to be strongly affected by taxation, because corporate status, with its limited liability and access to capital markets, is viewed as a *sine qua non* for large public companies that seek broad ownership. Indeed, in the UK there are no perfect substitutes for corporate status outside the corporate sector. But elsewhere, particularly in the US, there are ranges of organizational forms that, while not perfect substitutes, offer attributes sufficiently similar to those of traditional corporations to make the choice of organizational form a serious one.

Figure 9.8 shows the share of US non-financial corporate income accounted for by 'S' corporations, the most important alternative to

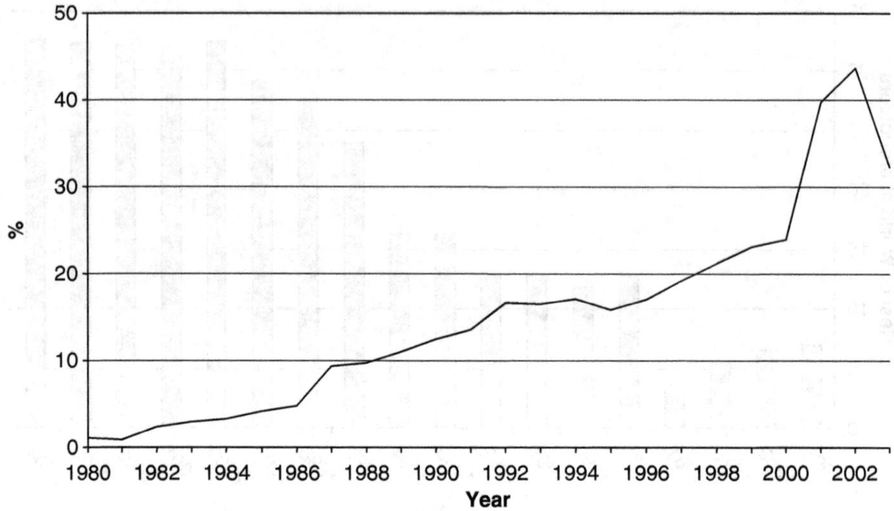

Sources: Internal Revenue Service, *Statistics of Income.*

Figure 9.8. S corporation share of US non-financial corporate income

traditional corporations. S corporations have legal corporate status but are taxed as 'pass-through' entities. Though an option only for companies with one class of stock and no more than one hundred shareholders, S corporations nevertheless now account for a significant part of corporate ownership. The upward jump in 1987 is consistent with incentives in the Tax Reform Act of 1986, the transition to S corporation status being largest among the smaller companies most likely to view this as viable (Auerbach and Slemrod (1997)). But the subsequent growth in S corporation elections may be due to a variety of factors including shifts in company size and industrial composition, and the literature to date (Gordon and MacKie-Mason (1997); Goolsbee (1998)) suggests relatively modest behavioural responses to tax incentives, and hence small deadweight losses, surrounding the choice of organizational form.

Implications for tax reform

A recurring theme in the discussion of the interaction of personal and corporate taxes is the importance of *heterogeneity*. Individuals sorting by tax rates may reduce the combined impact of corporate and individual taxes; firms financing with retained earnings may face a lower cost of capital than is faced by new corporations; individual taxes may influence the cost of capital more for domestic companies that rely solely on domestic investors as a source of funds than for those capitalized internationally; and smaller firms with simpler ownership structures may have a greater ability to avoid the traditional corporate form if it is advantageous from a tax perspective to do so.

This heterogeneity in behavioural responses suggests a need for flexibility in the design of tax reforms not emphasized in the Meade Report, to allow treatment to vary among firms and individuals according to circumstances. We might wish to treat domestic companies differently from multinational companies, new companies differently from existing ones, and small companies differently from large ones,[17] and we might wish to vary the extent of double-taxation relief among individual investors.

9.5. OPTIMAL PROPERTIES OF CORPORATION TAXES

This section discusses what the aims of a corporation tax should be in closed and open economies. In open economies, one must distinguish between the perspectives of a country acting unilaterally and one acting in coordination with other countries.

The first and most important question to address is 'Why *corporate* taxes?' To the extent that corporate taxes play a role that could be occupied by taxes on individuals, why tax corporations at all? From a positive perspective, corporate taxes may exist in part because of the political advantage of imposing taxes whose burdens are difficult to trace through to individuals. But there are also several potential normative justifications for taxing corporations.

First, corporations may offer an easier point of tax collection, even if the aim is to impose a tax on individuals. It may be easier, for example, to impose a tax on consumption using a tax on corporate cash flows rather than a personal consumption tax. Second, the base of taxation may be most easily measured at the corporate level. For example, if the aim is to tax rents generated by corporate activities, there is no advantage in tracing the receipt of these rents to individuals rather than taxing them directly. Third, taxing corporations may expand the scope of possible tax bases. If a country wishes to tax foreign shareholders of domestic corporations, for example, this may be legally possible and administratively feasible only through a tax on the corporations directly.

[17] Crawford and Freedman (Chapter 11) deal with the particular issues of designing tax regimes for small companies.

Thus, there may be a role for taxes on corporations, but the role will depend on the characteristics of the optimal tax system. For example, if there is no benefit to taxing foreign shareholders, then there will be no advantage to imposing taxes on domestic corporations in order to do so. Thus, we must first lay out the characteristics of a desired tax system before assessing the advantages of particular forms of corporate taxation. We begin by considering the simpler case of the closed economy, in which there is no issue of international coordination and taxes on saving and investment have equivalent effects.

Since Meade a literature has developed on the optimal tax rate on capital income in a closed economy. Various celebrated papers, beginning with Judd (1985) and Chamley (1986), argue that the optimal capital income tax rate in a dynamic setting is zero, though others find conditions under which it is positive. A second strand of the literature has emphasized the dispersions in effective tax rates that typically accompany capital income taxation and the distortions associated with this differential taxation.[18] Although the message of this literature reinforces arguments against a classical corporate tax system, it is consistent with the Meade approach of aiming for a zero effective marginal tax rate on corporate source income. Such a tax falls on projects which earn an economic rent, and on old capital (which has not received cash flow treatment of expenses). In a closed economy, taxes on rents are non-distortionary, as are taxes on old capital, to the extent that such taxes are not anticipated. Thus, there is an argument for imposing corporate taxes in a closed economy even if capital income taxes are not desirable. To the extent that capital income taxes remain part of the optimal tax system, corporate taxes can play a role as a collection mechanism, although the additional distortions associated with corporate taxation, discussed in Section 9.4, must be taken into account.

In an open economy, one must be more specific regarding the manner in which capital income taxes are imposed. Where it may be optimal to distort the saving decisions of residents, a country may wish to impose residence-based capital income taxes. But the literature, starting from the production efficiency theorem of Diamond and Mirrlees (1971) and developed in various contexts in the years since the Meade Report, suggests that small open economies should eschew source-based capital income taxation. Such a tax simply raises the pre-tax required rate of return and reduces the stock of capital, shifting none of the burden to foreigners but resulting in more deadweight loss than a tax on the domestic factors that bear

[18] See, for example, King and Fullerton (1984) and Auerbach (1983).

the tax. Just as source-based capital taxes should be avoided, the returns from outbound investment by residents should be taxed at the same rate as their returns on domestic investment; foreign taxes should be treated as an expense. This is a direct implication of imposing taxes on a residence basis.

These results, however, hold exactly only for small open economies acting unilaterally. Moreover, they apply to taxes on individual residents, where such residence is taken as given. When one shifts to a consideration of corporate taxes, the picture becomes cloudy, because a corporation's residence may differ from that of its shareholders and may also be much more easily adjusted in response to taxation. To the extent that corporations are internationally mobile, taxes based on corporate residence may have undesired effects similar to taxes based on source. Thus, the distinction between source-based and residence-based taxes is less clear for corporate income taxes than for taxes on individuals, and residence-based taxes are less obviously superior.

Open-economy considerations also affect what it takes to accomplish a zero rate on business activities. While the Meade flow-of-funds tax would accomplish this objective in a domestic-only context, the discrete location and profit-shifting possibilities imply that a small open economy might wish to have a zero tax rate on average returns and on moveable profits, an outcome possible only by eliminating source-based taxes entirely. In this case, source-based taxes might be justified only to the extent that there are location-specific economic rents, though such taxes might still be unattractive if they had to apply economy-wide.

If small open countries coordinate, then the range of policies expands. Coordinated source-based taxation, for example, could serve as a substitute for residence-based taxation if the latter approach were not feasible, although to an extent limited by different national revenue objectives and constraints. Hence, the role for source-based taxes may be stronger than for the small open economy acting on its own.

The most complex open-economy analysis applies to the choices made by a country for which the small-economy assumption does not hold. For such countries acting unilaterally, tax policies that serve the national interest need not further the objective of economic efficiency. Just as the optimal tariff for a large country is positive, the optimal source-based capital income tax is positive, for each action improves the country's terms of trade with the rest of the world. This strengthens the argument for policy coordination, which is also more difficult to analyse because of the variety of equilibrium concepts applicable when large countries interact.

9.6. ALTERNATIVE TAX SYSTEMS

This section considers a number of potential tax systems in the light of Sections 9.4 and 9.5 drawing on the organization of Table 9.1 The two broad questions to be considered are what should be taxed, and where should it be taxed? Each of the subsections below investigates options within a specific type of location: source, residence, and destination.

9.6.1. Source-based taxation

We begin with source-based taxation, on the grounds that this is the conventional approach to taxing corporations. However, in addition to the question considered above, whether it is desirable to tax corporate income at source, there is also a definitional problem that affects source-based taxation, whether applied to income or some other base. Attempting to define the 'source' of profit is actually very difficult, and in some cases impossible. We can begin with a simple example. Consider an individual resident in country A who wholly owns a company which is registered, and which carries out all its activities—employment, production, sales—in country B. Then country B is clearly the source country. In this simple example, country A is the 'residence' country. Conventionally, we can also drop sales from the list of activities in B. Suppose that the company exports all of its output to country C: then country B remains the source country. We refer to country C as the 'destination' country.

Now add a holding company in country D, so that our individual owns the shares in the holding company, which in turn owns the shares in the subsidiary located in B. Typically D would be thought of as a form of residence country as well: the residence of the multinational group. But in practice that may depend on the activities undertaken in D: typically, it would be seen as the place of residence only if management and control were exercised from D.

Returning to the source country, things rapidly become less simple. Suppose instead that this multinational has also two R&D laboratories in countries E and F, a subsidiary which provides finance in G, with the final product marketed by another subsidiary in H. Each of these activities is a necessary part of the whole which generates worldwide profit. There are now potentially five source countries: B, E, F, G, and H. A conventional definition of 'source' would require the contribution made by each subsidiary to worldwide profit to be calculated, with these contributions determined using 'arm's length pricing'—the price that would be charged by each subsidiary for its services were it dealing with an unrelated party. Of course, this procedure is difficult in practice since in many cases no such arm's length price can be observed; transactions between subsidiaries of the same corporation are not replicated between third parties.

But there is also a more fundamental problem with this approach: the arm's length price may not exist even conceptually. As an example, suppose that each R&D laboratory has invented, and patented, a crucial element of the production technology. Each patent is worthless without the other. One measure of the arm's length price of each patent is therefore clearly zero—a third party would not be prepared to pay anything for a single patent. Another possible measure would be to identify the arm's length price of one patent if the purchaser already owned the other patent. But if both patents were valued in this way, then their total value could easily be larger than the value of the final output. More generally, suppose that this multinational is a monopolist supplier of the final good. Then not only are there no other actual potential purchasers of the patents, but if there were, then the value of the patents would be different (and generally lower, as more competition is introduced in the industry).

So identifying how profit is allocated on a source basis between countries B, E, F, G, and H is not only extremely difficult in practice; there are clearly examples where it is conceptually meaningless. This is a fundamental problem of any source-based tax. Although it is a problem with which the world has long since learned to live, allocating profit among source countries is in practice a cause of great complexity and uncertainty. Having raised this issue, though, we will now consider specific forms of source country taxation, identifying more specific tax bases.

Standard corporation tax, on the return to equity

We begin with the most common form of corporate income taxation, which exists in the vast majority of developed countries: a source-based tax levied on the return to equity. Income is allocated among source countries on the basis of arm's length pricing.

The inefficiencies introduced by such a tax are well known, and have been largely outlined above. Because relief is given for debt finance, but not equity finance, it generates an incentive to use financial instruments which, for tax purposes at least, have the form of debt. In an international context, this creates an incentive to borrow in high-tax-rate jurisdictions (and lend to them from low-tax-rate jurisdictions), although governments try to limit this through the use of thin capitalization and interest allocation rules (which in turn generate further distortions). The welfare costs associated with these distortions are, however, hard to pin down. Ultimately, greater use of debt is likely to generate higher levels of insolvency and bankruptcy. That generates direct costs of bankruptcy, and also possibly indirect costs in terms of the effect on competition in specific markets. The costs of the industry which exists to exploit these differential effects also represent a welfare cost; though ironically, the more successful this industry is in creating financial instruments which are effectively equity, but are treated for tax purposes as debt, the lower will be tax-induced bankruptcy. The welfare costs of shifting profits between jurisdictions to reduce the overall tax liability are also hard to value, as the technology of profit-shifting is difficult to specify.

A standard source-based income tax also affects the location and scale of investment, as discussed in Section 9.4.1. As reviewed in Section 9.5, standard analysis indicates that a small open economy should not have a source-based tax on the return to capital located there. If there are economic rents that are specific to a particular location, it may in principle be possible for the government to capture those rents through taxation without inducing capital to shift out of the country. However, this is more a justification for a flow-of-funds tax, discussed below, since that is structured to tax economic rent but not the return to capital. In any case, more realistically, it seems infeasible to design a tax system which captures only location-specific rents. It may be possible to have a tax system which captures part of all economic rents, but this creates a trade-off between capturing the location-specific rent, and inducing some capital and mobile rents to flow abroad.[19]

Formula apportionment

One approach to dealing with the difficulty of determining the source of income is to allocate income to countries using measurable quantities that are viewed as proxies for income generating activities. This approach, referred to as formula apportionment, is practiced by US states in determining state corporate tax liabilities and has been proposed for the EU as well. Under formula apportionment, the worldwide (or, in the case of US states, domestic US) income of a company operating across boundaries is divided according to a simple formula based on the fractions of measured activities located in each jurisdiction; many US states use a three-factor formula that assigns equal

[19] From an international perspective, Keen and Piekkola (1997) also show that if governments cannot fully tax away economic rent, then it is in principle optimal to allow capital-importing countries to use source-based taxes as an indirect way of taxing pure rents.

weights to shares of assets, payroll, and sales in the jurisdiction, although some states assign greater, even total, weight to the sales factor.

Within a group of jurisdictions that agreed to adopt a system of formula apportionment, the calculation of income for any source jurisdiction would be simplified, and profit-shifting under source-based taxation would be reduced, since the location of profits would be determined by formula rather than by accounting and financial arrangements. Even within this group, though, formula apportionment would not eliminate the incentive to shift capital out of a high-tax jurisdiction, as long as assets are a factor in assignment of income among jurisdictions. The exact incentives faced by individual companies would depend on the extent to which policies were coordinated among countries.[20] Such coordination would potentially relate not only to the apportionment formula but also to the base used to determine taxable income. Absent policy coordination with respect to base and apportionment formula, governments would have incentives to compete in these dimensions. With a uniform tax base and apportionment formula, the incentive to engage in tax competition with respect to the choice of tax rates may even be strengthened. While differences in tax bases remain, the impact of differences in the tax rate may be uncertain, or at least more difficult to discern. If tax bases were uniform, the impact of the tax rate would be much clearer. Further, since countries would no longer be able to compete over the tax base, all competition would take place through the tax rate.

The European Commission has proposed a form of formula apportionment within the EU. This is subject to the advantages and disadvantages described. But in addition, it should be noted that the problems of source-based taxation remain if there is a boundary to the region in which formula apportionment applies—that is, with respect to any transactions between the group of jurisdictions with formula apportionment and the rest of the world. This is why we discuss formula apportionment in the context of a source-based tax: its main effect is not to eliminate the problem of defining source-based taxation, but simply to extend the boundaries over which source-based taxable income is computed.

Corporate flow-of-funds tax

The Meade Committee proposed two flow-of-funds taxes—the R base and the R + F (equivalently the S) base—which were designed to remove

[20] See McLure (1980) and Gordon and Wilson (1986) for a discussion of the effects of formula apportionment on business location decisions.

two distortions present in the standard corporation taxes summarized above: they do not affect decisions as to the scale of investment, and they do not discriminate between investment financed by different sources of finance. As noted above, they achieve this by leaving a marginal investment (one with a zero net present value) untaxed. The tax effectively is raised only on economic rent—that is, projects with a positive net present value.

As noted above, though, a source-based flow-of-funds tax leaves some distortions in place, in particular with respect to two important location decisions. Companies making discrete location choices will normally consider alternative locations on the basis of a comparison of the post-tax net present value. In general this would be affected by a flow-of-funds tax. Also, the question of the location of the 'source' of the profit is not resolved by a 'source-based' flow-of-funds tax. Indeed, the incentives to shift profit may be greater under a flow-of-funds tax to the extent to which a revenue-neutral reform which introduced a flow-of-funds tax would require a higher statutory tax rate (this is discussed further below). In turn, this would create greater incentives for shifting profits between jurisdictions. It may also induce the most profitable firms to move abroad, leaving the domestic economy with the less profitable firms.[21]

Three further well-known problems should also be mentioned. The first concerns transition effects. If a flow-of-funds tax were introduced without an appropriate phasing-in period (which could be very long), then existing capital would be more heavily taxed than new investment. To some extent that might be regarded as efficient, if inequitable. However, treating competing companies unequally might introduce distortions to competition and hence welfare costs, for example, if companies face financial constraints on their activities.

Second, the neutrality of the tax with respect to investment depends crucially on the tax rate being constant over time: indeed, it requires that investors believe that the tax rate will not change in the future. If investors expect future returns to be taxed at a different rate from that at which current investment is relieved, then marginal investments will be taxed (or subsidized). However, this is not only true for flow-of-funds taxes: no realistic tax can be neutral with respect to the scale of investment if the tax rate is expected to fluctuate.[22]

Third, a pure flow-of-funds tax requires the tax to be symmetric: tax payments must be negative when there are taxable losses. For a conventional

[21] See Bond (2000). [22] See Bond and Devereux (1995).

investment, which involves initial capital expenditure, followed subsequently by a return, this implies that the initial investment is effectively subsidized. Governments are typically reluctant to provide such subsidies, especially through a general tax system—and with some reason, since they would enhance the possibility of fraud. The next form of tax we consider is designed to lessen this problem.

We also raise one further question, which applies to this form of tax along with others considered here (and which was also addressed by the Meade Committee): would the international tax treaty system create problems for a single country introducing this form of tax on its own? The basic advantage of the flow-of-funds tax—the zero effective marginal tax rate—applies only if there is no other tax levied on the income stream from the investment. But for inbound investment, the capital-exporting 'residence' country may seek to tax the remittance of profit. Under existing tax treaties, any such residence-based tax would normally be moderated by a credit for tax already paid in the source country. If such a credit were given in respect of the flow-of-funds tax as well, then the residence-based tax would affect the overall effective average and marginal tax rates on such inbound investment, but these effects would not be too large as long as the statutory rates in the two countries were similar. However, if the capital-exporting country refused to give a credit for the flow-of-funds tax, then the overall effective average and marginal tax rates on inbound investment could be very large, reflecting both source- and residence-based taxation. Such a situation could substantially diminish or remove the benefits from reforming the tax in this way, at least with respect to inbound investment from such capital-exporting countries.

Revenue consequences of a flow-of-funds tax

In this chapter we do not provide a costing of alternative reforms to the taxation of corporate income. However, since an important focus of discussion is on the flow-of-funds tax, on a source (and below) destination basis, it is worth making some brief comments.

First, an important element of the cost in terms of tax revenue concerns the treatment of existing capital. On introduction of a flow-of-funds tax for new investment, the remaining value of such existing capital could be immediately expensed, or alternatively, it could be depreciated as under the existing system or simply denied depreciation deductions entirely.[23]

[23] In this case there would need to be anti-avoidance rules to prevent 'old' capital becoming 'new' and hence qualifying for immediate expensing.

We have noted above the efficiency issues surrounding this distinction; but there are clearly revenue implications as well. The same issue arises with respect to outstanding debt: would interest on such debt continue to be deductible for tax? These choices would clearly be very important for revenues for a lengthy transition period. A second factor likely to be important is the treatment of financial services: there may be significant differences in revenue from an R-base compared to an R + F base. A third issue is that we would expect the introduction of a flow-of-funds tax to have behavioural effects: to provide a complete measure of the revenue consequences of reform it would be necessary to take into account these effects.

One way of attempting to identify the broad revenue effects of moving to a flow-of-funds base is to identify the various components of the existing tax and estimate how they would change. Consider a move to an R-base, for example. Then the most significant effects would be that (i) depreciation allowances would be abolished and replaced by immediate expensing, and (ii) deductibility of nominal interest payments would be abolished. The first of these would tend to reduce revenues, while the second would tend to raise revenues. So, as a matter of principle, it is not clear in which direction revenues would move. It is clear that the reform would be less costly the lower is investment, the higher are nominal interest rates (and hence the inflation rate), and the more that companies use debt. More generally, we might expect the cost of such a reform to depend on when it was introduced, and to vary over time depending on broad economic conditions. As a result of these considerations, we do not propose to present our own estimates of the cost of introducing such a reform at any point in time.

However, we can get some idea of the cost from a recent study carried out using US data by Gordon, Kalambokidis, and Slemrod (2004), which draws on an earlier paper by Gordon and Slemrod (1988). They estimate the cost of introducing a source-based R-base tax in the US in two years, 1983 and 1995, following the procedure described above of identifying changes to particular elements of the tax base in each year. They found that introducing the change in 1983 would have increased tax liabilities of non-financial corporations by $23 billion (of which $14 billion was accounted for by eliminating the investment tax credit), or by more than half of the actual tax liabilities of these corporations, whereas introducing the change in 1995 would have reduced tax liabilities by $18 billion, or by 16.3% of actual tax liabilities. Several factors account for the difference between the two years, notably that the investment tax credit was repealed in 1986 and the ratio of interest payments to new investment fell from 37% in 1983 to only 20% in 1995. The authors also attempt to control for these and other business cycle effects to make the two years more comparable: the adjustment has little impact in 1983, but reduces the cost in 1995 to approximately zero. Although the costs of implementing an R-base in the UK may clearly differ, these estimates suggest that they may not be very large.

Allowance for corporate equity

A variant of the flow-of-funds tax was initially proposed by Boadway and Bruce (1984) and developed by IFS (1991). There are two possible versions. One is closest to the R-base: it would eliminate the deduction for interest and, instead of giving up-front relief for all investment expenditure, would use an arbitrary depreciation schedule but exactly compensate for the delay in receiving depreciation allowances by giving additional relief. A version closer to the R+F base would be to continue to allow interest to be deducted, but would introduce a separate allowance for the cost of equity finance (the Allowance for Corporate Equity, ACE). The size of the ACE is designed to compensate exactly for the delay in receiving depreciation allowances. In each case, in an uncertain environment the rate of relief required for neutrality is the risk-free rate, as long as the relief is certain to be received by the company at some point.[24] Various forms of the ACE tax have been used: Croatia has experimented with it, and Belgium has recently introduced it. Brazil and Italy have also used variants.

Either variant of the ACE system avoids the government's problem under the pure flow-of-funds tax of paying a proportion of up-front investment costs. Given that the timing difference between receiving relief and paying tax on the return is reduced, the ACE system also lessens (although likely does not remove entirely) the sensitivity of investment to tax-rate changes. It is also more likely—though not certain—that capital-exporting countries would be prepared give a tax credit for the ACE than for a flow-of-funds tax, since the ACE more closely resembles a conventional corporate income tax. However, all other criticisms of source-based flow-of-funds taxes also apply to these variants.[25]

[24] See Bond and Devereux (1995, 2003).

[25] If the corporation tax is based on economic rent, there is a question as to the appropriate personal taxation of income from the corporation. The Meade Committee and IFS (1991) envisaged a tax on economic rent at the corporate level being introduced in combination with different forms of consumption tax treatment at the personal level, so that the overall marginal tax rate on savings was zero. An alternative approach would be to combine a corporate tax on economic rent with a residence-based individual tax on the normal return, as proposed recently by Kleinbard (2007).

Comprehensive Business Income Tax

The differential treatment of debt and equity can be eliminated in two ways. One is to give equity the same treatment as debt—this is essentially the route taken by the ACE system, and which results in a tax only on economic rent. The other is a reform in the opposite direction: to remove the deductibility of interest from taxable income. This was proposed by the US Treasury (1992), and is called the Comprehensive Business Income Tax (CBIT). The CBIT results in a single tax on all corporate income, whether the source of finance is debt or equity.

The original proposal envisaged it would be introduced at a rate roughly equal to the top marginal personal tax rate on capital income. This would in principle make personal taxes on corporate source income redundant, at least in a closed economy. Other things being equal, corporate taxable income would be higher under a CBIT than under a conventional tax. Offsetting this, however, would be a reduction in personal taxes on corporate source income if such taxes were abolished. In fact, probably a large proportion of interest income is untaxed—for example, if it is received by tax exempt pension funds. Overall, a revenue neutral reform would therefore enable a cut in the statutory corporation tax rate (although this may imply a significantly lower rate than the top marginal personal income tax rate).

If it is assumed that there were such a cut, then the effective tax rate on equity-financed investment would generally fall, and the effective tax rate on debt-financed investment would generally rise, relative to a standard corporation tax. The net effect would be to reduce distortions to the scale and location of equity-financed investment, but to increase the distortions to the scale and location of debt-financed investment (assuming that the debt is issued and deductible in the same country as the investment). A lower tax rate will probably have a greater net impact on the effective average rate of tax, and hence on location decisions. The lower tax rate would also reduce the incentives to shift profit at the margin to another jurisdiction.

There would, of course, be transitional problems in moving to a CBIT: companies relying heavily on debt would be significantly disadvantaged by such a reform. Any such reform would therefore have to be phased in slowly to give companies time to adjust their financial position.

Dual income tax

A variant of the CBIT is the dual income tax, which is used in some Scandinavian countries.[26] The basic idea of a dual income tax is to have a low tax

[26] See Sørensen (1994, 2005a) and Nielsen and Sørensen (1997).

rate on all capital income, while keeping a progressive labour income tax. If the dual income tax were imposed solely at the corporate level, then it would have exactly the same structure as the CBIT.

However, the original proposals differ in the tax rate which they envisage on capital income. Tying the CBIT rate to the highest rate of personal income tax has the advantage of minimizing distortions to organizational form: businesses would be indifferent to paying income tax or a CBIT corporation tax. However, a high tax rate is likely to discourage inward flows of capital and profit. By contrast, proponents of the dual income tax point to the need to encourage inward international capital flows as a reason for keeping a low tax rate on capital income. In a pure version of the system, the corporate income tax rate is matched to the lowest marginal personal income tax rate so that only labour income above a certain level is taxed at a higher rate. That, though, raises the problem of distortions to organizational form: an owner-manager would rather take his return in the form of capital income than labour income.[27] (Although this problem is not unique to the dual income tax; it applies whenever capital income and labour income are taxed at different rates.)

A further difference from the CBIT is an important distinction in implementation. Instead of levying a single tax rate on all corporate income, dual income taxes tend to give relief for interest paid at the corporate level, as with a conventional corporation tax, and instead tax it at the personal level, possibly using a withholding tax, typically set at a lower rate for non-residents. However, this means that interest paid to non-residents is typically taxed at a lower rate than interest paid to residents. That reintroduces a distinction between debt and equity which is avoided under the CBIT.

9.6.2. Residence-based taxation

In general, identifying a residence country is more straightforward than identifying a source country. However, unfortunately this does not imply that residence-based taxes would be more straightforward to administer. There are two possible forms of residence: the residence of the ultimate individual shareholder, and the residence of the legal corporation. We discuss these in turn.

[27] To prevent such income shifting, Norway has introduced a personal residence-based tax on that part of the taxpayer's realized income from shares which exceeds an imputed rate of interest. This is in principle neutral, since it exempts the normal return from tax. At the margin, the total corporate and personal tax burden on corporate equity income is close to the top marginal tax rate on labour income. See Sørensen (2005b).

Residence-based shareholder tax on accrued worldwide profit

Although the legal residence of some individuals may be open to debate, for the vast majority of individuals, their country of residence is easy to identify. Moreover, the vast majority of individuals remain relatively immobile. Levying a tax on corporate source income at the level of the individual shareholder therefore has important conceptual advantages. In particular, since the tax base would not depend on where capital or profit were located (i.e. where the source country is), then the location of capital and profit would not be distorted by this tax.

Moreover, the effective incidence of a residence-based tax can be expected to be quite different from that of a source-based tax. A tax levied on the residents of a small open-economy country will reduce the post-tax rate of return they earn on world markets: it will not affect the pre-tax rates of return. Hence the effective incidence of the tax would be on the investors. As discussed in Section 9.5, this is what underlies the economic argument favouring residence-based taxes over source-based taxes for small open economies.

Such a tax, in its pure form, is unworkable. Any individual country would be seeking to tax corporate income accruing to its residents from throughout the world; either the company or the shareholder would have to provide details of that income. The government would have no jurisdiction over companies which were otherwise unconnected with that country. The shareholder might own shares in a large number of companies worldwide: it would be extremely costly to collect and provide detailed information on all of them. For companies which the investor continued to hold, it would be necessary to identify the portion of the profit generated, and a tax return based on the home government's taxable income definitions would need to be drawn up. For companies which the investor had sold, it would be necessary to identify dividends and capital gains earned during the period in which shares were held.

There would also be a problem of liquidity: it might be necessary to sell part of the asset in order to meet the tax liability. Of course, some of these problems would be eased if the tax were levied only on income received from foreign investments: but that would be a very different tax, which could be avoided by not returning the income to the owners, but allowing the investment to accumulate abroad.

Of course, these problems exist only to the extent that UK residents have direct portfolio holdings of foreign securities. In the past, this would not have been of such great concern as international portfolio diversification lagged well behind what economists might have expected given its apparent risk-pooling advantages. But international diversification has been growing, as illustrated above in Figure 9.7. This limits the attractiveness of residence-based shareholder taxation as an option for the future.

Residence-based corporation tax on accrued worldwide earnings

An alternative notion of residence is the residence of the company which is the ultimate owner of a multinational. Of course, a form of residence-based corporation tax is currently common: the UK and the US, for example, both seek to tax flows of foreign dividend income paid by foreign subsidiaries to parent companies. However, the notion of residence here is rather less clear-cut. To prevent tax avoidance, countries that seek to tax such income typically have rules to determine whether or not the company is resident for tax purposes; these rules are usually based on the notion of whether the multinational company is managed from that location.

The notion of residence-based corporation tax which we aim to discuss here, though, is one that taxes the worldwide earnings of the multinational as it accrues, rather than as it is repatriated to the parent company. As with a residence-based shareholder tax, taxing only repatriations may generate a strong incentive for the company to reinvest abroad, without returning retained earnings to the parent. Even when countries attempt to implement a tax on repatriations, they typically give credit for taxes paid abroad. There are various ways of giving such credit, but the net effect is that skilled tax managers can arrange the group's financial affairs to prevent significant liabilities to such home country tax.[28] Thus, application of the 'residence principle' to corporations, in practice, bears a strong resemblance to source-based taxation.

In principle, true residence-based corporate taxation, that is, a residence-based, accruals-based corporation tax, has one significant advantage. The home country tax authorities need only identify the worldwide taxable income of the multinational company. There would be no need to identify 'where' the profit was made; all that would matter would be the aggregate for the whole multinational. As a consequence—if all countries adopted such a tax—there would be no incentive for companies to shift profits between subsidiaries in different countries to reduce tax liabilities. Nor would the tax affect the location of capital investment.

However, there are also two significant problems with such a hypothetical corporation tax. The first is feasibility. In this respect, some of the

[28] The recent US experience of a temporary reduction in such taxes provides evidence that this is partly due to simply leaving the funds abroad.

problems of the residence-based shareholder tax are also relevant. A multinational company may have hundreds, or even thousands, of subsidiaries and branches around the world. Correctly identifying—and where necessary, checking—the taxable income in each of these locations would be challenging, even if ultimately the taxable income is consolidated into a single measure.[29]

Second, as discussed in Section 9.5, unlike shareholders, the ultimate holding company of a multinational company is, in principle, mobile. There have certainly been instances of holding companies moving location to take advantage of more favourable treatment elsewhere.[30] The rules mentioned above are relevant here: the original country of residence may not recognize that the holding company has actually moved unless its management and control has moved. But the mobility of the holding company raises a question of legitimacy. Suppose there is a holding company residing in the UK which earns profit throughout the world. Suppose also that the relevant economic activity does not take place in the UK, the shareholders do not live in the UK, and the consumers of the final products do not live in the UK. What right would the UK have to tax the worldwide profit of that company? It is hard to think of a convincing rationale. And in any case, if the UK attempted to impose a high tax rate then it seems very likely that the holding company would move to another location.

In short, while true residence-based taxation, at either the individual level or the corporate level, offers potential advantages, neither system is feasible to adopt. The partial approach currently practiced in the UK, which focuses on the corporate level and lies somewhere in between residence- and source-based taxation, lacks obvious advantages other than its feasibility.

9.6.3. Destination-based taxation

In our view, there are significant problems in attempting to tax corporate income on a source basis or a residence basis. Although the international tax system is intended to be based on a combination of source- and residence-based taxation, in many cases it is not clear what 'source-based' taxation is. What is clear is that the existing tax system creates considerable inefficiencies in the way it is implemented.

29 Of course, such problems exist even under the current approach to residence-based taxation to the extent that foreign profits are taxed immediately (as is true in the US for foreign branches).

30 See, for example, Desai and Hines (2002).

We therefore now turn to a more radical proposal: a destination-based tax.[31] The term 'destination-based' taxation is taken from the literature on indirect taxes, which has debated the merits of destination-based taxes, based on where the final consumer lives and purchases a good or service, compared to an origin-based (i.e. source-based) tax, based on where the good or service is created.[32]

Corporate cash flow tax

Given the difficulties in implementing taxes on a source or residence basis which are both feasible and non-distorting, it is worth considering whether a tax on corporate income could be levied on a destination basis. If that were possible then the tax would avoid distorting the location of capital and profit.

However, while it is clearly possible to identify final sales taking place in a country, those sales may be based on imported goods. The cost of producing those imported goods would have been borne elsewhere. A crucial issue is how costs can be set against income. Further, clearly a single plant in one country, say A, could supply final goods to a large number of other countries: how can the costs borne in A be allocated against income generated elsewhere? One option would be to take a simple formula: say to allocate costs to foreign countries in the same proportion as the value of final sales across those countries. This would effectively be a form of formula apportionment, as discussed above in the context of source-based taxes, where the formula was based only on final sales. This, and other possibilities, would require a significant degree of cooperation between tax authorities in identifying the size of costs and the value of goods sold in possibly a large number of other countries.

A more plausible alternative would be to organize the tax in the same way as a destination-based VAT. Indeed, value added as measured by VAT is equal to the sum of economic rent and labour income. In a closed economy, a VAT which also gave relief for labour costs would be equivalent to an R-based cash flow tax. All real costs, including labour costs, but not financial costs, would be deductible from the tax base. In an open economy, a destination-based VAT which also gave relief for labour costs would be a destination-based,

[31] This was first proposed as a form of corporation tax by Bond and Devereux (2002), who analyse the impact of the tax on location and investment decisions, although many of the business tax issues were analysed in the broader context of consumption taxation by Grubert and Newlon (1995, 1997).

[32] See Crawford, Keen, and Smith (Chapter 4) for related discussion in the context of VAT.

R-based, flow-of-funds tax. Since it would be equivalent to an R-based tax, it would not affect financial policy, nor would it affect the scale of investment. And since it would be levied on a destination-basis, it would not affect the location of capital or profit.

How would such a destination-based cash flow tax allocate costs between countries? It would relieve those costs in the exporting country in which they were incurred. Just as for VAT, an exporting company would not be taxed on its exports (although the import would be taxed in the destination country). Any VAT a company had already paid on intermediate goods would be refunded. A destination-based cash flow tax would need additionally to give a refund to reflect the cost of labour. A company which exported all its goods would therefore face a negative tax liability, reflecting tax relief for the cost of its labour.

On the face of it, this does not seem very feasible. Although countries would not be subsidizing exports (since the export price would be unaffected), they might face negative tax payments in the case where domestic costs (including labour costs) exceed domestic sales, for example for companies which predominantly export their output. Offsetting that, of course, is the fact that they would be taxing imports. The country's overall revenue position would therefore depend on the balance of trade in any given year. However, there are administrative ways of avoiding negative tax payments, if these are seen as problematic. One is to make offsetting adjustments to other taxes, for example payroll taxes withheld: instead of paying a rebate, the amount repayable could be set against the company's other tax liability. A second approach would be to enact the tax by increasing the rate of VAT: but since this would be a tax on labour income as well as economic rent, an offsetting reduction to taxes on labour income would be needed.

It should be clear that such a combination of taxes would not distort the location of capital or profit, while an origin-based tax, without border adjustments, would. It is worth noting, however, that the economic literature on VAT has identified conditions under which a destination-based VAT and an origin-based VAT would in other respects have exactly the same real effects. This raises the question of how similar origin-based and destination-based cash flow taxes would be with respect to other real decisions. Under certain conditions, these taxes would have similar incentive effects. These conditions include that there must be a single tax rate on all goods and no cross-border shopping or labour mobility between countries, conditions that are not met in practice.[33] Further, even if these conditions hold, the two taxes

[33] See, for example, Lockwood (2001).

also differ with respect to the wealth effects working through the impact on the owners of domestic and foreign assets.[34] We return to this difference below.

A destination-based cash flow tax would thus have desirable properties: the scale and location of investment, and the use of different forms of finance, would all be unaffected by the tax. There would also be no incentive to shift profits to low tax-rate jurisdictions, an advantage which applies even if the above conditions for equivalence hold. Offsetting this is the underlying need for the source country to give relief for the cost of labour, even if the final good is exported and hence not taxed in that jurisdiction.

A characteristic of the destination-based corporate cash flow tax is that it relinquishes the claim to domestic location-specific production rents. By imposing a tax based on destination, a country foregoes any attempt to tax rents that accrue to companies as a result of operating in its jurisdiction (source-based rents) as well as rents that might accrue as the result of residence. The corporate cash flow tax, like a VAT, is a tax on domestic consumption. (Since labour income is not taxed, it differs from VAT in being a tax on domestic consumption from non-labour income.) It therefore imposes no burden on the consumption of those abroad who benefit from local rents. On the other hand, it does impose a tax on the location-specific rents at home and abroad that accrue to domestic consumers. Thus, a country with considerable location-specific rents might lose by adopting a destination-based tax, but even in this case the loss might be offset by the advantages already discussed.

Potential problems with implementing this proposal arise in transition. As noted above, the distinction between old and new investment is a general problem in moving towards a tax based on economic rent, whether a flow-of-funds tax or an ACE. A related concern arises with the destination-based tax. That is, the transition could generate important valuation effects. Compared to a source-based tax, a destination-based tax alleviates tax on exports and imposes a tax on imports. With flexible exchange rates, such border adjustments should lead to a revaluation of the domestic currency, thereby creating positive windfalls for foreign owners of domestic assets and negative windfalls for domestic owners of foreign assets.[35] With fixed exchange rates or within a

[34] See Auerbach (1997), Bond and Devereux (2002).

[35] If the home country's international asset position is in balance, net windfalls will equal zero but the distributional effects will remain. These wealth effects are closely related to those already discussed that affect existing domestically owned domestic assets. To see this, note that the international accounts identity implies that the capital and current accounts balance. Thus, a deduction for exports and a tax on imports is equivalent to a tax deduction for foreign investment and a tax on gross investment income earned abroad plus a tax on inbound investment and a tax deduction

common currency area, such revaluations would still occur in the presence of fully flexible prices, through an increase in the relative domestic price level. The situation would become more complicated with fixed exchange rates and sticky prices, with the destination-based tax potentially providing an output stimulus via a reduction in the real exchange rate.

A further question is whether a destination-based flow-of-funds tax would be creditable against any tax levied by a capital-exporting country. Since a destination-based tax appears less similar to a conventional corporate profits tax than a source-based flow-of-funds tax, then arguably it is even less likely to be creditable. Suppose the UK introduced a destination-based flow-of-funds tax, but no other countries followed suit. A foreign-owned company which operated in the UK but which exported all its output would have no positive UK taxable income (and, indeed, would probably have a UK taxable loss). The UK tax regime itself would be neutral with respect to the location decision of the multinational; while source-based taxes in other countries would generate an advantage to the UK. But a residence-based tax in the residence country of the multinational might outweigh this advantage.[36]

It is also worth commenting on the likely overall revenue implications of implementing this tax. We have discussed above the likely costs of introducing an R-base on a conventional source basis. Compared to this, a destination-based tax would give relief for exports, but would tax imports. Over the long run, we might expect the balance of trade to balance: in this case, the revenue implications would be the same as for the source-based tax. Clearly, though, in the shorter run, revenues would be higher or lower depending on whether the trade balance was in deficit or surplus.

Taxing financial income

Like Meade's R-base flow-of-funds tax, a VAT-style destination-based flow-of-funds tax would not tax financial income. If only real flows were included in the tax base, then economic rent generated through an interest rate spread would be excluded.

However, Meade's R + F base does tax the economic rent generated on the interest rate spread.[37] As outlined in Section 9.2, the R + F base includes

for gross domestic earnings repatriated by foreign owners. Hence, border adjustments amount to the imposition of a positive cash flow tax on outbound investment and a negative cash flow tax on inbound investment, leading to taxes on existing domestically owned capital abroad and subsidies of existing foreign-owned domestic capital.

[36] It is even possible that the 'taxable loss' arising in the UK would become taxable in the residence country, further diminishing the benefit of the destination-based flow-of-funds tax.

[37] A 'generalized' version of the R + F base, along the lines of the ACE system, is analysed by Bond and Devereux (2003).

flows of debt finance in the tax base. Specifically, inflows of debt and interest receipts are taxed, while debt repayments and interest payments receive tax relief. In effect, this is therefore a tax on the net present value of net lending by the corporate sector. As such, it should in principle be neutral with respect to real and financial decisions.

It would be possible to introduce the R + F base on a destination-basis, in a similar way to introducing the R-base on a destination-basis. This would mean that only domestic transactions would be included in taxable income: border adjustments would apply to transactions with non-residents. For example, borrowing from a foreign bank would not generate taxable income; neither would its repayment be relieved from tax. Conversely, lending to a foreign company would also not generate tax relief, and the return from such lending would not be taxable. This mirrors the exemption of exports in that sales of goods to non-residents would also not be taxed. However, tax would be levied on the economic rent generated by domestic borrowing and lending by banks.

Introducing such a destination-based R + F tax raises three issues worth discussing.

First, there is again a similarity to VAT. In most countries, financial services are exempt VAT. Under the credit-invoice system, effectively a final tax is paid by banks on their inputs. No further charge is levied on transactions with the banks' customers. The resulting distortions have been the subject of a wide literature, including a literature on how VAT could be levied on financial services.[38] The most well-known proposals for doing so are effectively a destination-based R + F base, as described here, applied to financial companies: the main difference from that proposed here is simply that for a VAT, labour costs would not be deductible. Variants on the pure R + F base have been proposed which are very similar to the ACE: instead of an immediate tax on borrowing, the tax charge could be carried forward with an interest mark-up to offset against the eventual relief on the repayment with interest.[39]

Second, the R + F base requires the tax system to make a distinction between debt and equity. (Of course, the R-base requires a distinction between real and financial flows.) The distinction is much less important than under conventional corporation taxes, though, because only the economic

[38] See, for example, Hoffman, Poddar, and Whalley (1987), Merrill and Edwards (1996), and Poddar, and English (1997). De la Feria (2007) provides a description of the current state of play in the EU.

[39] This is the 'truncated cash-flow method with tax calculation account' of Poddar and English (1997).

rent arising from debt transactions would be taxed. However, as already discussed, there would be an incentive for a company to issue equity and debt to related parties and to make deductible payments to debt rather than non-deductible payments to equity. Care would also be required to impose appropriate tax treatment for hybrid instruments, such as equity which could be converted into debt. Issuing equity would not yield a tax charge (unlike issuing debt), but repaying the investment as debt, with interest, would receive tax relief. In this instance, the appropriate treatment of such a hybrid instrument would be that the act of conversion from equity to debt would be taxable.

The third issue concerns the UK in particular: currently the UK generates considerable revenue from corporation tax levied on the profits of resident financial companies. Part of this stems from the international activities of financial companies resident in the UK. A destination-based R + F base would raise revenue only on economic rent generated on lending within the UK. Introducing such a tax may therefore have a negative impact on UK taxable income.

Destination-based income taxation

Given the advantages of a destination-based corporate tax over a source-based tax, it is worth considering whether a similar approach might be taken in the context of an income-based tax, rather than a flow-of-funds tax. To rely on the previous analysis as much as possible, consider the conversion of a destination-based flow-of-funds tax into a destination-based income tax, accomplished by providing only a fractional deduction for the purchase of investment goods.[40] The company's tax base would be higher than under a pure flow-of-funds tax, as expected, but it would now also have an incentive to understate the prices of investment goods produced by a subsidiary, foreign or domestic, since it would get to deduct only part of the cost of the investment. It is unclear how big a problem this is. To the extent that most capital expenditures are at arm's length, then a destination-based approach to income taxation might be feasible, but, feasibility aside, it is not clear under what circumstances it would be desirable to impose an income tax on a destination basis. That is, one would need to consider why a country might wish to tax on a destination basis the capital income (as opposed simply to economic rent) associated with its domestic activities.

[40] This is the approach suggested in the domestic context by Auerbach and Jorgenson (1980).

9.7. CONCLUSIONS

This chapter has considered the design of taxes on corporate income. We began with the proposals of the Meade Committee (1978) for a flow-of-funds tax, and analysed how these proposals fare thirty years later, in the light of important developments in economies and economic thought.

We considered two principal dimensions in the choice of a tax on corporate income. The first dimension is the base of the tax. Here we compared a standard corporation tax, levied on the return to shareholders with two alternatives: a tax on economic rent, as proposed by the Meade Committee, and a tax on the return to all capital, such as under the comprehensive business income tax and the dual income tax. The second dimension is geographic: where should the income be taxed? Here we contrasted the typical approach of source-based taxation to the alternatives of residence and destination bases.

The 'optimal' tax system depends partly on why the tax is levied. If it is intended to be a substitute for taxing the capital income of domestic residents, then its form could be very different from that in which it is intended to capture the location-specific rent earned by non-residents. Given the increasing cross-ownership of shareholdings across countries, using a source-based tax on corporate income as a substitute for a residence-based tax on shareholders seems increasingly problematic. In open economies, much domestic economic activity is owned and controlled by non-residents; conversely, much of the accretion to wealth of residents takes place abroad. The argument for taxing source-based economic rent depends on the extent to which that rent is location-specific. At one extreme (equivalent to a closed economy) all rent is location-specific and can therefore be captured in tax without distorting investment. But at the other extreme, it is possible that little or no rent is location-specific: companies could earn equivalent profit by locating their activities elsewhere. In the latter case, a source-based tax on rent (such as proposed by the Meade Committee) could divert economic activity abroad, where it could face a lower tax rate.

One important aspect of the Meade proposals was to avoid a distinction in the tax system between debt and equity. Meade considered two proposals, each of which effectively eliminated the distinction. Avoiding this distinction has since become an even more important issue, as the boundaries between the two forms of financial instrument have become increasingly blurred. That consideration points to a tax which falls either on the whole return to investment, or only on economic rent. However, this is not straightforward either, since in either case the tax base still requires that distinctions be made either between real and financial income flows or between debt and equity. There is no obvious way simultaneously to avoid both distinctions. Differentiating between real and financial flows also creates additional problems in taxing the income of financial companies.

Moving from predominantly source-based corporate taxation to residence-based taxation is not an attractive option. Taxing corporate income in the hands of the parent company is in any case more like source-based taxation, since the location of the parent is not fixed. So true residence-based taxation would have to be at the level of the individual investor; but in a globalized world, this is scarcely feasible.

An alternative which we have put forward for serious consideration is a destination-based tax, levied where a sale to a final consumer is made. In fact, we formulate a simple—though far-reaching—extension of the flow-of-funds taxes of Meade. Specifically, we suggest that one might improve on Meade's proposed taxes by adding border adjustments: imports would be taxed, but tax on exports would be refunded. The result is a destination-based cash flow tax, essentially a destination-based VAT, but with labour costs deductible. We believe that there is a good case for implementing such a tax on an R + F basis, rather than on an R-basis, on the grounds that this would also tax the economic rents generated by banks on lending to domestic borrowers.[41]

Such a tax would leave discrete location choices unaffected by the tax, and would also considerably lower the opportunity for companies to shift profits between countries. One implication of such a tax is that a country introducing it would need to give relief for labour costs borne in the production of untaxed exports. The neutrality advantages of such a tax to a system are somewhat less clear if the normal return to domestic capital is to be taxed.

REFERENCES

Altshuler, R., and Auerbach, A. J. (1990), 'The Significance of Tax Law Asymmetries: An Empirical Investigation', *Quarterly Journal of Economics*, **105**, 61–86.

——and Goodspeed, T. (2002), 'Follow the Leader? Evidence on European and US Tax Competition', *Departmental Working Papers, 200226*, Rutgers University, Department of Economics.

Auerbach, A. (1979), 'Wealth Maximization and the Cost of Capital', *Quarterly Journal of Economics*, **93**, 433–46.

——(1983), 'Corporate Taxation in the United States', *Brookings Papers on Economic Activity*, vol. **1983**, 451–505.

[41] Whether the R + F base would apply only within the financial sector, as others have proposed in the context of existing VATs, or to all businesses is an issue that requires further consideration.

——(1997), 'The Future of Fundamental Tax Reform', *American Economic Review*, **87**, 143–6.

——(2002), 'Taxation and Corporate Financial Policy', in Auerbach, A., and Feldstein, M. (eds.), *Handbook of Public Economics*, **3**, 1251–92.

——(2006), 'The Future of Capital Income Taxation', *Fiscal Studies*, **27**, 399–420.

——and Hassett, K. (2007), 'The 2003 Dividend Tax Cuts and the Value of the Firm: An Event Study', in Auerbach, A., Hines, J., and Slemrod, J. (eds.), *Taxing Corporate Income in the 21st Century*, 93–126.

——and Jorgenson, D. (1980), 'Inflation-proof Depreciation of Assets', *Harvard Business Review*, September/October, 113–18.

——and King, M. (1983), 'Taxation, Portfolio Choice and Debt–equity Ratios: A General Equilibrium Model', *Quarterly Journal of Economics*, **98**, 588–609.

——and Slemrod, J. (1997), 'The Economic Effects of the Tax Reform Act of 1986', *Journal of Economic Literature*, **35**, 589–632.

Berle, A., and Means, G. (1932), *The Modern Corporation and Private Property*, New York: Macmillan.

Black, F., and Scholes, M. (1973), 'The Pricing of Options and Corporate Liabilities', *Journal of Political Economy*, **81**, 637–54.

Boadway, R., and Bruce, N. (1984), 'A General Proposition on the Design of a Neutral Business Tax', *Journal of Public Economics*, **24**, 231–9.

Bond, S. (2000), 'Levelling Up or Levelling Down? Some Reflections on the ACE and CBIT Proposals and the Future of the Corporate Tax Base', in Cnossen, S. (ed.), *Taxing Capital Income in the European Union: Issues and Options for Reform*, Oxford: Oxford University Press.

——and Devereux, M. P. (1995), 'On the Design of a Neutral Business Tax under Uncertainty', *Journal of Public Economics*, **58**, 57–71.

——(2002), 'Cash Flow Taxes in an Open Economy', *CEPR Discussion Paper 3401*.

——(2003), 'Generalised R-based and S-based Taxes under Uncertainty', *Journal of Public Economics*, **87**, 1291–311.

Bradford, D. (1981), 'The Incidence and Allocation Effects of a Tax on Corporate Distributions', *Journal of Public Economics*, **15**, 1–22.

Chamley, C. (1986), 'Optimal Taxation of Capital Income in General Equilibrium with Infinite Lives', *Econometrica*, **54**, 607–22.

Cummins, J., Hassett, K., and Oliner, S. (2006), 'Investment Behaviour, Observable Expectations and Internal Funds', *American Economic Review*, **96**, 796–810.

De la Feria, R. (2007), 'The EU VAT Treatment of Insurance and Financial Services (again) under Review', *EU Tax Review* **2007.2**, 74–89.

Desai, M. A., and Hines Jr., J. (2002), 'Expectations and Expatriations: Tracing the Causes and Consequences of Corporate Inversions', *National Tax Journal*, **55**, 409–40.

Devereux, M. P., and Griffith, R. (1998), 'Taxes and the Location of Production: Evidence from a Panel of US Multinationals', *Journal of Public Economics*, **68**, 335–67.

Devereux, M. P., Griffith, R., and Klemm, A. (2002), 'Corporate Income Tax Reforms and International Tax Competition', *Economic Policy*, **17**, 451–95.

——— (2004), 'Why has the UK Corporation Tax Raised so much Revenue?' *Fiscal Studies*, **25**, 367–88.

——Lockwood, B., and Redoano, M. (2008), 'Do Countries Compete over Corporate Tax Rates?', *Journal of Public Economics*, **92**, 1210–35.

——and Sørensen, P. B. (2005), 'The Corporate Income Tax: International Trends and Options for Fundamental Reform', *EPRU-Analysis No. 24*. <http://www.econ.ku.dk/epru>.

Diamond, P., and Mirrlees, J. (1971), 'Optimal Taxation and Public Production I-II', *American Economic Review*, **61**, 8–27 and 261–78.

Fazzari, S., Hubbard, R. G., and Petersen, B. (1988), 'Financing Constraints and Corporate Investment', *Brookings Papers on Economic Activity*, **1988**, 141–95.

Feldstein, M., and Horioka, C. (1980), 'Domestic Saving and International Capital Flows', *Economic Journal*, **90**, 314–29.

Goolsbee, A. (1998), 'Taxes, Organizational Form and the Deadweight Loss of the Corporate Income Tax', *Journal of Public Economics*, **69**, 143–52.

Gordon, R., Kalambokidis, L., and Slemrod, J. (2004), 'Do we *Now* Collect any Revenue from Taxing Capital Income?', *Journal of Public Economics*, **88**, 981–1009.

——and MacKie-Mason, J. K. (1997), 'How Much do Taxes Discourage Incorporation?', *Journal of Finance*, **52**, 477–505.

——and Slemrod, J. (1988), 'Do we Collect any Revenue from Taxing Capital Income?', *Tax Policy and the Economy*, **2**, 89–130.

——and Wilson, R. (1986), 'An Examination of Multijurisdictional Corporate Income Taxation under Formula Apportionment', *Econometrica*, **54**, 1357–73.

Graham, J. R. (1996), 'Debt and the Marginal Tax Rate', *Journal of Financial Economics*, **41**, 41–73.

Grubert, H., and Newlon, T. S. (1995), 'The International Implications of Consumption Tax Proposals', *National Tax Journal*, **48**, 619–47.

——— (1997), 'Taxing Consumption in a Global Economy', Washington DC: American Enterprise Institute.

Harberger, A. (1962), 'The Incidence of the Corporation Income Tax', *Journal of Political Economy*, **70**, 215–40.

Haufler, A., and Schjelderup, G. (2000), 'Corporate Tax Systems and Cross Country Profit Shifting', *Oxford Economic Papers*, **52**, 306–25.

Hoffman, L. A., Poddar, S. N., and Whalley, J. (1987), 'Taxation of Banking Services under a Consumption Type, Destination-based VAT', *National Tax Journal*, **40**, 547–54.

Horstman, I., and Markusen, J. (1992), 'Endogenous Market Structures in International Trade', *Journal of International Economics*, **32**, 109–29.

IFS (1991), *Equity for Companies: A Corporation Tax for the 1990s*, IFS Commentary C026. London: Institute for Fiscal Studies.

Jensen, M. (1986), 'Agency Costs of Free Cash Flow, Corporate Finance, and Takeovers', *American Economic Review*, **76**, 323–9.

Judd, K. (1985), 'Redistributive Taxation in a Simple Perfect Foresight Model', *Journal of Public Economics*, **28**, 59–83.

Keen, M., and Piekkola, H. (1997), 'Simple Rules for the Optimal Taxation of International Capital Income', *Scandinavian Journal of Economics*, **99**, 447–61.

King, M. (1974), 'Taxation and the Cost of Capital', *Review of Economic Studies*, **41**, 21–35.

—— Fullerton, D. (1984), *The Taxation of Income from Capital: A Comparative Study of the U.S., U.K., Sweden and West Germany*, Chicago: University of Chicago Press.

Kleinbard, E. (2007), 'Designing an Income Tax on Capital', in Steurele, C. E., Burman, L. E., and Aaron, H. J. (eds.), *Taxing Capital Income*, Washington, DC: Urban Institute Press.

Lockwood, B. (2001), 'Tax Competition and Tax Co-ordination under Destination and Origin Principles: A Synthesis', *Journal of Public Economics*, **81**, 279–319.

McLure, C. (1980), 'The State Corporate Income Tax: Lambs in Wolves' Clothing', in Aaron, H., and Boskin, M. (eds.), *The Economics of Taxation*, Washington, DC: Brookings Institution.

Markusen, J. (2002), *Multinational Firms and the Theory of International Trade*, Cambridge, Mass.: MIT Press.

Meade, J. (1978), *The Structure and Reform of Direct Taxation: Report of a Committee chaired by Professor J. E. Meade for the Institute for Fiscal Studies*, London: George Allen & Unwin. http://www.ifs.org.uk/publications/3433.

Merrill, P. R., and Edwards, C. R. (1996), 'Cash-flow Taxation of Financial Services', *National Tax Journal*, **49**, 487–500.

Miller, M. (1977), 'Debt and Taxes', *Journal of Finance*, **32**, 261–75.

Nielsen, S. B., and Sørensen, P. B. (1997), 'On the Optimality of the Nordic System of Dual Income Taxation', *Journal of Public Economics*, **63**, 311–29.

Poddar, S. N., and English, M. (1997), 'Taxation of Financial Services under a Value-Added Tax: Applying the Cash Flow Approach', *National Tax Journal*, **50**, 89–111.

Sinn, H-W. (1991), 'The Vanishing Harberger Triangle', *Journal of Public Economics*, **45**, 271–300.

Sørensen, P. B. (1994), 'From the Global Income Tax to the Dual Income Tax—Recent Tax Reforms in the Nordic Countries', *International Tax and Public Finance*, **1**, 57–79.

—— (2005a), 'Dual Income Taxation—Why and How?', *FinanzArchiv*, **61**, 559–86.

—— (2005b), 'Neutral Taxation of Shareholder Income', *International Tax and Public Finance*, **12**, 777–801.

US Department of the Treasury (1992), *Integration of the Individual and Corporate Tax Systems: Taxing Business Income Once*, Washington, DC: U.S. G.P.O.

Warren, A. C. (2004), 'U.S. Income Taxation of New Financial Products', *Journal of Public Economics*, **88**, 889–923.

Commentary by Harry Huizinga

Harry Huizinga is Professor of International Economics at Tilburg University. He received an A.B. in economics from Princeton University in 1984 and a PhD in economics from Harvard University in 1988. He was an Economic Advisor in the Directorate-General for Economic and Financial Affairs of the European Commission in the period 2000–03. He has published widely in the areas of public finance and financial economics, and has on several occasions been a visiting scholar to the IMF and a consultant to the World Bank.

Corporate tax policy amounts to choosing the appropriate tax base and the desired tax rate. At the time of the Meade Report (Meade, 1978), the UK economy was still relatively closed. Hence, there was little concern about how corporate tax policy could cause an international relocation of company residence, real investment, or reported profits. In this environment, the Meade Report proposed corporate tax base definitions that amounted to taxing economic rents. By effectively allowing a full expensing of capital expenditures, the tax system would not distort the marginal investment decision. In the absence of international tax interdependence, a relatively high tax rate could apply to this base. In the twenty-first century, companies and their profits have become far more internationally mobile. This prompts a re-evaluation of the appropriate corporate tax base as well as the rate.

In an integrated world, each country has to face the choice whether to tax corporate income on a residence basis or on a source basis. With residence-based taxation, capital income, say in the form of dividends, is taxed in the country where the parent company of a multinational firm resides or where the ultimate private or institutional shareholders reside. With source-based taxation, capital income is instead taxed in the country where it is generated. In this chapter, Auerbach, Devereux, and Simpson argue that residence-based taxation is difficult to maintain in an internationally integrated economy. First, it is difficult to maintain residence-based taxation of corporate shareholders, as such taxation—to the extent that it leads to international double taxation of corporate income—can be avoided by a movement of the firm's tax residence abroad. Second, taxing the income of ultimate shareholders is equally cumbersome, as it is hard for the tax authority to obtain information on the foreign dividend and capital gains income of domestic residents. Given these problems with residence-based taxation, countries are increasingly left to tax corporate income at source.

Auerbach, Devereux, and Simpson review the appropriate definition of the tax base in this environment from the perspective of UK national tax policy. While the UK to a large extent retains autonomy over its corporate tax base definition, it at the same time is a member state of the European Union. As such, the UK is subject to the existing body of EU tax directives and other forms of EU tax policy, and it is likely to be important in shaping future EU policy. Depending on one's view, one can see European tax policy as a constraint on UK policy or as a way to improve Europe's tax system by means not available to individual member states. Evidence for the latter view comes from the fact that European capital income tax policy as a generalization brings back elements of residence-based taxation in EU tax policies through its various Directives. At the same time, it aims to promote an 'orderly', non-discriminatory residence-based tax system, as evidenced by pronouncements of the European Court of Justice (ECJ) on capital income taxation. In my comments below, I will summarize the main elements of EU capital income tax policy affecting the UK and other EU member states.

As indicated, the internationalization of the economy also affects the appropriate tax rate. As Auerbach, Devereux, and Simpson point out, tax policy makers have to be aware that in an open economy a single tax rate can affect an entire sequence of decisions by corporations that in the end affect the profits that are reported in the countries where the firm operates. The tax rate first potentially affects the countries where the firm operates. The average tax rate, as affected by the headline tax rate, is especially relevant in this regard. Second, the organization form taken by a multinational firm, and in particular the international location of its parent company and subsidiaries, can be expected to be affected by the international tax system. In this regard, firms are interested in avoiding international double taxation where they can. The UK has a system of worldwide taxation, which in itself makes it less attractive as a location of company headquarters in the form of the parent firm. Third, the firm has to decide on the allocation of real productive assets among its establishments in different countries. This choice is affected by marginal tax rates. Next, the overall financing of the firm is affected by the tax system. Given the deductibility of interest expenses, the firm is interested in locating its debt in high-tax countries. Finally, the firm can engage in the international shifting of accounting profits so as to report fewer profits in high-tax countries.

In this environment, it is important to know how the tax rate affects each of the various decisions made by the firm that ultimately affect reported profits and hence tax liabilities. Knowledge about these issues ultimately has to come from empirical research. Auerbach, Devereux, and Simpson summarize important parts of the relevant empirical literature. However, much of the literature they review is for US rather than European firms. For instance, they review evidence on the relationships between capital structure and organizational forms on the one hand, and taxation on the other hand for US firms. UK firms, however, make a main share of their investments in Europe and continental European firms are of course key investors in the UK. Hence, evidence on tax sensitivities for European firms should also be relevant for the case of the UK. In the final part of my comments, I will review some recent evidence on tax sensitivities in the open economy based on European data to help shape the view on how sensitive profits are to tax policy in today's Europe.

1. THE ROLE OF EU TAX POLICY IN SHAPING UK TAX POLICY

The EU Treaties do not call for the alignment of direct taxes such as the corporate income tax, as direct tax policy differences are not deemed directly to affect the proper functioning of the common market. Moreover, as a matter of principle the Treaty of Maastricht does not rule out internationally discriminatory tax practices. Specifically, Article 58, paragraph 1, allows member states to 'distinguish between tax payers who are not in same situation with respect to their place of residence or with regard to the place where their capital is invested'. However, the scope for discrimination is limited by paragraph 3 of the same Article of the Maastricht Treaty that proscribes 'arbitrary discrimination'. As a further potential restriction on national capital income tax policies, the Treaty of Maastricht elevates the free movement of capital to treaty level.

Going beyond the treaty, the EU can adopt directives in the area of capital income taxation that would be directly binding in all member states. The requirement of unanimity among member states, however, has proven to be an important barrier to the adoption of EU tax directives. As a result, to date relatively few directives in the area of corporate income taxation have been adopted in the EU. In the relative absence of such directives, the European Court of Justice has taken on a heightened role as an arbiter on whether national tax policies are consistent with EU treaties. The lack of explicit legislative action has further prompted the EU commission to try to use 'suasion' to nudge national tax policies in a direction it favours.

What has been the effect of EU tax policies on tax policy in individual member states such as the UK so far? The various extant bits of EU tax policy importantly bear on the main issue of what is the appropriate tax base in an open economy. As indicated, economic openness appears to move the tax system towards a more source-based system. The overall impact of EU tax policy appears to be to slow down and in some instances to reverse this trend, thereby strengthening elements of residence-based taxation. At the same time, EU tax policy seems to work towards a relatively non-discriminatory, residence-based tax system.

To support this view, we next review some main elements of EU capital income tax policy to date. To start with directives, the Parent–Subsidiary Directive of 1990 eliminates non-resident withholding taxes on dividend payments among related businesses in different member states. The elimination of withholding taxes on intra-firm dividend payments applies, if the parent owns at least 25% of the stock of a foreign subsidiary. In 2003, the European Council adopted a revision of the Parent–Subsidiary Directive that extended its application in several ways. Specifically, the Directive was to apply to a wider range of companies (to include, for instance, companies that have the newly created legal form of a 'European Company') and it reduces the required minimum shareholding rate of the parent company gradually from 25% to 10%. Analogously to the Parent–Subsidiary Directive, the Interest and Royalties Directive of 2003 eliminates non-resident withholding taxes on intra-firm interest and royalty payments. Non-resident withholding taxes are source-based taxes and hence both Directives effectively cut back the scope of source-based capital income taxation in the EU.

Along similar lines, the Merger Directive, also adopted in 1990, eliminates the taxation of capital gains realized by corporations and shareholders at the occasion of an intra-EU merger or acquisition. Such capital gains taxes can be seen as deferred taxes on income generated at source in the target country, even if they only apply to resident companies and shareholders. In 2005, a revision of the Merger Directive was adopted to extend its scope.

The EU Savings Directive of 2005 embodies the international exchange of information on cross-border interest accruing to individuals as the main principle to enable residence-based taxation of such income in the EU. Three EU member states, Austria, Belgium, and Luxembourg, are allowed to levy source-based non-resident withholding taxes on interest instead, but only on a temporary basis till 2010. The Savings Directive covers bank interest as well as interest on government and corporate bonds, except some grandfathered issues. To enable exchange of information, financial institutions have to keep track of the nationality of bank and other interest recipients. This represents a substantial administrative burden for EU financial institutions. The EU Savings Directive thus materially affects the UK, which is the home to Europe's major financial centre. At present, the Directive does not cover dividends. Hence, the Directive provides some scope for arbitrage between interest and dividend income streams. If this proves to be important, it may make sense to expand the scope of the Directive in the future to include dividends.

With only a limited coverage of EU tax directives, decisions of the European Court of Justice take on a heightened importance in shaping tax policy in the EU. The court has made decisions with wider ramifications in the area of dividend taxation of individual as well as corporate shareholders. Affecting individual shareholders, the ECJ's judgment in the Verkooijen case of 2000 concerns the taxation of inbound dividends as part of portfolio income. The Netherlands at the time exempted the first 1,000 guilders of dividends from personal income taxation, but the exemption only applied to domestic dividends. The Court ruled that this did not conform with the EC Treaty, and that the exemption should apply to foreign inbound dividends as well. Generally, this ruling is taken to imply that personal income tax systems should not discriminate against inbound dividend income.

In the corporate tax area, the Court similarly has ruled in several instances that residence-based taxation of corporate shareholders should not afford a more favourable tax treatment to income from domestic subsidiaries than from foreign subsidiaries. In a case involving the UK, the ECJ ruled in 2005 in the Marks & Spencer case that this company's foreign losses could be offset against the company's UK profits, if these losses cannot be used in another member state against realized or future profits. The Court thus ruled against the UK's 'group relief' legislation that previously had prevented UK companies from offsetting foreign losses against UK profits. Pursuant to the ECJ decision, foreign losses can be claimed, even if the foreign subsidiary has never paid any dividends to the UK parent. Thus, this ruling opens the possibility that the residence-based taxation of foreign-source corporate income generates negative tax revenues in the UK and elsewhere.

In the Lankhorst-Hohorst case of 2000, the ECJ addressed German thin capitalization rules that limit the tax deductibility of interest payments by subsidiaries to their parent companies. In the German case, these thin capitalization rules only applied to interest paid by subsidiaries to their non-German, non-resident parent companies. The ECJ ruled that this violates non-discrimination principles as laid down in the freedom of establishment provision in the EC Treaty. This ruling has had far-reaching implications for thin capitalization policies throughout Europe. The UK, which has had a thin capitalization rule since 1988, saw itself forced to extend its thin capitalization rule to apply to domestic subsidiaries also in 2004.

In 2004, the European Commission (2003) published a communication that analyses the implications of case law of the ECJ for the international taxation of dividend income. With regard to outbound dividend payments, an implication appears to be that it is illegal to levy a higher withholding tax on dividends accruing to foreign shareholders than to domestic shareholders. With regard to inbound dividend payments, countries with imputation systems—providing their residents with tax credits for corporate taxes paid by domestic companies—equally have to provide credits for corporation taxes paid by foreign companies. Thus if the UK had retained its previous imputation system, it would be liable to pay tax credits for corporation taxes paid by firms in countries with potentially much higher corporate tax rates than the UK such as Germany. This may be a reason that the UK has abolished its imputation system.

In a non-legislative effort to limit harmful tax competition, EU member states agreed on a code of conduct regarding corporate income taxation in 1997. The code aims to protect the corporate tax base of member states and to bring about a fair international division of that base. It outlines several criteria to identify harmful tax competition. Harmful measures, for instance, may involve relatively low taxes that are ring-fenced in the sense that they are available only to non-residents or apply only to activities undertaken by non-residents. Other harmful measures are those that potentially shift the tax base without affecting the location of real activity. To identify harmful tax practices in the EU, in 1998 Ecofin established the Code of Conduct Group, chaired by the British Paymaster-General Dawn Primarolo. In 1999, this group published its report, which enumerated sixty-six harmful tax measures. Sweden and the UK interestingly were the only two countries that were not found to have harmful corporate tax practices. Hence, the restrictions on corporate tax policy laid out in the Code of Conduct do not appear to limit UK corporate tax policy.

2. THE BEHAVIOUR OF INTERNATIONAL FIRMS AND UK TAX POLICY

As Auerbach, Devereux, and Simpson outline, firms in open economies face a sequence of choices as to the location of production, physical investment, and the allocation of profits. In addition, the firm has to decide on its debt–equity ratio and, if it has foreign establishments, on the international assignment of its debts. Finally, the firm has to decide on its organizational form. In an open economy, this involves the location of its headquarters and consequently of its tax residence. Each of these choices is potentially affected by the tax rate and other aspects of the tax system. For tax policy, it is important to know how sensitive each of the firm's decisions is to the tax rate and other parts of the tax system. Estimates of tax sensitivities can be obtained by empirical research. To inform the UK tax debate, ideally such estimates stem from the investigation of European data. Much evidence as reviewed by Auerbach, Devereux, and Simpson—for instance, on the debt–equity ratio and organizational form—instead has been based on US data. In the remainder, I will discuss some recent studies on company choice and taxation in open economies with an emphasis on European studies.

Desai and Hines (2002) examine the role of taxation in so-called corporate inversions. In these dealings, the corporate structure is inverted in the sense that the previous US parent becomes a subsidiary of one of its earlier foreign subsidiaries. These inversions serve to eliminate US worldwide income taxation of all previous foreign subsidiaries. In fact, international double taxation is avoided (not counting US dividend withholding taxes) if the new parent resides in a country with a territorial tax system. Examining multinationals newly created through international mergers and acquisitions (M&As), Huizinga and Voget (2008) similarly find that the parent–subsidiary structure reflects international double taxation. Using their estimation results, Huizinga and Voget simulate how the change in a country's tax rate affects the proportion of M&As that select that country as the parent country. On average, an increase in the corporate tax rate by one percentage point reduces the proportion of firms taking up tax residence in a country by 0.36 percentage points. For the UK, the impact of a one percentage point increase in its tax rate on the proportion of multinationals taking up residence in the UK is estimated to be relatively large at 0.53 percentage points, reflecting the UK system of worldwide taxation.

De Mooij and Nicodème (2006) examine the relationship between incorporation and tax rates with European data. The impact of tax rates on incorporation is significant and large and it implies that the revenue effects of lower corporate tax rates partly show up in lower personal tax revenues rather than lower corporate tax revenues. This form of income shifting is found to have raised the corporate tax-to-GDP ratio by some 0.2 percentage points since the early 1990s.

Auerbach, Devereux, and Simpson mention that foreign ownership of companies may be a reason why corporate taxes have not declined much. Foreign ownership implies that part of the incidence of corporate taxation, in so far as there are rents, is on the foreign owners. They show that the percentage of shares listed in the UK and owned by foreigners has increased from around 5% at the time of the Meade Report to around 30% in 2004. Can the current degree of foreign ownership in the UK explain the relatively low UK corporate tax burden relative to other European countries? Huizinga and Nicodème (2006) consider a measure of the corporate tax burden based on tax payments as a share of assets. Their evidence, relating foreign ownership shares of subsidiaries to average tax burdens for a set of European countries, suggests that this is indeed the case. Figure 1 summarizes their data. The figure shows that there is an overall positive relationship between the foreign ownership share of corporate assets and the average tax burden. The foreign

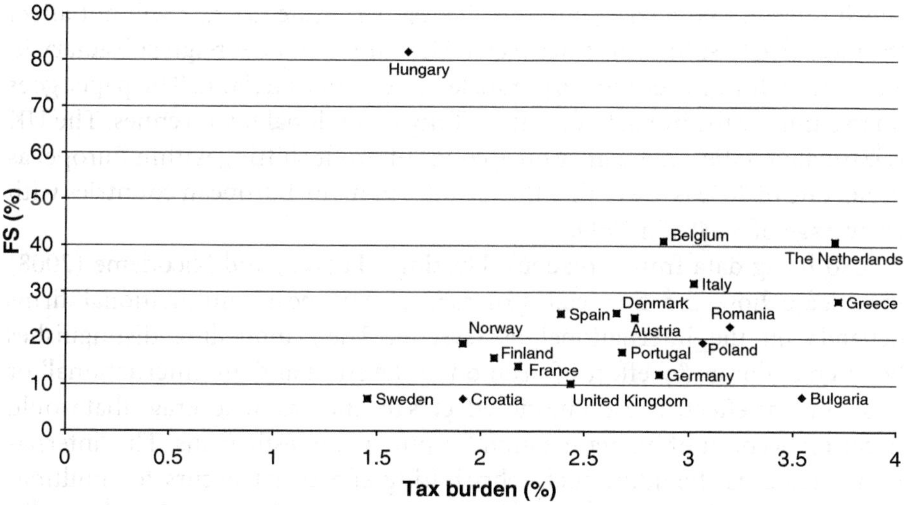

Notes: FS is the average country-level foreign ownership share over the years 1996–2000, where the country-level foreign ownership share in each year is the asset-weighted average of foreign ownership shares for firms in that country.

Tax burden is the average country-level tax burden over the years 1996–2000, where the country-level tax burden in each year is the asset-weighted average of tax burdens for firms in that country, and the tax burden for each firm measures corporate tax as a percentage of assets.

Sources: Huizinga and Nicodème (2006).

Figure 1. The tax burden and the foreign ownership share (1996–2000)

ownership share for the UK is seen to be relatively low at 10.3%, while the tax burden is also relatively low at 2.4%. Hence, the relatively low degree of foreign ownership in the UK can in part explain a relatively low tax burden. At present, there still is considerable room for foreign ownership to increase in the UK to levels already seen in many other European countries. This could imply upward pressure on the corporate tax level in the UK in the future.

Next, there are a few studies of the extent of international profit shifting by European firms. Using sectoral data in OECD countries, Bartelsman and Beetsma (2003) find that value added reported is negatively related to statutory tax rates. Their estimation suggests that at the margin more than 65% of the additional revenue from a unilateral tax increase is lost due to a decrease in the reported income tax base. Huizinga and Laeven (2008) investigate profit shifting by European multinationals using firm-level data on the location of the parent firm and of foreign subsidiaries from the Amadeus database. They find an average elasticity of the reported tax base with respect to the statutory tax rate of 0.45, while the corresponding elasticity is estimated to be somewhat smaller at 0.30 for the UK. This relatively small elasticity reflects the fact that the UK levies corporate income tax on a worldwide basis, which implies that a change in the UK top corporate tax rate will not affect the incentive to shift profits between a UK parent and a foreign subsidiary in a country with a lower top corporate tax rate such as Ireland. The paper goes on to simulate the impact of profit shifting on national tax revenues. The UK is estimated to be a net gainer on account of profit shifting within Europe, as its tax rate of 30% is lower that the tax rates in many European countries with an average of 34.4% in 1999.

Also using data from Amadeus, Huizinga, Laeven, and Nicodème (2008) investigate how the financial structure of European multinational firms depends on the international tax system. Their modelling distinguishes between a 'domestic' effect of taxation on leverage and an 'international' or debt-shifting effect. The 'domestic' effect is the increase in leverage that would occur on account of higher taxation for purely domestic firms. The 'international' effect is the additional debt-shifting effect that occurs for multinational firms on account of international tax rate differences. For domestic, stand-alone firms, the estimation implies that a 10 percentage points increase in the overall tax rate (generally reflecting corporate income taxes and non-resident dividend withholding taxes) increases the ratio of liabilities to assets by 1.8 percentage points, which is a rather small effect compared to the sample standard deviation of this leverage ratio of 21 percentage points. For multinational firms, the leverage ratio is more sensitive to taxation on account of international debt shifting. To illustrate this, one can take the example of a multinational with two equal-sized establishments in two separate countries. A 10 percentage points overall tax increase in one country is then found to increase the leverage ratio in that country by 2.4 percentage points, while the ratio in the other country decreases by 0.6 percentage points.

Parent companies in the UK on average have a liability ratio of 0.57, which is less than the average of 0.62 for the entire sample of parent firms in Europe, while foreign subsidiaries in the UK have a leverage ratio of 0.62 on average just equal to the European average. On the whole, subsidiaries located in the UK are found to have an incentive to shift debt out of the UK, which reflects the UK's relatively low tax rate in the EU.

3. CONCLUSION

International economic integration makes it more difficult for the UK to operate a residence-based corporate tax system with a reasonably high corporate tax rate. Two developments, however, potentially restrict the 'degradation' of the corporate income tax system. First, European tax policies tend to work towards maintaining or restoring residence-based capital income taxation. Second, increased foreign ownership in the UK and elsewhere prevents a 'race to the bottom' in corporate income tax rates. In the future, deeper economic integration may render it increasingly difficult to raise significant corporate tax revenues. In that instance, further European tax policy cooperation may be called for to enable the UK to implement an effective corporation tax.

REFERENCES

Bartelsman, E. J., and Beetsma, R. M. (2003), 'Why Pay More? Corporate Tax Avoidance Through Transfer Pricing in OECD Countries', *Journal of Public Economics* **87**, 2225–52.

Desai, M. A., Foley, C. F., and Hines, J. (2004), 'A Multinational Perspective on Capital Structure Choice and International Capital Markets', *Journal of Finance*, **59**, 2451–88.

—— and Hines, J. Jr. (2002), 'Expectations and Expatriations: Tracing the Causes and Consequences of Corporate Inversions', *National Tax Journal*, **55**, 409–40.

European Commission (2003), 'Communication on Dividend Taxation of Individuals in the Internal Market', Com (2003) 810 final, Brussels.

Huizinga, H., and Laeven, L. (2008), 'International Profit Shifting Within Multinationals: A Multi-country Perspective', *Journal of Public Economics*, **92**, 1164–82.

—— —— and Nicodème, G. (2008), 'Capital Structure and International Debt Shifting', *Journal of Financial Economics*, **88**, 80–118.

—— and Nicodème, G. (2006), 'Foreign Ownership and Corporate Income Taxation: An Empirical Evaluation', *European Economic Review*, **50**, 1234–44.

—— and Voget, J. (2008), 'International Taxation and the Direction and Volume of Cross-border M&A's', forthcoming in *Journal of Finance*.

Meade, J. (1978), *The Structure and Reform of Direct Taxation: Report of a Committee chaired by Professor J. E. Meade for the Institute for Fiscal Studies*, London: George Allen & Unwin. http://www.ifs.org.uk/publications/3433.

Mooij, R. de and Nicodème, G. (2006), 'Corporate Tax Policy, Entrepreneurship and Incorporation in the EU', CESifo Working Paper No. 1883.

Commentary by Jack M. Mintz

Jack Mintz is Palmer Chair in Public Policy at the University of Calgary. He is an Associate Editor of *International Tax and Public Finance*, of which he was the founding Editor-in-Chief, and of the *Canadian Tax Journal*, and is a Research Fellow of CESifo, Munich, and of the Oxford University Centre for Business Taxation. Widely published in the field of public economics and a regular contributor to print media, he was touted by *Tax Business* magazine in 2004 as one of the world's most influential tax experts. Dr Mintz has acted as a consultant to the World Bank, the IMF, the OECD, the governments of Canada and several Canadian provinces, and various businesses and non-profit organizations.

The primary focus of 'Taxing Corporate Income', written by three eminent authors, is to reconsider the Meade Report's (Meade, 1978) recommendation to tax corporate rents in light of evolving changes to the UK economy since 1978. Wisely, the authors focus on the impact of global economic integration on company taxation policy. I would agree that one cannot consider company taxation without thinking about international issues.

After examining a rich array of possible tax bases, the authors come to an almost stark conclusion that little will work properly in raising revenue as businesses will shift income to low-tax jurisdictions—whether the tax is based on income or on rents on a source basis. Eventually, international considerations will force governments to move towards a corporate tax that exempts exports and taxes imports, based on the destination principle.

I believe that we are far from that point yet. Despite the rapid growth in cross-border investments since 1990,[1] corporate income tax revenues as a share of GDP have been remarkably robust among OECD countries in the past twenty-five years (see Mintz and Weichenrieder (2007)). Governments are not about to abandon a tax base that raises almost 10% of their needs today.

[1] In 1990, cross-border investment flows of foreign direct investment among OECD countries was about US$200 billion, rising to over US$2 trillion by 2000, falling back to over US$600 billion by 2004 (all numbers expressed in 2000 dollars). See Organization of Economic Cooperation and Development, *Statistics* (2006).

I think this reflects a reality that capital markets are not quite as internationally integrated as sometimes assumed. Many financial studies show investor 'home bias' remains partly a result of regulations that limit the cross-border ownership of shares.[2] Further, while one cannot ignore the open economy in evaluating corporate policy in today's economy, one cannot forget the possible arbitrage between corporate and personal tax bases within the domestic economy. Smart tax arbitragers will work out schemes to shift labour into capital income or develop tax structures that allow businesses to escape paying tax when differential taxes apply—not just at the international level but also within the domestic economy.[3]

Indeed, I am not even sure it is right to emphasize only a 'corporate tax' when businesses have developed enterprise groups with corporations, unlimited liability corporations, limited liability partnerships, and trust arrangements to run business organizations. My preference has been to refer to business taxes rather than corporate taxes to keep in mind the complexity of business relationships in today's environment. Consistent with the chapter, however, I shall focus on corporations that are by and large the most important form of business organization in the UK economy.

The question in my view is whether a better tax base can be developed for corporate taxation that would improve the efficiency and fairness of the tax system. In my view, the Meade (1978) and the US Treasury (1977) reports got the essential argument right—eliminating the inter-temporal distortion of taxes by replacing a corporate income tax with a cash flow tax can arguably be efficient, fair and simple. This argument has not changed and has led to several tax reforms based on including cash flow taxes in the resource sector (Australia and Canada) and a deduction for the imputed cost of equity financing such as in Croatia, Belgium, and Italy.

The important contribution of Auerbach, Devereux, and Simpson is that they make a case for a destination-based cash flow tax in order to deal with international issues, a point that received little attention at the time when the

[2] See, for example, Helliwell (1998) and Helliwell and McKitrick (1999) who suggest that investment and savings rates are correlated among countries although within Canada there is no such correlation. Recent deregulation in the European Union making it easier for investors to trade across member state boundaries will likely increase capital market integration.

[3] A perfect example of how arbitrage can lead to distortions in the corporate sector was the conversion of corporations into income trusts in Canada that led to 17% of the stock market being capitalized in the form of trusts that distributed most of their cash flows to their investors. The incentive to create an income trust was to eliminate the non-integrated part of the corporate income tax for taxable investors, tax-exempts, and foreign investors but at the cost of adopting a business structure which required taxable income to be fully distributed to minimize taxes. Further announced conversions by two large telecommunications companies led to government action to put a special tax on publicly traded trusts after 31 October 2006. See Mintz (2006). Arbitrage was especially driven by pension funds and foreign investors.

Meade Report was written. I will return to this point below as I do believe that good reasons exist for an origin-base approach but practicality would push governments to some extent to exempt exports and tax imports under a cash flow tax or value-added tax, which is similar except that payroll costs are included in the tax base.

1. THE PURPOSE OF THE CORPORATE TAX

Going back to the Canadian Carter report (Canada (1966)), the purpose of the corporate tax has been twofold: (i) to be a backstop to the personal income tax, and (ii) to tax foreigners on their income earned in Canada. The Canadian Technical Committee on Business Taxation (Canada (1997)) added the concept that the corporate profit tax could be a surrogate for user fees when such levies are not applied in full for administrative or equity reasons.

Under a rent tax, as developed by the Meade Report, the basic purpose of the corporate tax remains the same in principle. Taxing rents can arguably be more efficient by removing the inter-temporal tax distortion on investments. A corporate rent tax could still be required as part of the overall expenditure tax. Otherwise, the rents could accrue to individuals as exempt income. Similarly, to ensure that rents accruing to foreigners are taxed, a corporate rent tax is needed. And, to the extent that corporate rents reflect benefits from public services provided to firms and priced below cost, a rent tax would also be appropriate to apply.

I would argue that the globalization of production does not change much the purpose of corporate taxation, whether on rents or income. Design issues are much more complex with respect to administration and compliance, for sure, and Auerbach, Devereux, and Simpson are spot-on in emphasizing its importance. However, despite the challenges imposed, the traditional arguments for corporate taxation do not disappear.

2. ORIGIN VERSUS DESTINATION-BASE CASH FLOW TAX

The authors argue for a destination-base cash flow tax on the presumption that it is too difficult to levy one on an origin-base principle. The origin-base cash flow tax would apply to exports and allow imports to be deducted from the tax base—this is the approach being currently used for the Italian IRAP and Hungarian regional taxes (which do not allow payroll taxes to be deducted from the base). The alternative, a destination-based cash flow tax, exempts exports and taxes imports.

A destination-base cash flow tax has the virtue of withholding worldwide rents according to consumption while an origin-base tax withholds rents according to production.

As sales taxes (equivalent to cash flow taxes on payroll[4] and economic rents), the two approaches can be equivalent in economic effects under certain conditions so long as all goods are taxable and cross-border ownership of rents do not occur. Under an origin-base tax, the exchange rate will be depreciated, reflecting the tax on exports and deduction given for imports compared to the destination-base tax. Otherwise, they will have differential effects—for example, all goods may not be taxable and rents may be claimed by non-residents (see Lockwood, de Meza, and Myles (1994)).

As the authors note correctly, origin-base taxes could result in potential transfer pricing problems although this argument can be overstated. For some products such as oil and gas, the application of the comparable uncontrolled pricing method—or its alternatives—is not a serious problem since quality differences are easily observable and priced in markets. However, rents arising from research, marketing, and branding (intangible income) are much more difficult to price for related-party transactions within multinational groups since comparable transactions are difficult to find. A destination-base cash flow tax avoids the transfer pricing issues since transaction values with the rest of the world do not get included in the tax base. However, a country does give up the right to tax rents at source, which it might wish to do for other reasons as specified below.

While transfer pricing reasons might push governments to move towards a destination-based tax, other arguments can be made for an origin-based tax that would need to be considered. Below are three arguments for an origin-based tax.

3. THE CORPORATE TAX IN RELATION TO THE PERSONAL TAX

If the Meade Report recommendations for an expenditure tax are adopted, an important question is whether a business level tax is required to ensure that expenditure is taxed at the personal level.

[4] It is assumed here that labour is immobile among countries.

Under the expenditure tax, two approaches can be used to tax consumption. The first is to allow individuals to deduct savings invested in registered assets from the tax base and add the withdrawals from registered assets to the tax base. The second is to exempt the yield on savings—no deduction is provided for savings and no tax is imposed on withdrawals. A very important point raised in the Meade Report is that both approaches are useful to apply since they allow individuals to average their expenditure base given that a progressive rate schedule would be used for personal tax purposes.

The corporate tax on rents would not be required for the registered asset approach but would be needed for the non-registered asset approach. Otherwise, taxes on business rents could be avoided if people own assets that give rise to rents in the non-registered form. Given that the corporate rent tax would need to be applied on a source basis, such rents would be double-taxed for owners of registered assets while singly taxed for owners of non-registered assets. Thus, some form of tax credit could be considered for owners of registered assets as an offset for the corporate rent tax. Presumably, the tax credit could be provided using the Australian approach of providing a credit for dividends equal to the actual tax paid at the corporate level.

So far so good. However, the world is not so simple. As the three authors review, one issue is whether the corporate tax should be applied to only real transactions (R-base equal to revenue net of employment compensation and capital expenditures) or real and financial transactions (the R + F base would include borrowings added and repayments of interest and principal deducted from the tax base). If some technical complexities associated with financial derivatives are left aside, the R + F base is certainly feasible to consider and has even been subject to analysis for a VAT applied to financial transactions. A different variation of the approach—the tax imposed on profits net of an imputed deduction for equity—shows that a rent tax can be levied at the corporate level including on financial transactions.

A further issue is whether the rent tax should be applied generally to corporations, partnerships, trusts, and other types of businesses. Business income earned by individuals would be subject to tax under the personal expenditure tax but within the business sector, different entities are possible to create that would not be a corporation but effectively operate on a similar basis. Corporate organizations could also be developed to attract investors with different tax preferences. If some business organizational forms are tax-free under the rent tax, they have the capacity to issue securities to attract certain tax-preferred investors. A more general approach to rent taxation ensures a level playing-field among different types of business organizations. Again, as experience has recently shown in Italy and Hungary, business value taxes (Bird and Mintz (2001)) applied to rents and payroll could be applied generally to corporations, non-profits, partnerships, and trusts.

Can we ignore the linkage between the personal and corporate side? Even in a small open economy, the absence of a business level tax would provide significant opportunities for persons to avoid the expenditure tax by leaving rents in the business level. In particular, labour income, including employee profit-based compensation, could be structured as stock grants to avoid personal taxes on labour earnings. Further, entrepreneurs controlling private and public corporations obtain significant earnings from their corporate investments that should be subject to a personal cash flow tax. One could require rules to treat all forms of compensation as taxable earnings although a corporate rent tax makes sure the tax is applied generally.

A rent tax should therefore be applied in a neutral manner without providing special exemptions, tax credits, or other tax preferences to certain business activities to avoid tax. Otherwise, rents available for personal consumption could escape taxation. In this sense, the rent tax should be broad in application, a principle equally applicable to a corporate income tax.

The other important question is whether a personal cash flow tax needs to be applied on an origin or destination basis. An advantage of a cash flow tax on earnings, compared to a destination-base sales tax such as VAT, is that an individual's consumption, whether at home or abroad, will be captured with a tax on earnings rather than sales taxes withheld domestically by businesses.

If international transactions are excluded from the cash flow base either for personal or corporate purposes or both, some earnings could be exempt. Some might be able to arrange labour compensation in foreign jurisdictions that might be exempt from tax and those with earnings from businesses (sole proprietorships or partnerships) could earn foreign-source rents that would escape personal cash flow tax. To the extent that the cash flow destination-base approach applies only to corporate earnings, individuals with foreign-source labour earnings or rents could avoid the personal cash flow tax on this income by having the corporation, owned on a non-registered basis, earn it instead.

Thus, origin-base cash flow taxes might be preferable to apply if the concern is to withhold earnings that would otherwise be avoided at the personal level.

4. THE CORPORATE RENT TAX AS A WITHHOLDING TAX ON FOREIGN INVESTORS

In many countries, including the UK, some industries earn origin-based rents especially from irreproducible factors of production, such as natural resources, and perhaps, protection from competition. In some recent work, I have found that countries with especially high corporate receipts are those with financial and petroleum industries (Mintz (2007)).

The Meade Report recommended a cash flow tax as the least distortive way to tax business profits. It is also an efficient withholding tax on rents accruing to non-residents, especially for the North Sea oil and gas developments, using the R-base, which has been adopted for royalty systems in some countries, as already mentioned. For the financial industry, the R-base is inadequate—instead, a more general treatment including financial flows is required.

To withhold rents from foreigners, an origin-base cash flow tax is necessary since earnings from exports are taxed (with a deduction provided for imports). A destination-base cash flow tax that exempts earnings from exports (and provides no deduction for imports) will not withhold rents earned from domestic production that accrues to foreign owners. Thus, an origin-base cash flow tax makes sense in minimizing inter-asset, inter-industry, and inter-temporal distortions although firm location might be affected.

5. THE CORPORATE TAX AS A SURROGATE USER FEE

Governments provide public services—including infrastructure, municipal services, and even political stability (rule of law)—that are beneficial to businesses operating in the jurisdiction. As user fees may not be assessed or charged below cost, a business will obtain origin-base rents from the use of under-priced public services. Similar to the argument that a rent tax should apply to origin-base rents, both domestic and foreign-owned businesses should pay tax on the rents accruing from under-priced factors of production.

Clearly, compared to a user fee, the rent tax is inferior since it would be better to charge for the service so that businesses more appropriately compare marginal benefits and costs when using various inputs in production. When roads and bridges are provided free, for example, businesses could arrange their production further from markets to minimize costs by substituting distribution for production expenditures. However, not all public services are easily priced for administrative reasons and, politically, governments might wish to under-price some services anyway.

In the absence of a perfect user fee system, an origin-base tax would be useful for this reason as well.

6. CONCLUSION

A practical case could be made perhaps for a general destination-base cash flow tax (such as existing value-added taxes), as recommended by the authors, but it would have quite important implications for the personal tax system and the tax treatment of rents earned at source in a jurisdiction. Without the origin-base approach to a cash flow tax, individuals might look to shift their consumption and earnings to foreign jurisdictions, a problem, which at this point, is not as serious with migration limitations.

I suspect that countries will muddle through with their tax systems. If we moved to the full adoption of the Meade Report, an origin-base tax should at least be considered for a variety of reasons to withhold rents. Given the latest robust corporate income tax collections among OECD countries, it is unlikely that a major shift will occur towards taxing businesses on the destination principle for tax policy considerations at least yet.

REFERENCES

Bird, R. M., and Mintz, J. M. (2001), 'Tax Assignment in Canada: A Modest Proposal', in Lazar, H. (ed.), *The State of Federation 1999/2000*, 262–92, Kingston Ontario: Institute of Intergovernmental Relations, Queen's University.

Canada (1966), Royal Commission on Taxation (Carter Report 1966), *Report*, Ottawa: Supply and Services.

—— (1997), 'Technical Committee on Business Taxation', *Report*, Ottawa: Finance Canada.

Helliwell, J. (1998), *How Much Do National Borders Matter?* Washington, DC: The Brookings Institution.

—— and McKitrick, R. (1999), 'Comparing Capital Mobility across Provincial and National Borders', *Canadian Journal of Economics*, 32, 1164–73.

Lockwood, B., de Meza, D., and Myles, G. (1994), 'When are Origin and Destination Taxes Equivalent?', *International Tax and Public Finance*, 1, 5–24.

Meade, J. (1978), *The Structure and Reform of Direct Taxation: Report of a Committee chaired by Professor J. E. Meade for the Institute for Fiscal Studies*, London: George Allen & Unwin. http://www.ifs.org.uk/publications/3433.
Mintz, J. M. (2006), 'Income Trust Conversions—Estimated Federal and Provincial Revenue Impacts', *Canadian Tax Journal*, **54**, 687–90.
—— (2007), *The 2007 Tax Competitiveness Report: A Call for Comprehensive Tax Reform*, C. D. Howe Institute Commentary No. 254, Toronto: C. D. Howe Institute.
—— and Weichenrieder, A. (2007), 'The Indirect Side of Direct Investment: Multinational Company Finance and Taxation', manuscript, CESIfo (forthcoming MIT Press).
Organization of Economic Cooperation and Development (2006), *Statistics*.
US Treasury (1977), *Blueprints for Basic Tax Reform*, Washington, DC: Treasury.

10

International Capital Taxation

*Rachel Griffith, James Hines, and Peter Birch Sørensen**

Rachel Griffith is a Deputy Research Director at the IFS and Professor of Economics at UCL. Her research interests are in the area of empirical microeconomics and firm behaviour. She is a Director of the *Review of Economic Studies*, on the Council of the Royal Economic Society and the European Economic Association, and a Research Associate of the Centre for Economic Policy Research.

James Hines is Richard A. Musgrave Collegiate Professor of Economics at the University of Michigan, where he is also Professor of Law and Research Director of the Office of Tax Policy Research. His research concerns various aspects of taxation. He is a Research Associate of the National Bureau of Economic Research, Research Director of the International Tax Policy Forum, and Co-editor of the *Journal of Economic Perspectives.*

Peter Birch Sørensen is Professor of Economics at the University of Copenhagen and a Research Fellow at CESifo, Munich. He is also International Research Fellow at the Oxford University Centre for Business Taxation, a former Editor of the *FinanzArchiv* and former Co-editor of *International Tax and Public Finance.* His main research area is the economics of taxation and tax policy, and much of his research has focused on international taxation and capital income taxation. He is currently serving as President of the Danish Economic Council and the Danish Environmental Economic Council. He has also served as a consultant on tax policy for the OECD, the European Commission, the IMF and several national governments.

* This chapter was finalized in early 2008 and descriptions of policy reflect the position at that time. The authors would like to thank the editors, Julian Alworth, Alan Auerbach, Richard Blundell, Michael Devereux, Malcolm Gammie, Roger Gordon, Jerry Hausman, Helen Miller, Jim Poterba, and Helen Simpson for comments on various drafts of this chapter. All shortcomings and viewpoints expressed are the sole responsibility of the authors.

EXECUTIVE SUMMARY

Globalization carries profound implications for tax systems, yet most tax systems, including that of the UK, still retain many features more suited to closed economies. The purpose of this chapter is to assess how tax policy should reflect the changing international economic environment. Institutional barriers to the movement of goods, services, capital, and (to a lesser extent) labour have fallen dramatically since the Meade Report (Meade, 1978) was published. So have the costs of moving both real activity and taxable profits between tax jurisdictions. These changes mean that capital and taxable profits in particular are more mobile between jurisdictions than they used to be. Our focus is on the taxation of capital and our main conclusions may be summarized as follows.

Income from capital may be taxed in the residence country of its owner, or it may be taxed in the source country where the income is earned. Ideally one would like to tax capital income on a residence basis at the individual investor level, exempting the normal return to saving as measured by the interest rate on risk-free assets that savers require to be willing to postpone consumption. Such a tax system would not distort people's behaviour as long as individuals did not change their country of residence in response, and as long as one could correctly identify the 'normal' rate of return. However, imputing corporate income and in particular the income from foreign corporations to individual domestic shareholders is widely seen as infeasible, given the large cross-border flows of investment.

An alternative might be to levy residence-based taxes on capital at the firm level, taxing firms on their worldwide income in the country where they are headquartered. But such taxes are complex and are likely to be rendered ineffective as companies would find it relatively straightforward to shift their headquarters abroad to avoid domestic taxation. For these reasons, and because they want to tax domestic-source income accruing to foreigners, governments rely mainly on the source principle in the taxation of business profits. Unfortunately source-based capital taxes also distort behaviour since they can be avoided by investing abroad rather than at home.

International cooperation could reduce these tax distortions, but extensive cooperative agreements are unlikely to materialize in the near future, for several reasons. First, national governments are jealously guarding their fiscal sovereignty vis-à-vis the OECD and the EU. Second, the analysis in this chapter suggests that the potential gains from international tax coordination are likely to be rather small and unevenly distributed across countries. Third, while it might be thought that the European Court of Justice could help to ensure a more uniform taxation of cross-border investment in Europe, recent court rulings do not suggest that its practice will necessarily make EU tax systems less distortionary.

Against this background this chapter discusses what the UK could do on its own to make its tax system more efficient and robust in a globalizing world economy. As far as the taxation of business income is concerned, we argue for a source-based tax which exempts the normal return from tax. This can be implemented by allowing firms to deduct an imputed normal return to their equity, just as they are currently allowed to deduct the interest on their debts. The case for such an 'ACE' (Allowance for Corporate Equity) system is that, in the open UK economy, imposing a source-based tax on the normal return to capital tends to discourage domestic investment. This reduces the demand for domestic labour and land, thereby driving down wages and rents. Exempting the normal return to capital from tax would increase inbound investment, thus raising real wages and national income in the UK.

Our proposal for a source-based business income tax implies that UK multinational companies would no longer be liable to tax on their dividends from foreign subsidiaries. This would allow abolition of the system of foreign dividend tax credits for UK multinationals. It would also improve the ability of UK companies to compete in the international market for corporate control, since most OECD governments already exempt the foreign dividends of their multinationals from domestic tax. With an ACE to alleviate the double taxation of corporate income, the existing personal dividend tax credit should likewise be abolished to recoup some of the revenue lost. Dividend income would then be taxed at the personal level like other savings income.

Since one of the purposes of the personal income tax is to redistribute income, it should be levied on a residence basis to account for all of the taxpayer's worldwide income. In practice, a residence-based tax is not easy to enforce because of the difficulties of monitoring foreign source income. We argue that this problem may be reduced if Britain offers to share the revenue from the taxation of foreign source income with the governments of foreign source countries when they provide information to the UK tax authorities that helps to enforce UK tax rules. Nevertheless, in a world of high and growing capital mobility there is a limit to the amount of tax that can be levied without inducing investors to hide their wealth in foreign tax havens. In part because of the threat of capital flight, but for a number of other reasons as well, we argue that personal capital income should be taxed at a relatively low flat rate separate from the progressive tax schedule applied to labour income, along the lines of the Nordic dual income tax.

Our proposal for a UK dual income tax assumes that the UK government will wish to continue levying some personal tax on the normal return to capital. If policy makers prefer to move towards a consumption-based personal tax, the equivalent of such a system could be implemented by exempting the normal return to saving from tax at the personal level, just as the ACE allowance exempts the normal return at the corporate level. Specifically, a consumption-based personal tax system could be achieved by exempting interest income from personal tax, and by allowing shareholders to deduct an imputed normal return on the basis of their shares before imposing tax on dividends and capital gains. Exemption for interest income would reduce the problem of enforcing residence-based taxation. Owners of unincorporated firms would be allowed (but not obliged) to deduct an imputed return to their business equity from their taxable business income, in parallel to the ACE allowance granted to corporations. The residual business income would then be taxed as earned income.

10.1. INTRODUCTION

This chapter assesses the role of international considerations in tax design, emphasizing issues related to capital taxation. Globalization carries profound implications for tax systems, yet most tax systems, including that of the UK, continue to retain many features that reflect closed economy conceptions. The purpose of the chapter is to review the tax policy implications of economic openness, assessing how tax provisions may be tailored to reflect the changing international economic environment. The chapter also considers the role of international tax agreements.

Institutional barriers to the movement of goods, services, and factors of production, and the costs of moving both real activity and taxable profits between tax jurisdictions have fallen dramatically since the Meade Report was published in 1978. It is now easier for firms to function across geographically distant locations, and cross-border flows of portfolio investment have increased substantially. These changes mean that both tax bases and factors of production are more mobile between jurisdictions. The political landscape has also changed. The extent to which national governments can unilaterally enact reform is constrained in a number of ways. As a member of the European Union, the UK is bound by the Treaty of Rome and the rulings of the European Court of Justice, and the large network of tax treaties fostered by the OECD also limits the extent to which individual countries can act on their own. Moreover, since the publication of the Meade Report theoretical advances have deepened our understanding of the strategic interactions between governments in tax setting behaviour, and empirical work has helped to highlight which of these theoretical considerations are most important.

Our focus is on the taxation of capital, which is widely held to be the most mobile factor. We start in Section 10.2 by taking a quick look at the current UK system of capital income taxation, seen in international perspective. In Section 10.3 we summarize some fundamental distinctions and results in the theory of capital income taxation in the open economy, and review some empirical evidence on how international investment and corporate tax bases respond to tax policies. We also consider how these policies have evolved in recent decades. While Sections 10.2 and 10.3 pay much attention to international market pressures on capital income taxes, Section 10.4 surveys various forms of international tax cooperation that may also constrain UK tax policy in the future. Against this background, Sections 10.5 and 10.6 discuss how the UK system of capital income taxation could be reformed to make it more robust and efficient in an integrating world economy.

10.2. THE UK TAX SYSTEM IN INTERNATIONAL PERSPECTIVE

The UK is a relatively open economy. Trade flows and inward and outward investment are large and growing and multinational firms account for a substantial amount of economic activity. Around 25% of domestic employment is currently in multinationals, with foreign-owned multinationals making up almost half of that, and about 50% of the shares in UK-resident corporations are now owned by foreigners (see Griffith, Redding, and Simpson (2004) for further discussion of the importance of foreign firms in the UK).

In this section we focus on three aspects of the UK tax system that are particularly important from an international perspective—the level of the statutory corporate tax rate in the UK compared to that in other countries, the taxation of the foreign earnings of UK-resident corporations, and the taxation of income earned in the UK by foreign investors. We also consider the role played by the network of bilateral tax treaties that Britain has signed.[1]

[1] In the UK the most important form of taxation of capital is the corporate income tax system, and that is our main focus here. There are also other forms of capital taxation, which include business rates, and at the individual level the council tax (a tax on property), taxes on financial assets (including pensions), capital gains tax, and taxes on inheritance. These are covered in other chapters of this volume. Auerbach, Devereux, and Simpson, Chapter 9, provides a detailed description of the

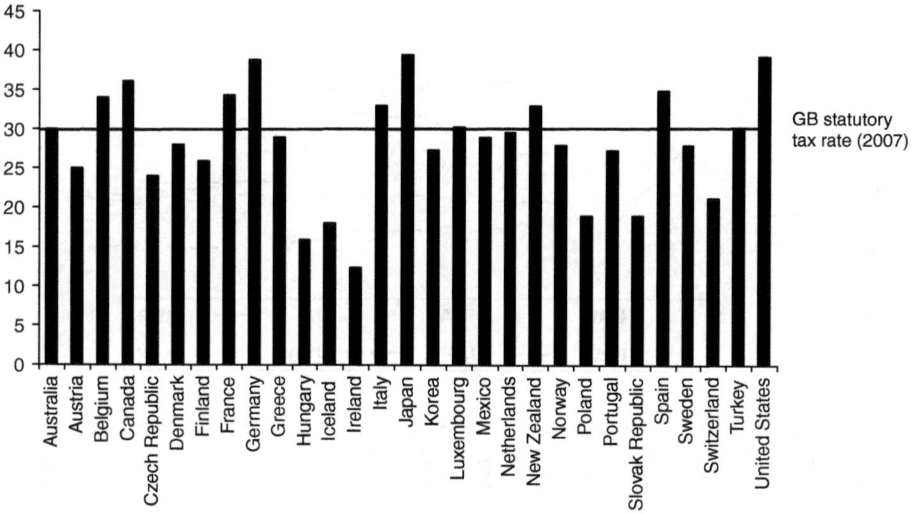

Source: OECD Tax Database.

Figure 10.1. Statutory corporate income tax rates, 2006–07

10.2.1. Corporate tax rates

In line with trends in other major economies, the statutory tax rate on corporate income in the UK has fallen substantially over the past two decades and currently stands at 28%. This lies above the (unweighted) average across OECD countries, but is the lowest amongst G7 countries (Figures 10.1 and 10.2).

At the same time as the tax rate was lowered, reforms have reduced the generosity of various allowances. This helps to explain why corporate tax revenues in the UK have held up so well, see Figures 9.3, 9.4, and 9.5 in Chapter 9.

The use of intangible assets created through R&D is a main activity of many multinational enterprises. As an exception to the trend towards reduced reliance on special allowances, the UK introduced an R&D tax credit for large companies in April 2002 which allows a 125% deduction of R&D expenditure from taxable profits.[2]

UK tax treatment of corporate income, and recent reforms. In this section we focus on those aspects of the corporate income tax system that are particularly relevant from an international perspective. It is worth noting that the provisions covering the taxation of international capital income are extremely complex and it is not possible for us to address their full complexity here.

[2] There is also an R&D tax credit for SMEs introduced in April 2000; the credit allows a 150% deduction from taxable profits, and is repayable to firms with no taxable profits.

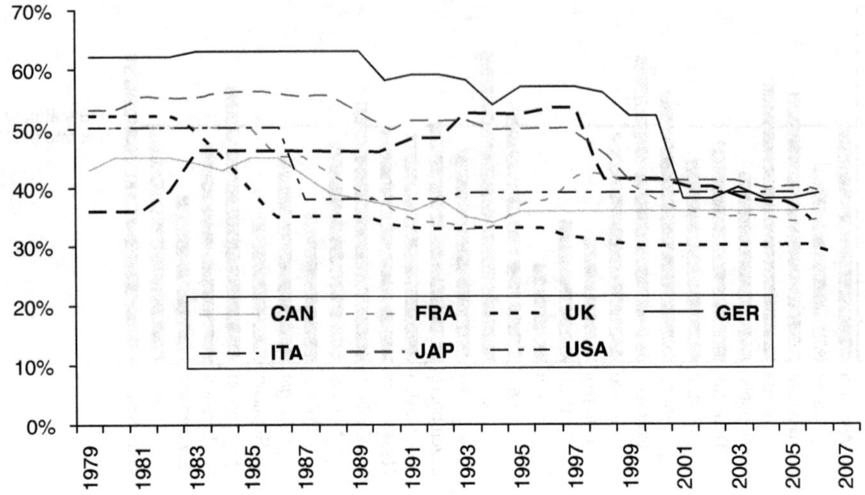

Figure 10.2. Statutory corporate income tax rates, G7 countries, 1979–2006

10.2.2. The tax treatment of foreign earnings of UK-resident corporations

The UK operates a worldwide system of corporate income taxation, which means that UK-incorporated companies are taxed on the total earnings from activities both in the UK and overseas. To avoid double taxation, UK companies are allowed to credit foreign taxes against their domestic tax liabilities. For example, if a UK firm has an investment in Ireland, it will pay corporate tax in Ireland at the Irish rate of 12.5%. When the profit is distributed as a dividend from the Irish subsidiary to its UK parent, the profit gross of the Irish tax is liable to UK corporation tax of 28%, but the UK gives a credit for the 12.5% paid in Ireland, so the tax bill due in the UK is 15.5%. The foreign tax credit is limited to the amount of liable UK tax on the foreign income, so if the foreign tax rate exceeds the UK rate, companies effectively pay the foreign tax on their foreign earnings.

Whereas the UK (along with the US and Japan) operates a credit system, most EU countries simply exempt dividends from foreign subsidiaries from the taxable income of domestic parent companies. Under an exemption system the foreign profits are thus only taxed in the foreign source country.

In general, resident companies are not subject to UK tax on earnings from their foreign subsidiaries until the profits are repatriated to the UK. However, reforms in 2000 and 2001 to the corporate tax regime for controlled foreign companies (CFCs) restricted the ability of UK-based groups to retain profits overseas without paying a full UK tax charge. The CFC rules mean that the retained profits of subsidiaries that are located in countries where the corporation tax is less than three-quarters of the rate applicable in the UK can be apportioned back to the UK and taxed as income of the parent.

Income from foreign subsidiaries may also take the form of interest or royalties. Since these items are normally deductible expenses for the foreign subsidiary, they are subject to UK tax in the hands of the UK parent company, with a credit for any withholding taxes paid abroad.

The CFC regimes in most OECD countries distinguish between 'active' business income and 'passive' income from financial investments. Typically the CFC rules are only applied to passive investment income retained abroad. By contrast, the UK CFC regime is based on an 'all-or-nothing' approach, applying to all of the income ('active' as well as 'passive') of the foreign subsidiaries falling under the CFC rules. The UK rules are seen by many observers as being fairly strict. In June 2007 the UK Treasury published some ideas for a reform of the regime for taxing foreign income, in part spurred by a recent ruling by the European Court of Justice on the UK CFC rules. In Sections 10.4.7 and 10.5.4 we shall return to this issue.

10.2.3. The tax treatment of UK earnings of foreign investors

Like many other countries, Britain imposes tax on income earned by foreign investors on capital invested in the UK. The profits of UK branches and subsidiaries of foreign multinational companies are thus subject to the UK corporation tax, and interest, dividends, and royalties paid to non-residents may be subject to UK withholding tax. However, withholding tax rates are constrained by EU tax law and by bilateral tax treaties. In particular, as a consequence of the EU Parent-Subsidiary Directive and the Directive on Interest and Royalties, no withholding taxes are levied on dividends, interest, and royalties paid to direct investors (controlling a certain minimum of the shares in the UK company) residing in other EU countries. In general, withholding tax rates on foreign portfolio investors tend to be higher than those on direct investors, but bilateral tax treaties frequently reduce withholding taxes to very low levels, indeed often to zero.

The average level of UK withholding tax rates on non-residents have tended to vanish in recent years. This is in line with a general international trend, illustrating the difficulty of sustaining source-based taxes on the normal return to capital in a world of growing capital mobility; a theme to which we shall return.

10.2.4. Tax treaties and the allocation of taxing rights

The UK has one of the world's largest networks of bilateral tax treaties with its trading partners. The benchmark for the negotiation of tax treaties is the *OECD Model Tax Convention on Income and Capital* which provides guidelines for the allocation of the international tax base between source and residence countries with the purpose of avoiding international double taxation. Since tax treaties typically reduce withholding tax rates on cross-border income flows significantly below the levels prescribed by domestic tax laws, a country with a wide-ranging network of tax treaties tends to become more attractive as a location for international investment.

The potential for international double taxation arises because national governments assert their right to tax income earned within their borders as well as the worldwide income of their residents. An investor earning income from abroad may therefore face a tax claim both from the foreign source country and from the domestic residence country. As far as active business income is concerned, tax treaties modelled on the OECD Convention assign the prior taxing right to the source country. According to the Convention, the residence country should then relieve international double taxation either by offering a foreign tax credit or by exempting foreign income from domestic tax. Importantly, residence countries using the credit method usually only commit to granting a credit for 'genuine' income taxes paid abroad. For example, the US government has signalled that it is not prepared to offer a foreign tax credit for cash flow type taxes paid abroad by US multinationals. Such a restriction on foreign tax credits may seriously reduce the incentive for foreign companies to invest in a country adopting a cash flow tax, thereby reducing the value of that country's network of tax treaties. In practice, this may be an important constraint on the options for tax reform available to the UK government.

A major issue in the assignment of taxing rights is how to allocate the worldwide income of multinational firms among source countries. According to UNCTAD, about one-third of international trade takes place between related entities in multinational groups, and the pricing of these transactions will determine how the total profit of the group is divided between source countries. The OECD Model Tax Convention prescribes that multinationals should apply 'arm's length' prices in intra-firm trade, that is, the prices charged should correspond to those that would have been charged between unrelated entities. The Convention leaves it to the domestic tax laws of the contracting states to detail how arm's length prices should be calculated. A main problem is that arm's length prices are often unobservable, since the specialized transactions within multinational groups frequently do not have a direct counterpart in the open market. For these situations the OECD has developed guidelines for setting transfer prices that will result in an 'appropriate' allocation of taxable profits between the related entities. However, these guidelines are often difficult to apply, and OECD member states do not always use identical formulae for calculating transfer prices. Moreover, when the tax authorities in one country have adjusted a transfer price that was deemed inappropriate, the authorities in the other country involved in the transaction do not always undertake an offsetting transfer price adjustment to ensure that profits do not get taxed twice, even though the OECD Model Tax Convention envisages such automatic adjustment, and the EU Arbitration Convention prescribes arbitration in the absence of agreement.

Because of the difficulties of defining arm's length prices, including appropriate arm's length royalty charges on intangible assets, multinationals will often have some scope for shifting profits from high-tax to low-tax countries by manipulating their transfer prices. At the same time the uncertainty whether tax administrators will accept a given transfer price adds to the investor risk of doing international business, and growing demands on multinationals to document how they calculate their transfer prices raise the costs of tax compliance. For these reasons transfer pricing problems are a major concern for taxpayers as well as tax administrators. The issue is particularly important for Britain as the home and host of so many multinational enterprises. Against this background Sections 10.5.5 and 10.5.6 will discuss some reform proposals involving reduced reliance on arm's length transfer pricing in the allocation of the international tax base.

10.3. THE EFFECTS OF CAPITAL TAXES IN AN OPEN ECONOMY: THEORY AND EVIDENCE

10.3.1. Some fundamental distinctions

What are taxes on capital and who pays them?

Capital taxes include taxes on (the return to) business assets as well as taxes on saving such as those falling on interest, dividends, and capital gains on the various assets held by households. Most tax systems, including that of the UK, make a distinction for tax purposes between capital held by individuals and capital held in the corporate sector. For example, in the UK property that is owned by individuals is usually subject to council tax, while property that is owned by an incorporated firm is subject to Non-domestic (or Business) Rates.

A distinction to be made when considering any tax, which is particularly important when considering capital taxes, is between who the tax is *levied* on and who the tax is *incident* on. The incidence of all taxes ultimately falls on individuals in their capacity as capital owners, workers, and consumers. For a variety of reasons it may be preferable to levy the taxes at the corporate level (for example, it may be administratively cheaper to collect), but this does not tell us who ultimately pays the tax. For example, in the UK personal income taxes are generally collected from employers via the PAYE system, but we think of the incidence of this tax as falling on the workers, not the owners of the firm.

It turns out to be very difficult to identify which individuals capital taxes are incident on. Work dating back to the seminal paper by Harberger (1962) has tried to estimate the incidence of the different taxes. The idea developed by Harberger was that, in order to work out who bears the burden of a tax, we need to have an economic model that describes how the tax will affect factor and product prices, and how different individuals will respond to these changes in price.

Harberger showed that in a closed economy with both individually owned and corporate owned capital, a tax levied on corporate income is borne by all capital (both that owned by individuals and that owned by incorporated firms). This is because, in response to the tax capital migrates from the corporate sector to the non-corporate sector until the returns in the two sectors are equalized. Thus, the tax on corporate income does not fall on shareholders, but on all owners of capital.

This work was based on a number of assumptions that have since been relaxed in the literature. A recent paper by Auerbach (2005) provides an excellent summary of this literature. For our purposes here one of the key assumptions to be relaxed was that the economy was closed. The challenge that globalization and increased mobility poses for the UK tax system is that corporate income can arise in the UK that is derived from any combination of UK or foreign-resident individuals holding shares (or debt) in UK or foreign-resident firms that operate in the UK, abroad, or in a range of countries. In addition, tax changes in one location will lead individuals to move real and financial capital between locations and can affect where they report income from capital.

We return below to what the literature tells us about tax incidence, and thus optimal tax setting behaviour by governments, when we take these considerations into account. But before we do so, it is useful to make a few more fundamental distinctions.

Source and residence based taxes

A fundamental distinction in the open economy is that between source-based and residence-based capital income taxes. Under the *source* principle (the return to) capital is taxed only in the country where it is invested. Source-based taxes are therefore taxes on investment. Under the *residence* principle the tax is levied only on (the return to) the wealth owned by domestic residents, whether the wealth is invested at home or abroad. Since wealth is accumulated saving, residence-based taxes are taxes on saving.

In an open economy with free international mobility of capital, the two types of taxes have very different effects on the domestic economy and on international capital flows. A small open economy does not have any noticeable impact on the international interest rate or the rate of return on shares required by international investors. Hence the cost of investment finance may be taken as given from the viewpoint of the small open economy. If the domestic government imposes a source-based business income tax, the pre-tax return to domestic investment will have to rise by a corresponding amount to generate the after-tax return required by international investors. Hence domestic investment will fall and capital will flow out of the country until the pre-tax return has risen sufficiently to compensate investors fully for the imposition of the source tax. Thus the incidence of a source-based capital tax falls entirely on the immobile domestic factors of production (land and labour). However, domestic saving will be unaffected, since a source-based capital income tax does not change the after-tax return that savers can earn in the international capital market.

On the other hand, a residence-based capital income tax (based on the residence of the individual taxpayer) will reduce the after-tax return available to domestic savers, thereby discouraging savings, but will leave the before-tax returns unaffected. Since a residence-based tax has no impact on foreign-located investors it will not raise the cost of domestic investment finance, so domestic investment will be unaffected. This means that the incidence of the tax is on the owners of capital. With unchanged investment and lower domestic saving, net capital imports will have to increase.

Types of neutrality

One of the guiding principles of taxation is neutrality: a well-designed tax system should not distort decisions (except where intended to do so). When we are confronted with the complexity of the global economy an important question becomes—what forms of neutrality are we most concerned about?

A pure source-based tax gives us *capital import neutrality* (CIN)—investment into the UK is treated the same for tax purposes regardless of the country of origin. CIN is achieved when foreign and domestic investors in a given country are taxed at the same effective rate and residence countries exempt foreign income from domestic tax.

A pure residence-based tax gives us *capital export neutrality* (CEN)—investments from the UK are treated the same for tax purposes regardless of the destination. While consistent residence-based taxation ensures CEN, this type of neutrality may also be attained even if source countries tax the income from inbound investment, provided residence countries offer a full credit for foreign taxes against the domestic tax bill.

So far we have treated the residence of the corporation and residence of the shareholder as synonymous. However, cross-border investment has increased dramatically over the past few decades, and in most OECD countries a large fraction of the domestic capital stock is now owned by foreign investors.

Ownership may have important implications for the assets (in particular intangible assets) that are used, and thus the productivity of firms. From this perspective it is important that the tax system satisfies Capital Ownership Neutrality (CON), that is, that it does not distort cross-country ownership patterns. As we explain in Section 10.5.1, CON can be achieved if *all* countries tax on the residence principle (i.e. tax worldwide income) and use the same tax base definition *or* if they *all* exempt foreign income from domestic tax.

In Section 10.5 we return to discuss the choice between alternative methods of international double tax relief and their implications for the various types of neutrality.

Normal returns and rents

Another fundamental distinction is the one between taxes on the *normal return* to capital and taxes on *rents*. Rents are profits in excess of the going market rate of return on capital. For debt capital the normal return is the market rate of interest on debt, which will vary with the level of risk, and for equity it is the required market rate of return on stocks in the relevant risk class.

In a closed economy a tax on the normal return to capital will tend to reduce the volume of saving and investment (if the elasticity of saving with respect to the net return is positive). However, according to the traditional view a tax on pure rents will in principle be non-distortionary in a closed economy.

This view assumes that investors can vary the capital stock in a smooth and continuous manner. In such a setting taxes on infra-marginal profits, or rents, have no impact on investment levels. As long as there are positive profits to be earned, investors will continue to invest. Recent analysis, however, has considered the possibility of 'lumpy' investments where investors must either commit a large chunk of capital or none at all (Devereux and Griffith (1998, 2002)). In these models taxes on pure rents may affect both the composition and level of investment.

In an open economy a source-based tax on rents may also reduce domestic investment if the business activity generating the rent is internationally mobile, that is, if the firm is able to earn a similar excess return on investment in other countries. It is therefore important to distinguish *firm-specific* or *mobile* from *location-specific* or *immobile* rents. A source-based tax is non-distortionary only if it falls on *location-specific* rents. Location-specific rents may be generated by the exploitation of natural resources, by the presence of an attractive infrastructure, or by agglomeration forces (see Baldwin and Krugman (2004)), whereas firm-specific rents may arise from the possession of a specific technology, product brand, or management know-how.

10.3.2. Optimal tax setting behaviour

One of the best-known results in the literature on optimal tax setting behaviour states that in the absence of location-specific rents, a government in a small open economy should not levy any source-based taxes on capital.[3] As already noted, a small open economy faces a perfectly elastic supply of capital from abroad, so the burden of a source-based capital tax will be fully shifted onto workers and other immobile domestic factors via an outflow of capital which drives up the pre-tax return. In this process the

[3] This result was originally derived by Gordon (1986) and restated by Razin and Sadka (1991). These authors did not explicitly include rents in their analysis, but their reasoning implies that a source-based tax on perfectly mobile rents is no less distortionary than a source tax on the normal return, as pointed out by Gordon and Hines (2002). The prescription that small economies should levy no source-based capital income taxes is usually seen as an application of the Production Efficiency Theorem of Diamond and Mirrlees (1971) which states that the optimal second-best tax system avoids production distortions provided the government can tax away pure profits and can tax households on all transactions with firms.

productivity of the domestic immobile factors will fall due to a lower capital intensity of production. To avoid this drop in productivity, it is more efficient to tax the immobile factors directly rather than indirectly via the capital tax.

This suggests that if governments pursue optimal tax policies, we might expect to observe a gradual erosion of source-based capital income taxes in the recent decades when capital mobility has increased. However, the literature has identified a number of factors that may offset the tendency for source-based taxes to vanish.

First, if firms can earn location-specific rents by investing in a particular location, the government of that jurisdiction may impose some amount of source tax without deterring investors. Moreover, when location-specific rents co-exist with foreign ownership of (part of) the domestic capital stock, it may seem that the incentive for national governments to levy source-based capital taxes is strengthened, since they can export part of the domestic tax burden to foreigners whose votes do not count in the domestic political process (see Huizinga and Nielsen (1997)). Mintz (1994) and others have suggested that increases in foreign ownership may be an important reason why governments choose to maintain source-based capital income taxes.

A second point is that the prediction that source taxes on capital will vanish assumes that capital is perfectly mobile. In practice, there are costs of adjusting stocks of physical capital so such capital cannot move instantaneously and costlessly across borders. Since adjustment costs tend to rise more than proportionally with the magnitude of the capital stock adjustment, the domestic capital stock will only fall gradually over time in response to the imposition of a source-based capital income tax (see Wildasin (2000)). In present value terms, the burden of the tax therefore cannot be fully shifted onto domestic immobile factors, and hence a government concerned about equity may want to impose a source-based capital tax, particularly if it has a short horizon.

A third factor that may help to sustain a source-based tax like the corporate income tax is that it serves as a 'backstop' for the personal income tax. The corporation tax falls not only on returns to (equity) capital but also on the labour income generated by entrepreneurs working in their own company. In the absence of a corporation tax, taxpayers could shift labour income and capital income into the corporate sector and accumulate it free of tax while financing consumption by loans from their companies. Still, while it is easy to see why protection of the domestic personal tax base may require a corporation tax on companies owned by *domestic* residents, it is not obvious why it requires a source-based corporation tax on *foreign-owned* companies whose shareholders are not liable to domestic personal tax. However, as pointed out by Zodrow (2006, p. 272), if foreign-owned companies were exempt from domestic corporate income tax, it might be relatively easy to establish corporations that are nominally foreign-owned but are really controlled by domestic taxpayers, say, via a foreign tax haven. Hence the backstop function of the corporation tax may be eroded if it is not levied on foreign-owned companies.

Finally, even though it may be inefficient to tax capital income at source, the voting public may not realize that such a tax tends to be shifted to the immobile factors, so levying a source-based corporation tax may be a political necessity, since abolition of such a tax would be seen as a give-away to the rich, including rich foreign investors. More generally, if there are political limits to the amount of (explicit) taxes that can be levied on other bases, it may be necessary for a government with a high revenue requirement to raise some amount of revenue via a source-based capital income tax, even if such a tax is highly distortionary.

In summary, while the simplest theoretical models predict that source-based capital income taxes will tend to vanish in small open economies, there are a number of reasons why such taxes may nevertheless be able to survive the ongoing process of international capital market integration. In the next section we consider some evidence which is relevant for the debate on the viability of capital income taxes.

10.3.3. Empirical evidence on corporate taxation in the open economy

Since the corporate income tax is the most important capital income tax, we shall mainly focus on trends in company taxation. In particular, we ask: How do multinational companies react to international tax differentials? How do national tax policies try to take advantage of these company reactions, and how do the policies of different countries interact? Finally, how have corporate tax revenues evolved as a result of changing government policies and private sector reactions to these policies?

The response of real investment to international tax differentials

How responsive is the international location of real investment to differences in (effective) national tax rates, and has it become more responsive over time?

The main approach of studies addressing this question has been to estimate the sensitivity of firms to changes in tax regimes. Hines (1999) reviews this literature and concludes that the allocation of real resources is highly sensitive to tax policies.[4] Devereux and Griffith (2002) discuss these findings and the literature on which they are based. They conclude that, while there is some evidence that taxes affect firms' location and investment decisions, it is not clear how big this effect is. Thus, while we can say that tax policy is important, we are unable to say precisely how strongly international real investment will react to specific changes in national tax policies.

The reaction of ownership patterns to tax differentials

As we explain in Section 10.5.1, the productivity of the assets used by multinational companies may depend on who owns them. If inter-jurisdictional tax differentials distort the pattern of ownership, they may therefore reduce economic efficiency. Hines (1996) compared the location of investment in the US by foreign investors whose home governments grant foreign tax credits for federal and state income taxes with the location of investment by those whose home governments do not tax income earned in the US. Investors who can claim credits against their home-country tax bill for state income taxes paid in the US should be much less likely to avoid high-tax states. Hines found foreign investor behaviour to be consistent with this hypothesis, indicating that the tax system does in fact influence the identity of the owners of assets invested in a particular jurisdiction. Desai and Hines (1999) also found that American firms shifted away from international joint ventures in response to the higher tax costs created by certain provisions of the US Tax Reform Act of 1986.

Taxation and international income-shifting

By lowering their corporate income tax rates, individual governments may try to shift both real activity and taxable corporate profits into their jurisdiction. There is ample evidence that international profit-shifting does indeed take place, despite the attempts of governments to contain it via transfer-pricing regulations and rules against thin capitalization. Thus, using different methods of identifying income-shifting, Grubert and Mutti (1991), Hines and Rice (1994), Altshuler and Grubert (2003), Desai et al. (2004), and Sullivan (2004)

[4] Devereux, Griffith, and Klemm (2002), de Mooij and Ederveen (2003), and Devereux and Sørensen (2006) also provide reviews of this literature.

all find evidence of significant tax-induced profit-shifting between the US and various other countries. Weichenrieder (1996) and Mintz and Smart (2004) find similar evidence for Germany and Canada, respectively, and Bartelsman and Beetsma (2003) use a broader data set to support their hypothesis of tax-avoiding profit-shifting within the OECD area.

Strategic interaction in tax rate setting

In so far as growing capital mobility of capital increases the sensitivity of capital flows to tax differentials, one might expect the tax policy of individual countries to become more sensitive to the tax policies pursued by other countries. There is a small but growing literature that tries to estimate whether individual governments cut their own tax rate in response to tax-rate cuts abroad. Devereux, Lockwood, and Redoano (2002) find evidence of such strategic interaction in corporate tax setting in the OECD between 1992 and 2002 and in the EU-25 between 1980 and 1995. Besley, Griffith, and Klemm (2001) also found evidence of interdependence in the setting of five different taxes in the OECD between 1965 and 1997, with a stronger interdependence the greater the mobility of the tax base. However, interdependence in tax setting might not reflect competition for mobile tax bases; it could also be the result of 'yardstick' competition where politicians mimic each others' tax policies to seek the votes of informed voters, or it could simply reflect a convergence in the dominant thinking regarding appropriate tax policies, for example, a growing belief across countries that a tax system relying on broad tax bases combined with low tax rates is less distortionary. This literature still has far to go in distinguishing between these explanations.[5]

Tax exporting

As discussed above, a government seeking to maximize the welfare of its own citizens will be tempted to 'export' some of the domestic tax burden to foreigners through a source-based capital income tax. Ceteris paribus, one would expect the incentive for such tax-exporting to be stronger the

[5] There are also a number of papers that have looked at policy interdependence across sub-national governments. Brueckner and Saavedra (2001) find strategic interaction in local property taxes in cities in the Boston metropolitan area and Brett and Pinkse (2000) obtain similar results using business property taxes of municipalities in British Columbia (Canada). Buettner (2001) finds interdependence for local business tax across German municipalities, while Esteller-Moré and Solé-Olé (2002) study Canadian income taxes and find evidence of interdependence across Canadian provinces. A paper that specifically finds evidence of yardstick competition is Besley and Case (1995) using income tax data for US states.

higher the degree of foreign ownership of the domestic capital stock. Recent empirical evidence provided by Huizinga and Nicodème (2006) confirms this hypothesis. Using firm-level data from twenty-one European countries for the period 1996–2000, they find a strong positive relationship between foreign ownership and the corporate tax burden. According to their benchmark estimate, an increase in the foreign ownership share by 1% raises the average corporate tax rate by between a half and 1%. However, as this is the only study that we know of that reports this result, it remains to be seen how robust it is.

Trends in tax rates

Statutory corporate income tax rates have fallen substantially in most OECD countries over the last decades. This would seem to support the hypothesis that growing capital mobility and the ensuing international tax competition puts downward pressure on source-based capital income taxes. However, statutory corporate tax rates remain far above zero, and corporate tax bases in almost all OECD countries have also expanded, through reductions in the generosity of allowances. Thus the *effective* corporate tax rates have fallen, but by much less than the statutory tax rates (see, inter alia, Chennells and Griffith (1997), Devereux, Griffith, and Klemm (2002), Griffith and Klemm (2004), and Devereux and Sørensen (2006)). This finding is based on an analysis of 'forward-looking' measures which use the methodology developed by Auerbach (1983) and King and Fullerton (1984) on the basis of Jorgenson's (1963) user cost of capital.[6]

Trends in tax revenues

Forward-looking measures of effective tax rates seek to illustrate the effect of the tax code on the current incentive to invest. However, these measures may not fully capture all of the special provisions of the tax code which affect the incentives to invest in particular sectors or assets. Some studies have therefore focused on 'backward-looking' measures of effective tax rates based on actual revenues collected. The actual taxes paid in any given year will be a function of past decisions over investment, the profitability of those investments, loss carry forward, and a range of other factors. Thus it is not clear that backward-looking measures of effective tax rates are very meaningful for evaluating the

[6] This was further developed by Devereux and Griffith (1998). For an overview and discussion of different measures, see Devereux et al. (2002), Devereux (2004), and Sørensen (2004a).

effects of changes in tax rules on investment incentives, although they do of course provide information on the ability of governments to collect revenue from capital income taxes. The backward-looking measures do not show any systematic tendency for the overall effective tax rate on capital income to fall (see Carey and Rabesona (2004)). This is consistent with the fact documented in Devereux and Sørensen (2006) that corporate tax revenues have remained fairly stable and have even increased as a percentage of GDP in several OECD countries.

How can the buoyancy of corporate tax revenues be reconciled with the tendency for average effective corporate tax rates to fall? Using data from OECD national income accounts, Sørensen (2007) finds that, while the total profit share has remained fairly stable, the share of total profits accruing to the corporate sector has in fact tended to increase significantly in several countries during the last two decades. The evidence presented by de Mooij and Nicodème (2006) suggests that part of the increase in the corporate share of total profits reflects tax-induced income-shifting from the non-corporate to the corporate sector.

To sum up, there is evidence that the location of real investment, the cross-country pattern of company ownership and in particular the location of paper profits react to international tax differentials. There is also evidence that national tax policies are inter-dependent, although the extent to which this reflects competition for mobile tax bases is unclear. Further, statutory corporate tax rates have fallen significantly in recent decades and forward-looking measures of effective tax rates have also tended to fall, but corporate tax revenues have been stable or even increased. Thus source-based capital income taxes seem alive and well.

10.4. INTERNATIONAL TAX COOPERATION

What has been the experience with international tax cooperation, and what does it say about the prospects for greater cooperation in the future? Do countries benefit from international cooperation, and if so, how much do they benefit and what costs do they incur from the constraints that cooperative agreements necessarily entail? In this section of the chapter we consider these controversial issues. We start by discussing the case for international cooperation on tax policy. We then describe the most important international and European initiatives to coordinate national policies in the area of capital income taxation.

10.4.1. Non-cooperative tax setting and the case for tax coordination

Since the publication of the Meade Report a large literature on the non-cooperative tax setting behaviour of governments has developed. This literature has focused on the international spillover effects which national tax policies can have, and which are not accounted for when governments choose their tax policies solely with the purpose of maximizing national welfare. For example, if one country lowers its source-based corporate income tax, it may attract corporate investment from abroad, thereby reducing foreign national income and foreign tax revenues. When this spillover effect is not accounted for by individual governments, there is a presumption that corporate tax rates will be set too low from a global perspective.[7]

The problem may be put another way: From a global viewpoint the elasticity of the capital income tax base with respect to the (effective) capital income tax rate is determined by the elasticity of saving with respect to the net rate of return. This elasticity is often thought to be quite low. However, from the perspective of the individual country, the elasticity of the capital income tax base is greatly increased by international capital mobility when taxation is based on the source principle. To minimize tax distortions, individual countries will therefore tend to set a rather low source-based capital income tax rate even though global capital supply might not be very much discouraged if all countries chose a higher tax rate. If the marginal source of public funds is a source-based capital tax, as assumed by Zodrow and Mieszkowski (1986), the result will be an under-provision of public goods relative to the global optimum. Alternatively, if governments can rely on other sources of public finance and if there are no location-specific rents, as assumed by Razin and Sadka (1991), capital mobility will tend to drive source-based capital income taxes to zero, causing a shift of the tax burden towards immobile factors such as labour. From a global efficiency viewpoint this is likely to imply an excessive taxation of labour relative to capital if labour supply is elastic, and it may also imply greater inequality of income distribution, as capital income tends to be concentrated in the top income brackets.

The reasoning above underlies the popular view that growing capital mobility will trigger a 'race to the bottom' in capital income tax rates through ever fiercer tax competition. But non-cooperative tax setting need not always drive capital income taxes below their globally optimal level. As noted in

[7] Oates (1972) provided an early analysis of the effects of fiscal externalities. Gordon (1983) elaborated these ideas, and many others have since contributed to the literature. See Wilson (1999) for a survey.

Section 10.3.2, source-based taxes on location-specific rents may be a way of exporting some of the domestic tax burden onto foreigners, and since growing capital mobility tends to increase the foreign ownership share of the domestic capital stock, it strengthens the incentive for tax exporting through a higher corporate tax rate. Hence one cannot say a priori whether effective corporate tax rates will become too high or too low as a result of increased capital mobility.

At any rate, both tax competition and tax exporting imply international fiscal spillovers, and unless the two effects happen exactly to offset each other, the existence of these fiscal externalities provides a case for international tax coordination. If tax competition exerts the dominant effect, global welfare may be improved through a coordinated rise in corporate tax rates. By contrast, if the incentive for tax exporting dominates, there is a case for an internationally coordinated cut in corporate tax rates.[8]

The fiscal spillovers described above would vanish if capital income taxation were based on a consistent residence principle. Thus, one form of international tax cooperation could be measures such as international exchange of information that could help national governments to implement the residence principle. However, a pure residence principle would require source countries to give up their taxing rights which is hardly realistic.

10.4.2. The case for tax competition

The theoretical models predicting welfare gains from tax coordination implicitly or explicitly assume that governments are benevolent, acting in the best interest of their citizens. To put it another way, these models assume that government policy decisions reflect a well-functioning political process ensuring a 'correct' aggregation of voter preferences.

Proponents of tax competition typically challenge this assumption. They argue that, because of imperfections in the political process, governments tend to tax and spend too much, and that this tendency may be offset by

[8] It should be noted that fiscal spillovers arise because governments are assumed to deviate from 'marginal cost pricing', i.e. the marginal effective tax on a unit of investment is assumed to deviate from the marginal cost incurred by the government in providing public goods and services to firms. If the source tax on capital were simply a user fee reflecting the government's marginal cost of hosting investment, a substantial body of literature has shown that international tax competition in tax rates and infrastructure services could well lead to an efficient level and allocation of investment (for a brief survey of this 'Tiebout' literature, see Wildasin and Wilson (2004, section 3)). However, our discussion assumes that governments will typically need to mobilize some net fiscal resources from the corporate income tax rather than just using it as a pure benefit tax.

allowing international tax base mobility, since this will make it more difficult to raise public funds.

An early and rather uncompromising version of this sceptical view of government was presented by Brennan and Buchanan (1980) who claimed that policy makers basically strive to maximize public revenues and to spend it on wasteful rent-seeking activities that do not benefit the general public. In popular terms, the government is seen as an ever-expanding 'Leviathan' that needs to be tamed, and one way of 'starving the beast' is to allow inter-jurisdictional competition for mobile tax bases, since this will reduce the revenue-maximizing tax rates.

More moderate advocates of tax competition argue that, because of the importance of lobbying groups for electoral outcomes, and due to asymmetric information between bureaucrats and politicians regarding the cost of public service provision, there is a tendency for governments to give in to pressure groups and to accept low productivity in the production of public services, resulting in inefficiently high levels of taxation and public spending. The claim is that lobbyism and asymmetric information imply a bias in the political process in favour of bureaucrats and other special interests. Since tax base mobility increases the distortionary effects of taxation, it may be expected to harden voter resistance to higher tax rates, thus forcing politicians to pay greater attention to the welfare of the ordinary citizen rather than serving special interests. In this way it is believed that tax competition will reduce the scope for rent-seeking and increase public sector efficiency.

In addition to these general arguments in favour of tax competition, the academic literature has pointed out two political economy reasons why tax competition in the area of capital income taxation may be beneficial even in the absence of rent-seeking and special interest groups (see Persson and Tabellini (2000, ch. 12). The first of these arguments focuses on redistributive politics: when tax rates are set in accordance with the preferences of the median voter whose income is below average, the median voter's interest in redistribution tends to imply an inefficiently high level of capital taxation, since capital income is normally concentrated in the higher income brackets. By making it harder to overtax capital, capital mobility and the resulting tax competition may offset this tendency.

The second argument in favour of capital income tax competition assumes that governments have short horizons and that they lack the ability to pre-commit to the tax policy which is optimal ex ante, before investors have made their decisions to save and invest. If international capital flows are constrained by capital controls, the supply of capital to the domestic economy will be inelastic once wealth has been accumulated, giving short-sighted governments a strong incentive to impose heavy capital taxes ex post. Anticipating this political incentive, investors will hold back their investments, so investment will be suboptimal due to the (correct) expectations that capital will be overtaxed ex post. In these circumstances an opening of the capital account and the ensuing international competition for mobile capital income tax bases may improve the government's ability to commit to a low-tax policy, since capital mobility offers investors a route of escape from excessive domestic taxation, thereby strengthening the credibility of the government's ex ante promise that it will not impose punitive capital taxes.

An entirely separate line of thought supporting tax competition notes that conformity to a common tax system and common tax rates is unlikely to represent an optimal configuration of national tax provisions. To the degree that national tax differences reflect sensible and purposive choices in response to differing situations and political preferences, tax coordination threatens to undermine the benefits that such choices may offer.

10.4.3. Quantifying the potential gains from tax coordination

The discussion above suggests that neutralizing tax competition through international tax coordination involves an economic cost if fiscal competition reduces 'slack' in the public sector and if coordination reduces the scope for tailoring the tax system to particular national needs. But tax coordination could also create benefits by internalizing international fiscal spillovers and by reducing tax distortions to the cross-country pattern of saving and investment. If these benefits could be quantified, policy makers would have a better basis for judging whether tax coordination is on balance likely to increase social welfare.

Some recent studies have constructed computable general equilibrium models in an effort to quantify the potential welfare gains from tax coordination, assuming a well-functioning political process that does not allow rent-seeking. The TAXCOM simulation model developed by Sørensen (2000, 2004b) was designed to estimate the potential gains from international tax coordination on a regional as well as on a global scale, recognizing that coordination among a subgroup of countries such as the EU is more realistic than coordination among all the major countries in the world. The TAXCOM model allows for elastic savings and labour supplies, international capital mobility, international cross-ownership of firms and the existence of pure profits accruing partly to foreigners, productive government spending on infrastructure as well as spending on public consumption, and an unequal distribution of wealth providing a motive for redistributive taxes and transfers. In the absence of tax coordination public expenditures are financed by a source-based capital income tax and by (direct and indirect) taxes on labour income. Fiscal policies are determined by the maximization of a social welfare function which may be seen either as the objective function of a benevolent social planner who trades off equity against efficiency, or as the welfare of the median voter who has a personal interest in some amount of redistribution from rich to poor.

Because it incorporates location-specific rents, the model includes an incentive for tax exporting, but at the same time capital mobility provides an incentive for countries to keep their source-based capital income taxes low. With plausible parameter values, including a realistic foreign ownership share of the domestic capital stock, the TAXCOM model implies that tax competition will drive capital income tax rates and redistributive income transfers considerably below the levels that would prevail in a hypothetical situation without capital mobility.

Sørensen (2000, 2004b) uses the TAXCOM model to simulate a number of different tax coordination experiments. The bulk of his analysis focuses on tax coordination within the 'old' European Union (the EU-15), assuming that tax competition will continue to prevail between the EU and the rest of the world, and allowing for a higher degree of capital mobility within the EU than between the Union and third countries. The model is calibrated to reproduce the observed cross-country differences in income levels and in the level and structure of taxation and public spending. On this basis Sørensen (op. cit.) estimates the welfare effect of introducing a common minimum source-based capital income tax in the EU-15 that would maximize the population-weighted average social welfare for the EU, taking the policies of the rest of the world (mainly the US) as given. His simulations suggest that introducing such a binding minimum (effective) capital income tax rate would raise social welfare in the EU by some 0.2–0.4% of GDP per annum. The gain would be somewhat higher for the Nordic countries and for the UK where the initial effective capital income tax rates are estimated to be relatively high,[9] whereas it would be smaller for continental Europe where initial effective capital income tax rates are low. The US would also gain some 0.1% of GDP

[9] This is based on the backward-looking effective tax rates of the type proposed by Mendoza et al. (1994). The relative tax rates for the UK and, say, Germany basically reflect the differences in revenue collected from corporate income taxes, rather than differences in the statutory tax rates, which as Figure 10.1 shows are higher in Germany than in the UK.

from EU tax coordination, since such coordination would imply less intensive tax competition from Europe.

These estimates assume that countries are free to adjust all of their social transfers in response to the pressures from fiscal competition. The estimated gains are not pure efficiency gains; rather, they reflect that national governments have greater scope for pursuing ambitious redistributive policies when the pressures from tax competition are reduced. However, since important parts of the social security system have a quasi-constitutional character, they may be difficult to change in the short and medium term. When tax competition puts downward pressure on public revenue, it may therefore be easier for governments to adjust via changes in discretionary spending on public services. If changes in public revenues are reflected in changes in public service provision rather than in changes in redistributive transfers, the simulations presented in Sørensen (2004b) indicate that the social welfare gain from tax coordination will be about 1.5 times as large as the gains reported above. Moreover, in this scenario the estimated gain will tend to reflect a pure efficiency gain, as tax coordination helps to offset an underprovision of public goods.

One limitation of the TAXCOM model described above is that it does not capture the asymmetries in the tax treatment of the many different types of capital income. Moreover, the model lumps the smaller EU countries into regions and thus does not fully disaggregate down to the level of the individual small country. The more elaborate OECDTAX simulation model of the OECD area developed in Sørensen (2002) seeks to overcome these limitations. This model includes private portfolio choices, endogenous corporate financial policies, a housing market, a distinction between foreign direct investment and foreign portfolio investment, explicit modelling of the financial sector, and a detailed description of the tax system. In particular, the model distinguishes between the corporate income tax and the various personal taxes on interest, dividends, and capital gains, and it allows for the various methods used to alleviate the double taxation of corporate income in the domestic and international sphere.

Brøchner et al. (2006) have recently used an extended version of the OECDTAX model to simulate the effects of a harmonization of corporate tax bases and/or corporate tax rates in the EU-25. Owing to the existing differences in national corporate tax systems, the cost of corporate capital varies considerably across EU member states, thus causing an inefficient allocation of capital within the Union, as the tax differentials drive wedges between the marginal productivities of capital invested in different member states. A harmonization of corporate tax bases and tax rates would cause a cross-country convergence of the costs of corporate capital. Hence capital would be reallocated towards member states where investment yields a higher pre-tax rate of return, which in turn would raise aggregate income in the EU.

In the model the broadness of the corporate income tax base is captured by a capital allowance rate which is calibrated to ensure that the initial general equilibrium produced by the model reproduces the observed ratios of corporate tax revenues to GDP, given the statutory corporate tax rates prevailing in the base year (2004). In the simulation summarized in Table 10.1, the capital allowance rates and the statutory corporate tax rates are assumed to be fully harmonized across the EU-25, at levels corresponding to their GDP-weighted average values in the EU in 2004. In most countries corporate tax harmonization implies a change in total tax revenue. In Table 10.1 these revenue changes are assumed to be offset by corresponding changes in total transfers to the household sector, to maintain an unchanged budget balance.

The bottom row in Table 10.1 shows that complete harmonization of corporate tax rates and tax bases at their GDP-weighted averages across the EU would leave total tax revenue in the union unchanged while raising total GDP in the union by some 0.4%. This rise in total income is driven by an improved allocation of capital, as investment is reallocated from countries with relatively low to countries with relatively high pre-tax rates of return. However, total welfare (measured by the population-weighted average welfare of the representative consumers in each country) only rises by about 0.1% of GDP because the higher economic activity requires an increase in factor supplies (e.g. an increase in work efforts) which is costly in terms of consumer utility.

The modest magnitude of the overall welfare gain is explained by the continued existence of other tax distortions to the pattern of saving and investment across the EU. Even if corporate taxes were harmonized, tax rules for household and institutional investors would still differ across member states. In particular, the taxation of corporate source income at the shareholder level would continue to differ across countries. Moreover, a significant part of the total capital stock is invested outside the corporate sector, particularly in housing capital. Corporate tax harmonization is therefore not sufficient to equalize the marginal productivity of different types of investment across the EU.

Although the aggregate effects of corporate tax harmonization are quite modest at the EU level, the effects on individual countries are often much larger and rather divergent, as indicated in Table 10.1. At the individual country level, the effects are driven mainly by the change in the overall level of

Table 10.1. Effects of harmonizing corporate tax rates and tax bases in the EU

Member state	Change in GDP (%)	Change in welfare (% of GDP)	Change in total tax revenue (% of GDP)	Change in corporate tax rate (%-points)	Change in capital allowance rate (%)
Austria	0.4	0.1	−0.1	−1.4	5.6
Belgium	2.4	0.5	−0.1	−1.4	51.2
Denmark	1.3	0.2	−0.1	2.6	66.1
Finland	1.2	0.1	−0.1	3.6	83.5
France	2.0	0.3	−0.3	−2.4	43.7
Germany	−2.1	−0.1	0.4	−5.4	−52.1
Greece	0.6	0.1	0.0	−2.4	2.1
Ireland	−1.3	−0.2	0.8	20.1	13.7
Italy	1.1	0.1	−0.3	−0.4	30.3
Luxembourg	3.4	0.5	−0.7	2.2	218.3
Netherlands	2.3	0.3	−0.4	−1.9	60.9
Portugal	0.8	0.1	−0.2	5.1	62.3
Spain	0.0	0.1	0.0	−2.4	−6.1
Sweden	0.7	0.0	−0.1	4.6	52.5
UK	1.9	0.2	−0.6	2.6	134.3
Cyprus	−1.4	−0.2	1.3	17.3	−7.8
Czech Rep.	2.0	0.1	−0.5	4.5	144.4
Estonia	−2.6	−0.1	1.5	6.5	−71.3
Hungary	0.3	−0.2	0.1	16.2	173.6
Latvia	−0.2	0.0	0.7	17.3	107.7
Lithuania	0.1	−0.1	0.5	17.5	190.5
Malta	−1.4	−0.1	0.3	−2.4	−36.9
Poland	−1.3	−0.3	0.7	13.5	−19.7
Slovak Rep.	−0.9	−0.2	0.8	13.5	7.5
Slovenia	−1.9	−0.2	0.7	7.4	−44.4
EU25	0.4	0.1	0.0		

Note: Statutory corporate tax rates and capital allowance rates are harmonized at their GDP-weighted average levels in 2004. The harmonized corporate tax rate is 32.6%. Government budgets are balanced by adjusting income transfers.
Source: Brøchner et al. (2006).

taxation implied by corporate tax harmonization. In rough terms, countries which are forced to increase their effective corporate tax rate experience a drop in GDP and welfare, whereas countries that are forced to reduce the effective tax burden on the corporate sector tend to experience an increase in total output and welfare. This simply reflects the distortionary character of the corporation tax.

This analysis highlights some fundamental dilemmas for any policy of tax harmonization. On the one hand, harmonization cannot generate any aggregate efficiency gain from an improved allocation of capital unless national tax systems differ from the outset. On the other hand, these initial differences in national tax policies inevitably mean that tax harmonization creates losers as well as winners. As long as decisions on EU tax harmonization require unanimity among the member states, it is thus inconceivable that any agreement could be reached without some kind of compensating transfers from the winning to the losing countries.

But this points to another dilemma: any compensation scheme must identify winners and losers. If losers are defined as those countries where tax revenues fall as a result of harmonization, the implication would be that countries suffering drops in GDP (and welfare) would compensate countries with gains in GDP (and welfare). If, on the other hand, losers are defined as those countries where GDP decreases as a result of the reforms, the implication would be that countries suffering drops in tax revenues would compensate countries with gains in tax revenues. Both options would undoubtedly be hard to accept for policy makers.

A further dilemma arises from the fact that the (sometimes significant) changes in member state revenues implied by tax harmonization can hardly be absorbed without a noticeable impact on the internal distribution of income and welfare within EU countries. Presumably, this makes tax harmonization even more controversial.

In summary, recent quantitative studies based on computable general equilibrium models suggest that the aggregate economic welfare gains from tax coordination within the EU are likely to be rather modest, amounting perhaps to 0.1–0.4% of GDP. Moreover, the aggregate gain is likely to be quite unevenly distributed, with some countries gaining considerably and others facing substantial losses in GDP and welfare.

It should be noted that these estimates may understate the potential welfare gains from tax harmonization since they do not account for the reduction in compliance and administration costs that would follow from a harmonization of corporate tax rules across the EU. Moreover, the alternative harmonization scenarios considered by Brøchner et al. (2006) indicate that the overall gain from tax harmonization would be more evenly distributed across countries if changes in corporate tax revenues were offset by changes in labour income taxes, or if harmonization took place only among the EMU member countries (exploiting the opportunity for Enhanced Cooperation among a subgroup of EU member states provided by the Nice Treaty).

On the other hand, tax harmonization suppresses differences in national policy preferences as well as the ability of national governments to differentiate their tax systems in accordance with cross-country differences in economic structures. The estimates in Table 10.2 do not include the costs of this loss of national autonomy. In conclusion, there is no doubt that individual member states would be affected very differently by a complete harmonization of corporate taxes, so full harmonization seems highly unlikely under the current unanimity rule for tax policy decisions at the EU level. In the following we shall therefore focus on the less far-reaching attempts at international tax cooperation that have been made in the OECD and in the EU in recent years.

10.4.4. OECD initiatives against harmful tax practices

The most ambitious multilateral tax agreement to date is an effort of the Organisation for Economic Cooperation and Development (OECD), the statistical arm of the thirty wealthiest countries that also offers guidance on economic policies, including fiscal affairs.

In 1998 the OECD introduced what was then known as its Harmful Tax Competition initiative (OECD (1998)), and is now known as its Harmful Tax Practices initiative. The purpose of the initiative was to discourage OECD member countries and certain tax havens (low tax countries) outside the OECD from pursuing policies that were thought to harm other countries by unfairly eroding tax bases. In particular, the OECD criticized the use of preferential tax regimes that included very low tax rates, the absence of effective information exchange with other countries, and ring-fencing that meant that foreign investors were entitled to tax benefits that domestic residents were denied. The OECD identified forty-seven such preferential regimes, in different industries and lines of business, among OECD countries. Many of these regimes have been subsequently abolished or changed to remove the features to which the OECD objected.

As part of its Harmful Tax Practices initiative, the OECD also produced a List of Un-Cooperative Tax Havens, identifying countries that have not committed to sufficient exchange of information with tax authorities in other countries. The concern was that the absence of information exchange might impede the ability of OECD members, and other countries, to tax their resident individuals and corporations on income or assets hidden in foreign tax havens. As a result of the OECD initiative, along with diplomatic and other actions of individual nations, thirty-three countries and jurisdictions outside the OECD committed to improve the transparency of their tax systems and to facilitate information exchange. As of 2007 there remained five tax havens not making such commitments,[10] but the vast majority of the world's tax

[10] These tax havens are Andorra, Liberia, Liechtenstein, the Marshall Islands, and Monaco.

havens rely on low tax rates and other favourable tax provisions to attract investment, rather than using the prospect that local transactions will not be reported.

It is noteworthy that the commitments of other tax haven countries to exchange information and improve the transparency of their tax systems is usually contingent on OECD member countries doing the same. Given the variety of experience within the OECD, and the remaining differences between what countries do and what they have committed to do, the ultimate impact of the OECD initiative is still uncertain. Teather (2005, ch. 9) argues that the OECD initiative has essentially failed to achieve its objective of reducing tax competition from tax haven jurisdictions because of the reciprocity clauses securing that tax havens will not have to follow the OECD guidelines until all OECD member countries are forced to do likewise. On the other hand, the OECD (2006) reports considerable progress in commitments to information exchange, though there remain many gaps, particularly among tax havens.

There is substantial uncertainty over the effects of low tax rate countries, particularly tax havens, on total corporate tax collections. Multinational firms report that they earn significantly more taxable income in tax haven countries than would ordinarily be associated with levels of local economic activity (Hines (2005)). While this suggests that tax havens drain tax base from high tax countries, it does not necessarily follow that tax collections fall in high tax countries, since the existence of tax havens changes the dynamics of tax competition by permitting high tax countries to distinguish the taxation of activities that are internationally mobile (and benefit from using tax haven operations) from activities that are not. This, in turn, facilitates taxing immobile activities at high rates, thereby maintaining corporate tax collections above the levels that would prevail in the absence of tax havens (Keen (2001)). Evidence from American firms indicates that the availability of nearby tax havens encourages investment in high tax countries (Desai, Foley, and Hines (2006a)), which suggests that tax havens contribute to economic activity, and thereby tax collections, in high tax countries.

The type of tax coordination being considered here differs from that of the previous section. The main objective for many jurisdictions is to fight evasion and potential round tripping transactions. This has not been an issue of as much concern in the UK as in many continental European countries such as Germany, France, and Italy. In part this may be because the fairly strict CFC regime in the UK deals with this problem, or because the UK operates a credit system for taxing foreign source income, while the other countries operate exemption systems.

10.4.5. The EU code of conduct on business taxation

Like the 1998 OECD initiative, the EU Code of Conduct for business taxation—agreed by the EU Council of Ministers in December 1997—was aimed at tackling 'harmful tax competition'. The Code was designed to curb 'those business tax measures which affect, or may affect, in a significant way the location of business activity within the Community' (European Commission (1998)). The Code defines as harmful those tax measures that allow a significantly lower effective level of taxation than generally apply. For example, the criteria used to determine whether a particular measure is harmful includes whether the lower tax level applies only to non-residents, whether the tax advantages are 'ring-fenced' from the domestic market, and whether advantages are granted without any associated real economic activity taking place. Rules for profit determination that depart from internationally accepted principles and non-transparent administrative practices in enforcing tax rules are also considered to be harmful.

The EU's Finance Ministers initially identified 66 measures that were deemed harmful (40 in EU Member States, 3 in Gibraltar, and 23 in dependent or associated territories), most of which were targeted towards financial services, offshore companies, and services provided within multinational groups. Under the Code, countries commit not to introduce new harmful measures (under a 'standstill' provision) and to examine their existing laws with a view to eliminating any harmful measures (the 'rollback' provision). Member states were committed to removing any harmful measures by the end of 2005, but some extensions for defined periods of time beyond 2005 have been granted.

The Code of Conduct Group established by the EU Council of Finance Ministers has been monitoring the standstill and the implementation of rollback under the Code and has reported regularly to the Council. Although the Code is not a legally binding document but rather a kind of gentlemen's agreement among the Finance Ministers, it does seem to have had some political effect in restraining the use of preferential tax regimes for particular sectors or activities.

The idea of the Code of Conduct is that if a country decides to reduce its level of business income tax, the tax cut should apply to the entire corporate sector and not just to those activities that are believed to be particularly mobile internationally. In this way the Code intends to increase the (revenue) cost to individual member states of engaging in international tax competition and to avoid intersectoral distortions to the pattern of business activity.

A recent theoretical literature has studied whether a ban on preferential tax treatment of the more mobile business activities will indeed enable national governments to raise more revenue from source-based capital income taxes.[11] In a provocative paper, Keen (2001) reached the conclusion that it will not. When countries are forced to impose the same tax rate on all activities, their eagerness to attract international investment will lead to more aggressive competition for the less mobile tax bases. In Keen's analysis, this will reduce overall tax revenue. In support of his argument that the Code of Conduct could intensify tax competition, Keen points to the example of Ireland. Under the Irish tax system prevailing until the end of 2002, manufacturing firms (mainly multinationals) paid a reduced corporate tax rate of 10%, whereas other firms (mainly domestic) paid the standard rate of 40%. When the Code of Conduct forced Ireland to move to a single-rate tax system, the country chose to impose a very low common rate of 12.5% from 2003.

However, Keen (2001) assumed that the aggregate international tax base is fixed and hence independent of the level of taxation. Janeba and Smart (2003) generalize Keen's analysis to account for endogeneity of the total tax base. Thus they allow for the possibility that lower corporate tax rates in the EU could increase the aggregate EU corporate tax base. In this setting a ban on tax discrimination that leads EU countries to compete more aggressively for the less mobile tax bases could attract capital from outside the EU. As shown by Janeba and Smart (op. cit.), it then becomes more likely that restrictions on preferential tax regimes will raise overall tax revenue. Haupt and Peters (2005) also find that a home bias of investors (i.e. a preference for investing at home rather than abroad) makes it more probable that a restriction on tax preferences granted to foreign investors reduces the intensity of tax competition and raises overall tax revenue.

Moreover, none of these studies account for the loss of economic efficiency occurring when tax preferences to particular sectors channel additional resources into those sectors, thus driving the marginal productivity of factors employed there below the level of productivity prevailing elsewhere. Overall, then, it seems likely that the EU's Code of Conduct does in fact help to avoid a counterproductive distortion of resource allocation within Europe.

10.4.6. The EU Savings Tax Directive

After many years of difficult negotiations, the EU's Savings Tax Directive was finally passed on 24 June 2005, taking effect from 1 July 2005. The

[11] Eggert and Haufler (2006, Part 3) offer a full survey of this literature.

Directive seeks to prevent international evasion of taxes on interest income by requiring that all affected countries must either levy a withholding tax on all interest payments to EU residents or automatically report the amount of interest paid to the recipient's national tax authorities so that they can tax it themselves under the residence principle. For countries opting for a withholding tax, the required tax rate is 15% for the first three years of operation of the system, 20% for the next three years, and 35% thereafter. The withholding tax must be deducted from interest payments by the payer (whether a bank or other entity), and 75% of the revenue must be transferred to the investor's home government. The recipient of the interest income is entitled to a credit for the withholding tax from his residence country and may be exempt from the withholding tax if he provides for information on his foreign source interest income to be transmitted to his residence country.

The adoption of the Savings Tax Directive was made contingent on its adoption by ten dependent/associated territories of EU member states (in the Channel Islands, the Isle of Man, and the Caribbean) as well as by the main non-EU European tax havens: Switzerland, Liechtenstein, San Marino, Monaco, and Andorra. In response to considerable diplomatic pressure from several EU member states, all of these jurisdictions ended up accepting the Directive during 2003–04.

The long-term goal of the Savings Tax Directive is to establish automatic exchange of information among all EU countries, but member states may opt for the alternative of a withholding tax during a 'transitional period', which will expire if and when all the dependent territories plus the five non-EU European tax havens, as well as the US, have committed themselves to information exchange upon request. Within the EU, Austria, Belgium, and Luxembourg opted for a withholding tax rather than information exchange in order to preserve their strict bank secrecy rules. However, the rather high withholding tax rate of 35% to be imposed after the first six years and the requirement that 75% of the revenue be transferred to the residence country are designed to induce these countries to switch to information exchange in the long run.

The Savings Tax Directive aims to help EU governments to enforce residence-based taxation of capital income. Effective implementation of the residence principle allows individual governments to choose their own preferred level of taxation without inducing residents to invest abroad rather than at home (or vice versa). This approach to tax coordination has the attraction that it does not sacrifice national tax autonomy, in contrast to tax harmonization. Enforcement of the residence principle also puts serious limits on tax competition, since investors can no longer take advantage of lower tax rates offered abroad unless they change their country of residence. For many EU member states, this brake on tax competition was an important motive for supporting the Savings Tax Directive.

However, the effectiveness of the Directive is likely to be very limited, for several reasons. First of all, investors still have plenty of opportunities to channel their wealth to safe havens outside the scope of the Directive. For example, in 2003 Hong Kong and Singapore experienced a massive influx of capital, apparently from European sources, as the adoption of the Savings Tax Directive began to seem a realistic possibility.

Second, the Directive leaves several obvious loopholes which have earned it the nickname of the 'fools' tax' in some circles (Teather (2005, p. 96)). The Directive applies only to interest, but not to dividends. If interest income from an EU source is paid out to a company that does not reside in an EU country, and the company subsequently distributes its interest income as a dividend to an EU investor, the latter can escape taxation so long as his dividend income is not reported. By channelling their funds via companies established in third countries—including the EU's dependent/associated tax haven jurisdictions—EU residents can thus avoid tax by having interest income transformed into dividend income.

Indeed, it may not even be necessary to undertake such transformation of income since the bank or other interest-paying entity could make its payment to a trustee based in a non-EU jurisdiction. The trustee could then pass on the payment free of tax to the ultimate investor residing in an EU country. It has also been suggested that redeemable preference shares—the return on which is essentially equivalent to interest, but legally considered a dividend—could be used to circumvent the Savings Tax Directive.

There are several other ways of avoiding the tax in addition to those mentioned above.

Although the Directive does appear to increase the transactions costs associated with international tax evasion, the cost increase is probably not significant relative to the amounts invested by large wealth owners whose income was probably already sheltered from the effects of the tax (through trusts, foundations, companies, etc.). The very limited (additional) tax revenues that have so far been collected under the Savings Tax Directive seem to confirm the impression that it is not very effective. Thus it is hard to avoid the conclusion that the Savings Tax Directive in its present form is mostly a symbolic gesture rather than a serious attempt to enforce the residence principle of capital income taxation.

10.4.7. The European court of justice: implications for member state tax policies[12]

While the European Commission has had rather limited success in its efforts to influence the rules for direct taxation within the EU, the European Court of Justice (ECJ) is gaining increasing influence on the evolution of capital income taxation in the EU. Under the EU Treaty, member states retain competence in matters of direct taxation, and the adoption of common rules of taxation within the EU requires unanimous agreement in the Council of Ministers. However, the Treaty also prescribes that national tax laws may not discriminate between the nationals of different EU countries, and they may not violate the 'four freedoms' of the EU internal market, that is, the free movements of goods, services, capital, and persons and the related freedom of business establishment within the Union. In recent years the ECJ has defended these Treaty provisions with increasing vigour, by striking down national tax rules that were deemed to discriminate on grounds of nationality or to jeopardize one of the four freedoms. With respect to capital income taxation, there are four areas where the ECJ has been or is expected to be particularly influential.

Integration of personal and corporate taxes

Over the years most EU countries have sought to alleviate the domestic double taxation of corporate income either by granting an imputation credit against the personal tax on dividends for (part of) the corporation tax on the underlying profit, or by some other means such as a reduced personal tax rate on dividends. However, these tax benefits have typically been granted only to domestic holders of shares in domestic companies. For example, imputation credits have been granted only against personal tax on dividends distributed from domestic companies and have not been extended to foreign holders of domestic shares. In a series of cases, the ECJ has ruled that such practices impede cross-border investment and therefore violate the EU Treaty. To respect Community law, member states with an imputation system must also provide a tax credit on dividends paid by foreign companies to resident shareholders, even though such a credit represents corporate tax paid to another government. In response to this ruling by the ECJ, several EU countries (including France, Germany, Ireland, Italy, and the UK) have replaced their imputation systems by various systems involving preferential personal tax treatment of dividends from domestic as well as from other EU

[12] This section draws heavily on Bond et al. (2006).

sources (e.g. in the form of a reduced tax rate or a dividend tax credit applying to all dividend income).

International tax base allocation

In their efforts to counter profit-shifting to low-tax countries, governments apply transfer pricing rules and thin capitalization rules which have in some cases resulted in cross-border transactions being taxed more heavily than equivalent domestic transactions. In several such cases the ECJ has not accepted the grounds that member states have stated to justify their application of anti-avoidance rules. In response to this, some EU governments have reacted by extending the scope of their transfer pricing rules and thin capitalization rules to cover transactions among domestic affiliates of a corporate group. In formal terms, this implies that domestic and cross-border transactions are treated the same, even though the anti-avoidance rules are only needed in a cross-border context where the affiliated firms face different tax rates. It remains to be seen whether the ECJ will accept this response to its rulings which has the unfortunate effect of increasing tax compliance costs for purely domestic firms. It should be added that the decisions of the ECJ in the area of tax base allocation have not consistently gone against the revenue interests of governments. In 2005 Marks and Spencer brought a case against the UK government involving tax relief against UK corporation tax for losses that had been made by some of its European subsidiaries. The ECJ ruling greatly limited the circumstances in which losses made by an overseas subsidiary can be set against profits made by the parent company, so that the revenue implications of this decision for the UK Exchequer are not serious.

Controlled Foreign Companies

Controlled Foreign Company (CFC) rules allow governments to tax the income of overseas subsidiaries located in low tax regime countries on a current basis, that is, without deferring tax until the foreign income is repatriated to the domestic parent company. For example, the profits of a foreign company in which a UK resident company owns a holding of more than 50% are attributed to the resident company and subjected to tax in the UK, where the corporation tax in the foreign country is less than three-quarters of the rate applicable in the UK. The resident company receives a tax credit for the foreign tax paid by the CFC. The UK tax on profits retained by the CFC may be waived if the parent company can show that neither the main purpose of the transactions which gave rise to the profits of the CFC nor the main reason for the CFC's existence was to achieve a reduction in UK tax by means of diversion of profits (the so-called 'motive test'). Cadbury Schweppes challenged the legality of these rules as they have been applied to two subsidiaries located in Dublin and taxed under the favourable Irish International Financial Services Centre regime. In a much publicized ruling of 12 September 2006, the ECJ concluded that the EU Treaty precludes the UK from applying its CFC rules except in the case of 'wholly artificial arrangements' designed to escape normal UK tax. The Court found that the UK CFC legislation constitutes a restriction on freedom of establishment within the EU, since the CFC rules involve a difference in the treatment of resident companies depending on whether they fall under this legislation or not. The fact that a CFC is established in an EU member state for the purpose of benefiting from more favourable tax treatment does not in itself suffice to justify such a restriction on the freedom of establishment. With this ruling the effectiveness of CFC rules within the EU could be seriously weakened. CFC rules are mainly required to reduce the incentives for multinationals to shift profits into tax havens outside the EU. Nevertheless, restrictions on their application within the EU could have significant revenue implications for some EU governments, by making it easier for multinationals headquartered in high-tax countries to route profits through other EU countries that have less effective CFC legislation against non-EU tax havens.

Credit versus exemption

The EU's Parent-Subsidiary Directive allows member states to eliminate international double taxation of EU multinationals through an exemption system or via a credit system. Nevertheless, on the occasion of the so-called Franked Investment Income case brought before the ECJ, the Advocate General appointed by the Court expressed a non-binding Opinion in April 2006 concluding that the current UK system of international double tax relief appears to be discriminatory on the ground that dividends from foreign subsidiaries are liable to tax, whereas dividends from domestic subsidiaries are not. However, the ruling on 12 December 2006 of the ECJ in this case indicates that the UK can apply different methods of double tax relief to dividends received from domestic and foreign subsidiaries, provided these different methods result in comparable tax charges. The case has been referred back to the UK High Court to decide whether or not this applies. The uncertainty regarding the compatibility of the current UK foreign tax credit system with EU law has prompted the UK government to consider possible reforms to the taxation of foreign profits. One option for radical reform would be to replace the credit system with an exemption system. In Section 10.5.3 we discuss the arguments in favour of the latter system.

10.5. TAXING INTERNATIONAL INVESTMENT: SOME OPTIONS FOR REFORM

A basic policy choice in international taxation is that between residence-based and source-based taxation. This also involves the choice between the credit method and the exemption method of international double tax relief. Another important question is whether and how the worldwide profits of multinational enterprises can be allocated among the different source countries in a manner that avoids the transfer pricing problems described in Section 10.2.4.

This section of the chapter addresses these issues from a UK perspective, taking account on the international constraints on UK policy formation described in Section 10.4. We start by discussing the choice between alternative methods of international double tax relief and then proceed to discuss possible solutions to the transfer pricing problem.

10.5.1. International double tax relief: which form of tax neutrality is more desirable?

Section 10.3.1 explained the concepts of Capital Export Neutrality (CEN) and Capital Import Neutrality (CIN) in relation to the taxation of income from cross-border investments. If effective capital income tax rates were completely harmonized across countries, both CEN and CIN would prevail. When tax rates are not harmonized, so that a choice between the two forms of neutrality has to be made, it has usually been argued that, from a global perspective, CEN should take precedence over CIN, implying a preference for the credit method of international double tax relief. The reasoning is that when investors face the same effective tax rate on foreign and domestic investment, the cross-country equalization of after-tax rates of return enforced by capital mobility is achieved when the pre-tax rates of return are brought into line. In this way a regime of CEN will tend to equalize the marginal productivities of capital across countries, as required for maximization of world income.[13]

[13] This may be seen as another application of the Production Efficiency Theorem of Diamond and Mirrlees (1971) to international taxation. Strictly speaking, however, the Production Efficiency

The time-honoured concepts of CEN and CIN were developed by Richman (1963). She also pointed out that from a national as opposed to a global perspective, neither the credit method nor the exemption method of international double tax relief seems optimal. From the viewpoint of the individual country, the addition to national income generated by investment abroad is the rate of return after deduction for the foreign source country tax. To maximize national income foreign investment should only be carried to the point where its marginal return *after* payment of foreign tax equals the *pre-tax* marginal return to domestic investment. Since capital mobility tends to equalize after-tax rates of return, this national optimum is attained when international double taxation is (partially) relieved through the *deduction* method. Under this method the residence country taxes foreign income *net* of foreign taxes at the same rate as domestic income. Such a tax system is sometimes said to imply National Neutrality (NN), by making foreign and domestic investment equally attractive from a national perspective.

In a world with little explicit tax coordination it may seem surprising that national governments hardly ever use the deduction method of international double tax relief in the area of foreign direct investment (FDI).[14] Indeed, the trend in developed countries has been towards increased reliance on the exemption method for corporate taxpayers (see Mullins (2006)). However, as argued by Desai and Hines (2003), this trend may be easier to grasp once one recognizes the importance of ownership of the assets utilized in FDI.

Desai and Hines point out that the assets developed by multinationals through R&D, marketing, and so on are often highly specific, so the productivity of these assets may depend critically on who owns and controls them. From this perspective it is important that the tax system does not distort the pattern of ownership. Building on earlier work by Devereux (1990), Desai and Hines (op. cit.) therefore suggest that the concept of 'ownership neutrality' should carry at least as much weight in the evaluation of the international tax system as the traditional concepts of CEN and CIN. A tax system satisfies Capital Ownership Neutrality (CON) if it does not distort cross-country ownership patterns. CON may be attained if all countries in

Theorem is relevant in an international context only if national government budgets are linked through a system of international transfers, as shown by Keen and Wildasin (2004). The optimality of production efficiency also rests on the assumption that governments can tax away pure profits. If they cannot, global optimality requires a compromise between CEN and CIN, as demonstrated by Keen and Piekkola (1997).

[14] In the area of foreign portfolio investment the deduction method is implicitly used since residence countries impose domestic personal tax on the foreign-source dividends paid out of after-tax foreign profits.

the world practise worldwide income taxation with unlimited foreign tax credits and if they all apply the same definition of the tax base. Under such a regime of worldwide income taxation multinationals will acquire the assets that maximize their pre-tax returns in the different countries, since this acquisition policy will also maximize their after-tax returns. Hence assets will be held by those companies that would be willing to pay the highest reservation prices for them in the absence of tax, that is, by those companies that can utilize the assets most productively. However, the same result may be obtained if all residence countries *exempt* foreign income from domestic tax and if they apply the same rules regarding the deductibility of financing costs or writing-off of cross-border acquisitions. In that case companies from all over the world face the same effective tax rate in each individual country, so again the assets invested in each country will be held by those companies that can earn the highest pre-tax (and hence the highest after-tax) return on them.

The point is that if global ownership neutrality is the policy goal, the exemption system (also referred to as a *territorial* tax system) is just as attractive as a system of worldwide taxation with foreign tax credits. Moreover, if optimization of the ownership pattern is the overriding goal, the territorial system is actually the preferred policy from the *national* viewpoint of an individual country, as argued by Desai and Hines (2003). If a country practises worldwide income taxation, its multinationals will tend to earn a lower after-tax return on operations in a foreign low-tax country than will multinationals headquartered in countries that exempt foreign income. Assets invested in low-tax countries will therefore tend to be taken over by companies based in territorial countries, even if those assets could be used more productively by companies based in countries with a worldwide system. By giving up the worldwide system and switching to territoriality, a country will increase the reservation prices that its multinationals are willing to pay for assets located in foreign low-tax countries, enabling domestic companies to take over assets that they can use more efficiently than companies based in other countries.[15]

Thus a policy of exemption will maximize the after-tax profitability of domestic multinationals. A country seeking to maximize the sum of its tax revenue and the after-tax profits of its companies will therefore opt for the exemption system if such a system does not reduce domestic tax revenue

[15] As already mentioned, this assumes that the home countries of foreign multinationals do not offer special tax advantages that reduce the costs of acquisitions. In practice this assumption may not always hold. For example, it seems that one of the reasons why Spanish firms have outbid other companies in recent years is their ability to write off goodwill for tax purposes.

raised from domestic economic activity. This condition will be met if any increase in outbound investment triggered by the switch to territoriality is offset by an equally productive amount of new inbound investment from foreign firms. Desai and Hines (op. cit.) argue that increased outbound FDI will indeed typically be offset to a very large extent by additional inbound investment. They point out that the bulk of global FDI takes the form of acquisitions of existing firms rather than new greenfield investment. Thus most cross-border FDI seems to involve a reshuffling of global ownership patterns rather than involving a net transfer of saving from one country to another.[16] The active market for corporate control also suggests that asset ownership may have important consequences for business productivity. In these circumstances a policy of territoriality may come close to maximizing national welfare. In the terminology of Desai and Hines, a tax system that exempts foreign income from domestic tax may be said to satisfy National Ownership Neutrality (NON).

The focus on the importance of ownership and the concept of NON may help to explain the trend in the OECD towards greater reliance on the exemption system in recent decades where FDI has tended to grow relative to total economic activity. Apparently governments feel that the exemption system is better suited than the worldwide system to promote the global competitiveness of domestic multinationals.

The above discussion of neutrality in the taxation of foreign source income assumes that recorded company profits represent a return to capital. The perspective on tax neutrality changes if a major part of company profits is really a reward for entrepreneurial creativity and effort and thus a form of labour income. In that case a main challenge for tax policy is to design the company tax such that entrepreneurial labour income earned in the corporate sector gets taxed in roughly the same way as labour income earned outside the sector.

Economists have long struggled to explain the so-called equity premium puzzle; that is, the huge difference between the average return to corporate assets and the risk-free interest rate. For example, in the US the average corporate profit rate has historically hovered around 9% whereas the real interest rate on Treasury Bills has averaged around 1.5%. If the difference between these two rates of return simply represents the risk premium required by corporate investors, it would seem to imply an implausibly high degree of risk aversion. Gordon and Hausman (Commentary on this chapter) argue that

[16] Becker and Fuest (2007) demonstrate that in these circumstances the exemption system is in fact optimal from a national perspective.

the equity premium mainly reflects the return to the efforts and innovative talents of corporate entrepreneurs. This group may include owner-managers as well as many other high-level corporate executives who hold shares in the company for which they work.

Part of the equity premium may indeed constitute a return to the labour of corporate entrepreneurs, but it seems unlikely that the equity premium puzzle can be fully explained by this hypothesis. For example, conventional asset pricing models suggest that plausible degrees of risk aversion would imply an equity risk premium of around 2%. With a risk-free real interest rate of 1.5%, the total real required return on corporate assets would then be 3.5%, leaving a difference of 5.5% between the observed 9% corporate profit rate and the required return to capital. If this 5.5% differential is really labour income accruing to corporate entrepreneurs and top executives, such entrepreneurial income would absorb between 11% and 17% of total corporate value-added in the realistic case where the ratio of corporate assets to value-added is between 2 and 3. This income comes on top of the wages and salaries and the various forms of stock compensation granted to corporate executives, since these expenses are deductible from corporate profits and are therefore not included in the recorded 9% average corporate profit rate mentioned above. Hence it seems to us that if one interprets the observed equity premium as mainly the labour income of corporate entrepreneurs, one will have to assign an implausibly high share of total corporate value-added to these individuals.

Against this background we believe that the main part of the observed equity premium is in fact a return to capital, at least in the large public corporations accounting for the bulk of the activities of multinational enterprises. However, in small closely held companies a large part of recorded company profit may well be a return to the labour of corporate entrepreneurs. The proposals for personal income tax reform presented in Section 10.6 are designed with this fact in mind, including provisions that will prevent corporate owner-managers from transforming high-taxed labour income into low-taxed capital income.

10.5.2. Obstacles to capital export neutrality and the effects of deferral

While the exemption system and the worldwide system with a foreign tax credit are in principle equally effective in promoting ownership neutrality from a global perspective, the worldwide system and the associated property of CEN does have the additional attraction that it does not distort the international location of real investment. However, there are two important reasons why countries relieving international double taxation through a foreign tax credit system do not in practice achieve CEN. The first reason is that residence countries limit the foreign tax credit to the amount of domestic tax payable on the foreign-source income. Many credit countries limit their credits on a country-by-country basis ('credit by source'), but some countries, like the UK and the US, only impose an overall limit on the credit equal to the total amount of domestic tax payable on total foreign income ('worldwide credit'). The reason for the limitation on credits is that governments are not willing to allow taxes levied abroad to erode the revenue from tax on domestic-source income. In the absence of limits on foreign tax credits the governments of source countries could appropriate the revenues of residence countries through high source country tax rates without deterring inbound investment. Because of the limitation on credits, investors are subject to the higher of the foreign and the domestic tax rate, whereas CEN requires that they should always face the same tax rate whether they invest at home or abroad.

The second reason for the failure of CEN under real-world credit systems is that residence countries usually defer domestic tax on the active business income of foreign subsidiaries until this income is repatriated in the form of a dividend to the domestic parent company. Profits retained abroad are thus only subject to the foreign corporation tax, so for retained earnings existing credit systems tend to work like an exemption system.

A foreign tax credit system with deferral is essentially a tax on repatriations (when the foreign tax rate is below the domestic tax rate so the limit on the credit is not binding). Some years ago Hartman (1985) argued that for mature subsidiaries with sufficient earnings to cover their need for investment funds through retentions, such a tax will be neutral. To see the argument, suppose a subsidiary may either reinvest a profit of £100 at a rate of return of 10% after foreign corporation tax or distribute the profit to its parent company, in which case the parent will have to pay an additional net tax of 10% of the dividend to its home country. If the profit is distributed immediately, the parent will receive a net income of £90 after domestic tax. If the profit is temporarily reinvested abroad and then paid out with the addition of the 10% return after a year, the parent will at that time receive a net income of $110 \times (1 - 0.1) =$ £99. By postponing repatriation, the multinational thus earns a net return of $(99 - 90)/90 = 10\%$ which is identical to the net return obtainable in the absence of the repatriation tax. Thus, provided the repatriation tax cannot be avoided so that equity is 'trapped' in the foreign subsidiary, this tax will be neutral towards the subsidiary's investment and distribution policy. This is an application of the so-called 'new view' of dividend taxation in the international context.

However, Hartman's analysis applies only to mature subsidiaries. Sinn (1993) extended the analysis to cover the entire life cycle of a foreign subsidiary, starting from the time it is established. He found that the repatriation tax will induce the parent company to inject less equity into the subsidiary initially. Over time, the subsidiary grows by reinvesting its earnings, thus benefiting from deferral, but in the long run the subsidiary's capital stock ends up at the same level as it would have reached in the absence of the repatriation tax, and the tax again becomes neutral, as in Hartman's analysis. Grubert (1998) confirmed the validity of the Hartman–Sinn results even when alternative repatriation vehicles such as royalties may be used.

The studies by Hartman and Sinn were based on the new view of dividend taxation according to which investors have no non-tax preference for distributed over retained earnings. In practice such a preference may exist. For example, in an international setting where domestic investors may have difficulties monitoring the activities and investment opportunities of overseas subsidiaries, they may value distributions from a subsidiary as a signal of its profitability or as a means of preventing overseas managers from using the funds in a way that does not benefit shareholders. According to this 'old view' of dividend taxation investors trade off the non-tax benefits from distributions against the (additional) tax cost of paying dividends, and a tax on repatriations will then affect the investment and distribution policies of multinationals.

If the new view of dividend taxation is correct, the repatriation taxes collected under existing systems of worldwide corporate income taxes are essentially lump-sum taxes, generating revenue at zero efficiency cost. But if the old view comes closer to the truth, the revenue comes at the cost of distortions to foreign investment and repatriations. On the basis of US data, Desai, Foley, and Hines (2001, 2002) estimate that 1% lower repatriation tax rates are associated with 1% higher dividends from foreign subsidiaries. Grubert (1998) also reports estimates indicating that repatriations are quite sensitive to their tax prices. The fact that repatriation behaviour depends on taxation is evidence in favour of the old view of dividend taxation.

Over the years several observers (including Gravelle (2004)) have called for the abolition of deferral in order to move existing systems of worldwide income taxation closer to a regime of full Capital Export Neutrality. Provided parent companies do not change their country of residence, abolition of deferral would reduce distortions to real investment decisions, eliminate the distortion to repatriation decisions, and reduce the incentives for international income shifting through transfer pricing and thin capitalization.[17]

However, in a world where most countries rely on territorial taxation, a country practising worldwide income taxation does not achieve national ownership neutrality, as already explained. Moreover, if the UK were to abolish deferral, UK-based multinationals would have a strong incentive to move their headquarters to countries offering credit with deferral or tax exemption of foreign income, in order to maintain their international competitiveness. The outcome might be a substantial UK loss of corporate headquarters and a resulting drop in the incomes of the less mobile UK factors of production. For these reasons we do not recommend a UK move towards worldwide income taxation without deferral.

10.5.3. The case for a UK move to territoriality

Following an earlier proposal by Grubert and Mutti (2001), the US President's Advisory Panel on Federal Tax Reform (2005) recently advocated that the US should move to a territorial basis for taxation of corporate income by exempting dividends paid out of active foreign business income from US corporation tax. Under this proposal passive and highly mobile income such as royalties and interest from foreign affiliates would still be taxed in the US on a current basis (i.e. without deferral) and a foreign tax credit would still be granted for any foreign tax paid on such income. Interest expenses and general administrative overhead expenses incurred in the US in generating exempt foreign income would not be deductible from the US tax base. Such expenses would be allocated to foreign income on a prorated basis, say, depending on the share of worldwide assets invested abroad.

The US Tax Reform Panel gave the following main reasons for proposing a territorial system: (1) to reduce the administrative complexity associated with the foreign tax credit system, (2) to move towards Capital Import Neutrality/Ownership Neutrality in order to improve the competitiveness of US firms in foreign markets, (3) to remove the distortionary incentive to retain profits in foreign low-tax countries implied by the current US tax on repatriations, and (4) to eliminate certain possibilities for abusing the current US system of worldwide income taxation.

[17] Distortions to real investment and incentives for income shifting would not be fully eliminated as long as foreign tax credits remain limited to the amount of domestic tax liable on foreign source income.

The first three reasons stated above also seem relevant in a UK context. In June 2007 the Treasury and HM Revenue and Customs (HMRC) set out proposals aimed at creating a more straightforward regime for taxing the foreign profits of UK companies.[18] The main proposal was for the UK to move from its current system of taxing foreign dividends after giving a credit for taxes paid to foreign governments to a system in which foreign dividends are exempt from UK taxation. This would bring the UK in line with most other European countries. In addition, it proposed overhauling the way in which the government tries to discourage companies from shifting profits to subsidiaries in countries with lower corporate tax rates.

The analysis in Section 10.5.1 suggests that the ownership neutrality implied by a territorial system could help UK multinationals to make more productive use of their assets. The current UK taxation of foreign income discourages UK firms from investing in low-tax countries more than do the tax systems of the firms in territorial countries with which they compete. With a switch to territoriality, UK multinationals may relocate some of their overseas activities from foreign high-tax to foreign low-tax countries to take advantage of increased after-tax profitability.

At the same time UK companies may also relocate some of their domestic activities to foreign low-tax countries in response to a move to territoriality, resulting in reduced rewards to local (UK) fixed factors of production and reduced UK tax revenues. Territoriality may also provide increased scope for income shifting through transfer pricing and through manipulation of royalty payments to take advantage of the asymmetric taxation of dividends and royalties.[19]

The extent to which these behavioural effects would occur will depend on the extent to which deferral makes the current system of international double tax relief equivalent to an exemption system. Using data for US multinationals, Grubert and Mutti (2001) found that the sensitivity of foreign real

[18] 'Taxation of the foreign profits of companies' <http://www.hm-treasury.gov.uk/media/E/B/consult_foreign_profits210607.pdf>.

[19] Thus British parent companies would be able to reduce their worldwide tax bill by repatriating income from subsidiaries in foreign low-tax countries in the form of non-deductible dividends which would be tax exempt in the UK, rather than deductible royalties that would be taxable in the UK. Similarly, British multinationals would save taxes by receiving royalties rather than dividends from subsidiaries in foreign high-tax countries. Note that whereas the UK government loses revenue in the former scenario, it gains revenue in the latter case, so while global tax revenue goes down, the net effect on UK tax revenue is in principle ambiguous, depending on whether the intangible assets owned by UK multinationals are mainly used in foreign high-tax countries or in foreign low-tax countries. As already mentioned, a move to a dividend exemption system may induce British multinationals to move some of their assets to foreign low-tax jurisdictions, in which case part of the global revenue loss would be borne by the UK government.

investment location to host country tax rates and the tendency to shift income to low-tax jurisdictions is practically the same whether a US company faces a binding limitation on its foreign tax credits—in which case it faces the same tax rates as under an exemption system—or whether the limitation on credits is non-binding. Although these estimates are not directly transferable to the UK context, they do suggest that the behavioural effects of a switch to exemption may be limited.

What would be the revenue implications if the UK moved to a territorial tax system? This is a difficult question to answer, in part because there are no official estimates of the UK corporation tax collected on foreign-source income (net of tax credits), and partly because a switch to territoriality would affect revenue through changes in company behaviour that are hard to predict.

If we look at countries that operate exemption systems we do not see any evidence that they collect systematically less revenue from corporate taxes. Table 10.2 shows corporate tax revenue as a share of GDP and statutory tax rates for countries that operate some sort of credit system, and for countries that operate exemption systems, either as a general policy or as a policy towards tax treaty partners.

Grubert and Mutti (1995) estimated that the average US corporate tax rate on foreign-source income is only 2.7%. Since the UK corporate tax rate is lower than that in the US, it also seems likely that the UK Exchequer collects very little net tax on the foreign income of UK multinationals.

In any case, the revenue and behavioural effects of a switch to exemption would depend critically on the exact design of any new system, including the rules for allocation of overhead and interest expenses between domestic income and foreign exempt income. Most of the exemption countries included in Table 10.2 allow full deduction for such expenses against domestic-source income, even if some of them may have been incurred to generate foreign income exempt from domestic tax. Such a lack of expense allocation obviously strengthens the incentive for multinationals based in high-tax countries to establish affiliates in foreign low-tax countries. To counteract this incentive, some exemption countries only exempt a certain fraction of foreign income (typically 95%) from domestic tax, as shown in Table 10.2.

While a lack of expense allocation could turn an exemption system into a direct subsidy to investment in foreign tax havens, a mechanical rule for expense allocation could also imply excessive taxation in some cases. To illustrate, suppose that the total interest expense of a multinational group is allocated between domestic and foreign income according to the location of

Table 10.2. Corporation tax revenue and statutory tax rate, 2004

Tax treatment of foreign source dividends	Corporate tax revenue as % of GDP	Statutory tax rate	Deductibility of costs related to tax exempt foreign dividends	Amount of tax exempt dividends (%)
Credit system				0
Ireland	3.6	13	-	0
United Kingdom	2.9	30	-	0
Greece	3.3	35	-	0
Canada	3.5	36	-	0
United States	2.2	39	-	0
Japan	3.6	40	-	0
Exemption system				
Switzerland	2.5	25	Yes	100
Norway	10.1	28	No	100
Sweden	3.1	28	Yes	100
Finland	3.6	29	Yes	100
Denmark	3.2	30	Yes	100
Luxembourg	6.1	30	Yes	100
Belgium	3.8	34	Yes	95
Austria	2.3	34	No	100
Netherlands	3.2	35	No	100
Spain	3.5	35	Yes	100
France	2.7	35	Yes	95
Italy	2.9	37	Yes	95
Germany	1.6	38	No interest deduction*	95

* Full deductibility in case the foreign subsidiary does not distribute profits.

Source: Yoo Kwang-Yeol (2003).

assets, as proposed by Grubert and Mutti (2001).[20] A multinational with 50% of its assets in the UK and 50% of its assets abroad and a total interest expense of £10 million would then only be allowed to deduct £5 million of its interest expense against its UK income, even if all the expense were incurred by the UK parent company and did not in any way reduce the foreign tax liability of the group. Such a system imposes an implicit domestic tax on foreign income, since additional foreign investment reduces the domestic tax benefits of deductions for existing UK administrative and interest expenses. Hence one might expect numerous disputes between taxpayers and tax administrators over expense allocation, so some of the alleged benefits of an exemption

[20] A similar interest allocation rule is already used under the current US foreign tax credit system for the purpose of calculating the limit on foreign tax credits.

system in terms of simplification and reduced compliance costs might be lost. If the UK were to adopt stricter limits on interest deductibility than other exemption countries, this would also violate the national ownership neutrality which is a main theoretical benefit of the system.

For these reasons we sympathize with the suggestion by HM Treasury (2007, pp. 25–6) that the UK should not adopt a general interest allocation rule of the type described above in case of a move to territoriality. As an alternative the Treasury proposes that the total interest deduction claimed by the UK members of a multinational group should be restricted by reference to the group's total consolidated external finance costs. If the UK subgroup has higher finance costs than the overall external finance costs of the entire group, the Exchequer will see this as an indication that interest expenses have been allocated to the UK subgroup with the purpose of reducing the entire group's worldwide tax bill. It is difficult to assess the extent to which such an anti-avoidance rule might compromise the policy goal of ownership neutrality, but the rule does seem to be a legitimate attempt to protect the UK tax base.

Mullins (2006) expresses concern that a switch to territoriality in the current credit countries may intensify global tax competition. Table 10.3 documents the important role played by the US and the UK in global FDI. If these countries were to abolish their foreign tax credit systems, and if the credit system has so far counteracted the incentive for source countries to set low tax rates to attract investment, there could indeed be a significant additional stimulus to tax competition. While there is no evidence that tax competition has so far eroded the corporate tax revenues of OECD countries, there is some evidence that *developing* countries have had difficulties maintaining their corporate tax revenues in the face of the global trend towards lower statutory tax

Table 10.3. The level and composition of outward FDI

Home country	FDI outward stock in % of GDP	Share of worldwide FDI outward stock (%)	Location of FDI outward stock: Share (%) invested in		
			Developed countries	Eastern Europe	Developing countries
United States	17.2	20.7	70.5	0.7	28.8
United Kingdom	64.8	14.2	90.3	1.1	8.6
France	38.1	7.9	93.3	2.1	4.6
Germany	30.8	8.6	86.3	5.9	7.8
Japan	7.9	3.8	73.0	0.4	26.6

Source: Compiled from Mullins (2006, tables 3 and 4).

rates (see Keen and Simone (2004)). Since several of these countries already have fiscal problems, a further downward pressure on their revenues would be unwelcome, and unfettered tax competition among all countries in the world may not necessarily be desirable from a global viewpoint.

As already mentioned, however, there is some evidence from the US that the effects of the current credit systems on investment location and income shifting are not significantly different from those one would expect to see under an exemption system. This suggests that a switch to territoriality in the UK and the US would not intensify global tax competition and stimulate international profit shifting to any significant degree.

In summary, a UK move from the current foreign tax credit system to a dividend exemption system would tend to improve the competitiveness of UK-based multinational companies in the international market for corporate control of firms located in foreign low-tax countries. A move to territoriality would also eliminate the tax distortion to repatriation decisions generated by the current system of credit with deferral. However, while in principle the exemption system is simpler, it is not clear that simplicity is borne out in the recent proposals by the UK Treasury to combine dividend exemption with a reform of the UK regime for taxation of Controlled Foreign Companies. The following section describes and discusses these proposals.

10.5.4. Reforming the UK regime for taxation of foreign profits[21]

In June 2007 the Treasury and HM Revenue and Customs (HMRC) set out proposals aimed at creating a more straightforward regime for taxing the foreign profits of UK companies, including proposed reforms to the Controlled Foreign Company (CFC) regime.[22]

The current 'Controlled Foreign Company' (CFC) regime

The UK normally taxes the profits of foreign subsidiaries only when they are remitted to the UK in the form of dividends. This means that UK multinational companies have the scope to defer UK taxation indefinitely by keeping the profits of their foreign subsidiaries offshore. To counter this the UK operates a Controlled Foreign Company (CFC) regime that limits the extent to which companies can defer UK tax by retaining profits offshore in a jurisdiction with a lower corporation tax rate.

[21] This section draws heavily on Gammie, Griffith, and Miller (2008).

[22] 'Taxation of the foreign profits of companies' <http://www.hm-treasury.gov.uk/media/E/B/consult_foreign_profits210607.pdf>.

In broad terms, a company is treated as a CFC if it is resident outside the UK, is subject to a tax regime with a significantly lower level of tax than the UK (less than 75% of the tax rate applied in the UK), and is controlled by UK residents. In such cases the UK resident company is taxed on the proportion of the profits of the CFC which can be attributed to the UK by virtue of the size of its shareholding (provided that such profits account for at least 25% of the total profits of the CFC).

The UK CFC regime has also been subject to challenge before the ECJ. In the *Cadbury Schweppes* case, it was argued that the UK's CFC regime treated investments in subsidiaries in other EU countries less favourably than investments in domestic subsidiaries (because foreign profits were subject to immediate taxation in the hand of the parent but domestic profits were not). The ECJ decided that the CFC regime did infringe Community law in this respect, as it impeded foreign investment. But the ECJ recognized that the UK might be able to justify its measures provided they were shown to be adequately targeted against attempts to avoid tax.[23]

Proposal for a Foreign Dividend Exemption

The Treasury and HMRC propose a dividend exemption system, whereby profits repatriated to a UK-resident company from abroad are not liable for UK corporation tax and therefore require no credit for tax paid overseas. The tax burden on foreign income would be determined by the corporate tax rate in the foreign jurisdiction where the overseas investment took place. The stated aims are to simplify the tax treatment of foreign profits, make the rules more certain and straightforward, and increase the competitiveness of the UK's tax system.

The proposed 'Controlled Company' regime

The dividend exemption system introduces an incentive for investors to move financial assets abroad to countries with a lower corporation tax rate, then to repatriate the returns as tax-free dividends and so benefit from the lower foreign tax rate. To protect the domestic tax base, the Treasury and HMRC propose replacing the existing CFC regime with a new 'Controlled Company' (CC) regime.

One of the big changes is that the current CFC regime applies to *entities* whereas the new CC regime applies to *income*. In order to understand

[23] Case C-196/04 *Cadbury Schweppes*.

the implications of this change it is first useful to define passive and active income. 'Active' income is income from commercial activities, while 'passive' income is mainly investment income such as interest, dividends (other than dividends flowing within the controlled group), royalties, and rents.

Under the CFC regime, both active and passive income are liable to UK taxation if a subsidiary is defined as a CFC. There are a series of exemptions from being defined as a CFC, including an exemption for active trading subsidiaries. Provided it does not compromise its exempt status, companies are able to mix passive with active income in a trading subsidiary (or trading subgroup) in order that the former goes untaxed in the UK.

In contrast, under the proposed CC regime all passive income would be liable to UK corporation tax. Most importantly, all of the passive income in 'active' subsidiaries would fall under the CC regime whereas this income is mostly not captured under the current CFC regime.

Alongside this there is a change to what is considered as passive and active income (although the terms active and passive income are not used in the existing system, the concepts are there). The biggest change is to treat mobile active income as passive income. 'Mobile' income is income that can be easily transferred to different parts of the company and can therefore be located outside the UK to reduce tax liability.

The controversial element of this proposal is the intention to tax 'active income to the extent that it is, in substance, passive income'. In particular, in the discussions that followed the publication of the proposals, it has become apparent that the Treasury and HMRC envisage this including income that is attributable to intangible assets (such as brands), even when they are employed in an active business. Under the new CC system, the passive income and mobile active income of a controlled subsidiary of a UK parent company would be apportioned to the UK parent and subject to UK tax on a current basis, with a credit for any foreign (and, presumably, UK) taxes paid.[24]

Another big difference between the regimes is that the current CFC rules apply to subsidiaries located in countries that have a tax rate that is 75% or less of the existing UK tax rate (so for the current UK rate of 30% this is 22.5%), while the new CC rules will apply to subsidiaries located in any jurisdiction.

[24] The apportioned income must represent at least 10% of the profits of the CC (a reduction from the 25% required under the CFC regime) before tax liability is triggered. Alongside this there are a series of exemptions for passive income that is the result of genuine active finance, banking, and insurance business.

An important feature of the proposed CC regime is that it applies to domestic as well as foreign subsidiaries of the UK parent, such that the passive income from UK subsidiaries would be treated the same as that from foreign subsidiaries. The implications for current UK corporation tax rules (e.g. for losses) of having the CC regime apply to domestic subsidiaries, the aim of which presumably resulted from concerns that the proposed CC regime would be incompatible with EU law unless it was extended to UK subsidiaries, were not explored in the Treasury's discussion document.

What impact might the proposed reform have?

A move from the current foreign tax credit system to a dividend exemption system should increase the after-tax profitability of UK multinationals by removing the disadvantage that they face relative to multinationals in other countries with exemption systems in the market for corporate control of firms located in foreign low-tax countries. A move to exemption would also eliminate the tax distortion to repatriation decisions generated by the current system of credit with deferral and move towards capital ownership neutrality. In practice how important these changes are depends in large part on the extent to which the current credit system is effectively an exemption system because of the ability to defer tax payments.

With regard to the details of the policy, the Treasury's proposed package appears to be handicapped by being designed to replicate an imperfect credit system by exempting some foreign dividends and moving from a CFC to a CC regime, rather than seeking real reform with a satisfactory policy underpinning. Actual exemption replaces effective exemption; foreign profits taxed under the current entity-based CFC regime are to continue to be taxed under an income-based CC regime; compliance with EU law would be secured by extending the CC regime to domestic transactions; and the system of interest relief would continue to subsidize foreign investment subject to some modest tightening of the rules.

At the very least it seems quite implausible that the measures would produce any real simplification in the system. In particular, given that the income-based CC regime (i) seems to have greater scope than the current entity-based CFC regime, (ii) extends to domestic situations, and (iii) requires detailed enquiry into the sources of a company's profits rather than the nature of the company itself, it is difficult to conclude either that it is administratively simpler or that it would be revenue neutral rather than revenue raising. At the same time the tightening of the existing interest deduction rules and the introduction of new interest restriction rules adds a further layer of anti-avoidance provisions to the plethora of anti-avoidance measures targeted at financing costs.

10.5.5. A common consolidated tax base for EU multinationals?[25]

Over the years the European Commission has made many proposals for coordination or partial harmonization of the corporate tax systems of EU member states. Although member states have adopted the directives on cross-border dividends, interest, and royalties which eliminate withholding taxes on such payments between associated companies in different EU countries, the more ambitious Commission proposals have failed to obtain the required unanimous support from member state governments.

In recent years the Commission has tried to promote the idea of introducing a so-called Common Consolidated Corporate Tax Base (CCCTB) for European multinational enterprises. Under a CCCTB system EU multinational groups could opt to have all of their EU-wide taxable profits calculated according to a common set of rules. This tax base would then be allocated across EU member states according to a common formula, and each member state would apply its own corporate tax rate to its apportioned share of the EU-wide tax base. Companies without international operations and multinationals not opting for the CCCTB would continue to have their profits computed and taxed according to the national tax rules of individual EU countries.

As mentioned in Section 10.2.2, current international tax law obliges the individual entities in a multinational group to calculate their taxable profits on a separate accounting basis, using different national tax rules, and to price intra-group transactions at arm's length, using the prices that would have been charged between independent parties. But because arm's length prices are so hard to identify for specialized products and services traded within multinational groups, taxation based on separate accounting becomes increasingly vulnerable to profit-shifting via distorted transfer prices as the volume of cross-border transactions within multinational groups increases. In reaction to this, national governments have introduced complex rules for the setting of transfer prices, and despite the efforts of the OECD to coordinate these rules, they sometimes differ across countries. Obviously this increases the costs of tax compliance for multinationals. The differences in transfer pricing rules also imply that national tax bases sometimes overlap,

[25] This section draws on Sørensen (2004c). See also McLure and Weiner (2000), Hellerstein and McLure (2004), and Weiner (2005) for a more detailed analysis of the issues involved in formulary apportionment of the corporate tax base.

whereas at other times the uncoordinated rules leave gaps in the international tax base.

Under a CCCTB, EU multinationals would no longer have to deal with all the different national tax rules within the EU. In particular, they would no longer have to deal with differing and sometimes inconsistent transfer pricing rules. Moreover, in principle the abolition of separate accounting would eliminate the possibility for multinationals to shift profits to low-tax countries within the EU through artificial transfer prices and thin capitalization.

However, the introduction of a CCCTB raises a large number of technical issues which are currently being scrutinized in a working group established by the Commission. One main issue is how to delineate those groups of companies whose income should be consolidated and apportioned among EU governments. Another important issue is the choice of the formula for apportionment of the tax base. One possibility would be to follow the practice under the state corporate income tax in the US where the tax base is allocated according to some weighted average of the proportion of the company's assets, payroll, and sales in each jurisdiction. But as shown by McLure (1980), the individual jurisdiction's corporate income tax is then effectively turned into a tax on or subsidy to the factors entering the formula for apportionment of the tax base.

If the corporation tax is really intended to be a tax on capital, it would thus seem natural to allocate the corporate tax base on the basis of the assets invested in the various countries. This raises another problem, however, since intangible assets—which are inherently difficult to measure—constitute an important and growing part of the total assets of many multinationals. In principle, one could calculate the value of a patented intangible asset by discounting the royalties paid for its use. But intra-company royalties and the associated asset value may be distorted as multinationals try to shift taxable profits from high-tax to low-tax jurisdictions. Thus, if intangibles are included, a system of formula apportionment based on asset values will be subject to some of the same transfer pricing problems as the current system of formula apportionment.

Moreover, the apportionment of profits would apply only to income generated within the EU, so separate accounting and the associated transfer pricing problems would continue to prevail for intra-company transactions between entities inside and outside the EU. This combination of formula apportionment within the EU and separate accounting between the EU and the rest of the world may have controversial implications. For example, suppose the US tax authorities decide to increase the transfer price of a product delivered from a US affiliate to its French parent company, thereby raising the affiliate's taxable profits in the US. Under current tax treaty principles, the French authorities should then undertake an offsetting downward adjustment of the taxable profits of the French parent company to prevent international double taxation. But under a European system of formula apportionment, a decision by France to reduce the (apportionable) profits of the French parent would also reduce the tax base of other EU countries, assuming that the French multinational operates on a European scale. Indeed, the main effect on the tax base may well be felt in the rest of Europe. A switch to a European system of formula apportionment could thus introduce a new and unwelcome type of fiscal spillover effect among EU member states.

From the viewpoint of the business community, one attraction of the Commission proposal for a CCCTB is that multinational companies can decide for themselves whether they want to subject themselves to the system. Presumably companies will only opt for the CCCTB if they can thereby reduce their overall tax bill, so introducing the system is likely to cause a revenue loss. From the viewpoint of tax administrators, a further drawback is that they will have to deal with the new system of CCCTB along with the existing national tax rules for companies not subject to the system. The coexistence of two different tax regimes—one applying to (some) multinationals and another one applying to all other companies—may also distort resource allocation within the corporate sector.

Thus, while the well-known problems associated with separate accounting and transfer pricing do provide a case for considering alternatives, the European Commission's proposal for a CCCTB raises a number of difficult technical and political issues.

10.5.6. Home state taxation versus a common consolidated tax base[26]

One obstacle to a CCCTB is the need for EU member states to agree on a common definition of the corporate tax base. As an alternative, Lodin and Gammie (2001) proposed a system of Home State Taxation (HST). Under HST EU multinationals are allowed to calculate the consolidated profits on their EU-wide activities according to the tax code of the residence country of the parent company. This tax base would then be allocated across member states through formulary apportionment, and each member states would apply its own tax rate to its allotted share of the base, as would be the case under a CCCTB. Hence the two systems raise the same technical issues of tax

26 This section draws on Sørensen (2004c).

base allocation, but from the perspective of national governments eager to maintain autonomy in matters of tax policy, the advantage of HST is that it does not require any harmonization. All that is needed is that member states mutually recognize the company tax systems of the other countries participating in the system (which could be only a subgroup of all EU countries). From the perspective of company taxpayers, one attractive feature of HST is that they will not have to familiarize themselves with a new common EU tax base and that the system is optional: no company will be forced to switch to the system, but those that make the switch are likely to experience lower tax compliance costs. Switching to a consolidated tax base will also enable companies to offset losses on operations in one country against profits made in another, and corporate restructuring within a consolidated group will meet with fewer tax obstacles (such as the triggering of capital gains taxation).

But the attractive flexibility of HST may also be its main weakness, since existing differences in national tax systems will continue to create distortions. In particular, unlike a CCCTB, HST will not attain Capital Import Neutrality and Capital Ownership Neutrality, since members of different multinational groups operating in any given EU country will be subject to different tax base rules if their parent companies are headquartered in different member states.

In auditing the foreign affiliates of the domestic parent company, the tax authorities of the home state will also depend on the assistance of the foreign tax administrators who may not be familiar with the home state tax code. Moreover, HST would invite member states to compete by offering generous tax base rules in order to attract company headquarters. Such competition would generate negative revenue spillovers, since a more narrow tax base definition in any member state would apply not only to income from activity in the home state, but to income earned throughout the EU (or the group of participating countries). Proponents of HST argue that the participating countries' mutual recognition of each others' tax systems will help to limit tax competition. However, any laxity in the auditing and enforcement effort of the home state tax administration would also have a negative spillover effect by reducing the revenues accruing to other member states, and such administrative laxity would seem hard to constrain through the mutual recognition of formal tax rules. Finally, the fact that companies may freely choose between HST and the existing tax regime is bound to create some loss of revenue as firms opt for the system promising the lowest tax bill.

For these reasons it is not obvious that Home State Taxation would be preferable to a Common Consolidated Tax Base, despite the greater degree of harmonization required by the latter system. The European Commission has in fact tried to promote HST as an option for small and medium-sized enterprises within the EU, but so far member states have shown little interest in the system.

10.5.7. Improving the current separate accounting regime

Realizing that Home State Taxation or a Common Consolidated Tax Base with formula apportionment may not be (politically) viable options for company tax reform, the European Commission has also taken some less ambitious initiatives to improve the working of the current system of tax base allocation based on separate accounting and the arm's length principle. Thus the Commission has persuaded EU member states to sign the Arbitration Convention designed to settle double taxation disputes relating to transfer price adjustments. As mentioned in Section 10.2.4, when the tax administration of one country adjusts a transfer price to increase taxable profits within its jurisdiction, the other country involved in the transaction between the affiliated firms does not always approve the new transfer price since the adjustment will typically reduce its tax base. Hence the multinational group may face some amount of double taxation of its total income. In such cases where member states fail to agree on a transfer price adjustment, the EU Arbitration Convention dictates a mandatory arbitration procedure. Unfortunately the Convention has not fulfilled expectations in the sense that relatively few cases reach the arbitration process. Hence there is a need for steps to make the arbitration procedure faster and less costly for taxpayers.

Partly in response to this need the European Commission has created the Joint Transfer Pricing Forum (JTPF), a consultative expert group established in 2002. One task of the JTPF was to propose measures that will make the Arbitration Convention work more smoothly. Another task has been the development of guidelines to promote so-called Advance Pricing Agreements whereby multinationals can obtain official approval of (methods of calculating) transfer prices before they engage in transactions. Finally, the JTPF has developed a Code of Conduct on Documentation intended to reduce the compliance burden for companies in relation to the documentation of their transfer prices. Overall the hope was that the JTPF could help to promote procedural changes and simplifications to the current transfer pricing regime that member states could adopt without the need for legislative initiatives, but so far progress in this respect has been slow.

An initiative that could potentially reduce the compliance burden for firms and the administrative burden for tax collectors would be the creation of a database with EU-wide data on arm's length comparable prices on various types of transactions. Such a database would ease the considerable burden for both tax authorities and multinationals related to finding and verifying comparables.

10.6. PROPOSALS FOR MORE COMPREHENSIVE REFORMS

In Section 10.5 we considered some options for reforming the taxation of cross-border income flows. In the present section of the chapter we present proposals for more comprehensive reforms of the UK tax system, motivated by the growing openness of the UK economy.

As emphasized in Chapter 9, a conventional corporate tax system tends to discriminate between corporate and non-corporate firms, between debt and equity finance, and between distributed and retained earnings. In addition, a source-based company tax tends to discourage domestic and inbound investment, as we explained earlier in this chapter. Below we present a proposal for a capital income tax reform that attacks all of these distortions. The proposal comes in two variants. The first variant assumes that UK policy makers wish to maintain a residence-based personal tax on the full return to capital. We refer to this variant as 'the income tax regime'. The second variant of our reform proposal assumes that policy makers only want to tax above-normal returns. This is referred to as 'the consumption tax regime'. Both regimes would exempt the normal return from tax *at the corporate level* through an Allowance for Corporate Equity (ACE). The difference between them is that the consumption tax regime would also allow a deduction for a normal return against the residence-based personal capital income tax. The following sections describe the proposals and the motivation for them in more detail.[27]

10.6.1. The rationale for an ACE in the open economy

The current UK corporate income tax falls on the full return to corporate equity invested in the UK, that is, the sum of the normal return and the 'pure' profit. Because it allows deductibility of interest payments, the

[27] To limit the scope of this chapter, we do not discuss more radical reform options such as the various cash flow taxes discussed in Chapter 9. The reform proposals presented here involve a less radical departure from current tax practices while still sharing some of the attractive neutrality properties of cash flow taxes.

current corporate tax system discriminates against equity finance. A so-called comprehensive business income tax (CBIT) like the one proposed by the US Treasury (1992) would end this discrimination by eliminating interest deductibility. Such a reform might have considerable merit in a closed economy, but in a small open economy like that in the UK it could cause significant problems. The prevalence of tax-exempt institutional investors holding debt instruments and the practical problems of enforcing residence-based personal taxes on interest income suggest that a large part of total interest income currently goes untaxed. By essentially introducing an interest income tax at source, the CBIT might therefore imply a significant increase in the cost of debt finance which could act as a strong deterrent to debt-financed inward investment.

As an alternative way of ensuring tax neutrality between debt and equity, we therefore favour the Allowance for Corporate Equity (ACE) proposed by the Capital Taxes Group of the Institute for Fiscal Studies (1991). Under the ACE system companies are allowed to deduct an imputed normal return on their equity from the corporate income tax base, parallel to the deduction for interest on debt. In this way the ACE seeks to avoid tax distortions to real investment and to ensure neutrality between debt and equity finance.

The theoretical case for an ACE in an open economy context follows from the analysis in Section 10.3.2. In that section we saw that, in a small open economy with near-perfect capital mobility, the burden of a source-based tax on the normal return to capital will tend to be fully shifted onto the less mobile domestic factors of production such as labour and land. Indeed, the domestic factors end up bearing *more* than the full burden of the source tax on capital, since the capital outflow generated by the tax reduces the productivity of (and hence the pre-tax return to) domestic production factors. The owners of these factors would therefore be better off if they paid the tax directly, since this would prevent the capital flight.

It is sometimes argued that since an ACE erodes the corporate income tax base, it creates a need for a higher statutory corporate tax rate which may induce multinationals earning mobile rents to flee the country so that domestic immobile factors will lose out anyway (see, e.g., Bond (2000)). However, since the owners of domestic factors already effectively pay the source tax on the normal return to corporate capital, there is no rationale for raising the statutory corporate tax rate to make up for the revenue loss from the introduction of an ACE. In the long term the abolition of the source tax on the normal return and the resulting stimulus to domestic and inbound investment will raise the pre-tax return to domestic immobile factors by *more* than the revenue loss from the ACE, so even if all of the lost revenue were recouped through higher taxes on these factors, their owners will still end up with higher net incomes than before. For this reason, and because of the opportunities for international income shifting through transfer pricing, we propose that the introduction of an ACE should not be accompanied by a rise in the statutory corporate income tax rate.

Apart from promoting domestic investment, the ACE has several other attractive features. One of them—originally pointed out by Boadway and Bruce (1984)—is that it offsets the investment distortions caused by deviations between true economic depreciation and depreciation for tax purposes. If firms write down their assets at an accelerated pace, the current tax saving from accelerated depreciation will be offset by a fall in future rate-of-return allowances of equal present value, since accelerated depreciation reduces the book value of the assets to which future rates of return are imputed. In fact, regardless of the rate at which firms write down their assets in the tax accounts, the present value of the sum of the capital allowance and the ACE allowance will always equal the initial investment outlay, so the ACE system is equivalent to the immediate expensing of investment allowed under a cash flow tax (Box 10.1).

Box 10.1. Investment neutrality under the ACE system

Under a conventional system of business income taxation, accelerated depreciation allowances distort the behaviour of firms as they effectively subsidize investment by allowing tax deferral. Accelerated depreciation can thereby induce low-productive investment that would not have been profitable in the absence of tax. On the other hand, if the depreciation allowed for tax purposes is less than the true economic depreciation of a particular asset type, the tax system will imply an artificial discouragement of investment in such assets.

One attractive feature of the ACE system is that it eliminates such distortions. Suppose, for example, that the tax code allows a company to bring forward 100 GBP of depreciation from year 2 to year 1, thereby reducing its tax liability in year 1 by 28 GBP (assuming a 28% tax rate). Since the retained profit reported in the company's tax accounts for year 1 is now 100 GBP lower, the base for calculating the ACE allowance for year 2 falls by a corresponding amount. If the imputed interest rate on equity is 10%, this raises the company's tax bill for year 2 by $0.28 \times 0.1 \times 100$ GBP. Furthermore, when the depreciation of 100 GBP is brought forward from year 2 to year 1, taxable profit in year 2 will increase correspondingly, triggering an additional tax bill of 0.28×100 GBP in that year. With a discount rate equal to the 10% interest rate imputed to the company's equity base, the net change

(cont.)

Box 10.1. (*cont.*)

in the present value of taxes paid by the company will therefore be

$$-0.28 \cdot 100 + \frac{0.28 \cdot (100 + 0.1 \cdot 100)}{1 + 0.1} = 0.$$

Thus the tax benefit from accelerated depreciation is exactly offset by the fall in the future ACE allowance, so the pace at which companies write down their assets does not matter for the present value of the taxes they pay.

Because an investment always triggers a total allowance (depreciation plus ACE) with the same present value as the initial investment outlay, the government in effect finances a fraction of the initial investment expense equal to the tax rate. This fully compensates for the fact that a similar fraction of the cash inflows generated by the investment is taxed away. Thus the ACE does not affect the profitability of investment, so companies will undertake the same investments as they would have carried out in the absence of tax.

Another attraction of the ACE is that the symmetric treatment of debt and equity eliminates the need for thin capitalization rules to protect the domestic tax base: since firms get a deduction for an imputed interest on their equity as well as for the interest on their debt, multinationals have no incentive to undercapitalize a subsidiary operating in a country with an ACE system. More generally, the ACE would solve the increasingly difficult problem of distinguishing between debt and equity for tax purposes. As explained in Chapter 9, financial innovations in recent decades have produced new financial 'debt' instruments allowing firms to take advantage of interest deductibility even though these instruments are in many ways equivalent to equity. Under an ACE system the base for the ACE allowance would be determined by a simple criterion that does not require the tax authorities to evaluate whether any given corporate liability is truly 'debt' or 'equity'. Under this criterion the ACE allowance would be imputed only to those liabilities on the company balance sheet to which no interest deduction is attached.

The neutrality properties of the ACE system will depend on whether the imputed rate of return on equity is set at the 'right' level. In principle it is not necessary to include a risk premium in the imputed rate of return, provided the tax reduction stemming from the ACE allowance is a 'safe' cash flow from the viewpoint of the firm (see Bond and Devereux (1995)). This requires full loss offsets, including unlimited carry-forward of losses with interest. With limitations on loss offsets, the imputed return should include a risk premium, but in practice the tax authorities would not have the firm-specific information necessary to choose the 'correct' risk premium. A practical solution might be to set the imputed rate of return equal to the average interest rate on UK corporate bonds, even if this would involve some sacrifice of tax neutrality (Box 10.2).

Box 10.2. Choosing the imputed rate of return under an ACE

A tax is neutral for investment and financing decisions if it falls only on the net cash flow to shareholders, since any investment behaviour that maximizes the present value of cash flows before tax will then also maximize the present value of after-tax cash flows.

The ACE system is in principle equivalent to such a neutral cash flow tax when the imputed rate of return equals the rate at which shareholders discount future ACE allowances: the system taxes cash returns to shareholders, but any injection of equity triggers a deduction of the same present value. For example, if shareholders inject an additional amount of equity E into the company, the company's ACE allowance will rise by the amount ρE in all future years, where ρ is the imputed rate of return to equity. If shareholders also discount the value of the future deductions at the rate ρ, the present value of the additional deductions under the ACE will be $\rho E / \rho = E$. In present value terms taxpayers thus receive exactly the same deduction as under a cash flow tax that allows them to deduct the amount E up front.

Thus, to obtain full tax neutrality under the ACE, the imputed rate of return must be equal to the rate at which shareholders discount the tax savings from the company's future ACE allowances. This discount rate will depend on the degree of riskiness attached to these tax savings. As a benchmark, consider a hypothetical case in which the tax law allows full loss offsets, meaning that companies can carry their losses forward indefinitely with an interest rate added, and that shareholders receive a tax credit for any remaining unutilized loss deduction in case the company goes bankrupt. In this case shareholders will receive the tax benefit from the ACE allowance with full certainty even if the company goes out of business, and so they will discount the tax savings from the ACE system at the risk-free rate of interest. To ensure tax neutrality, it is then sufficient to set the imputed rate of return equal to the risk-free rate proxied, say, by the interest rate on short-term government bonds.

In practice the tax law does not allow full loss offsets. In most countries business losses can only be carried forward for a limited number of years, and never with interest added, and unutilized losses existing when a firm goes out of business cannot always be offset against other taxable income. Hence there will be some risk attached to the deductions for ACE allowances. The risk will differ across companies depending on how much they are affected by the restrictions on loss offsets. A substantial part of the risk is likely to stem from the probability

(cont.)

Box 10.2. (*cont.*)

that the company goes bankrupt. This risk will be reflected in the rate of interest at which the firm can borrow, so setting the imputed rate of return equal to the interest on the company's long-term debt would presumably ensure rough neutrality of the ACE.

However, for administrative reasons it is necessary to use a common imputed rate of return for all companies rather than applying firm-specific rates (even if this involves some sacrifice of neutrality). In countries with a well-developed market for corporate bonds, the discussion above suggests that the average interest rate on such bonds would be a natural benchmark for choosing the imputed rate of return to equity under the ACE.

The ACE allowance is calculated as the 'normal' rate of return times the firm's equity base, defined as the difference between total investment and total borrowing. The present value of such an allowance equals investment minus borrowing. This in turn equals the net deduction to which the firm would be entitled under the source-based R + F cash flow tax discussed in Chapter 9. Thus the ACE system may be seen as a practical way of implementing an R + F tax which avoids some of the problems associated with the transition to a genuine cash flow tax.

An alternative to an ACE allowance could be to allow a deduction for an imputed return on the firm's total real asset base while at the same time abolishing the deduction for actual interest payments. The present value of such an 'asset allowance' would equal the firm's total real investment and would thus be equivalent to the deduction granted under the source-based R-base cash flow tax also discussed in Chapter 9.[28] Hence the choice between an equity allowance (ACE) and an 'asset allowance' involves some of the same issues as those involved in choosing between the R-base and the R + F base cash flow tax. We tend to favour the ACE over a real asset allowance because an R + F type tax includes the financial sector in the tax base.

10.6.2. The mechanics of the ACE and the transition from the current system

The ACE allowance is the product of the imputed rate of return and the company's equity base. Once the system is in place, the equity base for the current year may be calculated as follows:

[28] Bond and Devereux (2003) offer a formal analysis of the relationship between the ACE and the various cash flow taxes.

Equity base in the previous year
+ taxable profits in the previous year (gross of the ACE allowance)
+ dividends received
+ net new equity issues
– tax payable on taxable profits in the previous year
– dividends paid
– net new acquisitions of shares in other companies
= Equity base for the current year

In rough terms, the increase in the equity base from one year to the next stems from new equity issues plus equity formed via retention of after-tax profits. Note that, to avoid 'double counting', the acquisition of shares in other UK companies does not add to the equity base of the acquiring company since the purchase price of these shares will be included in the equity base of the company that issued the shares. Nor does the purchase of shares in foreign companies add to the equity base for tax purposes. Under the dividend exemption system proposed in Section 10.5.3, this treatment of foreign share purchases ensures that investments in foreign assets that do not attract UK tax will not erode the UK tax base. Note, however, that dividends received from foreign companies add to the equity base in so far as they are reinvested in the UK. This reflects the principle that all domestic investments—including those financed through reinvestment of income earned abroad—should qualify for the ACE allowance.

When a holding company finances investment in subsidiary companies by debt (or by a combination of debt and equity), its equity base calculated in the above manner will become negative, generating a negative ACE allowance and a corresponding addition to taxable profit. In this way the ACE system guarantees tax neutrality between debt and equity also for holding companies, since the negative ACE allowance offsets the amount of interest that the holding company is allowed to deduct from taxable profits. This ensures that holding companies have no tax incentive to finance acquisitions by debt rather than equity, since a switch between debt and equity finance does not affect taxable profits (provided the interest rate used to calculate the ACE allowance corresponds to the interest rate on the debt).

An important issue is how to calculate the initial equity base at the time of introduction of the ACE system. To minimize the revenue loss and to prevent windfall gains to the owners of 'old' capital already installed, we propose that the initial equity base be set equal to zero for tax purposes so that the ACE allowance would be granted only for *additions* to the equity base undertaken after the time of reform. As explained in Box 10.3, this transition rule may have to be supplemented by an anti-avoidance provision to prevent abuse.

Box 10.3. The transition to an ACE

To minimize the revenue cost of improved investment incentives, we propose that the ACE allowance be granted only for additional equity built up after the time of reform. Could a corporate taxpayer get around this transition rule and benefit from allowances on the existing equity by liquidating an existing company and starting up a new company in the same line of business? To evaluate this risk, it is useful to consider a simple example:

Suppose a company holds assets with a current market value of 100 when the ACE is introduced. Suppose further that the company earns a constant 10% rate of return on these assets; that it has no debt, and that the corporate income tax rate is 28%. If the company does not add to its equity base after the introduction of the ACE, it will receive no equity allowance under the proposed transition rule. It will then earn a constant after-tax profit of $(1 - 0.25) \times 10 = 7.2$ after the reform.

Suppose instead that the owners liquidate the existing company only to start up a new identical company right after in order to transform 'old' equity into 'new' equity that will attract the ACE allowance. Suppose in addition that the assets of the old company have already been fully written off in the tax accounts. Liquidation is normally treated as a realization of assets, so the old company will have to report a capital gain of 100 during its last year in business. This will be taxed at 28%, leaving 72 units of assets to be injected as equity into the new company. Given the assumed 10% rate of return on the business activity considered, the new company will thus earn a profit of 7.2. If the normal return imputed to equity is also 10%, the company's ACE allowance will be $0.1 \times 72 = 7.2$. Hence taxable profit will be zero, so the shareholders will end up with the same net profit as in the case where the old company stays in business.

If the business activity in this example earned a return above the imputed return under the ACE, say, 20%, it is easy to calculate that the after-tax return to shareholders would be 12.4% if the activity were carried out by a newly established company entitled to ACE allowance, whereas it would be 14.4% if the old company stayed in business. Thus there would be no incentive for tax avoidance through liquidations and new start-ups.

On the other hand, if the assets have not been fully written down in the tax accounts, the capital gains tax in case of liquidation will be smaller than indicated in our example, leaving some room for tax avoidance through the transformation of old into new companies after the introduction of the ACE. However, the scope for such behaviour will be limited by the transactions costs involved. There may nevertheless be a need for special anti-avoidance rules to ensure taxation of the revenue from liquidation in cases where an old company is wound up and replaced by a new one in the same line of business. In designing such rules, valuable experience may be gathered from Italy where transition to an ACE-type system (with a reduced tax rate on the normal return) was made in 1997 without offering any tax benefit to existing equity.

With such a transition rule the revenue loss from an ACE would be small over the short and medium term. Moreover, since the ACE ensures relief of the double taxation of dividends at the company level, the introduction of the system should be combined with an abolition of the existing personal dividend tax credit, that is, dividends should be subject to full personal income tax. This would further limit the revenue loss.

10.6.3. The 'income tax regime': a dual income tax for Britain

The ACE system exempts the normal return to capital from tax at the firm level because a source-based capital income tax tends to get fully shifted onto domestic production factors through the international mobility of capital. However, since individuals are much less mobile across borders than capital, there is no similar case for exempting capital income from tax at the level of the individual resident investors, assuming that all of their worldwide income can be taxed. In the next section we shall discuss some reasons why policy makers might nevertheless want to exempt the normal return from tax at the personal level (see also the extensive discussion by Banks and Diamond, Chapter 6 on the choice of the personal tax base), but in the present section we assume that the government wishes to include the normal return to saving in the personal tax base. We also assume that it wishes to impose a progressive tax on earned income. In such a setting we will argue that capital income should be subject to personal residence-based taxation along the following lines:

(1) All income categorized as 'capital income' should be taxed at a relatively low flat rate below the top marginal tax rate applied to earned income. Capital income would include interest, dividends, realized capital gains, rental income, and imputed returns to the assets of unincorporated firms. Ideally, an imputed return to owner-occupied housing should also be included, at least if deductibility for mortgage interest is allowed. To stimulate saving for retirement, policy makers may wish to leave the return to such saving out of the tax base, in line with current practice.

(2) If the corporate income tax rate is t^c and the top marginal tax rate on labour income is t^L, the capital income tax rate t^r should be set such that $(1 - t^r)(1 - t^c) = 1 - t^L$ to prevent tax avoidance through income shifting (see below).

(3) The owners of unincorporated firms should be allowed to impute a return to their business equity. This imputed return would be taxed as capital income, while the residual business income would be taxed as earned income. Proprietors who prefer to avoid the compliance cost of documenting their business equity may opt to have all of their business income taxed as earned income.

This proposal for a capital income tax reform involves a separation of 'capital income' from labour income. As elaborated in Chapter 6 on the personal tax base, economic theory provides no compelling reason why capital income should be taxed at the same rate as labour income. According to our proposal, the capital income tax rate should be flat and well below the top marginal tax rate on labour income, along the lines of the Nordic Dual Income Tax.[29] The UK tax system already includes an important element of dual income taxation, since the National Insurance contribution is not levied on capital income. From this perspective our proposal for a UK Dual Income Tax does not involve a radical break with current tax practice.

Our reasons for advocating a relatively low tax rate on capital income are pragmatic. One major reason is the high and growing international mobility of portfolio capital combined with the practical difficulties of enforcing taxes on foreign source capital income. The well-known 'home bias' in investor portfolios may enable the government to impose some amount of capital income tax without inducing a significant capital flight, but if the tax rate becomes too high, too many taxpayers may try to hide their assets from the domestic tax authorities by investing them abroad. The difficulty of collecting tax on foreign source income stems from the fact that source country authorities have little or no incentive to provide the necessary information to the authorities of the residence country. To improve this incentive, thereby

[29] The rationale for the Nordic Dual Income Tax is explored in Sørensen (1994, 2005a, 2005b) and Nielsen and Sørensen (1997). Sijbren Cnossen's preferred version of the system is described in Cnossen (2000). Elements of dual income taxation have been introduced in several European countries; see the survey by Eggert and Genser (2005). Variants of a dual income tax for Germany have recently been proposed by Sinn (2003, ch. 6) and by the German Sachverständigenrat (see Spengel and Wiegard (2004)). Keuschnigg and Dietz (2007) propose a 'growth oriented dual income tax' for Switzerland which combines an ACE with a flat personal capital income tax along the lines of our proposal. However, in contrast to our proposal, the tax system advocated by Keuschnigg and Dietz would require a distinction between the distributed and retained profits of non-corporate firms.

strengthening tax enforcement, we propose that the UK government should unilaterally declare that it will offer foreign source countries a share of the revenue from any UK tax collected on foreign income as a result of information provided by the source country. However, as long as the administrative ability to monitor foreign source capital income remains relatively weak, the prudent policy is to adopt a relatively low capital income tax rate to prevent capital flight.

Another justification for a low capital income tax rate is that the tax is typically levied on all of the *nominal* return to capital, including the inflation premium that simply serves to preserve the real value of nominal assets. The lack of inflation adjustment means that the capital income tax may become punitive even at low rates of inflation. For example, suppose the nominal interest rate is 4%, the rate of inflation is 2%, and the capital income tax on the nominal return is 50%, leaving a 2% nominal after-tax return. The *real* after-tax return would then be $2 - 2 = 0$, so the effective tax rate on the real return would be a confiscatory 100%. Thus, even if the policy aim is to tax the real income from capital just as heavily as labour income, the tax rate on nominal capital income should be well below the labour income tax rate even at moderate inflation rates. To illustrate, if the top marginal tax rate on labour income is 40% and the government wishes to impose the same effective tax rate on real capital income, the tax rate applied to nominal capital income should be 20% when the nominal return is 4% and the inflation rate is 2%.[30]

A third pragmatic reason for setting a low tax rate on capital income is that some types of income from capital are difficult to tax for administrative or political reasons. For example, this applies to imputed returns to owner-occupied housing and to many types of capital gain. By choosing a low tax rate on those forms of capital income which can in fact be taxed, the government reduces the inter-asset distortions to the savings pattern that arise when some types of capital income go untaxed. Moreover, a low tax rate may make it easier to broaden the tax base to minimize the inter-asset distortions. For example, when the Nordic countries introduced the dual income tax, the lowering of the capital income tax rate was accompanied by a tightening of capital gains taxation (see Sørensen (1994)).

The case for a *flat* tax on capital income (rather than a progressive tax schedule with rising marginal tax rates) likewise rests on pragmatic arguments. For example, it is well known that capital gains taxation based on the realization principle generates a 'lock-in' effect which hampers the

[30] The capital income tax liability would then be $0.2 \times 4\% = 0.8\%$ which is 40% of the real pre-tax return of 2%.

reallocation of capital towards more productive uses, since taxpayers can defer their tax liability by postponing the realization of accrued capital gains. Progressive taxation of realized gains exacerbates this lock-in effect because the taxpayer may be pushed into a higher tax bracket in the year of realization. A flat uniform tax on capital income avoids this additional distortion.

Moreover, a proportional tax on capital income eliminates the marginal tax rate differentials that may give rise to ownership 'clientele' effects under the current system. For example, under a progressive capital income tax investors in high-income brackets may choose to specialize in holding assets whose returns accrue mainly as (tax-favoured) capital gains. As we have argued previously, the productivity of assets may depend on who owns them, so by reducing tax distortions to ownership patterns, a switch to proportional capital income taxation may help to increase the average social (pre-tax) asset returns.

Proportional (as opposed to progressive) taxation of capital income also eliminates the opportunities for certain forms of tax arbitrage exploiting differences in the marginal tax rates faced by different individuals. In particular, the scope for tax avoidance through transfers of wealth among family members is reduced significantly when all taxpayers face the same tax rate on income from capital.

Further, a flat tax rate simplifies tax administration by allowing the tax on interest and dividends to be collected as a final withholding tax. However, since we are proposing a residence base for the dual income tax to minimize the risk of capital flight, the withholding tax will not be imposed on capital income paid to non-residents (i.e. such income will be taxed only in so far as existing bilateral tax treaties allow this).

A tax system involving different marginal effective tax rates on income from labour and capital potentially opens the door to tax avoidance through income shifting between the two tax bases. In particular, labour income generated within the corporate sector may be transformed into dividends and capital gains on shares if the latter forms of income are taxed more lightly. As stated in point (2) above, we therefore propose that the tax rate structure should (roughly) satisfy the condition $(1 - t^r) \times (1 - t^c) = 1 - t^L$. In that case the total corporate and personal tax burden on dividends and capital gains above the normal return would always be at least as high as the marginal tax rate on labour income so that no gain could be made by transforming labour income into capital income, despite the low personal tax rate on capital income.

The proposal in point (3) to tax the imputed return to the equity of unincorporated firms as capital income aims to ensure the greatest possible degree of tax neutrality between wage earners and the self-employed and between corporate and non-corporate firms. To avoid discrimination against savings invested in non-corporate business assets, the normal return to such assets should be taxed at the same rate as the normal return to the savings undertaken by wage earners. This will also guarantee that domestic savings invested in the corporate sector are not favoured relative to savings channelled into the non-corporate sector. Non-corporate business income above the imputed normal return would be taxed as labour income, at a top marginal rate equal to the top marginal tax rate on above-normal returns from the corporate sector, regardless of whether such income is distributed in the form of wages and salaries or in the form of dividends and capital gains.

For the purpose of calculating the imputed rate of return, the tax code must separate the 'business' assets and debts of proprietors from their 'private' assets and debts. Business assets could be defined as the depreciable assets recorded in the firm's tax accounts plus acquired goodwill and other acquired intangible assets whose cost price can be documented. If the recorded business debt exceeds the value of the firm's assets, it is an indication that the proprietor has transferred 'private' (i.e. non-business) debt to the business sphere in order to take advantage of the deduction for interest on business debt. An imputed return to the excess of recorded business debt over business assets should then be added to the proprietor's taxable labour income and deducted from his taxable capital income to prevent tax avoidance through the transformation of labour income into capital income.[31]

The application of these rules requires that proprietors are able and willing to document their business assets and liabilities. Hence this tax regime should not be mandatory for all unincorporated firms, but should be an option for entrepreneurs who wish to take advantage of the opportunity to have part of their business income taxed as capital income.

As indicated, the proposed tax rules would ensure rough neutrality with regard to the choice of organizational form. With a progressive tax schedule for labour income and the relationship $(1 - t^r) \times (1 - t^c) = 1 - t^L$, where t^L is the top marginal labour income tax rate, there would be a tax incentive to distribute rents from the corporate sector in the form of wages and salaries as

[31] A slightly simpler set of rules—which could be allowed as an option—would be to impute a return to *all* of the proprietor's business assets (and not just to the equity base) and tax the residual business income *before* interest as labour income. Taxable capital income would then equal the imputed return to business assets minus all of the proprietor's interest expenses. The residual business income before interest is taxed as labour income. The advantage of these rules—which correspond to current Norwegian tax practice—is that they do not require a distinction between 'private' debt and 'business' debt. Sørensen (2005b) provides more details on alternative ways of taxing income from self-employment under a dual income tax.

long as these rents are no larger than the top bracket in the labour income tax schedule. For corporate rents above that limit the tax consequences would be the same whether the income is realized in the form of shareholder income or as labour income. In principle companies can thus ensure that labour income and rents earned in the corporate sector are taxed in exactly the same manner as the rents and labour income in the non-corporate sector that are taxed progressively as earned income.

One important proviso to this conclusion is that corporate-source labour income and rents which are realized as capital gains on shares may be under-taxed because of the deferral of tax on accrued gains until the time of realization. To offset the compound interest gain from tax deferral in a rough manner, policy makers could decide to make a schematic upward adjustment of realized taxable gains that would increase systematically with the length of the holding period, in line with the proposal by Vickrey (1939).[32] This would eliminate the potential tax advantage to corporate-source labour income and rents which are realized in the form of stock compensation.

10.6.4. The 'consumption tax regime': exempting the normal return from tax

While the above proposal for a low flat capital income tax rate aims to reduce the inter-asset distortions caused by the existing non-uniform taxation of income from capital, significant inter-asset distortions would remain in so far as policy makers decide to maintain the current tax privileges for retirement savings and investment in owner-occupied housing. Even if expenses on mortgage interest payments are non-deductible, the wealth accumulated through saving in home equity would be favoured relative to other forms of

[32] To eliminate the interest gain from tax deferral, one can show that a capital gain realized after a holding period of n years should be adjusted upwards through multiplication by the factor

$$\frac{g\cdot(1+r)^n}{(1+g)^n-1}\left[\frac{1-\left(\frac{1+g}{1+r}\right)^{n+1}}{1-\left(\frac{1+g}{1+r}\right)}\right],$$

where r is the after-tax interest rate and g is the average annual percentage capital gain. If the asset was bought at the price A_b and sold n years later at the price A_s, the deemed annual capital gain would be calculated from the equation

$$A_s=(1+g)^n A_b.$$

Given knowledge of the buying and selling prices and the length of the holding period, tax administrators could thus use standard tables to calculate the adjustment factor needed to offset the deferral advantage.

saving if the imputed rent on owner-occupied housing is left out of the capital income tax base.

If UK policy makers do not wish to tax the returns to retirement saving and investment in owner-occupied housing, there may be a case for exempting the normal return to other forms of saving as well. This would avoid inter-asset and inter-sectoral distortions, and it would also eliminate the intertemporal tax distortion to the choice between present and future consumption by effectively moving Britain towards a consumption-based tax system. If this is the policy goal, we propose that it could be implemented through the following measures which would still be combined with an ACE at the corporate level:

(i) Dividends and realized capital gains on shares would be subject to a flat residence-based shareholder income tax, but only in so far as the income exceeds an imputed normal return to the shares. If the realized income from shares in any year falls short of the imputed return (henceforth denoted the Rate-of-Return Allowance, RRA), the unutilized RRA may be carried forward and deducted from future shareholder income. The RRA for the current year is imputed to the basis value of the share, defined as the acquisition price of the share plus any unutilized RRAs carried over from previous years.

(ii) If the corporate income tax rate is t^c and the top marginal tax rate on labour income is t^L, the shareholder income tax rate t^r would be set such that $(1 - t^r)\ (1 - t^c) = 1 - t^L$ to prevent tax avoidance through the transformation of labour income into shareholder income.

(iii) In general interest income would be exempt from personal tax. However, when the interest rate charged on a loan from a personal taxpayer to a company exceeds a normal interest rate on long-term bonds, the excess interest income would be deemed to be shareholder income and would be taxed as such.

(iv) The owners of unincorporated firms could opt to deduct an imputed normal return to their business equity from their taxable business income. The residual business income would then be taxed as labour income. Interest expenses would be deductible, but only in so far as the recorded debt does not exceed the recorded business assets. Alternatively, proprietors could opt to have all of their business income taxed as labour income. In the latter case only interest on business debt would be deductible.

A tax system along these lines extends the philosophy of the ACE to the personal income tax. It leaves the normal return to saving untaxed, whether savings are invested in interest-bearing assets, shares, business assets, or owner-occupied housing. The proposed shareholder income tax ensures that rents as well as labour income disguised as capital income get taxed at the top marginal personal labour income tax rate. Since unutilized Rate-of-Return-Allowances (RRAs) may be deducted from the base of the shareholder income tax in subsequent years and may also be added to the basis of the share, unutilized RRAs are effectively carried forward with interest. This ensures that the present value of the shareholder's deduction remains equal to the initial investment outlay regardless of when he realizes his income from the share. As demonstrated by Sørensen (2005a), this feature implies that the shareholder income tax is equivalent to a neutral cash flow tax. Sørensen (op. cit.) also shows that the shareholder income tax satisfies the properties of the retrospective capital gains tax proposed by Auerbach (1991) and the generalized cash flow tax described by Auerbach and Bradford (2004); that is, tax designs that are known to be neutral towards realization decisions even though they do not involve taxation of unrealized gains. The shareholder income tax thus avoids the distortionary lock-in effect associated with conventional realization-based taxation of capital gains.

Just as financial innovations have tended to blur the distinction between debt and equity, the distinction between shareholder income and interest income may not always be clear-cut. The rule described in point (iii) above is designed to ensure that controlling investors in closely held companies cannot avoid the shareholder income tax through the transformation of labour income into interest income.

Our proposal in point (iv) extends the ACE to the non-corporate business sector on an optional basis. The delineation of business assets and debts and the calculation of the imputed return would proceed in the same manner as under the income tax regime described in the previous section.

10.6.5. Would the proposals work in practice?

The novel features of the reform proposals above are the ACE system, the (optional) rules for splitting the business income from non-corporate firms, and the shareholder income tax. Compared to other and more radical proposals for tax reform, the advantage of our proposals is that they have already been tested in practice.

To date, the most important experiment with an ACE has been the Croatian profit tax which allowed a deduction for an imputed return on the equity of all business firms from 1994 to the beginning of 2001.[33] At that time the ACE allowance was abolished, apparently reflecting a desire to gain revenue in order to set a lower headline profit rate, and possibly also because it was felt that, in the specific Croatian context, the ACE tended to favour large state-owned enterprises with overvalued assets. In a careful review of the Croatian tax experiment, Keen and King (2002) argue that the abolition of the ACE did not reflect any irremovable technical flaw in the system. On the contrary, Keen and King conclude that in many ways the system worked rather well so that in this sense the ACE passed its first practical test. Interestingly, an ACE has recently been introduced in Belgium in an attempt to maintain the status of Belgium as an attractive location for international holding and financing companies (so-called 'coordination centres') without offering special tax benefits to such activities (see Gérard (2006) and Sørensen (2008)). Austria and Italy have also experimented with an ACE-like system in recent years, but they applied a reduced rather than a zero tax rate on the normal return. These countries abandoned the ACE as they lowered their standard rate of corporate income tax to the rate previously imposed only on the normal return.[34]

The rules for splitting the income of the self-employed into capital income and labour income are now a well-established part of the tax code in the dual income tax systems of Norway, Sweden, and Finland. The Nordic experience shows that such rules are indeed workable as far as unincorporated firms are concerned. The Nordic attempts to split the income of 'active' shareholders who work in their own closely held company have been less successful because of the difficulties of separating 'active' from 'passive' shareholders. Our reform proposals avoid this problematic distinction which is made redundant by the proposed tax rate structure under our income tax regime and by the shareholder income tax under our consumption tax regime.

From the beginning of 2006 Norway has introduced a version of the shareholder income tax as a replacement for the previous income splitting rules for active shareholders. The Norwegian experiment indicates that a shareholder income tax can in fact be implemented, although a final evaluation of this ACE type tax at the shareholder level must await the accumulation of further experience.[35]

[33] Rose and Wiswesser (1998) describe the Croatian profit tax in the context of the wider Croatian experiment with a consumption-based tax system in the 1990s. For an account of a Brazilian experiment with an ACE type profit tax, see Klemm (2006).

[34] For a review of the Italian experience with an ACE-type system, see Bordignon et al. (2001).

[35] See Sørensen (2005a) for a detailed discussion of the background for and practical implementation of the Norwegian shareholder income tax.

REFERENCES

Altshuler, R., and Grubert, H. (2003), 'Repatriation Taxes, Repatriation Strategies and Multinational Financial Policy', *Journal of Public Economics*, **87**, 73–107.

Auerbach, A. (1983), 'Taxation, Corporate Financial Policy and Cost of Capital', *Journal of Economic Literature*, **XXI**, 905–40.

——(1991), 'Retrospective Capital Gains Taxation', *American Economic Review*, **81**, 167–78.

——(2005), 'Who Bears the Corporate Tax? A Review of What we Know', NBER Working Paper 11686.

——and Bradford, D. (2004), 'Generalized Cash Flow Taxation', *Journal of Public Economics*, **88**, 957–80.

Baldwin, R. E., and Krugman, P. (2004), 'Agglomeration, Integration and Tax Harmonisation', *European Economic Review*, **48**, 1–23.

Bartelsman, E., and Beetsma, R. (2003), 'Why Pay More? Corporate Tax Avoidance Through Transfer Pricing in OECD Countries', *Journal of Public Economics*, **87**, 2225–52.

Becker, J., and Fuest, C. (2005), 'Optimal Tax Policy when Firms are Internationally Mobile', CESifo Working Paper No. 1592.

——(2007), 'Corporate Tax Policy and International Mergers and Acquisitions—Is the Tax Exemption System Superior?', CESifo Working Paper No. 1884.

Besley, T., and Case, A. (1995), 'Incumbent Behavior: Vote Seeking, Tax Setting and Yardstick Competition', *American Economic Review*, **85**, 25–45.

——Griffith, R., and Klemm, A. (2001), 'Empirical Evidence on Fiscal Interdependence in OECD Countries', Mimeo, Institute for Fiscal Studies.

Boadway, R., and Bruce, N. (1984), 'A General Proposition on the Design of a Neutral Business Tax', *Journal of Public Economics*, **24**, 231–9.

Bond, S. (2000), 'Levelling Up or Levelling Down? Some Reflections on the ACE and CBIT Proposals, and the Future of the Corporate Tax Base', in Cnossen, S. (ed.), *Taxing Capital Income in the European Union—Issues and Options for Reform*, Oxford: Oxford University Press.

——and Devereux, M. P. (1995), 'On the Design of a Neutral Business Tax under Uncertainty', *Journal of Public Economics*, **58**, 57–71.

——(2003), 'Generalised R-based and S-based Taxes under Uncertainty', *Journal of Public Economics*, **87**, 1291–311.

——Gammie, M., and Mokkas, S. (2006), 'Corporate Income Taxes in the EU: An Economic Assessment of the Role of the ECJ', IFS mimeo.

Bordignon, M., Giannini, S., and Panteghini, P. (2001), 'Reforming Business Taxation: Lessons from Italy?', *International Tax and Public Finance*, **8**, 191–210.

Brennan, G., and Buchanan, J. (1980), *The Power to Tax. Analytical Foundations of a Fiscal Constitution*, Cambridge: Cambridge University Press.

Brett, C., and Pinkse, J. (2000), 'The Determinants of Taxes in British Columbia', *Canadian Journal of Economics*, **33**, 695–714.

Brøchner, J., Jensen, J., Svensson, P., and Sørensen, P. B. (2006), 'The Dilemmas of Tax Coordination in the Enlarged European Union', CESifo Working Paper No. 1859.

Brueckner, J., and Saavedra, L. A. (2001), 'Do Local Governments Engage in Strategic Property-tax Competition?', *National Tax Journal*, **54**, 203–30.

Buettner, T. (2001), 'Local Business Taxation and Competition for Capital: The Choice of the Tax Rate', *Regional Science and Urban Economics*, **31**, 215–45.

Carey, D., and Rabesona, J. (2004), 'Tax Ratios on Labor and Capital Income and on Consumption', Chapter 7 in Sørensen, P. B. (ed.), *Measuring the Tax Burden on Capital and Labor*, Cambridge, Mass.: MIT Press.

Chennells, L., and Griffith, R. (1997), *Taxing Profits in a Changing World*, London: IFS.

Cnossen, S. (2000), 'Taxing Capital Income in the Nordic Countries: A Model for the European Union?', in Cnossen, S. (ed.), *Taxing Capital Income in the European Union—Issues and Options for Reform*, Oxford: Oxford University Press.

Conyon, M., and Sadler, G. (2005), 'How does US and UK CEO Pay Measure Up?', presented at the Royal Economic Society's 2005 Annual Conference at the University of Nottingham on Monday, 21 March.

De Mooij, R., and Ederveen, S. (2003), 'Taxation of Foreign Direct Investment: A Synthesis of Empirical Research', *International Tax and Public Finance*, **10**, 673–93.

—— and Nicodème, G. (2006), 'Corporate Tax Policy, Entrepreneurship and Incorporation in the EU', CESifo Working Paper No. 1883.

Desai, M., Foley, C., and Hines, J. (2001), 'Repatriation Taxes and Dividend Distortions', *National Tax Journal*, **54**, 829–51.

—— —— —— (2002), 'Dividend Policy Inside the Firm', NBER Working Paper No. 8698, Cambridge, Mass.

—— —— —— (2004), 'Economic Effects of Regional Tax Havens', NBER Working Paper No. 10806.

—— —— —— (2006a), 'Do Tax Havens Divert Economic Activity?', *Economics Letters*, **90**, 219–24.

—— —— —— (2006b), 'The Demand for Tax Haven Operations', *Journal of Public Economics*, **90**, 513–31.

—— and Hines, J. (1999), '"Basket" Cases: Tax Incentives and International Joint Venture Participation by American Multinational Firms', *Journal of Public Economics*, **71**, 379–402.

—— —— (2002), 'Expectations and Expatriations: Tracing the Causes and Consequences of Corporate Inversions', *National Tax Journal*, **55**, 409–40.

—— —— (2003), 'Evaluating International Tax Reform', *National Tax Journal*, **56**, 487–502.

—— —— (2004), 'Old Rules and New Realities: Corporate Tax Policy in a Global Setting', *National Tax Journal*, **57**, 937–60.

Devereux, M. P. (1990), 'Capital Export Neutrality, Capital Import Neutrality and Capital Ownership Neutrality and all that', IFS Working Paper, London: Institute for Fiscal Studies, June.

Devereux, M. P. (2004), 'Measuring Taxes on Income from Capital', Chapter 2 in Sørensen, P. B. (ed.), *Measuring the Tax Burden on Capital and Labor*, The MIT Press.

——and Griffith, R. (1998), 'Taxes and the Location of Production: Evidence from a Panel of US Multinationals', *Journal of Public Economics*, **68**, 335–67.

————(2000), 'The Impact of Corporate Taxation on the Location of Capital: A Review', *Swedish Economic Policy Review*, **9**, 79–102.

————(2002), 'Evaluating Tax Policy for Location Decisions', *International Tax and Public Finance*, **10**, 107–26.

————and Klemm, A. (2002), 'Corporate Income Tax Reforms and International Tax Competition', *Economic Policy*, **35**, 451–95.

——Lockwood, B., and Redoano, M. (2002), 'Do Countries Compete over Corporate Tax Rates?', CEPR Discussion Paper No. 3400.

——Griffith, R., and Klemm, A. (2004), 'Why has the UK Corporation Tax Raised so much Revenue?', *Fiscal Studies*, **25**, 367–88.

——and Sørensen, P. B. (2006), 'The Corporate Income Tax: International Trends and Options for Fundamental Reform', *European Economy. Economic Papers*, No. 264, European Commission.

Diamond, P., and Mirrlees, J. (1971), 'Optimal Taxation and Public Production: I—Production Efficiency', *American Economic Review*, **61**, 8–27.

Eggert, W., and Genser, B. (2005), 'Dual Income Taxation in EU Member Countries', *CESifo DICE Report*, **3**, 41–7.

——and Haufler, A. (2006), 'Company-tax Coordination Cum Tax-rate Competition in the European Union', *FinanzArchiv: Public Finance Analysis*, Mohr Siebeck, Tübingen, **62**, 579–601.

Esteller-Moré, A., and Solé-Olé, A. (2002), 'Tax Setting in a Federal System: The Case of Personal Income Taxation in Canada', *International Tax and Public Finance*, **9**, 235–57.

European Commission (1998), EU Code of Conduct for Business Taxation. <http://www.ec.europa.eu/taxation_customs/taxation/company_tax/harmful_tax_practices/index_en.htm>.

Gammie, M., Griffith, R., and Miller, H. (2008), 'Taxation of Companies' Foreign Profits', in Chote, R., Emmerson, C., Miles, D., and Shaw, J. (eds.), *The IFS Green Budget: January 2008*, Commentary 104, London: Institute for Fiscal Studies.

Gérard, M. (2006), 'Belgium Moves to Dual Allowance for Corporate Equity', *European Taxation*, **4**, 156–62.

Gordon, R. H. (1983), 'An Optimal Taxation Approach to Fiscal Federalism', *Quarterly Journal of Economics*, **98**, 567–86.

——(1986), 'Taxation of Investment and Savings in a World Economy', *American Economic Review*, **76**, 1086–102.

——(1992), 'Can Capital Income Taxes Survive in Open Economies?', *Journal of Finance*, **47**, 1159–80.

——and Hines, J. R. Jr. (2002), 'International Taxation', in Auerbach, A. J., and Feldstein, M. (eds.), *Handbook of Public Economics*, vol. **4**, Amsterdam: North-Holland, 1935–95.

Gravelle, J. (2004), 'Issues in International Tax Policy', *National Tax Journal*, **57**, 773–7.

Griffith, R., and Klemm, A. (2004), 'What has Been the Tax Competition Experience of the Last 20 years?', *Tax Notes International*, **34**, 1299–316.

——Redding, S., and Simpson, H. (2004), 'Foreign Ownership and Productivity: New Evidence from the Service Sector and the R&D Lab', *Oxford Review of Economic Policy*, **20**, 440–56.

Grubert, H. (1998), 'Taxes and the Division of Foreign Operating Income Among Royalties, Interest, Dividends, and Retained Earnings', *Journal of Public Economics*, **68**, 269–90.

——and Mutti, J. (1991), 'Taxes, Tariffs and Transfer Pricing in Multinational Corporate Decision Making', *Review of Economics and Statistics*, **73**, 285–93.

————(1995), 'Taxing Multinationals in a World with Portfolio Flows and R&D: Is Capital Export Neutrality Obsolete?', *International Tax and Public Finance*, **2**.

————(2001), *Taxing International Business Income: Dividend Exemption Versus the Current System*, AEI Studies on Tax Reform, American Enterprise Institute, Washington, DC.

Harberger, A. (1962), 'The Incidence of the Corporation Income Tax', *Journal of Political Economy*, **70**, 215–40.

Hartman, D. (1985), 'Tax Policy and Foreign Direct Investment', *Journal of Public Economics*, **26**, 107–21.

Haufler, A., and Schjelderup, G. (2000), 'Corporate Tax Systems and Cross-country Profit Shifting', *Oxford Economic Papers*, **52**, 306–25.

Haupt, A., and Peters, W. (2005), 'Restricting Preferential Tax Regimes to Avoid Harmful Tax Competition', *Regional Science and Urban Economics*, **36**, 493–507.

Hellerstein, W., and McLure, C. E. (2004), 'The European Commission's Report on Company Income Taxation: What the EU can Learn from the Experience of the United States', *International Tax and Public Finance*, **11**, 199–220.

Hines, J. R. (1996), 'Altered States: Taxes and the Location of Foreign Direct Investment in America', *American Economic Review*, **86**, 1076–94.

——(1999), 'Lessons from Behavioral Responses to International Taxation', *National Tax Journal*, **52**, 305–22.

——(2005), 'Do Tax Havens Flourish?', Chapter 3 in Poterba, J. M. (ed.), *Tax Policy and the Economy*, vol. **19**, National Bureau of Economic Research and the MIT Press.

——and Rice, E. (1994), 'Fiscal Paradise: Foreign Tax Havens and American Business', *Quarterly Journal of Economics*, **109**, 149–82.

HM Treasury (2007), 'Taxation of the Foreign Profits of Companies: A Discussion Document', HM Treasury and HM Revenue & Customs, June 2007.

Huizinga, H., and Nicodème, G. (2006), 'Foreign Ownership and Corporate Income Taxation: An Empirical Evaluation', *European Economic Review*, **50**, 1223–44.

Huizinga, H., and Nielsen, S. B. (1997), 'Capital Income and Profit Taxation with Foreign Ownership of Firms', *Journal of International Economics*, **42**, 149–65.

IFS Capital Taxes Group (1991), *Equity for Companies: A Corporation Tax for the 1990s*, London: The Institute for Fiscal Studies.

IFS Green Budgets, various years <http://www.ifs.org.uk/budgets/gb2006/06chap9.pdf>.

Janeba, E., and Smart, M. (2003), 'Is Targeted Tax Competition less Harmful than its Remedies?', *International Tax and Public Finance*, **10**, 259–80.

Jorgenson, D. (1963), 'Capital Theory and Investment Behavior', *American Economic Review*, **53**, 247–57.

Keen, M. (2001), 'Preferential Tax Regimes can Make Tax Competition Less Harmful', *National Tax Journal*, **54**, 757–62.

—— and King, J. (2002), 'The Croatian Profit Tax: An ACE in Practice', *Fiscal Studies*, **23**, 401–18.

—— and Piekkola, H. (1997), 'Simple Rules for the Optimal Taxation of International Capital Income', *Scandinavian Journal of Economics*, **99**, 447–61.

—— and Simone, A. (2004), 'Tax Policy in Developing Countries: Some Lessons from the 1990s, and some Challenges Ahead', in Gupta, S., Clements, B., and Inchauste, G. (eds.), *Helping Countries Develop: The Role of Fiscal Policy*, Washington: International Monetary Fund.

—— and Wildasin, D. (2004), 'Pareto-efficient International Taxation', *American Economic Review*, **94**, 259–75.

Keuschnigg, C., and Dietz, M. (2007), 'A Growth-oriented Dual Income Tax', *International Tax and Public Finance*, **14**, 191–221.

King, M., and Fullerton, D. (1984), *The Taxation of Income from Capital: A Comparative Study of the United States, the United Kingdom, Sweden and West Germany*, Chicago: Chicago University Press.

Klemm, A. (2006), 'Allowances for Corporate Equity in Practice', paper presented at the 2006 CESifo Venice Summer Institute workshop on 'The Future of Capital Income Taxation'.

Lodin, S. O., and Gammie, M. J. (2001), *Home State Taxation*, IBFD Publications.

McLure, C. E. (1980), 'The State Corporate Income Tax: Lambs in Wolves' Clothing', in Aaron, H., and Boskin, M. (eds.), *The Economics of Taxation*, Washington, DC: Brookings Institution.

—— and Weiner, J. M. (2000), 'Deciding Whether the European Union Should Adopt Formula Apportionment of Company Income', in Cnossen, S. (ed.), *Taxing Capital Income in the European Union—Issues and Options for Reform*, Oxford: Oxford University Press.

Meade, J. (1978), *The Structure and Reform of Direct Taxation: Report of a Committee chaired by Professor J. E. Meade for the Institute for Fiscal Studies*, London: George Allen & Unwin. http://www.ifs.org.uk/publications/3433.

Mendoza, E. G., Razin, A., and Tesar, L. (1994), 'Effective Tax Rates in Macroeconomics: Cross-country Estimates of Tax Rates on Factor Incomes and Consumption', *Journal of Monetary Economics*, **34**, 297–323.

Mintz, J. (1994), 'Is There a Future for Capital Income Taxation?', *Canadian Tax Journal*, **42**, 1469–503.

—— and Smart, M. (2004), 'Income Shifting, Investment and Tax Competition: Theory and Evidence from Provincial Taxation in Canada', *Journal of Public Economics*, **88**, 1149–78.

Mullins, P. (2006), 'Moving to Territoriality? Implications for the U.S. and the Rest of the World', *Tax Notes International*, **4** (September).

Nielsen, S. B., and Sørensen, P. B., (1997), 'On the Optimality of the Nordic System of Dual Income Taxation', *Journal of Public Economics*, **63**, 311–29.

Oates, W. (1972), *Fiscal Federalism*, New York: Harcourt Brace Jovanovich.

OECD (1998), 'Harmful Tax Competition: An Emerging Global Issue', OJC 002/1, 6 January.

OECD (2006), 'The OECD's Project on Harmful Tax Practices: 2006 Update on Progress in Member Countries', Paris: OECD Centre for Tax Policy and Administration.

Persson, T., and Tabellini, G. (2000), *Political Economics. Explaining Economic Policy*, Cambridge, Mass.: MIT Press.

President's Advisory Panel on Federal Tax Reform (2005), *Simple, Fair, and Pro-Growth: Proposals to Fix America's Tax System*, Washington: U.S. Government Printing Office.

Razin, A., and Sadka, E. (1991), 'International Tax Competition and Gains from Tax Harmonization', *Economics Letters*, **37**, 69–76.

Richman (Musgrave), P. B. (1963), *Taxation of Foreign Investment Income: An Economic Analysis*, Baltimore: Johns Hopkins Press.

Rose, M., and Wiswesser, R. (1998), 'Tax Reform in Transition Economies: Experiences from the Croatian Tax Reform Process of the 1990s', in Sørensen, P. B. (ed.), *Public Finance in a Changing World*, Basingstoke: Macmillan.

Sinn, H.-W. (1993), 'Taxation and the Birth of Foreign Subsidiaries', in Heberg, H., and Long, N. (eds.), *Trade, Welfare and Economic Policies: Essays in Honor of Murray C. Kemp*, Ann Arbor: University of Michigan Press.

—— (2003), *Ist Deutschland noch zu Retten?*, Berlin: Econ Verlag.

Spengel, C., and Wiegard, W. (2004), 'Dual Income Tax: A Pragmatic Reform Alternative for Germany', *CESifo DICE Report*, **2**, 15–22.

Sullivan, A. (2004), 'Data show Dramatic Shift of Profits to Tax Havens', *Tax Notes*, 1190–200.

Sørensen, P. B. (1994), 'From the Global Income Tax to the Dual Income Tax: Recent Tax Reforms in the Nordic Countries', *International Tax and Public Finance*, **1**, 57–79.

—— (2000), 'The Case for International Tax Coordination Reconsidered', *Economic Policy*, **31**, 431–61.

Sørensen, P. B. (2002), 'The German Business Tax Reform of 2000—A General Equilibrium Analysis', *German Economic Review*, **3**, 347–78.

Sørensen, P. B. (2004a), 'Measuring Taxes on Capital and Labor: An Overview of Methods and Issues', Chapter 1 in Sørensen, P. B. (ed.), *Measuring the Tax Burden on Capital and Labor*, Cambridge, Mass.: MIT Press.

—— (2004b), 'International Tax Coordination: Regionalism versus Globalism', *Journal of Public Economics*, **88**, 1187–214.

—— (2004c), 'Company Tax Reform in the European Union', *International Tax and Public Finance*, **11**, 91–115.

—— (2005a), 'Neutral Taxation of Shareholder Income', *International Tax and Public Finance*, **12**, 777–801.

—— (2005b), 'Dual Income Taxation—Why and How?', *FinanzArchiv/Public Finance Analysis*, **61**, 559–86.

—— (2007), 'Can Capital Income Taxes Survive? And Should They?', *CESifo Economic Studies*, **53**, 1–57.

—— (2008), 'A Note on the Belgian Experience with the Allowance for Corporate Equity', Mimeo, Department of Economics, University of Copenhagen, February 2008.

Teather, R. (2005), *The Benefits from Tax Competition*, Hobart Paper 153, London: The Institute of Economic Affairs.

U.S. Treasury (1992), *Integration of the Individual and Corporate Tax Systems—Taxing Business Income Once*, Washington, DC.

Vickrey, W. (1939), 'Averaging Income for Tax Purposes', *Journal of Political Economy*, **47**, 379–97.

Weichenrieder, A. (1996), 'Fighting International Tax Avoidance: The Case of Germany', *Fiscal Studies*, **17**, 37–58.

Weiner, J. M. (2005), *Company Tax Reform in the European Union*, New York: Springer.

Wildasin, D. (2000), 'Factor Mobility and Fiscal Policy in the EU: Policy Issues and Analytical Approaches', *Economic Policy*, **31**, 337–78.

—— and Wilson, J. D. (2004), 'Capital Tax Competition—Bane or Boon?', *Journal of Public Economics*, **88**, 1065–91.

Wilson, J. D. (1999), 'Theories of Tax Competition', *National Tax Journal*, **52**, 269–304.

Yoo K.-Y. (2003), 'Corporate Taxation of Foreign Direct Investment Income 1991–2001', OECD Economics Department Working Papers No. 365.

Zodrow, G. (2006), 'Capital Mobility and Source-based Taxation of Capital Income in Small Open Economies', *International Tax and Public Finance*, **13**, 269–94.

—— and Mieszkowski, P. (1986), 'Pigou, Tiebout, Property Taxation and the Underprovision of Local Public Goods', *Journal of Urban Economics*, **19**, 356–70.

Commentary by Julian S. Alworth*

Julian Alworth is Chairman of European and Global Investments (Dublin) and of European Investment Consulting (Milan) as well as an Associate Fellow at the Saïd Business School (Oxford). His research focuses on taxation and corporate decision making, the effects of taxation on financial markets, portfolio performance measurement, and risk measurement problems for defined contribution pension plans. His writing in these areas notably includes *Finance, Taxation and Financial Decisions of Multinationals*. He worked for many years at the Bank for International Settlements and has been consultant to a number of international organizations and private sector companies.

Our understanding of the impact of taxes on economic decisions in an open economy has increased very significantly over the past three decades. As in many other areas of public finance a great deal of empirical evidence has been gathered and the modelling of economic decision making has become more sophisticated, allowing for a more focused identification of the variables in play. Moreover, the behaviour and goals of governments have been analysed more carefully and this has allowed a richer account of interactions between various jurisdictions.

The chapter by Griffith, Hines, and Sørensen (GHS), three prominent contributors to the literature in this area, represents both a very comprehensive summary of our knowledge and a useful guide to potential policy prescriptions that follow from the analysis. My comments will be divided into three parts. The first concerns the overall framework employed by the authors. In the second I shall refer more directly to some of the specific analyses carried out by the authors whereas my third set of remarks will address their policy prescriptions.

* I am grateful to Stuart Adam for a number of comments and to Giampaolo Arachi for numerous discussions on the topics discussed in this commentary especially in Section 2.

1. OVERALL FRAMEWORK

GHS choose to frame their discussion within the traditional juxtaposition of residence versus source. There are many areas in which this analysis is essential and leads to useful benchmarks, such as that derived in a Diamond–Mirrlees optimal tax-setting that a government in a small open economy should not levy any source-based taxes on capital. The residence vs source and credit vs exemption dichotomies also lead to important insights in respect of intertemporal and interjurisdictional efficiency, and provide useful guidelines for what is ultimately at stake in the international domain, the assertion of tax jurisdiction and the division of taxable income.

This framework, however, has for some time proved to be inadequate as a policy guide in the face of numerous changes in the way economic activity is increasingly conducted. The problems with this approach stem from a number of developments and factors:[1] (i) international business is increasingly being conducted in ways that are not clearly associated in economic terms with a national jurisdiction;[2] (ii) there is a lack of coordination across jurisdictions in respect of the tax treatment of distributions out of a company whether in the form of dividends, interest, royalties, and other payment flows; (iii) a coherent basis for distinguishing between the return to capital and labour income[3]—particularly in the service sector—is becoming difficult to establish; (iv) the location decision of the overall controlling interest of a business (both head office and shareholder location) has become endogenous. As a result where and at what rate mobile individuals and companies choose to be taxed have become decision variables.

It is almost impossible to take account of all of these changes in an analytical framework because there are inevitably too many variables at play. While the tax credit or the exemption system seem adaptable to solve some of these problems both inevitably collapse when taking account of all these developments together. For example, taxation on the basis of residence (a pure credit system without deferral) can be adapted to solve problems (i)–(iii) but is not helpful for (iv) if businesses and individuals are allowed to change

[1] Bird and Wilkie (2000) draw attention to some of these developments.

[2] For example, what is the 'source jurisdiction' of the production of telephone services over the Internet? Should it be the location of the servers used for transferring the calls or should it be the jurisdiction of the 'user'?

[3] The recent UK and US debates regarding 'carried interest' in the private equity and hedge fund worlds is a case in point. This is not a small closely held company issue which appears to be the main concern of GHS. For a discussion of the scale of this phenomenon see Graham, Lang, and Shackelford (2004).

residence freely. By contrast, a territorial system cannot easily cope with (i) or (ii) although (iv) would probably not be of great concern.

These difficulties are endemic in a world of free trade and capital mobility. If there is no perfect unilateral tax arrangement that achieves neutrality in an open economy the issue becomes one of finding a non-neutral tax system that is least distortionary along some clearly established dimensions. The prime objective of the analytical framework should be to establish clear terms of reference, trade-offs, and priorities as to what a tax system should and can achieve given the existing constraints and the degree of complexity that one is willing to accept to achieve those objectives. Hence, if the credit system without deferral is too costly to implement or complex this should be quantified and analysed, and it should be possible to establish parameter values sufficient to warrant the abandonment of all CFC regimes. Furthermore, recognizing the inherent imperfection of the systems from the outset helps to identify those areas that are most clearly in need of anti-abuse or other forms of back-up provisions.

Since no system is watertight to a number of potential objections, analysis should be framed in terms of the least costly or most effective approach taking account when possible of potential foreign reactions. GHS rarely apply this cost–benefit approach systematically to the analysis of various alternative regimes. Indeed, what is generally disconcerting about most of the literature, and this is not the fault of GHS alone, is that the past thirty years of theory and empirical work rarely appear to inform the policy process except in a very distant fashion. Neither the costs or benefits of gradualism nor those associated with grand reform proposals are examined taking account of potential imperfections.

2. SPECIFIC ANALYTICAL ISSUES[4]

It has been common in recent years to argue that the corporation tax is the archetypal source-based tax and that the existence of rents is the basis for the tax. In many sections of this chapter, GHS argue that source-based taxes can be justified if they fall on *location specific* and *immobile rents*. While I believe there is a sense in which this notion is helpful, I find it extremely misleading as a general guide to policy particularly in an open economy world such as the one in which we are currently living.

[4] This section is the result of joint work with Giampaolo Arachi.

2.1. A simple model

In a static context, in the absence of a market for assets and in the absence of risk, a rent or pure profit is defined as the extra return on an asset over the normal return in a market. In a simple model of monopolistic firm the rent is the infra-marginal profit. The world is, however, not static. Assets are traded and the value of assets reflects the capitalized value of the future stream of returns and business is risky. The assumption of market valuation of assets as shown below is very important. The moment assets are valued in a capital market streams of returns with differing profiles but identical risk characteristics will be valued differently.

Assume two water wells are discovered one day on two different lots of land. Each can generate perpetual streams of income valued at R and 2R. The owner of the second well would clearly receive a yearly rent of R in excess of the owner of the first well. Note, however, that the owner of the first well would also be in a position of earning a rent of R if the cost of taking the water out of the ground were nil and if the land was valued at nil before the discovery of the well. Now assume that there is a market for wells. If the value of the riskless interest rate is R/100, the market value of the two wells would be 100 and 200. Hence, the owners will experience a capital gain at the moment of discovery, equal to the present value of the perpetual stream of net income, and from that instant onward they would both earn the same rate of return R/100 which incidentally is also the riskless rate. Clearly any subsequent purchaser of any of the two wells would earn the same rate of return R/100. In other words, the rent has vanished or rather been capitalized into the price of the assets. Once the rents have been capitalized owners will only earn the normal interest rate.

This example illustrates two issues with rents. The first is that rents are a relative measure. It is necessary to know the capital value of assets to be able to measure the exact amount of the rent. And secondly in the absence of risk if rents are capitalized there are no extra-normal returns to be earned in a well-functioning capital market. It is difficult to identify a 'rent' in a well-functioning capital market and its measurement is a question of valuation.[5]

2.2. A tax on rents

A tax on pure rents would be easy to apply before the lots were sold. The normal return on land is nil, under the assumptions that the land was worthless

[5] Valuation is important for determining the rent element.

before the discovery of the wells and that the water could be taken out of the ground at no cost. Hence any cash flow generated by the wells represents a rent and can be taxed. With a rate equal to 50% the owner of the first lot will pay an annual tax equal to 0.5R and his net wealth will decline to 50. The owner of the second lot will pay R and his net wealth would decline to 100.

But the tax base on rents as such would vanish if the land were sold prior to the introduction of the tax or if allowance were provided for capital losses to the owners of the wells. Notice that the first lot can still be sold at price 100. The buyer will earn a normal return equal to R which would go untaxed. Likewise, the second lot can still be sold at price 200 as the buyer could earn a (untaxed) normal return equal to 2R.

Revenues could be secured by levying a tax on capital appreciation at the time of discovery of the well. Assuming a tax rate equal to 50%, the owner of the first well would pay 50 while the owner of the second well would pay 100 leaving them exactly with the same net wealth they have under a tax on pure rents. Notice that if the capital gains tax is levied upon accrual, it can effectively substitute for the direct tax on rents. However, it is well known that it is quite difficult to implement accrual taxation as it could be hard to price an asset before it is sold and also because the taxpayer may have liquidity problems. There are two alternatives. The first one is to implement some kind of retrospective taxation on realized capital gains following the approach developed by Auerbach and Bradford (Auerbach (1991), Bradford (1995), Auerbach and Bradford (2004)). The second is to apply both a tax on pure rents and a tax on realized capital gains.

2.3. Taxing extra-normal returns on cross border investments

The previous analysis shows that it is quite difficult to introduce ex novo a tax on pure rents for firms whose value is actively traded because capital values already reflect past innovations in returns and also because 'new rents' tend to be capitalized quickly albeit imperfectly. The capitalization effect might be particularly relevant for cross-border investments. It is well known that most FDI is in the form of M&A. Brakman et al. (2006) calculate that 78% of all FDI, in value terms, are M&A while greenfield investment accounts for just 22% of total FDI value. Within M&A, 97% of deals are acquisitions. Further, the share of M&As has risen sharply in the last decades as shown by Table 1.

Table 1. Greenfield investment and M&As (as a percentage of GDP, weighted averages)

	Net FDI flows (%)	FDI Inflows (%) Total	Greenfield	M&A total	M&A privatization	FDI outflows (%)
INDUSTRIAL COUNTRIES						
1987–89	−0.28	0.99	0.23	0.76	0.01	1.27
1990–94	−0.41	0.76	0.26	0.50	0.02	1.17
1995–99	−0.60	1.74	0.26	1.48	0.06	2.33
2000–01	−0.19	3.67	0.46	3.21	n.a.	3.86
DEVELOPING COUNTRIES						
1987–89	0.46	0.86	0.77	0.09	0.01	0.40
1990–94	0.79	1.43	1.14	0.30	0.08	0.65
1995–99	1.83	2.80	1.87	0.93	0.31	0.97
2000–01	2.53	3.63	2.10	1.53	n.a.	1.10
LATIN AMERICAN COUNTRIES						
1987–89	0.64	0.74	0.65	0.08	0.01	0.10
1990–94	0.93	1.15	0.68	0.47	0.20	0.23
1995–99	2.72	3.21	1.58	1.63	0.74	0.49
2000–01	3.38	3.78	1.82	1.97	n.a.	0.40

Source: Calderon et al. (2004).

In particular, as shown by Table 2, the UK has been, on average, the second largest acquiring and target country after the US since 1986.

These considerations have important implications for the way we think of the incidence of taxes in an open economy. The first one is that it is unlikely that a source-based capital income tax may be justified as a way for exporting the tax burden on foreign investors even if there are rents. Assume that foreign investors may earn a net of tax riskless rate equal to R/100. If a tax is levied on wells' gross income, R and 2R, at a 50% rate, foreigners will be ready to pay no more than 50 for the first well and 100 for the second one. Hence the tax is entirely capitalized in the market value of the assets and will be borne by the original owners in the form of a lower sales price for the asset. The tax is shifted onto foreigners only to the extent that they have bought the land before the discovery of the wells (as in Huizinga and Nielsen (1997)). However, beside anecdotal evidence on recent M&As in Europe, the findings in Calderon et al. (2004) suggest that M&As do not precede a rise in profitability but rather that they respond to the arrival of new business opportunities as measured by the increases in the growth rate of the target country.

Table 2. Ten largest M&A countries; acquiring and targets, 1986–2005

Country	Annual average acquiring flows 1986–90	1991–95	1996–2000	2001–05	1986–2005
a. Ten largest acquiring M&A countries, 1986–2005 (constant 2005 $ billion)					
1 United States	41.1	42.3	142.3	118.0	85.9
2 United Kingdom	37.2	27.0	200.3	76.7	85.3
3 France	17.0	13.2	85.6	34.9	37.7
4 Germany	6.4	10.7	68.7	31.5	29.3
5 Netherlands	4.3	8.1	39.8	32.8	21.2
6 Canada	13.3	7.5	29.9	24.1	18.7
7 Switzerland	6.1	8.0	28.8	15.8	14.7
8 Spain	2.0	2.9	27.1	24.5	14.1
9 Australia	8.2	3.7	14.1	21.4	11.9
10 Japan	16.0	3.7	13.7	8.9	10.6
b. Ten largest target M&A countries, 1986–2005 (constant 2005 $ billion)					
1 United States	86.5	44.6	238.4	99.6	117.3
2 United Kingdom	29.6	22.7	119.7	92.7	66.2
3 Germany	4.1	7.9	83.3	40.3	33.9
4 Canada	11.3	6.9	37.6	22.2	19.5
5 France	5.8	12.9	28.9	26.1	18.4
6 Netherlands	3.0	5.7	29.4	20.6	14.7
7 Australia	4.1	8.4	18.0	13.5	11.0
8 Italy	3.8	5.8	10.4	21.8	10.5
9 Sweden	1.7	4.9	23.7	10.3	10.2
10 Spain	3.1	5.0	11.1	11.8	7.8

Source: Brakman et al. (2006).

The second is that a tax on extra-returns (like a cash flow tax or the ACE) would hardly discourage the location of profitable firms to the extent that the ownership of these firms can be traded in the capital market. As we have shown in the previous section, a tax on extra-returns would affect neither the net return that an external investor may earn through the firm nor (as a consequence) the price he is willing to pay. In other words, if rents are quickly capitalized in share prices, extra-returns will arise only to compensate for risk. A perfectly symmetric cash flow tax or ACE would leave both investors and the governments unaffected (Kaplow (1994)). This suggests that the emphasis should be shifted from rents to risk and that some provisions that may affect the volatility of post-tax income may be far more relevant for the location of international investment than statutory tax rates and double taxation agreements. One source of risk is the treatment of losses, in particular in the case of a business restructuring. Another one is given by the transfer pricing rules, where the lack of an international authority for settling the disputes among countries may give rise to highly volatile 'retrospective' double taxation, as illustrated by the recent case *GlaxoSmithKline v. IRS*.

Finally, I think it is important to recall that the corporate tax is not the instrument typically used in industries where location rents are prevalent, such as mining and oil industries; specific taxes are the norm. They take the form of 'royalties' payable to the host country and/or taxes based on a redefinition of corporate income that is far from that found in financial accounts. These taxes also tend to vary according to the nature of external shocks and are the object of very specific negotiations. For example, the recent sharp rise in oil prices has led to renegotiation of these arrangements in many countries.

3. POLICY ISSUES

The taxation of international investment is composed of many moving parts that interact with one another. As noted by GHS, taxes are known to affect strongly profit and investment location but there is little agreement on the size of elasticities. The effects of the tax system on inward and outward investments, moreover, cannot be considered in isolation from developments in other jurisdictions. Apparently minor changes in legislation in other countries may impact significantly on the effects of domestic tax provisions (Altshuler and Grubert (2006)) and other jurisdictions may alter their tax rules in response to policies enacted by domestic tax authorities.

Policy prescription in a world with few empirical benchmarks is difficult[6] and GHS are very guarded in their suggested agenda for reform. Accordingly they divide their prescriptions into 'gradualist' and 'grand' schemes.

The 'gradualist' approach can be summarized as follows:

(1) Move towards an exemption system.
(2) Revise the current CFC regime in such a way as to tax on a current basis only passive or 'mobile' income.
(3) Create an EU-wide data base on arm's length prices for comparable transactions.

In many ways they endorse the major proposals set forth in HMRC (2007). In particular GHS do not believe that a shift to exemption would entail any

[6] See De Mooij and Ederveen (2003) for a survey of the literature on the response of foreign direct investment to changes in taxes.

material change to current revenues.[7] They also support the other changes suggested by HMRC in respect of the current CFC regime and backstop provisions.

An important area not touched upon by GHS and HMRC (2007) concerns the extent to which participation exemption should extend to corporate capital gains resulting from the sales of assets. Currently in the UK capital gains are taxed albeit allowing for a revaluation of the original cost basis. Experience from other countries suggests that much of the attraction of using the UK as a basis for carrying out acquisitions would hinge on exemption from tax of the sales of foreign assets.[8] Another important element that is not considered by the authors is the impact of exemption for the tax treatment of shareholders in the parent company. Would there not be an incentive for domestic closely held companies to reincorporate abroad and establish a UK holding company? While in theory this would have been possible in the past the move towards exemption reduces the cost of such structures considerably. Given the growing evidence on the impact of taxes on organizational choice (De Mooij and Nicodème (2008)), one would expect that exemption would result in a significant reshuffling of company identities. Finally, the authors do not consider the importance of UK foreign direct investment in the world economy: it is not a small open economy as far as other capital importing jurisdictions are concerned. While moving towards exemption can make sense for most countries, the UK and US are special cases. Since these two countries account for such a large share of foreign direct investment, they may be playing a backstop role for source countries. If exemption were adopted the overall global incidence of taxes could change very markedly.[9]

The authors also take issue with the EU proposal for a common consolidated tax base (CCCTB). Many of their arguments such as the difficulties of a coexistence of formula apportionment within the EU and separate accounting between the EU and the rest of the world are well taken. However, GHS do not consider the increasing degree of integration occurring between

[7] GHS prefer exemption to credit without deferral apparently for three reasons. The first is that ceteris paribus in the absence of income shifting both the exemption and credit system can ensure neutrality in respect of company ownership. The second is that unlike the credit system with deferral an exemption system does not result in a penalty for repatriations. Thirdly, exemption is administratively simpler and may foster the competitiveness of British companies in the M&A arena.

[8] This would also require careful implementation of backstop provisions. Otherwise the funding costs of a foreign acquisition could be tax deductible in the UK and the proceeds of the sale as exempt.

[9] Altshuler and Grubert (2006) discuss how changes in the US tax system affected the distribution of tax revenues between Germany and the Netherlands following changes in US legislation regarding hybrid entities.

EMS countries. This may not concern the UK in the foreseeable future but if pressure for CCCTB were to grow in this group of countries particularly from the business sector, it would be in the interest of the UK to participate actively in the design of such a system. Opposition to CCCTB may simply not be an option.

The 'grander schemes' considered by the authors entail moving towards an allowance for corporate equity (ACE) along the lines suggested by IFS nearly two decades ago. GHS believe that a move towards ACE would entail revenue losses but that in the long run the reduction in taxes on normal returns would result in a significant increase in investment and therefore indirectly in some recovery of lost revenue. Implicitly they also appear to assume that any remaining revenue loss could be recovered by taxes on other (less mobile) factors of production (which presumably already bear the bulk of the burden of the tax) without sacrificing all the gain in production efficiency.

The exact impact of moving towards ACE, like the shift from the current tax system to a cash flow tax, would probably require one to have a greater understanding of the underlying responses to tax changes (through both profit shifting and investments) before agreeing fully with this conclusion. The recent decade has witnessed a massive increase in the mobility of both skilled and unskilled labour. While there is no hard evidence on the tax sensitivity of these international labour flows, the discussion arising out of the new regime on non-domiciled residents suggests some degree of responsiveness.[10] More generally, skilled labour and capital inputs have become increasingly complementary as a result of the growth of the services sector (whose share of the economy is likely to continue to expand). Under these circumstances the only factor of production bearing the tax burden would be immobile unskilled labour. An explicit tax on this factor would be difficult to justify.

One important aspect of the introduction of ACE that is not discussed by GHS is how it would interact with an exemption system. With a credit system (without deferral) ACE would operate as in a closed economy. With an exemption system, there would be a strong incentive to capitalize UK companies as 'holding companies' for international investments and exploit the current network of double taxation treaties.[11] As already mentioned,

[10] See, for example, <http://business.timesonline.co.uk/tol/business/economics/article3340849.ece> and <http://www.ft.com/cms/s/0/499bbd1c-edf7-11dc-a5c1-0000779fd2ac,dwp_uuid=05a3b658-ac95-11dc-b51b-0000779fd2ac.html>.

[11] The introduction of participation exemption in Italy including the exemption from capital gains was in part justified as a way to compete with the use of Luxembourg as a centre for locating holding companies. It is interesting to note that a political backlash against this capital gains exemption occurred at the time of the takeover of Banca Antonveneta by ABN-AMRO when a number of Italian investors were able to escape untaxed.

further consideration also needs to be given to the impact of these changes on the treatment of corporate capital gains. Moreover, as recently highlighted by the discussion surrounding the possible replacement of the tax credit system with an exemption system, there are a significant number of complications in implementing such a change under the current company system; it is not a foregone conclusion that ACE would not face the same issues.

4. CONCLUSIONS

Much has been learned in recent decades regarding the behaviour of companies in an international environment and GHS provide an excellent overview of many of the broad implications for policy in a stylized world. However, once one moves away from the ideal prescriptions a number of issues emerge regarding implementation and these have remained largely unaddressed. It is these rather problematic and at times messy areas that typically give rise to complications in the tax system and lead to an increase in compliance costs. They are generally also the ultimate driver for change rather than efficiency gains which are extremely difficult to quantify in the case of multinational companies.

REFERENCES

Altshuler, R., and Grubert, H. (2006), 'Governments and Multinational Corporations in the Race to the Bottom', *Tax Notes*, **110**, no. 8, 27 February.

Auerbach, A. (1991), 'Retrospective Capital Gains Taxation', *American Economic Review*, **81**, 167–78.

—— and Bradford, D. F. (2004), 'Generalized Cash Flow Taxation', *Journal of Public Economics*, **88**, 957–80.

Bird, R., and Wilkie, J. S. (2000), 'Source- vs. Residence-based Taxation in the European Union: The Wrong Question', in Cnossen, S., *Taxing Capital in the European Union: Issues and Options for Reform*, Oxford.

Bond, S. (2000), 'Levelling up or Levelling Down? Some Reflections on the ACE and CBIT Proposals, and the Future of the Corporate Tax Base', in Cnossen, S. (ed.), *Taxing Capital Income in the European Union: Issues and Options for Reform*, Oxford: Oxford University Press.

Bradford, D. F. (1995), 'Fixing Realization Accounting: Symmetry, Consistency and Correctness in the Taxation of Financial Instruments', *Tax Law Review*, **50**, 731–85.

Brakman, S., Garretsen, H., and van Marrewijk, C. (2006), 'Cross-border Mergers & Acquisitions: The Facts as a Guide for International Economics' (October 2006). CESifo Working Paper Series No. 1823.

Calderon, C. A., Loayza, N., and Serven, L. (2004), 'Greenfield Foreign Direct Investment and Mergers and Acquisitions: Feedback and Macroeconomic Effects', World Bank Policy Research Working Paper No. 3192.

De Mooij, R., and Ederveen, S. (2003), 'Taxation and Foreign Direct Investment: a Synthesis of Empirical Research', *International Tax and Public Finance*, **10**, 673–93.

—— and Nicodème, G. (2008), 'Corporate Tax Policy, Entrepreneurship and Incorporation in the EU', *International Tax and Public Finance*, **15**, 478–98.

Graham, J. R., Lang, M., and Shackelford, D. (2004), 'Employee Stock Options, Corporate Taxes and Debt Policy', *Journal of Finance*, **59**, 1585–618.

HM Treasury and HM Revenue & Customs (2007), *Taxation of the Foreign Profits of Companies: A Discussion Document*, London: HMT and HMRC.

Huizinga, H., and Nielsen, S. B. (1997), 'Capital Income and Profit Taxation with Foreign Ownership of Firms', *Journal of International Economics*, **42**, 149–65.

Kaplow, L. (1994), 'Taxation and Risk Taking: A General Equilibrium Perspective', *National Tax Journal*, **47**, 789–98.

Commentary by Roger H. Gordon and Jerry Hausman

Roger Gordon is Professor of Economics at the University of California, San Diego. He is also currently the Editor of the *Journal of Economic Literature*, a Past Editor of the *Journal of Public Economics* and the *American Economic Review*, a Research Associate of the National Bureau of Economic Research and the Centre for Economic Policy Research, a Fellow of the Econometric Society and the American Academy of Arts and Sciences, and an honorary doctorate recipient from the University of St Gallen. His research focuses on diverse topics in public finance.

Jerry Hausman is the MacDonald Professor of Economics at MIT. Professor Hausman received the John Bates Clark Medal from the American Economic Association in 1985 for the most outstanding contribution to economics by an American economist under 40 years of age. He also received the Frisch Medal from the Econometric Society and the Biennial Medal of the Modeling and Simulation Society of Australia and New Zealand. Professor Hausman's research concentrates on econometrics and applied microeconomics. His applied research has been into the effects of taxation on the economy, telecommunications, regulation, and industrial organization.

The authors of this chapter are all leading experts on international taxation. Rachel Griffith (along with Michael Devereux) has examined how taxes affect the location decisions of multinationals.[1] James Hines, often jointly with Mihir Desai, has documented a wide variety of behavioural responses of multinationals to the existing tax code.[2] Peter Birch Sørensen is well known for his work on the dual income tax and on tax coordination.[3] He also has a recent overview of capital taxes in an open economy that provides a more detailed examination of many of the issues that come up in the current chapter.[4]

[1] See, for example, Devereux and Griffith (2003).
[2] For a summary of this research, see Hines (1999) or Gordon and Hines (2002).
[3] See, for example, Nielsen and Sørensen (1997) and Sørensen (2004).
[4] See Sørensen (2006).

Given this expertise, the current chapter not surprisingly provides an informed and balanced summary of results from the recent academic literature on the many types of behavioural responses of multinationals to the existing tax treatment of cross-border capital investments, the welfare effects of tax competition, and the merits/demerits of possible tax reforms. As a result, in this commentary our objective will not be to raise questions about their assessment of the past academic literature but rather to argue that the emphasis on *capital* taxes both in the chapter and in the past academic literature is misplaced. As we argue below in Section 1, the data make clear that corporate profits, and particularly the profits of multinationals, largely do *not* represent capital income. We then argue in Section 2 that the current tax treatment in the UK (and in other countries) of income from multinationals also makes no sense if the underlying tax base represents capital income. If this chapter, owing to this focus on capital taxes, cannot come close to explaining either observed profit rates or existing tax structures, then it inevitably will be missing some of the key pressures affecting the design of the tax structure, and will not be taking such pressures into account when considering possible tax reforms.

In Section 3, we argue that the best available explanation for observed corporate income is that it largely represents the return to the efforts of both entrepreneurs and corporate managers that (in part for tax reasons) they choose to retain within the firm, and ultimately receive as realized capital gains on their shares in the firm. Section 3 then lays out what the existing tax literature implies about the appropriate tax treatment of multinational income to the extent it represents such labour income. To a reasonable degree, the current tax treatment of multinationals does approximate such a tax treatment.

Section 4 then discusses how this tax treatment should change if the domestic tax system undergoes any of several plausible major tax reforms. Section 5 considers the case for tax coordination across countries, while Section 6 provides a brief discussion of some omitted issues.

1. WHAT IS THE SOURCE OF REPORTED CORPORATE INCOME?

Most of the past academic literature presumes that the corporate tax base reflects the return to capital invested in the corporate sector, so that the main effect of the tax is to discourage capital investment in the domestic corporate sector. Yet Gordon and Slemrod (1988) find that the corporate tax base would be considerably *larger*, and overall tax revenue a bit higher, if the normal return to capital were exempted from tax (in present value) through allowing all investment to be expensed while making all personal and corporate financial income from capital (dividends, interest, and capital gains) non-taxable (and in the case of interest not tax deductible).[5] This analysis suggests that the corporate tax base comes almost entirely (or even more than entirely) from sources other than capital income. Gordon, Kalambokidis, and Slemrod (2004a) then argue, on the basis of this evidence, that the effective tax rate on capital is also very low.

Intuitively, if profits simply represent the normal income to capital, then the profit rate should equal the real risk-free interest rate plus a risk premium sufficient to compensate for the risk inherent in corporate investments, and plus of course the resulting random return. The average real risk-free interest rate in the US (represented by the T-bill rate) equalled 1.4% during the period 1959–2003,[6] while the average corporate profit rate in the US reported in Auerbach (2006) and Auerbach and Poterba (1987) was 8.9% during the same time period. If this difference between the average return to corporate capital and the real interest rate represents a risk premium, then the corporate profit rate should be no more or less attractive than a risk-free return on the same capital stock. Yet the corporate profit rate exceeded the real interest rate in every year but two (1981–82) during this sample period, and even then was lower on average by only 2.5% whereas during the rest of the sample period the profit rate on average was 8% above the real interest rate. We cannot make sense of the size of the observed profit rate solely due to risk.

If reported corporate profits do not represent a normal return to savings in corporate capital, then what are they? A conventional answer here is that they represent 'rents' accruing to corporations on their infra-marginal investments. In order to understand the economic effects of taxation of such 'rents', the key issue is where do these rents come from?

One type of 'rent' is profits earned from resources extracted from the land. If the price paid for the land when it was purchased reflected the present value of these rents, then the business would still be earning just a normal rate of profit. If the firm bought the land before the presence of the resources was known, and then discovered them from say exploratory drilling, then the

[5] Gordon, Kalambokidis, and Slemrod (2004) find that overall tax revenue would be only very slightly lower if the same tax reform had been conducted in 1995. Similar findings have been reported for Denmark by Sørensen (1988) and for Germany by Becker and Fuest (2005).

[6] Here, we used data reported in the Economic Report of the President for the 3-month T-bill rate for the nominal interest rate, and the December to December percentage change in the CPI as a correction for inflation.

'rents' represent a stochastic return to this investment in exploratory drilling. Such activity can then explain why corporate profit rates are so risky, but not why their ex post distribution is so much more attractive than a market interest rate. If the manager or other employees have expertise, though, in where oil might be found, then the firm can earn an above normal return on its investments in land and drilling. This extra return represents a return to the labour effort of the manager and employees, though, not a return to capital.

This example is generic. A key objective of any business manager (or entrepreneur) is to identify activities that generate such rents, for example, products that are not 'commodities'. If the manager is successful, the resulting above-normal corporate profits (now and continuing into the future) represent a return to the current ideas and effort of the manager, so are one form of labour income. In part for tax reasons, the present value of these extra profits is often left within the firm rather than paid out to the manager (or entrepreneur) as wages and salaries.[7] The innovator ultimately receives this income in the form of long-term capital gains, and for tax purposes this income shows up as continuing above-normal corporate profits.[8]

In a closely held firm, for example, compensation paid in the form of company stock is often valued for tax purposes at the par value of the stock, so at a minimal level, implying that employees avoid taxation at ordinary rates on their compensation while the firm foregoes a deduction for wage and salary payments. If the employees' tax obligations on wages and salaries (less any future capital gains taxes paid when the shares are sold) exceed the tax savings the corporation could receive from being able to deduct wage and salary payments, then there is a joint saving in personal and corporate tax payments from not paying wages but instead using stock compensation. Reported corporate profits are then higher, since there is no longer a deduction for wage and salary payments to these employees.

Gordon and Slemrod (2000) in fact find that reported corporate profit rates are very sensitive to the difference in the tax rate that would be paid on wages and salaries and that paid (through both corporate taxes and personal capital gains taxes) if the funds instead are retained. As a result, observed

[7] If these retained profits would be shared with other shareholders, the manager can be compensated with new share issues (or stock options). The manager is then taxed on the fraction of compensation taking this explicit form, perhaps at a favourable rate if the shares are undervalued for tax purposes or if the market valuation of the shares does not completely reflect the future value of the above-normal profits.

[8] Entrepreneurs face a tax incentive not to pay out as wages and salary the profits resulting from their ideas and effort to the extent that the effective taxes paid on wages and salaries exceed those paid on profits that are retained and ultimately realized in the form of capital gains.

corporate profit rates should be high during time periods when the corporate tax rate is low relative to personal tax rates, consistent with the recent growth in reported corporate profit rates as corporate tax rates have fallen.

Recent papers examining which firms become multinationals find that these firms tend to be much more profitable than are firms that simply operate in the domestic economy.[9] These firms presumably have developed particularly valuable new products or particularly efficient new processes, so have a comparative advantage over foreign firms in the same industry. The profits resulting from these new products or processes again should represent the return to the effort, skill, and imagination of scientists or entrepreneurs employed by the firm, and in (large) part show up for tax purposes as higher corporate profits, accruing to the firm on its operations throughout the world, and not just in the UK.

How plausible is it that the size of the observed corporate profit rate can be explained on the basis of income attributed to the ideas and efforts of the entrepreneurs? Put rhetorically, how plausible is it that the additional annual income to Microsoft attributed to the ideas and efforts of Bill Gates are an important fraction of the above-normal rate of return reported by Microsoft? Very plausible. The value of the shares he now holds in the firm or previously sold represents the ex post present value of his contributions to the firm beyond what he has been paid in salary, and the corporate income accruing to these shares represents labour income generated by Gates.[10]

2. TAXATION OF MULTINATIONALS IF PROFITS ARE ONLY CAPITAL INCOME

In thinking through the appropriate tax treatment of the profits of multinationals, a key distinction in the academic literature is between a 'residence-based' and a 'territorial' corporate tax. Under a territorial tax, profits are taxable to the extent that they arise from capital invested in the domestic economy regardless of the location of the owner of this capital. Under a

[9] See Helpman (2006) for a recent survey of this large and growing literature.

[10] Reported corporate profits are higher whenever the income ultimately accruing to innovators is never deducted by the corporation as a business expense. On the basis of US tax law, stock compensation and non-qualified options issued to executives are both a deductible expense, so do not explain higher corporate profits (as long as the value assigned to this compensation reflects its market value). The corporate income accruing to the founding shares in the firm, though, does measure a return to entrepreneurial effort.

residence-based tax, profits would be taxable whenever they are owned by a domestic resident, regardless of where the capital is located.

Unless a country has market power in the world capital market, then the past academic literature argues that the country should not make use of a territorial corporate tax. In response to such a tax, investors simply shift their investments abroad until the pretax domestic return to investment has risen by enough to offset the tax. That capital is paid more pretax to compensate for the tax means that workers are paid less, if the firm is to continue to break even. While a territorial corporate tax and a tax on labour income are both ultimately paid by workers, a territorial corporate tax is less attractive on efficiency grounds since it discourages capital investments as well as labour supply.

At least on the basis of the evidence reported in Hines and Hubbard (1990) for the US, the existing attempt to impose domestic corporate taxes on foreign-source income has been largely ineffective. Firms can postpone tax indefinitely through deferring any dividends to the domestic parent, and then repatriating heavily during occasional years when the tax rate at repatriation is low, as occurred in the US recently. Alternatively, firms can simultaneously repatriate profits from both more highly taxed as well as more lightly taxed countries so that no domestic tax is owned at repatriation, given worldwide averaging. This chapter presumes that the UK tax also in practice approximates a territorial corporate tax. Yet, the academic literature suggests that a country loses from use of a territorial corporate tax, making the existence of the tax puzzling.

A residence-based tax, in contrast, attempts to tax residents on any income they receive from their savings, regardless of the type or location of the asset. Since capital gains are normally taxed at a much lower effective tax rate than dividends or interest income, assets generating non-trivial capital gains would be tax favoured unless there is some compensating tax provision. Since much of the income from corporate equity takes the form of capital gains, the corporate tax can serve as such a compensating tax provision, ideally leading to an effective tax rate on corporate capital equal to that on other types of assets.[11] A corporate tax is then an important backstop to any personal tax on income from savings.

To implement a residence-based tax on corporate income, though, a country would need to tax corporate profits to the extent that they are owned by domestic residents, regardless of the location of the investment. If domestic

[11] Given the existing dividend imputation scheme in the UK, the corporate tax is partially rebated on income paid out as dividends, so that dividend income is only subject to personal taxes. As a result, the corporate tax focuses mainly on income generating accruing capital gains to shareholders.

firms are entirely owned by domestic residents, then this approach means taxing at accrual their foreign as well as their domestic profits.[12] To the extent that domestic firms have foreign owners, the corporate tax rate should be reduced proportionately.[13] Conversely, when domestic residents buy shares in foreign corporations, to that extent the corporate profits of the foreign firms should be taxable. If foreign subsidiaries located in the UK have no domestic shareholders, then they should be tax exempt.[14]

None of these tax provisions are seen in the UK, or anywhere else. In some cases, enforcement problems can be offered as an explanation. For example, if profits received by foreign subsidiaries located in the UK were tax exempt, then domestic shareholders may try to appear to be foreign shareholders, for example, by buying domestic equity through a Swiss financial intermediary, so as to avoid tax. If this threat from tax evasion is large enough, then foreign shareholders in the domestic economy should be taxed to some degree, trading off the benefits from reducing evasion with the costs from reducing investment in the domestic economy.

Yet there is no apparent pressure to adopt any of the above tax provisions, even though these are the provisions that avoid any distortions to the location or form of capital that residents choose to invest in. Of course, the current tax treatment in the UK may just be very badly designed. However, its stability over time and the use in many other countries of the same basic tax structure should raise questions about whether the tax structure in fact creates such large distortions. The inference we would draw is that this tax structure is responding to a variety of other pressures not taken into account in the above discussion. Without taking these pressures into account, it is hard to be confident when making policy recommendations based on the above framework.

3. TAXATION OF MULTINATIONALS IF PROFITS ARE LABOUR INCOME

If corporate profits represent labour income, through for example stock compensation replacing wage payments either for highly paid regular employees

[12] Alternatively, if the foreign profits are only taxed at repatriation, then the tax rate should be adjusted so as to replicate the effective tax rate that would have arisen with a tax at accrual. See Auerbach (1991) for a derivation of the appropriate rate.

[13] Formally, this is true only if the country has no market power in the international market for corporate equity.

[14] The argument here is the same as that against a territorial corporate tax.

or for entrepreneurs, then how should the corporate tax best be designed, given that labour income is otherwise taxable under the personal tax?

To focus this discussion on the issues left out of the chapter, we assume that there are no domestic taxes on income from savings, and full expensing of new investment (equivalent to use of an ACE).[15] The question becomes how the tax system should be designed so as to tax labour income at the same rate, regardless of the form of compensation, to avoid distorting the form of compensation. Since wages and salaries are taxable personal income to the employee,[16] distortions are avoided only to the extent that other forms of compensation are ultimately taxed at the same rate.

There are many ways to accomplish this outcome. If the corporate rate (together with future individual tax liabilities on the resulting capital gains) equals the maximum personal tax rate due on wage and salary income, as proposed in this chapter, then employees in the highest tax bracket will be indifferent between wage and stock compensation,[17] while all other employees face a tax advantage from receiving wage compensation. Since use of stock compensation is largely confined to top executives, this approach should provide a reasonable approximation to a level playing field.[18]

If this approach is used to avoid distortions to the form of compensation, how would it deal with cross-border economic activity? Passive portfolio investments by domestic residents in foreign firms would not include any 'labour' income, so should be treated the same as any other capital income. If capital income faces very low effective tax rates, then this foreign-source portfolio income should face low effective rates as well. Given existing crediting arrangements, this outcome largely corresponds to existing practice.

If foreign subsidiaries locate in the UK, then their highly paid employees face the same tax incentive as highly paid employees of domestically owned firms to receive compensation in the form of stock rather than wages and salaries. These incentives would be avoided if the profits of the subsidiary are taxed at the same rate as applies to other firms operating in the domestic economy, consistent with the observed tax treatment.[19]

[15] Gordon, Kalambokidis, and Slemrod (2004a) argue that the US tax system as of 1995 came close in practice to exempting capital income from tax.

[16] In the US at least, wage and salary income is also subject to payroll taxes and State as well as Federal income taxes.

[17] Similarly, entrepreneurs will be indifferent on tax grounds between wage payments and retention of accumulating profits.

[18] Bonuses tied to stock prices rather than stock compensation can then be used to provide incentives to employees for whom wage compensation is favoured on tax grounds.

[19] The subsidiary might well shift these profits abroad to avoid domestic tax. However, if the profits must ultimately be repatriated (the same issue faced in other contexts below), then they will

To avoid having this taxation of foreign subsidiaries located in the UK discourage capital investment in the UK, capital investment can be expensed (or equivalent), consistent with the treatment under an ACE.[20] To avoid discouraging foreign firms from using their intellectual capital in the UK, royalty payments would need to be deductible (as they are in the UK).

The sticking point here is determining the size of royalty payments for tax purposes, given the pressures faced by both the tax authorities and the firm in negotiating over their size. The multinational presumably would like to maximize the size of these deductions, subject to the constraint that enough profits remain within the subsidiary to allow it to provide outside shareholders an adequate rate of return on their invested funds. If subsidiaries with profitable technologies are fully mobile across possible host countries, then tax competition implies that tax rates will be pushed down to the point that host country governments just break even by allowing entry of foreign subsidiaries. The country breaks even if it collects no more in taxes than it would if the domestic factors employed by the firm instead were reallocated elsewhere, consistent with it allowing full deduction for the market royalty rate for any proprietary technology used by the subsidiary. If a subsidiary using a profitable technology gains from locating in a particular host country, however,[21] then the host country government does have an incentive to tax the location-specific profits of the multinational, for example by imposing a withholding tax on royalty payments made to the foreign parent firm.[22] We therefore expect full deductibility of royalty payments when firms are fully mobile across countries, but conflicts over the determination of royalty payments and some net taxation when firms are not fully mobile.

Our key concern with the proposal in this chapter concerns the proposed tax treatment of income earned by the subsidiaries of domestic multinationals operating abroad. Under the proposal, this income will be exempt from domestic tax. Yet this income includes a return to the ideas and effort of the entrepreneur and other firm employees, introducing a tax distortion favouring the use of ideas abroad, violating for example the proposed 'capital ownership neutrality'.

If these profits face corporate tax at accrual at the same rate as applies to domestic firms, then the tax treatment of labour income would be neutral.

be subject to the domestic corporate tax as well as personal capital gains taxes on any shares owned by domestic employees, so face a domestic tax rate comparable to that on wage and salary income.

[20] We have argued above that any country that is small relative to world capital markets has an incentive to exempt capital investments from tax.

[21] For example, a retailer like Walmart profits from setting up operations in each possible host country, so is not indifferent (taxes aside) to the location of its subsidiaries.

[22] This is true up to the point that the subsidiary would choose to shut down.

This treatment of course differs from the current law, which taxes foreign-source profits at repatriation, as well as from the proposed exemption treatment.

However, taxation of the income from foreign subsidiaries at repatriation is equivalent to taxation of their earnings at accrual if funds sent abroad are immediately deductible for tax purposes while all repatriations are taxable in full (and all realized capital losses deductible in full). This assertion is simply an application of the argument that taxing pension income when received is equivalent in present value to taxing the initial wage income that is withheld to invest in the pension plan: in either case, individuals are fully taxed on all compensation payments they receive, whether in the form of wage payments or pensions. The current treatment of pension income introduces no distortions to the form of compensation as long as the individual's tax rate is constant over time and as long as the rate of return earned on funds invested through a pension plan is equivalent to the rate of return that could be earned on other savings.[23]

This cash-flow tax treatment of transactions with foreign subsidiaries of domestic multinationals differs from current law because funds sent abroad are not currently deductible at the date when they are sent abroad but instead are deductible when invested capital is finally repatriated. In practice the amount of funds sent abroad by multinationals is likely to be small relative to the size of their operations, since largely they are providing intellectual capital to their foreign subsidiaries, so that this difference between current law and a neutral law should be minor.

An immediate complication, though, is that if the home country imposes the same effective tax rate on foreign-source entrepreneurial income as on other sources of labour income but also the host country taxes these profits, then the overall effective tax rate on foreign-source entrepreneurial profits exceeds that on other types of labour income. Here, existing tax provisions allowing a credit for taxes paid abroad help restore neutrality in the effective tax treatment of different forms of labour income from the perspective of the individual, even if not from the perspective of the home versus host country governments.

Neutrality requires that foreign-source income ultimately be taxed at the domestic tax rate, regardless of which government receives the revenue. The effective tax rate could be higher, in spite of the credit, if the foreign tax rate faced by the multinational exceeds the domestic tax rate. Given the ease of shifting profits to countries with low tax rates (such as tax havens), few

23 Recall that we continue to assume no domestic taxes on income from savings.

multinationals should face a tax rate on foreign-source profits above the domestic rate. The effective tax rate could end up being well below the normal domestic corporate tax rate, however, if firms can retain funds abroad until they have an opportunity to repatriate them when their domestic tax rate is temporarily low. For example, the US in 2003 allowed multinationals to repatriate profits subject to a tax rate of only 5%, so that the overall corporate tax rate on these profits could have been as low as this 5% if the income had previously accrued within a tax haven. This outcome can yield a very low ex post tax rate on these foreign-source earnings, and the anticipation of such opportunities generates an ex ante tax incentive encouraging use of entrepreneurial ideas abroad.[24]

Another potential problem is that firms may never need to repatriate profits earned abroad, so never face domestic tax on these earnings. Firms can continue to face attractive activities abroad into the indefinite future. Even if they need to raise further funds for domestic investments, multinationals may be able to borrow using foreign assets as collateral, so draw on these funds without formally repatriating them. Firms may well find a variety of other ways of implicitly repatriating the funds, for example, having the foreign subsidiary invest directly in the project that the parent firm hopes to finance. Deferral of tax until repatriation can at times mean that the tax is never paid, again introducing a distortion favouring foreign activity and favouring the creation of intellectual capital.[25]

This distortion is larger the lower the effective corporate tax rate paid abroad on these foreign-source profits. In particular, by shifting profits into a tax haven and never repatriating them, the firm can face little or no taxes on their foreign-source earnings. The UK responds here by making foreign-source profits immediately taxable at the domestic tax rate if they arise in a country with a corporate tax rate less than three-quarters of the UK rate. Not only does this approach reduce a distortion to the location of use of intellectual property but it also preserves the domestic government's tax base. Since not all countries with a corporate tax rate below the domestic rate fall under this provision, though, some distortions still remain.

[24] Funds can also be repatriated when the firm has domestic tax losses. Discretion over the timing of repatriations allows for greater shifting of income across time periods, so greater tax smoothing than is allowed under existing provisions on tax loss carry-forwards and carry-backs. With full tax smoothing, though, marginal profits are still taxable at the domestic corporate tax rate.

[25] Desai et al. (2002) report though that foreign subsidiaries of US multinationals paid out 54% of their profits in dividends during 1982–97, compared to a pay-out rate of 40% for all US firms included in the Compustat database. These figures do not suggest any systematic tendency to retain profits abroad.

If domestic multinationals face a tax when foreign-source earnings are repatriated, another way to avoid this tax is to shift their headquarters abroad before this repatriation occurs. This relocation avoids tax unless the move is viewed to entail a constructive repatriation of all existing foreign assets.

Equivalently, domestic inventors can set up a firm abroad to produce on the basis of their invention, so that the return to the inventor's intellectual property is not part of the domestic tax base. If the resulting income of the inventor accrues in a tax haven, then the inventor is simply taxed at domestic capital gains rates rather than the much higher tax rate on wage and salary income. One way for governments to close this loophole is to treat as labour income for tax purposes all receipts from foreign firms where the individual has had a past relationship, allowing any funds sent abroad to be fully tax deductible in order to avoid distorting savings incentives.

Of course, trying to treat differently for tax purposes any shares owned in firms where the individual has had a past relationship introduces administrative complications. This distinction is really unnecessary. If the same treatment were extended to all investments, allowing a deduction when any funds are invested and a tax on all funds received in return, then this treatment introduces no distortions for any passive 'marginal' investments. This outcome is precisely what is currently done with pension contributions. With a pension-type treatment of all savings, we end up with a personal consumption tax.

Under a personal consumption tax, since entrepreneurs and inventors ultimately face full taxation at labour income tax rates on any returns they receive from their intellectual property, whether in the form of capital gains, dividends, or wages, there is really no remaining need for the corporate tax, at least as a backstop for the personal tax on labour income. There may still be possibilities of tax avoidance through bequeathing shares at death, where labour income taxes have not yet been paid on the accumulated value. The response here that preserves a level playing field would be to treat any remaining funds never paid out to the shareholder during his or her life as taxable at labour income tax rates at the date of death. Another problem can be the monitoring of funds received from abroad. This potential problem may require information exchange between governments, or monitoring of funds from abroad deposited in domestic financial institutions.

Inventors and entrepreneurs can also avoid domestic tax on the returns to their intellectual capital by moving abroad before these profits are received.[26]

[26] We have been told that this is a serious problem in the Netherlands, where business owners often move abroad (typically to Belgium) before selling their businesses.

To the best of our knowledge, this problem has not to date been addressed in the UK or the US. To do so would involve constructive receipt of any earnings or capital gains that have accrued on business activity at the date when the individual moves abroad.

Another issue that arises with intellectual capital as well as with past investments in physical capital is the temptation governments may have to seize existing assets. Calling a firm's intellectual property 'rents' reflects this temptation. Past efforts at developing intellectual property or past savings to finance physical capital investments cannot be undone, so that these existing assets can be taxed at very high rates without any immediate loss of the tax base. However, the threat of this happening again in the future can badly discourage future investments in intellectual or physical capital in the country.[27] Here, governments cannot easily commit not to impose such windfall taxes in the future, and at best can build up a reputation for grandfathering existing assets when tax policy is changed. Losing this reputation through a one-time seizure can be very costly.[28]

4. IMPLICATIONS OF POSSIBLE DOMESTIC TAX REFORMS FOR THE TAX TREATMENT OF CROSS-BORDER ACTIVITY

In Section 3, we argued that the current tax treatment of foreign-source income is broadly consistent with what we would expect if the implicit aim is to impose a neutral tax on the labour earnings of domestic residents, regardless of the form of compensation and regardless of where the ideas are employed.

To what extent would current tax provisions need to be modified under any of a number of plausible reforms to the domestic tax system? How do international considerations affect the merit of any of these proposals?

A common proposal is to reduce the effective tax rate on income from savings. One possible means of accomplishing this reform would be to exempt dividends, interest income, and capital gains from personal tax, and to allow expensing for new capital investments. In our discussion above, we have assumed that the effective tax rate on income from savings is already very low, implying that any changes would be minor. However, any reduction in the tax rate on capital gains does reduce the effective tax rate on entrepreneurial

[27] This is referred to as a time-inconsistency problem in the economics literature.

[28] Note that even an increase in the personal tax rate involves a partial seizure of the return on intellectual capital not yet paid out to the inventor.

income that is ultimately received in the form of capital gains. To leave the effective tax rate on this form of labour income unchanged could then require a rise in the domestic corporate tax rate.

This chapter proposes to shift to a territorial corporate tax. Under such a tax, foreign-source earnings generated by the ideas of domestic residents become free of domestic corporate tax, so would only be subject to foreign corporate taxes and domestic personal capital gains taxes. To the extent that foreign-source earnings had previously been subject to domestic corporate taxes at repatriation, this reform also reduces the effective tax rate on the foreign-source earnings of domestic entrepreneurs. The resulting change may be limited, however, since the effective domestic corporate tax paid at repatriation has been small, owing to the existing credit.

What would be the effects of a shift to use of formula apportionment, a frequently proposed reform in the EU? Under such a proposal, the profits earned by a domestic multinational would be taxable at a weighted average corporate tax rate, with the weights based on the fraction of activity (property, payroll, or sales) located in each of the countries where a firm does business. Only a fraction of these profits would be taxable in the entrepreneur's home country, so that most of the earnings from the entrepreneur's intellectual capital would escape domestic taxes. Whether these earnings still face a comparable tax rate depends on where the firm does business. Making use of intellectual property in countries with low corporate tax rates is encouraged, and if the resulting weighted average corporate tax rate is below the domestic rate then there is a resulting tax distortion affecting forms of compensation. Distortions should be less than with a territorial tax or with the existing corporate tax, however, since shifting property, payroll, or sales to a tax haven should be more costly than shifting accounting profits.[29]

Another possible reform supported in this chapter, given its successful use in Scandinavia, is a dual income tax. Under such a tax, corporate income is first taxable under the corporate income tax, with the same issues as elsewhere about the domestic tax treatment of foreign-source income. Individual receipts from dividends, interest payments, and capital gains, are then taxable as 'capital income' as long as in total they are less than some fraction of the invested capital. In principle, any excess is taxable as 'labour income', though at least in Sweden any excess capital gains are instead treated as half capital income and half labour income. In practice, capital losses are instead treated as negative capital income.

[29] Formula apportionment introduces its own additional distortions, however, as described in Gordon and Wilson (1986).

To what degree does such a dual income tax distort an individual's incentives to become an entrepreneur, and if so to receive compensation as wages and salaries versus dividends or accruing capital gains in shares owned in the firm? Given the option to pay out profits as wages and salaries, the effective tax rate on positive entrepreneurial income should at most equal the personal tax rate on wages and salaries. To avoid introducing an incentive to retain earnings within the firm, converting wage into capital gains income, the chapter proposes setting the corporate tax rate so that corporate taxes plus any further capital gains taxes are equivalent to the labour taxes that would otherwise be due on this income.

For domestic firms, this proposal could work appropriately. Multinationals, however, can avoid the domestic corporate tax by reporting the income abroad. Under the proposal, corporate income reported abroad, perhaps through use of transfer pricing, is taxed as capital gains under the domestic tax code, unless the individual's overall return to 'savings' is so high that the excess is again taxed as labour income.[30]

Note, though, that taxing all earnings to labour effort as labour income requires allowing losses attributed to ideas that work out poorly to be deductible from other labour income as well as imposing tax on profits at labour tax rates. When capital income is reclassified as labour income only when it exceeds a normal rate of return, this approach does not treat losses resulting from entrepreneurial effort appropriately, discouraging risk-taking.

What are the international tax implications of a shift from the income tax towards greater use of a VAT? Under a VAT, real goods shipped abroad are tax deductible while any goods imported from abroad are fully taxable. Under the tax treatment proposed above for intellectual capital used abroad, funds sent abroad would be tax deductible while all repatriated funds would be fully taxable. In theory, the two approaches are equivalent in present value.[31] A VAT therefore should lead to neutral incentives as long as all of the consumption of an entrepreneur/inventor occurs in the home country. A VAT, though, is a proportional tax, while the income tax allows much more flexibility in the rate structure. To preserve some semblance of the progressivity available under the income tax, VATs normally impose higher tax rates on goods consumed mainly by the rich.

[30] Neutral incentives require that the 'normal' rate of return equal a risk-free interest rate. At least in Sweden, the 'normal' rate of return taxable as capital income has been set much higher, leading to a reduced tax rate on a sizeable fraction of entrepreneurial income.

[31] This difference is analogous to the difference between an R-base and an F-base, using the terminology of Meade (1978).

5. TAX COORDINATION

One issue discussed at length in this chapter is tax coordination across countries. What pressure is faced for tax coordination, if the role of the corporate tax is to impose a neutral tax on all forms of compensation for labour effort?

Given substantial differences in the maximum tax rates on labour income across EU countries, neutrality requires differences in corporate tax rates as well. Any shift towards equal corporate tax rates leads to a subsidy to non-wage compensation in countries with high personal tax rates and a penalty on non-wage compensation (incentive pay) in countries with low personal tax rates.

If foreign-source earnings from intellectual capital can be kept abroad indefinitely, however, then the threat of tax evasion through use of tax havens remains. A variety of policies can then provide means of lessening the gains from such tax evasion. One approach would be a minimum corporate tax rate. Another would be information sharing, allowing the home country to tax profits reported in a tax haven at accrual. If entrepreneurs are taxed at death on the accumulated value of unrepatriated assets, information sharing again would be needed to help assess the value of these assets.

These pressures, though, largely become moot if countries shift to use of a VAT or a dual income tax. They may become somewhat less pressing through use of formula apportionment.

As discussed in a variety of recent papers, for example, Keen and Ligthart (2004), information sharing can only be expected to occur if the host country has an economic incentive to provide such information. These issues are nicely discussed in this chapter, and are as relevant when information sharing is needed to enforce taxes on labour income as they are when the underlying source of income is capital income.

6. OMITTED ISSUES

The chapter starts with the sentence, 'This chapter assesses the role of international considerations in tax design, emphasizing issues related to capital taxation.' Our concerns with the chapter arise from this choice to focus on capital taxation. By our reading of the evidence, the key issues driving the current design of international tax provisions relate to the taxation of labour income, and more specifically income from entrepreneurial effort and imagination.

Taxation of labour income raises a quite different set of enforcement issues from taxation of capital income. Deferral of taxes, for example, is not a concern, only their present value. Taxation of income at repatriation can therefore work fine, as long as foreign-source earnings are ultimately repatriated. In general, current tax provisions seem reasonably well designed to try to implement a neutral tax rate on income earned by domestic workers, managers, and entrepreneurs, regardless of the source of their income or the form in which it is received. To preserve a neutral tax treatment of labour income, the substance of the current provisions dealing with cross-border flows should therefore be preserved rather than replaced with an exemption system.

One question omitted from the above discussion, though, is whether entrepreneurial income *should* be taxed at the same rate that applies to wage and salary income. If labour effort that generates intellectual capital also generates positive externalities to others, since the protection of intellectual property is inherently limited, then a case can be made that entrepreneurial activity should be encouraged. Externalities plausibly arise from attempted innovations, whether successful or unsuccessful, so any tax subsidies should be linked specifically to entrepreneurial *risk-taking*. Only the most successful projects will result in foreign-source income. Allowing a lower tax rate on this foreign-source income, while leaving unchanged the tax treatment of less successful projects under the domestic tax system, then provides one mechanism for increasing the incentives for engaging in more risky entrepreneurial projects.[32]

Another issue largely neglected in the above discussion is the effects of existing tax structures on migration decisions. When migrants choose a country in which to locate, they are in part choosing both a tax structure and a package of public services. The fiscal structure then discourages entry of individuals who are net payers, and encourages entry by individuals who are net recipients, relative to what these same individuals face in otherwise equivalent locations. Migration within the EU, while less for example than that between US states, is still non-trivial. The fiscal pressures are presumably greatest for those at the extremes of the income distribution. The richest individuals would be attracted to countries with the least progressive tax structure while the poorest individuals would be attracted to the countries with the most generous social safety-net expenditures. These migration pressures have largely been neglected in past discussions of the optimal personal tax rate

[32] Cullen and Gordon (2007) discuss other ways in which the tax system can encourage more entrepreneurial risk-taking.

schedule. Even after the thorough discussion of the taxation of international capital flows in this chapter and our more limited discussion of the taxation of the return to entrepreneurial activity earned abroad, there are many further issues for tax policy arising from cross-border activity.

REFERENCES

Auerbach, A. J. (1991), 'Retrospective Capital Gains Taxation', *American Economic Review*, **81**, 167–78.

—— (2006), 'Why have Corporate Tax Revenues Declined? Another Look', N.B.E.R. Working Paper No. 12463.

—— and Poterba, J. M. (1987), 'Why Have Corporate Tax Revenues Declined?', *Tax Policy and the Economy*, **1**, 1–28.

Becker, J., and Fuest, C. (2005), 'Does Germany Collect Revenue from Taxing the Normal Return to Capital', *Fiscal Studies*, **26**, 491–511.

Cullen, J. B., and Gordon, R. H. (2006), 'How Do Taxes Affect Entrepreneurial Activity? A Comparison of U.S. and Swedish Law', published in Swedish in *Entreprenörskap och Tillväxt*, edited by Braunderhjelm, P., and Wiklund, J. Stockholm: Forum för Småöretagsforskning.

—— —— (2007), 'Taxes and Entrepreneurial Risk-Taking: Theory and Empirical Estimates for the U.S.', *Journal of Public Economics*, **91**, 1479–505.

Desai, M. et al. (2002), 'Dividend Policy Inside the Firm', N.B.E.R. Working Paper No. 8698.

Devereux, M. P., and Griffith, R. (2003), 'Evaluating Tax Policy for Location Decisions', *International Tax and Public Finance*, 107–26.

Gordon, R. H., and Hines, J. R. Jr. (2002), 'International Taxation', in Auerbach, A. J. and Feldstein, M. (eds.), *Handbook of Public Economics, Vol. 4*, 1935–95, New York: Elsevier.

—— Kalambokidis, L., and Slemrod, J. (2004), 'Do we now Collect any Revenue from Taxing Capital Income?', *Journal of Public Economics*, **88**, 981–1009.

—— —— —— (2004a), 'A New Summary Measure of the Effective Tax Rate on Investment', in Sørensen, P. B. (ed.), *Measuring the Tax Burden on Capital and Labor*, Cambridge, Mass.: MIT Press.

—— and Slemrod, J. (2000), 'Are "Real" Responses to Taxes Simply Income Shifting between Corporate and Personal Tax Bases?', in Slemrod, J. (ed.), *Does Atlas Shrug? The Economic Consequences of Taxing the Rich*, Cambridge, Mass.: Harvard University Press.

—— —— (1988), 'Do we Collect any Revenue from Taxing Capital Income?', *Tax Policy and the Economy*, **2**, 89–130.

—— and Wilson, J. D. (1986), 'An Examination of Multijurisdictional Corporate Income Taxation under Formula Apportionment', *Econometrica*, **54**, 1357–73.

Helpman, E. (2006), 'Trade, FDI, and the Organization of Firms', *Journal of Economic Literature*, **44**, 589–630.
Hines, J. R., Jr. (1999), 'Lessons from Behavioral Responses to International Taxation', *National Tax Journal*, **52**, 305–22.
—— and Hubbard, R. G. (1990), 'Coming Home to America: Dividend Repatriations by U.S. Multinationals', in Razin, A., and Slemrod, J. (eds.), *Taxation in the Global Economy*, Chicago: University of Chicago Press.
Keen, M., and Ligthart, J. E. (2004), 'Information Sharing and International Taxation', CentER Discussion Paper No. 2004–117.
Meade, J. (1978), *The Structure and Reform of Direct Taxation: Report of a Committee chaired by Professor J. E. Meade for the Institute for Fiscal Studies*, London: George Allen & Unwin. http://www.ifs.org.uk/publications/3433.
Nielsen, S. B., and Sørensen, P. B. (1997), 'On the Optimality of the Nordic System of Dual Income Taxation', *Journal of Public Economics*, **63**, 311–29.
Sørensen, P. B. (1988), 'Wealth Taxation, Income Taxation, and Savings', Blue Mimeo 163, Department of Economics, University of Copenhagen.
—— (2004), 'International Tax Coordination: Regionalism vs. Globalism', *Journal of Public Economics*, **88**, 1187–214.
—— (2006), 'Can Capital Income Taxes Survive? And Should They?', CESifo Working Paper No. 1793.

11

Small Business Taxation

*Claire Crawford and Judith Freedman**

Claire Crawford is a Senior Research Economist at the IFS. Her research covers a wide range of issues, from the impact of the tax system on small businesses and entrepreneurship to the evaluation of large-scale labour market interventions. She is particularly interested in the determinants of educational attainment, and has recently completed work considering the roles of month of birth and non-cognitive skills.

Judith Freedman is KPMG Professor of Taxation Law at Oxford University, Director of Legal Research at the Oxford University Centre for Business Taxation and joint editor of the *British Tax Review*. Previously, she worked at the City law firm of Freshfields and then at the LSE. Her work has focused on business taxation and the law of business organizations, with one special interest being small businesses. She participated in the ESRC Small Business Initiative and was a member of the Company Law Review Steering Group's Small Private Company Working Group. She is a member of HMRC's Panel of International Academic Tax Expertise on Business and of the IFS's Tax Law Review Committee.

* The authors would like to thank Stuart Adam, Steve Bond, Michael Devereux, Malcolm Gammie, Graeme McDonald, Jonathan Shaw, and many others who commented and assisted with aspects of this chapter.

EXECUTIVE SUMMARY

This chapter considers how small, owner-managed businesses are currently taxed and how this might be improved. The focus is on the difficulties created by taxing different legal forms of business in different ways. Differences in tax treatment across a spectrum from employees to the self-employed (unincorporated firms) and on to companies (incorporated firms) create opportunities for taxpayers to reduce their tax liability and their social security contributions by converting income from labour into income from capital.

'Small business' has many different meanings in different contexts. Whilst this chapter does not attempt to cover every issue that could be considered to fall under the heading 'small business' taxation, it does deal with some topics that provide essential background to the main structural issues discussed. The authors explain why they reject the case for blanket tax incentives for small businesses as such, although they accept that there may be exceptional cases of market failure or issues of compliance costs where specific reliefs are warranted and can be targeted effectively. Otherwise, for both efficiency and equity reasons, steps towards increasing simplicity and reducing distortions in the tax system generally are likely to be of more help to all (including small businesses) than are special measures.

The structural issues addressed are a problem in many jurisdictions, but have been brought to the fore in the UK in recent years by the introduction, reduction, and subsequent withdrawal of a 'starting rate' of corporation tax, and by the different and increasing rates of social security contributions (known in the UK as National Insurance contributions (NICs)) levied on the employed and the self-employed. These developments have highlighted the tax advantages available through self-employment and, more importantly, incorporation. For many taxpayers there is no choice other than to be an employee. For larger businesses wishing to raise external capital, incorporation is generally essential for commercial reasons. Thus the incentive to select between employment, self-employment, and incorporation is relevant only for owner-managed businesses at the smallest end of the business sector. Nevertheless, the distortions in the system affect many. Not only do large numbers of employees feel unfairly treated but attempts to counteract these incentives can lead to anti-avoidance provisions targeted at the self-employed and owner-managers of small companies that increase costs and cause difficulties beyond the group at which they are aimed. Moreover, they impact on the design of the entire corporate tax system.

It is important to consider the entire spectrum of legal forms when considering reforms: simply treating the self-employed more like employees, for example, could increase the difference in treatment between incorporated and unincorporated businesses. Total alignment of tax and NICs treatment across the spectrum is difficult to achieve in a straightforward manner because there are real differences between legal forms: a self-employed contractor does not have the same legal rights and obligations as an employee, and an unincorporated business owner becomes a shareholder and probably a director and an employee on incorporation, rather than a direct owner of the underlying business. Nevertheless, this chapter argues that the aim should be to align effective tax rates for these groups after taking into account capital investment. Attempts by the UK government in recent years to advantage incorporation in the belief that this will encourage entrepreneurship have not proved to be a success. The authors maintain that the tax system should not discriminate between legal forms and proceed on this basis.

One suggestion frequently made as a step towards equal tax treatment of owner-managed businesses is that some sub-category of incorporated firms should be treated as if they were unincorporated for tax purposes, but this does not solve the problem at the employee/self-employed boundary. Moreover, it would only address the differences at the incorporated/unincorporated boundary if such treatment were to be mandatory, which would give rise to the problem of defining the firms to which this compulsion should apply. The chapter reviews the difficulties encountered in defining a sub-group of companies in a number of jurisdictions (including the UK, Norway, and Sweden), and, on this evidence, concludes that it is unlikely that a general, workable, and non-arbitrary definition could be devised. Approaches that seek to treat particular types of firm differently from others are rejected, therefore, in favour of reforms that can be applied to all firms, and the chapter then moves on to consider a number of potential solutions that adopt this approach.

Alignment of effective tax rates across different legal forms in the UK could be achieved either by adapting the existing system, or by adopting more radical reforms. If the structure of the current UK tax system were to be broadly maintained, neutrality could be increased across the spectrum by aligning NICs rates for the employed and self-employed, whilst at the same time increasing the small companies' corporation tax rate even to the point of aligning it with the main corporation tax rate (thus raising the effective tax rate on dividend income). This latter move appears to be in tune with the direction of recent UK government thinking.

Neither of these reforms completely addresses the fact that, for the reasons discussed in this chapter and elsewhere in this book, it is often argued that the return to capital should be more lightly taxed than the return to labour. Various radical alternatives could be adopted in order to deal with this. One solution would be the combination of a shareholder income tax with a rate of return allowance (RRA), and a corporation tax with an allowance for corporate equity (ACE). Such a system would exempt the normal rate of return to capital from taxation at both the corporate and the personal levels, while providing a mechanism for taxing above normal returns to capital and labour income at the same progressive rates, regardless of whether they are described as dividends, capital gains, or salary.

Thus, while it remains the case that alignment or equalization of the effective tax rates applied to different legal forms is necessary to tax small owner-managed businesses in a sensible way, this can be achieved without prejudicing the capacity of the tax system to distinguish coherently between normal returns to financial capital and labour income. Furthermore, the approach proposed has the advantage that it does not require the use of arbitrary definitions and difficult distinctions between different types of firm.

11.1. INTRODUCTION

This chapter addresses a focused set of structural issues concerning the way in which small, owner-managed businesses are taxed. This may sound limited, but in fact these issues are highly complex and pervade the design of the entire tax system. They affect the interaction between taxation of income from labour and that of income from capital. They are at the interface between the taxation of incorporated and unincorporated firms and also go to the heart of the relationship between personal and business taxation. These issues therefore have great significance for many of the areas examined by this Review, because it is impossible to design a sensible personal or corporate tax system without taking them into account. This is the reason for this special study.

This structural focus means that this chapter will not attempt to cover every issue that could be considered to fall under the heading 'small business taxation'. Some additional material which is key to an understanding of small business issues and provides important background to the structural focus is dealt with in Section 11.6. 'Small business' has many different meanings in different contexts. The chapter focuses on structural issues surrounding the taxation of business activity across a spectrum that starts with employment and then moves through self-employment (either sole proprietorships or partnerships, that is, unincorporated businesses), to small, owner-managed companies (incorporated businesses). This focus delineates the scope of this chapter.

11.1.1. The key structural question

Across the spectrum of activity described above, the practicalities and substance of taxation vary significantly. At one end of the spectrum there are standard, full time, permanent employees who appear to require very different tax treatment from incorporated businesses with a number of shareholders at the other end. Nevertheless, there are boundaries within this spectrum. On either side of these boundaries, between the employed and the self-employed, and between the incorporated and unincorporated business, there are activities which may be, or may seem, very similar economically but are based on different legal relationships, rights, and obligations. One solution might be to treat employees through to companies across this whole small business spectrum in exactly the same way for tax purposes, taxing them on the same receipts and at the same rate, but this is not achievable in a completely straightforward way for two reasons. First, differences in legal form have real practical consequences. Receipts vary in nature: an employee's wage cannot be equated with the receipts of a business and so business receipts will require the application of rules from which to derive a profit figure. Even once profit has been calculated, the existence of a company may mean that receipts can be paid out either as wages or as dividends, with different legal implications. Aligning overall rates of tax on income across this spectrum may require analysis of the tax levied at both corporate and personal levels. Secondly, there is a trend towards taxation of labour income at a higher rate than that levied on income from capital that leads away from neutrality between the taxation of different types of business. It may be that the requirements of small business taxation weigh against this trend, but, as discussed by Griffith, Hines, and Sørensen in Chapter 10, there are theoretical and pragmatic arguments to support a differential. If a differential is to be maintained between the tax rates on income from capital and income from labour, however, it follows that there will be an incentive to convert labour income into income from capital if possible.

One of the consequences of incorporation of a business, however small, is the scope it offers for conversion of labour income (earnings from employment or self-employment) into income from capital (dividends or capital gains). This can alter the tax consequences with no change in economic activity. To the extent that this is considered undesirable, this is sometimes dealt with by special tax rules that partially counteract the legal characterization, for example, by treating incorporated firms as if they were unincorporated, or by deeming all corporate income to be earned income. These provisions may bring their own difficulties, however, especially in relation to when they should be applied.

Some observers question the simple dichotomy between labour income on the one hand and income from capital on the other. Whilst income from employment is clearly labour income, income from self-employment and that derived through an incorporated business may be a mixture of labour income, income from capital and—possibly—a return to risk-taking or 'entrepreneurship'. Apart from the fact that risk and entrepreneurship are not easily measurable, it is not entirely clear whether income representing a reward for these factors should be taxed as a return to capital or in the same way as labour income (or in some other way). There are issues of equity and also of the creation of incentives for risk-taking. There are pragmatic and political questions which mean that the tax treatment of this type of return will not necessarily be identical with that of either labour income or income from capital.

In order to accommodate the structural problems described above, any proposed new system in which capital income is to be taxed at a lower rate than labour income needs to ensure that the way in which this is achieved cannot be exploited by recharacterizing labour income as capital income. The mechanism for determining the nature of the return needs to be built into the system and applicable to all firms in order to make it equitable and practical.

There is little discussion in the Meade Report (Meade, 1978) of these problems. They have become more significant in the UK over recent years due to changes in levels and relationships between personal and corporate tax rates, and increases in NICs which are paid on earned income at different rates by the employed and self-employed and not at all on corporate dividends or capital gains. Increased diversity in working practices and easing of corporate law regulatory burdens for incorporated firms have also added to this mix. These developments, together with at times low or even nil corporation tax rates, have led to increasing numbers of self-employed and incorporated firms. Incorporation offers opportunities to convert highly taxed labour income into less highly taxed corporate income which, on distribution, carries a tax credit and is free from NICs. Profits retained in the company may be sheltered from higher tax rates and re-invested, eventually leading to a capital gain on the sale or liquidation of the company rather than income tax at the top rate. These issues are not unique to the UK[1] and have real implications for the structure of personal and corporation taxes more generally and so to the fundamental design questions studied in this Review.

11.1.2. Outline of chapter

For the reasons given, the focus of this chapter is on issues relating to the integration of corporation tax and income tax which links it to some of the questions of tax system design dealt with in other chapters. Following this introduction (Section 11.1), Section 11.2 of this chapter deals with definitional issues and discusses the nature of the small business sector. Section 11.3 analyses the different types of business organization which exist in law. It describes the structural tax issues which arise as a result of the differences in rules for different legal forms of business, with special reference to the difficulties currently experienced in the UK system. Section 11.4 discusses the various alternative options that have been put forward and comments on the extent to which the structural issues would be solved or alleviated by these proposals. Section 11.5 concludes.

The Note to the chapter (Section 11.6) makes reference to important issues which have arisen in debates forming part of this Review. It addresses the question of when, if at all, the tax system should favour small firms. Whilst it is not the aim of this chapter to discuss the details of different types of support and incentives for small firms, this question is relevant to the structural issues which are the focus because rules which give rise to non-neutralities are often justified on the ground that small businesses, or particular sub-categories of them, require special incentives. Therefore this justification is analysed in order to consider the structural issue fully. Issues relating to capital gains tax and inheritance tax are referred to briefly in this context, as are compliance cost issues. Some of these questions are also dealt with extensively elsewhere in this volume but they are examined in Section 11.6 in so far as they are relevant to the key focus of the chapter.

[1] Although the difference between rates of social security for the employed and self-employed may be more extreme in the UK than in some other systems. This is particularly true once account is taken of the fact that employers pay NICs on their employees' earnings, while no equivalent is levied on the self-employed.

11.2. DEFINITIONS AND NATURE OF SECTOR

11.2.1. A problematic definition

The term 'small business' is used in many different ways. To some it may call to mind a one-person service provider or unincorporated self-employed contractor; to others the term might refer to a company listed on the Alternative Investment Market rather than the London Stock Exchange. What is meant by 'small' is relative and will depend on the purpose of the definition. It may relate to qualitative characteristics rather than size. The *Committee of Inquiry on Small Firms* (Bolton (1971)) favoured a qualitative, or what it called an economic definition, albeit in tandem with statistical definitions looking at different measures for different sectors. As explained above, this chapter focuses on structural issues, but these need to be set in the context of a review of the make-up of the business population in order to understand their significance.

11.2.2. Qualitative and quantitative definitions

The structural focus of this chapter might suggest a need to define firms that are small in some qualitative sense for tax purposes: independent firms that are managed by their owners in a personalized way. They could have a significant turnover or profit levels and still fall within this definition, so might properly be called owner-managed rather than small; however, the use of the term 'small' for such firms is widespread and embedded.

This definition is of limited value for practical and therefore taxation purposes. Objective and easily measurable criteria are often needed in legislation. Quantitatively, size may be measured by profit, turnover, balance sheet, number of employees, number of owners, or some combination of these, as can be seen in the various examples in Appendix 11A. Each measure will give a very different picture—for example, quite large businesses in terms of number of employees may make low or negative profits. In terms of tax design, whether a business is owner-managed and controlled may have greater relevance to how the business should be taxed than quantitative size, as owner control affects the nature of income and scope for choice in the characterization of payments out of a corporation.

There is a long history in both UK company law and tax law of trying to define special types of small company, with little success.[2] Attempts to define

[2] For example, the Companies Act 1947 introduced a definition of exempt private companies which was described by the Jenkins Committee (Board of Trade (1962)) as producing

a sub-category of owner-managed companies have always resulted in highly complex definitions which have been difficult to apply. Whilst prima facie an owner-managed company may seem to be a very different entity from a large listed company, it is very difficult to capture the exact point at which the tax or company law treatment should change in such a way that the test is not open to manipulation, not least because it is so difficult to define the concept of control, which may be obtained through voting rights but also in other ways. It is equally difficult to separate out passive investors from those working in the company, since whilst this is obvious in many cases, in others it will change from time to time and shareholders may be working for the company in a whole variety of ways and for varying periods and portions of time. The distinction between companies listed on a recognized stock exchange and those which are not is occasionally used for tax purposes,[3] but this only distinguishes a small percentage of companies from the majority and so will not be particularly helpful in tackling the structural problem discussed in this chapter.

The legal definition of a 'close company' for tax purposes in the UK (which is not to be confused with the use of that term in the economic literature) is one which attempts to achieve this kind of qualitative distinction, but involves several complex sub-definitions (see Appendix 11A) and is not straightforward to apply. For this reason, whilst some of the 'solutions' to the small business taxation problem, in which 'small' businesses would be treated differently to 'large' businesses (from a tax perspective), appear prima facie attractive they are likely to be unworkable in practice.

11.2.3. 'Small' as a proxy for other characteristics

Confusingly, the term 'small business' is sometimes used as a proxy for other characteristics which governments may wish to target through the tax system, such as new firms, 'entrepreneurship', growth, and job creation. Using size as a means of targeting these groups is inaccurate because size does not relate directly to these characteristics.

Despite the rhetoric sometimes found in the small business literature and in political references to small businesses to the effect that they are the 'engine

'hideous complications and capricious results' and the category was abandoned in the Companies Act 1967.

[3] For example, Section 691 Income Tax Act 2007 (anti-avoidance provision not applying to listed companies). The UK companies' legislation distinguishes public companies, which may offer their shares to the public, and private companies, which may not, but the public/private divide is not necessarily associated with size. Whilst most, but not all, public companies are large, privately owned companies may also be very substantial.

of the economy', there is considerable academic debate about the extent to which small businesses are significant to job creation or growth. Whilst some are, many are not. As the figures below show, many are (and remain) very small indeed and are what might be termed 'non-entrepreneurial life-style businesses'. Distinguishing ex ante between those that will create employment and growth and those that will not is notoriously difficult, and even then there is no evidence that the provision of tax incentives would make much difference to the chances of growth.[4]

In Section 11.6 of this chapter the authors explain their view that the tax system should only be used to provide assistance to the small business sector in limited circumstances, in particular if and when assistance can be clearly targeted to meet a specific market failure. Section 11.6 comments on the difficulties in achieving this, which are in part related to the definitional issues discussed in this section. Here it is simply noted that it is a mistake to equate 'small businesses' with any particular economic or social characteristics when devising tax policy.

11.2.4. Make-up of the 'small business' sector

The majority of businesses in the UK and in other economies are 'small' by any measure.

Employment

In 2006, there were an estimated 4.5 million private sector businesses[5] in the UK, of which over 99% were firms with fewer than fifty employees and 96% were firms with fewer than ten employees (referred to as micro-businesses).[6] Most businesses in the UK have no employees (other than the owner in the case of incorporated firms). The number of businesses with no employees increased from just over 2.5 million (68%) in 1996, to over 3 million (73%) in 2006. By contrast, the number of businesses with at least one employee did not rise at all between 1996 and 2006, falling as a percentage of the total from 32% in 1996 to 27% in 2006 (see Section 11.3 for details).[7] Thus

[4] Attempts have been made to predict which firms will grow based on such factors as the characteristics of the owners. Even these have limited predictive value ex ante and they could certainly not provide the basis for differential tax regimes (see Storey (1994) at p. 158).

[5] This includes all legal forms, i.e. incorporated and unincorporated businesses.

[6] Micro-businesses accounted for 33% of employment and 23% of turnover in 2006.

[7] Source: DBERR SME statistics 2006, accessed via: <http://stats.berr.gov.uk/ed/sme/smestats2006.xls>.

a disproportionate amount of the increase in the number of businesses in recent years has been of businesses with no employees: this has relevance to the later discussion of the way in which the tax system appears to affect behaviour.

Other size-related categories[8]

The number of employees is not the only test which reveals how very small most businesses in the UK are. Almost 91% of companies paid the small companies' rate of corporation tax (or less[9]) in 2005–06.[10] Further, approximately two-thirds of all businesses were not required to register for Value-Added Tax (VAT) in 2006—indicating that approximately two-thirds of all businesses had annual turnover of less than £60,000 (the registration threshold in 2005–06).[11] Finally, two-thirds of companies registered with Companies' House were audit exempt in 2005–06 (that is, their annual turnover was less than £5.6 million).[12]

Legal form

Legal form or structure (discussed in Section 11.3) is not a reliable measure of size or of qualitative characteristics per se. Figure 11.1 shows the number of businesses in the UK in 2006, by number of employees and legal form. This illustrates that while sole proprietorships and partnerships are less likely to have employees than companies, it is still the case that 39% of companies do not have any employees at all (aside from the owner-manager) and 86% have fewer than ten employees.[13] So a reduced corporation tax rate for small companies does not necessarily target businesses providing employment.

[8] For further information on size-related criteria, see Appendix 11A.

[9] A lower rate was also available to companies whose profits were less than £10,000 pa at this time (see Appendices A and B).

[10] Authors' calculations from <http://www.hmrc.gov.uk/stats/corporate_tax/11-3-corporation-tax.pdf>. Note, however, that a very large company could make profits within this range.

[11] Authors' calculations from <http://stats.berr.gov.uk/ed/vat/VATStatsPressReleaseNov2007.pdf>.

[12] Source <http://www.companieshouse.gov.uk/about/miscellaneous/DTIReport20056.pdf>.

[13] Around 89% of sole proprietorships and 63% of partnerships have no employees. The category 'with no employees' comprises sole proprietorships and partnerships comprising only the self-employed owner-manager(s), and companies comprising only one employee-director (see <http://stats.berr.gov.uk/ed/sme/smestats2006-meth.pdf> for more details).

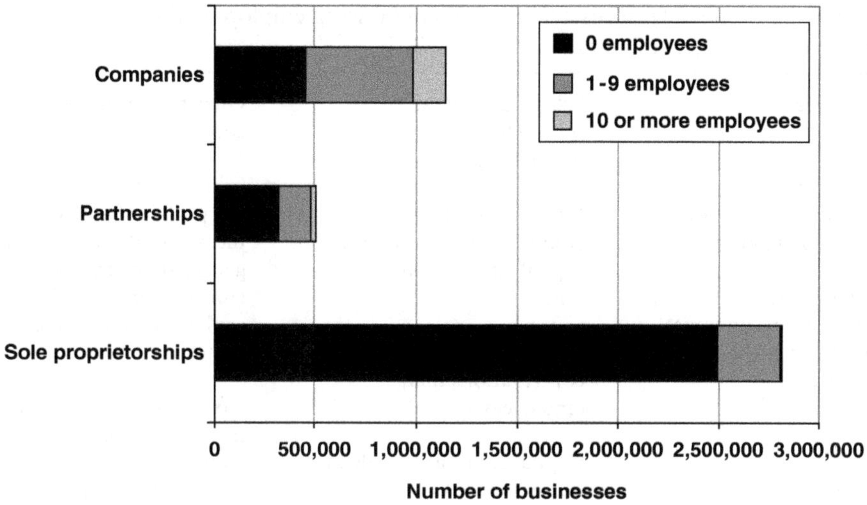

Note: Authors' calculations from DBERR SME Statistics, 2006.

Figure 11.1. Number of businesses in the UK in 2006, by number of employees and legal form

11.3. STRUCTURAL ISSUES: LEGAL FORM, BOUNDARIES, AND DISTORTIONS (WITH SPECIAL REFERENCE TO THE UK)

As outlined in the introduction, the approach taken in this chapter requires the legal forms of organization used by small businesses to be examined, and for consideration to be given to the link between legal form, the nature of the economic activity involved, and the consequent tax implications. The ideal would be that the legal form of a business should make no difference to its tax treatment (that is, complete neutrality would be achieved) but this cannot always be achieved in a straightforward way. Further consideration of the legal position may make this clear.

11.3.1. Two boundaries

There are two boundaries at which tax distortions can take place, as described in Table 11.1. The first is between the incorporated and unincorporated firm, and the second between the employed and self-employed.[14] To complicate

[14] Self-employed workers are all unincorporated businesses in tax terms, although they may not be considered to be businesses in economic terms. For the purposes of this chapter, self-employed workers and unincorporated businesses are synonymous unless otherwise stated.

Table 11.1. Some differences in tax treatment between employees, the self-employed, and owner-managers of companies in the UK[16]

Employee	Self-employed (sole proprietorship or partnership)	Owner-manager of company
Income tax on wages (return on labour) Social security contributions on wages (employee and employer)	Income tax on profits (mixed return on labour, capital and economic rents) Lower social security contributions than employees Capital gains tax on sale of business assets	Corporation tax on income profits and capital gains paid by company (mixed return on labour, capital, and economic rents) Tax on dividends (credit for corporation tax plus additional payment by higher rate taxpayer at personal level) Income tax and social security contributions on wages as employees (but flexible level chosen by owner-manager) Capital gains tax paid by shareholders on sale of shares

matters further, the worker's choice may be between employment and incorporation, rather than between employment and self-employed status. Horizontal equity[15] issues arise at each borderline and across the piece. Reducing the distortion at one boundary could make it worse at the other and so the whole spectrum must be considered as one issue in any proposals for reform. Thus, whilst bringing the tax treatment of the employed and self-employed closer together might be one solution at that end of the spectrum, if this meant that the difference between the unincorporated and incorporated firm increased, it might not be advisable; further, it might not even solve the problem at the boundary being tackled, since movement can take place between all three categories.

[15] Horizontal equity means that people with a similar ability to pay taxes should pay the same amount.

[16] This table is only designed to provide an indication of differences in tax treatment. Further details can be found in Appendix 11C.

11.3.2. Overview of legal form

The majority of small firms in the UK trade in one of three main forms: as sole traders, as partnerships[17] (both types of unincorporated firm), or as companies limited by shares (limited liability companies).[18] In addition, a new form, limited liability partnerships (LLPs) were introduced in the UK in 2001 (see Freedman (2004) for more details). LLPs are in some senses closer to companies than partnerships, but for the most part, they are taxed as partnerships. These forms are the key legal structures to be found in other jurisdictions, although there are important variations across systems. Although most large firms will be incorporated, it does not follow that most incorporated firms are large. Legal status is not a proxy for size. In addition, incorporation does not necessarily relate to qualitative characteristics such as separation of ownership and control, since single-person firms may incorporate and there are some large unincorporated partnerships.[19] Nevertheless it is true to say that most businesses which contemplate growth and the raising of external finance will incorporate. Incorporation does not encourage growth so much as anticipate or even follow on from growth. As will be shown, much of the recent increase in the number of incorporations has been in the form of companies with no employees other than the owner-manager himself and these companies will typically also have only one or two shareholders.

Unincorporated firms

In the UK, sole traders are not regulated by any special legal provisions regarding legal form[20] and the business has no separate legal personality. In particular, the business and personal assets of a sole trader do not need to be kept separate (although accounts are required for tax purposes for profits over a de minimis level). This has serious implications for any tax rules that require detailed records of assets belonging to the business and strict separation of business and personal assets. This is not merely a practical detail. The sole trader has personal liability for all debts and activities of his business so that his own assets and those of the business are mixed as a matter of law and it is conceptually difficult to treat them differently.

[17] Partnerships may be general or limited. Limited partnerships are unincorporated but registered and one partner must have unlimited liability, although that partner may itself be a limited liability company.

[18] UK limited liability companies should not be confused with US limited liability companies (LLCs), which are unincorporated and organized on a flexible partnership basis.

[19] Although many professional partnerships are now LLPs.

[20] Apart from the minimalist Business Names Act 1985 which governs the use of business names.

Similar rules apply to general partnerships. These may be governed by purely oral or written agreements and can arise quite informally. The relationships between the partners are governed by the Partnership Act 1890, which also lays down some mandatory provisions regulating the relationship between the partners and outsiders. General partners remain liable to the full extent of their personal assets and these may well be mixed with their business assets.[21]

Limited liability partnerships (LLPs) are a hybrid form which combine transparent partnership treatment for tax purposes with a corporate form and have a measure of limited liability like companies. They are required to be registered and were introduced to cater for the needs of professional firms. There has been some speculation that they might be utilized by small traders but they have not yet become popular for this purpose, not being designed with this in mind, and because, to date, they have not been attractive to most ordinary small businesses from a tax point of view. If the benefits of incorporation were to be eroded by higher corporation tax rates for small companies, this could change.[22] Hybrid forms are also important in the USA, which has limited liability partnerships and limited liability companies (LLCs). The creation of these US hybrid forms by state legislatures was tax motivated to a considerable degree (Carney (1995)).

Incorporated firms

In contrast to unincorporated firms, UK limited liability companies must be registered in order to have legal existence and they are governed by a complex and detailed piece of legislation.[23] The company has legal personality, that is, it is a legal entity distinct from its shareholders. In law it is capable of enjoying rights and of being subject to duties which are not the same as those enjoyed or borne by its shareholders, even if there is only one shareholder.[24] The shareholders are owners of the shares and not the underlying assets of the business. Although called limited liability *companies*, it is actually the liability of the shareholder that is limited rather than that of the company, which is liable to the full extent of its assets. The legislation governs the

[21] Limited partnerships must be registered but there are very few of these: only 14,400 at the end of March 2007 (see <http://www.companieshouse.gov.uk/about/pdf/companiesRegActivities2006_2007.pdf>).

[22] The total number of LLPs registered in the year ending March 2008 was 32,066, with new registrations in 2007–08 being 9,198 compared with 372,400 new limited companies registered in that period. Source: www.companieshouse.gov.uk/about/pdf/companiesRegActivities2007_2008.pdf.

[23] Companies Act 2006.

[24] For further explanation of corporate personality, see Davies (2003) at p. 27.

relationship between the shareholders, directors, and creditors. The underlying scheme assumes separation of ownership and control and the need to monitor management.

It has been suggested that 'the corporation is primarily a method of solving problems encountered in raising substantial amounts of capital' (Posner (1986)). This may be correct in terms of economic theory, and firms which need substantial capital clearly need to incorporate, but the reality is that a company may be, and frequently is, a one-person firm with very little (if any) capital. Most companies are very small indeed and have few shareholders.

In the UK, from the time of the 1855 Limited Liability Bill, Parliament was keen to make the corporate legal form widely accessible and there was no minimum capital requirement—as there is in some jurisdictions—so that the very smallest one-person businesses used the corporate form from its inception (Freedman (1994)). Furthermore, incorporation with limited liability in the UK has become steadily simpler and less costly as a matter of government policy which is to 'think small first' and remove unnecessary regulation from small companies (DTI (2005)). So, for example, the statutory audit requirement has been gradually removed from companies with profits below certain levels (see Appendix 11A), requirements about meetings have been relaxed and the 2006 Companies Act introduces further reforms (DBERR (2007)). The ethos of easily available incorporation has been strengthened by these changes (Freedman (1994)), which, supported by the tax changes described below, have contributed to increased popularity of the corporate form in the UK in recent years.

Nevertheless, incorporation can be inappropriate for firms where there is no actual separation of ownership and control, especially if the legal protections are mandatory and involve burdensome compliance, which in some jurisdictions can be very costly. Even under the relatively relaxed UK regime, there are financial protections around the corporation in the form of accounting requirements and restrictions on the way in which corporate funds can be utilized in order to protect shareholders, and these may be unnecessary for a one-person company. There may be costs of incorporation which are sometimes hidden—arising only, for example, on the break-up of a business relationship, where it may be more difficult for a shareholder to extricate himself from a company than it would have been for a partner to end a commercial partnership. Despite the drawbacks, very small businesses which intend to remain owner-managed may have commercial reasons for using the corporate form: they may wish to obtain limited liability (although this can be illusory in the case of small firms without outside shareholders since creditors will often insist on personal guarantees) and they may require corporate form for status or other business practice reasons (Freedman and Godwin (1992)). Corporate form may also facilitate borrowing by making the provision of security easier because floating charges[25] are available to corporate and not individual borrowers (Davies (2003)).

Employed and self-employed boundary

Certain types of employee, at the margins, may be engaged in activities that are economically very similar to those of self-employed contractors. The different legal status of these relationships creates important differences between the rights and duties in each case, however. In the UK, subject to any special legislative provisions, the nature of the relationship will be decided on the basis of the contractual rights and liabilities between the worker and the person or body to which he is supplying services. The boundary is defined in law through a series of decided cases based on certain characteristics or 'badges' of employment status. These badges include such matters as the degree of control over the worker, the level of risk he undertakes, the amount of equipment he provides and whether he is integrated into the business in any way. Each factor varies in importance depending on the circumstances.[26] The case law has made some movement to recognize that the tests of control and provisions of equipment are now less important than they once were in defining employment. The test does not offer a clear dividing line, however, and is very fact based (Freedman (2001); Redston (2002)). This limits the amount of guidance provided by the court decisions. While this keeps the law flexible and ensures that it can develop with changing conditions, it also makes it uncertain and difficult in terms of administration and compliance. Whilst in many cases it is obvious whether a person is an employee or self-employed, so that there is no room for argument, at the margins the law offers some opportunities for (perfectly legal) arrangement of the contractual duties so that the relationship falls on one or other side of the employment status boundary.

The advantage often lies with arranging affairs so as to avoid creating an employment relationship. Employment is costly for the employer both in terms of the NICs he must pay, and because of the obligations imposed by employment law. His compliance costs may also be increased. The employee is also subject to NICs, at a rate which is substantially higher than for the self-

[25] A floating charge is a form of borrowing secured on the assets of the company without being fixed on any one asset, so that assets can be dealt in despite the existence of the charge unless and until it is converted into a fixed charge as a result of a default.

[26] For a full discussion of the case law, see chapter 3 of Freedman (2001).

employed without the benefits available to employees being commensurately higher (see Appendix 11C, and Adam, Browne, and Heady, Chapter 1).[27] The employee suffers deduction of tax at source under the Pay-As-You-Earn (PAYE) system (see Shaw, Slemrod, and Whiting, Chapter 12, for details). This cumulative withholding tax reduces opportunities for evasion, but also makes tax planning more difficult for an employee than for the self-employed. The UK system has very restrictive rights to deduct expenses for employees, partly because the cumulative PAYE system attempts to operate to a high degree of accuracy, with most employees not completing a tax return (Freedman and Chamberlain (1997)). To make this feasible, the system keeps the availability of tax deductions for employees to a minimum by requiring them to satisfy a strict test of being *incurred wholly, exclusively, and necessarily in the performance of the duties of the employment.*[28] A self-employed person has to show only that the expenses are *incurred wholly and exclusively for the purposes of the trade.*[29] There are also significant differences between the employed and self-employed in the rules for travel expenses.[30] In view of these tax and other issues there is an incentive for those engaging workers to treat them as self-employed contractors where that is feasible. For the worker there may also be tax savings in self-employment and higher payments for work done to compensate for the lack of job security and other benefits. This is balanced by a loss of employee benefits, pensions in particular, and employment rights. In some cases the decision to operate as a self-employed contractor rather than an employee may be that of the worker, but there are certain industries—notably IT and publishing—where the clients insist on self-employed status, leaving the worker very little choice (Harvey (1995); Stanworth and Stanworth (1997); Boyle (1994); Freedman and Godwin (1992)).[31]

[27] The employed may have greater entitlement to some social security benefits than the self-employed. In particular, employees have state second pension rights that the self-employed do not enjoy. Many employees 'contract out' of these pension rights in exchange for a rebate on their NICs and those of their employers; however, even for contracted out employees, there is still a significant difference between the rate of NICs they and their employers pay, and that which is paid by the self-employed, which other relatively small differences in benefit entitlement do not account for. Table A3.1 of HM Treasury (2007) shows that the reduction in NICs for the self-employed *beyond that attributable to reduced benefit eligibility* was £1.8 billion in 2006–07. See Appendix 11C for more details.

[28] Section 336 Income Tax (Earnings and Pensions) Act 2003 (ITEPA).

[29] Section 34 Income Tax (Trading and Other Income) Act 2005 (ITTOIA).

[30] Broadly, costs of travel from home to work are not deductible; from one workplace to another they are. It may be easier for a self-employed person to claim that their home is their work base. The rules for employees are strict but have been relaxed to some extent legislatively in ss 337–42 ITEPA.

[31] Movement from employment to other modes of working is not only tax motivated. Changing work patterns are driven by a number of economic factors (Atkinson and Storey (1993)). Non-standard working and self-employment are increasing and together made up almost 40% of the

Pressure on the self-employed to incorporate: personal service companies

Where a person decides to set up a business, he/she may go on to consider incorporation, perhaps without going through the self-employed stage at all. This will convert the worker back into an employee, but as an employee of his own company he will have the ability to control how much he receives through (tax-disadvantaged) wages and how much by way of dividends or sometimes capital gains. His choice of legal form may be to obtain limited liability or one of the other commercial benefits described above, or for tax reasons or a mixture of the two. For this reason the boundaries of employment/self-employment and self-employment/incorporation must be studied together: consideration of alignment at one boundary must take into account the impact on the other.

It will often be the person or business to whom or which the services are being provided (the client) that will insist that the worker supplies his services through a company. For the client this incorporation route has the advantage of shifting the onus of proving status to Her Majesty's Revenue & Customs (HMRC) on to the worker. Not all incorporations by single taxpayers are at the behest of the client, of course. Within the UK system as it currently stands, the taxpayer may achieve significant tax advantages by being incorporated, as well as some commercial advantages in certain circumstances. Neverthless, various anti-avoidance tax provisions have been introduced to try to prevent workers supplying services from using incorporation to convert labour income into capital income. These provisions (notably the personal service company (PSC) legislation) are intended to apply where the taxpayers involved are economically closer to employees than to 'true' businesses, but the definitional difficulties have made these attempts contentious and complex and, until 2007 at least, not very effective.

11.3.3. How the tax system may affect choice of legal form

General issues

The relative effective tax rates paid on income earned in the corporate and non-corporate sectors often favour one legal form over another. Which form is favoured will depend on all the circumstances of the taxpayer, particularly in a system which has a progressive personal income tax, and on the structure of the tax system.

EU-25 workforce in 2005 (European Commission (2006)). This is forcing consideration of change in employment law as well as highlighting the problem of tax differentials.

Thus, in the USA, there has been a tax penalty on incorporation for those intending to distribute profits as a result of the classical system of dividend taxation which taxes dividends both at the corporate level (via corporation tax) and at the personal level (via income tax). This was tackled in 1958 by way of Subchapter S to the Internal Revenue Code which permits partnership or pass-through treatment for US corporations satisfying certain conditions ('S' Corps).[32] Thus many US firms may now choose incorporation without tax penalty and, in practice, the S Corp may have some tax advantages over unincorporated structures: for example, despite the pass-through treatment, the majority of the S Corp's profits escape various employment, social security and healthcare payments, and taxes, so the S Corp offers an opportunity to escape both labour taxes and the double taxation of corporate dividends. This led to an estimated loss of $5.7 billion in employment taxes in 2000 (US Treasury (2005); Winchester (2006); Keatinge (2007)). Indeed, this Treasury report describes the S Corp form as 'a multibillion dollar employment tax shelter for single owner businesses'. It is significant that in 2000, nearly 80% of all S Corps were either entirely or majority owned by a single shareholder. Since 1997, under the check-the-box regulations,[33] US entities other than corporations may elect to be treated for tax purposes either as a corporation or on a pass-through basis. The LLC hybrid form can also give limited liability with partnership tax treatment. These developments give many US businesses a choice of tax treatment regardless of legal form, but they also increase the opportunities for tax planning. Indeed, the growth in popularity of S Corps described by Auerbach, Devereux, and Simpson, Chapter 9, may be partially explained by these tax advantages.

In the UK, by contrast, the imputation system and now the system of tax credits have over recent years attempted to integrate the corporate and personal tax systems to some extent, so that the problem is often the reverse of that in the US: there is a tax advantage for many in incorporating so they would not generally elect for pass-through treatment even if it were to be available (which it is not).[34] The US literature on the impact of effective tax rates on choice of legal form—which in any case gives mixed messages—therefore has to be applied to the UK situation with care. Thus, while

[32] Sub-chapter S treatment can be chosen by companies with up to 100 shareholders. A series of other complex provisions must also be satisfied: for example, the only shareholders permitted are individuals, estates, and certain exempt organizations and trusts. In practice, the S Corp need not be small in financial terms, nor in market or geographic scope (McNulty (1992)). The tax election makes no difference to the corporate status of the firm for the purposes of corporation law.

[33] Treasury Decision 8697.

[34] There would be some circumstances in which pass-through treatment would be advantageous, of course, notably where there were losses (which could be deducted against higher personal taxes).

MacKie-Mason and Gordon (1997) consider that non-tax factors are likely to dominate tax factors in the choice of legal form by businesses, Goolsbee (2004) is critical of this and other earlier time-series studies and uses cross-sectional data for US states and industries to suggest that the impact of the difference between the effective tax rates paid on income earned in the corporate and non-corporate sectors on the degree of incorporation might be larger than previously estimated. A recent paper by De Mooij and Nicodeme (2007) using European data supports this suggestion, finding that the tax gap between personal and corporate tax rates does exert a significant positive effect on the degree of incorporation.

Of course, it is difficult to transfer these results to a different legal system where the other legal factors may carry greater or lesser weight. In particular, the existence of the Subchapter S election complicates the US picture. The true position is that the impact of taxation on choice of legal form no doubt depends on the precise balance of all the circumstances and factors (Freedman and Godwin (1992)). As will be shown, however, the recent increase in incorporation levels in the UK following the reduction of corporate tax rates supports the suggestion that the impact of taxation on legal form is strong.

It is fundamental to the arguments in this chapter that the tax system should not distort decisions about the best choice of legal form from a commercial point of view. Some commentators have suggested that it could be advantageous to encourage incorporation through the tax system as a means of promoting proper account keeping and similar business methods, as a benefit both for the firms themselves and for the revenue authorities (Sanger (2005)). Given the existence of audit exemptions for small companies and the informal way in which many are run, it is not entirely clear that incorporation does assist the revenue authorities very greatly in this way, although registration of the existence of the business may be helpful. VAT registration is probably more useful to the revenue authorities than incorporation per se, except that the UK has a high registration threshold relative to other jurisdictions (see Section 11.6, and Shaw, Slemrod, and Whiting, Chapter 12). Well-designed requirements to produce accounts for tax purposes would be as helpful as the accounting requirements for small companies, as well as being more relevant. The advantages to the revenue authorities and businesses alike achieved by the requirements of incorporation are unlikely to be as great as those which could be obtained more directly by requirements relating specifically to tax returns.

The incentive to incorporate in the UK

It has been explained above that NICs bear more heavily on the employed than on the self-employed in the UK.[35] There is also a tax and NICs (collectively referred to as 'tax' hereafter unless the context makes the contrary clear) advantage in incorporation. Technically, incorporation results in the taxpayer becoming an employee of his own company but it still gives tax advantages as he can take money out of the company in a form other than wages. Clearly most taxpayers are straightforward employees and have little choice about this but there is a group for which there appears to be some flexibility and who are increasingly choosing self-employment or incorporation.

The main tax advantages of incorporation as compared with employment and self-employment are threefold. First, corporate tax rates are lower than income tax rates, especially where the small companies' rate applies (and when the corporation tax starting rate used to apply) (see Appendices I and II for details). This means that shareholders of owner-managed companies, in particular those in the higher tax rate bracket, may shelter income for investment by the company, having paid only corporation tax on it at a lower rate than income tax. Eventually they will have to pay income tax if they take any gains as dividends, but if they sell or liquidate the company they may be able to convert some part of their income to a capital gain, which is generally taxed at lower rates.[36] Second, incorporation provides an opportunity to convert income from labour into income from capital, which enables shareholders to take income from the company in the form of dividends or capital gains not subject to NICs. Third, incorporation may offer the opportunity for an owner to split shareholdings with other family members so that the whole of the income is taxed at a lower rate than would be the case if it was all received by one shareholder.[37] This is considered objectionable by HMRC where the business of the company is essentially to supply the services of one of the shareholders, whilst the other or others do substantially less or no work for the company. This division of income across individuals is referred to as 'income splitting'.

[35] The Labour Force Survey reports that the number of individuals running their own business (including, under their definition, both the self-employed and some owner-managers of companies) has been increasing at a faster rate than the number of employees in the UK in recent years. Between 1998 and 2006, the number classifying themselves as self-employed in the UK increased by 10%, from 3.4 million in 1998 to 3.7 million in 2006; this can be compared with a rise of 8% (from 23 million in 1998 to 25 million in 2006) in the number of employees over the same period.

[36] For the most part, the companies on which this chapter focuses will not have this option since they will need to pay out much of the corporate income for living purposes.

[37] Of course the situation is rarely as simple as this.

To give an example of the interaction between these factors, in the case of a one-person company the lowest possible tax rate combined with benefits entitlement is achieved by the company paying the single owner-manager a low salary (equivalent to their personal allowance (tax free threshold)). The company then either retains profits which are taxed only at the small companies' corporation tax rate, or pays them out by way of dividends, which are not subject to NICs and which also carry a credit for corporation tax paid. For example, in 2008–09, applying this method means that an incorporated owner-manager whose business makes £25,000 gross annual profits pays only 16.1% (£4,035) of this in tax, compared with 27.0% for an employee and 21.9% for a self-employed individual earning the same amount (see Appendix 11C for details). To improve their tax position further, the owner-manager could also give shares in his company to other family members and distribute dividends accordingly.

These three advantages are subject to highly contentious anti-avoidance provisions. The UK government has attempted to prevent the conversion of labour income into dividend income by legislation which targets personal service companies (PSCs) and managed service companies (MSCs). Income splitting has been attacked by the use of anti-avoidance legislation aimed at settlements and new legislation has been under consideration, as discussed below. The government argues that a considerable amount of revenue is at stake, and that there are also fairness issues.[38]

Special anti-avoidance provisions to tax the income of certain types of PSC[39] as if it were employment income were introduced in 2000 (at the same time as the low starting rate of corporation tax, presumably in partial recognition of the fact that the low rate might exacerbate distortions) and instantly met with much discontent.[40] These anti-avoidance rules aim to look through the existence of the corporation for tax purposes. They apply where a worker provides his services to a client through a PSC, and where that worker would have been treated as an employee of the client for tax and NICs purposes had the arrangement been made directly between the worker

[38] The introduction of legislation to deal with PSCs was expected to increase NICs revenue by £220 million per year from 2002 (Inland Revenue (1999)). The introduction of legislation to deal with MSCs was expected to yield £350 million in 2007–08, £450 million in 2008–09, and £250 million in 2009–10 (HMRC (2007)). The introduction of legislation to deal with income splitting (now delayed) was expected to yield revenue of £25 million in 2008–09, £260 million in 2009–10, and £200 million annually thereafter (HMT/HMRC (2007)).

[39] In fact the rules also apply to intermediaries which are partnerships but for the purposes of this chapter all intermediaries shall be referred to as PSCs. The rules are sometimes called the 'IR35' rules after the press release that announced them (see now ITEPA Part 2, Chapter 8).

[40] Including an unsuccessful judicial review: *R (on application of Professional Contractors Group Ltd) v IRC* [2001] STC 629. For a detailed discussion of IR35, see Redston (2002).

and the client. The application of these rules depends, therefore, on a finding that there would have been a contract of employment between the client and the individual undertaking the work had there not been a PSC involved. This places heavy reliance on the finding of a legal relationship of employment, on which the law can be very unclear in borderline cases.

Where these rules apply, the client pays the PSC gross. Salary paid by the PSC to the worker is subject to PAYE and NICs rules in the usual way. In addition, to the extent that the PSC does not pay out its entire earnings as salary, the PSC is treated as paying a further salary of this retained sum to the worker. Benefits in kind paid to the PSC are taxed in the same way as employee benefits and the restrictive employee deduction rules are applied to expenses. Relief is given to prevent double taxation, and a small deduction is allowed for expenses of running the PSC.

The impact of the tax liabilities is on the individual worker and not the client, however, so that there has been no reduction of the incentive to large businesses to insist that those providing services to them incorporate. Initially the legislation was designed to put some of the onus onto the clients and this might have altered behaviour but, following business complaints, the liability was placed on the PSC itself.[41]

Thus it is that some workers find themselves in a situation in which they must incorporate in order to obtain work, or are starting up with only one client with a view to development, but, in these circumstances, are vulnerable to this complex anti-avoidance legislation. Arguably, the involvement of the problematic employee status test in the determination of whether IR35 applies has made the legislation unworkable, unenforceable, and uncertain in its application (Tiley and Collison (2007), p. 492; Lee (2007), p. 142; Gretton (2008)).[42] Taxpayers covered by this provision also pay tax as employees but without the benefits of employment. This could be the worst possible outcome, since it remains a trap for the unwary and increases compliance costs and encourages costly structuring to avoid the legislation, but is unlikely to raise very much revenue.

[41] Contrast the Construction Industry Scheme in force from April 2007, where the onus is on contractors to check the employment status of sub-contractors—but in this sector the main engagers are large and there is union pressure for compliance. Even here implementation had to be deferred to ensure that the industry was ready.

[42] The Professional Contractors Group (a lobbying trade group) claim that of the 1,431 IR35 tax investigations known to that body, tax was found to be owing in only four cases in 2007 (see: <http://www.pcg.org.uk/cms/index.php?option=com_content&task=view&id=3183&Itemid=427>). HMRC have been more successful since then, however, for example in the case of *Dragonfly Consultancy Ltd v HMRC* [2008] EWHC 2113 (Ch).

The lack of success of the PSC legislation led to the managed service company (MSC) legislation in the Finance Act 2007 (see HMRC (2006); Lagerberg (2007)). The MSC legislation does not rely on the problematic definition of employee. It overrides the PSC provisions, but the latter remain on the statute book in case there are situations in which the MSC legislation does not apply and they do. The MSC legislation was introduced to deal with specialized intermediaries (MSC providers) who were offering mass marketed packaged service companies to large numbers of individuals. From April 2007, PAYE is payable and most provisions relating to taxation of employment income are applied to a deemed employment payment by an MSC to the worker. An MSC is defined broadly as one whose business consists wholly or mainly of providing the services of an individual to other persons, the payments for which are mostly paid to the individual or his associates (note that this does not refer to the concept of an employee, unlike the PSC legislation.) Further, the way in which the payments are made would result in the individual or associates receiving more than if they had been payments of employment income (once tax and NICs are taken into account) and an MSC service provider is involved with the company. There are elaborations of these definitions in the legislation.

The existence of a provider giving straightforward legal or accountancy advice is not intended to convert a PSC into an MSC but there has been some discussion of this and the full extent of the provisions remains to be tested (Lagerberg (2007)). The mischief being addressed directly by this test is that small business owners were being encouraged by MSC providers to incorporate to take advantage of the incentives within the tax system, but the legislation still tackles the symptom and not the cause of the problem, despite moving away from the problem of defining employment. Opportunities were open to MSC providers only because of the structure of the tax system and this has not changed. To target those who have set up companies because they have had this idea presented to them as part of a mass marketed package, whilst leaving the more sophisticated unchallenged, makes little sense in terms of tax policy. It will not necessarily treat taxpayers equitably across the board and it may penalize those who most need advice and assistance.

A key problem with both the PSC and MSC legislation is that it applies only to certain categories of companies, which then have to be defined. This adds to the burdens of all small businesses, penalizes taxpayers who simply utilize incentives built into the tax system through differential rates, and potentially inhibits genuine entrepreneurialism. If it is desired to tax income from incorporated firms as labour income, then it would be preferable to achieve this through structural changes to the tax system that avoid definitional problems.

This may mean that rates of tax on labour income and capital income need to be aligned across the board rather than in particular cases only. Some argue against this on the basis that lower tax rates should be used as a reward for the loss of the benefits of employment. The authors reject this and argue that if business owners do take greater risks and have less security than employees, which will be so in some cases but not all, then that should be reflected by the market in the prices charged for their services rather than by the tax system.

As explained above, incorporation also facilitates income splitting for tax purposes. The income of one person can be shared with family members (who become shareholders of the company) and lower rates of tax can be achieved by paying out salaries within the personal allowances of these family members or dividends in respect of their shares. This raises objections from HMRC where the profits of the company arise mainly from the work of one family member but are nevertheless split with others. Of course, there may be practical difficulties in determining the relative contributions. To counter what it perceives as an abuse, HMRC has attempted to use anti-avoidance provisions (the 'settlements provisions') under which it can assess dividends as income of the settlor in some circumstances (the settlor in these cases being the family member providing most of the work).[43] This has proved highly contentious and HMRC has been largely unsuccessful in litigation in the case of *Jones v Garnett (Arctic Systems)*.[44] The House of Lords came to their decision on the facts of this particular case, which leaves many questions unresolved.[45] The decision was immediately followed by an announcement of the intention to legislate against such 'income splitting'[46] and a consultation document on the topic (HMT/HMRC (2007)). The negative reaction to these proposals has resulted in their indefinite deferral, although the issue remains under review (HM Treasury (2008)).

The proposals in the consultation document would have required the parties and ultimately the courts to evaluate whether income has been foregone by one individual in favour of another. The proposed test was complex and fact dependent, leading to justified criticisms that it would be heavy in compliance and administration costs and yet would probably raise little revenue. Extra-statutory guidance was looked to as the solution but this is unsatisfactory. The tests involved looking at the market value of work done but, as pointed out by Redston (2007), raised very difficult questions of the

[43] Formerly s 660A of part XV of the Income and Corporation Taxes Act 1988 and now in chapter 5 of part 5 to Income Tax (Trading and Other Income) Act 2005.

[44] [2007] UKHL 35.

[45] For a comprehensive discussion of the issues in the case, see Gammie (2007); Loutzenhiser (2007).

[46] *Jones v Garnett: Ministerial statement* (26 July 2007).

value of each person's work, balancing value against volume of work done, balancing work done with capital contributions, and accounting for changes in the fact patterns over time.[47]

There are many interacting issues to consider here. This is a question that needs addressing in a holistic way, looking at the rules on family taxation, small business taxation, and capital transfers between spouses in the round. An outright gift of other types of income bearing property may generally be made to a spouse, so that investment income may be split in this way. The government's objection is to splitting what is perceived to be the equivalent of labour income, but where the equity lies depends upon whether the comparator is truly labour income or investment income. The fundamental issue is once again that income from labour is being recharacterized as income from capital.[48] A system which treated all the income from companies in the same way as labour income (unless it represented a return to capital) would remove part of, although not all, the advantage of income splitting, since some of the advantage lies in being able to use the personal allowances and lower personal income tax bands. To deal with this, it would be necessary to consider the nature of independent taxation of spouses and civil partners and the role of their personal allowances. It would be possible to make their allowances and even their lower rate bands transferable to their partner, but this would bring other problems. It is not clear that it is appropriate to try to prevent the use of these allowances through a complex business tax measure which is guaranteed to alienate small business owners.

The incentive to incorporate in the UK: changing tax rates and statistical evidence[49]

Small business owners have, quite rationally, taken advantage of the potential benefits of incorporation described above. Government has at times increased these benefits, with the intention of providing incentives for entrepreneurship, which it has associated with incorporation. So, for example, the Paymaster General stated in 2002 that the government

[47] It is understood that similar tests operate in other jurisdictions such as the USA, the Netherlands, and Sweden, but that there are operational difficulties in all these and that such a test is likely to be of value only in extreme cases.

[48] Redston (2007) argues that it is not right to compare the small businessman and the employee in tax terms. 'One could just as easily argue that [small business proprietors] should have paid holidays and fixed working hours. With respect, these conditions have nothing to do with the tax system, whereas rates of tax clearly do.'

[49] For a more detailed discussion of these developments, see Freedman (2006) and Freedman (2007).

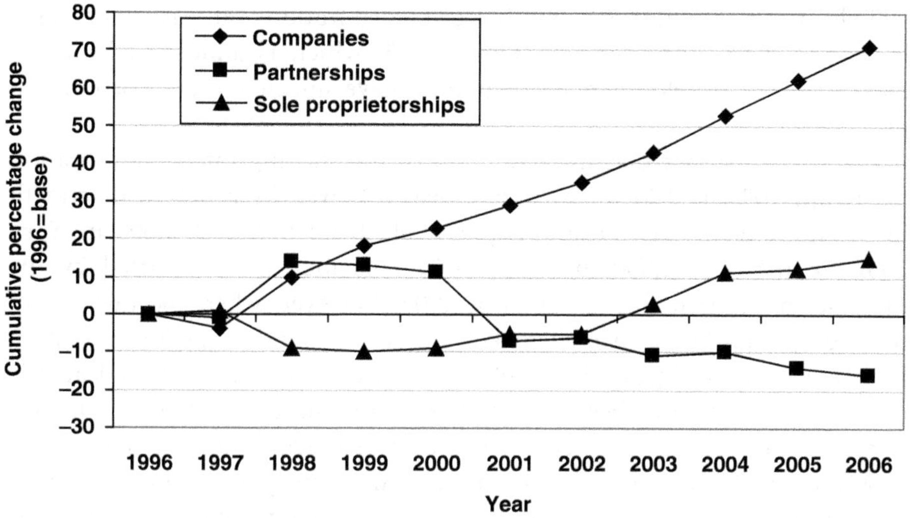

Note: Authors' calculations from DBERR SME Statistics, 1996 to 2006 accessed via http://stats.berr.gov.uk/ed/sme/.

Figure 11.2. Cumulative percentage changes in the number of businesses in the UK from 1996 to 2006, by legal form

recognises that businesses growing beyond a certain size will often be companies. We believe that cutting corporation tax is an effective way of targeting support at small and growing businesses ... Surely small businesses will not look a gift horse in the mouth. We want to create growth and economic activity, and to sustain entrepreneurial activity.[50]

For example, the tax advantages of incorporation were increased in 2000 when a 10% rate of corporation tax was introduced[51] for companies with profits of £10,000 or less (the 'corporation tax starting rate'). These advantages reached their height in 2003–04 when the starting rate of corporation tax was 0%.[52] In this year, an incorporated owner-manager whose business made £25,000 gross profits would have paid only 9% of this in tax. The potential for distortion was recognized by many at the time (see, for example, Blow et al. (2002)) and, not surprisingly, incorporations did indeed increase (Figure 11.2).

[50] House of Commons Standing Committee F, 16 May 2002, cols. 114–15.

[51] Announced in 1999 and included in the Finance Act 2000.

[52] The rate was reduced to 0% in 2002–03, but a 1 percentage point increase in the NICs rate for employees and the self-employed above the higher rate threshold was introduced in 2003–04, such that this was the year in which the advantage was greatest.

This upward trend in the number of incorporations (at least since 1997) is examined in more detail in Figure 11.3, which is annotated by reference to some developments which may have affected the incorporation rate.

Figure 11.3 shows that the reduction of the starting rate of corporation tax (from 10% to 0%) in April 2002 was followed by a period of growth in the number of incorporations per week, from just over 5,000 in April 2002 to just over 8,000 in April 2003. This increase is dwarfed by the increase in the first four months of 2007, however, when the number of new companies being formed rocketed from just under 7,000 per week in December 2006 to just under 13,000 per week in April 2007. This dramatic change seems to have been a response to the announcement in December 2006 that the government would be introducing legislation to tackle MSCs in April 2007, since it was thought for a time that forming individual companies rather than using umbrella vehicles would escape the new provisions. This may have been a short-term increase, but it does suggest a very clear impact of the tax and legislative system on choice of legal form.

Of course, if the observed increase in incorporations was primarily a response to tax and other legislative changes, then one might expect there to be higher growth in the number of companies with relatively few employees than in the number of companies with relatively more employees. Figure 11.4 shows the cumulative percentage changes in the number of companies with 0, 1 to 9, or more than 10 employees in the UK between 2000 and 2006. As anticipated, the rate of growth has been greatest for companies with no employees—increasing by approximately 50% (from just over 300,000 in 2000 to just over 450,000 in 2006).

Government complained that the increase in incorporations was due to 'self-employed individuals adopting the corporate legal form where the change is made for tax reasons rather than as a step to growth' (HMRC (2004)). This was the inevitable result of the policy pursued: small businesses did not 'look a gift horse in the mouth'. Whilst businesses that intend to grow are likely to incorporate in order to raise external finance and to obtain limited liability, it does not follow that encouraging incorporation through the tax system will necessarily encourage growth. Rather, non-entrepreneurial and life-style businesses will quite reasonably utilize the advantages of incorporation so created. Finally, the encouragement of incorporation in this way was accepted by government to be misconceived. Following some complex and unpopular changes in 2004 designed to reduce

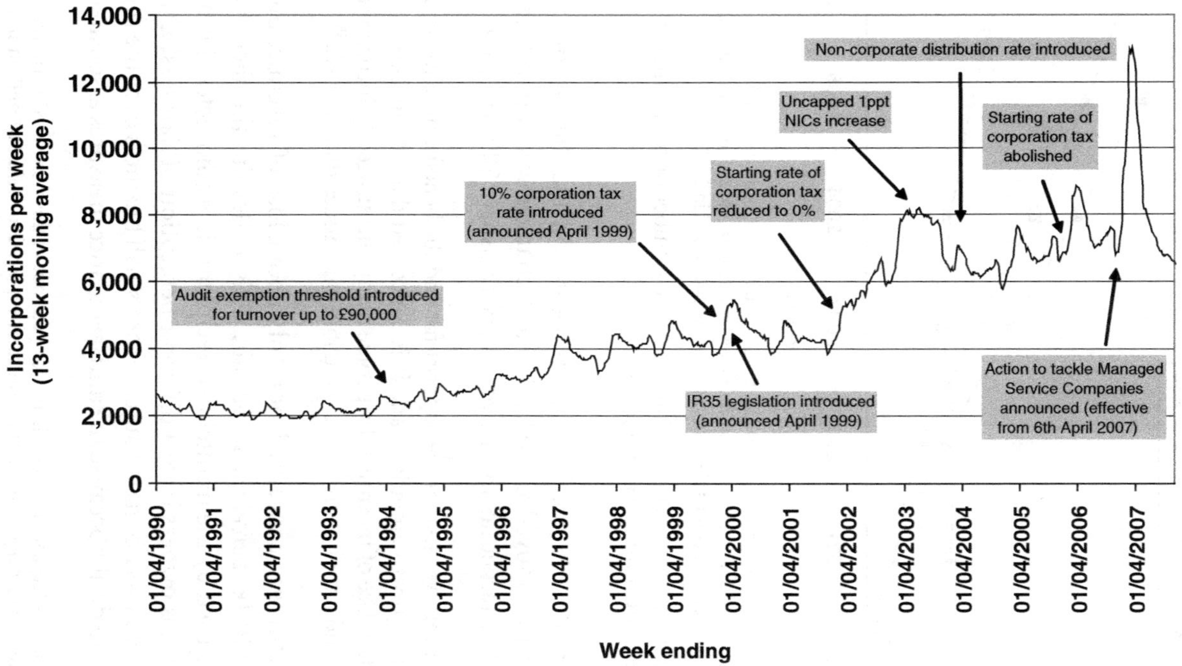

Note: Authors' calculations from statistics provided to the authors by Companies House, 1990 to 2007.

Figure 11.3. Number of incorporations per week in Great Britain (13-week moving average, not seasonally adjusted)

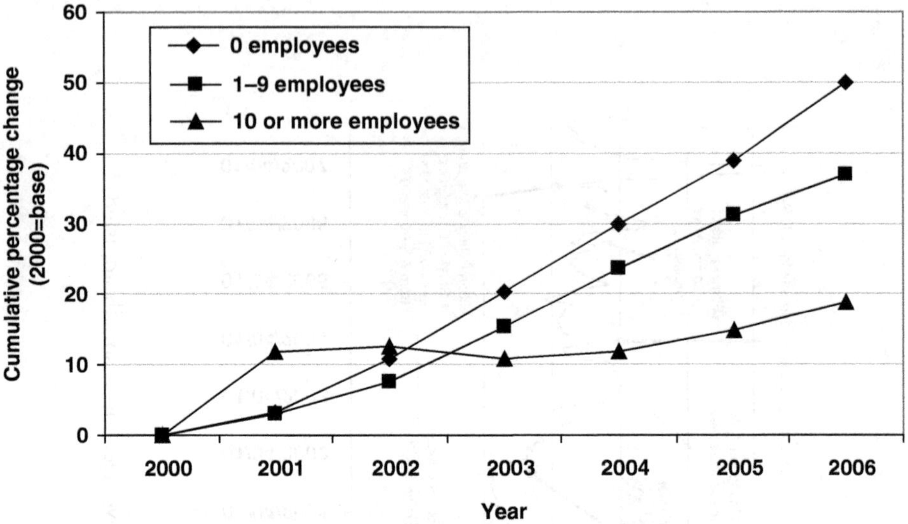

Note: Authors' calculations from DBERR SME Statistics, 2000 to 2006 accessed via <http://stats.berr.gov.uk/ed/sme/>. Note that it is not possible to make comparisons with earlier periods because the definition of companies with no employees changed in 2000.

Figure 11.4. Cumulative percentage changes in the number of companies in the UK from 2000 to 2006, by number of employees

the advantage of the 0% rate,[53] both this legislation and the corporation tax starting rate were removed in 2006.[54] These changes were announced as a measure to 'better target tax incentives' (HM Treasury (2005)) and to

> refocus growth incentives so that the support for and the benefits of reinvestment go to businesses with growth ambitions and it is concerned that any incentives should be perceived as fair. Use of incentives by people being encouraged to incorporate and reduce their tax and national insurance contributions erodes that fairness.[55]

Thus government was concerned not only about loss of revenue, but that incentives should be *perceived to be* fair. This is despite the fact that the incentives were used by the unintended recipients in a completely legal manner. Small business owners have a different perception of 'fairness', although interestingly there was no major outcry from small business over the removal of the 0% rate, no doubt because the anti-avoidance measures associated with

[53] Essentially this was legislation to tax dividends paid out of this non-taxed corporate income through the so called 'non-corporate distribution rate', expected to yield £10 million in 2004–05, £340 million in 2005–06, and £490 million in 2006–07 (HMRC (2004)).

[54] Income tax rates remained broadly constant over this period.

[55] HMT (2006). It was estimated that there were 720,000 companies with profits of less than £50,000 pa at that time, equivalent to 63% of all companies (although this provides no information about which companies would be winners or losers from the change).

it had deprived it of some of its value and were very complex.[56] The objective of targeting growth companies through a tax relief available to all companies below a particular size threshold was always likely to fail and this has now been recognized by government. Nevertheless, incorporation still brings tax advantages.

The 2007 Budget made an attempt to deal with these continuing advantages, proposing to raise the small companies' corporation tax rate from 19% in 2006–07 to 22% in 2009–10 (although the 2008 Pre-Budget Report announced that the increase to 22% would be delayed by one year; this was due to the economic climate rather than a change of direction (HM Treasury (2008)). This increase in corporation tax for the majority of corporations was accompanied by a decrease in the mainstream corporation tax rate and in the basic rate of income tax (and an elimination of the starting rate of income tax). As shown in Appendix 11C, this has the effect of reducing the tax advantage associated with incorporation. This appears to offer an improvement to the current UK situation of apparent tax-driven incorporation, but a radical cut in corporation tax rates generally to below the basic income tax rate, as is favoured by some as a reaction to the general downward trend in corporation tax rates internationally, would of course undermine this.

11.3.4. Conclusion on UK experience to date

The above figures indicate that the impact of the UK tax system on choice of legal form has been significant. This is important, because it may distort commercial decisions; more fundamentally, it reveals a lack of equity in the tax system, since taxpayers with similar accretions to their economic power are taxed differently. This problem has been exacerbated in the UK by the promotion of incorporation in an attempt to encourage growth. Predictably, this has been ineffective and has caused further problems.

The government has now declared its intention to encourage 'all businesses who invest to grow' without distortion[57] by introducing an annual investment allowance for the first £50,000 of expenditure on plant and machinery from 2008–09. In part this is to compensate for the loss of the starting rate of corporation tax, but it will be available to both incorporated and

[56] This is an example of complex deregulation (explained in Section 11.6). Indeed, these changes had been proposed by several small business organizations, including the Forum for Private Business, which pointed out that the compliance cost of the anti-avoidance provision outweighed the savings from the nil rate and ACCA—see 'Abolition of nil rate discussed' <http://www.bytestart.co.uk/content/news/1_12/abolition-of-nil-rate-cor.shtml>.

[57] HM Treasury (2007)—Press Notice 1.

unincorporated firms. This is a move away from a size or legal form linked incentive towards one targeted at the activity to be encouraged, which is positive, and to a limited extent it introduces a cash flow treatment for very small firms.[58] It is inevitable that any such incentive will further increase the advantages of being self-employed or incorporated over employment by a third party, so that this new allowance may exert more pressure to leave employment, but it would not be possible to devise any attempted incentive to enterprise which would not do this. The usefulness of this relief depends in part on straightforward implementation, but the proposals contain anti-avoidance provisions and there is a risk that these will increase.[59]

The UK experience lends strong support to the argument that the tax system should not seek to favour one legal form over another. Where the tax system does favour one form, structural solutions (such as rate changes) need to be sought for creating parity, rather than provisions which rely on definitions of sub-categories of businesses which will be difficult to apply and enforce.

11.4. OPTIONS FOR REFORM

11.4.1. Objectives of reform

As discussed in Section 11.3, in the UK, differential tax and NICs treatment of individuals across the spectrum of employment and small business activity generally creates an incentive to be self-employed rather than an employee, and to be incorporated rather than self-employed. For many there is no choice other than to be employed, but for a significant group at the margins, it is possible to structure their affairs in alternative ways. The tax incentive to incorporate arises primarily as a result of the opportunities to convert highly taxed labour income into less highly taxed capital income by incorporating. For reasons explained above and in Section 11.6, the authors' starting point is that the tax system should be neutral as to the choice of legal form, which should be made on the basis of commercial factors. Tax differentials do

[58] A flow of funds tax was also proposed for 'small' businesses by the President's Panel (2005). However, their proposal raises issues of definition that are not involved with the UK's less extensive provision.

[59] The point was made by business in the consultation process that complexity of anti-avoidance provisions needed to be avoided, and the government claims that it has used a 'light touch', but will, however, keep the matter under review to ensure the safeguards in place are proving effective in maintaining the balance between simplicity and control of abuse (HMT/HMRC (2007a)).

influence choice of legal form and will not always target 'entrepreneurial' businesses efficiently; furthermore, they create costs for business and revenue authorities. When taxpayers quite rationally take advantage of these differentials, revenue authorities often fail to go to the heart of the structural issues and instead react with complex provisions which attempt, often unsuccessfully, to confine the tax advantages to a sub-category. This in turn gives rise to dissatisfaction amongst taxpayers whose co-operation is important for the purposes of administration and for political reasons.

The authors do not believe that entrepreneurship should or can be encouraged by advantaging incorporation through the tax system. The solution to creating a structurally neutral system does not lie in producing special provisions for 'small' businesses: the difficulties of arriving at a non-arbitrary and enforceable definition of those 'small' businesses to which the tax system would be neutral with respect to legal form seem insurmountable. Those options that rely on such definitions are therefore considered only briefly before moving on to discuss in more detail reforms that would equate effective tax rates on income from the corporate and non-corporate sectors *for all businesses.*

11.4.2. Specific provisions for 'small' businesses

This section discusses a number of ways in which it might be attempted to reduce inequalities between effective tax rates applied to 'small' incorporated and unincorporated businesses, using a variety of definitions of 'small'.

Deterring or preventing incorporation

One way to tackle the small business taxation problem might be to prevent or inhibit 'small' businesses (however defined) from incorporating (for example, by way of an increased minimum capital requirement, as suggested by Murphy (2007)). This would mean that many very 'small' businesses would remain unincorporated and so be taxed under the personal tax system, thus eliminating opportunities for re-characterization of income. Alongside the difficulties of arriving at a suitable level of minimum capital requirement, such an approach is unlikely to be politically acceptable in the UK.[60]

[60] Indeed, following the decision of the European Court of Justice in *Centros* (C-212/97) that private companies operating in other member states could incorporate in the UK to avoid having minimum capital, other countries (e.g. the Netherlands) are abolishing their own minimum capital requirements. The associated suggestion by Murphy (2007) that small businesses should be encouraged to use the LLP legal form falls into the same category: whilst there is a tax advantage to

Mandatory pass-through treatment

Another route to alignment for 'small' businesses would be to tax certain incorporated firms as if they were unincorporated and to make such pass-through treatment mandatory in these cases. This would not achieve alignment across the board without first aligning the NICs treatment of employed and self-employed persons, preferably by integrating NICs and income tax.[61] Following this, all or part of the income of owner-managed companies would need to be treated as labour income, regardless of whether it was paid out by way of salary or not. This would essentially align tax rates on labour and capital income for this group. Very roughly, this is the approach of the UK PSC and MSC provisions, except that since NICs are not currently aligned for employees and the self-employed, the treatment of income of the PSC or MSC as employment income makes the owners worse off than if they had operated through unincorporated firms. Furthermore, the current UK provisions only apply to some, not all, owner-managed companies, and determining to which companies they should apply has been fraught with difficulty. Mandatory pass-through treatment thus does not seem to provide a viable solution to the small business taxation problem because of the need for difficult and potentially arbitrary or manipulable definitions. Furthermore, the effect of such legislation is to tax all profits of owner-managed companies as labour income, regardless of the investment of capital.

Optional pass-through treatment

Some commentators have argued for the *option* of pass-through or partnership treatment to be made available to owner-managed companies in the UK, as it is in the US (by making a Subchapter S 'S-Corp' election). As discussed above, the popularity of this legal form in the US is the result of aspects of the US tax system which differ from those in the UK as well as the ability to escape some labour and social security taxes. Far from increasing alignment between legal forms, it provides greater opportunities to obtain tax advantages by using one form rather than another. Under a system with a lower corporate tax rate than income tax rate, and especially one with a tax credit system for dividends (as in the UK), pass-through treatment would normally only be an attractive option for companies if they were loss making. Businesses in the UK can already opt to set up as an LLP (which essentially combines

incorporation it is unlikely that there will be sufficient advantages to the use of an LLP to make this attractive.

[61] See below and Adam and Loutzenhiser (2007) for a more detailed discussion of these issues.

limited liability with the ability to set off business losses against other personal income), but the numbers doing so are small,[62] suggesting no great demand for such treatment and thus for a pass-through option.

Special rules for companies with 'active' owners

The Nordic countries face similar difficulties with the taxation of small businesses to those found in the UK as a result of their dual income tax system—which combines a relatively low, flat rate of tax on capital income with progressive taxation of labour income. To deal with this problem, many have (at least at some point in time) adopted special rules for the treatment of the income of what have been defined as 'active' shareholders. These systems differ from simply treating all of the income of such shareholders as labour income (as under the UK PSC and MSC provisions) by making an allowance for the investment of financial capital in a business. In Sweden, for example, distributions from closely held corporations[63] are taxed at a reduced rate up to an imputed return on the acquisition price of the shares; above this return, they are taxed at the same rate as labour income.[64]

Although this seems more acceptable than treating all of the income of owner-managed companies as labour income, the same issues of definition arise: whatever classification of owner-managed businesses (or active shareholders) is chosen, it is likely to be somewhat arbitrary, creating horizontal inequity for very similar companies falling either side of the boundary.[65] Furthermore, there is a trade-off between the simplicity (in terms of implementation and adherence) of a clearly stated boundary between those to whom the rules apply and those to whom they do not, and the ability of small businesses to practice tax avoidance by moving to the most advantageous side of that boundary.

Rejection of definition-based approaches

The definitional problems of these kinds of approaches have been clearly demonstrated in practice, by the problems experienced with defining PSCs

[62] See note 22 above.

[63] Defined for this purpose as companies with one or 'a few' active owners, although the definition of active is itself problematic. In Sweden, for example, an active shareholder is one whose activity 'has a significant influence on the income generated by the company', with case law relied upon to delineate active shareholders further (Sørensen (2008)).

[64] Norway also adopted a similar approach between 1992 and 2006 (see Lindhe, Södersten, and Oberg (2002) and Sørensen (2007) for more details).

[65] Of course, this is also a problem under the current system.

and MSCs in the UK, and by reactions to the approaches attempted by some of the Nordic countries. For example, in Norway, which used to have a system of subjecting income to mandatory division into components of income from capital and income from labour in a similar way to Sweden (described above), there was a reduction in the percentage of companies to which the system applied, from 55% in 1992 to 32% in 2000, as taxpayers began to learn about the definition of 'active' shareholder (Sørensen (2007)). Small business owners (or their advisors) have reacted rationally to what are somewhat arbitrary classifications by seeking out the most tax-favoured position available to them, suggesting that whatever rules are in place will not eliminate the problem of tax-motivated incorporation entirely. In dealing with the issue of the taxation of owner-managed companies, therefore, it seems to the authors that the best solution will be one that does not rely on defining sub-categories of company or types of shareholder.

11.4.3. Alignment for all businesses

This section first considers how alignment of effective tax rates could be achieved by making changes within the current structure of the UK tax system, before moving on to suggest ways in which this could be improved upon through more radical reforms.

Changes broadly retaining the current UK income and corporation tax systems

To the extent that it is proposed to retain a tax on the normal return to capital—that is, the minimum return required for an investment to be worth undertaking—it seems likely that it will be argued that this should be relatively low in relation to the rate on labour income. There are various reasons for this, but the idea has wide support (see Griffith, Hines, and Sørensen, Chapter 10). In brief, the reasons for a relatively low tax rate on capital income are threefold, the first two being largely pragmatic whilst the third has a basis in theory. First, there is the high and growing international mobility of portfolio capital, combined with the practical difficulties of enforcing taxes on foreign-source capital income. Second, it is administratively and politically difficult to tax some types of income from capital, such as imputed returns to owner-occupied housing, so keeping a low rate of tax on income from capital generally minimizes distortions. Third, if tax is levied on the whole nominal return to capital, including the inflation premium, the effective rate of tax is in fact higher than it seems, due to the lack of inflation adjustment. Whilst the first of these reasons is of little direct relevance to most owner-managed domestic businesses of the kind discussed here, if the arguments in favour of maintaining a tax differential are accepted for general reasons, then the problem of distortion in the case of small businesses will remain.

The authors' preferred approach to tackling this issue—alignment of effective tax rates across all legal forms—requires that, in the context of the current system, a contrary approach should be taken: that is, that income from capital should, as a matter of equity, be taxed at the same rate as income from labour.[66] Indeed, this is the direction in which the UK government appears to be moving. Changes announced in Budget 2007 have certainly lessened the distortions to choice of legal form created in recent years, as shown in Appendix 11C.[67] The distinction between income tax and NICs, however, means that the small companies' rate now lies above the basic rate—a somewhat complicated way of achieving the desired result, and one that is not easily understood by the small business community (though it has some logic). Furthermore, there is a continued need for the complex, costly, and unpopular PSC and MSC legislation, because the tax differentials have not been eliminated entirely. These difficulties could be at least partially ameliorated through the integration of income tax and NICs—which would be a bold and desirable move, but which may be politically difficult at the present time (see Adam and Loutzenhiser (2007) for more details).[68]

A less radical approach would be to align the rate of NICs paid by the self-employed with that paid by employees. Such a move would eliminate some of the NICs differential between employees and the self-employed but importantly would exclude employer contributions. Moreover, the self-employed would still be subject to more favourable rules governing expenses claims than employees unless changes could be made in that respect also (see Freedman and Chamberlain (1997)).[69] These changes alone, however, would do nothing to reduce the tax advantage associated with being incorporated

[66] Indeed, some would take the view that income from capital should be *more* heavily taxed than that from labour, as was the case in the past with the investment income surcharge, but practical considerations would make this difficult even if it was desirable.

[67] In fact, the tax incentives evident in the proposed 2009–10 system look broadly similar to those found in 1996–97. See Crawford (2008) for more details.

[68] This means that NICs would be subsumed into income tax, such that a higher composite rate would apply to all labour income—whether for employees or the self-employed—and dividend income (although the credit for corporation tax already paid on dividend income would remain in place). There are some complications in deciding which NICs rate (contracted in or contracted out—and, if the latter, salary-related or money purchase scheme) would be most appropriate for the purposes of integration. See Appendix 11C for more details.

[69] It is difficult to quantify this particular tax advantage. Further, this is a problem that applies across all of the alternative approaches discussed in this chapter. It might not be possible to make

rather than employed[70] (and, indeed, would increase the tax incentive relative to being self-employed), highlighting the importance of considering the whole spectrum of employment and small business activity in tax design.

The distortions evident at the boundary between incorporation and (self-) employment could be reduced through the alignment of the small companies' rate of corporation tax (21% in 2008–09) with the mainstream rate of corporation tax (28% in 2008–09). The result of aligning the small companies' rate and the main rate of corporation tax at 26%, and of equating the NICs rate of the self-employed with that of employees (referred to as the incremental approach), can be seen in Appendix 11D.[71] These figures show that such an approach would eliminate most (but not all) of the tax incentive to incorporate. Clearly this would have a cost to those currently paying the small companies' rate, but this would balance the potential NICs savings through paying dividends rather than salary. As discussed in Section 11.6, there is no clear economic rationale for a distortion in the tax system in favour of those with low profits. Although this approach could reduce effective tax rate differentials between incorporated and unincorporated businesses, it might not be seen as acceptable because it would involve taxing returns to capital at the same rate as labour income (inclusive of NICs). The next section moves on to consider alternative reforms in which alignment of effective rates can be achieved after eliminating the normal return to capital, thus addressing the argument for a lower tax on income from capital.

Changes moving away from the current UK income and corporation tax systems

This section proceeds on the basis that there might be radical reforms to the current UK income and corporation tax systems as a whole, not just for small businesses. Much will depend on the detailed implementation of any such reform and so the overriding point is that in any consideration of these new approaches, thought should be given to the structural issues affecting small businesses described above.

major changes to the employee expenses rules without an increase in the number of employees filing tax returns or even a universal tax return—see Shaw, Slemrod, and Whiting in Chapter 12.

[70] This approach does not create a single composite income tax rate, such that the taxation of dividend income remains unchanged.

[71] That is, Class 2 and Class 4 NICs are abolished and the self-employed are moved onto the employees' Class 1 contribution schedule. For the purposes of these calculations, the 'contracted out' rate for employees is used (see Appendix 11C for details). The differences between the employed and the self-employed would be reduced still further through the integration of income tax and NICs.

A shareholder income tax with a rate of return allowance?

Assuming that the UK will continue to maintain a large gap between the rates of tax on income from capital and income from labour (a variant of a dual income tax system), the authors propose the adoption of a system along the lines of that developed in Norway. It was explained above that Norway has a dual income tax system, in which the corporation tax rate is equal to the capital income tax rate, which, in turn, is equal to the lowest labour income tax rate. There is also a higher (progressive) labour tax rate. To combat the incentive this produces to convert labour income into capital income, Norway adopted a residents' shareholder income tax with a rate of return allowance (RRA) in 2006. This facilitates alignment of the effective tax rate on the income of an individual from a corporation with that of labour income, whilst leaving normal returns to capital taxed at a lower rate, whether or not they are distributed. This meets concerns that the taxation of the whole of the distributed profits of a company as if they were labour income does not recognize the investment of shareholders, and also permits a lower effective tax rate on the normal return to capital than on labour income, which may be a attractive active for non-small business reasons.

The RRA exempts all shareholder income (including both dividends and realized capital gains, which are treated identically) below an imputed normal rate of return on the share basis (the RRA) at the personal level, as this income has already been subject to corporation tax (at a rate corresponding to the capital income tax rate) and should therefore not be taxed further.[72] The share basis in any given year is defined as the sum of the original share cost plus all unutilized RRAs from previous years: this is equivalent to carrying forward retained profits (postponed capital gains tax liabilities) with a normal return, to ensure that only capital gains in excess of the normal return are subject to taxation at the higher labour income rate.

Above the RRA, income is taxed at the capital income tax rate—which, in combination with the corporation tax rate (which has already been paid on this income), corresponds to the top marginal rate of taxation on labour income. In Norway, this top marginal rate excludes social security contributions (of 6%), but in a UK version, the authors would recommend that alignment should occur at a rate that takes into account both income tax and NICs—which could best be accomplished through integration. This is important because it is this equivalence that eliminates the ability of small

[72] If losses are fully deductible (which is necessary to ensure the neutrality of the shareholder income tax with respect to investment and financing decisions), then there is no need to include a risk premium in the RRA. See Sørensen (2007) for a more detailed discussion of the implementation issues surrounding the shareholder income tax.

business owners to convert highly taxed labour income into less highly taxed capital income.

The authors recommend that, as in Norway, unincorporated businesses are taxed on an imputed return to business assets at the capital income tax rate, with the remainder taxed at the labour income tax rate.[73] This gives an equivalent treatment to that for incorporated firms because the corporate and capital income tax rates are the same under the dual income tax system (and would also need to be equal under any UK version of the shareholder income tax that was adopted). Such an approach must be optional for unincorporated firms, however, as it requires detailed bookkeeping; those who do not wish to maintain such detailed records may instead opt to have the whole of their income taxed as labour income.

Of course, the equivalence of the combined corporate and capital income tax rates with the top marginal rate on labour income means that there will be a tax incentive to remain unincorporated for businesses whose profits do not exceed the higher rate threshold. This could be overcome, possibly with some additional complexity, by taxing capital income (including both dividend income and realized capital gains) above the RRA according to the same progressive rate schedule as that used for labour income. This could be achieved for the dividend income of domestic taxpayers, for example, either with a credit for corporation tax already paid and a correspondingly higher tax rate applied to grossed up dividends (as under the current system), or without a credit (and a correspondingly lower rate of tax applied to cash dividends). The administrative workings of this approach would depend on the relative tax rates, but clearly as much as possible would need to be done through withholding, as now, with adjustments for higher rate taxpayers who complete self-assessment forms in any event.[74]

The appeal of the Norwegian shareholder income tax for the taxation of small businesses is that it provides a mechanism for dealing with the fact that different types of income are taxed at different rates, and that it uses investment of capital (rather than legal form) as the basis for reducing the tax burden. Furthermore, it applies to all shareholders in all types of

[73] The imputed return to business assets can be calculated either on a 'net assets' basis or a 'gross assets' basis, each of which has advantages and disadvantages: while the net assets method is preferable because it does not distort marginal investment decisions, the gross assets method is preferable because it is less prone to tax arbitrage. See Sørensen (2007) for a more detailed discussion of these issues.

[74] In Norway, deduction of the RRA (at corporate level) is permitted for all shareholders resident within the EEA (and not just domestic shareholders) before any withholding taxes on dividends are imposed. This is necessary to comply with European legislation, and would also be necessary were such a system to be adopted in the UK.

company, thus circumventing the need to define 'active' shareholders or owner-managed companies or some other category of businesses to which special tax treatment would apply. It does not eliminate the ability of incorporated owner-managers to 'split' their income with family and friends in order to minimize their tax burden, although the fact that they will be paying the labour income tax rate on all income may reduce the advantages. Since income splitting is the product of a progressive, independent tax system, rather than of the choice of tax rates applicable to different legal forms, it is not surprising that it cannot be entirely dealt with in this way.

A potential problem with this approach is that only returns to financial capital are taxed at the capital income tax rate. One complaint in the UK already is that the entrepreneurialism of service companies and consultancies is insufficiently recognized, and there is a view that returns to entrepreneurialism, risk, ideas, and 'self-generated goodwill'[75] should be taxed at a lower rate than labour income. This could be achieved, for example, via a cap on the amount of income subject to taxation at the labour income tax rate (with any income beyond this cap taxed at a lower rate, that is, the tax rate on capital income only).[76] Alternatively, these types of input could be valued and treated in the same way as tangible capital investments. On the other hand, there is also an argument that the rewards for 'effort' in whatever form (be they bonuses awarded by employers, the above-normal returns made from an individual's investment portfolio, or the higher profits made by self-employed persons or persons providing their services through companies) should be taxed equally (and, possibly, at a different rate to the normal return on investment in capital). As a matter of general principle, however, it is the authors' view that returns to forms of input other than capital should be considered to be rewarded by the market and should not be given any special treatment by the tax system. If, however, a government wished to recognize such input by favourable treatment for pragmatic or policy reasons then this could be done, though not without introducing additional complexity and opportunities for manipulation, as seen in other jurisdictions.

Combining the RRA with an allowance for corporate equity?

The current UK tax system, like many others around the world, is one in which the normal return to capital is taxed, with consequent implications for

[75] Such as the name of the business, customer lists, etc. This is only a problem with self-created intangibles, since the value of acquired intangible assets is included in the basis value (acquisition price) of the shares and hence in the base for calculating the RRA.

[76] In Norway, there was previously a system for taking into account self-generated goodwill; however, it was quickly abandoned, after it was found that almost 80% of 'active' shareholders were reporting *negative* labour income for tax purposes (Sørensen (2005)).

the level of investment.[77] Companies' choice of financing methods may also be distorted, as a result of the differential treatment of debt and equity for tax purposes: while interest payments on loans (made to the company) are not subject to corporation tax, dividends (the return to equity) are.[78] This has led many commentators and others writing in this volume to argue for the removal of these distortions.[79]

Whilst the introduction of a shareholder income tax (along the lines described above) would exempt the normal return to capital (invested in the corporate sector) from taxation at the personal level, it would do nothing to eliminate the distortions outlined above: this would require a separate solution.

Many commentators have argued for the introduction of an Allowance for Corporate Equity (ACE). Under an ACE system, companies would be given an allowance—reflecting the opportunity cost of equity finance—to be deducted from taxable profits (in the same way that interest payments currently are). This allowance would be calculated by multiplying cumulative past injections of new equity and past retentions of profits by some appropriate interest rate,[80] representing the return that could have been obtained had these funds been invested elsewhere (see Bond, Devereux, and Gammie (1996), Devereux and Freeman (1991), and IFS Capital Taxes Group (1994) for more details). The equivalent for unincorporated businesses would be to exempt an imputed normal return to business assets.

The combination of an ACE with an RRA-based shareholder income tax would eliminate the distortions to choice of legal form (as outlined above). It would also remove the incentive to choose debt-financing over equity-financing. Under such a system, the normal return to capital would be exempt from taxation at both the corporate and the personal levels. This would be appropriate only in a system in which all forms of income from capital were exempt from personal tax up to the normal rate of return (that is, a consumption-based personal tax system). This combination of an ACE and RRA has various general difficulties, not least that it would narrow the tax

[77] To give the same post-tax return, the gross return required for an investment to be worth undertaking is higher than if there were no tax, making some investments that would have been profitable without the imposition of the tax not worth undertaking thereafter.

[78] This is further complicated by the availability of hybrid financial instruments, blurring the distinction between debt and equity (for tax purposes).

[79] For a more detailed discussion of these issues, see Auerbach, Devereux, and Simpson in Chapter 9 and Griffith, Hines, and Sørensen in Chapter 10.

[80] For example, this might be the risk-free interest rate on government bonds.

base in the case of larger companies, but in the case of very small businesses with little or no equity finance the base would be largely unaffected.[81]

11.5. CONCLUSIONS

The central small business taxation problem examined in this chapter is the structural one of lack of neutrality between different legal forms of doing business. In practice this is a problem only for owner-managed businesses at the smallest or micro end of the business sector, but this is an important group. Not only does it make a contribution to the economy but the small business community is vociferous and forceful when it comes to tax policy, and it can punch above its weight and create a sense of distrust in the tax system even if the actual number of people affected by a change is relatively small. In terms of being able to achieve sensible tax reform, this means that the concerns of the community need to be addressed, not necessarily by the tax response they have requested, but at least by a reasoned underlying policy rationale. Moreover, the issue of how to tax small businesses has an impact on the structure of both personal and business taxation more generally. In order to investigate this problem thoroughly, this chapter has considered the whole spectrum of activity from employment via self-employment to incorporation.

In most systems there are tax differences between these various forms of doing business. Total alignment has been difficult to achieve straightforwardly because there are real legal differences between these forms, even though they may be carrying out what appear to be very similar economic activities. While some commentators argue that tax advantages for incorporation are desirable in order to encourage entrepreneurship, the authors reject this notion. The chapter explains why neutrality between legal forms is desirable and proceeds on that basis.

In Section 11.6, the authors also explain why they do not accept the case for blanket tax incentives for small businesses as such, although there may be exceptional cases where some targeted reliefs are warranted. It is suggested that small (or in fact any) businesses should be provided with tax incentives

[81] A similar overall result to an ACE plus a shareholder income tax might be achieved via a cash flow corporation tax plus a personal expenditure tax, although there are operational differences. Under this combination the normal return to capital would be exempt at both the corporate and personal levels. Much would depend on the detailed implementation of such a combination: in particular, a mechanism would be needed to provide for alignment of tax rates, in the same way as under an ACE plus shareholder income tax system.

only where there is a clear case for targeted assistance to meet a market failure, but that otherwise, simplicity and an overall tax structure free from distortions that allows decisions to be made on commercial grounds will be the most desirable approach for both efficiency and equity reasons.

If a system broadly along the lines of the current UK tax system were to be retained, the obvious key to increasing neutrality between the employed, self-employed, and incorporated firms would be to align effective tax rates applicable to income from the corporate and non-corporate sectors as far as possible. Alignment would be aided considerably by the integration of income tax and NICs to create a composite rate on labour income, which would eliminate the most significant tax differences between employees and the self-employed, although it is accepted that this has political difficulties. At the other end of the spectrum, a simple route towards reduction of the tax incentive to incorporate would be the removal of the small companies' corporation tax rate, a relief for which there is little economic justification. This move would appear to be in tune with the direction of recent UK government thinking, and would bring the cumulative corporation tax and dividend income tax rates into approximate line with labour income tax rates. The removal of the small companies' rate could be seen as an attack on entrepreneurship in the current climate, however, and would have to be fully explained as part of a wider efficiency and simplification package. An accompanying reduction in the main corporation tax rate would assist although, as always where there are losers, acceptance by the small business community would not be immediate.

One suggestion frequently made is that a sub-category of small incorporated firms should be treated as if they were unincorporated for tax purposes. This does not solve the problem of the employee/self-employed boundary. Further, it only solves the incorporated/unincorporated boundary problem if it is mandatory, since otherwise corporate or non-corporate tax treatment can be chosen for purely tax reasons. Mandatory non-corporate tax treatment could, however, give rise to the problem of defining the firms to which this compulsion should apply. This chapter has reviewed the difficulties encountered in trying to do this in the UK in the case of a sub-category of owner-managed companies. The authors consider it unlikely that a workable and non-arbitrary definition could be devised for general application and so reject the treatment of particular types of firm differently from others.

Under the radical alternatives discussed in this chapter, there is a mechanism for exempting the normal rate of return to capital from taxation at either the corporate or the personal level, or both. It remains the case that alignment or equalization of tax rates across legal forms is necessary to achieve a sensible system for taxing small owner-managed businesses but, under these systems, this can be achieved whilst at the same time recognizing that, for the reasons discussed in this chapter and elsewhere in this book, the return to capital should be more lightly taxed than the return to labour. This has the major advantage of distinguishing between returns to capital and labour income in a coherent way that does not require the use of arbitrary definitions and difficult distinctions between different types of firm. Thus it is not necessary to tax owner-managed companies, or companies in which all the shareholders are 'active' differently from others where some are passive. These are notoriously difficult definitions to devise and a system which does not require them is vastly superior to one that does. One issue is that these systems recognize actual capital invested but not the contribution of ideas, risk-taking, and other forms of entrepreneurship. The chapter suggests (without recommending) ways in which this could be dealt with if required as a political matter.[82]

The authors recommend consideration of a rate of return allowance, a system that facilitates the taxation of normal returns to capital at a lower rate of tax than labour income, whilst providing a mechanism for taxing above normal returns at the labour income rate, whether they are described as dividends, capital gains, or salary. This could be combined with an allowance for corporate equity if it was desired to exempt the normal return to capital at both the personal and corporate levels.

11.6. SHOULD TAX SYSTEMS FAVOUR SMALL BUSINESSES? A NOTE TO THE CHAPTER

There is a strong assumption in government (often found in the speeches of politicians) and more generally in the business community, that small businesses should be provided with tax incentives and reliefs. The reasons for this preference relate to the sense in which the concept of small business is being used. As seen in Section 11.2, the range of ways in which this definition is used deprives it of any real general meaning. Even if it makes sense to target new firms or growth or entrepreneurship in some circumstances, targeting *size* per se is likely to lack rationale and therefore effectiveness. Politicians and policy makers too easily slip from rhetoric about entrepreneurship or growth to proposals about reliefs or incentives for *all* small businesses.

[82] Many of the owner-managed firms discussed in this chapter have little or no capital investments so this is an issue of importance to them.

This may be inevitable, due to the difficulty of targeting firms with more elusive characteristics; nevertheless this is a process that can create distortion in the tax system without necessarily being of clear economic benefit.

Proponents of tax measures favourable to small businesses, or to some small businesses, put forward several possible rationales for their view. Broadly, these include (i) the need to counteract market failures; (ii) the desirability of countering inherent disadvantages of being small such as the regressivity of compliance costs[83] and the asymmetry of taxable profits and losses; (iii) the need to ensure that small businesses can survive family and other events which might threaten to break them up. Overriding all these is the argument that small businesses are important to the economy in terms of creating wealth, stimulating competition, and creating jobs, and that this in itself justifies tax favourable provisions.

There are two distinct issues here. First, are claims for the importance of the small business sector justified? The objective here is not to decide upon this, but merely to note that there are issues surrounding the question. The second, and more important, question is: even if the importance of the small business sector is accepted, as it must be (to some extent), does it necessarily follow that it requires financial support, or that the tax system is an appropriate way to provide any such support as is appropriate? In particular, is it possible to target tax reliefs so as to support the possible rationales set out above? This note discusses these points to the extent needed to provide context for the structural review. Many (though not all) of the distortions present in tax systems as they relate to small businesses are the result of tax preferences. It is important, therefore, to consider the justification for such preferences. The authors argue that there are only limited circumstances in which small businesses and their owners should be advantaged through the tax system.

11.6.1. Significance of the small business sector

There is a large literature on this issue of which only a brief note is possible in the space available. The small business sector is important in so far as it creates jobs, generates wealth, and contributes to innovation. Small firms provide work for their owners, at least, and contribute to local economies. They carry out functions that it would not be economic for large firms to carry out and some of them have 'spillover' (external) effects which help to

[83] Regressivity of compliance costs is well established in the literature. The term here is used in the same sense as in Meade (1978), Appendix 22.1.

develop markets (Bannock, 2005). These attributes of small firms need to be recognized but not overstated.

Some of the earlier work purporting to show the importance of small businesses for job creation, specifically the work of Birch (1979), has been severely criticized (see Harrison (1997); Storey (1994); Davis, Haltiwanger, and Schuh (1996); de Rugy (2005)). The matter is not settled, but it is clear that only a minority of small firms generate jobs. Professor Storey has shown that 'most small firms do not grow and a handy rule of thumb is that over a decade 4% of small businesses create 50% of the jobs in small firms. The typical small firm is unlikely to survive for a decade and will create few additional jobs beyond those with which it started' (Storey (1995)). It is also the case that some small businesses are poor employers and may be inefficient (Curran et al. (1993); Storey (1994); Harrison (1997)), although workers may also find compensating factors in a small business environment (Curran et al. (1993)). Small firms have many functions in society and the job creation debate may to some extent miss the point (Bannock (2005)), but, to the extent that job creation by small firms is used to justify tax preferences, it is worthwhile pointing out that the issue is not beyond doubt.

As illustrated in Section 11.2, small firms, under the various definitions used, are numerous, but the businesses of most concern when discussing structural issues must be viewed in the context of their economic contribution. For example, in 2005–06, while almost all companies (91%) paid the small companies' rate or below, they generated only 13% of all corporation tax paid.[84]

The authors do not deny the importance of parts of the small firm sector but it is clear that it is heterogeneous and not susceptible to generalizations. There is a serious issue of targeting. When advocates of small business reliefs propose special measures they generally give the figures for all small businesses in existence, yet those of importance to the economy in terms of likely growth and job creation make up a much smaller number. Focusing such measures on size will not necessarily encourage growth of firms that do not intend to grow and which will be able to take the benefit of a relief without any need to grow. Reliefs aimed at all small businesses are available, inevitably, to so-called life-style businesses and to the type of small business which some suggest are not 'genuine businesses' but rather 'disguised employees'. The creation of poorly targeted reliefs and exemptions may result in the reorganization of business activity in order to create 'small businesses' at least

[84] Authors' calculations from <http://www.hmrc.gov.uk/stats/corporate_tax/11-3-corporation-tax.pdf>.

partly in order to obtain the tax advantages. The introduction of such reliefs may thus result in tax driven behaviour which is entirely rational but which policy makers may subsequently castigate as tax avoidance, as in the case of incorporation to obtain the benefit of the UK nil rate band for all small companies (see Section 11.3 for more details).

In any event, even if the sector is very important as a whole, the conventional wisdom that small business is the engine of the economy and the fountainhead of job creation is not, in itself, a justification for tax preferences targeted at size as opposed to other attributes (Holtz-Eakin (2000); Slemrod (2004); de Rugy (2005)). For example, it has been argued that new firms may increase total factor productivity in the industry because they are potential market entrants (Aghion et al. (2004); Disney et al. (2003)) but whilst this might be an argument for encouraging *new* entrants, or at least not setting up barriers to them, it is not necessarily an argument for providing relief to *small* firms per se as opposed to a group of firms with some other characteristic, such as innovation. For the sake of efficiency, some small firms need to fail. As Holtz-Eakin has pointed out, it is hard to know whether levels of business failure are the 'right' levels, and even harder to determine which firms to target for success or failure (Holtz-Eakin (2000)).

The areas in which it has been argued that there is a justification for providing tax reliefs for small firms are now discussed.

11.6.2. Possible rationales for tax preferences for small firms

The OECD (OECD (1994)) has commented that, from a strict economic efficiency viewpoint, all special provisions for small businesses need to be justifiable in terms of market failure or malfunction, although it recognizes that there may be objectives beyond pure economic efficiency, such as income distribution, which might justify special tax and other provisions for small firms. Even where there does appear to be a rationale for assisting small firms or some class of them, however, there are many problems with ensuring that these objectives are satisfied through business tax reliefs and incentives based on size of firm, or through structural reliefs related to legal form, rather than by more direct subsidies and other regulatory policies. There may be problems at European Community level with giving subsidies, which can amount to prohibited state aid, but targeted tax reliefs will face similar difficulties, whilst more general tax reliefs will not be well targeted.[85]

[85] Specific tax relief is as much subject to EU state aid rules as a subsidy (Article 87(1) of the EC Treaty (2006)). Tax relief which is not specific, such as a general reduction in capital gains tax, is

The OECD recommends that countries must first decide what problems are faced by small businesses and then, if they consider the problems are sufficient to warrant government action, they should consider the relative merits of preserving a neutral tax system (in so far as one exists) and using direct expenditures to pursue small business policy objectives, since non-tax measures will often be better targeted than tax measures. In a later report (OECD (1997)) it concludes that the tax system has a potential role in limiting the cost disadvantages faced by small businesses in complying with tax legislation, encouraging the creation of *new* small businesses and ensuring the continuation of small businesses when control passes from the founder of the firm to another person. Beyond that, the OECD concludes that since there is no such thing as a specific tax imposed on small businesses per se, as opposed to taxes on wider target groups, it is not necessarily helpful to attempt to provide special relief for small firms through the tax system.

Balanced against the possible role for small business reliefs, the following potential difficulties must be considered. In addition to the problem of targeting, referred to above, the provision of tax reliefs and exemptions for small businesses may be inefficient. They may distort the choice of business organization, commercial decisions about forms of expenditure, timing and method of change, and transfer into other hands. In addition, they may result in economic inefficiency if they interfere with the market and result in the allocation of resources to small, less efficient, firms rather than to larger, more efficient, ones. Reliefs might even result in barriers to growth at the margins if restricted to businesses below certain thresholds. Small business reliefs often create complexity in the system, especially when coupled with anti-avoidance provisions. For this reason a simple and neutral system of business taxation might be preferred, even by small businesses, to a more complex system that seeks to favour some small firms (Freedman (2006)).

The possible rationales are now examined in more depth.

Market failures

There may be market failures that affect some small firms, such as asymmetric information—for example, on markets or products—monopoly power of large firms making entry into the market difficult, or difficulties in raising finance due to size. These may be used as a justification for general tax

not state aid, even if it would favour some sectors above others. A Commission notice (European Commission, 1998) discusses the criteria for deciding what tax measures amount to state aid. Essentially, the test is whether the measure derives generally from the basic or guiding principles of the tax system in the member state concerned (Case 173/73 *Italy v Commission* [1974] ECR 709).

reliefs or for specific schemes to promote investment in small firms. These schemes, it is argued, will assist not only the firms themselves but the market more generally because of spillover effects from the innovative activity of the smaller firms (Gordon (1998); Aghion et al. (2004); Disney et al. (2003)).

Apparent market inefficiencies may, however, be examples of the market getting it right. If small businesses lack finance in some circumstances this might be because they do not have a good product or idea. Similarly, if the market rewards are not sufficiently high to compensate for undertaking risky activities, they may not be worth undertaking (see Adam (2008) at p. 226). Attempting to fine tune firm financing through the tax system could have unintended consequences. Thus, the OECD argues that tax measures are most likely to improve on the free market outcome in situations where the nature of the market failure is clear, but, of course, judging whether there is a market failure is the central difficulty that has to be addressed. It might be thought that the market is at least as likely to make sound judgements about the likelihood of the success of small business as are politicians. In addition, there needs to be evidence that the failure is significant, and a tax measure must be available that tackles the source of the inefficiency, has a significant effect on the behaviour in question, and does not produce major distortions elsewhere. This will be quite a rare combination of circumstances.

Although capital market failures are often cited as a problem for small firms, it seems that in the UK there has been little evidence of any general failure in the case of small businesses. Research in 2005 showed that 79% of small businesses seeking external finance were successful on their first attempt (IES (2005)). To the extent that there were difficulties, these were most likely to be experienced by early stage businesses to attract small amounts of risk capital (Bank of England (2004)). This suggested that the principal finance gap was for new and start-up businesses rather than small businesses as such (Graham Review (2004)). As a result of these findings, there has been an attempt to target tax assistance in raising external finance to those firms which do experience a problem, through the Enterprise Investment Scheme, Venture Capital Trusts, and the Corporate Venturing Scheme.[86] These seek to meet the perceived 'equity gap' for unquoted trading companies,[87] although there has been discussion about how well targeted they are, and the jury is still out on their effectiveness (see Boyns et al. (2003); Cowling et al. (2008)). Non-tax-based assistance is given through the Small Firms Loan Guarantee, which has been remodelled following the Graham Review to focus on firms

[86] See <http://www.hmrc.gov.uk/manuals/vcmmanual/index.htm>.

[87] See <http://www.hmrc.gov.uk/manuals/vcmmanual/vcm10020.htm>; HMT (2003).

within their first five years of business rather than small firms generally. This is consistent with the position taken here that the focus should not be on size but on other characteristics.[88] Current economic problems may result in a particular strain on small firms requiring credit due to their lack of reserves. This can only be dealt with by increased availability of credit. The Enterprise Finance Guarantee Scheme has been introduced to do this in the UK.[89] Some tax assistance has also been introduced to assist with cash flow problems, such as extended time limits for payment of taxes under the HMRC Business Payment Support Service and extended loss carry back of up to £50,000 for all businesses for a limited period.[90] While these provisions may be of more help to small businesses than to others, it is notable that that is not the way they are targeted.

In the UK, the abolition of taper relief from capital gains tax on business assets (available since 1998, when indexation and retirement relief were abolished) was announced in the 2007 Pre-Budget Report. This was greeted with strong protests from the business lobby, including small businesses, despite the fact that the removal of the relief was accompanied by the introduction of a generally applicable relatively low rate of capital gains tax. The government reacted by proposing a new entrepreneurs' relief (HMRC (2008)). This is not confined to small businesses as such, but is clearly directed towards them, given its limits and conditions. There is little or no evidence that this new relief is justifiable by any need to address a market failure.[91] The IFS has shown that the business cycle is far more important in determining the number of new VAT registrations than the introduction of capital gains tax reliefs (Adam (2008)). The new relief will introduce complexities and inequities, while the same low rate for all *without exception* (as originally proposed) would have been more efficient, more equitable, and much simpler.

One area often cited as being in need of intervention through tax incentives is investment in R&D. In the UK, the R&D credit was initially introduced for SMEs (small and medium-sized enterprises) in the Finance Act 2000 but was soon extended to all companies in the Finance Act 2002, although the relief is still more generous for SMEs.[92] The availability of a cash credit to SMEs and not to large companies may be justified on the basis that smaller

[88] For a similar point from a US perspective see de Rugy (2005).

[89] See www.berr.gov.uk/whatwedo/enterprise/enterprisesmes/info-business-owners/access-to-finance/sflg/page37607.html.

[90] See www.hmrc.gov.uk/pbr2008/loss-relief-583.pdf.

[91] Although it was in part at least a response to criticism that the change of rate affected taxpayers retrospectively.

[92] This measure does not extend to unincorporated SMEs, presumably for administrative and accounting reasons, since there is no principled justification for this.

companies have fewer possibilities for balancing costs against profits from other activities, but the larger amount of relief available to small companies is less easy to explain in the absence of evidence of greater credit constraints or spillover benefits in these cases. The evidence as to whether the UK R&D tax credits address the real limitations on innovation seems to be equivocal (Abramovsky, Griffith, and Harrison (2006); PWC (2006)). The extension of the relief to large companies is an example of the provision of reliefs for small companies fuelling demands by larger businesses. It is often the case that reliefs introduced for small companies result in pressure for extension to larger companies (what Alt, Preston, and Sibieta, Chapter 13, call 'policy creep'). Such pressure is not surprising if there is no very clear rationale for limiting the relief according to size. Furthermore, the fact that the relief is more generous to SMEs may mean that just as a business expands and needs most help its credit reduces (Alt et al., Chapter 13). This also illustrates one way in which small business tax reliefs might create barriers rather than remove them.

If such reliefs are to exist for all businesses, then the additional help required by smaller firms may lie in the need for assistance in accessing the schemes (Derregia and Chittenden (2006)). This relates directly to the size of the firm because smaller firms are less likely to have staff with specialist expertise and time to understand and prepare claims subject to complex requirements. Indeed, concern about take-up by SMEs of the R&D credit led to the announcement in 2006 of additional assistance for small businesses to make claims (HMRC (2006a)). This is closer to a compliance cost rationale, discussed below.

Inherent size disadvantages

A strong rationale for providing tax reliefs to small firms is that they are important in countering the inherent disadvantages of being small. The primary case is in relation to the regressivity of compliance costs.

Compliance costs

Compliance cost work in various countries has established that the costs of complying with tax and other regulatory burdens fall disproportionately on small businesses which have fewer staff and less expertise and time to devote to understanding and applying such regulation, the necessary information gathering being a fixed cost (Meade (1978); Sandford, Godwin, and Hardwick (1990); Chittenden, Kauser, and Poutziouris (2003); Evans (2003); KPMG

(2006); and see Shaw, Slemrod, and Whiting, Chapter 12, for a further discussion of the literature). Economies of scale and methods of organization utilized by larger firms are not available to smaller firms. This is widely accepted as being a problem that may legitimately be addressed by reliefs and exemptions, and by removing certain reporting and disclosure requirements from small firms (OECD (1997)).

Slemrod (2004), however, argues that greater non-compliance on average by small businesses (than employees) may offset their regressive compliance cost burden. Such evidence as exists in the UK points to sole traders and partnerships being the groups with the highest levels of non-compliance (as compared with employees and also with directors of companies).[93] There are clearly greater opportunities for non-compliance by the self-employed than there are for employees and others with income from which tax is deducted at source. This might mean that some parts of the small business sector are paying a lower overall rate of tax than other taxpayers as a result of non-compliance. This does not mean that policy makers should not seek to give relief from compliance costs where it is possible to do so without creating further problems, because there is unlikely to be a correlation between the tax savings of those prepared to reduce their taxes through non-compliance and those who suffer most through the regressivity of compliance costs (Gentry (2004)). Overall there should be a benefit to society through increased efficiency and greater revenue collection if compliance is encouraged by making it less costly. If this simplification also makes enforcement easier and so reduces opportunities for non-compliance, or encourages voluntary compliance, this will be an added bonus.

Trade-off between compliance cost and evasion: the VAT threshold Some attempts to reduce compliance and administrative costs may increase opportunities for evasion. An example of this might be the VAT registration threshold, which is set higher in the UK than anywhere else in the OECD. This creates opportunities for evasion by making it easier to stay below the threshold artificially (through receipt of cash payments, for example)[94] but may also reduce other forms of evasion which rely on VAT registration, such as carousel fraud (Crawford, Keen, and Smith, Chapter 4).

[93] See NAO (2003), Table 7. Although the text to this table refers to non-compliance, the figures on which it is based are the percentage of cases generating additional tax yield upon a random enquiry. There was generally little evidence of negligence or fraud, so that these cases may have been the result of accidental understatement of profits as opposed to deliberate non-compliance. See also HMRC (2007a). The different levels of compliance amongst different groups are largely the result of different opportunities for non-compliance amongst these groups.

[94] See the *Sunday Telegraph*, 'Middle class criminals cost millions in taxes' (24 February 2008), <http://www.telegraph.co.uk/news/main.jhtml?xml=/news/2008/02/24/nclass124.xml>.

There are some good administrative and compliance cost-saving reasons for a high registration threshold (Warren (1993);[95] Crawford, Keen, and Smith, Chapter 4), but the effect of too high a level may be a disincentive to grow beyond the level of the threshold and/or encouragement of methods of evasion used to stay below the threshold level. Chittenden, Kauser, and Poutziouris (2003) reported that the Small Business Research Trust (in 1998) found that, overall, 15.3% of VAT-registered firms expressed the view that the registration threshold was a significant problem for them, and that 18% of non-registered businesses stated that they intentionally avoided growth so that their turnover remained below the VAT-registration limit. Moreover, a high threshold may cause more significant disparities between firms which do have to register and those which do not, and can create a sense of unfairness. Thus there may be a loss of efficiency in that competition is hindered and more efficient larger small firms are put at a disadvantage. This is a matter which has been stated to cause concern by some small business groups (HM Customs & Excise (1999)). There is clearly a trade-off between these issues and the administrative and compliance cost considerations.

Complex deregulation: VAT schemes for small businesses Attempts to reduce compliance costs may also inadvertently increase them because the reliefs themselves introduce complexities (Freedman (2006)). The proliferation of thresholds below which special treatment is available can be confusing and some reliefs can require a considerable amount of advice and calculation before it can be decided whether they are advantageous.

These problems may be illustrated by some of the VAT simplification schemes which currently have a low rate of take-up and different thresholds.[96] A flat rate scheme was introduced in 2002 (available in 2007–08 to businesses with a turnover of £150,000 or less (excluding VAT) or £187,500 (including VAT)). Under this scheme, VAT is paid on a percentage of turnover. This is intended to reduce accounting work for individual transactions, although proper business records are still needed for the purposes of taxation on income, so it is questionable how much time is saved. The scheme is meant to be revenue neutral but is likely to be utilized only where there is a likelihood of saving and therefore might involve time-consuming comparisons (Benneyworth (2006); St John Price (2006)). Businesses with a turnover of

[95] The threshold was increased in 1977 to decrease the number of registered traders and thus administrative costs (Warren (1993)).

[96] These schemes are described at <http://customs.hmrc.gov.uk/channelsPortalWebApp/channelsPortalWebApp.portal?_nfpb=true&_pageLabel=pageVAT_InfoGuides&propertyType=document&id=HMCE_CL_001208>.

up to £1,350,000 (excluding VAT) may also opt for cash accounting (avoiding bad debt problems) and annual accounting (to smooth their cash flow).[97]

The National Audit Office (NAO) reports that take-up rates for VAT schemes are low: 22% for the cash accounting scheme, 16% for the flat rate accounting scheme, and 1% for the annual accounting scheme (NAO, 2006).[98] The NAO report remarks that the ICAEW (Institute of Chartered Accountants in England and Wales) consider that the simplification schemes should not be used as a substitute for simplifying the whole tax system. In a similar vein the CIOT (Chartered Institute of Taxation) has commented that some of its members consider that

> Stability is more important than more simplification schemes and simplification of the system is more beneficial than more schemes to counteract the complexity.[99]

These schemes are targeted at real needs and so are better than some, but they are examples of complex deregulation,[100] with a variety of thresholds, some of which are not easily ascertainable in advance for firms, and with detailed anti-avoidance provisions. Businesses may need professional advice before they can be sure that they should use the schemes and, as the reliefs apply only to VAT and not income or corporation tax, they do not reduce the need for record keeping more generally. Indeed, on one view, reduction of record-keeping requirements may not actually assist small firms because the tax requirement bolsters a commercial need, for example, to keep proper accounts. Some, such as Truman (2006), have argued for a move to cash accounting for income tax for the very smallest firms to reduce complexity, but small business owners might not find this helpful ultimately, because properly drawn accounts have an important management function.[101] Moreover, the end result could be a good deal of anti-avoidance regulation which might make for more complexity rather than less in the long run.

[97] The schemes are available until turnover reaches £1,600,000.

[98] There are certain pitfalls and traps for the unwary, particularly in the flat rate scheme—see Freedman (2007) for further discussion.

[99] See CIOT & ATT (2005) at p. 10. However, there were clearly different views on the committee since they also state the alternative view that the VAT cash accounting scheme could be extended to direct taxation to make it more popular.

[100] A concept explained further in Freedman (2003a); see also Dean (2005).

[101] The UK government issued a consultation paper in November 2008 which included discussion of such a move to a cash flow basis or, as an alternative, a move to harmonise the accounting and tax accounts of small corporations. The latter proposal risked creating an even greater divide between incorporated and unincorporated firms. The proposals for a cash flow basis were lacking in detail but were more than purely administrative and amounted to a change of the tax base, with full deduction of capital expenditure on plant and machinery and no deductibility of interest. As such they went far further than the proposals of Truman and others. It is not clear why such a radical change of the tax base was considered under the heading of tax simplification and only for small companies. For more details, see: http://www.hm-treasury.gov.uk/d/pbr08_simplificationreview_267.pdf. The ideas were not met

Asymmetry of profits and losses

It is arguable that losses bear more heavily on small businesses than on others. Tax is paid immediately on taxable profits, but relief for tax losses may have to wait until the business generates sufficient taxable profits to absorb past accumulated losses. This is less of a problem for mature firms, which are likely to be generating profits from existing business and so can claim immediate relief for any loss on the new investment against other profits. This option is not open to new firms without existing taxable profits, so that there is discrimination against investment spending by new firms, or by small firms during a high-growth phase in which investment spending is high relative to current profits. This may suggest that rules should be devised to permit some corporations to have some level of pass-through treatment for tax purposes so that the owners can set their business losses against other sources of income. The arguments here seem stronger in the case of new corporations than those which are simply small. In the case of high-risk investments, the fact that loss relief is of more use to firms where there are other investments against which to set the relief is likely to favour investment by mature firms as compared with start-up firms (see Chennells, Dilnot, and Emmerson (2000), chapter 8).

Keeping the small business intact

Another potential rationale that is in fact frequently adopted by governments is that used to justify special assistance to small businesses in relation to transfers, particularly from one generation of a family to another. It is argued that retirement or death might lead to the break-up of a business and therefore closure with consequent loss of employment and wealth generation (European Commission (1994)). On this view, not only should there be relief available on the death of a business owner but he should be encouraged to part with his business whilst alive in order to keep it intact and secure a sensible succession. European Commission (1994) takes it as given that there are advantages of intergenerational succession but provides no evidence (Bjuggren and Sund (2002)).

The UK has a number of tax reliefs aimed at easing the sale or transfer of businesses. In addition, there is a general capital gains tax uplift on death for all property and this is accompanied by business property relief on certain business assets and 100% exemption from inheritance tax.[102] As discussed

with any enthusiasm from the representative bodies and have now been rejected by the government. See http://www.hm-treasury.gov.uk/d/simplificationreview_responses.pdf.

[102] For the details of this relief, see <http://www.hmrc.gov.uk/manuals/ihtmanual/IHTM25022.htm>; see also Boadway, Chamberlain, and Emmerson in Chapter 8 for a discussion of this issue. They put the cost of business property relief alone at £350 million pa.

above, during the lifetime of the business owner capital gains tax may (from 6 April 2008) be removed or reduced by entrepreneurship relief, which reduces the rate of capital gains tax on some sales of businesses or sales of business assets following the cessation of a business.

The basis for these reliefs on transfer is not clear. First, as Boadway, Chamberlain, and Emmerson, Chapter 8, point out, the effects of the reliefs can be arbitrary, with 100% relief available for those who meet the inheritance tax provisions, for example, and none at all for those who do not. Second, the nature of the conditions means that the reliefs may be utilized for tax planning purposes so that the primary aim of holding the relevant asset may not always be a purely business objective. Third, the relief is available even if the business is not being maintained as a going concern by the person or persons inheriting it, so that it does not meet the test of being well targeted if the objective is to encourage continuity. It would be possible to provide relief as a deferral only whilst the business continues if the aim is to prevent break-up,[103] though it is not at all clear that this would be desirable since sometimes the continuity of the business in the most commercially efficient way will be best achieved through a sale to an outsider.

Transfer of a business to the second generation is not necessarily better than the purchase of a business by a third party. Some have argued that intergenerational succession is efficient because it preserves the benefits of knowledge idiosyncrasy (inherited knowledge) as well as being part of a transaction cost reducing social network (Bjuggren and Sund (2002)). This may be outweighed, however, by the inefficiency of having family disputes and poorly planned succession. Business owners frequently do not plan succession effectively and may even be reluctant to relinquish control (Handler (1994)). Children are often not interested in succession or, if they are interested, they are not the best managers. For example, Bloom and Van Reenen (2006) find that family-owned firms in which the position of the CEO is filled by the eldest male child are particularly poorly managed, with consequent implications for firm performance.[104] In light of the mixed evidence in this area, the best approach would seem to be not to give a tax preference to the passing on of businesses on death as opposed to lifetime sales, in order to allow the commercial considerations to govern.

There may be political and social reasons for favouring transfers within families and thus politicians may ultimately decide to support these through the tax system, but there does not seem to be any very clear economic

[103] Boadway et al., Chapter 8, point out that this could distort decisions and create compliance costs. It might, however, prevent people from buying and holding business assets purely as a tax planning device.

[104] This is supported in a publicly traded firm context by Perez-Gonzalez (2005).

rationale for doing so; indeed, the result of giving reliefs from capital taxes to small businesses seems likely to be distortion and demands for further reliefs.

11.6.3. Political economy considerations

The introduction of special reliefs for small businesses is often based on strong political considerations. Business lobby groups are vociferous and, although small businesses have less economic power than large businesses, experience suggests that the small business community can be very visible and often will be championed by the media. The result can be the introduction of reliefs which then become entrenched into the system and are hard to remove even if found to be unhelpful, although the experience with the abolition of the nil rate of tax in the UK does show that business will broadly support simplifying measures where the reliefs have become very complex. Reliefs initially introduced for small businesses can result in pressure to extend them to all businesses, as described by Alt, Preston, and Sibieta, Chapter 13. Thus, while it is not suggested that small business lobby groups can or should be ignored completely, in the long run a clear policy based system that can be explained to taxpayers and shown to be equitable and simple to operate may be more successful politically than one which responds to lobbyists and creates complexity, resulting in anti-avoidance provisions and confusion amongst users about the objectives of the system.

APPENDIX 11A

Legal size-related definitions

11A.1. UK Corporation Tax

Small companies' relief—Income and Corporation Taxes Act 1988 Section 13: A special rate of corporation tax applies where profits do not exceed £300,000 in an accounting period, with marginal relief between £300,000 and £1,500,000 (provisions exist to prevent splitting between associated companies). For the rates see Appendix 11B.

Small companies starting rate: This special rate applied between 2000–01 and 2005–06 to companies whose profits did not exceed £10,000, with marginal relief between £10,000 and £50,000.

Close companies—Income and Corporation Taxes Act 1988 Sections 414–417: A close company is one which is under the control of five or fewer participators or of participators who are directors. Owing to wide definitions of 'participator', 'associates', 'associated company', and 'control', companies with a large number of shareholders may be close companies. Accordingly it is necessary to remove certain quoted companies from this definition by a statutory exception.

Enhanced allowance for R&D expenditure: The definition follows the text of a Commission Recommendation 2003/36 (FA 2000, Sch 20, para 2(1)) (see <http://www.hmrc.gov.uk/manuals/cirdmanual/cird91400.htm> from which this summary is taken).

Recommendation 2003/361/EC defines enterprises as micro, small, or medium by reference to various ceilings relating to staff headcount, annual turnover, and balance sheet totals. To fall within a particular category an enterprise **must** meet the 'staff headcount' test and **at least one of** the 'turnover' or 'balance sheet total' tests.

Table 11A.1. Definitions of enterprise size according to the European Commission.
Ceilings within recommendation 2003/361/EC.

Enterprise category	Staff headcount	Turnover	Balance sheet total
Medium sized	<250	not exceeding €50 million	not exceeding €43 million
Small	<50	not exceeding €10 million	not exceeding €10 million
Micro	<10	not exceeding €2 million	not exceeding €2 million

If the accounting period is not equal to one year, the figures are annualized. These ceilings are not necessarily calculated solely by reference to the enterprise itself. Where an enterprise is not autonomous it may be necessary to take account of the headcount, turnover, and balance sheet totals of other enterprises to which it has connections.

11A.2. UK VAT

Registration threshold: From 1 April 2008—£67,000 annual turnover.

Eligibility for simplified systems: Annual accounting and cash accounting: £1,350,000 annual taxable turnover. Flat rate scheme: turnover under £150,000 (excluding VAT) or £187,500 (including VAT).

11A.3. Companies Act 2006

A company is 'small' if it satisfies two of the following:

- A turnover of not more than £6.5 million;
- A balance sheet total of not more than £3.26 million;
- Not more than fifty employees.

11A.4. Audit Exemption for Small Companies

1993 exemption introduced for turnover less than £90,000 (with reduction of burden up to £350,000).
1997 threshold raised to £350,000.
2000 threshold raised to £1 million.
2004 threshold raised to £5.6 million.
2008 threshold raised to £6.5 million.

APPENDIX 11B

UK tax rates over time

Table 11B.1. Corporation and basic income tax rates in the UK, 1982–2009

Financial year starting	Basic rate of income tax in April commencing that year (%)	Rate of corporation tax (%)	Small companies' rate (%)	Starting rate (CT) (%)
1982	30	52	38	
1983	30	50	30	
1984	30	45	30	
1985	30	40	30	
1986	29	35	29	
1987	27	35	27	
1988–89	25	35	25	
1990	25	34	25	
1991–95	25	33	25	
1996	24	33	24	
1997–98	23	31	21	
1999	23	30	20	
2000–01	22	30	20	10
2002–05	22	30	19	0[105]
2006	22	30	19	Abolished
2007	22	30	20	
2008–09	20	28	21	

105 In 2004–05 and 2005–06, the 0% rate only applied to retained profits and those distributed to corporate shareholders. Other distributed profits were subject to the non-corporate distribution rate of 19%.

APPENDIX 11C

Calculations of tax incentive to incorporate

Given that small businesses face a choice over the legal form that they adopt, it is worth considering how the UK tax system influences that decision. In this appendix, the situation in 2008–09 is described, and then it is shown how these incentives have changed over the period 1996–97 to 2008–09. For simplicity, the examples consider the position of a 'one-man' business making either £25,000 or £75,000 per annum—with the individual concerned able to choose between employment, self-employment, and incorporation.[106]

11C.1. 2008–09

Income tax: Income tax operates via a system of allowances and bands of income that are taxed at different rates. Individuals have a personal allowance, which is deducted from income to give taxable income. In 2008–09, income tax is charged at 20% (basic rate) on the first £34,800 of taxable income and 40% (higher rate) on all taxable income above £34,800.[107]

National Insurance: National Insurance contributions (NICs) entitle individuals to certain 'contributory' state benefits (see Golding (2006) for details). Employees pay Class 1 NICs of 11% on earnings between the primary threshold (roughly equivalent to the personal allowance for income tax) and the upper earnings limit (roughly equivalent to the higher rate income tax threshold), and 1% on earnings above this limit. If the employee 'contracts out' of the State Second Pension (S2P), the 11% rate is reduced by 1.6% (to 9.4%) to reflect their reduced S2P entitlement.

Employers pay Class 1 NICs of 12.8% for each employee who earns above the secondary threshold (equivalent to the primary threshold). Where the employee has 'contracted out' of S2P, the employer's NICs rate below the upper earnings limit is reduced by 3.7% (to 9.1%) if the employee is enrolled in a salary-related pension scheme.[108]

Self-employed individuals pay two different types of NICs: Class 2 contributions are paid at a flat rate of £2.30 per week, and Class 4 contributions are paid at a rate of 8% between the lower profits limit (roughly equivalent to the personal allowance) and the upper profits limit (roughly equivalent to the higher rate threshold), and

[106] It is assumed that the incorporated individual chooses to pay themselves a salary equal to the personal allowance (roughly equivalent to an 18-hour week on the national minimum wage), with the remainder of the profits from the business extracted in the form of dividend payments. The possibility of extracting profits in the form of capital gains is not considered.

[107] All bands and allowances are given in 2008–09 terms.

[108] There is a different rebate rate if the employee is enrolled in a money purchase scheme, but this rate is related to age, with younger employees receiving a smaller rebate than older employees.

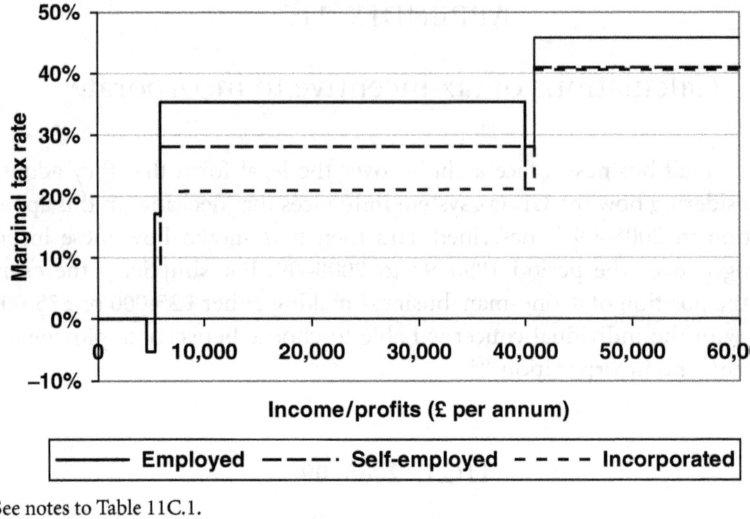

Note: See notes to Table 11C.1.

Figure 11C.1. 2008–09 marginal tax rates, by legal form

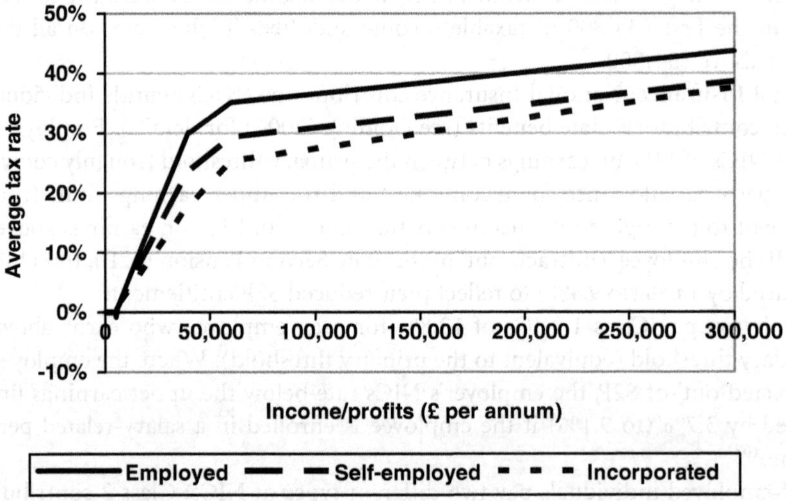

Note: See notes to Table 11C.1.

Figure 11C.2. 2008–09 average tax rates, by legal form

a rate of 1% for profits above this limit. The payment of Class 2 and 4 NICs does not entitle the individual to S2P. The other differences between the employed and self-employed (mainly that the self-employed are not entitled to contribution based jobseeker's allowance) are less significant than the S2P difference.

Table 11C.1. Tax and NICs to be paid in the UK in 2008–09, by legal form

	£25,000 income/profits per annum			£75,000 income/profits per annum		
	Employed	Self-employed	Incorporated	Employed	Self-employed	Incorporated
Salary	£23,396.63	£25,000.00	£6,013.49	£68,268.79	£75,000.00	£6,013.49
Income tax	£3,472.33	£3,793.00		£17,933.52	£20,626.00	
Class 1 employee	£1,673.56		£39.55	£3,520.33		£39.55
NICs Class 1 employer	£1,603.37		£21.51	£6,731.21		£21.51
NICs Class 2		£119.60			£119.60	
NICs Class 4 NICs		£1,565.20			£3,118.00	
Corporation tax			£3,974.34			£14,474.34
Dividend tax			£0.00			£3,404.03
Total tax and NI	£6,749.26	£5,477.80	£4,035.40	£28,185.05	£23,863.60	£17,939.43
Net receipts	£18,250.74	£19,522.20	£20,964.60	£46,814.95	£51,136.40	£57,060.57
Total tax and NI as a % of gross income/profits	27.0%	21.9%	16.1%	37.6%	31.8%	23.9%
Increase in net receipts compared to employed		£1,271.46	£2,713.86		£4,321.45	£10,245.62

Notes:

(1) All rates and allowances are in 2008–09 terms.

(2) The tax calculations for the employed individual take into account both employer and employee NICs, i.e. they reflect the combined tax and social security cost of being an employee (rather than being self-employed or incorporated). 'Contracted out' NICs rates are used in these calculations—with the employers' rate being the one relevant to salary-related pension schemes. This gives a better comparison than the 'contracted in' rate which carries an entitlement to S2P. Other entitlement differences are smaller.

(3) It is assumed that the incorporated individual pay themselves a salary equal to the personal allowance (after taking employer NICs into account, which is roughly equivalent to an 18-hour week on the national minimum wage), with the remainder of the profits from the business extracted in the form of dividend payments, on which corporation tax and dividend tax must be paid.

Table 11C.2. Total tax and NICs to be paid in the UK over time, by legal form

	£25,000 profits per annum			£75,000 profits per annum		
	Employed (%)	Self-employed (%)	Incorporated (%)	Employed (%)	Self-employed (%)	Incorporated (%)
1996–97	29.2	23.4	20.1	37.1	31.6	26.6
1997–98	28.4	22.6	17.7	36.5	31.1	24.3
1998–99	28.5	22.6	17.7	36.6	31.1	24.3
1999–2000	28.3	22.3	15.8	37.2	31.0	23.3
2000–01	27.4	22.2	12.6	36.9	31.0	23.2
2001–02	26.9	22.0	12.4	36.7	31.1	23.2
2002–03	26.6	22.0	8.9	36.5	31.1	22.3
2003–04	27.8	22.8	8.9	37.8	32.0	22.5
2004–05	27.9	22.9	14.7	37.9	32.0	22.6
2005–06	27.9	22.9	14.7	37.9	32.0	22.6
2006–07	27.9	22.8	14.7	37.9	32.0	22.6
2007–08	27.8	22.8	15.5	37.8	32.0	23.2
2008–09	27.0	21.9	16.1	37.6	31.8	23.9
Incremental approach	26.9	22.4	19.9	37.4	32.2	27.0

See notes to Table 11C.1. The incremental approach is discussed in Appendix 11D below.

Note: See notes to Table 11C.1.

Figure 11C.3. Total tax and NICs as a percentage of gross income/profits for a business making £25,000 p.a. in the UK over time, by legal form

Corporation tax: There is a small companies' rate of corporation tax (of 21%), which is paid on all profits below £300,000 per year.
Dividend tax: Dividend income is taxed at a rate of 10% up to the higher rate threshold for income tax and at 32.5% above this threshold. However, this is offset by a dividend tax credit—to reduce the distortion arising from the double taxation of dividends (once at the corporate level and once at the personal level)—which reduces the effective tax rates to 0% and 25% respectively.

11C.2. 1996–97 to 2008–09

Table 11C.2 illustrates how the proportion of gross income/profits paid out in tax and NICs by an employed, a self-employed, and an incorporated individual whose business makes either £25,000 or £75,000 per year has changed over time in the UK. Figure 11C.3 illustrates the same figures graphically for a business making £25,000 gross income/profits per year.

APPENDIX 11D

Proposed incremental approach

The 2008–09 tax system (described in Appendix 11C) is used as the basis for these calculations, with the following additional changes:

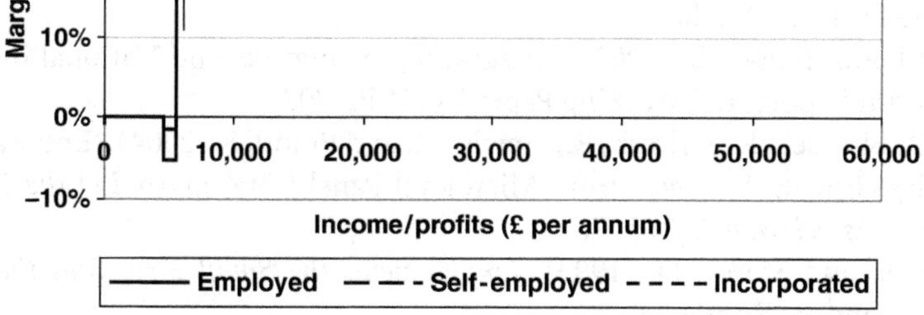

Note: See notes to Table 11C.1.

Figure 11D.1. Marginal tax rates under incremental approach, by legal form

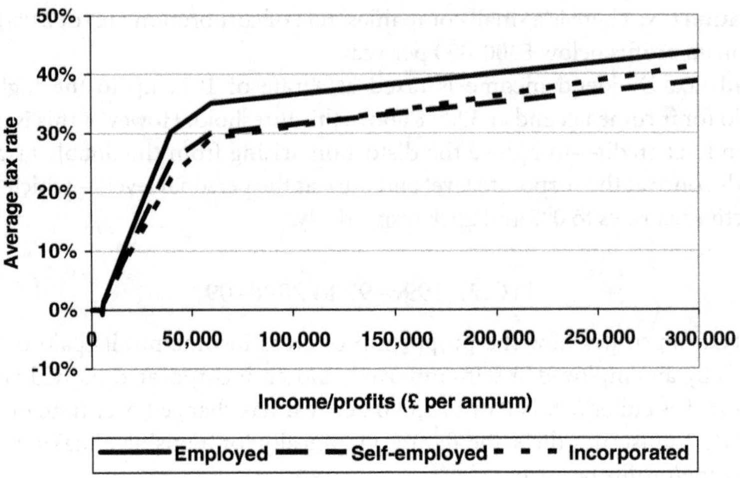

Note: See notes to Table 11C.1.

Figure 11D.2. Average tax rates under incremental approach, by legal form

Alignment of higher rate threshold and upper earnings limit: This is scheduled to be introduced in 2009–10.
National Insurance: Class 2 and Class 4 contributions are essentially abolished, with self-employed individuals now charged Class 1 employee contributions.
Corporation tax: A single rate of corporation tax is imposed at a rate of 26%.

REFERENCES

Abramovsky, L., Griffith, R., and Harrison, R. (2006), *Background Facts and Comments on 'Supporting Innovation: Enhancing the R&D Tax Credit'*, IFS Briefing Note No. 68.

Adam, S. (2008), 'Capital Gains Tax', in Chote, R., Emmerson, C., Miles, D., and Shaw, J. (eds.), *The IFS Green Budget: January 2008*, Commentary 104, London: Institute for Fiscal Studies.

—— and Loutzenhiser, G. (2007), 'Integrating Income Tax and National Insurance: An Interim Report', IFS Working Paper No. WP21/07.

Aghion, P., Blundell, R., Griffith, R., Howitt, P., and Prantl, S. (2004), 'Entry and Productivity Growth: Evidence from Microlevel Panel Data', *Journal of the European Economic Association*, 2, 265–76.

Atkinson, J., and Storey, D. (1993), *Employment, the Small Firm and the Labour Market*, London: Routledge.

Bank of England (2004), *Finance for Small Firms—An Eleventh Report.*

Bannock, G. (2005), *The Economics and Management of Small Business: An International Perspective*, London: Routledge.

Benneyworth, R. (2006), 'Watch Out—Flat Rate VAT Disaster!', AccountingWeb, 27 November 2006.

Birch, D. (1979), *The Job Generation Process*, MIT Program on Neighborhood and Regional Change, Cambridge, Mass.

Bjuggren, P., and Sund, L. (2002), 'A Transaction Cost Rationale for Transition of the Firm within the Family', *Small Business Economics*, **19**, 123–33.

Bloom, N., and Van Reenen, J. (2006), 'Measuring and Explaining Management Practices across Firms and Countries', London: LSE Research Online.

Blow, L., Hawkins, M., Klemm, A., McCrae, J., and Simpson, H. (2002), '*Budget 2002: Business Taxation Measures*', IFS Briefing Note No. 24.

Board of Trade (1962), *Report of the Company Law Committee*, Cmnd 1794, London: HMSO.

Bolton, J. (Chairman) (1971), *Report of the Committee of Inquiry on Small Firms*, Cmnd 4811, London: HMSO.

Bond, S., Devereux, M., and Gammie, M. (1996), 'Tax Reform to Promote Investment', *Oxford Review of Economic Policy*, **12**, 108–17.

Boyle, E. (1994), 'The Rise of the Reluctant Entrepreneurs', *International Small Business Journal*, **12**, 63–9.

Boyns, N., Cox, M., Spires, R., and Hughes, A. (2003), '*Research into the Enterprise Investment Scheme and Venture Capital Trusts*', Cambridge: Public and Corporate Economic.

Carney, W. (1995), 'Limited Liability Companies: Origins and Antecedents', *University of Colorado Law Review*, **66**, 855–80.

Chennells, L., Dilnot, A. and Emmerson, C. (eds.) (2000), *The IFS Green Budget, Commentary 80*, London: IFS.

Chittenden, F., Kauser, S., and Poutziouris, P. (2003), 'The Impact of Tax Regulation on Small Firms in the UK, USA, EU and Australia and New Zealand', *International Small Business Journal*, **21**, 85–106.

CIOT & ATT (2005), 'Working Towards a New Relationship: Priorities for Reducing the Administrative Burdens of the Tax System on Small Businesses' http://www.tax.org.uk/attach.pl/3606/3434/WorkingTowardsNewRelationship%20Final280605.pdf.

Cowling, M., Bates, P., Jagger, N., and Murray, G. (2008), *Study of the Impact of the Enterprise Investment Scheme (EIS) and Venture Capital Trusts (VCTs) on Company Performance*, HMRC Research Report 44.

Crawford, C. (2008), 'Corporation Tax and Entrepreneurship', in Chote, R., Emmerson, C., Miles, D., and Shaw, J. (eds.), *The IFS Green Budget 2008*, London.

Curran, J., Kitching, J., Abbott, B., and Mills, V. (1993), *Employment and Employment Relations in the Small Service Sector Enterprise—A Report*, London: Kingston University.

Davies, P. (2003), *Gower and Davies' Principles of Modern Company Law*, 7th edn., London: Sweet & Maxwell.

Davis, S., Haltiwanger, J., and Schuh, S. (1996), 'Small Business and Job Creation: Dissecting the Myth and Reassessing the Facts', *Small Business Economics*, **8**, 297–315.

DBERR (2007), 'Companies Act 2006: A Summary of what it means for Private Companies' <http://www.berr.gov.uk/files/file42262.pdf>.

De Mooij, R., and Nicodeme, G. (2007), 'Corporate Tax Policy, Entrepreneurship and Incorporation in the EU', Tinbergen Institute Discussion Paper TI 2007-030/3.

De Rugy, V. (2005), 'Are Small Businesses The Engine of Growth?', American Enterprise Institute Working Paper No. 123.

Dean, S. (2005), 'Attractive Complexity: Tax Deregulation, the Check-the-Box Election and the Future of Tax Simplification', *Hofstra Law Review*, **405**.

Derregia, M., and Chittenden, F. (2006), *The Role of Tax Incentives in Capital Investment and Research and Development Expenditure Decisions by Small and Medium Enterprises*, London: ICAEW.

Devereux, M., and Freeman, H. (1991), 'A General Neutral Profits Tax', *Fiscal Studies*, **12**, 1–15.

Disney, R., Haskel, J., and Heden, Y. (2003), 'Restructuring and Productivity Growth in UK Manufacturing', *The Economic Journal*, **113**, 666–94.

DTI (2005), *Company Law Reform*, Cm6456, London: HMSO.

EC Treaty (2006), 'Consolidated Versions of the Treaty on European Union and of the Treaty Establishing the European Community', *Official Journal C321E* of **29** December 2006.

European Commission (1994), Commission Recommendation of 7th December 1994 on the Transfer of Small and Medium-sized Enterprises (94/1069/EC).

—— (1998), Commission Notice on the Application of State Aid Rules to Measures Relating to Direct Business Taxation (98/C 384/03).

—— (2006), 'Modernising Labour Law to Meet the Challenges of the 21st Century (Green Paper)', COM(2006) 708, Brussels.

Evans, C. (2003), 'Studying the Studies: An Overview of Recent Research into Taxation Operating Costs', *eJournal of Tax Research*, **1**, 64.

Freedman, J. (1994), 'Small Businesses and the Corporate Form: Burden or Privilege?', *The Modern Law Review*, **57**, 555–84.

—— (2000), 'Limited Liability: Large Company Theory and Small Firms', *The Modern Law Review*, **63**, 317–54.

—— (2001), 'Employed or Self-employed? Tax Classification of Workers and the Changing Labour Market', London: TLRC Discussion Paper, IFS.

—— (2003), 'Small Business Taxation: Policy Issues and the UK', in Warren, N. (ed.), *Taxing Small Business: Developing Good Tax Policies*, Conference Series No. 23, Sydney: Australian Tax Research Foundation.

—— (2003a), 'One Size Fits All—Small Business and Competitive Legal Forms', *The Journal of Corporate Law Studies*, **3**, 123–48.

—— (2004), 'Limited Liability Partnerships in the United Kingdom: Do They Have a Role for Small Firms?', in McCahery, J., Raaijmakers, T., and Vermeulen, E.

(eds.), *The Governance of Close Corporations and Partnerships: US and European Perspectives*, Oxford: Oxford University Press.

—— (2006), 'Why Taxing the Micro-Business is not Simple—A Cautionary Tale from the "Old World"', *Journal of the Australasian Tax Teachers Association*, **2**, 58–77.

—— (2007), 'Small Business Taxation—The Indefinable in Pursuit of the Unachievable?', The ICAEW Faculty Hardman Memorial Lecture 2006 <http://www.icaew.com/index.cfm?route=146986>.

—— and Chamberlain, E. (1997), 'Horizontal Equity and the Taxation of Employed and Self-Employed Workers', *Fiscal Studies*, **18**, 87–118.

—— and Godwin, M. (1992), 'Legal Form, Tax and the Micro Business', in Caley, K., Chell, E., Chittenden, F., and Mason, C. (eds.), *Small Enterprise Development Policy and Practice in Action*, London: Paul Chapman Publishing.

Gammie, M. (2007), 'Reflections on *Jones v Garnett*', *British Tax Review*, **6**, 687–92.

Gentry, W. (2004), 'Comment on Small Business and the Tax System', in Aaron, H. and Slemrod, J. *The Crisis in Tax Administration*, Washington DC: Brookings Institution Press.

Golding, J. (2006), *Tolley's National Insurance Contributions*, London: LexisNexis Butterworths.

Goolsbee, A. (2004), 'The Impact of the Corporate Income Tax: Evidence from State Organizational Form Data', *Journal of Public Economics*, **88**, 2283–99.

Gordon, R. (1998), 'Can High Personal Tax Rates Encourage Entrepreneurial Activity?', *IMF Staff Papers*, **45**, 49.

Graham, T. (2004) *Graham Review of the Small Firms Loan Guarantee: Recommendations*, London: HMSO.

Gretton, S. (2008), IR35—The Lottery Workers 2 v HMRC 2 <http://www.accountingweb.co.uk>.

Handler, W. C. (1994), 'Succession in Family Business: A Review of the Research', *Family Business Review*, **VII**, 133–57.

Harrison, B. (1997), *Lean & Mean*, New York: Guilford Press.

Harvey, M. (1995), *Towards the Insecurity Society: The Tax Trap of Self-Employment*, London: Institute of Employment Rights.

HM Customs and Excise (1999), *Review of the VAT Registration Threshold*, London: HM Customs and Excise.

HMRC (2004), *Regulatory Impact Assessment (RIA)—Corporation Tax: The Non-Corporate Distribution Rate*, London: HMRC.

—— (2006), *Tackling Managed Service Companies*, London: HMRC.

—— (2006a), Research and Development Press Release <http://www.gnn.gov.uk/environment/fullDetail.asp?ReleaseID=241316&NewsAreaID=2&NavigatedFromDepartment=False>.

—— (2007), Full Regulatory Impact Assessment—Managed Service Companies <http://www.hmrc.gov.uk/ria/full-ria-man-serv-coys.pdf>.

—— (2007a), Developing Methodologies for Measuring Direct Tax <http://www.hmrc.gov.uk/pbr2007/mdtl-direct.pdf>.

HMRC (2008), *Capital Gains Tax: Relief on Disposal of a Business (Entrepreneurs' Relief)*. London: HMRC.

HM Treasury (2003), *Bridging the Finance Gap: Next Steps in Improving Access to Growth Capital for Small Businesses*.

—— (2005), *Pre-Budget Report December 2005*, Cm 6701, London: TSO.

—— (2006), *Budget 2006: Regulatory Impact Assessments*. London: TSO.

—— (2007), *Budget 2007, HC 342*, London: TSO.

—— (2008), *Pre-Budget Report November 2008*, Cm 7484, London: TSO.

HMT/HMRC (2007), *Income Shifting: A Consultation on Draft Legislation*, London: HMSO.

—— (2007a), *Business Tax Reform: Capital Allowances Changes*, Technical Note.

Holtz-Eakin, D. J. (2000), 'Public Policy Toward Entrepreneurship', *Small Business Economics*, **15**, 283–91.

IES (2005), *Annual Survey of Small Businesses: UK*, Brighton: Institute for Employment Studies, CN: 6622b.

IFS Capital Taxes Group (1994), *Setting Savings Free: Proposals for the Taxation of Savings and Profits*, London: Institute for Fiscal Studies.

Inland Revenue (1999), 'Regulatory Impact Assessment, National Insurance: Service Provision Through Intermediaries', The Welfare Reform and Pensions Bill <http://www.hmrc.gov.uk/ria/amendedria.pdf>.

Keatinge, R. (2007), *Self-Employment Tax Issues in LLCs Taxed as Partnerships*, Suffolk University Law School Research Paper No. 07–33.

KPMG (2006), *Administrative Burdens: HMRC Measurement Project*, KPMG Publication No. 300–808.

Lagerberg, F. (2007), 'Managed Service Companies: What Next?—Section 25 and Schedule 3', *British Tax Review*, **5**, 459–43.

Lee, N. (2007), 'Revenue Law—Principles and Practice', 25th edn. Haywards Heath, West Sussex: Tottel Publishing.

Lindhe, T., Södersten, J., and Oberg, A. (2002), 'Economic Effects of Taxing Closed Corporations under a Dual Income Tax', *ifo Studien*, **48**, 575–610.

Loutzenhiser, G. (2007), 'Income Splitting and Settlements: Further Observations on *Jones v Garnett*', *British Tax Review*, **6**, 693–716.

MacKie-Mason, J., and Gordon, R. (1997), 'How Much do Taxes Discourage Incorporation?', *Journal of Finance*, **52**, 477–505.

McNulty, J. (1992), *Federal Income Taxation of S Corporations*, New York: Foundation Press.

Meade, J. (1978), *The Structure and Reform of Direct Taxation: Report of a Committee chaired by Professor J. E. Meade for the Institute for Fiscal Studies*, London: George Allen & Unwin. http://www.ifs.org.uk/publications/3433.

Murphy, R. (2007), *Small Company Taxation in the UK: A Review in the Aftermath of the 'Arctic Systems' Ruling*, Tax Research UK.

NAO (2003), *Tackling Fraud against the Inland Revenue*, HC 429, London: HMSO.

—— (2006), '*Helping Newly Registered Businesses Meet Their Tax Obligations*', HC 98, London: HMSO.

OECD (1994), *Taxation and Small Businesses*, Paris: OECD.
—— (1997), *Small Businesses, Job Creation and Growth: Facts, Obstacles and Best Practices*, Paris: OECD.
Perez-Gonzalez, F. (2005), 'Inherited Control and Firm Performance', Columbia University Working Paper.
Posner, R. (1986), *Economic Analysis of Law*, 3rd edn. Boston: Little, Brown & Co.
President's Panel (2005), *Simple, Fair and Pro-Growth: Proposals to Fix America's Tax System*, Report of the President's Advisory Panel on Federal Tax Reform.
PWC (2006), *Enterprise in the UK: Impact of the UK Tax Regime for Private Companies*, PricewaterhouseCoopers.
Redston, A. (2002), *IR35: Personal Service Companies*, 2nd edn., Accountancy Books.
—— (2004), 'Small Business in the Eye of the Storm', *British Tax Review*, **5**, 566–81.
—— (2007), 'Income Sharing: The Nelsonian Option', *British Tax Review*, **6**, 680–6.
St John Price, A. (2006), 'Pros and Cons of the VAT Flat Rate Scheme', Accounting Web<http://www.accountingweb.co.uk/cgi-bin/item.cgi?id=162459&d=1032&h=1019&f=1026>.
Sandford, C., Godwin, M., and Hardwick, P. (1990), *Administrative and Compliance Costs of Taxation*, Bath: Fiscal Publications.
Sanger, C. (2005), *Taxline*, London: ICAEW.
Slemrod, J. (2004), 'Small Business and the Tax System', in Aaron, H., and Slemrod, J., *The Crisis in Tax Administration*, Washington DC: Brookings Institution Press.
Sørensen, P. (2005), 'Neutral Taxation of Shareholder Income', *International Tax and Public Finance*, **12**, 777–801.
—— (2007), 'The Nordic Dual Income Tax: Principles, Practices and Relevance for Canada', *Canadian Tax Journal*, **55**, 557–602.
—— (2008), 'The Taxation of Business Income in Sweden', Draft Report prepared for the Swedish Ministry of Finance.
Stanworth, C., and Stanworth, J. (1997), 'Reluctant Entrepreneurs and Their Clients: The Case of Self-Employed Freelance Workers in the British Book-Publishing Industry', *International Small Business Journal*, **16**, 58–73.
Storey, D. (1994), *Understanding the Small Business Sector*, London: Routledge.
—— (1995), 'A Symposium on Harrison's "Lean and Mean": A Job Generation Perspective', *Small Business Economics*, **7**, 337–40.
Tiley, J., and Collison, D. (2007), *Tiley & Collison: UK Tax Guide 2007–08*, UK: LexisNexis Butterworths.
Truman, M. (2006), 'What's in a name?', Taxation <http://www.taxation.co.uk/Articles/2006/11/23/51297/What's+in+a+name.htm>.
US Treasury (2005), 'Actions are Needed to Eliminate Inequities in the Employment Tax Liabilities of Sole Proprietorships and Single Shareholder S Corporations', Memorandum for Deputy Commissioner for Services and Enforcement, Reference No. 2005-30-080.
Warren, N. (1993), 'The UK Experience with VAT', *Revenue Law Journal*, **3**, 75–99.
Winchester, R. (2006), 'Working for Free: It Ought to be Against the (Tax) Law', *Mississippi Law Journal*, **76**, 227.

12

Administration and Compliance

*Jonathan Shaw, Joel Slemrod, and John Whiting**

Jonathan Shaw is a Senior Research Economist at the IFS. His research focuses on the evaluation of education and labour market programmes, the incentive effects of taxation, and the compliance costs of remitting taxes and claiming benefits. He co-edited the *IFS Green Budget* in 2008 and 2009. He is currently working on estimating the impact of tax credits on work and education choices.

Joel Slemrod is Paul W. McCracken Collegiate Professor of Business Economics and Public Policy and Director of the Office of Tax Policy Research at the University of Michigan. His research has focused on the evaluation of tax systems and their consequences, with emphasis on the issues raised by avoidance and evasion. He is a Past President of the National Tax Association and Editor of the *National Tax Journal*, and is now a Co-Editor of the *Journal of Public Economics*. He is a co-author of *Taxing Ourselves: A Citizen's Guide to the Debate over Taxes*, now in its fourth edition.

John Whiting OBE has been a tax partner with PricewaterhouseCoopers since 1984. He was the co-deviser and developer of the PwC Total Tax Contribution framework, and his current responsibilities include advising PwC and clients on tax policy developments and leading PwC's client tax training activities. John is a Past President of the Chartered Institute of Taxation and chairs their Management of Taxes Committee. His policy work involves regular contact with the UK tax authorities, Ministers and Shadow Ministers, and Parliamentary Committees. He was awarded the OBE in 2008 for public service. John won the LexisNexis 'Tax Writer of the Year' award in 2004 and confesses to having been the inaugural recipient of the 'Tax Personality of the Year' accolade.

* We gratefully acknowledge helpful comments from Stuart Adam, Chris Evans, Malcolm Gammie, John Hassseldine, Richard Highfield, David Massey, Alan Plumley, Anne Redston, and Shlomo Yitzhaki, as well as valuable input from Kate Bedwell.

EXECUTIVE SUMMARY

Assessing how much tax people owe and ensuring it is paid is a costly activity for both taxpayers and the government. Yet modern 'optimal tax theory' has for the most part ignored these costs and has focused on those created by distorting people's behaviour (distortion costs). But it is possible to adapt the standard framework to reflect administration and compliance costs, and include real-world features of tax administration such as penalties for tax evasion, enquiry rates, and obligations to report information to the tax authority.

Part I of this chapter presents a simplified model of this type. The optimal policy is to use a mix of tax instruments determined so that the cost to society of raising an extra pound of revenue is the same for each instrument used. This would give tax instruments that raise revenue relatively efficiently a more prominent place in the tax system than those which raise revenue in a more costly way.

This model generates several valuable insights.

- First, the optimal mix of tax instruments cannot be determined by looking at only a subset of the costs of taxation. A tax instrument that looks attractive when considering only distortion costs may have little role to play because it imposes high administrative or compliance costs.
- Second, it is marginal costs that matter when making incremental policy adjustments. Most publicly available data relate to average or total costs.
- Third, while enforcement activity by the tax authority is a true resource cost to society, any additional revenue such activity brings in is not a resource gain, but a transfer from private citizens. As a result, the superficially appealing rule that the tax authority should maximize tax revenue net of administrative costs is not optimal because it involves too high a level of enforcement.

An important question is what determines each of the costs of taxation. Increases in the probability of punishment or the size of the penalty should reduce evasion, though the latter has not been convincingly established empirically. If citizens are dutiful, evasion can also depend on the context and factors such as tax morale and dissatisfaction with the tax system. This implies that the tax authority should be careful not to alienate taxpayers when carrying out enforcement activity.

Administrative and compliance costs depend on a wide range of factors, including the complexity of the tax, characteristics of the tax base, structure of tax rates, frequency of reform, and organization and efficiency of the tax authority. Taxes should therefore be kept as simple and stable as possible. In other areas, there is a trade-off between administrative and compliance costs: for example, whether it is the tax authority or taxpayers who have responsibility for calculating tax liability. Providing help and guidance increases administration costs, but reduces compliance costs.

In order to achieve a high level of compliance at modest cost, modern tax systems rely heavily on taxing market transactions, and involve extensive withholding and information reporting requirements. As a result, businesses (as opposed to individuals) play a central role in tax collection.

Part II of the chapter addresses some current UK policy issues.

HM Revenue and Customs has a number of public performance objectives, including targets for reduced non-compliance and for improved accuracy and customer satisfaction. The difficulty with these targets is that they do not give a good sense of the ultimate goal, nor of the trade-offs and priorities involved. The government's work on cutting the burden of regulation gets closer to measuring marginal costs than most previous attempts, but excludes some things normally considered part of compliance costs and focuses on businesses rather than all taxpayers.

HMRC is already taking steps to improve the operation of PAYE, but the time is perhaps right for a more fundamental rethink of how income tax is collected in the UK. The need for paper communication could be much reduced by an online coding system, something that deserves further investigation. Other changes could help reduce the frequency with which PAYE withholds the wrong amount of tax, but at the cost of more burdensome information reporting requirements. A more radical alternative would be to move to a system of universal self assessment. This would allow PAYE to be simplified substantially, reduce employer compliance costs, and cut the number of errors that lie unnoticed for several years. Such a move is likely to be unpopular because of the additional burden placed on individual taxpayers. In part, this could be mitigated if HMRC pre-populated tax returns. And, were it possible to integrate tax credit claims into the tax return, some of the poorest taxpayers may benefit from such a change.

Another issue that has received much recent attention is tax avoidance. The perception remains that tax avoidance is a continuing source of considerable revenue leakage, complexity, and cost. Ultimately, tackling avoidance is part of the process of defining the tax base. This is easier where the tax base reflects a clear economic principle and avoids artificial and ambiguous boundaries. Governments are likely to have to continue to deploy a variety of measures to counteract avoidance and monitor the borders of the tax system where clear boundaries do not exist.

The overriding conclusion is that the UK's tax system is not doing too badly. But, as commercial life continues to change rapidly, there is increasing pressure for the tax system to adapt. The question is whether it can adapt quickly enough. If not, it runs the risk of imposing unnecessary burdens while simultaneously allowing revenues to escape taxation so that the tax burden is shared in a more capricious and inequitable fashion.

I. TAX SYSTEMS AND IMPLEMENTATION

12.1. INTRODUCTION

How taxes are administered and enforced matters—witness the debacle surrounding the introduction of tax credits in 2003. Most of modern tax theory, however, completely ignores administration and enforcement. The policy formation process is not much better, too often addressing implementation only after reform has been determined, rather than as an integral part of the decision-making process.

In this chapter, we step outside the usual framework for tax analysis to consider the administration and enforcement of the tax system. In essence, our primary focus is not what determines tax liability, but how that liability reaches the government's pocket. Our conclusions are of central relevance to the Mirrlees Review itself, since a number of the reforms being considered will require changes to the way in which taxes are administered and enforced.

The remainder of Part I introduces a simple theoretical framework that clarifies the key issues and trade-offs that exist. Part II applies this framework to current policy issues in the UK and offers some recommendations. Part III concludes. Although we range broadly over these issues, some we touch on only peripherally. We also assume that the net revenue required is fixed—the policy issue is how best to raise this given amount. Box 12.1 defines some key terms.

Box 12.1. Definition of key terms

We use the term **remit** to mean transmit funds to the tax authority (by writing a cheque, for example).[1] The agent ultimately liable for a tax—the **statutory bearer**—need not be the agent with responsibility for remittance. **Withholding**

(cont.)

[1] Our use of the term should be distinguished from the UK tax system offering the 'remittance basis' for the non-domiciled that allows an individual—usually someone resident in the UK but not domiciled in the UK—to be taxed on non-UK income only if it is brought into the UK.

Box 12.1. *(cont.)*

refers to the situation where some or all of tax liability must be remitted by someone other than the statutory bearer (the most obvious example of this is employers remitting on behalf of employees).

We say that an individual **bears the burden** of a tax to the extent it makes him or her worse off (causes a loss of utility). The loss of utility can occur either because a tax reduces the return an individual receives on his labour or capital, or because a tax increases the prices of the good and services a taxpayer wishes to purchase with his income (or both). To the extent that taxes reduce the rate of return to investing in or running a corporate business, this burden must be traced beyond the impact on the profitability of a legal entity to its impact on the utility of the owners or suppliers of capital to the business.

Who ultimately bears the burden of a tax is generally different from both the agent who remits the tax and the statutory bearer of the tax. This is because a tax system causes changes in pre-tax prices, thereby shifting the burden away from the statutory bearer. For example, a tax on labour earnings will in general increase the pre-tax wage, so that the after-tax wage does not fall by as much as the tax rate. Thus the burden of the tax is shared between the employer, who faces a higher cost of labour than otherwise, and the employee, who receives a lower after-tax wage rate than in the absence of the tax.[2] The response of prices and wages to taxation may not happen in the short run, especially in the presence of inflexible prices (due, for example, to long-term contracts). However, because prices are ultimately set by the interaction of supply and demand, the tax system will, in the long run, affect prices and these effects will determine ultimate incidence.

In the long run, what matters for the impact of a tax system is what actions trigger tax liability, who must remit that liability, and the expected penalties for the failure to remit. Aside from framing issues, what a tax is *called* is not relevant; for example, other things equal, whether a tax is labelled an employer tax or an employee tax will not matter.

We employ the traditional distinction between evasion and avoidance: that of legality. **Evasion** is the use of illegal means to reduce tax liability—false statements on a tax return, for example—whereas **avoidance** is the reduction of liability through legal channels—such as setting up a company so that self-employment income (subject to income tax) can be relabelled as dividends (subject to corporation tax). If uncovered, evasion can be punished through fines or imprisonment, whereas avoidance cannot. In reality, however, the dividing line is not always clear; where this is the case we will clarify as necessary.

[2] In the case of a tax on labour income, exactly how this burden is shared depends critically on the relative elasticity of the demand for and supply of labour: the less elastic is labour demand and the more elastic labour supply, the greater the proportion of the burden borne by employees.

12.2. ANALYSIS OF TAX SYSTEM DESIGN

In this section, we show how standard tax theory can be extended to incorporate tax implementation concerns. We begin with a description of the costs of taxation, followed by the extended theoretical framework itself and an outline of its policy implications, and concluding with a discussion of caveats and broader issues that the model does not fully address.

12.2.1. The costs of taxation

Taxes impose costs. From an individual taxpayer's point of view, the most obvious of these is the tax revenue itself, which serves to reduce the taxpayer's purchasing power relative to what it would have been without the tax. Of course, from society's point of view, the lost purchasing power is not a cost—it is a transfer from individuals to the government, which can be used to provide public goods or redistribute towards individuals deemed worthy of support.

But taxes have other costs—costs that are true losses to society. We can distinguish three of these: distortion costs, administrative costs, and compliance costs.

Distortion costs arise because taxpayers' decisions, including but not limited to how much to work and what to buy, are distorted by taxes. As a simple example, an employee might be unwilling to do an hour of overtime given a post-tax wage of £12, but would willingly work late for his pre-tax wage of £20. If so, the tax has *distorted* the employee's choice over how many hours to work. It is a cost because, had the tax authority agreed not to tax the hour of overtime, the employee would have done the extra hour and been better off as a result (otherwise he wouldn't have been willing to stay late) while tax revenue is unchanged. The change in behaviour occurs because taxes change the relative price of activities so that they do not represent the relative social costs, and is sometimes referred to as the real substitution response. This is to be contrasted with evasion and avoidance, which are efforts to reduce tax liability *without* changing work and consumption decisions (illegally in the former case, legally in the latter).

A different type of distortion cost is the risk exposure cost of tax evasion. An individual who evades part of his liability exposes himself to risk because he doesn't know whether he will be caught and penalized. Assuming he is risk-averse, this is costly: the individual would prefer to remit with certainty an amount equal to his expected tax liability. If the government is effectively risk-neutral, the social cost of the risk exposure is equal to the amount the individual would be willing to pay in order to eliminate the exposure.

Administrative costs are costs incurred by the tax authority in establishing and operating systems to manage all aspects of taxation. **Compliance costs**, in contrast, are incurred directly by taxpayers in complying with their tax-related obligations, and by third parties involved in the tax remittance process (such as employers who are required to remit tax on behalf of their employees).

Why administrative and compliance costs exist may be obvious, but it is worth making explicit. Even if all taxpayers were scrupulously honest, an administrative system would still be required to provide information about tax liabilities and to record and check payments, and taxpayers would still need to spend time and money finding their way through the increasingly complex maze of tax laws. But, of course, not all taxpayers are honest; nor are taxpayers obliged to arrange their affairs in a way that suits the tax authority. As a result, some taxpayers go to considerable lengths (avoidance or evasion) to reduce the size of their tax bill; this expense also constitutes compliance costs.[3] In response to avoidance and evasion, all tax authorities judge it worthwhile to expend resources to limit their deleterious consequences.

12.2.2. Optimal taxation

The costs of taxation having been described, the crucial next step is to realize that not all tax policy instruments impose the same costs per pound of revenue raised. All costs (apart from the loss of purchasing power, of course) can vary depending on the characteristics of the tax and its implementation, as can the distribution of costs across individuals. This explains why economists have spent, and continue to spend, so much time trying to find the 'best' tax system (the one that minimizes total costs, subject to distributional concerns).

In its search for the best tax system, modern optimal tax theory—begun by Mirrlees (1971) and Diamond and Mirrlees (1971)—has, for the most part, focused on distortion costs, ignoring both administrative and compliance costs as well as evasion. However, as a description of reality, the assumption that tax liability can be ascertained and collected costlessly is patently untrue.

[3] It might be argued that one should distinguish between unavoidable compliance costs (that arise in complying with tax obligations), and voluntary compliance costs (that result from attempts by the taxpayer to reduce his tax liability). In practice, it is very hard to separate the two (it depends on the intentions of the taxpayer). Moreover, both are an equally wasteful use of resources from society's point of view.

Accounting for evasion and for administrative and compliance costs in normative models is, therefore, important. It turns out that the standard optimal tax framework can be extended straightforwardly to incorporate the other costs of taxation, and to address details of tax system implementation, such as penalties for tax evasion, enquiry rates, and obligations to report information to the tax authority, and so on. We will outline a simplified model of this type below. But before doing this, we spend a few paragraphs describing the normative framework that forms the basis for the model we present—a basis common to most optimal tax models.

12.2.3. Normative framework

The standard normative framework for evaluating tax policy assumes that the best tax system is the one that is best for citizens' well-being (or welfare), as they judge it. This means that the *process* that generates welfare levels is irrelevant except insofar as it affects those welfare levels. Whether a tax system is 'fair' depends on its effect on the distribution of welfare across individuals, not on the process that generates this distribution. This assumption may seem unreasonable given the possibility that the welfare of some individuals has been achieved illegally (through evasion). This is something we discuss in more detail later.

Individuals are assumed to make decisions based on what will maximize their level of well-being, as they judge it, given prices and their resources. We recognize that there are situations in which behaviour appears to violate this assumption. We address the issues this raises where appropriate.

To determine how society makes trade-offs across individuals, a social welfare function is used. A social welfare function (implicitly) assigns a weight to each individual's welfare describing how important that welfare is from society's point of view. These weights may differ according to the level of welfare: the higher the weight on low-welfare individuals relative to high-welfare individuals, the more egalitarian is the social welfare function, and the more the society is willing to sacrifice aggregate welfare in favour of a more equal distribution of welfare across individuals. We will presume that the degree of egalitarianism is determined by the political system.

12.2.4. Raising revenue efficiently

As mentioned above, optimal tax theory can be straightforwardly extended beyond the traditional focus of enquiry—the choice of rates and bases—to address the policy instruments related to tax system implementation. In describing this extended framework, it is helpful to ignore distributional issues initially, and introduce them later, allowing us to focus first on how to raise revenue most efficiently (i.e. at minimum cost to society).

Assume the tax authority has to raise a fixed amount of revenue in order to fund public spending. Revenue is raised using a combination of tax instruments; the task of the tax authority is to choose which tax instruments to use (and how much to use each of them) in order to raise the required revenue at minimum cost to society. This choice will depend on the **efficiency cost** of each tax instrument, which describes how costly it is to raise revenue using that instrument. Efficiency cost incorporates all of the costs of taxation identified above—administrative and compliance costs, distortion costs including the risk bearing cost of tax evasion, plus the loss of purchasing power (it is convenient for this exercise to treat lost purchasing power like all the other costs).

What does the optimal policy look like in this model? It turns out that an optimal policy will equalize the Marginal Efficiency Cost of Funds (*MECF*) of any and all tax instruments that are employed.[4] The *MECF* of a particular tax instrument is defined as the marginal (additional) cost to society of raising an extra pound of tax revenue using that tax instrument. The higher is a tax instrument's *MECF*, the less efficient is the tax instrument at collecting revenue. The equalize-*MECF* principle holds because, if it is violated, the same revenue could be raised at lower social cost by reducing reliance on high-*MECF* tax instruments and increasing reliance on low-*MECF* instruments.[5] As shown in Slemrod and Yitzhaki (1996), the *MECF* of a given tax instrument, i, is equal to:

$$MECF_i = \frac{1 + x_i + c_i}{1 - a_i}$$

where a_i and c_i are marginal administrative and compliance costs per pound of revenue raised, and x_i is the distortion cost per pound raised (including risk exposure costs). The numerator is the social cost of the tax change per pound raised; the denominator is how much of that pound is left once administrative costs have been accounted for. Because c_i is added in the numerator and a_i is subtracted in the denominator, the key conceptual

[4] The *MECF* analysis applies to incremental policy changes, but the intuition applies to non-incremental policy changes, as well.

[5] In the more general model where the level of public spending is chosen optimally, it will also be true that the common value of the *MECF* for all tax instruments is equal to the social marginal benefit of public spending. This suggests that the level of public spending should depend, in part, on the efficiency of the tax instruments available to collect the revenue.

difference between compliance costs and administrative costs is explicit: only the latter uses revenue raised from taxpayers.

Three important implications of the model derive immediately from the form of the *MECF*. First, what matters for the evaluation of potential incremental policy changes are marginal costs, not total or average costs. This stands in contrast to much of the empirical evidence on administrative and compliance costs (discussed later), which concerns total costs. Second, since the *MECF* depends on all costs of taxation, policy reforms cannot be evaluated with reference to only a subset of the costs. A reform that looks attractive when considering only distortion costs may be very unattractive when administrative and compliance costs are taken into consideration. Third, to the extent that a trade-off exists between administrative and compliance costs, administrative costs should receive a slightly higher weight because administrative costs must themselves be met through taxation, which entails further administration, compliance, and distortion costs.

Since the optimal policy rule requires that the *MECF* be equalized for all tax instruments employed, it should be clear that tax instruments with a high *MECF* will, all else equal, have a less prominent place in the tax system than those with a low *MECF*. Some high-*MECF* tax instruments should not be used at all.

In this context, it is worth noting that the *MECF* of one tax instrument may depend on the setting of other tax instruments. This implies that the optimal setting of one tax instrument cannot be determined without reference to the settings of other tax instruments. For example, the optimal progressivity of the tax system given a sub-optimal level of enforcement may be below the overall optimal level of progressivity.

Another implication of the equalize-*MECF* rule relates to the appropriate amount of resources to devote to increasing the probability that evasion is detected. One superficially intuitive rule—to increase the probability of detection until the increase in revenue thus generated equals the marginal administrative cost (so that $a_i = 1$)—is incorrect.[6] This is clear from the *MECF* formula: if $a_i = 1$, then the *MECF* of increasing administrative resources is infinite, which can never characterize an optimal policy. The problem with the intuitive rule is that, although the cost of hiring more auditors is a true resource cost, the revenue brought in does not represent a net gain to the economy, but rather is a transfer from private (non-compliant) citizens. The correct rule will involve a lower probability of detection than the one implied by the superficially intuitive rule.

[6] This is formally demonstrated in Slemrod and Yitzhaki (1987).

This reasoning also makes clear that in general it is not optimal to expend resources to eradicate tax evasion, just as it is generally not optimal to station a police officer on every corner in an attempt to eliminate street crime. This is relevant for our later discussion of 'tax gap' measures, because the actual tax gap may be greater than or less than the optimal tax gap.

Finally, from one country's perspective, expending resources to crack down on cross-border income shifting is particularly attractive, because any revenue collected does not come with an offsetting utility loss to the taxpayer, as the taxpayer would have paid some tax to another tax authority. By ignoring the fiscal spillovers, this policy is very attractive from one country's point of view, but not necessarily from a global welfare perspective.

12.2.5. Distributional concerns

Implementation is not only a question of how to raise funds with minimal resource cost—the distributional consequences of how a tax system is implemented are also relevant. If distributional concerns are allowed for, the optimal policy now involves equating the marginal cost of funds, MCF_i, of each tax instrument.[7] The *MCF* is just the *MECF* (described above) reweighted to reflect distributional consequences:

$$MCF_i = DC_i \times MECF_i$$

where DC_i is Feldstein's (1972) distributional characteristic of the tax instrument that describes *who* bears the utility changes caused by a change in the tax instrument. A higher value of *DC* indicates that utility changes are concentrated among individuals with a higher marginal social welfare weight (generally lower-income individuals), reflecting the additional social cost of using a tax instrument with adverse distributional consequences (assuming a preference for equality, all else equal). Since the optimal policy now involves equating the *MCF* of each tax instrument rather than the *MECF*, it will—not surprisingly—involve lower reliance on tax instruments whose burden is concentrated among the poor, and more on those whose burden is concentrated among the rich.

As we will see later, evasion and compliance costs vary across the income distribution. At this stage, it is worth noting that systematic variation between individuals at *different points* in the distribution can be approximately offset by changing the structure of tax rates (making income tax more progressive, for example). In contrast, variation in evasion and compliance costs between

[7] This is shown in Mayshar and Yitzhaki (1995).

individuals at the *same* point in the distribution cannot be offset by changes in tax rates; this issue of horizontal equity is discussed below. Administrative costs have no distributional implications as, in effect, they can be spread across the whole population as desired.

12.2.6. Caveats and broader issues

Like every economic model, the *MECF* framework is highly stylized. Inevitably, there will be some issues that the *MECF* framework does not capture adequately. We discuss a number of these in this section.

Private costs and social costs

A central assumption of the model just presented is that the private costs of taxation are equivalent to the social costs. In some cases, however, the private cost is clearly not identical to the social cost. One example of this is when the behaviour of taxpayers directly affects people other than the taxpayer concerned and the tax authority (an 'externality'). Another example is fines for tax evasion. A fine is viewed as a cost by the individual, but from society's point of view fines collected serve to reduce the amount of revenue that would otherwise have to be collected. This benefit is ignored by the individual—hence the divergence between private and social cost. Note that an increase in fines can look like an attractive policy option indeed: unlike employing additional inspectors, the increase in tax collections due to increased deterrence is achieved with no resource cost. As discussed later, there are reasons unrelated to efficiency cost minimization that make it undesirable to increase fines for tax evasion without limit.

Welfare discounts for tax evaders

One notable aspect of the standard normative approach, raised by Cowell (1990, p. 136), is that it does not allow for the possibility that there should be a specific social welfare discount applied to the utility of those who are found to be guilty of tax evasion and thus 'are known to be anti-social', as opposed to the welfare weight applied to the innocent or uninvestigated (who may or may not be anti-social). If no such discount is applied, non-compliant taxpayers do not per se receive a lower welfare weight than compliant taxpayers. Resolving this issue is a matter of political philosophy rather than economics, and here we can only note that accepting this alternative perspective of discounting the welfare of non-compliers would suggest higher penalties for detected evaders and more resources spent on detecting evasion. It does not, though, in itself restore the logic behind expanding resources until the marginal revenue raised is equal to the marginal resource cost of raising that revenue.

Horizontal equity

The possibility of tax evasion raises the more general issue of horizontal equity—the extent to which a tax system results in the same tax burden among individuals at the same level of well-being. It is often invoked as a desirable criterion for judging tax policy that cannot be captured by the standard framework. Indeed, not only does our optimal policy fail to eliminate horizontal inequity caused by evasion (doing so would require 'excessive' anti-avoidance spending), it commonly involves creating *additional* horizontal inequity through the use of random audits and by making tax liability depend upon 'tags' (relatively immutable characteristics of individuals that are correlated with well-being).[8]

The problem with accepting horizontal equity as an explicit criterion is, as Kaplow (1989, 1995) demonstrates, that it means abandoning the Pareto principle (that any reasonable rule should accept a policy that makes some people better off and no one worse off). This doesn't seem to be a very desirable move. Even if one is willing to make this sacrifice, it is not clear how horizontal equity should be traded off against other objectives.

Privacy and taxpayer rights

Because the collection and evaluation of information is a critical aspect of implementing all taxes, the question arises of whether the government and other third parties to the tax system can be trusted with this information. Can the government be relied upon to keep it safe, make appropriate use of it in policy, and forego using it inappropriately by, say, selling it or exploiting

[8] Akerlof (1978) is the seminal article on the use of tags in tax, and other, policy. To see the potential efficiency benefits of tagging, imagine that having blue eyes is positively correlated with ability, and therefore well-being. Levying a tax on blue-eyed individuals would achieve a progressive distribution of the tax burden without the distortion costs associated with, say, graduated income tax rates (the possibility of a tax-reducing behavioural response to an eye colour tax is somewhat limited!). It is horizontally inequitable because an individual with brown eyes would have a lower tax burden than a blue-eyed individual at the same level of well-being.

it for political purposes? Concern over access to private information leads to tax data being fiercely protected in most countries.[9]

Much of this boils down to a question of privacy and whether our model adequately captures the value individuals place on it. Following Lessig (1999), it is helpful to distinguish three separate aspects of privacy. In the first, the concern is the burden of intrusion—what he calls the utility conception: a police search of one's home or car is, to be sure, a hassle. This hassle is, in principle, captured as compliance costs and taken into account by the tax authority in policy making. The second aspect is privacy as dignity—even if a search is not bothersome or costly, it is an offence to one's dignity. Again, in principle, the value of offences to citizens' dignity would be captured in a utility-based measure of compliance costs, although practically speaking this is much more difficult to quantify than the hassle of a search. The third aspect of privacy is its potential use as a way to constrain the power of the state by restricting the scope of regulation that is practically possible. We note that studies that attempt to measure compliance costs do not account for taxpayers' dislike of sharing private information.

If the government cannot be relied upon to take privacy adequately into account when devising policy, steps may be needed to limit the information the government can collect and use. One way this may be achieved is by relying on business-based taxes that do not make use of information about individuals, such as a VAT (value added tax). Particular methods of collection can also act to constrain the use of information. The UK Pay As You Earn (PAYE) system used to withhold income tax is an example of this, since it works well only with a fairly simple tax base. Whether PAYE has been a constraint on policy—and if so, whether this has been beneficial—is an issue to which we will return in Part II of this chapter.

The downside of privacy is that it can make achieving other aims more difficult. In particular, the efficiency of the tax system may be harmed if the use of certain types of information is disallowed. Fairness also commonly requires information: tax allowances for pensioners and the disabled, for example, rely on information about age and disability. Ultimately, a balance must be struck between protecting the privacy of citizens and achieving other aims of the tax system.

Tax systems inevitably impose obligations on taxpayers. But is there a balance: do taxpayers have rights against the tax authority? In the case of a

[9] It is important to distinguish the collection of information to implement policy, to monitor and prosecute taxpayers, and for statistical purposes (to inform policy). We note that in many countries data collected for statistical purposes cannot be used to prosecute an individual for tax non-compliance.

dispute, taxpayers can sometimes ask for some form of internal review, where the tax authority undertakes to have someone not connected with the case look at the issues. Of course, this lacks the independence of a real appeal: recourse to the courts is usually how this is achieved.

In exercising their rights, taxpayers face two issues. The first is knowledge of the routes available. To some degree, this could be addressed by a taxpayers' Bill of Rights, setting out the standards of service taxpayers can expect and the courses of action available in case of a dispute, alongside a list of the responsibilities of taxpayers. But even with one of these, taxpayers may still have little idea of their options. The second issue faced by taxpayers is that, even with an understanding of options open, taxpayers often need time and money to take advantage of them. This is particularly the case with court proceedings, which can be both lengthy and expensive.

Transparency

The way a tax system is implemented can have an important effect on transparency, which has value to a polity not captured by the model we have presented, in that it facilitates an open dialogue about the wisdom of the policies in place and possible alternatives. Getting taxpayers involved in the remittance process (by requiring them to fill in tax returns, for example) is usually good for transparency because they gain some understanding of the calculations involved and see the size of the cheque sent to the tax authority. In contrast, complexity is the enemy of transparency: it contributes to the attractiveness of using tax advisers and computer software, leaving individuals with little idea what is going on.

12.3. DETERMINANTS OF EVASION, AVOIDANCE, AND ADMINISTRATIVE AND COMPLIANCE COSTS

The previous section described how the modern theory of optimal taxation can be extended to incorporate administrative and compliance costs and the risk-bearing cost of tax evasion, to address tax system implementation. In this setting, we saw that the marginal efficiency cost of funds (*MECF*) of each tax instrument played a central role in determining the best choice of tax instruments (the combination that raises the required revenue at lowest cost). We also derived a formula that showed how the *MECF* incorporates all the costs of taxation: administrative and compliance costs, distortion costs including the risk bearing cost of tax evasion, plus lost purchasing power. In this section we address what determines the size of each of these costs by focusing on evasion and avoidance as well as administrative and compliance costs and discussing the relationships and trade-offs that exist between each of them.

12.3.1. Tax evasion and deterrence

The canonical economic model of tax evasion (the 'deterrence model') presumes that the taxpayer's actions are not motivated by morality or duty, but are restrained only by the possibility of punishment. The seminal formulation is due to Allingham and Sandmo (1972), who, in the context of an income tax, modelled the punishment as a fixed probability that any income understatement would be detected and subjected to a proportional penalty over and above payment of the outstanding tax liability.[10] The risk-averse taxpayer chooses a report in order to maximize expected utility, so that the choice of whether and how much to evade is akin to a choice of whether and how much to gamble. If, and only if, the expected pay-off to this gamble is positive, a risk-averse taxpayer will chance some evasion, with the amount depending on the expected pay-off and the taxpayer's risk preferences.[11] The key result for policy is that increases in either the probability of punishment or the penalty rate will reduce evasion.[12] Perhaps surprisingly, the relationship between the tax rate and the level of evasion is a priori ambiguous, depending on the taxpayer's risk preferences and whether the penalty for detected underreported income is tied to the tax liability evaded.[13]

Once an evader has been identified, imposing a financial penalty is (almost) costless from society's perspective because it is a transfer rather than a resource-using deterrent like hiring more tax inspectors. As a result, a government concerned with maximizing the expected utility of a representative

[10] The penalty may include damage to one's reputation.

[11] Like all economic models that are highly stylized, it is not meant literally in the sense that each taxpayer sits at his or her desk and solves a constrained maximization problem. It does, however, suggest that individuals weigh the potential gains from evasion with the costs and chances of being caught. The relevance of the model is ultimately an empirical question, resting on whether it can explain observed patterns of behaviour.

[12] Of course, what matters for decisions is the *perceived* probability of detection and attendant penalties rather than objective values.

[13] The relationship between the tax rate and the level of evasion is ambiguous because, when penalties are proportional to the tax understatement, a tax rate increase raises both the reward to the successful evasion of a given amount of taxable income and the penalty for its detection. See Yitzhaki (1974).

citizen will want to set the penalty as high as possible to deter evasion—this has been well known since Becker (1968). But this argument ignores the possibility that the tax administrator might abuse the system, and the fact that individuals (and the tax authority) make honest mistakes. It also flies in the face of the common notion that the level of punishment should in some sense 'fit' the crime.

In contrast to penalties, increasing the probability of detection is costly (it requires more tax inspectors, computers, etc.). A large theoretical literature has explored the extent to which the probability of detecting a given act of evasion can be raised above the average audit coverage rate by exploiting the statistical relationship between what is revealed on tax returns and non-compliance. Sophisticated 'risk-management' techniques of this sort are used in many countries (including the UK).

Perhaps the most compelling empirical support for the deterrence model in an income tax setting is the clear evidence that the non-compliance rate is lower for those acts of non-compliance with a higher likelihood of being caught. Klepper and Nagin (1989), for example, show that, across line items of the US income tax form, non-compliance rates are related to proxies for the traceability, deniability, and ambiguity of items, which are in turn related to the probability that evasion will be detected and punished. In contrast, the relationship between non-compliance and the penalty has not been convincingly established.

The deterrence model, and most subsequent extensions and empirical analyses, focus on evasion by *individuals*. Understanding non-compliance by *companies*, however, may require a different framework. This is particularly relevant for large firms, where tax reporting decisions are usually delegated to someone other than the firm's owner or shareholders (creating the potential for misaligned incentives) and where attention focuses not on (illegal) evasion but on (legal) avoidance or the blurry border between the two.

12.3.2. Duty, obligation, and tax evasion

The deterrence model of tax evasion presumes that individuals (and firms) are entirely amoral, and remit taxes only when a cost–benefit calculation indicates they should; the fact that evasion happens to be *illegal* is irrelevant aside from the effect penalties have on the cost–benefit comparison. Arguably, though, a non-trivial segment of individuals (and maybe even firms) would remit the taxes they owe due to a sense of obligation or duty even in the absence of any enforcement. Indeed, some have argued that duty and obligation are central to understanding taxpaying behaviour because evasion seems to be a winning proposition for many more people than actually do evade. From this perspective, the puzzle is not to explain why people evade, but rather why people don't evade more.

For three reasons, this argument for dismissing the deterrence model is not persuasive. Most important, it often relies on assuming that the probability of an act of evasion being detected is equal to the fraction of returns that are audited in a given year. For the bulk of income subject to tax in developed countries, this will be a vast understatement of the true probability because of the efficacy of risk-management techniques (discussed above), information reports, and withholding (discussed below). Second, it does not put a value on reputational damage to the taxpayer, something that may in practice be quite important. Third, to the extent that past years' returns may be audited, the relevant probability is the probability of being caught over a number of years rather than in a single year.

While the usual argument dismissing the deterrence model is not persuasive, there are certainly reasons to doubt that it is the end of the story. Some experimental evidence finds that subjects respond not only to the probability of detection and the stakes in a tax evasion game, but also to the context provided to them (which shouldn't matter according to the deterrence model). There is also evidence that dissatisfaction with the tax system is related to non-compliance (again, it should not be in a deterrence framework).[14]

Frey (1997) argues that punitive enforcement policies may crowd out the 'intrinsic' motivation of such people by making them feel that they pay taxes because they have to, rather than because they want to. Feld and Frey (2002) argue that where the relationship between the individual and the tax authority is seen as involving an implicit contract sustained by trust, individuals will comply due to high 'tax morale'. To sustain citizens' commitment to the contract, the tax authority must act respectfully toward citizens while at the same time protecting the honest from the free rider. It does this by giving taxpayers the benefit of the doubt when it finds a mistake, by sanctioning small violations more mildly, and by sanctioning large and basic violations (e.g. the failure to file a return) more heavily.[15]

[14] Scholz and Lubell (1998) found, after controlling for attitudes about tax fairness, civic duty, political efficacy, tax duty, opportunity for evasion, and being in a high non-compliance occupation, that high scores on two trust measures ('You can generally trust the government to do what is right,' and 'Dishonesty in government is pretty rare') significantly decrease the likelihood of non-compliance.

[15] Some survey evidence also provides support for this view, for example Torgler (2003) and Slemrod (2003) show there is a positive relationship across countries between survey-based attitudes

If perceptions matter for tax compliance, a natural question is to what extent tax compliance behaviour can be manipulated by the government to lower the cost of raising resources. Appeals to patriotism to induce citizens to pay their taxes are common in recent times. That such campaigns are successful during ordinary (non-war) times in swaying taxpayers from their otherwise selfishly optimal compliance strategy has not, though, been compellingly demonstrated.[16]

Given that businesses have a central role in tax remittance, an important question is whether arguments about honesty and dutifulness also apply to companies. If the tax director views paying taxes as a civic virtue and can determine policy, corporate evasion or aggressive avoidance may take on an ethical dimension and become responsive to non-deterrence aspects of the tax system.

12.3.3. Tax avoidance

Discussion of tax evasion leads naturally into the subject of tax avoidance. The starting point is that avoidance is legal, unlike evasion. Evasion reflects the mechanisms that are used to assess and collect tax and the ease with which those mechanisms can be controlled and monitored. Avoidance, in contrast, reflects the choice of tax base and the ease with which the concepts it involves can be described in legislation in a way that offers the fewest opportunities to taxpayers to reduce or eliminate their tax liabilities by modifying their behaviour—or the tax characterization of behaviour—in some way. In this respect, avoidance activity can provide an indication of the extent of distortion or non-neutralities that a particular tax base may entail. That said, the boundary between avoidance and evasion may not always be clear. In particular, where there is uncertainty about the correct taxation of particular arrangements or activities, the 'success' of particular avoidance may depend upon the tax authority not becoming fully aware of what the taxpayer has done so that the correct taxation of the arrangements or activities in question are never challenged and never have to be justified.

Every tax system is likely to generate some avoidance activity because every system involves the creation of boundaries of one sort or another—between what is taxed and what is not, between taxpayers with different tax

toward tax evasion on the one hand and professed trust in government, and Slemrod (2003) finds that the same relationship holds across individuals within the US and Germany.

16 In a randomized field experiment with Minnesota taxpayers in a peacetime setting, Blumenthal, Christian, and Slemrod (2001) find no evidence that either of two written appeals to taxpayers' consciences had a significant effect on compliance.

characteristics—that will then lead to tax arbitrage. If a tax system can avoid creating unnecessary and difficult-to-police boundaries it is likely to be more robust against avoidance than one that does involve such boundaries. Any system, however, is likely to involve a variety of instruments to minimize or impede avoidance activity. In Part II we outline the different approaches that have been adopted in the UK and make a number of observations on their relative success.

12.3.4. Administrative and compliance costs

In this section, we discuss the determinants of administrative and compliance costs. It is convenient to take the two together because many issues are common to both. Most work in this area has been empirical, attempting to measure how big administrative and compliance costs are for different taxes, and how they vary by size of taxpayer.[17] Surprisingly little of this empirical work has tried directly to answer the question we are most interested in: what features of a tax or tax system *cause* high costs? Nevertheless, we can list a number of important factors.

Administrative and compliance costs are generally lower for simpler taxes—those with fewer rates, borderlines, and reliefs. Less effort is required to understand how to comply, the mechanics of fulfilling obligations takes less time and there is less for the tax authority to have to record and monitor. If there is overlap between the bases of different taxes, the use of common definitions and procedures across taxes reduces costs by decreasing the number of calculations that have to be made (this has been one of the main motivations behind moves towards alignment of income tax and National Insurance in the UK in recent years). Complexity and lack of clarity in tax law in general will make for higher administrative and compliance costs.[18]

The characteristics of the tax base are particularly important for administrative costs. The important issue is the ease with which the tax base can be disguised, hidden, or relabelled. Two characteristics are likely to be particularly relevant: physical size and mobility (it is harder to tax diamonds than installed windows, for example), and whether there is compulsory registration (as there is for car owners and holders of driving licences).

[17] Evans (2003a) is a helpful introduction to recent work on the administrative and compliance costs of taxation.

[18] See section 1.7 of Evans (2003b) for a discussion of simplicity and complexity.

The structure of tax rates affects administrative and compliance costs for at least two reasons. First, average costs per pound of revenue collected are likely to fall as the tax rate increases because the cost of complying or inspecting a tax base does not depend on the tax rate (except to the extent that people are more inclined to avoid or evade when the tax rate is higher). Second, variations in tax rates can lead to large increases in administrative and compliance costs. To see this, consider two commodity taxes. If the tax rate is the same for both taxes, only total sales of the two commodities need be reported to and monitored by the tax authority. But if the tax rates differ, even fractionally, sales must be reported and monitored separately, implying considerably higher costs.

In recent years, tax systems in developed countries have moved towards giving small taxpayers the option of calculating their liability against a simplified scheme. The idea is to reduce administrative and compliance costs in cases where the risk of losing tax revenue is low. In practice, providing this sort of choice often turns out to be counter-productive, at least for compliance costs: taxpayers end up calculating their liability against all available schemes to make sure they choose the best one.

A major component of compliance costs is the cost of understanding which tax-related obligations apply to the taxpayer, and what needs to be done to comply with them. In this regard, stability is a highly desirable feature of a tax system, since learning what to do is much more costly the first time than on subsequent occasions. As Sandford (1995) points out, stability is helped if governments get legislation right the first time, which in turn underlines the importance of proper consultation beforehand (the zero per cent starting rate of corporation tax is a classic example of where the government got it wrong[19]). This argument also favours large one-off reforms over incremental changes that require new tax obligations to be understood multiple times. On the other hand, incremental reform might be preferable from the point of view of minimizing the chance of serious breakdown in the new procedures.

Whether the tax authority or the remitter is responsible for calculating tax liability obviously affects compliance costs: the greater is the reliance on the remitter to calculate liability, the higher are compliance costs and the lower administrative costs. Of course, administrative costs also depend upon the organization and efficiency of the tax authority.

Responsibility for remittance is important because there are economies of scale in tax administration and compliance: costs tend to be lower when the

[19] See <www.hmrc.gov.uk/ria/ria-corporation-tax.pdf>.

tax authority has to deal with fewer, larger remitters. The number of taxpayers (those with statutory liability) will also have some bearing on costs (more taxpayers means more calculations), but it is unlikely to be as important as the number involved in remittance. Administration and compliance is likely to be less costly if remitters understand the tax concerned, and have in place systems that are able to provide the necessary information without much additional work. For this reason it is less costly to tax a transaction that involves a large company, which may well need documentation for its own purposes, than to tax a small business, which may not require the same level of documentation.

There is a trade-off between administrative and compliance costs in regard to the provision of help and guidance: comprehensive user-friendly documentation and telephone support is costly to provide but makes it easier for taxpayers to comply.

Note, as mentioned above, administrative costs have no distributional consequences: they are met out of tax revenue so can effectively be spread across the population as desired. In contrast, compliance costs can have quite marked distributional consequences. These will depend on the ultimate incidence of compliance costs, not on where they fall in the first instance (i.e. on remitters). Ultimate (and long-run) incidence depends on the extent to which prices and wages adjust to shift the burden away from the remitter—the logic is similar to that for the incidence of the tax itself. A limited amount of empirical work has been done to try to estimate the incidence of taxes; to our knowledge, none of this has incorporated the effect of compliance costs (although one might imagine incidence to be similar). This is obviously an extremely important question if we are to understand the distributional consequences of compliance costs.

From the above discussion, it should be clear that, although some factors tend to move administrative and compliance costs in the same direction, others (such as who has responsibility for calculating tax liability) will move them in opposite directions. In fact, there is considerable potential for transferring between administrative and compliance costs. In this case, it is important to consider administrative and compliance costs together rather than targeting one separately from the other.

As a final point, so far we haven't drawn a strong distinction between compliance costs that are unavoidable (those incurred in meeting tax-related obligations) and those undertaken voluntarily (planning to reduce tax liability). Both represent social costs, because they use up resources that could otherwise have been put to valuable purposes. From a policy perspective, however, there may be an important difference: while reducing unavoidable compliance costs should help to reduce the overall costs imposed by the tax system, cutting voluntary compliance costs may facilitate avoidance and evasion and therefore increase the amount of avoidance and evasion that individuals find it beneficial to undertake. As a result, the tax authority may wish to concentrate on reducing unavoidable compliance costs (though distinguishing between the two is likely to be challenging!).

12.4. ENFORCEMENT SYSTEMS

The previous section discussed some of the factors that affect non-compliance and administrative and compliance costs. In this section, we consider a number of common strategies used to achieve a high level of compliance at modest administrative and compliance cost. In particular, we discuss: taxing market transactions, information reporting, and withholding. We also discuss the role of business and IT in tax implementation.

12.4.1. Taxing market transactions

Basing tax liability on market transactions—those between a willing buyer and an unconnected willing seller—has several advantages. First, in a market transaction information can potentially be obtained from either party, which provides a natural check on its accuracy. A second property is that market transactions tend to be better documented, and the more documented a transaction, the lower is the cost of gathering information on it. Finally, market transactions establish arm's-length prices, which greatly facilitate valuing the transaction. VAT, for example, relies almost entirely on market transactions, while taxing capital gains on a realization basis rather than the theoretically preferable accruals basis takes advantage of the measurement advantage of market transactions.

Where no suitable market transaction exists, implementing a tax can become quite costly. An example of this involves subsidiaries of a multinational corporation that deal with one another and are based in different countries. Without appropriate safeguards, there is considerable scope for taxable income to be shifted to relatively low-tax jurisdictions through the manipulation of prices used for transactions between subsidiaries (transfer prices). To avoid this happening, the tax authority needs to ensure 'arm's-length' prices are used; this can be extremely complicated if the subsidiaries do not deal with outsiders (where prices won't be artificially manipulated).

12.4.2. Information reporting

Information reporting relates to the requirement that certain transactions incurring tax liability be reported to the tax authority by the party that does not have statutory liability for the tax. It provides the tax authority with information that can be compared against the amount of tax actually remitted, allowing suspect returns to be identified and chased up. Evasion now requires coordination between the party providing the information report and the party responsible for remittance, but—and here is the key—their incentives and willingness to falsify the data are unlikely to be the same (incentives can even work in opposite directions).

Thus, a working system of information reporting discourages non-compliance by increasing the risk of detection for a given amount of tax authority resources. It forms a central element of all modern tax systems. In common with all other OECD countries, the UK requires information reporting on wages and salaries. Information reporting is also required for various other areas.

A rather different requirement to report information to the tax authority is the obligation introduced in the UK to disclose tax avoidance schemes shortly after they are first marketed. The aim is essentially to improve the tax authority's ability to combat what is seen as unacceptable planning: the tax authority has the chance to take early legislative action and (importantly, though this aspect receives less emphasis) gets to understand who is promulgating and using such schemes.

12.4.3. Withholding

Withholding refers to the situation where some or all of a tax liability must be remitted by someone other than the statutory bearer. It facilitates administration by allowing the tax authority to take advantage of economies of scale that exist in dealing with a smaller number of larger remitters who, for other reasons, have sophisticated record-keeping and accounting systems. It also acts as a safeguard, ensuring that some tax is remitted even when the statutory bearer fails to file a return or otherwise disregards their tax obligations. Tax systems often contain an indirect incentive for accurate and well-documented withholding. For example, to be sure of being able to deduct wage payments from taxable profits, businesses need to have their payment records in order, otherwise the deduction will be at risk of challenge.

Withholding is usually restricted to businesses and government agencies. Individuals in their capacity as employees and consumers are usually excluded—they are too numerous and not sufficiently capable as a class to be suitable withholding agents. To be able to withhold the appropriate amount of tax, the withholding agent must have an ongoing relationship with the statutory bearer of the tax, or, alternatively, the withholding scheme must be sufficiently simple to avoid the need for such a relationship.

In the first instance, the (compliance) costs associated with withholding fall on the withholding agents themselves, but they generally count as business expenses that can be deducted from taxable income (reducing tax liability), so get partially transferred to the government. Who bears the ultimate burden of compliance costs depends on the same demand and supply forces as determine the incidence of taxes themselves (see earlier discussion). A few countries provide explicit compensation to withholding agents. Most do not, but effectively compensate withholding agents by allowing a time lag between when tax liability is triggered and when remittance is due (interest can be earned on the tax liability in the intervening period), but this will be no more or less effective in relieving the burden than would be a tax rate cut equivalent to the interest gained during the time lag.[20]

Withholding for income tax is widespread among developed countries: it is required for wages and salaries in all but two of the thirty OECD countries, and for interest in twenty-one of the OECD countries. The use of withholding for other sources of income varies across the OECD.

12.4.4. The role of business and IT

The discussion of information reporting and withholding highlights the central role of business in the *implementation* of modern tax systems—in remitting tax revenue and in information reporting. On our calculations, almost 90% of UK tax revenue is remitted by business (Table 12.1). The impetus behind the role of business has been elegantly stated by Richard Bird, who wrote: 'The key to effective taxation is information, and the key to information in the modern economy is the corporation. The corporation is thus the modern fiscal state's equivalent of the customs barrier at the border.'[21] Collecting taxes from businesses saves on administrative and compliance costs because of the economies of scale inherent in tax remittance and because

[20] In fact, Sandford et al. (1989) find that this cash-flow benefit can exceed compliance costs for large companies.

[21] Bird (2002).

Table 12.1. Remittance responsibility in the UK tax system: 2006–07

	Receipts (£m)	Remitted by business (£m)	Proportion
HMRC-administered taxes			
Income tax:			
PAYE	124,799	124,799	1.00
Self Assessment, net of repayments	20,306	0	0.00
Other receipts[1]	8,331	4,868	0.58
Tax credits[2,3]	−4,435	−3,992	0.90
Other repayments[2,4]	−5,673	−5,514	0.97
National Insurance[5]	87,273	84,504	0.97
Corporation tax	44,308	44,308	1.00
Petroleum revenue tax	2,155	2,155	1.00
Capital gains tax	3,813	0	0.00
Inheritance tax	3,545	0	0.00
Stamp duties	13,392	13,392	1.00
VAT	77,360	77,360	1.00
Other indirect taxes[6]	48,485	48,485	1.00
Subtotal	**423,659**	**390,366**	**0.92**
Non-HMRC-administered taxes			
VED	5,100	1,020	0.20
Business rates	21,000	21,000	1.00
Council tax	22,200	0	0.00
Other taxes and royalties[7]	13,900	13,900	1.00
Subtotal	**62,200**	**35,920**	**0.58**
Total	**485,859**	**426,286**	**0.88**

Notes (figures in brackets are fractions assumed to be remitted by business):

1. Other receipts category comprises tax deduction scheme for interest (TDSI) (1.00), other tax deducted at source (1.00) and others (0.00).

2. Repayments are classified not according to how repayments were made but according to the tax for which they are repayments.

3. Tax credits comprise the negative tax part of WTC/CTC expenditure (0.90), MIRAS (0.90), LAPRAS (0.90), and other (0.90). The 0.90 for WTC/CTC is based on an estimate of the number of self-employed recipients. The 0.90 figure for all other tax credits is the proportion of gross income tax receipts remitted by business.

4. Other repayments comprise individuals (1.00), personal pension contributions (1.00), pension fund and insurance companies (1.00), charities (0.90), overseas (1.00), PEPs and ISAs (0.90), and other (0.90). Again, 0.90 is the proportion of gross income tax receipts remitted by business.

5. Class 1 National Insurance contributions (1.00), Class 2–4 contributions (0.00).

6. Other indirect taxes comprise (all 1.00): fuel duties, tobacco duties, spirit duty, beer duties, wine duties, cider and perry duties, betting and gaming duties, air passenger duty, insurance premium tax, landfill tax, climate change levy, aggregates levy, and customs duties and levies. A small fraction of customs duties may be attributable to individuals, but it is not easy to assess how much.

7. The main components of other taxes and royalties (all assumed 1.00) are VAT refunds to central government and local authorities, rest of the world taxes on products, national lottery distribution fund, and fossil fuel levy.

Sources: <http://www.hmrc.gov.uk/stats/tax_receipts/table1–2.pdf>, <http://www.hmrc.gov.uk/stats/t_receipt/table2–8.pdf>, <http://www.hmrc.gov.uk/stats/t_receipt/table2–9.pdf>, Appendix 6 of <http://www.gad.gov.uk/Documents/Social_Security_Uprating_Order_07.pdf>, Table C6 of Budget 2008 <http://www.hmtreasury.gov.uk/media/9/9/bud08_completereport.pdf> and authors' calculations.

businesses often already have record-keeping and accounting systems in place that simplify the process of tax remittance and information reporting.

One of the greatest changes in the three decades since the Meade Report (Meade, 1978) is the growth of information technology, now a completely indispensable part of the operation and management of taxes. IT cuts the cost of processing, reduces the risk of errors, helps to expose non-compliance, and may reduce the amount of information that needs to be collected. Its downside is that new IT systems can be extremely difficult and costly to implement and, because taxpayers no longer get involved in tax calculations themselves, lead to growing ignorance about the tax system.

12.5. IMPLEMENTATION GUIDELINES

Before turning to some key implementation issues in the UK tax system, it may be helpful to summarize the discussion so far. Getting administration and enforcement right are central to making a tax system work. We have shown how standard optimal tax theory can be extended to address these issues. In such a framework, the characteristics of the optimal policy have a number of important implications. In particular:

- The optimal mix of tax instruments cannot be determined by reference to a subset of the costs of taxation: all costs affect the optimal policy mix, and must therefore be considered together. In particular, this means considering administrative and compliance costs alongside the more traditional distortion costs.
- For incremental policy adjustments, what matters are marginal costs, not total or average costs.
- The optimal policy does not involve eradicating tax evasion. Nor does it involve maximizing revenue net of administrative costs. The correct rule involves lower enforcement spending than either of these alternatives require.

A number of conclusions also follow from our discussions of the determinants of different costs of taxation and of effective enforcement systems:

- Whilst increasing the probability of detecting non-compliance is costly for the tax authority, it does seem to be associated with reduced evasion. In contrast, the effectiveness of higher fines has not been convincingly established.

- When enforcing, authorities should be careful not to alienate taxpayers and thereby reduce the extent to which they comply out of a sense of duty rather than a fear of the consequences of being caught.
- Taxes should be kept as stable and simple as possible to minimize administrative and compliance costs and minimize non-compliance.
- Where possible, it is best to rely on market transactions between arm's-length parties, where information from one side can be easily checked against information from the other.
- Information reporting and withholding are key mechanisms for achieving a high level of compliance at modest administrative and compliance cost. For the same reason, it is generally sensible to maximize reliance on a small number of financially sophisticated entities (i.e. large firms).

II. ADMINISTRATION AND ENFORCEMENT ISSUES IN THE UK TAX SYSTEM

Having provided an analytical framework for addressing administration and enforcement issues and having discussed what procedures are of practical use in implementing a tax system, we can now assess how the UK tax system measures up. How good is its administration and enforcement and how can it be improved?

The big picture is that the UK tax system makes broad use of the key administration and enforcement mechanisms. It has a wide range of information reporting and withholding requirements, prime among which are the obligations on employers to withhold income tax from employees' wages and inform HMRC of wages and benefits-in-kind and of leavers and joiners. The UK system relies heavily on remittances by businesses, with approximately 88% of all tax revenue being remitted by businesses (Table 12.1).[22]

Table 12.2 details the administrative costs, compliance costs and non-compliance for the main UK taxes. Note that these are average costs rather than the marginal costs as would be required to evaluate an incremental

[22] This is very similar to the proportion found for the US by Christensen, Cline, and Neubig (2001), who calculate that in 1999 businesses 'paid, collected, and remitted' 83.8% of total taxes to all levels of government.

Table 12.2. Administrative and compliance costs and non-compliance for major UK taxes (2006–07 unless stated)

Tax[1]	Number of taxpayers[2] (millions)	Revenue raised[3] (billions)	Administrative costs (% of revenue)[4] (%)	Compliance costs (% of revenue)		Non-compliance (% of true liability)[7] (%)
				Sandford/ Inland Revenue[5] (%)	KPMG[6] (%)	
PAYE	36.0	£ 124.8	0.7	1.3	0.4	1.4
NICs	28.3	£ 87.3	0.4			
ITSA	9.5	£ 20.3	4.5	N/A	N/A	14.6
CT	0.9	£ 44.3	0.8	2.2	1.5	14.7
VAT	1.9	£ 77.4	0.6	3.7	1.4	14.2

Notes:

1. PAYE is Pay As You Earn, NICs National Insurance contributions, ITSA income tax self-assessment, CT corporation tax, and VAT value added tax.

2. Number of taxpayers (source unless stated: <http://www.hmrc.gov.uk/stats/tax_receipts/table 1-4.pdf>). PAYE: number of individuals under PAYE including individuals who also self-assess. 2005–06. Source: communication from HMRC. NICs: 2005–06. Source: <http://www.dwp.gov.uk/asd/tabtool.asp>. ITSA: source: Bourn (2007b). CT: 2005–06. VAT: number of registered traders at 31 March 2007.

3. Revenue raised (source unless stated: <http://www.hmrc.gov.uk/stats/tax_receipts/table1-2.pdf>). PAYE: includes revenue raised from self-assessment taxpayers through PAYE. Source: <http://www.hmrc.gov.uk/stats/t_receipt/table2-8.pdf>. ITSA: excludes revenue raised from self-assessment taxpayers. Source: <http://www.hmrc.gov.uk/stats/t_receipt/table2-8.pdf>.

4. Administrative costs (source: HMRC autumn report 2007) Includes direct collection costs (staff salary costs and other operating expenditure) and overheads (IT costs, accommodation, other non-cash costs, stock losses, corporate overheads and, where applicable, a share of Valuation Office costs).

5. Sandford/IR compliance costs (source unless stated: Sandford et al. (1989)). Excludes cash-flow benefit. PAYE and NICs: 1995–96. Source: Inland Revenue (1998). CT: 1986–87. VAT: 1986–87.

6. KPMG compliance costs (source: KPMG (2006)) Estimates are for 2005 and cover 'administrative burdens', which exclude tax planning, dealing with change, and understanding which tax obligations are relevant. PAYE and NICs: denominator is 2005–06 PAYE income tax and estimated Class 1 and 1A receipts (£113.9 billion and £82.2 billion respectively). CT: denominator is 2005–06 corporation tax receipts (£608 million). VAT: denominator is 2005–06 VAT receipts (£72.9 billion).

7. Non-compliance (source unless stated: <http://www.hmrc.gov.uk/pbr2007/mdtl-direct.pdf>): PAYE and NICs: Includes only small and medium-sized employers (no more than 500 employees). 2003–04. This ignores tax recovered through compliance work and non-payment. If these are taken into account, the figure falls to 1.2%. ITSA: 2001–02. This ignores tax recovered through compliance work and non-payment. If these are taken into account, the figure falls to 12.6%. CT: Includes only small and medium-sized companies (no more than 500 employees). 2003. This ignores tax recovered through compliance work and non-payment. If these are taken into account, the figure falls to 12.5%. VAT: Source: <http://www.customsandrevenue.eu/pbr2007/mitl.pdf>.

policy change. With the exception of income tax self-assessment, administrative costs (including overheads) are always less than 1% of revenue.[23] Compliance costs are usually at least as large as administrative costs, but

[23] Two important reasons why administrative costs for self-assessment are much higher than for other taxes are that much of the income tax liability of some self-assessment taxpayers is collected through PAYE, and that individuals who have to self-assess tend to have fairly complicated financial affairs.

much depends on which of the two sets of figures are consulted. The KPMG estimates (Section 12.6.4) are more recent (they relate to 2005) but exclude a number of things normally considered part of compliance costs such as tax planning, dealing with change, and understanding which tax obligations are relevant.

For PAYE/NICs, ITSA, and corporation tax, the column headed 'non-compliance' contains figures from HMRC random enquiry programmes. Note that random enquiries are not able to capture losses to the informal economy and, for PAYE/NICs and corporation tax, include only small and medium-sized companies (no more than 500 employees). The figure for VAT is an estimate of the VAT gap—the difference between the theoretical liability and actual tax revenue—so does include losses to the informal economy. Most striking are the estimates for ITSA, CT and VAT, all of which are above 10% of true liability. In contrast, the figure for PAYE/NICs is only 1.4%. No estimates are available for distortion costs and avoidance.

OECD (2007) gives some sense of how UK administrative costs compare with other countries. The overall UK figure for 2004 of 0.97% of revenue is close to the OECD median, but considerably higher than the US figure of 0.56%. It is important to note, however, that international comparisons of administrative costs are fraught with difficulties because ratios can vary for all sorts of reasons other than efficiency.

Getting estimates of compliance costs that are comparable across countries is even more difficult. Our sense is that overall compliance costs are lower in the UK than in the US, but it is impossible to place this in a comparative OECD context. A PricewaterhouseCoopers–World Bank study (2007) suggests that the UK compares favourably with many other countries. Using a mid-sized case study company, it ranks each of 175 countries according to the 'ease of paying taxes' (a combination of total tax rate, compliance time, and the number of tax payments required). The UK comes 12th, ahead of a number of obvious competitors—the USA at 63rd, Germany at 73rd, and France at 92nd.

Space constrains us from providing an exhaustive discussion of all of the current administration and enforcement issues in the UK tax system. Many are addressed in other chapters in this volume—VAT and missing trader fraud in Chapter 4 (Crawford, Keen, and Smith), tax credit administration in Chapter 2 (Brewer, Saez, and Shephard), international cooperation in Chapter 10 (Griffith, Hines, and Sørensen), and issues relating to small businesses in Chapter 11 (Crawford and Freedman). In the following sections, we concentrate on just three issues: HMRC's objectives and targets, the future of PAYE, and tax avoidance.

12.6. HMRC

Tax administration in the UK is undergoing considerable change. The UK was one of very few countries to start the twenty-first century with two tax authorities. In 2005, these were amalgamated to form Her Majesty's Revenue and Customs (HMRC). The resulting department is now undergoing a process of rationalization and modernization to improve its efficiency and ability to meet taxpayers' needs.

HMRC assesses its performance using a wide range of indicators. Along with other government departments, it has committed to a number of targets to improve performance and cut costs. The aim of this section is not to comment on the likelihood that HMRC will meet its targets; rather it is to assess some of the indicators and targets themselves in the light of the principles for tax administration outlined in Part I of this chapter.

12.6.1. Performance targets

At the outset, it is worth noting the potential problems with concrete performance targets in government. Unlike in a private business, where the ultimate objective is usually relatively unambiguous, the overall objective for a government department is less tangible. In principle, it should make decisions to enhance the well-being of the citizens, but that is not plausibly measurable. Nevertheless, some subsidiary objectives that are well-defined—for example, minimizing the cost of achieving a well-defined and easily measurable subcategory of output—should be pursued regardless of whether the ultimate objective is profits or social welfare.

What is different for the tax authority compared to most other government departments is the availability of something that has the superficial appearance of a quantitative output measure—revenue collected. Note, though, that in Part I of this chapter we showed that aiming to maximize revenue net of resource expenditures was the wrong objective because it failed to recognize that tax revenue is a transfer rather than a real resource gain.

HMRC has a large set of quantitative performance targets. At the time of writing, HMRC had not released details of their targets for the period 2008–09 to 2010–11 but has indicated that they will be similar in substance to those for the years 2005–06 to 2007–08—so we concentrate on these in this section. For the period 2005–06 to 2007–08, HMRC had three core objectives, the first two of which are directly relevant to the topic of this chapter:

- Improve the extent to which individuals and businesses pay the tax due and receive the credits and payments to which they are entitled.
- Improve customer experience, support business, and reduce the compliance burden.

These two objectives were underpinned by a number of quantitative targets, including targets to:

- Reduce the scale of VAT losses to no more than 11% of the theoretical liability.
- Reduce the illicit market share for cigarettes to no more than 13% and for spirits by at least a half, and hold the illicit market share for oils at no more than 2%.
- Reduce underpayment of direct tax and National Insurance contributions due by at least £3.5 billion a year.
- Increase to at least 90% the proportion of small businesses that find it easy to complete their tax returns, and to at least 85% the proportion of individuals who find their self-assessment statements, PAYE coding notices, and tax credit awards easy to understand.
- Increase the percentage of self-assessment returns filed on time to at least 93%.
- Increase to at least 95% the rate of accuracy achieved in administering SA, PAYE, Tax Credits, and NICs.
- Increase to 35% the percentage of SA tax returns and to 50% the percentage of VAT returns received online.[24]

Alongside these performance targets, HMRC was on course to achieve a substantial monetary saving between 2005–06 and 2007–08 and has agreed to a real terms reduction in its budget of 5% each year over the period 2008–09 to 2010–11, as part of the government's efficiency savings programme.

At first sight, these targets look like a list of 'good' things that HMRC aims to get a bit better at. They do not give a good sense of what is optimal, nor of the priorities and trade-offs involved. For example, why not reallocate resources and aim to reduce VAT losses to 12% (rather than 11%), and direct tax and NI contributions underpayment by £3.75 billion (rather than £3.5 billion)? And do the compliance-cost-reducing initiatives reflect the same trade-offs as the enforcement-increasing policies?

[24] See <http://www.hmrc.gov.uk/psa/psa2005-2008.htm>.

A potential pitfall of targets is that they may not be consistent with one another—in particular, can improvements in performance be achieved alongside real-terms cuts in the HMRC budget? HMRC has claimed that operational changes will enable both to be met, but this view does not seem to be shared by the Treasury Committee, who suggested that the failure of HMRC to meet many of their 2007–08 targets may be linked to the need to make efficiency savings (House of Commons Treasury Committee (2008), p. 51).

12.6.2. The tax gap

HMRC has published estimates of the size of the tax gap—the difference between the amount of tax collected and the theoretical liability—for VAT and illicit market share for spirits, tobacco, and diesel (HMRC (2007)). For income tax, random enquiry programmes have provided information about tax 'at risk' (this is only part of the tax gap—it only covers individuals who file a tax return). Bourn (2003, p. 8) concluded that 'there are benefits in terms of overall risk management in having an aggregate estimate of the shadow economy if a reliable practical technique can be found'. Although we are sympathetic with the latter view because a tax gap study can inform resource allocation decisions in key ways, it is important to realize that measures of the total tax gap and its components do not *directly* inform policy. This is because policy choices are generally marginal and depend on the relative effectiveness of alternative policies in raising revenue relative to the resource cost of doing so. For example, learning that the non-compliance rate for self-employed individuals is higher than that for multinational corporations does not necessarily imply that it is optimal to beef up enforcement on the self employed at the expense of the multinationals. Rather, an *MECF*-type calculation should, in principle, be relied on.

12.6.3. Administrative costs

Each year, HMRC's annual and autumn reports list the cost of collection per pound collected for each of the main taxes, and overall. For 2006–07, the overall ratio is listed as 1.13 pence per pound (HMRC (2007b), p. 31).[25] For each of several enforcement operations, it also lists the additional tax and penalties collected and estimated cost/yield ratios. These ratios range from

[25] How overhead costs are allocated is critical to this assessment. See notes to Table 12.2 for which overheads are included.

2.0 : 1 to 98 : 1. Critically, they are average, rather than marginal, figures, and it is marginal costs that matter for evaluating policy initiatives.

The text accompanying the yield/cost ratios in the 2004–05 annual report says that they 'are used as one of a number of factors to help management make considered judgment on the allocation of resources' (p. 106). The only other factor listed is the need 'to maintain an effective presence in all areas where there may be non-compliance'. Potential policy reforms cannot be satisfactorily evaluated without considering all costs of taxation—deadweight costs, administrative costs, and compliance costs. The danger of evaluating policies on the basis of their yield/cost ratios is that it ignores any distortion costs and compliance costs induced. If the ratio of distortion and compliance costs to administrative costs varies across policies, then ranking by their administrative cost will lead to misallocation.

Focusing on yield/cost ratios also risks obscuring the fact that additional yield is a transfer from private (albeit non-compliant) citizens while administrative costs are a real resource cost. Even if marginal ratios can be inferred from the averages presented and distortion and compliance costs are negligible, it is not optimal from society's point of view to expand enforcement up to the point where the ratios are equal to one.

12.6.4. Compliance costs

The government has embarked on an ambitious programme to quantify and cut the burden of regulation. As part of this, HMRC commissioned KPMG to undertake a large-scale study of the 'administrative burdens' of HMRC regulation on business, the results of which are presented in KPMG (2006). Following publication of the KPMG report, the government committed to reductions in various aspects of the burden (dealing with forms and returns and dealing with audits and inspections).

These developments suggest a growing awareness of the importance of compliance costs in the policy-making process, something that has been neglected in the past. Particularly welcome is the fact that the KPMG report attempts to provide a detailed breakdown of costs that can be useful in targeting their reduction. This comes closer to measuring marginal compliance costs than most previous work, which tended only to suggest that total compliance costs were high.

An important note of caution is in order, however. Administrative burdens exclude a number of things normally considered part of compliance costs, such as costs of tax planning, dealing with change, and understanding which tax obligations are relevant. Moreover, the focus is on business rather than all taxpayers, and only a subset of administrative burdens is currently being targeted. The danger is that compliance costs that do not count as targeted administrative burdens are neglected or—to the extent that burdens from targeted areas can be transferred—are increased (for example by shifting obligations from business to individuals).

It is also not clear how closely tied to the policy-making process the targeting of administrative burdens is. Since 2000, the means by which compliance costs have formally entered policy deliberations is through mandatory impact assessments (IAs). An IA sets out the costs, benefits, and risks of the proposed reform, and compares alternative options with the aim of improving policy-making. But doubts have been expressed over both their quality and the extent to which they have any meaningful impact on legislation.

In the context of compliance costs, the impact assessment that accompanied the new tax credits in 2003 provides a good example of difficulties that have been experienced. The impact assessment suggested that the new tax credits would reduce employer compliance costs by up to £11 million per year. But this estimate excluded what turned out to be the most burdensome part of paying tax credits via employers—amendment notices. The reason for this exclusion was that it could 'only be estimated once the system is up and running' (2.17 TC IA). The result was an inaccurate estimate of the overall impact on compliance costs (even allowing for the fact that some of the burden was the result of unforeseen difficulties with the HMRC tax credit computer system).

In summary, efforts to quantify and cut the administrative burden of HMRC regulation and the fact that compliance costs form part of the evaluation of proposed policy changes are both welcome. But desirable reforms cannot be identified accurately without consideration of their incremental impact on *all* compliance costs (as well as administrative and distortion costs), as indicated by the *MECF* framework.

12.7. THE FUTURE OF PAYE

How tax is collected is important because it has implications for the costs it imposes and because it affects what tax designs are feasible. In this section, we examine the way income tax is collected in the UK, assess the performance of the primary withholding mechanism (PAYE), and consider some options for reform. We do not address the issue of whether income tax and National Insurance should be integrated; we refer the interested reader to Adam and Loutzenhiser (2007). A description of how UK income tax works is contained in Chapter 1 (Adam, Browne, and Heady).

12.7.1. Collection of income tax in the UK

Withholding is an extremely effective way of collecting income tax because it reduces the risk of non-compliance and takes advantage of the economies of scale in tax remittance. But withholding the correct amount of tax is far from straightforward. Individuals often have more than one income source, and income is received at varying frequencies. Since income tax is progressive and liability depends on annual income aggregated across all sources the amount of tax that should be withheld from one income source may depend on how much income there is from other sources. But withholding happens separately for each income source, and withholding agents (e.g. employers) may not know anything about each other.

Two main ways to address this problem have been devised. The first involves giving withholding agents fairly complicated instructions about what to withhold so that the correct liability is collected from the majority of taxpayers; for the remainder, some form of end-of-year reconciliation is necessary. The alternative approach is to rely on a compulsory end-of-year tax return. Since there is then no need for withholding to get the right answer, the withholding process (but not necessarily the tax liability computation process) can be drastically simplified, with any additional inaccuracy introduced being cleaned up by the tax return.

The UK takes the former approach. Income tax due on employment earnings and private and occupational pensions (the most important sources of income for most people) is withheld via a system known as Pay-As-You-Earn (PAYE). PAYE is an extremely important part of income tax collection, accounting for over 80% of income tax revenue. The way PAYE works is discussed in detail below. Tax on interest income is withheld by banks and other financial institutions under the assumption that it is not subject to the higher rate of tax. There is also withholding on royalties, payments, and certain rents. Withholding does not exist for dividends (a form of imputation tax credit is used instead); nor is there any kind of withholding for self-employment profits, state pensions, or taxable benefits (although withholding for government transfers involves a different set of issues).

Small tax liabilities on sources where there is no withholding can be collected via adjustments to PAYE; non-PAYE withholding is *never* adjusted for this purpose. Relying on PAYE to collect tax liabilities incurred elsewhere works because the majority of individuals liable for income tax have substantial amounts of income that come under PAYE.

PAYE and other withholding cannot always collect an individual's full tax liability. In cases where withholding is likely to get the answer wrong, individuals have to complete a self-assessment tax return.[26] Currently, around nine million taxpayers (approximately one third of the total number liable for income tax) are required to self-assess. The majority of these individuals do not come under PAYE at all (the main group is the self-employed). A substantial minority, however, do come under PAYE, but have to self-assess because PAYE and other withholding cannot be guaranteed to get the answer right (this might be the case for individuals with substantial foreign income or income from property).

Tax returns are issued to these taxpayers shortly after the end of the tax year. The filing deadline is 31 October (almost 7 months later) for paper returns and 31 January (almost 10 months later) if the taxpayer files online. Tax liability (beyond that already withheld) is typically remitted in three instalments. The first two (one on 31 January in the year of assessment, one on 31 July following the end of that year) are usually estimated on the basis of the previous year's liability. The balance is due on 31 January after the end of the tax year, coinciding with the deadline for tax returns.

Each year, there are a number of individuals who are not required to self-assess but who end up having had the wrong amount of tax withheld. This might happen as a result of changes in circumstances (becoming unemployed shortly before the end of the tax year, for example). For these individuals, HMRC is responsible for calculating the adjustment that is required, informing the taxpayer and negotiating a payment schedule. Underpayments are often collected via adjustments to future PAYE withholding; overpayments are refunded lump sum.

For PAYE, employers do not automatically have access to all the information they need to calculate how much tax to withhold (they may not know age, disability, or income from other sources, for example). HMRC provides employers with a summary of this information in the form of a tax code, one for each job (or pension) of each individual. A tax code is a combination

[26] Details of who has to file a return can be found at <http://www.hmrc.gov.uk/sa/guidelines.htm>.

of numbers and letters that describes the tax-free entitlement for that job (or pension) and the rate at which income should be taxed. Since HMRC is responsible for calculating tax codes, it must keep track of individuals and their employers during the year.

The amount of tax withheld in any given week or month depends on earnings in the whole tax year to date. In each week or month of the year, tax allowances and tax bands are scaled down according to the proportion of the year that has elapsed ($^1/_{52}$ for week one, $^1/_{26}$ for week two, etc., or $^1/_{12}$ for month one, $^1/_6$ for month two, etc.). These rescaled allowances and bands are used to calculate *total* tax liability for the year so far based on *total* earnings so far. The amount of tax remitted in a given week or month is equal to total tax liability for the year so far less the amount of tax already remitted. This type of withholding is known as cumulative withholding. Its advantage is that, when earnings vary across the year, it is much more likely that the correct amount of tax will have been deducted at the end of the tax year than under a non-cumulative system that treats each pay period in isolation. Its disadvantage is that it requires employers to know what happened earlier in the year. If an individual changes jobs, information needs to be passed between employers about total earnings and tax remitted so far this year (achieved under PAYE using P45 forms).

Most employers must remit the tax due once a month (small employers can remit quarterly). This happens roughly three weeks after the end of the month to which the tax relates. Remittances cover National Insurance contributions and student loan deductions as well as income tax, and employers simply remit the total due across all their employees (there is no breakdown by employee and tax). At the end of the tax year, however, employers do provide such a breakdown, allowing all the calculations and remittances to be checked by HMRC.

In 2005–06 there were around 1.7 million active PAYE schemes covering around 36 million individuals.

12.7.2. An assessment of PAYE

Over recent decades PAYE has been the object of sustained criticism arguing that it is becoming less able to cope and needs to be reformed. Here we discuss the problems with PAYE and its advantages over alternative systems, addressing accuracy, flexibility, administrative and compliance costs, and non-compliance.

Accuracy

In conjunction with other withholding, PAYE is designed to collect the right amount of tax over the tax year for most taxpayers. In around 30% of cases, however, the amount of tax remitted during the year does not tie up with the end-of-year information sent to HMRC by employers (Bourn (2006)). Addressing these occurrences has a high administrative cost for individuals outside self-assessment. There are also cases where the wrong amount of tax has been withheld but the error is not uncovered. Bourn (2007a) suggests this may apply to 0.8 million taxpayers for 2006–07.

Inaccuracy in PAYE can be traced to four main issues:

- Errors made by HMRC.
- Errors made by employers.
- Breakdown in the transmission of information.
- Inertia or lack of understanding from employees.

We discuss these issues in turn. The most common error made by HMRC is failing to calculate tax codes correctly. Bourn (2006) reports that 8% of tax codes were incorrect in the 2005–06 tax year. Many of these errors are the result of HMRC failing to bring together income from different sources—the current PAYE computer system is spread across twelve databases and is based around jobs rather than individuals.[27] The task becomes more difficult when income from other sources is not known for certain when tax codes are calculated. Tax codes then have to be based on estimates, which may turn out to be incorrect. HMRC hopes that modernization already underway will eliminate many of these errors.

Inaccuracies also arise because of errors made by employers. Bourn (2007b) reports that 1.4% of end-of-year returns for 2006–07 had to be sent back to employers for correction. There is also some evidence that employers do not always follow instructions to amend tax codes (Bourn (2006)), but the extent of this is not known.

The third source of inaccuracies is the transmission of information breaking down. PAYE requires information faster and in greater quantities than a non-cumulative withholding system meant to approximate tax liability. But Bourn (2006) reports that around 70% of employees starting a new job do not immediately provide their new employer with a P45 containing their National Insurance number, and more than 70% of employees who are asked

[27] See HMRC 2005–06 annual report p. 27. PAYE modernization plans include moving PAYE onto a unified database.

for information about their earnings history fail to return the necessary form. In such cases, guesses often have to be made, frequently resulting in the wrong amount of tax being withheld.

The final source of inaccuracies is employees. Few check the coding notices HMRC sends them, so errors often lie dormant. They also forget to notify HMRC of relevant changes—or simply don't understand the need so to do. But whether it is fair to blame individuals for failing to deal with errors and exceptions in a system that is designed to do everything for them is a moot point.

These problems are being exacerbated by changes in the economic environment. For example, there are a growing number of individuals with multiple employment or multiple income sources. Internal HMRC estimates suggest that, in 2005–06, approximately 13% of individuals under PAYE had more than one PAYE income source. Job changes have become more frequent, with 20% of jobs lasting less than one year, and 5% less than three months (Bourn (2006)). Approximately 16.5 million income sources terminated during 2005–06. There is also more part-time and temporary work and remuneration has become more complex (particularly the growth of benefits in kind).

Flexibility

Although in some ways PAYE has proved to be adaptable, there have been complaints over a number of decades that it lacks flexibility and therefore constrains tax policy. As long ago as 1972, a Green Paper on tax credits (quoted in Barr, James, and Prest (1977), p. 47) said that PAYE 'has been found to lack flexibility and governments of both political parties have found it difficult to adapt it to accommodate changes that they have felt desirable'.

PAYE is argued to constrain tax policy because end-of-year adjustments and recoding are costly exercises, so any policy change that threatens the ability of PAYE to withhold the correct amount of tax without the need for extensive recoding is likely to be prohibitively expensive. Three examples will suffice: a graduated structure of rates, payment of tax credits by employers, and some form of expenditure tax.

It has often been claimed that PAYE won't work well with a highly graduated structure of tax rates because there needs to be a single wide tax band covering the vast majority of taxpayers. The reason is multiple income sources. If secondary income sources all fall within a wide basic rate band, it is possible to guess with reasonable accuracy the rate at which each income source should be taxed, avoiding large numbers of end-of-year adjustments. But the greater the number of tax rates and the narrower each band, the less likely it is that all secondary income sources fall within a single band and the more difficult it is to guess what rate each source should be taxed at. So, if withholding needs to collect exactly the right amount of tax from a large number of individuals, there is a constraint on the number of different tax rates there can be for the majority of taxpayers. It is worth noting that a lower rate band (below the basic rate) existed in 1978–79 and 1979–80 and again between 1992–93 and 2007–08, so there is evidently some flexibility in the schedule of rates. But even with the lower rate band in place, the vast majority of taxpayers still had the basic rate as their marginal tax rate.

A second example is the payment of tax credits through the pay packet. Between 2000 and 2006, the vast majority of employees eligible for tax credits received them from their employers rather than directly from the government. HMRC told employers the amount employees were entitled to, and employers were required to add this amount to salary payments. The funds for employers to do so came from the tax they had withheld from their employees. Although the payment of tax credits made use of some of the machinery of PAYE, it never involved adjustments to tax codes. The Regulatory Impact Assessment (RIA) for the 1999 Tax Credits Act said: 'The option of delivering tax credits through the PAYE coding system was considered, but was rejected on the grounds that PAYE codes could not deliver the necessary accuracy and reliability. Nor would they provide transparency for employees' (Inland Revenue (1999), p. 5).

Following persistent administrative problems, payment of tax credits via employers was abandoned in 2006. The government's stated reason for doing so was reducing compliance costs on employers (HMRC (2005)), but the cost incurred by the government was probably also a contributory factor. Payment via employers was primarily symbolic (intended to demonstrate that tax credits were a reward for work), and effectively added an additional link in the payment chain without simplifying administration.

The final example of a constraint imposed by PAYE concerns a progressive expenditure tax of the kind proposed in the Meade Report, in which deposits into savings accounts (and purchases of assets) are deducted from taxable income and withdrawals from such accounts are added to taxable income, similar to the treatment of pension funds now. As with the graduated rate structure, the issue relates primarily to the difficulty of taxing multiple income sources when there is more than one marginal tax rate. Currently, not all higher-rate taxpayers are required to self-assess. For those that are not, income outside PAYE may be taxed at the wrong rate (for example, interest on bank accounts, where withholding is correct for basic-rate taxpayers), but the tax revenue at stake is likely to be fairly small. This is not true of an expenditure tax, where all deposits must be given tax relief and all withdrawals taxed, not just the interest. Here, the sums involved are presumably too large to ignore.

These arguments suggest that PAYE may have kept the UK tax system simpler than it would otherwise have been. Income tax in the UK is certainly less complex than in the US (which has simple non-cumulative withholding and universal self-assessment) but this need not be due solely to PAYE. And, as discussed below, the government's incentive to keep the rules simple in other respects may be limited because it does not directly bear the major cost of operating PAYE. If the tax system has been kept simpler, it is not clear whether this means the tax system is better: this depends on whether the policy-making process takes full account of complexity created.

While it is impossible to know how binding the constraint imposed by PAYE has been, it seems reasonable to suggest that it has become less binding over time. In part this is because PAYE has become increasingly computerized, reducing the cost of recoding and end-of-year adjustments. But it is also due to a reduced appetite for policies likely to cause problems for PAYE for reasons unrelated to administrative ease. For example, there has been a move away from a highly graduated schedule of rates (for example, in 1976–77 there were ten non-zero tax rates on earned income; in 2008–09 there are only two), partly for political reasons, but also due to concern over the distortionary effects of high marginal rates on top incomes.

Administrative costs

As Table 12.2 indicates, in 2006–07, the cost to HMRC of administering PAYE (including overheads) was 0.74% of income tax revenue collected through PAYE. Historically, the UK has fared badly in international comparisons of administrative costs. More recent estimates, however, put UK costs on a par with many other OECD countries (see, for example, OECD (2007)). Moreover, there is a growing recognition that such comparisons can be misleading because cost-of-collection ratios depend on all sorts of things other than the efficiency of the tax authority. These include the number of taxpayers, tax rates and structures, the scope of the tax authority, the extent of enforcement activities, broader economic conditions, and differences in measurement methodology.

Because PAYE is a cumulative system that aims to collect the right amount of tax from the majority of taxpayers without an end-of-year adjustment, within-year costs are high and end-of-year costs low relative to a non-cumulative system of withholding. Whether overall administrative costs would be lower in the UK with an alternative collection mechanism is unclear.

Compliance costs

For most taxpayers under PAYE the correct amount of tax is withheld and remitted by employers without taxpayers having to file an annual return. Consequently, compliance costs of PAYE fall, in the first instance, on employers.[28] The Inland Revenue (1998) investigated the compliance costs of PAYE and National Insurance for 1995–96 (widely known as the 'Bath study'). Total compliance costs were estimated to be £1.32 billion, or 1.3% of the PAYE and (Class 1 and 1A) NI revenue collected.[29]

The KPMG (2006) study referred to above measured 'administrative burdens' on a basis substantially narrower than compliance costs as normally defined. In particular, costs are estimated for a 'normally efficient business', and exclude costs associated with tax planning, dealing with change, and understanding which tax obligations are relevant. It is not surprising, therefore, to find that the burden on employers of PAYE and NICs is estimated to be substantially lower than the Bath study found: £759 million in 2005, or 0.4% of PAYE and (Class 1 and 1A) NI revenue.

Both the Bath study and the KPMG report find that compliance costs relative to the size of the employer are much higher for small firms than large ones. For example, the Bath results suggest that average compliance costs for employers with 1–4 employees were £288 per employee in 1995–96, compared with less than £5 for employers with 5,000 or more employees.[30] The Bath study also estimated the 'cash-flow benefit' of the PAYE/NIC system, and found it to exceed compliance costs for large employers (those with more than 1,000 employees). This benefit arises because PAYE and NIC remittances

[28] Compliance costs may be shifted to some degree according to the same supply-and-demand logic that applies to the shifting of explicit tax liabilities. Consequently, it cannot be presumed that compliance costs reduce after-tax profits pound for pound relative to what they would have been in the absence of compliance costs.

[29] This £1.32 billion includes £93 million for statutory maternity and sick pay.

[30] Authors' calculations based on KPMG (2006) and data from the Small Business Service reveal that the KPMG results imply average costs for employers with 1–9 employees of £173 per employee, compared to around £6.50 for employers with 250 or more employees. It wasn't possible to reproduce the same firm size bandings as the Bath study. The Carter Review of Payroll Services (2001) states that intermediaries can provide a monthly payroll service for employers with up to four employees for £200–£250 per year, and that the marginal cost for additional employees is low.

are due about three weeks after employees are paid, so firms can earn interest on the tax liability in the intervening period.[31]

Tellingly, the Bath study concluded that the high fixed compliance costs in some cases deterred small business owners from taking on their first employee. Sandford concluded that when small firms compete with large firms they are placed under a 'state-created competitive disadvantage' (Sandford (1989), p. 200). Whether this disadvantage for small businesses is socially inefficient, though, is not clear because it might to some extent reflect the higher cost of raising revenue from small businesses.

From the employer's point of view, there is little doubt that the compliance costs of PAYE are higher than those of a simple non-cumulative system. But the size of the difference may be small, particularly given that most employers now run a computerized payroll, either in-house or outsourced. It is worth emphasizing that the P45 forms used to keep track of pay and tax to date when individuals change jobs do not cause a great deal of extra work for employers. Under a non-cumulative system, employers typically still need to give the employee notice of pay and tax deducted (so they can complete their tax return) and send a copy to the tax authority (for information reporting purposes) (Inland Revenue (1979)).

Whiting (2002, p. 44) argues that, because much of the cost of operating PAYE falls in the first instance on employers, the government has little incentive to keep the tax system simple. As a result, the tax system becomes complex with high compliance costs. It is impossible to tell how much this has happened in reality, but, as noted above, the US hasn't managed to avoid a complex tax system despite having universal self-assessment. The fact that taxpayers covered by PAYE incur almost no direct compliance costs mean that most of them are largely unaware of the tax system. Few understand what their tax code means or how their tax liability is determined. This can lead to less disciplined policy-making because individuals are not in a position to criticize bad policy.

Non-compliance

Information from HMRC's employer compliance random enquiry programme indicates that £0.9 billion of income tax and National Insurance was understated on returns from small and medium-sized employers in 2003–04 (HMRC (2007c)). This is equivalent to 1.4% of the total true liability, considerably lower than the figure for self-assessment (see Table 12.2) but very

[31] The cash-flow benefit is not a social cost but instead a transfer from the government to the employer equal to the time value of the money held by the employer.

similar to comparable US data (despite the fact that the US operates non-cumulative withholding). No UK figures are available for non-compliance among large employers.

12.7.3. A decade of self-assessment

Self-assessment—under which individuals whose full income tax liability cannot be collected through PAYE and other withholding have to complete a tax return—has been in place for a little over a decade. Before we consider options for reforming PAYE, it is worth spending a few paragraphs analysing how successful self-assessment has been. Self-assessment was introduced from tax year 1996–97, replacing the previous system of assessments made by tax inspectors. It was hailed as 'the biggest change [in tax administration] since the introduction of PAYE over 50 years earlier'[32] (Inland Revenue (2002a)). While it certainly was a big change, the difference for individuals who file their tax return in time for HMRC to calculate the tax liability is actually not that great. Indeed, under the old system of HMRC assessments, taxpayers were often obliged to provide information about their sources of income on a form not dissimilar to the current tax return.

Perhaps the most fundamental change brought about by self-assessment is the increased responsibility taxpayers are expected to take for their own tax affairs (Green (1996)). HMRC no longer issues estimated assessments; instead, the onus is on taxpayers to file and remit on time. HMRC also has much more extensive enquiry powers, including the ability to conduct audits randomly (previously there needed to be grounds for suspicion), and taxpayers are statutorily required to keep business records for a period of six years.

Eliminating old-style assessments and appeals, combined with transferring to the taxpayer some responsibilities that previously lay with HMRC, was projected to provide an administrative saving of £500 million by 2007–08. In 2006–07, the cost to HMRC of administering self-assessment (including overheads) was 4.46% of revenue collected directly through self-assessment.[33]

While many taxpayers and tax advisers acknowledged that self- assessment was a necessary modernization, there was a widespread feeling that not

[32] Paragraph 4 of IR memorandum submitted to the Treasury Sub-committee in 2002. <http://www.publications.parliament.uk/pa/cm200102/cmselect/cmtreasy/681/2030601.htm>.

[33] This is considerably higher than the figure for PAYE, but comparing the two figures is misleading. This is both because individuals under self-assessment tend to have more complicated tax affairs than those who are outside self-assessment and because some self-assessment taxpayers have most of their liability collected through PAYE.

enough effort had been put into making the process as simple as possible for taxpayers. As far as we are aware, no comprehensive study of self-assessment's implications for compliance costs has been undertaken.[34]

The self-assessment return is long (often up to twenty pages) and complex, though a shorter four-page return for those with simple tax affairs was eventually rolled out starting with the 2004–05 tax year. Other improvements over time have included better taxpayer statements and some removal of those with very simple affairs from the system altogether. Around 90% of tax returns are filed on time under the current system—much better than the 50% under the old system (Inland Revenue (2002b))—though many arrive very close to the 31 January deadline. The time between the end of the tax year and the final due date for tax payment is, at 10 months, the longest of any OECD country bar Finland.[35]

On the basis of data from the 2001–02 random enquiry programme (the latest year for which there is information), HMRC estimates that 33% of returns under-declare tax liability and that £2.8 billion of tax is not disclosed, equivalent to 14.6% of the £19.2 billion net receipts from self-assessment in 2001–02 (HMRC (2007c)). Around three-quarters of this is accounted for by 5% of returns; errors contained in many of the other returns may have been unintentional. As the self-assessment random enquiry programme only covers registered taxpayers, it does not provide any estimate of unpaid tax on income from the informal economy or other undisclosed income. It is unclear how these figures compare with the previous system, because there was no random enquiry programme that could provide statistically reliable estimates of unpaid tax. In 2006–07, HMRC accurately calculated the tax due for 96.5% of self-assessment returns.[36]

Overall, self-assessment was indeed a necessary modification to the tax system. Perhaps too much was expected of it too soon, with insufficient

[34] KPMG (2006) includes estimates of the burden of self-assessment for businesses, but excludes groups such as employees and pensioners who have to self-assess. Some idea of the amount of time involved in completing tax returns can be gained from the BMRB evaluation of the 2002–03 short tax return pilot (Inland Revenue (2004)). It found that median total compliance time was reduced from 162 minutes (for the main return) to 120 minutes (for the short return). Obviously, these results cannot be generalized across all self-assessment taxpayers because those eligible for the short return are likely to have simpler affairs than those who aren't. Also, the results do not include the cost of advisors.

[35] Proposals to shorten this period in the Carter Review (2006) were widely attacked, not least because there was no parallel attempt to simplify or streamline the reporting system which might justify a shorter timescale. The only change that got implemented involved moving forward the filing date for paper returns to 31 October for 2007–08 returns onwards.

[36] The annual reconciliation process that forms part of self-assessment uncovers a large number of other errors before they are able to have an impact on final tax remitted.

expectation of the need for continuous improvement. Now that more effort is being put into that improvement process, it is delivering more.

12.7.4. Policy options

In this section we consider ways in which some of the problems described above could be addressed. The first set of reforms attempt to improve the ability of withholding arrangements to collect the right amount of tax. The second set is a radical alternative: drastic simplification of PAYE combined with universal self-assessment. Throughout, we assume that there is no change to the way income tax is assessed.

Improvements to current withholding arrangements

HMRC has already begun to modernize PAYE in ways that should considerably improve its accuracy. But these changes are unlikely to remove the need for large quantities of paper communication, such as HMRC sending tax codes to employers, and employees taking P45s from their old employer to their new one. In principle, it would be possible to develop an online computer coding system that would allow much of this to be done electronically. Withholding agents could be required to register any employee they take on and, in so doing, would be provided with a tax code to use based on information about all income sources of the individual. Without pay-period information reporting, employers would still need to provide information about pay and tax to date when an employee changes jobs, but this could be done through the computer system without the need for employees to carry the information manually between employers. This sort of arrangement has the potential to reduce the cost of communication considerably, but the extent to which it improves the accuracy of PAYE depends on how often employees are to blame for the P45 failing to turn up. For any such computer system to be possible, security issues would need to be addressed: if employers are able to find out information about employees by registering them, there is obviously potential for personal data to be compromised. This is particularly pertinent given the controversy over lost Child Benefit records in 2007, but with careful consideration, it should be possible to address this issue satisfactorily.

A second possible change is to make other withholding non-flat-rate. Currently, withholding is designed to get the answer right for basic-rate taxpayers. Non-PAYE withholding (such as that on interest income) happens at the basic rate—so the right amount of tax is withheld if this income falls in the basic rate band, but the wrong amount is withheld if it does not. For individuals outside self-assessment, adjustments are often made to the PAYE code to resolve the difference. Potentially, the need for such adjustments could be reduced if withholding on other sources of income was not done at a flat rate. But this could only be achieved at the cost of requiring banks and other withholding agents to tailor withholding to individual circumstances. Information would need to be passed between HMRC and these other withholding agents each year. Were this combined with some sort of online computer system as envisaged above, it may not be too burdensome, though it is certainly administratively more complicated. Any decision would need to weigh any administrative savings against the additional compliance costs imposed.

A final possibility would be to move to monthly information reporting. Currently, information reporting happens annually as part of the end-of-year employer return. During the year, employers just remit the total tax, National Insurance and student loan repayments they owe (based on their own calculations) without any breakdown of what the money covers. This reduces within-year compliance costs for employers, but means that tax codes are not updated to reflect changes in circumstances, so often the wrong tax is withheld. If employers had to report information each time they remit tax liability (usually monthly), this information could be used to modify tax codes and reduce the number of cases where the wrong amount has been withheld at the end of the year. Although the majority of OECD countries have annual information reporting for employers, a substantial minority have monthly reporting, including Finland, Japan, and New Zealand. In the US it is quarterly (OECD (2007)).

Given HMRC is already moving towards requiring electronic transactions from employers, monthly information reporting may not be much of an additional burden assuming it takes the same form as information that has to be provided at the end of the year in any event. Currently, medium and large employers (50+ employees) must file end-of-year returns electronically, and from April 2011, this will apply to all employers. Although there are no published plans to make electronic remittance compulsory, it would not be surprising if this happened at some point. Nevertheless, the burden may be greater on small employers because their computer systems may not be so easily adapted to cope.

It is important to realize, however, that if PAYE is to withhold more accurately on the basis of monthly information reporting, it will require more frequent coding instructions to employers. Individuals whose circumstances change frequently may end up with different tax codes every month. Again, the extent to which this is a burden depends on how computerized the system is. In principle, it need not make that much difference if payroll software can be automatically linked up to the coding instructions provided by the online coding system. The extent to which such a change would reduce the number of cases where the wrong amount of tax is withheld over the course of the year depends on how common it is for circumstances to change once tax codes have been calculated.

Of these three reforms, an online coding system seems the most clearly beneficial, and we recommend it should be investigated further. Any move in this direction must, however, be tempered by the knowledge that the history of large-scale government IT projects is far from glorious. Both of the other reforms are more marginal and a proper assessment of their value would require detailed operational information. Nevertheless, it seems unlikely that either would be viable in the absence of an improved computer system.

Universal self-assessment and simple non-cumulative withholding

A radical alternative would be to extend self-assessment across the whole population. For this to result in any administrative savings it would need to be combined with a drastically simplified system of withholding. In the words of a 1979 Inland Revenue review of PAYE (1979, p. 24): 'Grafting self-assessment on to the present PAYE system would be pointless; it would secure the worst of both worlds—no savings on in-year work, but much more end-of-year effort—and call for many more staff, not less.' It would need a non-cumulative system of withholding in which the tax authority is not responsible for calculating tax codes (so it need not keep track of employees and employers during the tax year). This is the system operated in the US.

Whether it would result in much of a reduction in employer compliance costs is debatable. The KPMG (2006) burdens report suggests that the majority of the cost to employers of operating PAYE was remitting tax liability and filing end-of-year returns, both of which would be largely unchanged under a non-cumulative system. Calculation of liability—one of the main things simplified by non-cumulation—did not form a large part of the total.

Self-assessment should improve the accuracy of tax calculations for some individuals and remove any constraints on policy imposed by PAYE. It may encourage individuals to take a greater interest in the country's tax system, but to a degree this will be mitigated if individuals rely on advisers and software to complete their returns. It may also create greater impetus to simplify the tax system (since a universal self-assessment return would have to be simpler than the current form), though this has not really happened in the US.

The main objection to universal self-assessment is the implications for compliance costs of compulsory tax returns. If PAYE works reasonably well for the majority of taxpayers, why force them to file a return because of the minority for whom PAYE does not work well?

One response to this is that, with the introduction of tax credits, many families effectively have to complete a tax return each year anyway. Around 6 million families receive tax credits, of which approximately 4 million also interact with PAYE. Were it possible to combine tax credit claims into a system of universal self-assessment (as happens in the US), the implications of self-assessment for tax credit recipients would not be that great. But achieving this would be difficult because, unlike the US, the UK has individual assessment for income tax but joint assessment for tax credits. And it still leaves perhaps 25 million individuals under PAYE who do not self-assess and do not receive tax credits, for whom universal self-assessment would be a considerable change.

A second response is pre-population. Over the last couple of decades, a number of Nordic countries have started sending out tax return forms that have been 'pre-populated' with information already held by the tax authority.[37] Typically this information comes from third-party information reports, such as salary information from employers. Taxpayers then need only check the pre-populated information and complete the parts of the tax return that are blank.

Pre-population has a number of obvious advantages (OECD (2007)). In particular, it offers the potential for substantial compliance costs savings because taxpayers have to spend less time completing their tax returns. It is also likely to lead to more accurate tax returns because taxpayer errors are avoided in pre-populated sections. This will reduce the administrative resources required to deal with incorrect returns. One disadvantage of pre-population is that it reveals what information the tax authority holds. Individuals may be less likely to report income missed by a pre-populated return because, if the tax authority doesn't know about it, they infer that their chances of being caught are small. It is unclear how important this is in practice. Successful pre-population is also very demanding. The information held by the tax authority must be accurate, and the tax authority must be able

[37] The US state of California piloted a pre-populated state income tax return in 2004 and 2005, and in 2008 two of the major Democratic presidential candidates proposed such a system for the federal income tax.

to link together all information relating to a given taxpayer soon after the end of the tax year. Historically, HMRC has not found this straightforward.

Given current policies, the value of universal self-assessment depends both on the feasibility of pre-population and on the extent to which withholding can successfully be made to collect the right amount of tax from more taxpayers with less need for manual intervention. Were the policy context to change—particularly were it to move in favour of some form of expenditure tax—the balance may swing in favour of universal self-assessment. But, in either case, the long-term benefits of such a change would need to be substantial to outweigh the considerable disruption caused by switching.

12.8. TAX AVOIDANCE

12.8.1. Some causes of avoidance

As we have previously noted, the origins of avoidance lie in the difficulty of defining what is sought to be taxed—the tax base. In defining the tax base, tax systems create boundaries, some inevitable and others as matters of the political or other choices that are made in designing the system. Avoidance and the difficulty of constructing adequate countermeasures reflect the ease or difficulty of finding objective and verifiable criteria to determine those boundaries in order to prevent taxpayers seeking to eliminate or reduce their tax liabilities by changing their behaviour in particular ways. Significant avoidance activity is often clustered around the least satisfactory areas of a tax system. Complexity and avoidance can go hand in hand and it may also be the case that avoidance is on occasion difficult to distinguish from illegal evasion. In particular, the harder the tax base is to identify and locate within a particular taxing jurisdiction, the more difficult it is likely to become to tax and, as a corollary to that, the greater the scope for taxpayers to avoid tax on the tax base of a particular taxing jurisdiction. At the same time the inability of revenue authorities to monitor and control satisfactorily taxpayer behaviour in such a situation means that there may be considerable scope for evasion by less scrupulous taxpayers.

Much of the UK government's anti-avoidance agenda has been focused on corporate taxpayers. Companies will, in general, seek to minimize their taxes (both on profits and on employee remuneration) plus the cost of this minimization. There is an acknowledged tension between their understandable perception of taxes as a cost to be minimized, and the tax authorities seeing companies as needing to act responsibly and constrain their planning actions carefully. It is unsurprising that tax avoidance has attracted considerable attention in areas such as the taxation of international companies, where several tax systems must interact and the scope for tax arbitrage, playing the rules of one system off against another, is considerable.[38] Another area is the taxation of financial companies, where financial innovation (such as the use of derivative instruments) has allowed transactions to be constructed in ways that attract a more favourable tax treatment, while having essentially the same economic effect as simpler transactions that would be taxed less favourably.

At the same time a key challenge facing tax authorities is how to evolve to address the changing methods of commerce. The UK's tax system has struggled to keep up technically with such issues as financial instruments and the general way business financing is carried out.[39] At the other end of the spectrum, the growth of e-business—exemplified by eBay—brings particular challenges to the tax collector. In principle there is nothing new in tax terms: it is still an issue of whether a taxable trade is being carried out or disposals subject to CGT are made. In days gone by the taxman tried to control cash sales at market stalls; more recently activities moved to car boot sales; now the business takes place in cyberspace. This presents greater challenges, however, as to how HMRC can police this effectively.

Another dimension is the position of intellectual capital, which is increasingly replacing physical assets as the basis of wealth creation. If a company owns a trademark or patent that can in principle be 'located' anywhere, leading to profits being diverted abroad, HMRC must solve the question of how it defines a tax base that it can monitor without leaving open opportunities for uncontrolled avoidance or evasion.

There is no simple answer to these issues. A combination of measures to refine or redefine the tax base and to counter the avoidance opportunities that would otherwise undermine the tax base entirely is needed, without at the same time inhibiting ordinary commercial behaviour. The UK as a member of the European Union is forced to operate within the constraints imposed by the EC Treaty freedoms. Claims that ordinary cross-border anti-avoidance rules breach these freedoms has led to a succession of cases before

[38] As noted in Section 12.1, the welfare consequences of a taxpayer's choice regarding to which jurisdiction to pay a given tax are quite different from the choice of whether to pay tax to a given jurisdiction.

[39] Though in some areas it has been commendably quick to adapt: the way that considerable effort has been put into devising a way of catering for Shari'a compliant financing products in FA 2005 and subsequent Acts is very creditable. The driver has been to make sure London is positioned as a centre of the developing Islamic international finance market.

the European Court of Justice that affect all states, undermining their ability to implement measures designed to protect domestic tax revenues against cross-border activity notwithstanding the ECJ's development of an abuse (of Community law) doctrine. In the international context cooperation between revenue authorities, both in terms of finding solutions and in working out ways of policing tax systems efficiently, is likely to be the only satisfactory way forward. National customs authorities have cooperated over many years because they are outward facing. By contrast, revenue authorities responsible for direct taxation have tended to be inward facing. The establishment of the Joint International Tax Shelter Information Centre (JITSIC) between Australia, the UK, the US, Canada, and Japan is, however, a significant step forward in sharing information between the revenue authorities of those countries in order to identify abusive products or arrangements and those marketing them.

12.8.2. Categorizing avoidance and identifying the tax gap

Tax avoidance is action ordinarily designed to reduce a taxpayer's tax bill in one way or another by legal means (in contrast to evasion which aims at the same objective by fraud, deceit, or other illegal means). Not all tax reduction is characterized as 'avoidance' but for present purposes we do not seek to differentiate 'avoidance' from other forms of tax mitigation, planning, or reduction. However, certain avoidance has been demonized of late in the UK and various other countries as being 'unacceptable'. This raises difficult questions: if the taxpayer is operating in accordance with the law, disclosing fully and meeting all compliance obligations, what is the problem if the result of actions taken is not to the tax authorities' liking? The rejoinder is usually that the result is not in accordance with the legislative intention. But what does the taxpayer have to go by, if not the language of the legislation? If the law can be overridden at the discretion of the tax authorities, where does that leave fairness and certainty?

In some cases the boundary between 'acceptable' and 'unacceptable' avoidance becomes a matter of proper disclosure, that is, that unacceptable avoidance is often down to incomplete disclosure—possibly bordering on evasion if the success of arrangements depends upon non-disclosure. Some of the controversy can be taken out of the debate if there is full and frank disclosure. In addition, initiatives in countries such as the US and UK to require speedier disclosure of tax planning schemes (see below) seek to ensure a better balance in the system or at least an acknowledgement that current intelligence is important in dealing with avoidance. Even with full disclosure, however, there remain arrangements that continue to generate controversy, being designed for no purpose other than to eliminate tax liabilities or that operate as a 'raid on the Treasury' by generating tax repayments or double reliefs for particular expenditure.

There is undoubtedly room for the view that the UK's tax system, with its reliance on legal 'form' rather than on economic or financial 'substance', is particularly open to avoidance.[40] At the time of the Meade Report, promoters of tax avoidance schemes were fond of citing the following judicial dictum to justify their schemes:[41]

> No man in this country is under the smallest obligation, moral or other, so to arrange his legal relations to his business or to his property as to enable the Inland Revenue to put the largest possible shovel into his stores. The Inland Revenue is not slow—and quite rightly—to take every advantage which is open to it under the taxing statutes for the purpose of depleting the taxpayer's pocket. And the taxpayer is, in like manner, entitled to be astute to prevent, so far as he honestly can, the depletion of his means by the Revenue.

Countries that have a doctrine of 'abuse of rights' or have legislated an overarching General Anti-Avoidance Rule ('GAAR') leave less scope for argument or, at least, the grounds for argument are somewhat different. The UK government consulted on an overarching statutory GAAR in 1998 but decided against adopting one. It has therefore been left to the judiciary to develop its approach to construing tax legislation to counter avoidance. Initially, the House of Lords dealt many artificial 1970s schemes a judicial blow when it decided in *W T Ramsay v IRC* (1981) 54 TC 101 that composite pre-planned tax avoidance schemes could be rendered ineffective if the legislation in question justified that approach. Subsequent decisions on the *Ramsay* doctrine, however, have illustrated the limitations of this judicial action against avoidance.[42] Furthermore, judicial sentiment on avoidance can change and few governments can delay counter-action against avoidance once discovered to await a judicial answer as to whether particular schemes are effective or not. Earlier legislative action is usually required to protect tax revenues.

Recent years have seen the UK government step up its efforts to reduce the amount of tax revenue that it perceives to be lost as a result of various forms of tax avoidance. As shown in Table 12.3, measures described as 'protecting tax

[40] The best-known case illustrating this is probably *The Duke of Westminster v CIR* (1935) 19 TC 490.

[41] *Ayrshire Pullman Motor Services and D M Ritchie v The Commissioners of Inland Revenue* (1929) 14 TC 754.

[42] See e.g. *Barclays Mercantile Business Finance Ltd v Mawson* (2002) 76 TC 446.

Table 12.3. Treasury estimates of amounts raised through measures announced since Budget 2002 aimed at 'protecting revenues' (£ billion 2008–09 terms)

	Year					
Announcement	2003–04	2004–05	2005–06	2006–07	2007–08	2008–09
Budget 2008	N/A	N/A	N/A	N/A	N/A	0.7
Between Budget 2007 and Budget 2008	N/A	N/A	N/A	N/A	0.1	0.2
Budget 2007	N/A	N/A	N/A	N/A	0.2	0.3
Between Budget 2006 and Budget 2007	N/A	N/A	N/A	0.3	1.0	1.0
Budget 2006	N/A	N/A	N/A	0.3	0.8	0.6
Between Budget 2005 and Budget 2006	N/A	N/A	0.2	0.6	0.8	0.8
Budget 2005	N/A	N/A	0.8	1.2	1.1	1.1
Between Budget 2004 and Budget 2005	N/A	0.3	1.2	1.3	1.3	1.3
Budget 2004	N/A	0.4	0.9	1.0	1.0	1.0
Between Budget 2003 and Budget 2004	0.0	0.3	0.5	0.7	0.7	0.7
Budget 2003	0.6	0.6	0.6	0.6	0.6	0.6
Between Budget 2002 and Budget 2003	1.1	0.9	1.1	1.1	1.1	1.1
Total	**1.7**	**2.6**	**5.3**	**7.1**	**8.8**	**9.4**
% of national income	*0.1*	*0.2*	*0.4*	*0.5*	*0.6*	*0.6*

Sources: Various Budgets. Only measures scored under 'protecting revenues', 'protecting tax revenues', or 'anti-avoidance measures' included. Nominal figures uprated to 2008–09 terms using the Treasury's latest estimates of money GDP. Where Treasury estimates are not published, the revenue raised is assumed to remain constant as a share of national income.

revenues' introduced since Budget 2002 alone are estimated to raise around £9.4 billion in 2008–09. Some revenue-raising anti-avoidance measures are always likely to be required to prevent additional tax leakage as new avoidance schemes are developed. But the government clearly wants to do more than just run to stand still, and hopes to reduce avoidance over time.

12.8.3. Legislative anti-avoidance techniques

UK governments have tried most legislative techniques to curb avoidance and in recent years the volume of anti-avoidance legislation has increased, due to the ingenuity of tax planners and a determination by the government and revenue authorities to stamp out what they perceive as avoidance, in turn informed by the disclosure regime (see below). The legislative assault on avoidance has mainly involved specific anti-avoidance measures in the standard detailed rule-based form. Increasingly, however, legislation has incorporated a general tax avoidance test based on the existence of an avoidance motive or purpose or the derivation of tax benefits; effectively 'mini GAARs' attached to specific parts of the tax code (e.g. VAT option to tax and various share schemes provisions) or so-called 'targeted anti-avoidance provisions' (TAARs—notably on capital losses).

These have met with varying degrees of success.[43] The UK government's latest idea is to introduce, probably starting in 2009, 'principles-based' anti-avoidance legislation designed to achieve a better balance of simplicity and revenue protection. The perception that continues to be conveyed by government and HMRC, however, is that avoidance remains a major issue requiring substantial legislative measures every year.

A less conventional approach has involved the threat of retrospective legislation,[44] in particular targeted at employment schemes that sought to eliminate tax and/or NICs on bonus payments. At the time the threat was made, specific measures were introduced to counter identified avoidance but, in a clear signal that the authorities were no longer prepared to tolerate the situation, the Paymaster General threatened retrospective action against schemes uncovered in the future. There is anecdotal evidence that this threat, coupled with the fact that it has been acted upon (see S92 FA 2006), has been largely successful in stopping the annual bonus scheme round, where each year a series of devices targeted at eliminating tax/NICs on 'city' bonuses appeared.

12.8.4. Tax avoidance disclosure

A major initiative, however, has been the introduction of a Tax Avoidance Disclosure (TAD) regime in 2004. The TAD regime was brought in initially for direct tax (income tax, corporation tax, and CGT) and VAT; it has since extended to SDLT and NICs. The direct tax provisions were recast in 2006 and were extended in 2007 with the grant of greater information powers. The TAD regime has two distinct objectives: to identify new schemes, so that it is possible to take early anti-avoidance action; and to show who is using the schemes so as to help HMRC adjust their risk assessments.

The hub of TAD is the requirement for promoters to notify new schemes within five days of making them available or when implementation has started. Whilst the target might be marketed schemes, bespoke advice can

[43] See TLRC (2008) for a detailed examination of the different approaches.

[44] See the statement by the Paymaster General accompanying the December 2004 Pre-Budget Report.

also be caught and one of the practical problems (on both sides) has been identifying what else has to be disclosed. Various provisions in the successive Finance Acts of 2005, 2006, 2007, and the Finance Bill 2008 can be traced to disclosures made under the TAD (though, curiously, no VAT changes to date). To that extent, the regime is clearly working in allowing HMRC to identify and counteract avoidance more quickly. Statistics of disclosures to the end of September 2007 (867 for direct tax, 702 for stamp duty land tax, and 852 for VAT) suggest that the system is certainly delivering substantial data to HMRC.[45]

At the same time, however, the added stimulus to introduce further anti-avoidance legislation and to tweak incessantly existing anti-avoidance provisions has contributed to the sense that the UK's tax system is too complex and lacks stability in the affected areas. This feeling has led to the government's current simplification reviews, one element of which has been its announcement of principles-based anti-avoidance legislation designed to replace longer and more complex provisions with shorter and simpler anti-avoidance provisions based on clear statements of the principle that they are designed to achieve. While there has been general support for the aims of the review, the consultation initiated in December 2007 generated significant criticism that the proposals would create unacceptable uncertainty and went beyond their intended scope. The essential problem is that avoidance is frequently concentrated on those areas of the tax system where there is no clear principle. Accordingly, finding a satisfactory alternative, simpler, legislative approach is unlikely to be straightforward. In the meantime TAD will continue to generate pressure for further detailed rule-based anti-avoidance measures.

12.8.5. 'Tax in the boardroom'

A further stratagem that the government has deployed against avoidance has been publicity. This has not quite amounted to 'naming and shaming' those involved, but there was clearly a campaign in 2005 to demonize avoidance and portray tax avoiders, both corporate and individual, in a very poor light.[46] Some observers saw a degree of irony in the welter of publicity in that evasion,

45 <http://www.hmrc.gov.uk/avoidance/avoidance-disclosure-statistics.htm>.

46 For example, in announcing the opening of a second JITSIC office in London in September 2007, the Financial Secretary spoke in terms of the need to stamp out avoidance because 'tax avoidance gives those who seek to cheat the system an unfair advantage over the vast majority of taxpayers who play by the rules'. However much governments and revenue authorities may dislike avoidance, legal avoidance *is* playing by the rules.

which is illegal, seemed to be overlooked almost as if it were regarded as less reprehensible than avoidance.[47]

HMRC also sought to raise awareness among senior management of large companies of the potential risks of being caught on the wrong side of what the authorities consider to be unacceptable tax avoidance. In autumn 2005, HMRC officials wrote directly to the chairmen of the UK's largest 500 companies, seeking to establish a dialogue over the management of tax issues and tax risk. There are certainly positive aspects to greater communication between tax collectors and taxpayers, which should lead to greater understanding of the other side's position. There was a perception in some quarters, however, that HMRC was seeking to exert pressure on companies by raising questions about their tax strategies at boardroom level.

HMRC's increased emphasis on 'tax risk' can also be perceived as an attempt to increase uncertainty among taxpayers about the border between acceptable and unacceptable forms of tax planning, and to foster increased nervousness about the reputational risk of being seen to fall on the wrong side of the divide. Promoting opacity and unpredictability may seem a clever way to raise revenue in the short run, but transparency and certainty have long been seen as hallmarks of a fair and efficient tax system.

12.8.6. Conclusion

The disclosure regime has been successful in enabling HMRC to take counteracting measures against avoidance more quickly. This success, however, has come at the cost of an outpouring of specific or 'targeted' tax avoidance rules that, on top of other recent legislative activity in the tax field, threatens to clog the system. Even if anti-avoidance provisions are of 'limited' application—consigning schemes to the history books or ensuring that they never work—they involve a continuing cost to taxpayers, and business in particular, in ensuring that their ordinary commercial and personal arrangements do not fall foul of particular provisions and so avoid unintended effects.

It is important for the integrity of the tax system that people should contribute their 'fair share' of tax revenues and that there should not be undue scope for particular individuals to reduce their share of those revenues. This is the basis of the Paymaster General's statement on employment liabilities. In this respect the tax system that existed in the UK at the time of Meade, with high nominal rates of tax offset by opportunities for avoidance by those

[47] The social responsibilities of corporations with respect to taxpaying are discussed in Slemrod (2004).

with access to specialist advice, represented a poor combination of disincentives and inequity. While the reduction in nominal tax rates since that time has lowered the benefits of specific avoidance, the essential link between avoidance and the tax base remains so that even at lower nominal tax rates avoidance emerges where the tax base is, for whatever reason, difficult to define. Business taxation is a particular illustration because the tax base—'profits'—is difficult to state and in today's conditions is global in nature. It is an inherently difficult tax base both to define and to identify with the UK. In this respect, it is difficult to achieve a coherent policy that, on the one hand, demands that businesses pay their 'fair share' of taxation without undue avoidance, and, on the other, aims for a globally competitive tax system. Ongoing targeted anti-avoidance provisions may contribute to the former objective while undermining the latter by clogging of the arteries of what aims to be a competitive tax system.

III. CONCLUSIONS

Administration and enforcement are often neglected in tax policy, but they are central to making a tax system work. In Part I of the chapter we showed how standard optimal tax theory can be extended to address these issues and described a number of important implications. Here, we highlight just two. First, the optimal mix of tax instruments cannot be determined without reference to all the costs of taxation (distortion costs and administrative and compliance costs). Second, for incremental policy adjustments, what matters are marginal costs, not total or average costs.

In Part II we addressed three main issues relating to the administration and enforcement of the UK tax system: the objectives and targets of HMRC, the future of PAYE, and tax avoidance.

The reorganization that created HMRC promises efficiency savings, and recent initiatives make it clear that HMRC takes both administrative and compliance costs into consideration, as is entirely appropriate. Moreover, HMRC is clearly concerned with both raising revenue as well as raising it equitably and accurately. The focus on setting and attaining a long list of quantitative targets, though, runs the risk of obscuring the trade-offs that are implicit in HMRC resource allocation decisions, and potentially making these decisions internally inconsistent. There is also a danger that different costs are not considered simultaneously, and that incremental policy changes are decided on the basis of average rather than marginal costs.

PAYE functions reasonably well for the majority of taxpayers whose circumstances are straightforward but struggles in more complicated cases, particularly for individuals with multiple income sources and frequent job changes. HMRC has already begun to modernize PAYE in ways that should considerably improve its accuracy, but we recommend that more fundamental changes should be considered. In particular, an online system of coding has the potential to remove the need for much of the paper communication currently required, reducing both the number of errors made and administrative costs. The case for universal self-assessment depends both on the extent to which modernization of PAYE manages to address its current shortcomings and on the feasibility of pre-populating tax returns.

Despite significant legislative and other activity designed to counter tax avoidance, the perception remains that tax avoidance is a continuing problem and a source of considerable tax leakage (as compared with the tax that government believes it should be collecting) as well as complexity and cost. In reality, while there is taxation there will be avoidance and the avoidance will tend to be concentrated on those parts of the tax system where lines are drawn between different activities, products, taxpayers, and taxing jurisdictions. A balance must be found between attempting to eliminate every avoidance opportunity and not inhibiting unnecessarily ordinary commercial and personal activities. And tackling avoidance must not mean that tackling evasion is neglected.

Ultimately, tackling avoidance is part of the process of defining the tax base. This will be easier where the tax base reflects a clear underlying economic principle, that does not attempt to tax close substitutes differently, that draws lines where satisfactory objective and independently verifiable criteria exist to distinguish what is intended to be taxed and what is not, and that avoids drawing unnecessary lines without those characteristics.

Beyond such design issues, governments are likely to have to continue to deploy a variety of measures to counteract avoidance and monitor the borders of the tax system where in reality no very clear boundaries exist. A significant problem in the UK has been the tendency to be reactive to avoidance—to address the symptom by negating the latest device without considering the underlying cause of the problem. As a result, taxpayers have revised their plans to circumvent or exploit the latest set of detailed anti-avoidance rules. The attempt to move away from a detailed rule-based approach and find a principles-based answer may signal a recognition that the process of refinement and complication is not ideal and that better methods may be needed to monitor the borders of the tax system.

The overriding conclusion has to be that the UK's tax system is, all things considered, not doing too badly. But it is undoubtedly creaking and as commercial life continues to change rapidly, there is increasing pressure for it to adapt. The question is whether it can adapt quickly enough. If not, it runs the risk of imposing unnecessary burdens while simultaneously allowing revenues to escape taxation such that the tax burden is shared in a more capricious and inequitable fashion.

REFERENCES

Adam, S. and Loutzenhiser, G. (2007), 'Integrating Income Tax and National Insurance: An Interim Report', IFS Working Papers, W07/21, December 2007.

Akerlof, G. (1978), 'The Economics of "Tagging" as Applied to the Optimal Income Tax, Welfare Programs, and Manpower Planning', *American Economic Review*, **68**, 8–19.

Allingham, M. G., and Sandmo, A. (1972), 'Income Tax Evasion: A Theoretical Analysis', *Journal of Public Economics*, **1**, 323–38.

Barr, N. A., James, S. R., and Prest, A. R. (1977), *Self-Assessment for Income Tax*. London: Heinemann Educational Books.

Becker, G. (1968), 'Crime and Punishment: An Economic Approach', *Journal of Political Economy*, **76**, 169–217.

Bird, R. (2002), 'Why Tax Corporations?', *Bulletin for International Fiscal Documentation*, **52**, 194–203.

Blumenthal, M., Christian, C., and Slemrod, J. (2001), 'Do Normative Appeals Affect Tax Compliance? Evidence from a Controlled Experiment in Minnesota', *National Tax Journal*, **54**, 125–38.

Bourn, J. (2003), *Tackling Fraud against the Inland Revenue*. Report by the Comptroller and Auditor General, NAO. 28 February.

—— (2006), *Comptroller and Auditor General's Standard Report on the Accounts of the Inland Revenue 2005–06*, NAO. 7 July.

—— (2007a), *HM Revenue & Customs: Accuracy in Processing Income Tax*. Report by the Comptroller and Auditor General, NAO. 6 July.

—— (2007b), *Comptroller and Auditor General's Standard Report on the Accounts of the Inland Revenue 2006–07*, NAO. 6 July.

Carter, P. (2001), *Review of Payroll Services*, November, London: Inland Revenue.

—— (2006), *Review of HMRC Online Services*, March, London: HM Revenue and Customs.

Christensen, K., Cline, R., and Neubig, T. (2001), 'Total Corporate Taxation: "Hidden", Above-the-Line, Non-Income Taxes', *National Tax Journal*, **54** September, 495–506.

Cowell, F. (1990), *Cheating the Government: The Economics of Evasion*. Cambridge, Mass.: MIT Press.

Diamond, P., and Mirrlees, J. (1971), 'Optimal Taxation and Public Production. I-Production Efficiency', *American Economic Review*, **61**, 8–27.

Evans, C. (2003a), 'Studying the Studies: An overview of recent research into taxation operating costs', *Journal of Tax Research*, **1**, 64–92.

—— (2003b), *Taxing Personal Capital Gains: Operating Cost Implications*. Australian Tax Research Foundation. Research Study No. 40.

Feld, L., and Frey, B. (2002), 'Trust Breeds Trust: How Taxpayers Are Treated', *Economics of Governance*, **3**, 87–99.

Feldstein, M. (1972), 'Distributional Equity and the Optimal Structure of Public Prices', *American Economic Review*, **62**, 32–6.

Frey, B. (1997), 'A Constitution for Knaves Crowds Out Civic Virtues', *Economic Journal*, **107**, 1043–53.

Green, S. (1996), 'Self-Assessment: A New Era for United Kingdom Taxpayers, But What About the Costs?', *British Tax Review*, **2**, 107–19.

HM Revenue & Customs. (2005), *The Abolition of Payment of Working Tax Credit via Employers: Regulatory Impact Assessment*, August, London: HMRC.

—— (2007), *Measuring Indirect Tax Losses—2007*, London: HMRC October.

—— (2007b), *Departmental Autumn Performance Report 2007*, London: HMRC December.

—— (2007c), *Developing Methodologies for Measuring Direct Tax Loses*, London: HMRC October.

House of Commons Treasury Committee. (2008), 'Administration and expenditure of the Chancellor's departments, 2006–07', Seventh Report of Session 2007–08, HC57, 7 March.

Inland Revenue (1979), *PAYE—Possible Future Developments*. March.

—— (1998), 'The Tax Compliance Costs for Employers of PAYE and National Insurance in 1995–9', *The Centre for Fiscal Studies*, University of Bath.

—— (1999), *Tax Credits Act 1999 and Accompanying Regulations: Regulatory Impact Assessment*. December London: Inland Revenue.

—— (2002a), *Memorandum submitted by the Inland Revenue*. House of Commons Treasury Committee. 6 March London: Inland Revenue.

—— (2002b), *Inland Revenue: Self Assessment Systems*. House of Commons Treasury Committee. 23 July London: Inland Revenue.

—— (2004), *Self Assessment Pilots 2003/4: Technical Report*. IR Research Report. 8, September London: Inland Revenue.

Kaplow, L. (1989), 'Horizontal Equity: Measures in Search of a Principle', *National Tax Journal*, **42**, 139–54.

—— (1995), 'A Fundamental Objection to Tax Equity Norms: A Call for Utilitarianism', *National Tax Journal*, **48**, 497–514.

Klepper, S. and Nagin, D. (1989), 'The Anatomy of Tax Evasion', *Journal of Law, Economics, and Organization*, **5**, 1–24.

KPMG LLP. (2006), *Administrative Burdens: HMRC Measurement Project*. 20 March.

Lessig, L. (1999), *Code and Other Laws of Cyberspace*. New York: Basic Books.

Mayshar, J. and Yitzhaki, S. (1995), 'Dalton-Improving Tax Reform', *American Economic Review*, **85**, 793–807.

Meade, J. (1978), *The Structure and Reform of Direct Taxation: Report of a Committee chaired by Professor J. E. Meade for the Institute for Fiscal Studies*, London: George Allen & Unwin. http//www.ifs.org.uk/publications/3433.

Mirrlees, J. (1971), 'An Exploration in the Theory of Optimum Taxation', *Review of Economic Studies*, **38**, 175–208.

OECD (2007), *Tax Administration in OECD Countries and Selected Non-OECD Countries: Comparative Information Series (2006)*. Centre for Tax Policy and Administration.

PricewaterhouseCoopers LLP and the World Bank (2007), 'Paying Taxes 2008—The Global Picture', November.

Sandford, C. (ed.) (1995), *Tax Compliance Costs: Measurement and Policy*. Bath: Fiscal Publications.

—— Godwin, M., and Hardwick, P. (1989), *Administrative and Compliance Costs of Taxation*. Bath: Fiscal Publications.

Scholz, J. T., and Lubell, M. (1998), 'Trust and Taxpayers: Testing the Heuristic Approach to Collective Action', *American Journal of Political Science*, **42**, 398–417.

Slemrod, J. (2003), 'Trust in Public Finance', in Cnossen, S., and Sinn, H.-W. (eds.), *Public Finance and Public Policy in the New Century*, pp. 49–88. Cambridge, Mass.: MIT Press.

—— (2004), 'The Economics of Corporate Tax Selfishness', *National Tax Journal*, **57**, 877–99.

—— and Yitzhaki, S. (1987), 'The Optimal Size of a Tax Collection Agency', *Scandinavian Journal of Economics*, **89**, 183–92.

—— —— (1996), 'The Cost of Taxation and the Marginal Efficiency Cost of Funds', *International Monetary Fund Staff Papers*, **43**, 172–98.

TLRC (forthcoming), *Tackling Avoidance: A Report by the Tax Law Review Committee on UK Anti-Avoidance Measures 1997 to 2008*.

Torgler, B. (2003), 'Tax Morale, Rule-Governed Behaviour, and Trust', *Constitutional Political Economy*, **14**, 119–40.

Whiting, J. (2002), 'Employment Taxes: Where Are We Going?', *British Tax Review 2002 No 1*, pp. 42–55.

Yitzhaki, S. (1974), 'A Note on "Income Tax Evasion: A Theoretical Analysis"'. *Journal of Public Economics*, **3**, 201–2.

Commentary by John Hasseldine*

John Hasseldine is Professor of Accounting and Taxation and Head of the Accounting and Finance Division at Nottingham University Business School. He is Co-Director of Nottingham University's Taxation Research Institute where his main research areas are tax administration and compliance. Originally a tax inspector in New Zealand, he now works closely with various tax administrations. In 1997 he received his doctorate in accounting from the Kelley School of Business at Indiana University.

1. INTRODUCTION

The Shaw, Slemrod, and Whiting chapter is an important milestone in the tax administration and compliance literature. A major contribution of the chapter's authors is the framework they have applied to the wide topic of tax system design and implementation. Through their detailed discussion of an extensive literature, a review is provided on important issues such as revenue raising, equity, privacy, taxpayer rights, and the concept of transparency. To these issues, they add the enforcement systems required to 'manage' non-compliance and the costs of these enforcement systems—to both the tax agency and taxpayers themselves. The authors are to be complimented on the rigour with which they buttress their discussion and their outline of an optimal approach to resource allocation.

The authors make a number of interesting remarks, which may not be entirely novel but certainly need to be stated. First, the difficulties imposed by the hard-to-tax sector (e.g. eBay) and challenges imposed by globalization must be addressed. Second, the authors note the importance of modernization of IT systems which in turn, partly dictates the efficiency of tax regimes such as PAYE and VAT. Then, owing to increasing complexity, the authors

* The helpful comments of Peggy Hite and Kevin Holland on an earlier version of this commentary are gratefully acknowledged.

suggest there is a need for strategic thinking on PAYE/NICs. Radical options such as universal tax returns must be considered because the risk that demographic and economic change will have an adverse impact on the system is increasing.

This commentary briefly discusses two further implementation issues that should be considered by any tax administration in the twenty-first century. The first analyses the current environmental context of tax administration and highlights the necessity for consideration to be given to the nature and implementation of monitoring of tax agencies and the level and nature of their public performance reporting. The second issue is a discussion of the importance of considering the internal management of tax agencies and how they might learn from each other through benchmarking efforts and surveys of best practice.

The chapter's authors observe that business plays a key role in the UK tax system. They calculate (Table 12.1) that 88% of UK tax revenue is remitted by business. This is a huge proportion and clearly emphasizes the importance of maintaining good relationships with advisors and businesses to facilitate compliance (HMRC (2006)). Further discussion of this point and the importance of a consultative approach appears in Section 2 of this commentary. The commentary then offers some brief concluding remarks.

2. CONSIDERING THE STAKEHOLDERS OF TAX ADMINISTRATIONS

2.1. The current environmental context of tax administration

The environment facing tax agencies has changed considerably in recent times (Tomkins et al. (2001)) with issues such as tax shelters, large-scale fraud, tax code complexity, customer service, e-commerce, and globalization requiring consideration and response. These issues affect not only taxpayers and the tax agency itself, but also other stakeholders such as tax practitioners, those involved in processes of tax policy and tax disputes—thus including industry associations, professional organizations, and ultimately every citizen. In addition, one can speculate that the actual process of tax policy formulation has become more politicized in recent years with the establishment of tax-focused pressure groups and more vocal employer representative groups.

The overriding question is how do environmental characteristics impact on tax compliance, and the behaviour of taxpayers, tax practitioners, and tax administrators? From a compliance view, traditional audits consume agency resources, because compliance enforcement measures and performance indicators need careful specification and monitoring (at aggregate, sector, and individual levels). Of course, these issues are not unique to the UK (Weisbach and Plesko (2007)) and other countries face similar pressures and uncertainty.

One well-publicized example is the strategic focus on responsive regulation adopted in Australia where the introduction of the Australian Tax Office's (ATO) Compliance Model (Braithwaite (2003; 2007)) has led to a culture shift, and arguably, can now be viewed as 'best practice'. Essentially the compliance model is a pyramid that conceptually represents taxpayers' motivational postures ranging from Commitment (at the base) through Capitulation, Resistance, and Disengagement (at the peak). Thus appropriate strategies for tax agencies include non-discretionary Command Regulation (at the peak), discretionary Command Regulation, enforced Self-Regulation to Self-Regulation (at the base, which is the desired state). Thus, the model is consistent with the customary goal of voluntary compliance, and at the base, tax agencies can focus on enabling efforts such as education and service delivery. At middle levels, strategies can include business examinations and record keeping reviews, then moving to the top levels there are audits (with/without penalty) and finally prosecution (Hasseldine and Hite (2007); Hasseldine et al. (2007)).

In the UK, following the merger of Customs and Excise with Inland Revenue, different working practices, powers, and penalties have meant an agenda of modernization of these areas. With the (stated) adoption of broad principles of legitimacy and mutual respect into the compliance environment (Feld and Frey (2007); Picciotto (2007)), a consultative approach has been adopted in the UK (e.g. see the work of the Powers committee at <http://www.hmrc.gov.uk/about/powers-appeal.htm>). Hence, consultative committees have become the rule, rather than the exception and this now applies to both the setting of policy and the provision of guidance to 'customers'—especially businesses and their advisers. A further principle is to minimize taxpayer burden, and so the application of risk management techniques in audit selection is being refined especially for large business (NAO (2007)). There is international evidence that tax administrations (e.g. HMRC (2007)) are seeking to understand firms' behaviour rather than simply focusing on technical aspects of the tax code.

2.2. Public performance reporting and the use of monitoring agencies

Many tax agencies have, for a variety of reasons, become more transparent in their public performance reporting and/or in the amount of oversight that they are subject to, for example, by internal or external bodies with an audit or accountability role. For example, in the US, there is a taxpayer advocate function within the IRS, as well as the Treasury Inspector General of Tax Administration. In addition the IRS Oversight Board was created as part of the 1998 IRS reforms designed to allow IRS to better serve the public and meet the needs of taxpayers. The IRSOB is a nine-member independent body charged to oversee the IRS in its administration, management, conduct, direction, and supervision of the execution and application of the internal revenue laws and to provide experience, independence, and stability to the IRS so that it may move forward in a cogent, focused direction (<http://www.treas.gov/irsob/>). Of course, there also remains an issue of oversight at the point of enactment of tax legislation (e.g. by US Congress or UK Parliament)—as estimated revenue gains/losses can be very imprecise with 'revenue neutral' policy and the resulting legislation complex.

Australia established a Board of Taxation in 2000 to advise the government on the formulation and development of tax policy. Several reviews have been undertaken and its work programme currently includes a scoping study on small business compliance costs and a review of the application of consistent self-assessment principles (<http://www.taxboard.gov.au>). Further, in 2003, an Office of the Inspector General of Taxation was established as an independent statutory office to review systematic tax administration issues and to report to government, in the interests of taxpayers, on recommendations that would improve the fairness, efficiency, and integrity of the tax system (McKerchar (2007)).

A further example in the spirit of responsive regulation of transparent public performance reporting, both generally (such as agency business plans), and in detail, is Canada. The Canada Revenue Agency publishes its internal audit reports on the Internet and discloses to stakeholders its public opinion research where executive summaries are published on the website and full reports are available on request.

The examples given in this section are in addition to any role played through a public sector audit function such as the Government Accountability Office in the US and the National Audit Office in the UK. Given the increasingly political nature of tax policy, and the frequent accusations of selectivity when tax-related statistics are used (e.g. by political parties), one possibility is the establishment of an independent body responsible for commissioning the collection and publication of certain tax statistics although overlap issues with the Office for National Statistics would need resolving.

In summary, just as large companies increasingly consider tax issues as part of corporate governance (KPMG (2004); PwC (2004); Ernst and Young (2006)), so too must tax administrations consider governance and reporting issues. One of the key reasons for this is if there is to be mutual trust and co-operation on the part of taxpayer, tax agent, and tax official, then tax administrations must act and report in a transparent manner. It is not a one-way street.

3. MANAGING TAX AGENCIES AND THE NOTION OF 'BEST PRACTICE'

3.1. Internal management of tax agencies

Gill's (2003) World Bank study sets out a useful framework for the main tasks of revenue administration requiring analysis. These tasks can be classified as: (1) operational areas; including: taxpayer registration; processing of customer information; monitoring of withholders/agents; information collection about taxable transactions—and audit/investigation work; risk analysis; recovery of tax arrears and debt management; legal and judicial matters; external relations and customer focus; and (2) organization and management tasks including: strategy; planning; monitoring; personnel management; IT systems management; internal control and asset management. Far less attention has been devoted in the academic literature to the latter broad category, although this is likely to be of concern to review agencies and oversight boards (such as the Public Accounts Committee in the UK).

As part of an edited volume on the 'crisis' in tax administration, Owens and Hamilton (2004) discuss, provide support for, and observe that:

- just simplifying the law does not work;
- policy simplification needs a stronger voice;
- the complexity of policy and law may need to be reduced;
- small business needs special consideration;
- new compliance approaches are needed;
- a new compact is needed;
- tax administrations are underfunded.

Recognizing the above is obviously a useful first step, but clearly these issues interact and the magnitude of the issues facing tax administrators is clearly huge. That having been said, progress is being made and the next section illustrates some of these efforts.

3.2. The notion of 'best practice' in tax administration

Until the Centre of Tax Policy and Administration of the OECD began serious work on the 'administration' side there was very little sharing of 'best practice' although there have been several surveys of administrative practices. For example, the OECD (2005b) Forum on Tax Administration (FTA) allows tax administrators to share information and experience, and identify effective strategies/measures for various areas of tax administration, for example, the 'Comparative Information Series' (OECD (2007a)). This report provides internationally comparative data on various aspects of tax systems and their administration in OECD and selected non-OECD countries in terms of international and organizational arrangements for tax administration; aspects of management approaches and practices; return filing, payment, and assessment regimes for the major taxes; selected administrative powers of revenue bodies; tax revenue collections; operational performance information; administrative practice.

Other reports to date include topics such as: compliance risk management (OECD (2004)); strengthening tax audit capabilities (OECD (2006a; 2006b; 2006c)); surveying trends in taxpayer service delivery using new technologies (OECD (2005a)); the use of pre-populated tax returns (OECD (2006d)); and a study on tax intermediaries (OECD (2008)).

In the future, more in-depth benchmarking and documentation of best practices seems highly likely and the European Organisation of Supreme Audit Institutions (EUROSAI) has already begun to collate and categorize the main indicators that tax administrations use to evaluate their performance. Such work will need to identify how to create new and better practices and will require collaboration between international and regional tax organizations and a willingness to share initiatives and results.

4. CONCLUDING REMARKS

Modern tax administrations are large, complex organizations and there is still only a relatively small scholarly literature in the field of tax administration per se. There are many knowledge gaps that tax agencies must seek to understand. For example, why do taxpayers comply? Why don't they comply? Why do simplified tax regimes often suffer from poor take-up rates? How can compliance costs be minimized?

In summary, there are a number of fundamental characteristics that are likely to be associated with leading tax administrations of the twenty-first century. These are:

- a professional approach to internal management issues (HR; strategic planning);
- attention to cost efficiency and effectiveness;
- responsive engagement with all stakeholders;
- successful introduction of technology applications;
- understanding what drives taxpayer and tax agent behaviour;
- sophisticated risk profiling and informed responses to taxpayer behaviour, including the areas of enforcement and service provision;
- transparency of governance and detailed performance reporting.

Attention to these, however, is not a panacea, and whatever the end-goal is, it will always be difficult for tax administrations to demonstrate to all stakeholders that they are doing well. Perhaps we should consider whether they are doing well enough and examine whether the glass is half-full or half-empty (McCaffery and Baron (2006))! Certainly, the Shaw, Slemrod, and Whiting chapter clearly spells out the lessons to be learned and areas where progress can be made, not only by HMRC in the UK, but by tax administrations worldwide.

REFERENCES

Braithwaite, V. (2003), *Taxing Democracy: Understanding Tax Avoidance and Evasion*, Aldershot: Ashgate.

—— (2007), 'Responsive Regulation and Taxation: Introduction', *Law and Policy*, **29**, 3–10.

Ernst & Young (2006), *Tax risk: External Change, Internal Challenge*, London: Ernst & Young.

Feld, L., and Frey, B. (2007), 'Tax Compliance as the Result of a Psychological Contract: The Role of Incentives and Responsive Regulation', *Law and Policy*, **29**, 102–20.

Gill, J. (2003), *The Nuts and Bolts of Revenue Administration Reform*. Washington DC: World Bank.

Hasseldine, J., and Hite, P. (2007), 'Key Determinants of Compliance and Non-compliance', *Tax Notes*, **22**, October, 379–88.

—— —— James, S., and Toumi, M. (2007), 'Persuasive Communications: Tax Compliance Enforcement Strategies for Sole Proprietors', *Contemporary Accounting Research*, **24**, 171–94.

HMRC (2006), *2006 Review of Links with Large Business* (Varney Review), London: HMRC.

—— (2007), *Large Groups' Tax Departments: Factors that Influence Tax Management*, London: HMRC.

KPMG (2004), *Tax in the Boardroom*, London: KPMG International.

McCaffery, E., and Baron, I. (2006), 'Thinking about Tax', *Psychology, Public Policy, and Law*, **12**, 106–35.

McKerchar, M. (2007), 'Tax Complexity and its Impact on Tax Compliance and Tax Administration in Australia', paper presented at IRS Research Conference <http://www.irs.gov/pub/irs-soi/07resconfmckerchar.pdf>.

National Audit Office (2007), *HM Revenue and Customs: Management of Large Business Corporation Tax*, London: NAO.

OECD (2004), *Compliance Risk Management: Managing and Improving Tax Compliance*, Paris: OECD <http://www.oecd.org/dataoecd/44119/33818656.pdf>.

—— (2005a), *Survey of Trends in Taxpayer Service Delivery using new Technologies*, Paris: OECD <http://www.oecd.org/dataoecd/56/41/34904237.pdf>.

—— (2005b), *Products of the Forum on Tax Administration*, Paris: OECD <http://www.oecd.org/dataoecd/54/45/34898052.doc>.

—— (2006a), *Strengthening Tax Audit Capabilities: General Principles and Approaches*, Paris: OECD <http://www.oecd.org/dataoecd/46/18/37589900.pdf>.

—— (2006b), *Strengthening Tax Audit Capabilities: Innovative Approaches to Improve the Efficiency and Effectiveness of Indirect Income Measurement Methods*, Paris: OECD <http://www.oecd.org/dataoecd/46/16/37590009.pdf>.

—— (2006c), *Strengthening Tax Audit Capabilities: Auditor Workforce Management—Survey Findings and Observations*, Paris: OECD <http://www.oecd.org/dataoecd/46/17/37589929.pdf>.

—— (2006d), *Using Third Party Information Reports to Assist Taxpayers meet their Return Filing Obligations: Country Experiences with the use of Pre-populated Personal Tax Returns*, Paris: OECD <http://www.oecd.org/dataoecd/42/14/36280368.pdf>.

—— (2007a), *Tax Administration in OECD and Selected Non-OECD Countries: Comparative Information Series*, Paris: OECD <http://www.oecd.org/dataoecd/37/56/38093382.pdf>.

—— (2008), *Study into the Role of Tax Intermediaries*, Paris: OECD.

Owens, J., and Hamilton, S. (2004), 'Experience and Innovations in other Countries', In Aaron, H., and Slemrod, J. (eds.), *Crisis in Tax Administration*, Washington DC: Brookings Institution Press, 347–79.

Picciotto, S. (2007), 'Constructing compliance: Game playing, tax law, and the regulatory state', *Law and Policy*, **29**, 11–30.

PricewaterhouseCoopers (2004), *Tax risk management*, London: PwC.

Tomkins, C., Packman, C., Russell, S., and Colville, I. (2001), 'Managing tax regimes: A call for research', *Public Administration*, **79**, 751–8.

Weisbach, D., and Plesko, G. (2007), 'A legal perspective on unanswered questions in tax research', *Journal of the American Taxation Association*, **29**, 107–13.

Commentary by Richard Highfield*

Richard Highfield is a Senior Advisor on tax administration matters at the OECD's Centre for Tax Policy and Administration. He is the initiator and author of many OECD papers on tax administration, including its Comparative Information Series on selected aspects of tax administration, that are intended to promote good practices in domestic tax administration. He moved to the OECD from the IMF, and before that worked for twenty-eight years in the Australian Taxation Office. His extensive practical work (covering over fifty countries) in strategic and operational tax administration matters provides him with a unique level of experience in national tax system administration.

INTRODUCTION

At the present time, the UK tax system is undergoing an unprecedented level of administrative reform aimed at achieving substantial improvements in overall efficiency and effectiveness. While it is by no means unusual for revenue bodies to be subject to major reform activity, a distinguishing feature of the UK situation is the existence of a comprehensive range of mandated outcome-oriented targets—all time-bound and expressed in quantified terms—for improvements to taxpayers' compliance, service delivery, and overall efficiency, and reduced administrative burdens on business. It is difficult to identify another revenue body in an advanced economy with a more daunting array of challenges!

Given these imperatives, the subject of the Shaw, Slemrod, and Whiting chapter and its timing assume a high degree of topicality and provide an ideal opportunity to explore the directions and rationale for the reform of tax implementation in the UK in a way that may inform a wide variety of interested observers.

* The comments made are provided in a private capacity and are based on a version of the chapter reviewed in August 2007.

Structure of the chapter

The chapter is structured in three parts. In Part I, the authors provide a description of the principles of optimal tax system design and implementation aspects. Part II discusses substantive issues in a UK context, with a focus on PAYE and income tax self-assessment and HMRC's administration. Part III provides a set of conclusions and recommendations.

I. TAX SYSTEMS AND IMPLEMENTATION

This part constitutes a major portion of the chapter and provides a good foundation for the main subject of the chapter. There are a few comments to be made.

At the end of Part I the authors suggest a number of general rules regarding tax system implementation that should be considered in an evaluation of the UK system. From this commentator's perspective, the rules suggested all sound quite reasonable. However, one can readily identify other important 'rules' or 'guiding principles' of an implementation nature. For example: (1) optimize the use of withholding taxes at source; (2) require the payment of tax as close as possible to the timing of the taxing event, while allowing for compliance cost considerations; and (3) arrange tax administration operations organizationally in a way that helps to minimize both administrative and compliance costs. As explained later, this commentator is of the view that the UK does (1) well, lags well behind international best practice on (2), and has recently taken important steps to address (3).

A theme permeating through much of the chapter is that policy developers and tax administrators should possess and use precise information on the *marginal administrative and compliance costs* of the various taxes administered to inform and guide policy decision-making. This would be great if it were readily achievable in practice but based on this commentator's experience it is invariably not the case, for the following reasons:

- Increasingly, revenue bodies are being organized on a 'functional' and/or 'taxpayer segment' basis, thus making it quite a complex exercise for them accurately to attribute aggregate administrative costs to each of the taxes administered. A further complicating factor is the rapidity of developments in the use of technology, which can quickly change the cost structure and aggregate costs—both administrative and compliance costs—of an individual tax. Very few revenue bodies attempt such cost attribution exercises across the range of taxes they administer and even fewer have reliable data that they are prepared to publish. The UK's HMRC is one of the few revenue bodies that quantifies administrative cost data for each of its taxes and publishes the results.

- Concerning compliance costs, here also there is a dearth of comprehensive and reliable information and to this day there remains some contention, particularly in academic circles, as to what in fact constitutes a 'tax compliance cost'. In their chapter, the authors note that HMRC's recent measurement work in this area focuses on the administrative burden resulting from tax regulations, a subset of what they consider constitute overall tax compliance costs.

There is also the political dimension to tax policy decision-making that is not acknowledged by the authors. At the end of the day, tax policy changes are decided by government and influenced to a fair degree by its programmes and political ideology. Regrettably, such decisions are sometimes made that give little or no regard to, or even fly in the face of, administrative or compliance cost considerations of the kind rightly emphasized by the authors. This factor, coupled with use of tax systems for a plethora of objectives unrelated to their primary revenue raising role, in part explain why tax systems in advanced economies have become so complex (read 'costly to administer'). While it is true that some advanced economies have introduced procedures requiring mandatory cost–benefit analyses to accompany new legislation, these very often must rely on, for the reasons indicated, 'guesstimates' and broad judgements. A further weakness, as noted by the authors, is that these analyses typically exclude the impacts of legislation on individuals who in many countries bear a fair proportion of the compliance burden.

II. ADMINISTRATION AND ENFORCEMENT ISSUES IN THE UK TAX SYSTEM

Taking a broad sweep tax system implementation in the UK in 2007 and comparing it with the position, say, in the mid-1990s, one can identify many positive developments. For example:

- The outmoded separate organization and administration of direct and indirect taxes has been dispensed with; in its place, a new revenue body has been established to deliver the many benefits that integrated and more client-oriented processes and approaches to tax administration can bring.

- Administration of NICs has been integrated with tax system administration to achieve increased efficiencies, a practice increasingly being adopted by many other countries.
- In line with international best practice, a separate Large Business Office has been established to deliver a range of tailored services for the largest UK taxpayers who are responsible for collecting the vast bulk of tax revenue.
- There is a strong administrative focus on improving compliance with tax laws (and, as a result, government revenues) using modern risk management techniques. Estimates of the size and composition of the tax gap have been made for the major taxes using a variety of approaches (although not all of this has been published), targets have been set for compliance improvement, and a range of strategies implemented to address key areas of risk. In line with the trend and impacts of globalization, the international dimension of taxpayers' affairs is, from all accounts, receiving special attention.
- Administrative costs have been reduced substantially—in 'cost of collection' terms, from around £1.70 (1995–96) to £1.13 per £100 collected (2006–07)[1]—and appear to be on a further downwards trend with further efficiencies projected up to 2011.
- Compliance costs—in the current EU jargon, 'administrative burdens'—are acknowledged as a key concern by both the government and the HMRC and are receiving special attention. Measurement exercises have recently been conducted to understand better the size and nature of the administrative burden of the major taxes, targets have been set for burden reduction, and a suite of measures has been identified to address burden concerns.[2]
- Progress has been made, particularly over the last 2–3 years, in the take-up of modern electronic services by taxpayers and their agents.

[1] This improved ratio results, in part, from the inclusion of new revenue lines (i.e. NICs and VAT) in the 'cost of collection' computation, as revenue collection operations have been further integrated. Notably, cost of collection ratios for income tax and NICs show improvements of over 20% since year 2000.

[2] See *Progress Towards a new Relationship: How HMRC is Working to Make Life Easier for Business* published alongside Budget 2006.

- A comprehensive review is well advanced to modernize HMRC's enforcement powers, deterrents, and safeguards and relevant legislation is currently being considered.

The conclusion that one draws from these observations is that tax system implementation in the UK is receiving considerable attention. However, these positive developments should not hide the fact that some critically important issues remain to be addressed. These issues (and a few others) and the ideas raised by the authors are discussed in the following paragraphs, starting with some comments concerning HMRC's administration of the tax system, moving then to consider the PAYE system on which the authors have principally focused, before looking briefly at some issues raised of other taxes, namely NI contributions (NICs), corporation tax, and value added tax.

HMRC

Section 12.6 of the chapter raises a number of issues and expresses a number of viewpoints on HMRC's administration of the tax system. A few comments are called for.

The organization of tax administration

The authors note the recent merger of the two predecessor revenue bodies into a single revenue and customs agency (HMRC) and the efficiency-related rationale for this reform. There are two aspects worthy of comment.

The merger of the two tax bodies was indeed long overdue and there was a strong case on efficiency grounds for the amalgamation, as acknowledged by the authors. An additional potential benefit from the merger, as highlighted by the O'Donnell Review that led to the government's decision, was that it would allow for substantial re-engineering of the way tax administration is conducted, thereby enabling substantial improvements in overall organizational effectiveness and taxpayers' satisfaction with the standard of administration.

A second issue concerns the inclusion of the customs portfolio within HMRC's responsibilities. The administration of customs laws raises many issues unrelated to mainstream tax collection and in these times of heightened risks from terrorism, illegal immigration, and drug trafficking one can well argue that there is a strong case, in a country with 60 million citizens, for a separate dedicated agency for customs administration. One can equally argue that administration of the tax laws (and the other non-tax roles that

HMRC has been given), with an organization of around 60,000–70,000 staff, is more than enough for a single government agency. While a few other OECD countries administer both tax and customs from within a single organization, the vast majority of countries do not and there is certainly no trend in this direction.[3]

Performance indicators

The authors note the setting of compliance improvement targets for VAT—expressed in terms of achieving a reduction in the estimated tax gap, so as to achieve a gap figure of no more than 11%—and direct taxes and NICs—expressed in terms of additional revenue (some £3.5 billion). On this matter, they question what appears to them as a lack of transparency concerning the reasoning behind these objectives and pose the question whether compliance cost-reducing initiatives reflect the same trade-offs as the enforcement-increasing policies. It is also possible that performance indicators and targets based solely on additional yield might prompt areas of the HMRC to concentrate on enquiries of taxpayers' affairs with firmer prospects of immediate payback at the expense of preventative work which might lead to more significant yield in the longer term.

These viewpoints justify a range of comments, in part drawing on this commentator's working experience with HMRC officials:

- There is a strong case to argue that one of the major goals of a revenue body is to achieve improved overall compliance with tax laws, noting that increased revenues flow from improved compliance in an overall sense. Objectives expressed in terms of increased compliance (even if in revenue terms) are a logical consequence of this primary goal and specific targets would seem to be appropriate as a means of gauging overall progress.
- The targets set are, in many respects, aspirational in nature and form part of a broader set of objectives used by HMRC to gauge progress in achieving improved performance.
- Progress towards the targets is to be made in each of years up to the target year, and is the expected outcome from the full range of HMRC's service,

[3] In line with the views expressed, it was announced on 14 November 2007 that the government had decided to create a new Home Office agency, the UK Border Agency. The new agency will report to both the Chancellor of the Exchequer, on fiscal issues, and the Home Secretary and will combine most of HMRC's Detection Directorate and some of those who support them along with UK Visas and the Border and Immigration Agency. Policy on customs and tax matters and associated processing will remain within HMRC. The UK Border Agency is expected to have around 25,000 staff in total and it will begin to operate on an interim basis from January 2008 while the necessary legislation is put in place (as per HMRC's *Departmental Autumn Performance Report 2007*).

education, and enforcement activities across all segments of taxpayers, not just from inquiries/audits, as implied by the authors. HMRC does not break down the overall targets and attribute them to individual functional areas within its operations and, in this sense, it appears unlikely that the targets per se would lead to the sort of behaviour suggested by the authors. HMRC has been extremely transparent in its work on VAT gap measurement, considerably more so than revenue bodies in other advanced economies, and it provides a report of its ongoing work each December with the government's pre-Budget papers. If one looks at HMRC's most recent report the improvement in compliance required to achieve a VAT gap target of 11% is around £3.0 billion, which is more or less in line with the target for improved compliance of direct taxes and NI contributions (i.e. £3.5 billion). In this sense, there appears to be some consistency from HMRC in the respective targets, although clearly each area of risk will be subject to its own set of strategies.

- HMRC is largely a 'trailblazer' among national revenue bodies with mandated targets of this nature; perhaps some time should be allowed to see if the approach has any validity as a performance enhancing tool for revenue bodies before conclusive judgements are made.
- The authors are most probably correct in questioning whether the same trade-offs have been made concerning compliance cost-reducing initiatives. In fact, it is more than likely that the targets were set quite independently, by different officials and at different points in time, of the process for setting compliance improvement targets.

Measuring compliance costs

The authors note the considerable work carried out by HMRC (with KPMG's assistance) to get a better handle on the incidence and nature of the administrative burden on business resulting from the tax system, and the setting of targets aimed at achieving burden reductions. However, they express concerns that little attention has been given to individuals/citizens in any of the measurement work and a related concern that, as a result of this omission, the opportunity might be taken to transfer some of the costs of business onto individuals as part of the burden reduction programme. Another issue stems from the fact that the burden measurement work undertaken using the Standard Cost Methodology (SCM) may not be statistically representative and therefore questions arise in relation to its accuracy and usefulness. A few comments are called for.

The authors are correct in their conclusion that the focus of the recent burden measurement work has been on business and not individuals. However, given that the measurement work did cover some 3 million unincorporated/self-employed individuals who pay income tax, it can be said that a portion of the individuals' population is covered. This does, of course, leave some 7 million other taxpayers (e.g. employees and investors) who file tax returns and pay taxes and as a result incur an administrative burden.

Concerning the possibility that measures taken to address business's administrative burden may result in some cost transfer to individuals, this does appear to be unfounded. In parallel with the conduct of the measurement studies, HMRC (and the Treasury) undertook a detailed study of measures that might be taken to reduce administrative burdens and achieve the targets set. The results of this study were published alongside Budget 2006.[4] A reading of the study indicates that the measures planned to reduce business's administrative burden should have no impact on citizens.

In relation to the use of the SCM, the published reports do acknowledge that because of the underlying methodological approach the aggregate costs are likely to be 'understated'. That said, the measurement of administrative burdens/compliance costs, regardless of the methodologies used, is generally always associated with various assumptions and elements of guesswork that give rise to some degree of inaccuracy or doubt. The quantification of burdens/costs resulting from tax regulations is by no means a precise science.

On the other hand, application of the SCM does have the clear advantage of providing detailed and precise information on the specific information obligations pertaining to each tax and, as a result, facilitates the identification of the most burdensome areas of regulation. Furthermore, there is currently considerable interest in, and use of, the methodology across Europe, potentially leading to some opportunities for cross-country benchmarking. In February 2007, the EU's ECOFIN Council mandated use of a modified SCM methodology as part of an EU-wide burden reduction effort to achieve savings of 25% by 2012.

The future of PAYE

Section 12.7 of the chapter describes the operation of the PAYE systems and the self-assessment regime applicable to those required to file annual

[4] See *Progress Towards a new Relationship: How HMRC is Working to Make Life Easier for Business.*

tax returns. It concludes with views on policy options to address perceived weaknesses in the PAYE and interest withholding arrangements.

As noted by the authors, substantial reliance is placed on the personal income tax and NI contributions for government revenue purposes.[5] In 2006–07, revenue from these taxes represented a little over 50% of the total receipts collected by the HMRC (or around 45% of all government tax revenue). Central to the efficient and effective collection of both PIT and NICs are the separate withholding arrangements administered by employers and financial institutions in respect of employment and interest income respectively. Applying the authors' data, these withholding mechanisms were responsible for almost 89% of all personal income tax and NICs collected in 2006–07.[6] This high degree of reliance on withholding no doubt contributes to achieving high levels of compliance and is to be applauded. On the other hand, such a heavy reliance on the private sector as 'tax collectors' heightens the need for withholding arrangements that impose the minimum of costs and disruption on business, while at the same time protecting the Revenue.

The UK system of PAYE has long been lauded worldwide for its ability to free the majority of employee taxpayers from the obligation to file an end-year tax return, as is the case in some other advanced economies. This is largely achieved through the operation of the *cumulative* withholding feature of the PAYE arrangements that requires employers to calculate and withhold taxes for each employee on a progressive (i.e. cumulative) basis throughout the year, taking account of all their employment income. In conjunction with a system of withholding tax at the basic rate from interest payments these arrangements enable around two-thirds of all personal taxpayers to be freed from the obligation to file an end-year tax return.

The UK approach to personal tax administration (i.e. complex PAYE withholding arrangements but return-free for most employees) stands in contrast to the practice seen in other Anglo-Saxon economies (e.g. Australia, Canada, and the US) and in some European countries. There, simpler PAYE withholding arrangements (generally involving a *non-cumulative* form of withholding) are used, but all employees are generally required to file an end-year tax return. Tax returns enable the revenue body to view information relevant to determining a taxpayer's full year tax liability and to calculate

[5] The OECD considers NICs as akin to personal income tax and, for comparative purposes, as a 'tax'.

[6] As shown in Table 12.1 of the chapter, employers withheld £124.8 billion PAYE and £84.5 billion NICs. Financial institutions withheld £4.9 billion tax in respect of payments of interest. Netting off £9.5 billion repayments attributed to business gives a total of £204.7 billion, 88.8% of the total of £230.6 billion personal income tax and NICs.

whether any taxes are due after all types of advance payments. As employees typically represent a large proportion of the personal taxpayer population, this universal requirement to file an end-year tax return results in a significant compliance burden. Not surprisingly, proponents of tax reform in many of these countries regularly call for a simpler approach, ideally that involves getting rid of tax returns for most employees.

At first glance, the return-free feature of the UK system appears highly attractive given that it avoids the compliance costs associated with end-year tax returns and the administrative costs of processing them. However, as highlighted by the authors, the PAYE arrangements are becoming increasingly difficult (read 'costly') to administer properly for both employers and HMRC and lack the flexibility needed to accommodate effectively some government policy demands. In support of their concerns, the authors note the following points:

- *Inaccuracy*: Reports from the National Audit Office (NAO) note that about 30% of cases require an end-of-year adjustment due to errors in coding and the way PAYE is operated, and roughly 0.8 million taxpayers may end having paid the wrong amount of tax.
- *Lack of flexibility*: There is an inability to easily accommodate new entitlements for taxpayers or new government policy measures, as evidenced by experience with the system of tax credits introduced in 1999. The authors note that initial attempts to pay tax credits via employers failed and new arrangements entailing the direct crediting of tax credits by HMRC to taxpayers' bank accounts were introduced in 2006. Somewhat perversely, these new procedures require claimants to file something akin to a tax return to support their claim.

A further difficulty raised concerns the operation of the flat rate withholding system on interest income, which for some taxpayers results in too much tax being withheld (and the need for repayment arrangements), while for others (i.e. above basic rate taxpayers) too little is withheld.

Against this background, the authors express doubts (as does this commentator) as to whether the existing arrangements, taken in their entirety, represent a more effective and efficient means of administering the personal tax for employees than arrangements of the kind seen in other countries. An additional consideration is that there have been developments in a number of countries entailing the use of pre-filled tax returns that offer a highly effective way to minimize the compliance costs associated with preparing end-year tax returns (see later comments).

Policy options for withholding

To address the issues identified, the authors canvass a set of policy changes to the PAYE and interest withholding arrangements. On the surface, their ideas have both pros and cons and each would need careful appraisal. One reservation, in this commentator's view, is that adoption of a number of the suggestions (e.g. monthly reporting by employers) would increase the compliance burden on business at a time when priority is being given to burden reduction. However, the authors have an alternative suggestion for the longer term to address the issues raised that is discussed in the next part of this commentary.

Long-term reform options

To address the many 'rough edges' and limitations of the current withholding mechanisms, and to simplify their administration, the authors raise the possibility of adopting a system of universal self-assessment, ideally supported by a system of pre-filled tax returns. The rationale for this idea is as follows:

1. A move to universal self-assessment would provide a simpler, less costly and more accurate means of establishing each taxpayer's proper end-of-year tax liability and its reconciliation with taxes withheld at source, as well as providing information to validate taxpayers' entitlements to tax credits.
2. To avoid the significant additional compliance costs that a system of universal self-assessment arrangements would otherwise impose, the introduction of a system of pre-filled tax returns, along the lines seen in a growing number of other countries, is suggested as an accompanying feature.

At first glance, this may appear a little unrealistic, given both the magnitude of the changes their adoption would entail and perhaps a general lack of awareness of the concept of pre-filled tax returns. However, this commentator believes that the suggestion has considerable merit and a strong underlying rationale, as explained in the comments that follow, and warrants detailed study.

Around fifteen of the thirty OECD countries generally require all personal taxpayers to file an end-year tax return. In most of these countries, this obligation results in a significant compliance burden for employee taxpayers, given the relatively large number involved and the tendency for complex tax systems. In the late 1980s, taking advantage of newly emerging technology and a strong desire to ease the compliance burden of personal taxpayers, Danish tax authorities piloted the first version of what is now known as a 'pre-filled tax return'. The system has undergone ongoing refinement since the initial version.

As the name implies, a pre-filled tax return is one prepared in the first instance *by the revenue body for the taxpayer*. Under these arrangements, information reports (e.g. covering wages, fringe benefits, interest, dividends, pensions, sales of assets, taxes withheld and certain deduction items such as child care, mortgage interest, and pension contributions) that must be reported on electronic media and contain a unique taxpayer identifier are captured and validated by the revenue body. This large information processing activity enables the revenue body to generate a (pre-filled) tax return that sets out amounts and sources of known income and deductions and the like, and provides a preliminary calculation of tax liability/refunds and so on. These returns are sent to taxpayers for vetting around 5–10 weeks after the end of the relevant fiscal year, either via the Internet and/or on paper, with taxpayers being normally required to indicate either that the return is complete or to provide further information. In a few countries, taxpayers need not respond if the return is correct. Once taxpayers' responses have been processed by the revenue body, formal notices and refunds, where applicable, are sent to taxpayers.

Compiling and presenting information in the form of a pre-filled tax return removes the need for many taxpayers to undertake the task manually, thus significantly reducing the burden that they would otherwise face to comply with the law. In countries where these systems are well established and based on a comprehensive array of third party reports, substantial benefits are being derived. For example, the Danish revenue body reported that for fiscal year 2006 around 70% of all personal taxpayers received a pre-filled return that was complete in all respects, thereby significantly reducing their compliance burden. Other taxpayers were assisted, but to a lesser degree.

Today, the use of pre-filled returns is well entrenched and operating very effectively in all Nordic region countries. In recent years, similar (but not as sophisticated) pre-filled return systems have been adopted by revenue bodies in Chile, Portugal, Spain, and France. The Australian Taxation Office has operated a limited form of pre-filling as part of its electronic return filing system for a number of years and plans to expand it significantly into a 'full production system' from July 2008. The Dutch revenue body plans to introduce pre-filled personal tax returns for the 2008 fiscal year.

Given the experience in the countries mentioned, and in light of what appears to be an emerging trend in personal tax administration, it is quite conceivable to this commentator that adoption of the authors' suggestions is both realistic and, potentially, the most effective overall solution to address the problems being experienced. However, this solution is one for the longer term. Implementing a system of universal self-assessment incorporating a system of pre-filled tax returns is a substantial undertaking that would take many years to implement fully. In addition to the planning needed, there are three prerequisite features that must be in place to enable such arrangements to operate effectively: (1) an extensive system of third party reporting to the revenue body; (2) the use of a unique high integrity taxpayer identifier by third parties so that reports can be readily and accurately matched with tax records; and (3) optimal use of technology by reporting bodies and the revenue body enabling rapid transmission, capture, and processing of information reports.

National Insurance Contributions (NICs)

The authors note that substantial reform of the NICs has eroded the link between NICs paid and social security benefits received to the point where it appears worth considering whether the case for separate NICs any longer exists. NICs are, after all, analogous to the personal income tax so it might well be asked whether there is a need for two personal income taxes. A related concern is that despite their convergence over time, in practice a number of differences exist between PAYE and NICs that unnecessarily complicate compliance (read 'add costs') for employers who collect the vast majority of NICs. For example, the definition of 'pay' differs for PAYE and NICs purposes, while PAYE operates on a cumulative basis but a different approach applies for NICs. They indicate that because of these sorts of complications businesses are regularly calling for reform as a matter of high priority.

Across the OECD, twenty-eight of the thirty member countries operate separate social security contribution (SSC) schemes; only two countries (i.e. Australia and New Zealand) do not administer separate SSC regimes, instead choosing to pay the various benefits out of general government revenue (and thus avoiding the costs of such schemes!). While there does not appear to be any worldwide trend to rationalize personal income tax and SSC regimes, this appears worthy of study in a UK context given the NICs' evolution and the potentially significant benefits that a unified approach could deliver.

If the idea of unification is put aside, further efforts to harmonize PAYE and NICs would also appear worthy of urgent consideration. Actions along these lines have recently been taken by the Dutch government in its efforts to reduce administrative burdens on business by 25% by 2007. From all accounts, this objective will be met and measures to harmonize SSCs and PAYE have reportedly made a fair contribution to this outcome.[7]

Corporation tax

Despite the fairly high profile of the corporation tax in the UK, it is a relatively small source of government revenue. In 2006–07, corporation taxes represented less than 10% of government receipts (see Table 12.1). The last published figures for OECD countries show UK corporate tax receipts in 2004 at some 2.8% of GDP, somewhat below the OECD (unweighted) average of 3.4%. Yet, despite the relatively low contribution of corporation tax to revenue its administration receives considerable attention within HMRC, in particular, from its enquiry programme. The revenue yield from these activities is significant and growing, an outcome in line with what is being observed in most other advanced economies.

One issue is the extraordinarily generous return filing and tax payment obligations that are a feature of the current UK corporate tax regime (and to an extent for the income tax). Compared to the position in most OECD countries, the timing of tax payments (including advance payments) for corporate taxpayers is lagged considerably, particularly for companies with profits less than £1.5 million, while companies are given up to twelve months to file their end-year tax return. While these arrangements clearly benefit companies by reducing their compliance burden they are 'substantially excessive' when contrasted with the practices applied in other advanced economies and clearly have a number of downsides. Deferring tax payments has a cost to the UK Exchequer (read 'taxpaying community') and may contribute to revenue losses as some taxpayers 'find other uses for their funds'. Furthermore, abnormally long filing periods also impede a revenue body's capacity to detect and deal with non-compliance behaviour in a timely manner, and must inevitably result in the deferred collection of some revenue arising from enquiry work, or worse, a loss of some revenue resulting from non-payment of belatedly imposed additional liabilities.

[7] See *Focus on Businesses, Dutch Progress Report on Reducing Administrative Burdens*, April 2006.

Value added tax

The VAT is a significant source of UK government revenue raising £77 billion in 2006–07, around 16% of all government revenue (as per Table 12.1).

While originally conceived as a simple single rate tax on consumption expenditure, VAT systems generally have evolved into a relatively complex (read 'costly') method for raising government revenue. The UK's VAT, with its multiple rate structure and various exempt goods and services, fits squarely into this category, notwithstanding a range of policy measures taken by the UK government to ease the compliance burden of smaller businesses. In these respects, the UK's VAT mirrors much of what is seen generally across Europe in VAT system design.

On a positive note, the UK's VAT is characterized by a quite generous (by EU standards) registration threshold and a number of concessions, also subject to generous thresholds, to smaller businesses that enable use of simplified approaches for determining VAT liabilities. These concessions, which include the cash basis of accounting and a flat rate scheme where VAT liabilities can be based on a set proportion of a business's turnover, are intended to ease their administrative burden. Yet, despite these concessions, the administrative burden of the VAT, as quantified by HMRC's own measurement research, is the highest of any tax administered in the UK.[8]

An additional challenge for HMRC and the government concerns the relatively high level of revenue leakage from the VAT system resulting from all forms of non-compliance, in particular, 'missing trader intra-community' or 'carousel' fraud. HMRC's own research of the VAT tax gap points to a high incidence of revenue leakage—some 14.2% of the theoretical tax base for 2006–07. For what was originally conceived as a self-policing tax, leakage of this magnitude constitutes serious erosion of the tax base and warrants close and sustained attention. To their credit, the HMRC (and the former Customs and Excise Department responsible for VAT administration until April 2005) have been very active and transparent in their administration of VAT over the last seven years and can point to overall progress in reversing a trend of serious and increasing compliance that was evident in the early 2000s.

In circumstances of significant administrative burden and high revenue leakage it is disappointing that the authors have not canvassed any ideas for VAT reform. Is it time, for example, at least to consider the feasibility of a

[8] HMRC's administrative burden measurement studies conducted in 2005–06 revealed that the VAT was by far the most costly tax for business to administer—some £1,020 million. The figures for other major taxes were £608 million (corporation tax), £759 million (employer taxes—PAYE and NICs), and £857 million business taxes.

major simplification of the VAT system, entailing a substantial broadening of the tax base and a single (but substantially lower) standard rate? (The same comment applies equally to all European VATs.) For example, a VAT system with a tax base modelled along the lines of New Zealand's GST and a basic rate of, say, 12.5%[9] would raise substantially more revenue than the existing VAT system, some of which could be used to compensate those adversely impacted by such a reform. More importantly, however, a VAT designed along these lines would be less relatively costly for business and HMRC to administer (read 'easier to administer') and would provide considerably less incentive for non-compliant behaviour (read 'easier for HMRC to administer'). While this idea would undoubtedly be met with strong political opposition, one can argue that the existing situation of high revenue leakage and compliance costs requires a radical response. Further tinkering is unlikely to get the job done!

III. CONCLUSIONS

The authors end with some brief conclusions. For his part this commentator would conclude as follows on some of the key issues raised by them.

First, he would strongly support in principle according a high priority to the modernization of HMRC's IT systems. Indeed, he would be surprised if such modernization did not already have the necessary priority within the Department.

Second, he would support the continued process of harmonizing the definitions and rules for PAYE and NICs purposes. The unification of personal tax and NICs is certainly worthy of consideration given the erosion of the contributory principle and the potential benefits flowing from a simpler system. In the longer term this commentator would support moving towards the adoption of universal self-assessment incorporating a system of pre-filled tax returns coupled with a rationalization of the reporting requirements for the tax credits system.

Third, he would suggest that it is simpler to subsidize smaller businesses for their use of payroll agents (such as the scheme that the New Zealand IRD administers) rather than a scheme under which HMRC carry out payroll and other compliance tasks for very small employers.

[9] The commentator acknowledges that existing EU rules do not permit VAT's having a standard rate of less than 15%. A reform along the lines suggested would, accordingly, require enlightenment at the EU level.

Finally, as regards the use of tax shelters with a cross-border dimension, this remains a complex and difficult area for all revenue bodies to tackle. With JITSIC, it is already receiving attention and this commentator would expect that the risks to revenue that it involves are already appreciated and receiving a high degree of priority within HMRC.

Commentary by Brian Mace*

Brian Mace is a member of the IFS Tax Law Review Committee. He is a former Policy Director in the Inland Revenue (now HMRC). Between 1984 and 2004 when he retired, he worked primarily on personal taxation, providing policy advice to successive ministers on income tax, employment, inheritance tax, capital gains tax and the tax treatment of pensions, savings, and charitable giving. In 1988–89 he led the Revenue team that implemented independent taxation of husband and wife. Later he had responsibility for teams introducing new policy measures such as ISAs, reforms to capital gains tax, and on-line filing by employers.

INTRODUCTION

The Shaw, Slemrod, and Whiting chapter focuses primarily on the way the tax system is run and not on the structure, balance, or incidence of UK taxes. Those issues are considered in other chapters. But as the authors acknowledge, the structure of a tax and how it is administered are matters which are closely inter-linked. The structure of a tax may largely determine the way it is administered (or preclude certain administrative options). Conversely existing administration structures may make certain policy options difficult to implement without radical change.

The chapter is in two main parts. Part I looks at the economic theory and other principles which may underpin attempts to optimize how taxes are implemented; Part II looks at specific issues of administration in the UK, concentrating on PAYE, self-assessment of income tax, and measures to curb tax avoidance. This Part also discusses a number of specific ideas for possible change.

* This commentary sets out the commentator's personal views and opinions and not those of any organization. It is based on a version of the chapter dated 23 May 2007.

The following commentary looks at a number of the issues considered in the chapter, drawing attention to the key conclusions and testing some of the ideas and proposals in a little more depth. It also seeks to identify some subjects and issues which the authors have not mentioned, or mentioned only indirectly, which might be worth further attention. In preparing this commentary I have had the benefit of reading the commentary prepared by my fellow commentator on the chapter, Richard Highfield. I agree with much, though not all, of what he says.[1]

I: TAX SYSTEMS AND IMPLEMENTATION

This part looks in turn at:

- the theoretical analysis of tax design, drawing on previous work by the authors and the economic literature more generally and taking that work forward in a number of places;
- determinants of evasion, avoidance, and administrative and compliance costs;
- enforcement systems;

and concludes with a section offering some particular implementation guidelines.

This part of the chapter provides a helpful background to the specific analysis of tax issues in the UK which follows in Part II. A few points, not in any particular order of importance, call for some comment.

(i) Although the authors acknowledge that the general theory is highly stylized I feel, like my fellow commentator, that the absence of any reference to the role of politicians in shaping tax policy and administrative structures is an important gap in the analysis. Tax administrators and others supporting ministers in charge of tax policy will naturally aim to cover the considerations described by the authors in the advice that they give to government. But politicians often have wider considerations which they wish to bring into the analysis. Not all of these are the product of expediency or ideology. In seeking election a government may have made commitments about the sort of tax measures which

[1] I have not duplicated my fellow commentator's analysis where I agree with what he says (for example, his very clear discussion of performance indicators) but have focused on subjects where I have particular experience or where my perspective on the chapter is different.

it will or will not consider. For example, the government may have pledged not to raise a particular tax rate or not to impose tax on certain sorts of transactions. If, subsequently, there is a need to raise taxes it may therefore be that the optimal measure to do so in economic theory is closed off. In these circumstances it is not unprincipled for the government to look for alternative, if theoretically sub-optimal, means to raise the revenue it needs. It is important to recognize that administrators do not have final control over the decisions which are taken about tax structures.[2]

(ii) The authors comment on the importance of IT in the administration of the tax system. In the UK the tax administration was relatively late, by international standards, in making full use of IT in a number of areas and has subsequently continued to lag behind. There are political and historical reasons for this. Plans to computerize the largest[3] administrative system, PAYE, on the basis of nine large centralized processing centres, which had begun in the late 1960s, were abandoned in 1971 when the then government decided that it wanted to look at more radical options for a system of tax credits or negative income tax. When those proposals were in turn put on one side following the change of government in 1974 work began on proposals to computerize PAYE using desk-top terminals in local offices. As a result of this rather disrupted development process it was not until the early 1980s that PAYE was fully computerized, though that particular project was completed on time and on budget.

(iii) Although IT is now fundamental to the operation of the tax system the authors note that there are cautions to be aware of. The chapter mentions two but there are arguably others. For example, although computer systems can be very efficient at handling large numbers of straightforward, similar transactions, they may be less effective where non-standard action is required. There are two aspects to this. First, it may be more difficult, perhaps impossible, for the non-standard action to be handled by the computer even with manual intervention by an operator. This is particularly true for very large administrative computer systems. Adjustments or tweaks which in a manual system can be readily applied to give a more satisfactory outcome in a particular case may not be practicable. Second, there is a mirror to the point made by

[2] And as my fellow commentator notes policy-makers may not have the necessary factual information about marginal costs and other matters to enable them to carry out the analysis which theory would require.

[3] Largest both in terms of the number of persons liable to the tax and in total revenue raised.

the authors that IT may lead to taxpayers being less well informed about the tax system and how it works. This may also apply to the staff in local tax offices who, because the computer does the work and calculation, may have less understanding of what the administrative structure is trying to achieve in principle and therefore be less able to devise ways of dealing with individual problems.

(iv) Another factor to bear in mind in the design of administrative systems for taxation is that long-standing taxes like income tax are not superimposed on the economic structure of a country. They are the products of a wide range of cultural, historical, economic, social, political, and other factors. The way the tax system works is often deeply embedded both in the economic structure of the country and in the national psyche.[4] Moving to a new system may require not just a change to administrative procedures and computers; it may also depend on changing culture and attitudes too. This may in turn require lengthy programmes of education or re-education before a radically new design can be fully accommodated and assimilated. And those transitional costs need to be factored into the balance of whether the benefits of the change are actually worthwhile. This is partly why international comparisons in taxation need to be treated with very considerable caution. Just because an approach works well in one country and may be technically feasible in another does not necessarily mean that it can in practice be easily translated from one to the other. The approach may be the result of particular cultural or social features in the first country which simply do not apply in the other.

(v) In Section 12.3.2 the authors comment on the factors that lead people to pay their taxes rather than evade them. I agree with their view that the data here are not sufficient to overturn the theoretical deterrence-based model on evasion which they support. But it is important not to underestimate the role which cultural factors play in affecting compliance. On the whole, UK citizens have been acknowledged to be generally compliant in meeting their tax obligations. This goes hand in hand with a culture in which most people pay their credit card and other bills on time even where the sanctions for not doing so are weak. I suggest this is one, though not the only, reason why the UK does not have relatively strong enforcement powers.

[4] For example, consider how in the UK the number of a tax form, 'P45', has come to represent leaving a job.

II: ADMINISTRATION AND ENFORCEMENT ISSUES IN THE UK TAX SYSTEM

GENERAL

Part II focuses on income tax self-assessment and the operation of PAYE. This is undoubtedly an important area given the high proportion of total revenue raised by income tax and through the PAYE system in particular. However, the issues here are in my experience well-trodden ground. That is not to say there are no problems with taxes and charges on individual income but, for reasons which I shall fill out later, I am not sure that this is where the critical pressure points lie in the UK tax system. Other issues include the following:

- Whether there are ways in which the current serious leakage of VAT through 'carousel fraud' might be addressed (though admittedly this may not be an issue which the UK can easily tackle on its own because of the EU rules which govern VAT).
- Whether the present administrative structure for tax credits—of which there has been a lot of criticism—could be improved.
- Whether the structure of the more recent 'environmental' taxes (landfill tax, air passenger duty, etc.) is appropriate, especially since charges like these seem likely to be a growth area for future taxation.
- The implications of European Court of Justice decisions for the structure of corporation tax.
- Whether the totality of the tasks which HMRC is currently undertaking is manageable, and organizationally sensible.

PAYE

The authors look at a number of aspects of the present PAYE system for deducting tax from employees' pay.

Accuracy

In Section 12.7.2 the authors refer to reports about accuracy in the operation of PAYE. This is undoubtedly a concern and it is right to stress the importance of finding ways to reduce these inaccuracies. In the light of current constraints on HMRC resources I feel this is likely to mean that individuals will have to take more responsibility for ensuring the correctness of their own tax bills. Nevertheless it is important to keep this issue in perspective. Bourn (2005) cites an internal HMRC report which estimated that around £575 million per annum of tax due had not been pursued by the department and that taxpayers were not being advised of around £295 million per annum of tax potentially repayable.[5] However, the total yield from PAYE in 2005–06 was £113,894 million[6] so the variances identified by HMRC were of the order of $\pm\frac{1}{2}$%.

Changes in working patterns and demographics

Employees

In recent years the number of individuals whose circumstances are less easily accommodated within PAYE has undoubtedly increased. Typically problems arise where the individual has a number of jobs either simultaneously or sequentially during a tax year. But in practice the number of such cases remains a relatively small proportion of the total number of employees. For example, figures from the labour force statistics show that in 2000 over 80% of employees had been in their current job for over a year and almost 70% for two years. And while the number of employees with multiple employments has increased substantially since the mid 1980s the number of employees who held more than one job in 2000 was still only 4% of the employed workforce. These figures are now slightly out of date but I do not believe that they will have changed significantly.

I feel the authors underestimate the effectiveness of PAYE. PAYE can and does work very successfully, and with little manual intervention, for an employee who has a single job throughout the tax year or who changes job not too close to the end of the tax year.[7] That still describes the vast majority of the working population in the UK.

Pensioners

Another group for whom PAYE works less well consists of pensioners who have several pensions from a number of past employments. This is a relatively

[5] Bourn (2005).

[6] <http://www.hmrc.gov.uk/stats/t_receipt/table2-8.pdf>.

[7] If the change of job happens too close to the end of the tax year the P45 process may not catch up with the employee in their new job before the end of the tax year and cumulation may therefore break down.

recent (but growing) phenomenon as those who took advantage of the extension of pension options in the 1970s and 1980s start to reach retirement age.

In principle PAYE should work well for pensioners.[8] Their pensions come from the same payers each year and apart from any annual uprating the sums paid do not fluctuate between pay-periods. But difficulties occur where the pensioner has more than one pension because manual intervention is necessary to co-ordinate the correct deductions, month by month, from each payment. Getting that right requires personal attention from the pensioner's tax office which is very resource intensive. In practice it may be necessary for pensioners to be proactive themselves in ensuring that the right deductions are made from their income or in completing a tax return at the end of the tax year to ensure that they pay the right amount of tax.

There is an irony in having a system which, having got a person's tax affairs right without tax returns for the whole of their working life, requires the person to start filing a return once they have retired. But there is no easy answer to that problem and unfortunately I believe it is unlikely that resources will be available either in HMRC or elsewhere in government to undertake the complex co-ordination work which would be necessary to get the right results within PAYE. However, one solution which might be worth examining is whether, if an individual has pensions from several sources, one of the pension payers could act in the lead as a sort of clearing house for all the others. If all the pensions due to an individual were channelled to the person through the lead payer that provider could aggregate all the amounts and apply PAYE to the total sum before then paying the correct net amount to the pensioner. Such a system would obviously require the agreement of both the pensioner and pension providers and would undoubtedly mean more work for the pension payer co-ordinating the payments. But the other pension payers could have less work to do and would simply have to pay pension without tax deductions to the lead provider. There might, therefore, not be much increase in the total compliance costs of pension payers overall.

Flexibility

The authors are concerned that PAYE imposes some inflexibility on the tax system and may prevent certain policies being introduced. As an example they

[8] And in practice more than half of those aged 65 or over are in any case not liable to income tax.

mention that when the present system of personal tax credits was introduced they could not be accommodated within PAYE. However, this seems a rather harsh analysis: after all even a Rolls Royce car cannot fly you to New York! Had the UK had a system of universal self-assessment in place at the time tax credits were introduced, the task of getting substantial numbers of credit recipients to complete returns of income as is now required would have been much simpler if not obviated altogether. But, just like PAYE, universal self-assessment could not have delivered what the government at the time wanted, that is tax credits paid with wages and responding 'in real time' to fluctuations in the employees wages or salary. That would require a much more sophisticated system along the lines of the tax credits or negative income tax envisaged by the then government in 1972. The authors point to the difficulties of asking employers to operate such a system. Indeed, it must be very doubtful whether any such system could ever be made to work in a structure where the tax credits due may depend not only on changes in the individual's own income but on changes in the income of their partner too.

Apart from the example of tax credits, the authors do not indicate which policy options they think might have been precluded because of constraints imposed by PAYE so it is not easy to know what weight to attach to this factor. I do not recall many, if any, occasions over the past thirty years when ministers have said they would have introduced a particular, attractive policy if only the structure of PAYE had not made it impractical.

One kind of policy which under PAYE could be introduced only at considerable administrative cost or by bringing a large number of individuals into self-assessment is a tax relief for a kind of personal expenditure incurred by a significant proportion of the taxpaying population.[9] Child care costs might be an example. But from a tax policy perspective that restriction might well be perceived as an advantage, rather than a disadvantage if the aim generally is to have simpler taxes with broader bases and lower rates. By contrast the tax structure in the US is complicated by a wide range of specific deductions for various sorts of expenditure which can be accommodated in the system with little administrative cost because all taxpayers are obliged to file a return. That is unattractive on wider policy grounds and I think the UK system is better in this respect.

I would not suggest that there is no case for more flexibility in the tax system. One policy which undoubtedly would be precluded by the structure

[9] In the past this problem has been partially overcome by giving the tax relief at source, allowing the individual to deduct the relief from the payment before making it. Tax relief for charitable donations by basic rate taxpayers continues to be given in this way.

of PAYE is a local income tax under which substantial numbers of local authorities were permitted to set their own, separate local income tax rates. The law already envisages that there might be a different basic rate of income tax for individuals living in Scotland if the Scottish Executive decides to introduce such a measure.[10] Even that would be likely to impose significant new burdens on some employers with additional risks of error. But a tax system in which there were, say, ten rates of local income tax would involve impossible burdens for employers and the risk of very large numbers of errors. Any future government that wished to introduce a local income tax would therefore have to find some alternative mechanism to PAYE (probably some form of end-of-year assessment) to collect it. But there is a 'chicken-and-egg' issue to be addressed here: until the tax system is more flexible some policies may be difficult to implement, but until those policies are identified as required options by government there is less incentive to change the administrative structure.

Compliance costs

I do not myself believe that the existence of PAYE has made the tax code itself more complicated. Over the last thirty to forty years many substantial changes have been made (for example, abolition of mortgage interest relief, abolition of child and other tax allowances, reduction in the number of income tax rates) which have simplified both the income tax and the basic operation of PAYE for both employers and employees. The taxation of employment income is certainly more complex than it was. In my view, that is primarily in response to the increasing sophistication in forms of remuneration for some employees, to which the tax code has had to respond. However, I think that overall the employer's task in running payroll has become much more complicated since PAYE was first introduced. Because of the success of employers in operating PAYE, governments have, perhaps understandably, been encouraged to require them to take on more and more tasks: deduction of earnings related NICs, payment of statutory sick pay, maternity pay and paternity pay, recovery of student loans. Moreover, these tasks go alongside the wider burdens which employers have had to shoulder such as health and safety requirements for their employees. In total these requirements are now undoubtedly too heavy, and ought to be reduced.

[10] Section 73 Scotland Act 1998.

NATIONAL INSURANCE CONTRIBUTIONS (NICs)

I believe it is reasonable to argue that, on its own, and with the use of IT, PAYE for most employers, including small employers, is only a little more complicated than a non-cumulative system of tax withholding from employees' pay. But NICs add an additional level of complexity with a choice from several rates and structures to apply depending on the employee's circumstances. Once the employee's situation has been established most of these otherwise variable factors remain constant from pay-period to pay-period. But the fact that NICs are calculated non-cumulatively and on a pay-period basis (rather than cumulatively and annually as for income tax under PAYE) means that employers have to apply two different charges to, broadly, the same earnings. This undoubtedly imposes an additional compliance burden especially for small employers. Finding a means to lighten that burden, by aligning or assimilating income tax and NICs has been at the top of the wish list for business and employers for some time. Unfortunately, I do not believe that such an approach is going to be fruitful, for two main reasons.

First, significant alignment between income tax and NICs can be achieved only at the price of correspondingly significant changes in the incidence of one or both of these charges, probably mainly NICs. But that means substantial numbers not only of gainers but also losers amongst employees, many of whom could be on low or relatively low incomes. These changes would not be for any reason of improved fairness towards the individuals affected but to produce a reduction in employer compliance costs. However worthy that objective it is hard to see a government finding those consequences easy to accept.

Secondly, NICs are not just a single charge on the employee's wages or salary. There are also (secondary) employer NICs, calculated broadly but not entirely on the same base as the employee charge, but remitted and paid[11] by the employer rather than deducted from the employee's pay. Any initiative to achieve a reduction in employer compliance costs through aligning tax and NICs really has to address both of the NICs charges. Even if the employee NICs charge could be fully aligned with income tax there might be little reduction in employers' compliance costs if the employer NICs charge was left in place. But replacing employer NICs with a new charge in a way

[11] In economic terms the cost of employer NICs is, of course, ultimately borne at least in part by employees since the charge reduces the total remuneration which an employer can afford.

that does not have largely capricious distributional effects is very hard to achieve.

These remarks may no doubt be criticized by some as defeatist. But it would be wrong to believe that 'fundamental studies' of the options in this area have not been undertaken within government over the years.

Recent studies

The Treasury has now published a study[12] which looks at the option of charging employee NICs on an annual basis and collecting them cumulatively. The study concludes that on balance the benefits of administrative alignment do not outweigh the costs.

The study could no doubt be challenged in a number of respects. For example, the work assumes that the structure of PAYE codes remains broadly as it is now but I think there might be scope for rather more compliance cost savings for employers if the structure of PAYE codes were changed in some respects (by making them offsets against the amounts of income tax and NICs payable rather than against income subject to tax and NICs before those charges are calculated).[13] And the study does not look at the more radical option of merging income tax and NICs. But I do not think either of these changes would affect the overall conclusion that the study reaches against the change. Indeed, the study indicates that the consequences of radical change to employer as well as employee NICs would have further, difficult distributional and compliance consequences.

In my view the only way to achieve radical simplification for employers in the task of operating PAYE and NICs would be gradually to phase out both employer and employee NICs over time (probably a decade or more) by systematically shifting the burden on to income tax, corporation tax, and possibly other new taxes. By that means the very difficult distributional consequences of the change could be managed in such a way that individuals and employers could adjust to them slowly. Such a plan would naturally face its own obstacles since among other things it would require some replacement for the existing contributory principle (though I do not think that issue is insuperable). It would also require some means of dealing with the present arrangement under which employees in company or other pension

[12] HM Treasury (2007).

[13] This further change would involve additional transitional cost for all employers and government which would have to be taken into account.

schemes pay a lower 'contracted out' rate of NICs. Crucially it would need a sustained commitment to the change by government over probably three general elections.

Issues for small employers

If PAYE and NICs are looked at in isolation, most concern about compliance costs is focused on small employers without computer support. The Treasury study just mentioned estimates that about 20% of employers currently rely on manual payroll though HMRC expect this number to fall significantly over the next three to four years.

Because of the complexity of PAYE and NICs combined there are very good reasons for encouraging all employers, however small, to make use of computerized payroll processing. Such processing can in fact be purchased quite cheaply, as the chapter notes (footnote 30). It has been suggested that HMRC might themselves offer a payroll service for small employers but, like my fellow commentator, I think it would be preferable to subsidize small employers to use commercial payroll schemes. It would not necessarily be right for HMRC to set up in competition with commercial payroll firms and employers ought to have agents who are independent of HMRC. There have been subsidies for employers to e-file their end-of-year and other returns for some time which is in itself an encouragement for employers to switch to computerized payroll.

CHANGES TO WITHHOLDING

The chapter suggests three changes to withholding in order to improve the operation of PAYE: an online computer system; varying withholding on non-PAYE income by reference to PAYE income and introducing pay-period information reporting. As my fellow commentator notes these changes would increase the compliance burdens on business when priority is being given to reducing that burden—an initiative which the authors also support. Moreover, I feel these changes may be pointing in the wrong direction. I think it is right to recognize that PAYE withholding cannot get everyone's tax deductions precisely correct during and at the end of the tax year without disproportionate and costly intervention by employers and other intermediaries or staff in local tax offices. I shall return below to what I think is a better strategy, and one with greater potential for the longer term.

SELF-ASSESSMENT

I share the authors' perception that while overall the introduction of self-assessment has been good some aspects of it have been less so. And as they point out there is still more that could be done.

One aspect of self-assessment which the authors mention is e-filing. This undoubtedly had its teething troubles when it was first introduced. But for individuals the system now works well and HMRC could do more to publicize its virtues.

The authors welcome the efforts made to remove people with simple tax affairs from self-assessment. However, it is worth asking whether striving too hard to keep people out of self-assessment is actually the right approach. As I noted earlier there is a real dilemma to be addressed here in relation to how best to deal with the tax affairs of the minority of employees and other individuals with which PAYE does not deal effectively. One solution might be to identify groups of taxpayers—such as those who have a series of employments during the year—who should be positively encouraged to take greater charge of their own tax affairs, maintain records of their own, and make use of self-assessment with e-filing at the end of the year to get their tax liability right.

THE LONGER TERM

The authors and my fellow commentator feel that the problems which have been identified with PAYE may provide a case for looking at a move over time to some sort of universal self-assessment system. However, I do not find the arguments put forward persuasive. This is partly because I think the circumstances in which PAYE does not work well are less common than is often suggested, as I have mentioned above.

The authors suggest several reasons why a system of universal self-assessment would have advantages. The change would require all employees to file a tax return each year which would mean either additional work for them or incurring the cost of paying an adviser to handle the task. For that price the chapter says that HMRC would save some work, employers' compliance costs might fall a little, some as yet unspecified policy changes—new stealth taxes?—would be facilitated, and taxpayers would understand their tax bills better. That does not sound a very easy proposal for a government to persuade people to accept. For a number of individuals, tax bills would be made more accurate. That might be sufficient to persuade some that the change was worthwhile, but they might also ask whether there was simpler way of achieving the same result. I believe that taxpayers whose affairs are unlikely to be correctly dealt with under PAYE should be encouraged to take more responsibility for their own tax affairs. But I do not think there is a very strong case for asking all employees to do this.

In putting forward the case for looking at a system of universal self-assessment the authors and my fellow commentator argue that the additional compliance costs of the large numbers of employees filing tax returns for the first time would be significantly reduced if tax returns were pre-populated by HMRC with information about the individuals' income and tax deductions. This approach has clearly worked well in other countries such as Denmark, and is certainly worth further examination in the UK.[14] But as the authors and my fellow commentator note there are a number of features, not yet present in the UK system, which are prerequisites for pre-population to work well. For example, the absence of a unique taxpayer identifier in the UK is a major hurdle to be overcome.

In practice I feel neither PAYE nor universal self-assessment provide an ideal way to collect income tax with low administrative costs, low compliance costs for *both* employers and employees, flexibility to accommodate a wide range of tax policies, and securing the flow of tax revenue to government. Each system has its advantages and disadvantages and I am not convinced that there is an objective basis for preferring one system over the other. However, once one particular system has been adopted by a country and has become embedded in its culture, it is very difficult to change to another.

Against this background I do not believe that a study of universal self-assessment is likely to prove productive at the present time. That is not to say that the existing system does not require change and development. My preferred strategy, as I have already indicated, would be to abandon the task of trying to make PAYE work for individuals for whom the work involves disproportionate costs either for employers or HMRC *but* to ensure the PAYE system is properly maintained for the majority of employees for whom it works satisfactorily. And there are a number of further initiatives such as an examination of whether returns can be pre-populated which are worth pursuing. A combination of these strategies would provide sufficient work for HMRC to handle in the short to medium term and would not close off options for wider change in the future.

[14] However, a policy which is successful in a country of $5\frac{1}{2}$ million people will not necessarily work so well in a country with more than ten times the population.

HMRC

Good tax administration requires adequate resources and funding. Running the tax system is never going to have the same priority within government as major spending programmes such as education, health, or defence. But it is important that tax administration is not starved of the relatively modest sums which it needs to maintain and renew itself. Efficient administrative systems and willing compliance are not easy to recover, once lost, and without them the funding for public spending generally may be put at risk.

HMRC is currently undergoing a large amount of change and is also trying to achieve a substantial reduction in the numbers of staff in the department—by about 12,500 at present with a further similar reduction to come over the next five years. This has led to concerns about staff morale. Managing change and down-sizing simultaneously is a very difficult combination of measures to handle. Some concern has been expressed in the media that the senior management of HMRC have recently been too focused on managing change and not sufficiently on the basic business of running the tax system.

The authors approve the merger of the Inland Revenue and Customs and Excise to form HMRC which took place in 2005. The merger was recommended in a report by the then Permanent Secretary to the Treasury, Gus O'Donnell,[15] and there was undoubtedly a case for making this change. But such mergers require amongst other things substantial amount of senior management time to carry out successfully. And while the changes may yield savings in the longer term they initially require investment to ensure that the full benefits of merger can be realized. For HMRC, it is not clear whether all the necessary investment has been put in.

REFERENCES

Bourn, J. (2005), *Comptroller and Auditor General's Standard Report on the Accounts of the Inland Revenue 2004–05*, London: National Audit Office.

HM Treasury (2004), *Financing Britain's Future: Review of the Revenue Departments*, March 2004 CM 6163, London: HMT.

HM Treasury (2007), *Income Tax and National Insurance Alignment: An Evidence-based Assessment*, London: HMT.

[15] HM Treasury (2004).

13

The Political Economy of Tax Policy

*James Alt, Ian Preston, and Luke Sibieta**

James E. Alt is Frank G. Thomson Professor and Director of Graduate Studies in Government and a faculty associate of the Institute for Quantitative Social Science at Harvard University, where he was Founding Director of the Center for Basic Research in the Social Sciences. He is a member of the American Academy of Arts and Sciences and was a Guggenheim Fellow 1997–98. His research has been mainly in the fields of political economy, fiscal policy, and comparative politics. His PhD is from the University of Essex.

Ian Preston is Professor of Economics at UCL and a Research Fellow at the IFS. His recent publications in the field of public economics notably include 'Electoral Bias and Policy Choice: Theory and Evidence' (with Tim Besley) in the *Quarterly Journal of Economics*, and his research interests also include consumer demand and household welfare, the distribution of income, immigration and the labour market, and public economics. He has been a managing editor of *Fiscal Studies*.

Luke Sibieta joined the IFS as a Research Economist in 2005. His research focuses on education policy and income inequality. He has written about many aspects of these areas, including trends in the incomes of the very rich, progress towards the UK government's poverty targets, school finance, and socio-economic differences in educational attainment. He also has a keen interest in using the tools of political economy to uncover the reasons behind changes in economic policy.

* The authors thank Stuart Adam, Lucy Barnes, Tim Besley, Ian Brimicombe, Alan Budd, Judith Freedman, Rachel Griffith, James Hines, Paul Johnson, Alison Post, James Poterba, Christopher Sanger, Guido Tabellini, Christopher Wales, and conference participants in Cambridge for their helpful comments and suggestions. British Social Attitudes Survey data are collected by the National Centre for Social Research and made available through the UK Data Archive.

EXECUTIVE SUMMARY

This chapter reviews major changes in British tax-setting institutions in the past thirty years and highlights four key points about the politics of tax policy, which are summarized below. The chapter also makes policy recommendations, such as for improving scrutiny and parliamentary accountability; these are also summarized below.

A 'passive' movement to the right

The chapter analyses whether changes in voter preferences and strategic party positioning could explain declines in statutory rates of income tax. What we discover is that electoral support has moved to the right, though voters seem to have followed rather than led the changing content of party manifestos. Voters have always favoured redistribution, particularly from those with the highest incomes to those with the lowest incomes. Whilst preferences for redistribution have been declining over time, it is notable that the large cuts in statutory rates of income tax took place at a time when attitudes to redistribution were at their most favourable, and when a majority of voters voted for parties who did not favour these cuts. Whether this move to the right will persist and to what extent it is now a fact of political life is hard to say.

Policy drift and persistence

Our case study of the R&D tax credit provides a number of lessons, the primary one being that enacting tax policy can create interest groups and constituencies in favour of that policy. Even when they did not lobby for the policy in the first place, like the large firms in our study, they will lobby both for persistence and extensions that allow policy to drift from its original motivation. Therefore, any potential tax reformer should remember that any new allowances enacted or favourable tax treatments provided to particular groups could prove difficult to remove and may be distorted into something different over time.

While the example of the R&D tax credit vividly illustrates policy persistence as well as drift, the past thirty years has seen other areas of specific tax privilege phased out, most notably the married couples allowance and mortgage interest tax relief. The timing of these reforms suggest that it is helpful to phase out changes gradually and during a period when it can plausibly be claimed that other taxes are being cut or rationalized.

Disconnected tax debates

The framing of tax policy debates can be crucial. Framing the VAT zero-rating of children's clothing in isolation has helped maintain it; framing the estate tax in isolation also helped those lobbying for its abolition in the US. Such framing could easily result from a lack of public understanding about the interconnectedness of the tax system.

However, in order to pursue sensible tax policy it is essential to see the tax system as a *system* rather than to consider its different elements in isolation. So disconnected tax debates may be particularly counter-productive for tax policy as compared with other areas of public policy. This has a lesson for the Mirrlees Review, which may need to combine tax reforms in different areas to provide a broad-based set of reform measures, making clear that there is give and take across different population groups.

Transparency and accountability

There is a limit to how well-informed the electorate can be expected to be for the purpose of holding the government to account and ensuring good quality tax policy. However, institutional reforms which improve transparency and public understanding would help avoid situations where government can make increasing use of tax policy instruments that are either ill-understood by voters—as in the case of the relationship between National Insurance contributions, NHS spending, and state benefit spending—or those that are less visible or transparent to voters—such as VAT or fiscal drag.

Do other institutions play an accountability role where the electorate leaves off? Parliament plays some role, but lacks informational resources to play it well, and is hardly involved at all in the crucial pre-legislative stage. External organizations provide some level of scrutiny and accountability, helping to improve tax legislation and making it more likely that the economic impact of proposals is fully thought through.

A proposal for greater scrutiny

A degree of parliamentary accountability through greater levels of pre-legislative scrutiny of tax policy would be highly desirable. Of course, a lack of effective parliamentary accountability extends to other areas of policy, beyond taxation, and is a general political concern. However, the degree of pre-legislative parliamentary scrutiny is even weaker for tax policy, since in other areas policy proposals are regularly published in White Papers or Green Papers. Although there is pre-legislative scrutiny of draft tax proposals by tax professionals and other interested parties, Parliament is rarely involved in this process.

The best vehicle for pre-legislative scrutiny is the select committee system. We leave it as an open question as to whether scrutiny of tax policy is best undertaken by the existing Treasury Select Committee or by a new select committee on taxation. But it is clear to us that ensuring higher levels of pre-legislative scrutiny should be a priority for government.

Alongside this, in order to undertake effective pre-legislative scrutiny, MPs require more resources. At present, much advice and support comes through external organizations, and this could be extended. However, another possibility is a formal in-house service akin to the Congressional Budget Office in the US, which could be explicitly charged with providing analysis of tax policy for MPs.

More broadly, we believe that serious thought should be given to instituting a body to oversee the public finances. A group of experts with genuine knowledge of the operation of tax systems could be put in place to offer advice and to audit revenue and spending figures. This body could be accessible and accountable to Parliament as well as to the executive with appointments appropriately scrutinized. As well as scrutinizing government plans, the body could offer advice to all parties, particularly around election times. To provide meaningful scrutiny and advice, any such body would require access to more data than is currently provided to Parliament. As well as providing more data to this body, providing more data to the public could improve external scrutiny, for example, by publishing all assumptions behind fiscal forecasts.

13.1. INTRODUCTION

After an authoritative and exhaustive economic analysis of options for tax reform, the Meade Report concluded that:

> We believe that the combination of a new Beveridge scheme (to set an acceptable floor to the standard of living of all citizens), of a progressive expenditure tax regime (to combine encouragement to enterprise with the taxation of high levels of personal consumption), and a system of progressive taxation on wealth with some discrimination against inherited wealth, presents a set of final objectives for the structure of direct taxation in the UK that might command a wide consensus of

political approval and which could be approached by a series of piecemeal tax changes over the coming decade.[1]

However, whilst some piecemeal changes such as changes to taxation of certain forms of saving did move the UK tax system towards these final objectives, there was no 'new Beveridge system' nor implementation of a wealth tax. In order that the Mirrlees Review would give greater consideration to which reforms 'might command a wide consensus of political approval', we were charged with writing a chapter that explicitly analysed the political economy of taxation.

Beyond considering what reforms might be politically feasible, we believe that the purpose of studying the political economy of taxation, ultimately, is that a good tax system has to be politically sustainable within the institutions of government, and political economy helps us understand political sustainability. Empirically, there are some policy outcomes that are hard to understand without political economy but less puzzling with it. Some British examples that will be discussed below include the passage and subsequent repeal of the poll tax, absence of VAT on children's clothing, and the co-existence of National Insurance and personal income tax. However, we will look closely at two cases: why lowered top and basic rates of income tax have proved sustainable in an era of rising income inequality and why a tax credit for research and development aimed originally at small finance-constrained companies has grown so much.

When looking at examples like these, it is not new to say 'it's political', but we are trying to do more than that. We want to be more systematic in studying politics, and to study it in ways that are consistent with the tools and methods of economics, in order to draw lessons. Looked at this way, our purpose might seem to be part of specifying the constraint set, but it is again more than this. In tax policy, distributional issues are central, so getting to sustainability is not going to be just an issue of getting good advice on efficiency from economists. Administration is also part of this, but sustainability is not just an issue of collectability. Tax policy should be credible, especially in a dynamic setting, so considering elections and information is critical. We analyse specific features of the political system that shape tax reforms to give insight into specific institutional remedies that can improve the quality of tax policy. In all these ways political economy makes us think more rigorously about constraints on policy, about what recommendations are feasible and sustainable.

Political economy research suggests three main conflicts of interest that tax policy resolves through institutional processes. The first is a *class-interest view*

[1] Meade (1978).

of politics: citizens have different views about taxation based on their position in the income distribution. In a world in which citizens have different views about how taxes should be levied, political systems affect whose interests are represented and how. The second is between *organized and unorganized interests*: organized interests typically have advantages in securing favourable policy outcomes in return for electoral contributions that can be used to persuade voters. One issue is whether electoral incentives are sufficient to limit any misappropriation of public money. The third conflict is that between *citizens and government*. Making economic activity taxable allows decision makers in governments to appropriate resources for their own objectives and to use them in ways that citizens may not like. Our case studies (below) emphasize these conflicts and issues.

This chapter will make much use of previous research on political economy, but will also consider attitudinal data from the British Social Attitudes (BSA) Survey and data on tax shares collated by the OECD. For the purposes of further understanding the political economy of taxation, we felt that it was important to gain insight from those at the heart of the process. Therefore, we conducted a series of interviews with individuals who have been intimately involved in the tax policy process over the past thirty years. These include former special advisors, senior civil servants, and individuals on the other side of the process in the business community. These interviews sometimes confirmed our own lines of enquiry, but also opened new ones. With their permission, we have included quotes from some of these individuals, since their own words often best described the features or problems of the process. In order to hide their identity, these individuals are referred to as Persons A–G. However, we owe a great debt of gratitude to *all* those whom we interviewed.

Section 13.2 will describe the process of how tax policy is made in the UK and how this has changed since the Meade Report was published. It will also compare the process with how tax policy is made in other countries, such as the USA and Germany, with different institutional frameworks. The main point to emphasize here will be the dominance of the executive over tax policy, particularly HM Treasury. Section 13.3 will discuss in turn interesting developments—from the point of view of political economy—in income tax, indirect taxation, corporate tax, and other forms of taxation in the UK, and beyond. It will also set the scene for more detailed analysis later on in the chapter.

With these observations in mind, we will move on towards using the theory of political economy to explain them. Section 13.4 will begin by seeing if the trends in income taxation can be explained through an examination of electoral interests and voter behaviour. This will encompass discussion of empirical information on voters' opinions and behaviour, the classical Meltzer–Richard model—where the position of the median voter is seen as crucial—and more recent developments in the field. Section 13.5 will then move on to discuss the nature of interest-group politics in the UK through a case-study of the R&D tax credit.

Section 13.6 will examine the level of transparency and accountability in the UK tax policy process. Section 13.7 will conclude by summarizing the chapter, discussing the implications of our conclusions for potential tax reformers, and presenting our recommendations for how the tax policy process could be changed for the better.

13.2. THE UK TAX PROCESS

13.2.1. Description and comparison of institutional frameworks

Exactly *how* is tax policy made in the UK? What follows is a concise overview of this process and how it differs from the experience in other countries.

We begin by selectively illustrating the specific UK political institutions relevant to tax policy. The first-past-the-post electoral system used for the House of Commons usually allows single parties to govern with significant legislative majorities. Ministers responsible for tax policy (those at the Treasury) will be selected from the ranks of the governing party's MPs by the Prime Minister. This power of patronage is a major reason why these large legislative majorities also tend to be cohesive, with government bills almost always being passed by a subservient House of Commons. One should also note that the British tax system is exceptionally centralized by international standards: little actual discretionary power is located anywhere outside central government. In 2003, over 95% of UK tax revenues were raised by central government—amongst major OECD countries, only Ireland had a greater share of tax revenues accruing to central government.

The key point is that Britain has a narrow base from which policy initiatives can be made: the only body that can put forward tax policy proposals to Parliament is the Treasury.[2] This is a tremendous advantage to the government and empowers ministers to propose tax measures in the annual Finance Bill following the Budget—a major event in the parliamentary calendar. The unelected House of Lords has no power to block finance bills. Council tax

[2] Very occasionally a tax-related provision turns up in some other bill (e.g. partnership law) but it would have to be cleared with the Treasury (Person A interview).

rates are set locally, and the Scottish Parliament can change the basic rate of income tax in Scotland by up to 3p, but the power to alter the tax system remains overwhelmingly the prerogative of central government.

It is hard to over-play the dominance of the executive over tax policy, the Treasury in particular. This is because as well as enormous agenda-setting powers, the resources available to the Treasury are vast when compared with those of most MPs. The Treasury can draw on much policy and practical expertise, as well as analysis conducted by HM Revenue and Customs (HMRC). MPs have many fewer resources at their command throughout the year. When discussing the annual Finance Bill, they must generally rely on outside organizations for advice. Parliament thus finds it difficult to provide effective scrutiny of tax measures, and measures are nearly always enacted unchanged in the annual Finance Bill that follows the Budget. As Person A put it,

> Debate on the Finance Bill is poorer because there is no expert support available to MPs. Typically an Opposition MP will be briefed by an accounting firm and will have a question to ask during the committee stage, the minister has been briefed by officials and gives an answer, but the individual MP is unable to evaluate the response and cannot pursue a sensible discussion. So debate is utterly meaningless.[3]

Such criticisms could be made of parliamentary scrutiny of other areas of policy, with executive dominance evident in many others areas of public policy. However, in contrast to other areas of policy, the House of Lords cannot amend the Finance Bill and therefore has limited powers of scrutiny. It is also the case that tax measures receive far less pre-legislative scrutiny than other areas of policy. This is because most departments first announce policy in White Papers, or produce consultation documents called Green Papers discussing policy options. White Papers and Green Papers tend to receive much scrutiny in and outside Parliament. The effectiveness of this scrutiny is another question, but tax policy doesn't even receive this level of pre-legislative scrutiny. However, it does have to be said that pre-legislative consultation of tax professionals is widespread and has become more so in recent years, which should surely help in the development of good tax policy.

The lack of effective parliamentary scrutiny could be a problem for many reasons. First, it may be a problem in its own right, since the House of Commons has a constitutional responsibility to provide effective scrutiny of tax measures, which it is clearly failing to do at present. Secondly,

[3] Person A interview. In fact, 'It has happened that the Minister picks the wrong answer off the list, but the MP doesn't know and is satisfied with the answer.'

effective scrutiny may prevent policy-makers from making policy mistakes, and improve the tax system.

What are the direct sources of ideas for tax policy reforms within the executive branch? The first source will be proposals from civil servants within the Treasury, crafted to meet particular ministerial objectives. These ministerial objectives could be quite narrow and particular, for example, Nigel Lawson's main aim was widely seen to be promoting tax neutrality. Or they could be more general and wide-ranging, such as Gordon Brown's stated agenda of organizing public finances 'to encourage work, savings, investment and fairness'.[4] How these goals are defined varies from minister to minister. They could be personal views or they could be crafted for manifestos to achieve maximum electoral support. Clearly external influences—such as think tanks, tax practitioners, and the media—could persuade politicians of suitable ministerial objectives for a tax system, but there is also room for external influences in generating tax policy ideas that meet given ministerial objectives.

A second source of tax policy proposals concerns measures to prevent tax avoidance. In administering the tax system, staff in HMRC are able to identify loopholes in the tax system that allow agents to avoid paying tax. They are then able to propose ways to close such loopholes, or other ways to protect revenues. There is also a clear opportunity here for other specialist tax practitioners to suggest ways to reduce tax avoidance.

A third source of tax policy is more political, that made directly by ministers and advisors. This could come from election manifesto promises implemented soon after election, like the windfall tax on privatized utilities in 1997, or the cutting of top marginal rates of income tax in 1979. It could also be tax policy made between elections directly by ministers and their advisors, with or against the advice of tax policy officials.

The way tax policy is made in the UK is very different to the situation in many other European countries, particularly those with systems of proportional representation and powerful veto players. For instance, in Italy where coalition governments are the norm, tax policy is made as a result of negotiations within coalitions, and third parties, such as trade unions, are often consulted much more than in the UK. A good recent example from Italy is the cut in income tax enacted by Silvio Berlusconi in 2004. Before this became possible, agreement was required between all members of the governing coalition, who sometimes had quite different priorities. For instance, the far-right National Alliance wanted more to be spent on the south

[4] Pre-Budget Report 1997.

of Italy, whilst the Christian Democrats were keen to protect the privileges of public sector workers.

The cuts in corporate and incomes tax undertaken by Gerhard Schroeder's government, starting in 2001, are an example from Germany which shows how important are veto players. Ganghof (2008) shows that despite an apparent preference for the introduction of a dual-income tax system over across the board cuts in corporate and income tax rates, the latter was instituted instead. The dual-income tax system was primarily a non-starter in Germany because the constitutional court had already let it be known that differential tax treatment of income and capital would most probably be ruled unconstitutional.

Steinmo (1996) has already identified the role of committees and legislative bargaining as being crucial to understanding how US tax policy has evolved over time. In comparison with the US, Michael Keen wrote:

> To the outsider, the most obvious contrast is in the degree of consultation in the formation of tax policy. In the United States, major tax policy initiatives are developed, marketed, analyzed, and negotiated ... In the United Kingdom, they are commonly announced.[5]

Put another way, in the UK the processes of analysis, negotiation, and marketing take place much more within the executive branch than in the legislature, or indeed in politicians' campaigns for election. The executive has extensive agenda power, and government proposals are rarely subject to significant amendment, let alone veto.[6] The centralization of revenues, lack of information and expertise in Parliament, rarity of coalition bargaining, and absence of any powers of initiative and referendum reinforces the familiar executive dominance of British politics.

It should be noted that such arrangements do have some benefits, particularly with regard to levels of government debt. By international standards (based on OECD and IMF data reviewed in Alt and Lassen (2006)) Britain has a relatively transparent budget process, which weakens political incentives to manipulate revenues (and spending) for purposes of electoral gain. At the same time, Britain only very infrequently has coalition governments, which have higher debt levels at least in bad economic times, due to the relative

[5] Keen (1999).

[6] A rare example of Parliament significantly affecting the course of tax legislation is the so-called Rooker–Wise Amendment, introduced in the 1977 Finance Bill Committee by two Labour backbenchers. This ensures that an Act of Parliament is required in order to increase income tax allowances by less than the increase in RPI, which means that the default option is that they be uprated in line with RPI. Note that this amendment was introduced at a time when the governing Labour Party did not have a majority.

inability of multiparty coalition governments to respond quickly to economic shocks (Roubini and Sachs (1989)). In part at least for these reasons, Britain has had a comparatively low level of debt for most of the period since Meade.

13.2.2. Changes in executive process since Meade

This section will discuss changes in the executive process since the Meade Report was published, together with a short introduction to the fiscal rules that were introduced ten years ago.

The classical view of how executive goals evolve into policy sees civil servants producing tax policy recommendations that seek to achieve these policy goals; the more visible a politician's policy goals are to civil servants, the better they can respond. The classical view prevailed into the 1990s, but the last decade saw significant changes: a comprehensive reorganization of policy development in the Treasury, a major increase in the importance of political special advisors, and the adoption of some fiscal rules.

First and foremost, the organization of policy planning in HM Treasury (HMT) and HMRC has changed dramatically. Previously, according to Person B, in HM Treasury during the early 1990s,

> There was one 'team' for fiscal policy with three branches: taxes, indirect taxes, and budget coordination, with at most 2–3 people per branch. It was a big challenge to get anything done. Revenue and Customs produced material that was very technically phrased, but HMT was deeply dependent on the others for input.[7]

Now, by contrast, following the O'Donnell Review (O'Donnell, 2004) which proposed the merger of the Inland Revenue and Customs and Excise to create HMRC, the heart of policy development is in HMT, and new ideas could even come from policy teams there.

> Policy teams reflect ideas from outside. The organization of teams is formally structured. There are three subdirectorates and 19 teams: 2 for strategy, 1 for budget delivery, but the other 16 are policy teams, organized either by tax (for example, corporate) or labour market or sector (property tax). The idea is to have any policy proposal contained within a team but real policy is too wide, so there is typically Department for Work and Pensions (DWP) involvement and also across other directorates.

The consequences are not all benign according to Person A:

> the reallocation weakened the link between HMT and assessment of what happened in the field. Now the process has a clear divide with policy in HMT, but real-world

[7] Person B interview.

experience is at HMRC and they don't communicate as well as if they were all in one organization. It also affects career structures: now, if you are interested in tax policy, you go to HMT. If you start there the chance you will understand what happens in the field or on the ground is low. Policy becomes divorced from an understanding of how it is affecting behaviour in the field.[8]

These organizational changes have thus increased the power of the Treasury over tax policy, which were already quite substantial, at the expense of HMRC. But it does have another very important consequence. Sometimes the teams are deliberately used in a competitive environment, to get different people giving different views. For instance, as the R&D tax credit was shepherded through the institutional process, the input from multiple departments:

gives ministers broader choice. It works well if the three have equal power. Revenue controls costings; Productivity team ... had the eyes and ears of Special Advisers and Ministers because innovation was valued; Tax Policy sat in the middle with the scorecard trying to balance; each had its own focus. No-one has to tell HMT to get lined up with Enterprise [productivity] and Policy [tax] because you need them to fight for you.[9]

Second, partly as a consequence of the first set of changes, the process is now far more 'political' than before, at the special adviser and ministerial level. Special advisers were a feature of the political process even at the time of the Meade Report, however, they have become more important over time, especially during the past ten years. As Person C described the process during Brown's Chancellorship:

you had enfranchisement of political advisors far deeper than would have been the case before ... Special advisors were the real motive forces. Some are brought in because they have specialist knowledge of a topic, acting as a key expert witness within HMT. In HMT they were far more part of the day-to-day work, and, while they couldn't instruct anyone in the Civil Service, given that they talked to ministers all the time, they were often considered to be the mouthpiece of the minister. One always wanted to talk to the Special Advisor to figure out where the minister was coming from[10] and you might have four meetings with a Special Adviser, then one with the Chancellor. The result was that you would get much clearer policy direction much earlier.

[8] Person A interview.
[9] Person C interview.
[10] Person C interview. This point applies equally to representatives of outside interests and to those within HMT crafting policy proposals.

This change has created a systematic demand for information that can only be provided by outside organizations. For example, in the case of the R&D Tax Credit that we examine below,

> HMT at the time was trying to build more direct contact with business. Previously, all contact had been via the Inland Revenue and the Department for Trade and Industry (DTI) . . . and Treasury wanted to have direct company input in order to resist its intentions being constantly trumped by 'this won't work' statements from the others who had such direct contact. Furthermore, the Inland Revenue suffered from a negative external reputation as the tax collector and HMT had the advantage that it was seen by business as a policy group, not just the people who take your money.
>
> Finally, the direct access to company ideas meant that the ideas were delivered 'unwashed' to special advisors, rather than being 'normalized' through the Budget process. This led to a large initial set of vibrant ideas, with special advisers being involved in the weeding out process.[11]

The period we review, and specifically Brown's Chancellorship, may have been the peak of special advisers' importance in tax policy-making. According to Person E:

> Nearly a year after the move of Gordon Brown from the Treasury it is clear that special advisers are no longer the absolutely key element in the policy making process that they were between 1997 and 2007.

Nevertheless, tax policy is more 'political' than it used to be, with a greater role for special advisers than at the time of the Meade Report. Partly as a result of this, there has also been a fusion of tax policy goals with other political goals. The fusion of legislative input with the desire for social engineering is usually used to explain why the US tax code is so much more complicated than the UK code:

> The British example shows that the American tax code could be much simpler if Americans were willing to reduce the extent to which [they] tried to administer social policy through the tax code (Gale (1999)).

However, as already stated, this difference may be eroding:

> Mr. Brown's penchant for fine-tuning taxes has doubled the size of the tax code to 8,300 pages . . . the second-longest in the world's 20 top economies, after India. (*Wall Street Journal*, 3/21/07, p. 1)[12]

Increased fusion of tax policy with other political goals, Treasury assuming responsibility for tax policy input, and the increased politicization of the

[11] Person C interview.

[12] Citing a report by the World Bank and PriceWaterhouseCoopers.

whole tax policy process mark significant recent, though by no means certainly permanent, changes in the British tax policy process.

Finally, another important institutional innovation in the past thirty years is the introduction of the fiscal rules. The Labour government chose to impose two fiscal rules in 1998. The first was known as the 'golden rule' which demanded that the current budget be balanced over an economic cycle. The second rule was known as the 'sustainable investment' or 'net debt' rule. This said that net debt should remain at 'a stable and prudent level', which the government chose to define as below 40% of GDP. These rules were instituted in order that there be transparent public finance goals to which the government could be held to account, thereby ensuring responsible management of the public finances. We do not discuss the fiscal rules in much more detail since they relate more to the difference between levels of public spending and taxation, rather than levels of taxation.

13.3. TAX POLICY IN PRACTICE

This section describes how tax systems have been reformed over the past thirty years in five broad areas—income, social security contributions, indirect, corporate, and property taxes. It will concentrate on drawing out which political forces and ideas have driven the process, with a particular focus on the UK, though also contrasting and comparing the cross-country experience.

13.3.1. Income tax

One of the main headline changes of the last thirty years has been the fall in statutory marginal tax rates, with the top rate falling by the most. In the UK, following their election victory in 1979, the Conservatives cut the top rate on earned income from 83% to 60%, and the basic rate from 33% to 30%. Over the 1980s, these continued to be cut, with the top rate falling to 40% in 1988.

The Labour Party opposed these cuts throughout the 1980s, stating in its 1987 general election manifesto that, 'We will reverse the extra tax cuts which the richest 5 per cent have received from the Tory government and allocate that money instead to the most needy.' However, by 1997 the Labour Party under Tony Blair had changed its tune, with its general election manifesto stating that, 'There will be no increase in the basic or top rates of income tax.'

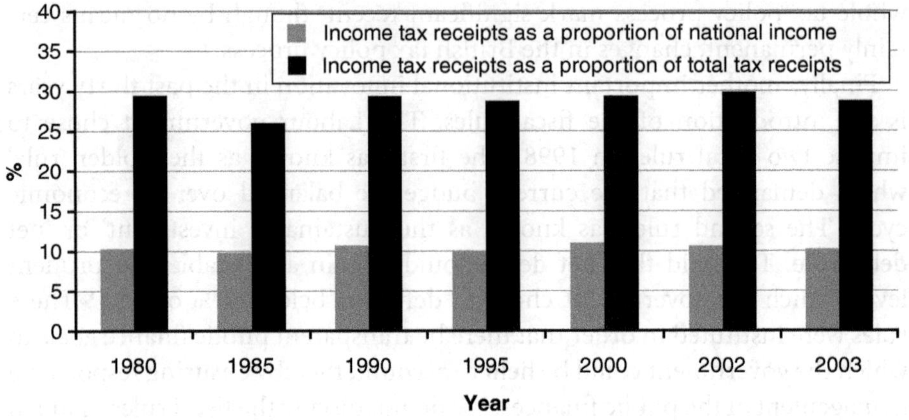

Source: OECD Revenue Statistics.

Figure 13.1. Income tax receipts as a proportion of GDP and total tax receipts

Drawing out the political reasons behind why statutory rates fell during the 1980s will be a key question for this chapter, as will why there has been a convergence on the status quo amongst the main political parties in recent years. We will attempt to answer these questions in Section 13.4 through an examination of voter preferences and models of political economy.

In contrast to the decline in statutory rates, it seems clear from Figure 13.1 that the overall burden of income tax—as measured by income tax receipts as a proportion of national income—has changed little over the past thirty years. This is because whilst statutory rates have been cut, thresholds and allowances have tended to rise in line with inflation, whilst earnings have risen more quickly, leading the number of higher rate tax-payers to grow from 674,000 in 1979–80 to 3.3 million in 2006–07—this process is known as 'bracket creep' or 'fiscal drag'. Moreover, certain major tax expenditures, such as mortgage interest tax relief, have been withdrawn, leading to a broadening of the income tax base. It is worth noting that 'fiscal drag' does not just affect income tax, it affects all taxes where the tax base grows faster than allowances and thresholds used for that tax. In fact, the Treasury estimates that 'fiscal drag' on all taxes contributes an additional 0.2% of national income to tax revenues every year.[13]

Looking at this from a political economy standpoint, it is odd how important the statutory rate has been in political debate relative to thresholds, given their joint importance in determining the tax burden. Income tax 'cuts'

[13] Paragraph A24 of HM Treasury, *End of Year Fiscal Report*, December 2003 <http://www.hm treasury.gov.uk/media/324/70/end_of_year_352%5B1%5D.pdf>.

appeared to be quite popular in the 1980s and how much you pay in income tax is quite observable and transparent. Yet the overall burden of income tax has hardly budged. This observation also raises the question of fiscal illusion—the idea that voters systematically underestimate the amount they are paying in tax. We will discuss how well informed the public are about the tax system in Section 13.6, together with a discussion of overall levels of transparency and accountability.

13.3.2. National Insurance contributions

The other major tax that is levied on earned income in the UK is National Insurance contributions (NICs). Over time the main NIC rates have risen for both employees and employers, rising from 6.5% in 1979–80 to 11% in 2006–07 for employee contributions (10% to 12.8% for employer contributions).

It is not clear that NICs should be treated as conceptually different from income tax, and whether a comparison with other countries' social security contributions is a valid one. This is because there is only a weak connection between contributions made and entitlement in the UK, compared with a much stronger one in other countries, particularly those in continental Europe. Moreover, in contrast to other countries where social security contributions are often earmarked for specific areas of public expenditure—a process known as hypothecation—NICs are not hypothecated in any meaningful sense. These two points suggest only minimal differences between paying income tax and NICs, something further underlined by a gradual alignment of their respective schedules.

Despite this, the fact that NICs and marginal rates of income tax have followed different trends over the past thirty years suggests that raising NICs is more politically acceptable than is raising income tax. Section 13.6 will discuss this issue further in the context of models of political economy where voters are imperfectly informed.

13.3.3. Indirect taxation

When VAT replaced purchase tax in 1973, it was not particularly controversial though it was considered complex and some believed it to be a source of price inflation. However, its structure has been a source of controversy, for instance, such controversy forced Labour to derogate from the EEC 6th VAT Directive in 1977 to maintain a zero rate for children's clothing.

Since 1979, the main rate was increased twice by the Conservatives: in 1979, from a two-tier system of 8% and 12.5% to a single higher rate of 15%, to help pay for lower statutory rates of income tax; and then again in 1991, from 15% to 17.5%, to help pay for reductions in the poll tax. Partly as a result of these changes, the proportion of GDP taken up by indirect tax receipts rose from 8.3% in 1979 to reach 11.2% by 2005. This overall change in the burden of indirect taxes does not tell us much about the change in its composition. There has in fact been a shift away from specific taxes on goods and excise duties towards the broadly based and uniform VAT. (More specific details can be found in Chapter 1 (Adam, Browne, and Heady).)

As already stated, the structure of VAT has been a more pertinent political issue than the main rate. All parties have attached a high salience to the zero-rating of children's clothing, food, and other items. Demonstrating this is the fact that the Labour Party has included a pledge in all of its recent general election manifestos: pledges along the lines of 'We renew our pledge not to extend VAT to food, children's clothes, books and newspapers and public transport fares' (taken from the 1997 Labour manifesto).

Similarly, the Labour Party made much political capital from the Conservatives' imposition of VAT on domestic energy at 8% in 1994, and from their role in preventing the Conservatives increasing this to 17.5% in 1995, as was the original intention. Labour then symbolically cut the rate to 5% in the summer budget of 1997, the first budget after the new Labour government had been elected. The taxation of petrol was, however, to prove even more costly for Labour. In response to high levels of tax on petrol, protests in September 2001 almost brought the country to a standstill and caused Labour to lose its lead in the polls for the first time since it was elected in 1997.

In our analysis of the role of interest groups in Section 13.5, we discuss how and why certain elements of indirect taxes have proved to be so politically controversial. Our discussion will emphasize the role that analysing individual taxes on their own rather than as part of the tax system has played in making these issues so controversial and reform so difficult. We will also extend this discussion to the present debate on council tax.

Coming back to this issue of why steady rises in the overall rate of VAT have proven to be politically sustainable, perhaps this is because it helped to pay for things voters valued more, such as lower rates of income tax or a lower poll tax. However, it is impossible to discuss VAT without reference to the increasing role played by the EU in this area. In fact we see that many current members of the EU have increased or introduced VAT over the past twenty-five years. This list includes founder members such as France, Germany, Italy, but also includes newer members such as Spain, Greece, and most of the former communist countries of Central and Eastern Europe. From Chapter 1 by Adam, Browne, and Heady, we also know that it is EU countries who raise relatively high proportions of revenue from indirect taxation. This is particularly the case when comparing major EU countries, such as Germany and France, with other major OECD economies, such as Japan and the USA.

In stark contrast to the largely uncontroversial raising of VAT in the EU, Canada, Australia, and Japan have all introduced a Goods and Services Tax (GST) or consumption tax over the past thirty years amid a wave of political controversy. One reason for the relatively controversial introduction of indirect taxes in Canada, Australia, and Japan could be the administrative differences between the operation of their indirect taxes and VAT in the EU.[14] More important though may be the increasing role of the EU in VAT policy, which has largely been to aid the creation of the Single Market. The 6th VAT Directive of the EU, introduced in 1977 (amended in various years and complemented by other directives since then), states that all EU countries must have a VAT rate above 15%, which goods can be granted reduced-rate status and that new exemptions for goods and services must be agreed to by the EU. This means that voters in current or aspirant members of the EU have to weigh the benefits of membership of the EU and the single market against any reservations about being forced to increase/introduce VAT. The intertwining of the issue of VAT with the issue of EU membership may thus largely defuse the introduction/extension of VAT as a potential political concern in a large number of European countries.

13.3.4. Corporation tax

Almost all major OECD countries show a very similar pattern in the timing and nature of reforms to their corporate taxation systems. One phrase can sum it up: 'Gradual cuts in the statutory rate of corporation tax, combined with base-broadening measures.' This has occurred across almost all

[14] Note that there has never even been a serious political attempt to implement a VAT in the US, where 90% of the states have retail sales taxes, a majority dating from the Depression. Exemptions and allowances vary widely across states. Increases in sales taxes are controversial, often occurring in response to fiscal crises, when it is often expedient to label them as temporary. For instance, Rhode Island's current 7% sales tax rate was raised 'temporarily' from 1 to 6% in the 1970s, and again 'temporarily' from 6 to 7% in the early 1990s to bail out the state's failed credit unions.

countries, no matter the political persuasion of governing parties nor the institutional setting. Moreover, there is little evidence to suggest that corporation tax has been a major issue in elections in any of these countries. Corporate tax receipts as a proportion of GDP have remained fairly constant in all major OECD countries. Base-broadening measures have largely offset the effect of falling statutory rates (see the chapters on taxing corporate income by Auerbach, Devereux, and Simpson, Chapter 9, and international capital taxation by Griffith, Hines, and Sørensen, Chapter 10, for more details).

The structure of corporation tax is complicated the world over. Cross-country comparisons are best illustrated in the separate chapters focusing on corporate tax and on international issues. However, in order to examine the role of interest groups in the development of corporate tax policy, we have chosen to conduct a detailed case-study of the development of the R&D tax credit in the UK (Section 13.5). Therefore, it is important to note the following facts.

First and foremost, the fact that Britain now has an R&D tax credit is not particularly surprising. Many governments offer R&D tax incentives to firms in research-intensive industries as part of a strategy to promote domestic innovation and competitiveness. As of 2006, R&D tax incentives are available in 18 of the 30 OECD countries, up from 12 countries in 1996.[15] These R&D incentives usually take the form of a tax relief, with the amount provided being determined by the extent of R&D activity undertaken.

Britain established a relatively generous credit by international standards. Billings and Paschke (2003)[16] confirm that the US provides one of the lowest incentives in the world for R&D. However, in a series of interviews, senior managers at leading pharmaceutical firms confirmed that from an investment perspective, the US continues to be the most attractive location; when asked to name potential future challenges to US leadership, not a single interviewee mentioned tax incentives as a significant consideration (Xu (2007)). Sedgley (2006) presents data that disputes any simple correlation between a country's share of OECD R&D spending and the generosity of its tax incentives (France and Germany, for instance, have less generous R&D tax incentives but higher shares of R&D than the UK). On the other hand, Berger (1993), Hall (1993), and Bloom, Griffith, and Van Reenen (2002) all present evidence that such credits can lead to increases in R&D.

It is also notable that international bodies have become increasingly important in the development of corporate tax policy, including the OECD and the

[15] Sedgley (2006), p. 42.

[16] Calculation methods are published in a paper in *Tax Notes International* in 2003.

EU. We note this fact, but leave it to Chapters 9 and 10 (Auerbach, Devereux, and Simpson; Griffith, Hines, and Sørensen) to discuss it in more detail.

13.3.5. Property and local taxation

The years since Meade saw one major attempt at innovation in property taxation. As already highlighted, less than 5% of total tax revenue is raised locally. Over recent history, practically all of this has been through various kinds of property taxes. As a result, it is thus quite difficult to separate out issues relating to property taxes and the degree of centralization in tax setting powers.

Up to and including the 1980s, local authorities funded part of their spending through a system called domestic rates. Every property had a 'rateable value', which was then multiplied by a tax rate called the 'rate poundage' set by each local authority to calculate the amount of domestic rates payable by residential households. There were rate rebates for poorer households. A similar scheme of rates also existed for business properties. The rest of local authority spending was funded through grants from central government, which were adjusted in order to equalize tax raising powers across local authorities.

By the late 1980s, 'rateable values' had not been adjusted since 1973 and thus were out of line with current patterns of property values. Domestic rates were also unpopular as some low-income households faced high rates bills, but had fairly modest incomes, for example, single pensioners. The unpopularity of rates can also be seen in the numerous instances of 'rate capping' during the 1980s, whereby the government prevented councils raising rates by more than a given amount.

The government also argued that this system was detrimental to local political accountability as

> All too often this accountability is blurred by the complexities of the national grant system and by the fact that differences arise among those who vote for, those who pay for and those who receive local government services.

In place of domestic rates, the government proposed to introduce a flat-rate charge for each adult in a household (with a few exemptions and rebates).[17] This charge was officially known as the community charge, but became known as the 'poll tax'. The intent of these proposals was to create

[17] Regarding non-domestic rates, they proposed equalizing rates on business properties across the country combined with a centralization of revenue collection. It also proposed replacing the scheme that equalized resources to correct for an uneven distribution of rateable values with a need-based assessment of spending requirements.

a system whereby each extra pound of local spending had to be funded through the poll tax rather than central government grants, with a view to increasing local political accountability by linking local government spending and local election voting. As well as improving political accountability, it was also argued that the community charge would be more equitable, since it would ensure that everyone contributed something to the provision of local services.

These proposals were included in the Conservative Party's general election manifesto in 1987. However, the Labour Party remained largely silent on the poll tax during the campaign in order to avoid reminding voters of the perceived profligacy of so-called 'loony Left' councils. Despite the opposition of the Chancellor at the time, Nigel Lawson, and an attempt by the Conservative MP Michael Mates to make the poll tax dependent on banded household income, the proposals were enacted and came into effect on 1 April 1990 (they came into effect one year earlier in Scotland). However, the poll tax proved to be very unpopular: there were riots in central London and many individuals were sent to court for refusing to pay the 'unfair' poll tax. The unpopularity of the poll tax is widely seen as a major contributory factor of the downfall of Margaret Thatcher that would follow later that year.

Why it was controversial is not that hard to explain. Most people felt its level and structure were deeply unfair, with many people being worse off by relatively large amounts. Many voters in social and economic groups C1 and C2 expected to be worst hit by the new poll tax (according to a poll conducted by NOP for the *Local Government Chronicle*). Moreover, the riots in Trafalgar Square were attended not just by the 'usual suspects', but also by these middle-income voters who expected to lose relatively large amounts from the poll tax. Therefore it is not surprising that many Conservative MPs felt their seats threatened. This fear almost certainly motivated many of them to vote for Michael Heseltine (who promised to get rid of the poll tax) against Margaret Thatcher in a leadership election in November 1990, resulting in her downfall.

What is surprising is how such a policy was even contemplated, let alone proposed and implemented. According to Butler, Adonis, and Travers (1994), it was a natural result of the set-up of British political institutions and nothing has changed to prevent such a blunder from happening again. According to them, apart from the already mentioned circumstance that Labour was unable to oppose the poll tax proposals effectively during the 1987 general election, the electoral system still guarantees safe legislative majorities, especially when the Opposition seems incapable of forming a government. Governing parties are still able to come up with policies without consulting outside the party or cabinet. Frequent cabinet shuffles still prevent most ministers from looking at policies from a considered long-term point of view. Governing parties are still largely able to force legislation through the Commons, even if their own backbenchers oppose it, through the promise of patronage. Finally, the House of Lords is still heavily restricted in its ability to scrutinize tax policy changes.

The experience of the poll tax thus provides very useful lessons for potential tax reformers. The UK institutional set-up permits a huge freedom of action for policymakers, with little effective scrutiny of tax policy after it has been announced. This may seem to be a blessing for a policymaker keen on reforming the tax system in a particular direction. However, insulation from effective scrutiny may allow them to implement deeply unpopular policies, resulting in severe punishment from a disgruntled public. For example, a brief legislative defeat over the poll tax might have been preferable to the rioting in Trafalgar Square. We will discuss measures that could improve effective scrutiny in Section 13.6 and in our final section on policy recommendations for the institutional process.

The poll tax was gradually unwound from 1991 onwards, with an increase in VAT in Budget 1991 paying for a reduction in average poll tax levels. The poll tax was then replaced with the council tax in 1993, which is not that dissimilar from the old domestic rates system though there are some important differences: council tax is calculated according to banded property values and there is relief for single occupants. Council taxes were originally set at a lower level than domestic rates, and now provide barely one-sixth of local authority expenditure. The net result of the poll tax experiment and changes to non-domestic rates has been a greater centralization of tax revenues. There is just as much uncertainty as to how increases in local taxation translate into greater local spending and, consequently, just as little local political accountability over local spending levels.

The council tax seems to be just as unpopular as domestic rates. For instance, when a YouGov poll for the Taxpayer's Alliance in August 2007 asked respondents which out of a set of potential tax reforms they favoured, the most popular was lower levels of council tax. Why council tax might be so unpopular will be discussed in relation to interest-group theory in Section 13.5, and with relation to voters' understanding of the tax system in Section 13.6 where we will also explore measures that could improve central and local political accountability.

13.4. INCOME TAXATION AND ELECTORAL INTERESTS: A CASE STUDY

Although personal taxes as a share of national income have remained at about the same level, a main headline change of the period since Meade has been the fall in statutory marginal tax rates in Britain (and elsewhere). This has happened over a period of rising and increasingly unequal pre-tax incomes in Britain. Nevertheless this increase in pre-tax income inequality has not been met by an increasingly progressive income tax structure. (See Adam, Browne, and Heady, Chapter 1). This is potentially puzzling to both political economists and optimum tax theorists: under fairly straightforward assumptions, in a system in which taxes and transfers are either chosen by a majority of rational self-interested voters or set by a benevolent social welfare maximizer, an increase in pre-tax income inequality would usually be offset by changes in taxation. The fact that this did not happen—and has frequently been observed not to happen in other contexts—suggests that we should look closely at the information, beliefs, and attitudes of voters, For example, did top rates come down and stay down because people changed their minds about the desirability of redistribution? We also need to consider how closely the politics of tax policy choice approximate majority voting. Political economists take note of wide institutional variation in how elections are conducted: majoritarian versus proportional representation is an aspect of this, along with the nature of parliamentary authority, accountability of the executive, whether politicians are term-limited, and whether there is scope for direct democracy.

Lowered top and basic income tax rates in Britain have proved politically sustainable for some time. In this section, we discuss this within the context of a fairly generalized model of political economy, relating changes in top and basic income tax rates to evidence and theory on voters, electoral interests and political parties. It is a case study: we discuss issues of theory and modelling at a fairly general level and tie this back to the policy and institutional issues in the UK. We stress the significance of voter loyalties to polarized parties, how the parties' manifesto pledges in turn affect voters' choices, and how voters connect the desirability of redistribution to their confidence in the government as their agent for public provision.

For this purpose we draw on the best source of consistent and reliable data on the evolution of attitudes in the UK, which is the British Social Attitudes survey. Since 1984 this has provided evidence on social attitudes of nationally representative samples of British residents and questions asked include several pertinent to the level and structure of taxation.

13.4.1. What taxes do voters want?

The standard model

Analysis of determination of tax rates under democracy begins with analysis of voter preferences. The standard model here proceeds from the same fundamentals as the optimum income tax literature. Voters like private consumption—and possibly also publicly provided goods—but not work. Taxation (interpreted broadly) determines individuals' private budget constraints linking the two and individual hours' choices then link tax schedules to realized utility at differing wage rates. The issue for political economy, as in the optimum income tax literature, is to study determination of the tax function from within some feasible set, restricted to satisfy the public sector budget constraint and possibly other administrative requirements.

Consider individual preferences over tax schedules. Self-interested individuals prefer tax schedules which maximize their own utility subject to the government budget constraint. Let us suppose for the moment (as in Romer (1975), Roberts (1977), and Meltzer and Richard (1981) for example) that the tax functions under comparison are linear and there are no publicly provided goods. We can think of there being two effects to positive tax rates. First, income is redistributed from the better off to the worse off and secondly, hours' choices are distorted and resources wasted in collection, creating a deadweight loss. The latter effect benefits no one but the former is to the advantage of those below mean pre-tax income[18] at the expense of those above it. Individuals whose wages are such that incomes would fall above the mean in the absence of taxes therefore favour zero taxes whereas those with lower wages are prepared to trade off the efficiency costs against the redistributive gains and therefore favour positive rates. Meltzer and Richard (1981) argue that desired tax rates will increase as one moves down the wage distribution. Eventually one reaches wage levels at which individuals would choose not to work at their desired tax rate and for all such individuals the best tax rate is simply that which maximizes the revenue available to fund

[18] Since the tax is linear and there is no other form of public spending, the government budget constraint requires the individual with mean pre-tax income to pay zero tax.

their government-provided post-tax income, a tax rate nonetheless less than 100% because of the incentive effects of taxation.[19]

With a linear tax schedule and a government budget constraint there is only one degree of freedom in tax setting and individuals are restricted to comparing taxes simply along the single dimension of the marginal tax rate. With more flexibility in feasible tax schedules the scope for individuals to design tax schedules which benefit them while placing the burden on others is increased. In particular, if we were to allow for, say, systems with two marginal rates then those on lower wages would be able to choose systems which have lower rates of tax on their own incomes but which make up revenue through higher rates on those on higher wages.

Some of the starker predictions of this sort of theorizing about individual preferences over tax setting—for example, no support for taxation at all from those above mean income—arise from a particularly crude assumption of self-interestedness. Even without our assuming altruism, the rich may believe that high levels of inequality would cause problems of crime and social unrest which would make their lives uncomfortable. If we allow for the possibility of altruistic concern as a complementary motivation then support for redistribution from better-off individuals becomes even less surprising. If we suppose, say, that individuals choose tax rates which maximize some weighted average of their own and other's utilities then a desire for positive tax rates will be present even at high incomes. The extent of altruism may differ between societies—and it has been argued, for example by Alesina, Glaeser, and Sacerdote (2001), that it is promoted by factors such as social and racial homogeneity—in which case the steepness with which desired tax rates decline with income should be greater in societies less disposed to altruism. Georgiadis and Manning (2007) point out that uncertainty about future income may have implications somewhat similar to altruism in inducing concern about tax rates at other points in the distribution. We return to discussion of the insurance role of taxation below.

Beliefs and attitudes on the distribution of income

The foregoing analysis suggests that support for taxation and redistribution should be related to position in the income distribution. For evidence

[19] These observations essentially all apply in the simplified model used by Bolton and Roland (1997) and subsequently by McCarty, Poole, and Rosenthal (2006) in which voters are interested solely in post-tax income, the redistributive gain is linear and there is a deadweight loss which is quadratic in the tax rate. The latter effect is therefore small relative to the former for small tax rates but becomes increasingly important for larger tax rates.

on this we turn to the BSA which has contained information on household income and on attitudes to redistribution throughout its duration. Information on income is banded and bands change with time but we can construct a measure of income position which is reasonably comparable across years by calculating for each respondent the number of other respondents placing themselves in lower income bands in the same year.[20]

One might worry, before using this measure, as to the extent to which individuals perceive their position in the distribution accurately. The BSA in 2004 asked respondents specifically what proportion of the population they believed to be less well off than themselves (Sefton (2005)) and it is interesting to compare this to actual position. Figure 13.2 shows that perception is strongly positively related to true position[21] though there is some evidence that those at the top underestimate how well off they are and those at the bottom underestimate how badly off they are[22] (in line with the observations of Taylor-Gooby, Hastie, and Bromley (2003) and Evans and Kelley (2004)) with the result that the perceived income distribution is a good deal flatter than the true distribution. We have checked using the 2004 data to see whether relating other survey responses to actual income position gives a misleading impression of relation to perceived position and there seems little evidence that this is an important issue.

BSA has asked a number of questions about support for income redistribution as an objective of government and we base analysis on the most consistent and longstanding of these.[23] Figure 13.3 shows how support for redistribution has evolved over time and also how it varies across the income

[20] As a measure of household living standard this is only rough since there are obvious arguments for adjusting for needs as reflected in household size and composition. Our measure of position is based crudely on gross household income without any such adjustment. It is questionable whether such an adjustment is needed in the current context anyway since it is position in the distribution of tax payments that matters and not position in the distribution of living standards. Since survey responses rates are known to vary with income we are careful to use weighting factors appropriately. Respondents in the same income band are assumed, for simplicity, to be half at higher incomes and half at lower.

[21] The figure shows a non-parametric regression of perceived position on the truth. Imprecision in measurement of true position means we should not expect a 45 degree line even if individuals knew the truth, but the deviation is sufficiently large to think there may well be considerable misperception.

[22] Hall and Preston (2000) present evidence from an earlier year's BSA showing that perception of hypothetical income-related tax payments is also reasonably accurate.

[23] Respondents are asked to place themselves on a scale from strong agreement to strong disagreement with the statement that 'government should redistribute from the better-off to those that are less well-off'. We create a binary variable whereby those 'agreeing' or 'strongly agreeing' are counted as approving redistribution.

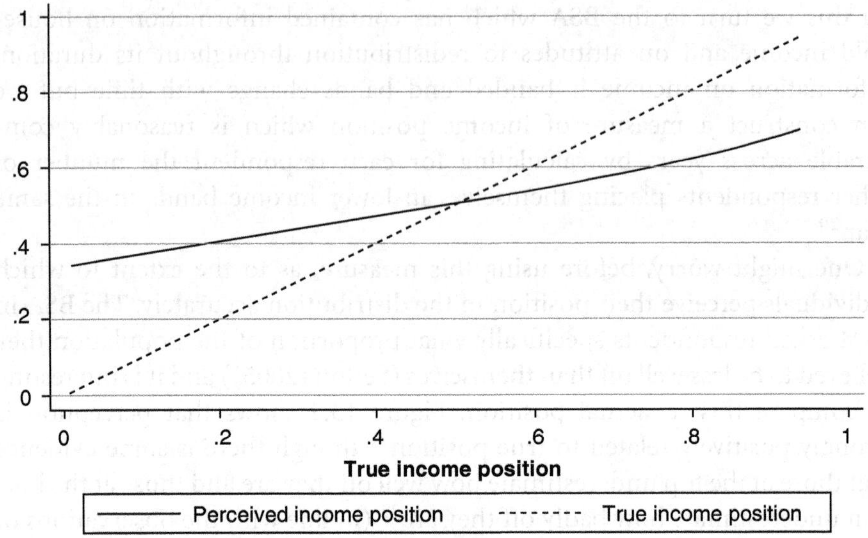

Figure 13.2. Income distribution: Perception and reality (BSA, 2004)

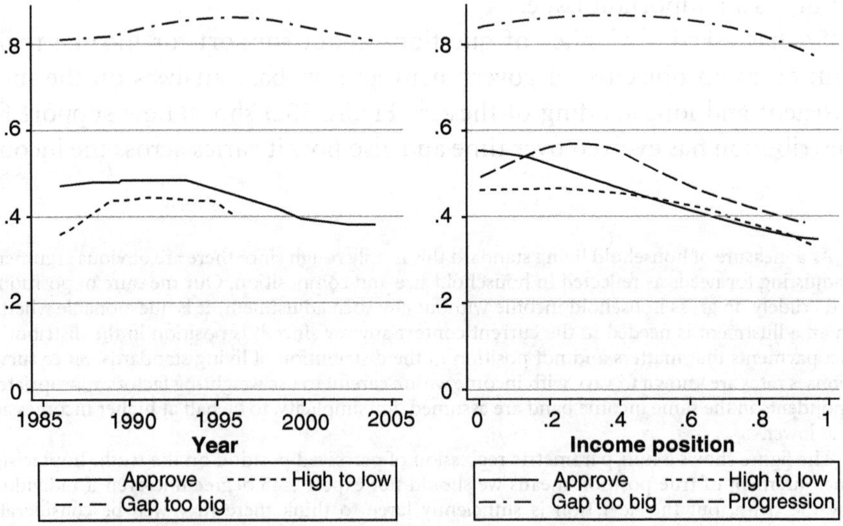

Figure 13.3. Support for redistribution (BSA, 1986–2004)

distribution.[24] The line in question is the unbroken line labelled 'Approve'. Approval close to 50% through the late 1980s and early 1990s drops somewhat in the mid-1990s but remains at over a third.[25] Georgiadis and Manning (2007) link this data to similar questions in British Election Surveys from ten years earlier, suggesting that support for redistribution was then considerably higher so that the decline is long term. They suggest that the decline over time can be linked to 'changing views about the workings of the economy, both in terms of the importance of incentives and the justness of the pre-tax distribution of resources' (p. 32), though cautioning that directions of causation between different attitudes are highly problematic to identify. Hills (2002) and Svallfors (1997) argue that declining support for redistribution may be a case of attitudes following policy making.

Sefton (2005) and Orton and Rowlingson (2007) point out that the proportion of the population expressing themselves as in support of government redistribution is consistently considerably smaller than the proportion who declare themselves in the same survey to view the gap between incomes of rich and poor as too large (labelled 'Gap too big'), which remains over 75% throughout the period. Plainly many individuals think either that governments should reduce the gap by other means (such as education policy or wage controls, say) or that ameliorating the gap is not the business of government.

The relationship to income is very clearly declining as one would expect, though it is notable that, even at the top end of the distribution, agreement with redistribution as an appropriate activity for government is, on average over the period, as high as a third of the population. Georgiadis and Manning (2007) point to correlations of attitudes with several other household characteristics—men, those in the middle years of life, those unmarried, and those without children and ethnic minorities, for example, are all more favourable than others to redistribution.

Beliefs and attitudes on taxation

Questions on the structure of taxation have not been asked in a consistent fashion over the entire period. An interesting set of questions, enquiring

[24] In this, as in similar figures below, the relationships are smoothed by taking running means. The relationship with year shows the evolution of the unconditional mean, whereas the relationship with income is taken after subtraction of year effects.

[25] By comparison the percentage disapproving of redistribution is typically between a quarter and a third over the period covered (though it exceeds the percentage approving for the first time in the final year).

Table 13.1. Opinions on taxes by self-assessed income group

Self-assessed income	No of respondents	Taxes on					
		High incomes		Medium incomes		Low incomes	
		Too high	Too low	Too high	Too low	Too high	Too low
High	460	36.8	19.1	37.8	5.5	71.0	1.5
Medium	8,472	17.5	44.6	33.9	4.0	78.2	2.2
Low	8,003	14.6	52.9	29.5	8.1	82.9	2.6

Table 13.2. Opinions on redistribution by self-assessed income group

Self-assessed income	No of respondents	Redistribute from		
		High to low	High to medium	Medium to low
High	460	16.1	3.0	4.2
Medium	8,472	37.8	9.0	2.8
Low	8,003	47.6	8.9	6.6

whether tax rates[26] on high, medium, and low incomes were too high, about right or too low, were asked in several years up to the mid-1990s. Individuals were also asked at the same time to assess their own income relative to these categories allowing us to draw inferences about how individuals saw their own tax rates. As Table 13.1 shows, not many individuals saw themselves as having a 'high' income but those that did were much less likely to see taxes on high incomes as too low—a rather popular view in the rest of the population. Those seeing their own incomes either as 'medium' or as 'low' were least likely also to see taxes on their own income group as too low, albeit that neither of these views was well supported in general.

Table 13.2 reports on the results of combining answers to different questions to draw inferences about attitudes to redistribution through taxes. If someone declares both that they believe taxes on high incomes are too low and that taxes on low incomes are too high it seems reasonable to think that they would support, at least to some extent, redistribution from high to low incomes[27]—we call this attitude 'High to Low'. Such individuals are more and

[26] The question is not specific as to whether it concerns average or marginal rates.

[27] The reverse opinion is too rare to be worth investigating. Although an appreciable number of individuals regard taxes as too high at the top end, these same individuals seldom regard low incomes as taxed too little.

more common the lower one looks in the self-assessed distribution. (Redistribution from high to medium incomes and from medium to low incomes also turn out to be most popular with recipients and least popular with those being taxed.) Figure 13.3 shows also that this alternatively defined measure of support for redistribution (labelled 'High to Low') varies negatively with actual position in the income distribution—in particular, that it declines sharply at high incomes. Tracking over time, we see that this view gained support in the mid-1980s—probably not coincidentally as marginal tax rates on high incomes were cut—but then showed hints of a decline (similar to that for the other measure considered earlier) in the mid-1990s at which point the question ceased to be asked.

Finally, a question asked only once, in 2004, offered respondents the alternative of funding a hypothetical increase in government spending by a flat additional tax payment, a proportional increase in taxes, or a progressive increase. Sefton (2005) reports that about half the population agreed with progression as an appropriate structure. The final line on Figure 13.3 shows that support for progression as indicated in responses to this question tended also to decline with income.

Altogether the clear income gradient in answers to these questions suggests that at least some of the preference for redistribution is linked, consciously or not, to self interest though the support for redistribution evident even in the richest groups of the population surveyed shows this is less than the whole of the picture.

Redistribution of pre-tax incomes earned with certainty is only one view of the purpose of progressive taxation and state welfare. Another view sees the goal of redistributive policy as providing insurance against uncertainty in incomes or in employment rather than or in addition to redistribution. Introducing such uncertainty raises new issues, for example as to how income risk and risk attitudes vary with income. Moene and Wallerstein (2001, 2003) show that self-interested support for state-provided insurance might in principle rise with income under reasonable assumptions about risk aversion. On the other hand, unemployment risk might be felt to decline with income, giving the well-off less reason to support welfare state redistribution. Indeed, Cusack et al. (2006) find that the demand for redistribution is related to exposure to labour market risk. Fong (2001) emphasizes the importance of beliefs about effort, luck, and opportunity of the less well advantaged in determining support for redistribution. Extending the Meltzer–Richard framework to a model in which taxed wage earners receive publicly provided goods but also face risks of temporarily joining a class of permanently unemployed in receipt of state benefits, Moene and Wallerstein (2001) demonstrate that how

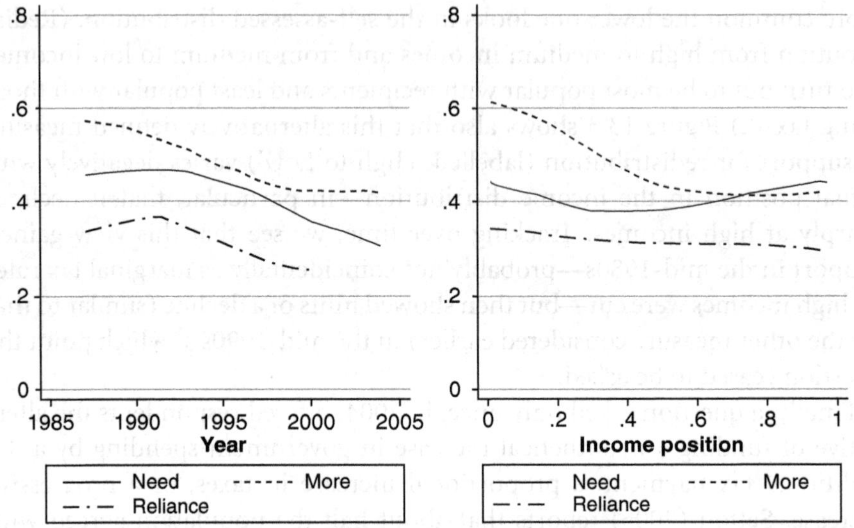

Figure 13.4. Support for social insurance (BSA, 1986–2004)

support for taxation varies with income depends upon assumptions made about the pattern of state spending.

Figure 13.4 presents a little more detail on attitudes within the BSA to welfare payments to the poor. While the evidence above suggests support for that aspect of redistribution which involves taking from the relatively rich, that need not mean comparable popularity for the distribution of funds through welfare spending to the relatively poor. The dashed line labelled 'More' shows support for increased payments to the poor.[28] This has fallen over time and is markedly lower among those with above average incomes. The other two lines are concerned with beliefs about the deservingness of the poor—that labelled 'Need' regards beliefs that the poor genuinely need the help given[29] and that labelled 'Reliance' regards the belief that self-reliance is not undermined by welfare state payments.[30] Again these views have become more negative over time though there is little evidence of any clear relationship to income within periods.[31]

[28] Specifically the question asks for agreement or disagreement with the opinion that 'the government should spend more money in welfare benefits for the poor, even if it leads to higher taxes'.

[29] Specifically the question asks for agreement or disagreement with the opinion that 'many people who get social security don't really deserve any help'.

[30] Specifically the question asks for agreement or disagreement with the opinion that 'the welfare state nowadays makes people less willing to look after themselves'.

[31] There are other questions in BSA relating social security to lack of self-reliance. Georgiadis and Manning (2007) draw attention to the association between these beliefs and support for

If we introduce expenditure on public provision of goods as another potential outlay of public funds then the demand for the goods provided becomes an issue in how voter attitudes differ. If taxes are raised proportionally to income and publicly provided goods are income elastic then this may be a reason for better-off voters to demand higher *levels* of taxes, for example. If there are different types of expenditure then not only will the composition of public spending be a source of political contention but expectations about how that contention is resolved will affect support for taxes and the way in which this varies with household characteristics.[32]

One question asked in almost every year of the BSA concerns whether or not the respondent would support an increase in the level of taxes and spending on health, education, and social benefits. For these particular items of spending, responses to this question provide the best long-term evidence on preferences regarding the size of the public sector and associated level of taxation. Figure 13.5 plots the proportion of respondents expressing themselves to be in favour of such a change over the period from 1986 to 2004. Those favouring an increase consistently exceed half of respondents and are at their highest, exceeding 60%, over the 1990s. There is little cross-sectional association with income, which may well be a consequence of the question grouping together goods of rather different income elasticities.

Given the apparent strength of support for increases in public spending over this period it is worth asking why politicians showed such reluctance to be seen favouring the associated increases in taxation. If the public doubts the likelihood of funds raised being spent as desired then this will obviously dampen support for tax increases. Hypothecation of tax revenues may be seen as a potential solution to the agency problem involved here but the essential fungibility of public funds makes credibility problems with any attempted promise to direct particular resources to particular uses inescapable. Even in a purely redistributive setting, there is the possibility that 'a fraction of total tax revenue that passes through the government's hands on the way from one set of citizen's to another is "lost" ... either through incompetence or venality' (Georgiadis and Manning (2007)). In the terms used earlier, such losses

redistribution and the apparently increasing strength of opinion that social security encourages dependence as evidence that declining support for redistribution is driven partly by changing views on incentive effects of the tax and welfare system. Unfortunately, BSA has little evidence regarding views on the incentive effects on high earners.

[32] Several papers, surveyed for example in Rubinfeld (1987), have sought to estimate demands for locally publicly provided goods using variation across localities in levels of provision and tax prices. Hall and Preston (2000) report on a largely unsuccessful attempt to separate tax price effects from income-dependent variation in demand for national public goods by randomization of tax instruments in questions in the BSA.

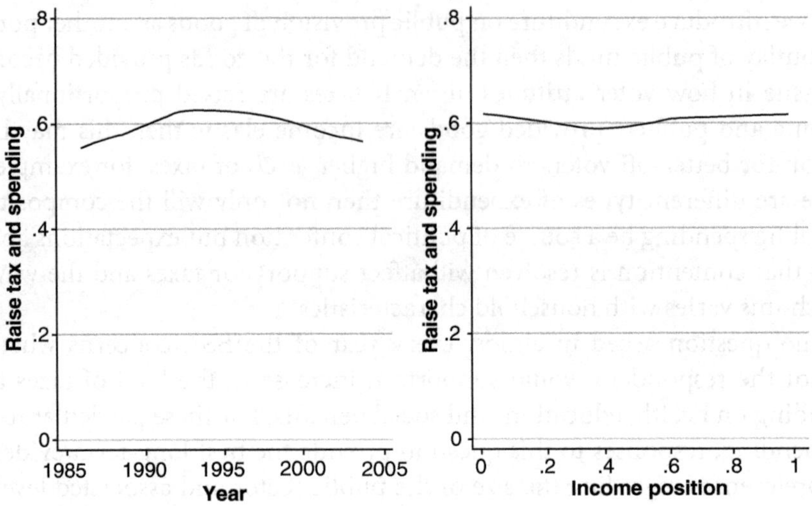

Figure 13.5. Support for public spending (BSA, 1986–2004)

would be viewed as another aspect of deadweight costs and declining trust in government competence or integrity interpreted as a perceived increase in those costs.

Unfortunately BSA asks no question addressing directly the issue of how effective the government is believed to be in directing public funds to desired uses but there are questions on trust. Specifically, for example, there is a question on whether the respondent trusts the party in government to put the interests of the country before those of the party.[33] Figure 13.6 shows a sharp and continuing decline in such trust, particularly over the 1980s and early 1990s. If this is reflective of a general erosion of confidence in government to use public money to deliver the public services demanded by voters then it may help explain why raising the headline rate of income tax is so politically difficult.

So what taxes do voters want?

Generally speaking, individuals favour redistribution, particularly that from 'high' to 'low' incomes. They also favour increases in public spending, and

[33] Specifically the question asks 'how much do you trust British governments of any party to place the needs of the nation above the interests of their political party'. We count someone as usually trusting government if they answer 'just about always' or 'most of the time' rather than 'only some of the time' or 'almost never'.

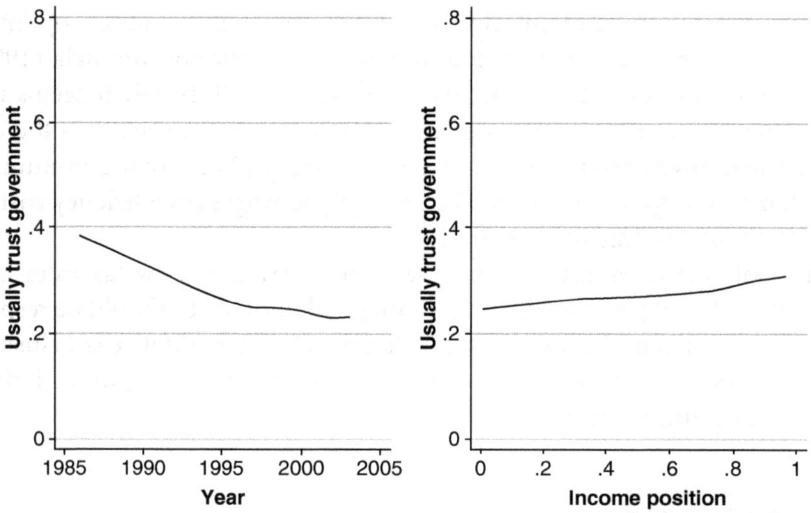

Figure 13.6. Trust in government (BSA, 1986–2004)

would like it to be funded on a progressive basis. It is also clear that preferences for redistribution decrease with income, as one might expect. However, it is also clear that preferences for redistribution have declined over the past twenty to thirty years.

We have already posited that declining levels of trust might explain why politicians have been reluctant to promise higher levels of public spending through increased levels of taxation, despite apparent public preference for such a policy. But we must ask other questions, such as why there were cuts in statutory marginal rates of income tax during the 1980s, a time when attitudes towards redistribution were at their most favourable. We attempt to answer this question through an examination of what we might expect politics to deliver, given different models of political economy. This involves consideration of the electoral system, party preferences, and the inherent multi-dimensionality of politics.

13.4.2. What taxes does politics deliver?

The foregoing analysis on individual preferences could serve as precursor to a standard treatment of the optimum income tax literature. Dependence of individual utilities on tax schedules is precisely the information needed for a hypothetical benevolent dictator to choose the tax schedule maximizing social welfare conceived as an appropriate aggregate of those individual utilities. In a general setting observations follow about the optimum structure of taxes and if we restrict ourselves to linear taxes we can compare optimum tax rates under different assumptions about the economy. Tuomala (1990), for instance, makes many comparisons of this type. Typically it seems true to say that optimum tax rates rise with the inequality of wages (as the case for redistributive correction becomes more pressing) and that optimum tax rates fall with responsiveness of labour supply to wages (as efficiency costs of redistribution become more acute).

The political economy literature seeks to investigate how tax rates arise from the political process. Since tax setting in democracies should be responsive to individual preferences it is not surprising that qualitative conclusions, at least of the simplest models, nonetheless have much in common with those regarding optimum tax setting.

Median voter models

The canonical model of political representation that has dominated political economy for fifty years is the case of two parties competing by announcing election strategies that they will carry out if they win office. The most stylized version of this model has no role for post-election politics with announcements being carried out after the election and parties whose sole motivation is to win. This approach was applied most influentially to the political economy of tax policy in Meltzer and Richard (1981), building on earlier work by Foley (1967), Romer (1975), and Roberts (1977).

The approach focuses on the rate of income tax as a single dimension of conflict between citizens who differ in their pre-tax incomes, as outlined above, the proceeds of taxation being spent on goods and services or income transfers which accrue uniformly to the citizens. As long as preferences are appropriately 'single-peaked', then competition between two parties, each of which cares only about winning, will result in the tax rate being chosen to suit the voter with median income. One simplistic interpretation of this is that we should expect the middle classes to have most political weight in determining tax policy outcomes.

The level of taxation, and thus the amount of redistribution, chosen by the median voter is determined by two things: (i) the distance between the median and mean income, and (ii) the extent to which increases in income taxation reduce pre-tax labour earnings through distortion of labour supply. To the extent that the difference between median and mean income can be regarded as indicative of the degree of inequality—as it is, for example, for a lognormal distribution—then these determinants are strikingly similar, at least qualitatively, to those that would determine optimum tax rates.

Another key implication of the theory which bears emphasizing is that both parties who compete to offer tax packages will offer the same policy. This is characteristic of the Downsian class of models in which this is based. There are periods in the UK in which such policy convergence seems plausible and there are clearly some important issues of tax policy where this is the case. For example, Labour in 1997 was committed to maintaining the 40% top rate of tax introduced by the Conservative Party in 1988. Likewise the Conservative Party in 2007 indicated a commitment to maintain Labour's spending plans (even before knowing what they were). But as a general proposition, there are sufficient differences in policy between parties—even in two-party systems—to make this a questionable intellectual foundation for studying political economy issues. We will discuss this further below.

This approach is hard to take to the data directly. First, the kind of tax system that it describes does not correspond very well to what we see in reality. Second, measuring the extent to which pre-tax income distributions are right skewed across countries on a consistent basis over time is also difficult. Most empirical work has tended to look across countries where it is difficult to believe that factors determining income distribution are not correlated with those affecting political choice over tax rates so that causation from the former to the latter is extraordinarily difficult to isolate. Moreover, the basic institutional structure which is needed to yield the median voter prediction—two vote seeking parties in a majoritarian system—seems implausible for many countries.

In any case the popularity of the model was never matched by the success of its empirical prediction that more pre-tax inequality should go hand in hand with more income-targeted redistribution (Perotti (1996)), even if there are historical instances where such a description might fit. Consequently, a significant literature extends the basic framework in a number of directions. For example Snyder and Kramer (1988) investigated voting on a progressive income tax in the presence of an untaxed alternative economy, but found difficulties in showing the existence of equilibrium. Voting behaviour in a Meltzer–Richard model also changes in the presence of social divisions including religion (Scheve and Stasavage (2006)), moral values (Roemer (1998)), Benabou and Tirole (2006)), race (Alesina and Glaeser (2004)), and the quality of jobs (Austen-Smith and Wallerstein (2006)).

Extending the median voter model to contexts in which tax and public spending choice acquire multiple dimensions requires heavy and unreasonable restrictions on voter preferences, on the nature of choice or on the political process. Moene and Wallerstein (2001) consider choice over both tax rates and targeting of benefits, demonstrating that equilibria may be found if one assumes issue-by-issue voting, for example, or party competition of a particularly restrictive kind. Bergstrom and Goodman (1973) discuss issues in public spending choice. However, existence of equilibrium is, in general, a challenging issue.

Hettich and Winer (1988, 1999) adopt a 'probabilistic voting' model to study tax policy. Here governments seek to maximize 'expected support' where the probability of any voter supporting them depends upon the difference between the value of benefits received and the costliness of taxes paid. More broadly we can interpret weight given to different voters' interest as reflecting 'relative political influence' (1988, p. 702), an idea underlying the treatment also in Georgiadis and Manning (2007). Models of this sort are notable for their explanation of income tax system complexity, with multiple brackets targeting particular constituencies being a prominent feature. While the ability to handle multidimensional issues in tax setting can be seen as an advantage, the extent to which this is achieved in this strand of literature by 'bypassing questions concerning the existence and stability of political equilibrium and the explicit derivation of government objective functions in a game-theoretic context' (Hettich and Winer (1988), p. 702) means important questions are left unresolved.

Party preferences and swing voters: passively moving rightwards

A weakness of the models considered so far is their treatment of parties as disinterested vote chasers. Iversen and Soskice (2006) show how recognizing parties as run by actors with specific interests can change conclusions. They present a model in which parties are tied to class interests, describing a world in which there are three classes but majoritarian political competition restricts the number of parties to two (according to Duverger's law). Median voters located in the middle class are forced to choose between parties representing coalitions of middle and lower class interests or middle and upper class interests. They vote for the latter because, uncertain about the class leanings of party leaders, they are more scared of lower class than upper class domination. The asymmetry arises because the middle class can ally with the lower class to defend itself against upper class expropriation but would stand alone defenceless against expropriation by the poor. There is an inherent tendency in their view for majoritarian systems, such as that of the UK, to deliver the median voter with less redistribution than they would prefer and less than would be delivered under alternative systems based on proportional representation.

Recognition that parties can represent particular interests, in some respects unconnected to issues of taxation, also opens up new perspectives on electoral competition over taxes. We can suppose that voters differ in their loyalties to the parties: some are more likely than others always to support the same party, while others can be persuaded by appropriately targeted policies. One useful way to think of this in a UK context is to maintain the idea that political competition is broadly organized between three main parties. These parties have core supporters who will be loyal to the parties under most circumstances. However, there are also groups of 'swing voters' who will vote for whichever party has a better policy stance on issues that it views to be salient. Some subset of these swing voters may view some kind of tax policy as being a salient issue. A party that has a large advantage over the other parties for non-tax reasons will find it less necessary to make tax promises that are designed to appeal to politically decisive voters. Such policies will be more important when there is a larger politically decisive group that is not loyal to one party.

Then there is the electoral system: we should also factor in that swing voters belong to Parliamentary constituencies. Some are safe in the sense that the outcome is determined by loyal voters while others are marginal in the sense of being potentially winnable by either main party. To win a majority in the House of Commons, electoral strategy will involve trying to appeal to swing voters in marginal seats. These will be the decisive voters in the sense that Meltzer and Richard cast the median voter as decisive, but the decisive voter will have to choose between alternatives proposed by the competing parties. These alternatives may or may not converge.

So are swing voters distinctive? BSA also collects data on party identification allowing us to separate out attitudes among those uncommitted to particular parties, who constitute about half of respondents, a proportion which has grown slightly over the period observed.[34] Figure 13.7 picks out attitudes on two of the dimensions discussed above. Generally speaking, trends in attitudes over time among both swing voters and party identifiers tend to move in very similar directions with attitudes of swing voters on most questions lying between Labour and Conservative identifiers in predictable ways. Attitudes to redistribution typify this, with swing voters less inclined to approve redistribution than either Labour or Liberal Democrat supporters but more so than the Conservatives and showing a time path of mean opinion very similar to that already seen for the overall population. Of all aspects

[34] Clearly, it would be interesting to analyse the opinions of uncommitted voters in marginal constituencies.

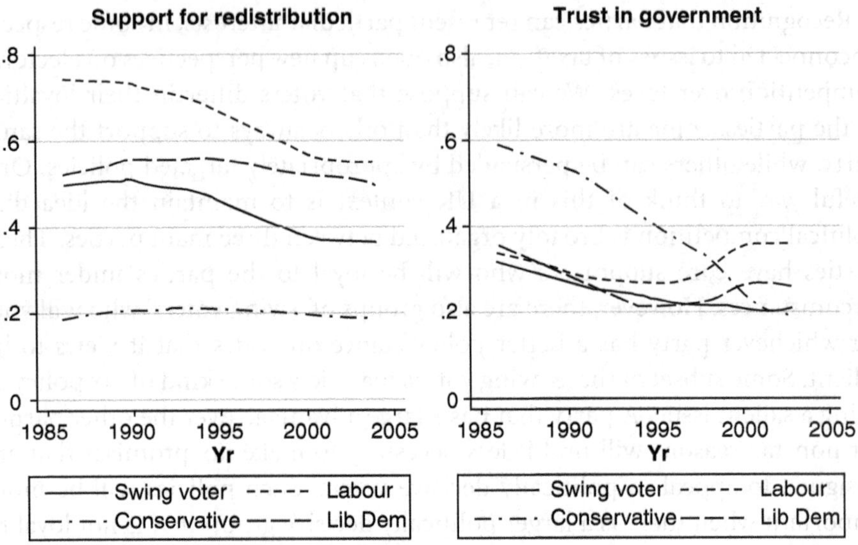

Figure 13.7. Opinions by party support (BSA, 1986–2004)

to attitudes considered above, the one exception to this rule, interestingly, is trust in government which is consistently weakest, and declining, among swing voters. Among committed voters, average trust in government appears to be driven largely by the identity of the party in power.

How will parties come up with their proposals in such a model? Parties will be reluctant to give election promises that compromise their core values if they can find something else that appeals to swing voters. As the electoral compromises reached will differ between parties we should not expect parties to converge on common tax policies and, even if voter opinions do not polarize, elites (parties) can, so the divergence between them may vary over time.

Table 13.3 summarizes each of the main parties' manifesto proposals on the basic and top rates of income tax at elections between 1979 and 2005. Where parties specified an exact value in their manifesto, we report this value; where they only give a preferred direction of change, we report whether this is less or more than the current value. If there is no evidence of a preference for change in either direction we report NC (for No Change).

Combining the information on party positions with the parties' shares of the votes allows us to construct a vote-weighted median position for each of the top and basic rates of tax by using weights equal to vote shares. If the tax issue in question were the sole issue on which voters decided then we could think of this as the position of the median voter. In practice, of course, there are many issues and the voter may have to make the best of

Table 13.3. Party position on income tax

	Actual	Labour	Lib Dem	Conservative	Other	Vote-weighted median
1979 vote shares		36.9	13.8	43.9	5.4	
Basic rate	33	NC	<33	<33		<33
Top rate	83	NC	50	<83		<83
1983 vote shares		27.6	25.4	42.4	4.6	
Basic rate	30	NC	NC	<30		30
Top rate	60	>60	>60	<60		>60
1987 vote shares		30.8	22.6	42.2	4.4	
Basic rate	27	29	NC	25		27
Top rate	60	>60	NC	<60		60
1992 vote shares		34.4	17.8	41.4	6.4	
Basic rate	25	25	>25	20		25
Top rate	40	50	>40	NC		>40
1997 vote shares		43.2	16.8	30.7	9.3	
Basic rate	23	23	24	20		23
Top rate	40	40	50	40		40
2001 vote shares		40.7	18.3	30.7	10.3	
Basic rate	22	22	23	<22		22
Top rate	40	40	50	<40		40
2005 vote shares		35.3	22.1	32.3	10.3	
Basic rate	22	22	22	NC		22
Top rate	40	40	50	NC		40

Source: Various manifestos 1979–2005, authors' calculations.

a bad job, choosing the most appealing of divergent party promises, so any such identification would be tenuous but the vote-weighted median remains an interesting indicator of where parties chose to stand on tax questions. So, for instance, in 1979, Labour proposed no change in the basic rate, but both the Conservative and Liberal parties favoured a cut. More than 50% of voters voted for the latter two parties, so the median voter in the pure tax policy dimension voted for a cut in the basic rate. Alternatively in 1992, the Labour party proposed a top rate of 50%, the Liberal Democrats a top rate higher than the current rate of 40% and the Conservatives proposed no change. Given that a majority of the population voted for either Labour or the Liberal Democrats, we know that the median voter in a pure tax policy dimension voted on this occasion for a rate higher than 40%.

What do we observe over time? First, it is worth noting that a non-median position has won the election on taxes quite a few times, something that is perhaps unsurprising under the UK's combination of three-party politics and plurality-based electoral system, demonstrating that the median voter is not necessarily the pivotal voter.

Secondly, one notes in Table 13.3 that the divergence in party tax proposals is also not constant over time. Although there has been policy divergence over the top rate in every election, disagreement over the basic rate was at its highest in the late 1980s and early 1990s, when tax policy was at its most salient as an electoral issue, but has declined since and more or less disappeared in the most recent election. There are circumstances under which this policy divergence or polarization advantages the right. In general how it affects the strengths of competing parties depends in a subtle way on how deadweight costs vary with tax rates.[35]

Thirdly, however, it is also the case that the median position has drifted rightwards over time so that parties in later years tend to compete in proposals centred around lower marginal tax rates. Moreover, the question of whom declining average tax proposals benefit is far clearer than that of whom declining polarization benefits: there seems to be good reason to think that they will be helpful to more left wing parties.[36] Finally, we note that Kim and Fording (1998, 2003) present evidence, based on expert analysis of party positions on taxing and spending, to suggest that the rightwards drift of the median that we observe in Britain since the 1970s has actually been OECD-wide.[37]

13.4.3. Summing up electoral interests and the representation problem

In summary, we have found some evidence of declining support for redistribution and social insurance, though on the whole attitudes towards redistribution, though declining, are still fairly positive and a majority of individuals favour higher top rates of tax. It is noteworthy that there is some evidence of a strong and ongoing decline in the number of people who place their

[35] In the linear-quadratic model, drawn from McCarty, Poole, and Rosenthal (2006) and discussed above, partisan advantage depends only upon the average tax rate offered. Polarization in tax proposals around an unchanging average offer polarizes party support in the sense that each party's supporters become more committed but doesn't lead anyone to switch sides. In a model where *marginal* deadweight costs were convex however, one would find greater polarization advantaging the right.

[36] If voters decide between competing tax proposals by balancing the redistributive gains (if below mean income) against deadweight costs (which harm everyone) and if marginal deadweight costs are increasing in tax rates whereas marginal redistributive gains or losses are not (as in the models of Bolton and Roland (1997) or McCarty, Poole, and Rosenthal (2006)) then differences in deadweight costs will assume more and more importance the higher is the average of the marginal tax rates offered by the parties, to the detriment of those proposing higher taxes.

[37] The Kim–Fording data also suggest two OECD-wide swings leftwards: an earlier one from 1950 to 1975 and recently from about 1990 to 2000. Their expert data is also consistent with our treatment of polarization in tax policy proposals, above.

trust in government, which may somewhat undermine support for taxation. It nonetheless seems difficult to claim that the trend towards lower statutory rates of income tax has been the result of a groundswell of support for such a policy.

Marginal tax rates proposed by the main parties at elections have evidently drifted downward in recent years and divergence between party proposals has recently declined markedly from a period of more intense competition over tax rates in the 1980s and early 1990s.

When we introduce the idea that voters are imperfectly informed about the tax system and party preferences, things naturally become more complicated, and we will discuss this more in Section 13.6. However, we speculate that the combination of a policy divergence from majority opinion and a lack of trust in politicians is a vicious circle, especially if voters are ill-informed about the tax system and true party preferences.

13.5. INTEREST GROUP POLITICS: A CASE OF POLICY PERSISTENCE AND DRIFT

Unlike the personal income tax, corporate taxation is not typically electorally salient. Perhaps the many who work for large corporations feel a (class) conflict with their employers or, as in the US, 'large corporations have not yet found any effective narrative for attacking corporate taxes' (Graetz and Shapiro (2005), p. 272). Perhaps corporate tax usually involves technical or complex aspects that elude public understanding.[38] Whatever the reason, the lack of an electoral connection opens the door to lobbying by special interests, often for closely targeted benefits. Nor does this happen just in the US:

> [A contrast with Britain] is the apparently greater vulnerability of tax policymaking in America to lobbying by special interest groups ... evident in the notoriously wide range of provisions favoring special groups that have typically characterized the US Tax Code ... But British tax policy is not immune to special pleading; the 1997 Budget brought special tax breaks for the film industry. (Michael Keen, 'A British Perspective on Tax Policy in the United States', in Slemrod (1999), pp. 505–6.)

[38] When the costs of a policy, though small, are easy enough to observe, then mixing even small but well-financed or organized groups with extensive media coverage can result in mobilizing the otherwise unorganized. This gives the issue increased potential electoral salience: this is the essence of Graetz and Shapiro's (2005) account of the evolution of support for estate tax repeal in the US. In the UK, the case of fuel tax protests makes a similar point.

We analyse the case of Labour's R&D tax credit to reveal both the opportunities for and limits on lobbying by special interests for favourable tax treatment in the UK. The R&D tax credit purports to support a socially desirable goal: its origin was a government intent on promoting innovation, to some extent initially impressed by the way this was done elsewhere. Any benefits of increasing aggregate innovation or investment are imperceptible to voters but larger to those firms actively involved in research and development. However, this policy does not appear to be the direct result of lobbying by concentrated, organized interest groups. The effects of lobbying appear to be more subtle. Development of policy subsequent to its introduction reveals important political forces, including *ex post* lobbying and provision of information by the industry, with the programme drifting and growing beyond the original intent and justifications that were offered for it.

We use a blend of quantitative, documentary, and interview evidence[39] that focuses particularly on the political behaviour of large firms and the transition of the R&D credit (initially predominantly aimed at and economically justified for small firms) from an SME credit to a larger programme of large company credits. How it happened, why it happened, what the politics of various decisions were is the substance. Nevertheless, puzzles remain. For instance, will the policy prove to be politically unsustainable, however good the original intentions?[40]

Section 13.5.1 provides a stylized model of policy persistence as a result of *ex post* lobbying (the full technical detail of which is not crucial for non-technical readers) and Section 13.5.2 provides the case study of the R&D tax credit. Section 13.5.3 provides examples of interest-group politics outside corporation tax, the zero-rating of children's clothing in VAT, together with one where the 'unorganized' suddenly became very organized and very vocal—the fuel tax protests in 2001.

13.5.1. The political economy of interest groups

The standard interest-group explanation of policy is that groups representing net beneficiaries of a policy form to advocate and/or defend it.

[39] As stated in the Introduction, we conducted a number of interviews with individuals involved in the tax policy process over the past thirty years. These interviews are an important source of information for our case study of the R&D tax credit. Although these individuals are not named in the case study, we do indicate which quotes came from the same people and the nature of their involvement in the tax policy process.

[40] Should they take power, the Conservatives appear likely to propose a scheme whereby businesses would be willing to give up the credit in exchange for a lower rate of corporation tax, an exchange several executives we interviewed indicated they would be happy enough to make.

Concentrated, organized groups have an advantage over unorganized interests (Olson (1965)) and a disproportionate advantage in seeking policies whose benefits are concentrated and costs widely dispersed (Wilson (1989)) because it is unlikely that those bearing the costs will find it worthwhile or possible to organize collectively to oppose the policy. This is the usual explanation for the success of special interests in seeking trade protection and subsidies as well as favourable regulation and tax treatment, in Britain as well as elsewhere.[41]

However, Noll and Cohen (1983) pointed out over two decades ago that firms affected by a regulation also frequently adjust to become its greatest defenders, even if they were not originally advocates. So far the R&D credit is a textbook case: frequently changed, with its tax cost rapidly growing in the years since it was introduced. Moreover, its principal beneficiaries were not active proponents of the credit before it began, and though they are quick to claim that it doesn't make a significant difference to their investment decisions,[42] they continue to be willing to suggest further extensions to the credit.

There is a puzzle here, which is this: if an interest group had the capacity and incentives to lobby to maintain a subsidy, for instance, they presumably would have the capacity and incentives to lobby to introduce such subsidies, so the existence of such subsidies cannot be used to explain their persistence. Coate and Morris (1999) describe the political economy conventional wisdom that once an economic policy is introduced, it is hard to remove, even if its original rationale no longer applies or is invalid.[43] Asking how policy introduction alters incentives in the political process for maintaining the new status quo, they write:

[T]he mechanism by which the introduction of the policy alters incentives in the political process in favor of the new status quo . . . [is that when] an economic policy

[41] For instance, Person F (interview) noted how lobbying for a special regime for shipping to encourage and retain UK ship-owners became the Tonnage Tax in Finance Act 2000. 'This was a result of direct lobbying by the industry. It benefited Greek ship-owners based in London, who also benefit from the personal tax rules for those not domiciled in the UK, as they only pay tax on money they bring into the country. A long running review on domicile by the then Inland Revenue never came to any conclusion, in part because of the perceived economic damage to the UK if such non-domiciliaries were to leave the country. Similar arguments have also been used, and widely reported, to criticize proposed changes to the rules governing non-domiciliaries from 2008 onwards—another good example of focused lobbying, by a special interest group.'

[42] Of course, a credit that works at the margin of choice can have real effects even if decision-makers are unconscious of its effects.

[43] Here Coate and Morris note that the standard explanation, which they regard as inadequate, is that 'interest groups representing net beneficiaries form to defend policies' (footnote added to quotation).

is introduced, agents will often respond by undertaking actions in order to benefit from it . . . increas[ing] their willingness to pay for the policy in the future.

This extra willingness to pay will be translated into political pressure to retain the policy and this means it is more likely to be operative in the future. We present a simple dynamic model which . . . combines an agency style model of political competition of the type pioneered by Robert Barro (1973) and John Ferejohn (1986), with a lobbying model of the form made popular by the recent work of Gene M. Grossman and Helpman (1994) . . . to point out that policy persistence . . . can be Pareto dominated . . . because voters forgo support for policies which provide temporary efficiency benefits, anticipating that they will persist once they have been implemented. (Coate and Morris (1999), p. 1327.)

The model's equilibrium sequence has policy first created without the support of the affected interest (in our case, the large firms did not lobby for the creation of the R&D tax credit), but once the policy exists, affected interests lobby and politicians respond by maintaining the policy in every period, even after the rationale for the original policy has disappeared.

The model combines agency and lobbying in an optimizing framework with political implications.[44] Politicians value re-election to a point, but firms' contributions can persuade politicians to do other things than carry out voters' most-preferred policy. In equilibrium, policies are either never implemented, or, if implemented, they persist, even if dominated by sequences (in the public, or voters', interest) in which a policy is implemented and then removed. However, the latter does not arise in equilibrium as long as voters have partial control, because firms, even if they did not contribute to creating the policy, adjust their behaviour so as to become willing to contribute enough to persuade politicians to maintain policy. If there are synergies between policies, so that firms can contribute to other policies favoured by the government, the policy in question may even expand. That is how some policies that favour a sector but are costly to citizens at large persist, indeed, even grow.

13.5.2. Policy evolution: the R&D tax credit

Tax incentives can potentially increase innovation by attracting investment by new firms, either by convincing large multi-national enterprises (MNEs) looking to expand globally to invest R&D resources or by helping small firms to emerge and establish themselves as business entities. Alternatively,

[44] In particular it lacks parties as well as the uncertainty about the results of elections that might make the implementation of post-election policy unpredictable *ex ante*.

tax incentives can fuel greater innovation by leading existing investors to increase their level of spending. In any case, R&D tax incentives provide tax relief to research-intensive companies for undertaking R&D, defined for tax purposes as projects that '[seek] to achieve an advance in overall knowledge or capability in a field of science or technology, not a company's own state of knowledge or capability'.[45]

Origins

Everyone seems to agree that the R&D tax credit was 'not something industry was lobbying for'.[46] New Labour came to power in 1997 with a Chancellor who believed that tax is a tool of social and economic policy.[47] His 1998 Budget speech announced that since '[e]ncouraging greater R&D investment is . . . crucial to higher productivity' the government would begin the consultations that by 1999 resulted in a small-company credit, seen as a measure 'to facilitate and directly influence the demand to innovate and undertake R&D' (p. 15). This measure was introduced in the 2000 Budget at an estimated cost of £100 million in 2001–02 and £150 million in 2002–03,[48] which compare with an initial cost estimate of £50 million per year.[49]

At the time, some believed there was observable evidence of an 'innovation deficit' in the UK. Griffith et al. (2006) show that in the 1990s affiliates of UK firms were disproportionately likely to place R&D in the US, in comparison with firms from Japan or Germany. Moreover, between 1987 and 1996 nearly half of the European Patent Office filings by the largest UK-based pharmaceutical firms were based on research conducted in the US, while 'for all other countries with major pharmaceutical industries . . . the large majority of patents came from the home country' (Gambardella et al. (2000), p. 42). Economic arguments for subsidizing R&D focus on externality issues associated with the inappropriability of technological spillover benefits from research and the inadequacy of other interventions, such as patenting legislation, fully to address the problem (see, for example, Griffith, Sandler, and Van Reenen (1996)).

At the same time it was also (and in many quarters continues to be) widely accepted that research supported the government's belief in the effectiveness of R&D tax credits (see Hall and Van Reenen (1999)), at least in the case

[45] As defined by HM Revenue and Customs in reference to DTI (now DBERR) Guidelines.
[46] Person F interview.
[47] Person C interview citing RedBook 7/97 sections 1.66–1.72 (HMT archive).
[48] See Budget 2000 Scorecard.
[49] Recollection of Person F (interview) confirmed by Person A (interview) and other decision participants.

of smaller firms that may be financially constrained and thus particularly unable to capture the economic returns that their research activities produce. Berger (1993) and Hall (1993) estimated that tax credits reducing the after-tax cost of R&D by 10% could increase R&D by 10–15%. Bloom, Griffith, and Van Reenen (2002) placed the long-run increase in R&D at 10% from a 10% reduction in costs, based on a study of several countries from 1979 to 1997, and noted that the benefits of such a tax credit increase from the short to the long run.[50]

Person A describes the sources of the R&D tax credit, including evidence surrounding the effectiveness of R&D tax credit in other countries:

> The source of the RDTC was atypical, it came from productivity policy built on work done at IFS, then it found favour with some advisors, who believed the benefits. It looked like a logical step to improve innovation and creativity . . . but [some] doubted it would work in the world. There was a need to understand whether firms will change their behaviour, and it was not convincing that firms would do R&D just because it is a bit cheaper. Firms do R&D because they need it for their business, not because it is a little cheaper. There were both formal and informal discussions, informal mostly with those with large R&D, aerospace and pharma, aerospace self-selected as leaders of the discussion; also informal (led by CBI) discussions with smaller firms.

Apart from a host of technical issues, the government faced two core choices. One was whether the basis of credit should be new increments of R&D spending or the total volume of spending. The other was what size companies would be eligible, since 'Increasing Innovation', the Budget 2001 consultation, specifically concentrated on the economic analysis of 'the difficulties that smaller companies have in accessing capital for R&D investment' (p. 19),[51] but while that case can be made for small firms, it is less clear for big.

But the goal of the policy was innovation, and R&D was to be substantially increased: later a 40% increase came to be the public target. Of course, big firms do most of the R&D. The 1999 BERD Survey shows that of the £8+ billion in current, private R&D expenditure undertaken in the UK in 1999, SMEs[52] did maybe 10% (Dilnot et al. (2002)). The other 90%, done by non-SMEs, was an attractive target for a government determined to do something

[50] Griffith, Redding, and Van Reenen (2001) provided further support. However, note that firms do not perceive financing, high costs, or appropriability problems to be more significant barriers to innovation in the UK than in the US (Abramovsky, Griffith, Harrison (2005b)). See also comments in *Supporting Growth in Innovation*.

[51] It also noted that the UK goes further and allows companies to write off immediately all R&D capital expenditure, including plant and machinery and scientific buildings but excluding land and dwelling houses.

[52] Throughout this discussion, as in eligibility for the credit itself, the definition of small and medium sized enterprises (SMEs) as having less than 250 employees follows EU concepts.

to encourage innovation. Since their contemplated scale of change would require an unimaginable fourfold increase in SME R&D, it would have to be done by larger firms.

In 2000, EU countries established the Lisbon Agenda to make the EU 'the most competitive and dynamic knowledge-driven economy by 2010'.[53] The Treasury's consultation paper, 'Increasing Innovation', came out shortly after in 2001, committed to

> Encouraging innovation ... a vital component of the Government's strategy for improving the UK's productivity performance and competitiveness ... The Government can help by ... giving business the platform from which to innovate. (p. x)

It proposed to extend the credit to larger firms, believing that of several available options, this one was 'the most appropriate instrument for helping boost the demand of businesses to innovate and undertake R&D' (p. 2) hoping to 'bring about a step change in the level of R&D and innovation' (p. 24).

Therefore, we see that the origins of the R&D tax credit seem to be a desire to raise levels of innovation and increase productivity. Moreover, the policy seems to have been based on evidence found in economic research. Its introduction was certainly not a case of industry lobbying for more generous tax treatment. We now move to discuss what informed the government's choice of a volume-based credit, and the decision to extend the credit to larger firms.

Volume versus incremental credits: an informed choice

Originally the intent was to introduce the credit in incremental form: this had the strong support of the DTI and influential figures in government. The incremental form was modelled on the US tax credit, first introduced in July 1981 as part of the Economic Recovery Tax Act and later renewed in the Tax Reform Act of 1986.[54] The US tax credit is administered on the incremental basis, rewarding relative increases in, rather than absolute levels of, R&D spending.[55]

[53] <http://www.euractive.com/en/agenda2004/lisbon-agenda/article–117510>.

[54] TRA86 made the significant change of incorporating it into the General Business Credit and removing it as a separate statistical line item. See Bronwyn Hall, 'Effectiveness of Research and Experimentation Tax Credits: Critical Literature Review and Research Design', Report prepared for the Office of Technology Assessment, Congress of the United States, 15 June 1995, p. 4. Over the next ten years, it continued to be renewed on a short-term basis, mostly through yearly Omnibus Budget Reconciliation Acts.

[55] Although the US is not the only country to use this system—France, Japan, and Korea have also implemented incremental schemes—it is nevertheless noteworthy as a contrast to the volume-based

The incremental system has been argued to distort dynamic incentives because companies have to invest more and more in R&D each year just to receive the same, or less, credit. They thus have less incentive to invest early in large quantities in R&D, because doing so will simply raise the base from which the incremental credit is calculated in subsequent years. It appears to have been clear already (see Griffith, Redding, and Van Reenen (2001) commenting on the 1999 consultations) that it was doubtful that the credit (which was announced in incremental form) would be cost-effective in the short run, though it always was in the long run. The volume-based system is intended to reward companies that show a long commitment to R&D and innovation.

In the end, the government chose to introduce a volume-based system, on the basis of internal discussions and on the advice of industry. Interviewees frequently cited similar economic logic as described above for why the government made this choice. Below Person A describes some of the reasoning behind why the government eventually chose the volume-based system.

> [Initially] HMT favoured an incremental credit over volume: in a simple model with one decision-maker, incremental looks better, but outside the one company model life is more complicated. The incremental approach takes away all the certainty with regard to the credit, where companies are linked they may take offsetting decisions by mistake. Business saw this as a problem too. Incremental had supporters, but not many in complex businesses.[56]

From Person D's point of view the R&D tax credit was born out of a broader agenda of putting the intellectual property tax regime right and agreed that industry certainly favoured the volume-based system:

> [We] heard Gordon Brown say 'Innovations are key to a knowledge-based economy, therefore, we need to incentivize the creation of knowledge', so they decided to introduce the R&D tax credit. In June 1998 came the Budget 98 document 'Innovating for the Future'. The government consulted the Intellectual Property Institute and business to discuss the position regarding all types of protected intellectual property: copyright, patents trademarks, know-how, etc., in order to understand the tax treatment in each case. They found that the tax treatment was inconsistent,

systems of other countries, including the UK. Because of their incremental nature, tax credits bear only a fraction of their face value. This is because each time they increase their spending, the base that they must spend to earn the same amount of credit increases. Based on some simple calculations, (Brown (1984), p. 3) concludes that 'the incentive is not the $25 face value of the credit, but just the value of getting $25 now rather than later. Assuming an interest rate of 10 percent, the discounted value of the credit is not $25, but only $4.29.'

56 Person A interview.

incomplete, and ambiguous and the cause of many disputes between taxpayers and the authorities. Company A was involved in the very thorough consultation, and favoured reform of the tax treatment of all intellectual property as well as a volume-based R&D tax credit.

Therefore, while some still favour an incremental system, we find it difficult to fault the government's choice of a volume-based system after both weighing up the economic arguments and listening to the advice of industry.

The large firms extension: policy drift and 'policy creep'

In 2002, the tax incentive was expanded to include a credit for large firms; this provided a 125% allowance but did not offer a cash repayment option. The allowance provides deductions from taxable income based on the actual expenditure amount. The large company scheme also allowed otherwise ineligible SMEs to claim under the large company scheme for qualifying expenditure where they act as subcontractor to a large company.

This did represent, in the eyes of people responsible for framing policy, a fundamental shift. According to Person C:

policy had always been talked about as restricted to SMEs, though the DTI was heavily pushing to include large firms, so there was a political aspect to decisions. The SMEs was a generous policy, but the government was unlikely to meet its targets through just SMEs. It was not exactly the targets that drove the decision to extend RDTC to large companies, but aggregate investment was a concern and the SMEs were not big enough. The Engineers' Employers Federation was key to the political push, with their continual focus and their power increasing over time. They definitely caused a sea change in the views of large company desirability.

The arguments put forward for large company R&D were more practical than economic—that the existence of a tax credit would 'get the UK onto the shortlist' and that, without a tax credit, we would not be getting our fair share of R&D. We needed to have special incentives for R&D when firms considered location. Pfizer can put its lab in Kent or Hannover, it won't even look at you if you can't check off the 'incentive' box on page 1.

Despite the practical nature of the arguments for the existence of the credit, the detailed discussion was still dominated by the externalities at the Research end of R&D. However, once the policy was in place, we saw a gradual erosion of this and a further shift in focus ('policy creep') onto Development, with people saying that, since this credit is practical in origin, we could easily alter the position to cover additional expenditure.

However, this extension was again not something that all industries were lobbying for. Recalling a meeting in June 2001 attended by representatives of ICI, AstraZeneca, BT, Reuters (for their IT-proprietary software), Logica, and Laporte, among others, Person D comments:

> [I] think the government was determined to bring in RDTC for large companies... There are many drivers of R&D investment decisions that come before tax efficiency. This was communicated to the government at the time and it was suggested that they could take the money available for the credit and invest it in science education instead for similar or greater impact. It was also suggested that securing contracts for UK based researchers would be more valuable as we were losing researchers to the US because of poor pay and unstable career prospects.

There can be no doubt that the government also attempted to tie any proposed broad-based tax credits to receiving assurances from industry that new incentives would be matched by new activity. In June 2001 Company A submitted that a volume-based system would be better for large firms. The firm also participates in a scheme to invest in research into disease areas that affect the developing world. In parallel there was growing political pressure for pharma to provide access to existing therapies to those poorest countries. Noting that this 'was a passion to a number of ministers', Person D remarks:

> A key aim for any government is to generate and conserve UK jobs. However, the vaccine credit can be obtained from qualifying investment located anywhere. To focus on a disease, companies need to access locations and people with the disease. The vaccine credit receives widespread political support, as part of the worldwide effort to provide access to improved therapies to developing nations. However, there is the complicating factor of security in pricing in developed markets and the effects of parallel trading.[57]

Therefore, the extension of the RDTC to large companies raises many issues. First, it reveals policy drifting from its predominant original justification, that is, boosting R&D through relieving small companies of credit constraints, in an attempt to meet a quantitative R&D target. This is not to say that such a change could not have been justified in terms of the general spillover benefits from R&D even in larger firms but just to note that there was an unmistakable shift in the nature of the policy. It also shows how even though no one really lobbied for the RDTC in the first place, once it was in place there was certainly lobbying for its extension to large firms from the DTI and some in industry like the EEF. So the extension to large firms is both an example of quantitative targets distorting policy—what one may call policy drift—and lobbying once the initial SME credit was in place—or as person C described it 'policy creep'.

[57] Person D interview. Documents in the file indicate that Company B also welcomed the Vaccine Credit, believing it should be more than 50% deductible against UK tax.

Policy operation: soliciting information and policy change

Securing information about company operations was always a problem for official assessment of the operation of the policy, though not because information was not being shared. People involved suggested that a greater problem was the need to make heroic assumptions about behavioural change while lacking information on bedrock R&D within companies. They found it very difficult to get a sense of the ratio of deadweight cost to RDTC spending. According to Person C:

The Inland Revenue has a significant amount of information, some of which is electronic, but tax returns are always a year behind, which doesn't help. Furthermore, the bulk of the information is in hard copy and was only really accessible as case studies of the largest companies. In addition, since HMT has no right of access to specific taxpayer data, the Inland Revenue needed to adopt strong precautions to make sure HMT couldn't identify individual companies.

So, although the Inland Revenue is a rich source, information was often not readily available. In cases like finance or shipping the clear way to get information is to go to the relevant tax inspector because the industry is regionally concentrated. The Inland Revenue was able to go back to companies to get a realistic amount of expenditure: very much on a case study plus estimate basis, not data for the whole population. For the SMEs, it was more of the same, but even more of a challenge since they publish less. That's why it was so important to talk to the companies.

Almost before the credit got out of the door, the government was thinking about altering it, and solicited firms' comments on its operations. As HMIR, 'R&D Tax Credits: responses to "Defining Innovation"', 12/2003, p. 1, put it, the respondents (virtually all larger firms or associations of firms) 'gave strong support for the R&D tax credit schemes and provided valuable insight into . . . how it might be improved'.

The UK government commissioned two consultation documents on the R&D tax credit, collecting feedback from firms and associations in order to assess the experiences of companies currently claiming the tax credit. However, even before reaching the document stage there were informal discussions involving CFOs about their business priorities and trying out ideas, mostly led by lower officials in HMT.

Almost exclusively large firms respond to the written consultations, because small firms cannot afford someone on the payroll to look after lobbying. The firms that do send in materials sometimes argue that policy as designed makes no difference to their behaviour, even while trying to tailor policy to their needs. The overall message that emerged from corporate responses was that, owing to a combination of unsatisfactory content and poor implementation, the tax credit was not substantively affecting their R&D investment decisions.

Why was this so? A variety of firms' responses argued, perhaps unsurprisingly, that the actual rate of the UK tax credit was not high enough. For example, the large-firm credit, designed to provide a 7.5% reduction, in practice covers only 60% of R&D expenditures. This really represents a 5% rate of relief which, according to the Confederation of British Industry, falls within the range of insignificant 'background noise'. Hence, Pfizer and GlaxoSmithKline (GSK), the world's leaders in pharmaceutical R&D, were sceptical that the tax credit offered any real incentive. GSK remarked:

> If the goal of the credit is to increase UK-based R&D expenditure, rather than maintain it, *the government should consider increasing the rate of relief.* This would then place the UK in a more competitive situation.[58] (Emphasis added.)

Pfizer stated:

> If the Government wishes the UK's tax credit system to act as a headline incentive for greater R&D investment in the UK, it needs to become more prominent in management's planning. *The current rate of the R&D tax credit is only at the margins of significance for our decisions on new investment and maintenance.* To become more prominent, significant increases in the current rate—doubling or tripling—would be required.[59] (Emphasis added.)

The Chemical Industries Association (CIA) further contends that the lack of a clear financial support and credit structure is symptomatic of a larger lack of clearly defined purpose and scope that plagues the UK government's actions with regard to innovation incentives:

> [A]re the tax credits meant to promote a 'new' culture within UK companies to invest more in R&D activities? If so, the current level of R&D tax credit that a company can gain is not seen as a real incentive to do more R&D. A rate of return greater than 5% is required if the credits are to have any meaningful impact within commercial enterprises.[60]

If the government's goal was to increase R&D spending in the UK, they certainly heard the opinion of affected parties that they would have to do more.

Virtually every company surveyed also argued that subjective and arbitrary application of policies resulted in a highly restrictive interpretation of the tax credit policy, contrary to the policy's original intent. AstraZeneca, for

[58] 'Supporting growth in innovation: Enhancing the R&D tax credit'. Comments from GlaxoSmithKline on the July 2005 consultation paper.

[59] 'Supporting Growth in Innovation.' Response dated 12 October 2005.

[60] CIA response to 'Defining Innovation' dated 14 October 2003.

example, claimed that the Inland Revenue's narrow interpretation of the term 'consumable stores' resulted in over-restriction of the definition of qualifying expenditures and the exclusion of expenditures that were clearly relevant to R&D.

Another alleged problem was limited accessibility: a combination of low awareness, ignorance of various benefits of submitting claims, complicated eligibility requirements, the possibility that credits would be temporary, and the costs and difficulty of the application process,[61] though a report prepared by the British Market Research Bureau for HMRC implied that the problem was not lack of familiarity.

There were other complaints about administration. The Cox Review (ch. 5: 'Providing Support and Incentive', p. 7) took very much a position frequently argued to us by firms' spokespersons. Cox suggested that 'Tax inspectors need to recognise that this is an incentive scheme to be encouraged, not an avoidance scheme to be policed.' Cox also felt that 'the UK continues to lag in international terms' and, echoing a view debated at the outset, that an incremental scheme would provide more incentive. Nevertheless, the credit seems to have flourished: Cox cites the 16,000 claims for the R&D Tax Credit 2000–01 to 2004–05 as 'above the original projection made by the Inland Revenue'.

So, the government also heard that they would have to change the definitions of what counted as R&D and they would have to improve the administration.

By and large, lobbying firms got nearly all of what they wanted, though many still want more. Significant changes include revised definitions broadening allowable costs of staff, consumables, and even clinical trials.[62] However, it would be inappropriate to characterize the entire consultation and policy refinement process as one of firms lobbying for more generous tax treatment. The consultation process is also one of policy improvement, as was the case with the choice of the volume-based system. However, over time the situation has changed from one where the R&D tax credit was 'not something industry was really lobbying for' to one where much of the affected industry is lobbying for quite specific changes to the credit. This is exactly what the Coate and Morris model predicts. The government when creating a tax credit also created an interest group, whose voice became louder over time.

[61] See, for example, the BAE response to 'Defining Innovation' dated 9 October 2003.

[62] For a time line and list of changes see HMRC's CIRD98900—R&D tax relief: legislative structure and time line.

The result and its implications

Those concerned with crafting sustainable policies can anticipate and take account of sources of policy drift that the R&D tax credit illustrates. Good intentions and even possible economic justifications are not enough. The case illustrates the ways that government goals interact in the process of policy formation and evolution. The need for information gives advantages to those who provide it, in ways that affect both the direction and details of policy. Sometimes, as with the vaccine credit, new activities that help achieve other government goals can be traded for policy benefits. Down the road, the supporting coalition for a policy can come to look quite different from the enacting coalition, even without anyone discovering they were wrong about anything. Nevertheless, the shape and size of policy may come eventually to bear little resemblance to what was on the table when the original justifications were argued out and beneficiaries chosen. It may well be that in British tax politics, in comparison with those at least in some other countries like the US, special interest politics are less important. Nevertheless, they may be growing in importance, and with consequences that a political economy analysis helps explain.

On goals, the government are on record as hoping that the R&D tax credit would raise Business Enterprise R&D by at least 40–50% (HM Treasury et al. (2004)), though this has not been achieved.[63] Sources converge in suggesting that at least three-quarters of the credit goes to large firms, and that this share is growing. 'Defining Innovation', the July 2003 consultative document (table 2.1, p. 6) appears to forecast about £600 million a year recurring cost for the credit (the last round of refinements may put the price up further) which is already a dozen times the size that participants recall being discussed when the first consultations were held.[64] The R&D tax credit certainly grew.

Did it achieve its objectives? That depends on a number of factors. It appears to be universally acknowledged that relieving financial constraints on research activity of small firms was a major initial goal, and indeed more than 90% of paid small-firm tax credit claims in the UK are in the form of cash repayment. But this is a small part of the actual credit. Arguments can be and are made for a general R&D credit to firms of all sizes, on grounds of addressing general externalities. Interviews with policy makers and industrialists revealed little evidence that such arguments had any prominence at

[63] See 'Science and Innovation Investment Framework 2004–2014' (HMT, DTI, DfES 7/2004) and Abramovsky et al. (2005a, 2005b).

[64] Echoing this, the July 2005 HMT/DTI/HMRC consultative document 'Supporting Growth in Innovation' mentions that in 2003–04 over 4,500 SME companies and almost 1,000 large companies claimed the credit, at just under £550 million in all (p. 13).

the time of the policy's introduction. Such arguments presuppose anyway that firms' behaviour is influenced by the credit and we found this idea to be treated with scepticism within large affected firms. For instance, Person F indicated that tax credits essentially represent 'free money', which firms will not turn down. Summing this up, Person D said that the large-firm credit

> was welcomed in the pharma community at large. For small firms [the SME credit] may be a competitive necessity. It's also good for levelling the playing field, and the UK is recognized as very competitive in this regard. But generally large firms will spend where they perceive they can gain in productivity and in high quality, innovative outputs and the tax incentive may or may not fit with that.

Against this, certainly taxes affect some decisions.[65] Defenders can also argue that decision-makers may not always be aware of the marginal influences affecting their choices or be best placed to evaluate comparison between policy regimes. Careful econometric observation of actual R&D outcomes should be a more reliable indicator. Indeed, the research that spawned the credit suggested that its main effects come very slowly, so it may be too soon to tell. So there is mixed evidence: the Cox Review on innovation was still a firm believer in the efficacy of the credits.

Finally, it also depends on whether the goal of policy was to encourage geographically specific R&D. If it concerned actual people doing research at actual seats in actual British workplaces, the case for the credit may be weaker. As Person D, the same person who recalled putting the case five years earlier that science-based contracts would have been a more powerful tool of policy, put it:

> If I were to ask the head of research about location decisions, he'd say: 'where are the best people?' It's not about labour and consumable costs, it's about intellectual power, scientific knowledge and innovation.

Abramovsky et al. (2007) provide evidence for co-location of pharmaceutical R&D labs and university research departments in Great Britain. The paramount importance of the quality of the scientific community in R&D location decisions features prominently in our interviews and those of Xu (2007). At the same time, Griffith et al. (2006) show that locating R&D in the US has a big productivity pay-off for UK firms. That result is consistent with two important ideas that affect evaluation of the R&D tax credit: first, that the main benefit of R&D is to create knowledge externalities which cross borders between countries and maybe companies, and second, that the very

[65] Person F, formerly Tax Director at Company B, did mention that he funded actual R&D in low tax jurisdictions.

nature of transmitting externalities means that the benefits of any investment decision may come through very slowly. But if the externalities are the benefit of R&D, and are biggest when the R&D is undertaken in the most advanced location, then indeed a good policy may be what Person D reports long advocating:

> We ask for the broadest definitions, because so much activity is on a global scale, we want to capture the entire investment made anywhere in the world.

The UK government has resisted this all along. The headline quality of giving tax credits in the UK to MNEs for their spending in other countries might just prove politically costly, even if the economic case for it can be made.

13.5.3. Lobbying outside corporate taxation

The costs of the R&D credit to the taxpayer are small, widely dispersed, and very hard to observe. Those facts alone help explain why the politics took the form they did. However, there is more to say about interest groups than that. When the costs of a policy, though small, are easy enough to observe, extensive media coverage can result in mobilizing the otherwise unorganized 'cause' groups, which are becoming increasingly prominent as a form of participation in British politics.[66] This gives an issue increased electoral salience, as the recent case of fuel tax protests shows. Moreover, in other cases the link between ideology and party politics creates circumstances in which the interests of unorganized groups are anticipated and represented by parties even without the galvanizing effect of mass protests. Zero-rating VAT on children's clothing and food is such a case. These two cases deserve a brief comment.

Between 1993 and 1999 excise duties on petrol were increased by a fixed proportion above inflation year on year by both Labour and Conservative governments in the name of reducing congestion and pollution. However, in September 2000, with unleaded pump prices at about 80p per litre and fuel duty at about 49p per litre,[67] protestors (mainly hauliers) who objected to this historic high in fuel duty blockaded petrol refineries. This caused nationwide petrol shortages, with many petrol stations running out, partly as a result of panic-buying. Eventually, the blockades ended with greater police protection for lorries leaving refineries, as the costs and inconvenience of shortages became more evident. Even though the fuel duty escalator had

[66] The poll tax case, mentioned above, also exemplifies this.

[67] <http://www.dtistats.net/energystats/qep411.xls>.

been halted before the protests, the government bore the brunt: this was the only time during Labour's first term that they fell behind the Conservatives in the polls.

Observing that this was an issue that threatened to change voting intentions quite strongly, the government reduced fuel duty in its Budget of 2001, just before the general election of that year. Since then it has been increased in nominal terms only four times: as a result it is much lower in real terms compared with the level in 2000. Why? Even if the economics of the issue are unchanged, if more voters are aware of the fuel duty, it is easier to mobilize their preconceptions than to create them in the first place,[68] and the reaction of 'swing' voters to higher levels of fuel duty could be highly costly in terms of public support.

Maintaining VAT exemptions for food and children's clothing has been an untouchable commitment of all major parties for many years. The commitment is usually justified on redistributive grounds: because these goods are perceived as essential items for poorer families with children taxing them would unfairly hit a deserving group in the population.

However, VAT is an ad valorem tax, so the main beneficiaries in absolute terms are those with higher absolute spending on these goods. The exemption subsidizes the rich parent buying designer clothes for their child as much as it does the poor family buying necessary items. If one really wanted to address redistributive concerns, it would make sense to end zero-rating of these goods and at the same time put the money 'saved' (the extra revenue collected) into increasing child benefits. This would benefit all families with the same number of children equally in absolute terms, but would benefit poorer households more in proportionate terms.

More generally, while it is clearly desirable that redistributing income taking account of needs should be one among several objectives met by the *overall* tax system it is not sensible to try to make every element of the system meet every objective.

Yet neither Labour, usually thought the most redistributive of the major parties, nor any of its rivals supports the change. Of course, one reason might be that the status quo is genuinely redistributive in relative terms when viewed in isolation. Perception of this may prevent voters from supporting more redistributive reforms that could be achieved with the same money. Second, eliminating zero-rating would be costly in a way immediately

[68] Graetz and Shapiro (2005) show that it is more expensive for ideologically motivated groups to frame the issue (in their case, abolition of the estate tax in the US) in the first place, but given sufficient resources (and perhaps a few lucky coincidences), large numbers of people can be persuaded to support a tax from which they derive no benefit.

apparent to a lot of people, even if the increase in child benefit were enacted simultaneously.[69]

Earlier we remarked that keeping the focus on an element of the tax system was also a key strategic element in the campaign organized by interest groups in the US that led to the abolition of the estate tax (the US equivalent of inheritance tax).[70] Keeping the focus on an element of the tax system viewed in isolation prevented voters from making many relevant comparisons. The recent skirmish over inheritance tax in Britain resembles some of the origins in that case:

> After a decade in which the threshold for inheritance tax rose at half the rate of house prices, stories began to appear (usually based on 'research' by banks) speculating about the number of home-owning families that would owe estate tax. This began modestly: 'A further 22% rise to 37,000 is expected by 2007, according to Halifax' (4 Aug 2005) but inflated rapidly when 'Halifax . . . said "house price rises meant the tax would be payable on 2.1 million homes"' (19 Nov 2005). Within months one could read that 'One in three UK homeowners will now be subject to a 40% inheritance tax, . . . a recent survey by Scottish Widows shows.' (16 Feb. 2006)[71]

At this point in the American case the Graetz–Shapiro analysis of careful, patient lobbying by groups shows how swing voters in the US were mobilized to the cause, to the point where even raised allowances eliminating 99% of citizens from the estate tax could not win in the legislature. The response by the UK Chancellor (an adjustment of thresholds which appeared to defuse the issue) reflects the lack of development of a comparable lobbying organization on the issue, perhaps because there have been no consultations to mobilize it. The inheritance tax also reflects the importance of insulation and centralization in British policy-making. One Chancellor can deflect lobbying; the next might change policy completely, just as a small, determined group of ministers were able to force through the poll tax.

13.5.4. What have we learned?

So what does our study of interest groups and taxation show? Its primary lesson is that enacting tax policy can create interest groups and constituencies for that policy. Even when they did not lobby for the policy in the

[69] If the changes are separated, questions about policy commitment could arise.

[70] See note 38 above. The estate tax was in fact not completely abolished, and will return after 2010 absent legislative action.

[71] All quotations taken from <http://news.bbc.co.uk>.

first place, they will lobby both for persistence and extensions that allow policy to drift from its original motivation. This is exactly what we see with the R&D tax credit. Lobbying for policy persistence from existing beneficiaries of a tax policy is a generalization of the widely understood phenomenon that losers from a reform are more vociferous than potential winners.

Outside corporation tax, we can see that the role of framing tax policy can be crucial. Framing the zero-rating of children's clothing in isolation has helped maintain it; framing the estate tax in isolation also helped those lobbying for the end of estate tax in the US. The lessons from the fuel tax protests are more difficult to generalize, but if anything we see that media attention can make the 'unorganized' very vocal indeed. One could also argue that focusing on the effects of the tax in isolation helped crystallize protest.

13.6. TRANSPARENCY AND ACCOUNTABILITY IN TAX SETTING

'Good' tax policy could be said to encompass a number of features: the ideal mix between different sources of taxation; the optimal size of government; and minimum wastage or misappropriation of public revenues. It is widely acknowledged that the making of good public policy in all areas of government—tax policy included—partly rests on the existence of a well-informed electorate that can hold the government to account. However, it is frequently claimed that the electorate is poorly informed about most areas of public policy, and that they are thus restricted in their ability to hold the government to account. This may allow politicians to follow their own agendas on tax policy, be this in terms of the overall size of government or the composition of tax revenues. For instance, one of the stated reasons for introducing the poll tax was to ensure profligate councils were held to account by local citizens. The 1987 Conservative general election manifesto stated that:

> We will reform local government finance to strengthen local democracy and accountability. Local electors must be able to decide the level of service they want and how much they are prepared to pay for it.

From a theoretical perspective, unlike redistributive taxation, it is harder to isolate a canonical model to represent the conflict of interest between politicians and voters. A related tradition in political economy that puts direct emphasis on elections is due to Barro (1973). He considers a world in which the promise of re-election can lead politicians to implement policies favoured by citizens. Thus, the problem of excessive taxation is held in check by the fact that political office is contestable. In effect political parties and/or politicians develop reputations that they lose if they do not fulfil them. Politicians who renege on their tax promises risk being voted out of office in this kind of framework. The models have found empirical support in evidence that some fraction of voters does appear to vote retrospectively, that is, looking at the records of incumbents on taxation and spending—see Paldam and Nannestad (1994) for a review of the literature. There is also evidence, consistent with these models, that politicians that are in the last period in office and hence cannot be re-elected behave differently in setting tax and spending policies compared to those who can run again—see, for example, Besley and Case (1995b).

Accountability models focus for the main part on debates about what drives the size of government rather than the composition of taxation. However, one key feature of the approach which does have implications for tax structures takes the information foundations of agency models more directly to heart. One of the reasons why politicians are able to run their own agendas which may not be in line with what voters want is based on the idea that voters are imperfectly informed. This builds on the quite reasonable fact that few voters are expert economists and, even if they were, they would lack the information needed to assess the incidence of many tax policies. Moreover, some forms of taxation may be less visible than other forms. This is important because Mani and Mukand (2007) show that public expenditure on public goods can suffer from a 'visibility effect'. This causes public expenditure to be distorted towards more visible forms of public goods, despite less visible public goods being of considerable public benefit. One could imagine a converse argument applying to taxation, such that less visible forms of taxation are over-used relative to the optimal tax structure.

Section 13.6.1 will discuss the implications of imperfect information, both in terms of voters' knowledge about the tax system, and in terms of the visibility of different elements of the tax system. Section 13.6.2 will discuss the role that political institutions and policy rules have played in terms of holding the government of the day to account: this will include a discussion of the role played by Parliament, fiscal rules, and external bodies. Section 13.6.3 concludes.

13.6.1. Role of information and transparency in shaping tax structures

Public understanding and hypothecation

It is unreasonable to expect voters fully to understand the tax system and its first- or second-order effects: that is, after all, what economists and accountants are employed for. However, a lack of understanding of the tax system and its elements may play a significant role in the shape the system takes. This is best understood when looking at the example of National Insurance contributions (NICs) and income tax.

Income tax and employee NICs (referred to as just NICs until we come to discuss employer NICs later in this section) are highly similar in their operation, such that NICs have increasingly come to resemble just another income tax over the years. They both tax earned income—though income tax also taxes savings and pension income. They are both withheld at source for employees (i.e. deducted from pay cheques), though collected via different administrative systems. There are some differences in that NICs are levied on weekly earnings, whilst income tax is levied upon annual income, and there are some other important differences for the self-employed. However, there is a common belief that there is a strong connection between NICs paid and state benefits, and that NICs pay for the NHS, making NICs distinct from income tax. Neither of these perceptions is based very convincingly on the reality.

In the UK, there has always been a weak connection between benefits and contributions. Furthermore, this connection has been weakened by a gradual alignment of the NIC schedule with the income tax schedule and the removal of the ceiling on NICs, such that NICs increasingly resemble just another income tax. Moreover, there is actually no meaningful connection between how much is spent on contributory state benefits or the NHS, and how much revenue is raised via NICs. Despite this there appears to be a general misperception that the NHS is funded via NICs (see Stafford (1998)).

Having first accepted the idea that NICs and income tax are highly similar, it may seem surprising that income tax rates and NICs have followed different trajectories over the past thirty years. This might not be so surprising if there are widespread misperceptions regarding the degree of hypothecation and the connection between contributions paid. This is because such misperceptions may make NICs more politically acceptable, since they are wrongly perceived to pay for things voters like and may benefit from later on in life.

However, as NICs only tax earned income, rather than that from savings and pensions, only the working-age population is likely to pay significant amounts. This means that rises in NICs, as opposed to income tax, exempts pensioners—a group that has a relatively high likelihood to vote in a general election. So, the greater relative reliance on NICs could also be the result of baser political motivations to tax relatively lightly a group in society with increasing political weight—pensioners.

Still, a situation where the public falsely believes that NICs are meaningfully hypothecated towards the funding of the NHS and contributory benefits is far from conducive to accountability. Whether a better situation is one with meaningful hypothecation is doubtful. Transparency might be enhanced but linking the revenue from particular tax instruments to spending on particular items would unhelpfully reduce discretion over the composition of public expenditure and unnecessarily complicate the tax system. An improvement in public information with respect to the current arrangements would improve transparency and accountability without these drawbacks.

Visibility

As already indicated, it seems like a reasonable conjecture that politicians that view voters as averse to increased taxation will tend to pick forms of taxation that are less visible to the decisive voters whose votes they care about. In the UK, this chimes with discussions about 'stealth taxation', the idea being that there has been a tendency in the last two administrations to pick low visibility forms of tax increase. Unfortunately, it is quite hard to assess the exact empirical validity of this proposition, in part because the effects of transparency are not quite as simple as 'more is better'.[72] However, we can point to some specific large-scale examples.

Examples of less visible forms of taxation would include most indirect taxes since they are typically not separated in prices perceived by consumers.[73] By contrast, pay slips are typically quite explicit about deductions for taxes and National Insurance. Things are more complicated, however, when the ultimate incidence of a tax is unclear. Consider, for example, employers' National Insurance contributions. In a competitive labour market, these will be borne by workers. However, few workers observe directly what is being paid by their employer and are likely to set aside the possibility that it is actually coming

[72] Partial transparency can create distortionary incentives in a variety of ways. For an example of a case where more transparency is not actually welfare-enhancing, see Besley (2006), ch. 3.

[73] This compared with most states sales taxes in the US, which are not included in the prices perceived by most consumers and are instead only included when consumers pay for their goods.

out of their pay packet since this requires an economic analysis of the market equilibrium.

An example of a relatively visible tax would be income tax paid by the self-employed, which has to be directly remitted by these individuals. Another would be council tax, which has to be paid by individuals directly, after the bill lands on their doorstep, ensuring maximum visibility. This could be a source of its public disfavour. However, unpopularity of the council tax may owe more to observed gaps between property values and property taxes due to infrequent revaluation as well as the opaqueness of the formulae under which local authorities receive grants from central government, both of which produce a disconnect between payment of taxes and receipt of services. Ironically, one of the arguments made in favour of the poll tax was that its transparent visibility would enhance accountability. However, as we discussed above, the policy was not sustainable in the face of public opposition, and the long-term consequence of the poll tax experiment turned out to be even greater centralization and further obscuring of the cost of local services.

Moreover, the way changes to taxation are perceived by the public or reported by the media may be important. Revenues from some taxes, such as income tax and VAT, keep pace with inflation as earnings and sales increase with inflation. However, excise duties and council tax must be 'raised' each year in line with inflation in order to prevent the revenues from being eroded by inflation. There is thus an incentive to place greater reliance on taxes that need not be 'raised' each year, which is exactly what we see in the UK, with relatively less reliance on specific indirect taxes over the past thirty years.

Similarly, governments of all stripes have partly relied on fiscal drag—or 'bracket creep'—over the past thirty years for growth in income tax revenues. If the government raised the top or basic rate of income tax, the effects are likely to be quite transparent and widely reported. However, it is not quite so obvious how much extra tax you pay when your earnings increase just enough to push you into the top income bracket because the government only increases the income tax threshold with prices, as opposed to earnings.

With all this in mind, we see that UK governments over the past thirty years have benefited from the growth in revenues associated with taxes (or elements of them) whose effects are not that transparent or well-understood—for example, rising rates of VAT, fiscal drag, and both employer and employee NICs. They have relied less on taxes whose effects are transparent or which require 'increases' each year to maintain their real value, for example, specific excise duties and top or basic rates of income tax. See Chapter 1, Figure 1.3 for trends in the composition of tax revenue over time.

13.6.2. Institutional constraints

We have speculated that the public is far from perfectly informed in matters of taxation and so cannot hold the government fully to account. Research conducted by Torsten Persson, Gerard Roland, and Guido Tabellini argues that some forms of institutional structures can improve the quality of governmental response to problems of imperfect information. For instance, Persson and Tabellini (2003) argue that presidential forms of government create a greater level of individual accountability. Obviously, the UK is not a presidential system and no such fundamental political change is under serious consideration, but are there other constraints on the executive that ensure accountability? We shall begin this section by discussing whether fiscal constitutions, such as fiscal rules, ensure greater levels of accountability. We will then move on to discuss the role played by Parliament and external bodies.

Fiscal rules

Scholars of political economy have put a lot of store by fiscal rules for governing the public finances. Among Public Choice scholars, like Brennan and Buchanan (1980), this is based on a belief that electoral mechanisms are insufficient by themselves to restrain government's power to tax. They advocate adopting a 'fiscal constitution' where governments are explicitly constrained.

In a broad sense, the need for explicit fiscal rules can be thought of as responding to explicit failures in governmental decision-making. Rules that govern macro-economic aspects of the public finances are usually motivated by the idea that voters are poorly informed about the true state of public finances. In principle, fiscal rules could also encompass specific tax measures—such as the tax base or the rate of income tax. However, while these are often the subject of electoral pledges, they are rarely embodied in rules. Most fiscal rules relate to the overall size of government.

The UK public finances are governed by the Code for Fiscal Stability, which says that the government must announce their fiscal objectives, and if they have any rules, how these will be defined. In 1998, the Labour government chose to impose two fiscal rules, neither of which related to the size of the state—instead they focused on measures of borrowing and debt. The first was known as the 'golden rule', which demanded that the current budget be at least in balance over an economic cycle. The second rule was known as the 'sustainable investment' or 'net debt' rule. This said that net debt should remain at 'a stable and prudent level', which the government chose to define as not more than 40% of GDP.

These are self-proclaimed rules and have no legal force. They also require the government to define important concepts, such as the dates of the economics cycle, and could thus be subject to manipulation. Nevertheless, according to Person E:

> However much mistrust there may be in the precise definition of the Golden Rule, there is no doubt that it played a very real role in constraining Gordon Brown as Chancellor. It set parameters around what was allowable, and by and large these parameters restricted and genuinely constrained policy.

Furthermore, the Labour government's decision to abandon these fiscal rules, when faced with a banking crisis in late 2008 and a large increase in the level of government borrowing, proved to be politically embarrassing. Such a situation added weight to the accusations from both main opposition parties that the government had been fiscally irresponsible.

Other countries have also adopted fiscal rules. For example, some states have adopted balanced budget rules that restrict the extent to which states can run budget deficits, which are easily verifiable but do restrict a state's ability to smooth tax and spending over the ups-and-downs of the cycle. There is also the Stability and Growth Pact, which forbids signatories from running budget deficits in excess of 3% of GDP except in exceptional circumstances. However, this has proven difficult to enforce in practice, especially in a context where it is fellow European leaders who decide on any possible sanctions.

Parliament

Going back as far as the thirteenth century, Parliament has had the constitutional responsibility of approving new taxes. How is it placed to hold the executive to account and perform scrutiny of tax policy in the twenty-first century?

Parliament has a number of routes through which it can scrutinize the government's tax policy. First, the Chancellor often comes before the Treasury Select Committee soon after the Budget and Pre-Budget Report. This gives members of the Treasury Select Committee the chance to ask the Chancellor questions about the announcements he or she has made about tax policy. There is also an opportunity for MPs to scrutinize tax legislation during debates on the Finance Act in the House of Commons and during the committee stage. However, the effectiveness of this scrutiny is questionable since MPs have few resources to draw upon, as we have already observed.

The House of Lords provides some scrutiny of the detail of tax policy, however its role is restricted as it cannot vote on money bills.

Neither is there any pre-legislative scrutiny, which is important to note given that tax reforms announced in the Budget, or Pre-Budget Report, are more often than not just enacted as announced. Therefore, since there is precious little evidence that Parliament is taking up the strain in terms of holding the government to account, do external bodies do the job any better?

External scrutiny

What roles do external bodies play in scrutinizing tax policy? One important source of scrutiny comes from tax professionals. HMRC regularly consults tax professionals before enacting legislation, either via formal consultations or informal approaches. The degree to which HMRC does this has also increased over the past thirty years. This has certainly helped improve the quality of tax legislation and more of the same could further improve matters. However, there is little explicit pre-legislative scrutiny from external economists.

Most of the external scrutiny from economists is provided immediately after tax policy announcements in the Budget or Pre-Budget Report. An important source of such scrutiny comes from pressure groups, accountancy analysts, and—excusing the authors' natural bias—the Institute for Fiscal Studies (IFS). The briefings provided by the IFS, for example, the day after Budget or Pre-Budget Report, have become a staple for economic journalists and the analysis of tax policy proposals is widely reported. Although such scrutiny rarely leads to changes in tax policy proposals, the knowledge that bodies like the IFS will provide detailed and careful analysis certainly provides strong incentives for the government to make sure the full implications of any proposal are fully thought through before they are announced.

However, such external scrutiny is limited by the availability of data. For instance, publishing more of the assumptions behind the fiscal forecasts would enable better external scrutiny and ensure greater credibility for the fiscal rules.

13.6.3. Summary

There is a limit to how well-informed the electorate can be expected to be for the purpose of holding the government to account and ensuring good quality tax policy. Nonetheless, the extent to which we observe government making increasing use of tax policy instruments that are either ill-understood by voters—as in the case of employer or employee NICs—or those that are less visible or transparent to voters—such as VAT or fiscal drag—should be seen as unwelcome.

Do other institutions pick up the accountability baton where the electorate leaves off? Parliament plays some role, but lacks the informational resources to play much of a role, and is hardly involved at all in the crucial pre-legislative stage. The fiscal rules appear to have lost credibility due to perceived fudging of the rules by government and little external scrutiny of assumptions. On a more positive note, external organizations do provide some level of scrutiny and accountability, ensuring improved tax legislation and that the economic impact of proposals is fully thought through.

Transparency is now part of the motherhood and apple pie of government policy making. Moreover, greater freedom of information and public discussion of these issues has certainly resulted in significant moves in this direction in recent years. We take it as a goal of transparent tax policy to make the analysis and data that is provided for debates about tax reform even more available to citizens.

13.7. CONCLUSIONS AND POLICY RECOMMENDATIONS

Following his attempts to create a fairer tax system, Jean-Baptiste Colbert, the French Minister of Finance under Louis XIV, observed that:

> The art of taxation consists in so plucking the goose as to obtain the largest amount of feathers with the least possible amount of hissing.

This quote neatly summarizes the conflicts inherent in tax design from both an economic and a political perspective, that is, we wish both to create a tax system that minimizes economic costs, such as deadweight loss, but also to create one that is politically sustainable within the machinery of government and society.

We conclude by summarizing the key themes our analysis has highlighted: a 'passive' movement to the right; policy drift as a result of lobbying; disconnected tax debates; the effect of an ill-informed electorate and minimal transparency; and finally we present our proposal to improve scrutiny and parliamentary accountability. Before we begin, it should be noted that many of the problems we identify are not unique to taxation, and neither are the solutions we recommend. Our recommendations should thus be seen in a wider context of the overall UK political process.

13.7.1. A 'passive' movement to the right

This chapter analyses whether changes in voter preferences and strategic party positioning could explain declines in statutory rates of income tax. What we discover is that electoral support has moved to the right, though voters seem to have followed rather than led the changing content of party manifestos. Voters have always favoured redistribution, particularly from those with the highest incomes to those with the lowest incomes. Whilst preferences for redistribution have been declining over time, it is notable that the large cuts in statutory rates of income tax took place at a time when attitudes to redistribution were at their most favourable, and when a majority of voters voted for parties who did not favour these cuts. Whether this move to the right will persist and to what extent it is now a fact of political life is hard to say.

13.7.2. Policy drift and persistence

Our case study of the R&D tax credit provides a number of lessons, the primary one being that enacting tax policy can create interest groups and constituencies in favour of that policy. Even when they did not lobby for the policy in the first place, like the large firms in our study, they will lobby both for persistence and extensions that allow policy to drift from its original motivation. Therefore, any potential tax reformer should remember that any new allowances enacted or favourable tax treatments provided to particular groups could prove difficult to remove and may be distorted into something different over time.

While the example of the R&D tax credit vividly illustrates policy persistence as well as drift, the past thirty years has seen other areas of specific tax privilege phased out, most notably the married couples allowance and mortgage interest tax relief. The timing of these reforms suggest that it is helpful to phase out changes gradually and during a period when it can plausibly be claimed that other taxes are being cut or rationalized.

13.7.3. Disconnected tax debates

The framing of tax policy debates can be crucial. Framing the VAT zero-rating of children's clothing in isolation has helped maintain it; framing the estate tax in isolation also helped those lobbying for its abolition in the US. Such framing could easily result from a lack of public understanding about the interconnectedness of the tax system.

However, in order to pursue sensible tax policy it is essential to see the tax system as a system rather than to consider its different elements in isolation. So disconnected tax debates may be particularly counter-productive for tax policy as compared with other areas of public policy. This has a lesson for the Mirrlees Review, which may need to combine tax reforms in different areas to provide a broad-based set of reform measures, making clear that there is give and take across different population groups.

13.7.4. Transparency and accountability

There is a limit to how well-informed the electorate can be expected to be for the purpose of holding the government to account and ensuring good quality tax policy. However, institutional reforms which improve transparency and public understanding would help avoid situations where government can make increasing use of tax policy instruments that are either ill-understood by voters—as in the case of the relationship between National Insurance contributions, NHS spending, and state benefit spending—or those that are less visible or transparent to voters—such as VAT or fiscal drag.

Other institutions like Parliament can have an accountability role, but as noted above limited information and pre-legislative involvement make it a small one. At the same time external organizations provide some level of scrutiny and accountability, which improves tax legislation and economic analysis of proposals. However, to the extent these are also interested parties, the costs of policy persistence and drift (analysed above in Section 13.5) have to be set against this.

13.7.5. A proposal to improve scrutiny

We are not the first to identify this lack of parliamentary accountability as a problem. In 2003, a Tax Law Review Committee working party chaired by Sir Alan Budd produced a report called 'Making Tax Law'. This report stated that,

> In the case of taxation, the unfortunate reality is that the House of Commons fails to scrutinise the rules (if not the levels) of taxation in any real sense at all. The truth of the matter is that the House of Commons has neither the time nor the expertise nor, apparently, the inclination to undertake any systematic or effective examination of whatever tax rules the government of the day places before it for its approval.

A degree of parliamentary accountability through greater levels of pre-legislative scrutiny of tax policy would be highly desirable. Of course, a lack of effective parliamentary accountability extends to other areas of policy, beyond taxation, and is a general political concern. However, the degree of pre-legislative parliamentary scrutiny is even weaker for tax policy, since in other areas policy proposals are regularly published in White Papers or Green Papers. Although there is pre-legislative scrutiny of draft tax proposals by tax professionals and other interested parties, Parliament is rarely involved in this process.

The best vehicle for pre-legislative scrutiny is the select committee system. We leave it as an open question whether scrutiny of tax policy is best undertaken by the existing Treasury Select Committee or by a new select committee on taxation. But it is clear to us that ensuring higher levels of pre-legislative scrutiny should be a priority for government.

Alongside this, in order to undertake effective pre-legislative scrutiny, MPs require more resources. At present, much advice and support comes through external organizations, and this could be extended. However, another possibility is a formal in-house service akin to the Congressional Budget Office in the US, which could be explicitly charged with providing analysis of tax policy for MPs.

More broadly, we believe that serious thought should be given to instituting a body to oversee the public finances. A group of experts with genuine knowledge of the operation of tax systems could be put in place to offer advice and to audit revenue and spending figures. This body could be accessible and accountable to Parliament as well as to the executive with appointments appropriately scrutinized. As well as scrutinizing government plans, the body could offer advice to all parties, particularly around election times. To provide meaningful scrutiny and advice, any such body would require access to more data than is currently provided to Parliament. As well as providing more data to this body, providing more data to the public could improve external scrutiny, for example, by publishing all assumptions behind fiscal forecasts.

REFERENCES

Abramovsky, L., Bond, S., Harrison, R., and Simpson, H. (2005a), 'Productivity Policy', Institute for Fiscal Studies, 2005 Election Briefing Note No. 6.

—— Griffith, R., and Harrison, R. (2005b), 'Background Facts and Comments on "Supporting Growth in Innovation: Enhancing the R&D Tax Credit" ', November 2005, IFS Briefing Notes, BN68.

—— Harrison, R. and Simpson, H. (2007), 'University Research and the Location of Business R&D', *Economic Journal*, **117**, C114–C141.

Alesina, A., and Glaeser, E. (2004), *Fighting Poverty in the US and Europe*, Oxford: Oxford University Press.

—— —— and Sacerdote, B. (2001), 'Why Doesn't the United States Have a European-Style Welfare State?', *Brookings Papers on Economic Activity*, **2**, 187–277.

Alt, J., and Lassen, D. (2006), 'Fiscal Transparency, Political Parties, and Debt in OECD Countries', *European Economic Review*, **50**, 1403–39.

Austen-Smith, D. (2000), 'Redistributing Income under Proportional Representation', *Journal of Political Economy*, **108**, 1235–69.

—— and Wallerstein, M. (2006), 'Redistribution and Affirmative Action', *Journal of Public Economics*, **90**, 1789–823.

Barro, R. J. (1973), 'The Control of Politicians: An Economic Model', *Public Choice*, **14**, 19–42.

Benabou, R., and Tirole, J. (2006), 'Belief in a Just World and Redistributive Politics', *Quarterly Journal of Economics*, **121**, 699–746.

Berger, P. (1993), 'Explicit and Implicit Effects of the R&D Tax Credit', *Journal of Accounting Research*, **31**, 131–71.

Bergstrom, T. C., and Goodman, R. P. (1973), 'Private Demands for Public Goods', *American Economic Review*, **63**, 280–96.

Besley, T. (2006), *Principled Agents*, Oxford: Oxford University Press.

—— and Case, A. (1995), 'Incumbent Behavior: Vote Seeking, Tax Setting and Yardstick Competition', *American Economic Review*, **85**, 25–45.

—— —— (1995b), 'Does Electoral Accountability Affect Economic Policy Choices? Evidence from Gubernatorial Term Limits', *Quarterly Journal of Economics*, **110**, 769–98.

—— —— (2003), 'Political Institutions and Policy Outcomes: Evidence from the United States', *Journal of Economic Literature*, **41** (March), 7–73.

—— and Preston, I. (2007), 'Electoral Bias and Policy Change: Theory and Evidence', *Quarterly Journal of Economics*, **122**, 1473–510.

Billings, B. A., and Paschke, R. (2003), 'Would H.R. 463 Improve the Competitiveness of the U.S. R&D Tax Incentives?', *Tax Notes*, **99**, 1509–38.

Bloom, N., Griffith, R., and Van Reenen, J. (2002), 'Do R&D Tax Credits Work? Evidence from a Panel of Countries 1979–1997', *Journal of Public Economics*, **85**, 1–31.

Bolton, N., and Roland, H. (1997), 'The Breakup of Nations: A Political Economy Analysis', *Quarterly Journal of Economics*, **112**, 1057–90.

Brennan, G., and Buchanan, J. (1980), *The Power to Tax: Analytical Foundations of the Fiscal Constitution*, Cambridge: Cambridge University Press.

Brown, K. (1984), *The R&D Tax Credit: Issues in Tax Policy and Industrial Innovation*, Washington, DC: American Enterprise Institute.

Budd, A. (2003), *Making Tax Law*, TLRC Discussion Paper No. 3.

Butler, A., Adonis, A., and Travers, T. (1994), *Failure in British Government: The Politics of the Poll Tax*, Oxford: Oxford University Press.

Coate, S., and Morris, S. (1999), 'Policy Persistence', *American Economic Review*, **89**, 1327–36.

Cusack, T., Iversen, T., and Rehm, P. (2006), 'Risks at Work: The Demand and Supply Sides of Redisitrubtion', *Oxford Review of Economic Policy*, **22**, 365–89.

Dilnot, A., Emmerson, C., and Simpson, H. (eds.) (2002), *The IFS Green Budget: January 2002*, Institute for Fiscal Studies, Commentary 87.

European Union (2001), 'Lisbon Agenda', <http://www.euractiv.com/en/agenda2004/lisbon-agenda/article-117510>.

Evans, M. D. R., and Kelley, J. (2004), 'Subjective Social Location: Data From 21 Nations', *International Journal of Public Opinion Research*, **16**, 3–38.

Ferejohn, J. A. (1986), 'Incumbent Performance and Electoral Control', *Public Choice*, **50**, 5–26.

Foley, D. K. (1967), 'Resource Allocation and the Public Sector', *Yale Economic Essays*, **7**, 45–98.

Fong, C. (2001), 'Social Preferences, Self-Interest, and the Demand for Redistribution', *Journal of Public Economics*, **82**, 225–46.

Gale, W. (1999), 'What Can America Learn from the British Tax System?', in Slemrod, J. (ed.), *Tax Policy in the Real World*, Cambridge: Cambridge University Press.

Gambardella, A., Orsenigo, L., and Pammolli, F. (2000), *Global Competitiveness in Pharmaceuticals: A European Perspective*, Report prepared for the Enterprise Directorate-General of the European Commission.

Ganghof, S. (2008), 'The Politics of Tax Structure', in Shapiro, I., Swenson, P., and Donno, D. (eds.), *Divide and Deal: The Politics of Distribution in Democracies*, New York: NYU Press.

Georgiadis, A., and Manning, A. (2007), 'Spend It Like Beckham? Inequality and Redistribution in the UK, 1983–2005', London School of Economics, March, manuscript.

Gerber, E. (1998), 'Pressuring Legislatures Through the Use of Initiatives', pp. 191–208 in Bowler, S., Donovan, T., and Tolbert, C. (eds.), *Citizens as Legislators: Direct Democracy in the United States*, Columbus: Ohio State University Press.

Graetz, M., and Shapiro, I. (2005), *Death by a Thousand Cuts*, New Jersey: Princeton University Press.

Griffith, R., Harrison, R., and Van Reenen, J. (2006), 'How Special is the Special Relationship? Using the Impact of U.S. R&D Spillovers on U.K. Firms as a Test of Technology Sourcing', *American Economic Review*, **96**, 1859–75.

—— Redding, S., and Van Reenen, J. (2001), 'Measuring the Cost-Effectiveness of an R&D Tax Credit for the UK', *Fiscal Studies*, **22**, 375–99.

—— Sandler, D., and Van Reenen, J. (1996), 'Tax Incentives for R&D', *Fiscal Studies*, **16**, 21–44.

Grossman, G., and Helpman, E. (1994), 'Protection for Sale', *American Economic Review*, **84**, 833–50.

Hall, B. (1993), 'R&D Tax Policy during the Eighties: Success or Failure', *Tax Policy and the Economy*, 7, 1–36.

—— and Van Reenen, J. (1999), 'How Effective are Fiscal Incentives for R&D? A Review of the Evidence', *Research Policy*, **29**, 449–69.

Hall, J., and Preston, I. (2000), 'Tax Price Effects on Attitudes to Hypothecated Tax Increases', *Journal of Public Economics*, **75**, 417–38.

Hettich, W., and Winer, S. (1988), 'Economic and Political Foundations of Tax Structure', *American Economic Review*, **78**, 701–12.

—— —— (1999), *Democratic Choice and Taxation*, Cambridge: Cambridge University Press.

Hills, J. (2002), 'Following or Leading Public Opinion? Social Security Policy and Public Attitudes since 1997', *Fiscal Studies*, **23**, 539–58.

Iversen, T., and Soskice, D. (2006), 'Electoral Institutions, Parties and the Politics of Class: Why some Democracies Distribute More than Others', *American Political Science Review*, **100**, 165–81.

Keen, M. (1999), 'A British Perspective on Tax Policy in the United States', in Slemrod, J. (ed.), *Tax Policy in the Real World*, 505–06, Cambridge: Cambridge University Press.

Kim, H., and Fording, R. C. (1998), 'Voter Ideology in Western Democracies, 1946–1989', *European Journal of Political Research*, **33**, 73–97.

—— —— (2003), 'Voter Ideology in Western Democracies: An Update', *European Journal of Political Research*, **42**, 95–105.

Kydland, F., and Prescott, E. (1977), 'Rules Rather than Discretion: The Inconsistency of Optimal Plans', *Journal of Political Economy*, **85**, 473–92.

McCarty, N., Poole, K. T., and Rosenthal, H. (2006), *Polarized America: The Dance of Ideology and Unequal Riches*, Walras-Pareto Lectures, Cambridge, MA: MIT Press.

Mani, A., and Mukand, S. (2007), 'Democracy, Visibility and Public Good Provision', *Journal of Development Economics*, **83**, 506–29.

Meade, J. (1978), *The Structure and Reform of Direct Taxation: Report of a Committee chaired by Professor J. E. Meade for the Institute for Fiscal Studies*, London: George Allen & Unwin. http//www.ifs.org.uk/publications/3433

Meltzer, A., and Richard, S. (1981), 'A Rational Theory of the Size of Government', *Journal of Political Economy*, **89**, 914–27.

Moene, K. O., and Wallerstein, M. (2001), 'Inequality, Social Insurance and Redistribution', *American Political Science Review*, **95**, 859–74.

—— —— (2003), 'Earnings Inequality and Welfare Spending: A Disaggregated Analysis', *World Politics*, **55**, 485–516.

Noll, R. G., and Cohen, B. M. (1983), *The Political Economy of Deregulation: Interest Groups in the Regulatory Process*, Washington, DC: American Enterprise Institute.

OECD (2006), *Revenue Statistics 1965–2005*, Centre for Tax Policy and Administration.

Olson, M. (1965), *The Logic of Collective Action*, Cambridge, MA: Harvard University Press.

Orton, M., and Rowlingson, K. (2007), *Public Attitudes to Economic Inequality*, York: Joseph Rowntree Foundation.

Paldam, M., and Nannestad, P. (1994), 'The VP-Function. A Survey of the Literature on Vote and Popularity Functions after 25 Years', *Public Choice*, **79**, 213–45.

Perotti, R. (1996), 'Growth, Income Distribution, and Democracy: What the Data Say', *Journal of Economic Growth*, **1**, 149–87.

Persson, T., and Tabellini, G. (2003), *The Economic Effects of Constitutions*, Cambridge, MA: MIT Press.

Roberts, K. (1977), 'Voting Over Income Tax Schedules', *Journal of Public Economics*, **12**, 157–201.

Roemer, J. (1998), 'Why the Poor Do Not Expropriate the Rich: An Old Argument in New Garb', *Journal of Public Economics*, **70**, 399–424.

Romer, T. (1975), 'Individual Welfare, Majority Voting, and the Properties of a Linear Income Tax', *Journal of Public Economics*, **4**, 163–85.

Roubini, N., and Sachs, J. (1989), 'Political and Economic Determinants of Budget Deficits in the Industrial Democracies', *European Economic Review*, **33**, 903–38.

Rubinfeld, D. L. (1987), 'The Economics of the Local Public Sector', in Auerbach A. L., and Feldstein, M. (eds.), *Handbook of Public Economics*, **2**, 571–645.

Scheve, K., and Stasavage, D. (2006), 'Religion and Preferences for Social Insurance', *Quarterly Journal of Political Science*, **1**, 255–86.

Sedgley, M. (2006), 'The State Giveth and the State Taketh Away: Supporting the Research-Based Pharmaceutical Industry in Europe and the UK', *Economic Affairs*, **26**, 39–47.

Sefton, T. (2005), 'Give and Take: Public Attitudes to Redistribution', in Park, A., Curtice, J., Bromley, C., Phillips, M., and Johnson, M. (eds.), *British Social Attitudes: The 22nd Report—Two Terms of New Labour: The Public's Reaction*, London: Sage.

Slemrod, J. (ed.) (1999), *Tax Policy in the Real World*, Cambridge: Cambridge University Press.

Snyder, J., and Kramer, G. (1988), 'Fairness, Self-Interest, and the Politics of the Progressive Income Tax', *Journal of Public Economics*, **36**, 197–230.

Stafford, B. (1998), *National Insurance and the Contributory Principle*, DWP In-house report No. 39.

Steinmo, S. (1996), *Taxation and Democracy: Swedish, British and American Approaches to Financing the Modern State*, New Haven, Conn.: Yale University Press.

Svallfors, S. (1997), 'Worlds of Welfare and Attitudes to Redistribution: A Comparison of Eight Western Nations', *European Sociological Review*, **13**, 283–304.

Taylor-Gooby, P., Hastie, C., and Bromley, C. (2003), 'Querulous Citizens: Welfare Knowledge and the Limits to Welfare Reform', *Social Policy and Administration*, **37**, 1–20.

Treasury, H. M. (2001), *Increasing Innovation: A Consultation Paper Budget 2001*, The Public Enquiry Unit, Inland Revenue.

—— (2003), *Defining Innovation: A Consultation on the Definition of R&D for Tax Purposes.*

—— (2005), *Cox Review of Creativity in Business: Building on the UK's Strengths* <http://www.hmtreasury.gov.uk/media/B91/B7/coxreview-chap5providing support.pdf>.

—— (2005), *Supporting Growth in Innovation: Enhancing the R&D Tax Credit,* <http://www.hmrc.gov.uk/consult_new/rd-taxcredit.pdf>.

—— DTI and DfES (2004), *Science & Innovation Investment 2004–2014*, <http://www.hmtreasury.gov.uk./spending_review/spend_sr04/associated_documents/spending_sr04_science.cfm>.

Tuomala, M. (1990), *Optimal Income Tax and Redistribution*, Oxford: Clarendon Press.

Wilson, J. Q. (1989), *Bureaucracy: What Government Agencies Do and Why They Do It*, New York: Basic Books.

Xu, R. (2007), 'Pipelines across the Pond: Pharmaceutical R&D Investment in the US and UK', Thesis, Department of Government, Harvard College.

Commentary by Peter Riddell

Peter Riddell is Chief Political Commentator of *The Times* and a Senior Fellow of the Institute for Government, having written about politics and economics for more than thirty years including from 1976 to 1981 as economics correspondent of the *Financial Times*. He has written six books on British politics, including two on the policies and performance of Margaret Thatcher and one on those of Tony Blair. He is currently Chair of the Hansard Society, holds two honorary doctorates of letters and is an Honorary Fellow of Sidney Sussex College, Cambridge.

The Alt, Preston, and Sibieta chapter has too much flimsy political science and not enough well-founded history. Its discussion of the political influences on tax policymaking would have been more convincing if the authors had examined what had happened rather than tested, and partly found wanting, some tendentious theoretical models. There are virtually no references to what Geoffrey Howe, Nigel Lawson, Kenneth Clarke, and Gordon Brown said, thought, and did. We do not have to speculate on why various tax decisions were made. There is ample evidence in what politicians said at the time, especially about what they believed (rightly or wrongly) about the attitudes of voters, and in more immediate, and extensive, opinion research by polling organizations, rather than just the British Social Attitudes Survey (valuable though that is). There have been two long periods of one-party rule in Britain, from 1979 to 1997 under the Conservatives, and since 1997 under Labour, when broadly consistent tax policies were followed (with notable exceptions, of course, such as the introduction and then abolition of the poll tax or community charge). This historical approach provides greater insights into the pressures to reduce marginal tax rates during the 1980s, then not to raise them again from the 1990s onwards, until the banking and financial crisis of 2008 onwards. Such an analysis would also place much greater emphasis on international influences on tax policy, especially during Labour's period in power, than this chapter does.

A major reservation about the chapter is over the discussion of voter preferences and median voter models. Their usefulness is limited because votes in general elections are not solely or even primarily determined by the public's views just on taxes and on the parties' tax policies. The pattern is, in practice, more complicated, because as the authors concede, public knowledge is imperfect, while attitudes on taxation form part of a much broader range of attitudes towards a governing party's competence in managing the economy. For instance, Gordon Brown's repeated emphasis, both before and after the 1997 election, on not raising the basic and higher rates of income tax was only partially about tax policy as such—and only a limited guide to the trend of the tax burden, as the chapter recognizes—and much more about convincing voters that it was safe for them to have, and then retain, a Labour government. The authors correctly link support for taxes to levels of public spending. But it is more a question of whether voters think their tax money is being well spent. The chapter says (on page 1236) that the BSA asks no question addressing directly the issue of how effective the government is believed to have been in directing public funds to desired uses. But this question has been asked frequently by the main polling organizations, such as ICM, Populus, and YouGov (all of whose work is readily accessible on their websites). This shows a consistent decline over the past five years in the number believing the increase in taxes has been well or efficiently spent. The trust question asked in the BSA, as mentioned in the chapter, is only a rough-and-ready proxy for this more specific question which is the key to attitudes to taxation. In this context, as discussed below, it is astonishing that this chapter does not discuss Gordon Brown's decision in 2002 to raise employer and employee National Insurance contributions specifically to finance a big increase in spending on the NHS.

1. THE CONSERVATIVE YEARS

The Conservatives came to power in May 1979 with a clear tax objective. As Margaret Thatcher (1993) put in her memoirs (p. 42): 'Lower income tax combined with a shift from taxation on earnings to taxation on spending, would increase incentives.' There was no dispute on this goal. Promises to cut taxation had featured prominently in Conservative campaigning and in its manifesto, cutting the top rate of income from 83 to 60% (the then European average) and also the basic rate, while undertaking an unspecified switch from direct to indirect taxation. Tory strategists believed that not just the wealthy but also skilled manual workers felt they were paying too much in direct taxes. As Professor Ivor Crewe pointed out (in Penniman (1981), pp. 284–97), taxes came third on the list of issues which members of the public said influenced their voting decisions (behind prices and unemployment). Moreover, amongst those saying the issue was important, the Conservatives enjoyed a lead of plus 61 points. The Tories' edge here and on law and order offset Labour's advantages on prices and unemployment. Moreover, crucially, voters believed that a Conservative government would succeed in achieving its promise to reduce income tax—by a margin of plus 49 points saying it would rather than would not. Tax, Crewe argued, was different from other economic questions.

> To promise a reduction in the income tax, as the Conservatives repeatedly did, is as clear, tangible, and accountable a campaign commitment as a party can make. The electorate felt that something ought to be done about process, jobs, strikes, crime and taxes, and on the first two it was marginally more inclined to put its trust in Labour; but only on taxes did the voters also believe that something could and would be done—and that it was the Conservatives who would do the doing.

Taxation was the most helpful issue for the party.

> A year before the election the Conservatives' lead over Labour as 'the better party to reduce taxation' was a mere two percentage points; by polling day, the Conservatives' lead was 42 percentage points. On no other issue did public concern and party popularity move so decisively—and swiftly—in the Conservative party's favour.

So the Conservative leadership regarded honouring the tax promise as a top priority, both because it was right and to show that their election manifesto was being implemented. The Howe–Lawson team never signed up in full to the theories of Art Laffer that cutting income tax would not reduce the tax yield, and might increase it as a result of stimulating economic activity. This was one of the main contrasts between the economic policies of the Thatcher and at least the first-term Reagan administration. While the Thatcherites agreed that, over the long term, cuts in marginal tax rates would raise incentives and activity, they thought the positive effects would take time to work through and would not immediately offset the revenue lost from any reduction in the basic rate or from raising thresholds. The sole exception was in cutting the previously very high top rate of 83% to 60%, which they believed would have favourable effects on revenue, not least through a reduction in tax evasions and avoidance. This positive effect would not, however, apply in the short term to a cut in the basic rate of income tax, which Howe believed, had to be from 33p to 30p in the pound. Howe (1994, p. 129) argued that:

the level of income tax payable by the average taxpayer had to be reduced substantially. Not just because his or her income was more highly taxed than that of most of our overseas competitors. Not just because he or she felt demotivated. But, most important of all, because it would be politically impossible to make the large cuts in top rates that were necessary without achieving some comparable reduction in the direct tax burden of the average citizen.

So with tax thresholds and allowances rising above the cost of inflation, the Treasury would have to find at least £4.25 billion from indirect taxes, notably by replacing the previous two rates of Value Added Tax of 8 and 12.5% by a unified one of 15%. The main downside of this big tax switch was in raising retail prices and on the retail prices index which, in turn, would affect the level of pay claims, especially at a time of double-digit inflation.

The intellectual and political drive for the tax change came from the Conservative Treasury team. But such a big change naturally also involved the Prime Minister. Howe noted (1994, p. 130):

the ambivalence which Margaret often showed when the time came to move from the level of high principle and evangelism to practical politics ... now that we had come to the point of decision, she expressed herself anxious, understandably, about the possible RPI effects. At our first bilateral meeting, on 22 May, she was inclined to stick at a VAT flat rate of 12.5 per cent. I argued that our first Budget provided 'our only opportunity to make a radical switch from direct to indirect taxation and thus honour the commitment on which our credibility depends'.

At a second meeting, two days later, the scale of the shift was agreed, with a later compromise on excise duties. Thatcher herself recalled (1993, p. 43): 'Income tax cuts were vital, even if they had to be paid for by raising Value Added Tax (VAT) in this large leap. The decisive argument was that such a controversial increase in indirect taxes could only be made at the beginning of a parliament, when our mandate was fresh.'

Important political influences were notable by their absence from this discussion. First, public opinion only played a background role: being seen to support the general proposition that income tax should be cut but no more. There were guesses about the impact of the direct to indirect tax shift but no more sophisticated assessment of public preferences. Second, there were no worries about the attitude of MPs or Parliament. It was assumed that even such a controversial package would be approved by MPs, as, indeed, it was later that summer. The key decisions were taken by only a small group of senior politicians and advisers, all committed Thatcherites, as shown by the dismay of some of what were then called 'wets', dissenters in the Cabinet such as James Prior and Sir Ian Gilmour: doubts shared by quite a number of civil servants and economists. The June 1979 Budget was essentially an ideological statement, underlined by the decisions to raise the tax burden in the spring 1981 Budget in order to reduce public borrowing and facilitate a cut in interest rates.

The second phase of the Thatcher era came with the appointment of Nigel Lawson as Chancellor in June 1983. He pursued the tax-cutting agenda, notably by slashing the top rate of income tax to 40% in his 1988 Budget and with further cuts in the basic rate. But the most striking aspect of his period as Chancellor was the priority he gave to tax simplification and neutrality. In his memoirs, the most comprehensive account of his period at the Treasury by any Chancellor, Lawson (1992, pp. 338–46) set out his broad approach:

1. To leave people more of their own money so that they could choose for themselves what to do with it.
2. So far as was practical, to reduce marginal tax rates, so that an extra pound of earnings or profits was really worth having.
3. To see that, as a general rule, people's choices were distorted as little as possible through the tax system.
4. But to be prepared, when it was sensible to do so, to promote tax reliefs designed to make the economy work better.
5. To ensure, so far as possible, that the tax system was both simple and acceptable (not least to married women).
6. To adopt an economic rather than a social approach.

Among the changes which Lawson introduced, or extended from the Howe years, were the abolition of the National Insurance surcharge on employers and the reduction of the bias against jobs in the corporation tax system, while savings were encouraged by the abolition of the investment income surcharge, the replacement of capital transfer tax by inheritance tax, and the launch of Personal Equity Plans.

Most of the Lawson era changes originated in the Treasury, in the mind of Lawson and his close advisers. Thatcher (1993, pp. 672–3) conceded that 'Nigel's Budgets were ... essentially his'. She added: 'We had some differences—not least about mortgage tax relief which he would probably have liked to abolish and whose threshold I would certainly have liked to raise. But Nigel did not generally like to seek or take advice. Doubtless he felt he did not need to. He was precisely the opposite of the collegiate style which Geoffrey Howe before him practised.' In the Lawson memoirs, there is virtually no mention of Cabinet colleagues on Budget decision-making and none of Parliament. His 1988 Budget caused considerable controversy in the Commons on the day, but his proposals were passed into law pretty smoothly despite the worries of some about fuelling an already strengthening consumer boom. This is leaving aside the battles between the Treasury and Thatcher over the replacement of domestic rates by the community charge, or poll tax, a rare occasion of a new tax being introduced despite the opposition of the Chancellor of the day.

The focus in this section of the commentary has been on marginal tax rates when as Alt, Preston, and Sibieta rightly point out, the trends in the tax burden are often very different and less spectacular. The tax share of national income rose by a couple of points during the Thatcher era, though it fell marginally during Lawson's time as Chancellor. Marginal tax rates for the average taxpayer fell by about 5 percentage points during the Howe and Lawson decade to 34%. The contrast with the smaller change in the relative tax share is not only because of the shift to VAT but also because of fiscal drag.

In the final phase of the Conservative years, from November 1990 until May 1997, there was much less emphasis on tax reform or simplification and much more on stabilization in response to the inflation, exchange rate, and fiscal crisis of 1991–93, which required substantial tax increases. The political and economic pressures were different from those of the Thatcher decade, not least because after the 1992 general election, the Major government had a precarious, and then non-existent, majority in the House of Commons. The relative freedom which Howe and Lawson enjoyed, at least in retrospect, was not shared by either Norman Lamont or, after May 1993, Kenneth Clarke. Even though the economy recovered steadily after Black Wednesday, the tax increases proved to be highly unpopular and were seen as breaking the 1992 election pledge, as the Labour opposition continually argued. Indeed, the gradual disappearance of the Conservatives' Commons majority, coupled with a rebellion by a number of euro-sceptic MPs led to the defeat in December 1994 of the government's proposal to raise VAT on domestic fuel from 8 to 17.5%. This was a very rare example of a government being defeated in the Commons on a Budgetary measure, but memories of the event acted as a constraint on what Clarke could do in his remaining period as Chancellor.

2. THE GORDON BROWN DECADE

The approach of Gordon Brown and New Labour to tax policy was a mirror image of the Tories' problems and loss of trust on economic competence and taxation from 1992 onwards. Brown, Tony Blair, and their key advisers were convinced that Labour's ambiguous message on taxation had been a major factor in their fourth successive election defeat in 1992. Philip Gould (1998, pp. 117–30) recorded the damaging impact of tax for Labour ahead of the 1992 election. A presentation he made in autumn 1991 showed that tax was the top reason for not voting Labour, with nearly two-thirds of voters agreeing that the party would raise taxes for everyone. The percentage was even higher amongst C2 skilled workers, reflecting their aspirations as much as their current position. Gould recorded that the presentation made the politicians angry. 'Tony Blair and Gordon Brown were frustrated that we were in a position where our policy was both untenable and highly unpopular; John Smith [then Shadow Chancellor], knowing what we said was all true, simply walked out.' Gould and other New Labour strategists believed that suspicions over Labour's tax plans had lost them the support of the key group of 'aspirational' voters, Middle England or Middle Britain if you like.

Tax, therefore, played a key part in the creation of New Labour. Gould recorded (1998, pp. 283–4) that

> Tax was central to our strategy of reassurance. If the election campaign had one crucial battle, one defining fight, it was over tax. We lost the 1992 election and won the 1997 one in large part because of tax. Tony Blair and Gordon Brown both believed the shadow Budget in 1992 had been a mistake: it revealed our hand and raised taxes for middle-income earners . . . Blair and Brown had a gut feeling that hard-working families paid enough tax; why should they pay any more?

So, both before and after Tony Blair became party leader in July 1994, Brown followed a double track approach: attacking the Tories for breaking their pledges by raising taxes and trying to reassure voters that Labour could be trusted on the economy, and particularly on taxation. This was not just about taxation but also involved taking a very tough line against new public spending commitments.

The key symbolic argument was about whether to introduce a new top rate of income tax. Blair and Gould were hostile, fearing that it would be seen as merely the start of higher taxes and would undermine voters' attitudes towards New Labour on taxation generally. Seeing it from the perspective of the Brown camp, and particularly that of Ed Balls, Brown's long-term economic adviser, Robert Peston described Brown's attitude (2005, pp. 253–4): 'The danger he foresaw of giving in to the party's opinion poll pundits—such as Gould—by closing down this tax option was that over time he would be forced to abandon his ability as a future Chancellor to raise any taxes, simply for fear of upsetting potential voters. He would be a neutered Chancellor.'

In the event, Brown was persuaded to announce in January 1997, only a few months before the last possible election date, that a Labour government would not increase the top rate of income tax for the next parliament. This was coupled with a promise not to raise the basic rate or broaden the scope of VAT.

This approach worked electorally. As Anthony King (1998, pp. 194–5) showed, nearly a half of 'lost' Tories, those who previously supported the party, said a reason for no longer supporting the party was because it promised to keep taxes down but had instead increased them. Similarly, Butler and Kavanagh (1997, p. 130) noted the view of Tory polling advisers that tax no longer worked as an issue to help them and to damage Labour because of Blair's successful campaign of reassurance.

Some of Labour's worries may have been exaggerated since, as King quoted (1998, p. 200), a big majority of voters polled by Gallup (72%) believed that government services such as health, education, and welfare should be extended, even if it meant some increases in taxes. This was up from 66% in 1992, and 61% in 1987. But the 1997 level was more than double the 34% of 1979, when 34% believed that taxes should be cut, even if it meant some reduction in government services such as health, education, and welfare. That figure had fallen to just 7% by 1997. These figures both explain the Thatcher opportunity in 1979 and underline the New Labour dilemma in 1997. Blair and his advisers were so scarred by the party's four election defeats that they may have been unnecessarily cautious in 1997. They were, however, sceptical about findings such as these and those in the BSA surveys, believing that voters were, in reality, much more worried about higher taxes.

In office, Gordon Brown addressed this dilemma by eventually both raising the growth of public spending, especially after 2000, and by increasing taxes. Throughout, Mr Brown honoured, and extended at both the 2001 and 2005 general elections, his 1997 pledge on not raising the higher rate of income tax or the basic rate (which was cut). Yet the tax burden rose steadily over the period, by more than three percentage points overall. This was partly as a result of what the Conservatives described, in their only effective slogan of the period, as 'stealth taxes'. These ranged from the high profile one-off windfall levy on privatized utilities and the lasting, and more damaging, changes to the tax treatment of dividends received by pension funds to various new charges on insurance premiums and airline flights. (For more details of these and other tax changes see both Peston (2005) and Robinson (2000).) But, for most of the time, Brown was reluctant to be seen as a tax raiser. He was, however, a substantial tax innovator, notably via the creation, and later extension, of tax credits, meant to reduce poverty among households with young children, and pensioners.

The big exception was the decision announced in the spring Budget in 2002, though taking effect a year later, to raise the National Insurance contributions paid by both employers and employees. This amounted to a substantial rise in taxes and, for employees, had the same effect as an increase in the basic rate of income tax. Blair and Brown were evasive on this issue during the 2001 election. But Brown announced the increase specifically to pay for an increase in the NHS Budget which he claimed was justified by a report by Sir Derek Wanless, a former chief executive of NatWest, which pointed to a large funding gap and ruled out alternative methods of funding health. It was only this specific link to the NHS that enabled Brown to announce the increase in tax. As Robert Peston (2005, p. 274) noted, the move would

> challenge one of the great givens of British politics since the advent of Margaret Thatcher in 1979, that direct taxes could not be increased in an explicit way without wreaking huge damage to the governing party (although they could be raised in inconspicuous 'stealthy' ways, by abolishing allowances or failing to raise thresholds). It was the first proper test of whether voters now had confidence in a British Government to spend their money wisely and Labour's sustained lead in opinion polls suggests they did (and do) have that confidence.

The key issue is not about taxation as such but about whether the public believes that the money is being well spent. That was the initial, favourable public response to the 2002 announcement and the 2003 tax increase. Tax was a neutral issue for Labour at the 2005 general election, partly also because voters did not believe Tory tax promises. However, voters became increasingly sceptical about whether the rise in taxes was being well spent. So, as repeated polls showed after 2005, there were increasing doubts about the effectiveness of the increased public spending, and complaints about waste and so on, and these affected attitudes to taxation as more people felt that taxes were too high. The crucial relationship was from attitudes to spending to views on taxation. One consequence was that the Tories recovered a lead, for the first time since 1992, as the best party on taxation.

In marked contrast to the situation in the Thatcher years, international influences had a much greater, and growing, impact on tax decisions by Brown. Howe and Lawson had often referred to international comparisons of tax rates, largely to justify cuts in the top rate down to European levels. But there were not specific international pressures, as there have been since 1997. First, these have appeared in EU pressures to harmonize tax policies as part of the single market. Brown has strongly resisted extensions of EU competence over taxation, whether corporate or over savings (the latter involving a long battle over withholding taxes). Second, Brown believed that taxation was an important part of competitiveness in a globalized world of mobility not only of capital but also of skilled workers, entrepreneurs, and investors. This applied particularly to Britain in view of the growing success, and importance to the Treasury and the economy, of financial services and the City. Hence, Brown became sensitive to arguments that measures might encourage bankers to leave Britain and invest elsewhere. These international pressures affected both higher rates of taxation and measures particularly affecting the City and foreign workers and investors. This was seen during the winter of 2007–08 in the arguments over the taxation of non-domiciled individuals, foreigners who worked in Britain but who could avoid tax on their foreign income and gains despite being resident in the UK (in some cases for many years).

3. THE TREASURY

Throughout the Brown decade, the key decisions were made in the Treasury, and generally only amongst a small circle of advisers and officials around Mr Brown himself. For much of the time there was little communication with 10 Downing Street, let alone the rest of the Cabinet, or with parliament, despite some moves towards greater openness noted below. At times, Blair acted as a voice of business arguing against measures that might deter investors and in so doing reinforced Brown's instinctive resistance to raising taxes.

These episodes underline not only the importance of the executive/Treasury, as argued in the Alt, Preston, and Sibieta chapter (though with qualifications noted below), but also the significance of the tax–public spending interaction. It has not just been the public's views of taxation, but more important has been the view of how money is being spent. This chapter's description of a dominant Treasury has largely been correct. What a Chancellor of the Exchequer wants, he can usually get. But a number of important qualifications need to be made. First, it should not always, or automatically, be assumed that the Treasury and the executive are the same. It is impossible to discuss this subject without, as noted above, considering the role of particular Prime Ministers and Chancellors. As I have argued, these relationships substantially affect the making of tax policy: for instance, the retention of mortgage tax relief throughout the Thatcher years; and her insistence, against the wishes of the Treasury, in pressing ahead with the replacement of rates by the poll tax. In the New Labour decade, Gordon Brown had virtual, but never entire, control over tax policy.

Moreover, it is misleading to brush aside the role of Parliament. The sentence on page 1210, 'this power of patronage is a major reason why these large legislative majorities also tend to be cohesive, with government bills almost always being passed by a subservient House of Commons', is an over-simplification. The role of Parliament on tax policy is unquestionably secondary, but it is not entirely insignificant. Parliamentary majorities are more cohesive than in a federal system, notably the USA with its formal separation of powers between the executive and the legislature. But this is as much because of party and ideological loyalties as because of the power of patronage. The collective self-discipline of party, and agreement with the thrust of most measures proposed by the government, is why the MPs of the ruling party vote for budgets and finance bills. However, as Professor Philip Cowley has shown, the image of a 'subservient' Commons is now out of date as both the frequency and scale of revolts by government backbenchers has increased sharply over the past decade, though admittedly less on tax than on other measures (see <http://www.revolts.co.uk>). Moreover, internal pressures within the ruling party can lead to changes, as happened in spring 2008 when protests by Labour MPs against the failure to compensate fully for the abolition of the 10p tax band forced £2.7 billion of tax relief.

Moreover, the assertion, on page 1211 of the chapter, that 'Parliament thus finds it difficult to provide effective scrutiny of tax measures, and measures are nearly always enacted unchanged in the annual Finance Bill that follows the Budget' is inaccurate. The proposals announced in a Budget in March are often amended by the time the subsequent Finance Bill becomes law the following July, and even on occasion between publication of the bill and its enactment. This is, admittedly, very seldom because of pressure from MPs or the Opposition as such, and is mainly because of broader political pressures or representations by specific interest groups to the Treasury or HM Revenue and Customs. In most cases, the result is detailed amendments, rather than major changes, or the abandonment of a measure. The committee and report stages of the annual Finance Bill are the occasion for such amendments, seldom the cause of them.

The main omissions in the institutional discussion are about the role of the Pre-Budget Report, the subsequent inquiries by the Treasury Select Committee of the Commons; the post-Budget investigations by the House of Lords Committee on Economic Affairs; and the many inquiries by the Treasury

Committee and the Public Accounts Committee of the Commons into the administration of the tax system, and particularly the serious difficulties with tax credits.

The Pre-Budget Report in the autumn, initially often dubbed the green budget, has been intended not just as a half-yearly review of the state of the economy and an updating of economic forecasts, but also as an opportunity to consult on proposed changes to the tax system. Consultatative papers would be produced, and at times draft clauses, ahead of the annual spring Budget. For instance, the Commons Treasury Committee, in its report of January 2007 (House of Commons paper 115, session 2006–07), discussed not only the broad outlook for the economy and for public finances, but also delays to improvements in the tax credits regimes, climate change and environmental taxation, missing trader intra-community fraud, and taxation of alternatively secured pensions, amongst other taxation issues. The committee noted, however, that 'it is important that the Pre-Budget Report retains a focus on consultation on fiscal measures that may be included in the forthcoming Budget. Although the 2006 Report is accompanied by a considerable volume of material on technical tax changes, there is less discussion on more substantive tax measures under consideration in the Budget.' The Treasury Committee's report on the 2007 Pre-Budget Report in late November 2007 (House of Commons paper 54, session 2007–08) contained lengthy discussion of the many taxation proposals which had been announced, notably the proposed major reforms to capital tax, the changes to inheritance tax thresholds, and the new rules for non-domiciled taxpayers. There was lively, and lengthy, debate in the Commons on each of these major tax changes, even though the objections and concerns of outside business and industrial bodies carried more weight in Whitehall, as noted above.

The role of the Lords Committee on Economic Affairs has been controversial. The Treasury has resisted the incursion by the Lords into issues traditionally the prerogative of the Commons, especially when a sub-committee was set up in 2003 to cover technical issues of tax administration, clarification, and simplification, but specifically not rates or incidence of taxation. This was intended to avoid encroaching on the financial privileges of the Commons. The Lords contains a number of experts in these areas and its reports are timed to appear before the report stage of the Finance Bill in the Commons, allowing amendments to be tabled. This has, however, proved to be a hurried and unsatisfactory process. The Treasury has at times resisted questioning by the committee on the grounds that ministers are accountable to the House of Commons where the substantive provisions are debated. (The Lords holds a formal debate on the Finance Bill but cannot amend it.)

Parliament is more effective in examining the implementation of policies. There have been several inquiries by the Public Accounts and Treasury committees of the Commons into the working, and many administrative failures, involved in the tax credit system, notably the repeated over-payments and therefore cost overruns.

However, the overall inadequacies of current parliamentary procedures for scrutinizing financial proposals, both on the expenditure and taxation side, were authoritatively examined in a report by the Hansard Society (Brazier and Ram (2006)). This report followed lengthy consultations both within Parliament and with practitioners. Amongst its main conclusions on the taxation side were that

- in the period between the Pre-Budget and the main Budget, parliamentary committees should take expert and public evidence on the government's plans, make a case for the priorities it wishes government to consider, and ensure the government provides full information and explanation for its proposals;
- the entire Finance Bill should be subject to pre-legislative scrutiny by a parliamentary committee;
- alternative options for reform include: the establishment of separate Tax Administrative or Taxation Committees in the House of Commons or a Joint Committee on Tax Administration. In addition, a Tax Law Commission could be established to overview the effectiveness of tax legislation and make proposals for change.

Many of these proposals have been echoed by George Osborne, the Shadow Chancellor, who has urged the publication of more information on technical tax changes at the time of the Pre-Budget report in the autumn, as well as allowing time for greater scrutiny by a new parliamentary committee which would hear evidence from tax specialists. This is among the ideas being examined in detail by a group headed by Geoffrey Howe, in turn echoing a speech along similar lines he made as Shadow Chancellor in the late 1970s.

4. CONCLUSIONS

Nonetheless, the Alt, Preston, and Sibieta chapter is substantially correct about the institutional balance in tax policymaking; and about the disconnected nature of the tax debate. The focus on headline rates of income tax has both obscured rational discussion of tax options and distracted attention from other tax changes, and the steady rise in the tax burden since the early 1990s. My qualification is over the chapter's discussion of a 'passive' movement to the right which is based too much on thin survey evidence and does not take sufficient, or even much, account of what has actually happened. This chapter's solutions are a mixture of the sensible on parliamentary scrutiny (reflecting those already made by a wide range of bodies inside and outside Parliament itself) to the slightly naive, about establishing 'a body to oversee the public finances' directly accountable both to Parliament and the executive. The authors do not consider whether there is a conflict of accountabilities here. There is certainly a case for greater transparency, auditing, and accountability, but tax decisions cannot be taken out of politics. They are the stuff of the party battle.

REFERENCES

Brazier, A., and Ram, V. (2006), *The Fiscal Maze—Parliament, Government and Public Money*, London: Hansard Society.

Butler, D., and Kavanagh, D. (1997), *The British General Election of 1997*, London: Macmillan.

Gould, P. (1998), *The Unfinished Revolution—How the Modernisers Saved the Labour Party*, London: Little, Brown and Company.

Howe, G. (1994), *Conflict of Loyalty*, London: Macmillan.

King, A. (1998), *New Labour Triumphs, Britain at the Polls*, New Jersey: Chatham House Publishers.

Lawson, N. (1992), *The View From Number 11—Memoirs of a Tory Radical*, London: Bantam Press.

Penniman, H. R. (ed.) (1981), *Britain at the Polls, 1979*, Washington DC: American Enterprise Institute.

Peston, R. (2005), *Brown's Britain*, London: Short Books.

Robinson, G. (2000), *The Unconventional Minister*, London: Michael Joseph.

Thatcher, M. (1993), *The Downing Street Years*, London: HarperCollins.

Commentary by Guido Tabellini

Guido Tabellini is Professor of Economics and Rector of Bocconi University. He obtained his degree in economics at Università di Torino and his PhD in economics at the University of California, Los Angeles. Before returning to Europe, he taught at Stanford and UCLA. His research interests include political economics and public choice, macroeconomics and international economics. Much of his recent research is summarized in two books co-authored with Torsten Persson: *Political Economics: Explaining Economic Policy*, and *The Economic Effects of Constitutions*.

1. INTRODUCTION

The political economy of tax policy is a huge topic, and the Alt, Preston, and Sibieta chapter does an excellent job of discussing some of the most relevant issues. It succeeds in linking real-world policymaking in the UK to the recent background literature in political economics. And it produces several novel insights that enhance our understanding of how tax policy is made in the UK.

This chapter contains a very rich and complete discussion of several issues, but essentially it develops three main themes. First, UK tax policy is very centralized, and it emanates from one key institution: the Treasury. Second, the political, economic, or ideological convictions of individuals in this key policymaking institution are the main drivers of UK tax policy; political opportunism, organized interests, or voters' demands seem to play a less important role. Third, voters don't understand the tax system well; from a positive point of view, this enables politicians to take advantage of this ignorance to pursue their political goals; from a normative point of view, voters' ignorance is undesirable and calls for much greater transparency in tax policy.

Here I briefly comment on each of these three themes, and conclude by raising an important general question that this chapter leaves unaddressed.

2. THE INSTITUTIONAL FRAMEWORK

The claim that UK tax policy emanates from the Treasury's office and reflects the will and opinion of key bureaucrats and policymakers in that institution is very convincing. The UK tax system is very centralized, the executive is controlled by a single party with absolute majority in Parliament, and the Chancellor has strong agenda setting prerogatives with regard to both the Cabinet and Parliament. Hence, the authors are right in insisting that, to understand the determinants of UK tax policy, we must start from the organization of the Treasury's office.

To someone trained in monetary economics like myself, this raises a natural question. Why is there such a big difference in the institutional framework of tax policy versus monetary policy? And is this difference desirable? In monetary policy, decisions are delegated to an independent and accountable agency, with very transparent decision-making procedures. Similar delegation has taken place with many regulatory policies. When it comes to taxation, instead, decisions are directly controlled by a political office, even to the smallest detail. Naturally, bureaucrats also operate inside the Treasury. But unlike in monetary policy, they do not enjoy independent decision-making power. Their influence on policy decisions has to be conquered through persuasion or by exploiting the inattention of their political principal. And outside observers have very little knowledge of how decisions are taken inside the Treasury and for what true reasons.

Of course, this is not a peculiarity of the UK. But we cannot simply dismiss this question with the answer that tax policy is 'too political' to be delegated to independent bureaucracies, or that representative democracy has developed precisely on the principle that there cannot be taxation without political representation. One can imagine alternative arrangements whereby political representatives choose general features of the tax code, but then delegate the execution to independent and accountable bureaucrats according to efficiency or other pre-established criteria, just as in regulation or other policy areas.

Personally, I doubt that there is a valid normative reason for current arrangements. There are several reasons of political expediency why office holders do not want to delegate control over any aspect of tax policy. But from a normative perspective, retaining full political control is likely to result in socially suboptimal outcomes under a robust set of assumptions.[1]

[1] Blinder (1997) advocated bureaucratic delegation over aspects of fiscal policy, and Alesina and Tabellini (2007, 2008) discuss political vs bureaucratic delegation in a more abstract setting.

The observation that voters don't have a full understanding of the tax system reinforces this conclusion, because it increases the need for a more transparent decision-making procedure. Sections 13.6 and 13.7 of the chapter, on institutional checks and balances over tax policy, briefly discuss the role of non-political or external institutions to audit revenue figures, or to offer advice. But their logic is one of oversight, rather than delegation of specific responsibilities.

Even retaining the focus on oversight, as opposed to delegation, the authors seem reluctant to advocate a greater role for an independent bureaucracy. They instead lean towards asking for greater accountability towards Parliament. I am sceptical that this would be effective, for two reasons. First, because in a Parliamentary democracy (unlike in a Presidential regime) there is no real separation of power between executive and legislative authority. The opposition of course would have the right incentives to question government choices in Parliament. But, and this takes me to the second reason, tax policy unavoidably hinges on many technical details that are bound to escape the attention of public opinion, and often also of elected representatives. Such details are better discussed by trained professionals, which calls for relying on independent and well-trained bureaucrats rather than political opponents in Parliament.

3. PASSIVE VOTERS AND IDEOLOGICAL POLITICIANS

Is tax policy mainly driven by the policymakers' convictions or by the wishes of the voters? This chapter leans towards the first answer. It presents two empirical arguments in support of this conclusion, one from voters' opinions and party manifestos, the other from a case study of how the R&D tax credit was enacted.

While I find the R&D case study interesting and persuasive, the interpretation of voters' opinions and party manifestos is very ambiguous and open ended. According to the opinion polls surveyed in this chapter, British voters are concerned about rising income inequality, but since the mid-1980s they are less supportive of redistributive policies and have less trust in government. A majority would also be prepared to pay more taxes if this extra tax revenue were used to increase public good provision.

What to make of this evidence, and how to relate it to actual tax policy, is not clear. If anything, these attitudes reveal that most voters would like a different mix of public spending (more public good provision and less redistributive transfers). But this is not surprising, since it is well understood that political competition induces politicians to under-provide public goods in favour of targeted redistribution to influential groups. Whether the observed reduction in statutory tax rates (but not in tax revenue, as the authors correctly remark) was a reaction to electoral concerns, or whether instead it was induced by the ideological agenda of partisan politicians, is hard to say on the basis of this evidence.

4. TRANSPARENCY OF FISCAL POLICY

We often take it for granted that more policy transparency is always good in a democracy. Implicitly this chapter seems to share this presumption. An interesting recent paper by Gavazza and Lizzeri (2006) clarifies that this simplistic view is incorrect.

The important distinction is between transparency of individual versus aggregate tax payments. Full transparency of individual tax payments means that the individual voter fully understands how much in taxes he is paying to the government. Full aggregate transparency means that he knows aggregate tax revenue (i.e. how much other tax payers are contributing).

Individual transparency, as defined above, generally improves government incentives. Intuitively, if voters fully understand how much they are paying to the government, they are more likely to demand something in return. Hence, individual transparency discourages corruption and wasteful redistribution, because it raises the political cost of government spending.

But aggregate transparency can be counterproductive, unless it is accompanied by a full understanding of how the government uses tax revenue. Suppose that voters are not sure about the true size of the budget deficit or surplus. In this case, as shown by Gavazza and Lizzeri (2006), transparency of aggregate tax revenues encourages 'fiscal churning'. The reason is that voters mistakenly interpret higher aggregate tax revenues as a higher budget surplus (rather than as more targeted redistribution to others). Thus, they reward the government if aggregate tax revenue is higher, which encourages politicians to have more distorting taxation than would be necessary to sustain the same amount of net redistribution (i.e. they encourage fiscal churning).

In general, wasteful redistribution is discouraged if voters observe the taxes that they individually pay, and the targeted benefits that others receive. On the contrary, wasteful redistribution is encouraged if voters observe the targeted benefits that they individually receive, and the taxes that others pay. Unfortunately, opportunistic politicians have strong incentives to provide the wrong kind of transparency. To maximize consensus, they want to increase the visibility of the individual gifts they provide, and to hide the individual costs; to appear virtuous, they also want to show that they collect large amounts of aggregate tax revenues and do not spend a lot. Hence, we should always expect to have the wrong kind of fiscal transparency. This is important, because it has implications for what the systematic distortions are that need to be corrected.[2]

5. WHAT SYSTEMATIC DEVIATIONS FROM OPTIMAL TAXATION?

The theory of optimal taxation has strong implications for how the tax structure ought to be designed, and how tax rates on different tax bases ought to react to shocks to government spending. Are there systematic deviations from these optimal prescriptions, and if so can they be explained by systematic political distortions? Perhaps this is the most important question in the political economics of tax policy.

Despite many contributions on politics and fiscal policy, this question has generally remained unaddressed in the literature. There is just one important exception: the time inconsistency problem. As is well known, lack of commitment imparts a systematic bias to tax policy. Whenever the elasticity of a tax base differs in the long-run from in the short run, a benevolent government that cannot commit neglects the long run elasticity. This implies over taxation of the tax bases that are more elastic in the long run, like any capital stock. Unfortunately, despite its many interesting insights, this chapter does not fill this gap in the literature, nor does it discuss the practical relevance of the time inconsistency problem with regard to the UK tax structure.

[2] There is evidence that voters often ignore how much they individually pay to support redistributive programmes. For instance, Boeri and Tabellini (2007) show that individual employees in countries in Continental Europe generally ignore by large margins the contribution rate that they or their employer pays into the social security system.

REFERENCES

Alesina, A., and Tabellini, G. (2007), 'Bureaucrats or Politicians? Part I: A Single Policy Task', *American Economic Review*, **97**, 169–79.

—— —— (2008), 'Bureaucrats or Politicians? Part II: Multiple Policy Tasks', *Journal of Public Economics*, **92**, 426–47.

Blinder, A. S. (1997), 'Is Government Too Political?' *Foreign Affairs*, **76**, 115–26.

Boeri, T., and Tabellini, G. (2007), 'Does Information Increase Support for Pensions Reform?' IGIER, mimeo.

Gavazza, A., and Lizzeri, A. (2006), 'Transparency of Economic Policy', mimeo, NYU.

Commentary by Chris Wales

Chris Wales is Managing Director of Lucida plc, an insurance company that specializes in longevity risk. Before setting up Lucida, he was a Managing Director at Goldman Sachs. In 2003–04, he was a Visiting Fellow at the Centre for Tax Law at Cambridge University. From 1997 to 2003, Chris was a member of the UK Council of Economic Advisers at HM Treasury and principal adviser on tax policy to the Chancellor of the Exchequer. Before 1997, he was a tax partner at Arthur Andersen. He is a member of the IFS Council and of the Advisory Board of the Oxford University Centre for Business Taxation. Chris has a PhD from Cambridge University in twelfth-century English history.

In this chapter, Professors Alt and Preston and Luke Sibieta make an important contribution to our understanding of the dynamics of the political economy of tax policy in the UK. They present a broad-based analysis of the subject, ranging across the institutional structure of policy-making, the influence of purely party political thinking on policy formation and the significance of the framework of scrutiny and accountability for legislative proposals. They provide an interesting and multi-perspective example of the tax policy-making process under Chancellor Brown that shows the interaction between economic theory, political intent, lobbying and consultation, and sheds some light on how relationships between the Chancellor's departments are perceived. The significance of the practical influence of the consultation process in shaping policy is well-illustrated.

In the comments that follow, I build on the analysis that the authors have presented with some thoughts of my own, drawing on my experience at HM Treasury as a member of Chancellor Brown's *Council of Economic Advisers* between 1997 and 2003, and as the individual with the most direct responsibility for tax policy in that period.

I argue that the democratic deficit in relation to tax policy-making, to which the authors allude, arises because:

- The public are ill-informed about the tax system and the education system does nothing to address that.
- Governments do not adequately present policy choices to the electorate and Opposition parties shy away from firm policy commitments in the run-up to general elections.
- There is an unnecessary imbalance of information relevant to tax policy choices between government and the rest of the population.
- The mechanisms through which the public can engage on tax policy issues are too limited and ill-defined.
- Standards of journalism on taxation issues are too low, partly because of the information deficit.

I set out an analysis of policy development that explains how the situation is exacerbated by the narrow base for tax policy-making in the UK and institutional weaknesses.

Finally, I comment on three other factors that affect tax policy-making in the UK: the nature of the electoral system; attitudes to radical change, which I illustrate briefly by reference to the balance between national and local taxation; and the absence of effective scrutiny and accountability for tax policy choices.

1. THE DEMOCRATIC DEFICIT

One of the key points that emerges from this chapter is the extent of the democratic deficit in relation to tax policy-making. How do policy-makers, including ministers, know what the people want and how do they present choice to a largely uninformed public? How do the people decide what they want? And if and when they do, what are the mechanisms through which they can communicate their views?

It would be difficult to identify any element in the education system in the UK that adequately prepares the general population to participate in a meaningful way in a debate about tax policy choices. Beyond a narrow group of specialists who are mostly practitioners working with existing legislation, there are frighteningly few individuals who have any real understanding of how the tax system works and of the likely consequences of making changes to it. The sums of money that are raised by taxation are unimaginably large for the average voter; and the relationship between tax and public spending is poorly understood. How many hospitals does inheritance tax fund? How many new teaching posts would a 1p increase in capital gains tax allow? How many voters can visualize a tax to GDP ratio of 40% and what it means to private sector wealth creation, the size of government, or the quality of public services? How many understand the impact of a change in that ratio to 35% or 45%; and how many can judge the impact of raising a given level of taxation through one set of instruments rather than another? Tax policy-making is a very specialist game.

To say this is not to criticize the general population but rather to highlight the difficulty of trying to engage, even at a headline level, on complex issues on which the vast majority are simply not informed. The problem exists in other policy areas as well but generally to a lesser extent. Most of us, for example, are not experts in education but we will have experienced the UK education system first hand and many of us will have seen it in relation to our own children as well. We are more likely to have experience-based views that we can articulate on the quality of teaching, the state of our schools and the relevance and rigour of the examination system, than on the efficacy of taxes on expenditure rather than income. We can more easily envisage the impact on education of proposals to introduce a system of specialist schools, than the effect on investment of reforming the taxation of North Sea oil production. Election manifestos map out the differences between the education policies of the parties and we can make reasonably informed choices. It is rare in the UK to have a broadly based debate about taxation policy, even at the time of a general election. In recent elections, there has been a reluctance to set out any detailed proposals and have them tested by the electorate.

So how *do* tax policy-makers know what the public want? And how do we break the circle of ignorance that makes sensible debate about tax policy all but impossible?

The first issue is information. One of the key issues is for government to be more open and a critical step in achieving that is to institute a policy of publishing more data in a quality and form that is usable by economists outside government. Data has historically been closely guarded by government and the very limited availability of data, even in an anonymized or aggregated form, makes it exceptionally difficult for those outside central government, including opposition parties, academic economists, and think-tanks to develop tax policy proposals with any degree of confidence. A publication programme for tax system data would make a major contribution to the development of ideas and it could, potentially, provide a mechanism through which to transform public debate.

The second issue is to publish policy choices well in advance of final decisions by the Executive. This is now done in some areas, particularly business taxation, where there is extensive consultation, at least with the largest companies, but the process needs to become much more widespread. Steps taken in the last ten years to require the publication of the rationale for significant policy proposals, the alternatives considered and the costs of compliance have made a contribution but they are published in any detail only very late in the decision-making process. The Freedom of Information Act provides only limited assistance. The publication of detailed analysis in support of tax policy changes proposed by government would do much to improve the trust and confidence of the electorate in government and the quality of public debate around policy options. This is a process that will become much easier the more often it is used.

The third issue is that there has to be a clearer mechanism through which the electorate can express its views on tax policy issues. The media have a role to play here. Standards of journalism around taxation policy are relatively low, a problem exacerbated by the limited access to relevant hard information. Wider publication of data should support higher standards among the most influential news media.

At present, when debate arises on tax policy issues, it is normally very narrowly focused. It is easy enough to get a reaction to a specific proposal put forward in isolation. But the discussion and the follow-up have to be handled with greater maturity and less political opportunism. We have learned in autumn 2007, for example:

- that inheritance tax is very unpopular even among those who are likely to be well beyond its reach—an echo of experience in the US;
- that the British public is happy to see a random amount of tax charged on a group of people with little in common save that they are perceived (whether rightly or wrongly) to be well off and more importantly to be demonstrably of foreign origin;
- that targeting simplification above policy purpose may sub-optimize outcomes and run into significant opposition as the recent round of capital gains tax proposals has demonstrated.

We have learned that environmental taxation is regarded by many as a good thing but we also know from the fuel tax disputes in 2000 that there are limits to public tolerance of heavier taxation, even when the underlying justification is powerful.

The challenge is to get a debate going about broader choices and to allow it time to mature. That is inextricably linked to the first two issues: the availability of quality data to support analysis by institutions (including the press) external to government and a willingness to put broad ideas out into the public for discussion. The result will be that ministers and other policy-makers will be much better equipped to make policy choices that reflect what the electorate really want.

2. SOURCES OF TAX POLICY

Today, the problem with achieving democratic inputs to the development of tax policy is a real one. Ministers are not tax policy experts. They are professional parliamentarians. Even Treasury ministers are unlikely to have wide experience of tax policy-making before taking office. Most that do will have gained it on the Opposition Front Bench where the skills required are somewhat different from those needed in office. Focus groups can be useful at the two ends of the spectrum: the very broad and the very narrow; but they are better for testing out ideas than for inspiring them. Policy-makers have little to go on in terms of broad attitudes towards taxation. Most media research is shallow and of limited value. The British Social Attitudes survey, cited by the authors, is interesting but of limited utility in forming anything other than high level policy thoughts. So where do ministers' ideas for tax policy come from? Essentially, there are three main sources.

The first is their own fundamental political beliefs. The second is the internal institutions of government. The third is external institutions.

Fundamental political beliefs provide a natural frame of reference within which tax policy options can be considered: the optimal balance between state and private provision with its implications for the need to raise revenues; the importance and direction of redistribution of wealth; and the desirability of using taxation instruments to achieve behavioural change. The political overlay to tax policy-making is essential. Policy cannot be made on economic principles alone. However, the political overlay is ultimately no more than that. It does not of its own generate tax policy proposals. The principal utility of political beliefs is in decision-making rather than policy generation.

Of much more direct significance to the development of policy options are the internal institutions of government. In the UK, ministers today rely substantially on HM Treasury and HMRC officials to generate policy proposals. Before the O'Donnell Review in 2003–04, the Treasury was more of a clearing house for tax policy than a policy initiator. Tax Policy, as a department, was a small sub-set of Budget and Public Finance that ensured that proposals from Inland Revenue and HM Customs & Excise were properly presented and considered by ministers and that worked with the relevant departmental officials on costing individual measures. Relatively little work was done by that group in bringing forward policy, although there were some notable exceptions, such as the development of the Climate Change Levy. It was mostly staffed by quite junior economists who had limited previous experience of working on taxation issues. An advantage of this approach was that policy proposals were largely put together in departments that had direct experience of dealing with taxpayers and taxpayer situations and that had a high level of expertise on both the policy purpose and legislative form of individual taxes. Weaknesses were that policy-making in the revenue departments was too narrowly focused on individual taxes, often with little thought given to the system as a whole and the overall economic purpose; and, at times, it was over-concerned with avoidance. As things stood in the late 1990s and early years of this century, the Treasury lacked senior economists with the experience, knowledge, and vision to provide the policy direction to harness effectively the skills and detailed understanding of Inland Revenue and HM Customs & Excise.

The implementation of the O'Donnell Review made substantial changes to the order of things. It was clearly desirable to strengthen the policy-making capability of the Treasury but the changes left a number of significant weaknesses:

1. The new structure put the Treasury firmly in control of all aspects of tax policy-making. The balance of views between the largely theory-based Treasury approach and the more experience-based approach of the revenue departments that was often evident in the pre-O'Donnell period effectively disappeared in 2004. The authors refer to 'the sheer dominance of the Treasury over the entire process'. It is difficult to find a democratic country where tax policy-making power is so concentrated.
2. The new structure did not involve the creation of any new senior posts for experienced economists to take responsibility for the structure of the tax system as a whole. The Treasury does not have a heavyweight economist with such a role. The reorganization removed some of the narrowness of focus that had previously resulted in policy being developed on a tax-by-tax basis but missed the opportunity to create one or more expert posts to co-ordinate between the directorates dealing, for example, with business and indirect tax, international tax, personal tax, and welfare reform. As a result, there is a continuing failure to develop policy on a fully joined-up basis. Despite the importance of

the overall design of the system, the structure of the tax policy-making departments clearly demonstrates that the lowest priority is given to system-wide coherence.

3. The strengthening of the tax policy capability of HM Treasury was achieved largely at the expense of the other revenue departments. The merger of Inland Revenue and HM Customs & Excise may have been a wise strategy (although the full benefits of the merger have yet to be realized) but denuding them of senior policy roles was not. The transfer of the policy-making function to the Treasury disconnected it from the underlying relationships with taxpayers and taxpayer issues and seems likely, in the longer term, to lead to a weakening in the policy-making process. The expertise necessary for the proper functioning of the Treasury as a policy-making unit was initially largely sourced from the revenue departments. It is not obvious where that will come from in the future, since HMRC has only a limited policy-making role and seems unlikely to generate a supply of experienced policy-makers in the future. Those with a policy inclination are more likely to join the Treasury at the start of their careers and will thus miss out on the experience in the field that was a strength of the previous system.
4. The O'Donnell changes also missed an opportunity to give a stronger role to the development of economics-led policy. The two revenue departments employed a substantial number of economists and statisticians. It would have been possible to bring these together, as part of the O'Donnell changes, into a new free-standing department, reporting to Treasury ministers—an *Office of Tax Analysis (OTA)*. An OTA would carry out research on tax policy options based on the full statistical information available to government and could, potentially, be an important engine room for the development of tax policy initiatives. It could give new prominence to economics-based policy development which is currently weak in the UK. It could have responsibility for the collection of tax statistics and act as the analysis and research team for HMRC and HM Treasury in relation to their tax proposals. It could also take responsibility for the publication of tax statistics and data for use by external organizations (including Parliament).

Given the extent to which Treasury ministers currently rely on the generation of policy proposals by HM Treasury and HMRC officials, these are issues that need to be addressed.

The difficulties with the internal institutions are compounded by the relative weakness of external institutions with a focus on taxation policy. The quality of policy initiatives is often closely related to the strength of external institutions and, in the taxation area, these have historically been quite weak. There are few institutions that have a forward-looking policy focus. The IFS is normally a commentator on government policy rather than a generator of policy proposals itself, the Mirrlees Review itself being a major exception. There are many organizations that focus on the detail of new legislation and its impact but most of these look at the economics and policy purpose only to a limited extent and rarely put forward specific proposals of their own. A number of business organizations, including, for example, the CBI and the ABI, LIBA, and the BBA, engage with the policy process but mostly from a relatively narrow standpoint and again, more as commentators and analysts of government proposals than as generators of policy ideas themselves.

There is evidence that some think-tanks have a more direct influence on ministerial thinking: for example, the Fabian Society, IPPR, and the Smith Institute under the present government. Both the Fabians and IPPR have engaged on the debate about the use of taxation instruments in relation to environmental policy, with some apparent success, but the Fabian attempt to initiate a debate around inheritance tax policy was notably less successful.

There are relatively few academic centres in the UK that engage directly on UK tax policy issues. This deficiency was partly addressed in the establishment of the Oxford University Centre for Business Taxation, funded by the Hundred Group of leading UK quoted companies. The Centre operates entirely independent of its funders, has a broad remit to address tax policy issues that affect business in the UK, and to publish its research findings. One of the main objectives in setting up the Centre was to provide a source of new research-based ideas that would provide Treasury ministers and officials with an alternative perspective and a wider range of policy options.

There remain, however, a relatively small number of institutions outside government that support the tax policy-making process and few of these have the kind of public profile that can generate a broadly based policy debate in which the public will engage.

In the short to medium term, it is very much in the hands of government to create an opportunity for the electorate to debate tax policy. By making data more readily available, by setting out the direction of taxation policy for a whole parliament, by publishing policy options in advance of the Executive making decisions, the government could extend significantly the opportunity for public discussion. At present, there is almost no transmission mechanism for public views on taxation. A systematic process of publication and the creation of opportunities for debate through the early publication of policy options could change that.

3. OTHER FACTORS AFFECTING THE DEVELOPMENT OF TAX POLICY IN THE UK

In this section, I comment on three other factors that affect the development of tax policy in the UK.

3.1. The electoral system

The authors comment on the significance of the electoral system in shaping tax policy. In the UK, unlike in most European countries, governments are normally strong and not dependent on the formation of policy-aligned coalitions. Political differences on the left and the right in the UK tend to be subsumed within what is essentially a two-party system. Fragmentation of parties is discouraged by an electoral system that delivers first-past-the-post victories at a constituency level and the potential of a large and absolute majority in Parliament to a party that may have taken as little as 40% of the votes cast. Fringe parties remain just that. Those that achieve even a handful of seats in Parliament have little or no influence. It is usually better to fight for specific policies within a major party than to form a new one. This is as true of taxation as it is of other policies.

In such a system, it might be logical to expect a greater degree of extremism and volatility in tax policy. Parties would seek to reward their own supporters rather than develop policies that appeal primarily to the median voter. As the authors note, this was evident in the period from 1979 through to the mid-1990s when the UK all but abandoned the progressive taxation of income for the better off; but has been much less of a feature of more recent government. The median voter is rarely the swing voter in UK elections but tax policy has been surprisingly skewed towards that median voter in the recent past.

Under the present Labour government, although there has been a redistribution of income from the better off particularly to the very poorest, the focus of policy seems to have been on the redistribution of opportunity rather than of wealth.

In fact, the extremes of the income spectrum have grown further apart in the last decade, mostly through an acceleration of earnings and wealth at the upper end of the scale and in spite of significant improvements in the absolute position of the bottom decile of the population. This has given rise to surprisingly little demand for redistribution through the taxation system. There are a number of possible explanations for this: a general growth in absolute levels of prosperity which have allowed the middle classes apparently to accept that they pay proportionately too much and the rich, too little; the absence of effective mechanisms through which to give prominence to the issue; or the absence of effective political leadership for the group most significantly affected by what is largely explicable as fiscal drag. Another relatively benign explanation would be that, like the US, the UK has become a society that is fundamentally optimistic and positive towards wealth creation. People see themselves as able to improve their economic status and therefore do not want to see high earners and wealth more heavily taxed. This would fit with the attitudes displayed towards inheritance tax.

3.2. The approach to radical change

Political parties are often even less radical in power than they seem likely to be in opposition, to the disappointment of many of their supporters. I have already commented on some of the reasons for this: their own lack of specialist expertise that leads them to rely heavily on the internal institutions of government for ideas and analysis; the relative weakness of external institutions providing serious input on tax policy; the structural weaknesses in the policy-making process that stress the importance of particular taxes over a system-wide approach; and the political drift to the centre right in pursuit of the median voter. However, there are other factors that also contribute to the 'sameness' of policy approach between governments of different political persuasion:

- the absence of a clear electoral mandate for specific reform proposals (recent exceptions include the windfall tax on the excess profits of the privatized utilities introduced in 1997);
- the natural conservatism of the Chancellor's departments (HM Treasury and HMRC);
- the normative effect of international influences (the EU, tax treaties, and the OECD);
- the limitations on modelling capability, including the inadequacy of computerized records, that inhibit the simultaneous implementation of major changes in more than one area;
- the perceived wisdom that an old tax is a good tax and that a new tax is a bad tax;
- the stifling effect of complexity and detail;
- a pre-occupation with avoidance;
- the generally negative role of the media.

The Labour administration of 1997 in which I was closely involved was moderately radical in its first years, introducing substantial changes in corporate and individual taxation, including the creation of the controversial tax credits system, a rebalancing of the capital gains tax system in favour of the entrepreneur, and putting forward a doctrine of structural simplification for the corporate sector that encompassed changes in the treatment of groups, the realization of gains on the sale of subsidiaries, the taxation of intangible property, and the abolition of advance corporation tax as well as a reduction in rates.

There is an assumption in government that the electorate has no appetite for radical change in tax policy and structures but the reality is that that appetite is untested. None of the major parties has campaigned for radical change, even though there are elements in each of the main parties that would be willing to do so.

This is not simply a question of the level of taxation. There are extreme views on both the right and the left about the size of the state that would, if implemented, create a major shift in the overall scale of tax revenues. However, there is a debate which is overdue in the UK about the balance between local and national taxation and to which the authors refer. They note that 'the British tax system is exceptionally centralized by international standards: little actual discretionary power is located anywhere outside central government. In 2003, over 95% of UK tax revenues were raised by central government.'

They draw a strong link between this imbalance and the fact that 'Britain has a narrow base from which policy initiatives can be made: the only body that can put forward tax policy proposals is the Treasury'. Against this background, a truly radical shift would be to give more substantial tax-raising powers to local government.

The logic of such a move is clear.

There is an enormous democratic deficit in local government. As much as 70–80% of the electorate regularly abstain from voting in local government elections. Even though local government spending has a major impact on the delivery of public services, the electorate is disconnected. There is a wide range of reasons for this but part of the problem is the perception that local government choices are not significant enough; and part is a direct result of the way in which local government spending is financed.

The financing structure for local government is seriously flawed. Central government grants and allocations mean that on average as much as 75% of local authority spending is financed out of general taxation. This places enormous stress on local authorities that want to increase spending. The council tax has to rise by a disproportionate amount to fund small increases. Similarly, the system rewards over-generously the authorities that seek to reduce spending.

This set of problems could be solved but it would require radical change, including the surrender of some of the taxing powers of central government. Three steps to make a real difference to the democratic deficit:

- Create larger local authorities. Local government units are small and fail to attract the calibre of officials who would normally seek Whitehall positions.
- Make a serious investment in raising skill levels in local government and attracting well-qualified management and workers There is not enough emphasis on raising the level of public sector skills and this has a significant effect on the quality of local service delivery.
- Give them meaningful tax-raising powers on which the local electors could decide.

The tax changes to support this could include:

- Allocating control over setting the basic rate of income tax to the local authorities, initially within limited ranges such as are set for the Scottish Parliament. This would give them a more dynamic revenue base. It would still need to be underpinned by a balancing system of grants but the aim would be to invert the ratio of locally to nationally raised taxes so that the minimum local funding proportion became around 75%. It would dramatically change the public perception of the role and significance of local government. The system works in other countries. Sweden is a classic example, where there are significant differences in the tax rates levied by different local authorities, each approved by the local electorate. In the US, there is significant choice at the local level and real examples of local populations voting, for instance, for much higher expenditure on education funded out of locally raised revenues. From an administrative perspective, the change to a tax system for basic rate taxpayers where the rate was set locally should not have to be complex. It can be driven by tagging PAYE information with address-based codes. But for a Treasury that has grown used to complete control over taxation structures and rates, this would involve a huge conceptual leap.
- Abolishing council tax in favour of a more broadly based, nationally set tax on land and property. Land and property is arguably under-taxed in the UK and the proposed changes in the capital gains tax rules

will weaken the existing scheme of taxation still further by reducing the effective rate of tax on second and third homes. Replacing the council tax with a nationally set tax would bring to an end the rather tenuous link between the taxation of land and property from the delivery of local public services and allow the tax to be levied on a basis that was fairer across the country as a whole rather than just within communities.

Alongside these changes, it is possible to see a much stronger case for removing inheritance tax, a significant element of which is land- and property-based. If the value of land was more effectively taxed on a current basis than it is today, the argument for taxing its value again on death would be weakened.

These would be radical changes and they would require not only careful modelling but a willingness on the part of central government to see some meaningful powers devolved to the regions. It was not apparent from the outcome of the Lyons Review (Lyons, 2004) that central government was ready for this level of devolution.

The changes would also require a serious level of public debate and a gradual transition. Moving tax-raising powers without first dealing with the issue of local government skills and the size of the new single-tier local government units that would be required would be a recipe for disaster, not improvement.

Governments face genuine difficulty in putting forward ideas for radical change. In taxation matters there is even more nervousness than in other policy areas. Part of this is an education and information issue, as discussed earlier on in this commentary. Part of it is to do with institutions: the development of radical policy ideas is much less sensitive if it is undertaken at one step removed from central government. Where there is an 'almighty' institution such as HM Treasury, with a stranglehold on tax policy initiatives, it is not surprising that the public assumes that if policy ideas are being generated within it, they are likely to come to fruition; but if they are generated, say, by the IFS or the Oxford University Centre for Business Taxation, it may be possible to achieve a more balanced public reaction. This does not mean that HM Treasury should not risk putting forward radical ideas at an early stage in their development; but it does mean that government should also look to external institutions to do some of the early development work.

3.3. The influence of current arrangements for scrutiny and accountability

One of the areas where the authors focus is on the issue of scrutiny and its relationship with the policy-making process. Scrutiny has two main functions: to improve proposals by a process of debate and amendment; and to hold the Executive accountable. As the authors note, 'scrutiny is even weaker for tax policy than it is for other areas'.

The problems of scrutiny outside the framework of central government have already been touched upon in this note. Consultation, particularly in the area of business taxation, has been dramatically improved in the last ten years and that has both enabled certain areas of tax policy-making to become more effective through drawing in external expertise, and highlighted the need for wider consultation on other aspects of tax policy-making. Wider access to relevant data and the early publication of the strategic direction of tax policy within a Parliament and of specific tax policy options and choices will further enhance the quality of public scrutiny.

This should not stop with the introduction of a tax or a taxation measure. There should be a formal process of post-legislative review. At present, there is normally no public process that seeks to establish whether a taxation measure has achieved either its intended behavioural impact or the expected revenue effect. Some changes cry out for such a review: the capital gains tax changes of 1998 and subsequent years, for example. Have they had a marked effect on entrepreneurial activity? Are gains now being realized onshore that would previously have been realized by individuals who have gone offshore for that purpose? Another case might be the research and development tax credits. Has the aggregate level of R&D expenditure increased (or was that always too susceptible to non-tax-related decisions of the aerospace and pharmaceutical companies to be a useful indicator)? Has there been a real shift in R&D expenditure by small companies? Or has the net effect of the changes been primarily the spawning of a new activity among accounting firms based on reclassifying expenditure to ensure that the maximum benefit can be claimed by their clients? A formal process of post-implementation review would improve the scrutiny of these kinds of changes and arguably ensure, in the long term, better value for public money.

There is also the issue of parliamentary scrutiny. Here the authors spend some time and point the way towards a potentially better state of affairs, albeit a little timidly.

The problem is, as I have argued elsewhere, that the present parliamentary system provides little or no effective scrutiny of taxation proposals. I do not believe the answer is, as some have argued, to have a technical Finance Bill separated out from the annual Finance Bill process. I believe the answer is structural change.

Parliament needs to be put in a position where it can have a meaningful and informed debate about taxation policy. It needs to be able to discuss the macro-economic issues, the impact of legislative proposals and, perhaps most importantly of all, the possible range of policy options. With the present structures it cannot. MPs are no more tax policy experts than ministers are and they have much more restricted access to information.

I would suggest three fundamental structural changes:

1. Parliament should set up a body of economists and lawyers dedicated to providing analysis to MPs serving on parliamentary committees such as the Finance Bill Committee and the Treasury Select Committee. It should have a similar remit to the Congressional Budget Office in the US and be resourced to a level where it can analyse proposals from the Executive and examine alternative policy options on behalf of Committees. Such an organization would transform the quality of debate on taxation policy within Parliament. Ideally, it would be provided with the necessary data to carry out its work by an Office of Tax Analysis.
2. Alongside the democratization of the House of Lords, its members should be given a more significant role in the scrutiny of tax proposals. The absence of a 'normal' review process in the House of Lords for Finance Bills creates a significant and unnecessary weakness in the process of parliamentary scrutiny for taxation policy measures. It is increasingly anomalous in the context of the changes in the composition of the House of Lords, the greater balance in party representation there and the undoubted qualification of some of its members to comment on tax policy.
3. The introduction of a requirement for the publication of a statement in Parliament at the start of an Administration setting out the intended strategic direction of tax policy for the life of the Parliament. Such a requirement would be likely to drive a greater openness in the preparation of election manifestos. It would facilitate a more thorough debate about policy objectives that would aid policy-development and the scrutiny process. It would inform external institutions about policy direction and enable them to make a more effective contribution; and it would create a greater climate of certainty among the public and the business community.

I believe that the implementation of these proposals, together with the formal requirement for a post-implementation review of major policy changes, would have a dramatic effect on the quality of scrutiny and provide a much better system of accountability than exists today.

4. FINAL THOUGHTS

As I indicated at the start of this note, the authors of this chapter on 'The Political Economy of Tax Policy' have raised some important issues in their work. In providing this commentary, I have attempted to draw out more directly some of the key points: the importance of access to information; the value of putting choices out for public scrutiny and debate; the need for structural changes to strengthen and empower the process of scrutiny. At the heart of the suggestions made in this note is the desire to see a greater engagement between government and the governed on taxation issues, and an informed engagement in which the current imbalances are addressed. Over the last decade there have been some significant improvements, but they have served to highlight the need to go further and to establish a much stronger and more democratic base for tax policy-making.

REFERENCES

Lyons, M. (2004), *Well Placed to Deliver: Shaping the Pattern of Government Service*, London: HM Treasury. <http://www.hm-treasury.gov.uk/consult_lyons_index.htm>

O'Donnell, G. (2004), *Financing Britain's Future: Review of the Revenue Departments*, Cm 6163, London: HM Treasury. <http://www.hm-treasury.gov.uk/bud_bud04_odonnell_index.htm>

Index